HANDBOOK
of
DEVELOPMENTAL PSYCHOLOGY

HANDBOOK *of* DEVELOPMENTAL PSYCHOLOGY

Edited by
Jaan Valsiner and Kevin J. Connolly

SAGE Publications
London • Thousand Oaks • New Delhi

First published 2003

SAGE Publications Ltd
6 Bonhill Street
London EC2A 4PU

SAGE Publications Inc
2455 Teller Road
Thousand Oaks, California 91320

SAGE Publications India Pvt Ltd
32, M-Block Market
Greater Kailash - I
New Delhi 110 048

British Library Cataloguing in Publication data

A catalogue record for this book is available from the British Library

ISBN 0 7619 6231 X

Library of Congress Control Number available

Typeset by Keystroke, Jacaranda Lodge, Wolverhampton
Printed in Great Britain by The Cromwell Press Ltd, Trowbridge, Wiltshire

Contents

Part Three: **Development in Early Childhood**

Part Four: **Development in Middle Childhood**

Part Five: **Development in Pre-Adolescence and Adolescence**

Part Six: **Development in Adulthood**

Introduction

The Nature of Development: The Continuing Dialogue of Processes and Outcomes

JAAN VALSINER AND KEVIN J. CONNOLLY

This book is about development. But what is development? The word, which is in common everyday usage, has an extensive range of meanings. We speak of the development of a film, a fertilized egg, a new engine design, a legal system, or a social policy (Nagel, 1957). The word 'development' is used widely – and wildly – in our everyday talk. What does it mean – and how can it illuminate our scientific understanding of the world?

Let us begin at the beginning – the common meanings of the term. An examination of two contemporary dictionaries produced more that a dozen meanings, including:

1 to bring into existence
2 to cause progress from simple to complex
3 to elaborate a theme
4 to unfold
5 to bring to a more advanced stage.

Each of these definitions is about change, but not all change is development. Development is a lifelong process; it begins at conception and continues until death. It is central to our understanding of human nature. It deals with historical phenomena, that is when previous events affect the manifestation of current or future events.

When it comes to scientific terminology, we need to provide a general elaboration of the meaning of the term. Development is identifiable only across time. It is impossible to consider a specific – infinitely small – time moment, and talk about an event taking place within that unit, in terms of development (or change). It takes the adjacency – or sequence – of two such infinitely small moments to set the stage for consideration of any change. Yet, as is clear from the common language meanings, change in itself does not equal development. *Development is a process of change with direction.* That direction need not be specified in concrete terms: it is sufficient to posit that such direction exists. The direction need not be a given: it does not entail progression (or regression) in relation to some ideal end state.

Development can be anchored in the past (direction of change: 'moving away' from some known state) as well as in the projected future ('moving towards' some ideal or desired state).

The developmental perspective in any science privileges a study of *processes* that occur in real time rather than arguments based on *products* (or outcomes) of such processes. Thus the metaphors of 'unfolding', 'becoming more complex' and 'elaborating a theme' are all familiar and widely used in developmental biology as well as in developmental psychology. In fact, the developmental approach is currently unifying or bringing about closer links between various sciences which build their knowledge on that approach. Increasingly the notion of 'developmental science' is in evidence (Cairns, Elder, & Costello, 1996). This focus grew out of the internal tensions in North American psychology between ideological perspectives oriented towards outcomes (needed for different administrative practices: see Danziger, 1997) and processes. In the USA, similarly to the former Soviet Union (Valsiner, 1988), the socio-political factors relevant in a given society at a given time determine the mindset of the researchers in the social sciences, and fortify it through consensus. Ideas of development have been repeatedly proposed – and then dismissed or set aside – in the history of child psychology in North America (see Cairns, 1998, for an overview). The emergence of developmental science is the most recent return to focus on developmental processes.

General Principles

The contributions to this book belong to developmental science. The authors were asked to write about issues of basic knowledge concerning development, as it is being created in their respective areas. A number of general principles necessary for development have been identified (Anderson, 1957; Michel & Moore, 1995). For development to occur, irreversible changes in organization are necessary; this in turn requires an open system. An open system is one having exchange relationships with its environment. The environment of the developing organism is its context. This idea of context is relative to the developing organism. It does not exist independently of that organism. Hence any investigator who studies development must necessarily take into account the context of the developing organism.

Development Is Characterized by Activity

Organisms are not only reactive, they are active in relation to their environment. They seek input which they then transform by their behaving – by acting upon the environment. In so doing organisms move towards both internal coherence within themselves, and coherence with their environment. An organism is a heterogeneous whole. It has many levels of organization: systems range from the components of cells to the whole organism operating in its environment.

Each system has emergent properties specific to its level of organization and some may also display properties of lower level systems. Different levels are mutually integrated (as will be seen in Gilbert Gottlieb's contribution, Chapter 1 in this volume). Developing systems grow and change in complexity. Increased complexity is brought about by the progressive reorganization of systems. This reorganization may result in a more capable, adaptive system (Anderson, 1957). At times, it is also adaptive for the system to operate at a lower level of organization reflecting an earlier state. Hence phenomena usually considered regressive can be part of the progressive development of the system. And, of course, there are the phenomena of destruction of the current system – its involution. Development entails the unity of evolution and involution.

Developing organisms become flexible so that they may operate at whatever level is necessary to meet the environmental conditions. The relevance of the irreversibility of time becomes obvious here: a developing system that encounters environmental conditions *X at a given moment* needs not merely to adapt to that (already) known state of the environmental demands, but to adapt in ways that *anticipate the possible changes* in these demands at a subsequent moment. For that, relative autonomy of the organism from its environment is necessary. In both phylogeny and ontogeny, one can discern the making of such autonomy. The highest level – known to us so far – of such autonomy is the self-reflexive mentation of an introspective kind in *Homo sapiens*.

Causality in Developing Systems

In considering causation it is important to appreciate that there are always two or more components involved in development; they may be within a system or between a system and its context. Development and the appearance of new emergent properties cannot arise in a single component or solely in the context; two or more components are always necessary. Hence the classical notions of linear causality (e.g. cause *X* leads to outcome *Y*) are inappropriate in the case of developing systems. Instead, developmental science operates with the notion of systemic causality (Valsiner, 2000). An outcome is a result of the systemic relationship between parts of a system: system $\{a\text{–}R\text{–}b\}$, where *a* and *b* are parts and *R* is their relation, leads to an outcome *Y*. Neither part *a* nor part *b* of the system, taken alone, results in the outcome. Neither does their formal combination (mixing) produce the desired outcome. Imagine trying to mix two gases (hydrogen and oxygen) in a vessel, hoping for water to result from the mixing. It is only when the particular structural and functional relationship between the parts of the system is in place that the systemic causality can be detected. All biological systems operate on the basis of systemic causality, perhaps the best example of which is the Krebs cycle (a basic biochemical circular reaction chain that guarantees the energetic maintenance of the organism).

Furthermore, the developing systems entail catalytic functions (Minch, 1998): different components of the system are synthesized in order to guarantee the transformation of incoming material into a new form, while reproducing the organismic systemic mechanism itself. The conceptual models of the life sciences differ from those of the physical sciences where non-organic phenomena are involved.

Thus, for causality to be discovered in developmental science, the identity of the components involved in a changed relationship must be specified. This task goes far beyond the inferential tools currently in wide use by psychologists, such as analysis of variance and factor analysis. The mathematical sophistication of developmental science increases with the search for more adequate formal models than traditional statistical ideas afford (see Nesselroade and Molenaar, Chapter 27 and van Geert, Chapter 28 in this volume).

Axiomatizing development

The study of transformation addresses issues that the study of things-as-they-are regards as superfluous, unnecessary or even error. The non-developmental perspective is based on the axiom of identity:

$X = [\text{is}] = X$

On the basis of this axiom, it makes good sense to ask questions of the kind, 'What *is* personality?', 'What *is* intelligence?', 'What *is* memory?' Once the identity of our research target is clear, there is no more doubt as to its organization. The law of the excluded middle from Aristotelian logic applies: if *X* is *X* it is true that *X* is not anything else but *X*, and there is nothing else between *X* and non-*X*. Questions of development are ruled out – or at least rendered uninteresting – from that axiomatic basis. Why ask a question of how *X* came to be *X*, if we already take it for granted that *X* is *X*, and the whole functioning of *X* is due to its essence ('*X*-ness')? The Non-developmental thought needs the projection of an essentialistic kind into the object it covers.

The developmental perspective requires us to rummage in the murky terrain of *what precisely is in the domain of the 'excluded middle'* – the domain of phenomena that are not yet developed, but are about to develop in the near future (Valsiner & van der Veer, 1993). Hence, the developmental perspective is based on the axiom of becoming. This axiom takes two forms:

$X \rightarrow [\text{becomes}]\ Y$
$X \rightarrow [\text{maintains itself as}]\ X$

Becoming and remaining are processes that guarantee both relative stability and change in the case of development. With regard to maintenance, the particular system that is maintained in its general form depends upon constant innovation of the form by new parts. Organisms maintain themselves by the processes of cell production and cell death, while the form (the structure of the organism) in general remains the same.

Developmental perspectives transcend discipline boundaries. We need to be aware of a misconception about development that is common in much of psychology. Development is *not* about children's (or adults') age-related changes in different kinds of measures of psychological variables. Child psychology need not be developmental psychology; nor does developmental psychology necessarily deal with children. A developmental perspective can be applied to adult development (see Lawrence and Dodds, Chapter 22 and Staudinger and Werner, Chapter 25 as well as old age (Rabbitt, Anderson, Davis, and Shilling, Chapter 24). The developmental perspective is shared across discipline boundaries, for example, with developmental biology and embryology. In the case of genetics we can also discern the juxtaposition of the developmental perspectives (focusing on issues such as cytological environments for gene expression, genetic regulation of the formation of new structures) with their non-developmental counterpart (genetic determinism of selected phenotypic features, fashionable through the fascination with the decoding of the genome: see Wahlsten, Chapter 2 and Gottlieb, Chapter 1.

Some disciplines could benefit from developmental perspectives – even if they currently do not explicitly include them. If there were a subdiscipline of 'developmental sociology' it would study the emergence and development of social units – communities, towns, countries – over historical time. Likewise, 'developmental anthropology' would look at the emergence of humans and the cultural development of the species and its societies. Developmental economics would consider economic processes and the history of economic cycles. In short, the developmental perspective is a general framework of science that focuses on understanding the directional change of the phenomena under investigation. It is the science of becoming.

Conceptions of Development

In broad terms there are two kinds of general explanation of development. The first, 'preformationism', presumes that everything is formed at conception and that it remains only for the individual to grow; in this scheme of things children were represented in the fertilized egg as miniature adults. Strictly this idea does not deal with development because no qualitative changes take place. A different but clearly related version of preformationism which does deal with development is the notion of predeterminism. Here provision is made for qualitative changes which are permitted over the life-span. Development is presumed to proceed in an orderly and preordained progression through a series of distinct stages. The pattern and interrelationship of these stages are predetermined.

Preformationism does not provide an explanation of development; features do not pre-exist, rather they come into existence as a consequence of developmental processes. Preformationist ideas are still evident in the widespread use of notions like '*a* gene *for* [function *X*]', 'genetic blueprint', 'genetic programme' and 'information specified in the genes'. All these presume to explain the origin of order and organization but they do not offer an account or description of the mechanism.

The alternative approach to understanding development, epigenesis, presumes that the organism's features are not present at conception but come into existence by the gradual production of parts from a single undifferentiated cell. Epigenesis refers to qualitative change which is not reducible to genome or genetic programmes and is based upon interaction within and between many levels of the changing organism and its external milieu. More complex structures arise as a result of interactions between features. Development thus always entails interactions between two or more components in a system.

Gottlieb (1997; and Chapter 1 has drawn a distinction between *predetermined* and *probabilistic* epigenesis. Predetermined epigenesis presumes that the development of behaviour in the foetus and newborn can be explained in terms of the structural maturation of the nervous system. Structure determines function: as the nervous system develops, behaviour appears as an epiphenomenon. Probabilistic epigenesis presumes that function facilitates neural maturation: structure and function have a bidirectional relationship in which each feeds into the other. The theoretical notion of probabilistic epigenesis provides developmental science with a general reference system where both structure of the organisms (at different levels) and their environments is unified with a functionalist developmental scheme.

Evolution and Development

The processes of psychological development that give rise to behaviour and mentality are products of evolution. These processes are also themselves subject to evolutionary pressures. If the environment changes, the outcome for individual development may produce marked effects; differential survival and advantage lead to changes in the gene pool linked to changes in behaviour. Oppenheim (1981) points out that babies and children have special faculties and patterns of behaviour which are suited to their habitat at a given period; these he calls 'ontogenetic adaptations'. Immature animals often live in markedly different environments to those of adults of the same species.

For example, consider a foetus, a newborn, and a preschool child. Each of these stages may have required the evolution of specific anatomical, physiological and behavioural mechanisms different from those used by an adult and which require modification before the adult stage is reached. A feature of many mammalian species and a particularly striking one in the case of our own species is the long childhood which forms a large part of our life history. This long childhood is presumably an adaptation made necessary by the complexity of the adult behaviour which an individual must acquire. Another ubiquitous and likely candidate as an ontogenetic adaptation is 'play' which seems to be an important antecedent of much later behaviour.

The idea of construction through the interaction of many factors applies to evolution as well as to development. Evolutionary change is a result of interactions and outcomes that are jointly constructed by populations and environments which commonly have interwoven histories. If we think of evolution as a change in developmental systems we cannot regard organisms as simply accommodating, or not, to their environment. Organisms are active; they select their environment and they change it (Lewontin,1978). Hence a careful consideration of the development of instrumental action (Smitsman and Bongers, Chapter 8 and Langer, Rivera,

Schlesinger, and Wakeley, Chapter 7) is central for any overview of developmental science.

METHODOLOGY

At the core of any science is its methodology. Methodology is the process through which knowledge is created in a given discipline. It entails a cyclical relation of general meta-theoretical assumptions, immediate perception of the phenomena (both introspectively and externally, in the human case), methods, and specific theories (Branco & Valsiner, 1997; Valsiner, 2000; 2001). Scientific knowledge does not result merely from data collection or from scholastic speculation. There must be some way of coordinating the general ways of thinking (deductive propositions) with empirical evidence (inductive inference), leading to the transformation of both. The scientific enterprise itself is a developmental phenomenon *par excellence*.

The specific ways of knowledge construction set a different emphasis for different parts of the methodology cycle. Particle physicists spend most of their time making sure that their experimental results are not equipment artifacts (Knorr-Cetina, 1999), whereas psychologists usually attempt to amass large quantities of consensually validated data and set their hopes on inductive generalization – for example, by way of meta-analyses – rather than dwell on the veridicality of each data point. Psychologists often see a dramatic difference between qualitative (Smith and Dunworth, Chapter 26) and quantitative perspectives (Nesselroade and Molenaar, Chapter 27). This contrast is an artifact of social divisions in psychology. Fortunately the newer formal models coming into developmental science from dynamic systems theory (Fischer, Yan, and Stewart, Chapter 21 and van Geert, Chapter 28) are rendering such opposition between the quantitative and qualitative perspectives obsolete. The basic knowing about the world is textured – or structural – and hence qualitative. Quantification is but a technical operation used for gaining new qualitative knowledge. It guarantees no objectivity: a science that practises unreflexive averaging of data is not much different from the fortune teller reading palms.

There are differences between non-developmental and developmental methodologies. The latter lead to the use of a number of characteristics of scientific methodology.

Structure and Fluidity within Units of Analysis

As the notion of the irreversible transformation of structures (which is the cornerstone of developmental perspectives) is assumed, then naturally the temporal frame that permits the representation of this emergent process needs to be present in the empirical data. This may entail the use of mutually overlapping temporal units for the detection of emergent processes. Consider a sequence entailing *A–B–C*. In order to create a developmental unit of analysis, at least two of these symbols (*A–B* or *B–C*) need to be considered.

Each of the parts of these units (*A* or *B* in *A–B*; or *B* or *C* in *B–C*) may be either clearly structured or 'fuzzy' (semi-formed). Development entails parts of semi-formed – and therefore difficult to classify – phenomena that may be natural parts of the units of analysis. This was clearly understood by the originators of the microgenetic methodology in the study of development (Sander, 1930). Development takes place through the integration and differentiation of quasi-formed parts of the organism. The units of analysis used in empirical work need to preserve that quality.

Developmental Science Studies Dynamically Transforming Structures, not 'Variables'

The talk about 'variables' is a relatively recent invention in psychology, as Kurt Danziger (1990; 1997) has demonstrated. In the case of a developmental focus on transformation of structures, psychological experiments cannot be seen as entailing the simple changing, by an experimenter, of 'independent' variables to check their effect upon the 'dependent' variables. In line with the strict developmental stance, the distinction between independent and dependent variables becomes impossible, as the relations between the experimental setting and the research participant entail dynamic feedback loops. An intervention (by the researcher, or by a change in the natural environment) into the development of the organism – the equivalent of an independent variable – is not simply responded to, it is reconstructed. This result (the equivalent of a dependent variable) becomes new input material (a new independent variable) for the organism on the next occasion, and so on. The ontological distinction of the independent and dependent variables becomes impossible in the case of the development of dynamic systems (see Fischer, Yan, and Stewart, Chapter 21 in this volume).

The Single Case: Definitive Source of Data

A particular person is studied in his or her negotiation process with the particular here-and-now setting. Generalizations in this perspective are made from single cases to the generic functioning of the personality system. This is in line with Gordon Allport's 'morphogenic analysis', which has been misconstrued in the disputes about idiographic versus nomothetic perspectives (Allport, 1962; 1966). The empirical task of the researcher is first to analyse the systemic functioning of a single case and, once the single case is explained, to aggregate knowledge of the ways in which the system works across persons into a generic model. The way to general knowledge proceeds from a single empirical case to a general model of the system, which is then further tested on another single case; necessary corrections are made to the model, which is tested again on data from an individual system; and so on.

If the hypothesized generic model of the single case (and based on one single case, say from the middle range of the sample distribution) is demonstrated to function in cases which are outliers in the distribution, the researcher is on her (or his) way towards basic knowledge. This strategy is well known in linguistics, where the adequacy of a theoretical proposition is tested on singular examples from language, looking for extreme cases that may refute the proposition. The finding of such contrary cases forces the reconstruction of the theoretical system, or at times it may lead to the abandonment of the system. There is a definite crucial role for empirical evidence in theoretical reconstruction – yet only in key moments in knowledge construction.

Envoi

The developmental approach is currently serving to unify the framework in which many branches of the life sciences are progressing. The 28 chapters of this book written by 49 individuals outline the way in which new questions and new theories are changing the landscape of developmental psychology. Our starting point was put well by an English mathematician, Alan Turing, half a century ago:

> Most of an organism, most of the time, is developing from one pattern to another, not from homogeneity into a pattern.

References

Allport, G.W. (1962). The general and the unique in psychological science. *Journal of Personality*, 30, 405–422.

Allport, G.W. (1966). Traits revisited. *American Psychologist*, 21, 1–10.

Anderson, J.E. (1957). Dynamics of development: systems in process. In D.B. Harris (ed.), *The concept of development*. Minneapolis: University of Minnesota Press.

Branco, A.U., & Valsiner, J. (1997). Changing methodologies: A co-constructivist study of goal orientations in social interactions. *Psychology and Developing Societies*, 9 (1), 35–64.

Cairns, R.B. (1998). The making of developmental psychology. In W. Damon (series ed.) & R. Lerner (ed.), *Handbook of child psychology, 5th edn: Vol. 1. Theoretical models of human development* (pp. 25–105). New York: Wiley.

Cairns, R.B., Elder, G.E., & Costello, E.J. (eds) (1996). *Developmental science*. New York: Cambridge University Press.

Danziger, K. (1990). *Reconstructing the subject*. Cambridge: Cambridge University Press.

Danziger, K. (1997). *Naming the mind*. London: Sage.

Gottlieb, G. (1997). *Synthesizing nature/nurture*. Mahwah, NJ: Erlbaum.

Knorr-Cetina, K. (1999). *Epistemic cultures: How the sciences make knowledge*. Cambridge, MA: Harvard University Press.

Lewontin, R. (1978). Adaptation. *Scientific American*, 239 (9),156–169.

Michel, G.F., Moore, C.L. (1995). *Developmental psychobiology*. Cambridge, MA: MIT Press.

Minch, E. (1998). The beginning of the end: On the origin of the final cause. In G. van de Vijver, S.N. Salthe, & M. Deplos (eds), *Evolutionary synthesis* (pp. 45–58). Dordrecht: Kluwer.

Nagel, E. (1957). Determinism and development. In D.B. Harris (ed.), *The concept of development*. Minneapolis: University of Minnesota Press.

Oppenheim, R.W. (1981). Ontogenetic adaptations and retrogressive processes in the development of the nervous system and behaviour: A neuroembryological perspective. In K.J. Connolly & H.F.R. Prechtl (eds), *Maturation and development*. London: Heinemann.

Sander, F. (1930). Structure, totality of experience, and Gestalt. In C. Murchison (ed.), *Psychologies of 1930* (pp. 188–204). Worcester, MA: Clark University Press.

Turing, A.M. (1952). The chemical basis of morphogenesis. *Philosophical Transactions of the Royal Society of London*, 237, 37–72.

Valsiner, J. (1988). *Developmental psychology in the Soviet Union*. Hemel Hempstead: Harvester.

Valsiner, J. (2000). *Culture and human development*. London: Sage.

Valsiner, J. (2001). *Comparative study of human cultural development*. Madrid: Fundación Infancia y Aprendizaje.

Valsiner, J., & van der Veer, R. (1993). The encoding of distance: The concept of the zone of proximal development and its interpretations. In R.R. Cocking & K.A. Renninger (eds), *The development and meaning of psychological distance* (pp. 35–62). Hillsdale, NJ: Erlbaum.

Contributors

Mike Anderson is associate professor of psychology at the University of Western Australia. Educated at Edinburgh and Oxford he works on the nature of intelligence and cognitive development. He has done work in developmental psychology, information processing and intelligence,and developmental psychopathologies. He was a senior scientist at the UK Medical Research Council's Cognitive Development Unit between 1983 and 1989. His publications include *Intelligence and development: A cognitive theory*, Blackwell, 1992; and *The development of intelligence*; Psychology Press, 1999.

David F. Bjorklund is professor of psychology at Florida Atlantic University, USA. He was educated at the University of North Carolina at Chapel Hill, from where he received his Ph.D. He has done work in different areas of cognitive development such as memory development, including eyewitness memory, and inhibitory functions. His most recent work addresses issues of developmental evolutionary psychology. Bjorklund's main publications include *Children's Thinking: Developmental Functions and Individual Differences,* Wadsworth, 2000; and *Developmental Evolutionary Psychology,* with Toni Pellegrini, 2002.

Raoul Bongers is currently a post-doc. at the Department of Movement and Perception in the Faculty of Sport Sciences at the University of Aix-Marseille, France. In 2001 he graduated in the Social Sciences at the University of Nijmegen, The Netherlands. His research concentrates on the control and coordination of perception and action and entails both psychological experiments and the modelling of behaviour. He works on tool use, pointing movements, interceptive actions, perceptual systems, and neural networks.

Harke A. Bosma is associate professor of developmental psychology at the University of Groningen. He received his Ph.D, from Groningen, for a study of identity development in adolescence. He has also done work in the area of parent-adolescent relationships. His main publications include *Identity and Development. An interdisciplinary Approach,* Sage, 1994; co-edited with TLG Graafsma, HD Grotevant, & DJ de Levita, and *Identity and Emotion. Development through Self-Organization*; Cambridge University Press, 2001; co-edited with ES Kunnen.

Angela U. Branco is professor of psychology at Universidade de Brasilia, Brazil, where she directs the Laboratory of Metacommunication and Social Interaction (LABMIS). Her main interests are in the ontogeny of cooperation in childhood, and the ways in which communcation and metacommunication are co-constructing human development. She is the editor of *Communication and metacommunication,* Greenwood, 2000.

Nancy Budwig is the Vice Provost and Dean of Research at Clark University. Her research on language development is based in a functionalist perspective, highlighting the ways in which language forms are acquired in tandem with learning to communicate. This work has aims to better understand the protracted nature of children's organization of linguistic forms and the functions they serve. In a further set of studies, she has focused on the role of language in socialization. Here emphasis shifts from language as the domain of study, to viewing language as a system through which the child comes to co-construct meaning. This research examines ways children's participation in language practice contributes to the construction of culturally relevant senses of personhood. Current research on language development and language socialization has drawn upon cultural comparisons of American, German and Hindi-speaking children interacting with their caregivers and peers.

Kevin J. Connolly is emeritus professor of psychology at the University of Sheffield. His principal research interests are in the genetics and evolution of behaviour, and in development; specifically in the development of skilled action, the acquisition of tool using skills and manual dexterity. He has also worked on maternal iodine deficiency during pregnancy and its consequences on the infant and the child, work undertaken in Papua New Guinea. He has held visiting academic appointments at Padua, Amsterdam, California, Hong Kong, Santiago and São Paulo. He has served as president of the British Psychological Society and as chairman of The Association for Child Psychology and Psychiatry. His recent books include; *The Psychobiology of the hand*, MacKeith/Cambridge University Press, 1998, and, with Margaret Martlew, *Psychologically speaking*: *A book of quotations,* British Psychological Society/ Blackwell, 1999.

Helen Davis is lecturer in psychology at Murdoch University, Western Australia. Educated at the University of Western Australia, she works on cognitive development and individual differences. Her main work has been in investigating the roles of speed, working memory capacity and inhibitory ability on cognitive task performance in children. She has also researched the nature of cognitive deficits associated with chronic fatigue syndrome. Her publications include 'Developmental and individual differences in fluid intelligence: Evidence against the unidimensional hypothesis.' *British Journal of Developmental Psychology*, 2001.

Agnes E. Dodds is a senior lecturer in the Faculty Education Unit of the School of Medicine, Dentistry and Health Sciences at the University of Melbourne, Australia. Her background is in educational psychology, multi-media education and staff development, distance education and music. She is responsible for the assessment and evaluation of the medical curriculum and she teaches in the schools of medicine and psychology. She gained her Master's degree from the University of Melbourne. Her current research interests include the development of the self in relation to the social world, the processes of obtaining and using medical knowledge and skill, and the relation of tertiary teaching to student learning.

Fraser Dunworth graduated in English at the University of London and then took an MA in English renaissance drama at York University. For some time he worked as an actor and as director of a theatre company. He then read psychology at Guildhall University in London after which he undertook training in clinical psychology at Sheffield University. His current research interests are in the use of qualitative methods to explore families' experience of mental health issues. At present Dr Dunworth practises as a clinical psychologist in the Child, Adolescent and Family Therapy Service at Chesterfield in North Derbyshire.

Kurt Fischer is Charles Bigelow Professor of Education and Director of the Mind, Brain, and Education Concentration at the Harvard University Graduate School of Education. Educated at Harvard he works on the organization of behavior and the ways it changes, especially cognitive development, social behavior, emotions, and brain bases. In his approach, called dynamic skill theory, he aims for a coherent framework to combine the many organismic and environmental factors that contribute to the rich variety of developmental change and learning across and within people. He has been visiting professor or scholar at the University of Geneva, University of Pennsylvania, University of Groningen, and the Center for Advanced Study in the Behavioral Sciences, Stanford. Fischer is the author of nine books and monographs.

Paul van Geert belongs to the neo-realist school of Flemish portrait painting – the skills of which he transfers successfully to building dynamic systems models of human development. In his professional affiliation he is professor of developmental psychology at the University of Groningen, He is particularly interested in theoretical problems of development, and has developed the sub-area of experimental theoretical developmental psychology that specializes in formal models-based reconstruction of basic processes of development. His books include *Dynamic systems of development*, Harvester Wheatsheaf, 1994.

Coby Gerlsma is senior lecturer at the Department of Clinical Psychology, University of Groningen. She has done work on parental rearing styles, expressed emotion, marital functioning, adult attachment and psychopathology Her publications include, Attachment style in the context of clinical and health psychology, *British Journal of Medical Psychology,* 2000 and, Recollections of parental care and quality of intimate relationships: The role of re-evaluating past experiences, *Clinical Psychology and Psychotherapy*, 2000.

Gilbert Gottlieb is research professor at the Center for Developmental Science at the University of North Carolina at Chapel Hill. He is currently exploring genetic correlations in longitudinal studies of human development, one study beginning in infancy and two others in adolescence. He is particularly interested in furthering the synthesis of developmental biological and developmental psychological thinking (developmental-psychobiological systems theory). This involves the concept of equifinality (the existence of different developmental pathways to the same endpoint), an understanding of structure-function bidirectionality, and delineating the various ways that experience or function operates at the genetic, neural, and behavioral levels of analysis. Among his recent books is *Individual development and evolution: The genesis of novel behavior*. Erlbaum. (Reprint of 1992 book.)

Peter Hepper is professor of psychology & director of the Fetal Behaviour Research Centre at Queen's University, Belfast, Northern Ireland. Educated at the Universities of Exeter and Durham he works on fetal behaviour and diagnosis, and kin recognition.

Hubert Hermans is professor of personality psychology at the Katholijke Universiteit, Nijmegen, The Netherlands. His early work was on achievement motivation and fear of failure. Later he developed a valuation theory and a self-assessment procedure—the 'Self Confrontation Method'. He is the founder of Society for Dialogical Science. His books include *The dialogical self*, 1993, with Harry Kempen.

Els Hermans-Janssen is an active psychotherapist and co-founder, with Hubert Hermans, of the 'Valuation and Self-Confrontation Method Foundation'. Her work is presented in the book, with Hubert Hermans, *Self narratives: the construction of meaning in psychotherapy,* Guilford Press,1995,

Claes von Hofsten is professor of psychology at Uppsala University, Sweden. He was educated at Uppsala and served as professor psychology at Umeå University before returning to Uppsala. He has been a fellow at the Center for Advanced Studies in the Behavioral Sciences at Stanford and at the Center for Cognitive Science at MIT. His research interests are mainly in the early development of action, perception, and cognition, on which he has published extensively.He has contributed to a large number of books on developmental psychology. He is *Honoris Causa* at Universite de Caen.

Brian Hopkins is professor of psychology at Lancaster University. Previously he has been professor in the Faculty of Human Movement Sciences, Vrije Universiteit Amsterdam. Educated at University of Leeds, his research interests are in pre- and postnatal development of movement and posture, the development of laterality, crying and preterm infants. Among his recent publications is his chapter *Understanding motor development: Insights from dynamical systems perspectives* in A. Kalverboer and A. Gramsbergen (Eds.), *Handbook on Brain and Behavior in Human Development.* Kluwer, 2001, and *Crying as a sign, a symptom, and a signal.* With R.G.Barr and J Green (eds) MacKeith/ Cambridge, 2000.

Thomas A. Kindermann is an associate professor of psychology at Portland State University, Portland, Oregon, USA. Educated at the University of Trier and the Free University Berlin, his research focuses on the developmental influences of social interactions across the life-span and on children's peer relationships. His publications include, *Development of Person-Context Relations,* with Jaan Valsiner, Erlbaum, 1995, and 'Strategies for the study of individual development within naturally existing peer groups', *Social Development* , 1996.

Hideo Kojima is emeritus professor at Nagoya University, Japan. Currently he is professor of psychology at Kyoto Gakuen University in Japan. His main work has concentrated on the history of cultural models of child-rearing. He is the originator of the notion of the 'Ethnological Pool of Ideas'. His books include *Family and education,* Tokyo: Daiichi Hoki, 1982, *Quests for tradition in childrearing in*

Japan, Tokyo: Shin' yo-sha, 1989) and *Development of school-aged children,* Tokyo, 1991.

Kurt Kreppner is senior research scientist at the Max Planck Institut für Bildungsforschung in Berlin, Germany. He is interested in the crisis of contemporary psychology, which moves in the direction of proliferation of empirically active but theoretically futile research traditions. He takes a family-systems view on human ontogeny, and has conducted a longitudinal study of family structures developing through childhood.

Jonas Langer is professor of psychology at the University of California at Berkeley. He works on cognitive development and how it evolved in primates. He has done work on the development and evolution of logical, arithmetic and physical concepts in monkeys, chimpanzees and humans. He has held visiting appointments at the University of Geneva, Rockefeller University, and the Comparative Psychology Department of the National Research Council, Rome. His publications include; *Theories of Development*, Holt, Rinehart & Winston, 1969, *The Origins of Logic: Six To Twelve Months*, Academic Press, 1980, and *The Origins of Logic: One To Two Years*, Academic Press, 1986.

Jeanette Lawrence is associate professor of psychology at the University of Melbourne, Australia. She gained her Ph.D. from the University of Minnesota. She teaches developmental psychology and the ethics of psychology. Her current research interests focus on the processes involved in the decisions and judgments made by adults and adolescents in their interactions with the social world. She has studied the sentencing behaviours of magistrates, the contributions of adults to each other across generations in families, and internalizing and externalizing processes. She is a past president of the Australasian Human Development Association.

Eduard Martí is professor of psychology at the Universitat de Barcelona,. Educated at the Université de Genève he works on cognitive development. He has done work in developmental and educational psychology and held visiting appointments at the Université de Fribourg and the Université Paris IX. Martí's main publications include *Construir una mente*, Barcelona, Paidós, 1997 and, Mechanisms of internalisation and externalisation of knowledge in Piaget and Vygotsky's theories. In A. Tryphon & J. Vonèche (eds), *Piaget-Vygotsky. The social genesis of thought*, London, Psychology Press, 1996.

Usha Menon is assistant professor of anthropology in the Department of Culture and Communication at Drexel University. She received her Ph.D. from the University of Chicago in 1995. She has written on different aspects of Hindu society and civilization based on extensive fieldwork experience in the temple town of Bhubaneswar, Orissa, India. One of her essays, 'Does feminism have universal relevance? The Challenges posed by Oriya Hindu family practice' appeared in the October 2000 issue of *Daedalus*. At present, she is working on Hindu-Muslim relations, doing research on the ways in which Indian muslims constitute and experience themselves.

Peter C.M. Molenaar is professor and head of the Department of Psychological Methodology and head of the Cognitive Developmental Psychology Group at the University of Amsterdam. His statistical interests include dynamic factor analysis, applied nonlinear dynamics, adaptive filtering techniques, spectrum analysis, psychophysiological signal analysis, artificial neural network modeling, covariance structure modeling and behavior genetical modeling. He has published widely in these areas, emphasizing applications to cognitive development (stochastic catastrophe analysis of stage transitions), brain-behavior relationships (real-time artificial neural network simulation of cognitive information processing), brain-maturation and cognition (equivalent dipole modeling of longitudinal registrations of electrocortical fields), genetical influences on EEG during the life span, and optimal control of psychotherapeutic processes.. He has been and is the Principal Investigator of 30 grants focusing on methodological issues.

John Nesselroade is professor of psychology at University of Virgina, USA. He is a renowned expert in the area of developmental statistical methodology, with a particular interest in intra-individual variability.

David Olson is university professor at Toronto University, Canada. He is one of the world's leading authorities on the connection between literacy and human cognitive development. He has been professor of human development and applied psychology at the Ontario Institute for Studies in Education for three decades. Professor Olson has been awarded honorary degrees by University of Göteborg in Sweden and by the University of Saskatchewan in Canada. He has been a Fellow at Wolfson College, Oxford, and at the *Wissenschaftskolleg* in Berlin, the German equivalent for Center of Advanced Studies, in the social sciences.

Anthony D. Pellegrini is professor of educational psychology at the University of Minnesota. Educated at Ohio State University, he works on play, dominance and bullying, early literacy and observational methods. He has been a visiting professor at the University of Sheffield, and Cardiff University. His publications include *Observing children in their natural worlds*, Erlbaum, 1996; *Applied child study:a developmental approach,* Erlbaum, 1998, *The child at school:interacting with peers and teachers*, Arnold, 2000.

Janette Pelletier is assistant professor at the Institute of Child Study, in the Department of Human Development and Applied Psychology, Ontario Institute for Studies in Education at the University of Toronto. Educated at the University of Toronto she works on issues related to early child development and education, including literacy development, school readiness and family involvement in early education. She has done work in the area of early writing among first and second language learners and school readiness intervention for diverse families. Her publications include *Children's* clever *misconceptions about print*, in J. Brockmeier, M. Wang & D. Olson (eds), *Literacy, narrative and culture*. Surrey, Curzon, 2002.

Patrick Rabbitt is research professor in gerontology and cognitive psychology, and director of The Age and Cognitive Performance Research Centre, University of

Manchester, UK, and Adjunct Chair, Department of Psychology, University of Western Australia, Perth, Western Australia. He has published extensively on cognitive performance and ageing and is a leading authority on reaction times.

Susan M. Rivera is an Assistant Professor at the University of California, Davis. She received her Ph.D. from the University of California at Berkeley. Her research is on the origins and development of symbolic representation in infants and children, using both classic behavioural and neuroimaging (fMRI) techniques. She also contrasts typical development with that of children with neurodevelopmental disorders including Autism and fragile X Syndrome. Some of Dr Rivera's recent publications include: The drawbridge phenomenon: representational reasoning or perceptual preference? *Developmental Psychology*, v35(2), 427-435 (Rivera, Wakeley, & Langer, 1999); and Functional brain activation during arithmetic processing in females with fragile X Syndrome is related to FMR-1 protein expression. *Human Brain Mapping.16(4),* 206-218 (Rivera, Menon, White, Glaser, Glover, and Reiss, 2002.)

Matthew Schlesinger is an assistant professor of psychology in the Brain and Cognitive Sciences Program at Southern Illinois University. He received his Ph.D. in developmental psychology from the University of California at Berkeley in 1995. His current research focuses on cognitive development in infants and young children, and neural network models of learning and development. Recent publications include 'The agent-based approach: A new direction for computational models of development', with Parisi, *Developmental Review*, 2001.

Louis A. Schmidt is an associate professor in the Department of Psychology at McMaster University, Canada. His research interests include the neural basis of emotion regulatory processes in infants and children and individual differences in affective style, particularly childhood shyness and aggression. He recently co-edited *Extreme fear, shyness, and social phobia: Origins, biological mechanisms, and clinical outcomes*, Oxford University Press.

Wolfgang Schneider is professor of psychology at the University of Würzburg, Germany. He was educated at the University of Heidelberg, where he also received his Ph.D. He has done work in several areas of cognitive development; memory development, the development of metacognition, and personality development. His work in educational psychology focuses on reading and writing and the prevention of disorders in these areas. His publications include *Memory development between 2 and 20*, with Michael Pressley; Erlbaum 1997, and, with David F. Bjorklund, a chapter on memory development in the most recent edition of the *Handbook of Cognitive Development,* 1998.

Sidney Segalowitz is professor of psychology and neuroscience at Brock University, Canada. He received his undergraduate degree at McGill University and Ph.D. at Cornell. His research interests focus on cognitive electrophysiological studies of attentional control and information processing in a lifespan context. His most recent books are two volumes, co-edited with Isabelle Rapin in *Child Neuropsychology*, in the *Handbook of Neuropsychology* series from Elsevier, Amsterdam 2003.

Val Shilling is a research fellow at the Brighton and Sussex Medical School, University of Sussex. Educated at Manchester University her doctoral work investigated age-related changes in inhibitory efficiency. Since leaving Manchester in 2000 she has researched the effects of cancer treatments on cognition.

Jonathan Smith is senior lecturer in the School of Psychology, Birkbeck College, University of London. Prior to this he taught at Keele and Sheffield Universities. He has developed a particular qualitative approach 'interpretative phenomenological analysis' (IPA) and its application to a range of areas in health and social psychology. IPA usually involves the systematic qualitative analysis of transcripts of semi-structured interviews conducted with participants. He has conducted an idiographic longitudinal study of identity change in the transition to motherhood, collecting a great deal of data from a small number of women during their pregnancy and immediately after the birth of their first child. His recent books include, *Rethinking methods in psychology,* with R. Harre and L.v. Langenhave, Sage, 1995.

Peter K. Smith is professor of Psychology and head of the Unit for School and Family Studies at Goldsmiths College, University of London. He is a Fellow of the British Psychological Society. He received his B.Sc. at the University of Oxford and his Ph.D. from the University of Sheffield. His research interests are in social development, play, school bullying, grandparenting, and evolutionary theory. He is co-author of *Understanding Children's Development*, Oxford: Blackwell, 2002, and co-editor of *The Nature of School Bullying* Routledge, 1999, *The Family System Test*, Brunner-Routledge, 2001, and the Blackwell *Handbook of Childhood Social Development* Blackwell, 2002, and editor of *Violence in Schools: The Perspective from Europe*, Routledge, 2002. He has written widely on children's play, especially pretend play training, and rough-and-tumble play.

Ad W. Smitsman is associate professor of psychology at The University of Nijmegen, The Netherlands. He received his Ph.D. from Nijmegen in 1980. He has published on; number and object perception in infants and older children, categorization, tool use, touch in visually handicapped and non-handicapped children and adults. His current work is on tool use, touch, and action.

Peter Stratton is a developmental psychologist and family therapist. He is senior lecturer in psychology at Leeds University, and director of the Leeds Family Therapy and Research Centre, a training and research clinic housed within the university psychology department. The clinic has an international reputation for its development of systemic approaches to family treatment, founded in psychological theory. This clinical work provides a background, and generates data for research into distressed human systems and for techniques of consultation to such systems. He led the team that developed the Leeds 'Attributional Coding System' which has been applied to a wide variety of research issues. He is the Editor of *Human Systems: The Journal of Systemic Consultation and Management.*

Ursula M. Staudinger is professor of psychology at the Dresden University. Prior to this she was senior researcher at the Max Planck Institute for Human Development. She received her Ph.D. in 1988 from the Free University of Berlin. She has co-edited several books, including Interactive Minds: life span perspectives on on social cognition, Cambridge University Press, 1996. She is a Fellow of the APA. Among her research interests are the study of plasticity and reserves in lifespan development, the social-interactive nature of human functioning, and the accumulation of self knowledge, life experience, life insight, and wisdom across the life span.

Jeffrey Stewart is a doctoral candidate at Harvard University Graduate School of Education. He has done work on emotion, phenomenal experience, consciousness, and the self. Stewart's publications include: Fischer, K. W., & Stewart, J. Into the middle of things: From dichotomies to grounded dynamic analysis of development: Commentary on Baillargeon & Smith. *Developmental Science*, 1999 and Fischer, K. W., & Stewart, J. (1999). Duncker's analysis of problem solving as microdevelopment. *From Past to Future*, 1999.

Jaan Valsiner is the founding editor of the Sage journal, *Culture & Psychology*, 1995. He is currently professor and chair of Department of Psychology, Clark University, USA, where he also edits a journal in the history of psychology – *From Past to Future: Clark Papers in the History of Psychology*. Among his recent books are, *Culture and human development*, Sage, 2000 and *Comparative study of human cultural development,* Madrid: Fundacion Infancia y Aprendizaje, 2001.

Douglas Wahlsten is emeritus professor of psychology at the University of Alberta. He received his Ph.D. from the University of California at Irvine. He has done research at the University of Waterloo and at the University of Alberta on neural and behavioral genetics in relation to theories of individual differences and development. He has published numerous journal articles and book chapters in volumes ranging from *Methods in Genomic Neuroscience* to *The General Factor of Intelligence,* R. Sternberg, E. Grigorenko (eds), Erlbaum, 2002.

Ann Wakeley is a doctoral candidate in Special Education at the University of California at Berkeley and San Francisco State University. She works on early mathematical development, cognitive and school related outcomes of premature birth, and cognitive development in infancy. Her publications include Wakeley, A., Rivera, S., & Langer, J. Can young infants add and subtract? *Child Development*, 2000.

Ines Werner is a doctoral fellow in lifespan development at Dresden University. She studied psychology at Dresden where she received her Diploma in Psychology in 1997. Her major interests are in the development of language and of wisdom.

Zheng Yan is assistant professor of educational psychology at the State University of New York at Albany. Educated at Harvard University he works on cognitive development and longitudinal methodology, particularly on the psychology of the Internet and dynamic growth modeling. He taught dynamic modeling methodology at Harvard Graduate School of Education. His publications include Yan, Z. & Fischer, K. Always under construction: Dynamic variations in adult cognitive development. *Human Development*, 2002. Fischer, K. & Yan, Z. (2002). Development of dynamic skill theory. In R. Lickliter & D. Lewkowicz (eds), *Conceptions of development: Lessons from the laboratory*. Psychology Press. 2002.

PART ONE: FUNDAMENTAL APPROACHES AND PRINCIPLES OF DEVELOPMENT

1

Probabilistic Epigenesis of Development

GILBERT GOTTLIEB

The current definition of *epigenesis* holds that individual development is characterized by an increase in novelty and complexity of organization over time. Thus, new structural and functional properties arise sequentially over the course of development. The emergence of these structural and functional novelties is a consequence of horizontal and vertical coactions among the parts, including organism–environment coactions (Gottlieb, 1991). The early formulation of epigenesis around the 1800s did not recognize the coactional nature of epigenetic causality but, rather, saw the epigenesis of the embryo as a consequence of a formative drive (review in Müller-Sievers, 1997). In the late 1800s, with the advent of experimental embryology, the causal role of interactions among the embryo's bodily parts in bringing about the epigenesis of form was placed on a firm empirical basis. Around 1900, the scope of embryology was extended to include the study of behavior (behavioral embryology). The conceptions of epigenesis gleaned from these early studies were eventually generalized to include postnatal behavioral and psychological development.

Our present understanding of the various defining features of epigenesis has been laboriously worked out over the past 200 years. The first part of this chapter begins with a brief recounting of that intellectual history. The second part of the chapter expounds on the more recent notion of the probabilistic character of epigenesis, in contrast to the concept of predetermined epigenesis which flourished into the 1960s and, in some quarters, even beyond that time.

The Triumph of Epigenesis over Preformation

The triumph of epigenesis over the concept of preformation ushered in the era of truly developmental thinking. Namely, to understand the origin of any phenotype, it is necessary to study its development in the individual. This insight has been with us since at least the beginning of the 1800s, when Etienne Geoffroy Saint-Hilaire (1825) advanced his hypothesis that the originating event of evolutionary change was an anomaly of embryonic or fetal development. The origin or initiation of evolutionary change was thus seen as a change in the very early development of an atypical individual. Although not a believer in evolution (in the sense that a species could become so modified as to give rise to a new species), Karl Ernst von Baer (1828) used the description of individual development as a basis for classifying the relationships among species: those that shared the most developmental features were classified together, while those that shared the fewest features were given a remote classification. Von Baer noticed that vertebrate species are much more alike in their early developmental stages than in their later stages. This was such a ubiquitous observation that von Baer formulated a law to the effect that development in various vertebrate species could be universally characterized as progressing from the homogeneous to the heterogeneous. As individuals in each species reached the later stages of their development, they began to differentiate more and more away from each other, so there was less and less resemblance as each species reached adulthood. In our century, it speaks to the generality of von Baer's law that the comparative developmental psychologist Heinz Werner (1957, p. 126) applied von Baer's notion to the psychological realm in his orthogenetic principle of developmental psychology: 'wherever development occurs it proceeds from a state of globality and lack of differentiation to a state of increasing differentiation, articulation, and hierarchical integration'. Getting truly developmental thinking into biology and then into psychology has been a slow and laborious process.

The Birth of Experimental Embryology

While von Baer's emphasis on the importance of developmental description represented a great leap forward in understanding the question of 'What?', it did not come to grips with the problem of 'How?' He and his predecessors evinced no interest in the mechanisms or means by which each developmental stage is brought about: it simply was not a question for them. It remained for the self-designated *experimental* embryologists of the late 1800s to ask that developmental question: Wilhelm His, Wilhelm Roux, and Hans Driesch. As His wrote in reference to von Baer's observations:

> By comparison of [the development of] different organisms, and by finding their similarities, we throw light upon their probable genealogical relations, but we give no direct explanation of their growth and formation. A direct explanation can only come from the immediate study of the different phases of individual development. Every stage of development must be looked at as the physiological consequence of some preceding stage, and ultimately as the consequence of the acts of impregnation and segmentation of the egg. (1888, p. 295)

It remained for Roux, in 1888, to plunge a hot needle into one of the two existing cells after the first cleavage in a frog's egg, thereby initiating a truly *experimental* study of embryology.

The arduously reached conclusion that we hold today – that individual development is most appropriately viewed as hierarchically organized system – began with Hans Driesch's being dumbfounded by the results of his replication of Roux's experiment. While Roux found that killing one cell and allowing the second cleavage cell to survive resulted in a half-embryo in frogs, Driesch (1908) found that detaching the first two cells in a sea urchin resulted in two fully formed sea urchins, albeit diminished in size. (When the detachment procedure was later used in amphibians, two fully formed embryos resulted as in Driesch's experiment with sea urchins.) Driesch came to believe there is some nonmaterial vitalistic influence (an 'entelechy') at work in the formation of the embryo, one that will forever elude our best experimental efforts, so he eventually gave up embryology in favor of the presumably more manageable problems of psychology.

Because Driesch had found that a single cell could lead to the creation of a fully formed individual, he gathered, quite correctly, that each cell must have the same prospective potency, as he called it, and could in principle become any part of the body. He thought of these cells as *harmonious-equipotential systems*. For Driesch, the vitalistic feature of these harmonious-equipotential systems is their ability to reach the same outcome or endpoint by different routes, a process that he labeled *equifinality*. Thus, in the usual case, two attached cleavage cells give rise to an embryo, whereas in the unusual case, you have two separated cleavage cells, each giving rise to an embryo. While to Driesch these experimental observations provided the most elementary or 'easy' proofs of vitalism, for those still laboring in the field of embryology today they continue to provide a provocative challenge for experimental resolution and discovery.

For the present purposes, it is important to note that, if each cell of the organism is a harmonious-equipotential system, then it follows that the organism itself must be such a system. Driesch's notion of equifinality – that developing organisms of the same species can reach the same endpoint via different developmental pathways – has become an axiom of developmental systems theory.[1] In a systems view of developmental psychology, equifinality means that (a) developing organisms that have different early or 'initial' conditions can reach the same endpoint and (b) organisms that share the same initial condition can reach the same endpoint by different routes or pathways (cf. Ford & Lerner, 1992). Both of these outcomes have been empirically demonstrated by the behavioral research of D.B. Miller (Miller, Hicinbothom, & Blaich, 1990) and R. Lickliter (Banker & Lickliter, 1993) in birds, and by Nöel (1989) and Carlier et al. (1989), among others, in mammals. The uniquely important developmental principle of equifinality is rarely explicitly invoked in theoretical views of developmental psychology, so it may seem unfamiliar to many readers. K.W. Fischer's theory of skill development in infancy and early childhood is one of the rare exceptions in that it explicitly incorporates the notion of equifinality: '[D]ifferent individuals will follow different developmental paths in the same skill domain . . . The developmental transformation rules predict a large number of different possible paths in any single domain' (1980, p. 513). (Also see Fischer, Yan, & Stewart, Chapter 19 in this volume.)

Microgenetic studies of human development are most likely to reveal equifinality because, under these conditions, the response of individuals to the same challenge is closely monitored and described for shorter or longer periods (e.g. Kuhn, 1995). An example of equifinality involved a study of language development in young hearing and deaf preschool children. Each group devised an arbitrary system of signs to refer to events and objects, but the hearing children achieved the outcome by using the language of their adult caretakers as their model, whereas the deaf preschool children, being born to hearing parents who did not know sign language, developed their own arbitrary set of gestures to communicate meaningfully with peers and adults (Goldin-Meadow, 1997).

As a final example, in lines of mice selectively bred for high and low aggression, individuals in the low line become as aggressive as the high line if they are tested four times from day 28 to day 235 of life (Figure 1.1) (Cairns, MacCombie, & Hood, 1983). Once again, the developmental pathways to the same endpoint are different. ('Testing' involves placing a high- or low-line mouse in a small chamber with a mouse from an unselected line and observing, among other things, who attacks whom how many times in a given time period.)

However, in these mouse experiments, equifinality does not mean there is a genetic pathway in the high line and an experiential pathway in the low line: the expression of aggression is genetically and experientially mediated in both lines. The crucial experience in the developmental pathway to high aggression in the high line is rearing in social isolation between days 21 and 45, whereas the crucial experience in the developmental pathway to high aggression in the low line is repeated testing from days 28 to 235. This latter finding raises a significant question: would the usual line difference in aggression at day 45 be erased if the low line were repeatedly tested before day 45 rather than after day 45?

In any event, one suspects that if close attention were paid to the intervening processes that mediate the same developmental outcome, equifinality might be found to be ubiquitous, especially in human behavioral and psychological development.

SYSTEMS VERSUS MECHANICO-REDUCTIVE AND VITALISTIC-CONSTRUCTIVE VIEWPOINTS

As our overview of the precursors to our present concept of the systems nature of development moves from the late 1800s to the 1930s, we encounter the insights of the systems or organismic embryologists, Paul Weiss and Ludwig von Bertalanffy, and the physiological geneticist Sewall Wright.

In his wonderfully lucid and historically complete opus on the topic of development, *Modern theories of development: An introduction to theoretical biology* (originally published in German in 1933), von Bertalanffy (1962) introduced the system theory, as he called it, as a way of avoiding the pitfalls of machine theory, on the one hand, and vitalism, on the

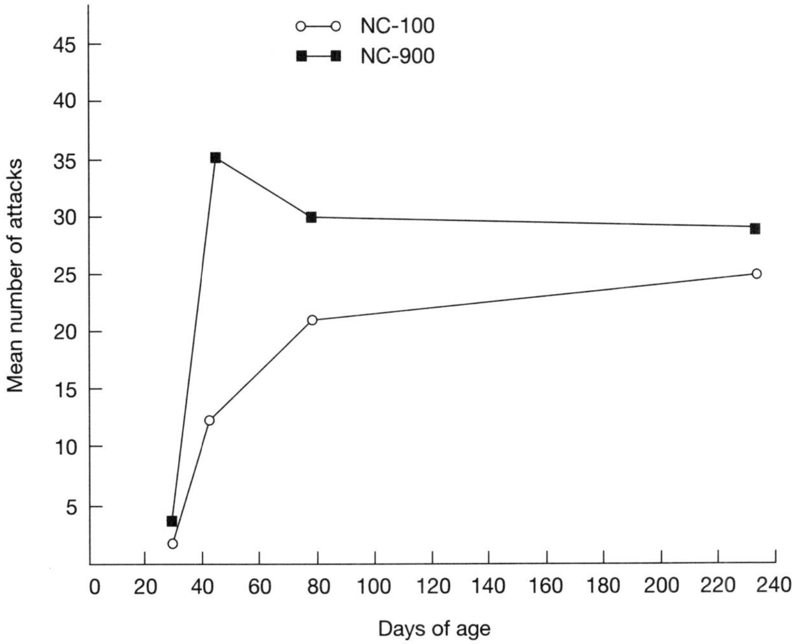

Figure 1.1 *Mean number of 5 second blocks in which subjects of the high-aggressive (NC-900) and low-aggressive (NC-100) lines attacked their test partners; the same subjects were repeatedly tested at days 28, 42, 72, and 235 (modified from Cairns, MacCombie, & Hood, 1983)*

other. The error of the machine theory of development, as von Bertalanffy saw it, was the attempt to analyze the various aspects of the development process into their individual component parts or mechanisms, conceived of as proceeding independently of one another. Von Bertalanffy believed that the fundamental error of the classical concept of mechanism, which was adopted wholesale from physics, lay in its application of an additive point of view to the interpretation of living organisms.

> Vitalism, on the other hand, while being at one with the machine theory in analyzing the vital processes into occurrences running along their separate lines, believed these to be coordinated by an immaterial, transcendent entelechy. Neither of these views is justified by the facts. We believe now that the solution of this antithesis in biology is to be sought in an *organismic* or *system theory* of the organism which, on the one hand, in opposition to machine theory, sees the essence of the organism in the harmony and coordination of the processes among one another, but, on the other hand, does not interpret this coordination as vitalism does, by means of a mystical entelechy, but through the forces immanent in the living system itself. (1962, pp. 177–178)

Nowadays, we make von Bertalanffy's point by distinguishing between theoretical and methodological reductionism. Theoretical reductionism seeks to explain the behavior of the whole organism by reference to its component parts – a derivative of the older additive, physical concept of mechanism – while methodological reductionism holds that not only is a description of the various hierarchically organized levels of analysis of the whole organism necessary but a depiction of the bidirectional traffic between levels is crucial to a developmental understanding of the individual.[2] For purposes of recognizing historical precedent, it is appropriate here to present the diagrams of Paul Weiss and Sewall Wright as they exemplify the strictly methodological reductionism of the hierarchically organized systems view of development. (I use what I hope is not an annoying plural form of system because the various levels of organismic functioning constitute within themselves systems of analysis: the organism–environment ecological system, the nervous system, the genomic system, for example. Von Bertalanffy himself later (1950) came to use the plural form in his conception of general systems theory.)

In Paul Weiss's (1959) diagram of the hierarchy of reciprocal influences, as shown in Figure 1.2, there are seven levels of analysis. The *gene* (DNA) is the ultimately reduced unit in an ever-expanding analytic pathway that moves from gene to *chromosome* – where genes can influence each other – from cell *nucleus* to cell *cytoplasm*, from cell to *tissue* (organized arrangements of cells that form organ systems – the nervous system, circulatory system, musculoskeletal system, etc.), all of which make

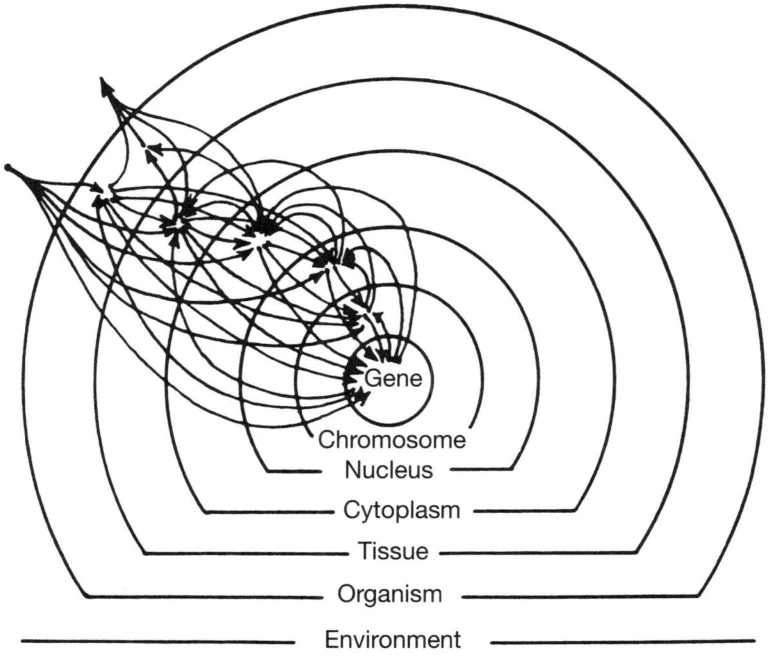

Figure 1.2 *Embryologist Paul Weiss's hierarchy of reciprocal influences from the lowest level of organization (gene) to the highest level (external environment) (from Weiss, 1959, copyright © 1959 by* Reviews of Modern Physics, *reprinted with permission)*

up the *organism* that interacts with the external *environment*. The entire schema represents a hierarchically organized system of increasing size, differentiation, and complexity, in which each component affects, and is affected by, all the other components, not only at its own level but at lower and higher levels as well. Thus, not only do the arrows in Figure 1.2 go upward from the gene, eventually reaching all the way to the external environment through the activities of the whole organism, but the arrows of influence return from the external environment through the various levels of the organism back to the genes.

While the feed-forward or feed-upward nature of the genes has always been appreciated, the feed-backward or feed-downward influences have usually been thought to stop at the cell membrane. The newer conception is one of a totally interrelated, fully coactional system in which the activity of the genes themselves can be affected through the cytoplasm of the cell by events originating at any other level in the system, including the external environment. It is known, for example, that external environmental factors such as social interactions, changing day length, and so on can cause hormones to be secreted (review by Cheng, 1979), and the hormones in turn result in the activation of DNA transcription inside the nucleus of the cell (i.e. 'turning genes on'). There are now many empirical examples of external sensory and internal neural events that excite and inhibit gene expression (e.g. Anokhin et al., 1991; Calamandrei & Keverne, 1994; Mauro et al., 1994; Rustak et al., 1990), thereby supporting the *bidirectionality* of influences among the various levels of analysis from gene to environment (to be discussed further below).

Weiss was an experimental embryologist, so it was probably merely an oversight that he did not explicitly include a developmental dimension in his figure. Another schematic of a systems view, also not explicitly developmental, was put forward by Sewall Wright in 1968. As shown in Wright's schema (Figure 1.3), once again, the traffic between levels is bidirectional and the activity of the genes is placed firmly inside a completely coactional system of influences. It is a small but important step to apply this way of thinking to the process of development (see Figure 1.4 later).

Before describing the concept of developmental causality and giving further examples of sensory influences on genetic activity, I would like to describe in a somewhat personal way my concept of the developmental manifold.

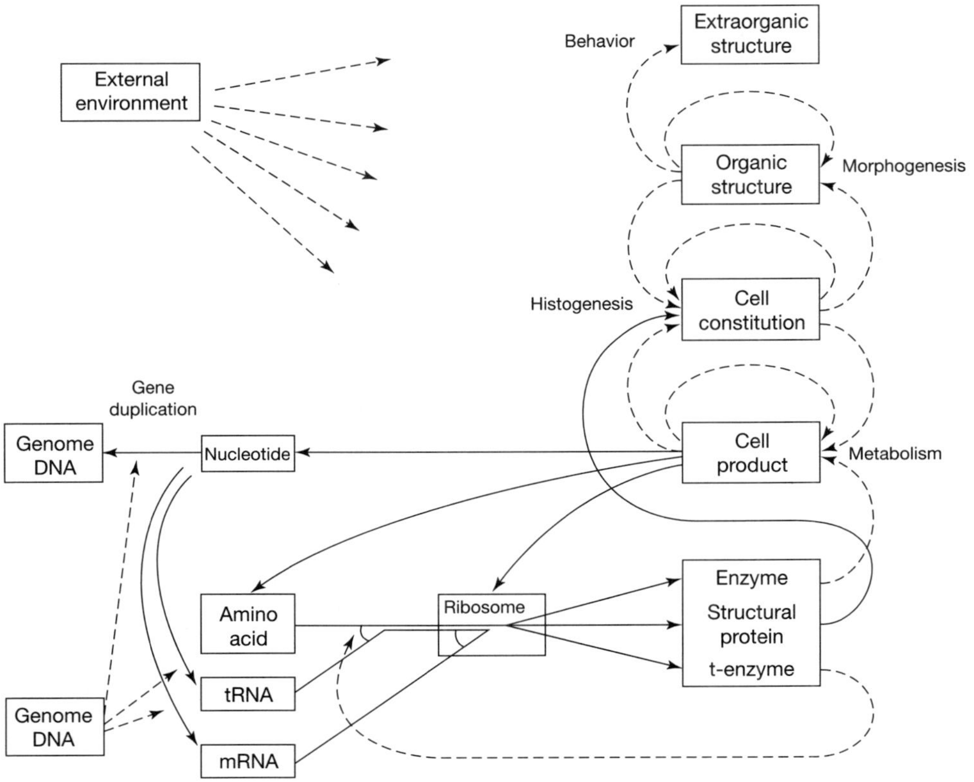

Figure 1.3 *The fully coactive or interactional organismic system, as presented by Sewall Wright, a physiologically oriented population geneticist (modified from Wright, 1968)*

The Developmental Manifold Concept

In 1971, my own research program with duck embryos and hatchlings paid off in what I believed to be a conceptually valuable way. (I hoped others would agree, but this agreement proved to be a rockier and longer road than I anticipated: Gottlieb, 1997.) In 1965, I had shown that ducklings and chicks hatched in incubators, and thus deprived of maternal contact, could nonetheless identify the maternal assembly call of their own species after hatching. The only vocal-auditory experience they had was exposure to their own and sib vocalizations prior to entering the test situation. In 1966, I was able to show that enhancing exposure to sib vocalizations lowered the latency and increased the duration of their behavioral response to their own species maternal call. However, it was necessary to devise an embryonic devocalization procedure to truly rule in the critical importance of the embryonic vocalizations in perfecting the perceptual selectivity of the response that was evident after hatching. With the help of John Vandenbergh, I was able to devise an embryonic muting operation that did not otherwise interfere with the health of the embryo and hatchling (Gottlieb & Vandenbergh, 1968). Now, the selectivity of the postnatal response to the species' maternal call could be examined in ducklings that had not experienced their own or sib vocalizations. Lo and behold, the devocalized mallard ducklings' usual auditory selectivity was not in place: they could not distinguish the mallard maternal call from the chicken maternal call. The control birds that had been allowed to hear their own embryonic vocalizations for 18–23 hours before being devocalized did show the usual preference for the mallard maternal call over the chicken maternal call (Gottlieb, 1971, pp. 141–142). This experiential influence is not attributable to any conventional or obvious form of learning because the embryonic and maternal calls have different primary acoustic features and do not sound at all alike to the human ear.

The outcome of these experiments led to the formulation of the developmental manifold concept.

> The present results indicate that the epigenesis of species-specific auditory perception is a probabilistic phenomenon, the threshold, timing, and ultimate perfection of such perception being regulated jointly by organismic and sensory stimulative factors. In the normal course of development, the manifest changes and improvements in species-specific perception do not represent merely the unfolding of a fixed or predetermined organic substrate independent of normally occurring sensory stimulation. With respect to the evolution of species-specific perception, natural selection would seem to have involved a selection for the entire developmental manifold, including both the organic and normally occurring stimulative features of ontogeny. (Gottlieb, 1971)

In 1987, West and King took the developmental manifold idea a step further by pointing out that, in addition to our genes, we inherit not only a fairly standard embryonic and fetal stimulative environment but also parents, peers, and the places they inhabit. They coined the term 'ontogenetic niche' to signify the species-typical ecological and social legacies that accompany genes. Thus, we inherit not only nature (genes) but also nurture (the usual prenatal and early postnatal environmental conditions that prevail in any given species).

A full understanding of the development (and evolution) of behavior will necessarily include genetic factors. Thus, from the beginning of my work in the early 1960s I was eager to include the genetic contribution and seized upon an early opportunity to collaborate with two neurologists, one of whom (George Paulson) was adept at brain dissection in birds and the other of whom (Stanley Appel) was running a laboratory in which protein synthesis in the nervous system was being studied. According to what was then already known, protein synthesis was the result of messenger RNA activity and mRNA activity was a consequence of DNA activity (DNA → mRNA → protein). So, protein synthesis could be used as an indirect measure of genetic activity. Accordingly, I prepared two groups of duck embryos for Paulson and Appel by exposing them for several days before hatching either to tape-recorded sib vocalizations or to extra visual stimulation by incubating them in a lighted incubator chamber. The control group was incubated in the dark and in acoustic isolation from other embryos. The point of the experiment was to look for enhanced protein synthesis in the auditory and visual parts of the brain in the treated groups.

Subsequently, Appel told us that both experimental groups showed an enhancement of protein synthesis in the synaptic regions of the brain stem, in which the auditory nucleii are located, and in the optic lobes of the brain, which mediate auditory as well as visual stimulation. This was a clear indication that the extra auditory and visual stimulation had enhanced gene expression in the embryo, meaning that genetic activity could be influenced by normally occurring exteroceptive sensory stimulation and thus result in an enhancement of neural maturation. The experiment was completed in 1965, and Paulson and I pleaded with Appel to complete the data analysis so we could share the results with interested colleagues by publishing them. Alas, overly hectic research, clinical, and other duties took precedence in Appel's life, so Paulson and I were frustrated in our desire to see this work to completion in the form of publication in a refereed journal. At the time there was only one other study in the literature implicating exteroceptive influences on genetic activity, a study involving the influence of vestibular-mediated learning on changes in nuclear RNA base ratios in vestibular nerve cells in rats (Hydèn & Egyhàzi, 1962). It was not until also found that the posterior brain region specialized for receptive language and semantic processing of words (Wernicke's area) is larger in those with more education, suggesting that exercise increases the size of the region. Of course, one could also construct an argument with the reversed causality, that an increased size in a particular brain region enables the specialized thinking associated with that region. In this case, more capacity in Wernicke's area would predispose the person to pursue more verbal pursuits such as higher education. The technology is now available to sort out this sort of causal quandary by means of human longitudinal studies.

The language areas mature later than the sensory and motor areas, but they do not grow as a single unit. There is also differentiation within the language areas themselves and this is reflected in the growth spurts and pruning schedules. In addition to differentiating cortical regions, we must also keep in mind that the cortex is made up of six layers of neurons, each layer serving a somewhat specialized function (see Figure 3.2). Layers four and five of both the anterior and posterior language regions are most involved in input and output of sounds and reach their plateau of connections between 6 and 24 months, after which thinning begins (Campbell & Whitaker, 1986). It is during this time that the baby normally begins to babble (at six to eight months) and by 10 months has started to acquire the accent of the familial language (Werker & Tees, 1984). By about two years, babies are starting to show some skill at verbal play, using words in a rote fashion without sophisticated grammar or full appreciation of the symbolic implications of words. By age three or four years, there is phenomenal word growth, and the child starts to use over 20 new words a day (Miller, 1981). At this age the child not only 'catches on' to what the language game is about but also has the building blocks of skills with which to take part. Interestingly, this is the period (four to six years) during which the topmost three layers of cortex in the language regions are growing fastest. These intracortical layers are specialized for communication within the region (Campbell & Whitaker, 1986), that is, they are solely involved in internal fine-tuning of information. While it is tempting to suggest that the various stages of language development occur because of the brain's growth spurts, without appropriate stimulation language cannot occur at all. Yet presumably it is also true that language development needs these appropriate brain growth spurts, and where one of the pair is lacking (e.g. in the adult language learner or in the linguistically deprived child), the process is never quite the same.

Late Frontal Lobe Maturation

Whereas there is some controversy concerning the extent to which the prefrontal cortex structurally matures later than other cortex, there seems to be consensus that this region matures later in some functional manner (Goldman-Rakic, Bourgeois, & Rakic, 1997; Huttenlocher & Dabholkar, 1997). Indeed, the controversy over whether frontal cortex increases in synaptic density later than other regions of the neocortex may come down to differences in the maturation rate of tissue in humans versus great apes.

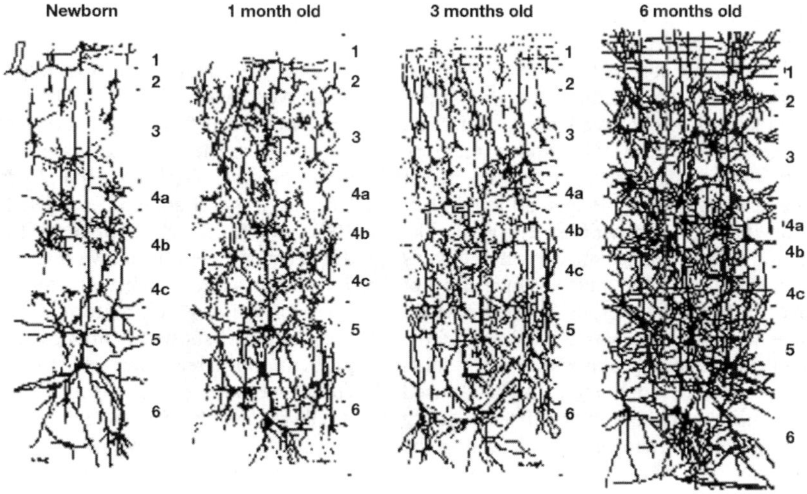

Figure 3.2 *Golgi stain preparations of visual cortex illustrating the multiple cortical layers and growth of neuronal processes in infancy (from Conel, 1939–67)*

In humans, this late frontal maturation applies to infancy and early childhood (Greenough, Black, & Wallace, 1987; Kolb & Fantie, 1989) and probably continues into adolescence and perhaps even young adulthood (Chugani, 1996; Kostovic et al., 1992; Stuss, 1992). For example, cerebral blood flow as measured by positron emission tomography (PET) is a reasonable reflection of synaptic activity. It rises after birth to adult levels by about 1 year, with the frontal region lagging slightly behind the posterior regions. However, cerebral blood flow continues to rise to almost double the normal adult level and then begins a dramatic reduction at about 8 years through the second decade after birth. Similarly, there is a thinning of the cortex (as shown on MRI) during adolescence (Jernigan & Tallal, 1990; Jernigan et al., 1991), especially in the dorsal (upper) frontal and parietal regions (Sowell et al., 1999), presumably due to the pruning process. Dopamine receptors, found in much of the cortex but especially in frontal lobe tissue, have also been shown (in rats) to dramatically reduce in number through adolescence (Andersen et al., 2000). Thus, it appears that there are greater than adult levels of connections, cerebral metabolism, and cortical thickness throughout adolescence. Synapse elimination during this period would be a reasonable mechanism for the dramatic increase in a wide variety of skills, with a gradual reduction in plasticity for most functions (Chugani, 1996).

Behavioral Inhibition, Self-Regulation, and Plasticity

While there may be controversy concerning the neurobiological evidence for the lateness of prefrontal cortex maturation, there is agreement that the prefrontal cortex and its connecting networks are critically involved in some of the functions that reflect maturation later in childhood and adolescence. In examining the functions associated with the dorsolateral prefrontal cortex, Goldman-Rakic and her colleagues demonstrated that adult monkeys with bilateral lesions of this area have considerable difficulty with certain types of working memory tasks. These tasks resembled some of the object permanence tasks devised by Piaget, although they were developed independently of Piaget's work. The interesting finding was that lesioned infant monkeys could do the task and their performance did not seem to be disturbed. However, the degree to which performance was affected was a function of the age at which the lesioning and testing was done. For example, Alexander and Goldman (1978) used a reversible paradigm that involved temporarily cooling the cortex, and showed that disabling the region temporarily incapacitated the memory function to a varying degree – none in infancy, some in childhood, and greatly in adolescence. Early lesioning, however, had an interesting developmental effect: The monkeys were kept in the lab after recovery from the surgery and, when tested at 24 to 36 months of age (adolescence in monkeys), they showed the performance loss that they did not show earlier! In other words, the animals had grown into the deficit (Goldman, 1974).

This 'sleeper effect' concept is now readily understood in terms of brain growth. Consider that the young brain does not rely on the frontal tissue for this function because the tissue itself is not properly connected yet, or because some other neurological functions need to be in place first (Goldberg & Bilder, 1987). Damage to this region will then have little effect. The reason we expect the effect of the damage to be minimal in infancy comes from a comparison of the effects of such lesions in adults. In infants the effect seems minor, and *we assume that the brain will show plasticity in development*, i.e. that whatever losses there are will be compensated for. This assumption of plasticity is pervasive in psychology and in our society. Sameroff and his colleagues articulated this notion as a 'self-righting' process or 'movement towards health', and espoused a continuity model where early events were explicitly not seen as having later effects unless some way of linking them over time could be specified (Sameroff & Chandler, 1975; Sameroff & Fiese, 2000). In their examples, children with early neglect or abuse are at risk later because the interactional repertoire first developed is counterproductive and is maintained as the world reacts to them as a negative influence, and they react back, continuing the cycle. This plasticity principle rests on the usually reasonable notion of the adaptive quality of growth: if the organism's growth is halted in one direction, then it will grow in some other direction. Growth implies taking advantage of new opportunities, with all the adaptability that this affords. However, the hidden assumption is also that all the necessary tools will be available for that growth. Goldman-Rakic's work shows that this assumption is not always warranted (Goldman, 1974).

Since Goldman-Rakic's studies on monkeys, much work has been done with children who have been victims of frontal lobe damage with a variety of etiologies. There are many fascinating case studies in this literature (Ackerly, 1986; Eslinger, Biddle, & Grattan, 1997; Grattan & Eslinger, 1992; Marlowe, 1992; Williams & Mateer, 1992). One well-documented case was of a woman who at the age of 7 years had surgery on her left frontal lobe to correct a congenital venous malformation. Even though she certainly showed some subsequent learning problems in school, her real psychological difficulties started at age 12, when puberty brought on its usual new agenda of social temptations, concerns and responsibilities. However, her mechanism for self-regulation and planning was awry. The difficulties she encountered appeared long after one would have expected recovery, and were considerably greater than the intervening psychological profile would have predicted (Grattan & Eslinger, 1992).

Another example comes from the United Kingdom. Two teenage boys, guilty of sociopathic delinquent behavior, were each reported to have acquired frontal lobe damage through a closed head injury at ages 4 and 6 years (Vargha-Khadem, Cowan, & Mishkin, 2000). Not only did they fail to show neural plasticity and recovery of function, their behavior deteriorated considerably. Without knowledge of the earlier brain injuries, we might be tempted to blame their unacceptable behavior on poor parenting or their peer group. But their problem was an inherent difficulty in self-monitoring and utilization of feedback that may only affect behavior seriously long after the lesion occurred. Two similar extreme American cases were documented in which young adults showed reasonable intelligence levels but high risk-taking and gross deficiencies in planning, empathy, and emotional self-regulation (Anderson et al., 1999). They had suffered serious frontal damage in infancy (in one case in a motor vehicle accident, and in the other due to surgery to remove a tumor) but both seemed to show immediate good recovery. Both families were stable, highly supportive and well educated. Yet by adolescence, both children had become unmanageable. These case studies reflect the more general association between antisocial personality disorder and loss of tissue in the prefrontal cortex (Devinsky, Morrell, & Vogt, 1995; Raine et al., 2000).

The implications of this model are considerable, since much of the difficulty in mapping out the causal relationships in child development center around the natural desire to leap from significant early events in the child's life to later outcomes, sometimes with an explanatory gap of years. Sometimes this is conceptualized as an early traumatic event influencing later psychological stability. While developmentalists are often at pains to uncover such influences that can affect a child's psychological maturation compared to peers, these may not be a new social situation or a new disease process, but rather a neurobiological one that was initiated much earlier. This process is unlike a 'slow virus' in that the mechanism is not one of pernicious activation long after the original event, but rather one of pernicious inactivity. The much-needed component in the module is lacking just when the growing brain needs it most.

Decentration

A major theme in all of cognitive development is what Piaget called decentration, the gradual loss of perceptually centered, egocentric thinking. There have been many ways of thinking about what leads to the child's growing ability to take more factors into account, or to see things from another perspective. These accounts involve building constructs about the process. Developments in cognitive neuroscience however have taken a different tack – partly dealing with constructs, but also just dealing with tissue. In a classic exposition on her position, Goldman-Rakic (1987) argues that certain sections of the prefrontal cortex are necessary for the representation (mental re-presentation) of experience, and that this is the basis for the development of working memory and ultimately for human cognition and problem solving. In this model, the prefrontal cortex has connections to posterior regions that code the actual sensory experiences involved in the memories, and these connections are necessary for the reactivation and maintenance of these memories. While there is some debate about the precise role of specific regions in the prefrontal cortex concerning the maintenance of thoughts in working memory versus the manipulation of information in working memory (D'Esposito et al., 1999; Pochon et al., 2001), there is consensus that there are cells in this region that are specialized for bridging thoughts across time in the absence of the original stimulus (Fuster, 1987; Hasegawa et al., 2000). It is natural then to suppose not only that these functions (of representation, anticipation, perspective-taking, etc.) grow because of experience, but also that they depend on the maturation of prefrontal cortex and the associated connections with that region.

An interesting newer application of the concept of decentration has been in the question of the basis for *theory of mind*, i.e. the child's coming to realize that others have a different perspective on the world. This function develops dramatically during early childhood and forms a major part of human interactions. It has also been recently shown to involve specifically medial prefrontal cortex (Gallagher et al., 2000). Autistic-spectrum individuals often show deficits on theory of mind tasks, and adults with Asperger's syndrome seem to have difficulty (compared to controls) in activating portions of the dorsolateral prefrontal cortex during a task that requires this perspective-taking (Happé et al., 1996). Much is being made of the richness of the constructs linked to the prefrontal cortex, and any theory of cognitive development will have to take the maturation and functioning of this region into account.

Exuberant Growth and Sensitivity to Experience

The notion that there is major brain maturation in early childhood accords well with what we know of changes in the child's functional capacity. In early infancy, there is considerable reorganization of primitive reflexes and this is reflected in the maturation of the electroencephalogram and in the increases in cortical glucose metabolism during this period (Chugani, 1994; 1996). Such increases in visual and sensory cortex correspond to improvements in visual and sensory integrative functions during the second and third month after birth (Bronson, 1974). This pattern of exuberant growth of neuronal processes followed by subsequent elimination extends over much of the period of dramatic cognitive growth in infancy, childhood and adolescence (Chugani, 1996). The advantage of such an extended dynamic growth period is increased sensitivity to the environmental factors that may shape the development, i.e. the child is sensitive to experience, allowing for structural changes in the brain to reflect influences of the experience even into complex thought processes. This may be the major hallmark of human development, and may separate us from other mammals.

An important aspect of the fine-tuning that experience has on brain structure is that the pruning is a marker of important advances in information processing. For example, primary auditory and visual sensory cortex reach maximal thickness with subsequent thinning during the middle of the first year after birth, and the electrocortical evoked potential matures in parallel with this change, at first rising in amplitude dramatically and then reducing to a reduced amplitude by the end of the first year (Vaughan & Kurtzberg, 1992). Failure to prune back connections in brain regions associated with conceptual and motor control appropriately during adolescence may be a source of a variety of developmental disabilities, such as ADHD (Andersen & Teicher, 2000) and schizophrenia (Hoffman & Dobscha, 1989). Sex differences in the pruning and growth processes may also be informative (Andersen & Teicher, 2000; De Bellis et al., 2001). With respect to ADHD, it is probably not the case that a simple biochemical trigger for pruning is missing in the affected child; rather, whatever conditions lead to the pruning process (so far unknown) are not properly set in place in the child with the disability. After all, the disability predates the obvious evidence of pruning in late childhood and adolescence. Since we are dealing here with a variety of unknown variables, we cannot know the extent of experiential influences on the pruning process. However, an important feature of the model of exuberant growth followed by experience-influenced pruning is that each individual develops uniquely.

The sculpting of the neural connections can be influenced by many factors. Panksepp (1998) has recently speculated that early rough-and-tumble play influences the maturation of frontal lobe systems that are responsible for impulse control, and cultural changes limiting such early play behavior are at the root of the increase in rates of ADHD. He shows in animals that rough-and-tumble play can serve as a mediator and therapy for impulse control (Panksepp, Burgdorf, & Gordon, in press). Whether these effects are due to dendritic pruning or changes in biochemical responses is not yet known, but either would support a model of experience altering some fundamental parameters of child development.

On the Dynamics of Brain Development in Normal and Abnormal Growth

It used to be very clear: genes direct brain growth, brain growth determines brain function, brain function determines psychological traits, state and potential. While these principles still hold, so do principles that move in the opposite direction (see Gottlieb, Chapter 1 in this volume). The challenge of developmental neuroscience is to delineate the mechanisms in both directions. Activity-driven growth certainly makes development complex, but such complexity is needed for the psychological development of the child.

The interplay between structure (dendritic growth, synaptogenesis, 'set points' of neurotransmitter and hormone levels, neuronal interconnections, growth of myelin, etc.) and function (communication among neurons, sensory input from the peripheral nervous system, modulation of the arousal system and its effects on experienced stress levels, etc.) is now known to be far too complex to be summarized by a flow of information in one direction only. The current challenge for developmental neuroscientists is to understand the parameters defining this interplay, and for developmental neuropsychologists to understand the implications of this interplay for the psychological growth and well-being of the child.

There has been the intuitive notion that the physical structure of the brain is dependent entirely on the development program outlined in the genome. We now know that this model of brain growth is far too simple, but it does naturally lead to the expectation that major functional characteristics of the brain, such as general intelligence, are highly constrained or even defined by the individual's genome. We do not have the space to go into the many ways in which this notion is wrong (see Elman et al., 1996; Greenough, Black, & Wallace, 1987; Johnson, 1997; Quartz & Sejnowski, 1997; Wachs, 2000) but we have given some examples and others are considered below. The variation in outcome after rehabilitation or treatment of developmental disabilities affords us examples of the mechanisms. For example, basic neural dysfunction may lead to experiential deprivation that in turn reduces opportunities to learn and to interact socially, which in turn prevent the development of strategies to overcome the original impairments, e.g. Munday and Crowson (1997) on autism and Brown and Pollitt (1996) on malnutrition and poverty. The success of early stimulation programs highlights the flexibility of the system. Such flexibility allows an initial impairment to lead to a serious disability and eventually a handicap (using the World Health Organization definitions of these terms) when untreated, but the same flexibility permits successful treatments too, especially for communication disorders (McLean & Cripe, 1997) and for cognitive functions in preterm infants (Brooks-Gunn, Liaw, & Klebanov, 1992). A prime example is the development of cognitive skills in deaf children, where the cognitive experience of language made available by the intervention of sign language affords enormous opportunities (Mayberry, in press) that the structure *per se* does not.

Top-Down Control

Since the 1960s, there have been many studies illustrating the now classic finding that activity is a necessity for the healthy development of the cortex, and that activity causes the cortical mantle to grow. There are many excellent reviews of this literature available (e.g. Diamond, 1988; Greenough, 1975; Rosenzweig & Bennett, 1996; Sur & Leamey, 2001), the main point of which is that mental and physical activity are major factors in the healthy robust growth of cortical tissue, and affect the connectivity of the cortex (Elbert et al., 1995). Gottlieb's (1976) insightful summary of some animal embryological work opened up to psychologists how the experience of function is critical for the development of physical structures. Only recently, however, has the technology of developmental neuroscience started to examine the mechanisms involved in activity-dependent growth (Thoenen, 1995).

The firing of neurons is a critical feature in their own growth, and accounts for the maintenance of synapses that might otherwise be withdrawn, or might even stimulate the growth of new synapses (Quartz & Sejnowski, 1997). For children to be directing their own mental growth, it would have to be shown that simply attending to one experience over others increases the neuronal activity in the brain region responsible for that experience (Singer, 1982). We now have such evidence. Thus, we can now say with confidence that *children's mental engagement furthers healthy maturation of the specific function in which the child is engaged.* Anyone working with children knows that at a functional level children spontaneously engage in challenging activities, and that this is probably a requirement for healthy mental growth. Indeed, Held and Hein (1963) showed many years ago that perceptual experience must be active to be an effective vehicle for learning. What is the nature of the newer evidence?

Attending Increases Neuronal Firing Selectively

Much of the work on attention-directing with humans involves visual stimuli for the simple reason that we know a great deal about the neural pathways for vision and manipulating spatial attention visually is easy. For example, cueing people to attend to one region of the visual field over another changes the activation of the visual cortex selectively and this is reflected in the scalp EEG. EEG alpha activity (a sign of reduced focal activation in the cortex) increases over the visual cortex corresponding to the to-be-ignored visual field even though the stimulus has not been presented yet (Worden et al., 2000). Similarly, when subjects are presented with a visual display containing both moving and stationary dots, the visual-movement region of the cortex (V5) either increases in activation or decreases depending on which set of dots is attended (see also Hopfinger, Buonocore, & Mangun, 2000; Macaluso, Frith, & Driver, 2000; O'Craven et al., 1997). Similarly, somatosensory cortex increases activation when a vibratory stimulus is attended to (Meyer et al., 1995). In this sense, practice makes perfect in that increased activation of a particular primary function fine-tunes the cortex at the most fundamental level, not just at the level of strategic planning; for example, practicing visual orientation identification improves coding in primary visual cortex even in adult brains (Schoups et al., 2001).

This alteration in the cortex may be mediated through the reward system: when a sound is followed by stimulation of dopamine neurons in the ventral tegmental area, a region activated by unexpected rewards and by novel stimuli, the cortical representation of that sound is increased, while the representation of nearby sound frequencies is reduced (Bao, Chan, & Merzenich, 2001). We are also starting to understand some of the details of this increased activation. Steinmetz et al. (2000) showed that attention synchronizes the neural firing (in somatosensory cortex) in monkeys, and the more challenging the task, the greater is the increase in synchronized firing. We will have to wait until the technology is developed to measure such neuronal coordination at the cellular level noninvasively to see whether children with attentional difficulties have problems with this particular mechanism, or whether this mechanism is one that requires maturation of the cortex and experience. Thus, circuits keep changing physically by growing connections, and the functioning of the brain alters the degree to which regions become activated, thereby feeding back on the growth pattern. With this neuronal growth model in mind, it is not surprising that early propensities lead to later talents. The system is built to take advantage of what experience has to offer to develop expertise in the world as it presents itself.

Brain Functions in Affective Development

The study of affective development has not been exempt from the controversies surrounding the study of cognitive development in the twentieth century. There are many similar threads in terms of history and ideas that exist between the view taken by developmentalists of affective and cognitive development. A major theme in the 20th century was the contrasting schools of thought that advocated a learning versus maturation approach. As with cognitive development, these two schools have given way to a third model of development, an interactionist approach which embodies the two former schools. We will start with a brief history of these three models in affective development.

Emotions as Innate, Universal, and Hard-Wired Phenomena

One view of affective development is firmly rooted in Darwinian (Darwin, 1872) thinking and the beliefs of the earlier functionalists such as James (1884) and Dewey (1894; 1895), namely, that emotions are innate, universal, and biologically programmed. The contemporary work of Izard (1971; 1994) is a good example of this point of view. Izard has shown that young infants exhibit the same pattern of facial expressions in response to distress and novelty independent of culture and learning. These patterns of facial expression are associated with distinct patterns of autonomic activity and are interpreted to reflect different underlying affective states. When an infant is distressed, there is an increase in heart rate and a constriction of the facial muscles; when an infant exhibits interest, there is a deceleration of heart rate and the facial muscles become more labile.

The development of fear is another example of how there may be a biologically preprogrammed time course for the emergence of particular emotions. Fear responses are routinely seen in children only after the second half of the first year. In a series of studies, Campos and his colleagues (Campos, Kermoian, & Zumbahlen, 1992) have shown quite convincingly that infants before 6 months of age will cross a visual cliff, but not at about 6–9 months. Campos and colleagues have also found that 9-month-old infants will not cross the cliff even if there is an incentive before them (i.e. the mother on the other end smiling and encouraging her baby to cross), suggesting that environmental input may not be able to modulate the infant's fear response. Campos and others speculate that in the second half of the first year of postnatal life a 'biological switch' is thrown that prevents the infant from crossing the visual cliff. The emergence of fear at this age may have important biological significance and evolutionarily adaptive value. The infant is beginning to walk and explore the environment and is likely therefore to encounter strangers and objects which may be harmful. The child's ability to experience and express fear may serve as a means by which to signal the caregiver of impending harm. Indeed, the emergence of stranger fear in infants around 9 months of age across cultures, and its coincidence with the onset of locomotion, suggest that the appearance of some emotions may be independent of learning, are preprogrammed and involve developmental maturation.

Emotions as Products of Learning

A second school of thinking on emotional development that contrasts with a maturation hypothesis is the learning model. The origins of this view date to early behaviorism and the influential studies of Watson (1925; Watson & Rayner, 1920). In the study of little Albert, Watson took a child who was not fearful of white furry objects and conditioned him to be so. Watson concluded that emotions, particularly fear, result from learning. This view, that infants at birth are like blank slates, dominated much of how emotional development and the treatment of disorders of emotion were seen during the twentieth century. A learning hypothesis regarding emotional development also serves as the foundation of attachment theory.

Attachment theory essentially proposes that mothers and primary caregivers influence how the child comes to view and understand his or her world (Ainsworth et al., 1978; Bowlby, 1969; 1973; 1980). The nature of the child's tie to mother and the nature of this early relationship set in motion the course of the child's social and emotional development and how subsequent peer and intimate relationships will be formed. Through learning, the child will begin to develop a sense of whether the world is a safe or a threatening place. For example, if babies cry when they are hungry and their basic needs are met, babies will develop a working model of the world as a safe place. If, on the other hand, their needs are not met, babies will come to view their world as an unsafe place. This working model of the world will then be borne out in terms of how they begin to form new relationships: infants will not trust others.

A number of developmentalists have attempted to instantiate Bowlby's theoretical claims empirically. Tronick, for example, suggests there exists a 'dance' between the mother and the child (Tronick & Giannino, 1987). If the dance is synchronized in a positive healthy manner (e.g. baby smiles, mother smiles back), the child will develop a working model of the world as a secure and safe place. In a series of studies, Tronick and his colleagues have utilized a still-face paradigm to measure infants' emotional responses to their mothers' behavior. When mothers present neutral facial expressions, the infant will soon begin to exhibit signs of distress and lose bodily control (e.g. begin to drool). These behavioral changes in the infant are yoked to the mother's behavior and taken to mean that environmental input is critical to the emergence of some emotions. Tronick and his colleagues propose that through this mother–child dance, children begin to learn which emotions to express in order to clue mother into their underlying feeling states. Furthermore, it is when this dance is synchronized that optimal social development occurs. Other child psychologists have used this theoretical framework and paradigm in an attempt to understand affective development in atypical populations.

In a series of studies, Field (1984; 1994) has noted that emotional development may be compromised in infants whose mothers are depressed. Depression is characterized by flattened affect and an inability to experience positive affect. One robust distinction between healthy and depressed mothers is in their facial expressions of affect. Mothers who are depressed tend not to exhibit facial expressions of positive affect. When depressed mothers were observed while interacting with their infants in the still-face paradigm, the infants tended to exhibit more signs of distress, irritability and negative affect compared with infants of healthy mothers. Recent studies have shown that these behavioral patterns are also paralleled by distinct physiological patterns. For example, infants of depressed mothers tend to exhibit a pattern of greater relative right frontal brain electrical activity (EEG) compared with infants of healthy mothers who exhibit greater relative left frontal EEG activity (Field et al., 1995). This pattern of greater relative right frontal EEG activity has also been found in adults who are depressed and anxious and may be reflective of an inability to regulate the experience of negative emotion (for a review see e.g. Davidson, 1993). Taken together, these data suggest that environmental input may significantly influence emotional responses in infants.

The notion that environmental input may influence emotional development has long been known from studies of animals. Animal work involving kindling suggests that deprivation and environmental insult can influence changes in brain chemistry and increase timidity and fear-related behavior. Schneider et al. (1998) found that nonhuman primates prenatally exposed to stress showed lasting influence on noradrenergic and dopaminergic activity for as long as 15 years; such animals were more jittery and startled more easily. There is in addition a wealth of data demonstrating that socially isolated nonhuman primates exhibit disturbances in endocrine activity, social behavior and later withdrawal (see Suomi, 1991, for a review). Human post-traumatic stress disorder studies also show the powerful influence that stress can have in altering brain physiology and possibly structure, and also emotional behavior (Yehuda et al., 1994).

Interactionist Approaches to Emotional Development

Researchers who subscribe to an interactional approach to development proffer that it is a combination of genetic blueprinting and environmental factors that influences development and developmental change. This belief provides the major theoretical platform today for how we view emotional development.

Developmental neuroscience has typically focused on easily measurable factors in development, especially vision, audition, and movement. However, human psychological development concerns much more, especially in the development of emotional and arousal self-control. Although there is well-documented evidence from converging sources including behavioral genetics studies, molecular genetics studies and animal studies to suggest that there may be a genetic contribution to systems (e.g. arousal and self-regulatory systems) that underlie affective development (for an extensive review see C.P. Schmidt, Polak, & Spooner, 2001), these genetic contributions are only actualized via the influence of particular social environments. Social interaction and affective arousal alter catecholamine levels, and engage the sympathetic nervous system. The role of the caregiver for the developing young child is to regulate these, by reducing overarousal, soothing negative affect, and increasing attentional engagement to objects in the environment, including other people. Presumably during this early period of considerable neural growth, plasticity and vulnerability, these systems can reach a more healthy or less healthy stasis. Reducing anxiety from an unacceptable level, or alternatively increasing excitement and arousal to an acceptable level, is a major responsibility. A lack of involvement or insensitive intrusiveness, such as happens sometimes with depressed mothers, can presumably alter the neural response in the child (e.g. Dawson et al., 1992). Without appropriate external stimulation and modulation, it is not clear how well a child can develop affective self-regulation. We do not know whether the affective system requires a relatively small amount of stable and healthy attachment to facilitate adequate emotional self-regulation or whether its healthy development can tolerate relatively large amounts of instability. However, the literature on emotional resiliency suggests that some children are capable of making do with amazingly small pockets of stability and emotional guidance in an otherwise neglectful context (Werner, 2000).

As can be seen in Figure 3.3, heightened levels of chronic stress can have deleterious effects on the central nervous system. The stress response involves altered activation of the hypothalamic–pituitary–adrenocortical system, resulting in increased levels of the catecholamine neurotransmitters dopamine and noradrenaline, and subsequently of ACTH and cortisol. While normal, everyday challenges may be beneficial for the development of the HPA system, what has been documented are the deleterious effects of chronic heightened stress. Such stress can be brought about by either neglect or abuse, with the result of either dampened HPA responsiveness or

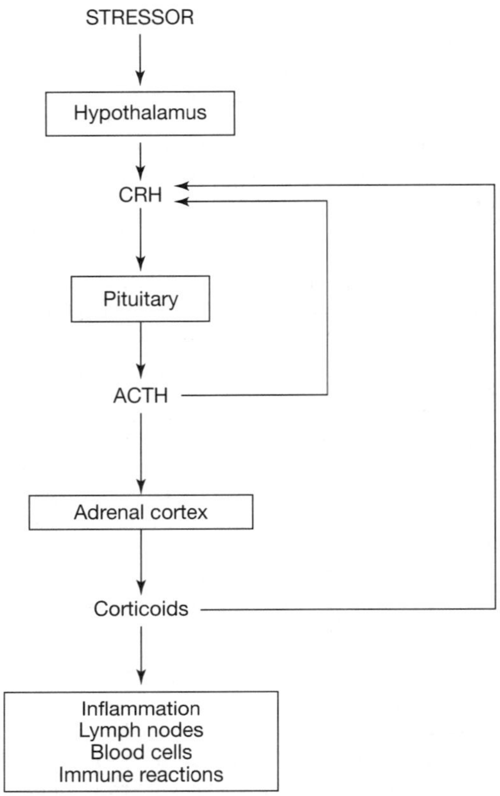

Figure 3.3 *HPA axis and stress–reactivity model (adapted from Goldberger & Breznitz, 1982)*

inappropriately heightened stress response, depending on a variety of complex factors (for summaries of the complexities, see Glaser, 2000; Gunnar, 1998). Inappropriately high levels of dopamine and noradrenaline are associated with dysfunction of the prefrontal cortex, a region acutely involved in emotional self-regulation (Arnsten, 1999; Schore, 1994). Of course, individual infants will differ in the amount of stress response shown, and their caregivers will vary in their proficiency in soothing. In this way, individual differences naturally arise not only from congenital variations in central nervous system structure, but also from the complexity of experiences during infancy. Such effects have been demonstrated in primates experiencing prenatal stress (Schneider et al., 1998).

Another implication of high levels of stress during infancy is the effect of cortisol on various aspects of nervous system function. High levels of cortisol have documented effects on the immune response, and more importantly for the discussion here, on the growth of the hippocampus (Sapolsky, 1996). High levels of cortisol (whether achieved through chronic stressors or through medication) atrophies hippocampal connections, although this is reversible if the levels are reduced. Survivors of severe childhood abuse show reduced hippocampal size, and this is associated with diagnosis of post-traumatic stress disorder (PTSD) (Bremner et al., 1997). Interestingly, the reduced hippocampal size may be a response that only appears later, in adulthood (De Bellis et al., 1999), and therefore may be linked to the normal generation of new cells in that region, which in these cases would be reduced.

Perry et al. (1994) have also demonstrated that children with post-traumatic stress disorder have overactive sympathetic nervous system responses, including raised heart rate which has been linked to lowered vagal tone, and inhibited social communication (Porges, 1995). Of even more concern is the report that boys who experienced severe neglect (with or without abuse) before age 3 also had lowered plasma levels of dopamine beta hydroxylase, which was correlated with reduced valuation of authority and rules of conscience (Galvin et al., 1997). The authors suggest that this represents a reduced development of the behavioral inhibition system, which is associated of course with the prefrontal cortex. Similarly, such children show signs of hypervigilance and hyperactivity, with heightened readiness to respond to perceived threats (Perry et al., 1995), traits that may be symptomatic of a reduced efficiency of the behavioural inhibition system (Koenen et al., 2001). Similarly, in a series of maltreated children and adolescents, brain size correlated with age of onset of the abuse and negatively with its duration, while tissue loss (ventricular size) correlated with intrusive thoughts, hyperarousal and dissociation (De Bellis et al., 1999).

A particularly interesting source of data concerns the brain responses of infants with depressed mothers. Activation patterns that represent affective valence appear to be reversed (Dawson et al., 1992) or at least altered in a major way (Dawson et al., 1999). Rather than showing a relatively greater EEG activation of the left frontal lobe relative to the right during interactions with the mother, these infants show the opposite, primarily because of a reduced left frontal activation. Right frontal EEG activation has been associated with negative affect and withdrawal tendencies, the left activation with positive valences and approach (Davidson, 1993). While it is not clear that the cortical organization for affect is altered in infants of depressed mothers, the heightened levels of activation would presumably have long-term effects on the connectivity patterns, i.e. they may grow to have a predisposition for depression which is not genetically transmitted yet is biologically transferred through activation patterns.

Today, and in the coming decades, the distinctions between maturational and learning hypotheses will be seen largely as academic. Most have now come to view the development of affective processes as resulting from a complex interaction of genes, biological context, and environmental influences. It is this integration that is now so evident in the emergence of new disciplines such as social and affective neuroscience which embody the notion that affective development results from the interplay between biology and experience.

Is the Brain Open to Change in Affective Development?

While historical accounts such as Freud's writings and Spitz's work with children who were orphaned suggested that personality was fixed by the age of six, recent neuroscience data appear inconsistent with this view, before and after the early school age years. Indeed, the idea that the affective system is open to change appears to be more the rule than the exception. Brain systems involved in affective processes are highly plastic during early postnatal life and beyond. Work by Meaney and his colleagues (Francis et al., 1999) noted that in rats, mothers licking their pups can influence the HPA system and behavior responses to stress. Studies by Kolb and his colleagues (for a review see Kolb et al., 1998) noted that brushing rat pups stimulates neural growth and behavioral changes in early postnatal development. Using this animal analog, Field (1984; 1994) has noted that touch therapy can contribute to positive emotional health in children born prematurely or born to cocaine-addicted mothers. Still many other studies have noted depression and then resiliency following traumas such as parental suicide, exposure to violence, non-normative events, natural disasters, and parental divorce (McFarlane, 1988; Quinton & Rutter, 1975; Saylor, 1993; Schaffer, 1998; Shepherd & Barraclough, 1976). Taken together, these data suggest that the affect system is open to considerable change, at least in early periods. An important challenge for the future is to chart the extent to which this system is flexible in later development. While no one doubts that emotional stability can be altered through major experiences (positively and negatively), it remains to be seen whether the same physiological systems are involved in change in later stages of development.

What Accounts for Change in Affective Development?

It is entirely reasonable to speculate that the plasticity which we observe in the affective system is due primarily to changes in cortical structure and function. The frontal cortex is known to play an important role in the regulation and expression of emotion. Many of the subcortical areas of the brain implicated in emotion, the forebrain limbic and brainstem areas involved in the regulation of autonomic function, are brain centers that are also important for the regulation of systemic physiology and such things as sleep/wake cycles, breathing and basic drive states. Damage to these areas typically results in the loss of function of these basic motivational systems and sometimes death.

Individual Differences in Resilience and Regulation of Stress

One way to examine whether there are individual differences in who might and might not be predisposed to stress is to examine individual differences in cortical brain mechanisms which appear to be a well-established locus for such individual differences. One popular measure of dynamic cortical brain activity is the EEG, which tells us something about the electrical activity of brain processes and their temporal resolution. It is a non-invasive measure affording use with infants and children and is relatively inexpensive.

Although frontal EEG measures have been used widely in studying emotional states in adults, few studies have used such measures in order to understand emotional processes in children. We are just beginning to explore fundamental questions posed by brain-based measures used to study affective processes in children: for example, (1) are measures of brain activity stable during development or do they change? (2) To what extent is alteration in brain activity reflected in behavioral and psychological change? (3) What is the causal relation between brain activity and affective processes? We are now in a position to attempt to answer some of these questions.

What Changes in Brain Electrical Activity Parallel Affective Changes?

A large literature has emerged over the last two decades that suggests that the pattern of frontal EEG asymmetry may reflect individual differences in affective style. For example, individuals who exhibit a pattern of relatively greater right frontal EEG activity during baseline conditions are likely to be anxious, shy, and depressed, while individuals who exhibit a pattern of relatively greater left frontal EEG activity during baseline conditions are likely to be sociable, outgoing, and extraverted (Schmidt, 1999). These EEG patterns and their relation to personality have been consistently found in adults and children during awake and conscious states. A fundamental issue needs to be considered: if the pattern of frontal EEG activity is to be considered a trait, in the usual sense of the term, there should be stability in measurement over time and across situations. The psychometric properties of frontal EEG activity in relation to temperament have recently begun to be explored in the literature and will have important implications for the study of brain development and emotional processes.

One study noted high stability in total frontal EEG power over time but modest stability in frontal EEG asymmetry measures over a three week time period (Davidson, 1993). Still other studies have noted that individuals who exhibit a stable pattern of high right frontal EEG activity over three weeks are likely to judge unpleasant film clips more negatively than those who exhibited an unstable right hemisphere pattern or stable high left frontal EEG activation. In another study, Schmidt and Tasker (2000) examined second-by-second stability of frontal EEG asymmetry in relation to individual differences in infant temperament. He collected 30 seconds of baseline frontal EEG activity and divided the 9-month-old subjects into three groups based upon the distributional characteristics of the asymmetry scores. The first group comprised infants whose mean EEG asymmetry showed greater right frontal activity with low variance, that is, infants in this group exhibited a stable pattern of higher right frontal EEG activity and little change. The second group comprised infants whose mean frontal EEG asymmetry score showed greater left frontal activity and whose variance was low. A third group comprised infants whose mean asymmetry score was around zero and whose variance was high. Schmidt then noted that the three groups were different in temperament and heart rate. The first group of infants exhibited significantly more distress to novelty as indexed by maternal report and had a higher resting heart rate compared with infants in the other two groups. Thus, studies with both adults and infants suggest that frontal EEG asymmetry may be stable and reflective of temperament. One question then becomes, can change in the pattern of frontal EEG activity tell us anything about emotional development? Further, does the pattern of change reflect innate developmental processes or is it due to alterations in an individual's environment? Such questions are important to other issues being raised in development, such as behavioral plasticity. Recent studies have begun to address these questions in research on personality in childhood.

Temperamental Inhibition

Temperamental inhibition is a construct that has received much attention over the past two decades due largely to the work of Kagan and his colleagues (Garcia-Coll, Kagan, & Resnick, 1984; Kagan, 1994). Temperamental inhibition reflects behavioral and physiological reactions to unfamiliarity. Children who display a long latency to approach novel social and nonsocial stimuli remain in close proximity to their mothers. They exhibit a high degree of distress in response to these stimuli and have been classified as behaviorally inhibited. Approximately 5–10% of healthy children exhibit such reactions to novelty and these children also display a number of distinct physiological and endocrine reactions during resting conditions and in response to stress, including greater right frontal EEG activity, high heart rate with little natural variability, and high cortisol levels. Some of these children develop shyness and internalizing problems during the preschool and early school age years (Hirshfeld et al., 1992). Some researchers have begun to investigate the degree of stability and change in temperamental inhibition in children and whether such behavioral change is paralleled by changes in physiological activity. We have recently found that children who remain behaviorally inhibited from 9 to 24 months of age are likely to exhibit a stable pattern of greater relative right frontal EEG activity compared with those who change from inhibited to uninhibited. Those children whose temperamental profile changed over this time span also showed change in their pattern of frontal brain electrical activity. These children switch from a pattern of greater relative right frontal EEG activity at 9 months to a pattern of greater relative left frontal EEG activity at 24 months. These findings suggest that temperamental inhibition and the pattern of frontal brain activity are not fixed but open to change. What the factors are that contribute to this change are still under consideration. It is reasonable to speculate though that the children whose temperamental profile changed from inhibited to uninhibited may have had parents and caregivers who noticed their children's inhibition and intervened, thus nurturing the needs of the children. These kinds of questions about how brain changes map onto changes in emotional regulatory styles during development and about which factors influence these changes are next on the research agenda. The ideas of Allport (1937) and Murray (1938) in the 1930s in which they posited that personality processes are linked to frontal lobe processes, which hitherto were only speculative, may now be explored.

CONCLUSIONS

It has often been pointed out that there have been three psychological jolts in western civilization that have forced our cultures from egocentrism. The first was the discovery that the Earth is not the centre of the universe, ushered in by Copernicus', Kepler's and Galileo's models of the solar system. The second was Darwin's articulation that humans are not divinely created but rather share much with the rest of the animal kingdom. The third was Freud's popularization of how we do not even clearly know our own minds. As we move ahead, developmental psychology is being heavily influenced by advances in neuroscience, leading to a fourth insight: that we cannot shape our minds as we would like because our minds are constrained by factors inherent in the central nervous system, and that we must recognize as immodesty the notion that we can construct ourselves without recognizing underlying biological principles. However, rather than seeing this as necessarily a depressing limitation on our growth and development, we can instead view it as both liberating and expanding. In this chapter, we have provided an overview of both of these perspectives. While we see both cognitive and affective development – the mainstay of developmental psychology – as having interesting parameters being set by neurological factors, new discoveries in developmental neuroscience also highlight the plasticity and adaptability of the system. Patterns of development are both biologically rooted in our brains and heavily influenced by experience, and the biological influences are manifested through experience. Indeed, developmental neuroscience is revealing an amazingly dynamic world in the growth of the child's mind and brain. We have outlined some of the history of these new insights, and their application to issues in child development, starting with cognitive and then affective processes. Discoveries and new technologies are evolving so rapidly that we can only speculate at this point as to which of the current thrusts will continue as the field rapidly develops.

Notes

1 We are using this term as a short-hand for developmental child psychology. While there is a considerable literature on adult developmental neuropsychology, we will restrict ourselves in this context to the period leading up to the end of adolescence. The term 'developmental' refers to all processes that lead to central nervous system change in the organism, whether the influence stems from the biological side (e.g. genetic, hormonal, nutritional) or the psychological side (e.g. perceptual, emotional, cognitive, motor). A neuroscience approach to development does not, in the final analysis, separate biological and psychological factors since all psychological states must have some instantiation in the brain. Some may be short-lived, like remembering someone's name for a moment, and some may be longer-lasting, like a changed anxiety reaction due to constant stress. This leads to less of a distinction among the constructs of learning, plasticity and development in neuroscience than it may in other fields (Stiles, 2000).

References

Ackerly, S.S. (1986). A case of paranatal bilateral frontal lobe defect observed for thirty years. In J.M. Warren & K. Ackert (eds), *The frontal granular cortex and behavior* (pp. 192–218). New York: McGraw-Hill.

Ainsworth, M.D., Blehar, M., Waters, E., & Wall, S. (1978). *Patterns of attachment: A psychological study of the Strange Situation*. Hillsdale, NJ: Erlbaum.

Alexander, G.E., & Goldman, P.S. (1978). Functional development of the dorsolateral prefrontal cortex: An analysis utilizing reversible cryogenic depression. *Brain Research*, 143, 233–249.

Allport, G.W. (1937). *Personality: A psychological interpretation*. London: Constable.

Andersen, S.L., & Teicher, M.H. (2000). Sex differences in dopamine receptors and their relevance to ADHD. *Neuroscience and Biobehavioral Reviews*, 24 (1), 137–141.

Andersen, S.L., Thompson, A.T., Rutstein, M., Hostetter, J.C., & Teicher, M.H. (2000). Dopamine receptor pruning in prefrontal cortex during the periadolescent period in rats. *Synapse*, 37, 167–169.

Anderson, S.W., Bechara, A., Damasio, H., Tranel, D., & Damasio, A.R. (1999). Impairment of social and moral behavior related to early damage in human prefrontal cortex. *Nature Neuroscience*, 2 (11), 1032–1037.

Arnsten, A.F.T. (1999). Development of the cerebral cortex: XIV. Stress impairs prefrontal cortical function. *Journal of the American Academy of Child and Adolecent Psychiatry*, 38 (2), 220–222.

Bao, S., Chan, V.T., & Merzenich, M.M. (2001). Cortical remodelling induced by activity of ventral tegmental dopamine neurons. *Nature*, 412, 5 July, 79–83.

Bartzokis, G., Beckson, M., Lu, P.H., Nuechterlein K.H., Edwards, N., & Mintz, J. (2001). Age-related changes in frontal and temporal lobe volumes in men. *Archives of General Psychiatry*, 58, 461–465.

Best, C.T. (1988). The emergence of cerebral asymmetries in early human development: A literature review and a neuroembryological model. In D.L. Molfese & S.J. Segalowitz (eds), *Brain lateralization in children: Developmental implications* (pp. 5–34). New York: Guilford.

Blakemore, C. (1991). Sensitive and vulnerable periods in the development of the visual system. *Ciba Foundation Symposium*, 156, 129–147.

Bowlby, J. (1969). *Attachment and loss: Vol. 1. Attachment*. New York: Basic.

Bowlby, J. (1973). *Attachment and loss: Vol. 2. Separation: Anxiety and anger*. New York: Basic.

Bowlby, J. (1980). *Attachment and loss: Vol. 3 Loss: Sadness and depression*. New York: Basic.

Bremner, J.D., Randall, P., Vermetten, E., Staib, L., Bronen, R.A., Mazure, C., Capelli, S., McCarthy, G., Innis, R.B., & Charney, D.S. (1997). Magnetic resonance imaging-based measurement of hippocampal volume in posttraumatic stress disorder related to childhood physical and sexual abuse: A preliminary report. *Biological Psychiatry*, 41 (1), 23–32.

Bronson, G. (1974). The postnatal growth of visual capacity. *Child Development*, 45, 873–890.

Brooks-Gunn, J., Liaw, F.R., & Klebanov, P.K. (1992). Effects of early intervention on cognitive function of low birth weight preterm infants. *Journal of Pediatrics*, 120, 350–359.

Brown, J. L., & Pollitt, E. (1996). Malnutrition, poverty and intellectual development. *Scientific American*, 274 (February), 38–43.

Burke, H.L., & Yeo, R.A. (1994). Systematic variations in callosal morphology: The effects of age, gender, hand preference, and anatomic asymmetry. *Neuropsychology*, 8 (4), 563–571.

Campbell, S., & Whitaker, H. (1986). Child maturation and developmental neurolinguistics. In J. Obrzut & G. Hynd (eds), *Child neuropsychology* (Vol. 1, pp. 55–70). New York: Academic.

Campos, J.J., Kermoian, R., & Zumbahlen, M.R. (1992). Socioemotional transformations in the family system following infant crawling onset. In N. Eisenberg & R.A. Fabes (eds), *Emotion and its regulation in early development*. San Francisco: Jossey-Bass.

Chapman, B., Godecke, I., & Bonhoeffer, T. (1999). Development of orientation preference in the mammalian visual cortex. *Journal of Neurobiology*, 41 (1), 18–24.

Chomsky, N. (1963). Formal properties of grammars. In R. Luce, R. Bush, & E. Galanter (eds), *Handbook of mathematical psychology* (Vol. 2, pp. 323–418). New York: Wiley.

Chomsky, N. (1965). *Aspects of the theory of syntax*. Cambridge, MA: MIT Press.

Chugani, H.T. (1994). Development of regional brain cludcose metabolism in relation to behavior and plasticity. In G. Dawson & K.W. Fischer (eds), *Human behavior and the developing brain* (pp. 153–175). New York: Guilford.

Chugani, H.T. (1996). Neuroimaging of developmental nonlinearity and developmental pathologies. In T.W. Thatcher, G.R. Lyon, J. Rumsey, & N. Krasnegor (eds), *Developmental neuroimaging* (pp. 187–195). San Diego: Academic.

Conel, J.L. (1939–67). *The postnatal development of the human cerebral cortex*. Cambridge, MA: Harvard.

Cowan, W.M., Fawcett, J.W., O'Leary, D.D.M., & Stanfield, B.B. (1984). Regressive events in neurogenesis. *Science*, 225, 1258–1265.

Darwin, C. (1872). *The expression of the emotions in man and animals*. Reprint, Chicago: University of Chicago Press, 1965.

Davidson, R.J. (1993). Cerebral asymmetry and emotion: Conceptual and methodological conundrums. *Cognition and Emotion*, 7 (1), 115–138.

Daw, N. (1995). *Visual development*. New York: Plenum.

Dawson, G., & Fischer, K.W. (eds) (1994). *Human behavior and the developing brain*. New York: Guilford.

Dawson, G., Frey, K., Self, J., Panagiotides, H., Hessl, D., Yamada, E., & Rinaldi, J. (1999). Frontal brain electrical activity in infants of depressed and nondepressed mothers: Relation to variations in infant behavior. *Development & Psychopathology*, 11 (3), 589–605.

Dawson, G., Panagiotides, H., Klinger, L.G., & Hill, D. (1992). The role of frontal lobe functioning in the development of infant self-regulatory behavior. *Brain and Cognition*, 20 (1), 152–175.

De Bellis, M.D., Keshavan, M.S., Beers, S.R., Hall, J., Frustaci, K., Masalehdan, A., Noll, J., & Boring, A.M. (2001). Sex differences in brain maturation during childhood and adolescence. *Cerebral Cortex*, 11 (6), 552–557.

De Bellis, M.D., Keshavan, M.S., Clark, D.B., Casey, B.J., Giedd, J.N., Boring, A.M., Frustaci, K., & Ryan, N.D. (1999). Developmental traumatology: Part II. Brain development. *Biological Psychiatry*, 45, 1271–1284.

DeCrinis, M. (1932). Die Entwicklung der Grosshirnrinde nach der Geburt in ihren Beziehungen zur intellektuellen Ausreifung dese Kindes. *Wiener Klinische Wochenschrift*, 45, 1161–1165.

D'Esposito, M., Postle, B.R., Ballard, D., & Lease, J. (1999). Maintenance versus manipulation of information held in working memory: An event-related fMRI study. *Brain and Cognition*, 41 (1), 66–86.

Devinsky, O., Morrell, M.J., & Vogt, B.A. (1995). Contributions of anterior cingulate cortex to behaviour. *Brain*, 118, 279–306.

Dewey, J. (1894). The theory of emotions: I. Emotional attitudes. *Psychological Review*, 1, 553–569.

Dewey, J. (1895). The theory of the emotions: II. The significance of the emotions. *Psychological Review*, 2, 13–32.

Diamond, A. (1990). The development and neural bases of higher cognitive functions. *Annals of the New York Academy of Sciences*, 608, 1–749.

Diamond, M.C. (1988). *Enriching heredity: The impact of the environment on the anatomy of the brain*. New York: Free Press.

Diamond, M.C., Scheibel, A.B., Murphy, G.M.J., & Harvey, T. (1985). On the brain of a scientist: Albert Einstein. *Experimental Neurology*, 88 (1), 198–204.

Driesen, N.R., & Raz, N. (1995). The influence of sex, age, and handedness on corpus callosum morphology: A meta-analysis. *Psychobiology*, 23 (3), 240–247.

Dronkers, N.F., Redfern, B.B., & Knight, R.T. (2000). The neural architecture of language disorders. In M.S. Gazzaniga (ed.), *The new cognitive neurosciences* (2nd edn, pp. 65–71). Cambridge, MA: MIT Press.

Elbert, T., Pantev, C., Wienbruch, C., Rockstroh, B., & Taub, E. (1995). Increased cortical representation of the fingers of the left hand in string players. *Science*, 270, 305–307.

Ellemberg, D., Lewis, T.L., Liu, C.H., & Maurer, D. (1999). The development of spatial and temporal vision during childhood. *Vision Research*, 39, 2325–2333.

Elman, J.L., Bates, E.A., Johnson, M.H., Karmiloff-Smith, A., Parisi, D., & Plunkett, K. (1996). *Rethinking innateness: A connectionist perspective on development*. Cambridge, MA: MIT Press.

Eslinger, P.J., Biddle, K.R., & Grattan, L.M. (1997). Cognitive and social development in children with prefrontal cortex lesions. In N.A. Krasnegor, G.R. Lyon, & P. Goldman-Rakic (eds), *Development of the prefrontal cortex* (pp. 295–335). Baltimore: Brookes.

Field, T. (1984). Early interactions between infants and their post-partum depressed mothers. *Infant Behavior and Development*, 7, 517–522.

Field, T. (1994). The effects of mother's physical and emotional unavailability on emotion regulation. In N. Fox (ed.), *The development of emotion regulation: Biological and behavioral considerations. With commentary by Joseph J. Campos et al.* (pp. 208–227). *Monographs of the Society for Research in Child Development*, Vol. 59, nos 2–3, serial 240.

Field, T., Fox, N.A., Pickens, J., & Nawrocki, T. (1995). Relative right frontal EEG activation in 3- to 6-month-old infants of 'depressed' mothers. *Developmental Psychology*, 31 (3), 358–363.

Filipek, P.A. (1999). Neuroimaging in the developmental disorders: The state of the science. *Journal of Child Psychology of Psychiatry*, 40 (1), 113–128.

Francis, D., Diorio, J., Liu, D., & Meaney, M.J. (1999). Nongenomic transmission across generations of maternal behaviour and stress responses in the rat. *Science*, 286 (5), 1155–1158.

Freeman, R., & Thibos, L. (1973). Electrophysiological evidence that abnormal early visual experience can modify the human brain. *Science*, 180, 876–878.

Frost, D.O. (1990). Sensory processing by novel, experimentally induced cross-modal circuits. *Annals of the New York Academy of Sciences*, 608, 92–112.

Fuster, J.M. (1987). Single-unit studies of the prefrontal cortex. In E. Perecman (ed.), *The frontal lobes revisited* (pp. 109–120). New York: IRBN Press.

Gallagher, H.L., Happé, F., Brunswick, N., Fletcher, P.C., Frith, U., & Frith, C.D. (2000). Reading the mind in cartoons and stories: an fMRI study of 'theory of mind' in verbal and nonverbal tasks. *Neuropsychologia*, 38, 11–21.

Galvin, M.R., Stilwell, B.M., Shekhar, A., Kopta, S.M., & Goldbarb, S.M. (1997). Maltreatment, conscience functioning and dopamine beta hydroxylase in emotionally disturbed boys. *Child Abuse & Neglect*, 21 (1), 83–92.

Garcia-Coll, C., Kagan, J., & Resnick, J.S. (1984). Behavioral inhibition in young children. *Child Development*, 55, 1005–1019.

Gardner, H. (1983). *Frames of mind*. New York: Basic.

Glaser, D. (2000). Child abuse and neglect and the brain: A review. *Journal of Child Psychology and Psychiatry*, 41 (1), 97–116.

Goldberg, E., & Bilder, R.M. Jr (1987). The frontal lobes and hierarchical organization of cognitive control. In E. Perecman (ed.), *The frontal lobes revisited* (pp. 159–187). New York: IRBN Press.

Goldberg, M.C., Maurer, D., Lewis, T.L., & Brent, H.P. (2001). The influence of binocular visual deprivation on the development of visual-spatial attention. *Developmental Neuropsychology*, 19 (1), 55–83.

Goldberger, L., & Breznitz, S. (1982). *The handbook of stress: Theoretical and clinical aspects* (pp. 12–13). New York: Free Press.

Goldman, P.S. (1974). An alternative to developmental plasticity: Heterology of CNS structures in infants and adults. In D.G. Stein, J.J. Rosen, & N. Butters (eds), *Plasticity and recovery of function in the central nervous system* (pp. 149–174). New York: Academic.

Goldman-Rakic, P.S. (1987). Circuitry of the prefrontal cortex and the regulation of behavior by representational knowledge. In F. Plum & V. Mountcastle (eds), *Handbook of physiology* (Vol. 5, pp. 373–417). Bethesda, MD: American Physiological Society.

Goldman-Rakic, P.S., Bourgeouis, J.-P., & Rakic, P. (1997). Synaptic substrate of cognitive development. In N.A. Krasnegor, G.R. Lyon, & P. Goldman-Rakic (eds), *Development of the prefrontal cortex* (pp. 27–47). Baltimore: Brookes.

Gordon, N. (1995). Apoptosis (programmed cell death) and other reasons for elimination of neurons and axons. *Brain Development*, 17 (1), 73–77.

Gottlieb, G. (1976). Conceptions of prenatal development: Behavioral embryology. *Psychological Review*, 83, 215–234.

Gould, S.J. (1981). *The mismeasure of man*. New York: Norton.

Grattan, L.M., & Eslinger, P.J. (1992). Long-term psychological consequences of childhood frontal lobe lesion in patient DT. *Brain and Cognition*, 20 (1), 185–195

Greenough, W.T. (1975). Experiential modification of the developing brain. *American Scientist*, 63, 37–46.

Greenough, W.T., Black, J.E., & Wallace, C.S. (1987). Experience and brain development. *Child Development*, 58, 539–559.

Gross, C.G. (2001). Neurogenesis in the adult brain: death of a dogma. *Nature Reviews Neuroscience*, 1, 67–72.

Gunnar, M.R. (1998). Quality of early care and buffering of neuroendocrine stress reactions: Potential effects on the developing human brain. *Preventive Medicine*, 27, 208–211.

Gur, R.C., Turetsky, B.I., Matsui, M., Yen, M., Bilker, W., Hughett, P., & Gur, R.E. (1999). Sex differences in brain gray and white matter in healthy young adults: Correlations with cognitive performance. *The Journal of Neuroscience*, 19 (10), 4065–4072.

Habib, M., Gayraud, D., Oliva, A., Regis, J., Salamon, G., & Khalil, R. (1991). Effects of handedness and sex on the morphology of the corpus callosum: A study with brain magnetic resonance imaging. *Brain and Cognition*, 16 (1), 41–61.

Happé, F., Ehleres, S., Fletcher, P., Frith, U., Johanddon, M., Gillberg, C., Dolan, R., Frackowiak, R., & Frith, C. (1996). 'Theory of mind' in the brain: Evidence from a PET scan study of Asperger syndrome. *NeuroReport*, 8, 197–201.

Hasegawa, R.P., Blitz, A.M., Geller, N.L., & Goldberg, M.E. (2000). Neurons in monkey prefrontal cortex that track past or predict future performance. *Science*, 290 (1 December), 1786–1789.

Heiervang, E., Hugdahl, K., Steinmetz, H., Smievoll, A.I., Stevenson, J., Lund, A., Ersland, L., & Lundervold, A. (2000). Planum temporale, plaum parietale and dichotic listening in dyslexia. *Neuropsychologia*, 38 (13), 1704–1713.

Held, R., & Hein, A. (1963). Movement-produced stimulation in the development of visually guided behavior. *Journal of Comparative & Physiological Psychology*, 56 (5), 872–876.

Hiemenz, J.R., & Hynd, G.W. (2000). Sulcal/gyral pattern morphology of the perisylvian language region in developmental dyslexia. *Brain and Language*, 74 (1), 113–133.

Hirsch, H.V. (1985). The role of visual experience in the development of cat striate cortex. *Cell Molecular Neurobiology*, 5 (1–2), 103–121.

Hirshfeld, D.R., Rosenbaum, J.F., Biederman, J., Bolduc, E.A., Faraone, S.V., Snidman, N., Reznick, J.S., & Kagan, J. (1992). Stable behavioral inhibition and its association with anxiety disorder. *Journal of American Academic Child and Adolescent Psychiatry*, 31s (1), 103–111.

Hoffman, R.E., & Dobscha, S.K. (1989). Cortical pruning and the development of schizophrenia: a computer model. *Schizophrenia Bulletin*, 15 (3), 477–490.

Hopfinger, J.B., Buonocore, M.H., & Mangun, G.R. (2000). The neural mechanisms of top-down attentional control. *Nature Neuroscience*, 3 (3), 284–291.

Hubel, D.H., & Wiesel, T.N. (1962). Receptive fields, binocular interaction and functional architecture in the cat's visual cortex. *Journal of Physiology (London)*, 160 (1), 106–154.

Huttenlocher, P.R. (1979). Synaptic density in human frontal cortex: Developmental changes and effects of aging. *Brain Research*, 163, 195–205.

Huttenlocher, P.R., & Dabholkar, A.S. (1997). Developmental anatomy of prefrontal cortex. In N.A. Krasnegor, G.R. Lyon, & P.S. Goldman-Rakic (eds), *Development of the prefrontal cortex* (pp. 69–83). Baltimore: Brookes.

Ingalls, S., & Goldstein, S. (1999). Learning disabilities. In S. Goldstein & C.R. Reynolds (eds), *Handbook of neurodevelopmental and genetic disorders in children* (pp. 101–153). New York: Guilford.

Izard, C.E. (1971). *The face of emotion*. New York: Appleton Century Crofts.

Izard, C.E. (1994). Innate and universal facial expressions: Evidence from developmental and cross-cultural research. *Psychological Bulletin*, 115, 288–289.

Jacobs, B., Schall, M., & Scheibel, A.B. (1993). A quantitative dendritic analysis of Wernicke's area in humans: II. Gender, hemispheric, and environmental factors. *The Journal of Comparative Neurology*, 327, 97–111.

James, W. (1884). What is an emotion? *Mind*, 9, 188–205.

Jernigan, T.L., & Tallal, P. (1990). Late childhood changes in brain morphology observable with MRI. *Developmental Medicine and Child Neurology*, 32, 379–385.

Jernigan, T.L., Trauner, D.A., Hesselink, J.R., & Tallal, P.A. (1991). Maturation of human cerebrum observed *in vivo* during adolescence. *Brain*, 114, 2037–2049.

Johnson, M.H. (1993). *Brain development and cognition: A reader*. Cambridge, MA: Blackwell.

Johnson, M.H. (1997). *Developmental cognitive neuroscience*. Cambridge, MA: Blackwell.

Kaas, J.H. (2000). The reorganization of sensory and motor maps after injury in adult mammals. In M.S. Gazzaniga (ed.), *The new cognitive neurosciences* (2nd edn, pp. 223–236). Cambridge, MA: MIT Press.

Kagan, J. (1994). *Galen's prophecy*. New York: Basic.

Kimelberg, H.K., & Norenberg, M.D. (1989). Astrocytes. *Scientific American*, 260 (April), 66–76.

Koenen, K.C., Driver, K.L., Oscar-Berman, M., Wolfe, J., Folsom, S., Huang, M.T., & Schlesinger, L. (2001). Measures of prefrontal system dysfunction in post-traumatic stress disorder. *Brain and Cognition*, 45, 64–78.

Kolb, B., & Fantie, B. (1989). Development of the child's brain and behavior. In C.R. Reynolds & E. Fletcher-Janzen (eds), *Handbook of clinical child neuropsychology* (pp. 17–39). New York: Plenum.

Kolb, B., Forgie, M., Gibb, R., Gorny, G., & Rowntree, S. (1998). Age, experience and the changing brain. *Neuroscience and Biobehavioral Reviews*, 22, 143–159.

Kostovic, I., Petanjek, Z., Delalle, I., & Judas, M. (1992). Developmental reorganization of the human association cortex during perinatal and postnatal life. In I. Kostovic, S. Knezevic, H.M. Wisniewski, & G.J. Spilich (eds), *Neurodevelopment, aging and cognition* (pp. 3–17). Boston: Birkhauser.

Lemke, G. (2001). Glial control of neuronal development. *Annual Review of Neuroscience*, 24, 87–105.

Lenneberg, E.H. (1967). *Biological foundations of language*. New York: Wiley.

Leonard, C.M., Lombardino, L.J., Mercado, L.R., Browd, S.R., Breier, J.I., & Agee, O.F. (1996). Cerebral asymmetry and cognitive development in children: A magnetic resonance imaging study. *Psychological Science*, 7, 89–95.

Luria, A.R. (1966). *Higher cortical functions in man*. New York: Basic.

Macaluso, E., Frith, C.D., & Driver, J. (2000). Modulation of human visual cortex by crossmodal spatial attention. *Science*, 289, 1206–1208.

Marlowe, W.B. (1992). The impact of a right prefrontal lesion on the developing brain. *Brain and Cognition*, 20 (1), 205–213.

Marshall, L.H., & Magoun, H.W. (1998). *Discoveries in the human brain*. Totawa, NJ: Humana.

Maurer, D., & Lewis, T.L. (2001). Visual acuity and spatial contrast sensitivity: Normal development and underlying mechanisms. In C. Nelson & M. Luciana (eds), *Handbook of developmental cognitive neuroscience* (pp. 237–251). Cambridge, MA: MIT Press.

Mayberry, R.I. (in press). Cognitive development in deaf children: The interface of language and perception in neuropsychology. In S.J. Segalowitz & I. Rapin (eds), *Child neuropsychology* (2nd edn). Amsterdam: Elsevier.

McFarlane, A.C. (1988). Recent life events and psychiatric disorders in children: The interaction with preceding adversity. *Journal of Child Psychiatry and Psychology*, 29, 677–690.

McGraw, M.B. (1946). Maturation of behavior. In L. Carmichael (ed.), *Manual of child psychology* (pp. 332–369). New York: Wiley.

McLean, L.K., & Cripe, J.W. (1997). The effectiveness of early intervention for children with communication disorders. In M.J. Guralnick (ed.), *The effectiveness of early intervention* (pp. 349–428). Baltimore: Brookes.

Meyer, E., Ferguson, S.S.G., Zatorre, R.J., Alivisatos, B., Marrett, S., Evans, A.C., & Hakim, A.M. (1995). Attention modulates somatosensory cerebral blood flow response to vicrotactile stimulation as measured by positron emission tomography. *Annals of Neurology*, 29, 440–443.

Miller, G. (1981). *Language and speech*. New York: Freeman.

Molfese, D.L. (2000). Predicting dyslexia at 8 years of age using neonatal brain responses. *Brain and Language*, 72, 238–245.

Molfese, D.L., & Molfese, V.J. (1997). Discrimination of language skills at five years of age using event-related potentials recorded at birth. *Developmental Neuropsychology*, 13, 135–156.

Moore, C. (1992). The role of maternal stimulation in the development of sexual behavior and its neural basis. *Annals of the New York Academy of Sciences*, 622, 160–177.

Morgan, A.E., & Hynd, G.W. (1998). Dyslexia, neurolinguistic ability, and anatomical variation of the planum temporale. *Neuropsychological Reviews*, 8 (2), 79–93.

Mower, G.D., Christen, W.G., & Caplan, C.J. (1983). Very brief visual experience eliminates plasticity in the cat visual cortex. *Science*, 221, 178–180.

Muller, K., Ebner, S., & Homberg, V. (1994). Maturation of fastest afferent and efferent central and peripheral pathways: No evidence for a constancy of central conduction delays. *Neuroscience Letters*, 166, 9–12.

Munday, P., & Crowson, M. (1997). Joint attention and early social communication: Implications for research on intervention with autism. *Journal of Autism and Developmental Disorders*, 27 (6), 653–676.

Murray, H.A. (1938). *Explorations in personality*. New York: Oxford University Press.

Nelson, C.A., & Luciana, M. (eds) (2001). *Handbook of developmental cognitive neuroscience*. Cambridge, MA: MIT Press.

O'Craven, K.M., Rosen, B.R., Kwong, K.K., Triesman, A., & Savoy, R.L. (1997). Voluntary attention modulates fMRI activity in human MT-MST. *Neuron*, 18, 591–598.

Panksepp, J. (1998). Attention deficit hyperactivity disorders, psychostimulants and intolerance of childhood playfulness: A tragedy in the making? *Current Directions in Psychological Science*, 7 (3), 91–98.

Panksepp, J., Burgdorf, J., & Gordon, N. (in press). Modeling ADHD-type arousal with unilateral frontal cortex damage in rats and beneficial effects of play therapy. *Brain and Cognition*.

Perry, B.D., Pollard, R.A., Blakley, T.L., Baker, W.L., & Vigilante, D. (1995). Childhood trauma, the neurobiology of adaptation, and 'use-dependent' development of the brain: How 'states' become 'traits'. *Infant Mental Health Journal*, 16 (4), 271–289.

Perry, B.D., Southwick, S.M., Yehuda, R., & Giller, E.L. (1994). Adrenergic receptor regulation in posttraumatic stress disorder. In E.L. Giller (ed.), *Biological assessment and treatment of posttraumatic stress disorder* (pp. 87–114). Washington, DC: American Psychiatric Press.

Peters, M. (2000). Contributions of imaging techniques to our understanding of handedness. In M.K. Mandal, M.B. Bulman-Fleming, & G. Tiwari (eds), *Side bias: A neuropsychological perspective* (pp. 191–222). Holland: Kluwer.

Piaget, J. (1947). *The psychology of intelligence/La psychologie de l'intelligence* (Vol. 20). Paris: Armand Colin.

Pieniadz, J.M., Naeser, M.A., Koff, E., & Levine, H.L. (1983). CT scan cerebral hemispheric asymmetry measurements in stroke cases with global aphasia: Atypical asymmetries associated with improved recovery. *Cortex*, 19, 371–391.

Pochon, J.-B., Levy, R., Poline, J.-B., Crozier, S., Lehericy, S., Pillon, B., Deweer, B., Le Bihan, D., & Dubois, B. (2001). The role of dorsolateral prefrontal cortex in the preparation of forthcoming actions: an fMRl study. *Cerebral Cortex*, 11 (March), 260–266.

Ponton, C.W., Moore, J.K., & Eggermont, J.J. (1999). Prolonged deafness limits auditory system developmental plasticity: evidence from an evoked potentials study in children with cochlear implants. *Scandinavian Audiology*, 28 (Suppl. 51), 13–22.

Porges, S.W. (1995). Orienting in a defensive world: Mammalian modifications of our evolutionary heritage: A polyvagal theory. *Psychophysiology*, 32 (4), 301–318.

Post, R.M., & Weiss, S.R.B. (1997). Emergent properties of neural systems: How focal molecular neurobiological alterations can affect behavior. *Development & Psychopathology*, 9, 907–929.

Quartz, S., & Sejnowski, T.J. (1997). The neural basis of cognitive development: A constructivist manifesto. *Behavioral & Brain Sciences*, 20 (4), 537–596.

Quinton, D., & Rutter, M. (1975). Early hospital admissions and later disturbances of behavior. *Developmental Medicine and Child Neurology*, 18, 447–459.

Raine, A., Lencz, T., Bihrle, S., LaCasse, L., & Colletti, P. (2000). Reduced prefrontal gray matter volume and reduced autonomic activity in antisocial personality disorder. *Archives of General Psychiatry*, 57, 119–127.

Ramon y Cajal, S. (1894). La fine structure des centres nerveux. Croonian Lecture, 8 March 1894. *Royal Society of London Proceedings*, 55, 444–468.

Rapin, I.R. & Segalowitz, S.J. (eds) (1992). *Child neuropsychology, Part I*. In F. Boller & J. Grafman (series eds), *Handbook of neuropsychology* (Vol. 6). Amsterdam: Elsevier.

Reynolds, C.R., & Fletcher-Janzen, E. (eds) (1997). *Handbook of clinical child neuropsychology*. New York: Plenum.

Rodier, P.M. (1980). Chronology of neuron development: Animal studies and their clinical implications. *Developmental Medicine and Clinical Neurology*, 22 (4), 525–545.

Rosenzweig, M.R., & Bennett, E.L. (1996). Psychobiology of plasticity: effects of training and experience on brain and behavior. *Behavioral Brain Research*, 78 (1), 57–65.

Rushworth, M.F.S., & Walsh, V. (1999). Special issue: TMS in neuropsychology. *Neuropsychologia*, 37, 125–252.

Sameroff, A.J., & Chandler, M.J. (1975). Reproductive risk and the continuum of caretaking casualty. In F.D. Horwitz, M. Hetherington, & S. Scarr-Salapatek (eds), *Review of child developmental research* (Vol. 4, pp. 187–244). Chicago: University of Chicago Press.

Sameroff, A.J., & Fiese, B.H. (2000). Transactional regulation: The developmental ecology of early intervention. In J.P. Shonkoff & S.J. Meisels (eds), *Handbook of early childhood intervention* (2nd edn, pp. 135–159). Cambridge: Cambridge University Press.

Sapolsky, R.M. (1996). Why stress is bad for your brain. *Science*, 273, 749–750.

Saylor, C.F. (1993). *Children and disasters*. New York: Plenum.

Schaffer, H.R. (1998). *Making decisions about children* (2nd edn). Oxford: Blackwell.

Scheibel, A.B., Fried, I., Paul, L., Forsythe, A., Tomiyasu, U., Wechsler, A., Kao, A., & Slotnick, J. (1985). Differentiating characteristics of the human speech cortex: A quantitative golgi study. In D.F. Benson & E. Zaidel (eds), *The dual brain* (pp. 65–74). New York: Guilford.

Schmidt, L.A. (1999). Frontal brain electrical activity in shyness and sociability. *Psychological Science*, 10, 316–320.

Schmidt, L.A. (in press). Special issue: Affective neuroscience. *Brain and Cognition*.

Schmidt, L.A., Polak, C.P., & Spooner, A.L. (2001). Biological and environmental contributions to childhood shyness: A diathesis stress model. In W.R. Crozier & L.E. Alden (eds), *International handbook of social anxiety: Concepts, research and interventions relating to the self and shyness* (pp. 29–51). Chichester: Wiley.

Schmidt, L.A., & Schulkin, J. (eds) (1999). *Extreme fear, shyness, and social phobia: Origins, biological mechanisms, and clinical outcomes*. New York: Oxford.

Schmidt, L.A., & Tasker, S.L. (2000). Childhood shyness: Determinants, development and 'depathology'. In W.R. Crozier (ed.), *Shyness: Development, consolidation and change* (pp. 30–46). London: Routledge.

Schneider, M.L., Clarke, S., Kraemer, G.W., Roughton, E.C., Lubach, G.R.,Rimm-Kaufman, S., Schmidt, D., & Ebert, M. (1998). Prenatal stress alters brain biogenic amine levels in primates. *Development and Psychopathology*, 10, 427–440.

Schore, A.N. (1994). *Affect regulation and the origin of the self.* Hillsdale, NJ: Erlbaum.

Schoups, A., Vogels, R., Qian, N., & Orban, G. (2001). Practising orientation identification improves orientation coding in V1 neurons. *Nature*, 412, 549–553.

Segalowitz, S.J., Menna, R., & MacGregor, L. (1987). Left and right hemisphere participation in reading: evidence from ERPs. *Journal of Clinical and Experimental Neuropsychology*, 9, 274.

Segalowitz, S.J., & Rapin, I.R. (in press). *Child neuropsychology* (2nd edn). In F. Boller & J. Grafman (series eds), *Handbook of neuropsychology*. Amsterdam: Elsevier.

Segalowitz, S.J., & Rapin, I.R. (eds) (1992). *Child neuropsychology, Part II*. In F. Boller & J. Grafman (series eds), *Handbook of neuropsychology* (Vol. 7). Amsterdam: Elsevier.

Segalowitz, S.J., Wagner, W.J., & Menna, R. (1992). Lateral versus frontal ERP predictors of reading skill. *Brain and Cognition*, 20, 85–103.

Shankle, W.R., Landing, B.H., Rafii, M.S., Schiano, A., Chen, J.M., & Hara, J. (1998). Evidence for a postnatal doubling of neuron number in the developing human cerebral cortex between 15 months and 6 years. *Journal of Theoretical Biology*, 191, 115–140.

Shepherd, D.M., & Barraclough, B.M. (1976). The aftermath of parental suicide for children. *British Journal of Psychiatry*, 129, 267–276.

Shors, T.J., Miesegaes, G., Beylin, A., Zhao, M., Rydel, T., & Gould, E. (2001). Neurogenesis in the adult is involved in the formation of trace memories. *Nature*, 410 (15 March), 372–376.

Singer, W. (1982). The role of attention in developmental plasticity. *Human Neurobiology*, 1 (1), 41–43.

Sowell, E.R., Thompson, P.M., Holmes, C.J., Batth, R., Jernigan, T.L., & Toga, A.W. (1999). Localizing age-related changes in brain structure between childhood and adolescence using statistical parametric mapping. *NeuroImage*, 9, 587–597.

Stanwood, G.D., Washington, R.A., & Levitt, P. (2001). Identification of a sensitive period of prenatal cocaine exposure that alters the development of the anterior cingulate cortex. *Cerebral Cortex*, 11 (May 2001), 430–440.

Steinmetz, P.N., Roy, A., Fitzgerald, P.J., Hsiao, S.S., Johnson, K.O., & Niebur, E. (2000). Attention modulates synchronized neuronal firing in primate somatosensory cortex. *Nature*, 404, 187–190.

Stemmer, B. (1999). Special issue. Pragmatics: Theoretical and clinical issues. *Brain and Language*, 68 (3), 389–590.

Stemmer, B., & Whitaker, H.A. (1998). *Handbook of neurolinguistics*. San Diego, CA: Academic.

Stiles, J. (2000). Neural plasticity and cognitive development. *Developmental Neuropsychology*, 18 (2), 237–272.

Stuss, D.T. (1992). Biological and psychological development of executive functions. *Brain and Cognition*, 20 (1), 8–23.

Suomi, S.J. (1991). Uptight and laid-back monkeys: Individual differences in response to social challenge. In S.E. Brauth, W.S. Hall, & R.J. Dooling (eds), *Plasticity of development* (pp. 27–56). Cambridge, MA: MIT Press.

Sur, M., & Leamey, C. (2001). Development and plasticity of cortical areas and networks. *Nature Neuroscience Reviews*, 2 (4), 251–262.

Thoenen, H. (1995). Neurotrophins and neuronal plasticity. *Science*, 270, 593–598.

Tronick, E.Z., & Giannino, A.F. (1987). The transmission of maternal disturbance to the infant. In E.Z. Tronick & T. Field (eds), *Maternal depression and infant disturbance*. San Francisco: Jossey-Bass.

Vargha-Khadem, F., Cowan, J., & Mishkin, M. (2000). Sociopathic behaviour after early damage to prefrontal cortex. Paper presented at the Society for Neurosciences, New Orleans.

Vaughan, H.G., & Kurtzberg, D. (1992). Electrophysiologic indices of human brain maturation and cognitive development. In M.R. Gunnar & C.A. Nelson (eds), *Developmental behavioral neuroscience* (pp. 1–36). Hillsdale, NJ: Erlbaum.

Wachs, T.D. (ed.) (2000). *Necessary but not sufficient : The respective roles of single and multiple influences on individual development.* Washington, DC: American Psychological Association.

Watson, J.B. (1925). *Behaviorism.* New York: People's Institute Publishing.

Watson, J.B., & Rayner, R.R. (1920). Conditioned emotional reactions. *Journal of Experimental Psychology*, 3, 1–14.

Werker, J.F., & Tees, R.C. (1984). Cross-language speech perception: Evidence for perceptual reorganization during the first year of life. *Infant Behavior and Development*, 7, 49–63.

Werner, E.E. (2000). Protective factors and individual resilience. In J.P. Shonkoff & S.J. Meisels (eds), *Handbook of early childhood intervention* (2nd edn, pp. 115–132). Cambridge: Cambridge University Press.

White, L.E., Coppola, D.M., & Fitzpatrick, D. (2001). The contribution of sensory experience to the maturation of orientation selectivity in ferret visual cortex. *Nature*, 411, 1049–1052.

Wiesel, T.N., & Hubel, D.H. (1963a). Effects of visual deprivation on morphology and physiology of cells in the cat's lateral geniculate body. *Journal of Neurophysiology*, 26 (6), 978–993.

Wiesel, T.N., & Hubel, D.H. (1963b). Single-cell responses in striate cortex of kittens deprived of vision in one eye. *Journal of Neurophysiology*, 26 (6), 1002–1017.

Wiesel, T.N., & Hubel, D.H. (1965). Comparison of the effects of unilateral and bilateral eye closure on cortical unit responses in kittens. *Journal of Neurophysiology*, 28 (6), 1029–1040.

Williams, D., & Mateer, C.A. (1992). Developmental impact of frontal lobe injury in middle childhood. *Brain and Cognition*, 20 (1), 196–204.

Witelson, S.F. (1985). The brain connection: The corpus callosum is larger in left-handers. *Science*, 229 (4714), 665–668.

Witelson, S.F., & Goldsmith, C.H. (1991). The relationship of hand preference to anatomy of the corpus callosum in men. *Brain Research*, 545 (1–2), 175–182.

Witelson, S.F., Kigar, D.L., & Harvey, T. (1999). The exceptional brain of Albert Einstein. *Lancet*, 353, 2149–2153.

Witelson, S.F., & Pallie, W. (1973). Left hemisphere specialization for language in the newborn: Neuroanatomical evidence of asymmetry. *Brain*, 96, 641–646.

Worden, M.S., Foxe, J.J., Wang, N., & Simpson, G.V. (2000). Anticipatory biasing of visuospatial attention indexed by retinotopically specific alpha-band electroencephalography increases over occipital cortex. *The Journal of Neuroscience*, 20, RC63.

Yeates, K.O., Ris, M.D., & Taylor, H.G. (eds). (2000) *Pediatric neuropsychology: Research, theory, and practice.* New York: Guilford.

Yehuda, R., Southwick, S.M., Perry, B.D., Mason, J.W., & Giller, E.L. (1994). Interactions of the hypothalamic-pituitary-adrenal axis and the catecholaminergic system in posttraumatic stress disorder. In E.L. Giller (ed.), *Biological assessment and treatment of posttraumatic stress disorder* (pp. 115–134). Washington, DC: American Psychiatric Press.

4

Historical Contexts for Development

HIDEO KOJIMA

My starting point is the belief that to understand the courses and processes of development and the nature and findings of developmental research it is necessary to situate them in the historical context of the social and cultural conditions of a society. In other words, this chapter is an attempt of two kinds of historical contextualization: first that of developmental phenomena, and second that of developmental research. Interest in the historical contexts of cultural and social conditions does not simply mean looking for the *difference* in these conditions at different historical periods, and relating them to people's lives and development in each period. Rather, historical *change and continuity* of the cultural and social conditions of a society should be described, and theoretical explanations for the processes of change and continuity are required.

My standpoint entails three components that are embedded and one that is embedding. They are person, immediate environment (Bronfenbrenner's microsystem and mesosystem: Bronfenbrenner, 1979; Bronfenbrenner & Morris, 1998), developmental research, and the cultural and social conditions within which human development proceeds and its research is conducted. Each should be characterized as a system with its own structure and functions.

All four systems change across time, though the time scales, i.e. meaningful units of time for understanding the changing phenomena, are not the same. For example, more or less different time scales for each system should be applied to the behavioral and psychological change of individual family members and to the changes in their family relationships in order to meaningfully describe their changing processes and outcomes. In addition, change in each component system is neither random nor endowed with complete freedom of movement. For example, yesterday's I and today's I may appear quite different on the surface, but the I-system of yesterday could not be replaced with a completely new I-system in a day or even in a year. Likewise, even after being subjected to some system-shaking events, the family system in a later phase may not be organized independently of the former system. That is because change in the organization of any system, i.e. a reorganization, is characterized not as mechanical replacement but as transformation. Thus each system has its own history of organization and reorganization that partly influences the trajectory of its future change. Furthermore, as far as each system is connected with others in a systemic way, change in one system will sooner or later influence other systems, and will be fed back to the change-triggering system later. From a developmental perspective, the relationship between the person and his or her immediate external environment has been characterized as an *enduring* reciprocal interaction of the person and environment. A number of models of this have been proposed (Magnusson & Stattin, 1998).

Then what kinds of interaction are to be expected between the third component system, i.e. developmental research, and the person and immediate environment components? Gergen's (1973) proposal in the field of interpersonal behavior and personality research is relevant here. Gergen, as will be described in a later section, focused his attention on the influence of social psychological research on individuals and their interpersonal behavior. He was concerned that the dissemination of psychological knowledge might modify the informed person's dispositions and pattern of behavior upon which the scientific knowledge is based, thus invalidating the original psychological knowledge. This recognition led Gergen (1973) to characterize social psychology as history because of the historical specificity of the findings. However, he appeared not to be directly interested in the reciprocal interactions between scientific research and individual persons.

In the study of human development, one of the potentially promising research themes to deal with reciprocal interactions between scientific research on the one hand and person–environment system on the other is parenting and associated belief systems (e.g. Goodnow & Collins, 1990; Harkness & Super, 1996; Sigel, McGillicuddy-DeLisi, & Goodnow, 1992). However, they have mainly been interested in describing parental belief systems and their psychological consequences for children. Nevertheless we can find a few cases (e.g. Goodnow & Collins, 1990, Chapter 4; Lightfoot & Valsiner, 1992) that have thoughtfully dealt with the constructive process by parents, focusing on the role of expert advice. These authors, however, dealt neither with the place of academic research itself nor with the potential indirect influence of parents on expert advisors. In my view, a further step is needed in order to place academic developmental research and the role of expert advisor separately in their interacting relations with the developing person and his or her immediate environment. This is one of the tasks of this chapter. The identification of four district social roles related to human development and the relations among them provides a starting point that will be dealt with in later sections. In connection with this task it is pertinent to review the relations between scientific psychology and common-sense psychology.

The main task of this chapter remains: to understand historical contexts for development. It is related to a part of the opening statement of this chapter, i.e. to situate person, environment, and developmental research within the historical contexts of the cultural and social conditions of a society. A number of thoughtful contributions have been made to the critical social or cultural history of developmental psychology (Bronfenbrenner et al., 1986; Riegel, 1976; Wertsch & Youniss, 1987; Valsiner, 1997). Though I am not familiar with the world-wide situation, I can find similar critical analyses of the Japanese situation (e.g. Hatano & Yamashita, 1987; Yamashita, 1977). Hatano and Yamashita (1987) analyzed the lives of two educational psychologists in Japan through the prewar, wartime, and postwar periods, by historically placing developmental research in its social and political contexts.

Needless to say, the two kinds of contextualization – that of developmental phenomena and that of developmental research – are closely related. The task of contextualization from historical perspective is a very complex one that requires, metaphorically speaking, integration of broad horizontal perspectives on inter-system relations and insightful vertical viewpoints on history. Even when the target of inquiry is restricted to a specific society within a limited span of historical time, the task is enormous for a single author. In the following section, I shall present some ideas that will help to construct what I hope is a promising approach to an inquiry into the complex problem of historical contexts for human development.

Historical Perspectives and Developmental Research: An Overview

Crossroads of Social/Cultural History and Developmental Psychology

The opening statement of this chapter is the primary message I took from a volume edited by Elder, Modell, and Parke (1993). This book comprises the outcomes of an organized program by developmental researchers and historians that lasted for more than six years. The book tells the story of a painstaking process of collaboration by developmental researchers and historians. It reports the lessons they learned and offers some concluding insights and perspectives for future research.

In 1983 a joint endeavor by some historians interested in human development and some developmental researchers interested in history was undertaken in the United States of America. The stage for this work was set by several factors, including the expansion of social/cultural history research, the development of life course studies, and a general acceptance of life-span views in developmental psychology. The joint activity therefore was based on the preceding conditions, and their attainment stimulated other research activities at the crossroads of cultural/social history and developmental psychology that went beyond the United States in the twentieth century. I will begin with the three tasks proposed by Elder, Modell, and Parke (1993) regarding the historical contributions to developmental psychology. Although my interpretation of the editors' intention may not be quite correct, I believe that some discussion on the proposals is a convenient starting point. The main tasks proposed (Elder, Modell, & Parke, 1993, pp. 246–247) are:

1 an examination of the adequacy of our current theories for explaining human development in earlier historical periods
2 a description of the social, economic, and political circumstances that may have conditioned the theoretical account of development in different historical periods
3 a consideration of whether folk theories (common expectations, beliefs, and explanations) of development change across time.

The first task embodies one way of answering the implicit assumption of universality of theories of human development that are independent of historical times. It is a question open to empirical scrutiny and potentially solvable once a target society, a range of historical periods to be covered, and the content domains dealt with by theories have been delimited. We could even decide which of the current theories are more adequate than others for the explanation of human development in earlier historical periods. In order to do that, however, we need multiple sets of historical data each of which contains the same set of relevant variables across the particular historical periods. The availability of this kind of hypothetical, ideal data sets assumes relative invariance of a theory of development over time. That is because the existence of the same kinds of data sets itself reflects the commonality of theory within which a set of concepts measured are to be placed. Furthermore this kind of historical comparison presupposes the already established empirical science of human development. Therefore a range of time to be dealt with in terms of this kind of comparative work should be relatively recent and narrow. In that case we will be able to obtain information on the degree of similarity of the theoretically selected inter-variable relations across historical time. If the results show similar or stable inter-variable relations over time, one can argue that the current theory is applicable to earlier periods and that the basic nature of the phenomenon has remained unchanged.

Another approach is direct comparison of theories in a specific domain across time. In order to do this, we should specify who theorizes and the social role of the theory constructor. We can meaningfully compare, for example, an academic account of the orienting reflex in the 1890s and a recent one (see a remark by White in Bronfenbrenner et al., 1986, p. 1225). Likewise, change and continuity of expert advice on child-rearing during the past century can be traced. The roles of academic researcher and of expert advisor are not to be defined independently of each other in a specific society. Therefore we need to analyze the relationships among related roles across historical periods. As is explained in a later section, the relationships among the four roles related to construction of child-rearing theories in Japan have, in my view, been basically similar for the past three centuries. Identification of theory constructors and understanding of the relations among them are the important points to be clarified before we embark on the first task proposed by Elder, Modell, and Parke (1993).

The second task proposed by Elder, Modell, and Parke (1993) is to place the theoretical accounts of development in different historical periods within their social, economic, and political contexts. Elder, Modell, and Parke noted a few empirical and theoretical studies on the interplay between the two classes of variables. Two case studies by Wertch and Youniss (1987), though they do not deal with historical changes, are interesting with regard to the formulation of social scientific issues within the context of nation building in the United States and the former USSR. Kojima dealt with the issue more directly. He described Japanese child-rearing theories as they appeared in the advice of experts from the mid seventeenth century (Kojima, 1986), relating them to cultural, social, and economic conditions in five historical epochs (Kojima, 1996a). In addition to those prescriptive theories, various descriptive sources (e.g. family diaries, survey of folk customs, and popular novels) were used to construct Japanese theories of child-rearing since the eighteenth century (e.g. Kojima, 1996b; 1999). These analyses revealed historical continuity of basic beliefs and values in Japanese ethnotheories on child-rearing and human development. This experience leads me to be particularly interested in the third task proposed by Elder, Modell, and Parke (1993).

They posed the third task in the form of a question, 'Do our folk theories change across time?' The answer they anticipated was 'Yes!', for they wrote: 'Just as we are increasingly aware of the non-universal nature of development and recognize the variability in agenda for children in different contemporary cultures, we recognize the same differences across historical time' (1993, p. 247). Of course it is an open question that can be answered either 'Yes' or 'No'. What draws my attention, however, is the authors' recognition of the possibility of continuity of folk theories (targets of task 3) as distinguished from academic theories (targets of task 1). For the latter they posed a question in a somewhat different way. They appear to implicitly recognize the possibility of differential ways of historical change for academic theories and folk theories of human development. In this chapter I will put emphasis on folk theories whose historical continuity and change have not been fully dealt with thus far.

Incidentally the above quotation refers to another distinction of the developmental question, i.e. 'nature of development' and 'the agenda for children'. These correspond roughly to the process or mechanism of development and the course of development, respectively. In my view these are the two basic questions that are posed by both academic and folk theories. The next section begins with questions concerning developmental research.

The Study of Developmental Problems

Wohlwill (1973) presented a systematic model for answering the major questions on the behavioral development of individuals. It consisted of five tasks for research on developmental change. These were:

1 the discovery and synthesis of developmental dimensions
2 the descriptive study of age changes
3 the correlational study of age changes

4 the study of the determinants of developmental change
5 the study of individual differences in development.

These are all directed to the investigation of the course of development, i.e. finding age functions of the quantitative or qualitative indices of development. The first task is concerned with the construction of dimensionalized scales with which to chart the course of development. Tasks 2 and 3 concern the descriptive study of the course of development. While task 2 deals with the course of development on a single dimension, task 3 is concerned with the structural changes of the relationships among multiple dimensions including across-occasion analyses of longitudinal data sets. Heritability indices as calculated in recent behavioral genetics studies (e.g. Plomin et al., 1997) can also be used as the R variables in developmental functions. Wohlwill (1973) characterized task 3 as an intermediate phase of research between the descriptive phase and that of the study of functional relationships aimed at the mechanisms of developmental change.

Wohlwill (1973) proposed the view that the age variable A in developmental functions $R = f(A)$, where R stands for an index of development consisting of single or multiple/structural dimensions, forms a part of the so-called dependent or outcome variable which is the object of the developmentalist's study. Therefore the strategy of the fourth task, searching for the variables on which the age-related changes depend, is either experimental intervention or the selection of subgroups classified in terms of differential experiential factors, both at a certain phase of development. By looking for the effects of these manipulated or selected variables on age functions that are to be monitored over a relatively extended period, we can proceed some way towards understanding the process of developmental change. The fifth and last task is concerned with individual differences in age functions and with the question of stability, i.e. the invariance or change of individual differences over the course of development.

Wohlwill's proposal for a programmatic approach to research on developmental change is still a very useful frame within which to locate developmental research. It is true that his proposal centers around the description of the course of development rather than the elucidation of the processes or mechanism of development. In my view, however, the fourth research question with regard to human subjects is very hard to empirically answer in any direct way at the present state of our theory and methodology. With regard to the process of developmental change, especially if one wishes to deal with the dynamic change of the target process during the course of development (Valsiner, 1997), we are still at the phase of diverse ways of theorizing, in both academic and folk psychology. Therefore with respect to the process or mechanism of development I will deal in later sections with only some aspects of theories. On the other hand, I will deal with models that have guided empirical studies on the course of development, extending the scheme proposed by Wohlwill and others.

In a sense, the fourth and fifth tasks listed by Wohlwill (1973) are an extension of Kessen's (1960) discussion of the design of developmental research. Included in Kessen's design are, shown schematically, $R = f(A)$, $R = f(A, P)$, $R = f(A, S)$, and $R = f(A, P, S)$, where R stands for an index of development, P for population variables like gender and dispositions of the subjects, and S for environmental variables. The effect of S on age functions is given by the function $R = f(A, S)$, by selection or manipulation, and is the chief concern of task 4. The effects of P and of the interaction $P \times S$ on age functions are the major concern of task 5, i.e. problems of individual differences. For the purpose of this essay a further step of elaboration is required. In both Kessen's and Wohlwill's formulations, historical time appears not to have been taken into account. Logically the historical time T may be contained as one of the variables, like $R = f(A, T)$. However, since Kessen and Wohlwill were dissatisfied with the treatment of age variables in developmental functions, a simple introduction of the historical time variable into a formula without specifying what is indexed by T does not further our understanding of development in different historical periods. Even when we are sure that R holds the same meaning across historical time, S is certainly different depending on T (e.g. changing moral values), and P may also be different (e.g. birth cohort difference in genetic factors).

From this viewpoint, it might be said that contributions by Schaie and Baltes on model building for analyzing long-term human development (e.g. Schaie, 1965; Schaie & Baltes, 1975; Baltes, Lindenberger, & Staudinger, 1998) started as a data analytic model expressed as $R = f(A, T)$. Reported findings based on this sequential model soon made the majority of developmentalists aware of the potential distortion of developmental functions, especially when they were inferred from cross-sectional age-difference data (i.e. the confounding of age changes and birth cohort differences). In addition, awareness of the inadequacy of developmental functions based on a single longitudinal data set led developmental researchers to be sensitive to the historical specificity of a given cohort, especially a series of historical events that the cohort encountered at specific phases of development. This awareness has finally developed into a set of theoretical and methodological process of life-span development incorporating organismic and environmental factors as well as the interaction among them (e.g. Baltes, Lindenberger, & Staudinger, 1998).

One aspect of the contributions by Elder (1998a; 1998b) in this domain can also be characterized as an $R = f(A, T)$ program where the cohort difference in the timing of life course transition (variable R) is the main concern. The ample evidence of cohort differences in the actual or perceived timing of life course transitions (e.g. Elder, 1998b), when interpreted in terms of the historical changes and cultural factors of a particular society (Hareven, 1991), has provided developmentalists with important information on contextual factors and their interactions with psychological variables. In this respect, Hareven's (1991) propositions on three features of timing – i.e. individual timing, synchronization of individual with collective (e.g. familial) timing, and the cumulative impact of life transitions – provide developmental researchers with an important framework in which to conceptualize the interrelationship among personal, interpersonal, social, and cultural timetables.

Historical Contexualization of Developmental Phenomena and of Developmental Research

In this section, the close interrelations between the two kinds of contexualization, i.e. of developmental phenomena and of developmental research, will be discussed from several aspects. The aim is to provide ideas and viewpoints with which to understand the phenomenon of human development and research into the historical contexts of cultural and social conditions of society. Some of the subsections consist of a general discussion of a particular issue, while others contain material from my interest in Japanese child-rearing. My intention is to present generalizable ideas.

Social Systems, Developing Individuals, and Developmental Research

As has been explained in the preceding sections, one of the two basic interests of developmental research is the description of the course of development. It is also one of the major concerns at the personal, interpersonal, and collective levels in such matters as a timetable of life course and a timetable of development and aging. Let me begin by presenting the organizational framework I have been using to deal with these problems (Figure 4.1).

The course of a given human life from birth to death must unfold in a specific cultural setting during a specific historical time. Therefore the basic conditions in which a society finds itself will necessarily influence the lives of individuals to a large extent, as well as how the human life course is viewed at both collective and individual levels. Included in these conditions are the ecological, demographic, economic, political, social, and religious factors which shape the lives of individuals. In turn, these factors are influenced by the actual lives led by the people in a society and by prevailing notions about the human life course.

Social Systems

A society's views on the process of human development and aging, i.e. a kind of collective social representation (Moscovici, 1990; Moscovici & Duveen, 2000), will have direct effects on the way people of different ages are treated in that society. For example, the idea that a six-year-old child is usually ready to begin formal education is directly linked to the decision to enter children into primary school at that age. Likewise, the various rites of passage in a particular society are closely interrelated with social ideas on human development and aging. These are examples at the social level of the close interrelation between commonly held ideas on age-related changes of human beings and the treatment of individuals.

Individuals

At the individual level, the actual process of development and aging is influenced by biological variables, including genetic and nongenetic factors. The individual's development and aging are also influenced by his or her own experiences. But because an individual's mode of experiencing differs according to developmental status, their development and experience are mutually related.

Social Systems and Individuals

Looking at the relation between the social system and an individual, we can clearly see that the social systems in which the life course unfolds and the individual's experience and development are also related. This is for two reasons. On the one hand, a society's ideas about the life course and the appropriate treatment of different age groups are partly based on people's actual age-related changes. On the other hand, the common beliefs and customs of the society will also have a constraining effect on the range of experiences that an individual has. In addition, a society's notions about the normative life course are realized in the form of a generally accepted timetable of the human life course that is shared by its members, and this timetable provides people with the basis for age-related role and status. Needless to say, the timetable is subject to certain modifications by the individual. We should emphasize that an individual has not only a timetable of his or her own, but also one for related persons, and that these timetables are mutually related. For

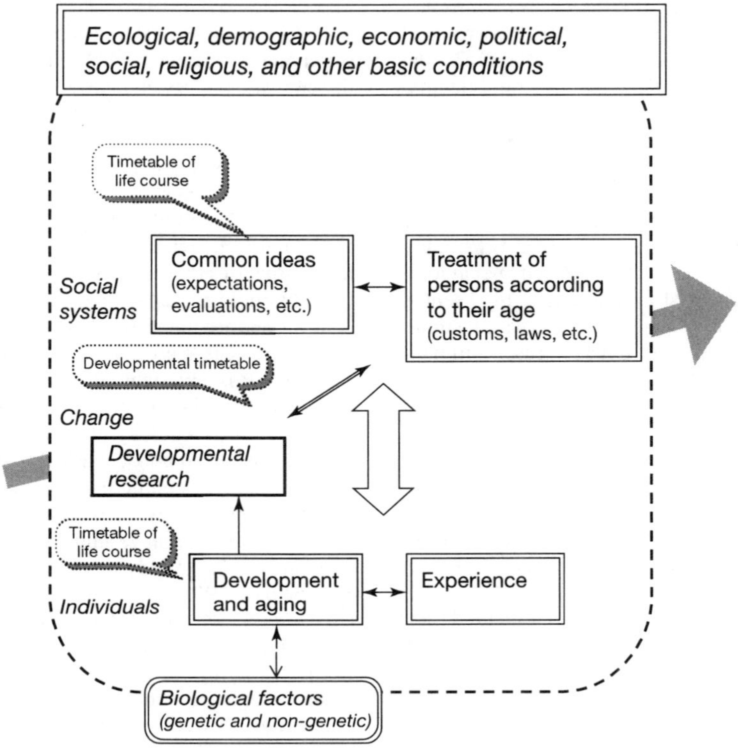

Figure 4.1 *Schematic representation of the relationship between social systems on age-related changes, individual development and aging, and developmental research (adapted from Kojima, 1991)*

example, the maternal role in a woman's timetable is closely related with her timetable for children. Her own timetable may also be influenced by that of her aged parent.

Developmental Research

Developmental research is placed in the context of these social and individual frameworks. Needless to say, the theories and findings of developmental researchers are based on the actual developmental processes of individuals. The developmental timetables that researchers make, i.e. age functions of indices of human development and aging, reflect the actual course of development that is going on in society. It is also true, however, that the conceptual and theoretical frameworks that researchers employ in order to observe developmental phenomena have been shaped by the social systems in which the researchers conduct their inquiries. Thus indices of development are selected or constructed by developmental researchers who are situated within society. Conversely research findings feed back into society and may affect society's notions and practices.

Finally, all three of these elements in Figure 4.1 – social systems, developing individuals, and developmental research – may change across historical periods, while still maintaining a considerable degree of continuity.

Folk Theories of Human Development: The Relations between Common Sense and Science

What is the relation between so-called common-sense psychology and scientific psychology? Baldwin (1967) once argued that what is called common-sense psychology may actually be a set of cultural conventions operating in the sphere of human relations. He argued that common-sense psychology, even if it does not overlap at all with genuine psychological mechanisms, is as important as language itself for purposes of analysis, because people understand each other's behavior in terms of how it accords with common-sense psychological theories. Such theories constitute a system of tacit assumptions that are reflected in the everyday actions of people, and people are thus led to acquire common-sense theories of their society.

If we pursue this line of thinking, we confront a fundamental question: what do the theories and findings of scientific psychology reflect? Do the research findings on human relations from scientific psychology reflect an understanding of actual psychological mechanisms, if there are such things, or do they merely represent an understanding of the cultural conventions that are reflected in common-sense psychology? If the latter is the case, the science of psychology has merely identified, or unwittingly rediscovered, the culturally defined behavioral conventions of society that are already represented in common-sense psychology and act as a constraint on people's daily behavior. In which case, common-sense psychology not only precedes scientific psychology, but also in a causal sense generates the laws found by the latter. In addition, if we admit the influence of the people's understanding of cultural conventions on their behavior, it follows that common-sense psychology, and subsequently the findings of scientific psychology, may differ from culture to culture, and also from one historical period to another.

On the other hand, it cannot be denied that scientific psychology has influenced common-sense psychology. If parents' ideas, theories, and skills relating to child development are mediated by expert advisors, they are likely to incorporate theories and findings from developmental research and thus the content of common-sense developmental psychology may gradually change. Eventually not only the research findings on parental belief systems, but also those on children's behavior and development, may change. In this case, what we have found is partly produced by ourselves.

This line of argument rests upon many presuppositions which should be questioned. Still, it is certain that we need to rethink the place of developmental research within society as well as the nature of the psychological understanding we are pursuing.

Developmental researchers tend to consider themselves engaged in the activity of constructing theories mainly through interacting with other academic researchers both past and present. Generally they are not aware of, or tend to disregard, the fact that the persons on whom our work is targeted are also engaged in thinking and even theorizing about human development and child-rearing. Therefore one difficulty for research at the present time is the realization that developmental theories actually interact with the common-sense psychology of ordinary people. As has been argued by a few psychologists, however, the conceptions and theories of academic researchers are influenced by common-sense psychology (e.g. Baldwin, 1967; Kelley, 1992). Conversely, it is quite evident that academic psychology has influenced common-sense psychology through the changing social representations and knowledge base of the relevant domain (e.g. Farr & Moscovici, 1984; Gergen, 1973; Moscovici, 1990). Arguing against transhistorical laws in social psychology, Gergen (1973) pointed out that the dissemination of psychological knowledge in general and of social psychology in particular alters the behavior it seeks to study. According to Gergen, the impact of psychological science on society occurs due to (1) the prescriptive bias of psychological theorizing, (2) the liberating effects of knowledge, and (3) the reactive resistance of people to psychological theories (based on prevalent cultural values). In addition, historical changes in people's acquired dispositions are induced by cultural changes.

Because it is inconceivable that common-sense psychology is invariant across time and universal across cultures, I prefer the term 'ethnopsychology' to denote the psychology of a particular society at a specific time. In addition, considering the interdependence between common-sense psychology and scientific psychology, as well as their dependence on a common language and their inbuilt thought structures (e.g. Baldwin, 1967; Kelley, 1992; Smedslund, 1997), it is probable that scientific psychology not only changes across time due to intra- and inter-disciplinary impetus but also differs from one culture to another. It was the American anthropologist LeVine who emphasized the close connection between empirical (i.e. scientific) psychology and folk (i.e. common-sense) psychology. He demonstrated that American psychologists and parents shared a common culture, with culture-specific beliefs diverging sharply from those of peoples elsewhere in the world. In his argument for the need to internationalize American child development research, he wrote:

> All empirical psychology is folk psychology to some degree, profoundly influenced by cultural assumptions that scientists share with nonscientists of the same background, and all folk psychology is empirical to some degree, embodying a folk wisdom effective in a specific milieu. The continuity in assumptions between child psychology as we know it in the United States and our beliefs, values, and ideologies concerning development affects every phase of research: the formulation of research problems, the organization and collection of data, and the interpretation of findings. (1980, p. 77)

Thus the scientific psychology of child development may vary depending on its cultural contexts. In addition to such variation, another source of variation has been developing. It is the intentional indigenization of psychology in terms of making knowledge culturally appropriate so that psychological knowledge can play a role in national development (Sinha, 1997). This position does not necessarily reject the ideal of universal psychology. In this connection it is of interest to note that the founders of the Japanese Society for Educational Research (founded in 1880) apparently believed in both universal laws of human evolution and the specificity of the social and historical conditions of Japanese society. Thus in a prospectus printed in 1891 to solicit from interested parents and teachers information about the development of children, they argued:

> Because Japanese children develop in a society whose organization and history are completely different from those of Western children, there is no doubt of the fact that their inheritance is different from that of Western children. Therefore research findings on Western children are not necessarily useful to us . . . We propose to conduct research with Japanese children and to make the findings a solid base for education in Japan.

This passage reflects their adoption of recapitulation theory and Lamarckism as universal principles of evolution. They believed, however, that the particular history of Japanese society had caused an accumulation of specific hereditary characteristics that was different from those of Western society, thus inducing a different unfolding process of ontogeny. I do not know whether this argument had been adopted from the West. However, aside from the historicism of the newly imported Western ideas the argument is consistent with the traditional Japanese notion – which might have originated in China (Kojima, 1992) – that different places yield different creatures (plants, animals, people's characteristics, and so on). Thus a familiar notion was reinforced by new ideas from the West, making their argument more persuasive and also expanding the time dimension beyond ontogeny to the history of the society.

Ideas and Skills in Society: Four Roles Related to Construction of Child-Rearing Theories and Practices

The question here is, 'Who were, and are, the constructors of theories of child-rearing?' My answer to this question is based on the differentiation of four social roles that are involved in some form of theory construction. These are roles of the layperson, the practitioner, the expert advisor, and the academic researcher. I will especially emphasize the interaction among these roles in the construction and reconstruction processes of theories of child-rearing that are placed within social and cultural contexts. The interaction between these roles is illustrated diagrammatically in Figure 4.2. In my view, the diagram is applicable not only to present-day Japan but also to eighteenth century Japan, with one limitation for the earlier period, namely that there was no empirical research in human development. I emphasize the interdependency among the four roles plus developing and aging individuals, without which present-day developmental psychology as a scientific discipline could not function within a society.

I will begin by introducing the distinction of the four roles related to child-rearing. However, its explication necessarily needs reference to another issue, that of the relation between culture and the individual's behavior and thought, because the two questions posed above are mutually interrelated.

What are the four social roles that can be identified in constructing theories and devising practices related to human development in general, and child-rearing in particular? These social roles are those of the layperson, the practitioner, the expert advisor,

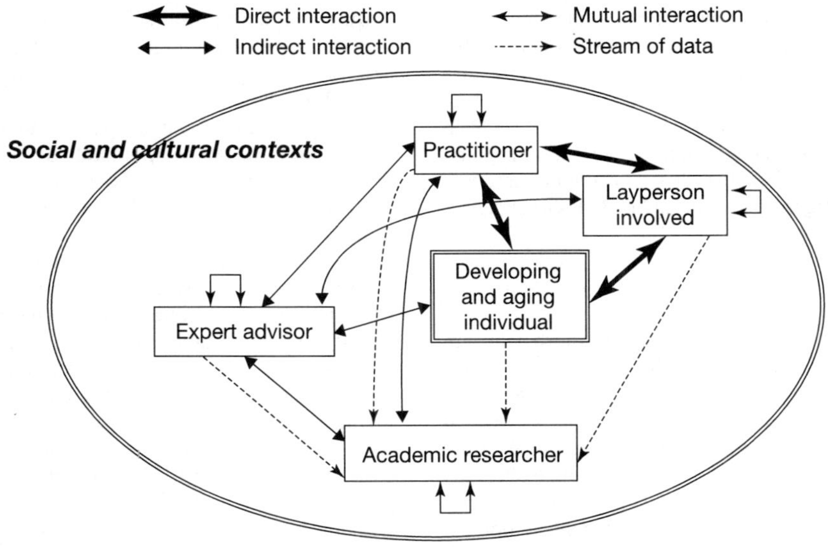

Figure 4.2 *Relations between the four roles (Kojima, 1998b)*

and the academic researcher. I have presented a model consisting of three social roles which omits the role of the practitioner (Kojima, 1998a), but now I believe a four-role model is more appropriate for discussing the Japanese child-rearing situation since the mid seventeenth century (Kojima, 1998b).

In the field of the sociology of knowledge, Schutz (1964) distinguished the man on the street, the well-informed citizen, and the expert. These three in his model represented persons. In addition, an ascending order of levels of knowledge among them was assumed. When applied to a certain realm, for example computer technology and the monetary system of a nation, Schutz's model fits very well. No one would question the fact that an expert knows best, and a well-informed citizen is more knowledgeable than the man in the street.

With regard to child-rearing, however, I believe that the distinction of roles without assuming any hierarchical ordering among them is more meaningful for two reasons. First, a technical breakthrough in child-rearing as described in science fiction is unlikely due to the biological and cultural constraints of human development, and thus a pool of ideas and skills for child-rearing is not monopolized for long by a selected few, but comes in time to be shared by many members from all ranks (Kojima, 1996a). In addition, a grandmother's wisdom can often be more effective than the professional practitioners' knowledge for solving a specific problem with children. Therefore I assume no hierarchy of practical knowledge among, for example, an experienced mother, a professional counselor, and an experimental child psychologist.

Secondly, it is not unusual for one person to play more than two social roles with regard to child-rearing. For example, it often happens that one person acts as an academic researcher, serves as an expert advisor in a newspaper column, and, as a father, worries about his son's problems. It may also happen that an expert writer of popular child-care books is accused by his sons because his parenting is divergent from his advice to the public. It is not an interesting research question to reveal what is going on in the mind of an individual who assumes multiple roles with regard to parenting? Now I will explicate each of the four roles.

Layperson Involved

The layperson's role is played by those who are directly involved in the daily practices of child-rearing without having any responsibility as a professional practitioner. The role of a parent is a typical case. Generally speaking, the expected goal of the parental role is to bring up the child to finally become a productive member of the particular society. Parents in general are responsible for the attainment of this goal, and the majority of them actually try to fulfill the responsibility.

Parents construct a set of working theories of child development and child-rearing through their experiences of daily interactions with their children, through social interaction with other family members, relatives, peers, and professional practitioners, and also through other sources of information such as expert advice conveyed by the mass media. Parental ideas or belief systems at the individual level are the main components of such working theories (e.g. Goodnow & Collins, 1990; Harkness & Super, 1996; Sigel, McGillicuddy-DeLisi, & Goodnow, 1992).

Personal theorizing by parents is motivated by the practical questions that they generate by themselves or are raised in social interaction with other people. Examples of such questions are, 'Why should I treat my child this way rather than in some other manner?', 'What will the results be if I continue the present treatment of my child?', and 'Why has my child developed this problem? Does he finally outgrow his interest in comics and begin to study hard?' These questions reflect the parents' need to understand the child-rearing process, to reason about it, and to justify or modify their own child-rearing practices. Parents' theories may range from the most unsophisticated and naive to the highly sophisticated and well-organized that are even superior to those of the so-called experts in the field. Still, whatever their level of sophistication, the parental role is always defined as that of laypersons directly involved in the child-rearing process, along with other family members and close friends.

Although some parents may have acquired a set of concepts and skills related to child-rearing before the birth of their child, it is typical that parental notions and theories are gradually constructed, tested, modified, and verified in the actual process of raising the child. In present-day Japan, parents, especially first-time parents, seek expert advice on child-rearing available from books, parents' magazines, and individual consultation with such professional practitioners as physicians, public health nurses, and clinical psychologists.

Along with these sources, parents are exposed to other sources of information and advice, including folk wisdom on the subject. For example, if a child's birth weight is somewhat lower than the average, a family member, a friend, or even a pediatrician will invoke the Japanese proverb, 'It is better to give birth to a smaller baby and help it to grow larger.' Incidentally, I have noticed that the net increase in height and body weight in the first three months after birth is sharper in Japanese infants than in Dutch infants. Another example is that if the infant seems inclined to sleep a great deal, the proverb 'A child who sleeps well grows well' will be mentioned to ease worrying parents. The proverb may reflect a generalization based on unsystematic observation without knowledge of the secretion of growth hormone during sleep. Invoking such proverbs not only serves to relieve the parents of any anxiety about their baby's birth weight or sleep pattern, but also enables them to interpret the baby's state and characteristics in a positive light. When I was analyzing a set of family diaries in early nineteenth century Japan (Kojima, 1996b), I found many examples of sayings about children which adults referred to in order to interpret the changes of children's behavior according to their age, or to understand each child's characteristics.

It is worth noting that ideas of this kind as represented by sayings are shared by the majority of people, because they are stored in the intrapersonal pool of cultural ideas. The component ideas in the personal pool of each individual have been accumulated during the individual's formative years, having been adopted from a bigger and more diversified cultural pool which I call the ethnopsychological pool of ideas (EPI) (see later). Though far less diversified than the collective EPI, the personal pool of cultural ideas contains heterogeneous and even mutually contradictory contents. Nevertheless the personal pool is not a simple hodgepodge of diverse elements but consists of more or less organized and locally consistent components. Parents may retrieve some of the components from this personal pool in order to use them in the problem-solving process of child-rearing.

Practitioner

The second role is that of practitioner in the capacity of professional specialist. In any society, special training and experience are required to become a socially recognized practitioner. In the realm of child-rearing in present-day Japan, such roles are typically performed by midwives, health care nurses, family doctors, teachers, and educational or psychological counselors. In addition, healers using folk remedies and minor religions have some clients, especially those who are suffering from intractable chronic illnesses and psychological problems.

Based on the demands of their clients, practitioners directly interact with the target persons: gathering information probably related to the problem, identifying the problem, and giving treatments. In the process of passing judgment and giving treatments, practitioners make full use of their personal theories and skills. These theories and skills have been constructed in each practitioner's mind through formal training in the particular field, and they have been modified through the individual's experiences in treating their cases – some of which were successful while others ended in failure.

Eventual success or failure of the treatment is the basic criterion for the evaluation of each practitioner. However, the credibility of a practitioner's judgment in each phase of treatment and its theoretical explanation to clients are also important for his or her reputation as a practitioner. An account lacking in credibility is the main reason for clients being distrustful of the practitioner. In order to make a practitioner's explanations and suggestions understandable and persuasive to a client, they should be based on a common theoretical ground with the client. On the other hand, however, if the explanations and suggestions made by a practitioner are no different from those of laypersons, the practitioner loses the confidence of the client. In this sense, an effective practitioner should understand the concepts, beliefs, values, and theories of the client and appropriately accommodate his or her theoretical explanations to the client's understanding. In some cases, the client's beliefs, values, and personal theory might become the direct target of treatment.

Expert Advisor

An expert advisor on child-rearing is the socially designated expert who provides advice, suggestions, and directions to the more or less generalized public through writings, informal or public talks, and in the context of indirect consultation. In my former three-role model (Kojima, 1998a), the tasks of giving advice and making suggestions to specific clients were also assigned to the expert's role. In the four-role model, however, direct involvement with specific clients has been assigned to the role of practitioners. Thus the interaction between an expert advisor and laypersons or practitioners is always indirect. An expert advisor does not directly interact with specific clients.

Take the example of an expert advisor who provides a specific advice-seeker with an answer through such forms of mass media as a newspaper, a magazine, radio, and TV. The expert answers the questions and gives advice to the person who is a member of the more or less generalized public. As explained below, it was in the middle of the seventeenth century that the role of expert advisor on child-rearing for the general public emerged in Japan. Before that period, a small number of experts such as priests and Confucians served the role of advisor for specific, privileged members of the society. In the sense that they directly served specific clients, these experts are categorized as practitioners in my four-role model.

Needless to say, expert advisors need their own theory to fulfill their role. Such theories are individually constructed by experts who refer to relevant academic research, the opinions of other experts, the questions probably raised by laypersons, and their own experiences. In societies in which academic inquiry into human nature and its development exists, the main task of an expert advisor is to act as an intermediary between laypersons or practitioners and academic scholars. The expert advisor converts academic knowledge into principles and methods that can be applied by laypersons and practitioners. Without the intervention of expert advisors, neither theoretical arguments nor empirical research findings in academia can be utilized by laypersons and practitioners to solve their own problems. The problems that laypersons and practitioners daily cope with take place in actual real-life situations that are more complex than the research conditions under which more abstract and purer scientific principles have been derived. An effective expert advisor should be knowledgeable about both the nature of academic research and the conditions of laypersons and practitioners. Therefore what an expert advisor suggests should be adjusted according to the characteristics of the intended audience and the actual conditions surrounding the audience.

Academic Researcher

Needless to say, all academic researchers, regardless of whether their academic activity involves empirical research or not, are engaged in the construction and reconstruction of their own theories.

Relationships among the Four Roles Concerning Child-Rearing

Let me explain the relationships between these four roles by taking some concrete examples. It is my argument that the diagram represented in Figure 4.2 is applicable to pre-industrial, industrial, and perhaps to post-industrial Japan. Let me begin with pre-industrial Japan.

Expert Advisors and Their Readers/Audience

In early modern Japan, that is, between the seventeenth and the mid nineteenth century, various kinds of child-rearing manuals were published by expert advisors (Kojima, 1986; 1996a). In these publications, a systematic explanation was developed with regard to three closely connected issues. They were (1) the nature of the child and of the developmental process, (2) the goals of child-rearing and education, and (3) the method of child-rearing and education. The sales point of each form of advice was the third issue, i.e. straightforward advice on the method. However, in order to make any form of advice persuasive and meaningful for readers to assimilate, an expert should construct a cohesive theory containing all three issues.

These pieces of advice were published not simply because of the writers' personal motive to enlighten people, and of promotion by the government for the purpose of effective social engineering. Laypersons (e.g. parents, relatives, and peers), practitioners (e.g. teachers of the three Rs and family doctors), and developing individuals needed these publications for ready reference as well as to construct their own implicit theories.

There are some pieces of evidence for this. According to recent research by Japanese historians, among the book collections of high-ranking farmers, village physicians, and village merchants from mid eighteenth to mid nineteenth century Japan, various kinds of popular manuals of child care, child-rearing, and education were to be found. It is also of interest that they also possessed health care manuals for women and for the elderly. It certainly reflects the fact that child-rearing, disease, and the life and death of the common people were important concerns of these people as laypersons and practitioners as well as of the central and local feudal governments.

While a developing individual, laypersons, and practitioners had direct mutual interactions with each other as shown by thick bi-directional arrows in Figure 4.2, the interaction between expert advisors and their readers or audience was more indirect and sporadic. Nevertheless the latter interaction was bi-directional in that not only did an expert advisor influence the reader/audience but the possible responses from the latter were taken into account by the former for the formulation of advice (Kojima, 1996a). The thin arrows that connect expert advisor with practitioner, layperson, and developing individual indicate this indirect nature of the interaction. Their unequal sized pointers indicate the dominant direction of the flow of discourse, i.e. from expert advisor to recipients.

In my analysis of expert advice on child-rearing and human development, I have tried to understand its construction as co-constructive discourse processes by expert advisors and their potential readers. The authors of advice documents often anticipated opposing views on the part of their readership. A few examples will follow but without giving references, which can be found in Kojima (1986; 1996a; 1996b; 1998a; 1999). The authors who claimed that most children were similar in their innate moral character and intellectual abilities anticipated in their writings a number of possible responses from their readers. Thus they argued, for example, against a certain view that attributed a son's bad conduct to his innate evil nature. Likewise, an eighteenth century physician recommended a contingent response on the part of care-takers to the smiling and vocalizing of young infants at sixty days after birth. This recommendation was placed in a cultural context in which some caretakers were likely to engage in vigorous over-stimulation of very young infants, believing this to be advantageous to the baby's development, or simply for fun.

Thus the advice of experts could be viewed as a communicative attempt to persuade the readers. In this sense the lay public was given a voice, participating indirectly in the process of advice construction. As a matter of fact, some of the advice developed out of the actual interactions between an expert and his followers or the audience.

Overt Social Interactions and Covert Processes among Laypersons

Some laypersons appeared to have developed implicit theories of child-rearing and development. As I have presented elsewhere (Kojima, 1996b), low-ranking warrior-class families in the nineteenth century were interested in the motor, social, cognitive, and language development of their children, and they shared knowledge on milestones of early development, and they communicated with each other on these matters. They had implicit theories, for example for explaining the pace of motor development that was slower than the norm. In addition, their daily effort to modify children's habitual behavior showed that they had developed some implicit theories on the self-regulation of conduct (e.g. Kojima, 1996b). Actual and imaginary interactions between the persons involved were quite evident. In the family diaries, not only interactions among family members, but also those involving relatives, neighbors, colleagues, and peers were amply recorded.

In addition to these actual interactions, I was able to reconstruct what was going on in the minds of parents and children who were involved in attempts to modify children's habitual behavior. During a period that spanned a few months, parents continually monitored the effects of their actions on children. Moreover, I was able to construct internal dialogues going on within the target child's mind during the period when his/her habitual behavior gradually changed through actual interactions with parents. Let me take an example of the treatment of a three-year-old girl who still sucked her mother's breast until the birth of her brother.

The parents began the behavioral modification process with external verbal suggestions by saying from time to time, 'Why do you still continue to suck your mother's breast?' or 'Why don't you stop sucking your mother's breast?' The child did not change her habitual behavior at all, but she was neither inhibited nor punished for that. Instead, the same kind of verbal suggestion was given. Through such interactions, the girl began not only to be aware of her behavior but to become conscious of the self-image of 'still sucking the mother's breast'. The girl seemed to be conversing with a self that was brought into her awareness through the daily interaction with her parents. That awareness was reflected by her behavioral change. That is, she ceased to make direct demands to her mother to let her suck. Instead she adopted a more indirect way to secure the opportunity. She said, 'Mom, I am sleepy now. Come to me!' When the father asked a question like 'Does milk really come out?' the girl answered, 'Yes, plenty of it!' Then there would be a time point when the girl became ready to discontinue this habitual behavior. She tried to persuade herself by making declarations to the parents, 'I have given the breast to the baby. It is dirty because the baby sucked it.' After that point, the girl never again sucked her mother's breast.

Academic Researchers in Early Modern Japan

Who were the academic researchers on children whose theory and knowledge on child-rearing were mediated by expert to practitioner and layperson? In pre-industrial Japan, the role was performed by two kinds of people. First, medical scholars conducted research on classic medical theory, tested its validity, and constructed their own theory. In particular, child-care and illnesses and growth of the child were the major concerns. Secondly, inquiry into human nature, goals of life, and ways of living and learning to accomplish the goals was fulfilled by Confucians as academic researchers in pre-industrial Japan. These medical and Confucian theories were referred to and quoted by expert advisors. The communication between academic researcher and expert advisor was not one-sided but bidirectional. Not all but many academic researchers also served the role of expert advisor. Kaibara Ekiken, the Confucian, physician, and naturalist in seventeenth to eighteenth century Japan, was a typical figure who served in both roles.

This was a period when no empirical research in the modern sense of the word was conducted on human development, and thus the streams of data from research targets to academic researcher (broken arrows) shown in Figure 4.2 were not channeled. However, expert advisors, practitioners, and laypersons developed their own more or less systematized theories and practices. In addition to mutual interaction within the same role, direct and indirect interactions among the roles were very active in the realm of child-rearing in pre-industrial Japan. It is my contention that in eighteenth century Japan not only can we find fertile soil for modern developmental science but we can clearly identify precursors of the science itself.

Figure 4.2 applies fully to the modern scene where professional academic research on child development and related domains emerged. It was around 1890 when the child study movement started in Japan. Using the Western framework of human development, academic researchers launched empirical studies of children. The data collected since then, however, have long been mainly concerned with development of the individual child, taken directly from children using observational, testing, survey, and experimental methods, or through reports by parents and teachers. It is only rather recently that researchers began to study social interactions involving the child (e.g. parent–child, and teacher–child, peers, and siblings), and it is also only recently that they have tried to understand naive psychology developed by laypersons (e.g. parental belief systems), practitioners (e.g. teacher's implicit theories), and children (e.g. theory of mind). Research by developmental psychologists on expert advice and its historical change dates back only to the 1970s in Japan.

Concerning the modern scene of child-rearing in Japan, my conclusion thus far is: with the exception of the establishment of academic developmental psychology and the flow of newly produced data, the structural aspect of Figure 4.2 appears not to have changed much from pre-industrial to industrial Japan. Of course, in some respects we find conspicuous changes from the pre-industrial to the industrialized period, including emphasis on maternal roles not only in child care but also in child discipline and education, progressive views on human development that are associated with intensified social competition. Nevertheless, my conclusion on the history of expert advisors' child-rearing theory in Japan during the past three centuries (Kojima, 1997) is very similar to what White characterized as 'old wine is being poured into new bottles' with regard to Western academic psychological theory (Bronfenbrenner et al., 1986, p. 1225).

Models of 'Culture and Human Behavior' in a Changing Society

The question here is, 'How does culture work in the theory construction process and in the actual practices of an individual?' I will present a model of the interrelationship between collective culture, intrapersonal culture, and an individual's actions (Figure 4.3, initially published in Japanese in Kojima, 1995). One important component of this model is the ethnopsychological pool of ideas (abbreviated as EPI, initially published in Japanese in Kojima, 1991) concerning child-rearing. The EPI is characterized as containing diverse, often mutually contradictory source materials on which the layperson's, the practitioner's, the expert advisor's, and the academic researcher's theories are to be constructed (Kojima, 1996a; 1997; 1998a; 1999). Thus the psychology of human development, which has been constructed by the four roles plus developing individuals, is based on a cultural pool of ideas and skills that I call the EPI. I will discuss historical continuity and change in the EPI concerning child-rearing in Japan over the past three and a half centuries.

The Concept of EPI

In spite of the above mentioned changes in modern Japan, the historical continuity of basic beliefs and values in ethnotheories of child-rearing for more than three centuries is evident. It is my contention that in Japan the collective ethnopsychological pool of ideas on child-rearing has maintained diverse, often mutually contradictory, components across historical periods to be utilized for constructing child-rearing theories by laypersons, practitioners, expert advisors, and academic researchers (Figure 4.3).

The pool tends to maintain once fashionable but then outmoded ideas. Even heterodox ideas and atypical practices that are processed in some forms of interaction (e.g. being debated, accused, or inhibited) in society tend to be retained as components of the collective pool of ideas. It has often happened in the Japanese history of child-rearing that these outmoded ideas and related skills are revived later to be utilized as components of new child-rearing and educational theories and practices. If one compares the representative, fashionable ideas that were drawn from the EPI across time, it appears that the older ideas were replaced by new ones. Nevertheless, the 'older' ideas are often maintained in the reservoir.

This does not mean that the EPI of child-rearing has remained unchanged. As is shown in Figure 4.4, the contents of EPI 1 at time 1 and EPI 2 at time 2 overlap considerably with each other. However, social change, interactions with other cultures, and

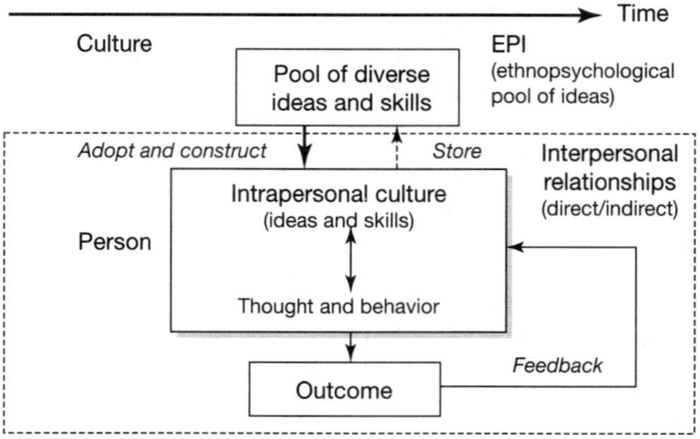

Figure 4.3 *A person's behavior and culture (Kojima, 1995)*

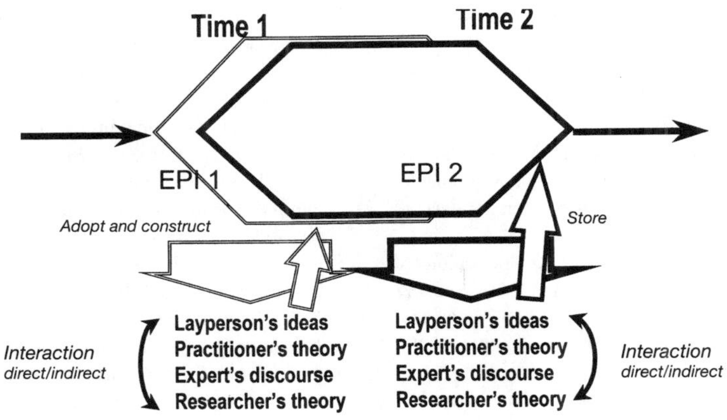

Figure 4.4 *Maintenance and change of EPI in a specific culture*

changing academic psychology may facilitate interaction processes among the four roles, introducing new components into the collective reservoir or causing the exclusion of some components from the reservoir.

Since 1991 when I first presented this concept, I have noted similar notions by other scholars, including Bell (1976; 1980), Cole (1992), Erikson (1976), and others. They are mainly concerned with ideas at the collective level. Some emphasize the timeless concern of humans for the meaning of human existence. For Cole, the past 'contains a fundamental human stock of ideas, images, beliefs, wishes, superstitions, feelings, dreams, hopes, and fears about aging' (1992, pp. xxvii–xxviii). Others focused attention on the dynamic nature of tension between the opposites. Cole himself wrote about the ability of early American culture to hold opposites in a creative tension. Erikson (1976) described the temporal variation of community members on an axis of variation and a balance of contrary tendencies. In his exposition of six different modes of child-rearing and mentality, Stone (1977) did not assume straightforward linear development; instead an unending dialectic of competing interests and ideas was assumed. My concept of EPI espouses the notion of conservation of the past but does not directly deal with tension and dialectic at the group level. This is because the EPI is characterized as the reservoir of ideas and other components to be utilized as source materials by the individual as theory construction. In addition I posit an intrapersonal mini reservoir that can hold mutually contradictory components. However, actual interaction with other persons, and intrapersonal interactions between roles, e.g. as a parent and as an expert advisor, may certainly give rise to the awareness of self-inconsistency. How an individual copes with the situation, and how the coping process is connected to interactions with the cultural reservoir, are among the issues that remain to be clarified. However, I believe that the concept is useful in dealing with individual construction processes in cultural historical contexts.

Concluding Remarks

The problem of culture and the development of mind, and the relationships between these that are mediated by social (both actual and symbolic) interactions, lie at the root of this chapter. For further understanding of the social interactions between the practitioners and those engaged in basic research, and of the construction of theories situated in the historical contexts of the cultural and social conditions of society, advances in both conceptual theoretical and methodological areas (Valsiner, 1998) are needed. If we can place theories of human development (e.g. Lerner, 1998), with necessary provision, at the cross-roads of historical and developmental disciplines, we can learn much from each other. For this purpose, active contributions from historically minded (not only history sensitive) developmentalists are badly needed.

References

Baldwin, A.L. (1967). *Theories of child development*. New York: Wiley.

Baltes, P.B., Lindenberger, U., & Staudinger, U.M. (1998). Life-span theory in developmental psychology. In W. Damon (series ed.) & R.M. Lerner (ed.), *Handbook of child psychology: Vol. 1. Theoretical models of human development* (5th edn, pp. 1029–1143). New York: Wiley.

Bell, D. (1976). *The cultural contradictions of capitalism*. New York: Basic.

Bell, D. (1980). *The winding passage: Essays and journeys, 1960–1980*. Cambridge, MA: ABT.

Bronfenbrenner, U. (1979). *The ecology of human development: Experiments by nature and design*. Cambridge, MA: Harvard University Press.

Bronfenbrenner, U., Kessel, F., Kessen, W., & White, S. (1986). Toward a critical social history of developmental psychology: A propaedeutic discussion. *American Psychologist*, 41 (11) , 1218–1230.

Bronfenbrenner, U., & Morris, P.A. (1998). The ecology of developmental process. In W. Damon (series ed.) & *Handbook of child psychology: Vol. 1. Theoretical models of human development* (5th edn, pp. 993–1028). New York: Wiley.

Cole, T.R. (1992). *The journey of life: A cultural history of aging in America*. Cambridge: Cambridge University Press.

Elder, G.H. Jr (1998a). The life course and human development. In W. Damon (series ed.) & R.M. Lerner (ed.), *Handbook of child psychology: Vol. 1. Theoretical models of human development* (5th edn, pp. 939–991). New York: Wiley.

Elder, G.H. Jr (1998b). The life course as developmental theory. *Child Development*, 69 (1), 1–12.

Elder, G.H. Jr, Modell, J., & Parke, R.D. (eds) (1993). *Children in time and place: Developmental and historical insights*. New York: Cambridge University Press.

Erikson, K.T. (1976). *Everything in its path: Destruction of community in the Buffalo Creek flood*. New York: Simon and Schuster.

Farr, R.M., & Moscovici, S. (eds) (1984). *Social representations*. Cambridge: Cambridge University Press.

Gergen, K.J. (1973). Social psychology as history. *Journal of Personality and Social Psychology*, 26, 309–320.

Goodnow, J.J., & Collins, W.A. (eds) (1990). *Development according to parents: The nature, sources, and consequences of parents' ideas*. Hove: Erlbaum.

Harkness, S., & Super, C.M. (eds) (1996). *Parents' cultural belief systems: Their origins, expressions, and consequences*. New York: Guilford.

Hareven, T.K. (1991). Synchronizing individual time, family time, and historical time. In J. Bender & D.E. Wellbery (eds), *Chronotypes: The construction of time* (pp. 167–182). Stanford: Stanford University Press.

Hatano, G., & Yamashita, T. (eds) (1987). *Kyoiku shinrigaku no shakaishi (Social history of Japanese educational psychology)* (in Japanese). Tokyo: Yuhikaku.

Kelley, H.H. (1992) Common-sense psychology and scientific psychology. *Annual Review of Psychology*, 43, 1–23.

Kessen, W. (1960). Research design in the study of developmental problems. In P.H. Mussen (ed.), *Handbook of research methods in child development* (pp. 36–70). New York: Wiley.

Kojima, H. (1986). Japanese concepts of child development from the mid-17th to mid-19th century. *International Journal of Behavioral Development*, 9, 315–329.

Kojima, H. (1991). *Jido shinrigaku eno shotai (Introduction to child psychology)* (in Japanese). Tokyo: Saiensu-sha.

Kojima, H. (1992). Current status, historical background, and problems of educational psychology in Japan. *Zeitschrift fuer Paedagogische Psychologie*, 6, 63–73.

Kojima, H. (1995). Kodomo no hattatsu ni taisuru bunka no hataraki (The function of culture in child development) (in Japanese). *Shoni Kango*, 18, 473–478.

Kojima, H. (1996a). Japanese childrearing advice in its cultural, social, and economic contexts. *International Journal of Behavioral Development*, 19, 373–391.

Kojima, H. (1996b). Zwei japanische Erziehungstagebuecher aus dem 19. Jahrhundert. In D. Elschenbroich (ed.), *Anleitung zur Neugier: Grundlagen japanischer Erziehung* (pp. 162–172). Frankfurt am Main: Suhrkamp.

Kojima, H. (1997). Problems of comparison: Methodology, the art of storytelling, and implicit models. In J. Tudge, M. Shanahan, & J. Valsiner (eds), *Comparisons in human development: Understanding time and development* (pp. 318–333). New York: Cambridge University Press.

Kojima, H. (1998a). The construction of childrearing theories in early modern to modern Japan. In M.C.D.P. Lyra & J. Valsiner (eds), *Construction of psychological processes in interpersonal communication (Child development in culturally structured environments, Vol. 4)* (pp. 13–34). Norwood, NJ: Ablex.

Kojima, H. (1998b). Genzaino hattatsu shinrigaku (Contemporary status of developmental psychology) (in Japanese). In H. Kojima & K. Miyake (eds), *Hattatshu shinrigaku (Developmental psychology)* (pp. 9–19). Tokyo: Hoso Daigaku Kyoiku Shinkokai.

Kojima, H. (1999). Ethnothérie des soins et de l'éducation des enfants au Japon: Une perspective historique. In B. Bril, P. Dasen, C. Sabatier, & B. Krewer (eds), *Propos sur l'enfant et l'adolescent: Quels enfants, pour quelles cultures?* (pp. 185–206). Paris: L'Harmattan.

Lerner, R.M. (1998). Theories of human development: Contemporary perspectives. In W. Damon (series ed.) & R.M. Lerner (ed.), *Handbook of child psychology: Vol. 1. Theoretical models of human development* (5th edn, pp. 1–24). New York: Wiley.

LeVine, R.A. (1980). Anthropology and child development. *New Directions for Child Development*, no. 8, 71–86.

Lightfoot, C., & Valsiner, J. (1992). Parental belief systems under the influence: Social guidance of the construction of personal cultures. In I. E. Sigel,, A. V. McGillicuddy-DeLisi, & J.J. Goodnow (eds) (1992). *Parental belief systems: The psychological consequences for children* (2nd edn, pp. 393–414). Hillsdale, NJ: Erlbaum.

Magnusson, D., & Stattin, H. (1998). Person–context interaction theories. In W. Damon (series ed.) & R.M. Lerner (ed.), *Handbook of child psychology: Vol. 1. Theoretical models of human development* (5th edn, pp. 685–759). New York: Wiley.

Moscovici, S. (1990). Social psychology and developmental psychology: Extending the conversation. In G. Duveen & B. Lloyd (eds), *Social representations and the development of knowledge* (pp. 164–185). Cambridge: Cambridge University Press.

Moscovici, S., & Duveen, G. (2000). *Social representations: Explorations in social psychology*. Cambridge: Polity.

Plomin, R., DeFries, J.C., McClean, G.E., & Rutter, M. (1997). *Behavioral genetics* (3rd edn). New York: Freeman.

Riegel, K.F. (1976). *Psychology of development and history*. New York: Plenum.

Schaie, K.W. (1965). A general model for the study of developmental problems. *Psychological Bulletin*, 64, 92–107.

Schaie, K.W., & Baltes, P.B. (1975). On sequential strategies in developmental process: Description or explanation? *Human Development*, 18, 384–390.

Schutz, A. (1964). The well-informed citizen: An essay on the social distribution of knowledge. In A. Brodersen (ed.), *Collected papers II: Studies in social theory* (pp. 120–134). The Hague: Martinus Nijhoff. Originally published 1946.

Sigel, I.E., McGillicuddy-DeLisi, A.V., & Goodnow, J.J. (eds) (1992). *Parental belief systems: The psychological consequences for children* (2nd edn). Hillsdale, NJ: Erlbaum.

Sinha, D. (1997). Indigenizing psychology. In J.W. Berry, Y.H. Poortinga et al. (eds), *Handbook of cross-cultural psychology: Vol. 1. Theory and method* (2nd edn, pp. 129–169). Boston: Allyn & Bacon.

Smedslund, J. (1997). *The structure of psychological common sense*. Mahwah, NJ: Erlbaum.

Stone, L. (1977). *The family, sex and marriage in England 1500–1800*. London: Weidenfeld & Nicolson.

Valsiner, J. (1997). *Culture and the development of children's action: A theory of human development* (2nd edn). New York: Wiley.

Valsiner, J. (1998). The development of the concept of development: Historical and epistemological perspectives. In W. Damon (series ed.) & R.M. Lerner (ed.), *Handbook of child psychology: Vol. 1. Theoretical models of human development* (5th edn, pp. 189–323). New York: Wiley.

Wertsch, J.V., & Youniss, J. (1987). Contextualizing the investigator: The case of developmental psychology. *Human Development*, 30 (1), 18–31.

Wohlwill, J.F. (1973). *The study of behavioral development*. New York: Academic.

Yamashita, T. (1977). *Han-hattatsu ron (Anti-developmentalism)* (in Japanese). Tokyo: Gendai Shokan.

PART TWO: PRENATAL AND INFANT DEVELOPMENT

5

Prenatal Psychological and Behavioural Development

PETER HEPPER

> A study of adult behaviour without consideration of its origin before birth is as incomplete as . . . the study of adult anatomy without reference to the embryology of the structures considered.
>
> (Carmichael, 1954)

Carmichael's words should ring loud and clear to all those studying psychology. To fully comprehend the behaviour of an individual at any particular point in time, some consideration must be given to the experiences that the individual has received up to that time. The prenatal period of development however has been largely ignored in these considerations. It is an oversight which greatly limits our ability to understand behaviour.

There have been few attempts to understand or explain behaviour in terms of events in the prenatal period. However, as research provides greater insight into prenatal development and behaviour a picture is forming that the prenatal period may be far more important than previously supposed. Indeed a full understanding of behaviour will only be achieved once its developmental origins are fully explored and understood. In this essay I shall review the current knowledge of behaviour in the prenatal period, and examine the evidence for the view that prenatal experience is important for future functioning and the extent to which such experiences influence the behaviour of the individual in the longer term.

Confusion over Age

Research examining prenatal behaviour faces an immediate problem since it is dealing with a period not accounted for in the normal ageing of the individual. Twelve months after birth the infant is celebrated for reaching its first birthday, 1 year old. Working backwards the individual, at birth, is aged 0, zero. This may seem reasonable given it marks the individual's first appearance into our world (the postnatal world). Such a view however fails to consider what happens in the period preceding this, zero being regarded as the start. Despite the acceptance that development is a continuous process, the calendar used to age individuals presents a problem when trying to extend this continuity back into the prenatal period. Conception occurred approximately 9 months prior to birth. The individual begins to move approximately 6–7 weeks after conception (or minus 7 months from birth), and at 24 weeks gestation responses to sound can be seen (minus 4 months). Placing such developments into the same time scale as developments after birth is difficult. The impression is created that development starts at birth, this being ground zero for development. As the evidence presented in this chapter will show, this is not the case.

Physical Development

The study of prenatal development can be conveniently divided into two broad areas: research examining physical development and research examining psychological development. The main emphasis here will be on psychological development.

The subject of prenatal development, or part of it, has its own discipline, embryology, and our understanding of the physical development of the human foetus has proceeded apace with large numbers of embryological, anatomical and physiological studies being undertaken. As a result the physical development of the human foetus is well understood. The availability of many detailed textbooks on virtually all aspects of physical development attests to this (Carlson, 1994; McLachlan, 1994; Moore, 1989). The physical processes that determine development and the embryological origins of adult structures are well understood and the induction of cell growth and specialisation are beginning to be broadly understood. This is in marked contrast to prenatal psychological development, which is poorly understood.

It is not my intention to discuss physical development *per se* other than to provide a brief outline of the basic terminology and key principles underlying development.

Development before birth is divided into three periods: the conceptual, the embryonic and the foetal. The conceptual period extends from fertilization to the establishment of the pregnancy, approximately 2 weeks later. During this period the fertilized egg (the zygote) travels down the fallopian tube and implants itself into the wall of the uterus (5–6 days after fertilization). During this time, first the cells divide to form a ball of cells (the morulla) and then, with the formation of a cavity within the morulla, this becomes the blastocyst. For the next 7 days the blastocyst burrows into the uterine lining, establishing a primitive placenta and circulation. After 2 weeks pregnancy is established. The next period of development, the embryonic period, begins during the middle of the second week with the formation of the bilaminar embryonic disc and finishes at the end of the eighth week. During this time all the major structures of the body are formed (heart, lungs, kidneys, liver, etc.). The individual is now called an embryo, and at the end of this period the physical appearance of the embryo is clearly human. The foetal period extends from 9 weeks after fertilization to birth and the individual is referred to as a foetus. Remarkable during this period is the phenomenal rate of bodily growth during the third and fourth month and body weight during the final months of pregnancy.

For clinical management pregnancy is divided into three equal length trimesters.

Different strategies regarding physical development are exhibited during the embryonic and foetal periods. The embryonic period is in some ways the most important period of development of our lives, for it is between the third and eighth week that all the major organs and structures begin to form. This is the time of specialization when specific organs form, e.g. heart, bone, skin, etc., initially in a rudimentary form. For example, the heart, although only two chambered, begins to 'beat' and blood is circulated around the embryo by the end of the third week. This enables the removal of waste and the acquisition of nutrients. Factors interfering with the formation of these structures may result in permanent major malformations (see discussion of teratogens below). During the foetal period development is largely concerned with the growth and differentiation of structures that emerged during the embryonic period. Very few new structures appear during the foetal period.

In general terms development proceeds in a cephalocaudal (head to toe) direction, such that at any particular time structures nearer the head will be more developed than structures nearer the feet. Also development proceeds from the basic to the more specialized. Thus the heart develops initially as a two-chambered structure, and its final four-chambered form develops subsequently.

Of particular interest in this essay is the brain and I shall outline its development in slightly more detail (see O'Rahilly & Müller, 1994). The brain is the most complex organ in the human body and befitting this it is one of the slowest to develop. It is the first organ to begin its development (at 18 days after fertilization) and one of the last to reach functional maturity around 4 years of age. In the 9 week foetus the brain comprises some 25% of the total body weight. The relative proportion of brain to body decreases as the foetus grows, being approximately 10% of body weight in the newborn, compared to 2% in the adult.

The brain begins its development at 18 days as a layer of cells on the embryonic disc, the neural plate. The neural plate folds to form the neural tube, which closes, beginning in its middle and progressing to each end. Failure of the neural plate to fold and form a tube correctly results in neural tube defects, e.g. spina bifida or anencephaly. By the end of the fourth week the neural tube has completely closed. The wall of the neural tube thickens and forms the brain and spinal cord.

During the fourth week the caudal (head) end of the neural tube develops to form three primary vesicles, the hindbrain, the midbrain, and the forebrain. In the fifth week the forebrain further subdivides into the telencephalon and diencephalon and the hindbrain divides into the metencephalon and myelencephalon. The relation of these embryonic structures to adult brain structure is well known (Figure 5.1a).

The myelencephalon forms the medulla oblongata which contains the centres for regulation of respiration and heartbeat. The metencephalon forms the cerebellum and pons. The cerebellum develops from the rhombic lips of the 5-week-old embryo. Initially these expand inwards but from the beginning of the fourth month these grow and expand rapidly outwards. The midbrain undergoes less change than

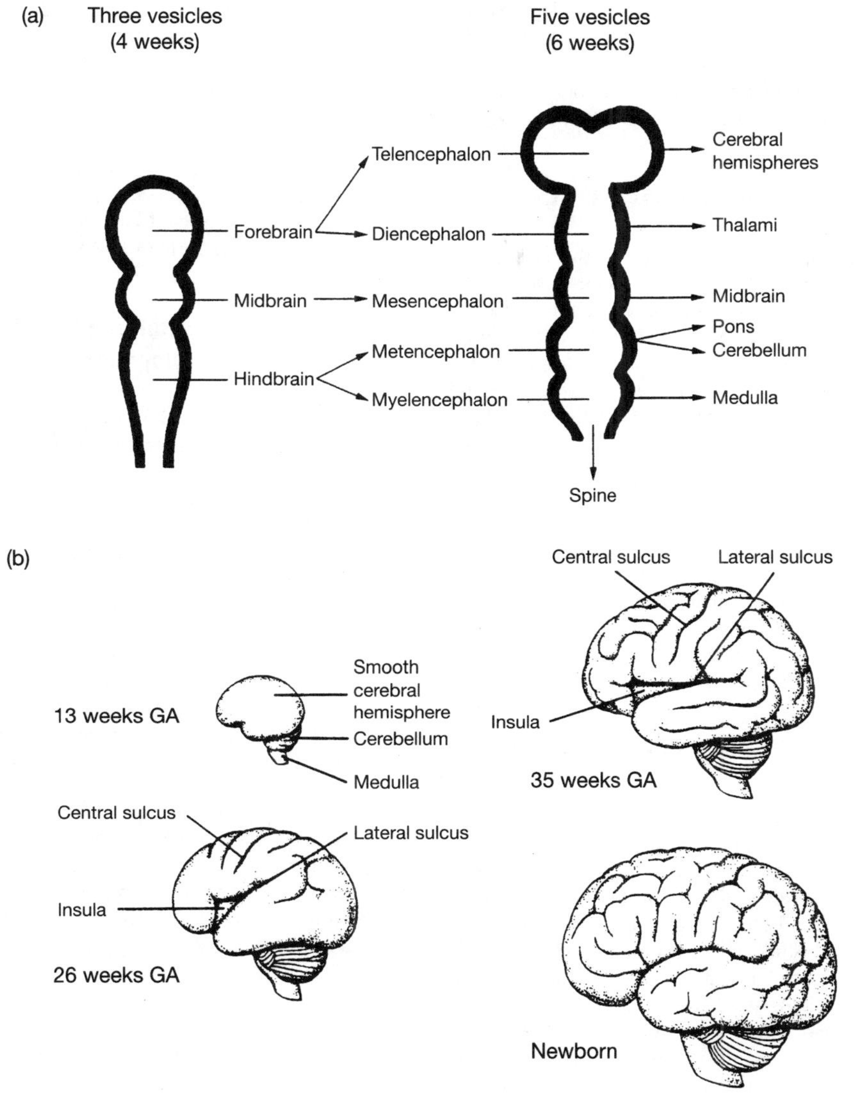

Figure 5.1 *(a) Diagrammatic representation of derivation of adult brain structures from embryological brain (from Moore, 1989). (b) Diagrammatic representation of growth of cerebral hemispheres and appearance of gyri and sulci during gestation (from Moore, 1989)*

virtually all other parts of the brain and forms the inferior and superior colliculi (concerned with the auditory and visual system respectively), the tegmentum and substantia nigra. The diencephalon forms the thalamus (a site where nerves from higher brain centres synapse with those from other regions of the brain and brain stem), the hypothalamus (which controls and regulates many functions, e.g. sleep, temperature, hunger, thirst, emotions, etc.) and the pineal body (which secretes melatonin). The telencephalon is particularly fascinating as it gives rise to some of the oldest and most primitive parts of the brain, the rhinencephalon (the olfactory centres), and some of the newest, the neocortex. In the early part of development the rhinencephalon forms the majority of the telencephalon but as the brain develops the neocortex becomes the region forming most of the mass of the brain. The cerebral hemispheres develop from the growth of the bilateral telencephalic vesicles. Initially these expand sideways but as growth continues they develop to the midline of the brain covering the diencephalon and mesencephalon. Initially the hemispheres are smooth in appearance but as growth continues the surface folds forming sulci (grooves) and gyri (convolutions), greatly increasing the surface area of the brain, without increasing the size of the brain cavity (see Figure 5.1b). Growth is particularly marked between weeks 28 and 30 (Dorovini-Zis & Dolman, 1977).

More Complications over Age

The terminology used to describe the age of the embryo or foetus before birth is also somewhat complex. Two different ages are commonly used to describe the maturity of the individual before birth: gestational age and conceptual age. Gestational age begins at the first day of the last menstrual period whilst conceptual age begins at fertilization. Thus gestational age will be 2 weeks greater than conceptual age for the same individual. For the remainder of this chapter, gestational age will be used. Reference will be made to the general principles of physical development where they are of relevance to understanding of prenatal psychological development; however, for convenience I shall use the term 'prenatal development' to refer to 'psychological' development before birth.

Prenatal Psychological Development

With apologies for the pun, the study of prenatal psychological development is very much an embryological science. Our understanding of psychological development and behaviour in this period lags far behind that at all other stages of the life cycle. The experimental study of prenatal abilities has only recently become a subject of sustained interest to some psychologists (Lecanuet et al., 1995; Nijhuis, 1992; Smotherman & Robinson, 1988). Theoretical considerations concerning the importance of the prenatal period are also absent and many theories of development do not extend into the prenatal period. There are a number of explanations for this: the lack of satisfactory methods with which to examine the foetus; an underestimation of the abilities of newborns; and seemingly persuasive arguments to explain the foetus's behaviour during this time.

Early studies of embryonic behaviour (e.g. Preyer, 1885) found that movement in chick embryos could be observed prior to the time that a reaction could be elicited using a tactile stimulus. This led to the view that the embryonic origin of behaviour was the result of the spontaneous firing of the nervous system. The development of movements was seen as a consequence of the development in the neuromotor system. Further studies confirmed this (e.g. Hamburger, 1963; Provine, 1972). With embryonic movement apparently consigned to following a designated course impervious to environmental influences, there was little interest in studying the phenomenon. However, other studies began to question this and demonstrated that stimulation played an important role in embryonic behaviour (e.g. Coghill, 1929, and recently Smotherman, e.g. Smotherman & Robinson, 1995). The area thus became of greater interest as external (environmental) factors were seen to influence prenatal behavioural ontogenesis and more research was undertaken (e.g. see reviews in Lecanuet et al., 1995; Nijhuis, 1992; Smotherman & Robinson, 1988).

Research Examining Prenatal Development

As with any new area of investigation, its opening researches need to address some basic questions. What, how, when and why does the foetus do the things it does? The study of prenatal development has barely scratched the surface of these questions. Our understanding of the 'how' question is probably the most advanced due to the volume of research on physical development. For example, an observation of foetal movements at around 8 weeks gestation ('when' and 'what' questions) can quickly be supported by data on the development of the muscles, nervous system, etc., to address the 'how' question.

In the absence of experimental data a broad spectrum of views has been presented regarding abilities before birth (Hepper, 1989). At one end of this range the prenatal individual is considered a passive organism subject largely to 'commands from its genes' to initiate and control development and growth. At the other extreme the individual is considered to be a fully interactive, sentient miniature adult possessing adult abilities and only requiring a period of growth. The latter is the psychological equivalent of the pre-formationist views of embryological development. Neither of these views is correct and a middle ground between the two extremes is more appropriate. Genes may trigger some aspects of development but experiential factors are crucial for normal development to proceed (see also Gottlieb, Chapter 1 and Wahlsten, Chapter 2 in this volume). A picture is emerging that reveals both the environment and the activity of the foetus playing crucial roles in its development. Development may be activity dependent (Miller, 1994; Provine, 1986) requiring appropriate interaction between behavioural activity, environmental cues and physical structures to ensure normal development.

In this essay I shall review the evidence regarding the development of prenatal psychological functioning, and how prenatal experiences and activity may influence the development of the individual with potential short-term and long-term impact. I shall concentrate on the prenatal period in the human; for a discussion of work with animals see Lecanuet et al. (1995) and Smotherman and Robinson (1988).

Historical overview

It would not be an exaggeration to say that for the greater part of the twentieth century psychological functioning during the prenatal period has been the subject of little consideration (see below). Certainly it has not figured highly on the agenda for experimental study. However that is not to say it has been ignored. Indeed the importance of this period has been warmly embraced by certain psychoanalytical traditions, which have argued that events during the prenatal and birth periods have an important impact on the psychological development of the individual. Freud (1933) considered a traumatic birth a possible cause of later anxiety although he did not believe in 'mental life' at birth. Rank (1929) believed reactions to birth to be the source of all psychological problems. He viewed the womb as a primal paradise which the individual lost at birth. How the individual dealt with this loss had long-term consequences. Many therapists report success through use of, for example, birth regression, to enable individuals to come to terms with adverse uterine or birth experiences and thus overcome their adult psychological problems (Chamberlain, 1988). Such views have not predominated or gained much credence due to lack of experimental evidence.

The best way to describe the experimental study of prenatal development during the early part of the century (until the late 1970s) is sporadic and infrequent. Two papers appeared in the 1920s demonstrating that the foetus reacted to external sounds (Forbes & Forbes, 1927; Peiper, 1925). The 1930s and 1940s saw a change in emphasis, perhaps reflecting current thinking in psychology, and two papers appeared reporting classical conditioning in the human foetus (Ray, 1932; Spelt, 1948). The 1930s also saw the beginning of work by Sontag examining the influence of various environmental factors, including maternal anxiety, on the development of the foetus (e.g. Sontag, 1962; Sontag & Wallace, 1934). However there was little other interest in studying the human foetus. Only in the late 1970s and 1980s was interest in the behaviour of the foetus renewed.

Theoretical interest in the role of the prenatal period came largely from outside the discipline of psychology with, for example embryologists and biologists speculating on the role of prenatal experiences for subsequent development (e.g. see Carmichael, 1954). One individual however stands out from this, Leonard Carmichael, who wrote extensively and championed research into prenatal development (Carmichael, 1941). He may be considered one of the first psychologists to use experimental data to support the view that the prenatal period was of importance for subsequent behaviour and functioning.

Two factors have triggered interest in the prenatal period in recent years. One is technological advances which provide safe, non-invasive access to the foetus *in utero*. The second is a new appreciation of the abilities of the newborn infant.

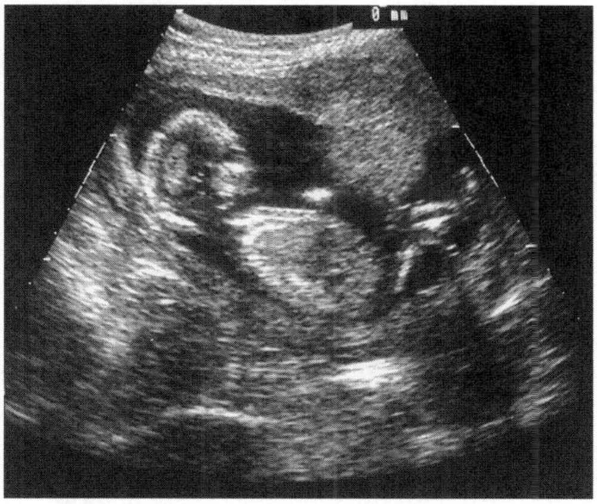

Figure 5.2 *Ultrasound picture of human foetus at 16 weeks gestational age (copyright Hepper and FBRC)*

A major factor that enabled a greater and more detailed study of the foetus was the availability of ultrasound imaging. Ultrasound technology has enabled the foetus to be observed, safely, in great detail and in real time (see Figure 5.2). Such is the resolution of the ultrasound machines available today that the opening and closing of the pupil of the eye can be observed. Prior to the availability of this equipment, early studies were performed on aborted foetuses (Hooker, 1952; Minkowski, 1928). Attempts were also made to measure foetal activity indirectly (Sontag & Wallace, 1934). Comparison of these data with those obtained from ultrasound reveals little similarity. Ultrasound technology provided the means to overcome the difficulty of observing the foetus and thus enabled the study of prenatal behaviour to proceed apace.

The second factor that has driven research in the prenatal period was a reappraisal of the abilities of the newborn infant. As greater newborn competencies and abilities were uncovered it became apparent that the newborn was not a passive organism at the mercy of its environment. Rather the newborn possessed functioning sensory systems, was able to learn and could thus exert a degree of control over its environment (Hepper, 1992). This raised the question of the developmental origin of these abilities. Whilst it is possible that they may have arisen at the moment of birth it is more likely they arose during the prenatal period. Interest in tracking the origins of behaviour thus stimulated research into the abilities of the foetus.

The Abilities of the Foetus

Study of the foetus has largely proceeded as a descriptive science, with investigators exploring and describing the activities of the foetus. Indeed description is the first and important goal in any new discipline. The following review outlines current knowledge regarding the behaviour of the foetus. Three broad areas will be described: the movements of the foetus, its sensory systems and its learning and/or memory abilities. Methodological problems will be considered where appropriate in each section.

Foetal Movements

Every woman who has been pregnant knows that the foetus moves. Maternal reports of movements provided the first indicator that the foetus was active in the uterus. Mothers report feeling the movements of the foetus (quickening) at around 18–20 weeks gestation in their first pregnancy. These first movements are often described as a 'fluttering' by mothers, who frequently report feeling movements earlier in their second pregnancy (Neldam, 1986). This may reflect the fact that mothers now know what the feelings are and recognize them sooner. However, there is much individual variation in the maternal perception of movements. Moreover, compared with movements observed via ultrasound, mothers feel only a small proportion of the movements that can be observed, about 5–10%.

The first study of foetal movement was performed by Preyer (1885) who 'observed' foetal movements by using a stethoscope placed on the mother's abdomen. With this method he 'heard' the foetus move at 12 weeks gestation and speculated that movements may be present before this. The study of aborted foetuses revealed movements present at around 8 weeks gestation (e.g. Hooker, 1952; Minkowski, 1928).

The first documentation of movements using ultrasound was made by Reinold (1971). He observed foetal movements beginning around 8 weeks gestation. Different authors have described these first movements differently, e.g. a twitch (Birnholz, Stephens, & Faria, 1978), vermicular movements (Ianniruberto & Tajani, 1981), a rippling (Goto & Kato, 1983), or a just discernible movement (de Vries, Visser, & Prechtl, 1982). Direct observation of these movements indicates that they are slow and originate in the back or spinal column. The back may flex or extend and this motion results in passive movements of the arms and legs.

Studies of behaviour have largely concentrated on describing the onset of particular movements (Kisilevsky & Low, 1998). The first movements are observed at 8 weeks gestation, and the next few weeks see the appearance of a variety of different movements (see Table 5.1). Most of the movements that the foetus will produce in utero are present by 20 weeks gestation (Prechtl, 1988). One of the major problems in the study of foetal movements is that the descriptive base has yet to move on from frequency counts and the timing of their onset. There is no doubt that the complexity of behaviour increases as the foetus matures but this has yet to be fully described and examined. Some have argued for a qualitative approach in order to describe the development of foetal movements to capture their complexity. Prechtl, for example, argues that the qualitative assessment of general movements (although these are not defined, e.g. Prechtl & Einspieler, 1997) provides the best and most suitable movement with which to assess the functioning of the CNS (Kainer et al., 1997; Sival & Prechtl, 1992). The fluency, complexity, speed and amplitude, it is argued, provide an accurate means of describing foetal movement. However, in the absence of a standardized pattern for describing all movements the development of foetal movement remains largely uncharted.

Eye movements and breathing movements have received specific attention. These are briefly discussed here to illustrate how the study of foetal movements may elucidate the origins of adult behaviour (eye movements) and indicate the

Table 5.1 *The gestational age at which behaviours are first observed in the foetus*

Behaviour	Gestational age (weeks)	Behaviour	Gestational age (weeks)
Just discernible movement	7	Leg twitch	10
Startle	8	Hand–face contact	10
General movement	8	Stretch	10
Hiccup	9	Rotation of foetus	10
Isolated arm movement	9	Jaw movement	10–11
Isolated leg movement	9	Yawn	11
Isolated head retroflexion	9	Finger movement	12
Isolated head rotation	9–10	Sucking and swallowing	12
Isolated head anteflexion	10	Clonic movement of arm or leg	13
Foetal breathing movements	10	Rooting	14
Arm twitch	10	Eye movements	16

Source: adapted from Birnholz, Stephens, and Faria (1978), de Vries, Visser, and Prechtl (1982; 1985).

importance of activity during the foetal period (foetal breathing movements).

Eye movements are first observed at around 16 weeks gestation (Birnholz, 1981). These first eye movements are slow, with rapid eye movements appearing around 23 weeks gestation (see review in Horimoto et al., 1993). Interestingly the co-ordination of eye movements necessary for focusing, i.e. both eyes move inwards together to focus on near objects whereas both eyes should move outward together to focus on a distant object, appears to be a property of the visual system as soon as the eyes move (Takashima et al., 1991). Thus it is possible to track the developmental origin of a behaviour that is present in individuals postnatally from its emergence in the uterus.

The foetus is unable to inspire air in its fluid-filled uterine environment, and thus the existence of foetal breathing movements is somewhat paradoxical. These movements – motion of the diaphragm and rib cage – would result in breathing after birth and hence are termed foetal breathing movements. Around 9–10 weeks gestation the first breathing movements are observed and appear regular in nature (de Vries, Visser, & Prechtl, 1985). Regular and irregular breathing movements are observed at 12 weeks gestation (de Vries, Visser, & Prechtl, 1985) and by 30 weeks of gestation foetal breathing movements are occurring around 30% of the time (Patrick et al., 1980). Towards the end of pregnancy foetal breathing movements increase during periods of activity – a marked parallel with breathing after birth. The existence of foetal breathing movements has suggested one functional explanation for the prenatal presence of certain movements: that is, these movements are so important for survival that they are practised before the time that they are needed to ensure they are functioning efficiently when required. It would make little sense for such a complicated and vital process as breathing to be switched on suddenly at birth; far better to practise beforehand. This is not to say there is any conscious effort on the part of the foetus to breathe. It appears that it is a property of the foetal neural pathways involved in respiration to trigger breathing movements to ensure all the necessary systems are operational and integrated before birth.

Once the foetus begins to move it remains active. However as it ages its movements become more concentrated into periods of activity followed by periods of inactivity. From about 20–22 weeks of gestation diurnal variation in foetal movements may be observed (James, Pillai, & Smoleniec, 1995).

The foetus's active–inactive cycle reaches its peak towards the end of gestation when certain individual movements become co-ordinated in their occurrence; these patterns of behaviour are termed 'foetal behavioural states' (Nijhuis et al., 1982). Behavioural states can be defined as a recognizable and well defined association of variables, stable over time, with clear transitions between each. Based on the observation of behavioural states in the newborn (Prechtl, 1974), four behavioural states have been identified in the foetus (Nijhuis et al., 1982). These states are termed 1F, 2F, 3F and 4F, where F represents foetal. The variables used to define behavioural states in the foetus are: the heart rate pattern; the presence or absence of eye movements; and the presence or absence of body movements (Nijhuis et al., 1982). The four states that have been defined are:

- State 1F: quiescence. The foetus exhibits occasional startles, no eye movements, and a stable foetal heart rate (pattern A, Figure 5.3). This state increases in occurrence from about 15% at 36 weeks of gestation and 32% at 38 weeks to 38% at term.
- State 2F. This state is characterized by frequent and periodic gross body movements, eye movements are present, and the foetal heart rate shows frequent accelerations in association with movement (pattern B, Figure 5.3). This is the most commonly occurring state, being observed around 42–48% of time in the foetus.
- State 3F. No gross body movements are observed, eye movements are present, and the foetal heart rate (pattern C, Figure 5.3) shows no accelerations and has a wider oscillation bandwidth than state 1F. This is a rare state to observe as it occurs only briefly. In fact its occurrence is usually represented by number of occurrences rather than as a percentage of time.
- State 4F. In this state the foetus exhibits continual activity, eye movements are present, and the foetal heart rate is unstable and tachycardia is present (pattern D, Figure 5.3). This state occurs about 6–7% of the time between 36 and 38 weeks gestation, increasing to 9% around 40 weeks gestation.

Periods when no states are identifiable, i.e. when variables do not truly associate, decrease with gestation, occurring around 20% of the time at 36 weeks gestation but only 5% at term. These states are observed from 36 weeks of gestational age (Nijhuis et al., 1982) and their emergence has been argued to represent a greater degree of integration between the various centres of the central nervous system.

Foetal Sensory Abilities

All of the senses that operate in adults have been found, in some degree, to function before birth. Studies of foetal sensation need to address two issues: first whether the foetus responds to a particular stimulus, and second what kind of sensory environment the foetus exists in.

Study of the foetus's sensory abilities must proceed with caution in regard to the conclusions that may be

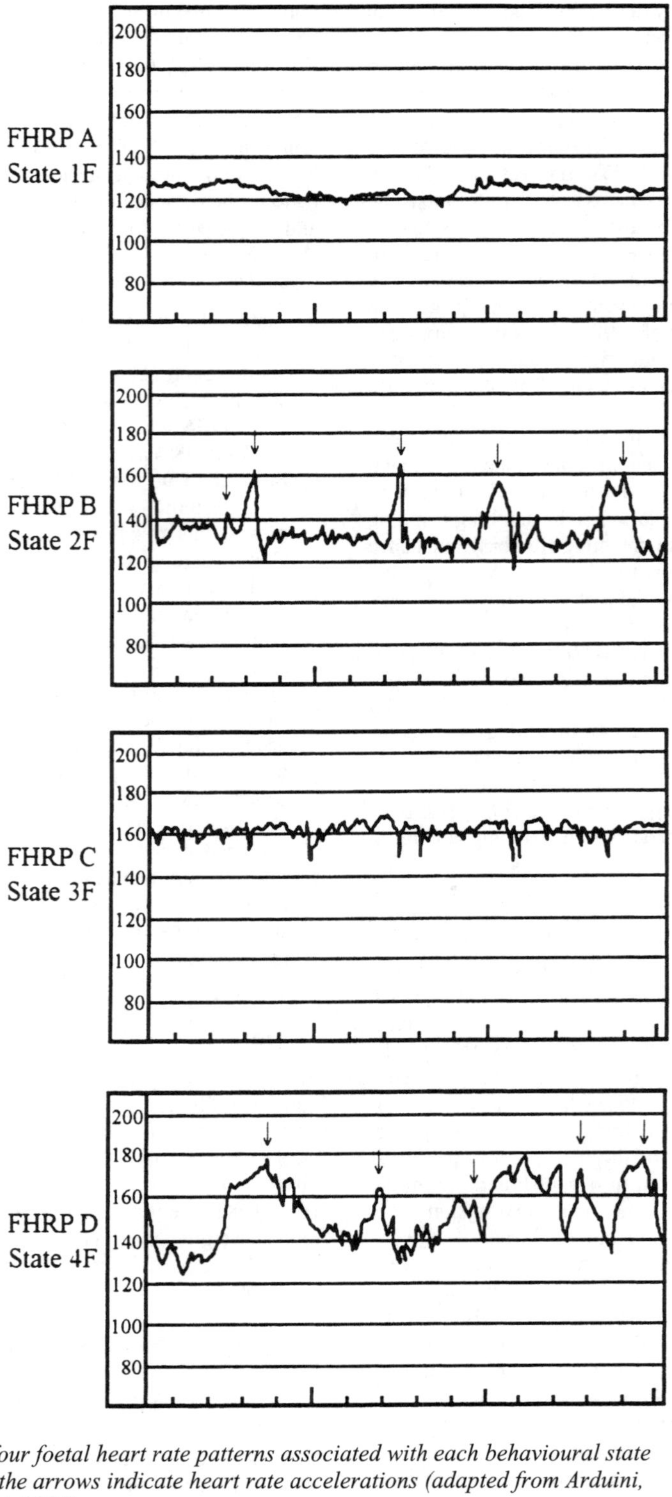

Figure 5.3 *The four foetal heart rate patterns associated with each behavioural state (1F, 2F, 3F, 4F); the arrows indicate heart rate accelerations (adapted from Arduini, Rizzo, & Romanini, 1995)*

drawn from such research. It is worth briefly drawing attention to some of the problems encountered in research on an organism that is removed from direct contact and unable to inform us of what we may be doing wrong.

First, one has to exert great caution in attempting to elucidate the actual developmental origin of a particular ability or response. To illustrate this I shall use a hypothetical study concerned with foetal hearing. To examine the hearing of the foetus we can only present a stimulus outside the mother's body and observe the foetus's reaction to it. The two most used responses to monitor effects in studies of the foetus have been movement and heart rate. For example, if a sound is presented and a change in heart rate or movement is observed it is inferred that the foetus has responded and can hear that stimulus (though see below). However, if the foetus does not respond we cannot conclude that it is unable to hear. For the foetus to exhibit a response to a sound stimulus it must have a functioning auditory system, a functioning motor system and a functioning link between the two. Immaturity in any one of these components would result in the failure to observe a response. Thus, whilst we can say the foetus does not respond to the sound, whether this is due to its auditory system not functioning cannot be established from this experiment. In general terms a lack of response on the part of the foetus does not necessarily mean the system under investigation is not functioning. Other explanations for a lack of response must be considered. A second reason for caution is an increased concern for the safety of the foetus in relation to a variety of environmental threats. Pregnant women who work in a noisy environment have been the subject of attention because of concern that the foetus's hearing may be damaged (Hepper & Shahidullah, 1994a). Sound passes through the abdomen of the mother and reaches the developing individual from the day of conception. The hair cells of the ear form at around 12 weeks gestation (Pujol, Lavigne-Rebillard, & Uziel, 1991) and are thus potentially at risk from this time to damage by high intensity stimulation. The fact that the foetus does not respond does not allow the conclusion that it is 'safe' from loud sounds. The potential for damage to the foetus is not necessarily linked to a functional response. Damage may be caused prior to the appearance of function in an organ whose structure is present earlier in gestation.

Second, care must be taken in interpreting the responses of the foetus. Again the exploration of foetal hearing may be used as an example. The sound stimulus is presented to the foetus, usually via a loudspeaker positioned on or near the mother's abdomen. It then passes through the mother's skin and other abdominal tissues to reach the foetus. If the foetus responds it is assumed that it is responding to the sound, but caution must be exercised. Sound is simply vibration; it may be that the foetus's response is mediated via cutaneous receptors in its skin. Studies of foetuses subsequently found to be deaf but with a perfectly normal cutaneous sensory system have shown this not to be the case (Shahidullah & Hepper, 1993a). However, the observation highlights the need for appropriate controls. The quality and intensity of the sound stimulus may be altered as it passes through the abdomen (Querleu et al., 1988). Certain sounds will be highly attenuated and hence may not be perceived by the foetus. Thus the stimulus that is detected by the foetus may be different from that presented in an experiment.

Third, it should not be forgotten that experimental studies of the foetus's response to certain stimuli are just that: experimental studies. Whilst every effort is made to choose appropriate stimuli, that is stimuli of ecological significance to the foetus, some studies present stimuli that the foetus will never experience naturally in the course of its development. An example is visual stimuli. Any natural visual stimulus, if experienced by the foetus, will probably appear as a diffuse glow on the abdomen and not a specific source. Yet responses can be elicited by shining a torch and forming a specific light point on the abdomen (Polishuk, Laufer, & Sadovsky, 1975). Experimentally it may be possible to stimulate and elicit responses from the foetus's visual system but in the normal course of pregnancy such stimuli are unlikely to occur (Hepper, 1992). To fully understand the role of prenatal experiences or behaviour for subsequent development, these experiences or behaviours must be ecologically valid. That is to say they must represent the natural environment of a foetus and not be exceptional conditions. While detailed research may be undertaken on the development of responsiveness to visual stimuli, such research has limited significance for elucidating the normal processes of development.

Audition

The most studied of human sensory abilities in the foetus is that of audition. This is largely explained by the fact that auditory stimuli are relatively easy to present to the foetus (Shahidullah & Hepper, 1993b). A number of different responses have been measured to assess the foetus's response to sound: a change in foetal heart rate (Gagnon, 1989; Read & Miller, 1977); a change in movement (Birnholz & Benacerraf, 1983; Shahidullah & Hepper, 1993b); or a change in behavioural state (Devoe et al., 1990; Visser et al., 1989). The measure used influences the observation of when the foetus first responds to sound. Thus an auditory stimulus elicits a reliable change in movements from as early as 20–24 weeks gestation (Shahidullah & Hepper, 1993b) whereas if heart rate is monitored a reliable response is found from 28 weeks gestation (Gagnon, 1989). The response of the foetus may be influenced by the type of sound used, its frequency, intensity and duration, and the foetus's behavioural state (Hepper & Shahidullah, 1994b). For example, louder intensities elicit a greater response. The foetus begins hearing in the low frequency part (250 Hz, 500 Hz) of the adult hearing range (20–20,000 Hz) and as it matures the range of frequencies it responds to increases (Hepper & Shahidullah, 1994c). Interestingly (see Figure 5.4) it appears that the foetus first starts to hear in the range of frequencies that would be encoded by the volley principle and later develops the ability to encode high frequency sound, encoded by the place principle (Hepper & Shahidullah, 1994c). The foetus is able to discriminate between pure-tone frequencies (Shahidullah & Hepper, 1994) and speech sounds, e.g. 'BABI' and 'BIBA' (Lecanuet et al., 1987).

The foetus will be exposed to a variety of auditory stimuli in the uterus. Noise from the mother's heartbeat, blood flow and digestive system between 20 and 70 dB will be present (Querleu et al., 1988). Sounds in the external environment will also penetrate to the uterus. The mother's skin and other tissues however attenuate sounds from the external environment. There is little attenuation around 125–250 Hz but as the frequency increases the attenuation becomes much greater, with sounds over 2000 Hz being attenuated as much as 40 dB (Querleu et al., 1989). As such these frequencies will probably not be experienced by the foetus. This attenuation will change the quality of external sounds as they reach the foetus, although certain aspects, notably the rhythm, will remain unaltered (see below for discussion on speech recognition and language).

Thus in the normal course of pregnancy, sound forms a part of the foetus's environment and experience and provides a stimulus to which the foetus responds.

Chemosensation

It is difficult to separate olfaction (smell) and gustation (taste) *in utero* since both receptor types are bathed in amniotic fluid and stimuli present in the amniotic fluid may stimulate both sensory systems. For this reason the foetal responses to smell and taste are usually considered under the same heading: chemosensation.

The foetus is able to discriminate between sweet and noxious substances added to the amniotic fluid. An increase in foetal swallowing is observed following the addition of saccharin to the amniotic fluid (De Snoo, 1937). In contrast a decrease in swallowing is observed when a noxious substance, lipiodol (iodinated poppy seed oil), is added to the amniotic fluid (Liley, 1972).

More evidence of a functioning chemosensory system has been obtained from observations of newborns. Newborns show a preference for the odour of their mother compared to that of another female (Macfarlane, 1975; Porter, 1991). Furthermore neonates orient to their own amniotic fluid (Schaal et al., 1991) which suggests that there is some experience of odours/tastes *in utero*. This evidence indicates the foetus has a functioning chemosensory system but when the system begins to operate is not known.

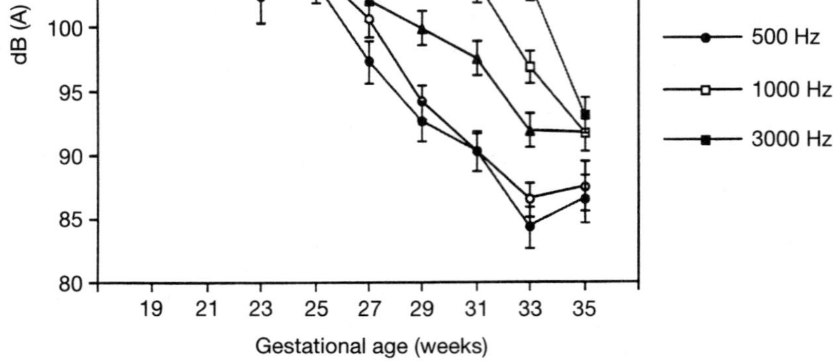

Figure 5.4 *The mean (± SE) intensity level required to elicit a response at each gestational age for each frequency examined (from Hepper & Shahidullah, 1994c)*

Chemosensory stimuli may be experienced by the foetus in a number of ways. Substances can diffuse into the amniotic fluid which the foetus swallows from around 12 weeks gestation. The quality of the amniotic fluid is influenced by the mother's diet. Chemical analysis of the amniotic fluid reveals a variety of substances which the foetus may experience as odours/tastes, e.g. lactic and citric acids, amino acids and fatty acids (which may smell rancid and pungent to adults: Schaal, Orgeur, & Rognon, 1995). Furthermore as the mother's diet changes the mix of these substances changes, providing the foetus with an ever-changing source of chemosensory stimulation (Schaal, Orgeur, & Rognon, 1995). The foetus may also experience substances via its bloodstream. As nutrients pass from the mother's blood supply to that of the foetus, flavours and 'smells' may also pass across and be experienced by the foetus. Garlic is one such blood-borne odorant which can be 'experienced' via its presence in the blood (Hepper, 1988). Substances which reach the foetus in this way may then be broken down and expelled from the foetus's body into the amniotic fluid as the foetus urinates. When swallowing the amniotic fluid the foetus may experience these stimuli.

Exactly when the foetus first responds to chemosensory stimuli is not known but the foetus lives in an environment of ever changing olfactory and gustatory stimuli, virtually from conception.

Somatosensory Stimuli

The somatosensory system comprises a number of different senses. There is evidence to suggest that they are all functioning in the human foetus.

Pain The question of pain perception in the human foetus has been the subject of much debate and conjecture. The fact that pain is a subjective phenomenon makes it much more difficult to assess whether the human foetus feels pain. Neural pathways responsible for the transmission of pain are formed around 26 weeks of gestation (Anand & Hickey, 1987; Fitzgerald, 1993). Behaviourally the foetus is seen to respond if pricked by the needle during amniocentesis or following foetal scalp blood sampling (Hill, Platt, & Manning, 1979; Ron, Yaffe, & Polishuk, 1976). Fetal stress responses are seen from 23 weeks gestation (Giannakoulopoulos et al., 1994). It has been argued that pain responses are present in the premature infant from around 24–26 weeks (Anand & Hickey, 1987). However whether, and to what extent, the foetus 'feels' pain is not known (Derbyshire & Furedi, 1996; Glover & Fisk, 1996; Lloyd-Thomas & Fitzgerald, 1996; Szawarski, 1996).

Temperature The foetus is unlikely in the normal course of events to experience a diverse range of temperatures. The temperature of the uterine environment is very carefully controlled by the mother, being maintained approximately 0.5–1.5 °C above that of the mother.

Anecdotal reports suggest that mothers feel more foetal movements as they take a hot bath. However, whether this reflects a response to temperature or to other factors is not known. During active labour a jet of cold water squirted at the face of the foetus at 4 °C elicited a change in foetal heart rate (Timor-Tritsch, 1986). However, whether this response was elicited by temperature or pressure is not known.

Touch The foetus will receive much tactile stimulation during its time in the uterus. As the foetus grows it is continually in contact with the walls of the uterus and when it moves the foetus will be constantly stimulated by this contact. The foetus will also be stimulated by its own body; it 'touches' its face from about 13 weeks gestation (de Vries, Visser, & Prechtl, 1985). Contact will be made with the umbilical cord. In the case of multiple pregnancies there will be much contact with the other foetus(es) to provide an extra source of cutaneous stimulation.

Of all the foetus's senses, touch is the first to develop. At 8 weeks gestation, if the foetus is touched on the lips it responds by moving (Hooker, 1952). Responsiveness to tactile stimuli then spreads to the cheeks, the forehead and the palms followed by the upper arms. By 14 weeks gestation most of the body, excluding the back and top of the head, is responsive to touch.

Proprioception Two senses are considered under this heading. The vestibular sense relates to the position of the body in space in relation to gravity, i.e. upright, upside down. The second, the kinaesthetic sense, relates to the position of the various parts of the body in relation to one another, e.g. legs straight, arm bent, and so on. Although it was once thought the foetus 'floated' in the amniotic fluid, this is now known not to be true. The foetus is of a heavier specific gravity than the amniotic fluid and will be subject to the forces of gravity. Furthermore as the mother moves around the foetus will be subject to forces of linear and angular acceleration The foetus moves around in the uterus from 8 weeks gestation; its arms, legs, fingers, mouth, etc. all move independently from one another and thus much information will be available from the kinaesthetic sense.

The foetus exhibits a 'righting reflex' from about 25 weeks gestation (Hooker, 1952) which may indicate a functioning vestibular system. Towards the end of gestation the foetus comes to lie in a 'preferred' position. From about 13 weeks gestation the foetus's hand makes contact with its mouth and the foetus may be observed sucking its thumb. However whether this is due to a 'decision' on the part of the foetus to suck its thumb or simply to chance is not known. Of course the foetus, in most cases, adopts a 'head down' position for birth and both vestibular and kinaesthetic senses are involved in this.

Thus the foetus will be exposed to a range of cutaneous stimuli and is responsive to some of them.

Vision

Of all the senses the visual sense is probably the most unlikely to be stimulated during the normal course of pregnancy (Hepper, 1992). Certainly when mothers wear clothes this will, for the most part, block out any light from reaching the foetus. Even if the mother's abdomen were exposed to light, e.g. sunbathing, or under artificial room lighting, the foetus will probably only experience a diffuse glow on the abdomen. Specific light sources will not be visible but a general change in the level of illumination may be sensed.

When a torch is shone onto the mother's abdomen the foetus has been observed to respond to that light, either by a change in its heart rate (Peleg & Goldman, 1980) or by moving (Polishuk, Laufer, & Sadovsky, 1975). The earliest responses are observed around 26 weeks gestation.

Thus the foetus will probably experience little visual stimulation during the course of pregnancy but if exposed experimentally to a light source it does respond, indicating some functioning visual sense.

Summary

The extent to which the foetus *senses* (i.e. encodes the information in the sensory stimulus) or *perceives* (i.e. interprets meaning from the information in the sensory stimulus, e.g. that the most frequently heard sound stimulus is in fact its mother's voice) its environment remains to be discovered.

Foetal Learning

A number of studies have examined the ability of the foetus to learn. These studies have perhaps received most attention because of the central importance attached to learning among the range of human abilities. Studies of learning can be conveniently divided into three categories and I shall deal briefly with each.

Habituation

Habituation can be defined as the decrement in response to a repeated stimulus and is considered a form of learning (Thompson & Spencer, 1966). The ability of the foetus to habituate was the first study of learning undertaken in the foetus (Hepper & Leader, 1996). Peiper (1925) sounded a loud motor car horn within a few feet of a woman during late pregnancy. He observed that the initial presentations of the sound elicited a large response from the foetus but as presentations continued the response waned until no response was observed.

More recent studies using foetal heart rate or foetal movements observed with ultrasound have confirmed that the presentation of a sound initially elicits a large reaction but repeated presentation results in a progressive decrease and eventual disappearance of the response (e.g. Leader et al., 1982). Habituation to sound is observed around 23 weeks gestation (Leader et al., 1984). This is the time that the foetus first begins to hear (Hepper & Shahidullah, 1994b). Habituation to an auditory stimulus may be first observed at this time because it is the time at which the foetus first becomes able to detect the stimulus. Habituation to sound cannot be observed earlier because the foetus is unable to detect the stimulus. Hooker (1952) reported habituation to a tactile stimulus much earlier in gestation, at 15 weeks. It may be that habituation, a property of the CNS, operates early in gestation and can be observed in different sensory modalities as they mature and start to function.

Exposure Learning

The majority of studies examining learning in the foetus can be grouped under the general heading of exposure learning. In these studies the foetus is repeatedly exposed to a stimulus, usually sound, and its response is examined at a later date. A variety of different stimuli have been presented to the foetus, either naturally or under experimental conditions, to examine whether the foetus can 'learn' them.

Mother's Voice Newborns prefer their mother's voice to that of an unfamiliar female voice after birth. Recordings from the uterus have revealed that the mother's voice forms a salient stimulus (Querleu et al., 1989). If newborns are given a choice between their mother's voice and that of an unfamiliar female, they prefer their mother's voice (DeCasper & Fifer, 1980; DeCasper & Spence, 1986). These studies utilized the newborns' aptitude for sucking to examine possible prenatal learning of the mother's voice. After establishing a baseline sucking rate for the newborn, two choices were presented: if the newborn sucked at a faster rate it would hear its mother's voice; if it sucked at a slower rate it would hear an unfamiliar female's voice. Newborns increased their sucking rate to hear their mother's voice. Moreover when the contingencies were changed, i.e. newborns now had to suck more slowly to hear their mother's voice, they did so.

Experimental investigations have confirmed prenatal learning by studying the response of the newborn to voices as they sounded inside and outside the uterus. The mother's tissues attenuate sound as it passes from the external world to the foetus *in utero* and thus these voices may sound different compared to outside the uterus. Fifer and Moon (1989) examined this. They used a slightly different procedure from DeCasper's studies although presentation of voices was contingent upon the newborn sucking in response to a predetermined signal. In their studies newborns were presented with a tape recording of 4 seconds of one syllable 'pæt', followed by 4 seconds of another syllable 'pst', followed by 'pæt' and so on. If the infant sucked during the presentation of e.g. the 'pæt' syllable, they heard the sound of their mother's voice as we would hear it; if they sucked during the presentation of the other syllable, 'pst', they heard the sound of their mother's voice filtered to sound as it would in the uterus (this was achieved by progressive attenuation of frequencies above 500 Hz). They found newborns sucked more frequently to the syllable that predicted their mother's voice as it sounded in the uterus. This provides strong evidence that the infant's preference for its mother's voice is acquired before birth.

Maternal Heartbeat The mother's heartbeat forms a major part of the foetus's sound environment and some investigations have examined whether the foetus learns this pattern. These studies have relied on natural exposure to the mother's heartbeat and examined the response of individuals after birth to heartbeat sounds. Newborns to whom a heartbeat sound was played at 72 beats per minute (bpm) gained more weight in the first few days of life and cried less than a control group to whom the sound was not played (Salk, 1960; 1962). At 16–37 months, infants who experienced the sound of the maternal heartbeat fell asleep faster than those who (a) did not hear this sound, (b) were exposed to a metronome at 72 single beats per minute, or (c) were played recorded lullabies. Only the sound of the maternal heartbeat reduced the time taken to fall asleep over that of the control no-sound condition (Salk, 1962). Whether this reflects prenatal learning or a 'genetic' preference for a beat of 72 bpm has yet to be determined (Hepper, 1989).

Music Some studies have examined whether the foetus 'learns' music played to it during pregnancy. Newborns of mothers who had watched a particular TV soap opera, 'Neighbours', during pregnancy stopped crying, became alert and exhibited a change in both heart rate and movements when played the tune after birth (see Table 5.2). Moreover at 36 weeks gestation, when the tune was played to them through a loudspeaker placed on the mother's abdomen, the foetuses responded to the tune. No response was observed at 30 weeks gestation, which indicates something about the onset of learning. No response was observed in newborns whose mothers did not watch the programme or who were played

Table 5.2 *Group means (SE) of heart rate, number of movements and behavioural state scores of foetuses whose mothers did (Neighbours group) and did not (control group) watch 'Neighbours' during pregnancy in baseline (no music played) and experimental (music played) conditions when tested postnatally and prenatally*

	Infants exposed to 'Neighbours' as foetuses (Neighbours group)		Infants not exposed to 'Neighbours' as foetuses (Control group)	
Experiment	Baseline	Experimental	Baseline	Experimental
Response to 'Neighbours' tune 2–4 days after birth:				
HR	138.93 (2.54)	124.8 (2.77)*	136.67 (2.3)	135.1 (2.9)
Movements	5.2 (0.6)	2.9 (0.6)*	4.5 (0.7)	4.1 (0.5)
State	3.7 (0.3)	2.9 (0.3)*	4.1 (0.3)	3.4 (0.4)
Response to unfamiliar tune 2–4 days after birth:				
HR	137.2 (2.65)	135.8 (2.24)		
Movements	4.1 (0.69)	3.8 (0.71)		
State	3.2 (0.39)	3 (0.49)		
Response to 'Neighbours' tune 21 days after birth:				
HR	119.25 (2.27)	119.75 (1.39)		
Movements	5.75 (0.59)	5 (0.46)		
State	3.375 (0.38)	3.375 (0.42)		
Response to 'Neighbours' tune 36 weeks gestation:				
Movements	7.2 (1.06)	11.4 (1.45)*	7.3 (0.87)	7.7 (0.90)
Response to 'Neighbours' tune 30 weeks gestation:				
Movements	9 (0.76)	8.5 (0.62)		

* Indicates a significant difference in score between baseline and experimental conditions.
Source: Hepper (1991).

other unfamiliar TV tunes (Hepper, 1991). The response was specific to the frequently heard tune during gestation. However by 3 weeks of age individuals only exposed prenatally to the music no longer showed any preferential or differential response to it.

Classical Conditioning

Perhaps reflecting the current *Zeitgeists* of the 1930s and 1940s, early studies of foetal learning examined classical conditioning. Ray (1932) paired a vibration (the conditional stimulus, CS) with a loud sound (the unconditioned stimulus, UCS). The paper reports no data and examined only a single foetus; however, the author concludes that the subject of the study had 'so far shown no ill effects from her pre-natal education'. In 1948 Spelt similarly paired vibration (CS) with a loud sound (UCS). He reported that during the last 2 months of pregnancy successful conditioning (i.e. the foetus moved in response to the presentation of the vibration which initially elicited no response) could be observed following 15–20 pairings of the UCS and CS. Little further examination of classical conditioning took place until Feijoo (1975; 1981) attempted to classically condition the foetuses of 23 women by pairing a 12 second burst of music (CS) with a period of relaxation (UCS). Evidence of successful conditioning was found before and after birth. Foetuses were quicker to move and exhibited a shorter response latency when presented with the sound after around 24 pairings. Playing the music after birth reduced crying in newborns. Although few in number these studies suggest that the human foetus is able to be classically conditioned.

Summary

The evidence suggests that the foetus is able to learn before birth and retain this information at least into the newborn period. Evidence of learning has implications for a wide variety of psychological functions in the foetus. That the newborn can respond to familiar music, heard only as a foetus, indicates that some form of memory is present at this stage. Though the quality of evidence is limited, studies of classical conditioning suggest that the foetus is able to associate events. Obviously in order to learn the properties of the stimulus the foetus must be capable of fine discriminations. For example, the auditory system must be sufficiently well tuned to discriminate its mother's voice from that of another female, or one piece of music from another. These psychological abilities imply that the foetus's nervous system is developed sufficiently to support them.

Finally it should be noted that when the foetus exhibits evidence of exposure learning it is simply learning a salient stimulus in its environment. It does not, for example, know who its mother is when learning her voice. Her voice simply provides a salient frequent stimulus. The foetus displays no evidence of learning its father's voice. It is able to discriminate its father's voice from that of another male, but exhibits no recognition of it (DeCasper & Prescott, 1984). This probably reflects simply a lack of exposure to the father's voice. Thus exposure learning is non-directional: the foetus learns those stimuli that are most salient. Evolutionary pressures may well have had a role in determining which stimuli are the most salient.

Functions of Prenatal Behaviour

The foetus is certainly not a passive organism in the uterus. It is active from 7 weeks gestational age. The foetus has functioning sensory systems and exists in an environment of ever changing stimuli which ensures a high level of sensory stimulation to which the foetus responds. The foetus is able to learn and by doing so demonstrates not only the ability to learn but also memory and association abilities. The question of what functions these abilities serve now arises.

The behaviours and abilities of the foetus may serve a number of general functions. First I shall consider the possible functions of prenatal behaviour for the foetus and newborn and then I shall extend these arguments to examine the potential long-term influences of foetal experience.

The Immediate Role for Prenatal Behaviour

The behaviour of the foetus may serve a number of functions which can be broadly divided into two categories, those that ensure its survival at the present time and those that prepare the individual for a future time (Michel & Moore, 1995). In the uterus the foetus experiences a very different environment to that which it will experience after birth. From this it follows that the individual would exhibit behaviour(s) that ensure its survival in the uterus; such behaviours have been called ontogenetic adaptations (Oppenheim, 1981; 1984). For the foetus these can be defined as those features or behaviours that are mainly adapted to the uterine environment as distinct from preparing the foetus for its extra-uterine life. These categories are not mutually exclusive and some behaviours or features of the individual may serve both functions. Oppenheim's (1981) discussion of ontogenetic adaptations is an important development in the study of behavioural ontogenesis. The emphasis placed on the continuity of development had tended to regard all behaviours as laying the foundations for future adult behaviour.

Behaviours were seen as preparing the individual for its future, adult, life. Little attention was paid to the need for the developing individual to successfully negotiate its current environment and little consideration was given to the possibility that some behaviours functioned to ensure survival. The concept of ontogenetic adaptations is concerned with the idea that the function of behaviours, or other features, must be assessed in two ways: first, whether they prepare the individual for some future demand; and second, whether they support the survival of the individual at the present point in development.

The behaviour of the foetus may be essential for its life in the uterus. The uterine environment is obviously different from that experienced after birth. For 38 weeks the embryo and foetus live in a fluid filled environment, dependent upon its mother's physiological systems to provide nutrients and oxygen and to remove waste. It is to be expected that the foetus will be adapted to this environment and many of its behaviours and abilities tailored to ensuring it successfully survives in its uterine environment. Some of its motor patterns and reflexes may be present to help during the process of labour and birth. Although the concept of ontogenetic adaptation is generally accepted there has so far been little study of foetal behavioural adaptations to the uterine environment (Michel & Moore, 1995).

The foetus may in some way be practising behaviours essential for its survival outside the uterus. I have already discussed this in the context of foetal breathing movements. The activities and experiences of the foetus may constitute an important preparation for extra-uterine life by ensuring that those behaviours essential for survival are well rehearsed and functional when needed.

The learning abilities of the foetus may be crucial for its survival and for development in the first weeks after birth by enabling it to recognize its mother, begin the process of attachment and exploration, and ensure that breast feeding takes place from birth.

The ability to learn and form a memory may be important for the development of maternal recognition and attachment (Hepper, 1992). The newborn is able to recognize its mother by her voice (DeCasper & Fifer, 1980) and her smell (Porter, 1991). This is important given the immaturity of the newborn's visual system (Slater & Johnson, 1998). At birth the newborn displays limited ability to focus the lens of the eye to form sharp visual images. By 3 months of age however this ability is nearly adult-like. The newborn has a poor ability to control the amount of light entering the eye. Taken together these attributes mean that the newborn's effective visual range is for objects about 8–20 inches away. Thus the auditory and olfactory systems provide the best opportunity for recognizing individuals in the newborn's environment. These senses also operate at a distance and need no direct 'line of sight' between newborn and mother in order to work. The baby in its crib may still recognize its mother, talking in the distance, even though there is no physical contact between them. Biologically it makes very good sense for the individual to learn the characteristics of its mother (even though as yet the newborn does not know this familiar stimulus as its mother). By learning about its most salient caretaker the foetus may be ensuring that it responds preferentially to the one individual 'primed' to look after the child at birth. Recognition of a familiar object may be important for the newborn and may mark the beginnings of attachment. It is difficult to imagine the world of a newborn infant. Whilst the newborn has functioning sensory and learning abilities it resides in a world where everything at birth is unfamiliar. When as adults we encounter unfamiliarity in our environment we become disoriented and confused. For the newborn nothing in its world can be said to be familiar with the exception of its mother. Given that the mother is the only familiar 'object' we might expect her to be the secure base from which the infant begins to explore and learn about its environment. The physical structure of the pregnant woman may have evolved to facilitate this recognition. Sounds around 125–250 Hz pass through the mother's abdomen with little attenuation and form a salient stimulus for the foetus *in utero* (Querleu et al., 1988). These are the same frequencies as the fundamental frequency of the human voice (Querleu et al., 1988). It may be an adaptation to ensure that the foetus learns about this particularly important stimulus. Learning to distinguish its mother's voice and smell prenatally may enable the individual to recognize its mother (a familiar stimulus) and form the ontogenesis of attachment, necessary for normal development.

A related area where prenatal learning may be important is for the acquisition of language. Newborns show a preference for their mothers' native language (Moon, Cooper, & Fifer, 1991). However whilst newborns can discriminate between their mother's native language and another language they are unable to discriminate between two unfamiliar languages (Mehler et al., 1988). The foetus is able to discriminate between different speech sounds in the uterus (Lecanuet et al., 1987). Recordings of the mother's voice made in the uterus reveal that the prosodic nature of speech clearly emerges (Querleu et al., 1988). Prenatal experience of language may begin the process of language acquisition.

Prenatal learning of maternal smell may be important in the establishment of breast feeding. It must be remembered that the biological system of mother and foetus and mother and newborn has evolved over many generations to ensure the survival of both mother and foetus/newborn. When this system was being established, alternatives to breast feeding were not available. To survive the infant must take nourishment. In the first few months of the newborn's life this is supplied by the mother's breast milk. Selected pressures will have been exerted to ensure that the newborn drank this fluid. The mother's diet flavours both her breast milk and amniotic fluid similarly (Mennella & Beauchamp, 1991a; 1991b). Evidence now suggests that the foetus learns about its chemosensory uterine environment and, as a newborn, it can recognize flavours or smells it has experienced *in utero* (Porter & Winberg, 1999). The mother's colostrum will taste and smell similar to the amniotic fluid and hence when put to the breast for the first time the newborn may recognize the fluid as familiar and show no hesitation in ingesting this fluid. Prenatal chemosensory learning may prime the individual to accept breast milk. It should be noted that the newborn possesses a well developed sucking response, practised from 12 weeks gestation (de Vries, Visser, & Prechtl, 1985), to ensure it is able to breast feed. Perhaps the priming of chemosensory familiarity also serves to ensure breast feeding proceeds with little difficulty.

These behaviours have relevance for the survival of the foetus and newborn in the short term. Some behaviours of the foetus however may not serve any proximal developmental function.

The Long-Term Influence of Prenatal Behaviour

In one respect the behaviour of the foetus has clear long-term implications: its activity is important for its structural development. The final structure of the joints of the body is influenced by the movements of the limbs. Where the movement of the limbs is restricted the joints do not form properly (Drachman & Coulombre, 1962; Drachman & Sokoloff, 1966; Moessinger, 1988) which results in a permanent effect on the individual. However this relates to structural development. Is there any evidence which suggests that the behaviour of the foetus can exert a long-term effect on more psychological aspects of the individual's function?

One important way in which foetal behaviour may exert a long-term effect is by influencing the development of the nervous system. There is now little doubt that the central nervous system develops, in part as a consequence of its experiences (Miller, 1994; Oppenheim, 1991; Provine, 1986). The activity of the nervous system shapes its final development. The most clear-cut evidence for this comes from studies of the development on the visual system. Here, for example, experience of stimuli in particular orientations is necessary for the formation of cells to detect the presence of these orientations. Thus the classic experiments (Blakemore & Cooper, 1970; Hirsch & Spinelli, 1970) demonstrated that cats reared in a visual environment composed only of horizontal bars were unable to detect vertical bars and vice versa. This was due to the absence of cells able to detect the presence of these vertical lines. In the period when these cells would normally form, the absence of experience of vertical lines provided no input from which to shape the receptive fields of these cells. The role of experience in the development of the CNS is clearly important.

The effect is not restricted to the visual system. Examples can be found for speech perception and emotional development (Nelson, 2000). It is likely that at certain particular periods during the formation of the nervous system, experiential influences are important for shaping its development.

The idea of 'critical' periods has vexed the study of development for many years (Bateson, 1979), when originally introduced into ethology. It was assumed they were controlled by an internal clock and only the passing of time determined the beginning and end of the period; 'experiences' necessary for development must occur during this time window, and if not the opportunity or necessity for those experiences to influence development was lost. It was realized that this concept did not fully explain the observed behaviour and it was replaced by the notion of sensitive periods (Bateson, 1979). A sensitive period differs from a critical period in that other (possibly many other) factors may influence the start and end of the period. For example, the period for imprinting in chicks may be extended by rearing them in the dark (Johnson & Horn, 1988). The key point is that it is not simply the passing of time that opens and closes the window or period of receptivity: many other factors may contribute to shorten or extend it.

There is no doubt that there are certain periods during which the individual is particularly vulnerable to the effects of external agents. For example, thalidomide exerted its effect on arm growth only during the period when the upper limbs were developing, between 24 and 42 days after fertilization. Outside this period it had little effect on arm development. This is an example of a very discrete sensitive period. The acquisition of language on the other hand has a very long 'sensitive' period. Although language is easily acquired simply through exposure early in development, it can also be acquired later on although the stimulation needed is much greater.

The activity generated within the foetus's CNS through its movements and sensory experiences is likely to be important for developing the CNS itself. The movements of the foetus may develop the neural structures associated with movements; the sensory experiences of the foetus *in utero* may affect the formation of the sensory system. Sensory experience in all of the senses, with the exception of vision, is a feature of the foetus's environment. Such experience may influence the formation, and hence subsequent function, of the nervous system, similar to that of visual experience after birth. Whether there are sensitive periods to mediate the effect of prenatal experiences and their possible influence on CNS development is not known.

It may be that activity or experience dependent development is a key element of the prenatal period. If experiential factors or foetal activity influence neural system development then the potential for long-term effects arising from prenatal experiences is a distinct possibility.

Adaptability is often seen as a key feature of child development. The existence of discrete sensitive periods for behavioural development in humans is doubtful. If such periods exist they are quite long: consider the period for the acquisition of language. Individuals may experience many adverse circumstances but the adaptability of our developmental process ensures that these can be overcome. Only in extreme long-lasting adverse circumstances does permanent damage result. For example, long-term poor mothering may have a detrimental effect on the individual but even very adverse early experiences may be ameliorated through subsequent 'good' mothering. Such a view of adaptability is appropriate and correct; however, this does not deny the fact that early experiences may permanently shape long-term functioning. However most of the 'theorizing' in this area has been concerned with the individual after birth. After birth the development of the CNS, which mediates behaviour, is much slower than during the foetal period. In 9 months a single cell has changed into an organism capable, to a certain extent, of interacting with its environment. The prenatal period is the fastest period of development of our lives. The number of functioning brain cells that the individual will ever possess and the interaction between cells and different parts of the brain may be extensively determined in these 9 months.

Evidence from two areas clearly indicates the potential influence of prenatal events for the future and it is worth revisiting these. The first is that of teratogens and the second is the comparatively new topic of 'programming'.

The existence of teratogenic influences on behaviour is now well established. A teratogen is any agent which results in an increase, or an increased likelihood of, congenital malformation in the foetus. Exposure to a teratogenic agent during development may exert a long-term effect on the development and functioning of the individual. Perhaps the best known example, and probably the one which most clearly demonstrated the potential for prenatal influences to affect long-term outcome, is that of thalidomide. Prescribed as a sedative, thalidomide's best known side effect was the disruption of the formation and growth of arms and legs, although it has also caused cardiac malformations. There are many teratogens, e.g. cigarette smoke, alcohol, warfarin, etc. That the prenatal environment may exert a long-term effect on the individual is no longer in doubt. Initially attention was paid to structural defects but more recently it has been realized that many teratogens affect the central nervous system, often in subtle ways that result in behavioural and psychological consequences. For example, it has been argued that alcohol produces a variety of behavioural effects at lower doses than those which result in structural defects (Roebuck, Mattson, & Riley, 1999). Alcohol acts on the foetal CNS, influencing its development and structure and resulting in the functional abnormalities observed later in life. If normal prenatal experiences similarly influence central nervous system development, should they not also be considered to exert a long-term influence?

The second area is that of 'programming' (Barker, 1992; Nathanielsz, 1999). This idea is concerned with how prenatal factors may influence subsequent health. Programming, or the 'foetal origins hypothesis', in general terms can be described as the process that results in a long-term change in function that occurs as a result of the environment experienced during the individual's prenatal life. It has been shown that low birth-weight may result in poor adult health. Babies of small size are at greater risk, for example, of diabetes, hypertension and coronary heart disease. Birth-weight is often linked to maternal diet and in cases of poor nutrition the birth-weight decreases. It is argued that the foetus adapts to this poorer nutrition by developing its body functions to cope with an environment providing poor nutrition. The foetus's functions are set to expect a poor nutritional environment as its normal environment and in consequence it develops its body to cope with this environment. One finding associated with decreased body size in babies is that of increased cholesterol levels in adults. Foetuses are preprogrammed to save their most important organ, the brain, and thus in times of reduced oxygenation or reduced nutrition, resources are redistributed to ensure the brain is adequately served, though as a consequence other areas of the body are deprived. Thus growth retarded babies may have a normal head circumference but small abdominal circumference. Such deprivation influences the development and functioning of organs in the body, e.g. the liver, the major organ in the abdomen and the organ responsible for regulating cholesterol levels. Experiences of poor nutrition may 'programme' a variety of functions including blood pressure, insulin response to glucose, and cholesterol metabolism. Although there has been a debate over the extent of programming before birth there is sufficient evidence to suggest that suboptimal conditions in the prenatal period may have long-term consequences for the efficiency of a variety of bodily functions. Two important points may be drawn from this work. First, prenatal experience plays a part in determining the *adult* performance of various organs, and second, *function* is permanently changed.

Both these areas of research indicate that there may be long-term consequences of prenatal experience. Is the same true for behavioural or psychological functioning? Could activity generated within the foetus's nervous system by either its environment or its behaviour help shape the structure and functioning of its central nervous system? Prenatal activity may play a greater role in postnatal behaviour than previously thought.

HANDEDNESS AND BRAIN ASYMMETRIES: CAUSE OR CONSEQUENCE?

One behavioural characteristic that has attracted considerable interest in its ontogenesis is lateralized behaviour, especially handedness. Approximately 90% of the human population exhibit a preference for the right hand, the remainder having a preference for their left hand. Handedness has been a focus of interest because of its relationship to brain asymmetries (Boklage, 1980; LeMay & Culebras, 1972; Previc, 1991; Witelson, 1992). However, asymmetries in the structure of the brain have yet to be mapped to handedness or asymmetric motor behaviour more generally. A variety of different theories concerning handedness have been proposed (e.g. Annett, 1985; Bakan, Dibb, & Reed, 1973; Behan & Geschwind, 1985; Iaccino, 1993; Porac & Coren, 1981; Satz, 1973). However a general assumption is made that structural asymmetries in the brain lead to motor asymmetries including handedness, although how is not known. Handedness is viewed as a consequence of asymmetries in the brain.

Recent evidence has thrown this conclusion into question. At 38 weeks gestation foetuses are more likely to have their head turned to the right (Ververs et al., 1994). More importantly there is also evidence of motor asymmetries in the foetus. Foetuses observed at 15–21, 28–34 and 36–40 weeks gestation were noted to suck their right thumb more than their left (Hepper, Shahidullah, & White, 1991). Foetuses at 10 weeks gestation moved their right arm more than their left (Hepper, McCartney, & Shannon, 1998), a bias which is maintained over the first half of pregnancy (McCartney & Hepper, 1999). It has yet to be tracked further. It is worth exploring this latter result in more detail because it has major implications for the development of handedness.

Although the foetus exhibits its first movements at around 7 weeks gestation, these movements involve the whole body (de Vries, Visser, & Prechtl, 1985). Individual limb movements emerge at 9–10 weeks gestation and are the first movements exhibited by the foetus which could show laterality. Thus the human foetus exhibits lateralized behaviour at its first opportunity to do so. Moreover the proportion of foetuses classed as right handers, i.e. those who exhibit more right arm movements overall, is around 90%, the same as the proportion of right handers in the adult population.

It is conventionally believed that hemispheric brain lateralization leads to later handedness and behavioural lateralization (Nowakowski, 1992). It is proposed that the development of brain asymmetries arises from genetic pre-programming with proximate mechanisms such as differential hemispheric cell growth or cell elimination (Nowakowski, 1992).

Two problems are posed by the existence of handedness at 10 weeks gestation. First, this predates any evidence available for anatomical asymmetries in the brain. Asymmetry of the Sylvian fissure is observed at 16 weeks gestation (Chi, Dooling, & Gilles, 1977) and in Heschl's sulcus at 31 weeks gestation (LeMay & Culebras, 1972). Of course this does not mean that asymmetries do not exist; they may have escaped detection. The second problem is more serious. At 10 weeks gestation motor function is under muscular or spinal control and not control by the brain (Hepper, 1994; Nijhuis, 1992). Thus even if brain asymmetries were found they would not be responsible for lateralized motor behaviour at this age.

This research is highly suggestive of another relationship between handedness and brain asymmetries, namely that handedness is the *cause* and not the consequence of brain asymmetries. Asymmetric motor behaviour may determine differential hemispheric development. There is much evidence that neural activity may influence brain organization (Greenough, 1986; Purves et al., 1994) and specifically that prenatal motor patterns may influence the development of neural connections in the central nervous system (Reigger-Krugh, 1993). It is entirely possible that foetal behavioural lateralization differentially stimulates the foetus's central nervous system and advances the development of neurological structures controlling right sided movements.

It remains to be determined how this initial motor asymmetry develops. Most likely it is under genetic control (Morgan, 1977). However it is these genetic factors that predispose the individual to exhibit more right sided movements, not brain asymmetries. The brain asymmetries arise from the differential movement of left and right arms.

This research indicates a key element of human behaviour, the laterality of motor function, which can be observed from early in gestation. The early appearance of handedness suggests that lateralized behaviour is a fundamental feature of prenatal behavioural development. Moreover this differential behaviour may have an important role in the development of subsequent asymmetries within the central nervous system.

More research is needed to examine whether this is the case. The evidence is persuasive and work in other areas indicates quite clearly that activity can influence the development of the central nervous system. Is it possible that a key element of central nervous system function, lateralization of function, has its roots in the prenatal period and results from the activity of the foetus at an early stage of its development? Time will tell. However, this research is the first to indicate that the experience and activity of the foetus may influence the long-term functioning of the individual. At a time when considerable attention is being paid to the genetic components of behaviour and huge sums of money are being spent to map the human genome, it should not be forgotten that the experiences and environment of the individual have a key role to play in determining the development of that individual (see also Wahlsten, Chapter 2 in this volume). Indeed the activity generated within the central nervous system of the foetus by its behaviour and features of the environment may have a major influence on the formation of the central nervous system and its subsequent functioning.

THE PRENATAL PERIOD AND FUTURE BEHAVIOUR

What does the prenatal period contribute to the development of the individual? The foetus is active during its time *in utero* and its behaviour enables it to adapt it to the uterine environment and ensure its survival. While in the uterus the foetus practises behaviours that are necessary for its survival after birth. Prenatal learning may play an important part in ensuring recognition of the mother which forms the beginnings of attachment.

The picture emerging is that prenatal development is a carefully orchestrated series of interactions. Whilst genes play an important part in triggering the process, its continuation is achieved by the interaction of the individual with its environment. Behaviour and activity generated by this interaction provide the foundation for the subsequent development of behaviour. How significant these interactions are in shaping the complete individual remains to be discovered. For those sensory systems where experience has been shown to be crucial for their normal development, prenatal sensory experience may be essential. Evidence suggests that prenatal experiences may influence the structure and functioning of the central nervous system during the prenatal period. This will have a long-term influence on the functioning of the central nervous system and the behaviours which it ultimately mediates. Experiential effects may not be as final or irreversible as, for example, those of teratogens, and further investigation is needed to tease out the role of the prenatal period for the individual. Indeed there are huge gaps in our knowledge of every aspect of the prenatal period and many questions remain to be answered, but the role of the prenatal period in shaping behaviour should not be overlooked.

The role of the foetus in the developmental process needs to be placed in context. The prenatal period is the most rapid period of development in the life span. The time periods in which key structures develop and are open to environmental influence are comparatively brief given the long time that these structures will serve the individual over a lifetime. Evidence from 'foetal programming' suggests some organs are programmed to function in a given way by their prenatal environment (Barker, 1992) The extent to which the brain is sensitive to certain experiential factors during this time remains to be discovered. It may be that the plasticity of development during this period means that the foetus is much more sensitive to experiential effects than at other times; alternatively this plasticity may confer on it some protection from experiential influences. Whatever the outcome the foetus's behaviour and environment make an important contribution to its development.

From a single cell to an interactive organism in less than 9 months: this much alone should indicate the importance of understanding development during the prenatal period. That during this time the individual is well adapted to, responds to, and learns about its environment only strengthens the case for a greater understanding and acknowledgement of the role of the prenatal period in development. As the most formative period of human life with the potential for long-term influences on psychological function through the shaping of the central nervous system, prenatal development may hold an important key to a greater understanding of behaviour.

Perhaps not a novel, but certainly an often overlooked, conclusion:

> The history of man for the nine months preceding his birth would, probably, be far more interesting and contain events of greater moment than for all the three score and ten years that follow it. (Samuel Taylor Coleridge, 1885)

ACKNOWLEDGEMENTS

I acknowledge the support of the Wellcome Trust. I thank the Editors for their helpful suggestions and careful reading of this manuscript.

REFERENCES

Anand, K.J.S., & Hickey, P.R. (1987). Pain and its effects in the human neonate and fetus. *The New England Journal of Medicine*, 317, 1321–1329.

Annett, M. (1985). *Left, right, hand and brain: The right shift theory*. Hillsdale, NJ: Erlbaum.

Arduini, D., Rizzo, G., & Romanini, C. (1995). Fetal behavioral states and behavioral transitions in normal and compromised fetuses. In J.-P. Lecanuet, W.P. Fifer, N.A.

Krasnegor, & W.P. Smotherman (eds), *Fetal development: A psychobiological perspective* (pp. 83–99). Hillsdale, NJ: Erlbaum.

Bakan, P., Dibb, G., & Reed, P. (1973). Handedness and birth stress. *Neuropsychologia*, 11, 363–366.

Barker, D.J.P. (ed.) (1992). *Fetal and infant origins of adult disease*. London: British Medical Journal.

Bateson, P.P.G. (1979). How do sensitive periods arise and what are they for? *Animal Behaviour*, 27, 470–486.

Behan, P., & Geschwind, N. (1985). Dyslexia, congenital anomalies and immune disorders: The role of the fetal environment. *Annals of the New York Academy of Sciences*, 457, 13–18.

Birnholz, J.C. (1981). The development of human fetal eye movements. *Science*, 213, 679–681.

Birnholz, J.C., & Benacerraf, B.R. (1983). The development of human fetal hearing. *Science*, 222, 516–518.

Birnholz, J.C., Stephens, J.C., & Faria, M. (1978). Fetal movement patterns: A possible means of defining neurologic developmental milestones *in utero*. *American Journal of Roentgenology*, 130, 537–540.

Blakemore, C., & Cooper, G.F. (1970). Development of the brain depends on the visual environment. *Nature*, 228, 477–478.

Boklage, C.E. (1980). The sinistral blastocyst: An embryonic perspective on the development of brain function asymmetries. In J. Herron (ed.), *Neuropsychology of left-handedness* (pp. 115–137). New York: Academic.

Carlson, B.M. (1994). *Human embryology and developmental medicine*. St Louis: Mosby.

Carmichael, L. (1941). The experimental embryology of mind. *Psychological Bulletin*, 38, 1–28.

Carmichael, L. (1954). The onset and early development of behavior. In L. Carmichael (ed.), *Manual of child psychology* (pp. 60–185). New York: Wiley.

Chamberlain, D.B. (1988). The significance of birth memories. *Pre- and Peri-Natal Psychology Journal*, 2, 136–154.

Chi, J.G., Dooling, E.C., & Gilles, F.H. (1977). Left–right asymmetries of the temporal speech areas of the human fetus. *Archives of Neurology*, 34, 346–348.

Coghill, G.E. (1929). *Anatomy and the problem of behavior*. Cambridge: Cambridge University Press.

Coleridge, S.T. (1885). *Miscellanies, aesthetic and literary*. London: Bell.

DeCasper, A.J., & Fifer, W.P. (1980). Of human bonding: Newborns prefer their mothers' voices. *Science*, 208, 1174–1176.

DeCasper, A.J., & Prescott, P.A. (1984). Human newborns' perception of male voices: Preference, discrimination and reinforcing value. *Developmental Psychobiology*, 17, 481–491.

DeCasper, A.J., & Spence, M.J. (1986). Prenatal maternal speech influences newborns' perception of speech sound. *Infant Behavior and Development*, 9, 133–150.

Derbyshire, S.W.G., & Furedi, A. (1996). 'Fetal pain' is a misnomer. *British Medical Journal*, 313, 795.

De Snoo, K. (1937). Das trinkende Kind im Uterus. *Monatsschr. Geburtsh. Gynaekol.*, 105, 88–97.

Devoe, L.D., Murray, C., Faircloth, D., & Ramos, E. (1990). Vibroacoustic stimulation and fetal behavioural state in normal and term human pregnancy. *American Journal of Obstetrics and Gynecology*, 163, 1156–1161.

de Vries, J.P.P., Visser, G.H.A., & Prechtl, H.F.R. (1982). The emergence of fetal behaviour: 1. Qualitative aspects. *Early Human Development*, 7, 301–322.

de Vries, J.P.P., Visser, G.H.A., & Prechtl, H.F.R. (1985). The emergence of fetal behaviour: 2. Quantitative aspects. *Early Human Development*, 12, 99–120.

Dorovini-Zis, K., & Dolman, C.L. (1977). Gestational development of the brain. *Archives of Pathology and Laboratory Medicine*, 101, 192–195.

Drachman, D.B., & Coulombre, A.J. (1962). Experimental clubfoot and arthrogyposis multiplex congenita. *Lancet*, 2, 523–526.

Drachman, D.B., & Sokoloff, L. (1966). The role of movement in embryonic joint development. *Developmental Biology*, 14, 401–420.

Feijoo, J. (1975). Ut conscientia Noscatue. *Cahier de Sophrologie*, 13, 14–20.

Feijoo, J. (1981). Le foetus Pierre et le loup: Ou une approche originale de l'audition prenatale humaine. In E. Herbinet & M.C. Busnel (eds), *L'Aube des sens* (pp. 192–209). Paris: Stock.

Fifer, W.P., & Moon, C. (1989). Psychobiology of newborn auditory preferences. *Seminars in Perinatology*, 13, 430–433.

Fitzgerald, M. (1993). Development of pain pathways and mechanisms. In K.J.S. Anand & P.J. McGrath (eds), *Pain research and clinical management* (pp. 19–38). Amsterdam: Elsevier.

Forbes, H.S., & Forbes, H.B. (1927). Fetal sense reaction: Hearing. *Journal of Comparative Psychology*, 7, 353–355.

Freud, S. (1933). *New introductory lectures on psychoanalysis*. New York: Norton.

Gagnon, R. (1989). Stimulation of human fetuses with sound and vibration. *Seminars in Perinatology*, 13, 393–402.

Giannakoulopoulos, X., Sepulveda, W., Kourtis, P., Glover, V., & Fisk, N.M. (1994). Fetal plasma cortisol and ß-endorphin response to intrauterine needling. *Lancet*, 344, 77–81.

Glover, V., & Fisk, N.M. (1996). We don't know: Better to err on the safe side from mid-gestation. *British Medical Journal*, 313, 796.

Goto, S., & Kato, T.K. (1983). Early movements are useful for estimating the gestational weeks in the first trimester of pregnancy. *Ultrasound in Pregnancy and Biology* (suppl. 2), 577–582.

Greenough, W.T. (1986). What's special about development? Thoughts on the bases of experience-sensitive synaptic plasticity. In W.T. Greenough & J.M. Juraska (eds), *Developmental neuropsychology* (pp. 387–407). New York: Academic.

Hamburger, V. (1963). Some aspects of the embryology of behaviour. *Quarterly Review of Biology*, 38, 342–365.

Hepper, P.G. (1988). Adaptive fetal learning: prenatal exposure to garlic affects postnatal preferences. *Animal Behaviour*, 36, 935–936.

Hepper, P.G. (1989). Foetal learning: Implications for psychiatry? *British Journal of Psychiatry*, 155, 289–293.

Hepper, P.G. (1991). An examination of fetal learning before and after birth. *Irish Journal of Psychology*, 12, 95–107.

Hepper, P.G. (1992). Fetal psychology: An embryonic science. In J.G. Nijhuis (ed.), *Fetal behaviour: Developmental and perinatal aspects* (pp. 129–156). Oxford: Oxford University Press.

Hepper, P.G. (1994). The beginnings of mind: Evidence from the behaviour of the fetus. *Journal of Reproductive and Infant Psychology*, 12, 143–154.

Hepper, P.G., & Leader, L.R. (1996). Fetal habituation. *Fetal and Maternal Medicine Review*, 8, 109–123.

Hepper, P.G., McCartney, G.R., & Shannon, E.A. (1998). Lateralised behaviour in first trimester human foetuses. *Neuropsychologia*, 36, 531–534.

Hepper, P.G., & Shahidullah, S. (1994a). *Noise and the fetus: A critical review of the literature*. Sudbury: HSE.

Hepper, P.G., & Shahidullah, S. (1994b). The development of fetal hearing. *Fetal and Maternal Medicine Review*, 6, 167–179.

Hepper, P.G., & Shahidullah, S. (1994c). Development of fetal hearing. *Archives of Disease in Childhood*, 71, F81–F87.

Hepper P.G., Shahidullah, S., & White, R. (1991). Handedness in the human fetus. *Neuropsychologia*, 29, 1107–1111.

Hill, L.M., Platt, L.D., & Manning, F.A. (1979). Immediate effect of amniocentesis on fetal breathing and gross body movements. *American Journal of Obstetrics and Gynecology*, 135, 689–690.

Hirsch, H.V.B., & Spinelli, D.N. (1970). Visual experience modifies distribution of horizontally and vertically oriented receptive fields in cats. *Science*, 168, 869–871.

Hooker, D. (1952). *The prenatal origin of behavior*. Kansas: University of Kansas Press.

Horimoto, N., Hepper, P.G., Shahidullah, S., & Koyanagi, T. (1993). Fetal eye movements. *Ultrasound in Obstetrics and Gynaecology*, 3, 362–369.

Iaccino, J.F. (1993). *Left brain–right brain differences: Inquiries, evidence and new approaches*. Hillsdale, NJ: Erlbaum.

Ianniruberto, A., & Tajani, E. (1981). Ultrasonic study of fetal movements. *Seminars in Perinatology*, 5, 175–181.

James, D., Pillai, M., & Smoleniec, J. (1995). Neurobehavioural development in the human fetus. In J.-P. Lecanuet, W.P. Fifer, N.A. Krasnegor, & W.P. Smotherman (eds), *Fetal development: A psychobiological perspective* (pp. 101–128). Hillsdale, NJ: Erlbaum.

Johnson, M.H., & Horn, G. (1988). Development of filial preferences in dark reared chicks. *Animal Behaviour*, 36, 675–683.

Kainer, F., Prechtl, H.F.R., Engele, H., & Einspieler, C. (1997). Prenatal and postnatal assessment of the quality of general movements in infant of women with type 1 diabetes mellitus. *Early Human Development*, 50, 13–25.

Kisilevsky, B.S., & Low, J.A. (1998). Human fetal behavior: 100 years of study. *Developmental Review*, 18, 1–29.

Leader, L.R., Baillie, P., Martin, B., Molteno, C., & Wynchank, S. (1984). Foetal responses to vibrotactile stimulation: A possible predictor of foetal and neonatal outcome. *Australian and New Zealand Journal of Obstetrics and Gynaecology*, 24, 251–256.

Leader, L.R., Baillie, P., Martin, B., & Vermeulen, E. (1982). The assessment and significance of habituation to a repeated stimulus by the human foetus. *Early Human Development*, 7, 211–219.

Lecanuet, J.-P., Fifer, W.P., Krasnegor, N.A. & Smotherman, W.P. (eds) (1995). *Fetal development: A psychobiological perspective*. Hillsdale, NJ: Erlbaum.

Lecanuet, J.-P., Granier-Deferre, C., DeCasper, A.J., Maugeais, R., Andrieu, A.-J., & Busnel, M.-C. (1987). Perception et discrimination foetale de stimuli langagiers, mise en évidence à partir de la réactivité cardiaque: Résultats préliminaires. *Compte-Rendus de l'Académie des Sciences de Paris*, 305 (3), 161–164.

LeMay, M., & Culebras, A. (1972). Human brain: Morphologic differences in the hemispheres demonstrable by carotid arteriography. *New England Journal of Medicine*, 287, 168–170.

Liley, A.W. (1972). The foetus as a personality. *Australian and New Zealand Journal of Psychiatry*, 6, 99–105.

Lloyd-Thomas, A.R., & Fitzgerald, M. (1996). Reflex responses do not necessarily signify pain. *British Medical Journal*, 313, 797–798.

Macfarlane, A.J. (1975). Olfaction in the development of social preferences in the human neonate. *Ciba Foundation Symposium*, 33, 103–117.

McCartney, G., & Hepper, P.G. (1999). Development of lateralized behaviour in the human fetus from 12 to 27 weeks' gestation. *Developmental Medicine and Child Neurology*, 41, 83–86.

McLachlan, J. (1994). *Medical embryology*. Wokingham: Addison-Wesley.

Mehler, J., Jusczyk, P., Lambertz, G., Halsted, N., Bertoncini, J., & Amiel-Tison, C. (1988). A precursor of language acquisition in young infants. *Cognition*, 2, 143–178.

Mennella, J.A., & Beauchamp, G.K. (1991a). Maternal diet alters the sensory qualities of human milk and the nursling's behavior. *Pediatrics*, 88, 737–744.

Mennella, J.A., & Beauchamp, G.K. (1991b). The transfer of alcohol to human milk: Effects on flavor and the infant's behavior. *New England Journal of Medicine*, 325, 981–985.

Michel, G.F., & Moore, C.L. (1995). *Developmental psychobiology*. Cambridge, MA: MIT Press.

Miller, K.D. (1994). Models of activity-dependent neural development. *Progress in Brain Research*, 102, 303–318.

Minkowski, M. (1928). Neurobiologische studien am menschlichen foetus. *Handbk Biol. ArbMeth*, 5, 511–618.

Moessinger, A.C. (1988). Morphological consequences of depressed or impaired fetal activity. In W.P. Smotherman & S.R. Robinson (eds), *Behavior of the fetus* (pp. 163–173). New Jersey: Telford.

Moon, C., Cooper, R.P., & Fifer, W.P. (1991). Two-day-olds prefer their native language. *Infant Behavior and Development*, 16, 495–500.

Moore, K.L. (1989). *Before we are born*. Philadelphia: Saunders.

Morgan, M.J. (1977). Embryology and inheritance of asymmetry. In S. Harnad, D.W. Doty, L. Goldstein, J. Jaynes, & G. Krauthamer (eds), *Lateralization in the nervous system* (pp. 173–194). New York: Academic.

Nathanielsz, P.W. (1999). *Life in the womb: The origin of health and disease*. New York: Promethean.

Neldam, S. (1986). Fetal movements as an indicator of fetal well-being. *Danish Medical Bulletin*, 33, 212–220.

Nelson, C.A. (2000). Neural plasticity and human development: The role of early experience in sculpting memory systems. *Developmental Science*, 3, 115–130.

Nijhuis, J.G. (ed.) (1992). *Fetal behaviour: Developmental and perinatal aspects*. Oxford: Oxford University Press.

Nijhuis, J.G., Prechtl, H.F.R., Martin, C.B., & Bots, R.S.G.M. (1982). Are there behavioural states in the human fetus? *Early Human Development*, 6, 177–195.

Nowakowski, R.S. (1992). Mechanisms of asymmetrical development of the human CNS. In I. Kostovic, S. Knezevic, H.M. Wisniewski, & G.J. Spilich (eds), *Neurodevelopment, aging and cognition* (pp. 100–111). Berlin: Birkhauser.

Oppenheim, R.W. (1981). Ontogenetic adaptations and retrogressive processes in the development of the nervous system and behaviour: A neuroembryological perspective. In K.J. Connolly & H.F.R. Prechtl (eds), *Maturation and development: Biological and psychological perspectives* (pp. 73–109). Philadelphia: Lippincott.

Oppenheim, R.W. (1984). Ontogenetic adaptations in neural development: Toward a more 'ecological' developmental psychobiology. In H.F.R. Prechtl (ed.), *Continuity of neural functions from prenatal to postnatal life* (pp. 16–30). London: Spastics International.

Oppenheim, R.W. (1991). Cell death during development of the nervous system. *Annual Review of Neuroscience*, 14, 453–501.

O'Rahilly, R., & Müller, F. (1994). *The embryonic human brain*. New York: Wiley-Liss.

Patrick, J., Campbell, K., Carmichael, L., Natale, R., & Richardson, B. (1980). Patterns of human fetal breathing during the last 10 weeks of pregnancy. *Obstetrics and Gynecology*, 56, 24–30.

Peiper, A. (1925). Sinnesempfindungen des Kindes vor seiner geburt. *Monatsschrift fur Kinderheilkunde*, 29, 237–241.

Peleg, D., & Goldman, J.A. (1980). Fetal heart rate acceleration in response to light stimulation as a clinical measure of fetal well-being: A preliminary report. *Journal of Perinatal Medicine*, 8, 38–41.

Polishuk, W.Z., Laufer, N., & Sadovsky, E. (1975). Fetal reaction to external light. *Harefuah*, 89, 395–397.

Porac, C., & Coren, S. (1981). *Lateral preferences and human behavior*. New York: Springer.

Porter, R.H. (1991). Mutual mother–infant recognition in humans. In P.G. Hepper (ed.), *Kin recognition* (pp. 413–432). Cambridge: Cambridge University Press.

Porter, R.H., & Winberg, J. (1999). Unique salience of maternal breast odors for newborn infants. *Neuroscience and Biobehavioural Reviews*, 23, 439–449.

Prechtl, H.F.R. (1974). The behavioural states of the newborn infant: A review. *Brain Research*, 76, 1304–1311.

Prechtl, H.F.R. (1988). Developmental neurology of the fetus. *Clinical Obstetrics & Gynaecology*, 2, 21–36.

Prechtl, H.F.R., & Einspieler, C. (1997). Is neurological assessment of the fetus possible? *European Journal of Obstetrics & Gynecology and Reproductive Biology*, 75, 81–84.

Previc, F.H. (1991). A general theory concerning the prenatal origins of cerebral lateralisation in humans. *Psychological Review*, 98, 299–334.

Preyer, W. (1885). *Die spezielle physiologie des embryo*. Leipzig: Grieben.

Provine, R.R. (1972). Ontogeny of bioelectric activity in the spinal cord of the chick embryo and its behavioural implications. *Brain Research*, 41, 365–378.

Provine, R.R. (1986). Behavioural neuroembryology. In W.T. Greenough & J.M. Juraska (eds), *Developmental neuropsychobiology* (pp. 213–239). New York: Academic.

Pujol, R., Lavigne-Rebillard, M., & Uziel, A. (1991). Development of the human cochlea. *Acta Oto-laryngologica* (suppl. 482), 7–12.

Purves, D., Riddle, D.R., White, L.E., & Gutierrez-Ospina, G. (1994). Neural activity and the development of the somatic sensory system. *Current Opinion in Biology*, 4, 120–123.

Querleu, D., Renard, X., Boutteville, C., & Crepin, G. (1989). Hearing by the human fetus? *Seminars in Perinatology*, 13, 409–420.

Querleu, D., Renard, X., Versyp, F., Paris-Delrue, L., & Crepin, G. (1988). Fetal hearing. *European Journal of Obstetrics, Gynecology and Reproductive Biology*, 29, 191–212.

Rank, O. (1929). *The trauma of birth*. New York: Harcourt Brace.

Ray, W.S. (1932). A preliminary report on a study of foetal conditioning. *Child Development*, 3, 175–177.

Read, J., & Miller, F. (1977). Fetal heart rate acceleration in response to acoustic stimulation as a measure of fetal well-being. *American Journal of Obstetrics and Gynecology*, 129, 512–517.

Reigger-Krugh, C. (1993). Relationship of mechanical and movement factors to prenatal musculoskeletal development. *Physical and Occupational Therapy in Pediatrics*, 12, 19–36.

Reinold, E. (1971). Beobachtung foetaler Aktivitat in der ersten Halfte der graviditat mit dem ultraschall. *Padiatrie und Padologie*, 6, 274–279.

Roebuck, T.M., Mattson, S.N., & Riley, E.P. (1999). Behavioral and psychosocial profiles of alcohol-exposed children. *Alcoholism: Clinical and Experimental Research*, 23, 1070–1076.

Ron, M., Yaffe, H., & Polishuk, W.Z. (1976). Fetal heart rate response to amniocentesis in cases of decreased fetal movements. *Obstetrics and Gynecology*, 48, 456–459.

Salk, L. (1960). The effects of the normal heartbeat sound on the behaviour of the newborn infant: Implications for mental health. *World Mental Health*, 12, 168–175.

Salk, L. (1962). Mothers' heartbeat as an imprinting

stimulus. *Transactions of the New York Academy of Science*, 24, 753–763.

Satz, P. (1973). Left handedness and early brain insult: An explanation. *Neuropsychologia*, 11, 115–117.

Schaal, B., Orgeur, P., Lecanuet, J.-P., Locatelli, A., Granier-Deferre, C., & Poindron, P. (1991). Chémo-réception nasale *in utero*: Expériences préliminaires chez le foetus ovin. *Comptes Rendus de l'Académie des Sciences (Paris)*, 113 (3), 319–325.

Schaal, B., Orgeur, P., & Rognon, C. (1995). Odor sensing in the human fetus: Anatomical, functional, and chemoecological bases. In J.-P. Lecanuet, W.P. Fifer, N.A. Krasnegor, & W.P. Smotherman (eds), *Fetal development: A psychobiological perspective* (pp. 205–237). Hillsdale, NJ: Erlbaum.

Shahidullah, S., & Hepper, P.G. (1993a). Prenatal hearing tests? *Journal of Reproductive and Infant Psychology*, 11, 143–146.

Shahidullah, S., & Hepper, P.G. (1993b). The developmental origins of fetal responsiveness to an acoustic stimulus. *Journal of Reproductive and Infant Psychology*, 11,135–142.

Shahidullah, S., & Hepper, P.G. (1994). Frequency discrimination by the fetus. *Early Human Development*, 36, 13–26.

Sival, D.A., & Prechtl, H.F.R. (1992). The relation between the quantity and quality of prenatal movements in pregnancies complicated by IUGR and premature rupture of membranes. *Early Human Development*, 30, 193–209.

Slater, A., & Johnson, S.P. (1998). Visual sensory and perceptual abilities of the newborn: Beyond the blooming, buzzing confusion. In F. Simion & G. Butterworth (eds), *The development of sensory, motor and cognitive capacities in early infancy: From perception to cognition* (pp. 121–141). Sussex: Psychology Press.

Smotherman, W.P., & Robinson, S.R. (eds) (1988). *The behavior of the fetus*. New Jersey: Telford.

Smotherman, W.P., & Robinson, S.R. (1995). Tracing developmental trajectories into the prenatal period. In J.-P. Lecanuet, W.P. Fifer, N.A. Krasnegor, & W.P. Smotherman (eds), *Fetal development: A psychobiological perspective* (pp. 15–32). Hillsdale, NJ: Erlbaum.

Sontag, L.W. (1962). Effect of maternal emotions on fetal development. In W.S. Kroger (ed.), *Psychosomatics: Obstetrics, gynecology and endocrinology* (pp. 8–14). Springfield, IL: Thomas.

Sontag, L.W., & Wallace, R.F. (1934). Preliminary report of the Fels Fund: Study of foetal activity. *American Journal of Diseases of Children*, 48, 1050–1057.

Spelt, D.K. (1948). The conditioning of the human foetus *in utero*. *Journal of Experimental Psychology*, 38, 338–346.

Szawarski, Z. (1996). Probably no pain in the absence of 'self'. *British Medical Journal*, 313, 796–797.

Takashima, T., Horimoto, N., Satoh, S., Maeda, H., Koyanagi, T., & Nakano, H. (1991). Characteristics of binocular movements in the human fetus at term, assessed with real time ultrasound. *Japanese Society Ultrasound in Medicine*, 59 (suppl. 2), 883–884.

Thompson, R.F., & Spencer, W.A. (1996). Habituation: A model for the study of neuronal substrates of behavior. *Psychological Review*, 73, 16–43.

Timor-Tritsch, I.E. (1986). The effect of external stimuli on fetal behaviour. *European Journal of Obstetrics, Gynecology and Reproductive Biology*, 21, 321–329.

Ververs, I.A.P., de Vries, J.I.P., van Geijn, H.P., & Hopkins, B. (1994). Prenatal head position from 12–38 weeks: 1. Developmental aspects. *Early Human Development*, 39, 83–91.

Visser, G.H.A., Mulder, H.H., Wit, H.P., Mulder, E.J.H., & Prechtl, H.F.R. (1989). Vibro-acoustic stimulation of the human fetus: Effect on behavioural state organisation. *Early Human Development*, 19, 285–296.

Witelson, S.F. (1992). Neuroanatomical bases of hemispheric functional specialisation in the human brain: Developmental factors. In L. Kostovic, S. Knezevic, H.M. Wisniewski, & G.J. Spilich (eds), *Neurodevelopment, ageing and cognition* (pp. 112–137). Berlin: Birkhauser.

6

On the Development of Perception and Action

CLAES VON HOFSTEN

INTRODUCTION

Actions Are the Origins of Actions

The basic thesis of this chapter is that perception and action are the complements of each other. No action could exist without perception and perception relies ultimately on action. Together they form functional systems around which adaptive behavior develops. These systems are associated with strong motives that drive development. According to this view, the starting point of development is not a set of reflexes triggered by external stimuli, but a set of action systems that are activated by the infant. To begin with they may be very primitive, but as long as there is a loop connecting the sensory side and the motor side, a window is open for refining the systems from activity and experience and gearing them to the environment. Thus, dynamic systems are formed in which the development of the nervous system and the development of action mutually influence each other in the process of forming increasingly complex and sophisticated systems. With development the different action systems become increasingly future oriented and integrated with each other and ultimately each action will engage multiple coordinated action systems.

Varieties of Perception–Action Systems

Perception and action appear to have coevolved. In the course of evolution, organisms have become equipped with increasingly advanced systems for extracting information about what the environment affords and increasingly advanced systems for utilizing these affordances to their benefit. The environment includes many different kinds of resources, and, consequently, a diversity of functional systems has evolved. Reed (1996) lists a number of such systems including those for basic orientation, those for locomotion of various kinds, those that fulfill the appetitive functions such as respiration, ingestion and thermoregulation, those for manipulating objects in the environment, and those for interaction with other animals. In historic time, humans have reconstructed the environment to better fit their different action systems. For instance, thermoregulation has been facilitated by the construction of houses and clothes, manipulation by the making of various tools, and locomotion by the construction of vehicles of various kinds.

Perception and Action are Mutually Dependent

No action, however prescribed, can be implemented in the absence of perception (Bernstein, 1967). Perception is needed both for planning actions and for guiding them toward their goals. However, not only does action rely on perception, it is also a necessary part of the perceptual process. For instance, active touch is required to haptically perceive the form of an object (Gibson, 1966). The hand must move over the object and feel its form, its bumps and its indentations. The clearest example of the necessity of action for functional perception is vision itself. Our visual field consists of a very small foveal area, not larger than the thumbnail at arm's length, surrounded by a large peripheral visual field over which acuity rapidly deteriorates with increasing angular eccentricity. Already at 10 degrees, acuity is only 20% of its foveal value. In spite of this, we have the illusion that we see equally clearly over our whole field of vision. A simple experiment shows that this is wrong. If one firmly fixates a word in a text it is hardly possible to even read the neighboring words. The illusion of an equally clear visual field is created by the fact that we move the fovea to every single detail that we want to inspect, and by doing this we can inspect it with optimal resolution.

The same principles hold for all modes of perceiving. Perception is always characterized by exploratory activities such as looking, listening, sniffing, tasting, and feeling (Gibson, 1966). It is equally true that all actions also have perceptual functions. Locomotion reveals the layout of the environment, manipulation reveals object properties, and social interaction is essential for person perception. One's movements also reveal information about the biomechanics of the body, the forces acting on it and how these change over the execution of a movement. Thus, by necessity, any action also involves perceptual actions. The special status of perceptual activities is that they do not need to be specifically attached to any immediate performative activity. Their immediate function may simply be to gather information about the world. However, viewed over a longer window of time they have very important implications for action because they improve the perceptual process and the planning of actions. Organisms have evolved elaborate memory systems for maintaining the information extracted over longer time periods and use it when organizing actions at later stages.

Actions Are Prospective

Actions have to fit the outside world and accurate spatial information is therefore necessary for scaling a movement and planning its trajectory (von Hofsten & Lee, 1994). Furthermore, actions are accomplished in real time and have to fit in with the stream of events in the outside world. Therefore, neural pathways have evolved for relaying sensory information to the motor system with as little delay as possible. In certain cases, these loops are organized entirely at the spinal level as in the case of the postural reflexes. However, when more sophisticated processing is involved, dedicated pathways in the brain can be distinguished for providing closer contact between perception and action (Goodale & Milner, 1992).

Actions are directed into the future toward events that have not yet occurred. Guiding them requires information about what is going to happen next. I will refer to this as prospective control or prospectivity of action. There is no alternative to prospective control. Time is irreversible and the only part of the action that is controllable is the one that has not yet been accomplished. Even a simple reach requires the ability to anticipate what is going to happen next both with the moving limb itself and with the object it is about to capture. If the object is out of reach, the action of attaining it will also involve global body movements that will further increase action time. If the object is moving, the whole action has to be directed towards a point further ahead where the hand and the object will meet (von Hofsten, 1980; 1983). This requires anticipation of the external object's movement.

Most actions involve movements of more than one body part. In manual actions, the two hands generally collaborate in achieving a goal. In looking, the movements of the head and the eyes collaborate in controlling gaze, and in talking, the mouth and lungs collaborate in producing the speech sounds. Actions involving more than one part of the body can only be accomplished if the movements of the different parts are timed and scaled to each other. This is only possible if each body part 'knows' what the other parts are going to do ahead of time, which in turn requires the movements of the different parts to be subordinate to one common system or mechanism. Precise timing also requires monitoring the movements of each part of the body prospectively.

Coordination and regulation of purposeful movements are only possible in relation to a stable context – that is, the posture of the body. The problem is that the movements themselves affect the equilibrium of the body. When a body part is moved, the point of gravity of the whole body is displaced which will push it out of equilibrium if nothing is done about it. Gravity is a strong force and when body equilibrium is disturbed, posture becomes quickly uncontrollable. Therefore, disturbances have to be foreseen or detected at an early stage if balance is to be maintained without interruption of ongoing activity.

In gearing actions to the environment, obstacles have to be avoided and encounters prepared. When walking in a cluttered terrain, a suitable ground support has to be found for each step and the encounter with the support has to be precisely timed. When reaching for an object, the subject must prepare for the encounter by opening the hand, orienting it appropriately, and closing it relative to the encounter with the object. Some events are irreversible and simply have to be dealt with ahead of time. As the foot is lowered toward the ground in a stepping movement, the quality of the ground must be foreseen, whether it is hard, soft, or slippery; if not, the smoothness of walking will be disrupted.

Information for Prospective Control

Access to information about future events is only possible in a world, like ours, that is governed by rules and regularities. In such a world, events project into the future and what is presently happening informs about what will happen next. Perception is designed to extract such information. Within a small time frame, this works very well because sensory variables have prospective properties. For instance, because of inertia, a moving object will only gradually change its acceleration, velocity and direction of motion. Therefore, sensing those variables gives a good basis for knowing how the object will move next. When an object or a surface is being approached, the inverse of the relative change of sensory magnitudes informs about the time to contact with it, given that approach velocity stays the same (Lee, 1974). Even more useful is the rate of change of this variable because it determines the mode of encounter, whether it is going to be hard or soft (Lee, 1976; 1992). Lee has shown that humans and animals use this parameter in situations where timing is crucial to control their approaches to objects and surfaces (Lee, Lishman, & Thompson, 1982; Lee, Reddish, & Rand, 1991; Lee et al., 1993).

Over longer time intervals it becomes increasing important to base predictions of what is going to happen next on knowledge of the rules and regularities that govern events. Although the imminent catching of a ball thrown towards a subject has to rely on prospective perception of its approach, it also helps to know something about the physical laws that govern object motion, like gravity and inertia. It also helps to know how the motion of the ball depends on different kinds of throws and different winds and how you should position yourself to optimize the chances of catching the ball. Most of this knowledge is tacit and can be expressed in action but not in scripts. However, script can also be of importance for action control. When dancing, the future movements of the partner must be anticipated if coordination is going to be maintained. Although the next step of the partner may be at least partly revealed by his or her postural adjustments and therefore perceived directly, it clearly helps to know the rules of dancing. Finally, when engaging in social communication, passes and facial gestures must be appropriately timed. It is crucial to know when information is going to be sent by the partner so that the message can be perceived and responded to. It is also important to know when the partner is going to end the pass so that one can prepare a response. Only then can communication flow smoothly. It helps to know something about social rules and the partner's mode of communication but direct perception of the partner's intentions is obviously crucial as well.

However, knowledge of the rules that govern events can never replace perceptual guidance of actions. As the prospective time interval increases, the relationship between current changes and future effects may become very complex and difficult to penetrate in detail. Indeed, as Bernstein (1967) has pointed out, the complexity of the active and passive forces acting on a limb during the production of a movement is so huge that it is impossible to totally program a movement in advance, however simple. Therefore, the global organization of actions relying on long term planning has to be supplemented with perceptual guidance that gives more precise information about upcoming events.

In traditional terminology a distinction is made between planned movements controlled by feedforward information and unplanned movements controlled by feedback information from the movement itself. But feedback and feedforward are deceptive concepts. Time is irreversible and what has been accomplished is only of interest for the ability to control the next part of the action. Therefore, the question is not whether a movement is controlled by feedback or feedforward, but rather how far into the future it reaches. The development of skill is a question of building both procedures for structuring actions far ahead in time and procedures for extracting the right kind of information for the detailed monitoring of actions.

Preparing the Child for Action

There are, in principle, three basic prerequsites for establishing an action system. First, there must be some functional prestructuring, however primitive, of the morphology of the body and perceptual and motor systems in relation to the task. Without such a prestructuring, there is no foundation on which to build the action system. Such internally originated prestructuring is also necessary for setting up interactions with the outside world. It is an old insight that without any initial perceptual structuring, information about the environment can never be acquired. It is equally true that without some initial structuring of the motor system, actions will never emerge. Other internally originated information may not be necessary for defining the system but could facilitate the learning of certain crucial skills at a time when the infant needs them for its survival. In order to understand the development of action, perception and cognition it is of crucial importance to investigate these different ways in which innate knowledge is expressed.

Secondly, perception and action must form one loop so that information can be fed back into the system. Loops are essential because they provide the possibilities for guiding the movements instead of just eliciting them. Loops are also necessary for modifying the system during ontogenesis towards more optimal functioning. When there is a loop, feedback can be provided and a window opened up for experience to affect and refine the behavior in question. Therefore, one of the most important aspects of phylogenetic adaptation is to set up loops that enable the growing organism to regulate its own behaviors.

Thirdly, there must be an urge for performing the actions in question. Irrespective of how sophisticated the perceptual–motor prestructuring is, and how many loops connect them, without a motivation to perform the action in question there will be no development. Even if there is a loop connecting the afferent and efferent parts of the system and even if the learning task is facilitated by some innate constraints, there will be no organized behavior without motives and certainly not any development. Motives focus the infants' interests on specific kinds of information and make certain actions pleasurable. By doing that they accomplish two important things. By directing attention to certain affordances of the environment they make sure that the infant learns more about them, and by making infants persist in certain activities they make it possible for the infant to eventually master those activities.

Morphological Prestructuring

The most obvious way in which the child has been prepared for action is the design of its body. It is clear that hands are made for grasping and manipulating objects, feet are made for walking, and eyes are made for looking. However, there is no grand plan for evolution. It just optimizes what is at hand. Therefore the same body part may look rather different in different species depending on its function. For instance, the limbs of horses, lions, and humans differ for obvious functional reasons. It is also true that different body parts may have evolved to serve the same function. The trunk of elephants and the human hand are both examples of how the morphology of the body has been altered in special ways in order to facilitate object manipulation.

What is less obvious but equally true is that each of these body parts is a part of a perception–action system that also includes specially designed perceptual and neural mechanisms. The designs of the body of any animal, its perceptual system, its effector system, and indeed its neural system have been tailored to each other for solving specific action problems. The changes in the morphology of the body also include adjustments of the perceptual system to improve extraction of information for controlling specific actions. For instance, the frontal positions of the eyes in primates give access to better information for controlling manual movements. It should be noted, however, that the same evolutionary change decreases the size of the visual field and decreases the ability to quickly detect predators. Precise manipulation is greatly facilitated by the evolution of detailed foveal vision, by the ability to precisely converge and accommodate the eyes on the point of interest and track objects over space, and by the evolution of direct cortico-motor-neuronal pathways that make it possible to control individual finger movements (Kuypers, 1973).

In lower vertebrates, it often appears as if action systems have evolved independent of each other. Thus the frog seems to possess independent perceptual mechanisms for extracting spatial information needed for catching flies and for negotiating barriers (Rozin, 1976). In higher vertebrates, movement patterns are more flexible and the perceptual skills more versatile. When a new skill evolves, the animal may reuse some of the mechanisms already evolved for other tasks instead of developing completely new ones. This leads to more general mechanisms and more generalized skills. A similar trend seems to be going on in ontogeny. The earliest appearing skills seem more task specific than those appearing later.

Prestructuring of the Motor System

Simply providing the hardware is not sufficient for establishing a perception–action system. In addition there needs to be some initial constraints on the movements produced in order to reduce the many degrees of freedom of the motor system (Bernstein, 1967). To facilitate control, the activation of muscles is therefore organized into functional synergies at the beginning of life. The earliest appearing organized movements of the human foetus are observed around the ninth week after conception and are expressions of such synergies. A timetable of the emergence of some of these movements is shown in Figure 6.1. It can be seen that some of these synergies are rather complicated, for example in breathing and swallowing. Synergies have both facilitating and constraining effects. For instance, the arm and finger movements of newborn infants are organized into extension and flexion synergies that make the arm and the fingers extend and flex together. These synergies simplify the control problem and enable newborn infants to direct movements of their arms in space. However, they prevents the neonate from grasping an object reached for because that would require them to flex the hand around the object while the arm is extended.

Prestructuring of the Perceptual System

Perception also requires some structuring to begin with in order to provide the necessary guidance for action. Infants must be able to perceive speech sounds when they are ready to produce them. Research in this area has shown that speech perception actually develops ahead of speech production (Menn, 1983). Before vision can guide looking, the visual field must be directionally structured, and before it can guide

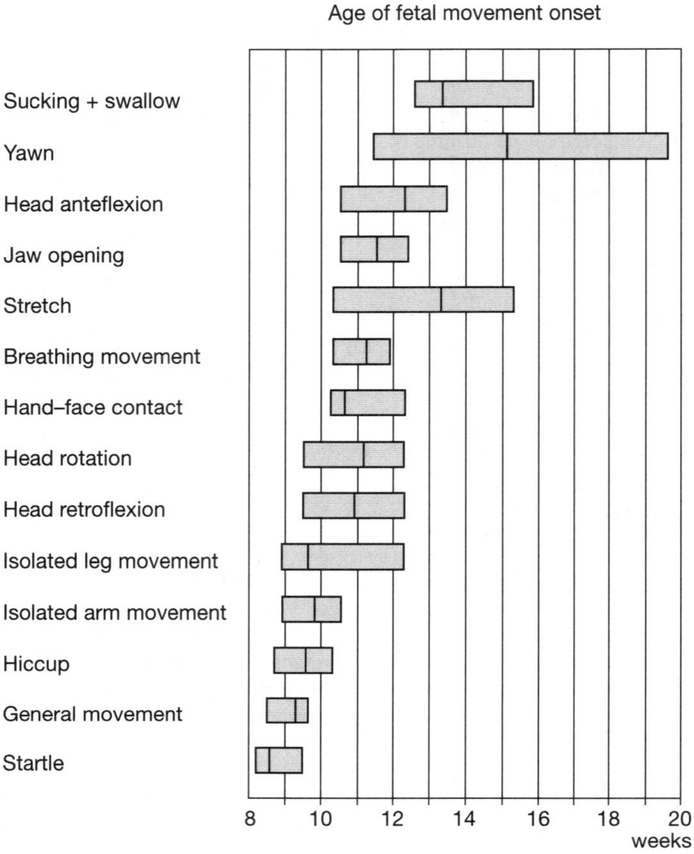

Figure 6.1 *A timetable of the emergence of the more important fetal movement patterns. The horizontal bars indicate the time period over which all fetuses started to show the particular movement patterns. The vertical line within each bar indicates the median age (after deVries, Visser, & Prechtl, 1982)*

object directed action, it must be able to divide up the perceptual field into object defining entities. Although little is known about when these processes of perceptual structuring start to emerge in development, some of the actions performed by newborn infants indicate that object perception is present at birth.

The early structuring of vision is accomplished prenatally and provides a beautiful example of the parsimony of the embryogenetic process. It may serve as an example of the more general principles of neural mapping. It is a two-stage process. The first stage is primarily determined by the genotype and the second stage by the activity of the fetus. First, an abundance of axons originating at the retinal level migrate to the thalamus (the lateral geniculate nucleus) and the superior colliculus under guidance of genetically determined chemical gradients where they will form topographies crudely corresponding to the retinal topography (Retaux & Harris, 1996). The resulting projections are, however, too fuzzy for extracting specific information about the world.

At the second stage of the mapping, structured activity at the retinal level will cause connections to be modulated through competitive interactions (von der Malsburg & Singer, 1988). Strong connections become strengthened (Hebb, 1949) and will successfully compete with the weaker connections for the limited synapse space available. This will transform the initial crude mapping into a detailed one. The structured activity at the retinal level could be determined by structured light after birth, but if this was the case for humans, neonates would be unable to use vision in any practical way because the fetus does not receive structured light. A simple but crucial change in the epigenetic process, however, has enabled the fine structuring to start much before birth. Shatz and colleagues (Shatz, 1992) showed in prenatal cats that waves of structured neural activity move back and forth over the retina. This is quite sufficient for launching the fine mapping process of the visual field.

Both stages of mapping are necessary. In a series of computer simulations of the mapping process, von der Malsburg and Singer (1987) found that if there were to be no initial mapping at all, many local maps would start to form. They would then compete with each other and prevent the overall structure from emerging. Some initial global mapping had to be present to act as a frame of reference for the more detailed one.

Forming Functional Systems

The various constraints set up by phylogeny will selectively sponsor the growth and structuring of pathways in the nervous system that are parts of functional systems which the child needs at birth (Anokhin, 1964). As a consequence of this selective, accelerated growth, neonates are prepared to sustain life in their new environment and to explore and adapt to it. Anokhin (1964) gives a number of examples of such accelerated growth. For instance, although the facial nerve is an isolated structure, it shows a marked disproportionate maturation of several fibers at birth. The fibers projecting to *M. orbicularis oris*, providing the most important movement in sucking, are already myelinated and the contacts with the muscle fibers are established at a stage when no other facial muscles have such marked organization. Similar accelerated growth can be observed in the *medulla oblongata*. The parts related to the functional system of sucking are ready to be used while, for instance, the parts that are the source of the frontal branches of the *N. facialis* are just beginning to differentiate. The fact that the morphogenesis of the nervous system primarily follows functional rules rather than structural ones was called 'the principle of systemogenesis' by Anokhin (1964).

Motivational Prestructuring

A nice example of the importance of motives for developing perception–action systems is the early development of reaching. Around 3–4 months of age, a normal infant will work systematically to get the hand to an object and grasp it. To start with the attempts are not very successful, but that doesn't seem to make much difference. The infants may stubbornly continue hour after hour with the same apparent goal: to grasp the object. It could hardly be the success of the activity that rewards the infant. Rather, the reward seems to be the activity itself, and through this activity the reaching system will assemble itself. This is the function of motivation in the development of action. It makes certain activities fun in a way that predates the child's mastery of those activities.

Moving one's body seems to be as motivating for the child as the attainment of the goal itself. This has interesting implications for the development of action. The pleasure of moving makes the child focused less on the final goal and more on its movement possibilities. It makes the child try many different procedures and introduces necessary variability into the learning process. From the variety of movement exemplars the child can then select the most optimal ones (Edelman, 1989).

Motivation drives development from the very start. The first appearing movements in the fetus are clearly not reflexes. They are spontaneously driven and most probably controlled by information that is fed back into the system through various proprioceptive loops. I propose that the function of fetal movements is to provide the necessary conditions for forming and calibrating the action systems that the infant needs at birth. The motor system most probably gets organized through their own activity in the same way as the perceptual system does.

The Action Systems of the Newborn Child

The behavior of the neonate has traditionally been discussed in terms of reflexes rather than actions. According to Sherrington (1906) a reflex is a hard-wired sensorimotor loop organized at a spinal or para-spinal level. Although reflexes may serve important functions for the subject, they are stereotyped, elicited, and once launched run their predetermined course. In other words, they cannot be considered goal-directed and they do not adjust to future states in a prospective way. This means, for instance, that reflexes are not adjusted in order to meet other goals or attain other advantages than those for which they were originally designed.

Like adults, neonates have reflexes. A slight hit below the kneecap elicits a stretch reflex in adults and newborns. However, most of the neonatal behaviors described as reflexes are not characterized by the properties described above. As I will show, neonatal movements are functional, initiated by the individual, goal-directed, prospective, and flexible in the sense that they can be altered to gain advantages. This is valid for such behaviors as rooting, sucking, looking, reaching and imitating. It even seems to be true for some of the basic postural adjustments like the asymmetric-tonic neck reflex (ATNR: see later) (van der Meer, van der Weel, & Lee, 1995). The neonate is clearly prepared for interacting with the external world and adapting to it.

Rooting

Rooting is traditionally described as a typical neonatal reflex. Rooting refers to the infant's search for the nipple of the breast. Mechanical stimulation in the area around the mouth makes the infant move his or her mouth toward the point of stimulation (Prechtl, 1958). However, rooting is more than a simple reflex. Odent (1979) showed that rooting does not just involve movements of the head and mouth but seems to include explorative movements of the whole body with all the senses involved. This requires a common spatial reference system for these sensory systems. Furthermore, rooting is not elicited when the infant touches itself (Rochat & Hespos, 1997), only when an external object is the source of stimulation. These facts speak in favor of a far more sophisticated organization of this behavior than suggested by the reflex notion.

Sucking

Sucking is probably the most precocious action of the newborn. This behavior may be the only one which is more skilled in the newborn than in the adult. Skilled sucking relies on a complex interaction of muscle contractions that are prospective in nature. Within a day or so after birth the sucking system functions with amazing accuracy (Craig & Lee, 1999). The *sucking* and *release* phases are beautifully sequenced and adjusted to each other, as can be seen in Figure 6.2. Such smooth functioning relies on adjusting the change in sucking pressure to the flow of milk that is different from suck to suck. In other words, the newborn infant has to sense the coming flow of milk and adjust the sucking pressure to it ahead of time.

Apart from using sucking to acquire food, neonates are also able to use it to gain other advantages, for instance, as a means to get access to the mother's voice (deCasper & Fifer, 1980) or to regulate a visual event (Kalnins & Bruner, 1973). DeCasper and Fifer found that, within a day from birth, neonates would alter their sucking rate in order to get access to their mother's voice. Kalnins and Bruner found that 5-week-old infants used sucking as a means to focus a picture. When high frequency sucking resulted in a clear focus, the subjects quickly detected this contingency and increased their sucking rate. When high frequency sucking resulted in a blur, sucking rate dropped instead. This shows that neonates can separate the perceived affordance of an event and the action used to fulfill what it invites. In other words, actions can be used as means rather than ends and they can be flexibly applied to a variety of problems.

Looking

In addition to the structuring of perception itself, perception is also mapped onto action at birth. Take, for instance, the simple functioning of the saccadic system for centering gaze on a target. The same is true for reaching as discussed above. The newborn 'knows' from the start how to move its arm to get to the proximity of the seen object. These initial maps between perception and action are not there just to enable the newborn infant to negotiate the surrounding world successfully. They are probably necessary prerequisites for precise mapping to occur.

It is important to appreciate that perceptual systems are also action systems and that perceiving always involves overt actions. For instance, the visual system is built to scan the world, focus on objects and events, and track objects over the visual field. The development of oculomotor control is as important to vision as the development of the receptor function itself. If a subject cannot control its eye movements, the visual system is useless (Jacobsen, Magnussen, & Smith, 1997). When a distinct visual stimulus is shown to an alert newborn, it will move its eyes to the stimulus (Haith, 1980). This presumes a preset mapping between position in the visual field and eye movement commands. In other words, the newborn 'knows' from the outset how to move its eyes to get to the target. Neonates have some ability to detect interesting parts of the optical array and direct gaze towards them. These are parts that contain much optical change, and define certain specific stimuli like faces (Johnson & Morton, 1991). Neonates are also prepared to visually explore their surrounding. They can also, to a certain degree, coordinate the movements of both eyes and converge them towards the object on which they are fixating (Haineline et al., 1992).

There are, however, also important restrictions in the use of the oculomotor system. Kremenitzer et al. (1979) found that neonates would smoothly track a 12° black disc, but only with low relative amplitude and only for approximately 15% of the time. Small targets are primarily followed with discrete saccadic steps. Bloch and Carchon (1992) used a red transparent ball covering 4° of visual angle and found only saccadic tracking in neonates. Similar findings were reported by Aslin (1981) who used a black bar 2° wide and 8° high moving sinusoidally in a horizontal path. Head movements are used in orienting gaze towards salient objects and events in the environment. For instance, neonates turn their head towards a human voice and other complex sound sources (Alegria & Noirot, 1978; Field et al., 1979; Mendelsson & Haith, 1976). They also have a tendency to use head movements in the tracking of an attractive target (Bloch & Carchon, 1992).

Imitation

Neonates tend to imitate facial gestures (Meltzoff & Moore, 1977). The most reliable observations have been obtained from mouth opening and protrusion of the tongue (see also Heimann, Nelson, & Schaller, 1989). Although contingent on the model's behavior,

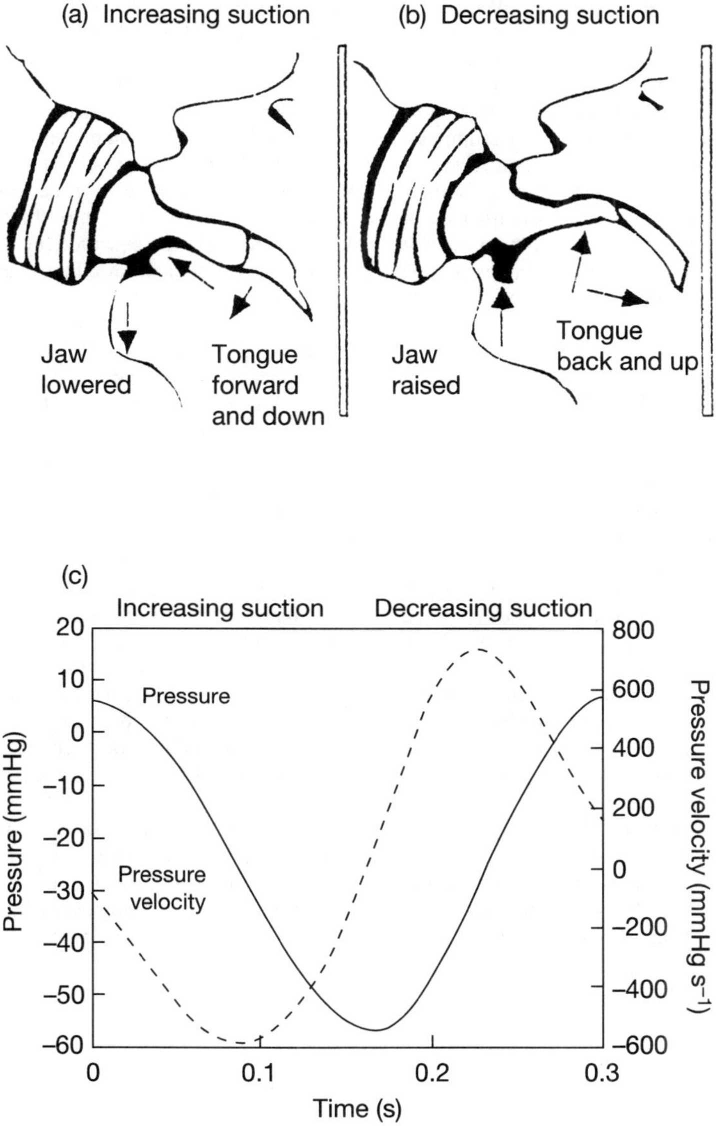

Figure 6.2 *A diagrammatic representation of the different movement processes that take place within an infant's mouth to bring about smooth changes in the intraoral pressure. (a) The increasing suction period, where the tongue moves forward and down as the jaw is lowered. The culmination of these processes brings about an increase in suction, which facilitates the flow of milk from the bottle into the mouth. (b) The decreasing suction period, where the tongue moves upwards and backwards as the jaw is raised. These movements help to propel the milk expressed during the increasing suction period to the back of the mouth, where it waits to be swallowed. (c) Actual record of sucking pressure from inside the mouth of a feeding infant (Craig & Lee, 1999, p. 372)*

this is not a reflex. The tongue protrusion of the model does not just elicit the tongue protrusion of the child. It changes the frequency and the appearance of spontaneously performed tongue protrusions. Neonatal imitation provides important information about newborn capabilities. It shows that neonates have a visual acuity good enough to identify the mouth among other facial features and that they can discriminate different mouth movements. It also shows that neonates apply differentiated and appropriate behaviors to the seen facial patterns. It makes sense for nature to invest in such innate abilities. Neonatal imitation has great social significance. It provides a means for social contact between the mother and her newborn child. However, it is also the embryo of a social communication system based on gestures.

Neonatal Reaching

Although successful reaching does not appear until around 4 months of age, the link between eye and the hand is already established in the neonate. Von Hofsten (1982; 1984) studied the arm and hand movements of neonates in the presence and absence of a large, colorful, and slowly moving object: a tuft made of yarn. He found that the newborns aimed their extended arm movements toward the object when fixating it. An example of such behavior can be seen in Figure 6.3. The immediate function of this reaching behavior cannot be to grasp and manipulate objects, because the infant does not yet control arm and hand movements independently (von Hofsten, 1984). On the contrary, the arm and the hand movements are coupled to each other in flexion and extension synergies. The successful grasping of an object necessitates flexion of the hand while the arm is extended. However, newborn reaching has another very important function. When the hand moves toward the object of interest it enters into the visual field and its movements may then become controlled by visual information. Closing the visual–manual loop in this way is of crucial importance for the development of manual control. This is precisely what is needed for developing the system. It makes it possible for the infant to explore the relationship between commands and movements, between vision and proprioception, and to discover the possibilities and constraints of manual movements.

Another kind of goal-directed arm and hand movement that neonates engage in is putting their fingers or their thumbs into their mouth. Such behaviors can also be observed prenatally. They are guided by proprioception rather than vision. These arm and hand movements are coordinated with mouth movements in a prospective way. Lew and Butterworth (1995) reported that neonates open the mouth in anticipation of the arrival of the hand rather than as a response to it. This pattern was especially distinct just before feeding.

Viewing their hands seems attractive in itself for neonates, and they will make an effort to continue to view one of their hands if they have it in sight. Van der Meer, van der Weel, and Lee (1995) placed neonates on their back with the head turned to one side. In this posture neonates extended the arm towards which their head was turned and flexed the other one. This posture is known as the asymmetric-tonic neck reflex (ATNR) or the fencing posture. Van der Meer, van der Weel, and Lee (1995) showed that this is not just a reflex. In the experiment, they gently pulled both arms downwards and found that the arm towards where the neonates turned resisted this pull but not the other arm. This could be either because the infants made an effort to keep the extended arm in the field of view, or because the turning of the head induced an increased tonus in the extended arm on the ipsilateral side as predicted by the reflex account. Then they put a TV monitor between the infant's face

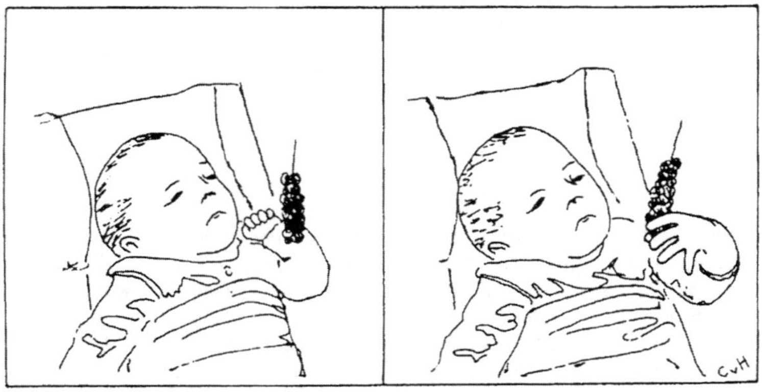

Figure 6.3 *A subject reaching for a target at 2 weeks of age. The left picture shows the starting position and the right picture the final position of the approach. Although the subject got the object in the hand it was never grasped*

and the extended arm. In the TV monitor the infant could see the other arm – the one on the contralateral side. In this case the infant resisted the pull of the contralateral arm but not the arm towards which they were turning. This result contradicts the reflex hypothesis and supports the hypothesis that the infants actively tried to keep the seen arm in the field of view.

On the Development of Action Systems

Action is at the heart of development. It involves all psychological functions including perception, cognition, motivation, and motor control. Action systems can best be described as dynamic systems consisting of many different subsystems that interact with each other in complex ways in development. Each of these has its own dynamics that determine development.

Developmental changes are self-organizing. When certain thresholds are attained, this can lead to radically new modes of functioning. Actions bring about developmental change. In addition, the CNS has its own dynamics that determine development and this determinant is especially important in infancy. As new pathways open up in the central nervous system and new connectivity emerges, new modes of control become possible. There are a number of such programmed changes in the CNS that have great impact on early action development, but it is important to note that these require external activity to be regulated appropriately. In order to extend the action repertoire and improve performance, the new modes of control must be integrated with the existing ones and geared to the environment. This is only possible if they are used in action. Two kinds of processes are distinguishable. The first has to do with coordinating muscle activations to make efficient movements and assembling those movements into functional synergies. The second has to do with acquiring prospective control. Below I will exemplify these different aspects of the developmental processes with reference to looking, postural control, reaching, and social communication.

Looking

Although each perceptual system has its own privileged procedures for exploration, the visual system has the most specialized one. The whole purpose of movable eyes is to enable the visual system to explore the world and to stabilize gaze on objects of interest. The development of oculomotor control is one of the earliest appearing skills and marks a profound improvement in the competence of the young infant. It is of crucial importance for the extraction of visual information about the world, for directing attention, and for the establishment of social communication. Controlling gaze may involve both head and eye movements and is guided by at least three types of information: visual, vestibular, and proprioceptive. How do young infants gain access to these different kinds of information, how do they come to use them prospectively to control gaze, and how do they come to coordinate head and eyes to accomplish gaze control? Two kinds of task need to be mastered: moving the eyes to significant visual targets and stabilizing gaze on these targets. Each of these tasks is associated with a specific kind of eye movement. Moving the eyes to a new target is done with high speed saccadic eye movements, and stabilizing them on the target is done with smooth pursuit eye movements. The second task is, in fact, the more complicated one. In order to avoid slipping away from the target it requires the system to anticipate forthcoming events. When the subject is moving relative to the target, which is almost always the case, the smooth eye movements need to anticipate those body movements in order to compensate for them correctly. When the fixated target moves, the eyes must anticipate its forthcoming motion.

Shifting Gaze

The ability to shift gaze is of crucial importance for the development of visual perception, because it turns the visual sense into an efficient instrument for exploring the world. The saccadic system for shifting gaze develops ahead of the system for smooth tracking. It is functional at birth and newborn infants are fairly skilled at moving gaze to significant events in the visual field. Tracking moving targets is then also primarily done with saccadic eye movements. Shifting gaze is preceded by an attentional shift which involves a process of disengaging attention to the current fixated target and moving the eyes to a new target. The ability to engage and disengage attention on targets is present at birth. However, as infants gets better at stabilizing gaze on an attractive target, they become less able to look away from it. This phenomenon has been termed 'obligatory attention' or 'sticky fixation' (Mayes & Kessen, 1989; Stechler & Latz, 1966). It has been suggested that it reflects the early maturation of a basal-ganglia/nigral pathway that induces a nonspecific inhibition of the superior colliculus (Johnson, 1990). The phenomenon of obligatory attention expresses itself rather dramatically in object tracking. Von Hofsten and Rosander (1996; 1997) found that 2- and 3-month-old infants almost never looked away from the moving object they were tracking smoothly even though each trial had a duration of 20 to 30 seconds. By about 4 months of age, however, the ability to disengage fixation and willfully steer attention emerges rapidly and the infant will then excel in looking around. At 5 months of age the subjects had a clear tendency to look away from the moving object and then return to it again. It is as if the infants looked away not because they were bored, but because they wanted to check whether anything else of importance was happening elsewhere.

Tracking Eye Movements

Several studies on eye movements indicate that newborn infants have only limited ability to track a moving target smoothly. Dayton and Jones (1964) found that neonates pursued a wide-angle visual display with smooth eye movements but the eye movements became rather jerky for a 'small' target. These results were supported by several other studies (Aslin, 1981; Bloch & Carchon, 1992; Kremenitzer et al., 1979). An example of a 4-week-old infant tracking a target with mainly saccadic eye movements can be seen in Figure 6.4. Rosander and von Hofsten (2002) also found that 1-month-old infants and younger tracked a large moving vertical grating in a smoother way than a small moving target. However, when the saccades were eliminated from the records the residual smooth tracking did not differ for the two targets. In other words, the reason why the tracking of a small target looks jerky is because infants make frequent catch-up saccades in an effort to be on target, which they do not need with a large target. The reason is simple. With a wide-field pattern of vertical stripes, the eyes are always on the target, however they move.

From about 6 weeks of age, the smooth part of the tracking improves rapidly. This was first observed both by Dayton and Jones (1964) and by Aslin (1981). Von Hofsten and Rosander (1996; 1997) recorded eye and head movements in unrestrained 1- to 5-month-old infants as they tracked a happy face moving sinusoidally back and forth in front of them. They found that the improvement in smooth pursuit tracking was very rapid and consistent between individual subjects. This is shown in Figure 6.5. Smooth pursuit starts to improve around 6 weeks of age and attains adult levels from around 14 weeks. As can be seen from Figure 6.5, one of the subjects improved performance from about 30% of smooth pursuit at 8 weeks to 90% at 10 weeks. The effect of target velocity depended on age. At 2 months of age the proportion of smooth pursuit in the slowest condition (0.2 Hz and 10° amplitude) was almost twice as high as it was in the fastest condition (0.4 Hz and 20° amplitude). At 4 months of age, the proportion of smooth pursuit was high in all conditions and approached adult values.

In order to stabilize gaze on a moving object during tracking, the smooth pursuit must anticipate its motion. Two such predictive processes have been observed in adult visual tracking (Pavel, 1990). One uses the just seen motion to predict what will happen

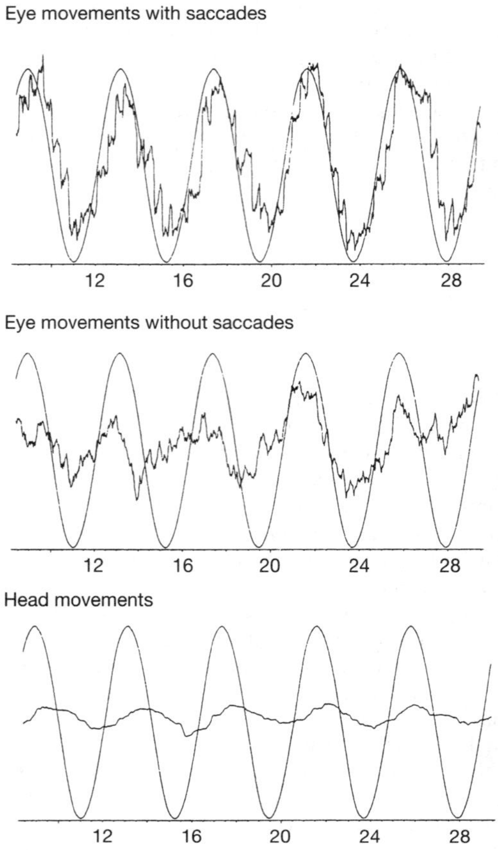

Figure 6.4 *An example of a 4-week-old infant tracking a target with mainly saccadic eye movements. Removing the saccades leaves a residual of smooth eye movements that are geared to the moving target. However, this smooth tracking component is associated with a lag. The head moves with the target as well. Also in this case is the tracking movement associated with a lag*

next through a process of extrapolation. Such predictions are in accordance with inertia which presumes that a motion with a certain speed and direction will continue with the same speed and in the same direction unless it is affected by a force, in which case the motion will change gradually. The extrapolation process is important in predicting object motion over small time windows but it cannot handle prediction over larger time frames. With increasing time there are growing possibilities that intervening events will alter the motion. Neither can it handle abrupt motion changes because such changes do not reveal themselves in the just seen motion. In order to investigate the development of these predictive processes, von Hofsten and Rosander (1997) studied visual tracking of two motion functions, one sinusoidal and one triangular.

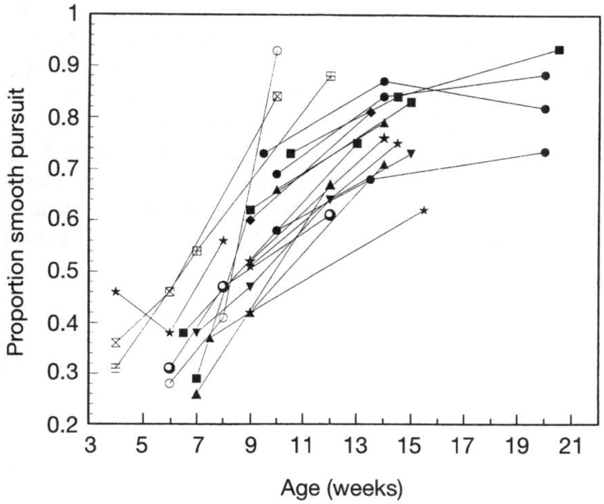

Figure 6.5 *Records of smooth pursuit development in individuals studied longitudinally. The measured property of smooth pursuit is the proportion of eye movement amplitude accounted for by smooth tracking of the moving object (smooth pursuit). Note that most of the development of smooth pursuit in these subjects occurs between 6 and 14 weeks of age*

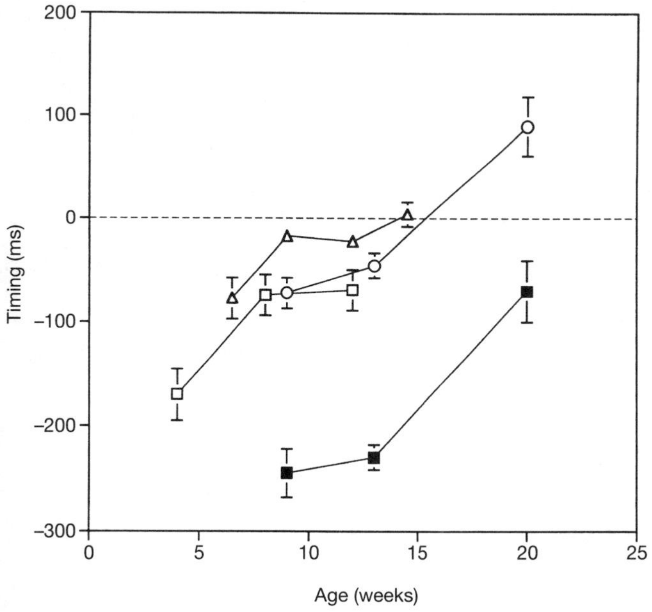

Figure 6.6 *Average lags of smooth pursuit eye movements in infants tracking a target moving back and forth in front of them. Sinusoidal target motion is depicted with open symbols and triangular motion with filled symbols (from von Hofsten & Rosander, 1976, squares; von Hofsten & Rosander, 1977, circles; and Rosander & von Hofsten, 2000, triangles)*

The sinusoidal motion can be predicted by extrapolation but not the triangular one. A triangular motion is characterized by constant velocity between the end points where the motion abruptly reverses.

In their different studies, von Hofsten and Rosander (von Hofsten & Rosander, 1996; 1997; Rosander & von Hofsten, 2000) found that the smooth eye tracking was not predictive at 1 month (see Figure 6.6). Between 1 and 2 months of age, the tracking lag of the sinusoidal motion diminished from almost 200 to 70 ms. However, the tracking of the triangular motion continued to lag more than 250 ms at that age. At 5 months, another major change took place. Then the tracking lag of the sinusoidal motion turned into a tracking lead, and the tracking lag of the triangular motion diminished substantially. The results indicate that the extrapolation mechanism functions at 2 months of age but that infants are not able then to predict abrupt events like the sudden reversal of the motion. At 5 months they are also able to predict such events if the abrupt change occurs periodically. Von Hofsten and Rosander (1997) used two amplitudes of triangular motion (10° and 20°) and found that the 5-month-old infants showed a lag with the smaller amplitude and a lead with the larger amplitude. This indicates that the infants were forming a general expectancy of where the object reversed its motion. The tracking reversed before the motion in the higher amplitude condition and after the motion in the low amplitude condition.

Von Hofsten and Rosander (1997) found that the amplitude of head tracking increased very much between 3 and 5 months of age. At 5 months the amplitude of head tracking was sometimes as large as the amplitude of the object motion. The problem was that the head still lagged the target at that age (by 0.3 s or more). In order to stabilize gaze on the target, the eyes must then lead. This creates a phase difference between the eye and the head tracking which may be so large that the eye tracking and the head tracking counteract each other. Instead of contributing to stabilizing gaze on the fixated moving object, head tracking may then reduce gaze stabilization. Figure 6.7 shows an example of a 5-month-old infant tracking a fast target with large head movements. It can be seen that the head lags substantially. The eye tracking record shows that in order to keep the gaze on the target, the eyes must

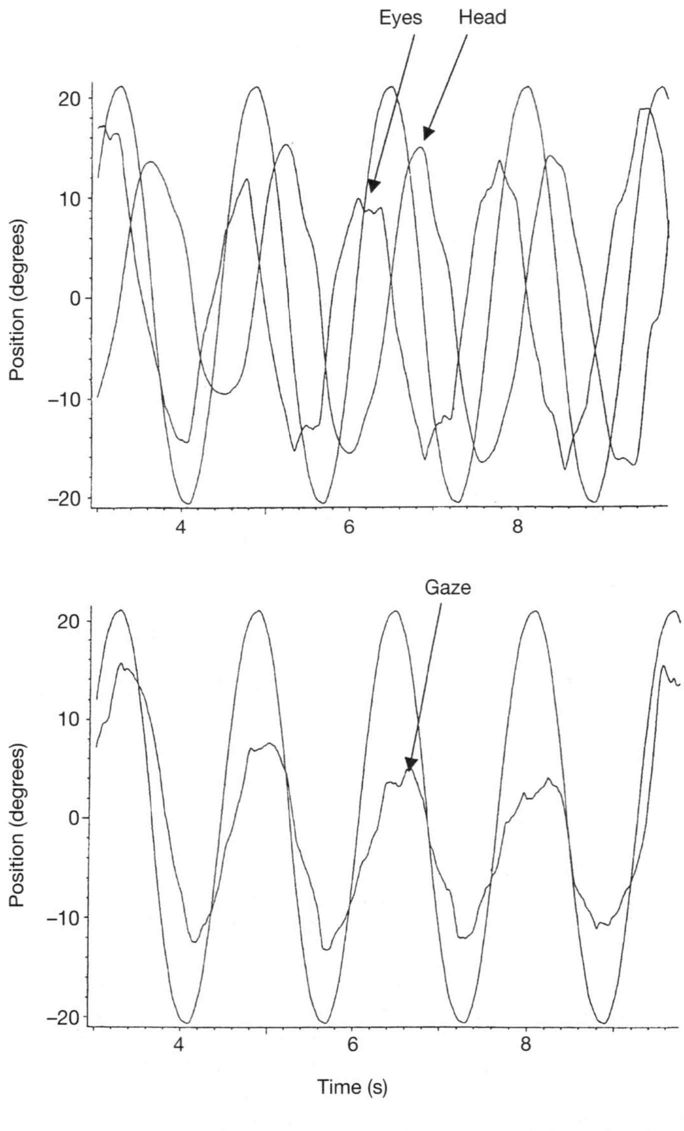

Figure 6.7 *An example of a 5-month-old infant tracking a fast target with large head movements. The target moved with 0.63 Hz which means that one cycle was completed in 1.6 s. The top diagram shows that the head lags substantially and that the eyes lead with about the same magnitude. The phase difference is so large that gaze amplitude suffers. Instead of contributing to smooth pursuit gain, the head movements counteract the smooth pursuit eye movements*

make large and fairly complicated movements to compensate for the head lag. In fact, the task would be much simpler if the head had not moved at all. The reason why infants persist in engaging the head can only be because they are internally motivated to do so. Just as in the early development of reaching, this is an expression of important developmental foresight because eventually the ability to engage the head will result in much more flexible tracking skills.

Compensatory Gaze Adjustments

Both visual and vestibular mechanisms operate to compensate for head movements unrelated to fixation. The visual one aims at stabilizing gaze on the optic array by minimizing retinal slip, while the vestibular one aims at stabilizing gaze in space. The visual mechanism is designed to work at slow optical changes and its performance begins to deteriorate at frequencies above 0.6 Hz (Benson & Barnes, 1978; Hydèn, 1983). The vestibular mechanism functions most optimally above 1 Hz where the gain approaches unity and the phase lag approaches zero (Barnes, 1993). Head movements unrelated to visual tracking are generally faster and more dynamic than the tracking itself, and the eye movements that compensate for those head movements are predominantly guided by vestibular information. This mode of control already functions at birth. These compensations are well geared to the performed head movements in terms of both amplitude and timing. Figure 6.8 shows an example of vestibularly controlled compensating eye movements in a 2-month-old infant. It can be seen from Figure 6.8 that the eyes lead rather than lag the movement of the head. This

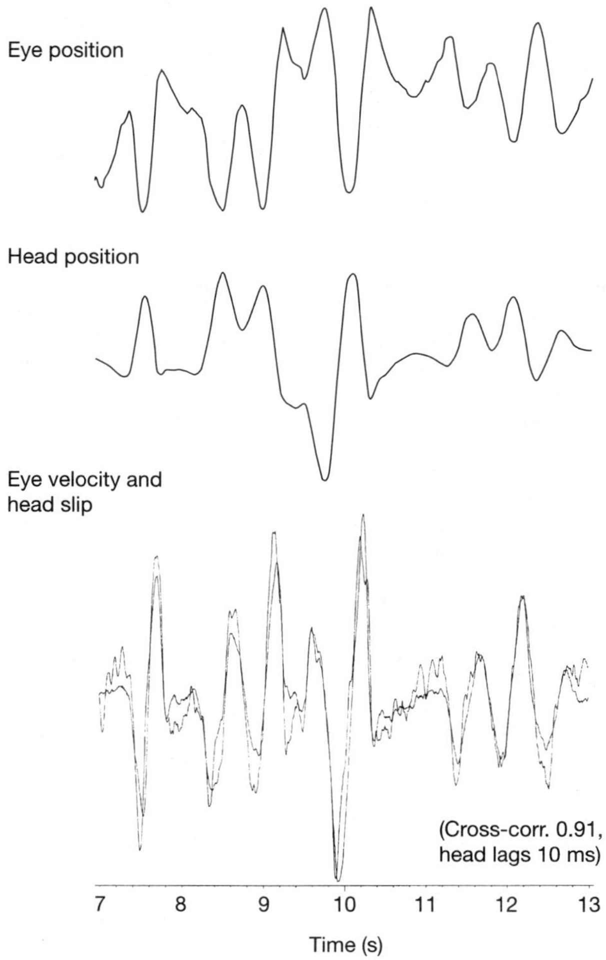

Figure 6.8 *An example of compensational eye movements in a 2-month-old infant who shook her head while closing her eyes. These eye movements are controlled by the vestibular system. On average, the eyes lead the head by 10 ms (unpublished data)*

demonstrates that the compensations are not a part of a reflex. Reflexes are elicited and will always show a lag. The prospective control of the eye movements is possible because the head movements are voluntary. The system knows ahead of time what the head will do and can use that information for controlling the eye movements.

Basic Orienting, Postural Control, and Locomotion

Basic orientation is a prerequisite for any other functional activity (Gibson, 1966; Reed, 1996) and purposeful movements are not possible without it. This includes balancing the body relative to gravity and maintaining a stable orientation relative to the environment. As Reed states, 'maintenance of posture in the real world involves much more than simply holding part of the body steady; it is maintaining a set of invariant activities while allowing other activities to vary' (1996, p. 88). Gravity gives a basic frame of reference for such orientational stability and almost all animals have a specialized mechanism for sensing gravity (in humans it is the otoliths). In addition, vision provides excellent orientational information, as does proprioception.

Gravity is also a potent force and, when body equilibrium is disturbed, posture becomes quickly uncontrollable. Therefore, any reaction to a balance threat has to be very fast and automatic. Several reflexes have been identified that serve this purpose. For instance, when one slips on a patch of ice, ongoing actions are interrupted, and a series of fast automatic responses are elicited that serve the purpose of regaining balance. However, disturbances to balance are better handled in a prospective way, because if the disturbance can be foreseen there is no need for an emergency reaction and ongoing actions can continue. Another threat to balance is one's own movements. When a body part is moved, the point of gravity of the whole body is displaced, which will push it out of equilibrium if nothing is done about it. In addition, one's own movements create momentum that pushes the body out of equilibrium. Therefore, the effects of one's own movements must be foreseen and prepared for in order to maintain ongoing activity.

At around 3 months, infants show the first signs of being able to actively control gravity. When in a prone position they will lift their head and look around. To hold the head steadily, its sway must be correctly perceived and used to control head posture. Such control seems to be attained over the first few weeks of head lifting. The next step in mastering postural control is controlling the sitting posture. This is normally accomplished around age 6 months and requires the child to control the sway of both head and trunk in relation to each other. This could be accomplished in a large number of ways because many different muscle groups affect the sitting posture. Woollacott, Debu, and Mowatt (1987) found that infants did not show a consistent postural response synergy while sitting until around 8 months of age. Hadders-Algra, Brogren, and Forssberg (1996) tested 5- to 10-month-old infants' postural adjustments when sitting on a platform and subjected to slow and fast forward and backward displacements. They found that from the youngest age onwards rather variable but direction specific muscle activation patterns were present. With increasing age the variation in muscle activation pattern decreased, resulting in a selection of the most competent patterns.

In upright stance, the body acts as a standing pendulum. The natural sway frequency of a pendulum is inversely proportional to the square root of its length. This means that the balancing task is much more difficult for a child than for an adult. For instance, a child who is only half the size of an adult will sway with a frequency which is 40% higher than that of the adult and will consequently have 40% less time in which to react to balance disturbances. In other words, when, by the end of the first year, infants start to be able to stand independently, they have mastered a balance problem more difficult than at any time later in life. When standing up, the prospective control of balance becomes extremely important. A nice example of how this mode of control emerges as the child gets to master upright stance is provided by Barela, Jeka, and Clark (1999). They examined how infants used a supporting contact surface (a handrail) during the acquisition of upright stance. The infants were studied at four developmental epochs: pulling to stand (10 months), standing alone (11 months), walking onset (12 months), and walking mastery (13.5 months). The subject's body sway, and the forces applied to the contact surface by the subject were measured. They found that both body sway and the forces applied to the contact surface decreased with increasing upright stance experience. Furthermore, the youngest subjects applied forces to the contact surface as a reaction to or a physical consequence of their body sway whereas the oldest infants applied forces to the contact surface in anticipation of body sway. These results can be seen in Figure 6.9.

Vision is quite superior in detecting small body displacements, and with it, the subject can be more efficient in using prospective control for controlling body sway. Lee and Aronsson (1974) showed that infants who have just attained upright stance are quite sensitive to peripheral visual information for body displacement. They positioned standing infants in a room with movable walls and ceiling (the moving room), and when they moved these surrounding structures the infants lost their balance in the direction predicted by the visual flow. With more experience of standing, children were not as easily overthrown

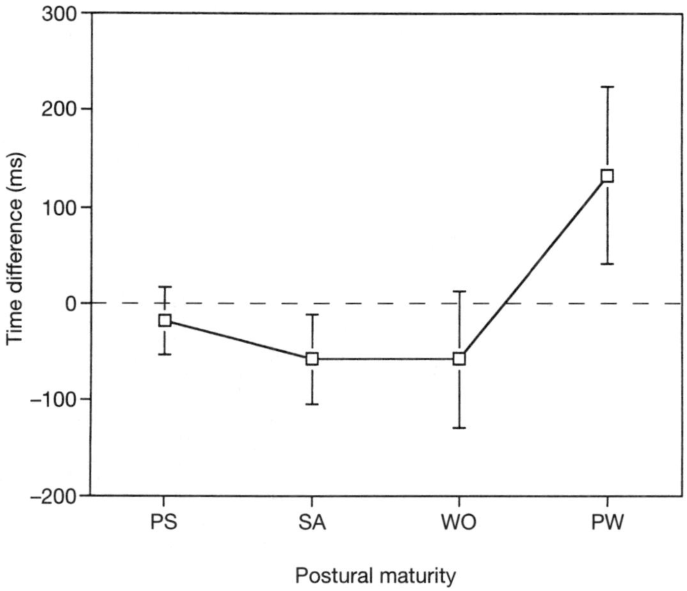

Figure 6.9 *Average time lag and SE of the applied force relative to body sway for the anterior–posterior direction collapsed across infants in each developmental period. PS = pull to stand, IS = independent stance, WO = walking onset, PW = post-walking. The dashed line depicts zero lag (after Barela, Jeka, & Clark, 1999)*

by the visual flow alone. Bertenthal, Rose, and Bai (1997) showed that the sensitivity to visual flow improves over the months after upright stance has been achieved. Visual information is especially important for dynamic postural control, that is, when maintaining balance while moving around. Therefore it is not surprising that walking independently is one of the clearest delays in the motor development of blind infants (Fraiberg, 1977). Fraiberg found that in a sample of blind children, 90% were delayed past the upper limits of sighted children as given by Bayley (1969) when walking independently across a room.

Special demands are associated with balance control during bodily activities. In order to maintain balance during limb movements, the subject must know about the contingencies between the limb movements, the reactive forces that arise during movement, and the displacement of the point of gravity. Adults seem to counteract such disturbances to the postural system in a precise way ahead of time. For instance, when adults prepare for pushing or pulling a handle in front of them, they will not simply activate the arm that is doing the job. Just before the arm muscles fire, the appropriate leg muscles that resist a displacement of the body are also activated (Cordo & Nashner, 1982). When the handle is pulled, for instance, the gastrocnemius muscle is activated around 50 ms before the pulling starts.

Von Hofsten and Woollacott (1990) studied anticipatory adjustments of the trunk in 9-month-old infants reaching for an object in front of them while balancing the trunk. The infants were seated astride one of the knees of the accompanying parent who was supporting the child by the hips (see Figure 6.10). Muscle responses were recorded from the abdominal and trunk extensor muscles as well as from the deltoid muscle of the reaching arm. The results showed that trunk muscles participated in the reaching actions of 9-month-old infants. It seemed to be the trunk extensors that primarily prepared for reaching, while the role of the abdominal muscles was less clear-cut. They participated in the reach, but less in its preparation and more as part of bending the body forward towards the end of the reach. This can be seen in Figure 6.10.

Witherington et al. (2002) examined the early development of anticipatory postural activity in support of pulling action while standing. A total of 34 infants between 10 and 17 months were tested. The task required infants to open a cabinet drawer to retrieve toys while a force resisting the pulling action was applied to the drawer. Before each trial an attractive toy was placed in the drawer that enticed the infant to pull the drawer to retrieve the toy. Displacements of the drawer, movements of the head and trunk, and activity of both gastrocnemius and biceps muscles were measured. It was found that the proportion of pulls involving anticipatory activity in the gastrocnemius muscles progressively increased between 10 and 17 months. The emergence of independent walking coincided with marked increases in anticipatory postural adjustments relative to pull

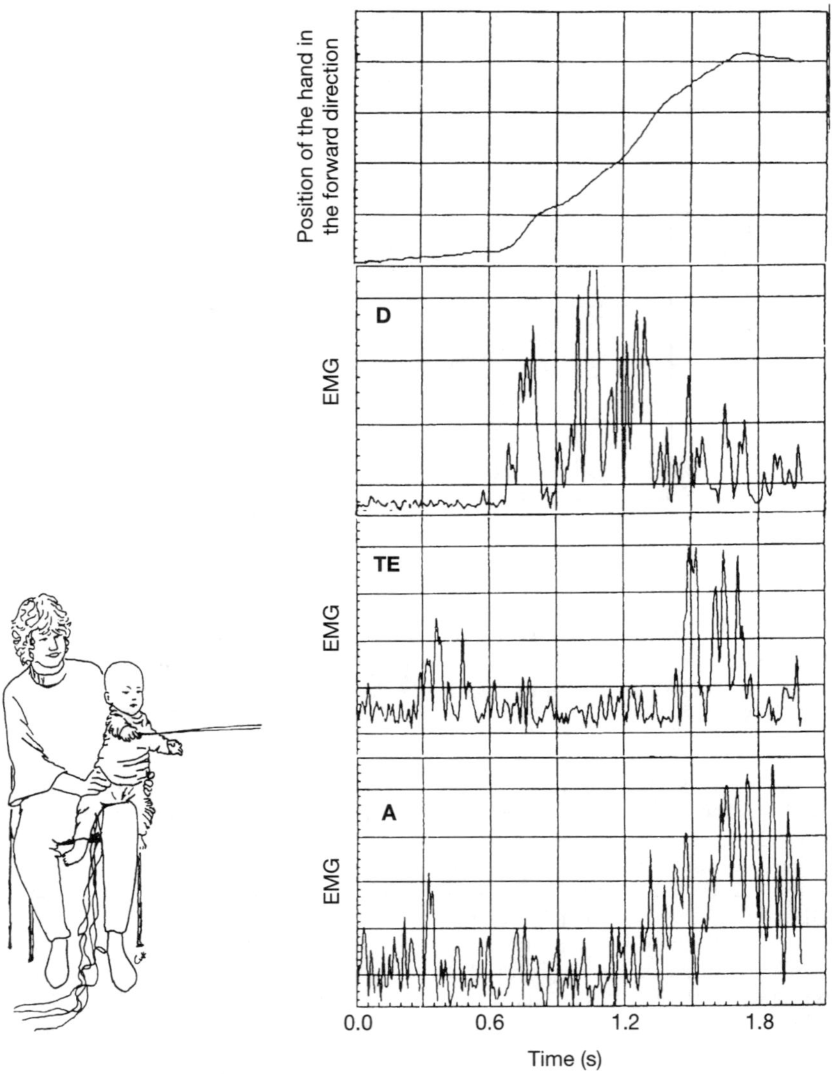

Figure 6.10 *Left: the experimental situation in von Hofsten and Woollacott, (1990 unpublished).*
Right: example of one infant's responses from the deltoid (D) of the reaching arm, the abdominal muscles (A) and the trunk extensor muscles (TE) plus records of the relative displacements of the reaching hand. In this specific example the reach was performed with the left hand. It can be seen that the trunk extensor muscles start increasing firing well before the deltoid muscle. The major activation of the abdominal muscles occurs at the end of the reach when the object is grasped

onset. Figure 6.11 shows that the frequency of postural activity initiated within 500 ms before and persisting past the pull onset increased from less than 40% of the trials in the pre-standing infants to over 80% in the experienced walkers. The most substantial developmental changes occurred between the pre-walking infants and the early walkers. Very specific anticipatory adjustments in the gastrocnemius muscle within 240 ms before pull onset increased from roughly one-third of the pulls to over 50%. This is also illustrated in Figure 6.11.

Because of its central role in movement production, postural control becomes a limiting factor in motor development. If the infant is given active postural support, goal-directed reaching can be observed at an earlier age than is otherwise possible. For instance, the neonatal reaching observed by von Hofsten (1982) was performed by properly supported

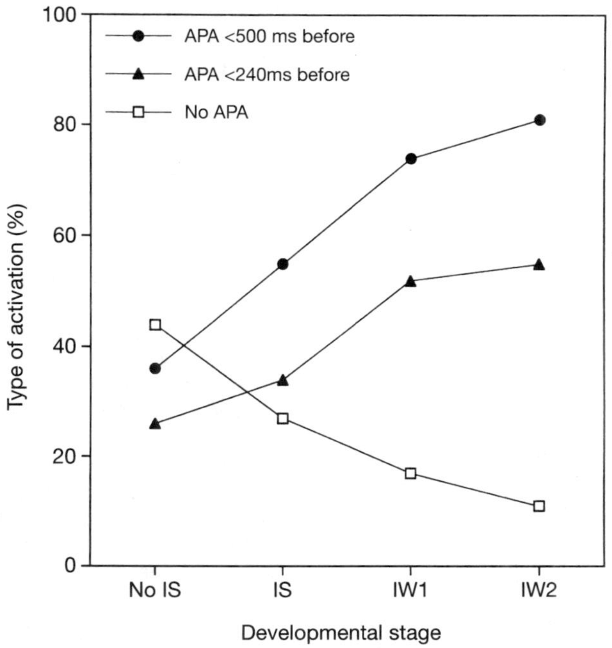

Figure 6.11 *Mean proportion of pulls (and standard error) involving anticipatory postural activity (APA) for four levels of standing and walking experience. The proportions of pulls in which the gastrocnemius muscle was activated within 500 ms (circles) or 240 ms (squares) before and persisting past the pull onset are depicted. The proportion of pulls involving no anticipatory postural activity is shown in comparison (triangles). The following developmental stages were distinguished: no IS = no independent standing experience, IS = 2 to 12 weeks of independent standing experience, IW1 = 4 to 12 weeks of independent walking experience, IW2 = 16 or more weeks of independent walking experience*

infants. For these reasons, development of reaching and other motor skills should be studied in the context of posture. However, only a few studies have seriously considered the influence of such contextual factors. Rochat and associates (Rochat, 1992; Rochat & Goubet, 1995) showed that the onset of self-sitting made infants transfer from two-handed to one-handed reaching. They suggested that this was because the newly attained posture could be easily disturbed and that two-handed reaching was more threatening to balance than one-handed. Rochat also observed that when infants sitting independently reached forward with one hand, the other one often moved backwards to preserve the point of equilibrium.

Reaching and Manipulation

Although newborns may extend their arms toward an attractive object in front of them, they never grasp it. The arm and the hand seem to be coupled in synergistic extension–flexion movements (von Hofsten, 1984). When the arm extends the fingers extend too, and when the fingers flex the arm also flexes. Von Hofsten (1984) found that the hand was either open or opened during the extension of the arm in about 70% of the extended arm movements. The opening of the hand did not seem to be a function of the act of reaching towards the object because the same thing happened when the child extended the arm without looking at the object. This pattern was also observed in young rhesus monkeys by Lawrence and Hopkins (1976). They found that newborn monkeys had difficulties in grasping an object they had reached for and, if they finally closed the hand around it, they had difficulties in releasing it after they had pulled it towards them.

Von Hofsten (1984) found that the synergistic arm–hand pattern changed dramatically at 2 months of age. The coupling was then broken, and instead of opening the hand, the child had a strong tendency to fist it during the extension of the arm (see Figure 6.12). At the same time the movements became more vigorous and appeared more voluntary, as if the child really tried to attain the object (von Hofsten, 1985). A few weeks later, the subjects were again observed

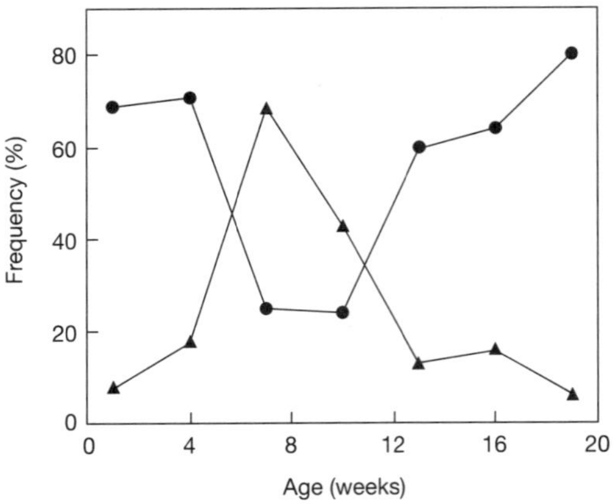

Figure 6.12 *Frequency of open hand (circles) and fisted hand (triangles) during pre-reaching movements performed by infants from 1 to 19 weeks of age (after von Hofsten, 1984)*

opening the hand during the extension of the arm but then only when the arm movement was visually directed toward the object. The infants then also started closing the hand when it was close to the object, suggesting that the global extension–flexion pattern had developed into a differentiated pattern where arm and hand were more independently controlled.

The transition from pre-reaching to reaching was studied by Thelen et al. (1993). They found that each infant had its own individual way of moving its arms: some moved them more slowly with rather damped movements, and some more vigorously. Overall, the early reaching attempts were characterized by much variability which casts doubt on the notion that early movements are stereotyped. During the transition from pre-reaching to successful reaching and grasping the movements became less variable as the infants came to control the intrinsic dynamics of their arms.

Studies of reaching kinematics (Berthier, 1996; von Hofsten, 1979; 1991) show that early reaches are rather segmented, in contrast to adult reaches which consist of a single bell-shaped velocity curve. Von Hofsten (1979) defined movement units as segments of the reach, each consisting of an acceleration and a deceleration phase. Early reaching consisted of several such segments but the number decreased rapidly with increasing age. Already after a few months of experience with reaching, the number of segments approached two units, one associated with the approach and one with the grasping act. Von Hofsten (1993) interpreted this development as reflecting increased prospectivity of the reaching action.

In the act of reaching for an object there are several problems that need to be dealt with in advance, if the encounter with the object is going to be smooth and efficient. The reaching hand needs to adjust to the orientation, form, and size of the object. The securing of the target must be timed in such a way that the hand starts to close around the target in anticipation of and not as a reaction to encountering the object. Such timing has to be planned and can only occur under visual control. Tactually controlled grasping is only initiated after contact, and will induce an interruption in the reach-and-grasp act. Thus, the emergence of prospective visual control of grasping is crucial for the development of manual skill.

From the age when infants start to reach for objects they have been found to adjust the orientation of the hand to the orientation of an elongated object reached for (Lockman, Ashmead, & Bushnell, 1984; von Hofsten & Fazel-Zandy, 1984). Adjusting the hand to the size of a target is less crucial. Instead of doing that, it would also be possible to open the hand fully during the approach which would lessen the spatial end point accuracy needed to grasp the object. Adults use this strategy when reaching for an object under time stress (Wing, Turton, & Fraser, 1986). The disadvantage is the additional time it takes to close a fully opened hand relative to a semi-opened hand. Von Hofsten and Rönnqvist (1988) found that 9- and 13-month-old infants, but not 5-month-olds, adjusted the opening of the hand to the size of the object reached for.

Von Hofsten and Rönnqvist (1988) also monitored the timing of the grasps. For each reach it was determined when the distance between thumb and index finger started to diminish and when the object was encountered. It was found that all the infants studied, including those that had just recently started to reach for objects successfully, started to close the hand before the object was encountered. For infants of 9 months and younger the hand first moved to the vicinity of the target and then started to close around it. For the 13-month-olds, however, the grasping action typically started during the approach, well before touch. In other words, at this age grasping started to become integrated with the reach to become one continuous reach-and-grasp act.

A remarkable ability of infants to time their manual actions relative to an external event is demonstrated in early catching behavior (von Hofsten, 1980; 1983; von Hofsten & Lindhagen, 1979; von Hofsten et al., 1998). Von Hofsten and Lindhagen (1979) found that infants reached successfully for moving objects at the very age they began mastering reaching for stationary ones. Eighteen-week-old infants were found to catch an object moving at 30 cm/s. Von Hofsten (1980) found that the reaches were aimed towards the meeting point with the object and not towards the position where the object was seen at the beginning of the reach. Von Hofsten (1983) also found that 8-month-old infants successfully caught an object moving at 120 cm/s. The initial aiming of these reaches was within a few degrees of the meeting point with the target, and the variable timing error was only around 50 ms. The studies show that infants predict the future position of a moving object, but they tell us little about the nature or limits of these predictions. Systematic study of the principles guiding predictive reaching requires manipulation of the spatial as well as the temporal properties of object motion.

Von Hofsten et al. (1998) presented 6-month-old infants with an object that moved into reaching space on four different trajectories: two linear trajectories that intersected out of reach at the center of the display, and two trajectories containing a sudden turn at the point of intersection. Shortly after the object had passed the intersection point it came temporarily within reach (see Figure 6.13). In order to catch the object, the reach had to be planned before the object arrived at the intersection. In two experiments, infants' tracking and reaching provided evidence for an extrapolation of the object motion on linear paths, in accord with inertia. This tendency was remarkably resistant to counter-evidence, for it was persistent even after repeated observations of objects whose trajectories suddenly turned at the point of intersection.

Systems for Social Interaction

Social interaction relies on perception–action systems, some of which are functioning at birth or shortly after. There is an important difference between these action systems and those used for negotiating the physical world. The fact that one's own actions affect the behavior of the person towards whom they are directed creates a much more dynamic situation than when actions are directed towards objects. In addition, anticipating what is going to happen next is less dependent on physical laws as in the object case and more dependent on knowledge of the rules and regularities that govern the other person's actions, which in turn is dependent on one's own social behavior and social conventions. In order to master social interaction it therefore becomes crucially necessary to perceive the intentions and emotions of the subject with whom one interacts and to know the conventions of social interaction. Intentions and emotions are readily displayed by elaborate and specific movements, gestures, and sounds which become important to perceive and control. Some of these abilities are already present in newborn infants and reflect their preparedness for social interaction. Neonates display distinct attractions towards people, especially to the sounds, movements, and features of the human face (Johnson & Morton, 1991; Maurer, 1985). They also engage in social interaction and turn-taking that among other things is expressed in their imitation of facial gestures. They also communicate emotions such as pain, hunger and disgust through innate display systems (Wolff, 1987). These innate dispositions give social interaction a flying start and open up a window for the learning of the more intricate regularities of human social behavior. Parents show a remarkable talent for responding to the infant's signals and turning them into sophisticated forms

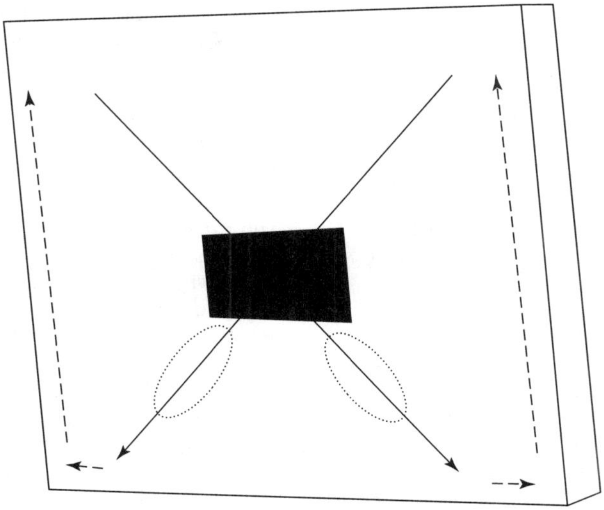

Figure 6.13 *A schematic view of the display screen showing the different motion paths used in von Hofsten et al. (1998), von Hofsten, Feng, and Spelke (2000), and Spelke and von Hofsten (2001). The dashed ellipses depict the areas where the object was within reach. The rectangle indicates the position of the occluder in von Hofsten, Feng, and Spelke (2000) and Spelke and von Hofsten (2001)*

of social interaction. Rochat and Striano (1999) suggested that this 'propensity to express empathy through the echoing of affects and feelings in highly scaffolding ways is part of normal parenting and . . . the primary source of intersubjectivity'.

One of the perception–action systems that serve social interaction is speech. Like other action systems, speech has both a perceptual and a productive side. Perception of certain aspects of speech seems to occur even in the womb, and newborn infants have been shown to prefer their mother's voice (DeCasper & Fifer, 1980). Because of the lowpass filtering of the human voice in the womb, it is presumably the prosody of the voice rather than any other more detailed property that neonates recognize. There is good evidence that infants have a sensitivity to prosodic structure, that this sensitivity is present in the newborn, and that it improves from then on (Juscyck, 1992). Also the phonemic structure develops early. By 4 months of age, infants seem to be able to distinguish between virtually any pair of stimuli that cross phoneme boundaries (Kuhl, 1994).

The research on early development of speech shows that the productive capabilities of speech clearly lag the perceptual ones (see e.g. Menn, 1983). Thus, human infants can perceive speech before they can speak or babble. On the other hand, phylogeny has prepared the human child for the task of speaking. The morphology of the human vocal tract has been altered relative to that of other primates in a way that facilitates speech (Carré, Lindblom, & MacNeilage, 1995). Babbling is, furthermore, dominated by the cyclical opening and closing of the mandible in a way that is also characteristic of sucking. MacNeilage and Davis (1993) argued that many of the articulatory regularities in the sound patterns of babbling and early speech can be attributed to properties of this mandibular cycle.

When the perception–action cycle of speech is closed, speech develops rapidly. Infants start spending much of their time awake exercising babbling sounds. They also discover the communicative value of speech sounds and use them in their social interactions long before they can articulate specific words.

Action and Cognition

All actions are directed into the future and the ability to control them requires the prediction of events that have not yet occurred. Events are governed by rules and, if the rules are known, prediction is possible. The motion of an object, for instance, can be predicted from the physical laws that regulate the motion. In such a case, a simple prediction is to assume that objects will continue to move in the same way as before. This assumption follows from the principle of inertia and is very reasonable for short time intervals. Von Hofsten et al. (1998) found that 6-month-old infants follow this rule when reaching for objects that moved on straight trajectories on a screen. However, when the on-line monitoring is interrupted because the object temporarily moves out of sight, the motion must often be predicted over longer time intervals. Also in this situation, infants tend to rely on the principle of inertia. Von Hofsten, Feng, and Spelke (2000) studied 6-month-old infants tracking an object that moved on the same four paths as in von Hofsten et al. (1998). The object was invisible for almost a second. This was accomplished by placing an occluder over the part where the paths intersected. At the very first trial, the infants were somewhat confused and simply turned the head to the middle of the screen, but on the following trials they moved the head over to the opposite side, whether they had been presented with objects that moved in a straight path or ones that abruptly turned behind the occluder. This effect is illustrated in Figure 6.14. Infants also learned to anticipate nonlinear motion. Figure 6.14 shows that after six trials with abruptly turning motion, they began to move to their reappearance point. As illustrated in Figure 6.7, 5-month-old infants learned to predict the turning of an object that moved back and forth with constant velocity and abruptly turned at the end points of the trajectory. The turning could only be predicted from knowledge of the periodicity of the motion, that is where or when it would turn (von Hofsten & Rosander, 1997). These findings suggest that infants form representations of objects and their motions that are biased by the principle of inertia and are also influenced by learning.

Spelke and von Hofsten (2001) studied the reaching activity of infants in the same experimental situation as von Hofsten, Feng, and Spelke (2000). They found infants' predictive reaching for a moving object was sharply disrupted when the object underwent a brief period of occlusion before it came within reach. In the presence of an occluder, most infants failed to reach for the object at all, while on average they reached every third trial when it was visible. Similar results were obtained by Jonsson and von Hofsten (in press) and Munakata et al. (1996). They also found that reaching was disrupted in the same way when the moving object was made temporarily nonvisible by darkness. However, in this situation reaching recovered more rapidly than in the occluder condition.

Why do infants fail to reach for an object whose path is temporarily occluded? One possible explanation is that infants' failure may follow from a shift in visual attention away from the nonvisible object (Baillargeon, 1993; Piaget, 1954). This explanation, however, received no support from the studies of reaching for occluded objects (Jonsson & von Hofsten, 2000; Spelke & von Hofsten, 2000). Visual attention to the object was as high in the presence of an occluder as in its absence and infants looked for the place where it would reappear. However, even

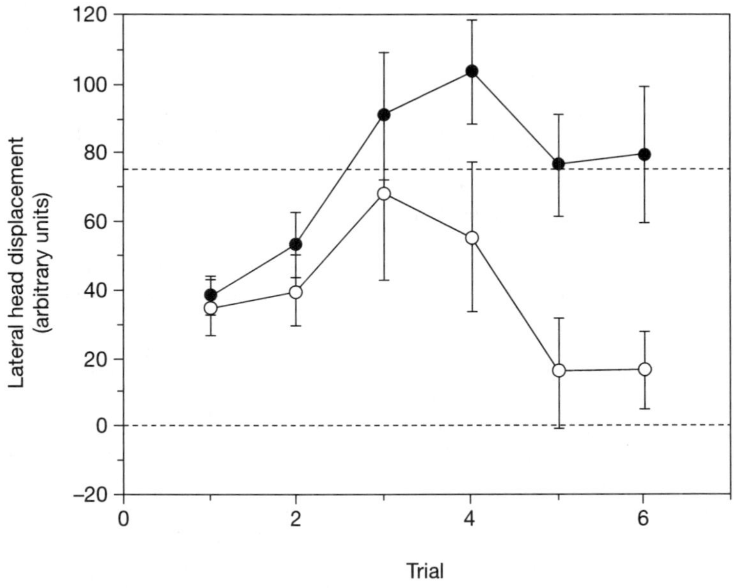

Figure 6.14 *Mean head position (and standard error) at reappearance for each of the six first trials of the experiment by von Hofsten, Feng, and Spelke (2000). Filled circles correspond to linear motion and unfilled circles correspond to nonlinear motion. Lower dashed line indicates head position directed toward the point where the object disappeared behind the occluder, and upper dashed line indicates head direction toward the reentrance point on the opposite side of the occluder. When the object reappeared on the same side of the occluder the head should ideally be directed in the same way as when the object disappeared*

when attention was high, occlusion sharply disturbed infants' reaching.

Some ability to represent objects and their motions under conditions of nonvisibility seems to be present before 6 months of age. Baillargeon (1986) found that 5-month-old infants looked longer at an event where an object moved through the space occupied by an occluded object. Spelke and associates (1992; 1994) presented infants with a visible object that moved out of view behind a visible occluder, and the occluder was then removed to reveal the object at one of several positions. Under certain conditions, infants looked systematically longer than baseline at outcome displays that presented the object in a position that it would not have entered if it had continued to move naturally behind the occluder. Such preferential looking experiments provide evidence that infants make inferences about object motions behind occluders. Secondly, studies of reaching in the dark (Clifton et al., 1991; 1993; Hood & Willatts, 1986) show that infants continue to orient to an object that is obscured by darkness. They also attempted to reach for the object and their reaching was found to be appropriate to the object's size, shape, and position.

Spelke and von Hofsten (2000) and Munakata et al. (1997) proposed that young infants represent both visible and hidden objects, but that their representations are less precise than the representations of older children. Precise representations are required for reaching: to reach for an object, the infant must know where it is, how big it is, what shape it is, and how it is moving. In contrast, determining that a hidden object exists behind a screen does not require this precision. This could explain how looking and reaching was differentially affected by temporary occlusion of the object of interest.

Object representations are weaker when an object is plunged into darkness than when it is visible, but they are stronger in the dark than in the presence of a visible occluding object, which competes with the hidden object for attention. The differing strength of object representations in darkness versus occlusion may account for the different findings of reaching experiments in the two situations.

When young infants participate in a preferential looking experiment involving an occluded object, they can draw on their imprecise representation of the object to determine that it exists behind the occluder, although they will fail to represent its exact shape, size, or location. When infants are presented with an occluded object in a reaching experiment, however, this same imprecise representation is not sufficient to guide object-directed reaching.

Conclusions

Actions originate in actions. Our biological system has prepared us for negotiating the surrounding world from the beginning of life, by setting up adequate foundations for our basic action systems. These foundations include some initial organization of the perceptual system for extracting significant structures in the environment and providing the information necessary for guiding the movements towards them. They also include some initial organization of the motor system to make it controllable. In order for a newborn to be able to direct reaching movements towards an object he or she must be able to perceive where the object is in space and to be able to organize the muscle contractions of the arm to make it move to that location. In order to imitate a tongue protrusion the newborn child must be able to correctly perceive the movements of the mouth and the tongue of the model, and be able to associate their own mouth and tongue movements to the perceived patterns. These are remarkable achievements considering the fact that vision cannot be used before birth.

To become adaptive instruments, perception and action must form loops by which information is fed back into the system. Loops are essential because they provide the possibilities for guiding the movements instead of just eliciting them. Loops are also necessary for modifying the system during ontogenesis towards more optimal functioning. When there is a loop, feedback can be provided and a window opened up for experience to affect and refine the behavior in question. Therefore, one of the most important aspects of phylogenetic adaptation is to set up loops that enable the growing organism to regulate its own behaviors.

Motivation is also essential for the establishment of action systems. Actions are not elicited or triggered by some sensory signal like reflexes; they are defined by a goal, initiated by a motivated subject, and guided by information. Motivation focuses infants' interests on specific kinds of information and makes certain actions pleasurable. But motivation does more than that. It makes infants curious and eager to explore the world. Activity is at the very center of it all and helps to organize infants' actions, structure their perception, build up their knowledge of the world, and ultimately contribute to the tailoring of their central nervous system. This is made possible by multiple loops that feed information back into the system.

The development of actions is multi-determined. It depends on the child's ability to control their movements, their perceptual abilities, their abilities to foresee what is going to happen next, and the dynamics of their nervous system. Take for instance the development of reaching and manipulation. It includes the development of postural control that frees the hands from the task of supporting the trunk, the development of binocular depth perception that defines the object position precisely in space, the increase in arm strength, and the development of independent control of the arm, hand, and fingers. In order to grasp an object at reaching distance, the movements of the arm and hand must be independently controlled. In order to manipulate an object in a precise way the fingers needs to be independently controlled.

Changes in the state of the nervous system in early development often result in dramatic effects on the organization of actions. The rapid synaptogenesis of the cerebral cortex around 2–3 months of age makes smooth pursuit eye movements and binocular depth perception go from an almost nonfunctional state to adult-like performance over just a few weeks, and the establishment of the direct cortico-motor-neuronal pathways at around 9 months enables the child to use the pincer grasp when prehending objects.

The acquisition of new action skills seems to proceed in two steps: first there is an increase in the variability of movement patterns, after which the variability decreases and merges on a few optimal procedures for action (Hadders-Algra, Brogren, & Forssberg, 1996; Thelen et al., 1993). This sequence resembles the steps in neuronal mapping where initially an abundance of connections are formed, after which the less useful connections are eliminated to leave only those that mediate information most reliably (Edelman, 1987; von der Malsburg & Singer, 1988). Edelman (1987) and Changeux and Danchin (1976) suggested that this sequence reflects the same underlying principles as those of evolution itself: production of variability and the selection of the fittest (the neuronal group selection theory). Sporns and Edelman (1993) suggested furthermore that similar principles hold for the establishment of new action skills. The increase in the variability of the produced movement patterns corresponds to proliferation of synapses in the neural structures engaged. The subsequent decrease in variability is due to an experientially driven selective process in which the less useful connections are eliminated. In the end only the most optimal neuronal patterns and movements remain.

An alternative interpretation (von Hofsten, 1997) presumes that the increase in variability is the result of a motivation to explore new domains of movement possibilities that have been opened up as a result of, for instance, the establishment of new neuronal pathways, improved perception, biomechanical changes, or improved mobility in other domains. When the new workspace is known to the child, efficient solutions will be found to specific tasks and this will tend to decrease the variability of the movements produced. Thus, the difference between these two viewpoints is that while the 'neuronal group selection theory' presumes that the observed decrease in variability is an irreversible neuronal event, the latter alternative explains the same phenomenon as an optimization of actions to specific task constraints. When the task space is known, it is always possible to find the smoothest and most economical route through it independently of the previous routes taken. If unexpected problems or obstacles are encountered, a different optimal route will be found that will lead to the goal. The knowledge gathered through systematic exploration of a task is structured into a frame of reference for action that makes planning possible. This is the basis of skill. The importance of practice and repetition is not to stamp in patterns of movement or to achieve a immutable program, but rather to encourage the functional organization of action systems (Reed, 1996).

Although perception and action are mutually dependent, there is an asymmetry between them. Perception is necessary for controlling actions and every action requires specific information for its control. Without perception there will be no action. The reverse is only partially true. Action is a necessary part of perceiving but only in a general sense. Specific actions are not required for producing specific percepts, and action does not tell perception what to perceive. It only provides opportunities for perceiving and guides the perceptual system to where the information is.

This has clear consequences for development. The ability to extract the necessary information must be there before actions can be organized. Only then can the infant learn to control the dynamics of their motor system and gear it to the appropriate information. Take, for instance, the speech system where infants' ability to perceive the phonemic and prosodic structure of speech develops much ahead of their ability to produce those sound qualities. The infant is still able to produce sounds and show joy in doing that but the sounds have a much simpler cyclical structure than suggested by their perceptual abilities.

I can see two processes of perceptual development. The first one is a spontaneous perceptual learning process that has to do with the detection of structure in the sensory flow. As long as there is variability and change in the sensory flow, the perceptual system will spontaneously learn to detect structure and differentiate invariants in that flow that correspond to relatively stable and predictible properties of the world. The second process is one of selecting information relevant for guiding action. Infants must already have detected that structure in the sensory flow before it can be selected for guiding action. It could not be the reverse. In other words, perception is not encapsulated in the actions to start with, as Piaget (1953; 1954) suggested. It is rather the other way around.

For an understanding of the development of perception, action and cognition it is of utmost importance to trace their origins in development. I have tried to do that in the present chapter. Piaget (1953) perhaps more than anyone else understood how important this was and his theoretical model makes a strong point of tracing the origins of action and cognition. With the dominating views and limited knowledge of his time, he ended up conceiving of the origins as reflexes and he came to undervalue the importance of perception. This was clearly a mistake. However, he showed significant insights into the developmental processes, how knowledge systems merge and differentiate and how they self-organize under the influence of the child's own activity. This is a lasting contribution.

There is, finally, an important independency in early development and that has to do with the modularization of actions. Abilities expressed in one context do not necessarily transfer to another, and the systems of representations underlying them do not seem to do so either. Just because an infant at a certain age can track an object predictively with his or her eyes does not imply that they track predictively with their head (von Hofsten & Rosander, 1997). With development, more generalized skills and more generalized systems of representations emerge form the complex interactions both within and between action systems. Little is still known about these developmental processes, but even in the adult the mind is still significantly modularized (Fodor, 1983).

REFERENCES

Alegria, J. and Noirot, E. (1978). Neonate orientation behavior towards human voice. *International Journal of Behavioral Development*, 1, 291–312.

Anokhin, P.K. (1964). *Systemogenesis as a general regulator of brain development. Progress in Brain Research*, 9.

Aslin, R.N. (1981). Development of smooth pursuit in human infants. In D.F. Fisher, R.A. Monty, & J.W. Senders (eds), *Eye movements: Cognition and visual perception*. Hillsdale, NJ: Erlbaum.

Baillargeon, R. (1986). Representing the existence and the location of hidden objects: Object permanence in the 6- and 8-month-old infants. *Cognition*, 23, 21–41.

Baillargeon, R. (1993). The object concept revisited: New directions in the investigation of infants' physical knowledge. In C.E. Granrud (ed.), *Visual perception and cognition in infancy*. Hillsdale, NJ: Erlbaum.

Barela, J.A., Jeka, J.J., & Clark, J.E. (1999). The use of somatosensory information during the acquisition of independent upright stance. *Infant Behavior and Development*, 22, 87–102.

Barnes, G.R. (1993). Visual–vestibular interaction in the control of head and eye movement: The role of visual feedback and predictive mechanisms. *Progress in Neurobiology*, 41: 435–472.

Bayley, N. (1969). *Bayley scales of infant development*. New York: Psychological Corporation.

Benson, A.J., & Barnes, G.R. (1978). Vision during angular oscillations: The dynamic interaction of visual and vestibular mechanisms. *Aviation Space and Environmental Medicine*, 49, 340–345

Bernstein, N. (1967). *The coordination and regulation of movements*. Oxford: Pergamon.

Bertenthal, B., Rose, J., & Bai, D. (1997). Perception–action coupling in the development of visual control of posture. *Journal of Experimental Psychology: Human Perception and Performance*, 23, 1631–1643.

Berthier, N.E. (1996). Learning to reach: A mathematical model. *Developmental Psychology*, 32, 811–823.

Bloch, H., & Carchon, I. (1992). On the onset of eye–head co-ordination in infants. *Behavioural Brain Research*, 49, 85–90.

Carré, R., Lindblom, B., & MacNeilage, P. (1995). Rôle de l'acoustique dans l'évolution du conduit vocal humain. *Comptes Rendus de l'Académie des Sciences (Paris)*, 320, Série IIb.

Clifton, R., Muir, D.W., Ashmead, D. H., & Clarkson, M.G. (1993). Is visually guided reaching in early infancy a myth? *Child Development*, 64, 1099–1110.

Clifton, R., Rochat, P., Litovsky, R., & Perris, E. (1991). Object representation guides infants' reaching in the dark. *Journal of Experimental Psychology: Human Perception and Performance*, 17, 323–329.

Cordo, P.J., & Nashner, L.M. (1982). Properties of postural adjustments associated with rapid arm movements. *Journal of Neurophysiology*, 47, 287–302.

Craig, C.M., & Lee, D.N. (1999). Neonatal control of sucking pressure: Evidence for an intrinsic tau-guide. *Experimental Brain Research*, 124, 371–382.

Dayton, G.O., Jones, M.H. (1964) Analysis of characteristics of fixation reflex in infants by use of direct current electroculagraphy. Neurology 14:1152–1156.

deCasper, A.J., & Fifer, W.P. (1980). On human bonding: Newborns prefer their mothers' voices. *Science*, 208, 1174–1176.

deVries, J.I.P., Visser, G.H.A., & Prechtl, H.F.R. (1982). The emergence of fetal behavior: I. Qualitative aspects. *Early Human Development*, 23, 159–191.

Edelman, G.M. (1987). *Neural Darwinism*. New York: Basic.

Field, J., Muir, D., Pilon, R., Sinclair, M., & Dodwell, P. (1979). Infants' orientation to sounds from birth to three months. *Child Development*, 51, 295–298.

Fodor, J. (1983). *The modularity of mind*. Cambridge, MA: MIT Press.

Fraiberg, S. (1977). *Insights from the blind*. New York: Basic.

Gibson, J.J. (1966). *The senses considered as perceptual systems*. New York: Houghton Mifflin.

Goodale, M.A., & Milner, D.A. (1992). Separate visual pathways for perception and action. *Trends in Neuroscience*, 15, 20–25.

Hadders-Algra, M., Brogren, E., & Forssberg, H. (1996). Ontogeny of postural adjustments during sitting in infancy: variation, selection and modulation. *Journal of Physiology*, 493, 273–288.

Haineline, L., Riddell, P., Grose-Fifer, J., & Abramov, I. (1992). Development of accommodation and convergence in infancy. *Behavioural Brain Research*, 49, 33–50.

Haith, M. (1980). *Rules that babies look by: The organization of newborn visual activity*. Hillsdale, NJ: Erlbaum.

Hebb, D.O. (1949). *The organization of behaviour*. New York: Wiley.

Heimann, M., Nelson, K.E., & Schaller, J. (1989). Neonatal imitation of tongue protrusion and mouth opening: Methodological aspects and evidence of early individual differences. *Scandinavian Journal of Psychology*, 30, 90–101.

Hood, B., & Willatts, P. (1986). Reaching in the dark to an object's remembered position: Evidence for object permanence in 5-month-old infants. *British Journal of Developmental Psychology*, 4, 57–65.

Hydén, D. (1983) The broad frequency-band rotatory test. Linkoping University Medical Dissertations, No 152. Linkoping, Sweden.

Jacobsen, K., Magnussen, S., & Smith, L. (1997). Hidden visual capabilities in mentally retarded subjects diagnosed as deaf-blind. *Vision Research*, 37, 2931–2935.

Johnson, M.H. (1990). Cortical maturation and the development of visual attention in early infancy. *Journal of Cognitive Neuroscience*, 2, 81–95.

Johnson, M.H., & Morton, J. (1991). *Biology and cognitive development: The case of face recognition*. Oxford: Blackwell.

Jonsson, B. and von Hofsten, C. (in press) Infants ability to track and reach for temporarily occluded objects. Developmental Science.

Juscyck, P.W. (1992). Developing phonological categories from the speech signal. In C.A. Ferguson, L. Menn, & C. Stoel-Gammon (eds), *Phonological development: Models, research, implications* (pp. 17–64). Timonium, MD: York.

Kalnins, I.V., & Bruner, J.S. (1973). The coordination of visual observation and instrumental behavior in early infancy. *Perception*, 2, 307–314.

Kremenitzer, J.P., Vaughan, H.G., Kurtzberg, D., & Dowling, K. (1979). Smooth-pursuit eye movements in the newborn infant. *Child Development*, 50, 442–448.

Kuhl, P.K. (1994). Learning and representation in speech and language. *Current Opinion in Neurobiology*, 4, 812–822.

Kuypers, H.G.J.M. (1973). The anatomical organization of the descending pathways and their contribution to motor control especially in primates. In J.E. Desmedt (ed.), *New developments in electromyography and clinical neurophysiology* (Vol. 3, pp. 38–68). New York: Karger.

Lawrence, D.G., & Hopkins, D.A. (1976). The development of the motor control in the rhesus monkey: Evidence concerning the role of corticomotoneuronal connections. *Brain*, 99, 235–254.

Lee, D.N. (1976). A theory of visual control of braking based on information about time-to-collision. *Perception*, 5, 437–459.

Lee, D.N. (1992). Body–environment coupling. In U. Neisser (ed.), *Ecological and interpersonal knowledge of the self*. Cambridge: Cambridge University Press.

Lee, D.N., & Aronsson, E. (1974). Visual proprioceptive control of standing in human infants. *Perception & Psychophysics*, 15, 529–532.

Lee, D.N., Davies, M.N.O., Green, P.R., & van der Weel, F.R. (1993). Visual control of velocity of approach by pigeons when landing. *Journal of Experimental Biology*, 180, 85–104.

Lee, D.N., Lishman, J.R., & Thompson, J.A. (1982). Visual regulation of gait in long jumping. *Journal of Experimental Psychology: Human Perception and Performance*, 8, 448–459.

Lee, D.N., Reddish, P.E., & Rand, D.T. (1991). Areal docking by hummingbirds. *Naturwissenschaften*, 78, 526–527.

Lew, A.R., & Butterworth, G. (1995). The effects of hunger on hand–mouth coordination in newborn infants. *Developmental Psychology*, 31, 456–463.

Lockman, J.J., Ashmead, D.H., & Bushnell, E.W. (1984). The development of anticipatory hand orientation during infancy. *Journal of Experimental Child Psychology*, 37, 176–186.

MacNeilage, P.F., & Davis, B.L. (1993). Motor explanations of babbling and early speech patterns. In Boysson-Bardies et al. (eds), *Developmental neurocognition: Speech and face processing in the first year of life* (pp. 123–127). Amsterdam: Kluwer.

Maurer, D. (1985). Infants' perception of faceness. In T.N. Field & N. Fox (eds), *Social perception in infants* (pp. 37–66). Hillsdale, NJ: Erlbaum.

Mayes, L.C., & Kessen, W. (1989). Maturational changes in measures of habituation. *Infant Behavior and Development*, 12, 437–450.

Meltzoff, A.N., & Moore, M.K. (1977). Imitation of facial and manual gestures by human neonates. *Science*, 198, 75–78.

Mendelsson, M.J., & Haith, M.H. (1976). *The relation between audition and vision in the human newborn. Monographs of the Society for Research in Child Development*, Vol. 41, serial 167.

Menn, L. (1983). Development of articulatory, phonetic and phonological capabilities. In B. Butterworth (ed.), *Language production and control* (Vol. 2, pp. 3–50). London: Academic.

Munakata, Y., Jonsson, B., von Hofsten, C., & Spelke, E.S. (1996). When it helps to occlude and obscure: 6-month-olds' predictive tracking of moving toys. Poster presented at the Tenth International Conference on Infants Studies, Providence, RI, April 1996.

Munakata, Y., McClelland, J.L., Johnson, M.H., & Siegler, R. (1997). Rethinking infant knowledge: Toward an adaptive process account of success and failures in object permanence tasks. *Psychological Review*, 104, 686–713.

Odent, M. (1979). The early expression of the rooting reflex. In L. Carneza & L. Zichella (eds), *Emotion and reproduction* (Vol. 20B). London: Academic.

Pavel, M. (1990). Predictive control of eye movement. In E. Kowler (ed.), *Eye movements and their role in visual and cognitive processes. Reviews of Oculomotor Research* (Vol. 4, pp. 71–114). Amsterdam: Elsevier.

Piaget, J. (1953). *The origins of intelligence in the child.* New York: Routledge.

Piaget, J. (1954). *The construction of reality in the child.* New York: Basic.

Prechtl, H.F.R. (1958). The directed head turning response and allied movements of the human infant. *Behaviour*, 13, 212–242.

Reed, E.S. (1996). *Encountering the world: Towards an ecological psychology*. New York: Oxford University Press.

Retaux, S., & Harris, W.A. (1996). Engrailed and retinotectal topography. *Trends in Neuroscience*, 19, 542–546.

Rochat, P. (1992). Self-sitting and reaching in 5- to 8-month-old infants: the impact of posture and its development on early eye–hand coordination. *Journal of Motor Behavior*, 24, 210–220.

Rochat, P., & Goubet, N. (1995). Development of sitting and reaching in 5- to 6-month-old infants. *Infant Behavior and Development*, 18, 53–68.

Rochat, P., & Hespos, S.J. (1997). Differential rooting reponses by neonates: Evidence for an early sense of self. *Early Development and Parenting*, 6, 105–112.

Rochat, P., & Striano, T. (1999). Socio-emotional development in the first year of life. In P. Rochat (ed.), *Early social cognition*. Mahwah, NJ: Erlbaum.

Rosander, K., von Hofsten, C. (2000). Visual–vestibular interaction in early infancy. *Experimental Brain Research*, 133, 321–333.

Rosander, K., von Hofsten, C. (2002) Development of gaze tracking of small and large objects. *Experimental Brain Research*, 146, in press.

Rozin, P. (1976). The evolution of intelligence and access to cognitive unconscious. *Progress in Psychobiology and Physiological Psychology*, 6, 245–279.

Shatz, C.J. (1992). The developing brain. *Scientific American*, September, 35–41.

Sherrington, C.S. (1906). *The integrative action of the nervous system*. New Haven, CT: Yale University Press.

Spelke, E.S., Breinlinger, K., Macomber, J., & Jacobson, K. (1992). Origins of knowledge. *Psychological Review*, 99, 605–632.

Spelke, E.S., Katz, G., Purcell, S.E., Ehrlich, S.M., & Breinlinger, K. (1994). Early knowledge of object motion: Continuity and inertia. *Cognition*, 51, 131–176.

Spelke, E.S., & von Hofsten, C. (2001). Predictive reaching for occluded objects by six-month-old infants. *Journal of Cognition and Development*, 2, 261–282.

Sporns, O., & Edelman, G.M. (1993). Solving Bernstein's problem: A proposal for the development of coordinated movement by selection. *Child Development*, 64, 960–981.

Stechler, G., & Latz, E. (1966). Some observations on attention and arousal in the human infant. *Journal of the American Academy of Child Psychiatry*, 5, 517–525.

Thelen, E., Corbett, D., Kamm, K., Spencer, I.P., Schneider, K., & Zernicker, R.F. (1993). The transition to reaching: Mapping intention and intrinsic dynamics. *Child Development*, 64, 1058–1099.

van der Meer, A.L.H., van der Weel, F.R., & Lee, D.N. (1995). The functional significance of arm movements in neonates. *Science*, 267, 693–695.

von der Malsburg, C., & Singer, W. (1988). Principles of cortical network organisations. In P. Rakic & W. Singer (eds), *Neurobiology of the neocortex* (pp. 69–99). London: Wiley.

von Hofsten, C. (1979). Development of visually guided reaching: The approach phase. *Journal of Human Movement Studies*, 5, 160–178.

von Hofsten, C. (1980). Predictive reaching for moving objects by human infants. *Journal of Experimental Child Psychology*, 30, 369–382.

von Hofsten, C. (1982). Eye–hand coordination in newborns. *Developmental Psychology*, 18, 450–461.

von Hofsten, C. (1983). Catching skills in infancy. *Journal of Experimental Psychology: Human Perception and Performance*, 9, 75–85.

von Hofsten, C. (1984). Developmental changes in the organization of pre-reaching movements. *Developmental Psychology*, 20, 378–388.

von Hofsten, C. (1991). Structuring of early reaching movements: A longitudinal study. *Journal of Motor Behavior*, 23, 280–292.

von Hofsten, C. (1993). Prospective control: A basic aspect of action development. *Human Development*, 36, 253–270.

von Hofsten, C. (1997). On the early development of predictive abilities. In C. Dent & P. Zukow-Goldring (eds), *Evolving explanations of development: Ecological approaches to organism–environmental systems* (pp. 163–194). Washington, DC: APA.

von Hofsten, C., & Fazel-Zandy, S. (1984). Development of visually guided hand orientation in reaching. *Journal of Experimental Child Psychology*, 38, 208–219.

von Hofsten, C., Feng, Q., & Spelke, E.S. (2000). Object representation and predictive action in infancy. *Developmental Science*, 3, 193–205.

von Hofsten, C., & Lee, D.N. (1994). Measuring with the optical sphere. In G. Jansson, S.S. Bergström, & W. Epstein (eds), *Perceiving events and objects* (pp. 455–467). Hillsdale, NJ: Erlbaum.

von Hofsten, C., & Lindhagen, K. (1979). Observations on the development of reaching for moving objects. *Journal of Experimental Child Psychology*, 28, 158–173.

von Hofsten, C., & Rönnqvist, L. (1988). Preparation for grasping an object: A developmental study. *Journal of Experimental Psychology: Human Perception and Performance*, 14, 610–621.

von Hofsten, C., & Rosander, K. (1996). The development of gaze control and predictive tracking in young infants. *Vision Research*, 36, 81–96.

von Hofsten, C., & Rosander, K. (1997). Development of smooth pursuit tracking in young infants. *Vision Research*, 37, 1799–1810.

von Hofsten, C., Vishton, P., Spelke, E.S., Feng, Q., & Rosander, K. (1998). Predictive action in infancy: Tracking and reaching for moving objects. *Cognition*, 67, 255–285.

von Hofsten, C., & Woollacott, M. (1990). Postural preparations for reaching in 9-month-old infants. Unpublished data.

Wing, A.M., Turton, A., & Fraser, C. (1986). Grasp size and accuracy of approach in reaching. *Journal of Motor Behavior*, 18, 245–261.

Witherington, D.C., von Hofsten, C., Rosander, K., Robinette, A., Woollacott, M.H., & Bertenthal, B.I. (2002). The development of anticipatory postural adjustments in infancy. *Infancy*, in press.

Wolff, P.H. (1987). *The development of behavioral states and the expression of emotions in early infancy*. Chicago: Chicago University Press.

Woollacott, M., Debu, M., & Mowatt, M. (1987). Neuromuscular control of posture in the infant and child: Is vision dominant? *Journal of Motor Behavior*, 19, 167–186.

7

Early Cognitive Development: Ontogeny and Phylogeny

JONAS LANGER, SUSAN RIVERA,
MATTHEW SCHLESINGER and ANN WAKELEY

Introduction and Brief History

Cognitive development has an evolutionary as well as an ontogenetic history. Its phylogenetic and ontogenetic roots predate the acquisition of language or symbolization. But its ontogeny already begins to be affiliated with cultural, especially language or symbol development during human infancy. Infants begin to use conventional symbolizing to represent and communicate knowledge.

Whether cognitive and symbolic development already begin to be affiliated in phylogeny is a controversial issue that is starting to be studied empirically. It was assumed that even the great apes only develop the subjective (e.g. affective vocal expressions and gestures of desire) and not the objective (e.g. deictive reference) aspects of language or symbolic processing (e.g. Kohler, 1926; Vygotsky, 1962; Werner, 1948; Yerkes & Learned, 1925). So it was proposed that attaching objective (notationally denotative) language to prerepresentational cognition during late human infancy is the proximate cause of our species' uniquely extended cognitive development and the evolution of cultural history (e.g. Cassirer, 1953; Kohler, 1921; S.K. Langer, 1942; Vygotsky, 1962).

An alternative evolutionary scenario in which culture is not uniquely human but evolved in great apes has been proposed by Whiten et al. (1999). They report multiple and diverse suites of behavior patterns (e.g. in using probes to extract food and fluids, and in aiming thrown objects) that differ between geographically distinct chimpanzee communities. These culturally varying behavior patterns are transmitted intergenerationally within each chimpanzee community.

The Origins of Knowledge

Traditionally it has been assumed that human infants, great apes, and other nonhuman primates' prerepresentational cognition includes elementary physical knowledge. Physical knowledge is about contingent causal, object, spatial and temporal relations. Contingent relations vary as a function of (i.e. are dependent upon) the physical circumstances or conditions determining their occurrences. So, physical phenomena are probabilistic (i.e. are conditional events that are always dependent upon circumstances). The cognitions that organisms develop about them include progressive knowledge about their contingency (e.g. whether one billiard ball launches a second depends upon whether they collide spatially).

Logicomathematical cognition, on the other hand, is about necessary qualitative or intensive (e.g. class) and quantitative or extensive (e.g. numeric) relations. Necessary relations are nonprobabilistic (i.e. are not conditioned by or dependent upon circumstances). The cognition that subjects develop about them include progressive knowledge about the certainty of these relations. The knowledge that subjects develop about quantitative relations such as numerical equivalence by commutativity is prototypical (e.g. spatially rearranging a set of objects necessarily conserves its number).

Since logicomathematical cognition is about necessary relations, it was therefore also traditionally assumed that even its most elementary beginnings, unlike physical cognition, requires representation in objective symbolic language. The minimalist view was that language is necessary (as a notational system) but not sufficient for constructing and using logicomathematical operations (e.g. Vygotsky, 1962; Werner & Kaplan, 1963). The maximalist view was that logic is nothing but a set of syntactic linguistic conventions (e.g. Carnap, 1960). Minimalist and maximalist shared the assumption that logic is symbolic logic (e.g. Cassirer, 1953; 1957).

A related traditional claim by the Gestaltists was that initial physical but not logicomathematical cognition is perceptual, with spatial perception being prototypical. Minimally, perception is a necessary but not sufficient condition for the development of logicomathematical cognition. Logicomathematical operations require re-representing perceptual knowledge in culturally transformed and communicable forms (Koffka, 1928; cf. its contemporary enrichment into representational redescription by Karmiloff-Smith, 1992). Maximally, logicomathematical cognition is nothing but the cultural explication of implicit configurational principles prefigured in perception that are made explicit by productive thinking (Wertheimer, 1945).

These traditional symbolist and perceptual views, whether minimalist or maximalist, converged on the assumption that only elementary physical cognition (e.g. of causal phenomena) is an original or primary development in both phylogeny and ontogeny. In contrast, even elementary logicomathematical cognition (e.g. of adding quantities) is a culturally derived or secondary development in human ontogeny only. Recent constructivist and neonativist research that we will review supports an alternative hypothesis: that elementary logicomathematical cognition is not a culturally derived ontogenetic development, but is an original development like physical cognition.

Constructivist and Neonativist Perspectives

The main theoretical differences between these recent research programs about the origins of cognitive development are twofold. Constructivism hypothesizes that newborns' initial state of both physical (e.g. Piaget, 1954) and logicomathematical (e.g. Langer, 1980; 1986) cognition is prerepresentational and, in gradual stages, becomes representational during infancy. Neonativism proposes a rich initial state that is already representational (e.g. Fodor, 1980) or rapidly becomes representational via innate 'fast learning' in the first few months (e.g. Baillargeon, 1987).

Of course, both constructivism and neonativism posit that no cognition can develop without infants interacting with the environment. According to neonativism, however, infants are innately endowed with cognitive as well as biological structures or organs that interact with the environment. The strong claim is that the innate cognitive structures comprise core representational reasoning and adult-like concepts, such as knowledge that partly occluded objects are continuous (e.g. Spelke et al., 1992; Spelke & Newport, 1998). The weaker claim is that they only comprise elementary representational concepts that must still undergo much developmental reorganization to become adult-like (e.g. Meltzoff & Moore, 1999).

Constructivism is more parsimonious. It does not assume that infants are innately endowed with cognitive structures. It only assumes that they are endowed with biological structures or organs that have psychobiological adaptive functions of assimilating, accommodating and organizing (Piaget, 1952a). So, even infants' initial prerepresentational or presentational knowledge (e.g. of object permanence) is not innate. It is progressively constructed by infants' psychobiological functions interacting with their environment.

The second major theoretical difference is about the proximate causes of the origins and initial development of cognition. Infants' constructive sensorimotor interactions with the environment are the predominant proximate cause of their cognitive development according to constructivism (e.g. Langer, 1980; Piaget, 1952a; Werner, 1948). Perceptual reflection of innate representational reasoning and knowledge is the predominant proximate cause according to neonativism (e.g. Spelke et al., 1992).

Both theoretical perspectives nevertheless agree that logicomathematical as well as physical cognition has a phylogenetic as well as an ontogenetic history. As far as we can ascertain, a neonativist account of the phylogenetic history has yet to be proposed. It simply assumes phylogenetic continuity (Spelke & Newport, 1998).

A constructivist account has been proposed. Only the psychobiological adaptive functions of assimilating, accommodating and organizing are invariant and continuous in phylogeny (Piaget, 1971). Cognitive structures are variant and discontinuous in phylogeny as well as ontogeny. Therefore, the ontogenetic history of cognition does not simply recapitulate its phylogenetic history (e.g. Antinucci, 1989; Werner, 1948). Instead, the evolution of cognitive development is heterochronic (Langer, 1989; 1996; 2000a; 2000b). On this account, ancestral ontogenetic covariations between cognitive structures, including importantly between the logicomathematical and the physical, were displaced in descendant species. This heterochronic evolutionary reorganization opened up cascading cognitive developmental opportunities (e.g. the possibility of constructing a logic of causal experimenting).

Developmental Progress

We return to this constructivist evolutionary hypothesis of heterochronic cognitive development in the conclusion. First, we will analyze the infantile origins and development of cognition in sensorimotor action and in perception. Analyzing cognitive development requires an operational definition or standard metric by which to determine or measure behavioral progress or advance with age, not just behavioral change. We will therefore follow the definition of progress proposed by Langer (1969, pp. 178–180) as synthesized into a twofold metric (Langer, 1990): cognition becomes progressively structured or organized (i.e. developed) as (1) one or more cognitive operations and/or relations become increasingly defined, generalized, powerful, etc.; and (2) the elements onto which the operation and/or relations are mapped, applied, etc., become increasingly constant and powerful.

Accordingly, we begin by analyzing the origins and development of constant given elements of cognition during infancy. Then we will analyze the origins and development of progressively structured cognitive operations during infancy, starting with their logicomathematical operations of qualitative classifying followed by their quantitative numerical operations. After this we will turn to analyzing their physical cognition manifest in their progressive causal and objectifying operations.

Constructing the Elements of Cognition

The elements of cognition constrain the knowledge that can be attained. The elements range from the concrete (e.g. things and actions) to the symbolic (e.g. words and numbers) on which cognition (e.g. qualitative classifying and quantitative adding) operates. To illustrate, composing at least 2 objects into 1 set is prerequisite to the logicomathematical cognition of single-category classifying (e.g. of 2 yellow objects as belonging to 1 category, the color yellow). The composed set is a sufficient element upon which cognition operates to predicate a single classificatory property. It is not, however, a sufficient element for 2-category classifying (e.g. the colors yellow and red). Composing 2 sets of objects is necessary. In turn, this is not a sufficient element for hierarchical classifying (e.g. yellow and red as subclasses of the superordinate class of colors). Composing at least 3 sets is required.

Since it provides elements for both logicomathematical and physical cognition, combinatorial action (such as composing sets of objects) has been proposed as constituting general purpose operations (Langer, 1980; 1993; 2000b; 2000c). Nevertheless, the forms of composing elements of physical and logicomathematical knowledge differ. So, for example, causal relations require spatiotemporal contact between the objects composed into a set. Class relations do not because proximity suffices. Moreover, we shall see later, classifying does not even require spatial proximity between objects.

Infants have two ways of composing elements for their cognition, sensorimotor activity and perception. Only the development of sensorimotor composing elements of cognition has been studied empirically. Perceptual composing has not. So we will review the findings on sensorimotor composing before speculating about how infants might perceptually compose elements of cognition and how their perceptual composing might compare with their sensorimotor abilities.

Sensorimotor Composing

Young infants are quite productive composers of sets by bringing two or more objects into contact or close proximity with each other (Langer, 1980; 1986). Their mean rate of production is already substantial at age 6 months, increases a bit during their first year, and with minor fluctuations remains stable during their second year (see Figure 7.1).

The constancy and power of the sets that infants' sensorimotor activity constructs increases with age. The core relevant measures are the number of objects composed per set and the number of sets constructed contemporaneously (i.e. in temporal overlap or simultaneity). Both increase with age (Grigorakis, 1999; Langer, 1980; 1986; Sugarman, 1983). At age 6 months, infants mainly compose minimal singular sets (i.e. sets of 2 objects only that do not overlap in time). By the end of their first year, infants just begin to construct minimal contemporaneous sets (i.e. 2 sets of 2 objects only that overlap in time) infrequently (see Figure 7.2). They only begin to compose a substantial number of two contemporaneous sets towards the middle of their second year. By the end of their second year, about half of the sets comprise 3 to 6 objects, with most having 3 or 4 objects. So, some are already more than minimal. These are 2 contemporaneous sets of 3 or 4 objects each. Moreover, some contemporaneous sets are even beginning to be multiple. These are 3 or 4 contemporaneous sets of 2 objects each.

Perceptual Composing

As far as we can determine, there has not been any empirical research on whether, how and when infants perceptually compose elements for their cognition. We do, however, have indirect evidence from habituation studies suggesting that newborns can

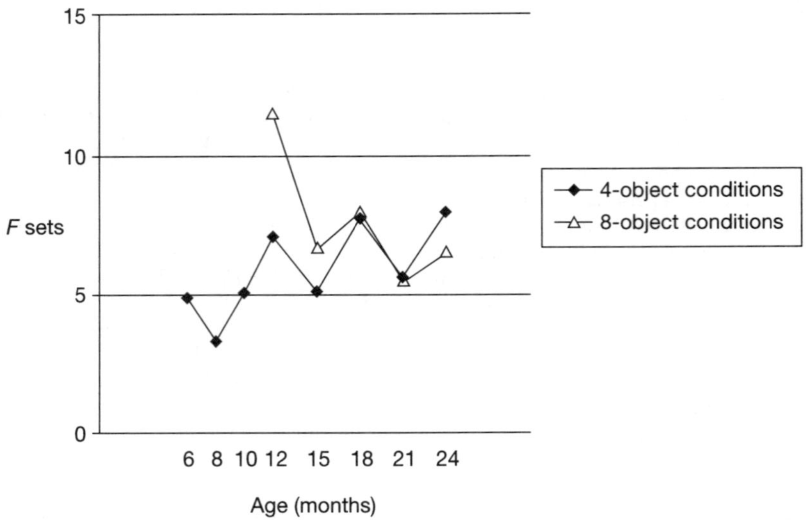

Figure 7.1 *Mean frequency of sensorimotor composing sets per minute (summarized from Langer, 1980; 1986)*

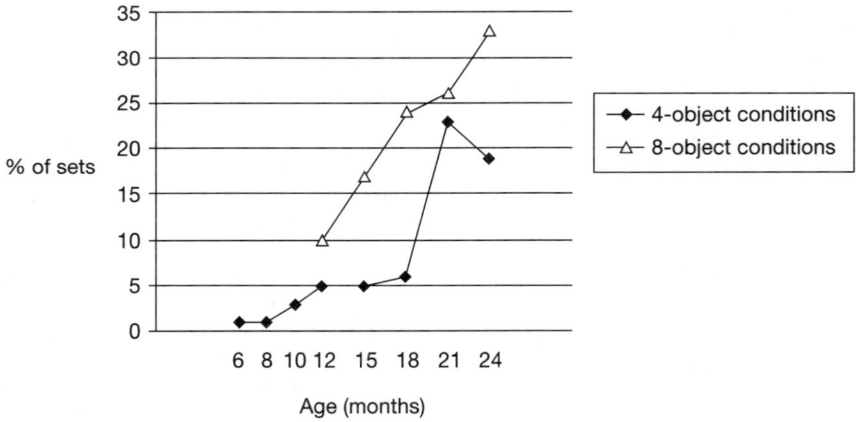

Figure 7.2 *Development in sensorimotor composing of contemporaneous sets (summarized from Langer, 1980; 1986)*

already perceive single sets of up to three objects if they are repeatedly shown the same number of objects. For example, after familiarization with repeated displays of 2 elements, newborns look longer at displays of 3 elements (Antell & Keating, 1983). This suggests that newborns can perceive 2-object sets as elements of their cognition with which to compare and discriminate subsequent displays of 3-object sets. So too, after familiarization with repeated displays of a partially occluded continuous (moving) object such that its middle part is not visible, newborns look longer at displays of a continuous object (e.g. Slater, Morison, Somers, et al., 1990). This suggests that newborns perceive (the single partly occluded continuous objects as) 2 discontinuous object sets as elements of their cognition with which to compare and discriminate subsequent displays of 1 continuous object.

Such findings indicate that newborns may already perceptually compose single sets of up to 3 objects as elements for their cognition when their environment prepackages sets for them (e.g. organizes and repeatedly shows them 2-object sets during habituation). The findings do not tell us whether and at what age infants can perceptually compose single sets as elements of cognition on their own, that is, when the sets are not prepackaged for them. This is precisely what infants do on their own when spontaneously composing objects into sets by their sensorimotor activity.

Comparing Sensorimotor and Perceptual Composing

So, it is not possible at this stage of our knowledge to make direct comparisons between infants' sensorimotor and perceptual composing of elements for their cognition; that is, whether they develop in parallel, whether one is more precocious than the other, whether one develops more rapidly than the other, etc. On the other hand, it seems most likely that the constancy and power of the elements that infants' perception can provide to their cognition is limited as compared to the elements provided by their sensorimotor activity (Langer, 1990; 1998). The reasons are manifold, but three seem central. First, the span of perceptual attention is restricted. It can only encompass minimal environmental features within any given fixation. For example, we shall see later that up to age 3 years infants cannot attend perceptually to more than 3 objects at a time. Second, the transformations that perception can impose upon the environment with which it interacts are restricted. Perception is restricted temporally to the near present. It is restricted spatially to selecting and combining objects within its immediate focal span. And, it is restricted to apprehending, not constructing, causal phenomena. Third, perception cannot externalize the elements it composes for cognition. Instead, it is dependent upon infants' limited mnemonic capacity.

In comparison, with age infants' sensorimotor composing becomes progressively expansive. The reasons are reciprocal to those that restrict infants' perceptual composing. Sensorimotor activity literally constructs its elements for cognition by transforming the spatial, and sometimes causal, relations between objects. And, all its compositions are externalized into actual sets of objects. So, infants' sensorimotor composing is relatively free of the spatiotemporal and causal phenomenal constraints plus attentional and mnemonic limitations under which their perceptual composing labors.

CLASSIFYING

We start with classifying because it is central to logical cognition about qualitative relations but also to much other knowledge (e.g. Langer, 1994b). Moreover, it is basic to the foundations of logic (e.g. Kneale & Kneale, 1962) and mathematics (Kramer, 1970). Boole (1854) even proposed an algebra of classes as the laws of thought.

Classifying requires combining 'into one whole of definite, distinct objects of our perception or our thought, which are called the elements of the set'. We need only update this early prescription by Cantor (1895) by adding the objects of our sensorimotor action to those of our perception and thought to cover contemporary theory and research on classifying. Research on its origins and development has, of course, focused on when and how infants' sensorimotor actions construct and perceptions apprehend qualitative or intensive relations by combining different, similar and identical distinct objects into class-consistent sets.

Sensorimotor Classifying

Infants' sensorimotor actions mostly compose only one set of objects at a time up to the middle of their second year (see Figure 7.2). Accordingly, their initial sensorimotor constructions comprise single categories only when presented with mixed arrays of objects or shapes embodying two or more classes, such as red and blue cups or circular and rectangular shapes; and have therefore been labeled first-order classifying (Langer, 1980). One way in which their sensorimotor actions construct single categories is by spontaneously grouping objects together in spatial contact or proximity even when no problems are posed and no instructions, training, feedback, rewards, reinforcement, etc., are given.

First-Order Classifying: Single-Category Grouping

Single-category sensorimotor classifying is not of a piece. Instead, it develops in a four-stage sequence (see Figure 7.3). At age 6 months, infants consistently (i.e. beyond chance expectation) compose single categories (or intensive relations) of *different* objects (Langer, 1980). For example, they consistently put together a circular and a rectangular shape instead of putting together circular shapes or rectangular shapes into single sets. Surprisingly, it seems that the initial qualitative relations that infants' sensorimotor acts construct predicate the differences objects embody instead of their identical or similar properties.

At ages 8 and 10 months, infants' categorizing is no longer consistent (Langer, 1980). It becomes *random*. Their single-set categorizing comprises an equal parts mixture of different objects (e.g. a circular and a rectangular shape) and identical objects (e.g. two circular shapes or two rectangular shapes). This may reflect a transitional stage between the stage of consistently constructing single-set categories of different objects at age 6 months and that of consistently constructing single-set categories of *identical* objects which develops by age 12 months (Grigorakis, 1999; Langer, 1980; Ricciuti, 1965; Starkey, 1981; Sugarman, 1983).

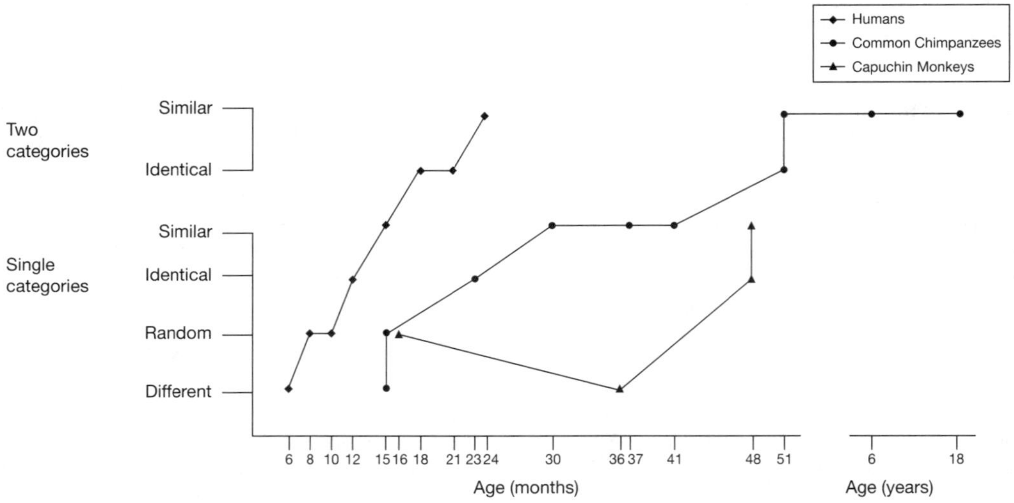

Figure 7.3 *Comparative development of sensorimotor classifying of objects into single and into two categories: onset age, rate and sequence*

The fourth stage of single-category classifying develops by age 15 months. Then infants begin to also compose together *similar* objects that are different in some properties and identical in others (Langer, 1986). To make this determination, infants may be presented with objects such as a red and a blue circular shape and a red and a blue rectangular shape. It is not until this age that infants consistently group together similar objects (e.g. a blue circular with a blue rectangular shape) instead of totally different (i.e. disjoint) objects (e.g. a blue circular with a red rectangular shape).

First-Order Classifying: Single-Category Manipulating

The origins and early development of infants' sensorimotor classifying are not limited to grouping objects together spatially. Simultaneously manipulating objects suffices (e.g. lifting an object with one hand while manipulating another object with the other hand). Classifying objects requires forming some minimal binary set relation. But it need not be spatial; temporal concurrence will do (Langer, 1980; Langer et al., 1998; Spinozzi et al., 1998; Spinozzi & Langer, 1999).

Accordingly, infants' ontogenetic trajectory of single-category classifying by manipulating objects simultaneously but spatially apart parallels their trajectory for grouping objects spatially (Langer et al., 1998). At age 6 months, infants predominantly produce serial one-at-a-time manipulations of one object only. However, when they produce parallel two-at-a-time manipulations of two objects, the objects are consistently different. By age 12 months, infants predominantly produce parallel two-at-a-time manipulations of two identical objects.

Infants' development from doing single things in series to doing two things in parallel manifests their progressive ability to split their sensorimotor manipulatory attention (Langer, 1980). When infants begin to split their manipulatory attention at age 12 months, their acts usually map different transformations onto the objects with which they are interacting (Langer et al., 1998). For example, one hand may put down an object it was moving while the other hand picks up another object. The first hand is transforming the state of the object it is manipulating from kinetic displacement to static placement while the second hand is transforming a static placed object into a kinetic displaced object.

By age 18 months, half of infants' parallel manipulatory transformations become identical or reciprocal (Langer et al., 1998). Transforming objects' states identically by manipulating them in the same way affords infants a way to begin constructing functional equivalence classes even when the objects do not belong to the same predicate class (Piaget, 1952a). For example, simultaneously throwing a doll and a cup transforms both into functionally equivalent 'throwables.' On the other hand, transforming objects' states reciprocally affords infants a way to begin constructing functional complementary or dependent classes (Langer et al., 1998). For example, pretending to feed a doll with a spoon makes them into dependent complements of a 'feeding' event hierarchy.

Constructing singular functional equivalence and complementary class relations by age 18 months is preceded ontogenetically, we have seen, by infants constructing singular predicate class relations first by difference at age 6 months, then by identity at age 12 months, and eventually by similarity at age 15 months. Infants assimilate objects to their sensorimotor action schemes while disregarding the objects' actual predicate properties when constructing functional equivalence and complementary relations. Conversely, infants accommodate to objects' actual predicate properties while disregarding their functional affordances when constructing difference, identity, and similarity relations. Accommodating to objects' predicate properties by age 15 months, then, seems to precede assimilating objects' affordances by age 18 months in infants' developing classificatory cognition. Neither (Piagetian) assimilation nor (Gibsonian) affordances have ontogenetic priority in the origins of constructive sensorimotor classifications; (Piagetian) accommodation does.

Second-Order Classifying: Two-Category Grouping

In the entire four-stage developmental sequence of first-order classifying, infants construct nothing more than one set with one class property at a time. This differentiates these four sequential developments from second-order classifying (Langer, 1986). Second-order classifying only becomes possible during infants' second year when they begin to compose two contemporaneous sets with some frequency (see Figure 7.2). Then, they begin, at age 18 months, to spontaneously compose contemporaneous sets in which the objects comprising each set are *identical* and the objects in the two sets are *different* (Gershkoff-Stowe et al., 1997; Grigorakis, 1999; Langer, 1986; Nelson, 1973; Ricciuti, 1965; Sugarman, 1983; see Figure 7.3). By age 24 months infants also construct two categories in which the objects comprising each set are *similar* and the objects in the two sets are *different* (Langer, 1986; see Figure 7.3). So, the development of second-order classifying involves a two-stage sequence of composing two sets and two class properties at the same time, beginning with identical properties and eventually with similar properties.

Toward the end of their second year, infants' two-category classifying begins to be extended to spontaneously correcting nonverbal counterconditions presented to them without any instructions, training, reinforcement, rewards, etc. To illustrate, in one condition infants were presented with two alignments, one comprising three rectangular and one circular ring and the other comprising three circular rings and one rectangular ring. At age 21 months some infants begin to correct such classificatory mistakes (Langer, 1986). By age 36 months all do (Sugarman, 1983). Some infants even rebuke the experimenter. For example, one 30-month-old remarked, 'No belongs this way' as she corrected the classificatory misplacements (Langer, 2000c).

Does infants' second-order classifying merely reflect a cognitively more natural and therefore primary way of partitioning objects into 'basic level' prototype-based categories? If it were more natural and primary, then basic level should precede predicate two-category classifying in infant ontogeny. It does not (Gopnik & Meltzoff, 1992). They seem to develop in tandem.

In sum, the research on how infants' sensorimotor actions *spontaneously construct* class-consistent sets has investigated their development in composing (different, identical or similar) objects and shapes with each other (spatially or temporally). At first infants create single class-consistent categories (in a four-stage sequence). At subsequent stages they begin to create two contemporaneous but different class-consistent categories.

Perceptual Categorizing

The research on infants' perceptual categorizing, on the other hand, has investigated their *provoked reactions* (visual, auditory, or tactile) to (different, identical or similar) stimuli (e.g. pictures of shapes, speech sounds or objects). So, perceptual categorizing involves infants orienting their sensory systems in a similar way to identical stimuli (indicating recognition) or similar stimuli (indicating generalization) but not to different stimuli (indicating discrimination). Because the behaviors manifesting infants' perceptual categorizing are often subtle (e.g. attentional shifts, scanning, etc.), a number of methods have been used to study it.

The major paradigms include habituation–dishabituation, preferential looking, and instrumental conditioning. Each of these paradigms works by first establishing a perceptual response to a series of stimuli from one category in order to determine whether infants will generalize this response to new (similar) members of the familiar category but not to novel (different) stimuli that do not belong to the familiar category. For example, after habituating to pictures of cats, 3-month-old infants respond similarly to pictures of novel cats while dishabituating (i.e. recover their interest or look longer) to pictures of dogs (Quinn, Eimas, & Rosenkranz, 1993). So, they generalize within one category while discriminating objects that do not belong to it.

Single Categories

Perceptual recognition and discrimination begin to develop during the neonatal period (see Bornstein, 1981, 1984, for reviews). For example, 2-week-olds begin to differentiate between objects that they do and do not prefer to suck on (Piaget, 1952a). Using a habituation paradigm, very young infants can be familiarized with (that is, will generalize between) similar stimuli belonging to single categories while discriminating stimuli that do not, such as cats versus dogs mentioned in the previous paragraph (see Cohen & Younger, 1983; Quinn & Eimas, 1986; and Reznick & Kagan, 1983, for reviews).

By age 4 months, infants perceive (i.e. generalize and discriminate) a fairly wide range of single categories. Importantly, this includes both basic level categories of highly similar stimuli such as dogs or chairs (e.g. Quinn, Eimas, & Rosenkranz, 1993) and superordinate level categories of less similar stimuli such as mammals or furniture (Behl-Chada, 1996). These findings on early infant perceptual categorizing are consistent with those on late infancy second-order sensorimotor classifying discussed above. Thus, basic level classifying does not seem to have developmental priority throughout infancy.

Two Categories

Perceiving two contemporaneous categories (e.g. triangles and squares) develops sometime between ages 4 months (Quinn, 1987) and 10 months (Husaim & Cohen, 1981). By age 10 months, infants also begin to perceive single categories based upon correlated features. They are more complex because membership in the category is determined by a set of correlated features, rather than a simple list of features. For example, around age 10 months infants begin to perceive categories based on correlated features (e.g. beaks and feathers) or feature combinations which reliably co-occur (Younger, 1990; Younger & Cohen, 1986). Thus, while young infants respond primarily to independent features, by age 10 months infants also begin to respond to invariant relations between features in a category.

During their second year, infants' perceptions extend to categories based upon increasingly complex correlated features. For example, 14-month-olds (but not 10-month-olds) integrate perceptual information over time to categorize objects according to their causal function (Madole, Oakes, & Cohen, 1993). By age 18 months, perceptual categorizing of object functions extends to causally related form–function correlations (Madole & Cohen, 1995). These categories are more complex than simple causal dependencies because they require recognizing more than the particular function of an object (e.g. lifting and pushing). They also require noting which particular features are meaningfully correlated with that particular causal function (e.g. shape is a necessary feature while color is irrelevant).

Relations between Sensorimotor and Perceptual Classifying

The findings on infants' developing perceptual categorizing are based upon measures of their attending to stimulus displays. In contrast we saw earlier that the findings on their developing sensorimotor classifying are based upon measures of their manipulating objects. The crucial difference is that sensorimotor activity transforms the objects of its manipulatory attention to construct classes while perception does not transform the objects of its sensory attention to apprehend categories.

Do they influence each other's development nevertheless? An initial investigation explored these questions using an A–B–A research design (Schlesinger & Langer, 1993). Either perceptual categorizing by infants intervened between their pre- and post-test sensorimotor classifying, or sensorimotor classifying by infants intervened between their pre- and post-test perceptual categorizing. The infants were 6, 10 and 12 months old. In the sensorimotor condition infants were presented with a mixed array of four shapes belonging to two form categories (i.e. two triangles and two crosses). A standard measure of sensorimotor classifying was taken, the sequence of infants' contact with each of the four objects over a period of 2½ minutes. In the perceptual condition, infants were visually habituated to one of the same two shape categories, and tested for dishabituation with a novel shape form.

A specific, limited interaction was found between the development of sensorimotor classifying and perceptual categorizing. Surprisingly, 6-month-olds did not perceptually discriminate between two categories of shapes unless they first had the opportunity to do sensorimotor classifying of comparable shapes. Conversely, prior perceptual categorizing had no effect on 6-month-olds' subsequent sensorimotor classifying.

These findings suggest unidirectional information flow from sensorimotor classifying to perceptual categorizing. However, this interaction appears to be limited to very early infancy (i.e. before age 10 months). No further interactions were found in 10- or 12-month olds. Thus, sensorimotor classifying and perceptual categorizing do not seem to influence each other during early infancy with one exception. The exception is both age related and unidirectional.

QUANTIFYING

Infants' developing logicomathematical cognition of quantitative relations parallels that of their qualitative relations. At first the qualitative relations that very young infants' logicomathematical operations construct are minimal, such as the single-category classifying considered in the previous section. Progressively, older infants construct increasingly powerful qualitative relations, such as two-category classifying. So too, very young infants' logicomathematical operations begin by constructing minimal quantitative equality and nonequality relations within single sets of up to 3 objects only. Progressively older infants construct increasingly powerful quantitative relations, such as one-to-one correspondence between 2 sets of 4 objects each.

This progress is found in infants' developing sensorimotor activity. Most importantly, towards the end of their second year infants' sensorimotor constructions of quantitative relations, such as correspondences between two sets, begin to break out of the bounds of very small numbers (of no more than 3 objects). Developments in perceptual quantifying remain constrained to very small numbers throughout infancy, indeed even into early childhood.

Sensorimotor Quantifying

Core operations with which infants' sensorimotor actions begin to construct quantitative or extensive relations include exchange by substituting, replacing, and commuting objects within single sets (Langer, 1980). All three operations produce quantitative equivalence. Substituting preserves the initial number and configuration of objects in a set that infants have composed by subtracting one or more objects from it followed by adding an equal number of different objects back in the same place. Replacing preserves the initial number and configuration by subtracting one or more objects followed by putting the same objects back in the same place (i.e. adding the subtracted objects). Commuting preserves the initial number of objects in a set that infants have composed by recomposing the set into a rearranged spatial configuration without adding or subtracting any objects.

First-Order Quantifying

Infants' three quantitative exchange operations develop in parallel (Langer, 1980; 1986; 1989). At age 6 months, some infants just begin to construct quantitative equivalence relations by exchange operations. But they only map exchange operations onto minimal single sets of two objects that they have composed. Therefore they have been labeled first-order. To illustrate, one 6-month-old dropped a doll into a ring shape, quickly lifted the doll out of the ring, and substituted a different doll by dropping it into the ring.

By age 8 months almost all infants construct quantitative equivalence by all three exchange operations on minimal sets only. In addition, some begin to invert their exchange operations (e.g. by resubstituting the initially subtracted object) to reconstruct their initial 2-object set. To illustrate, after substituting one object for another, they subtract the substitute object, and then add back the initially subtracted object into the 2-object set.

By age 10 months all infants construct quantitative equivalence by all three exchange operations on minimal sets. All also repeatedly invert their exchange operations, such that they reconstruct their initial 2-object sets. Thus, all infants now generate minimal quantitative equivalence relations that are systematically reversible.

By age 12 months all infants construct reversible quantitative equivalence relations by all three exchange operations on minimal sets which they then negate by their inverse exchange operations. In addition, almost half begin to extend all three exchange operations to constructing quantitative equivalence in single 3-object sets that they have composed. Some even begin to invert their exchange operations to reconstruct their initial 3-object set.

Second-Order Quantifying

Three major developments mark infants' sensorimotor progress in constructing quantitative relations during their second year (Langer, 1980; 1986). First, they extend their three exchange operations to constructing quantitative equivalence in increasingly larger single sets that they have constructed. Most are extended to their 3- and 4-object sets by age 24 months, some even to their 5- to 8-object sets. Usually they exchange 1 object only, sometimes 2 or 3.

Second, infants begin to construct quantitative relations between contemporaneous sets by correspondence operations. This includes constructing equivalence relations between sets by composing them in one-to-one numerical, temporal and spatial correspondence. Its origins may reach back to age 10 months when some infants begin to compose 2 sets of 2 objects each in one-to-one correspondence. To illustrate, one infant did this by his right hand placing a yellow cross ring on top of a green rectangular ring while his left hand placed a yellow rectangular ring on top of a green cross ring. By age 12 months, more than half of infants compose 2 sets of 2 objects in one-to-one correspondence; and by age 15 months all do. Constructing equivalence by one-to-one correspondence is extended to composing 2 sets of as many as 4 objects each by two-thirds of infants at age 24 months. Some infants at this age also begin to compose 3 sets of 2 objects each in one-to-one correspondence; and some begin to compose 4 sets of 2 objects each in one-to-one correspondence.

Third, infants begin to construct quantitative relations between contemporaneous sets by their three exchange operations. By age 24 months more than half of infants do this. When preserving equality, infants construct sets in one-to-one correspondence and then apply an exchange operation to them. To illustrate, some construct 2 stacks of 2 objects in one-to-one correspondence, then substitute the topmost objects for each other such that the 2 stacks remain in one-to-one correspondence. By mapping such exchange operations onto their correspondence operations, infants begin to construct second-order quantitative relations of equivalences upon equivalences. Alternatively, when preserving nonequality, infants apply exchange operations to numerically unequal contemporaneous sets that they have constructed. To illustrate, they may construct a stack of 2 objects next to a stack of 3 objects, then substitute the topmost objects for each other such that the 2 stacks preserve their initial nonequivalence relation. Then they begin to construct second-order quantitative relations of equivalences of nonequivalences.

An important consequence of developing such second-order logicomathematical operations is that infants begin to apply them to novel problems (Langer, 1986). For example, we have already noted in the previous section that 2-year-old infants begin to apply substituting operations to reconstruct misclassified sets presented to them into correctly classified sets; and that all 3-year-olds do this. Such behavior opens up cascading possibilities for constructing new and more powerful cognitions. It culminates during middle childhood, according to constructivist theory, in the development of concrete operational logicomathematical structures of number, seriation and classes (Inhelder & Piaget, 1964; Piaget, 1952b; 1972).

Perceptual Quantifying

In contrast to constructivism, neonativism assumes that human infants have an innate concept of number that is the foundation for their later number development. The richest assumption is that this includes the innate ability to quantify elements in perceptual displays, to mentally represent numbers and their ordinal relations, and to calculate exactly the results of simple addition and subtraction with objects (e.g. Wynn, 1992a; 1992b; 1995). Unlike true arithmetic, however, these numerical representations are limited to physical entities (e.g. objects). Only positive integers are represented, and the calculations could probably not even extend to simple multiplication and division (Wynn, 1995).

The research has used procedures such as visual habituation and preferential looking to measure infants' reactions to the numeric features of perceptual displays. For example, in a typical number discrimination study using a habituation procedure, infants repeatedly see displays in which the number of elements is unchanged, although other features such as size or spatial configuration of the elements may vary. These are followed by test displays of a novel number of elements. If the infants attend to and remember the number of elements in the habituation displays, it is assumed that their attention (looking) should decline over repetitions (i.e. they should habituate to the familiar number). And, if they recognize the change in number, they should show renewed attention to the novel test display(s).

Discriminating between Very Small Numbers of Objects

Young infants may discriminate quantitative equivalence from nonequivalence in perceptual displays of single sets as long as the set sizes are very small (up to a maximum of 3 elements). For example, they may look longer at novel displays that differ from familiar displays by one more or one less for contrasts such as 2 versus 3 but not 4 versus 5 (Strauss & Curtis, 1981), or even 4 versus 6 (e.g. Starkey & Cooper, 1980). One incompletely controlled study found that newborns may be able to do this (Antell & Keating, 1983). The more typical finding is that at age 6 months infants discriminate between very small numerosities in both static (e.g. Starkey, Spelke, & Gelman, 1990; Strauss & Curtis, 1981) and moving displays (van Loosbroek & Smitsman, 1990) and in sets of items presented simultaneously (e.g. Starkey & Cooper, 1980) or sequentially (Canfield & Smith, 1996; Wynn, 1996).

Even 6- to 8-month-olds, however, do not discriminate between small numbers of objects when their contour length and area are controlled (Clearfield & Mix, 1999; 2001; Feigenson, Carey, & Spelke, 2002). Since some of the previous research confounded the number with the contour length and with the area of the objects presented, their findings that 6-month-olds discriminate number are questionable. Infants may be discriminating continuous quantity only, not number.

Similar questions have arisen about infants' ability to perceptually detect quantitative equivalence between very small numerosities across different sensory modalities by age 6 to 8 months. In one study, infants looked longer at numerically corresponding than at numerically noncorresponding visual displays when listening to sequences of up to three sounds (Starkey, Spelke, & Gelman, 1983; 1990). In two nonreplications, however, infants looked longer at the numerically noncorresponding visual displays (Mix, Levine, & Huttenlocher, 1997; Moore et al., 1987). Moreover, when rate and duration of sound sequences were varied randomly, infants did not look longer at either the corresponding or the noncorresponding visual displays (Mix, Levine, & Huttenlocher, 1997).

Perceptually discriminating quantitative nonequivalence between very small numbers of objects is not uniquely human, or even uniquely primate. Indeed, similar and in some cases superior abilities have been found in a variety of different species. Even avian species (notable for their small brains) such as pigeons, jackdaws, parrots, and ravens are not restricted to detecting very few objects. They can perceptually discriminate from five to seven elements (Koehler, 1951). In addition, perceptual discrimination as high as sixteen has been observed in trained, food-deprived rats (Mechner, 1958). Human infants' discriminatory abilities do not develop beyond three objects even by age 3 years (Starkey & Cooper, 1995).

Perception of ordinal quantitative relations between two paired sets of very few objects does, however, appear to develop during infancy. At age 7 months, infants still cannot discriminate equal paired sets from unequal paired sets (Cooper, 1984). By ages 10 to 12 months they do. And by ages 14 to 16 months they discriminate very small ordinal (less than and greater than) relations between paired sets. As with quantitative discrimination, the ability to order quantities of objects is not a uniquely human perceptual competence since it is also found in at least one species of monkeys (Brannon & Terrace, 1998).

Discriminating between Correct and Incorrect Adding and Subtracting

Infants' knowledge of adding and subtracting objects has been investigated by testing their perceptual discrimination of correct and incorrect resultants with very small sets. These studies use a violation-of-expectation procedure. One to 3 objects is first shown to infants, then screened from view. The infants then see 1 object added to or subtracted from the screened set. The screen is then removed revealing, on alternating trials, either a correct or an incorrect number of objects. The assumption is that if infants are able to calculate the effect of the addition to and subtraction from the screened set of objects, they should expect to see the correct result. Therefore, they should pay greater attention to the unexpected, incorrect result since it is surprising.

Neonativists claim that this method measures infants' ability to remember the number of objects out of sight (i.e. how many are behind a screen), perform a numeric transformation on that represented set, and then calculate exactly (e.g. Dehaene, Dehaene-Lambertz, & Cohen, 1998; Wynn, 1992; 1998). A more parsimonious alternative account that does not require representational numerical reasoning has been proposed and successfully simulated using a non-numeric computational model (Simon, 1997; 1998).

Even though the neonativist claim includes that adding and subtracting objects may be innate, the youngest infants for which evidence has been presented are already 5 months old. Wynn (1992) tested 5-month-old infants' perceptual discrimination of correct and incorrect results of adding and subtracting Mickey Mouse dolls in three experiments. In two experiments infants saw an addition (1 + 1 = 1 or 2) or a subtraction (2 – 1 = 1 or 2). In both experiments, infants tended to look longer at two dolls when it was the incorrect result in the subtraction condition. However, in the addition condition they tended to look longer at one doll when it was the incorrect result only in the second experiment. These results provide, at most, only weak evidence since these problems could be solved by recognizing the ordinal direction of the transformation or by simply expecting that the transformation will result in a change (Simon, 1997; 1998; Wynn, 1992). Accordingly, Wynn (1992) conducted a third experiment in which both the correct and incorrect results presented a change in the initial display and were in the correct direction (1 + 1 = 2 or 3). Infants looked longer at the incorrect result (three dolls). Wynn concluded that young infants calculate the exact results as well as the ordinal direction of simple transformations performed on small sets of items, and that evidence of these abilities suggests that they are innate.

Several studies have attempted to replicate Wynn's (1992) addition (1 + 1 = 1 or 2) and subtraction (2 – 1 = 1 or 2) problems. Replication attempts with 5-month-old infants (Koechlin, Dehaene, & Mehler, 1997; Moore, 1997; Simon, Hespos, & Rochat, 1995; Wakeley, Rivera, & Langer, 2000), 8- and 10-month-old infants with the addition problem only (Uller et al., 1999), and 12-month-olds (Arriaga et al., 1999) have found variable results. The findings range from longer looking at the incorrect results (Simon, Hespos & Rochat, 1995: Uller et al., 1998), longer looking only in particular subgroups or experimental conditions (Koechlin, Dehaene, & Mehler, 1997; Moore, 1997), to no systematic preference for the correct or incorrect result (Arriaga et al., 1998; Wakeley, Rivera, & Langer, 2000).

Importantly, Wynn's (1992) third experiment (1 + 1 = 2 or 3) has not been replicated with infants. Moreover, although cited as evidence of exact calculation, infants may have looked longer at the incorrect result due to a simple perceptual preference for looking at more dolls (as found, for example, by Koechlin, Dehaene, & Mehler, 1997, and Xu & Carey, 1996). Accordingly, we conducted a subtraction counterpart (3 – 1 = 1 or 2) experiment (Wakeley, Rivera, & Langer, 2000). Here too, both the correct and incorrect results were designed to be in the correct direction. But since the incorrect result was smaller than the correct result, the design also eliminated the potential confound of infants' perceptual preference for looking at more objects. Infants did not look longer at the incorrect result.

Other studies using different equations and somewhat different procedures have also found that infants look significantly longer at incorrect results in some conditions but not in others (e.g. Wynn, 1995; Wynn & Chiang, 1998). These variable results together with the limited range of equations that have been presented to infants raise more questions than answers about the phenomenon. They suggest that infants' perceptual reactions to even the most minimal adding and subtracting objects are quite variable and that their numerical competencies are very limited if any.

Moreover, there is a paucity of developmental data. An exception is a series of studies that provide support for a non-numeric account (Uller et al., 1999; see also Simon, 1997; 1998). Eight- and 10-month-olds were tested on an addition problem (1 + 1 = 1 or 2) in three conditions which varied when and how the initial set was screened from view. When the initial set was placed directly behind a screen ('screen first' condition), instead of being placed on the stage and then screened from view ('object first' condition), only 10-month-olds looked longer at the incorrect result. However, 8-month-olds looked longer at the incorrect result in a 'screen first' condition with two screens (the initial set was placed behind one screen and a second object was 'added' behind the second screen). They needed the visible markers of one screen for each object to discriminate when an object was missing from the display. It seems that infants were keeping track of the individual objects that were placed in the display rather than forming a numerical representation of the objects. Additionally, the greater success of the 10- than the 8-month-olds in the single 'screen first' condition suggests that all these studies are measuring infants' developing cognition about objects instead of innate numerical reasoning.

This conclusion is reinforced by the findings on 7-month-olds' differential looking time when the surface area of objects added to each other is controlled (Feigenson, Carey, & Spelke, 2002). Then infants looked longer at the result which is numerically correct but quantitatively incorrect in surface area than at the result which is numerically incorrect but quantitatively correct in surface area.

Detecting the Ordinal Direction of Adding and Subtracting

The conclusion that infants' early numerical competencies are very limited is further reinforced by the toddler and early childhood developmental data. One set of studies followed Wynn's (1992) procedure with one modification (Houdé, 1997; Vilette, 1996; Vilette & Mazouz, 1998). Since the subjects were older, the dependent measure was verbal. The children were asked whether the results they saw were 'right' or 'wrong.'

Vilette (1996; Vilette & Mazouz, 1998) presented 2½- and 3½-year-old children with 2 + 1 = 2 or 3, 3 – 1 = 2 or 3, and 2 + 1 – 1 = 2 or 3 problems. The 2½-year-olds' performance was at chance level on all three problems. The 3½-year-olds were successful on the addition problem, but their performance was still at chance on the subtraction and the addition followed by subtraction problems. Houdé (1997) only presented addition problems with smaller set sizes to somewhat older children (ages 2 years 8 months and 3 years 10 months). The children were presented with 1 + 1 = 1 or 2 (the same as Wynn's, 1992, experiments 1 and 2 addition condition), and 1 + 1 = 2 or 3 (the same as Wynn's experiment 3). The younger children responded correctly on the 1 + 1 = 1 or 2 problem, but not on the 1 + 1 = 2 or 3 problem. In contrast, the older children solved both problems correctly. Thus, the younger children were only successful when the incorrect solution was in the wrong ordinal direction of the transformation and, therefore, did not require precise addition.

These findings are consistent with studies that use different procedures. They have also found that very young children only know the ordinal effects. The ability to calculate exactly simple addition and subtraction problems develops gradually throughout the toddler and preschool years. By their second year children know the ordinal effect of simple addition and subtraction on very small numbers of objects, that addition yields more and subtraction yields less (Sophian & Adams, 1987; Starkey, 1992). However, calculating the exact results of addition and subtraction develops gradually during early childhood (Huttenlocher, Jordan, & Levine, 1994; Starkey, 1992). To illustrate, in one set of experiments, children (ranging in age from 18 to 48 months) saw a very small number of balls put into a 'searchbox' apparatus followed by either adding balls to or subtracting balls from the hidden set (Starkey, 1992). The children were then asked to reach in and retrieve the correct number of balls. Most of the solutions were in the correct *direction* of the transformation but few were exactly correct at the younger ages. Overall, 81% of the children's solutions were ordinally correct (i.e. were in the correct *direction* of the transformation), indicating that they knew that addition resulted in more and subtraction resulted in less. The percentage of numerically exact solutions increased significantly from only 49% at age 24 months to 62% at age 48 months.

Similarly, in another study young children saw an addition or subtraction performed on a hidden array and were then asked to use objects in front of them to construct the correct result (Huttenlocher, Jordan, & Levine, 1994). Two- to 2½-year-olds were not reliably able to produce the correct result of even the easiest problems (1 + 1; 2 –1). However, their answers did not appear to be simply random. Instead, they tended to vary systematically with the numerosity of the correct result. For example, they put out more objects when the correct result was 3 than when it was 1. Again, this is consistent with an expectation of the ordinal effect of adding and subtracting objects. Like Starkey (1992), Huttenlocher, Jordan, and Levine found that the ability to calculate *exactly* the results of these simple problems improved from ages 2 to 4 years. In this study, as in Starkey (1992), children's success was generally limited to problems with very small set sizes (i.e. three or less).

Comparing Sensorimotor and Perceptual Quantifying

Infants' developing quantification in perception and in sensorimotor action has not been compared directly. The different measures used (observations of infants' spontaneous constructions and tests of their provoked constructions versus perceptual reactions to displays that are prepackaged for them) make this comparison difficult because of the possibly different implications of these different behaviors. However, there are some parallels and discrepancies in the findings suggestive of the course of development during infancy.

Infants' quantitative sensorimotor manipulations and perceptions are limited to very small numbers of elements during their first year. While still remaining within the range of very small numbers, during their second year infants' perception develops from discriminating equality from inequality relations between 2 sets to discriminating ordinal relations (less than, more than) between them (Cooper, 1984). This is a major advance over the kinds of equivalence (same) and nonequivalence (different) perceptions to which infants are limited during their first year. Furthermore, findings on toddlers using a variety of methods indicate that young children begin to know the ordinal effect of addition and subtraction (that addition results in more and subtraction results in less) during their second year (Huttenlocher, Jordan, & Levine, 1994; Sophian & Adams, 1983; Starkey, 1992; Vilette 1996; Vilette & Mazouz, 1998). Still, infants' performance in these studies suggests that this is a fragile developing competence.

Unlike in perception, the number of the sets and their sizes that infants' sensorimotor actions construct and operate on begin to exceed the limits of very small numbers during their second year (Langer, 1986). This includes beginning to construct 4 corresponding sets of 2 objects and 2 corresponding sets of 4 objects by age 24 months. Moreover, they also begin to map exchange operations onto their corresponding sets, thereby constructing second-order equivalence on equivalence relations, and onto their ordered sets, thereby constructing second-order equivalence on nonequivalence relations.

These developmental data do not support the hypothesis that infants are innately endowed with representational quantifying competencies including adding and subtracting exactly. Instead, quantifying abilities develop throughout infancy. Quantifying is constructed by infants' perceptions and sensorimotor actions. However, only the development of sensorimotor quantifying begins to exceed the limits of very small numbers of objects during late infancy and early childhood.

CAUSING

Physical cognition, including causing and objectifying which we will consider in this and the next section, develops in parallel with logicomathematical cognition during infancy. Genetic parallels, however, involve formal differences as well as formal similarities between developmental series (Langer, 2000d; cf. Werner, 1948). A major formal difference already indicated in the introduction is that physical cognition is about contingent, not necessary phenomena.

Physical cognition requires structuring means–ends transformations by infants creating, orienting to or solving some goal, object or problem. So, the physical relations they construct between their own sensorimotor or perceptually observed means–ends transformations are coordinated dependencies or functions (e.g. effects are dependent functions of causes: Langer, 1980; 1986; Piaget et al., 1977). For example, causal means–ends transformations construct contingent energy relations between objects, such as when one object is pushed against another and makes it move. Infants' means–ends transformations have therefore been proposed as basic functions that construct physically possible and impossible contingent dependency relations (Langer, 1980; 1986).

Causality is at the heart of physical cognition. From the start, much and perhaps most neonatal sensorimotor acts produce causal effects in their physical environment. Even much prenatal sensorimotor activity produces causal effects (Hepper, Chapter 5 in this volume). This includes legs, arms and fingers extensions; head and body rotations; and even coordinations within and between body parts such as contact between the head and a hand resulting in mouth–finger sucking (see Michel & Moore, 1995, for a review). Thus, while the precise onset age for cognizing causality remains indeterminate, its precognizant sensorimotor foundations may already begin to be constructed by prenatal sensorimotor activity. So far, we have no behavioral indications of any prenatal reactions that could be foundational to infants' developing perception of causality.

Sensorimotor Causing

Newborns' sensorimotor actions that produce effects in their physical environment have been hypothesized to mingle two undifferentiated primitives of constructive causal cognition (Piaget, 1952a; 1954). Of course, they are not yet intentional or conscious. One primitive is a *dynamic internal feeling of efficacy*, that is, that effects (ends) are dependent upon or a function of subjects' efforts or actions (means) upon objects. Efficacy's mature cognitive developmental issue will become knowing that effort, in the form of work and energy, causes physical effects. The other primitive is a *kinetic external impression of phenomenal datum*, that is, that effects are dependent upon or a function of spatiotemporal contact and movement relations between objects. Phenomenalism's mature cognitive developmental issue will become knowing that spatiotemporal and kinetic conditions determine whether effort produces physical effects. Therefore, physical causality is irreversible (e.g. constrained by the arrow of time). Irreversible causal functions are formally different from reversible logicomathematical operations (see Piaget, 1974).

Direct Causing

The initial stage, then, is marked by minimal sensorimotor acts to maintain desired goals. At most, newborns make rudimentary sensorimotor efforts at maintaining goals only briefly and only when their means are in direct contact with their ends. For example, if their mouth happens to contact a hand they can preserve the contact for as much as 10 minutes while they suck their hand (Piaget, 1952a). Both causal primitives, efficacy and phenomenalism, become increasingly evident (albeit still in intermingled forms) in the behavior of neonates as they progressively coordinate their hand with their mouth movements to suck on their hand (Butterworth et al., 1985).

At first, the causal relations neonates construct are probably accidental; but they rapidly notice and reproduce them. For instance, between ages 1 and 3 months infants elaborate (a) accidental kicking of their crib, which shakes the crib, which swings a mobile hanging from the crib above them, into (b) well-directed and repeated kicking of their crib in order to see the mobile swing (Piaget, 1954; Rovee & Rovee, 1969; Watson, 1985). A critical limitation of their causal constructions during this early period is that there must be direct physical connection between infants (as causal agents) and the effects they produce. Consequently, much of infants' earliest causal actions are interactions with their own body (e.g. moving the hand to the mouth, sucking the fingers, etc.).

At their origins, then, all the causal functions or dependency relations that infants construct are direct and immediate. Their sensorimotor activities (means) directly and immediately cause effects (ends). These include both types of functions that have been proposed as fundamental, causing (affirming) effects to occur and causing (negating) effects to be annulled (Langer, 1980; 1986). Direct production of effects occurs, for example, when infants kick their crib causing it to move. Direct negation of effects occurs when infants act to cancel them. To illustrate, by age 4 months infants can reach to and grasp a desired object that is moving in front of them (e.g. Crichton & Lange-Küttner, 1999). Thereby, infants directly negate an effect (i.e. the movement of the object) that they observed (usually so as to go on to producing or affirming a different effect).

Indirect Causing

Direct and immediate contact between infants' sensorimotor acts and new causal effects is no longer necessary between ages 3 and 6 months. They also begin to construct indirect and mediated causal chains. To illustrate, once they happen fortuitously to hit an overhanging toy with a stick in their hand, 4-month-olds can reproduce this behavior, quickly becoming proficient at using the stick to hit its target (Piaget's, 1952a, 1954, sensorimotor stage 3 rudimentary secondary circular reactions). So too, once they happen to have done it, 4-month-olds can already continue grasping and pulling a chain attached to an overhanging rattle that makes a noise. They begin, systematically and intentionally, to use instrumental intermediaries to reproduce new causal results of their prior acts.

This does not mean that very young infants fully comprehend the necessary role of spatial contact or intermediaries in the production of causal chains. The proof is that after repeatedly pulling on a string tied to a rattle above them so that it shakes, they continue pulling on the string even when the string has been visibly detached from the rattle. Nondifferentiation between what is physically possible and impossible was therefore labeled *magicophenomenalism* by Piaget.

Constructing and using instrumental intermediaries to cause effects become increasingly intentional and systematic means–ends behavior between ages 6 and 12 months. The manifestations are varied. First, infants begin to generate causal relations between objects, by producing a variety of exploratory actions on them and observing the consequences (Langer, 1980). In a typical construction of a causal chain, an infant might first put a block in a cup, then empty the cup, drop the block on the floor, and finally cover it with a blanket. It is important to note that these causal actions not only inform infants' causal knowledge, but also play a critical role in the development of other knowledge domains. For example, sequences of causal actions generate spatial transformations (such as containment or occlusion) on objects (which disappear and reappear, displace each other, etc.). These actions also provide pragmatic logical categories for objects, as they are assimilated (or not) into particular causal action schemes (e.g. rollables, pushables, throwables).

Another manifestation is that their construction and use of instrumental intermediaries to cause (affirm) or negate effects become progressively objective, most especially determining what is physically possible and impossible. One of the first instruments infants master to cause (affirm) an effect is the support (see Figure 7.4; Bates, Carlson-Luden, & Bretherton, 1980; Piaget, 1952a; 1954; Schlesinger & Langer, 1999; Uzgiris & Hunt, 1975; Willats, 1984; 1999). At age 6 months infants still pull a cloth whether or not it supports a toy, in order to entrain the toy and retrieve it. Their magicophenomenalism indicates that they efficaciously exploit the contingency between pulling the support and retrieving the toy, while neglecting the necessary spatiotemporal relations

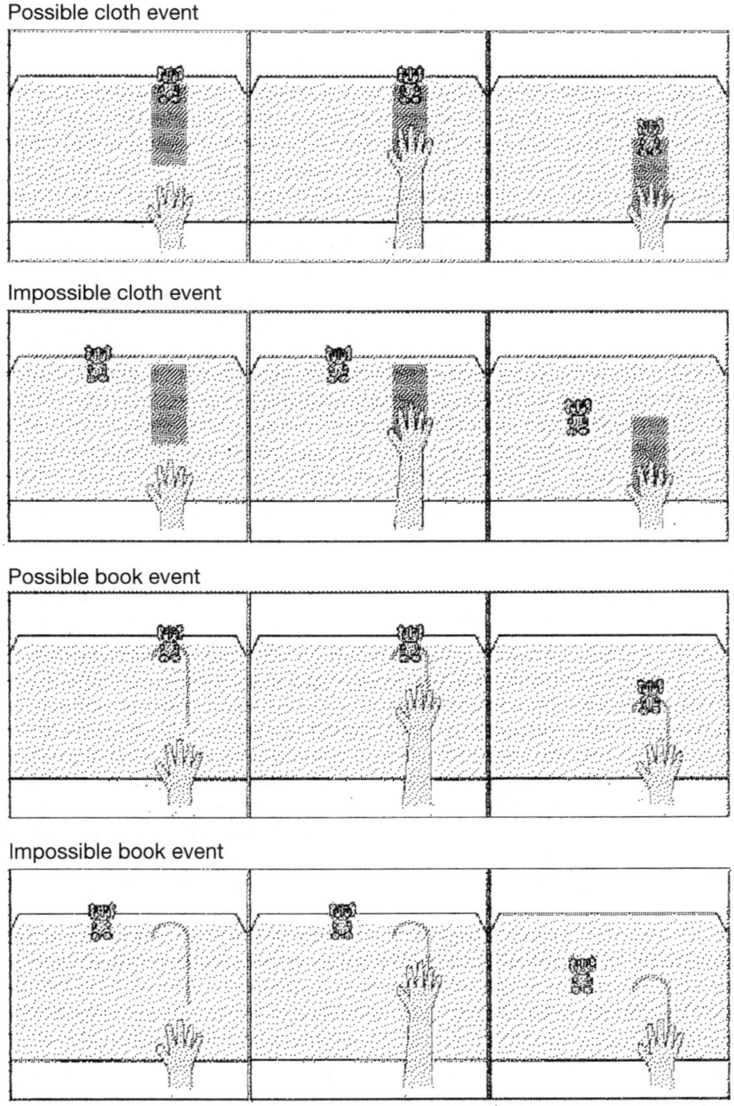

Figure 7.4 *Schematic representation of the possible and impossible cloth and hook tool-use events used to test both sensorimotor and perceptual cognition of causality in 8- and 12-month-olds (Schlesinger & Langer, 1999)*

(e.g. contact of the cloth and toy). By age 8 months infants no longer pull a cloth support when the goal is placed beside rather than on the cloth. Instead they make social pleas for assistance, discard the cloth, or turn their attention elsewhere (Schlesinger & Langer, 1999; Uzgiris & Hunt, 1975).

Initial objectification of intermediaries in negating mediate causality develops at the same time. As just noted, 8-month-olds begin to discard (negate) intermediaries such as a cloth when it does not work. At this stage (Piaget's, 1952a, 1954, stage 4 consolidated secondary circular reactions) they also begin to remove (negate) simple obstacles that are in the way of their achieving their causal ends.

The decline in magicophenomenalistic behaviors near the end of infants' first year is marked by their increased attention to the spatiotemporal relations between cause and effect, as well as the particular features of the objects involved in the causal event. In general, infants' sensorimotor construction of causal chains becomes progressively less subjective and more objective. As objectification increases infants construct and use more sophisticated tools. For example, by age 12 months, infants will pull a cane to entrain a toy in order to retrieve it if it is placed in the crook of the cane (possible), but not if it is placed to the side of the cane (impossible) (see Figure 7.4; Bates, Carlson-Luden, & Bretherton, 1980; Schlesinger & Langer, 1999). A related development during the same period is the ability to solve multi-step causal problems. For example, 12-month-olds will remove a barrier, pull a cloth which supports a string, and then pull the string in order to retrieve a toy (possible) (Willats, 1990). When the toy and string are not connected (impossible), infants will play with the barrier instead of pushing it aside.

Experimenting with Possible and Impossible Causing

A major feature of infants' progressively objectified causal actions during their second year is the gradual appearance of systematic exploratory behaviors. In contrast to their earlier action sequences, infants now begin to vary their actions on objects in an ordered or structured pattern (e.g. Piaget's, 1952a, 1954, sensorimotor stage 5 tertiary circular reactions). For example, an infant might drop a block from successively higher points or bang it harder and harder (Langer, 1986). These causal sequences form quasi-experiments on actions or objects. Their systematic form affords infants the opportunity to judge the critical features of objects and actions that determine what is causally possible and impossible (Langer, 1985).

At age 15 months infants already experiment with what is possible and impossible. For example, after standing cylinders upright (possible) they may try to do the same with a spoon and find out that it is impossible (Langer, 1986). By age 18 months they successfully differentiate between such simple possible and impossible conditions and undertake more advanced experimenting, e.g. turning over a cylindrical Fisher-Price doll that they have stood on its base (possible) and trying to stand it on its head, thereby disconfirming a new impossible condition.

Determining some possible and impossible conditions such as *what* can and cannot stand, it has been hypothesized (Langer, 1994a), is prerequisite to developing the ability to work out the parameters of these conditions in order to understand *how* they work. This is apparent in the test of stability constructed by one 21-month-old (Langer, 1986). He followed up standing a cylinder upright by tilting it a bit before letting go so that it fell over. He immediately replicated his test and observed the same result, i.e. that tilting minus support causes falling. Explorations in understanding what is causally possible and what is causally impossible, and how it works, progresses to experimenting with covarying functions or dependency relations by the end of infants' second year. To illustrate, one 24-month-old experimented extensively with reciprocally manipulating two spoons to lift and transport a cylinder (see Langer, 1986, pp. 292–298, for details).

From First- to Second-Order Causing

In sum, infants' sensorimotor activity begins to construct indirect and mediate causal functions by using instrumental intermediaries during the second half of their first year. To begin with they are subjective (e.g. magicophenomenalistic) but they become progressively objective. This includes both fundamental types of causal functions, producing and annulling effects. As we have seen, infants use instrumental intermediaries to cause effects, e.g. use one object to push another. They also use instrumental intermediaries to negate effects, e.g. use one object to block another object that is rolling in front of them (Langer, 1980).

Infants' sensorimotor construction of mediate causal dependencies develops markedly during their second year (Langer, 1986). This includes generating ordered effects that are correlated indirect functions of seriated causes, e.g. pushing one object harder and harder into a second object so that it moves further and further. The mediate functional dependency may be formalized as one-way ratio-like causal relations, such as 'moving further' is a dependent function of 'pushing harder'. This is what differentiates first-order from second-order indirect causal functions that develop during infants' second year (see Langer, 1986, for detailed definitions and formalization).

Second-order functions are integrative means–ends transformations. They coordinate elementary first-order means–ends functions to each other. This produces a second structural level of more powerful functions. Effects are indirectly dependent upon the causes in first-order functions. In contrast, the effects begin to be proportional to the causes in second-order functions. So, the expected structural developmental difference is that first-order functions are featured by indirect ratio-like relations, while second-order functions are marked by indirect analogical or proportional-like relations.

Older, like younger, infants use one object as an instrument with which to push a second dependent object. But beginning at age 18 months, when the effect is that the dependent object rolls away, then infants may also transform the instrument into a means with which to block the dependent object (Langer, 1986). Infants thereby transform the end or goal from rolling to stopping. As soon as the dependent object stops rolling infants transform the same instrumental object back into a means with which to make the dependent object roll away again. And so on.

Thus, older infants begin to covary their transformations of both means and ends. These covariations form coordinate proportional-like dependencies between causes and effects. These protoproportions map previously constructed first-order dependencies onto each other. The products are second-order causal functions, such as 'moving is a function of pushing, as stopping is a function of blocking'.

Constructivist theory proposes that sensorimotor cognition begins to become representational when infants start producing hierarchical mappings upon mappings (Langer, 1986; 1994a). The conceptual origins of representational causal cognition are infants' second-order sensorimotor mappings of one causal function onto another (e.g. the just described second-order covarying dependency between means and ends). Then the referents of the causal functions are no longer limited to the concrete objects forming the dependency relations. The referents become dependency relations. Since relations are more abstract than objects, the referents are becoming abstract. Causal cognition is no longer limited to the concrete but can begin to be abstract and reflective, that is, begin to construct representational and thoughtful understanding of how things work as well as what works. Then infants can begin to reconstruct the nonvisible causes of visible effects and anticipate future effects of present causes (Piaget's, 1952a, 1954, sensorimotor stage 6 representational cognition).

Perceiving Causality

Most research on infants' causal perception, like that on infants' developing causal action, focuses on mechanical phenomena (e.g. collisions and support). Some research has also begun to study infants' perception of other types of causal events (e.g. animate agents and intentionality: Gergely et al., 1995; Woodward, 1998). It is therefore noteworthy that the onset age for perceptually discriminating possible versus impossible intentional causal phenomena is 9 months (Csibra et al., 1999). Six-month-olds cannot make this discrimination. We have seen that by age 9 months infants are already constructing fairly advanced intentional indirect causal functions. For example, they have developed to Piaget's (1952a; 1954) stage 4 sensorimotor causal cognition; so they have progressed to their second stage of intentional causality in which they purposefully vary the ends they are trying to achieve while keeping their means constant. So far then, the data indicate that the onset age of infants' developing cognition of intentional causality in sensorimotor action precedes its onset in perception; and that its rate of development in sensorimotor action is more rapid than in perception.

This comparative developmental conclusion seems applicable to infants' cognition of mechanical causal phenomena too: sensorimotor action leads perception. The earliest age at which any evidence of infants perceiving causality has been reported is between 3 and 6 months when they are already in Piaget's stage 3 secondary circular reactions. Even at that relatively late age, causal perception is limited to detecting spatiotemporal cues or features that are relatively salient and perceptually accessible. Infants begin to attend to the gross spatial relations between the cause and effect, as well as their relative timing (Leslie, 1982; Leslie & Keeble, 1987). For example, 3-month-olds look longer at an impossible support event in which a box is pushed completely off its support but fails to fall, compared to a similar possible event. It is not until around age 6 months, however, that infants begin to notice and use the relative amount of contact between the box and its support (during partial support events) as a perceptual cue (Baillargeon, Kotovsky, & Needham, 1995). A similar developmental pattern emerges with respect to the visual complexity of the causal events. Thus, 7-month-olds perceive causality in launching events when they are presented as relatively simple computer-animated displays, but not when the events are videotaped displays of real objects (Oakes, 1994; Oakes & Cohen, 1990).

Between ages 6 and 15 months, infants become increasingly sensitive to the spatiotemporal cues that differentiate possible and impossible causality. While 7-month-olds' perception of causality is limited to linear (i.e. straight-line) direct launching between two objects, 10-month-olds also perceive causality in nonlinear launching (Oakes, 1994). However, 10-month-olds still do not perceive causality in indirect 3-object chained launching (Cohen et al., 1999). By age 11 months infants also attend to the relative sizes of the two objects in a collision as an indirect cue for the magnitude of the launching force (Kotovsky & Baillargeon, 1994). By age 12 months infants begin to perceive causality in indirect 3-object chained entraining (see Figure 7.4; Schlesinger & Langer, 1999) and by age 15 months in indirect 3-object chained launching (Cohen et al., 1999). These findings are consistent with Michotte's conclusion that entraining is 'the basic form of the causal impression' while launching is 'only secondary in relation to it' (1963, p. 265). Not consistent with Michotte's conclusion, on the other hand, are findings that 6-month-olds perceive causality in direct 2-object launching but not yet in direct 2-object entraining (Bélanger & Desrochers, 2001).

We have found no research on how causal perception may develop further during the rest of infants' second year. Several negative findings during the first year, however, suggest possible further developments. For example, both 7- and 10-month-old infants do not perceive causality in collisions of bouncing objects (Oakes & Kannass, 1999). Although 10-month-olds perceive 2-object direct launching of real objects as causal, their causal perception is disrupted if the colliding objects vary from trial to trial (Cohen & Oakes, 1993). Similarly, 12-month-olds discriminate between possible and impossible 3-object indirect 'support' entraining when a cloth is used to pull a toy but not 'surround' entraining when a cane is used instead (see Figure 7.4; Schlesinger & Langer, 1999).

Comparing Sensorimotor and Perceptual Causality

While concluding, contra neonativism and pro constructivism, that the development of causal cognition in sensorimotor action is more precocious than in perception, we recognize that it is based upon comparisons of independent data sets that were not generated to test this conclusion. Testing this conclusion requires directly comparing infants' developing sensorimotor actions with their perceptions when interacting with the same causal phenomena. To this end we will examine the findings on infants' developing cognition of causal entraining. It is the only form of causality that comes with a well-documented database on both perceptual and sensorimotor activity by infants during their first year. Moreover, it is one of the only two forms of causality inherent to and a primitive of perception according to Michotte's (1963) Gestalt-like theory and empirical findings. Entraining occurs when a moving object (the causal agent or actor) contacts a stationary object (the patient) causing it to move together with the agent object, i.e. to be entrained or carried off.

The earliest age at which infants have been found to perceive direct 2-object causal entraining is 4 months (Leslie, 1984). At that age they discriminate possible (i.e. with contact) from impossible (i.e. without contact) direct entraining. But they only discriminate when the causal agent is an animate object (a hand picks up a doll) and not when it is an inanimate object (a white oblong picks up a doll). This is 3 months after the onset of infants' sensorimotor construction of entraining, e.g. using their hands to transport objects they happen to have grasped at age 1 month (Piaget, 1952a).

Moreover, there does not seem to be any basis in neonativist theory to account for infants' initially perceiving direct 2-object causal entraining by animate agents only and not by inanimate agents. If knowing about direct causal entraining is an innate module, as proposed by Leslie (1984; 1994), then infants should apply it equally to animate and inanimate causal agents. It is predictable by constructivist theory. As already noted in the previous paragraph, infants' most immediate, direct and perhaps predominant relevant constructive sensorimotor interaction with their environment is of themselves as the agent causing direct entraining from at least age 1 month. Therefore, it is expected that after 3 months of their own animate construction of direct entraining they would most likely develop the perceptual ability to discriminate possible from impossible entraining first when the causal agent is animate.

The earliest age at which infants have been found to develop the perception of indirect 3-object chained causal entraining is 12 months (see Figure 7.4; Schlesinger & Langer, 1999). Then they discriminate possible (a hand pulls a cloth which supports a toy) from impossible (a hand pulls a cloth which is proximate to a nearby toy) support. In their experiments, Schlesinger and Langer (1999) compared 8- and 12-month-olds' developing sensorimotor actions with their developing perceptions on possible and impossible, supporting cloth and surrounding cane entraining. Infants' discriminatory causal action developed before their discriminatory causal perception between possible and impossible indirect 3-object chained entraining for both support and surround.

These comparative developmental findings reinforce our conclusion about the relative precocity of infants' sensorimotor causal cognition. They support the constructivist hypothesis that infants' sensorimotor causality develops before and may inform their developing perception of causality. They counter neonativist claims that infants' causal cognition is expressed in their perceptions before their sensorimotor actions, and that measures of sensorimotor actions underestimate infants' knowledge (e.g. Leslie, 1994).

Objectifying

The actions that infants develop construct progressive knowledge about the physical existence or permanence of objects, and about the essential physical properties of objects such as their continuity and solidity. Because of space limitations we will focus mainly on object permanence. The reasons are twofold. First, without object permanence there can be no constant given elements for cognition. So, by considering how infants develop object permanence we bring our discussion back full circle to where it began on how infants construct the elements of their cognition. Second, some knowledge of objects' existence is prerequisite to any cognition of their physical properties. To illustrate infants' developing cognition of these properties we will extend our focus to aspects of just one, object continuity.

Focusing on infants' developing cognition of object permanence and continuity also reflects the central contemporary empirical arena for the debate between constructivist and neonativist theories on the origins of cognitive development. Constructivism hypothesizes that infants' initial cognition of object permanence and continuity is presentational and develops into representational cognition over the course of their first 2 years. Neonativism hypothesizes that very young infants' initial cognition of object permanence and continuity is already representational.

The Origins of Sensorimotor Objectifying

In his classical longitudinal research on infants' developing sensorimotor construction of reality, Piaget (1952a; 1954) discovered six progressive stages in their objectifying sensorimotor actions. They start out by being modifiable reflex-like actions at the first stage. These actions construct presentational knowledge about the permanence and continuity of here-and-now objects. During four transitional stages their objectifying actions become circular reactions, developing from primary to secondary to tertiary. These actions progressively construct anticipatory and recognitory knowledge about the permanence and continuity of objects that are less and less in the here-and-now. By the final sixth stage infants' objectifying actions become initial representational operations. These operations construct evocative symbolic knowledge recalling the existence and continuity of not-here-and-not-now objects.

At the beginning of the first stage newborns' sensorimotor actions already begin to pursue, if only barely, objects with which they have had direct contact. They root after a nipple that has escaped their sucking by minimally groping or searching for it; they visually pursue or follow an object to which they have been attending as long as its motion is minimal; and so on. By the end of their first stage, 1-month-olds' rooting and visual pursuit become quite systematic. For example, Piaget's (1952a, pp. 27 and 28, observations 7 and 8) longitudinal quasi-experimental observations of his three children found that by age 21 days Laurent's search activity had developed to successfully overcoming loss of direct sensorimotor contact with his goal objects. So too, by this age Laurent visually tracked objects back-and-forth until they left his visual field (e.g. disappeared behind something). Thus neonates act as if objects exist and are continuous as long as they interact with them.

During stage 2 primary circular reactions, from ages 1 to 3 months, infants begin to develop some object expectancies and recognition. In addition to visually tracking objects until they disappear, they now also visually search for their reappearance at the place they disappeared (Piaget, 1952a; 1954). Thus, they now anticipate the existence and continuity of objects that are momentarily invisible (i.e. no longer present spatially and temporally) and recognize them when they reappear.

By stage 3 initial secondary circular reactions, from ages 3 to 6 months, infants' object expectancies and recognition begin to be extended spatially as well as temporally. They begin to anticipate where disappearing objects are going and recognize their reappearance as long as (a) their trajectories are straightforward and (b) their nonvisibility is minimal (e.g. by going behind something at one end and coming out at the other end). So, too, infants now expect and recognize that objects are continuous even when they are partly hidden (e.g. they will retrieve a doll when they can only see its feet). Thus, they are able to reconstruct both (1) whole invisible moving objects from following a visible part of their trajectories, and (2) whole invisible stationary objects from observing a visible part of their totality (Piaget, 1954).

The Origins of Perceiving Objects

These findings – that infants' constructive cognition of objects develops in three stages during their first 6 months – underestimate infants' competence according to neonativism. Neonativism claims that sensorimotor actions require relatively complex behavioral coordinations not yet available to very young infants. So, sensorimotor measures of infants' cognition necessarily underestimate their competence that is revealed by measuring simpler perceptual behaviors.

Accordingly, neonativist research has comprised cross-sectional perceptual experiments designed to support two core hypotheses. These are that 'young infants, like adults, represent the existence and properties of hidden objects' (Baillargeon, 1995, p. 367) and that these representational cognitions of object permanence and continuity are innate (e.g. Spelke et al., 1992). We will consider each in turn, permanence then continuity.

Permanence

Key to the hypotheses that infants' knowledge of object permanence is innately representational are perceptual measures of their preferential looking at kinetic events involving occluded solid objects that appear to violate physical laws (Baillargeon, 1987; Baillargeon, Spelke, & Wasserman, 1985). A habituation paradigm was used to create these events. In both experimental and control conditions infants were first habituated to a screen repeatedly rotating back-and-forth 180°. In the experimental condition, an obstructing box was introduced in the way of the rotating screen during the post-habituation test trials. This permitted presenting alternating possible and impossible variants of the habituation event during the post-habituation test trials. In the possible post-habituation variant the screen repeatedly rotated back-and-forth 112° only, thus appearing to stop at the point of contact with the by now no longer visible obstructing box. In the impossible post-habituation variant the screen repeatedly rotated back-and-forth 180°, thus appearing to pass through the by now no longer visible obstructing box. The control condition post-habituation test trials were identical except that no obstruction was introduced. In the post-habituation trials, infants looked longer at the 180° than at the 112° repeated back-and-forth screen rotations in the experimental condition but not in the control condition.

The conclusion drawn from these findings was that young infants innately represent the obstructing box as permanent (e.g. Spelke et al., 1992). They know that it continues to exist when it is not visible in the apparently impossible 180° rotations by the screen. That is why they are surprised and look longer when the screen does so anyway.

The habituation paradigm used in these studies, however, confounded apparently impossible screen rotations with degrees of its movement. In the experimental condition test trials, the 112° and 180° back-and-forth screen rotations differ not only in their apparent physical possibility and impossibility. The 112° rotations also present less movement to the infants than the 180° rotations. Thus, infants may be looking longer at the 180° rotations because they prefer more movement (e.g. Gibson, 1988; Piaget, 1952a), not because the rotations are apparently impossible.

Baillargeon (1987) discounted the significance of this disparity in amount of movement between the two displays because she found no looking time differences in the control condition in which no obstructing box was present. Infants looked equally long to the post-habituation 112° and 180° rotations after having been habituated to 180°. However, if there were no difference in infants' intrinsic interest between the two rotations, post-habituation 112° rotations should have captured infants' attention more because they are novel while post-habituation 180° rotations are familiar. The fact that they looked equally long to both 112° (novel) and 180° (familiar) post-habituation rotations indicates that infants prefer 180° rotations which present more movement, and that their perceptual preference for more motion was only partially suppressed by prior familiarization with repeated 180° rotations in the habituation phase.

To disconfound apparent impossibility from degree of rotations, Rivera, Wakeley, and Langer (1999) replicated Baillargeon's (1987) procedures but omitted habituating the infants to 180° rotations before testing them in the experimental and control conditions. Without prior habituation infants still looked longer at 180° than at 112° repeated back-and-forth rotations when an obstructing box appeared to make the 180° rotations impossible and the 112° rotations possible, just like Baillargeon (1987) found with prior habituation. But, infants also looked longer at 180° than 112° rotations when no obstructing box was present to make the 180° rotations appear impossible. And, the magnitude of infants' longer looking at 180° than 112° rotations was the same whether the 180° rotations appeared possible or impossible. Therefore, infants' longer looking at 180° than 112° rotations was due to perceptual preference for more motion only and not due to representational reasoning about object permanence.

Without prior habituation, Rivera, Wakeley, & Langer (1999) also found the same interaction effect of rotation condition with order that Baillargeon (1987) and others have found with prior habituation. Infants only looked longer at 180° rotation when it was presented first, both when the 180° rotation appeared impossible and possible. Therefore, the preference could not index any innate representational knowledge about object permanence since it would require claiming that such interaction effects (i.e. rotation condition with order) are encoded in our genes. These findings, then, disconfirmed the claim that the perceptual measures uncovered innate representational object permanence that sensorimotor measures underestimated.

Continuity

Studies of preferential looking are also key to hypotheses that infants' cognition of object continuity is innately representational. The perceptual measure used to determine if their cognition is representational was whether infants dishabituated to 1 object (e.g. a rod) or 2 objects (e.g. the top and bottom pieces of a rod) after being habituated to a single moving object whose middle was not visible (e.g. a rod whose top and bottom pieces were visible but whose center was occluded by a nearer object; Kellman & Spelke, 1983). Infants were credited with representational knowledge of object continuity if they dishabituated to 2 objects since this indicated that they experienced the habituation display as one continuous object even though its middle was not visible. Conversely, infants were only credited with presentational knowledge of object continuity if they dishabituated to 1 object since this indicated that they experienced the habituation display as two discrete objects.

Kellman and Spelke (1983) found that 4-month-olds dishabituated to 2 but not 1 object. On this basis, they concluded that infants are innately endowed with a representational concept of object continuity (see also e.g. Spelke, 1985). However, subsequent findings on younger infants lead to the opposite conclusion. Newborns dishabituate to 1 but not 2 objects (Slater et al., 1990; 1994; 1996). By this perceptual measure, then, infants are born with only presentational not representational knowledge of object continuity. At age 2 months, infants are in transition from presentational to anticipatory and recognitory knowledge of object continuity. They still dishabituate to 1 but not 2 objects unless the occluder is very narrow and most of the singular object in the habituation display is showing (Johnson & Aslin, 1995). This developmental course is insured by infants' ordinary experience during their first 4 months. Their experience includes numerous, varied and repeated sensorimotor and perceptual interactions with continuous singular objects that are partly and temporarily hidden (by infants themselves as well as by their environment) only to re-emerge intact.

So, by this perceptual measure infants' initial cognition about object continuity develops from presentational to transitional to some anticipatory and recognitory knowledge. These findings parallel those found by the sensorimotor measures in which infants' initial cognition about object continuity develops from their stage 1 presentational to their stage 3 anticipatory and recognitory knowledge in which they reconstruct an invisible whole object from a visible part. Thus, the ontogenetic findings from both measures support the hypothesis that infants' initial cognition of objects develops stage-wise from presentational to anticipatory and recognitory knowledge. They do not support the hypothesis that it is innately representational.

Further, while (big brained) newborn children are not representational about object continuity by perceptual measures, (small brained) newborn domestic chicks (*Gallus gallus*) are (Lea, Slater, & Ryan, 1996; Regolin & Vallortigara, 1995). To make this determination, newly hatched chicks were imprinted to a single moving rod whose top and bottom pieces were visible but whose center was occluded by a nearer object. In postimprinting test trials, chicks preferred approaching a single rod over two rod pieces. By this perceptual measure, then, newborn chicks are innately endowed with a representational concept of object continuity. But newborn children are not. So, the phylogenetic history of cognition is not simply continuous as proposed in Spelke and Newport's (1998) neonativist account.

The A-not-B Error

Beyond infants' first three stages of developing object cognition, constructivist theory has discovered that infants' anticipatory and recognitory object permanence continues to develop in two further stages from ages 6 to 15 months (Piaget, 1954). During sensorimotor stage 4 infants can reconstruct whole invisible stationary objects even when no part remains visible as long as they observe the disappearance (e.g. when the total objects are covered so that no parts remain visible). However, if they find an object in one place A and it is visibly displaced to another place B, infants produce what Piaget labeled the A-not-B error. That is, even though they may attend to the displacement infants nevertheless search for the object at A, the initial locus of their success. Much follow-up research has not only replicated this error but explored its parameters. Infants make A-not-B errors more frequently when (a) the delay between the placement and searching is increased (e.g. Diamond, 1985; Diamond & Goldman-Rakic, 1989; Fox, Kagan, & Weiskopf, 1979; Gratch & Landers, 1971); (b) the visual distinctiveness of the locations is minimized (e.g. Bremner, 1978; Bremner & Bryant, 2001; Butterworth, Jarrett, & Hicks, 1982; Carranza, Brito, & Escudero, 1990); and (c) the numbers of trials and locations are increased (e.g. Cummings & Bjork, 1983; Piaget, 1954; Sophian, 1985; see Marcovitch & Zelazo, 1999, for a meta-analytic review).

Piaget (1954) attributed infants' A-not-B errors to a combination of defects in their memory, spatial localization and objectification. A wide range of complementary accounts have been proposed subsequently that are compatible with Piaget's. One attributes infants' A-not-B errors to defects in short-term memory and motor inhibition caused by their dorsolateral prefrontal cortex immaturity (Diamond, 1985; 1990; Diamond & Goldman-Rakic, 1989; Diamond, Zola-Morgan, & Squire, 1989). Another account attributes infants' A-not-B errors to competition between their 'latent' memory traces for A and their 'active' memory traces for B (Munakata, 1998; Munakata et al., 1997).

All these accounts assume that infants are in the process of developing a concept about the permanence of objects. Another account, labeled dynamic systems theory, challenges this assumption (Smith et al., 1999). On this account infants' behaviors are patterns of activity emerging within each infant's unique physical situation and history. The A-not-B error is caused by a so-called 'attractor space' around the A location that is created by infants' previous reaching patterns to A (see van Geert, Chapter 28 in this volume, on 'attractor space'). No developing object concept is attributed to infants, only an 'error . . . created by the in-task dynamics, by the emergence of each reach out of memories for preceding reaches, and by the continuous coupling and co-evolvement of reaching and looking' (Smith et al., 1999, p. 240).

From Presentational to Representational Objectifying

Neither dynamic systems theory nor neonativism provides an account of the further course of infants' developing cognition of objects during their second year. Constructivism does. Since its findings are well known we can be brief. It begins with overcoming the A-not-B error at stage 5 (tertiary circular reactions) from ages 10 to 15 months (Piaget, 1954). This stage is the culmination of infants' developing anticipatory and recognitory presentational cognition of object permanence. For example, during this stage infants become able to anticipate where disappearing objects are going and recognize their reappearance across multiple occlusions as long as their displacements between occlusions are visible. So it is predictable that if an object emerges with different features from the one which disappeared behind the occluder, infants will now recognize that it is a different object and that there must have been two different objects (Xu & Carey, 1996).

During the final sixth sensorimotor stage from ages 15 to 24 months infants develop evocative recall or representational cognition of object permanence

Table 7.1 *Heterochronic primate phylogeny*

Ontogenetic measures	Cognitive domains	Phylogenetic findings
Onset age	Physical (e.g. causing)	Similar in all species
	Logicomathematical (e.g. classifying)	Earlier in humans
Offset age	Physical	Later in humans
	Logicomathematical	Later in humans
Extent of progress	Physical	Greater in humans (e.g. theoretical)
	Logicomathematical	Greater in humans (e.g. formal)
Velocity or rate	Physical	Accelerated in humans
	Logicomathematical	Accelerated in humans
Stage sequence	Physical	Similar in all species
	Logicomathematical	Similar in all species but with exceptions
Structural organization	Within and between domains	Asynchronic in monkeys to synchronic in humans

(Piaget, 1954). They know that objects that are not-here-and-not-now continue to exist even when their displacements are also not visible. This sensorimotor representation of object permanence, according to constructivist theory, is the first step towards developing representational concrete operations about the conservation of objects' properties such as their length and weight during childhood; and, ultimately, hypotheticodeductive formal operations about the conservation of objects' properties such as their motion by inertia beginning in adolescence (Inhelder & Piaget, 1958).

The Evolution of Cognitive Development: The Heterochrony Hypothesis

How did this rich early cognitive development by human infants evolve? To study its evolutionary antecedents constructivist theory has focused on the comparative sensorimotor development of logico-mathematical and physical cognition in primates. The research has discovered primate conceptual universals. But it has also discovered that their ontogenetic covariation is progressively displaced or heterochronic in primate phylogeny (Langer, 2000a; 2000b). The evolution of primates' conceptual universals is marked by diverging ontogenetic onset and offset ages, velocity, and stage sequencing and organization, plus discontinuous developmental extent (as outlined in Table 7.1).

The Comparative Development of Sensorimotor Classifying

Primates' development of constructive logical classifying is paradigmatic. So it will serve as our illustrative data set (see Figure 7.3). Comparative developmental data on sensorimotor classifying, described earlier, by different samples of children provide the baseline for comparing its development in modern nonhuman primates. The human samples include 8- to 21-month-old Aymara and Quecha Indian children in Peru (Jacobsen, 1984) and 6- to 30-month-old infants exposed *in utero* to crack cocaine (Ahl, 1993). The Indian children were raised in impoverished conditions as compared to the mainly Caucasian middle class San Francisco Bay Area children (Langer, 1980; 1986; 1998). Nevertheless, no differences were found in onset age, velocity, sequence, extent, or organization of cognitive development during infancy in these different human samples; though the crack cocaine babies manifested many other behavioral dysfunctions, especially emotional. Only velocity and sequence were studied in autistic children from ages 5 to 8 years (Slotnick, 1984). The sequence was not affected, but the rate of development was severely retarded.

In comparison, when presented for example with objects from two form classes (such as cups and rings), juvenile capuchin (*Cebus appela*) and macaque (*Macaca fascicularis*) monkeys (see Figure 7.5 for a cladistic map of primate phylogeny) develop single-category classifying only (such as rings: Spinozzi & Natale, 1989). Bonobo (*Pan paniscus*) and common (*Pan troglodytes*) chimpanzees' development progresses from single- to two-category classifying, but no further (Spinozzi, 1993; Spinozzi & Langer, 1999; Spinozzi et al., 1998; 1999). For example, presented with objects from three form classes (e.g. cups, rings and sticks) chimpanzees only

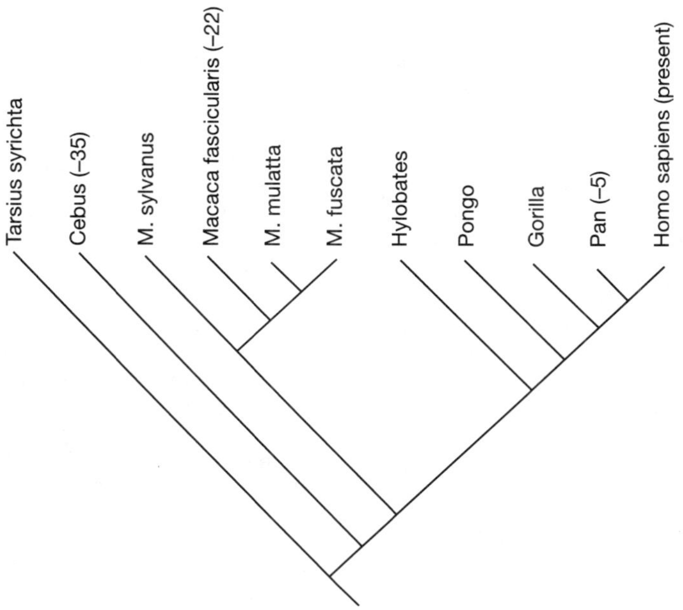

Figure 7.5 *Primate phylogeny (millions of years ago in geological time given in parentheses for compared species)*

construct two categories (e.g. cups and sticks). Humans' development progresses from single- to two- to multiple- to hierarchic-category classifying (Langer, 1980; 1986; 1998; Langer et al., 1998).

In toto, the extent of classificatory development is discontinuous in primate phylogeny (see Figure 7.3). Monkeys do not progress beyond single-category classifying. Chimpanzees do not progress beyond two-category classifying. Humans progress to multiple-category classifying and beyond.

These studies have also found the following major divergences in primates' classifying development (see Figure 7.3). The onset age for the origins of classifying by primates is youngest in humans, intermediate in chimpanzees, and oldest in monkeys. The velocity with which classifying develops is fastest in humans, intermediate in chimpanzees, and slowest in monkeys. The stage sequence of classificatory development is similar in humans and chimpanzees, but the sequence is different in monkeys. The offset age when primates stop developing any more classificatory cognition is youngest in monkeys, intermediate in chimpanzees, and oldest in humans.

Cross-Fostering

These comparative data support the originalist hypothesis that elementary constructive cognition, including logical cognition such as classifying, is a primary and initial development in all primates (Langer, 1980; 1986; 1989; 1994a). It does not require human language or enculturation. For example, preverbal human infants and nonverbal monkeys and chimpanzees develop at least first-order single-category classifying. Moreover, nonverbal chimpanzees even develop second-order two-category classifying.

This raises the question of the role that human enculturation and language (symbolic) rearing plays in the development of constructive cognition. The answer has been sought by studying the comparative sensorimotor development of logical and arithmetic cognition by bonobo and common chimpanzees who have been cross-fostered by humans. So far, the findings lead to the hypothesis that enculturation and language rearing may have a quantitative but, with few exceptions, not a qualitative effect (Potí & Langer, 2001; Potí et al., 1999; Spinozzi & Langer, 1999; Spinozzi et al., 1999). Again, the findings on comparative classifying development are paradigmatic.

The quantitative advance made by the cross-fostered chimpanzees in their classifying remains within the second-order level developed even by chimpanzees who have not been cross-fostered. Chimpanzees not cross-fostered also constructed two contemporaneous class-consistent categories of objects when presented with 6 objects such as 3 sticks and 3 rings (Spinozzi, 1993). But almost all included only some of the objects, e.g. groupings of 2 sticks and 2 or 3 rings. By comparison, many 2-category constructions by the cross-fostered chimpanzees were exhaustive (e.g. included groupings of all 3 sticks and all 3 rings: Spinozzi et al., 1999). Testing the hypothesis that such quantitative advances within a cognitive developmental level are caused by human enculturation and language rearing will require additional research to separate these variables from increasing age. They are confounded in the research so far.

Cross-fostered chimpanzees' lack of qualitative progress is also well illustrated by their comparative sensorimotor development of classifying. They, like chimpanzees not cross-fostered and unlike human children, did not progress beyond the second-order level of two-category to the third-order level of three-category classifying. This is a crucial cognitive developmental difference since three categories are the minimal necessary conditions for constructing hierarchic classifying (see Langer, 1998, for a detailed discussion). Hierarchic classifying requires a minimum of two subordinate and complementary subclasses that are integrated by a third, a super-ordinate class that subsumes the other two.

This finding is representative. Cross-fostering which leads to acquiring language comparable to about the 2- to 3-year-old human child's level (as measured by Greenfield & Savage-Rumbaugh, 1990; Savage-Rumbaugh et al., 1993) does not engender qualitative development to a higher level of most constructive cognition. Nor does human enculturation. Nor does the combination of language and enculturation. They do not extend most of nonhuman primates' cognitive development beyond their 'natural' qualitative level (see Langer, 2000b, for a summary discussion of the potential importance of the few exceptions found in Potí et al., 1999, and Spinozzi & Langer, 1999).

Precocial Human Brain and Cognitive Development

These findings are paradigmatic of the other constructivist findings on the comparative origins and development of logical, arithmetic, and physical cognition by primates. The comparative developmental findings on onset and offset ages plus velocity in particular disconfirm the neoteny (or progressive temporal retardation) hypothesis about the evolution of primate cognitive development (proposed e.g. by Bjorklund, 1997; Gould, 1977; 1984; Montague, 1989). Instead, they support the hypothesis that it is precocial or progressively accelerated in descendant primate species (proposed by Langer, 1989; 1993; 1994a; 1998). The comparative composite emerging from the findings is earlier onset, accelerated velocity, later offset, and progressive extension of human cognitive development.

Humans' comparatively precocious, accelerated and extended cognitive development parallels their precocial brain maturation. The human brain is already larger than that of other primate species at birth, as measured by the log encephalization quotient or the fraction of the body devoted to brains (Deacon, 2000). In addition, human brain development is extended into adolescence and young adulthood, a later offset age than for other primate species (e.g. Gibson, 1990; 1991; Paus et al., 1999; Purves, 1988; Sowell et al., 1999). This includes comparatively prolonged glial cell growth, myelination of axons, synaptogenesis, and dendritic growth in the cortex. The result is great expansion of the human brain especially in the neocortex (e.g. Deacon, 2000; Finlay & Darlington, 1995).

Consistent with humans' precocial and extended brain ontogeny, the comparative onset age of cognitive development is early and the comparative offset age is late. The offset age for humans is young adulthood between ages 25 and 30 years (Kuhn et al., 1977). The findings (that require further research to become definitive) suggest that the offset age of cognitive development is no more than age 6 years in bonobo and common chimpanzees (Potí et al., 1999; Spinozzi et al., 1999). Thus, evolution has provided humans with the most ontogenetic time and speed to develop the brain and cognition most extensively.

Compared to other primates, the origins of human cognitive development are predominantly precocial not neotenous. Its onset and velocity are accelerated while its terminus is delayed and extended. At the same time, human (nonbrain) physiological maturation such as dentition (see e.g. Smith, 1992) and attendant noncognitive behavioral development, such as locomotion and dependence, are predominantly neotenous (as suggested by Werner, 1948, and others such as Gould, 1977). Precocial brain and cognitive development together with neotenous physiological and noncognitive behavioral development lead to the further hypothesis that humans' ontogenetic 'window of opportunity' for cognitive development is wider than chimpanzees' which is wider than monkeys' (see Langer, 1998, 2000a, 2000b, for more detailed presentations of this hypothesis).

The Phylogenetic Reorganization of Cognitive Ontogeny

The comparative cognitive development of primates is inconsistent with a simple recapitulatory evolutionary account, as already anticipated for all of mental development by Werner (1948). Instead, it is consistent with an evolutionary theory of organizational heterochrony in the timing of cognitive development that is marked by major phylogenetic changes in ontogenetic covariation between cognitive features (see McKinney & McNamara, 1991, for comprehensive definitions of heterochrony). Heterochrony provides a heuristic evolutionary theory about the possibilities opened up and the constraints

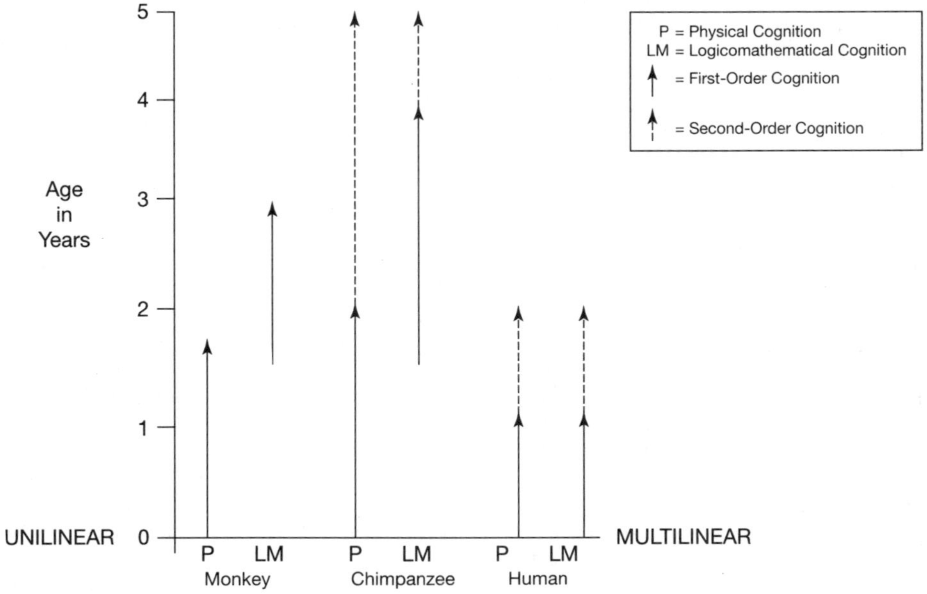

Figure 7.6 *The heterochronic 'folding over' of cognitive ontogeny in primate phylogeny from unilinear to multilinear early development*

imposed on the origins and development of cognition in primate phylogeny (for the detailed proposal see Langer, 1989; 1996; 2000a; 2000b).

To investigate how heterochrony works as an evolutionary mechanism, constructivist research has also been studying the comparative structural organization of cognitive development in these primate species. The research is discovering striking divergences in developmental sequencing within and between cognitive domains in primates; and therefore in the structural organization of their cognitive development (see Table 7.1 and Figure 7.6). Our comparative focus here will be limited to between-domains structural developmental organization (detailed in Langer, 2000a; 2000b). For comparative analyses of within-domains structural developmental organization see e.g. Langer (1989).

Physical, logical and arithmetic cognition develop in parallel in human children. The onset age is the same for all three cognitive domains. Their onset is during very early infancy and probably the neonatal period. And, importantly, they develop in synchrony. The other extreme is found in monkeys. They show almost total asynchrony between their development of physical, logical and arithmetic cognition. Since they are out of developmental phase with each other, they are not likely to be open to similar environmental influences and to each other's influence.

To comprehend the significance this disparity in developmental synchrony has for the ontogeny of cognition in primate phylogeny requires sketching some illustrative findings. Monkeys develop their core physical cognition (such as of causal relations) before they develop their core logicomathematical cognition (such as of classes). The development of their physical cognition is well under way or completed by the developmental onset of their logicomathematical cognition. To illustrate, capuchins develop simple causal cognition, such as about using a support as an entraining tool to get a goal object, by age 9 months (Spinozzi & Potí, 1989). They develop more advanced causal cognition, such as about using a stick as an entraining instrument to get a goal object, by age 18 to 20 months (Natale, 1989). Thus, capuchins' causal cognition is well developed by the onset of their logicomathematical cognition, such as classifying, that they only begin to develop at around age 15 months (Spinozzi & Natale, 1989).

In chimpanzees' ontogeny, physical and logicomathematical cognition constitute partially overlapping developmental trajectories. While already well under way, chimpanzees' development of physical cognition is not completed before the onset of their logicomathematical cognition. Physical and logicomathematical cognition constitute partially asynchronic developmental trajectories. We can therefore expect that these cognitive domains may eventually begin to be partially open to similar environmental influences and to each other's influence – but beginning relatively late in chimpanzee ontogeny as compared to humans.

From the start of human ontogeny, physical and logicomathematical cognition constitute contemporaneous developmental trajectories that become progressively interdependent. Synchronic developmental trajectories permit direct interaction or information flow between cognitive domains. Mutual and reciprocal influence between logicomathematical and physical cognition is readily achievable since humans develop them simultaneously and in parallel.

In the heterochronic evolution of primate cognitive development, the unilinear growth trajectories of physical *followed by* logicomathematical cognition evolved into multilinear growth trajectories of physical *at the same time as* logicomathematical cognition. The sequential pattern of physical followed by logicomathematical cognition in the ontogeny of monkeys became 'folded over' and, hence, concurrent trajectories: (a) first to form descendant partially multilinear cognitive development midway in chimpanzee ontogeny; and (b) eventually to form fully multilinear cognitive development from the start in human ontogeny.

Heterochronic reorganization of cognitive development opened up multiple cascading possibilities for full information flow between logical (e.g. classificatory), arithmetic (e.g. numerical) and physical (e.g. causal) constructions by human infants (e.g. making it possible for them to construct a 'logic of experimentation'). Hence their comparatively rich early cognitive development. The possibilities opened up for further development vary accordingly and, one of us has proposed (Langer, 1989; 1993; 1998), reciprocally constrain the 'direction' of progressive cognitive ontogeny in primate phylogeny. Humans' synchronic and rich early cognitive ontogeny opens up comparatively unlimited, permanent, and cascading possibilities for further intellectual development. On this evolutionary hypothesis about the descent of cognitive development, human cognitive development is the initial source of the history of ideas that can be transmitted between generations to construct our cultural intellectual heritage.

REFERENCES

Ahl, V.A. (1993). Cognitive development in infants prenatally exposed to cocaine. Unpublished doctoral dissertation, University of California at Berkeley.

Antell, S.E., & Keating, D.P. (1983). Perception of numerical invariance in neonates. *Child Development*, 54, 695–701.

Antinucci, F. (ed.) (1989). *Cognitive structure and development of nonhuman primates*. Hillsdale, NJ: Erlbaum.

Arriaga, R.I., Joyce, K., Pathmarajah, M., Walthall, A., Treynor, W., & Langer, J. (1999). Do 11-month-olds know more about addition than 5-month-olds? Poster presentation, Western Psychological Association, Irvine, California.

Baillargeon, R. (1987). Object permanence in 3½- and 4½-month-old infants. *Developmental Psychology*, 23, 655–664.

Baillargeon, R. (1995). A model of physical reasoning in infancy. In C. Rovee-Collier & L. Lipsett (eds), *Advances in infancy research* (Vol. 9, pp. 305–371). Norwood, NJ: Ablex.

Baillargeon, R., Kotovsky, L., & Needham, A. (1995). The acquisition of physical knowledge in infancy. In D. Sperber, D. Premack & A. J. Premack (eds), *Causal cognition: A multidisciplinary debate* (pp. 79–116). Oxford: Clarendon.

Baillargeon, R., Spelke, E.S., & Wasserman, S. (1985). Object permanence in 5-month-old infants. *Cognition*, 20, 191–208.

Bates, E., Carlson-Luden, V., & Bretherton, I. (1980). Perceptual aspects of tool using in infancy. *Infant Behavior and Development*, 3, 127–140.

Behl-Chada, G. (1996). Basic-level and superordinate-like categorical representations in early infancy. *Cognition*, 60, 105–141.

Bélanger, N.D., & Desrochers, S. (2001). Can 6-month-old infants process causality in different types of causal events? *British Journal of Developmental Psychology*, 19, 11–21.

Bjorklund, D.F. (1997). The role of immaturity in human development. *Psychological Bulletin*, 122, 153–169.

Boole, G. (1854). *An investigation of the laws of thought*. New York: Dover.

Bornstein, M.H. (1981). Two kinds of perceptual organization near the beginning of life. In W.A. Collins (ed.), *Aspects of the development of competence* (pp. 39–91). Hillsdale, NJ: Erlbaum.

Bornstein, M.H. (1984). A descriptive taxonomy of psychological categories used by infants. In C. Sophian (ed.), *Origins of cognitive skills* (pp. 313–338). Hillsdale, NJ: Erlbaum.

Brannon, E.M., & Terrace, H.S. (1998). Ordering of numerosities 1 to 9 by monkeys. *Science*, 282, 746–749.

Bremner, A., & Bryant, P. (2001). The effect of spatial cues on infants' responses in the AB task, with and without a hidden object. *Developmental Science*, 4, 408–415.

Bremner, J.G. (1978). Spatial errors made by infants: Inadequate spatial cues or evidence of egocentrism? *British Journal of Psychology*, 69, 77–84.

Butterworth, G., Henshall, C., Johnston, S., Abd-Fattah, N., & Hopkins, B. (1985). Hand to mouth activity in the newborn baby. Paper presented at the British Psychological Society Meetings, Belfast.

Butterworth, G., Jarrett, N., & Hicks, L. (1982). Spatiotemporal identity in infancy: Perceptual competence or conceptual deficit? *Developmental Psychology*, 18 (3), 435–449.

Canfield, R.L., & Smith, E.G. (1996). Number-based expectations and sequential enumeration by 5-month-old infants. *Developmental Psychology*, 32, 269–279.

Cantor, G. (1895). Beiträge zur Begründung der transfiniten Mengenlehre, i. *Mathematische Annalen*, xlvi, 481–512.

Carnap, R. (1960). *The logical syntax of language*. Paterson, NJ: Littlefield & Adams.

Carranza, J., Brito, A., & Escudero, A. (1990). The absence of the second container in the A-not-B error. *Archives de Psychologie*, 58 (226), 275–282.

Cassirer, E. (1953). *Philosophy of symbolic forms: Vol. 1. Language*. New Haven, CT: Yale University Press.

Cassirer, E. (1957). *Philosophy of symbolic forms: Vol. 3. Phenomenology of knowledge*. New Haven, CT: Yale University Press.

Clearfield, M.W., & Mix, K.S. (1999). Number versus contour length in infants' discrimination of small visual sets. *Psychological Science*, 10, 408–411.

Clearfield, M.W., & Mix, K.S. (2001). Amount versus number: Infants' use of area and contour length to discriminate small sets. *Journal of Cognition and Development*, 2, 243–260.

Cohen, L.B., & Oakes, L.M. (1993). How infants perceive a simple causal event. *Developmental Psychology*, 29, 421–433.

Cohen, L.B., & Younger, B.A. (1983). Perceptual categorization in infants. In E.K. Scholnick (ed.), *New trends in conceptual representation* (pp. 197–219). Hillsdale, NJ: Erlbaum.

Cohen, L.B., Rundell, L.J., Spellman, B.A., & Cashon, C.H. (1999). Infants' perception of causal chains. *Psychological Science*, 10, 412–418.

Cooper, R.G. (1984). Early number development: Discovering number space with addition and subtraction. In C. Sophian (ed.), *Origins of cognitive skills* (pp. 157–192). Hillsdale, NJ: Erlbaum.

Crichton, M.T., & Lange-Küttner, C. (1999). Animacy and propulsion: Tracking, waving and reaching to self-propelled and induced moving objects. *Developmental Science*, 2, 318–324.

Csibra, G., Gergely, G., Biro, S., Koos, O., & Brockbank, M. (1999). Goal attribution without agency cues: The perception of 'pure reason' in infancy. *Cognition*, 72, 237–267.

Cummings, E.M., & Bjork, E.L. (1983). Search behavior on multi-choice hiding tasks: Evidence for an objective conception of space in infancy. *International Journal of Behavioral Development*, 6 (1), 71–87.

Deacon, T. (2000). How flexible is the neurodevelopmental clock? In S.T. Parker, J. Langer, & M.L. McKinney (eds), *Biology, brains and behavior: The evolution of human development*. Santa Fe, NM: School of American Research Press.

Dehaene, S., Dehaene-Lambertz, G., & Cohen, L. (1998). Abstract representations of numbers in the animal and human brain. *Trends in Neuroscience*, 21 (8), 355–361. Erratum in *Trends in Neuroscience*, 1998, 21 (12), 509.

Diamond, A. (1985). Development of the ability to use recall to guide action, as indicated by infants' performance on AB. *Child Development*, 56 (4), 868–883.

Diamond, A. (1990). Development and neural bases of AB and DR. In A. Diamond (ed.), *The development and neural bases of higher cognitive functions* (pp. 267–317). New York: National Academy of Sciences.

Diamond, A., & Goldman-Rakic, P. (1989). Comparison of human infants and rhesus monkeys on Piaget's AB task: Evidence for dependence on dorsolateral prefrontal cortex. *Experimental Brain Research*, 74, 24–40.

Diamond, A., Zola-Morgan, S., & Squire, L.R. (1989). Successful performance by monkeys with lesions of the hippocampal formation on AB and object retrieval, two tasks that mark developmental changes in human infants. *Behavioral Neuroscience*, 103 (3), 526–537.

Feigenson, L., Carey, S., & Spelke, E. (2002). Infants' discrimination of number vs. continuous extent. *Cognitive Psychology*, 44, 33–66.

Finlay, B.L., & Darlington, R.D. (1995). Linked regularities in the development and evolution of mammalian brains. *Science*, 268, 1578–1584.

Fodor, J. (1980). On the impossibility of acquiring more powerful' structures. In M. Piattelli-Palmarini (ed.), *Language and learning: The debate between Jean Piaget and Noam Chomsky* (pp. 143–149). Cambridge, MA: Harvard University Press.

Fox, N., Kagan, J., & Weiskopf, S. (1979). The growth of memory during infancy. *Genetic Psychology Monographs*, 99 (1), 91–130.

Gergely, G., Nadasdy, Z., Csibra, G., & Biro, S. (1995). Taking the intentional stance at 12 months of age. *Cognition*, 56, 165–193.

Gershkoff-Stowe, L., Thal, J., Smith, L.B., & Namy, L.L. (1997). Categorization and its developmental relation to early language. *Child Development*, 68, 843–859.

Gibson, E.J. (1988). Exploratory behavior in the development of perceiving, acting, and the acquiring of knowledge. *Annual Review of Psychology*, 39, 1–41.

Gibson, K.R. (1990). New perspectives on instincts and intelligence: Brain size and the emergence of hierarchical mental constructional skills. In S.T. Parker and K.R. Gibson (eds), *'Language' and intelligence in monkeys and apes* (pp. 97–128). Cambridge: Cambridge University Press.

Gibson, K.R. (1991). Myelination and behavioral development: A comparative perspective on questions of neoteny, altriciality and intelligence. In K.R. Gibson & A.C. Petersen (eds), *Brain maturation and cognitive development* (pp. 29–63). New York: de Gruyter.

Gopnik, A., & Meltzoff, A.N. (1992). Categorization and naming: Basic level sorting in eighteen-month-olds and its relation to language. *Child Development*, 63, 1091–1103.

Gould, S.J. (1977). *Ontogeny and phylogeny*. Cambridge, MA: Harvard University Press.

Gould, S.J. (1984). Relationship of individual and group care. *Human Development*, 27, 233–239.

Gratch, G., & Landers, W.F. (1971). Stage IV of Piaget's theory of infants' object concepts: A longitudinal study. *Child Development*, 42 (2), 359–372.

Greenfield, P.M., & Savage-Rumbaugh, E.S. (1990). Grammatical combination in *Pan paniscus*: Process of learning and invention in the evolution and development of language. In S.T. Parker & K.R. Gibson (eds), *'Language' and intelligence in monkeys and apes: Comparative developmental perspectives* (pp. 540–578). Cambridge: Cambridge University Press.

Grigorakis, K. (1999). Numerical architectures in early manipulatory classification. Unpublished PhD thesis, University of California, Berkeley.

Houdé, O. (1997). Numerical development: From infant to the child. Wynn's (1992) paradigm in 2- and 3-year-olds. *Cognitive Development*, 12, 373–391.

Husaim, J.S., & Cohen, L.B. (1981). Infant learning of ill-defined categories. *Merrill-Palmer Quarterly*, 27, 443–456.

Huttenlocher, J., Jordan, N.C., & Levine, S.C. (1994). A mental model for early arithmetic. *Journal of Experimental Psychology*, 123, 284–296.

Inhelder, B., & Piaget, J. (1958). *The growth of logical thinking from childhood to adolescence*. New York: Basic.

Inhelder, B., & Piaget, J. (1964). *The early growth of logic in the child*. London: Routledge & Kegan Paul.

Jacobsen, T.A. (1984). The construction and regulation of early structures of logic. A cross-cultural study of infant cognitive development. Unpublished doctoral dissertation, University of California at Berkeley.

Johnson, S.P., & Aslin, R.N. (1995). Perception of object unity in 2-month-old infants. *Developmental Psychology*, 31 (5), 739–745.

Karmiloff-Smith, A. (1992). *Beyond modularity: A developmental perspective on cognitive science*. Cambridge, MA: MIT Press.

Kellman, P.J., & Spelke, E.S. (1983). Perception of partly occluded objects in infancy. *Cognitive Psychology*, 15, 483–524.

Kneale, W., & Kneale, M. (1962). *The development of logic*. Oxford: Oxford University Press.

Koechlin, E., Dehaene, S., & Mehler, J. (1997). Numerical transformation in five-month-old human infants. *Mathematical Cognition*, 3, 89–194.

Koehler, O. (1951). The ability of birds to count. *Bulletin of Animal Behavior*, 9, 41–45.

Koffka, K. (1928). *The growth of the mind*. London: Routledge & Kegan Paul.

Kohler, W. (1921). *Intelligenzpruefungen an Menschenaffen*. Berlin: Springer.

Kohler, W. (1926). *The mentality of apes*. NY: Harcourt, Brace.

Kotovsky, L., & Baillargeon, R. (1994). Calibration-based reasoning about collision events in 11-month-old infants. *Cognition*, 51, 107–129.

Kramer, E.E. (1970). *The nature and growth of modern mathematics*. New York: Hawthorne.

Kuhn, D., Langer, J., Kohlberg, L., & Haan, N. (1977). The development of formal operations in logical and moral judgment. *Genetic Psychology Monographs*, 95, 97–188.

Langer, J. (1969). *Theories of development*. New York: Holt, Rinehart & Winston.

Langer, J. (1980). *The origins of logic: Six to twelve months*. New York: Academic.

Langer, J. (1985). Necessity and possibility during infancy. *Archives de Psychologie*, 53, 61–75.

Langer, J. (1986). *The origins of logic: One to two years*. New York: Academic.

Langer, J. (1989). Comparison with the human child. In F. Antinucci (ed.), *Cognitive structure and development of nonhuman primates* (pp. 229–242). Hillsdale, NJ: Erlbaum.

Langer, J. (1990). Early cognitive development: Basic functions. In Hauert, C.A. (ed.), *Developmental psychology: Cognitive, perceptuo-motor, and neuropsychological perspectives* (pp. 19–42). Amsterdam: North Holland.

Langer, J. (1993). Comparative cognitive development. In K. Gibson & T. Ingold (eds), *Tools, language and cognition in human evolution* (pp. 300–313). New York: Cambridge University Press.

Langer, J. (1994a). From acting to understanding: The comparative development of meaning. In W.F. Overton & D. Palermo (eds), *The nature and ontogenesis of meaning* (pp. 191–213). Norwood, NJ: Erlbaum.

Langer, J. (1994b). Logic. In V.S. Ramachandren (ed.), *Encyclopedia of human behavior* (Vol. 3, pp. 83–91). San Diego: Academic.

Langer, J. (1996). Heterochrony and the evolution of primate cognitive development. In A.E. Russon, K.A. Bard, & S.T. Parker (eds), *Reaching into thought: The mind of the great apes* (pp. 257–277). Cambridge, MA: Cambridge University Press.

Langer, J. (1998). Phylogenetic and ontogenetic origins of logic: Classification. In J. Langer & M. Killen (eds), *Piaget, evolution and development* (pp. 33–54). Mahwah, NJ: Erlbaum.

Langer, J. (2000a). The descent of cognitive development. *Developmental Science*, 3, 361–378.

Langer, J. (2000b). The heterochronic evolution of primate cognitive development. In S.T. Parker, J. Langer, & M.L. McKinney (eds), *Biology, brains and behavior: The evolution of human development* (pp. 213–233). Santa Fe, NM: School of American Research Press.

Langer, J. (2000c). The mosaic evolution of cognitive and linguistic ontogeny. In M. Bowerman & S. Levinson (eds), *Language acquisition and conceptual development* (pp. 19–44). Cambridge: Cambridge University Press.

Langer, J. (2000d). Comparative mental development. *Journal of Adult Development*, 7, 23–30.

Langer, J., Schlesinger, M., Spinozzi, G., & Natale, F. (1998). Developing classification in action: I. Human infants. *Human Evolution*, 13, 107–124.

Langer, S.K. (1942). *Philosophy in a new key*. Cambridge, MA: Harvard University Press.

Lea, S.E.G., Slater, A.M., & Ryan, C.M.E. (1996). Perception of object unity in chicks: A comparison with the human infant. *Infant Behavior and Development*, 19, 501–504.

Leslie, A.M., & Keeble, S. (1987). Do six-month-olds perceive causality? *Cognition*, 25, 265–288.

Leslie, A.M. (1982). The perception of causality in infants. *Perception*, 11, 173–186.

Leslie, A.M. (1984). Infant perception of a manual pick-up event. *Cognitive Development*, 2, 19–32.

Leslie, A.M. (1994). ToMM, ToBy, and agency: Core architecture and domain specificity. In L. Hirschfeld & S. Gelman (eds), *Mapping the mind: Domain specificity in cognition and culture* (pp. 119–148). New York: Cambridge University Press.

Madole, K.L., & Cohen, L.B. (1995). The role of object parts in infants' attention to form–function correlations. *Developmental Psychology*, 32, 637–648.

Madole, K.L., Oakes, L.M., & Cohen, L.B. (1993). Developmental changes in infants' attention to function and form–function correlations. *Cognitive Development*, 8, 189–209.

Marcovitch, S., & Zelazo, P.D. (1999). The A-not-B error: Results from a logistic meta-analysis. *Child Development*, 70, 1297–1314.

McKinney, M.L., & McNamara, J.K. (1991). *Heterochrony: The evolution of ontogeny*. New York: Plenum.

Mechner, F. (1958). Probability relations within response sequences under ratio reinforcement. *Journal of the Experimental Analysis of Behavior*, 1, 109–121.

Meltzoff, A.N., & Moore, M.K. (1999). A new foundation for cognitive development in infancy: The birth of the representational infant. In E.K. Scholnick, K. Nelson, S.A. Gelman, & P.H. Miller (eds), *Conceptual Development. Piaget's Legacy*. Mahwah, NJ: Erlbaum.

Michel, G.G., & Moore, C.L. (1995). *Developmental psychobiology*. Cambridge, MA: MIT Press.

Michotte, A. (1963). *The perception of causality*. New York: Basic.

Mix, K.S., Levine, S.C., & Huttenlocher, J. (1997). Numerical abstraction in human infants: Another look. *Developmental Psychology*, 33, 423–428.

Montague, A. (1989). *Growing young*. New York: McGraw-Hill.

Moore, D., Benenson, J., Reznick, J.S., Peterson, M., & Kagan, J. (1987). Effect of auditory numerical information on infants' looking behavior: Contradictory evidence. *Developmental Psychology*, 23, 665–670.

Moore, D.S. (1997). Infant mathematical skills? A conceptual replication. Poster session presented at the biennial meeting of the Society for Research in Child Development, Washington, DC, April.

Munakata, Y. (1998). Infant perseveration and implications for object permanence theories: A PDP model of the AB task. *Developmental Science*, 1 (2), 161–211.

Munakata, Y., McClelland, J.L., Johnson, M.H., & Siegler, R.S. (1997). Rethinking infant knowledge: Toward an adaptive process account of successes and failures on object permanence tasks. *Psychological Review*, 104, 686–713.

Natale, F. (1989). Causality II: The stick problem. In F. Antinucci (ed.), *Cognitive structure and development in nonhuman primates* (pp. 121–133). Hillsdale, NJ: Erlbaum.

Nelson, K. (1973). Some evidence for the primacy of categorization and its functional basis. *Merrill-Palmer Quarterly*, 19, 21–39.

Oakes, L.M. (1994). Development of infants' use of continuity cues in their perception of causality. *Developmental Psychology*, 30, 869–879.

Oakes, L.M., & Cohen, L.B. (1990). Infant perception of a causal event. *Cognitive Development*, 5, 193–207.

Oakes, L.M., & Kanass, K.N. (1999). That's the way the ball bounces: Infants' and adults' perception of spatial and temporal contiguity in collisions involving bouncing balls. *Developmental Science*, 2, 86–101.

Paus, T., Zijdenbos, A., Worsley, K., Collins, D.L., Blumenthal, J., Giedd, J.N., Rapoport, J.L., & Evans, A.C. (1999). Structural maturation of neural pathways in children and adolescents: *In vivo* study. *Science*, 283, 1908–1911.

Piaget, J. (1952a). *The origins of intelligence in children*. New York: International Universities Press.

Piaget, J. (1952b). *The child's conception of number*. London: Routledge & Kegan Paul.

Piaget, J. (1954). *The construction of reality in the child*. New York: Basic.

Piaget, J. (1971). *Biology and knowledge*. Chicago: University of Chicago Press.

Piaget, J. (1972). *Essai de logique opératoire*. Paris: Dunod.

Piaget, J. (1974). *Understanding causality*. New York: Norton.

Piaget, J., Grize, J.B., Szeminska, A., & Vinh Bang (1977). *Epistemology and psychology of functions*. Dordrecht: Reidel.

Potí, P., & Langer, J. (2001). Spontaneous spatial constructions by chimpanzees (*Pan troglodytes, Pan paniscus*). *Developmental Science*, 4, 474–484.

Potí, P., Langer, J., Savage-Rumbaugh, E.S., & Brakke, K.E. (1999). Spontaneous logicomathematical constructions by chimpanzees (*Pan troglodytes, Pan paniscus*). *Animal Cognition*, 2, 147–156.

Purves, D. (1988). *Body and brain: A trophic theory of neural connections*. Cambridge, MA: Harvard University Press.

Quinn, P.C. (1987). The categorical representation of visual pattern information by young infants. *Cognition*, 27, 145–179.

Quinn, P.C., & Eimas, P.D. (1986). On categorization in early infancy. *Merrill-Palmer Quarterly*, 32, 331–363.

Quinn, P.C., Eimas, P.D., & Rosenkranz, S.L. (1993). Evidence for representations of perceptually similar natural categories by 3-month-old and 4-month-old infants. *Perception*, 22, 463–475.

Regolin, L., & Vallortigara, G. (1995). Perception of partly occluded objects by young chicks. *Perception and Psychophysics*, 57, 971–976.

Reznick, J.S., & Kagan, J. (1983). Category detection in infancy. In L.P. Lipsitt (ed.), *Advances in infancy research* (Vol. 2, pp. 79–111). Norwood, NJ: Ablex.

Riccuiti, H.N. (1965). Object grouping and selective ordering behavior in infants 12 to 24 months. *Merrill-Palmer Quarterly*, 11, 129–148.

Rivera, S.M., Wakeley, A., & Langer, J. (1999). The drawbridge phenomenon: Representational reasoning or perceptual preference? *Developmental Psychology*, 35, 427–435.

Rovee, C.K., & Rovee, D.T. (1969). Conjugate reinforcement in infant exploratory behavior. *Journal of Experimental Child Psychology*, 8, 33–39.

Savage-Rumbaugh, E.S., Murphy, J., Sevcik, R.A., Brakke, K.E., Williams, S.L., & Rumbaugh, D.M. (1993). *Language comprehension in ape and child. Monographs of the Society for Research in Child Development*, Vol. 58, nos 3–4.

Schlesinger, M., & Langer, J. (1993). The developmental relations between sensorimotor classification and perceptual categorization in early infancy. Paper presented at the Meeting of the Society for Research in Child Development, Chicago, March.

Schlesinger, M., & Langer, J. (1999). Infants' developing expectations of possible and impossible tool-use events between the ages of 8 and 12 months. *Developmental Science*, 2, 196–206.

Simon, T.J. (1997). Reconceptualizing the origins of number knowledge: A 'non-numerical' account. *Cognitive Development*, 12, 349–372.

Simon, T.J. (1998). Computational evidence for the foundations of numerical competence. *Developmental Science*, 1, 71–78.

Simon, T.J., Hespos, S J., & Rochat, P. (1995). Do infants understand simple arithmetic? A replication of Wynn (1992). *Cognitive Development*, 10, 253–269.

Slater, A., Johnson, S.P., Brown, E., & Badenoch, M. (1996). Newborn infants' perception of partly occluded objects. *Infant Behavior & Development*, 19 (1), 145–148.

Slater, A., Johnson, S.P., Kellman, P.H., & Spelke, E. (1994). The role of three-dimensional depth cues in infants' perception of partly occluded objects. *Early Development and Parenting*, 3, 187–191.

Slater, A., Morison, V., Somers, M., Mattock, A., Brown, E., & Taylor, D. (1990). Newborn and older infants' perception of partly occluded objects. *Infant Behavior and Development*, 13, 33–49.

Slotnick, C. (1984). The organization and regulation of block constructions: A comparison of autistic and normal children's cognitive development. Unpublished doctoral dissertation, University of California, Berkeley.

Smith, H. (1992). Life history and the evolution of human maturation. *Evolutionary Anthropology*, 1, 134–142.

Smith, L.B., Thelen, E., Titzer, R., & McLin, D. (1999). Knowing the context of acting: The task dynamics of the A-not-B error. *Psychological Review*, 106 (2), 235–260.

Sophian, C. (1985). Perseveration and infants' search: A comparison of two- and three-location tasks. *Developmental Psychology*, 21, 187–194.

Sophian, C., & Adams, N. (1987). Infants' understanding of numerical transformations. *British Journal of Developmental Psychology*, 5, 257–264.

Sowell, E.R., Thompson, P.M., Holmes, C.J., Jernigan, T.L., & Toga, A.W. (1999). *In vivo* evidence for post-adolescent brain maturation in frontal and striatal regions. *Nature Neuroscience*, 2, 859–861.

Spelke, E.S. (1985). Perception of unity, persistence, and identity: Thoughts on infants' conceptions of objects. In J. Mehler & R. Fox (eds), *Neonate cognition: Beyond the blooming, buzzing confusion* (pp. 89–113). Hillsdale, NJ: Erlbaum.

Spelke, E.S., & Newport, E.L. (1998). Nativism, empiricism, and the development of knowledge. In W. Damon (ed.), *Handbook of Child Psychology* (Vol. 1, pp. 275–340). New York: Wiley.

Spelke, E.S., Brieinlinger, K., Macomber, J., & Jacobson, K. (1992). Origins of knowledge. *Psychological Review*, 99, 605–632.

Spinozzi, G. (1993). The development of spontaneous classificatory behavior in chimpanzees (*Pan troglodytes*). *Journal of Comparative Psychology*, 107, 193–200.

Spinozzi, G., & Langer, J. (1999). Spontaneous classification in action by a human-enculturated and language-reared bonobo (*Pan paniscus*) and common chimpanzees (*Pan troglodytes*). *Journal of Comparative Psychology*, 113, 286–296.

Spinozzi, G., & Natale, F. (1989). Classification. In F. Antinucci (ed.), *Cognitive structure and development of nonhuman primates* (pp. 163–188). Hillsdale, NJ: Erlbaum.

Spinozzi, G., & Potí, P. (1989). Causality: I. The support problem. In F. Antinucci (ed.), *Cognitive structure and development of nonhuman primates* (pp. 113–120). Hillsdale, NJ: Erlbaum.

Spinozzi, G., Natale, F., Langer, J., & Brakke, K. (1999). Spontaneous class grouping behavior by bonobos (*Pan paniscus*) and common chimpanzees (*Pan troglodytes*). *Animal Cognition*, 2, 157–170.

Spinozzi, G., Natale, F., Langer, J., & Schlesinger, M. (1998). Developing classification in action: II. Young chimpanzees (*Pan troglodytes). Human Evolution*, 13, 125–139.

Starkey, D. (1981). The origins of concept formation: Object sorting and object preference in early infancy. *Child Development*, 52, 489–497.

Starkey, P. (1992). The early development of numerical reasoning. *Cognition*, 43, 93–126.

Starkey, P., & Cooper, R.G. (1980). Perception of numbers by human infants. *Science*, 210, 1033–1035.

Starkey, P., & Cooper, R.G. (1995). The development of subitizing in young children. *British Journal of Developmental Psychology*, 13, 399–420.

Starkey, P., Spelke, E., & Gelman, R. (1983). Detection of intermodal correspondence by human infants. *Science*, 222, 179–181.

Starkey, P., Spelke, E., & Gelman, R. (1990). Numerical abstraction in human infants. *Cognition*, 36, 97–128.

Strauss, M.S., & Curtis, L.E. (1981). Infant perception of numerosity. *Child Development*, 52, 1146–1152.

Sugarman, S. (1983). *Children's early thought: Developments in classification*. New York: Cambridge University Press.

Uller, C., Carey, S., Huntley-Fenner, G., & Klatt, L. (1999). What representation might underlie infant numerical knowledge? *Cognitive Development*, 14, 1–36.

Uzgiris, I.C., & Hunt, J.McV. (1975). *Assessment in infancy: Ordinal scales of psychological development*. Urbana, IL: University of Illinois Press.

Van Loosbroek, E., & Smitsman, A.W. (1990). Visual perception of numerosity in infancy. *Developmental Psychology*, 26, 916–922.

Vilette, B. (1996). De la 'proto-arithmétique' aux connaissances additives et soustractives. *Revue de Psychologie de l'Education*, 3, 25–43.

Vilette, B., & Mazouz, K. (1998). Les transformations numériques et spatiales entre deux et quatre ans. *Archives de Psychologie*, 66, 35–47.

Vygotsky, L.S. (1962). *Thought and language*. New York: Wiley and MIT.

Wakeley, A., Rivera, S., & Langer, J. (2000). Can young infants add and subtract? *Child Development*, 71, 1525–1534.

Watson, J.S. (1985). Bases of causal inference in infancy.

In L. Lipsitt & C. Rovee-Collier (eds), *Advances in Infant Behavior and Development*. Norwood, NJ: Ablex.

Werner, H. (1948). *Comparative psychology of mental development*. New York: International Universities Press.

Werner, H., & Kaplan, B. (1963). *Symbol formation*. New York: Wiley.

Wertheimer, M. (1945). *Productive thinking*. New York: Harper.

Whiten, A., Goodall, J., McGrew, W.C., Nishida, T., Reynolds, V., Sugiyama, Y., Tutin, C.E.G., Wrangham, R.W., & Boesch, C. (1999). Cultures in chimpanzees. *Nature*, 399, 682–685.

Willats, P. (1984). The stage-IV infant's solution of problems requiring the use of supports. *Infant Behavior and Development*, 7, 125–134.

Willats, P. (1990). Development of problem-solving strategies in infancy. In D.F. Bjorkland (ed.), *Children's strategies: Contemporary views of cognitive development*. Hillsdale, NJ: Erlbaum.

Willats, P. (1999). Development of means–ends behavior in young infants: Pulling a support to retrieve a distant object. *Developmental Psychology*, 35, 651–667.

Woodward, A.L. (1998). Infants selectively encode the goal object of an actor's reach. *Cognition*, 69, 1–34.

Wynn, K. (1992a). Addition and subtraction in human infants. *Nature*, 358, 749–750.

Wynn, K. (1992b). Evidence against empiricist account of the origins of numerical knowledge. *Mind and Language*, 7, 315–322.

Wynn, K. (1995). Origins of numerical knowledge. *Mathematical Cognition*, 1, 35–60.

Wynn, K. (1996). Infants' individuation and enumeration of actions. *Psychological Science*, 7, 164–169.

Wynn, K. (1998). Psychological foundations of number: Numerical competence in human infants. *Trends in Cognitive Sciences*, 2, 296–303.

Wynn, K., & Chiang, W.-C. (1998). Limits to object knowledge in 8-month-olds. Paper presented at the Eleventh International Conference on Infant Studies, Atlanta, GA, April.

Xu, F., & Carey, S. (1996). Infants' metaphysics: the case of numerical identity. *Cognitive Psychology*, 30, 1–43.

Yerkes, R.M., & Learned, B.W. (1925). *Chimpanzee intelligence and its vocal expression*. Baltimore: Williams & Wilkins.

Younger, B. (1990). Infants' detection of correlations among feature categories. *Child Development*, 61, 614–620.

Younger, B., & Cohen, L.B. (1986). Developmental change in infants' perception of correlations among attributes. *Child Development*, 57, 803–815.

8

Tool Use and Tool Making: A Developmental Action Perspective

AD W. SMITSMAN and RAOUL M. BONGERS

Introduction

The last 20 years have seen an increase in the number of studies on the development of action inspired by a dynamic systems view and the perspective provided by ecological psychology (see Bertenthal & Clifton, 1998; Ulrich, 1997; see van Geert, Chapter 28 in this volume, for an overview). Most of these studies addressed relatively simple systems that were confined to the bodily organizations of infants and toddlers, and actions such as reaching, grasping and locomotion. However, children's developing action systems also involve organizations that extend the body. Human action systems include various types of environmental objects and artifacts called tools, which enhance the individual's capacity to act. After the first year of life, tool use and later tool making become fundamental components for the action systems which children develop.

In this chapter we will expand on the insights from the dynamical systems perspective and ecological psychology to provide an action framework for tool use and tool making. The framework addresses the goal directed organizations of postures and movements, called action systems (Pick, 1989), that an actor configures to regulate the relationship with the environment. Bodily and environmental resources sustain these organizations. We will argue that tool use and tool making originate from the opportunity that environmental objects furnish to modify bodily resources for a goal. As a consequence, using a tool allows the actor to regulate relationships with the environment that were beyond control of the actor. Thus, the action problem that motivates tool use involves the control of a relationship with the environment. Tool making extends the perception–action cycles that tool use involves. Some of the cycles will now involve activities to make the implement suitable to its task. These activities may even encompass other persons than the tool user him/herself. Nevertheless, the difference between tool use and tool making is gradual, and not a fundamental one. To realize this, one should note that it is not the implement that determines whether it will be a tool, but the way that it is used (see Ingold, 1997, 1993b for a more elaborate discussion on this issue).

To start with we will show how accomplishments such as reaching, grasping and walking enable young children to modify an action system and how tool use and tool making result from their exploitation of new resources as they become available. Subsequently we will discuss different views on tool use and redefine tool use and tool making from an action perspective. We will also highlight the processes from which tool use and tool making evolve. To further clarify the different action problems a child is faced with in tool use and tool making, we will use the concept of action system. Finally, we will discuss the invariant spatio-temporal structures that children learn to regulate when using a tool and discuss some research to clarify the arguments we present.

Origins of Tool Use and Tool Making: Modification of an Action System

Around the end of the first year of life, the human infant has attained important milestones with respect to the capacity for action. By about this time, infants are able to reach, grasp, and manipulate objects. Moreover, they are able to sit independently, and are taking their first walking steps. The increased postural control and flexibility in sitting that develops around the end of the first year greatly enhances the capacity of reaching towards objects at different locations and distances. It also enhances the capacity of grasping and manipulation (Berthenthal & von Hofsten, 1998; Thelen & Spencer, 1998). The attainment of upright bipedal locomotion by the beginning of the second year (Bril & Breniere, 1992; 1993; Clark & Phillips, 1993) further frees the hands and extends the infant's span in both space and time, and in a variety of manual encounters with the surrounding environment.

What is the importance of these motor milestones for the child's developing capacities? Confining the significance of these accomplishments to the immediate goals they serve greatly underestimates their contribution to future developments that take place, at least for the human infant. Goals such as obtaining objects and moving from one place to another, which are usually attained by actions such as reaching, grasping and locomotion, are of great value to the child. But more important perhaps is that actions such as reaching and grasping also enable children to modify their existing capacity for action (Lockman, 2000; Smitsman, 1997). These actions set the stage for the development of new skills that involve tool use. For example, by grasping a stick, the child gains a reaching system that permits touching objects at a greater distance. Also, it allows the child to safely approach objects which might otherwise have been too dangerous. Of course, the new opportunities for action that the environment furnishes only emerge when the child grasps a stick that it can handle in mass, size and shape. Given that such is the case, new opportunities for the arm plus stick can be discovered by exploring surrounding surfaces. One should note that in order to grasp the object, the child does not need to understand in advance how a hand-held object affects the relationship with the surrounding layout. Rather, understanding emerges from action when the child explores opportunities the environment may afford to the modified system. Therefore, the change in capacity for action emerges from the way the object modifies the system.

The example of stick use indicates that, in principle, the boundary of a child's bodily resources for action is a flexible one (Lockman, 2000; Smitsman, 1997). It shows that taking advantage of implements can modify these resources. This means that the capacity for action may expand, depending on whether and which implement the actor assembles from the environment to become part of the action. For instance, a heavy object allows the child to exert greater force on surfaces when hitting, but reduces the capacity of the arm to wield and point, and consequently to precisely aim at the target. More generally, by assembling environmental elements, a capacity may expand for some tasks and diminish for others. What happens to an action system depends on the fit of a newly assembled element, existing (bodily) components, the fit of the changed system and the context for the task. An element that does not fit existing components will only perturb behavioral organizations. Therefore, whether an environmental element becomes a tool depends on how it affects an action system and the system's relationship with the environment. Thus, a tool cannot be considered independently from an action system of which it forms a part and its impact on the relationship of the system with the environment.

In defining tool use and its origins we did not attribute a particular significance to some components above others. Hands, body and brain are equally important (Connolly & Elliott, 1972). In our view, no particular component is especially responsible for the emergence of tool use; this position accords with a dynamical systems view of action (Thelen & Smith, 1994), which is discussed below. Indirect support for this view also comes from ethological studies that compare tool use in different species, for instance in apes (McGrew, 1993). McGrew's comparison revealed that the frequency of tool use in apes, as observed in different studies, was unrelated to factors such as brain size, several measures of intelligence, and ecology (ground living or arboreal). In our opinion, the causal mechanisms for the emergence of tool use have to be found in the way different components interact to regulate the relationship with the environment. The second remark concerns the means for expanding the capacity to act. Resources may be assembled in various ways from the animate and inanimate environment. Manipulation forms a powerful means for a child in making environmental objects a part of him/herself. But other activities, manual as well as nonmanual, may serve similar purposes. Tool use is not confined to manual activities, graspable objects or the manipulation of objects. Animate objects may become tools as well by manual, facial and vocal gestures (Acredolo & Goodwyn, 1988; Sugarman, 1984). By pointing, a child may activate a caregiver to grasp an object beyond her reach. We will consider every implement as a tool that, coupled to an action system, enhances the capacity of the system for a goal. To simplify discussion for this chapter, we will mainly focus on the use of graspable solid objects.

The examples of stick use employed serve to highlight the fundamental relation that exists between tool use and action. Tool use emerged to solve action problems in the first place. Action problems refer to problems actors face in regulating a relationship with the environment. They include finding the appropriate components (e.g. bodily resources, tools, environmental resources) for the action system and coordinating them such that an intended goal can be ascertained. However, tool use also creates action problems. Implements challenge the child to configure new behavioral organizations and to explore and exploit new environmental opportunities that may arise in relation to these behavioral organizations. The development of action is challenged by action problems that arise to regulate the relation with the environment (Bertenthal & Clifton, 1998; Goldfield, 1995; Gottlieb, 1992; 1997; Reed & Bril, 1996; Thelen & Smith, 1994: Smitsman, 2000). To conclude, in order to understand what tool use and tool making involve, we need to address the action problem that motivated tool use and tool making. Moreover, we hypothesize that the way the action problem arises and is solved is akin to the way developmental processes proceed. Therefore, we also need a developmental perspective to unravel the underlying mechanisms that motivate and support tool use and tool making. These mechanisms concern the child as well as the environment. Tool use and tool making are embedded in an environment that is inanimate as well as animate, cultural as well as social. In tool use and tool making human actors become, in a manner of speaking, creators of themselves as well as of their environment. In the following paragraphs we will discuss each of these issues in more detail, but first we will briefly discuss some old and new perspectives and issues with respect to action and tool use.

Old and New Perspectives and Issues

The Cognitive View

Earlier studies of tool use and tool making did not focus on action itself, or the actor's relationship with the environment. Instead, guided by the assumption that objects and movements with those objects formed the units of action in tool use, the issues concerned the demands that tool use would impose on the brain to orchestrate those movements (K.R. Gibson, 1977; 1981; Greenfield, 1991; Koslowski & Bruner, 1972; McCarty, Clifton, & Collard,1999). This view reduced tool use to a form of object manipulation that differed in complexity from simpler forms such as reaching, grasping and holding, which involved only one object as the goal of action (Bard, 1993; Parker & K.R. Gibson, 1977; Piaget, 1954). The greater complexity would result from the fact that an object, originally the target, served as the means to act on another target object in tool use. Insight into such means–end relationships was taken to form the core for tool use to evolve. Assuming that means–end relationships would also be a key to intelligence, psychologists, anthropologists, ethologists, archeologists and paleontologists have studied tool use and tool making in hominids and lower species, and in developing children (see Berthelet & Chavaillon, 1993 for an overview on these issues). Despite these efforts, satisfactory answers were not found. Ethologists demonstrated tool use in nearly every species (Beck, 1980), leading to the conclusion that intelligence could not be unraveled by studying tool use. As a result, the interest in tool use has waned.

The narrow focus on object manipulation and means–end relationships has reduced insight not only into what could be conceived as examples of intelligent behavior (see e.g. van de Grind, 1997 for elaborate discussions on this issue) but also into tool use and its origins. As with respect to tool use, it has also led to fruitless discussions about whether animals show tool use when, instead of manipulating an object, they take advantage of environmental surfaces in some other way. For instance, inspired by Piaget's (1954) views on object manipulation, scientists (e.g. Parker & K.R. Gibson, 1977) began to distinguish tool use from what they called proto-tool use. They considered, for instance, the actions of a bird, such as a seagull that drops an oyster on a rock to break the shell, to be a case not of tool use but of what they called proto-tool use. Indeed the bird does not manipulate an object, for instance a heavy stone to hit the oyster. This would have been regarded as tool use, but might have perturbed the animal's behavior. The bird is not bound by definitions of tool use and has found another, perhaps more satisfactory way to open the oyster; namely carrying the lighter and more easily graspable oyster and then dropping it above surfaces that will break the oyster's shell on dropping.

Although tool use is widely spread over the animal kingdom, it is certainly true that tool use and tool making in man considerably outweigh those activities in lower species. But, given the generality of their occurrence in the animal kingdom, one may question whether this justifies the conclusion that a large complex hominid brain is sufficient for tool use to evolve. Whether and how tool use evolves in a species depends just as much on local circumstances (McGrew, 1993: Sugiyama, 1993). In order to better understand how tool use emerges and develops, it would make more sense to address the action problem that challenges tool use and tool making, and the underlying bodily and environmental resources that are available to solve the problem. Fundamental questions that are still waiting to be studied concern: what are the mechanisms that underlie tool use and tool making in man and other species? What can we learn about tool use and, more importantly, about action and its development, from studying these mechanisms? These are questions for which no satisfactory answers are yet available. Presumably there are no simple answers to these questions, such as a larger brain resulting in a greater complexity of brain architecture, or a greater dexterity as the result of erect locomotion. All such factors might have contributed to the evolution of tool use in hominids and man, as new theoretical perspectives and research on action and its development suggest, in combination with recent studies on tool use in hominids (McGrew, 1993). These results are also important for understanding the development of tool use in the child. To investigate whether and how tool use arises and is sustained, we have to take into account many circumstances, some haphazard and others more systematic. It would be too simplistic to confine questions solely to the cognitive orchestration of means–end relationships involved in the manipulation of objects. Instead, it would be more sensible to address both the body and the brain and the environment that surrounds them for studying tool use and tool making.

An Action Perspective

During the last 10 to 15 years the study of motor development, or *action* development as it is now called, has seen new stimulating insights. These insights have led to a resurgence of interest in the study of action, especially in infancy, and they also hold promise for the study of tool use and tool making. Inspired by Bernstein's (1967) views on motor coordination and control, James Gibson's (1966; 1979/1986) ecological approach to perception, and Eleanor Gibson's (1969; 1988; 1997) related approach to perceptual development, new and challenging questions about action and its development have been addressed. The focus has shifted to the dynamic nature of action and its regulatory function with respect to the relationship with the environment (see Bertenthal & Clifton, 1998; Goldfield, 1995; Hopkins & Butterworth, 1997; Thelen & Smith, 1994). Therefore, action is studied embedded in the environment (Reed, 1996), where the action system is constrained for the specific task at hand (Beek & Bingham, 1991; Newell, 1986; 1996). The assembly of goal directed, time dependent organizations of bodily, brain and environmental resources makes the regulatory function of action possible. James Gibson (1979/1986) referred to the environmental resources that support those organizations as *affordances*: 'The affordances of the environment are what it offers the animal, what it provides or furnishes, either for good or ill' (1979/1986, p. 127). In Gibson's definition, affordances denote the meaning of the animate and inanimate environment for behavior. However, this meaning is not constructed by the active engagement with the environment, but rather forms the cause for such an engagement, just as the body and the components that compose the body do. Therefore, in Gibson's view, affordances have to be perceived in the first place to guide action. They also entail goals that the environment furnishes the actor. For example, an object of a mass, shape, and size that fits the hand of a child and the strength of its arms for lifting may become a goal for grasping and manual exploration. For a child who discovers this goal, it forms a challenge to develop the behavioral skills to take advantage of the affordances that graspable objects furnish. E.J. Gibson (1988) therefore argued that affordances form the targets of infants' exploratory behavior, and the basis for the development of actions.

The concept of affordance is of central concern to the ecological approach. The concept expresses the mutuality between resources that are available in the environment and those that are provided by the body and the brain. Turvey and Shaw (Shaw & Turvey, 1981; Turvey & Shaw, 1979) have called the bodily resources *effectivities*. The concept of affordance also expresses the tight connection of perception and action that is needed to take advantage of those resources. Gibson was right in underscoring the significance of this concept for understanding action and perception. When we consider the dynamic nature of the behavioral patterns that underlie action, we see that their stability depends as much on properties supplied by the body as on properties that are furnished by the environment. In dynamical systems terms, affordances form a niche for the actor of regions for the establishment of stable behavioral organizations (Reed & Bril, 1996). For instance, postural balance for walking, and a propelling force to alternately move the center of mass of the body over the feet, depend as much on neuromuscular and intersegmental synergies of the actor as on the gravity field and the support surface on which to walk. The typical step cycle that characterizes bipedal locomotion will destabilize at changes of any of these components at a critical value, irrespective of whether they belong to the actor or the environment. Given the variability of the environment and the need for an agent to preserve the stability of the ongoing activities, Gibson's claim that affordances are perceived properties of the environment enables understanding of how the guidance of action is possible under continuously changing circumstances. It leaves research with the more difficult question of how we perceive affordances and the information that specifies affordances to the individual (Michaels & Beek, 1995; Smitsman, 1995; Stoffregen & Bardy, 2001). This question is of importance to understand how behavior may become goal directed as a result of the availability of information to the senses and the coordinated activity of those senses to gather this information that guides action.

Affordances and Tool Use

James Gibson used tool use as the prototypical example to highlight the concept of affordance. Tool use most clearly illustrates that the environment is perceived relationally, and not as composed of single particles that bear no relationship to the actor. An affordance denotes an opportunity to engage in a particular relationship, and so do tools (Reed, 1996). Tools are affordances. Although tools are often also objects, i.e. bounded entities, as affordances they exist only as a relationship to an action system: a time dependent organization of postures and movements that is configured to serve a particular category of goals, such as locomotion or manipulation. Therefore, the discovery of a tool involves more than just the discovery of an object with a particular function. Instead, it involves the discovery of an opportunity for relating an object to an action system and the awareness of its relationship with the environment that evolves by embedding the object in the system.

It does not require a big step to acknowledge that awareness of the opportunity to embed an object in an action system implies awareness of what happens to the capacity of the system when the opportunity is realized. The detection of environmental affordances implies co-perception of the 'self', as having the means to take advantage of these affordances (Fogel, 1993; Neisser, 1993; Reed, 1996). Sticks not only afford grasping, but when grasped they change the geometric, dynamic and even information gathering properties of the system for touching and manipulating environmental surfaces. Thus, an object that affords grasping also affords a particular modification of the action system and a different engagement with the surrounding layout. As a consequence, perceiving a graspable object entails the possibility of discovering a way of modifying the capacity for the action system relative to new affordances that become available when the system is modified. Although the new affordances emerge in relation to the modified system, they are not constructed by modifying the system. Affordances are environmental properties with reference to an action system. When the action system changes, the relationship with the environment changes and therefore also the environmental properties that embody this relationship, irrespective of whether these changes occur due to growth, accidents, or on purpose as in tool use. In all such cases, existing affordances may disappear and new ones may emerge.

Discovery of new affordances is possible because the relationship with the environment is continuous and because opportunities for action do not exist in isolation but are embedded in other relationships that the actor has with the environment. Therefore, realization of an opportunity always affects the other relationships. One cannot hold a stick in one's hand without changing the relationship of the body to the surroundings, as we argued before. In our view, tool use and tool making find their origin in the actor's discovery of how different relationships are nested for achieving an action. Perceiving a hammer means that one perceives the 'graspableness' of an object, which involves a relationship to the hand, as nested within a relationship of the object plus hand to another target object, be it a nail, a stone or any other object to be hit. This nested structure encompasses several properties that concern the shape, size, mass and material of which the tool object is composed. However, these properties imply the hand as well as the target to be hit. Hammers therefore have a handle to make them graspable. For hitting, a head may be attached to the long axis of the handle, which varies in shape, size and material and in how it is attached to the handle depending on whether a nail, a stone, or a piece of wood has to be hit. It should be noted that the tool emerges in the action of the hand. A stick may also be used even for hitting different target objects. The different tools it entails arise from the way the stick is manipulated. Ingold (1997) refers to aborigines from New Zealand who used a very limited number of tools for an enormous variety of tasks. Their skill in tool use arises from the different ways they were able to use these tools. This example shows how gradual the difference is between tool use and tool making.

Affordances refer to the complementary environmental part of a relationship for which an actor forms the other part, or the actor's bodily properties, called effectivities by Shaw and Turvey (1981). A tool points, however, to an actor as well as to an environmental target. One might argue that the duality that qualifies affordances therefore turns into a threefold relationship when a tool is involved (van Leeuwen, Smitsman, & van Leeuwen, 1994). Although such seems superficially the case, we like to argue that this view mistakenly conceives a tool as an object whose existence indeed does not imply an actor. However, the duality that characterizes the affordance–effectivity relationship continues to exist when the action system involves tool use. Tools on the contrary do not exist without an actor. Their existence implies the activities of an actor. The above example from Ingold (1997) concerning tool use by aborigines from New Zealand most clearly illustrates that tools are made in the practice of using the tool which involves perceiving and acting. Perceiving an object as a tool means, therefore, perceiving the object as a component of the 'self', or of another 'self', when another individual is using the tool. Ingold (1997) pursues this argument one step further by stating that objects become tools not by design but by the practice of the tool user. A final argument against postulating a discontinuity in the kind of relationship with the environment when tool use takes place is that nesting of relationships also occurs when actions do not involve tool use. For instance, in reaching, activities of looking and of head and trunk movements are nested within the act of reaching. They prepare the extension of the arm in ensuring an unimpeded reach. The difference with tool use is not the nesting of the activities, but the fact that an external object complements the action system. Postulating a difference between tool use and nontooling activities means essentially a denial of the flexible boundary of the action system, and the reality of affordances.

In sum, tool use and tool making indicate that individuals are able to detect opportunities for action. Those opportunities are nested within other opportunities. This insight must guide their activities of tool use as well as tool making. In both cases, activities of using the tool form the kernel of the efforts that take place. In the case of tool making, modifications of the object have to anticipate the use of the tool to become meaningful. The cycle of activities may be more elaborate in the case of tool making and even extend to other actors, but it cannot exist independently of the use of the tool. For activities to become tool making they need to anticipate tool use. In tool use an object is transformed into a tool (see Ingold, 1997 for a more elaborate discussion on tool use, tool making and technology).

Embedding Tools in an Action System

Coupling an implement to an action system modifies the system. Tool use takes advantage of this fundamental fact. The way in which the coupling is achieved and how the new system will function may vary considerably, depending on the properties of the implement and the goal the actor intends to achieve. For activities such as scooping, slicing, or hammering, the tool is coupled to a limb, which is the hand. The interaction with the environment is regulated by manual activities that are directed at mechanical events at the interface of tool and environment. Thus, the tool becomes the new end effector, instead of the hand. Tool use may also involve other objects, activities, events and ways of coupling, without an object that is held and literally attached to the body. For instance, animate objects can be more easily and safely used as instruments by exploiting their capacity to perceive and act. Another difference concerns the goal of tool use. In the foregoing cases, events that occur at the interface of the tool and the environment formed the goal of action. The tool user takes advantage of the tool to regulate those events. However, tool use can also take place without having the events at the interface of tool and environment as the final goal for action. Action in fact encompasses many goals, nested within cycles of activities that take place over time and space. Tools may serve any of these cycles and goals. For instance when a chair is used to ensure a stable posture for playing the piano, or working at a computer, the chair functions as a tool. It enhances the capacity of the action system for performing these tasks. It is a tool although the ultimate goal of the activities concerns not the chair but the interface of the hands and the computer or piano. A nice example of tool use serving a subgoal comes from one of Köhler's (1925) famous studies on tool use in chimpanzees. Köhler showed how a chimpanzee discovered how to displace a box to a position below a suspended banana in order to reach the banana that otherwise would remain beyond reach. By selecting and moving the box, the animal organized a reach that encompassed the box and extended the limits of the body for reaching. The animal's solution of the action problem shows awareness of the bodily limits and affordances that are available (a box for displacement and for providing a stable posture and position that brings the banana within reach) for enhancing capacity. The reach itself was not achieved by regulating an interaction between the box and the banana – another and perhaps less successful solution to modify the reaching system. The inventiveness of the animal's solution would remain unnoticed if one confined the reaching system to activities of the limb that is used for reaching and tool use to the object this limb manipulates. By adapting the relation between the feet and the floor to regulate the relation between the hand and the banana, the animal has indeed found a smart solution to solve the action problem. These relations are controlled at the level of the interacting surfaces of body, box and floor, and banana.

Regulation of Topologies

Events at the interface of tool and environment take place for the tool user at different levels. At the level of surfaces and materials, they are characterized geometrically by a particular topology. Here we loosely define a topology as a spatial arrangement of surfaces of tool and goal object that is maintained over time. At the lower level, patterns of energy underlie and sustain the topology as we will exemplify below. The tool user can regulate these patterns of energy by arranging the topology that is needed for tool and target object. J.J. Gibson has therefore called such events *ecological events*: 'ecological events, as distinguished from microphysical events and astronomical events, occur at the level of substances and surfaces' (1979/1986, p. 93). At the level of their surfaces and materials, tool and target as well as their topological arrangement contain information to regulate the patterns of energy that are needed for a tool using action. Topologies differ according to the kind of tool using action that takes place. For instance the topology differs for scooping slicing, nailing, raking and piercing. Therefore, the topology that needs to be established may provide information to determine the object to be used as a tool for the target object and how it should be used In the case of tool making, the topology determines how an object has to be modified to become a tool for a task. For instance, when scooping a liquid is the goal, a concavity is needed that can be differently oriented depending on whether the liquid has to be scooped, transported or poured. For slicing, a sharp edge is needed that can be pressed against the skin of, for example, an apple at a range of angles. The blade of a knife is not necessarily needed to realize a cutting edge. A thin nylon string, tightly stretched between two hands also presents a sharp edge and may suit as well or even better for slicing soft substances such as cheese, or cake according to 3 to 5-year-old children, as Smitsman and Bosman (1985) showed.

To further highlight what such a topology may entail and how it is regulated, the example of windsurfing may be illustrative. It leads us away from ordinary examples of stick use, scooping or hammering. On the other hand, the system is also composed of graspable objects that need to be connected to limbs to become tools: the board to the feet and the sail via the bar to the hands. Moreover, sailing has a long history in the evolution of human tool use. The principles that were used in the past are still the same. Windsurfing rests on a surfer's ability to take advantage of energy systems such as the hydrodynamics of water and the aerodynamics of airflow by regulating topologies of surfaces: the sail to the wind and the board to the water surface. The topology of a surfboard and water, regulated by the human body, can create a hydrodynamic system that allows a surfer to be pulled over the water surface and to stand stable when pulled. The topology of the surface of a sail and wind regulated by both hands can generate the required aerodynamic systems that provide the pulling force to the action system on which its stability and speed depends. If we look at the surfer, the whole body is involved. The feet, supporting his posture, regulate the topology of board surface and water surface. The hands, supported by the rest of the body, regulate the topology of sail and wind. The system is also nonlinear. Beyond a critical value of angles of sail to wind, the aerodynamic systems break down. The same occurs for the hydrodynamic system in relation to the topology of board surface and water surface. Postures and movements of the surfer form the variable means that serve to maintain the topologies and underlying dynamics that are needed. Evidently, surfers have to be able to vary postures and movements to preserve a topology and its underlying dynamic organization. The variability of the whole system has to be exploited to find a way of achieving the task, a situation that characterizes not only wind surfing but also other forms of tool use and skilled action (see Manoel & Connolly, 1997). In different kinds of tool use, realization of a topology often involves the whole body and not just the hands. One often observes craftsmen using both hands, knees, trunk and even feet to preserve a required topology in a slicing task, such as in carving a piece of wood.

To summarize, reduction of tool use to object manipulation considerably underestimates the variety of tool use in human and other species. It leads and has led to fruitless and muddling discussions and useless distinctions about what tool use entails. Finally, the idea that the secret of tool use concerns the regulation of means–end relationships for objects that are external to the actor creates an unwarranted dichotomy between actor and environment. Moreover, it bypasses the generality of nested relationships in action and fails to address what 'means for acting' truly are. Action requires the coordination of several components that encompass different body segments, neuromuscular synergies and environmental affordances into postures and movements. This does not change when one uses a tool. What changes are the geometrical dynamical and information gathering properties of the action system. Therefore, fundamental questions with respect to tool use and tool making concern the opportunities to enhance the capacity of action for a task that are offered by the animate and inanimate environment, and children's ability to explore and select new behavioral organizations that exploit the changes in capacity. The study of tool use in particular may reveal how the repertoire may evolve when children discover how to take advantage of affordances that are offered by their animate and inanimate surroundings to enhance their capacity. In the following paragraphs, we will place these developmental processes in the broader perspective of evolutionary processes that create new forms.

Tool Use, Tool Making, and Evolutionary Processes

Evolutionary Processes

The term *evolutionary processes* in the broad sense used in this chapter denotes historical processes that involve the emergence of new patterns or forms (Goldfield, 1995; see Thelen & Smith, 1994; Gottlieb, Chapter 1 in this volume). Examples of these processes are found in biological evolution which takes place at the level of the species, as well as in ontological development which takes place at the level of the individual. Moreover, evolutionary processes also take place at the level of a society and shape the material and nonmaterial culture within the society. Tools that became available over the history of a society are the result of such processes. New patterns thus include the behavior of an organism, biological and material components such as tools that sustain action, and the natural and cultural environment that provides affordances for action. All these components are present in tool use and tool making. Therefore, we need to understand how these components interact and evolve in order to understand how tool use and tool making evolve and are sustained in individuals.

Tool use and tool making evolved over generations and continue to change individuals' lives. Their evolution is part of the history of a society and also shaped this history (see Ingold, 1993a). Nevertheless, regardless of the difference in time scale and level at which new patterns emerge, their causal mechanisms may be rather similar. These mechanisms include changes in bodily resources and/or environmental affordances, the need to preserve continuity in attaining vital goals by inventing new ways of acting to take advantage of changed resources (Goldfield, 1995; Gottlieb, 1992; 1997; Reed, 1996; Sameroff, 1983; Thelen & Smith, 1994; see Gottlieb, Chapter 1 in this volume). Even biological evolution, which rests on changes of a particular biological resource, the genotype, was perhaps initiated by changes in the phenotype (Gottlieb, 1992). In considering the phenotype, Gottlieb (Chapter 1 in this volume) argues that given the fact that a sexually mature individual is needed to transmit genetic mutations to the next generation, an atypical individual must lie at the basis of evolution. Irrespective of how the atypical individual emerged (by genetic mutation or whatever), being atypical implies a discontinuity in resources and consequently in the relationship with the environment for the individual and a pressure to develop new behavior patterns. Dynamic systems theory (Goldfield, 1995; Thelen & Smith, 1994) shows that an organism's continued existence depends on the capacity to select stable, goal directed behavioral organizations for goals such as gathering food, moving from one place to another, or socially interacting. It also shows that the stability of these organizations depends on the fit that exists between an organism's biological resources (e.g. body segments, neuromuscular synergies) and environmental properties, earlier called affordances for a goal. The fit will change when components change, irrespective of whether they belong to the environment or the organism. Changes in components lead to discontinuities in the relationship and a challenge for the individual in the development of new behavioral forms. Developmental research confirms such a hypothesis. During early development, bodily components, change rapidly in size, mass and shape and in their relationship with other components putting pressure on the exploration of new behavioral forms for vital goals. Research on the development of action (Bertenthal & Clifton, 1998; Goldfield, 1995; Thelen & Smith, 1994) shows that actions such as crawling, walking, reaching and grasping largely develop during the first year of an infant's life due to the rapid changes in the biological resources available to the infant and its exploration of new opportunities using these resources.

Developmental Processes and Tool Use

Tool use implies evolutionary processes as briefly described. First, tools provide new resources with which the infant can act and in doing so change the relationship with the environment. Unlike growth, in tool use resources become available instantaneously and temporarily. They arise at once and as long as the implement is part of the action system. Regardless of the different time courses of a change, actions have to be developed to take advantage of this change. Actions develop more gradually than resources become available. Therefore action development may function as a rate limiting factor for the emergence of tool use in children (Thelen & Smith, 1994). Second, earlier behavior patterns for the same goal become destabilized when a tool is part of the action system. An infant who, for instance, begins to eat with a spoon encounters an action problem. The problem involves the loss of earlier eating patterns using only the hands and the need to discover new patterns that regulate the topology of the spoon for the transport of food to the mouth. Third, to take advantage of the new resource, new patterns of arm movement and body posture have to be selected and fine-tuned for the phases of scooping, transporting and emptying of the spoon into the mouth. This means that the child has to discover (1) how to rotate the spoon in order to get food into the bowl, (2) how to keep the bowl in the correct orientation during transport, and (3) how to empty the spoon into the mouth. Research by Steenbergen et al. (1997) on young children's scooping behavior showed that activities indeed concerned the topology of bowl and food. Arm and finger postures and movements varied to preserve the topology. Children gradually discover how to use a spoon for eating, as the work of Connolly (1980; Connolly & Dalgleish, 1989; 1993) shows. It takes time to develop behavioral fine-tuning which can stabilize the new eating patterns and make action more efficient. Destabilization of earlier patterns, exploration, selection and the fine-tuning of new patterns, all form essential ingredients of a developmental process that is required to make a tool part of an action system.

For the child, tool use becomes an important if not a major part of the behavioral repertoire that develops after the first year of life. After the first year of life, changes in resources still originate from bodily growth, but they are complemented and augmented by all kinds of objects that become available to be used as tools for action. One can think of hardly any later developing action for which tools do not form a central component of the actions. Rogoff (1990) nicely illustrates how, through a process of apprenticeship, artifacts available within a culture become part of children's daily actions as they grow up. Tools are part of what Reed and Bril (1996) have called the *zone of promoted action*. This term refers to the hypothesis that caregivers may select which affordances they offer children depending on the children's age. In selecting tools caregivers constrain how a child's capacity to discover and exploit the new opportunities that the environment provides will be expanded, and which behavioral organizations develop to take advantage of those opportunities. The underlying mechanisms for new actions are constituted by the modifications achieved on children's action systems.

Evolution of Tools and the Cultural Environment to Use Tools

Action skills in tool use develop within the individual child when she grows up, but they also evolve within the society that she grows up in when new tools become available. The development of the individual child's skill in tool use cannot be considered independently from the society that evolves new artifacts for tool use and new skills to use those artifacts. Today, the widespread availability of computers and new information technology in western societies continues to challenge the development of new actions for their members, adults as well as children. Perhaps most of our actions today rest on artifacts. A major part of these became available over many generations. Moreover, new affordances were created to fit those skills, a process that over generations gradually changed competencies, beliefs and values, and the environment to sustain these. This also extends to ways of living, travelling and communicating. Thus the competencies that children develop are in essence cultural, which means that they are sustained by an environment that is cultural as well as by tools that are cultural. It also means that their persistence will depend on the availability of those tools and the environment that provides affordances to use those tools.

Tools, and the environment that complements those tools, express the material culture of a society, but they also affect the nonmaterial culture. Tool use and tool making modified the actions of individuals, but also the social interactions that took place while these tools were being used, such as their beliefs and values (Ingold, 1996). The study of tool use and tool making may highlight how culture evolves, is sustained and is transmitted to future generations. A nice illustration of how tools evolved and how their evolution mutually affected action skills, social interactions, and surroundings is the invention of utensils most people use for daily eating. These utensils have shaped dinner settings, furniture, social interactions during dinner in eating patterns and table manners, but also interactions in gathering and preparing food. Although utensils have been used for eating perhaps as long as the history of mankind, utensils we use today for dinner, such as forks for transporting a variety of food to the mouth, have a rather short history. They first became available in the sixteenth century in France and the seventeenth century in England (Petroski, 1993). Petroski reports that for a long time eating was done with a single knife, which was used for a variety of purposes, among which was cutting. When cutting of, for instance, meat needed to be supported by other means, another knife was often used for that purpose. This was the case when one needed to cut off hot roasted meat that would burn the fingers if touched directly. The second knife was used to stabilize the meat against rotation when cutting. Later, a two-tined fork followed the knife, which better prevented meat from rotating. However, these forks were not made for and not well suited to scooping and transporting. Three and subsequently four-tined forks evolved much later, when table manners changed in France and England and using the hands was no longer acceptable (Petroski, 1993).

Tools did not simply put pressure on the activities of their users and makers to further enhance those activities. They also put pressure on the environment to change, in order to support those tools and skills. No other species has modified its action skills and surroundings for those skills to such an extent as the human species (Reed, 1996). An example of how tool use may modify the surroundings is the invention of wheels for vehicles (Smitsman, 2000). Wheels do not work well on bumpy uneven terrain, so their use for new vehicles that could roll instead of jump or step required the creation of relatively even terrain roads on which they could operate efficiently. This motivation resulted finally in the transformation of the terrain into endless highways on which no species can survive other than the one that uses the new vehicles. In sum, when we consider the evolution of tool use and tool making in humans, we may conclude that this process has led not only to new actions, but also to the transformation of the natural environment into an 'artificial' environment that can support those skills. Humans continuously reshuffle the environment, and create new affordances for the behavioral systems that their artifacts necessitate.

The extent and variety of tool use in humans considerably outweigh those of other species, and an intriguing question is what enables humans to use tools on such a large scale. The answer may shed light on differences between humans and other species, but more importantly perhaps is the insight it may provide into the development of action in humans itself. The answers given to such questions generally refer to the evolution of the body and the brain in relation to the development of speech, which modified social interactions (see e.g. Ingold, 1993a; 1999; Paillard, 1993). The action perspective discussed above may hint at a more fundamental answer on this issue. It suggests that tool use can only take place for an individual, human or nonhuman, who can take advantage of changes that environmental objects may bring about on action systems. In the course of activities such as gathering food and exploration, objects may become temporarily connected to an animal's body. In this way opportunities for exploiting such changes may arise for all species. Occasionally, animals do find a way to take advantage of changes that objects may cause on an action system, given the widespread examples of tool use among the animal kingdom. Nevertheless, finding a new way of organizing activities that take advantage of changes that temporarily and perhaps haphazardly occur to an action system, requires flexibility in the organization of behavior. The flexibility is needed to adapt to the changes that occur in the system, but also to vary behavior such that new patterns can be created (Manoel & Connolly, 1997). Selection implies variability in the organization of action. Therefore, the answer to tool use has to be found in the causes of the greater variability or flexibility in the human action system compared to that of other species. The reasons for this variability may be many. The greater size and complexity of the brain may be one reason. But the neuromuscular and limb-segmental organization of the body and the changing natural environment and material culture must also contribute to this flexibility. To investigate why and how tool use and tool making develop, we have to take into account the organism *and* its environment, the various component features involved and the way in which they interact.

Tool Use and Action Systems

In the foregoing paragraphs, we have described tool use as activities by which an actor takes advantage of environmental elements, also called affordances, by coupling them to action systems composed of bodily components. By doing this, goals can be attained that otherwise would be impossible or very difficult. The individual changes the boundary between body and environment, making environmental elements functionally a part of the body, or the 'self', where we conceive the 'self' as an agent or acting individual (see e.g. Fogel, 1993; E.J. Gibson, 1997; Neisser, 1993; Reed, 1996). In the next section, we will further delineate the processes involved in the control of new systems, and young children's ability to take advantage of the opportunity to change a system. But before addressing these issues, we will discuss the concept of an action system as it has been presented by Reed (1982; 1988; 1996) and its significance for understanding tool use and tool making. To start with, we will make some preliminary remarks about which elements can become a tool and the role those elements may fulfill for an action system.

The concept of action system refers to broad categories of goals, such as locomotion and ingestion, that need to be fulfilled for any individual of a species (Pick, 1989). The concept uses functional criteria defined according to the goals of action for distinguishing actions instead of criteria that are based on bodily and other components for action. According to Reed, functional criteria are to be preferred above criteria based on body segments and their postures and movements. This is because functional criteria specify the relationships with the environment that have to be regulated at the different levels of a system's activities. Relationships form the constants the actor has to preserve by employing postures and movements and components involved as the variable means to achieve this task. Using relationships as the criterion for distinguishing actions makes the concept of action system also very useful for addressing tool use, which most notably exploits the flexibility of the actor to configure behavior differently in order to preserve a relationship. Functional criteria highlight the different goals that tool use enables, and the flexibility and continuity in attaining these goals with and without the use of tools. For instance, the goal of locomotion as self-initiated and self-regulated displacement of the body with respect to a surface stays the same irrespective of whether it is achieved by walking, crawling, rolling over the ground, cycling or wind surfing. Compared to walking, cycling greatly extends the capacity for travelling in terms of larger distances in shorter periods of time. However, self-initiated and self-regulated displacement of the body and the keeping of postural balance during displacement are still needed, although the movements and postures involved somewhat differ. They differ because a relationship of rolling wheels to the road has to be preserved instead of stepping feet to the road. In sum, defining action in a functional way makes it clear just how tool use extends the capacity for an action system. Such a definition allows us to address the kind of relationship that the actor regulates in using a tool, instead of focusing on the movements, postures and components involved without considering what these components and activities are used for.

Other reasons for using the concept of 'action system' that are related to the foregoing discussion are the following. First, the concept allows us to consider tool use as part of a larger system instead of as composed of single isolated activities. Considering the larger system of perception action cycles within which tool use is embedded allows us to better clarify the functions that tool use serves. Action is often composed of many components that are orchestrated into perception–action cycles that serve several goals. Tool use may only serve some of these goals but nevertheless ensure that these other goals are ascertained. Such was the case when one of Köhler's chimpanzees prepared for the reach toward the banana by displacing a box to a position from where the banana came within reach of the animal. Second, considering the action system that encompasses tool use enables us to investigate in which respect the system's organization needs to be adapted to take advantage of the tool and in which respect there is continuity in the way an action is performed before tool use becomes part of it. For instance, incorporating a tool into a system does not necessarily mean that a whole sequence of activities has to be reordered in time and space. Tool use alters the relationships that have to be regulated by the sequence of activities, or some of these relationships, but it does not necessarily change their order over time. In studying the origins of tool use in infancy, researchers, taking a skill integration perspective, have overlooked this simple fact (Bruner, 1973; Connolly, 1980; Connolly & Dalgleish, 1989; 1993; Koslowski & Bruner, 1972). Guided by this perspective, they suggested that the difficulty would be for young children putting the sequence of activities properly together in using a tool like a spoon for eating. From the perspective of an action system, however, it is questionable whether such would indeed be the case. This is because the action system, and thus the sequence of postures and movements that characterizes the system, may already be well ordered before tool use starts. Actions such as eating are well organized before tool use becomes part of the action in infants. Before an infant begins to use utensils for eating, it has grasped food thousands of times, transported the food to the mouth and emptied the hands into the mouth. It has used the hands for these purposes, but the sequence does not change when a spoon is used instead of the hands. Even in neonates, this sequence already exists in a rudimentary form (Butterworth & Hopkins, 1988). It further develops at about 4 months of age, at the time successful reaching emerges (Lew & Butterworth, 1997; Thelen et al., 1993). Thus, when an infant starts to use a spoon, it presumably does not have to build up a new sequence or grammar, except perhaps for extending the sequence with the act of grasping the spoon. There is continuity in the way actions are achieved without and with a tool (see also Lockman, 2000).

A final reason why the concept of action system will be useful for understanding tool use is that it broadens our view of tool use, and helps us to distinguish different types of tools and forms of tool use, and tool making, according to the systems that they serve. The concept of action system allows us to realize that tools are involved not only in manipulation but also in other systems. The action systems that Reed (1996) distinguishes involve the goals of ingestion, perception, social interaction, locomotion, manipulation, play and basic orienting. The latter system involves activities that orient postures and movements of the other systems to gravity and the surrounding surfaces, and that includes postural control. The capacity to act is limited for all these goals and can be expanded by taking advantage of affordances in the environment. That means that in principle we can find tool use for each of the systems. Tool use for manipulation will be different from tool use for social interaction and play, because the relationships involved differ as well as the components for which these relationships have to be regulated. For example, a person may use dress or decoration of the body to impress other individuals, taking advantage of other people's capacity to attend and to be impressed. We can also speak of intellectual tools (Waddington, 1977). Symbol systems such as drawing systems and number systems evolved presumably as tools in order to preserve information of importance for regulating social interaction over time (Reed, 1996; Smitsman, 2000). Toys evolved for children as tools to play scenarios of daily life. These toys, in the first place, need to be manageable for children in a play session. They do not necessarily need to be like the objects they represent during play.

In considering the diversity of tool use, we begin to realize how tool use has enabled humans to expand the capacity to act over space and time and broaden the circumstances and forms under which vital goals could be obtained. We can find tools in an enormous diversity for any system. There are tools for basic orienting such as chairs, for the expression of internal feelings such as clothes and decorations, for exploration such as microscopes and telescopes, and for locomotion such as vehicles. Tool use enabled humans to expand the manner of transport in a variety of ways that also exploit the media of other species such as fish and birds that would be inaccessible without tools. Tools also enabled humans to explore the environment and gather information at a macro and a micro scale far beyond the scale of our senses. Modern sciences evolved due to tools that became available in the form of instruments, procedures and techniques for research. The diversity and significance of tool use for human action and understanding force us to consider these diverse forms in order to better understand what these abilities entail and how they develop.

Tool Use and Tool Making: Solutions to a Control Problem

What precisely does the action problem entail in tool use? Basically, the kinds of problem a child has to solve in tool use are comparable to the kinds of problem that arise when actions would not involve tool use. A basic characteristic of all actions is the problems of coordination and control that have to be solved. The coordination problem refers to the need to attune the action to environmental affordances, which form the goal of the action. At a lower level, it involves selecting the appropriate organization of postures and movements along with the neuromuscular synergies to realize the goals that have been selected. The control problem refers to the need to stabilize the selected organization against perturbations from the inside and outside while flexibly adapting it to variable task demands (Goldfield, 1995; Kelso, 1995; Thelen & Smith, 1994). Tool use has to be understood in relation to these problems.

It forms a clever solution to the control problem. Stabilization of a selected organization is possible only within limits of the different components that have been selected for the organization of the action. These limits are determined by the geometrical, dynamical and information gathering characteristics of these components. By embedding a tool in the system these limits can become scaled up. For instance, stretching and leaning too far forward in a reach will finally result in loss of postural control. The distance an actor can reach is limited due to the geometrical and dynamical characteristics of the arm, trunk and legs. A stick held in the hand modifies the geometrical characteristics of the arm. A box to step on will do the same for the legs. In sum, tool use gives the individual the opportunity to solve a control problem by changing the limitations of the components of the action system that caused the control problem. By doing this it extends the capacity for action.

Although tool use and tool making are intended to solve control problems for the actor, they also create new problems for the control and coordination of action. To continue with the stick as an example: the stick has length as well as mass and inertia that directly affect forces in the arm, shoulder, trunk, legs, and feet. This means that the tool user has to adapt movements and postures to compensate for the changed dynamics of the system. In addition, the changed geometry and dynamics of the system also directly affect the relationship with the environment, which forms the goal of an action. The regulation of processes at the tip of the stick, assuming that the tip forms the interface with the environment, imposes new coordination and control problems that greatly constrain how postures and movements must be adapted. Moreover, their solution may differ greatly from those achieved in using the hand as the end effector. The dynamics and geometry of a stick differ from those of the human hand. Objects cannot be grasped by means of a stick and, therefore, displacing an object implies a new type of topology of stick and target object that often involves additional surfaces to support the target object against gravity. Both the new topology and the additional surface of support for the target show how fundamentally the relationship with the surrounding changes even for such a simple task as using a stick. Tool use can only successfully take place if the actor can solve such problems, which involves finding the appropriate topology for regulating the tooling action and adapting postures and movements to establish and sustain the topology. Modification of the tool can make problems more readily soluble when adaptation of postures and movements is difficult to achieve. Thus, tool use presents a challenge for flexibly using the body as well as tool making when flexibility is difficult to achieve. One might speculate that cultures may differ in the direction they take to solve these problems. Perhaps cultures such as those of the aborigines from New Zealand have taken the road of flexibly adapting the body to generate a variety of tools out of a small set of different objects, whereas western societies have taken the road of adapting the objects.

Having discussed control problems that challenge tool use and, as its extension, tool making, we are now in a better position to define both more clearly. There have been many definitions of tool use (see Connolly & Dalgleish, 1993, for a brief summary), and fewer of tool making. All these definitions highlight a particular feature of tool use and tool making. However, these definitions generally bypass the control problem that evokes tool use and tool making in the first place. Taking into account the control problem, we prefer to define tool use and tool making as activities that solve a control problem of action by coupling one or more environmental elements to the action system. By using environmental elements to solve a control problem, tool use and tool making extend the boundary of the body and enhance its capacity to act.

YOUNG CHILDREN'S PERCEPTION AND REGULATION OF TOPOLOGIES

Discrimination of Objects and Topologies of Objects

One of the first questions that arise in studying the development of tool use in young children is whether and when young children begin to distinguish among different topologies that contain information for specifying different tool using actions. When will they be able to anticipate outcomes of object interactions in seeing a topology arise and for which kind of events? Such ability is needed to guide activities in tool use, which requires regulation of these topologies.

We are accustomed to assume that objects themselves form the primary focus of interest to young children and infants. However, from an early age infants also pay attention to what happens to the relationship between objects. The narrow focus on objects as units of perception may cause us to forget that in fact the primary units of perception and action are relationships (E.J. Gibson, 1988; J.J. Gibson, 1979/1986). Affordances concern relationships between the actor and the environment, but solid objects form relationships too, namely between surfaces. The unity and 'boundedness' that specify solid objects mean that the relationship of surfaces, both geometrically and functionally, remains constant during motion, while the relationship between the surfaces that compose the object and surfaces that surround the object instead changes. Preservation of the arrangement of surfaces during motion occurs for rigid objects as well as flexible objects. Therefore, unity defined as nonchanging relationships provides information to perceive solid objects (Gibson, 1979/1986). The significance of motion for infants' perception of the unity of an object illustrates that the object is detected as a relationship that *does not* change amidst relationships that *do* change (see e.g. Kellman & Banks, 1998; Spelke, 1990). However, the changing relationship with other surfaces also entails important information. According to Gibson, the change specifies what is happening with the object, such as whether it moves away, towards or alongside another surface. Thus, in attending to a moving object there is information to perceive the object and to simultaneously perceive what happens to the relationship of the object with other surfaces that surround the object. Gathering this information should enable infants to perceive an object as well as the event that takes place with the object. Moreover, it allows the infant to guide object manipulation such that an intended interaction will take place for objects, given they can handle those objects. Michotte (1951/1991) has shown that interactions between objects are perceived not as sequences of independent motions for each of the objects separately, but as *relationships* of the motion of one object to that of another object. Studies pursuing Michotte's line of research in infants show that 7-month-old infants also perceive such relationships (Leslie, 1984; 1988; Oakes, 1994).

Earlier we argued that object interactions can be geometrically described in terms of a topology of their surfaces that arises over time. This topology differs according to the kind of interaction that takes place. For instance, pushing, pulling, entering, lifting, slicing each involve different topologies of surfaces for the interacting objects. Entering involves a moving solid object in the process of being enclosed by a concave shaped surface arrangement. Lifting requires a surface of support to push another object against the direction of gravity. These topologies emerge as higher order structures from the confluence of the lower level mechanical and geometrical characteristics of the object and forces exerted on the objects. In fact, they form dynamic nonlinear organizations in which surfaces of objects and their surroundings may become ordered over time. For instance, a small change in direction of approach (a continuous variable) may occur, changing entering into colliding (a different type of topology) for an object whose size fits a concavity. Assuming that the number of organizations that can arise over time is limited, it can be hypothesized that infants will attend to these organizations at some age and use them as information to discriminate the kind of event that takes place and to anticipate its outcome. Moreover, when young children begin to manipulate objects, gathering such information may enable them to guide their activities in selecting an object for an intended event and handling it such that the event occurs. To make a particular event happen for objects, their surfaces and those of their surroundings need to satisfy the topology that characterizes the event. Discrimination among topologies enables the child to successfully solve control and coordination problems for tool use. Finally, it may also enable her to modify an object such that it better fits the topology for a target object, improving control on the target. In the later case, the tool using child becomes a tool maker.

When do infants begin to discriminate topologies for interacting objects and anticipate the outcomes of such interactions based on the topology they perceive? Spatial arrangements of surfaces are already important properties of the surroundings that infants attend to before the second half of the first year, as Rovee-Collier's (1996) research shows. Different studies revealed that spatial characteristics of the surroundings form a fundamental ingredient of infants' recollection of mobiles, which they earlier learned to set into motion through kicking while a string connected their feet to the mobile.

A more direct answer to the above question comes from recent research on infants' perception of object interactions such as those that result in containment or support (Aguiar & Baillargeon, 1998; Sitskoorn & Smitsman, 1995; 1997). These studies show that infants attend to the topology that the surfaces of one object form with another object and perceive the event that occurs and its outcome. In a containment event, the concavity of one object forms an enclosure with another object, or substance. The specific topology depends on the objects' geometrical properties and their motion: an enclosure occurs only for an object whose dimensions fit the concave geometry of a container. Sitskoorn & Smitsman (1995) showed that at about 5–6 months of age infants perceive whether the width of a concavity is sufficient to contain another object, and by 12 months of age whether a trajectory to enter is appropriate for containment (Sitskoorn & Smitsman, 1997). This research shows that, by the second half of their first year of life, infants attend to topologies that specify object interactions, and anticipate the event that will take place and its outcome.

Tool Use: Regulation of Topologies

In tool use, however, children have to regulate topologies when objects interact and not just anticipate them. Regulation involves selecting appropriate objects to become tools and stable organizations of behavior in using these objects as tools. Reaching, grasping, manipulation, and postural control have to be sufficiently developed in order to find such stable organizations, which may not happen before the end of the first year of life (Bertenthal & von Hofsten, 1998). Holding an object while making it interact with another object may easily perturb the movement of the arm and the posture of the body, especially when the system is still fragile. Thus the object that is selected for tool use needs to satisfy not only the topology that is required, but also the action skill of the child in handling the object. In a manner of speaking, selection of the object has to anticipate the topology for which it will be used as well as the tool user.

To get an idea of how an object may affect postures and movements, one may imagine elongated objects of varying mass, distribution of mass, shape, length and rigidity. When, for the sake of clarity, we confine the action system to the arm, it will not be difficult to accept that variation in an object's shape, size and mass will affect the stability of postures and movements of the arm. This means that the stability of movements and postures in using an object for activities such as piercing, waving, and hitting will vary, depending on how the masses are distributed over the object. For instance, precise pointing will be very difficult to perform with a stick that has most of its mass at the tip, compared to a stick with its mass mostly in the handle. Precise aiming will further deteriorate for an elongated object that is asymmetrically shaped compared to a symmetrically shaped one. On the other hand, forceful hitting may be more easily performed when mass is located at the tip. So, depending on how an object that is held has been shaped, a topology may be more or less easily discovered for the limb that holds the object.

One may guess that inexperienced tool users such as young children have difficulty in selecting an object for use as a tool that suits the task. The ability to perceive the kind of object that is needed and the ability to use it, presumably, develop together with the discovery of the kind of topology that has to be established. For instance the discovery of the topology for cutting and slicing may create the need for a sharp edge as well as the need to orient the edge appropriately to another surface for cutting or slicing. On the other hand, action skills to hold and manipulate an object perhaps constrain the discovery of these topologies. There must be a mutual process in which on the one hand goals select implements, and on the other hand the available stable behavioral organizations select goals for using implements.

How do young children discover and regulate the topology that is needed for a task, and which characteristics of the action system and task enable them to do so? There is very little systematic research with which to answer these questions. Familiar tasks that have been studied in young children are eating by means of a spoon (Connolly & Dalgleish, 1989; 1993) and reaching by means of a stick, hook, string or in other ways to bring a distant target nearby (Bates, Carlson-Luden, & Bretherton, 1980; Brown, 1990; Buhler, 1930; Koslowski & Bruner, 1972; Richardson, 1932). Connolly and Dalgleish (1989) provide detailed information about the grip patterns and sequence of movements in 12- to 24-month-old children in using a spoon for eating. Connolly and Dalgleish (1993) extended the first study by investigating four children individually at weekly intervals over the first 6 months of the second year of life on the same task, using the behavior categories developed for the first study. Although both studies provide detailed observations of young children's behavior and individual differences in behavior, they do not explicitly address how the behavior relates to the topology that a child needs to regulate using a spoon. Nevertheless, some of Connolly and Dalgleish's (1993) data suggest that the relation of food to spoon formed the goal of children's activities especially in the second half of the period over which the infants were studied. They observed enhanced visual monitoring as well as bimanual activities to maintain the bowl in the proper orientation during transport, suggesting that infants were not just holding the spoon on its trajectory to the mouth, but were engaged in activities intended to keep the food in the spoon during transport. However, the studies provide little insight into the characteristics of the action system that needed to be available for children to handle the spoon and the changes with respect to these characteristics that would make performance more efficient and smooth.

Other tasks involved using a tool (e.g. a stick or string) to retrieve an object which was beyond reach of the arm. Bates, Carlson-Luden, and Bretherton (1980), Brown, (1990), Koslowski and Bruner (1972) and Richardson (1932) showed that the position of the tool relative to a target object formed an important property for young children to perceive the opportunity of the tool to bring the target nearby. A revealing example of difficulties that beginning tool users may face in discovering the relevant parameters to assemble the action system comes from one of Köhler's (1925) famous studies on tool use in chimpanzees. Although the example does not apply to young children, it may illustrate problems that young children also face. In one investigation, Köhler reports that Sultan, one of the animals in his study, used everything he could find in his cage from cups to hats and cloth to hit a banana beyond his reach. Apparently, the animal was aware of the fact that the action system needed to be modified geometrically and dynamically. It explored a variety of possibilities to change the system and establish a topology that would solve the action problem. In one such attempt, Sultan used a cloth. Köhler reported that the banana came accidentally landed on the cloth after Sultan hit it fiercely by means of the cloth. The behavior of the chimpanzee then changed dramatically, according to Köhler's report. Instead of the earlier furious attempts, the animal pulled very carefully on the cloth to ensure that the banana would stay on it. Köhler's observations indicate that the animal's attention was directed at the interface of cloth and banana. When a topology or a Gestalt, to use Köhler's terms, emerged that the animal could regulate, he adapted his behavior to preserve the arrangement. These observations show that Sultan's exploration and pulling behavior was directed at the finding and maintaining of a topology instead of the manipulation of an object. Other results of Köhler's study, involving the use of a stick, confirm this hypothesis. In the case of the stick, the particular spatial arrangement of stick and target, a banana, was the major factor in whether the animal would select the stick to get the banana, and not whether the stick had been used successfully before. In advance, the stick was only grasped when both stick and banana were located in the animal's visual field, but not when the stick was placed beyond the visual field, for instance at the back of the animal's cage. After experience with the task, the animal's regulation became more flexible and mobile. Regulation of the topology, which includes selection of the tool, became possible over a greater variation of spatial arrangements for the elements. Köhler's results would be difficult to interpret from a perspective that only focuses on separate objects instead of relationships between objects. The results become understandable when we consider the spatio-temporal arrangement of objects as a unit of perception and action as Köhler did. Such units can be formed and annihilated because objects can be manipulated and displaced in space.

The findings of Butterworth and Grover (1999) on pointing in infants and van Leeuwen, Smitsman, and van Leeuwen (1994) on toddlers' use of a hook underscore the significance of spatio-temporal arrangements as units of perception and action. Although pointing does not involve tool use, but is used to direct another person's attention to features of the environment, the pointing finger and the target of pointing form a spatio-temporal unit. Discovery of this unit reveals the target of pointing. Butterworth and Grover found that with age infants become more flexible in sampling information to detect this unit. Their research showed that the angle that a pointing finger made with the line of sight of the infant formed an important variable for the infant to detect the target of pointing. With age, this angle could deviate further from the line of sight of the infant. The study of van Leeuwen, Smitsman, and van Leeuwen (1994) extended the earlier studies on tool use, such as those of Bates, Carlson-Luden, and Bretherton (1980), Brown (1990), Köhler (1925), and Richardson (1932). In their study, young children of about 1–3 years of age were facing a cookie placed beyond their reach on a table in front of them. To get the object, a hook was placed on the table. The handle was within reach of the child and the crook varied in its spatial orientation with respect to the cookie (Figure 8.1).

The topology of crook and cookie had a marked effect on whether a child discovered the opportunity a hook provides for displacing an object towards the place where the child was seated. When the cookie was placed inside or nearly inside the crook (Figure 8.1a, b), children easily discovered how to pull the crook to bring the target nearby. However, when the crook was facing away from the target, such that it first had to be rotated to enclose the target (Figure 8.1d, e), children of 1 and several of 2 years of age largely ignored the hook, and reached for the target with the hand. Another finding underscored that the spatial arrangement of hook and target formed the unit of children's perception and action. Children who had used the hook successfully in the easy orientations ignored it in the more difficult orientations, indicating that for them the tool function of the hook depended on its spatial relation to the cookie. To further investigate this hypothesis, the hook was presented in the most difficult orientation, but the position towards which the target needed to be displaced was changed. The new end position for the target was no longer where the child was seated, but a 90 degrees clockwise as well as anti-clockwise change with respect to the original position. To control displacement of the target it was sufficient to displace the hook to the side until it touched the target and then to push the target further to the side towards its end position. For controlling the push the long handle could be used and, in fact, the crook was not needed. Results showed that the earlier most difficult

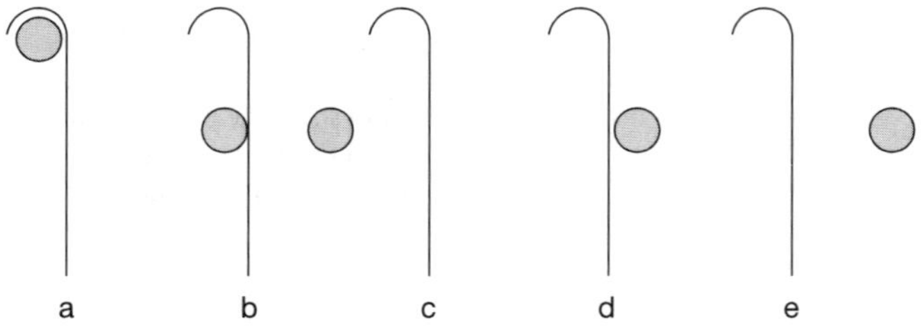

Figure 8.1 *Different spatial positions of a target object and a hook (after van Leeuwen, Smitsman, & van Leeuwen, 1994). Both objects were presented on a tabletop, the hook within reach and lying in front of the child, and the target object beyond reach in five different positions with respect to the hook. In position (a), the crook encloses the target object, the appropriate topology for bringing it nearby. The other positions require additional activities to establish the topology, varying from a displacement (b) and (c) to a displacement and a reorientation (d) and (e)*

orientation no longer formed a problem for young children. They solved the problem but did not use the crook to solve the problem. Direction of displacement of hook or stick toward a target is an important variable a child has to regulate to ensure that the appropriate topology for a controlled displacement of the target arises. Results indicate that with age children are better able to control this variable. Finding the relevant variables and discovering how to regulate them, presumably, enables children also to apprehend the control problem that is solved in using a hook instead of a stick for displacing targets over a larger variety of directions. This would mean that even when young children made use of the crook, they still did not fully apprehend its control function.

To discover the relevant variables for regulating a topology for tool use, the child's attention should be focused on what is happening to the relationship of tool and target object during action. The relationship of tool and body is also important, but is embedded within the former relationship. Therefore, grip and hand position with respect to the tool should vary to regulate events at the interface of tool and target. To investigate whether action is directed at the topology of tool and target and whether manual activities vary to preserve a topology, Steenbergen et al. (1997) perturbed the system. They gave children, aged about 2–3 years, different spoons to scoop rice. Some of the spoons made it very difficult to keep the bowl in the proper orientation for scooping and transporting, because the long axis of the bowl was orthogonal to the long axis of the handle. For these spoons, the handle was bent 90 degrees either to the side, or upwards or downwards (Figure 8.2).

As might be expected when the stability of a system is perturbed, grip patterns became variable, as well as the position of the hand on the handle where the spoon was held. These results differed from those of Connolly and Dalgleish (1989; 1993), who showed a growing preference for particular grips. However, their study did not perturb the stability of the system by presenting awkward spoons. More importantly, the variability Steenbergen et al. discovered was functional. Children varied grip pattern and position on the handle to keep the scoop in the proper orientation, indicating that the topology of scoop and rice formed the goal of children's activities. Spoons could still be easily held when children ignored the relationship of the hand to the spoon. However, instead, they preferred more difficult movements and postures to regulate the topology of bowl and rice

To better understand how tool use can take place and develop, we need to study the way an implement affects the action system. To investigate this question, Bongers, Smitsman, and Michaels (submitted) varied the geometry and dynamics of the action system in a series of studies. Toddlers and adults were given several sticks to displace an object to the side. The object was positioned on a small platform in front of the child or adult at hip height. Sticks varied in length, weight (mass homogeneously distributed) and mass distribution in different experiments. With respect to the distribution of mass, additional mass was invisibly placed either at the tip or at the handle (i.e. near the hand). Differences between sticks that varied in distribution of mass were not visible. Adults and toddlers had to walk toward the platform with the stick held upwards at an angle of 45° to the horizontal. They were asked to stop walking at a distance at which they judged the target on the platform in front of them to be within reach and displaceable with the tip of the stick. The important measure was the body distance to the target, measured by the position of the feet at the onset of displacement. To guarantee an unimpeded reach, the distance participants selected should anticipate the changed length that was

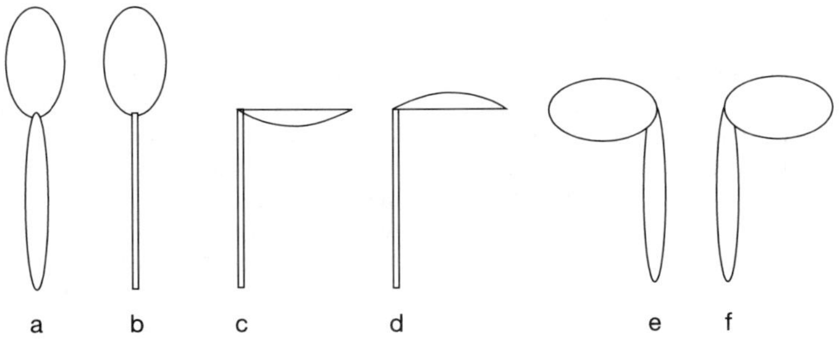

Figure 8.2 *Six different spoons for scooping that vary in position of the bowl with respect to the handle (after Steenbergen et al., 1997). Spoon (a) represents an ordinary spoon. The other spoons form different variations of this spoon. In spoon (b), the handle has been rotated over its longitudinal axis by 90°; the long axis of the bowl still extends the long axis of the handle. For the other spoons the long axis of the bowl has been made orthogonal to the long axis of the handle, by bending the bowl either to the left or right with respect to the handle (c and d), or backwards or forwards (e and f). Spoons (a) to (d) are frontal views, (e) and (f) are side views*

available to the system for reaching and the changed load that would arise on extending the arm and leaning forward when reaching. Bongers, Smitsman, and Michaels (in press) were interested in the parameters of the action system that were employed to select a distance, such as length, torque, or inertia or combinations of these. Results showed that both children and adults adapted the distance to reach according to the changed geometry of the action system (i.e. length), but only adults adapted also to the changed dynamics, i.e. the mass and mass distribution. Remarkably, changes in mass and mass distribution, which are both changes in the underlying dynamics of the system, affected the distance adults selected to perform the task differently. Increased mass led to a shorter distance and increase of mass only at the tip of the stick to a longer distance. The important result for the present discussion was that action remained directed at regulation of the relationship of the new system between hand, stick and environment, for toddlers as well as adults. Both selected a position that enabled them to touch the target with the tip of the stick. However, for toddlers this position did not always make reaching comfortable, given that increased torque at arm and shoulders due to heavy sticks did not lead to shorter distances. Apparently fine-tuning of a modified system requires a lengthy period of experience given the differences between toddlers and adults.

Planning of the Action

Performing a tool using action, geometrically specified by a particular topology and afforded by properties of the tool and target object, requires planning of the activities. Several activities have to be carried out and not all can be performed at the same time. The tool user has to know in advance how and where to start, in order to ensure that the topology will arise. Even for a simple task such as scooping, the emergence of a 'scooping device' depends on the part of the spoon that has been grasped and the grip that has been selected. At a minimum, the planning of the reach should leave the bowl free for scooping. For other tasks, such as screwing or piercing, the bowl might be the place to grasp the object, leaving the handle or its tip free for tool use. Thus, the relationship with the target determines how the action is planned, including where the object is held. Planning is also needed to ensure that a tool is used. Young children may directly reach toward the food on the dinner table without first grasping a spoon or fork. One can eat food comfortably using the hand, as Indian children are taught to do (Rogoff, 1990).

How do young children plan an action that involves using a tool? Steenbergen et al. (1997) showed that at least 24-month-old children perceived the affordance of a spoon for scooping. They regulated the action accordingly. To investigate the planning of infants and toddlers, McCarty, Clifton, and Collard (1999) presented 9-, 14-, and 19-month-old children with spoons in two different orientations, the bowl being filled with food. In one orientation the bowl was pointing to the left side of the infant, and in the other orientation the handle was pointing to the left. Spoons were presented in the frontal parallel plane at midline and within reach of the child. By varying the orientation of the filled spoon, children were forced to vary the hand for grasping the spoon to ensure that a grip was used that enabled transporting the food toward the mouth and emptying the bowl into the mouth. Such would become very difficult when the grasp was directed at the handle, and the bowl was pointing away from the thumb instead of the little finger when grasped. Results showed that 9-month-old infants and also most of the 14-month-old infants used the preferred hand instead of the hand closer to the handle of the spoon. Moreover, they also often grasped the spoon at the bowl instead of the handle. By the age of 19 months, the children anticipated the demands made by transporting the spoon to the mouth. It is unclear what made younger infants reach the way they did and what made toddlers change their manner of reaching. Several possibilities, separately or in combination, may have caused this change, for instance heightened level of activation in seeing food, the need to prevent postural imbalance in crossing the midline when reaching, hand preference, in addition to not knowing how to make use of a spoon. Each of these may lead to inadequate planning of the action, which is the question the McCarty, Clifton, and Collard's (1999) study addressed. The authors discussed the planning of the action in terms of emerging action plans for the sequence of movements that is needed to realize the goals that are involved. However, their model ignores what it is that enables children to discover what these goals are, and the underlying dynamics that ensures these goals will become and stay part of the action planning when performing the task. As we have argued, the sequence follows from perceiving the relationships that have to be regulated. Circumstances of the task, such as the kind of object that is presented, how and how often it is presented, in addition to how the child is seated, may affect the relationships that children will attend to. These may also affect whether a relationship which they have attended to will remain part of the action planning when the task is performed.

Thelen et al. (2001) recently presented a more dynamic planning model that perhaps better suits the action planning in tool use. They describe action planning in dynamic systems terms to explain infants' search behavior in object permanence tasks. Although the object permanence task does not involve tool use, problems the child faces in planning the action may be related to those of tool use. Moreover, Piaget (1954) also conceived a relationship between object permanence and tool use, although not precisely in terms of planning. Application of Thelen et al.'s model to the study of tool use may provide new insights into why such a relationship may exist. To highlight some central ideas from their model we will briefly describe the object permanence task they used. In the object permanence task studied by Thelen et al., the so-called A-not-B task, an experimenter hides an object a couple of times in front of the child at a place called A. After repeating the process successfully several times, the experimenter chooses another place, B, in front of the child to hide the object. Although 8-month-old infants search successfully even on the first trial at place A, they often do not shift to place B when the experimenter hides the object at B, even if they gaze at the new hiding place. They continue searching at place A. In Thelen et al.'s planning model, there is a space of all possible directions to reach. A dynamic field spans the space of directions. Selective attention of the child for one particular direction depends on the activation level of the field. In their model, activation level is a probabilistic variable that measures how well something is able to attract the attention of a child. The higher the activation level, the more chance of attracting the child's attention. Places of the field that have high activation level strongly attract the attention of the child, whereas places with a low activation level remain unnoticed. Activation of different areas of the field varies over time in a continuous fashion. Whether one direction is more attractive than another is dynamically regulated. It depends on the level of activation of a particular area compared to the other areas at a particular moment. The activation level itself depends on many circumstances. One such circumstance is what has happened in the past, such as repeatedly hiding at place A, which will heighten the activation level for A. Another concerns activities in the present. Not all activities have the same activation level. In general, activities that are novel or more attractive than routines have a heightened activation level. Shifting the position of the object from location A to location B will increase activation for B, and repeatedly hiding it in the same fashion will after a while decrease the attention level for the 'hiding game'. In addition, objects can have different levels of salience: a toy often becomes more interesting when it makes noises or is brightly colored. Thelen et al.'s model shows that continuation of search at A may occur because the activation level for B is not high enough to compete with location A, given the fact that the children have had to attend many times to location A before shifting to location B.

The idea of a dynamical planning field provides a new perspective on the planning of action in tool use. One of the explanations for infants' continued search at place A in the object permanence task, when the experimenter switches to hide the object at B, has been the inability to inhibit earlier responses (Diamond, 1991; see Willats, 1997 for a more elaborate discussion and alternatives). The idea of a developing inhibitory capacity might be attractive for someone who considers the selection of a particular goal as the result of inhibition of other competing goals. However, such an explanation will be useless for tool use. In tool use several goals have to become ordered over time. Achievement of this ordering over time can hardly result from a developing inhibitory ability, because to become coupled to one another over time, goals have to stay part of the planning of action instead of being inhibited. Also questionable is the notion that new order emerges from an action plan that already contains the order. Such a plan defers the question of how the order arises instead of explaining it. Hence, when a relationship exists between tool use and object permanence, as Piaget (1954) amongst others suggested, then perhaps a model that addresses the underlying dynamics of the planning of action and the properties that sustain activation for goals may be more promising. For instance, in grasping a spoon, the relation of the food to the bowl of the spoon and the mouth has to remain as a goal of action, although the child plans the reach toward the handle. Considering planning in a more dynamic way may also open interesting vistas for understanding how several goals are sustained in the planning, while the circumstances of the task affect which particular subgoal activities will be directed. Planning has to be dynamic to ensure that goals become adequately but flexibly spread over time and action can be adapted to future circumstances. These circumstances may lead to subgoals temporarily disappearing from the planning, or to a subgoal turning into a final goal – a situation that may happen to an infant as well as an adult. In seeing attractive food inside the bowl of a spoon, which may afford touching for an infant, she may forget the spoon and reach directly toward the food. A comparable situation may also occur for an adult who, for instance, has to eat with chopsticks for the first time. In lifting food with the tips of the chopsticks the food may push the chopsticks out of the hand. The accident may draw attention away from the relation between food and chopsticks and toward the relation between chopsticks and hand. During such a period, the chopsticks may become the target of the activities and the hand the boundary of the action system with respect to the environment. In such a moment the chopsticks will lose their meaning as a tool. To conclude, the examples show that planning of actions in using a tool presumably does not develop in an all-or-nothing fashion. Circumstances that lead to planning problems for young children may also be present for experienced tool users like adults. Differences between ages may arise because these circumstances may be more likely at some age than at others.

Concluding Remarks

In this chapter, we have presented a framework for tool use that combines a dynamic system's perspective of action with an ecological psychology view of the relation of action to the environment. This relation is a given by the mutuality of environmental opportunities or affordances and bodily organizations and exists due to the coupling of perception and action, which enables actors to take advantage of those affordances. We have argued that tool use and its extension, tool making, rest on an actor's ability to discover these affordances. In this respect, tool use does not differ from any other action that does not involve tool use. The dynamic systems view that we have discussed conceives of action at the macro level as composed of dynamic organizations of postures and movements that serve to regulate an actor's relationship with the environment for a variety of purposes. At the micro level, these postures and movements self-organize due to the complex interaction of several bodily components forming the dynamic, geometric and information gathering properties of the action system – the so-called underlying dynamics and environmental components that provide affordances to the system. We have argued that tool use results firstly from self-regulated modification of the underlying dynamics of an action system, taking advantage of the affordances that implements provide, and secondly from new behavioral organizations that emerge, challenged by these modifications. Taking the stance that evolutionary processes, including development, are generally motivated by changes of the underlying dynamics of action systems at the level of individuals, we have argued that tool use involves such processes. Moreover, within a society that provides all kinds of artifacts for all kinds of activities to individuals that grow up within the society, these processes challenge the creation of new actions. The presence of new artifacts not only motivates the development of new behavioral organizations, but also challenges changes of the environment to furnish affordances for the new behavioral organizations when such affordances fail. It may lead to new 'artificial' environments. In addition, it may motivate the production of new artifacts or tool making to optimize a fit of an artifact with an actor.

To highlight how young children learn to take advantage of those artifacts, we have discussed the action problems that tool use solves and the new action problems it creates. Tool use solves an action problem, in that it extends a child's limits to control a relationship with the environment. However, to extend the boundary of control, the child has to adapt postures and movements to regulate events that now mostly occur at the interface of tool and environment. We have suggested that these events can be geometrically described by a particular topology of surfaces of tool and target that differs according to the kind of tool use that takes place. Energy systems (i.e. forces) that arise at a lower level sustain the topology and ensure that the tool use intended is what takes place. The tool user regulates those systems by taking advantage of the surfaces and substances of tool and target for preserving the topology that is needed. As a consequence, the topology that arises and the surfaces and materials of tool and target that give rise to the topology contain information for regulating the tool use action that is intended. Regulation of these processes imposes new control and coordination problems for the tool user. We have argued that the study of tool use must unravel these problems. In particular it needs to address the action variables that enable children to regulate a topology for a tool and a target, exploiting the changed underlying dynamics of the action system as a consequence of the tool that is used. It also needs to investigate how these action variables enable children to select tools that indeed solve control problems for them. Finally, studying tool use requires a developmental perspective that addresses the fundamental mechanisms that cause the emergence of new patterns of behavior and the loss of existing patterns – something that occurs at all ages, instead of at a particular age for the tool user.

Acknowledgments

The authors are grateful for the valuable comments of Kevin Connolly, Nienke Smitsman and Jaan Valsiner on earlier drafts of this chapter.

References

Acredolo, L., & Goodwyn, S. (1988). Symbolic gesturing in normal infants. *Child Development*, 59, 450 – 466.

Aguiar, A., & Baillargeon, R. (1998). Eight-and-a-half-month-old infants' reasoning about containment events. *Child Development*, 69, 636–638.

Bard, K.A. (1993). Cognitive competence underlying tool use in free-ranging orang-utans. In A. Berthelet & J. Chavaillon (eds), *The use of tools by human and non-human primates*. New York: Oxford University Press.

Bates, E., Carlson-Luden, E., & Bretherton, J. (1980). Perceptual aspects of tool-using in infancy. *Infant Behaviour and Development*, 3, 127–140.

Beck, B.B. (1980). *Animal tool behavior: The use and manufacture of tools by primates*. Hillsdale, NJ: Erlbaum.

Beek, P.J., & Bingham, G.P. (1991). Task-specific dynamics and the study of perception and action: A reaction to von Hofsten (1989). *Ecological Psychology*, 3, 35–54.

Bernstein, N. (1967). *The coordination and regulation of movements*. Oxford: Pergamon.

Berthelet, A., & Chavaillon, J. (1993). *The use of tools by human and non-human primates*. New York: Oxford University Press.

Bertenthal, B.I., & Clifton, R.K. (1998). Perception and action. In W. Damon, D. Kuhn, & R.S. Siegler (eds), *Handbook of child psychology: Vol. 2. Cognition, perception, and language*. New York: Wiley.

Bertenthal, B., & von Hofsten, C. (1998). Eye, head and trunk control: The foundation for manual development. *Neuroscience and Biobehavioral Reviews*, 22, 515–520.

Bongers, R.M., Smitsman, A.W., & Michaels, C.F. (in press). Prospective control in toddlers' tool use reflects geometric, but not kinetic, properties of tools.

Bril, B., & Brenière, Y. (1992). Postural requirements and progression velocity in young walkers. *Journal of Motor Behavior*, 24, 105–116.

Bril, B., & Brenière, Y. (1993). Posture and independent locomotion in early childhood: Learning to walk or learning dynamic postural control? In G.J.P. Savelsbergh (ed.), *The development of coordination in infancy*. Amsterdam: Elsevier.

Brown, A.L. (1990). Domain-specific principles affect learning and transfer in children. *Cognitive Science*, 14, 107–133.

Bruner, J.S. (1973). Organization of early skilled action. *Child Development*, 44, 1–11.

Bühler, K. (1930). *Die geistige entwicklung des Kindes* (6th edn.,). Jena: Fischer.

Butterworth, G., & Grover, L. (1999). The origins of referential communication in infancy. In P. Lloyd & Ch. Fernythough (eds), *Lev Vygotsky. Critical assessments: Thought and language* (Vol. II, pp 3–30). New York: Routledge.

Butterworth, G.E., & Hopkins, B. (1988). Hand–mouth coordination in the new-born baby. *British Journal of Developmental Psychology*, 6, 302–314.

Clark, J.E., & Phillips, S.J. (1993). A longitudinal study of interlimb coordination in the first year of independent walking: A dynamical systems analysis. *Child Development*, 64, 1143–1157.

Connolly, K.J. (1980). The development of competence in motor skills. In C.H. Nadeau, W.R. Halliwell, K.M. Newell, & G.L. Roberts (eds), *Psychology of motor behaviour and sport 1979*. Champaign, IL: Human Kinetics.

Connolly, K.J., & Dalgleish, M. (1989). The emergence of tool-using skill in infancy. *Developmental Psychology*, 6, 894–912.

Connolly, K.J., & Dalgleish, M. (1993). Individual patterns of tool use by infants. In A.F. Kalverboer, B. Hopkins, & R. Greuze (eds), *Motor development in early and later childhood: Longitudinal approaches* (pp. 174–204). Cambridge: Cambridge University Press.

Connolly, K.J., & Elliott, J.M. (1972). The evolution and ontogeny of hand function. In N. Blurton Jones (ed.), *Ethological studies of child behavior* (pp. 329–383). Cambridge: Cambridge University Press.

Diamond, A. (1991). Neuropsychological insights into the meaning of object concept development. In S. Carey & R. Gelman (eds), *The epigenesis of mind: Essays on biology and cognition* (pp. 67–110). Hillsdale, NJ: Erlbaum.

Fogel, A. (1993). *Developing through relationships: Origins of communication, self, and culture*. New York: Harvester Wheatsheaf.

Gibson, E.J. (1969). *Principles of perceptual learning and development*. New York: Appleton-Century-Crofts.

Gibson, E.J. (1988). Exploratory behavior in the development of perceiving, acting, and the acquiring of knowledge. *Annual Review of Psychology*, 39, 1–41.

Gibson, E.J. (1997). An ecological psychologist's prolegomena for perceptual development: A functional approach. In C. Dent-Read & P. Zukow-Goldring (eds), *Evolving explanations of development: Ecological approaches to organism–environment systems* (pp. 23–45). Washington, DC: APA.

Gibson, J.J. (1966). *The senses considered as perceptual systems*. Boston: Houghton-Mifflin.

Gibson, J.J. (1979/1986). *The ecological approach to visual perception*. Boston: Houghton-Mifflin.

Gibson, K.R. (1977). Brain structure and intelligence in macaques and human infants from a Piagetian perspective. In S. Chevalier-Skolnikoff & F.E. Poirier (eds), *Primate bio-social development*. New York: Garland.

Gibson, K.R. (1981). Comparative neuro-ontogeny: its implications for the development of human intelligence. In G. Butterworth (ed.), *Infancy and epistemology*. Brighton: Harvester.

Goldfield, E.C. (1995). *Emergent forms: Origins and early development of human action and perception*. New York: Oxford: Oxford University Press.

Gottlieb, G. (1992). *Individual development and evolution: The genesis of novel behavior*. New York: Oxford University Press.

Gottlieb, G. (1997). *Synthesizing nature–nurture: Prenatal roots of instinctive behavior*. Mahwah, NJ: Erlbaum.

Greenfield, P.M. (1991). Language, tools and brain: The ontogeny and phylogeny of hierarchically organized sequential behavior. *Behavioral and Brain Sciences*, 14, 531–595.

Hopkins, B., & Butterworth, G. (1997). Dynamical systems approaches to the development of action. In J.G. Bremner, A. Slater, & G. Butterworth (eds), *Infant development: Recent advances*. East Sussex: Psychology Press.

Ingold, T. (1993a). Technology, language, intelligence: A reconsideration of basic concepts. In K.R. Gibson & T. Ingold (eds), *Tools, language and cognition in human evolution* (pp. 449–472). Cambridge: Cambridge University Press.

Ingold, T. (1993b). The reindeerman's lasso. In P. Lemonnier (ed.), *Technological choices: Transformation in material cultures since the Neolithic* (pp. 108–125). London: Routledge.

Ingold, T. (1996). Situating action: V. The history and evolution of bodily skills. *Ecological Psychology*, 8, 171–182.

Ingold, T. (1997). Eight themes in the anthropology of technology. *Social Analysis*, 1, 106–138.

Ingold, T. (1999). 'Tools for the hand, language for the face': An appreciation of Leroi-Gourhan's *Gesture and*

Speech. Stud. Hist. Phil. Biol. & Biomed. Sci., 30, 411–453.

Kellman, P.J., & Banks, M.S. (1998). Infant visual perception. In W. Damon, D. Kuhn, & R.S. Siegler (eds), *Handbook of child psychology*: Vol. 2. *Cognition, perception, and language*. New York: Wiley.

Kelso, J.A.S. (1995). *Pattern formation: The self-organization of brain and behavior*. Cambridge, MA: MIT Press.

Köhler, W. (1925). *The mentality of apes*. London: Kegan.

Koslowski, B., & Bruner, J.S. (1972). Learning to use a lever. *Child Development*, 43, 790–799.

Leslie, A.M. (1984). Spatiotemporal continuity and the perception of causality in infants. *Perception*, 13, 287–305.

Leslie, A.M. (1988). The necessity of illusion: Perception and thought in infancy. In L. Wesikrants (ed.), *Thought without language*. Oxford: Clarendon.

Lew, A.R., & Butterworth, G. (1997). The development of hand–mouth coordination in 2- to 5-month-old infants: Similarities with reaching and grasping. *Infant Behavior and Development*, 20 (10), 59–69.

Lockman, J.J. (2000). A perception–action perspective on tool use development. *Child Development*, 71, 137–144.

Manoel, E. de J., & Connolly, K.J. (1997). Variability and stability in the development of skilled actions. In K.J. Connolly and H. Forssberg (eds), *Neurophysiology and neuropsychology of motor development*. London: MacKeith.

McCarty, M.E., Clifton, R.K., & Collard, R.R. (1999). Problem solving in infancy: The emergence of an action plan. *Developmental Psychology*, 35, 1091–1101.

McGrew, W.C. (1993). Brains, hands, and minds: Puzzling incongruities in ape tool use. In A. Berthelet & J. Chavaillon (eds), *The use of tools by human and non-human primates*. New York: Oxford University Press.

Michaels, C.F., & Beek, P. (1995). The state of ecological psychology. *Ecological Psychology*, 7 (4), 259–278.

Michotte, A. (1951/1991). The perception of the 'Tool effect'. In G. Thines & A. Costall (eds), *Michotte's experimental phenomenology of perception* (pp. 87–102). Hillsdale, NJ: Erlbaum.

Neisser, U. (1993). The self perceived. In U. Neisser (ed.), *The perceived self: Ecological and interpersonal sources of self-knowledge* (pp. 3–21). Cambridge: Cambridge University Press.

Newell, K.M. (1986). Constraints on the development of coordination. In M.G. Wade & H.T.A. Whiting (eds), *Motor development in children: Aspects of coordination and control* (pp. 341–360). Dordrecht: Nijhoff.

Newell, K.M. (1996). Change in movement and skill: Learning, retention, and transfer. In M.L. Latash & M.T. Turvey (eds), *Dexterity and its development*. Mahwah, NJ: Erlbaum.

Oakes, L.M. (1994). The development of infants' use of continuity cues in their perception of causality. *Developmental Psychology*, 30, 869–879.

Paillard, J. (1993). The hand and the tool: The functional architecture of human technical skills. In A. Berthelet & J. Chavaillon (eds), *The use of tools by human and non-human primates*. New York: Oxford University Press.

Parker, S.T., & Gibson, K.R. (1977). Object manipulation, tool use and sensorimotor intelligence as feeding adaptations in rhesus monkeys and great apes. *Journal of Human Evolution*, 6, 623–641.

Piaget, J. (1954). *The construction of reality in the child*. New York: Basic.

Pick, H.L. (1989). Motor development: The control of action. *Developmental Psychology*, 25 (6), 867–870.

Petroski, H. (1993). *The evolution of useful things*. London: Pavilion.

Reed, E.S. (1982). An outline of a theory of action systems. *Journal of Motor Behavior*, 14 (2), 98–134.

Reed, E.S. (1988). Applying the theory of action systems to the study of motor skills. In O.G. Meijer & K. Roth (eds), *Complex movement behavior: The motor action controversy* (pp. 45–86). Elsevier.

Reed, E.S. (1996). *Encountering the world: Toward an ecological psychology*. New York: Oxford University Press.

Reed, E.S., & Bril, B. (1996). The primacy of action in development. In M.L. Latash & M.T. Turvey (eds), *Dexterity and its development* (pp. 431–451). Mahwah, NJ: Erlbaum.

Richardson, H.M. (1932). The growth of adaptive behaviour in infants. *Genetic Psychology Monographs*, 12, 195–359.

Rogoff, B. (1990). *Apprenticeship in thinking: Cognitive development in social context*. New York: Oxford University Press.

Rovee-Collier, C. (1996). Shifting focus from what to why. *Infant Behavior and Development*, 19, 385–400.

Sameroff, A.J. (1983). Developmental systems: contexts and evolution. In P.H. Mussen (ed.), *Handbook of child psychology*, Vol. 1, W. Kessen (ed.), *History, theory, and methods* (pp. 237–294). New York: Wiley.

Shaw, R.E., & Turvey, M.T. (1981). Coalitions as models of ecosystems: A realist perspective on perceptual organization. In M. Kubovy & J.R. Pomerants (eds), *Perceptual organization*. Hillsdale, NJ: Erlbaum.

Sitskoorn, M.M., & Smitsman, A.W. (1995). Infants' perception of dynamic relations between objects: Passing through or support. *Developmental Psychology*, 31, 437–447.

Sitskoorn, M.M., & Smitsman, A.W. (1997). Perception of dynamic object relations in infancy. *Infant Behavior and Development*, 20, pp. 141–150.

Smitsman, A.W. (1995). Information through action: Comments on Michaels and Beek. *Ecological Psychology*, 4, 279–283.

Smitsman, A.W. (1997). The development of tool use: Changing boundaries between organism and environment. In C. Dent-Read & P. Zukow-Goldring (eds), *Evolving explanations of development: Ecological approaches to organism–environment systems* (pp. 301–329). Washington, DC: APA.

Smitsman, A.W. (2000). Slumbering talents: where do they reside? In C.F.M. van Lieshout & P.G. Heymans (eds), *Developing talents across the life span*. Hove: Psychology Press.

Smitsman, A.W., & Bosman, A.M. Th. (1985). Some consequences of Gibson's affordance concept to the study of meaning and its development in children. Paper presented at the Third International Conference on Event Perception and Action, Uppsala, June.

Spelke, E.S. (1990). Principles of object perception. *Cognitive Science*, 14, 29–56.

Steenbergen, B., van der Kamp, J., Smitsman, A.W., & Carson, R.G. (1997). Spoon handling in two- to four-year-old children. *Ecological Psychology*, 2, 113–129.

Stoffregen, T.A., & Bardy, B.G. (2001). On specification and the senses. *Behavioral and Brain Sciences*, 24, 195–261.

Sugarman, S. (1984). The development of preverbal communication: Its contribution and limits in promoting the development of language. In R.L. Schiefelbusch & J. Pickar (eds), *The acquisition of communicative competence*. Baltimore, MD: University Park Press.

Sugiyama, Y. (1993). Local variation of tools and tool use among wild chimpanzee populations. In A. Berthelet & J. Chavaillon (eds), *The use of tools by human and non-human primates*. New York: Oxford University Press.

Thelen, E., Corbetta, D., Kamm, K., Spencer, J.P., Schneider, K., & Zernicke, R.F. (1993). The transition to reaching: Mapping intention and intrinsic dynamics. *Child Development*, 64, 1058–1098.

Thelen, E., Schoner, G., Scheier, C., & Smith, L. (2001). The dynamics of embodiment: A field theory of infant perseverative reaching. *Behavioural and Brain Sciences*, 24, 1–86.

Thelen, E., & Smith, L.B. (1994). *A dynamic systems approach to the development of cognition and action*. Cambridge, MA: MIT Press.

Thelen, E., & Spencer, J. (1998). Postural control during reaching in young infants: A dynamic systems approach. *Neuroscience and Biobehavioral Reviews*, 22, 507–514.

Turvey, M.T., & Shaw, R.E. (1979). The primacy of perceiving: An ecological reformulation of perception for understanding memory. In L.G. Nillson (ed.), *Perspectives on memory research: Essays in honor of Uppsala University 500th anniversary*. Hillsdale, NJ: Erlbaum.

Ulrich, B.D. (1997). Dynamic systems theory and skill development in infants and children. In K.J. Connolly & H. Forssberg (eds), *Neurophysiology and neuro-psychology of motor development* (pp. 319–345). London: MacKeith.

Van de Grind, W.A. (1997) *Natuurlijke intelligentie: Over denken, intelligentie en bewustzijn van mensen en andere dieren*. Amsterdam: Nieuwezijds.

van Leeuwen, L., Smitsman, A.W., & van Leeuwen, C. (1994). Affordances, perceptual complexity, and the development of tool use. Journal of Experimental Psychology: Human Perception and Performance, 20, 174–191.

Waddington, C.H. (1977). *Tools for Thought*. London: Cape.

Willats, P. (1997). Beyond the 'couch potato' infant: How infants use their knowledge to regulate action, solve problems, and achieve goals. In G. Bremner, A. Slater, and G. Butterworth (eds), *Infant development: Recent advances* (pp 109–133). Hove: Psychology Press.

9

Social Relations and Affective Development in the First Two Years in Family Contexts

KURT KREPPNER

Development in Context: Basic Issues

The first two years in human development are characterized by a sequence of dramatic changes in all relevant domains such as neurophysiological, sensorimotor, or cognitive functioning. There is no period in later life which could be compared to this phase of rapid and tremendous changes in the child. The entire spectrum of human development with all its various components is included in this process. Aside from neuronal differentiation and increment of cognitive competence during the first two years, perhaps the most obvious and amazing changes can be observed in the child's growing ability to establish, maintain, and reorganize relationships. Changes in social competence and emotional expressiveness are the areas where parents first tend to realize the 'human' conditions associated with the child's growth. The first laughing, repeated when the mother is approaching the baby, regular reactions to different kinds of voicing, and the increment of mutual adaptation during everyday rituals like feeding, bathing, changing diapers, and so forth, soon form a specific emotional bonding of the parents – and siblings – for this new member of the family. A relationship is being established with a certain rhythm of mutuality, a series of contingent behavior patterns, associated with a specific emotional tone. For the infant, the members of the family and the way they approach the new member constitute his or her proximal context, and define the character of the relationships which provide the essential basis for the child's possibilities to explore the world and to build up meaning. During the first months, every concrete interaction with other family members may be associated with repeated occurrence of fundamental affects and basic visceral reactions in the infant. Spitz (1957) has proposed a differentiation of affective exchange modes between infant and caretaker during the first 4–6 months. During this period, the infant changes from a holistic in-depth reaction which does not differ among the inputs from different sense organs to a more and more sense-organ-specific reaction to stimulation. Spitz has called these two basic ways of perceiving 'coenesthetic' (holistic perception) and 'diacritical' (differentiated). Mother–infant interactions and communication during the first months are characterized by the coenesthetic way of perception. From the third to fourth month on, the more differentiated mode of diacritical perception by using the various sense organs is smoothly being established. During the early months, the exchange of emotion between infant and caretaker is believed to range between the two principal alternatives of eliciting either positive or negative holistic reactions in the child. According to Lazarus (1991), congruent transactions between child and caregiver produce a positive tone and incongruent transactions a negative tone. This description of a global characteristic of an affective tone which defines a relationship appears to be a rather basic concept with regard to repeated action–reaction cycles. Recurring experiences of the two alternative inner states (positive or negative affective tone) will soon be associated with environmental conditions, particularly with the appearance of a specific person. If these feelings are bound to a person and his or her actions, a relational experience is shaped in the child at a stage where he or she is still in a state where the sense organs are just starting to differentiate among various stimulations.

The child experiences relationships with other persons, and the developmental process unfolds within the limits of these relationships. Here the various possibilities are experienced to communicate about subjects, events, or persons, perhaps quite differently with the various family members such as mother, father, sibling, or grandparent. The family members approaching the infant set the frame in which the child can make his or her relational experiences, including the exchange of expressions and the feeling of having positive or negative affect. Even during the first months in the family, the infant encounters the various members' idiosyncratic ways of establishing and maintaining a relationship.

In a more general perspective, it should be realized that the mode of exchange between infant and outside world is also shaping a segment of the world which is more and more becoming the infant's 'proximal environment'. William Stern (1935) has conceptualized this segment of proximal environment as the 'personal world' in which the specific kind of exchange between a person and the outside world is formed. The 'personal world' is part of both the individual and its environment where concepts and perceptual patterns of the person meet with the specific structures of the environment; it provides the range of possibilities to initiate a new or participate in an ongoing interaction, or to communicate affective signals. By creating such an arena for exchange, Stern – following ideas of his colleague von Uexküll (1920) – defined the ecological niche of a person. This arena of exchange was taken as essentially influencing a person's formation of cognitions about the world; this 'proximal environment' is also believed to be highly relevant for the formation of inner representations, although not identical with it. It is exactly that part of the wider environment that is identical neither with the set of experiences and inner representations nor with the 'objective' environment. Stern conceptualized a third location between experiencing (subjective side) and physical description of environmental conditions (objective side), the necessary condition for characterizing the person's activities in an environment, the *gelebte Welt* (the world a person is living in), which is different from both *erlebte Welt* (experience) and *objektive Welt* (objective world). He put the focus on the process of 'interaction' between person and environment where the person, by his or her actions in the proximal space, reconciles the incongruities between expectancy sets and the results of actions which, in turn, create new experience and new sets of expectancies:

> The personal world is not identical with that set of experiences we call 'world view'. This experienced 'world' is but a segment of the world in which the individual really exists or 'lives' [*gelebte Welt*]. Objective events can only become part of an individual's experience by the fact that they fit into his or her world in which he or she exists. The relationship we have to explore, therefore, is not two-pronged (objective world, subjective experience) but three-pronged (transpersonal objective world, world of individual's existence, experienced subjective world). Between the physical stimulus and the experience of perception lies the integral situation of stimulation in which the individual exists. Between the sociological unit 'family' and the experience of one's family lies the individual's vital and introceptive connectedness with the family. (1935, p. 124, translated by K.K.)

From an infant's perspective, early relationships format this 'personal world': they generate the part of the environment which becomes essential for the subject's inner representation of the world, and at the same time they provide the arena for the subject's growing and unfolding possibilities to actively shape the environment. Again, William Stern has emphasized the subject's own activity to have an impact on the proximal part of the environment which he had called 'personal world':

> By the permanent exchange between person and world, not only the person is being shaped, but also her or his world. The 'environment' of an individual does not consist just of that part of the objective world which is accidentally surrounding this individual and therefore affects him or her. Environment is rather that portion of the world that the individual actively brings close to him or her as he or she is both receptive and sensitive to this portion. At the same time, the individual tries to shape this piece of world which is fitting his personality. (1935, p. 125, translated by K.K.)

Thus, parent–infant relationships and their quality appear to strongly form the basic accumulation of two major experiences in the child: first, the frequencies of either positive or negative emotional states, and second, the linking of the regulation of these inner states with other persons. Inner states are not merely experienced as being either escalating, de-escalating, or even changing when being together with another person (e.g. a specific member of the family); they are basic components for constituting models or blueprints for modes to approach the wider social context. In sum, the family's idiosyncratic ways of communicating about objects, situations, and feelings set the context for the infant's earliest experiences, particularly linking emotional states to other persons. Thus the development of a child cannot be thought of as occurring without being affected by environmental conditions. Development is neither just the unfolding of a genetic endowment nor the process of being imprinted by stimulation. It is rather a complex interplay between genetic endowment and environmental factors, bound to a specific relational context characterized by a particular emotional climate.

Family, Relations, and Early Social-emotional Experiences

The family as an institution of infant development, characterized by a specific communication culture and a particular emotional climate supporting or impeding the unfolding of the child's various skills and abilities, has been discussed in modern developmental psychology as a relevant factor only since the late sixties and the beginning of the seventies. The role of the quality of mother–infant and father–infant relationships as a crucial aspect for emotional and social development became more systematically studied when psychoanalytic, ethological, and evolutionary concepts were linked together. Observational research has obviously played a relevant role as this methodological approach generated a new and more holistic approach for understanding infant development. Although the family as an institution had been investigated under economic and historical perspectives, individual human development was not directly associated with the qualities of a family. When, for example, Sir Francis Galton (1883) studied pedigrees of British families, the intention was to find out how certain – mostly intellectual – abilities are transmitted across generations. There was no intention to classify families according to their state of inner harmony or to their offspring's possibilities to unfold their capacities by growing up in a positive emotional climate. Even when William Stern (1935) tried to reconcile dispositional and environmental concepts in his personalistic psychology, he did not directly address the family as the place where person-specific environment is being experienced.

Family as the institution in which specific modes of relationship and communication are being established was first conceptualized by Ernest Burgess in 1926, who began to think about families in a dynamic, perhaps even systems-oriented way. He tried to categorize families according to salient characteristics, for example their religious or ethnic origins. Although failing in this attempt, he detected another aspect which he assumed could serve as a promising candidate for successfully classifying families with regard to their potential to provide an appropriate environment for development and adaptation, the quality of relationships among family members. Burgess' idea of the family as a 'super-personality' (1926, p. 5) can be taken as a precursor of the later conception of the family as a developing unit (Duvall, 1977). Of course, different cultures may have different socialization goals, and therefore family environments for infants may look rather dissimilar. Culturally preformed values, belief systems, traditions and developmental ideals may format many concrete interaction patterns inside the family for the child. However, at the same time, albeit perhaps appearing different on the surface, we do believe that some basic human conditions exist which, beyond cultural multiformity, foster or impede a child's development.

The Concept of Emotional Climate

A basic concept to describe differing qualities of relationship formats in which children grow up, the notion of 'emotional climate', is often used to elucidate particular characteristics which are mainly associated with global and mostly nonverbal aspects of affective exchange in the family. Families differ according to their emotional climates and form contexts in which, for example, the regulation of affect is cultivated or not, and communication about emotions is easy or difficult. The infant grows up in a socio-emotional niche which has been and is continuously constructed by the family members. Sometimes, however, the concept of 'emotional climate' is misunderstood as an incidental and perhaps more or less marginal feature of a relationship. For a child's emotional development, the climate of the relationship with the primary caretakers, the parents, is an essential attribute. Every relationship between two persons can be qualified according to its particular emotional tone. Exploration of the world, and exchange about controversial issues, are dependent on the emotional climate of the relationship in which they occur.

Although the concept of emotional climate in a relational context has been emphasized only in more recent research, it has a remarkable tradition in developmental psychology. For example, the scholar Erasmus Desiderius (Rotterdamus) (1518), when writing for mothers and how they should care for their children, emphasized in a chapter entitled 'The happy mother' the importance of love and attention for successful learning and the growth of social competence in children: 'The prime condition of all learning is the reciprocal love between teacher and taught' (Erasmus, 1518; in Niestroj, 1987, p. 35). Here, the relationship between 'teacher and taught' can be taken as another example where the emotional climate is influential for the creation of meaning. Even without exchange with another person, an individual creates different meanings about objects depending on their subjective emotional state and imagination. In his 'war landscape' Kurt Lewin (1917) has explored the different meanings of a landscape for a farmer, a soldier, or a person who just walks through it. Stern's (1935) concept of a 'personal space' focused on a holistic understanding of inner representation, dependent on experiences in the proximal environment and modes of inner processing, where perceptions are linked to emotional states. In the tradition of Dilthey, Felix Krueger (1924; 1928) emphasized the structural and holistic aspect of all experiences on the one hand, and the importance of emotion for the processing and structuring of experiences on the other. He created a new and dynamic notion of perception, where the individual actively creates his or her meanings in a process. At the beginning of this process, an unstructured and diffuse affect is primarily dominating the experience and influencing the modality of structuring the end product; at the end of this process, a well-structured concept might exist in the individual's inner representation. In this holistic approach, creation of meaning is always associated with an emotional environment, and inner representations are linked to an emotional tone.

Recent studies in infant development have emphasized the general importance of affect for individual development, as the infant's basic experiences through communications with other members in the family are believed to be mainly emotional:

> Affect is increasingly viewed as a central socialization process (Gottman, Fainsilber-Katz, & Hooven, 1996; Parke, 1994). The study of affect has assumed a variety of forms, including the development of emotion regulation (Bridges & Grolnick, 1995; Eisenberg & Fabes, 1994), the development of emotional production and understanding, and the role of emotion in the enactment of the parenting role (Dix, 1991). (Parke & Buriel, 1998, p. 467)

Family members have to invest energy and emotion in relationships in order to maintain or, if necessary, to renegotiate them. This process is realized by communication. The style of communication and the modality in which it is possible to talk about the world, others, or oneself has an impact on the child's capacity to understand social meanings of exchange modes, and to regulate own feelings. Recent research seems to indicate that the way a family talks about relationships and family history may provide a promising diagnostic tool for the quality of the family relationship (Fiese et al., 1999).

Importance of Parent–Parent Relationship

The relational context of a family is constituted not only by the mother–child and the father–child relationships, but also by the spouses' way of communicating with each other. The relationship between the spouses is an integral part of the family; it has been established in a long process before the child was born and is now, after the arrival of a child, in a period of difficult adaptation (Cowan & Cowan, 1987; 1992). The spouses have to reorganize their former relationship (as a couple without a child); they have to transform it into a relationship inside the family characterized by both 'marital' and 'parental' aspects. The experience of seeing the partner in a new relationship with the child where oneself is not participating – for the father the mother–child relationship, for the mother the father–child relationship – implies the reorganization of the former relationship between marital partners only. Moreover, the rapid changes of the infant's development with regard to the different functions demand permanent parental monitoring in order to adapt to the child's new competences and ways to express own needs and intentions. The notion of the family as an intergenerational institution for maintaining the members' motivation and for creating a common meaning system has been formulated by family researchers like Ira Reiss (1965), Bell and Vogel (1968), and Rodgers (1973). Two parents with a child form a complex relational context which constitutes the family. The course of development therefore not only is embedded in the dyadic parent–child relationships but has to be seen as taking place within the relational framework inside the entire family. However a caveat should be made concerning the generalization of family formats and their implications for child development across different cultures. Divergent normative family forms, e.g. monogamous versus polygamous families, may cause environments for infants which are structurally difficult to compare and have seldom been systematically studied under these developmental perspectives. Most of the studies which shape our picture of healthy or deprived developmental pathways are based largely on European or Euro-American standards of family contexts. It should be left open to further in-depth studies within other non-European and non-Euro-American cultures to discover both general and specific patterns of child care and developmental contexts.

Basic Course of Development during the First Two Years

Particularly during early development, a family's emotional climate and its culture of communication about objects, events, inner states, and conflicts are believed to be essential for a child's differential developmental pathway. Fundamental conditions for differences are, according to Malatesta et al. (1989), the varying abilities to properly express emotions in a relationship, mutual attention or lack of contingency. Being able to express emotions, to learn to exchange information about inner states with relevant others, is also always connected with other strands of development. As the studies of Malatesta et al. have shown, the so-called catch-up effect of motor and cognitive skills reported from infants during their early steps of development are not found for either emotional expression or social skills. Catch-up effect means a compensatory realignment process (mostly initiated by an intervention) aimed at correction of deviations which have occurred during earlier development. However, the effect has only been observed after intervention in areas such as motor and cognitive development. Corrections seem much more difficult if the deviations took place in the area of social and emotional development. Two conclusions can be drawn from this area-specific difference in developmental compensation.

First, early development of social competence and emotional expressiveness may be essential for the further course of individual social and emotional developmental pathways. Second, if development is seen as a holistic process, different functional aspects such as cognition or motor development cannot be considered separately. Table 9.1 gives a systematic overview of the first two years in the life of a child covering both relevant functions (horizontal) and transition periods (vertical). The two-year period has been subdivided into eight phases; changes occur during all developmental phases for all major functions of locomotor and sensorimotor development. The four other aspects all belong to the social-emotional realm, although terms like 'relational sensitivity' or 'relational competence' could perhaps better characterize aspects of developmental differentiations in the child which in this table are labeled as 'intersubjectivity' and 'individuation'. These last two terms focus on the child as a developing individual expressing own intentions toward others and the understanding of others' intentions.

As the table shows, tremendous changes and progress are made in all relevant functions during the first 24 months in the child's life. Under a holistic perspective of infant development, a formal separation of single functions such as locomotor or sensorimotor development from affective or social development appears to be obsolete. Rather it seems necessary to consider all the different functions at the same time when the relational network in a family as the basic context for individual development is being analyzed.

Brief Historical Overview

Through history one can easily find the tradition of being confronted with fundamentally diverging views on the handling of child care and visions about child development at different time periods. Perhaps this may be helpful in finding some orientation in today's controversial discussion between the two camps, where one is still emphasizing exclusively the importance of genetic endowment, and the other is underlining the eminent role of environment for human development. Without a deeper look into the history of developmental psychology, our understanding of current concepts may remain rather shallow or shortened. For long periods in history, development in infants during the first years was believed to be largely a matter of nature, triggered by biological factors alone. Over the last 500 years of child care, however, the idea of natural growth was often confronted with the vision of the education

Table 9.1 *Ontogenetic changes in the child*

Months	Locomotoric development (Gesell)	Sensorimotoric development (Piaget)	Affective development (Sroufe)	Social development (Sander)	Intersubjectivity (Trevarthen)	Individuation process (Mahler)
0–1		Reflexes	Absolute stimulus barrier			Symbiotic phase
2–3		Primary circular reactions	Orientation to external world	Initial regulation of basic activities (sleeping, eating eliminating)	Primary intersubjectivity	
4–7	Turning of body, sitting	Secondary circular reactions	Showing positive affect	Reciprocal exchange in relationship		Phase of differentiation
8–9	Crawling	Coordination of secondary circular reactions	Active participation in relationship	Initiative in relationship	Secondary intersubjectivity	
10–12	Standing	Tertiary circular reactions	Attachment	Focalization, exploration		
16–17	Toddling, walking	Combination of schemata, Internalization	Control of emotional expressions	Self-assertion		*Rapprochement* and triangulation
18–21			Emergence of self-concept			
22–24		Symbolic representation				Consolidation of individuality

and creation of a new human being. For example, as early as during the flourishing of humanism, the quality of relationship between caregiver and child was strongly accentuated as a prerequisite for creating better and more future-oriented conditions for infant development.

Early Knowledge about the Relevance of Relationship Quality

Already 400 years ago, the importance of the quality of mothers' talk for infants' language acquisition and cognitive growth had been clearly formulated. For example, Luis Vives (1531/1912) stressed the relevance of the quality of the mother–child relationship as the basic component for promoting the child's development. The infant was primarily seen as being dependent on the relationship with the primary caregiver, and the humanists emphasized the importance of this early relationship with mothers as they intended to teach them how to introduce new humanistic ideas into the next generation. By giving instructions to mothers they hoped to overcome the mental procrastination of the prevailing scholastic schools. Thus, Luis Vives wrote about the role of the mothers:

> For the babe first heareth her mother and first beginneth to inform her speech after hers. For that age can do nothing itself, but counterfeit and follow others, and is cunning in this thing only . . . Let [the mother] give her diligence, at least wise because of her children, that she use no rude and blunt speech lest theat manner of speaking take such root in the tender minds of the children, and so grow and increase together with their age, that they cannot forget it. Children will learn no speech better, nor more plainly express, than they will their mother's. They inquire everything to her; whatsoever she answereth, thy believe and regard, and take it even for the Gospel. Oh mothers, what an occasion for you unto your children, to make them whether you will, good or bad! (1531/1912, pp. 124–125)

In order to underline the importance of the quality of the relationship between mother and child, another humanist, Erasmus Desiderius (Rotterdamus) (1518/1965), pointed to the dangers of alienation when daily routines of child care were left to nurses. He depicted a vivid scenario of derailing the mother–child relationship and directly warned mothers in his *colloquia familiaria*:

> Do you really believe that a wet-nurse can make as little fuss about the unpleasantness of infant care as the natural mother; that she can show the same care and concern when the nappies are full, when the child has to pee, when it screams or is ill? Only when she loves the infant as much as the mother will she concern herself with all that. But then it may happen that your own child will love you less; it has to divide its love between two mothers. And you too will not be drawn with the same love to your child, the moment you see that your growing child doesn't feel it has to obey your commands. And you may become cooler in your affection when you are forced to realize how your child is taking after its wet-nurse. For the prime condition of all learning is the reciprocal love between teacher and taught.

This citation may bring to mind even some of today's controversial discussions about the advantages and disadvantages of day care centers for development during early childhood. Not only is the relevance of establishing a good relationship between mother and child by providing continuous care echoed in Erasmus' arguments, but also the danger of the infant's alienation from the mother when exposed too extensively to another caretaker. This citation also echoes the concept of 'quality time' as frequent advice for managing and maintaining a well-functioning parent–child relationship. Quality of relationship, however, has lived on in history as a relevant aspect in child education.

The intense relationship between teacher and student for successful education was, for example, later emphasized by Jean Jacques Rousseau. In his book *Emile* (1762) he demanded that educators should realize that abilities in children develop in different stages and also that teachers should have a development-sensitive view on children. In contrast to the humanist period, the mother–child relationship or the family as an institution with specific relational qualities for the child's development was no more at the center of interest in Rousseau's time. Heinrich Campe (1785), strongly influenced by Rousseau's ideas to teach children at an early age by confronting them – according to their developmental stage – with nature, underlined the role of early stimulation more than the importance of a warm and well-functioning relationship. He rather favored the idea of keeping children from being too pampered by their caretakers and preferred a more autonomy-oriented and skill-promoting mode of interaction between parents and children. Dietrich Tiedemann (1787) observed carefully the first three and a half years in the life of his son and registered the development of single perceptional and cognitive skills. His diary represents the first systematic report about an infant's developmental progressions. Tiedemann, however, was less interested in documenting real interaction patterns between parents and child. Instead, he meticulously depicted the natural mental development of an average child in order to gain some comparative information for further research. Tiedemann, like Campe, worked in the tradition of both Rousseau and John Locke, starting out from the importance of early education to provide the child with appropriate stimulation.

This view on child care and child development changed after Darwin's (1859) conception of the evolution of species. Biologists became more and more attracted to intense study of the course of child development; they hoped to learn more about evolutionary processes by observing the natural growth in children. As a result of these intentions, children's developmental progress during the first years of life was systematically observed and described in the diaries of various scientists such as Preyer (1893), Shinn (1900), Scupin and Scupin (1907), and Stern (Stern & Stern, 1907). A more and more sophisticated observational methodology using the newly developed cinematograph as a medium to preserve developmental stages and to analyze developmental progress in the work of Bühler (Bühler & Hetzer, 1927), Lewin (1926; 1927), and Gesell (1928; 1935) in the first half of this century led to a better understanding of developmental processes.

Nature and Nurture as Two Factors Affecting the Individual's Course of Development

Although the controversial issue of nature and/or nurture and their role for individual development has been debated for centuries without a satisfying solution, it seems as if many of today's research programs are still haunted by the idea of finding a final solution. Nativism and empiricism are two positions which have led to very different models for understanding the growth during early stages of development of a person. Whereas under a nativistic perspective an individual is born with a set of dispositions or a genetic endowment which is believed to dominate the course of development, the individual is born as a *tabula rasa* under the empiricist perspective. Here, a person's development is directed by experience alone, and only sensations and perceptions of reality lead to an inner representation.

Youniss (1999) argued for new life in the old field of developmental psychology, beyond this controversy, by pointing out that the well-known antinomies of nature–nurture, biology–society, individual–culture had led to false research strategies in the field. Referring to the work of Klaus Riegel (1975), Youniss argued for a more unified view on humans, as they are always influenced both by their endowment and by their cultural history. Youniss also replicated the argument of Toren (1993) who claimed that 'humans are biologically social creatures whose initiating biology is socially shaped so that it becomes futile to try to separate what is biological from what is social. The person is defined by a social history which is shared with others in the culture' (Youniss, 1999, p. 147).

Plasticity and Activity

William Stern (1935) had already tried to reconcile the different views by conceptualizing development as a process of 'convergence' of a person's genetic endowment such as various dispositions on the one hand and environmental factors influencing the path of development on the other. In Stern's view, the individual's set of dispositions is in permanent interaction with the culture-specific environment during development. This process of convergence is responsible for creating a unique personality. An individual's endowment, the dispositions of a person, are always linked to the environment, and the dispositions' development depends on the specific environmental conditions in which a person grows up. Stern favored the idea of plasticity and activity. In his concept of the person as a *unitas multiplex* he tried to integrate the two controversial positions by creating an active, Gestalt-shaping individual whose developmental course is dependent on the multitude of dispositions on the one hand, and on the specific conditions of the environment on the other. Long before systemic concepts were common in psychology, Stern proposed a concept similar to a transactional model of individual development. The question of how endowment and cultural environment interact during human development was a favorite topic in discussions at Stern's institute at the University of Hamburg. Stern, the developmental and person-oriented psychologist, Cassirer, the neo-Kantian philosopher, and von Uexküll, the biologist with a holistic and vitalistic view on the interplay between nature and nurture, developed a new dynamic thinking about the interaction between the developing organism and its environment (see Kreppner, 1997). Cassirer (1944) emphasized the ability of the human species to handle and transmit symbols and signs as a basic difference with other species. For him, the use of symbols and signs opened a new dimension for creating meaning in communication.

What Is Human in Human Development? The Role of Culture and the Transmission of Symbols by Communication

Comparative research studying differences in developmental pathways between humans and other species is not new. For example, Kellogg and Kellogg (1933) tried to find out whether a common environment could reduce species differences between chimpanzees and human infants in early development. More recently, differences in species-specific development were studied under a language acquisition perspective. In particular, increased joint activities to use gestures and words were registered to occur between mothers and infants when both are engaged with a common object (Bakeman & Adamson, 1984). Furthermore, the concept of joint attention between mother and infant was also a major focus in a number of studies on the process of language acquisition in interaction (Akhtar, Dunham, & Dunham, 1991; Tomasello & Farrar, 1986). A comparison study between chimpanzees and infants revealed marked differences in the use of gestures as a tool to understand other persons as intentional agents with whom they may share experience even at an early age (Tomasello & Camaioni, 1997). It may well remain an open question whether this differential characteristic of the acquisition of early symbolic communication skills should be understood as a process of social learning or as a kind of inborn device. Without deciding this still unanswered question, a number of studies further explored the onset of differences between chimpanzees and human infants (Carpenter, Nagell, & Tomasello, 1998). During the age between 9 and 15 months, differences between the two species seem to become more and more manifest. The sharing of attention, referring to a common meaning in a communication, the ability to recognize another person's intentions from his or her behavior or expression, early imitation of behavior, and acquisition of language occurred in human infants but not in apes during this developmental period.

> The reason that they [chimpanzees] have not created cultures of the human kind is that it appears as though they do not understand their conspecifics as intentional agents like themselves who experience the world in ways similar to the ways in which they themselves do. Thus, in their communication with conspecifics, apes do not point to distal entities in the environment, they do not hold up objects for others to see and share, and they do not actively give or offer objects to other individuals. (1998, pp. 131–132)

In human development, shared attention is always linked to a functioning relationship between child and parent, and the essential prerequisite to create a functioning relationship is the possibility to exchange and to regulate emotions. This perspective on the eminent role of emotional exchange in a relationship for the course of individual development has been emphasized, for example, by Saarni, Mumme, and Campos (1998). These authors summarize the knowledge about the links between emotional development and other functions of development that has been gathered during the last 15 years (1998, p. 238). The communication and regulation of emotions between parent and infant have been elaborated as central aspects for a child's growing competence in establishing and maintaining relationships.

Productive Research: A New Look at the Child and A Dynamic View of the Family Context

Dramatic changes in looking at children and developmental processes have occurred during the last 15 years. As Harter (1998) notes, a major shift can be observed from a function-oriented to a more holistic view of the child. Furthermore, the new concept of the 'competent child' influenced the design of infant research conducted during the 1970s and 1980s. Experiments with infants, even a few days after birth, showed very early participation in interactions with caretakers and revealed phenomena which had remained unnoticed in previous studies. For example, the newborn's obvious capacity to engage in interactions immediately after birth was documented in studies which showed the child's ability to imitate basic expressions of others (Meltzoff & Moore, 1983) as early as a few days after birth.

In general, results in new experimental studies covering the first 18 months in the life of a child underlined the importance of the infant's relatedness to primary caregivers. Furthermore, the intense observation of the developing infant within a dyadic relationship or, under a family perspective, within a complex relational network, elucidates the process of the growing self, that is, how patterns of repeated affective exchanges are linked to recurring experiences in joint actions with others, structuring the otherwise chaotic world around a child who is increasingly exploring the differences between a still diffuse self and other persons.

Activity of Babies and the Impact of Infant-Caregiver Relationship on Early Development

The quality of relationship between infant and mother as well as between infant and father became a salient issue during the late 1960s and 1970s, when researchers into human infancy began to look at everyday interactions between parents and children and detected the bidirectional exchange even in early infant–parent interactions (Bell, 1968; Escalona, 1973; Rheingold, 1969). Another series of studies documented the specific impact of fathers on infants. Infants showed specific reactions to fathers' play which was different to mothers' stimulations (Lamb, 1975; 1976; Pedersen, 1975; 1980). Furthermore, evidence was also found that mother–child interaction changes in quality and quantity when the father is present (Clarke-Stewart, 1978; 1980; McHale & Rasmussen, 1998). A new interest emerged in investigating not only single parent–child dyads but also the entire family encompassing the parent–parent or marital relationship (Belsky, 1981; Pedersen, Anderson, & Cain, 1980).

The linking of connectedness and the growth of autonomy in early childhood to the quality of the child–caregiver relationship has created new perspectives for studying developmental processes associated with the emergence of self in the child. The quality of relationship between child and caregiver, and the kind of information conveyed in this relationship, are considered to be relevant components for children's abilities or inabilities to organize their own behavior and to regulate their emotions when interacting with others. For example, Harter (1998, p. 553) claims in her review that today a far more integrated view on cognitive, social, and emotional aspects of a child's developmental pathway is prevailing compared to former more isolated concepts in this area.

From I-Self to Me-Self

The discrimination between I-self and Me-self (in the terms of G.H. Mead, 1934) during the second half of the second year is seen as a developmental shift which brings the child to a new level of consciousness (Lewis, 1994). The self as an object (Me-self) can be communicated to others. This concept is akin to the notion of a child's 'internal working model' (Bowlby, 1969; 1973; 1980), a concept describing the inner representation of a relationship in the child. The continuous dynamics in building up such a model during the first two years of life has been discussed extensively by Pipp (1990; 1993), who distinguishes later representational working models – such as the emerging Me-self during the second half of the second year – from earlier sensorimotor working models. These earlier models are believed to contain episode-like sequences of interactions which are routinely repeated at certain everyday situations such as feeding, bathing, changing diapers, putting to bed. These emotionally highly loaded rituals activate a set of behavior patterns in the child and generate expectations of behavior patterns in the caregiver. In a similar approach, early expressions of a growing self are formulated by Neisser (1991) who has proposed the notion of an 'ecological self', in which the experience of the I-self as an agent on the environment is indicated. This shift in early self-development is fostered by a growing history of reciprocity experienced in the relationships with relevant others. The development from an I-self to a Me-self is further promoted by the increased experience of being able to initiate patterned behavior sequences when being together with others, and to vary elements in these sequences.

Widening the Perspective on the Child's Relational Context: A Dynamic View of the Family

New ideas about conceptualizing the family as a dynamic unit were first proposed by Ernest Burgess (1926). He defined families as interacting units or 'superpersonalities' and claimed that their modes of communication could be used as a criterion for differentiation. During the 1940s and 1950s, new concepts taken from systems theory, cybernetics, and information theory in combination with old approaches such as psychoanalytic theory formed an entirely new perspective on the complexity and reciprocity of human behavior and its development within the relational network and communication culture of the family. Why was this research so important for a new understanding of development in the family? Children's sensitivity for the quality of relationship, and their handling of ambiguities in communications with their parents, became a center of attention and interest. Harry Stack Sullivan (1953), for example, extended the application of family systems theory and psychoanalysis to psychotics. He claimed that even schizophrenics could be understood if it was possible to establish a social relationship with these patients; he argued that schizophrenics suffer from early disturbed social relationships. Although research with schizophrenics was not successful in terms of communication analysis and the double bind concept, the role of communication in the family, the way of handling information between the family members, became a general issue, even in infancy research.

The Concept of Family Development

One of the most influential theoretical achievements for finding new access to the linking of family and developmental research was the expansion of family systems theory by adding a time dimension. This new approach was elaborated when the family's role of conveying pathological symptoms between generations was debated under a perspective of the normative needs of children in their families during the various stages of their development. A new theory was first formulated by Evelyn Duvall and Reuben Hill (1948). These authors began to conceptualize a developmental perspective on the entire family. The roots of this concept, aside from being inspired by Burgess' (1926) ideas, reach back to David Havighurst's (1953) developmental task concept. During its developmental course, a family has to accomplish a number of 'family developmental tasks' which describe the conditions to master a specific developmental period. These periods are largely defined by the children's developmental stages. During the 1970s and 1980s, the perspective on the course of a family through life changed when researchers focused no longer on single stages but rather on the intervals between the different stages, the so-called 'transition periods'. Cowan (1991) brought up the topic of transition competence in families directly. By introducing his new concept he depicted a family's capacity to handle periods of change and uncertainty during the child's developmental course.

Different Methodological Approaches for Describing Active Development in a Complex Relational Context

The Ethological Approach

The growing knowledge about the sensitivity of infants to social relationships and to variations in communicative contexts had considerable effects on the designing of empirical studies as well as on the selection of methodological approaches. Researchers like Clarke-Stewart (1978) who started from a behavioral framework and a focus on the micro-analysis of single behaviors ended up by investigating more molar behaviors. They became more and more interested in the description of recurring interaction patterns. The intense observation of mother–child interactions and, later, of even more complex communication patterns within the family led to the establishment of new categories which focused more on the dynamics of exchange process and relational aspects than on the description of isolated single behaviors. Such attempts were the detailed analyses of interaction rituals like 'greeting behavior' in very young infants interacting with their mothers (Papoušek & Papoušek, 1977), or 'secondary intersubjectivity' (Trevarthen & Hubley, 1978), a behavior in 8-month-olds checking the affective reaction of the caretaker when exploring objects. The openness for creating new categories in many observational studies helped to focus more on relation-oriented behaviors during data collection. A good example of this openness for registering new aspects when observing mother–child interactions is the description of the lengthy process of category generation by Richards and Bernal:

> Our recording of categories grew out of our observations rather than being imposed on them by some pre-determined theoretical position. At first we watched without making any attempt to record. Later we began to note features of behavior that recurred regularly. (1972, p. 181)

With the use of video recordings, this open approach in observational studies was even more extended. For example, different perspectives could now be taken into account during one recorded situation when behaviors of persons in a complex relationship or holistic aspects of the character of a relationship were to be analyzed (Kreppner, 1991). As the original situation in all its complexity was 'frozen' on video-tape, a variety of different categories describing multiple aspects of behaviors and relationships could be applied. For example, when two or more partners are observed while communicating with each other, reciprocity in the regulation of emotional expressions in a family network can be studied in full detail.

The Use of Experiments

As reciprocity was observed in interactions even between newborns and their caretakers in everyday situations (Bell, 1968) and as babies' ability was shown to imitate facial expressions of caretakers even a few days after birth (Meltzoff & Moore, 1983; 1989), experiments were conducted which aimed at the study of infants' early capacity to actively influence the partner in a relationship. It has been found, for example, that from the third month infants are able to initiate emotional exchange in an ongoing relationship when mothers had been instructed to exhibit a 'still face', that is, a completely straight face in front of their children (Tronick, 1989; Tronick & Cohn, 1989). Another example of a new approach to apply a combination of ethological methodology and comparative analysis is the 'strange situation test' (Ainsworth et al., 1978). Observations of systematic changes in child behavior in a standardized situation sequence varying presence and absence of the mother and a strange person led to an experimental procedure now very common to measure the quality of relationship between children and their parents at about one year of age. In the 'strange situation test' the one-year-old child is confronted with a series of situations in a lab in which he or she is together with the mother, with a strange person, or alone. Differences in attachment quality were systematically investigated and classified by Mary Ainsworth in her Baltimore experimental study. When the mother enters the room after the separation period, the reaction of the child is classified according to the *rapprochement* to the mother and the ongoing exploration behavior. Three major children classifications were found, A, B, and C. Children are classified as A, 'insecure-avoidant', when they seem to ignore their mothers on reentry and appear to continue to play with a toy. These children do not seek proximity to or contact with the mother and, if picked up, exhibit little or no tendency to cling, but also do not show active resistance to contact with the mother. Children are classified as B, 'secure', when they actively greet the mother on her return, let her pick them up for a while and then carry on playing. These children may or may not be friendly with the stranger, but they are clearly more interested in interaction with the mother than with the stranger; they are distressed during the absence of their mothers. Finally, children are classified as C, 'ambivalent-insecure', when they cannot be comforted by their mothers and cling to them at the same time, giving the impression of being ambivalent. These children also do not continue to play or to explore and appear either more aggressive or more passive than other children. There have been sub-classifications such as two subclasses for A, four for B, and two for the C classification (see Ainsworth et al., 1978, pp. 234–251). Furthermore, an additional D classification was introduced to cover behaviors of children who do not fit into the classifications A, B, or C. These children sometimes showed a kind of bizarre behavior such as a frozen expression on the face, extensive grimacing etc. Still another example of how experimental methods were applied to investigate how infants react to maternal affective expressions when confronted with critical situations is the visual cliff experiment (Sorce et al., 1985). Here, infants were exposed to a cliff covered with glass. Children crawling to the cliff's rim stopped and looked at their mother's face. Mothers were standing at the other side of the cliff. When they signalled danger and fear by facial expression, children did not continue to crawl over the cliff. When mothers encouraged their children by exhibiting positive emotion and encouragement, babies crossed over the cliff. This experimental setting is a simulation of an event in which an infant is encountering an uncommon or even dangerous situation during exploration. It is assumed that this situation triggers a 'check back' gaze to the mother and that the (manipulated) facial expression and emotional reaction influence the child's behavior. In sum, experiments were adopted to the growing knowledge about the infants' relational competence and became more and more sophisticated. In contrast to traditional experiments which continued to follow the common practice of isolating single variables describing skills and abilities, these approaches tried to systematize and standardize everyday situations with interacting infants and caregivers in their homes.

The Use of Narratives

Of course, infants cannot talk about their life histories in the way that adults do. However, during observations, the child's communications and speech acts during the period of language acquisition are highly relevant when, for example, the general emotional climate in a family is to be studied. As is known from analyses with the Adult Attachment Interview (AAI) (George, Kaplan, & Main, 1985; Main & Goldwyn, 1991), adults differ in the styles in which they talk about their own childhood and about their families of origin. These different styles are taken as indices for specific relational experiences and attachment patterns in early childhood. Narratives have gained new interest in developmental psychology over recent years as they are assumed to open new windows to understand how individuals evaluate and interpret everyday events and how children are influenced by their parents' modes to communicate about events and situations. Parents' way of talking about the world, the family and relationships form the basic reservoir from which the child later builds his or her specific models to understand the world and the meaning of relationships. Therefore, investigating the communication context in which a child grows up is an important source of information about possible different developmental pathways. In general, the results of a number of studies (Fiese et al., 1999) show that not differences in content, but rather differences in the modalities of talking about content such as coherence and relationship beliefs, are the relevant distinguishing aspects when narratives in families were analyzed.

Some Formative Studies and their Results

Early Exchanges between Parents and Children and Children's Differential Reactions to Emotional Signals during the First Year

Even before birth, the emotional climate in a family and the quality of the relationship between parents may influence the child's well-being. Babies from the seventh gestational month onwards can acquire experience about the vocal interactions of the mother with her environment, as studies by DeCasper et al. (1994) have illustrated. Within the family context these interactions are exchanges of the mother with her husband or with other children in the family, the future siblings. The emotional tone of the mother's voice and the variation of pitch are known to the yet unborn child. Within three days after birth, children can identify the mother's speech from others (De Casper & Fifer, 1980; Fifer & Moon, 1995). From these results it can be concluded that already at birth the infant is accustomed to a certain spectrum of vocal exchange which might strongly differ not only from culture to culture, but also within one culture from family to family.

New experimental research with very young children further illuminates the vividness of infants' reactions to different emotional signals from caretakers. As already mentioned above, imitations of caretakers' behaviors as early as a few days after birth have been reported from experiments conducted by Meltzoff and Moore (1983). Haviland and Lelwica (1987) found that 10-week-old babies respond differently to mothers' expressions of happiness, show more mouthing to sadness, and no mouthing or interest in response to anger. Moreover, as the still face experiments of Cohn and Tronick (1983) have illustrated, infants do actively participate in nonverbal communication by trying to initiate facial expressions in the mother in order to continue an ongoing communication. Six-week-olds exhibited up to nine different forms of facial expressions to bring the interaction partner back to communication. Around seven months of age, infants were even able to classify and imitate facial expressions across different instances (Field et al., 1982). Facial expression and emotional tone of voice may be highly relevant cues for the discrimination of emotional states in others, but indicators like body posture and gestures also represent relevant sources of information for the child. Five-month-old babies were exposed to varying voices (Fernald, 1989; 1993); these infants exhibited appropriate emotional responses to the vocalizations, independently of the spoken language. Three- to six-month-old infants were able to decode sensitively the rhythm and tempo of recurrent social events in an established relationship (Field, 1995, Tronick, 1989). Infants' attempts to repair mutuality lacking in a relationship with the caretaker during the first months has also been reported from studies conducted by Daniel Stern (1977; 1985). Furthermore, Trevarthen (1984) could show that infants are sensitive toward dyadic synchrony and asynchrony in social interactions at a very early age.

From Emotional Attachment to Internal Representations of Relationships

The rapid growth of different locomotor and sensorimotor skills during the first two years increases the child's autonomy, agency, and efficiency and establishes a set of expectations about the other's reactions in certain situations. Specific attachment patterns are being formed by the child according to his or her experience with parental reactions to emotional expressions and specific social behaviors. Representations of interactions and communications form an 'episodic' memory (Tulving, 1972) which enables the child to build up 'procedural knowledge' (Pipp, 1993) or specific 'working models' (Main, Caplan, & Cassidy, 1985) relevant for the acquisition of social skills (Erickson, Sroufe, & Egeland, 1985). Perhaps the most spectacular shift in the child's social development is the move from primary to secondary intersubjectivity (Trevarthen & Hubley, 1978), when the child is about eight months old. During this phase, infants are beginning to test their parents' limits when they transgress rules or norms. It seems as if a new format of actively negotiating the parent–child relationship emerges during this phase which is also marked by the child's highly increased mobility (crawling, standing, walking). The combination of growing physical and psychological competence empowers the child to effectively begin to explore the quality of the relationship and to experience continuity or discontinuity in a well-established relationship. During this period, however, parents change their behavior toward the child as well. In a longitudinal approach, families with a second child were observed every month during the first 24 months after the arrival of a second child (Kreppner, 1988; 1991). Trajectories of both parents' socialization activities (control of situation and transmission of rules) over the two year period directed toward the second child followed a rather systematic course. Parents' behavior and communication changed according to the child's major developmental shift when reaching secondary intersubjectivity at 8–9 months or understanding of language between 12 and 16 months. These trends mirror a systemic change in parents' socialization practices during the first and second year. It is assumed that families vary during these transition periods in how they handle the child's new skills and interests (Kreppner, 1990).

These developmental pathways, widely considered to be normative processes, may vary in different cultures. As attachment studies across cultures have shown, different mean frequencies in attachment categories were found for children growing up, for example, in northern Germany (Grossmann et al., 1985) or Japan (Miyake, Chen, & Campos, 1985). Expectancies of growing up in environments where the mother usually is not permanently present (as in northern Germany) compared to an environment where permanent closeness or presence of the mother is the rule, as in Japan, may have an impact on the development of different behavior patterns in expressing emotions such as during the reunion phase in the attachment experiment (strange situation test). Newer studies exploring differences in attachment development have found amazing links to divergent sleeping arrangements in kibbutzim (Aviezer et al., 1994; 1999). The emotional availability of the parents even during sleeping times seems to be of eminent importance for the securely attached child. Furthermore, longitudinal studies have shown that securely attached children later exhibit a greater degree of social competence and fewer problem behaviors when compared to insecurely attached children (Grossmann, 1988; LaFreniere & Sroufe, 1985; Wartner et al., 1994).

Growing Sensitivity to Differences in the Relationships with Mothers and Fathers, and in the Quality of the Relationship between the Parents

Towards the end of the second year the child begins to insist on realizing own goals, manifesting his or her own will even against the intervention of others. Thus, the intention to separate from the parents or, in relational terms, to renegotiate the degree of autonomy in the extant relationship with the parents becomes obvious. Experience of clear differences in the relationships the child has with mother and with father may lead to a more and more distinct sense of self, the self in divergent relationships (Abelin, 1971), during the end of the second year. It is assumed that the child acquires a new sense of self by facing the different relationships within the family. Clarke-Stewart (1978), Belsky (1981), and Belsky and Rovine (1990) have pointed to the complex interaction process in family triads. Mothers step back and exhibit less stimulation toward the child with a father present compared to being in a dyadic situation. However, the child shows a growing sensitivity not only for the complexity and diversity of the family's relational network in general, but also for the quality of the relationship between the two parents in particular. A number of newer studies including children at different ages – and also toddlers at the end of the second year – emphasize this family-specific aspect as a crucial factor for differential individual pathways in development (Cummings & Davies, 1994; Emery, 1988; Erel & Burman, 1995; Grych & Fincham, 1990). Moreover, as Parke and Buriel (1998) have illustrated, the quality of relationship between parents also seems to be highly relevant for the quality of the father–child relationship in a family (Belsky, Gilstrap, & Rovine, 1984; Belsky & Volling, 1986; Dickie, 1987). During the first months after a child's arrival, the quality of relationship between parents is also a relevant indicator for the family's well being. As Cowan and Cowan (1987; 1988; 1992) have put it, the sometimes difficult rhythm of communication between father and mother during this period can be characterized as a 'parental gavotte', a dance with movements of both partners oscillating between pulling and pushing, creating a series of mutual misunderstandings. The Cowans found in their study that the quality of relationships between the partners during pregnancy is predictive for both the parents' and the child's well-being during the first year after birth. The more satisfaction both parents had experienced in their marital relationship during pregnancy, the less they suffered from postnatal stress and problems in caring for the child.

Consequences of Malfunctioning Parental Relationships for the Infant's Development

Infants' experiences with permanent parental fights and negative emotional exchanges increase the likelihood of children's later personal difficulties, adaptability, and feelings of insecurity (Cummings & Davies, 1994; Cummings, Davies, & Simpson, 1994; J.S. Cummings et al., 1989; Davies & Cummings, 1994; 1998; Davies, Myers, & Cummings, 1996). Although many of these studies have investigated children at a later age, i.e. at preschool or school age, the impact of the quality of the parents' relationship on the child's social and emotional development during the early years should not be underestimated. Development of children's antisocial behavior (Emery, 1982), internalization problems (Fainsilber-Katz & Gottman, 1993), and the entire gamut of emotional and cognitive responses to marital conflict (Cummings & Davies, 1994; Gottman & Fainsilber-Katz, 1989) has proven the influential power of the quality of marital relationship for children's well-being. There are numerous indications for associations between children's concrete experiences and marital discords such as angry and withdrawing fathers (Fainsilber-Katz & Kahen, 1993) or over-critical and intruding mothers (Gottman, 1994).

Moreover, observation of differences in mothers' and fathers' parenting styles created new insights into possible consequences for a child's development when confronted with two instead of only one model of parenting style within the family. It is not the difference between two models but the parents' mutual support and acceptance of their different ways of handling the child which appears to be extremely important for a child's well-being. Belsky, Crnic, and Gable (1995) demonstrated that a consistent and supportive pattern of co-parenting proved to be a relevant aspect for children's coping ability in stressful situations. The exchange between parents and children about emotions, both positive and negative, was another aspect that emerged as a new factor in understanding differences in the development of children (Gottman, Fainsilber-Katz, & Hooven, 1996). As conflictual parent–parent relationships have been shown to produce spillover effects for parent–child relationships, children's behaviors after divorce cannot solely be attributed to the act of divorce alone. Rather, impairment in development can be seen as a product of children's experiences in their families long before parents separate or divorce, as they grow up in a context of a deteriorating parent–parent relationship. Thus, behavior problems, maladjustments, poor social skills, and – particularly during adolescence – disengagement from the family as well as an increased orientation towards peer groups is more prevalent in children from divorced than from nondivorced families (Block, Block, & Gjerde, 1986; Cherlin et al., 1991; Hetherington, 1979). Moreover, academic achievement and antisocial behavior appear also to be strongly influenced by family status (Zill, 1994).

In sum, two major aspects that have been reported here seem to indicate a new approach to a more relationship-oriented research in early childhood. First, results from studies in infancy which revealed a high degree of sensitivity for other persons even in very young infants also signal very early competence in children to actively maintain and manage relationships. Second, children's reactions to their parents' malfunctioning marital relationship, that is, to the kind of negative communication they perceive when the parents talk to one another, point to children's high degree of sensitivity for the quality of relationships in which they do not directly participate. It seems that it is the general emotional and communication climate in a family which affects the children's differential developmental pathways. In the long run, these empirical results from studies focusing on family relationships instead of personal characteristics or global environmental aspects may lead to a new assessment and understanding of the infant's relational context in the family.

Social-emotional Developmental Pathways During the Early Years: Quality of Relationship with Primary Caretaker as a Basic Start

From the Infant's Holistic Interchange with the Caretaker to Competent Management of Family Relationships

As early as during the newborn period, that is, during the first three to four months, the co-regulation of fundamental functions is experienced within the relationship with the primary caregivers. As the infant is not in a total state of disorganization or random behavior after birth, the character of mutual exchange in terms of nonverbal signs defines the quality of relationship. The modality by which the caretaker meets the infant's basic needs constitutes a rhythm of interaction and communication which Sander (1975) has labeled 'initial regulation'. It incorporates the establishment of predictable formats for ritual interactions like feeding, bathing, changing diapers, and sleeping habits. These physiological regulations cannot be separated from basic psychological regulations encompassing the entire gamut of social, emotional, and cognitive exchange (Sroufe, 1995).

During the next six months, from nine to about 15 months, the child experiences an enormous increase in his or her competencies concerning various aspects and functions. Acquisition of language and the more and more elaborate knowledge of the others' intentions in the family lead to the ability to share common perspectives. According to Emde (1988), these increments in competence are responsible for a new kind of self-development. Depending on the experienced quality in family relationships, growing and enriched or restricting and poor working models facilitate or impede the infant's early self-development, the shift from an 'I-self' to a 'We-self', a precursor of the 'Me-self'. Moreover, during this period the child is on his or her way to becoming a fully fledged member of the family. The shared experiences comprise both emotional and cognitive components and represent blueprints for the child to actively format relationships (Main, Kaplan, & Cassidy, 1985; Sroufe & Fleeson, 1986), and to develop new forms of affect regulation, oriented to the family-specific way of expressing emotions and talking about them. The transfer of these relational experiences inside the family to the world outside the family may lead to new, either positive or negative experiences when establishing social relationships.

The Interplay between Different Developmental Functions: Locomotoric, Affective, Social, and Self Development

Zumbahlen and Crawley (1996) have shown that mothers seldom express anger or fear to their children prior to 8 months. Development of locomotion, however, changes dramatically the caretakers' attribution of responsibility. The growth of locomotion increases the need for caretakers' vigilance to assure the child's safety (Campos, Kermoian, & Zumbahlen, 1992). Under a relational perspective, these functional developments tend to bring vivid variation in a child's experience of autonomy and dependency in a family context. As a consequence, the development of locomotory activities including grasping, crawling, and walking should be related to basic changes in the infant's emotionality and capacity to manage relationships (Emde, Gaensbauer, & Harmon, 1976). The acquisition of walking during the end of the first year has already been linked to major affective changes by authors like Spitz (1965) or Mahler (Mahler, Pine, & Bergman, 1975). Encouragement or discouragement of the child to explore the world according to the new acquired skills is one of the most important issues for the development of a new autonomy–dependency balance in the child's relationship with the parents.

Even shortly after birth, infants seem to have some competence for actively maintaining relationships. Moreover, infants very early seem to recognize emotional nuances in everyday interactions. According to Spitz (1965), a highly differentiated and elaborated communication between caretaker and child begins at about 3–4 months, a format of exchange which he labeled 'diacritical' communication. This format has been described more analytically by Saarni, Mumme, and Campos (1998) in their list of the ingredients for early emotional communication:

1 sensitivity to the hedonic tone of communication
2 ability to discriminate one emotional signal from another
3 appreciation of discrete meanings of different emotional displays
4 appreciation of the referential nature of emotional signals
5 awareness that emotional reactions are subjective.

Thus, the child shows during the two year period a growing competence to react to emotional signals and to maintain and negotiate extant relationships within the family. The testing of this relationship as described by Trevarthen and Hubley (1978) at the age of about 8–9 months, when new interests have developed to actively initiate and vary the character of a relationship, appears to be a critical crossroads for the child's further development. It is a period where the child encounters the parents' ability to deal with developmental changes, their 'transition competence', that is, to react in a flexible way to the child's new skills and demands. Later, at about 15–18 months, again the renegotiation of the balance between autonomy and dependency represents another landmark in a child's social development. Here, an even more complex developmental process can be studied, a crucial pathway to the development of identity, 'Me-self', and self-organization of the infant. This period is characterized by the establishment of a new perspective in the child, the awareness of being consistent or inconsistent in different relationships.

Toward a Better Understanding of the Development of Emotional and Relational Competence

The Role of Developmental Sensitivity in Early Parent–Child Relationships

In newer approaches dealing with the role of emotion for early development, the importance of the general emotional climate in which a child grows up has been increasingly underscored. Saarni, Mumme, and Campos (1998) try to describe this broader concept, including also the communication about feelings and emotional issues, as being essential for setting a certain kind of 'culture' in the family relationship. They define culture as:

> a set of traditional, explicit and implicit beliefs, values, actions, and material environments that are transmitted by language, symbol, and behavior within an enduring and interacting group of people. (1998, p. 247)

During infancy, this 'group of people' is clearly constituted by the members of the family. Furthermore, the possibility to convey norms and values, to communicate with one another about objects and events, and to exchange feelings and experience is largely determined by the quality of relationship among the members of the family. The general emotional tone in interactions, the modes of negotiating mundane issues in everyday life, as well as world views or more general issues such as religion or politics, is taken as a major prerequisite for conveying the basics of culture between generations. The emotional quality of the infant–parent relationship as well as the growing competence of the child to manage a relationship increase the likelihood that shifts between developmental levels can successfully be mastered within the family's relational network. Whereas during early development the attempts to balance a relationship are carried out between two rather unequal partners, the infant adapts more and more to the family-specific communication patterns. During the course of the second year, the child begins to contribute by own activities to overcome misunderstandings when she or he starts to articulate needs firmly, and, for example, creates new communicative skills that fit the caretakers' capacity to understand.

The art of establishing, maintaining, and negotiating relationships consists in the ability to initiate interactions, to sensitively react to the partner's attempts to define the relationship, and to compensate misunderstandings. Within the family context, developmental changes engender new abilities and also new demands of the child. Major developmental shifts may challenge extant, well-established relationships and create serious crises in family life. As developmental changes occur with an extraordinary speed during the first two years, the likelihood is high that parents and child find themselves trapped in mutual misunderstandings. Parents' expectations regarding the child's abilities at a certain level of development often do not meet the child's actual competence. Here, perhaps a more serious perceptual problem is being raised which sometimes may lead to confusing conclusions not only in parents but also in observers of parent–infant interaction. The infant's attempts to change a once established level of interaction with the parents, and the parents' reactions to keep the child on the level they consider to be still adequate, would need a 'meta-level' knowledge in both parents and observers to recognize the nonfitting behavior patterns during periods when children move from one level to the next higher level of their individual developmental course. Even well-trained researchers with a detailed blueprint of age-specific behavior patterns cannot always detect such mutual misunderstandings, as tiny deviations from repeating patterns might be caused by a multitude of possible reasons. Only the comparison of concrete family-specific interaction patterns over time, e.g. by condensing a longer time period by linking a number of different video recordings, could reveal these transitional phenomena.

Variations in Emotional Exchange and Implications for Individual Development

The modalities of emotional exchange in a relationship vary largely across families, sometimes even within one family. As nonverbal exchanges of emotional signals between parents and children occur long before the child's language acquisition, that is, before culture-based formats enter the child's mind, the quality of this emotional and relational exchange may be taken as a foundation upon which later and more elaborate formats of communication are built.

Emotional availability, adequate stimulation, and coherent behavior may be associated with the development of an emotionally and socially competent child, whereas the experience of emotional unavailability in early developmental stages, incontingent reactions, and incoherent behavior patterns may lead to ambivalent emotional reactions in social relationships and ineffective exploration. Parental under- or over-attuning to the child can be linked to fragmentation of attention, uncertain mutuality, ambivalent emotionality, and insecure relationship. The classification of the quality of attachment in the child – secure, avoidant, ambivalent – can be taken as an example of the attempt to differentiate across diverse types of relationship quality between parents and children.

Research conducted so far still seems far from being able to show exactly the mechanisms of transmission in parent–child relationships on the level of single variables. As Sroufe and Rutter (1984) in their initial article on developmental psychopathology claimed, a holistic, activity-oriented, and function-flexible perspective of continuity and change on a variety of different developmental pathways could help to better understand the early onsets of disorders. Progressive adaptation and transformation were labeled as the two most fundamental processes of development. This sounds promising, but still most research on continuity and change during development is focused on single characteristics and personality oriented outcomes. A genuinely relational perspective could perhaps be even more helpful for designing future research.

Conclusions

The following four conclusions are formulated as statements. They intend to direct future research in the area of early childhood to focus on relationships more than on persons.

1 Early developmental processes in the child should be studied under a holistic and integrative perspective.
2 The emotional quality of the communication between caretaker and infant is regarded as a basis for establishing a functioning relationship and a common communication culture in the family.
3 During the first two years, the competence to actively maintain and manage a relationship as well as the capacity to gain self-confidence are particularly developed during phases in which the child acquires new skills and abilities and the parents have to sensitively deal with these developmental shifts. Families differ according to their competence to master these developmental transitions.
4 The family's entire relational network is to be studied when differential context influences on the child's developmental pathway are investigated.

A holistic, activity-oriented, and function-flexible perspective does not exclude the possibility of conducting intense research on infants' principal ability to react to specific sensory stimulations and to construct activity patterns in distinguished functional areas. A holistic and integrative perspective on development may keep researchers' eyes open for cues which might be relevant for the recognition of early differentiations in a child's individual developmental course. Affection, stimulation, coherence and patterning of action–reaction cycles within a relationship are basic experiences in a child's life. Case's conception of the infant experience as 'small islands of sensory-affective coherence in what appears otherwise as a rather vast and uncharted spatio-tempered sea' (1991, p. 215) may lead us to a better understanding of the importance of the quality of early relationship to developmental progress. The amount of affectivity distributed to the child, the sensibility by which the caretaker meets the infant's needs, and the contiguity of action–reaction pattern are components for a growing sense of mutuality and also for a feeling of security and self-trust. Under a family perspective, the complexity of an infant's experience with regard to relationship quality should include not only parent–child but also parent–parent relationships. The child's experience with the parents' modes of emotional exchange and the quality of mutuality in a family's relational network are aspects which may open a new and wider landscape to the exploration of the variety of developmental pathways.

References

Abelin, E.L. (1971). The role of the father in the separation–individuation process. In J. McDevitt & C.F. Settlage (eds), *Separation–individuation: Essays in honor of Margaret S. Mahler* (pp. 229–253). New York: International Universities Press.

Ainsworth, M.D., Blehar, M.C., Waters, E., & Wall, S. (1978). *Patterns of attachment.* Hillsdale, NJ: Erlbaum.

Akhtar, N., Dunham, F., & Dunham, P.J. (1991). Directive interactions and early vocabulary development: The role of joint attentional focus. *Journal of Child Language*, 18, 41–49.

Aviezer, O., Sagi, A., Joels, T., & Ziv, Y. (1999). Emotional availability and attachment representations in Kibbutz infants and their mothers. *Developmental Psychology*, 35, 811–821.

Aviezer, O., van Ijzendoorn, M.H., Sagi, A., & Schuengel, C. (1994). 'Children of the Dream' revisited: 70 years of collective early child-care in Israeli Kibbutzim. *Psychological Bulletin*, 116, 99–116.

Bakeman, R., & Adamson, L. (1984). Coordinating attention to people and objects in mother–infant and peer–infant interactions. *Child Development*, 55, 1278–1289.

Bell, N.W., & Vogel, E.F. (eds.) (1968). *A modern introduction to the family*. New York: Free Press.

Bell, R.Q. (1968). A reinterpretation of the direction of effects in studies of socialization. *Psychological Review*, 75, 81–95.

Belsky, J. (1981). Early human experience: A family perspective. *Development Psychology*, 17, 3–23.

Belsky, J., Crnic, K., & Gable, S. (1995). The determinants of coparenting in families with toddler boys: Spousal differences and daily hassles. *Child Development*, 66, 629–642.

Belsky, J., Gilstrap, B., & Rovine, M. (1984). The Pennsylvania Infant and Family Development Project: I. Stability and change in mother–infant and father–infant interaction in a family setting at one, three, and nine months. *Child Development*, 55, 692–705.

Belsky, J., & Rovine, M. (1990). Patterns of marital change across the transition to parenthood: Pregnancy and three years postpartum. *Journal of Marriage and the Family*, 52, 5–19.

Belsky, J., & Volling, B.L. (1986). Mothering, fathering, and marital interaction in the family triad during infancy: Exploring family systems processes. In P. Berman & F. Pedersen (eds), *Man's transitions to parenthood: Longitudinal studies of early family experiences*. Hillsdale, NJ: Erlbaum.

Block, J.H., Block, J., & Gjerde, P.F. (1986). The personality of children prior to divorce: A prospective study. *Child Development*, 57, 827–840.

Bowlby, J. (1969). *Attachment and loss: Vol. I. Attachment*. London: Hogarth.

Bowlby, J. (1973). *Attachment and loss: Vol. II. Separation*. London: Hogarth.

Bowlby, J. (1980). *Attachment and loss: Vol. III. Loss, sadness, and depression*. New York: Basic.

Bridges, L.J. & Grolnick, W.S. (1995). The development of emotional self-regulation in infancy and early childhood. In N. Eisenberg (ed.), *Review of personality and social psychology* (pp. 185–211). Newbury Park, CA: Sage.

Bühler, C., & Hetzer, H. (1927). Inventar der Verhaltungsweisen des ersten Lebensjahres (Inventory of behaviors during the first year). *Quellen und Studien zur Jugendkunde*, 5, 128–250. Jena: Gustav Fischer.

Burgess, E. (1926). The family as a unity of interacting personalities. *Family*, 7, 3–9.

Campe, J.H. (1785). *Über die früheste Bildung junger Kinderseelen* (*On the earliest education of young children's minds*). Ed. B.H.E. Niestroj, Frankfurt: Ullstein, 1985.

Campos, J.J., Kermoian, R., & Zumbahlen, M. (1992). Socioemotional transformations in the family following infant crawling onset. In N. Eisenberg & R. Fabes (eds), *New directions in child development: Emotion and its regulation in early development* (Vol. 5, pp. 25–40). San Francisco: Jossey-Bass.

Carpenter, M., Nagell, K., & Tomasello, M. (1998). *Social cognition, joint attention, and communicative competence from 9 to 15 months of age. Monographs of the Society for Research in Child Development*, Vol. 63, no. 4, serial 255.

Case, R. (1991). Stages in the development of the young child's first sense of self. *Developmental Review*, 11, 210–230.

Cassirer, E. (1944). *An essay on man: An introduction to a philosophy of human culture*. New Haven, CT: Yale University Press. German edition *Versuch ueber den Menschen*, Hamburg: Felix Meiner, 1996.

Cherlin, A.J., Furstenberg, F.F. Jr, Chase-Lansdale, P.L., Kiernana, K.E., Robins, P.K., Morrison, D.R., & Teitler, J.O. (1991) Longitudinal studies of effects of divorce on children in Great Britain and the United States. *Science*, 252, 1386–1389.

Clarke-Stewart, K.A. (1978). And daddy makes three: The father's impact on mother and young child. *Child Development*, 49, 466–478.

Clarke-Stewart, K.A. (1980). The father's contribution to children's cognitive and social development in early childhood. In F.A. Pedersen (ed.), *The father–infant relationship* (pp. 111–146). New York: Praeger.

Cohn, J.F., & Tronick, E.Z. (1983). Three-month-old infants' reaction to simulated maternal depression. *Child Development*, 54, 185–193.

Cowan, C.P., & Cowan, P.A. (1987). Men's involvement in parenthood: Identifying the antecedents and understanding the barriers. In P.W. Berman & F.A. Pedersen (eds), *Men's transition to parenthood* (pp. 145–174). Hillsdale, NJ: Erlbaum.

Cowan, C.P., & Cowan, P.A. (1992). *When partners become parents: The big life change for couples*. New York: Basic.

Cowan, P.A. (1991). Individual and family life transitions: A proposal for a new definition. In P.A. Cowan & M. Hetherington (eds.), *Family transitions* (pp. 3–30). Hillsdale, NJ: Erlbaum.

Cowan, P.A., & Cowan, C.P. (1988). Changes in marriage during the transition to parenthood. In G.Y. Michaels & W.A. Goldberg (eds), *The transition to parenthood: Current theory and research* (pp. 114–154). Cambridge: Cambridge University Press.

Cummings, E.M., & Davies, P.T. (1994). *Children and marital conflict: The impact of family dispute and resolution*. New York: Guilford.

Cummings, E.M., Davies, P.T., & Simpson, K.S. (1994). Marital conflict, gender, and children's appraisals and coping efficacy as mediators of child adjustment. *Journal of Family Psychology*, 8, 141–149.

Cummings, J.S., Pellegrini, D.S., Notarius, C.I., & Cummings, E.M. (1989). Children's responses to angry adult behavior as a function of marital distress and history of interparental hostility. *Child Development*, 60, 1035–1043.

Darwin, C. (1859). *On the origin of species*. London: John Murray.

Davies, P.T., & Cummings, E.M. (1994). Marital conflict and child adjustment: An emotional security hypothesis. *Psychological Bulletin*, 116, 387–411.

Davies, P.T., & Cummings, E.M. (1998). Exploring children's security as a mediator of the link between marital relations and child adjustment. *Child Development*, 69, 124–139.

Davies, P.T., Myers, R.L., & Cummings, E.M. (1996). Responses of children and adolescents to marital conflict scenarios as a function of the emotionality of conflict endings. *Merrill-Palmer Quarterly*, 42, 1–21.

DeCasper, W., & Fifer, W. (1980). Of human bonding: Newborns prefer their mothers' voices. *Science*, 208, 1174–1176.

DeCasper, W., Lecanuet, J.P., Busnel, M.C., Granier-Deferre, C., & Maugeais, K. (1994). Fetal reactions to recurrent maternal speech. *Infant Behavior and Development*, 17, 159–164.

Dickie, J.R. (1987). Interrelationships within the mother–father–infant triad. In P.W. Berman & F.A. Pedersen (eds), *Men's transition to parenthood* (pp. 113–143). Hillsdale, NJ: Erlbaum.

Dix, T. (1991). The affective organization of parenting: Adaptive and maladaptive processes. *Psychological Bulletin*, 110, 3–25.

Duvall, E. (1977). *Marriage and family development*. New York: Lippincott.

Duvall, E., & Hill, R. (1948). Report of the committee on the dynamics of family interaction. Mimeographed manuscript. Washington, DC: National Conference on Family Life.

Eisenberg, N., & Fabes, R.A. (1994). Emotion regulation and the development of social competence. In M. Clark (ed.), *Review of personality and social psychology* (pp. 119–150). Newbury Park, CA: Sage.

Emde, R.N. (1988). Die endliche und die unendliche Entwicklung (Finite and infinite development). *International Journal of Psycho-Analysis*, 69, 24–42. Also *Psyche*, 1991, 9, 745–779 and 10, 890–913.

Emde, R.N., Gaensbauer, T., & Harmon, R. (1976). *Emotional expressions in infancy: A biobehavioral study*. New York: International Universities Press.

Emery, R.E. (1982). Interparental conflict and the children of discord and divorce. *Psychological Bulletin*, 92, 310–330.

Emery, R.E. (ed.) (1988). *Marriage, divorce, and children's adjustment*. Newbury Park, CA: Sage.

Erasmus Desiderius (Rotterdamus) (1518/1965). *The colloquies of Erasmus*, edited and translated by C.R. Thompson. Chicago: Chicago University Press.

Erel, O., & Burman, B. (1995). Interrelatedness of marital and parent–child relations: A meta-analytic review. *Psychological Bulletin*, 118, 108–132.

Erickson, M.F., Sroufe, L.A., & Egeland, B. (1985). The relationship between quality of attachment and behavior problems in preschool in a high-risk sample. In I. Bretherton & E. Waters (eds), *Growing points of attachment theory and research* (pp. 147–166). *Monographs of the Society for Research in Child Development*, Vol. 50, nos 1–2, serial 209.

Escalona, S.K. (1973). Basic modes of social interaction: Their emergence and patterning during the first two years of life. *Merrill-Palmer Quarterly*, 19, 205–232.

Fainsilber-Katz, L.F., & Gottman, J.M. (1993). Patterns of marital conflict predict children's internalizing and externalizing behaviors. *Developmental Psychology*, 29, 940–950.

Fainsilber-Katz, L.F., & Kahen, V. (1993). Marital interaction patterns and children's externalizing and internalizing behaviors: The search for mechanisms. Paper presented at the Biennial Meetings of the Society for Research in Child Development, New Orleans.

Fernald, A. (1989). Intonation and communicative intent in mothers' speech to infants: Is the melody the message? *Child Development*, 60, 1497–1510.

Fernald, A. (1993). Approval and disapproval: Infant responsiveness to vocal affect in familiar and unfamiliar languages. *Child Development*, 64, 657–674.

Field, T.M. (1995). The effects of mothers' physical and emotional unavailability on emotion regulation. *Monographs of the Society for Research in Child Development*, Vol. 59, no. 5, serial 242, pp. 208–227.

Field, T.M., Woodson, R., Greenberg, R., & Cohen, D. (1982). Discrimination and imitation of facial expressions by neonates. *Science*, 218, 179–181.

Fiese, B.H., Sameroff, A.J., Grotevant, H.D., Wamboldt, F.S., Dickstein, S., & Fravel, D.L. (1999). *The stories that families tell: Narrative coherence, narrative interaction, and relationship beliefs. Monographs of the Society for Research in Child Development*, Vol. 64, no. 2, serial 257.

Fifer, W., & Moon, C. (1995). The effects of fetal experience with sound. In J.P. Lecanuet, W. Fifer, N. Krasnegor, & W. Smotherman (eds), *Fetal development: A psychological perspective* (pp. 351–366). Hillsdale, NJ: Erlbaum.

Galton, F. (1883). *Inquiries into human faculty and its development*. London: Macmillan.

George, C., Kaplan, N., & Main, M. (1984). Attachment interview for adults. Unpublished manuscript, University of California, Berkeley.

Gesell, A. (1928). *Infancy and human growth*. New York: Macmillan.

Gesell, A. (1935). Cinema as an instrument for parent education. *Parent education*, 2, 8–9.

Gottman, J.M. (1994). *What predicts divorce?* Hillsdale, NJ: Erlbaum.

Gottman, J.M., & Fainsilber-Katz, L. (1989). Effect of marital discord on young children's peer interaction and health. *Developmental Psychology*, 25, 373–381.

Gottman, J.M., Fainsilber-Katz, L., & Hooven, C. (1996) *Meta-emotion: How families communicate emotionally*. Mahwah, NJ: Erlbaum.

Grossmann, K., Grossmann, K.E., Spangler, G., Suess, G., & Unzner, L. (1985). Maternal sensitivity and newborns' orientation responses as related to quality of attachment in northern Germany. In I. Bretherton & E. Waters (eds), *Growing points of attachment theory and research* (pp. 233–256). *Monographs of the Society for Research in Child Development*, Vol. 50, nos 1–2, serial 209.

Grossmann, K.E. (1988). Longitudinal and systemic approaches in the study of biological high- and low-risk groups. In M. Rutter (ed.), *The power of longitudinal data: Studies of risk and protective factors for psychosocial disorders* (pp. 138–157). Cambridge: Cambridge University Press.

Grych, J.H., & Fincham, F. (1990). Marital conflict and children's adjustment: A cognitive-contextual framework. *Psychological Bulletin*, 108, 267–290.

Harter, S. (1998). The development of self-representations. In W. Damon & N. Eisenberg (eds), *Handbook of child psychology, 5th edn: Vol. 3. Social, emotional, and personality development* (pp. 553–617). New York: Wiley.

Havighurst, R.J. (1953). *Human development and education.* New York: David McKay.

Haviland, J.M., & Lelwica, M. (1987). The induced affect response: 10-week-old infants' responses to three emotional expressions. *Developmental Psychology*, 23, 97–104.

Hetherington, E.M. (1979). Divorce: A child's perspective. *American Psychologist*, 34, 851–858.

Kellogg, W.N., & Kellogg, L.A. (1933). *The ape and the child: A study of environmental influence upon early behavior.* New York: McGraw-Hill.

Kreppner, K. (1988). Changes in dyadic relationships within a family after the arrival of a second child. In R.A. Hinde & J. Stevenson-Hinde (eds), *Relationships within families: Mutual influences* (pp. 143–167). Oxford: Oxford University Press.

Kreppner, K. (1990). Differences in parents' cooperation patterns after the arrival of a second child. Paper presented at the International Conference BABY XXI, Lisbon, Portugal, October.

Kreppner, K. (1991). Observation and the longitudinal approach in infancy research. In M. Lamb & H. Keller (eds), *Infant development: Perspectives from German-speaking countries* (pp. 151–178). Hillsdale, NJ: Erlbaum.

Kreppner, K. (1997). Cultural psychology and the problem of exchange between individual and environment: Is there a common concept? *Culture and Psychology*, 3, 405–422.

Krueger, F. (1924). *Der Strukturbegriff in der Psychologie.* Jena: Fischer.

Krueger, F. (1928). Das Wesen der Gefühle. *Archiv für die gesamte Psychologie*, 65, 91–128.

LaFreniere, P.J., & Sroufe, L.A. (1985). Profiles of peer competence in the preschool: Interrelations between measures, influence of social ecology, and relation to attachment history. *Developmental Psychology*, 21, 56–69.

Lamb, M. (1975). Father: Forgotten contributors to child development. *Human Development*, 18, 245–266.

Lamb, M.E. (1976). *The role of the father in child development.* New York: Wiley.

Lazarus, R. (1991). *Emotion and adaptation.* New York: Oxford University Press.

Lewin, K. (1917). Kriegslandschaft (War landscape). *Zeitschrift für angewandte Psychologie*, 12, 440–447.

Lewin, K. (1926). Filmaufnahmen über Trieb- und Affektäußerungen psychopathischer Kinder (verglichen mit Normalen und Schwachsinnigen) (Cinema on expressions of drive and affect in psychopathological children compared to normal and mental deficient children). *Zeitschrift für Kinderforschung*, 32, 414–447.

Lewin, K. (1927). Gesetz und Experiment in der Psychologie (Law and experiment in psychology). *Symposion*, 1, 375–421.

Lewis, M. (1994). Myself and me. In S.T. Parker, R.W. Mitchel, & M.L. Boccia (eds), *Self-awareness in animals and humans: Developmental perspectives* (pp. 20–34). New York: Cambridge University Press.

Mahler, M.S., Pine, F., & Bergman, A. (1975). *The psychological birth of the human infant.* New York: Basic.

Main, M., & Goldwyn, R. (1991). Adult attachment classification system. Unpublished manuscript, University of California, Berkeley, Department of Psychology.

Main, M.B., Kaplan, N., & Cassidy, J. (1985). Security in infancy, childhood, and adulthood: A move to the level of representation. In I. Bretherton & E. Waters (eds), *Growing points of attachment theory and research* (pp. 66–104). *Monographs of the Society for Research in Child Development*, Vol. 50, nos 1–2, serial 209.

Malatesta, C.Z., Culver, C., Tesman, J.R., & Shepard, B. (1989). The development of emotion expression during the first two years of life. *Monographs of the Society for Research in Child Development*, Vol. 54, nos 1–2, pp. 1–104.

McHale, J.P., & Rasmussen, J.L. (1998). Coparental and family group-level dynamics during infancy: Early family precursors of child and family functioning during preschool. *Development and Psychopathology*, 10, 39–59.

Mead, G.H. (1934). *Mind, self, and society from the standpoint of a social behaviorist.* Chicago: University of Chicago Press.

Meltzoff, A.N., & Moore, M.K. (1983). Newborn infants imitate adult facial gestures. *Child Development*, 54, 702–709.

Meltzoff, A.N., & Moore, M.K. (1989). Imitation in newborn infants: Exploring the range of gestures imitated and the underlying mechanisms. *Developmental Psychology*, 25, 954–962.

Miyake, K., Chen, S., & Campos, J. (1985). Infant temperament, mother's mode of interaction, and attachment in Japan. In I. Bretherton & E. Waters (eds), *Growing points of attachment theory and research* (pp. 276–297). *Monographs of the Society for Research in Child Development*, Vol. 50, nos 1–2, serial 209.

Neisser, U. (1991). Two perceptually given aspects of the self and their development. *Developmental Review*, 11, 197–209.

Niestroj, B.H.E. (1987). Modern individuality and the social isolation of mother and child. *Comparative Civilizations Review*, 15, 23–40.

Papoušek, H., & Papousek, M. (1977). Mothering and the cognitive head-start: Psychobiological considerations. In H.R. Schaffer (eds), *Studies in mother–infant interaction* (pp. 63–85). New York: Academic.

Parke, R.D. (1994). Progress, paradigms, and unresolved problems: A commentary on recent advances in our understanding of children's emotions. *Merrill-Palmer Quarterly*, 40, 157–169.

Parke, R.D., & Buriel, R. (1998). Socialization in the family: Ethnic and ecological perspectives. In W. Damon & N. Eisenberg (eds), *Handbook of child psychology, 5th edn: Vol. 3. Social, emotional, and personality development* (pp. 463–552). New York: Wiley.

Pedersen, F.A. (1975). Mother, father, and infant as an interaction system. Paper presented at the Annual Convention of the American Psychological Association, Chicago.

Pedersen, F.A. (1980). *The father–infant relationship*. New York: Praeger.

Pedersen, F.A., Anderson, B.J., & Cain, R.L. (1980). Parent–infant and husband–wife interactions observed at age five months. In F.A. Pedersen (ed.), *The father–infant relationship* (pp. 71–86). New York: Praeger.

Pipp, S. (1990). Sensorimotor and representational internal working models of self, other, and relationship: Mechanisms of connection and separation. In D. Cicchetti & M. Beeghly (eds), *The self in transition: Infancy to childhood* (pp. 243–264). Chicago: University of Chicago Press.

Pipp, S. (1993). Infants' knowledge of self, other, and relationship. In U. Neisser (ed.), *The perceived self: Ecological and interpersonal sources of self-knowledge* (pp. 41–62). Cambridge: Cambridge University Press.

Preyer, W. (1893) *Die geistige Entwicklung in der ersten Kindheit*. Anleitung für Mütter zur Führung von Kindertagebüchern. Leipzig: Grieben.

Reiss, I.L. (1965). The universality of the family: A conceptual analysis. *Journal of Marriage and the Family*, 27, 343–353.

Rheingold, H.L. (1969). The social and socializing infant. In D.A. Goslin (ed.), *Handbook of socialization theory and research* (pp. 779–790). Chicago: Rand McNally.

Richards, M.P.M., & Bernal, J.F. (1972). An observational study of mother–infant interaction. In N. Blurton-Jones (ed.), *Ethological studies of child behaviour* (pp. 175–197). Cambridge: Cambridge University Press.

Riegel, K.F. (1975). Toward a dialectical theory of development. *Human Development*, 18, 50–64.

Rodgers, R. (1973). *Family interaction and transaction: The developmental approach*. Englewood Cliffs, NJ: Prentice-Hall.

Rousseau, J.J. (1762). *Emile* (2 vols). Trans. A. Bloom, New York: Basic, 1979.

Saarni, C., Mumme, D.L., & Campos, J.J. (1998). Emotional development: Action, communication, and understanding. In W. Damon & N. Eisenberg (eds), *Handbook of child psychology, 5th edn: Vol. 3. Social, emotional, and personality development* (pp. 237–309). New York: Wiley.

Sander, L.W. (1975). Infant and caretaking environment: Investigation and conceptualization of adaptive behavior in a series of increasing complexity. In E.J. Anthony (ed.), *Explorations in child psychiatry* (pp. 129–166). New York: Plenum.

Scupin, E., & Scupin, G. (1907). *Bubis erste Kindheit: Ein Tagebuch über die geistige Entwicklung eines Knaben in den ersten drei Lebensjahren*. Leipzig: Grieben.

Shinn, M. (1900). *The biography of a baby*. Boston: Houghton Mifflin.

Sorce, J.F., Emde, R.N., Campos, J., & Klinnert, M.D. (1985). Maternal emotional signaling: Its effect on the visual cliff behavior of 1-year-olds. *Developmental Psychology*, 21, 195–200.

Spitz, R. (1957). *Die Entstehung der ersten Objektbeziehungen: Direkte Beobachtungen an Säuglingen während des ersten Lebensjahres* (*The first object relationships: Direct observations of infants during the first year*). Stuttgart: Klett.

Spitz, R. (1965). *The first year of life: A psychoanalytic study of development of object relations*. New York: International Universities Press.

Sroufe, L.A. (1995). *Emotional development: The organization of emotional life in early years*. New York: Cambridge University Press.

Sroufe, L.A., & Fleeson, J. (1986). Attachment and the construction of relationships. In W. Hartup & Z. Rubin (eds), *Relationships and development* (pp. 51–71). Hillsdale, NJ: Erlbaum.

Sroufe, L.A., & Rutter, M. (1984). The domain of developmental psychopathology. *Child Development*, 55, 17–29.

Stern, C., & Stern, W. (1907). *Die Kindersprache: Eine psychologische und sprachtheoretische Untersuchung* (*The language of children: A psychological and linguistic study*). Leipzig: Barth.

Stern, D.N. (1977). *The first relationship: Infant and mother*. London: Open Books.

Stern, D.N. (1985). *The interpersonal world of the infant*. New York: Basic.

Stern, W. (1935). *Allgemeine Psychologie auf personalistischer Grundlage* (*General psychology from the personalistic standpoint*). Den Haag: Martinus Nijhoff.

Sullivan, H.S. (1953). *The interpersonal theory of psychiatry*. New York: Norton.

Tiedemann, D. (1787). Beobachtungen über die Entwickelung der Seelenfähigkeiten bei Kindern (Observations on the development of the mental faculties of children). *Hessische Beiträge zur Gelehrsamkeit und Kunst*, II, 313–315 and III, 486–488.

Tomasello, M., & Camaioni, L. (1997). A comparison of the gestural communication of apes and human infants. *Human Development*, 40, 7–24.

Tomasello, M., & Farrar, M.J. (1986). Joint attention and early language. *Child Development*, 57, 1454–1463.

Toren, C. (1993). Making history: The significance of childhood cognition for a comparative anthropology of mind. *Man*, 28, 461–478.

Trevarthen, C. (1984). Emotions in infancy: Regulators of contact and relationships with persons. In K. Scherer & P. Ekman (eds), *Approaches to emotions* (pp. 129–162). Hillsdale, NJ: Erlbaum.

Trevarthen, C., & Hubley, P. (1978). Secondary intersubjectivity: Confidence, confinding and acts of meaning in the first year. In A. Lock (ed.), *Action, gesture and symbol* (pp. 183–229). London: Academic.

Tronick, E.Z. (1989). Emotions and emotional communication in infants. *American Psychologist*, 44, 112–119.

Tronick, E.Z., & Cohn, J. (1989). Infant–mother face-to-face interaction: Age and gender differences in coordination and the occurrence of miscoordination. *Child Development*, 60, 85–91.

Tulving, E. (1972). Episodic and semantic memory. In E. Tulving & W. Donaldson (eds), *Organization of memory* (pp. 382–403). New York: Academic.

Vives, J.L. (1531/1912). *On education*. Translation of *De tradendis disciplinis* from *De disciplinis libri XX* (1531) by F. Watson. Cambridge: Cambridge University Press.

von Uexküll, J.J. (1920). *Theoretische Biologie* (*Theoretical biology*). Berlin: Springer.

Wartner, U.G., Grossmann, K., Fremmer-Bombik, E., & Suess, G. (1994). Attachment patterns at age six in south Germany: Predictability from infancy and implications for preschool behavior. *Child Development*, 65, 1014–1027.

Youniss, J. (1999). Giving the discipline new life and overcoming fruitless dualities. *Human Development*, 42, 145–148.

Zill, N. (1994). Understanding why children in stepfamilies have more learning and behavior problems than children in nuclear families. In A. Booth & J. Dunn (eds.), *Stepfamilies. Who benefits? Who does not?* (pp. 97–106). Hillsdale, NJ: Erlbaum.

Zumbahlen, M., & Crawley, A. (1996). Infants' early referential behavior in prohibition contexts: The emergence of social referencing? Paper presented at the meetings of the International Conference on Infant Studies, Providence, RI.

PART THREE:
Development in Early Childhood

10

The Role of Language in Human Development

NANCY BUDWIG

Over the last few decades developmental psychologists have made increasing use of the study of language in their attempts to understand development. One finds two major ways language has been viewed in such endeavors: a view of 'language as method' and an alternative view of 'language as mechanism' (see Budwig, 1999; 2000a; 2000b). The first view of language, quite popular in psychological theorizing, presupposes a representational view of meaning (see Budwig, Wertsch, & Uzgiris, 2000; Reddy, 1993, for review). According to this view language provides a useful method for the researcher; language can be thought of as a powerful tool that assists in better understanding underlying conceptual or social developments. Here the view is offered that the study of language affords the researcher access to otherwise hard to examine notions. This view of language as method has been used extensively by many developmental psychologists, including researchers interested in theory of mind questions (see Bartsch & Wellman, 1995; Dunn, Bretherton, & Munn, 1987; Wellman, 1990), as well as in the study of self (Lewis & Brooks-Gunn, 1979).

While this is a dominant view of language, others exist and have begun to gain significance in developmental theorizing and research. One alternative view considers language in terms of a functional perspective highlighting the role of language as a mechanism that children draw upon in their construction of meaning (see Bruner, 1990; Budwig, 1999; 2000b; Nelson, 1996; Schieffelin & Ochs, 1986; Wertsch, 1991, among others). Here emphasis is placed on the idea that language provides children with a powerful tool to apprehend, represent, and transform their worlds. Note though that the issue is not simply one of providing a tool for the researcher or a tool for the child. In the most general terms, this distinction has to do with whether language is viewed as a tool for revelation or a tool for the construction of reality. To this extent, those highlighting the more dynamic view of language also recognize that researchers themselves are involved in meaning construction as they conduct their investigations in and through language. It is this second view of language that I shall explore in this essay.

This chapter is organized into four sections. First we will consider historical aspects of developing the view of language as mechanism position. Although much emphasis has been placed on the influence of Vygotsky and Whorf, in this chapter I shall discuss the work of Stern, Bühler, and Sapir. In the following section I examine guiding assumptions and stable empirical findings from the emerging field of language socialization. A third section of this chapter will focus on an exploration of what these findings tell us about development. Finally, I will turn to a discussion of my own sense of where work in this area is heading and make some specific recommendations about how theory and research can best proceed.

Some Early Figures Influencing the Study of Language, Thought, Culture, and Development

The view that language encodes reality is one of many alternative ways to view the interface between language and thought. The idea that language might not only mirror but also provide a means for constructing reality has a long history (Taylor, 1985). For instance, Herder (1966) argued that language not only provides speakers with words that designate, but also provides the possibility for reflective awareness.

To this end, Herder claimed language is not only designative but also expressive. Humboldt (1836/1988) added to this anti-designative view by stressing the idea of language as activity. Language can be viewed as both ergon (language as form) and energeia (language as formation). Language as activity is continually structured through ongoing acts of communication. In this section I review the work of three thinkers who each made a unique contribution to current attempts to discuss the interface between language, thought, culture and development.

Stern's Legacy: The Notion of Development and Individual Variation

William Stern (1871–1938) can be considered a leading figure in contributing to the buildup of developmental psychology in German-speaking countries (see Cairns, 1998). Stern is well known for establishing and directing the Psychological Institute at Hamburg University, where he worked until 1933 when he was expelled from Germany by the Nazis and moved a year later to the US for the remainder of his life. Stern's writings spanned many domains of developmental psychology: he is acknowledged for contributing to discussions of the IQ, studies of language development, and personality development (see Cairns, 1998; Kreppner, 1994; Lamiell, 1996; Stern, 1906; 1911; 1918; Valsiner, 1998a).

The idea that the study of language and its development was central to psychological issues and in particular developmental issues took shape in the late 1800s. Stern argued (based on extensive diary reports that he and his wife Clara collected of their three children) that the process of language development shared much in common with general principles of development. As he has noted (see Stern, 1935/1938; Stern & Stern, 1907/1928, currently being translated into English as Stern & Stern, in progress), there are at least three reasons why the study of language development is central to developmental studies: first, Stern claims that 'it is to speech alone that man owes the power of all real thought' (1935/1938, p. 141); second, Stern argues that language is acquired with such relative ease and speed; and third, children's speech is not simply some imperfect version of an adult telos, but has a form of its own.

In connecting the study of language with that of other domains of development, Stern highlighted the interconnectedness of an individual's functioning. Stern's personalistic epistemology is at the heart of this work. Central to his theorizing about human functioning was the notion that psychological elements themselves are not defining elements but rather must be viewed in terms of the entire structure of person, environment, and person–environment relations (see Kreppner, 1994; Stern, 1911). Language is part of a larger whole, a piece that cannot be studied in and of itself: 'All development of single functions is unfailingly dependent on the development of the whole' (1935/1938, p. 50). In keeping with this holistic framework, Stern focused on general principles of development. In addition to viewing development in terms of growth, Stern proposed that development is also marked by 'an increase of differentiation in function' (1935/1938, p. 54). Such a view of development places emphasis on the child's active and constructive efforts to organize and reorganize language, as part of the more general differentiation process. This allows for two further points concerning development that will be central to thinking about the role of language more broadly in human development. First, Stern has emphasized that the process of acquiring language is *protracted*, and second, he has focused on the extent of variation in his own three children's language development based on their different contexts of learning. That is, Stern expected not only that children raised in different communities or stemming from different backgrounds would differ, but that even children raised in the same family would exhibit individual variation.

A flavor of Stern's emphasis on protracted differentiation and individual variation is given in his discussion of the process of acquiring self-reference forms. Stern and Stern (1907/1928) noted that their children went through an extended phase of using their own name and the first person (German) nominative form *Ich* side by side. Early use of the form *Ich* was restricted in usage. Stern and Stern referred to this early limited use of pronominal forms as 'the primitive form of the "child-*I*"' (1907/1928, p. 273). Only much later would it take on its full range of adult meaning. In addition to the path of development being protracted, and filled with children's own attempts to construct personal meaning systems, the routes followed by his children were said to differ in significant ways. For instance, the Sterns noted that Hilde, their oldest child, began using her own name to refer to herself and only slowly began to use the pronominal form *Ich*, while their second and third born children Gunter and Eva began by referring to themselves with the pronominal form *Ich*. Stern and Stern argued that the different pathways could be accounted for in terms of the distinct speech contexts provided to only children – who speak primarily to adults – and children who are raised with older siblings (see Deutsch et al., 1997; Stern & Stern, 1907/1928, p. 273, for further discussion).

Stern's holistic view of development contrasts to the prevailing view that has been to treat language as something of a mirror that simply represents underlying cognition. Stern's work is central in that it reminds us of the close connection between cognitive, language, and affective development in young children. This clearly points to placing more emphasis on the role of language in the study of human development. Stern's work is also quite critical with respect to our current understanding of the way in which language can be thought of as impacting on human development. Stern was clear that the unit of analysis was not to be simply a teleological view of the adult system which then would be evaluated in terms of whether a child had acquired it. Much like an ethnographer, Stern was concerned with finding children's own ways of patterning language forms and meanings. Both the idea that children's meaning systems differ from the input they receive and the claim that children, even those raised by the same caregivers, develop distinct meaning systems, will be points we shall return to later in this chapter. These suggestions raise issues that make complex any theory of how language can be viewed as playing a central role in human development.

Bühler's Contribution: Towards a Functional Theory of Language

While William Stern put forward the idea that young children's contrasting use of linguistic forms was a sign of their primitive or child-like functioning, Bühler suggested that all speakers' use of language is linked up with contexts of use. Bühler argued, 'the language signs function in the commerce of people as instruments that guide practical behavior' (1932, p. 104). Although Bühler, a psychologist whose writing spanned from the early 1900s until the late 1930s, has been explicitly cited and praised by scholars in the neighboring disciplines of linguistics and anthropology, his work has received little attention from psychologists (but see Brock, 1994; Sinha, in press; Valsiner, 1998b, for exceptions). Jakobson directly noted the significance of Bühler's work for linguists by claiming that it was 'for linguists probably the most inspiring among all contributions to the psychology of language' (1973, p. 41). Most contemporary volumes on functional linguistics or linguistic anthropology at least briefly discuss his ideas. In fact, many of the 'new' ideas that developmental psychologists claim to have imported from neighboring disciplines can partially be traced to Bühler (see Budwig, 1998; Sinha, in press).

Bühler's interest in language was fueled by his involvement in the development of a new form of psychology that began in Würzburg called *Denkpsychologie*. Within this context, Bühler began to explore the idea that language must be viewed in terms of both its structure and its function. In developing a new theory of sentence types Bühler highlighted the importance of distinguishing three functions of language: *Darstellung* (representation), *Kundgabe* (expression), and *Appell* (appeal or arousal). Regardless of which of these functions he took as central, and he wavered on this across his publications, the thrust of his work was devoted to the idea that language is action (see Nehrlich & Clarke, 1996, for further discussion). Of central focus then to psychological theorizing was this idea that in using talk speakers not only perform actions but also are able to get others to act in particular ways.

Nehrlich and Clarke (1996, p. 224) argued that Bühler was the most celebrated pragmatic thinker in Germany and an influential addition in a chain of thinkers that extends from Humboldt to Habermas. Although most of the emphasis in both psychology and related disciplines has been on Bühler's notions of language functioning, it is important to keep in mind that Bühler also made important contributions to thinking about the connections between linguistic forms and the semantic and pragmatic functions they serve. First, Bühler has contributed to the development of the notions of fields which we will see link forms with meanings in ways that are similar to discussions currently taking place in cognitive linguistics (see Tomasello, 1998). A second central contribution of Bühler is his discussion of deixis and in particular, the ways 'pointing words' orient speaker and listener in terms of context. This discussion can be viewed as paving the way for much work currently going on in cultural and linguistic anthropology, work that has played a pivotal role in the development of the language socialization framework.

Bühler introduces his field-theoretic approach to language when outlining the relationship between words or lexical items on the one hand, and fields on the other:

> But just as the painter's colors require a painting surface, so too do language symbols require a surrounding field in which they can be arranged. We call this the *symbolic field* of language. (1934/1990, p. 170)

This view is clearly a precursor to the notion put forward more recently by individuals working in cognitive linguistics such as Lakoff (1987), Fillmore and colleagues (see Goldberg, 1996; Palmer, 1996, for review), and Langacker (1987) in which it is argued that the use of particular lexical items invokes a particular perspective or vantage point. To this extent, Bühler's discussion of the construct of the symbolic field suggests that particular linguistic arrangements provide distinct slants on event construal. To this extent, Bühler argued that language cannot simply be viewed as representing a given reality, but rather linguistic forms in conjunction with symbolic fields help structure the nature of experience. For Bühler, language (viewed as a system consisting of lexical and syntactic units) plays a central role in constructing the world. Language, therefore, can be viewed as more than a mapping of an 'out there' experience. Through the complex linkage of sign and symbolic field, language plays a significant mediating role in the construction of reality (see also Sinha, in press).

A second central contribution made by Bühler concerns his discussion of deixis. For Bühler, deictic words can be described as follows:

> To put it briefly: the formed deictic words, phonologically distinct from each other just as other words are, are expedient ways to guide the partners. The partner is called by them, and his gaze, and more generally, his searching perceptual activity, his readiness for sensory reception is referred by the deictic words to clues, gesture-like clues and their equivalents, which improve and supplement his orientation among the details of the situation. That is the function of the deictic words in verbal contact, if one insists upon reducing this function to a single general formula. (1934/1990, p. 121)

The idea here, that language use itself creates context, has more recently been discussed by a range of cultural and linguistic anthropologists under terms such as 'shifters' (Silverstein, 1976), 'frames' (Goffman, 1974), 'contextual cues' (Gumperz, 1982), and 'deictic fields' (Hanks, 1996).

What is central for the current purpose is Bühler's insistence that the construction and understanding of meaning rest not only on naming and symbolizing but also on indexing. Bühler likened deictic forms in language to other signs (e.g. arrows on signposts) but also recognized their specialness in the sense that concrete speech events are just that: events. They are grounded in time and space. To this extent, Bühler argued, deixis in language requires not just locations but also roles such as the communicative roles of speaker and listener to guide in the interpretive processes involved in using and understanding such forms.

Although Bühler's work has received little direct discussion in psychological circles, it seems that studies of human development have come to rely on ideas that interestingly enough can be traced to his theory of language. Bühler can be viewed as having an impact on the study of human development in at least two ways. Only the first of these ways is directly acknowledged. For the other, the road is less direct, and interestingly, in contrast to Bühler's aim to develop a *two-field theory* (i.e. indexing and naming), in developmental circles there has been next to no attempt to link the two avenues together (see Budwig, 1998, for further discussion).

The first and only direct connection to Bühler's work can be found in Werner and Kaplan's *Symbol formation* (1963/1984). When discussing the development of symbolic abilities, Werner and Kaplan draw heavily on Bühler's discussion, noting though some limitations of Bühler's perspective. In particular they note that his view of language can be seen as 'agenetic' to the extent that he focuses on 'ideal structure' (see Werner & Kaplan, 1963/1984, p. 52), while their own approach is characterized as developmental. Bühler, for instance, has noted ways case markers and other linguistic markers are often used in languages to mark specific formula-like schemata. The use of transitive verbs for example 'call for' the filling in of two slots in the syntactic model, that is a 'subjective' and an 'objective' case. What is central here is that for Bühler meaning consists of more than the sum of individual words. Meaning is always related to the broader symbolic fields in which individual words are placed. Werner & Kaplan elaborated this model by discussing how speakers move from rather concrete action fields to more abstract frames. They argue that this shift can be best viewed as part of a more general developmental process, namely children's desire to conceive of the world first in terms of 'formula-like schemata' and only later in terms of more freedom from the concrete perceptual-motor contexts. The view that children go from more concrete meanings to more abstract ones also has been discussed by Slobin (1985) and colleagues (see Budwig, 1995, for review). Such treatments focus on Bühler's notion of representation and the symbolic field of language, but leave aside his discussion of other language functions and the issue of deixis.

It is exactly this second aspect of Bühler's theory, the deictic and non-representational functions of language, that can indirectly be linked to researchers working within the rapidly growing area of language socialization. To anticipate our discussion in the next section, language socialization research is guided by the belief that in learning to use language children are simultaneously socialized into cultural ways of being (Miller & Hoogstra, 1992; Schieffelin & Ochs, 1986). A guiding assumption is that deictic forms index culturally appropriate ways of acting, feeling, and knowing, and that these indexicals simultaneously provide individuals with ways of co-constructing cultural meanings (Budwig, 2000a; 2000b; Goodwin, 1990; Ochs, 1996). Indexicals are said to play a central role in this process:

> A linguistic index is usually a structure (e.g. sentential voice, emphatic stress, diminutive affix) that is variably used from one situation to another and becomes conventionally associated with particular situational dimensions such that when that structure is used, the form invokes those situational dimensions. (Ochs, 1996, p. 411)

Extending Bühler's claims that deictic forms 'are expedient ways to guide the partners' (1934/1990, p. 121), one can see that the sort of claim made by language socialization researchers is that experts, in their use of particular indexicals, give 'clues' to novices about how to 'orient' themselves in given situations.

Sapir's View of the Interconnection between Language, Personality, and Culture

Sapir was born in Germany in 1884, but was raised in the United States from the age of five. While at Columbia University he met up with Boas who encouraged him to study anthropology. Later Sapir did for anthropology and linguistics what Bühler did for psychology: he attempted to unite the study of psychological issues and the study of languages. Sapir (1929/1970) noted with pleasure that psychologists were beginning to concern themselves more and more with linguistic data. It was Sapir's belief that the psychologists, while perhaps having little to contribute to an understanding of linguistic behavior, nevertheless had much to offer the linguist interested in psychology:

> But the feeling is growing rapidly, and justly, that the psychological explanations of the linguists themselves need to be restated in more general terms, so that purely linguistic facts may be seen as specialized forms of symbolic behavior. (1929/1970, p. 71)

Sapir echoes Bühler's belief in the idea that language is not best viewed as a mirror of reality. On the one hand, Sapir suggests that language provides a guide for the observation and interpretation of reality. Discussing examples of abstract metaphoric use of syntactic frames (which look quite close to Bühler's discussion of symbolic fields), Sapir makes the following claim about language: 'it does not as a matter of actual behavior stand apart from or run parallel to direct experience but completely interpenetrates with it' (1929/1970, p. 8). In developing his position about the relationship between language, thought, and society he claimed:

> The fact of the matter is that the 'real world' is to a large extent unconsciously built up on the language habits of the group. No two languages are ever sufficiently similar to be considered as representing the same social reality. The worlds in which different societies live are distinct worlds, not merely the same world with different labels attached. (1929/1970, p. 69)

If Bühler was interested in developing a broad theory of language that could be used to better understand broad psychological issues, Sapir was interested in exploring the implications of the connection between such a view of language, culture, and personality.

Sapir thought language was particularly well suited for the study of culture for several reasons. First, Sapir he claimed that 'The content of every culture is expressible in its language' (1933/1970, p. 6). In addition, he argued that language allows one to go beyond that which one has experienced. But Sapir was also clear to note that there is no exact one-to-one correspondence between one's language and one's culture:

> There is no general correlation between cultural type and linguistic structure . . . The cultural significance of linguistic form, in other words, lies on a much more submerged level than on the overt one of definite cultural pattern. (1933/1970, pp. 34–35)

Sapir also held a multifunctional view of language. In addition to recognizing how language functions within the spheres of 'thought, communication, and expression' (1933/1970, p. 15), he also recognized it as a powerful resource for enculturation and individuation. In fact he boldly claimed, 'Language is a great force of socialization, probably the greatest that exists' (1933/1970, pp. 15–16). He elaborated three main reasons for this. First, language provides a mechanism for indexing social solidarity. Members of the same group – and here he was clear that he did not mean language typology but rather social network (e.g. family, undergraduate members of a college, etc.) – develop idiosyncrasies that function to mark the group as such. Second, Sapir believed that language socializes to the extent that it helps create rapport among individuals. Third, and most important, in and through language, communities have ways of passing on cultural stock. Proverbs, prayers, and other forms of discourse preserve culture. Note though that Sapir never linked the specific linguistic devices to acts of socialization, a trend we will see that has become dominant in current work in the area of language socialization. At the same time that Sapir recognized the resourcefulness of language as a means of enculturation, he also noted the role language plays in what he referred to as individuation. He argued: 'In spite of the fact that language acts as a socializing and uniformizing force, it is at the same time the most potent single known factor for the growth of individuality' (1933/1970, p. 19).

Sapir recognized though the dangers of viewing socialization and individuation as distinct. For Sapir, both required a view of the individual that is quite active:

> There is no real opposition, at last analysis, between the concept of a culture of the group and the concept of an individual culture. The two are interdependent . . . An automatic perpetuation of standardized values, not subject to the constant remodeling of individuals willing to put some part of themselves into the forms they receive from their predecessors, leads to the dominance of impersonal formulas. (1924/1970, pp. 101–102)

This view led Sapir to develop a stance about development that portrays the novice as active in the process. Sapir's views on the connection between development and culture can be found in his lectures which took place during the 1930s on this theme (see Sapir, 1934/1993, Chapter 10). When discussing 'the adjustment of the individual in society' he clearly portrays a view of culture that is actively constructed by the child:

> Culture is then not something given but something to be gradually and gropingly discovered. We then see at once that elements of culture that come well within the horizon of awareness of one individual are entirely absent in another individual's landscape. (1934/1993, p. 197)

Elaborating on this, Sapir goes on to argue, in a style that echoes what has been previously claimed by Stern, his views of individual difference:

> Even within the same family, each child's world is a different kind of a thing because the fundamental emotional relationships were differently established depending on his status as first or second child. (1934/1993, p. 197)

To this extent Sapir claims that the notion of 'cultural patterning' is something of an 'illusion', leading him instead to emphasize a pluralistic concept of culture that is continually negotiated and co-constructed by individuals.

The Modern Day Study of Language Socialization

Theoretical Perspectives

While much of the work by Stern, Bühler, and Sapir anticipated the modern day view of language socialization, it was not until more recently that a framework for understanding the intersection between developing language, thought and culture was formulated. Much of the delay can be attributed to altering conceptions of development as well as more representational conceptions of language that dominated during the 1960s and 1970s. But with the recent resurgence of interest in developing a cultural psychology there has been a growing need for a more complete understanding of the role of symbolically mediated experiences in the process of human development. Drawing on prior theorizing by figures such as Stern, Bühler, and Sapir and guided by renewed interest in the interdependent relation between language, thought, culture, and development, modern day research on language socialization is guided by a shared belief in several principles. First, when appealing to the socializing power of language, researchers are adopting a view of language that focuses on its situated use. Second, language is viewed not only in terms of structure but also in terms of function. A third tenet shared by modern theorists concerns the active role of participants, including children, in the dynamic construction of meaning. We will briefly discuss these principles and their application to several domains of research after first providing a broad definition of how the modern day view on language socialization is defined. Ochs and Schieffelin (1984, p. 277) have articulated it best by drawing on two claims:

1 The process of acquiring language is deeply affected by the process of becoming a competent member of a society.
2 The process of becoming a competent member of society is realized to a large extent through language, by acquiring knowledge of its functions, social distribution, and interpretations in and across socially defined situations (i.e. through exchanges of language in particular social situations).

In sum, language socialization theorizing rests on the assumption that processes of socialization and communicative development go hand in hand.

Situated Use of Language

In suggesting that language plays a powerful role in childhood socialization, theorists within this perspective assume that language encompasses a constitutive as well as a representational function. The idea that language plays a fundamental role in the social construction of meaning depends on the idea that language be viewed as a highly organized activity. Borrowing from work in sociolinguistics and the ethnography of communication, speaking is viewed as a form of social action. As Schieffelin and Ochs have argued, 'vocal and verbal activities are generally socially organized and embedded in cultural systems of meaning' (1986, p. 164). This holds true not only for adult interactions but also for those taking place between infants or young children and their caregivers (see Cook-Gumperz, Corsaro, & Streeck, 1986; Schieffelin & Ochs, 1986). Work starting from a situated view of talk has highlighted the extent to which language interactions can be viewed as highly structured units that universally segment the ongoing stream of action into orderly sequences related to culturally sanctioned ways of organizing social life.

Talk also has been said to play a pivotal structuring role in the apprehension of reality. The habitual organization of language plays a fundamental role not only in the understanding of context, but also in its very determination (see Shweder et al., 1997). Context thus can best be viewed as something that is emergent, rather than something that is external to or surrounding in some physical sense the very act of speaking (see Duranti, 1997; Duranti & Goodwin, 1992; Miller, 1996).

The study of language as practice has provided a useful approach for better understanding how socialization takes place. The claim is made that children and significant others socially construct meaning in and through regular participation in language practices. The study of the situated use of language provides also a powerful methodological tool for the study of such socialization processes. The study of situated practices provides a way to examine the tacit and routine organization of social space and is often better than interviewing because researchers can identify regularities that participants themselves may not have conscious access to (Budwig, 2000b; Shweder et al., 1997).

Language Structure and Language Function

In talking about verbal activities as socially organized units of practice, sociolinguists have highlighted a variety of ways of examining organizational units of language. Researchers working in the area of language socialization have primarily examined two of these many ways. Some have relied on the examination of narrative units while others have looked at lexical and grammatical forms in terms of the notion of contextual cues.

Drawing upon narrative as a unit of analysis, Miller's program (Miller, 1996; Miller et al., 1990) is amongst the most elaborate. For example, Miller has examined regularities in how personal stories are told by caregivers in different communities. She has investigated the particular way stories are organized and she suggests that this provides the child with a powerful message about issues such as the construction of self. Although the communities studied differed in important ways in terms of the versions of reality that were 'carved out' in the process, Miller claims that all caregivers, both as co-narrators with their children, and in their narratives *about* their children, provided a public space for the construction of meaning. Language in this way not only provides a resource for the child to represent reality. In its social uses it also provides a mechanism for the ongoing construction of such a world. Central here is the assumption that language is to be viewed in terms of rather large discourse chunks, namely narratives. Narratives provide a structured space that makes accessible a variety of language functions, that in turn can be utilized by participants to construct ways of being in the world.

Similarly, though at a more local unit of analysis, others have relied on specific lexical or grammatical forms and the role they play in language socialization. The idea here, expressed well by Ochs, is that such forms when used habitually come to be indexical of larger meaning units:

> A linguistic index is usually a structure (e.g. sentential voice, emphatic stress, diminutive affix) that is used variably from one situation to another and becomes conventionally associated with particular situational dimensions such that when that structure is used, the form invokes those situational dimensions. (1996, p. 411)

Such forms come to be what Gumperz has called contextualization cues – a set of forms that give an indication as to how a specific situation or interaction is proceeding and is expected to continue. To this extent, context is dynamically produced through the regular use of language forms (regardless of how small or large such units are) used to achieve specific functions.

The Role of the Child as an Active Contributor to the Meaning Making Process

One might assume that such a view of the regular and conventional use of forms to achieve specific functions could easily lead to a rather passive view of the child in this process given that the child, as novice, has yet to master the conventions of these very forms. Researchers studying language socialization have been explicit in suggesting that meaning making is a dynamic process in which the child plays an active role. Gaskins, Miller, and Corsaro claim: 'Meaning creation is a collective process, embedded in institutional activities and mediated by language and other semiotic systems. At the same time, it is an individual process' (1992, p. 11). Miller (1996, p. 184) highlights the negotiated and mutual aspects of participation in discourse practices, and Schieffelin and Ochs suggest that 'individuals (including young children) are viewed not as automatically internalizing others' views, but as selective and active participants in the process of constructing social worlds' (1986, p. 165). Ochs and Schieffelin (1984) further emphasize the dynamic and interpreted aspects of meaning construction. First, they suggest that the same individual might interpret language differently over time. In addition, they note that there may be individual variation in how meanings are interpreted by individuals who share a language. Cook-Gumperz (1986, p. 55) goes the furthest in articulating the process by which an individual child organizes and reorganizes inferences based on the regular use of particular linguistic devices, clarifying how the child actively structures and revises hypotheses based on further assessments of social outcomes. Nevertheless, as we shall see, little empirical work has systematically examined these points. To date, researchers in the area of language socialization have primarily articulated this view of the child as actively involved in sorting out interpretive stances towards linguistic form–function pairs in the ongoing assessment of meaning at the theoretical level.

Domains

While work on language socialization has examined many ways in which language plays a central role in childhood socialization, three main areas have received most attention. These include personhood, affect, and gender identity. In considering prior work in these areas, our discussion will be organized around the type of unit of analysis utilized by the investigators. Three sorts of research focus can be found, namely on the role of narrative practices, on the importance of social acts and the organization of conversational routines, and finally on the role that particular linguistic form–function pairing plays in socialization processes.

Socialization of the Person

One of the first studies to suggest variation in the language socialization practices of caregivers described a typology of socialization based on ethnographic studies of American middle-class, Samoan, and Kaluli caregiver–child interactions (see Ochs & Schieffelin, 1984). This work pointed out the limitations of developmental research that focused exclusively on American middle-class assumptions about the goals and enactment of early communicative interchanges between babies and their caregivers since they found these did not apply world wide. Their ethnographic work highlights a variety of ways caregivers organize early interactions with their children, consistent with their different goals for their babies' development. In describing in rich detail the variety of interaction styles found, Ochs and Schieffelin simultaneously outlined a beginning sense of the variation to be identified with regard to what it means to be a person in different social-historical contexts. Their distinction between language practices that emphasize adapting situations to children, as opposed to communities that adapted children to situations, later came to be known as individualist and collectivist senses of the person. Refining the specifics of the rich variation to be found has been documented in numerous studies that have focused on a variety of communities and units of analysis (Harkness, Raeff, & Super, 2000). All come together on the point that these early communicative practices provide the child with an entry way into figuring out culturally sanctioned ways of being a person.

Miller's work on the role of narrative practice in the socialization of a person has illustrated the varied and systematic organization of the stories children overhear and co-participate in telling (see for instance Miller & Hoogstra, 1992; Miller et al., 1992; 1997). Examining the content, form, and function of narrations about focal 2-year-old children (half Taiwanese, half middle-class European American), mounting evidence suggests that storytelling is a dominant activity in both communities, but one which is carried out in distinct ways leaving children with a different sense of self. The Chinese caregivers were more likely to use storytelling about the focal child to emphasize moral and social standards and ways children connected to a larger social order. In contrast, the middle-class American caregivers engaged in storytelling that routinely emphasized the children's autonomy and agency. Similar follow-up work has also highlighted the importance of narrative practices for demonstrating cultural differences among American caregivers. Wiley et al. (1998) further examined families from two European American communities – one working class and the other middle class. While caregivers in both communities encouraged the children to have autonomous selves by granting them extensive rights to speak as well as offering them limited rights to 'author' their reporting of past experiences, the researchers also pointed out that the two communities differed in how they promoted autonomy. For instance, middle-class children were given the sense that they had 'natural rights', while the practices of the working-class families made clear that their children had to earn and defend their rights.

These same themes of the cultural variation of personhood also can be found in the vast literature examining interactional routines in terms of the social organization of conversation. Eisenberg's (1992) examination of middle-class American mothers highlights the way conversational practices encourage an autonomous self. For instance, mothers provided justifications for refusing to affirm the children's requests, and tended to also use delay techniques rather than explicit negatives when avoiding compliance with their children's requests. Furthermore, Tardif and Wan (2001), in a longitudinal study of Chinese caregiver–child dyads, reports that that the Chinese caregivers were even more positive than the American middle-class caregivers studied by Eisenberg. Both groups were indirect but the Chinese caregivers made use of a variety of indirect strategies and expected their children to refuse making use of similar indirect styles in a way not reported for American middle-class children. It is important to note that in studying the dyads, Tardif and Wan point out that the children were not simply mimicking the adult strategies for indirectness. While they picked up on the idea that indirectness was central to the presentation of self, they nevertheless did not make use of identical verbal means as their caregivers who had more sophisticated verbal resources. At the onset of the study the children were said to make use of silence as one way to achieve the indirect refusal stance, while over time the children began utilizing the devices their caregivers made use of when refusing.

While the Chinese dyads gave precedence to indirectness, Bhatia (1998; 2001) has emphasized the directive nature of person reference in Indian caregiver–child dyads. As was the case with Miller, who studied working-class and middle-class Americans, Bhatia focused his analysis on socio-economic differences in the Indian sample of preschoolers growing up in Delhi. Bhatia notes that the social acts engaged in, and in particular, the heavy use of directives to control the behavior and actions of the children, downplayed the children's autonomy. The upper class children, while participating in dialogues dominated by directives also heard person references within the context of declarative utterances which Bhatia suggests offers the child a framework for understanding the negotiated sense of personhood. His work highlights the complex interplay between forms of personhood and cultural and class based interaction patterns.

The importance of not aligning language communities with a global assessment of kinds of personhood emphasized is found in the work of others (see Lin, 1993; Vinden, 2001; Wiley, 1997). Vinden found that American caregivers of various socioeconomic backgrounds differed in the request language used and that this variation played a contributing role in accounting for theory of mind development in their preschool children. More specifically, some caregivers, frequently the more educated parents, were more likely to provide their children with a range of perspectives as they controlled their children's behavior through the use of control acts. In contrast, other caregivers were more likely to use bare imperatives that introduced no perspective into the discourse. Vinden suggests that such language based request routines play an especially important role in children's development of mind.

Lin (1993) examined the ways caregivers and their toddlers organized interaction within two religious communities around New England. One group of caregivers affiliated with conservative religious groups (e.g. Fundamentalists), while the other group were described as 'liberal' (e.g. Unitarians, reformed Jews, and Quakers). Indeed Lin's study revealed that even some American caregivers will engage in non-autonomy supporting conversational activities with their toddlers. The conservative caregivers as a group were more likely to engage in what Ochs and Schieffelin described as parent-centered discourse, while the liberal caregivers' style was clearly the more child-centered. This was displayed in the organization of turn taking and topic continuity in the following way: the child-centered dyads organized interaction so that the children initiated more turns, while in the parent-centered dyads the caregiver controlled the organization of turn initiations and topic focus (see also Hoff-Ginsberg, 1991, for a similar analysis based on SES background). Lin, like Tardif and Wan (2001), notes some individual variation which she suggests might be accounted for by age differences in particular children, suggesting the need for future developmental analyses to better understand the interplay between cultural presentations of self in interaction and issues of development. Wootton (1997) has provided precisely such a developmental analysis of one middle-class child growing up in England.

Thus far I have discussed ways in which investigators examining personal narratives, as well as the social organization of conversation, have isolated patterns that have been noted to play a role in the socialization of personhood within the everyday interactions of caregivers and their preschool children. One last kind of work, namely by researchers adopting an indexical approach to language, shows yet another way language is said to play a critical role in the co-construction of personhood in the early years. Here the underlying idea is that the regular use of linguistic forms comes to index or call up larger frames. Researchers in this tradition have focused in particular on the ways speakers index one another when using self and other reference terms (see Budwig, 2000a; 2000b; Budwig & Chaudhary, 1996; Budwig & Wiley, 1995; Moissinac & Budwig, 2000). Budwig and colleagues have shown how subtle variations in the selection of name versus personal pronouns ground interactions in different ways. For instance, Budwig and Chaudhary (1996) have noted how Hindi-speaking caregivers of varying socioeconomic levels appeal to a similar range of forms to address their children, but with different frequencies and for distinct functions. For instance, although all Hindi-speaking caregivers tended to use imperatives to their children with no person reference form (null), the upper-class caregivers used other self-reference forms to mark distinct ways to situate the child within the ongoing interaction. For instance, these caregivers switched from the null form to nominal forms (child's name) when making declarations about the relation between the child and a given state in the world, and used terms of endearment when the interactive goal was one of highlighting the dyads' social connectedness. In contrast, even though the lower-class caregivers occasionally used variations in forms, in all contexts the regulative view of the child was portrayed. It is suggested that the upper-class children could use the regularities in form shifts to build up a more varied sense of self (self to be controlled, self as agent, self as interconnected) in their ongoing interactions with caregivers in ways not available to the lower-class children.

Similarly, Moissinac and Budwig (2000) have noted how caregivers from (former East) Berlin, Germany and Berkeley, California distinctly used desire verbs to anchor the child in ongoing play activities. For example, the American caregivers tended to use desire verbs when making inquiries about their child's current state (*Do you want a tea cup?*) or to access permission from their children to act in particular ways (*Do you want me to pour tea?*). German caregivers were unlikely to refer to their children's individual states or seek permission with desire verbs. Rather, they used desire talk as a way to invite their children into constructing joint activities together and these caregivers were equally as likely to appeal to themselves or the child when using desire verbs. Budwig (2000a) has argued that these same children do not mimic their caregivers, although she notes that the children's use of self-reference forms and other linguistic devices is sensitive to the language patternings of their caregivers. The American children were extremely interested in building a grammar of personal agency, while the German children were more focused on anchoring self in relation to normative ways of being.

Issues of personhood have also been linked to the indexical use of other areas of language by a variety of speakers, showing that at least by the preschool years children are sensitive to categories of personhood as marked by phonological, lexical and grammatical variations. Andersen's (1986; 1996) work on role and status markers in the pretend play of young Anglo-American children shows their sensitivity to the ways such devices index power and status roles. Comparini (1999; Comparini & Bhatia, 2000) has shown that usage of formal and familiar second person pronouns in the conversations taking place in Mexican caregiver–child dyads is also used productively to negotiate within the flow of ongoing social activities. In other words, such relationships are not static. And Platt (1986) has shown how the use of deictic verbs such as 'come' and 'go' in Samoan is already patterned around social status categories in young children's usage, indicating their budding understanding of the hierarchical nature of social norms of status in the community. At many levels of linguistic analysis, specific formal devices have been linked to particular ways of constructing persons when communicating in everyday activities.

Whether a researcher examines personal narratives, the social organization of conversations, the regular use of self and other reference forms, desire verbs, or markers of social status, the general point to be made is that such analyses contribute to a better understanding of the socialization of personhood. This body of work suggests that all communities interact with young children in a variety of ways such that the children come to co-construct culturally sanctioned ways of being in the world. Second, this work highlights the complex nature of the process in that some studies stressed rich between-cultural variation, others stressed within-cultural variation, and still others pointed to the protracted nature of children's organization and reorganization of cultural ways of being.

The Socialization of Affect

One of the major tasks all children face is learning the culturally sanctioned ways of understanding and expressing affect. Each society has ways of feeling, and one aspect each child must develop is an understanding of and social ability to verbally and non-verbally display and understand the relationship between context and affective forms of communication. Several investigators studying the development of preschool age children in a variety of communities have highlighted aspects of this process, revealing an early competence at enacting and understanding socioculturally situated emotional stances. Such work has involved all three methods described above, namely investigations of narrative, the social organization of conversation, and indexicality. A basic theme running through such research is a distinction made between what Ochs (1986a) calls 'hot affect' and what can be referred to as a more harmonious/empathetic affective stance. More specifically, caregivers from many different communities spend a good amount of time interacting with their young, socializing a style of interaction that their community values. For instance, the Kaluli (Schieffelin, 1986; 1990), the Samoan (Ochs, 1986b; 1988), Mexican and Mexicano (Comparini, 2000; Eisenberg, 1986) and working-class American families studied by Miller and colleagues (Miller, 1986; Miller & Sperry, 1988) have been noted to socialize an interaction style called 'hot' or affect loaded, while other communities emphasize through interaction a valuing of more muted or harmonious affective states, such as the Japanese (Clancy, 1986). We turn now to give a brief overview of such work by illustrating this basic distinction in affective stance that is socialized during the preschool years.

Caregivers who spend time engaging in affect loaded practices such as teasing and shaming are known to value their children's ability to assert and protect themselves from particular actions of others. That is, the caregivers reported that children are justified in showing anger and aggression in some situations such as engaging in self-defense, but are unjustified when engaging in something like self-indulgence (see Miller & Sperry, 1988). Communities vary in how direct they are in socialization practices engaged in concerning affect loaded talk. For instance, Kaluli caregivers have been observed to provide explicit instruction early on when interacting with their infants, but gradually they begin to use more implicit forms of affect expression (Schieffelin, 1986). Kaluli children likewise show an early competence at using simple forms that have been directly taught, but take a few years to master the rhetorical and grammatical complexity of using more sophisticated ways of teasing and shaming. In contrast, reports of three working-class children growing up in South Baltimore (Miller & Sperry, 1988) suggest that mothers did less explicit marking of teasing episodes, but nevertheless their responses to children's anger revealed patterned responses that suggested to the children information about how and when to feel angry. Indeed the mothers were noted to often promote anger through teasing routines. And indeed Miller and Sperry (1988) found that although there was an absence of direct reference to emotional states in the preschool children's talk, they nevertheless were able to communicate anger and aggression in culturally sanctioned ways by drawing upon a rich range of verbal and nonverbal resources by the age of three.

A particularly interesting case study can be found in communities that adopt an affect loaded communicative style that provide a language rich in structures (lexical, prosodic, grammatical) marking affect. Samoan, as reported by Ochs (1986b; 1988), represents such a case study. Ochs noted two broad kinds of categories of affect marking in Samoan, 'those that specify affect and those that intensify affect' (1986b, p. 264). Ochs' ethnographic research provides evidence that by the time children utter their first word they are able to mark affect and indeed often give preference to an affectively loaded form compared to a more neutral form in the acquisition process. For instance, the Samoan children studied by Ochs made rich use of the sympathy marked first person pronominal form before using a more neutral way of self-reference. Goodwin's (2000) work on peer group organization highlights that one of the important tasks continuing well into adolescence is learning to mark affective stance in loaded ways when interacting with peers.

In contrast to the affectively loaded communicative routines found in many communities, others seem to favor conformity and place more value on indirect modes of communicating affect. Japanese caregivers have been noted to adopt exactly such a view (see Clancy, 1986). Like the Kaluli caregivers, the Japanese mothers were often quite explicit in their training, for instance telling their children what others felt as a method of empathy training or exercising numerous politeness routines designed to make their children more empathetic to others. In addition, they used many communicative strategies involving means of indirectly directing, challenging, and refusing their children's behaviors. And by the age of two, although children were allowed to use direct strategies of communicating negative affect to their mothers, this was indirectly and directly corrected when displayed to members outside the family.

In summary, research on expressing affect has highlighted that there is no one kind of universal affect that is socialized in all communities. Some communities value communications in which there is rich expression of a charged affective stance, while other communities use social harmony as the ideal and prefer more indirect strategies of expressing affect. Regardless of the community children are raised in, two things are clear from the literature. First, all children engage with more experienced others in a range of practices that provide both direct and indirect indications of culturally sanctioned ways of feeling in particular contexts. Second, children as young as two are quite able to engage in modified ways in such practices, showing a starting point that is quite flexible to the conventions of the community.

Gender Socialization

Thus far I have examined how young children before the age of 4 come to position self in relation to others and adopt culturally sanctioned ways of feeling in ongoing communicative routines with primary caregivers. What this leaves unaccounted for is the way in which gender comes to be socialized and how this interacts in complex ways with how the self is anchored and the way affect is expressed and experienced. We turn now to review a few studies that have focused on the role of language in the socialization of emotion talk and what it means to be a person from the perspective of gender identity.

An extensive literature has highlighted differences in the ways in which caregivers talk differently to their sons and daughters (Eisenberg, 1999; Fivish, 1993; Gleason et al., 1996). This work has been used to argue that already by the end of the first year of life, children are treated in linguistically distinct ways by caregivers. For instance, Gleason et al. (1996) have argued that middle-class American boys receive far more prohibitions from their caregivers than girls of a similar age. It has also been noted that the mothers of girls talk more about emotions than the mothers of boys (see Dunn, Bretherton, & Munn, 1987; Fivish, 1993). It has been suggested that such different routines provide an early origin for male and female communicative styles.

While there are some well-documented cases of English-speaking caregivers using different language practices with boys and girls, few studies have examined caregiver–child interactions in a comparative light during the preschool years (see Ochs, 1988; Schieffelin, 1990). In fact, most of the literature concerning gender and the language practices of young children has focused on peer based interactions often taking place in the English-speaking nursery school setting.

Nicolopoulou and colleagues (Nicolopoulou, 1997; Nicolopoulou, Scales, & Weintraub, 1994; Richner & Nicolopoulou, 2001) have gathered stories from English-speaking preschool children (from a variety of geographic regions and SES backgrounds) as part of naturally occurring storytelling practices in the school setting. Such work has revealed that boys and girls elaborated two quite distinct narrative styles, characterized in part as representing different images of persons based on gender. For instance, girls tended to embed characters in an interpersonal framework and over time developed these female characters to take nuanced conceptions of responsible agents working in a network of interdependent relations. In contrast, the boys created stories of persons who were individual agents often acting in antagonistic ways, and over time developed such characters to be more 'stable, autonomous, and self-conscious' (Richner and Nicolopoulou, 2001, p. 393). Richner & Nicolopoulou make the important point that both the character types constructed and the developmental pathways traveled were distinct for boys and girls, leading them to claim that such stories are important for the social construction of personhood.

This is not to imply that gender is something static that one brings to activities. Much of the peer gender socialization work follows up on the claim that enacting gender is a highly fluid and situated activity socially constructed in everyday routines. To this extent, gender is an emergent product of social interaction more than a property that individuals bring to communicative routines. Danby and Baker (2001) illustrate this emergent property and in particular the social organization involved in 'escalating terror' in their analysis of preschool boys' play in a nursery school. Drawing upon a number of conversational strategies (including how talk is chained, how turns are managed, and also how deictic pronouns are used in patterned ways to include and exclude membership), Danby and Baker highlight the numerous resources involved in the ongoing negotiation of masculinity.

Kyratzis' (2001) work on American middle-class preschoolers' same sex group play also highlights the fluid and contextual nature of gender construction, while at the same time pointing out that emotion talk is differently enacted by the young boys and girls she studied. She notes that the children made use of a range of lexical, grammatical, and prosodic features that reflexively construct emotion stances in ways that were not modeled by adults. For instance, boys used silence to enhance suspense, and distinct lexical and prosodic features to constitute a rough and assertive self, while the girls used such devices as pitch and hyperbole to give a sense of intimacy and solidarity. Kyratzis points out that such findings highlight the very active role children play in producing gendered models of being in the world (see also Corsaro & Rosier, 1992, for a similar point). Kyratzis, like Richner and Nicolopoulou (2001), suggests that these models transform themselves over time, and nuances in one aspect of gendered talk concurrently alter other aspects. For instance, Kyratzis suggests that as the preschool boys develop more refined gender-scheme knowledge, they seem to simultaneously downplay prior agreed upon notions, like the importance of marking scaredness. That gendered emotion talk was interactively achieved and not something brought statically to the interactions by individuals was highlighted by Kyratzis' analysis of the transformative role particular children have in the development of play activities, suggesting the degree to which gendered enactments are influenced greatly by situational factors.

In summary, work on gender socialization, while limited in the range of communities studied, nevertheless has introduced much new knowledge about the role of peers in the socialization process, as well as highlighting the protracted nature of socialization over time.

Explanations of Development

One of the basic goals of research on language socialization has been to show the interconnection between language development and the acquisition of culture. A central claim of such work is that in acquiring language the child is simultaneously acquiring a world view. In the review of Stern, Bühler, and Sapir we saw that although some general notions of this sort can be found in the literature, until recently a general framework has been lacking. Stern, for instance, was clear about the need to understand language in terms of general developmental principles and highlighted that children learning the same language, even those in the same family, might find alternative pathways to the same endpoint of language development. Nevertheless the view he adopted of language was highly referential, failing to realize language in terms of the rich functional variation discussed by Bühler. At the same time Bühler, who has been celebrated as one of the greatest pragmatic thinkers of our time (see Nehrlich & Clarke, 1996), had a more universal understanding of the relation between grammar and world view in his discussion of symbolic fields. His model, like much of current cognitive linguistic theorizing, presupposed a sort of universal vantage point, rather than recognizing the rich variation in ways members of different communities view the world. It is here that Sapir had much to offer. He has been noted to discuss the rich variation in world views, views which he suggests stem from differences in the language patterns of members of distinct communities. While he was clearly aware of the interpenetration of language and culture in socialization processes, he offered little in the way of specifics about the nature and direction of ways in which language habits play a significant role in socialization processes. More recently, theories of language socialization have contributed to our understanding of how young children come to orient themselves in relation to others within broader meaning systems. Nevertheless, I will argue that at present our understanding is primarily at the level of developing a theoretical framework, and much of the specifics of the process remain to be articulated.

At least three changes have taken place that simultaneously led to renewed interest in developing the framework called language socialization. First, as noted above, there was a resurgence of interest in broadening the view of language simply in terms of its representational function, to incorporate more dynamic conceptions of language, including viewing language as constitutive of reality. Second, there was increasing recognition by investigators of early language and communicative development that some of the universal assumptions held about caregiver–child interaction may be limited to particular western groups. Finally, around this time cultural psychologists were pointing out that constructs such as self, personhood and affect were cultural constructions related to symbolically mediated processes. Researchers such as Ochs and Schieffelin (1984) outlined the implications of the three developmental stories they found in their ethnographic observations of growing up in white middle-class American, Samoan, and Kaluli families. In the same article they laid the foundations for a modern day language socialization approach to development by arguing for the reciprocal relations between acquiring culture and language.

Although there has been a resurgence of interest in studying the interface between language, thought, culture and development since the 1980s, it is interesting that the bulk of the work to date within this framework has been non-developmental in a strict sense. That is, much of the groundwork done from a language socialization perspective was dedicated to shifting the gravity in problem setting, rather than problem solving. The main issue addressed in much of the literature written in the 1980s and into the 1990s involved showing the rich cultural variation in cultural practices concerning personhood, affect and the like. That is, the preliminary work made the point that caregivers' interactions with their children varied greatly from community to community. Such work also emphasized that young children were ready and able to adapt to any of the systems made available to them.

Over this period researchers began to produce a theoretical framework suggesting an active view of the child, though it is important to note that research often failed to produce evidence for this claim. The framework outlined a view suggesting that there was more involved in development than simply presenting children with socially organized conversational structures that provide immediate access to cultural patterns and social regularities. Such work emphasized the importance of children's active involvement in such verbally rich environments in order that socialization take place. In this sense, it becomes clear that at a theoretical level, the idea of the child is a quite active one. Events are not simply framed through language for the child to passively acquire ready made categories. The claim is made that children must 'come to identify these contexts and their internal organization' (Schieffelin & Ochs, 1986, p. 167). There have been several warnings in the literature not to adopt static views of development that assume all children within a culture receive similar linguistic input or work with linguistic input in a similar way (see Lieven, 1997, for review) or are said to be socialized in identical ways. Nevertheless the literature provides few specific illustrations about the relationship between categories provided in caregivers' discourse and the ways children come to be actively involved in reproducing culture (see Briggs, 1992; Corsaro & Miller, 1992; Wootton, 1997, for some important exceptions).

One of the reasons little research has examined the specifics of the developmental process is precisely that the framework provides a sophisticated view of how that process must be conceived. More specifically, language socialization theorists suggest there is a dynamic tension between ongoing negotiation of context by speaker and hearer through the use of contextualization cues and the background stock individuals bring with them based on their own unique interactional experiences. This view of development is well articulated in an overview by Cook-Gumperz:

> It is this interpretive process which guides children's acquisition of language within the conversational context, and which gives them the basis for the situated understanding of social processes. For it is by such means that interactional histories are developed on which children draw their background social knowledge. (1986, pp. 55–56)

To this extent, language and the interactional routines of one's culture do not determine as much as *play an invitational role* in development. The habitual use of particular linguistic symbols lends itself to tacitly constructed framings of experience. Clearly to find ways to account for the complexities of such an approach towards development is not an easy task. The majority of work reviewed above has clearly illustrated the range and variability found in cultural practices that children from different communities experience. Furthermore there is increasing knowledge about the ways children of different ages make use of language, but an elaboration of the connection between such variations and a framework for understanding the specifics of the developmental processes of children in these diverse communities has yet to be produced.

While the bulk of the language socialization work has yet to tackle the complexities of explaining development, in the last few years some burgeoning work has begun looking more specifically at developmental processes (see for instance the collection of articles in Budwig, 2001). For instance, Richner and Nicolopoulou (2001) have analyzed the development of conceptions of persons within a narrative framework. Their findings highlight that although already by age three gender specific styles could be found, with increasing age boys and girls developed such styles in unique ways. Their findings make the important point that not only does development push towards new interpretations of meaning, but also the trajectories of development may differ as well. For instance, in their analysis the boys' and girls' construction of personhood followed distinct paths because of the prior ways each gender had constructed such notions, thereby providing an extremely dynamic account of developmental processes.

While such work highlights the ways particular prior meanings play a role in the content of subsequent ones, my own longitudinal studies (Budwig, 2000a; 2000b) have suggested that there may be some complex yet organized ways interpretive processes develop over time, regardless of content area. Such work has shown that although children and adults do not always imbue forms with the same meaning, children nevertheless seem to be influenced by broader cultural themes. That is, while the specific form–function patterns may differ between caregiver and child, the children's patternings nevertheless appear to be influenced by overarching meaning systems created by their caregivers. Furthermore, such longitudinal work has highlighted that although children of different communities develop at one level in distinct ways, at another level of analysis, regularities in the nature of the patternings of all the children studied regardless of the community examined could be found. For instance, my work has shown that there is a preference for children of diverse communities to begin with rather general and diffuse categorizations of forms and functions and move towards form–function pairings that are more nuanced and hierarchically integrated. This view, introduced into the developmental literature by Werner (1957) under the heading of the orthogenetic process, has been summarized by Werner and Kaplan as follows:

> We assume that organisms are naturally directed towards a series of transformations – reflecting a tendency to move from a state of relative globality and undifferentiationedness towards states of increasing differentiation and hierarchical integration. (1963/1984, p. 7)

This principle was introduced into the study of children's language development by Slobin (1973) who suggested that old forms are transformed to meet new functions, and new forms are first utilized for old functions (see Budwig, 1995, for further discussion). Thus it appears there may well be variation at the level of content and meanings developed by children from different communities, while at the same time overarching similarities in the directionality of the developmental process.

A third recent insight that adds to our understanding of the construct of development within a language socialization context involves the longitudinal role of subtle variation of group membership on developments witnessed over time. Kyratzis' (2001) longitudinal examination of peer culture highlights the extent to which particular children's participation over time influenced other group members, reminding us of the need, pointed out by Stern long ago, to carefully examine not only culturally situated and internally driven aspects of development but also situationally produced factors that make this process so complex.

To summarize, most of the discussions of development within the language socialization area are primarily at the level of theorizing. Currently there is general consensus that any account of development will need to integrate an active view of the child. Nevertheless, at the present time there is scant research describing the specifics of such developmental processes. I shall now consider 'blind spots' in this field and make suggestions for future work.

Blind Spots and New Directions

A critical review of literature dealing with the relation between language, thought, culture and development has highlighted the immense progress as well as some remaining issues for future consideration. As pointed out by Shweder et al. (1997), the idea that language as a symbolic system plays a central mediating role in human development is not new. At various phases in the history of psychology, language was viewed as more centrally related to issues of development including an extremely rich phase around the turn of the last century. Nevertheless I have also argued that there has been significant development in the specificity about this process. Although much progress can be seen, both between the early and modern phases, as well as over the last two decades which have marked a real resurgence of interest in this theme, there remains much work to be done. I will turn now to two central issues in need of further discussion. First, I consider the issue of integrating in a systematic fashion some of the threads developed over the last two decades, and second, I will close by addressing the need for much work in the empirical study of the specifics of developmental processes.

Integrating Prior Work on Language Socialization

A review of the research conducted over the last two decades has highlighted some important developments in our understanding of the relationship between language, thought, culture, and development. One of the most significant developments over the last two decades has been the attempt to develop a framework that aims to better understand the role of semiotic mediation in human development. Such work has also made use of a number of different units of analysis in efforts to better understand the role language plays in socialization processes. Although one finds a large amount of cross-citation between authors working within the language socialization framework, and extensive pockets of collaboration, our knowledge could be strengthened if more consideration was given to the joint implications of such work. Two examples will be discussed that point the way towards both some blind spots and some areas for future research.

This review has pointed to the need for more cross-fertilization between different research areas. Most notably, we find that much of the research conducted on personhood and affect has been conducted in the home setting with children interacting with their caregivers between the age of first words and their third birthday. The strength of such work though lies in the ability to draw cultural comparisons since broadly similar work has been conducted in a variety of communities. At the same time, the work in the area of gender socialization has primarily taken place with children growing up in the English-speaking world (predominantly but not exclusively in middle-class America). These children have been studied in the preschool setting most notably when engaged in multiparty interactions with their peers. Thus we end up knowing very little about the role of peers in personhood and affect development, and simultaneously we know very little about the role of language in gender socialization outside the school setting, and in particular in non-western cultures.

A second related need is to consider the affordances of various units of analysis in the study of language socialization. As noted above, different studies, stemming from a generally similar overarching theoretical perspective, have made use of distinct methodological means of analysis. For instance we saw that in some studies of personhood, affect, and gender socialization researchers made use of narrative analysis, while in others researchers examined the social organization of conversation by examining turn taking, speech acts, etc. A third kind of unit used by many researchers has entailed adopting an indexical approach, thereby examining the habitual patterning of specific linguistic elements and the active role such units play in the negotiation of meaning. All these methods appear equally able to assess ways in which caregivers in different communities provide distinct input concerning personhood, affect, and gender socialization. At the same time, such methods enable us to draw conclusions about whether children are sensitive to such distinctions. Nevertheless, there are large theoretical differences among them when it comes to understanding processes of development. That is, although researchers using these various approaches (a narrative approach, a conversation analytic approach or an indexical approach) share some important theoretical assumptions about language socialization, at the same time they actually align with some subtle, but important, distinctions about the implications for conclusions drawn about development. For instance, a narrative approach is much more focused on children arriving at central cultural themes through a content analysis of narrative functioning. In contrast, an indexical approach suggests particular ways children can latch on to cultural meanings – using specific patternings of linguistic structure and functions as anchorings. Currently what approach is used has more to do with disciplinary training than interests in answering particular kinds of development questions. It would seem important in the future to consider selection of unit of analysis with more attention given to the kinds of claims such approaches allow concerning issues of development. It also would seem appealing to cluster the study of a given issue using multiple methods (see for instance Bamberg, in press, for an example pertaining to masculinity formation).

To work in these ways though is not without its own set of problems. First, more collaboration between researchers could lead to issues of divergent interpretations of data. Comparini (2000) has already identified instances in that two seemingly identical verbal routines were interpreted in different ways by researchers. In a review of prior work done on the organization and meaning of teasing routines, Comparini points out that different researchers have isolated similar forms of parental involvement which they conclude are aligned with similar speech act types (e.g. threats, challenges) but in a curious way are said to serve *different* socializing functions. For instance, Comparini (2000) noted that Eisenberg (1986) suggested that teasing routines contribute to inviting the child to participate in a community that values relational views of self and other, while she notes that Miller (1986) argues that such routines function to prepare the child for the tough realities of existing as a person outside the family unit, thereby contributing to the development of an assertive self. Thus, as soon as we begin broadening our analysis to include communities that use similar routines, we might begin to find the need to make our discussion of meaning making more complex. This would allow us to be able to account for how children interacting in these different communities come to understand similar routines in distinct ways.

In a related way, examining particular children in a variety of communicative settings will on the one hand lead us to deepen our understanding of developmental processes, but at the same time make more difficult attempts to generate general patterns of development. Here the issue will become one of recognizing the lack of apparent unity in one particular member's construction of a domain. Take for example the claim that American middle-class caregivers place a premium on harmonious individuated selves, while Miller's working-class American sample has been noted to use conflict and teasing routines to bring about a more assertive and at times confrontation self. What remains to be explained is how such middle-class children come to interact in the confrontational ways that Miller reports for the working-class caregiver–child dyad. Goodwin (2000) has highlighted exactly such a presentation of self between upper-middle-class girls in her ethnographic observations of middle-school girls' peer interactions. In summary, as we begin to branch out in our analysis of a given child to include that same child interacting in a range of communicative situations and with a variety of others, we will find that new problems emerge, namely those of explaining the various ways selves are enacted in everyday interactions. This will become especially true as the range of activities and partners becomes larger as development proceeds. Future research would do well to attend to these complexities by devising some large scale comparative longitudinal projects of individual children growing up in a variety of cultures using a similar variety of methodological units of analysis. While samples of convenience have worked well for the initial outline of a language socialization framework, the time is ripe for a team approach with a conscious attempt to reflexively pursue a common set of issues, targeting communities that pose potentially interesting comparative and developmental questions.

The Problem of Development

While such comparative work will clearly assist in a better understanding of development, it should be obvious that there is no simple solution for the developmental problem alluded to above. One of the chief limitations of the language socialization paradigm is a lack of understanding of how children actively contribute to the meaning making process, while at the same time orientating themselves in ways that are in synchrony with culturally sanctioned meaning systems. At present we are lacking dynamic ways to approach such a problem. Looking over the available literature, one finds most researchers approaching the tension between cultural invitation and child productivity in a similar fashion. Despite some overtures recognizing the dynamic nature of the socialization process, most researchers report data based on an assessment of individuals. That is, most studies of expert–novice interaction begin with a discussion of cultural patterns as illustrated by caregiver practices, and follow with a section on children's sensitivity to or unique use of similar patterns. Such analyses are limited because the dynamics of the interaction process often get lost.

The issue is not one unique to language socialization. Most cultural psychologists have been limited by existing tools of analysis. Note for instance Valsiner's description of the primary developmental issue as discussed by cultural psychologists:

> Human beings develop their psychological functions in the context of environments organized by their social others. The developing child internalizes many aspects of his or her social experiences and at the same time expresses these internalized experiences in socially shared interaction . . . The internalization and externalization process leads to the construction of a personal culture – a unique system of signs, values, habits, and preferences – that is guided, but not determined, by the collective culture of the society. The collective culture is not static but undergoes development of its own, which can be partially influenced by the personal cultures of individuals. Cultural transmission – the transfer of the collective culture from one generation to the next – is a bidirectional process in which every new generation reconstructs new solutions to the problems of organizing social life. (1989, pp. 70–71)

To date, attempts by developmental psychologists to find analytic tools with which to document this sort of theoretical perspective have been missing. It is important to note that the problem of accounting for development is not unique to language socialization; it is currently one of the central problems for anyone looking at development as a dynamic and bidirectional process. Having said this, it would seem that the language socialization framework, with its partial roots in the fields of linguistic anthropology and conversation analysis, is uniquely positioned to make progress in this arena specifically because linguistic anthropologists and conversation analysts have been struggling to account for the dynamics of social interaction and symbolic processes for quite a long time. Finally, I will suggest two directions that I believe hold promise for making progress on this complex issue: first, the need to bring cognition (back) into the picture in new ways; and second, the need to consider how analysis of co-occurrence patterns might provide some assistance.

By the late 1970s, there had occurred a shift away from viewing language exclusively in terms of its representational function towards one of viewing it in terms of its more social functioning. This ultimately led to the adoption of a functional account of language which in turn has contributed to the (re)development of theoretical frameworks that positioned language as a central mechanism of socialization. In so doing, an anti-cognitive view has developed. At this point, it might be wise to reconsider some views about thinking as originally discussed by Bühler and Sapir, both of whom had quite a lot to say about basic conceptual vantage points. Such discussions currently are at the forefront of cognitive linguistic work (see Budwig, 1998; Tomasello, 1998; 1999). The time is ripe to reconsider how current thinking about distributed cognition (see Hutchins, 1995; Lave,1988) with its emphasis on thinking about cognition located outside individual minds (see also Slobin, 1997, for a related discussion for language development) might successfully be linked with approaches to language socialization. One intriguing question is whether linking work in the area of distributed cognition with work in the area of language socialization might provide a means to better understand the specifics of developmental processes. Language symbols (whether at the broad level of narrative genre or at the local level of specific morphological forms) provide cognitive artifacts that could play a role in the dynamic process of meaning making in ways yet poorly understood (see Amin, 1998; 2001, for some initial attempts in this direction).

A second suggestion that might contribute to a better understanding of the dynamics of development would be to rethink the specifics of the meaning making process. Much work has concentrated locally on understanding individual meaning making patterns within and across communities (e.g. person reference). To date though, few researchers have attempted to link up such findings. More than a decade ago, Eli Ochs concluded her 1988 book by drawing a distinction between direct and indirect indexicality. She suggested that certain habitual patterns linking a specific form and current communicative function can come to be used indexically to create novel meaning patterns. This raises the possibility that broader vectors of indexicality link up in powerful ways such that regularities could cut across multiple levels of form–function pairings emphasizing certain dominant social and cultural categories. As researchers begin to look at given speakers in terms of a range of indexical patterns, and build up knowledge of recurring ways indexicality takes place, this might provide an entry also into the process by which novices come to produce meaning. The suggestion here is that speakers most likely are not only marking individual notions that are socially relevant to their communicative needs, but also marking some in multiple ways. This might provide partial solutions both to the speed with which children appear to be able to negotiate meaning, and also to an understanding of why different participants will come to imbue similar forms and speech events with distinct meanings.

General Conclusions

In this chapter I have summarized a view of language that has slowly been gaining attention in the field of developmental psychology, namely a view grounded in the assumption that language is multi-functional. Such a view challenges the dominant way of viewing language found in developmental theorizing – namely a view of language that focuses on its representational function. The addition of other functions highlights ways language can be viewed to play a dynamic role in development. Language not only provides a tool for representing reality but can be granted a role in its very production.

In reviewing work in the area of language socialization, I have suggested that such work to date has outlined a promising theoretical framework and introduced new interpretive methods that provide exciting resources to developmental psychologists. In the coming years, the field would do well to take stock of available findings and chart out a course of research based on the variety of findings currently available. One key issue that I have identified as needing attention concerns the development of sophisticated methods to carefully examine developmental processes. A particular suggestion for future research is reconsideration of how to link the notion of cognition back into the examination of language socialization. A second suggestion reviewed above concerns thinking about how the notion of vectors of indexicality might assist in our attempts to better understand processes of development. Exciting challenges lie ahead for those working on language socialization.

Acknowledgments

I wish to thank the editors for constructive feedback on an earlier version of this chapter. Jeff Della Rovere provided useful technical assistance. In addition, members of the SCLDLIPS research group at Clark University provided a lively forum for discussing issues related to this chapter. The chapter was completed while I was a visiting researcher at the Max-Planck-Institute for Evolutionary Anthropology, Leipzig, Germany. The support of the Institute is gratefully acknowledged.

References

Amin, T. (1998). A 'participatory role' for cognitive units. *Clark Working Papers on Developmental Psychology*, 1, 17–25.

Amin, T. (2001). Language-based construal in high school physics. Unpublished doctoral thesis, Department of Psychology, Clark University, Worcester, MA.

Andersen, E.S. (1986). The acquisition of register variation by Anglo-American children. In B.B. Schieffelin & E. Ochs (eds), *Language socialization across cultures* (pp. 153–164). Cambridge: Cambridge University Press.

Andersen, E.S. (1996). A cross-cultural study of children's register knowledge. In D.I. Slobin, J. Gerhardt, A. Kyratzis, & J. Guo (eds), *Social interaction, social context, and language* (pp. 125–142). Mahwah, NJ: Erlbaum.

Bamberg, M. (in press). Narrative and narrative methods. *Theory and Psychology*.

Bartsch, K., & Wellman, H. (1995). *Children's talk about the mind*. New York: Oxford University Press.

Bhatia, S. (1998). The role of language in the construction of the object and person world: An analysis of Indian caregivers' everyday communicative practices. Unpublished doctoral thesis, Department of Psychology, Clark University, Worcester, MA.

Bhatia, S. (2001). Social acts, class and the construction of personhood in Indian families. *Early Education and Development*, 12 , 433–454.

Briggs, J.L. (1992). Mazes of meaning: How a child and a culture create each other. In W. Corsaro & P.J. Miller (eds), *Interpretive approaches to children's socialization: New directions for child development* (pp. 25–50). San Francisco: Jossey-Bass.

Brock, A. (1994). Whatever happened to Karl Bühler? *Canadian Psychology/Psychologie Canadienne*, 35, 319–326.

Bruner, J. (1990). *Acts of meaning*. Cambridge, MA: Harvard University Press.

Budwig, N. (1995). *A developmental-functionalist approach to child language*. Mahwah, NJ: Erlbaum.

Budwig, N. (1998). Bühler's legacy: Full circle and ahead. *From Past to Future*, 1, 36–48.

Budwig, N. (1999). The contribution of language to the study of mind: A tool for researchers and children. *Human Development*, 42, 363–368.

Budwig, N. (2000a). Language, practice, and the construction of personhood. *Theory and Psychology*, 10, 769–786.

Budwig, N. (2000b). Language and the construction of self: Linking forms and functions across development. In N. Budwig, I. Uzgiris, & J. Wertsch (eds), *Communication: An arena of development* (pp. 195–214). Stamford, CT: Ablex.

Budwig, N. (ed.). (2001). *Language socialization and children's entry into schooling. Early Education and Development*, 12.

Budwig, N., & Chaudhary, N. (1996). Hindi-speaking caregivers' input: Towards an integration of typological and language socialization approaches. In A. Stringfellow, D. Cahana-Amitay, E. Hughes, & A. Zukowski (eds), *Proceedings of the 20th Annual Boston University Conference on Language Development* (Vol. 1, pp. 135–145). Somerville, MA: Cascadilla.

Budwig, N., Wertsch, J., & Uzgiris, I. (2000). Communication, meaning, and development. In N. Budwig, I. Uzgiris, & J. Wertsch. (eds), *Communication: An arena of development* (pp. 195–214). Stamford, CT: Ablex.

Budwig, N., & Wiley, A. (1995). What language reveals about two year olds' categories of person. In L. Sperry & P. Smiley (eds), *Conversational reflections of self and other knowledge* (pp. 21–32). San Francisco: Jossey-Bass.

Bühler, K. (1932). *Das Ganze der Sprachtheorie, ihr Aufbau und ihre Teile*. Kafka.

Bühler, K. (1990). *Theory of language: The representational function of language* (trans. D. Goodwin). Amsterdam: Benjamins. Original work published 1934.

Cairns, R. (1998). The making of developmental psychology. In W. Damon & R. Lerner (eds), *Handbook of child psychology, 5th edn: Vol. 1. Theoretical models of human development* (pp. 25–105). New York: Wiley.

Clancy, P.M. (1986). The acquisition of communicative style in Japanese. In B.B. Schieffelin & E. Ochs (eds), *Language socialization across cultures* (pp. 213–250). Cambridge: Cambridge University Press.

Comparini, L. (1999). The use of directives in conflict talk between Mexican preschoolers and their mothers. Paper presented at the International Association for the Study of Child Language, San Sebastian, Spain.

Comparini, L. (2000). Constructing self and other: A language socialization approach to Latina mother–child conflict talk. Unpublished doctoral thesis, Department of Psychology, Clark University, Worcester, MA.

Comparini, L., & Bhatia, S. (2000). Indexing self and other relationships through directives: The construction of class, social roles, and authority in Indian and Mexican-American caregiver–child interactions. In S.C. Howell, S. Fish, & T. Keith-Lucas (eds), *Proceedings of the 24th Annual Boston University Conference on Language Development* (pp. 208–219). Somerville, MA: Cascadilla.

Cook-Gumperz, J. (1986). Caught in the web of words: Some considerations on language socialization and language acquisition. In J. Cook-Gumperz, W. Corsaro, & J. Streeck (eds), *Children's worlds and children's language* (pp. 37–64). New York: Mouton de Gruyter.

Cook-Gumperz, J., Corsaro, W., & Streeck, J. (eds) (1986). *Children's worlds and children's language*. New York: Mouton de Gruyter.

Corsaro, W., & Miller, P.J. (eds) (1992). *Interpretive approaches to children's socialization: New directions for child development*. San Francisco: Jossey-Bass.

Corsaro, W., & Rosier, K. (1992). Documenting productive–reproductive processes in children's lives: Transition narratives of a black family living in poverty. In W. Corsaro & P.J. Miller (eds), *Interpretive approaches to children's socialization: New directions for child development* (pp. 67–91). San Francisco: Jossey-Bass.

Danby, S., & Baker, C.D. (2001). Escalating terror: Communicative strategies in a preschool classroom dispute. *Early Education and Development*, 12 (3), 343–358.

Deutsch, W., Wagner, A., Burchardt, R., Jahn, K., & Schultz, N. (1997). From Adam('s) and Eve('s) to mine and yours in German singletons and siblings. In E. Clark (ed.), *Proceedings of the Twenty-Eighth Annual Child Language Research Forum* (pp. 85–94). Stanford, CA: CSLI.

Dunn, J., Bretherton, I., & Munn, P. (1987). Conversations about feeling states between mothers and their young children. *Developmental Psychology*, 23, 132–139.

Duranti, A. (1997). *Linguistic anthropology*. Cambridge: Cambridge University Press.

Duranti, A., & Goodwin, C. (eds) (1992). *Rethinking context*. Cambridge: Cambridge University Press.

Eisenberg, A. (1986). Teasing: Verbal play in two Mexicano homes. In B. Schieffelin & E. Ochs (eds), *Language socialization across culture* (pp. 182–198). Cambridge: Cambridge University Press.

Eisenberg, A. (1992). Conflicts between mothers and their young children. *Merrill-Palmer Quarterly*, 38, 21–43.

Eisenberg, A. (1999). Emotion talk among Mexican-American and Anglo-American mothers and children from two social classes. *Merrill-Palmer Quarterly*, 45, 267–284.

Fivish, R. (1993). Emotional content of parent–child conversations about the past. In C. Nelson (ed.), *Memory and affect in development: The Minnesota Symposia on Child Psychology*. Hillsdale, NJ: Erlbaum.

Gaskins, S., Miller, P., & Corsaro, W. (1992). Theoretical and methodological perspectives in the interpretive study of children. In W. Corsaro & P.J. Miller (eds), *Interpretive approaches to children's socialization: New directions for child development* (pp. 5–23). San Francisco: Jossey-Bass.

Gleason, J., Ely, R., Perlmann, R., & Narasimhan, B. (1996). Patterns of prohibitions in parent–child discourse. In D. Slobin, J. Gerhardt, A. Kyratzis, & J. Guo (eds), *Social interaction, social context, and language: Essays in honor of Susan Ervin-Tripp*. Mahwah, NJ: Erlbaum.

Goffman, E. (1974). *Frame analysis: An essay on the organization of experience*. New York: Harper & Row.

Goldberg, A. (1996). *Constructions: A construction grammar approach to argument structure*. Chicago, IL: Chicago University Press.

Goodwin, M.H. (1990). *He-said-she-said: Talk as social organization among black children*. Bloomington, IN: Indiana University Press.

Goodwin, M.H. (2000). Constituting the moral order in girls' social organization: Language practices in the construction of social exclusion. Paper presented at the American Anthropological Association, San Francisco, November.

Gumperz, J. (1982). *Discourse strategies*. Cambridge: Cambridge University Press.

Hanks, W. (1996). Language form and communicative practices. In J. Gumperz & S. Levinson (eds), *Rethinking linguistic relativity* (pp. 232–270). Cambridge: Cambridge University Press.

Harkness, S., Raeff, C., & Super, C. (eds) (2000). *Variability in the social construction of the child*. San Francisco: Jossey-Bass.

Herder, J.G. (1966). *Essay: On the origin of language* (trans. A. Gode). New York: Frederick Ungar. Original work published 1772.

Hoff-Ginsberg, E. (1991). Mother–child conversation in different social classes and communicative settings. *Child Development*, 62, 782–796.

Humboldt, W. von (1988). *On language: The diversity of human language-structure and its influence on the mental development of mankind* (trans. P. Heath). Cambridge: Cambridge University Press. Original work published 1836.

Hutchins, E. (1995). *Cognition in the wild*. Cambridge, MA: MIT Press.

Jakobson, R. (1973). *Main trends in the science of language*. London: Allen & Unwin.

Kreppner, K. (1994). William L. Stern: A neglected founder of developmental psychology. In R.D. Parke, P.A. Ornstein, J.J. Rieser, & C. Zahn-Waxler (eds), *A century of developmental psychology* (pp. 311–331). Washington, DC: American Psychological Association.

Kyratzis, A. (2001). Emotion talk in preschool same-sex friendship groups: Fluidity over time and context. *Early Education and Development*, 12, 359–392.

Lakoff, G. (1987). *Women, fire, and dangerous things: What categories reveal about the mind*. Chicago, IL: University of Chicago Press.

Lamiell, J.T. (1996). William Stern: More than the I.Q. Guy. In G.A. Kimble, C.A. Boneau, & M. Wertheimer (eds), *Portraits of pioneers in psychology* (Vol. 2). Washington, DC: American Psychological Association.

Langacker, R. (1987). *Foundations of cognitive grammar* (Vol. 1). Stanford, CA: Stanford University Press.

Lave, J. (1988). *Cognition in practice*. New York: Cambridge University Press.

Lewis, M., & Brooks-Gunn, J. (1979). *Social cognition and the acquisition of self*. New York: Plenum.

Lieven, E. (1997). Variation in a crosslinguistic context. In D. Slobin (ed.), *The crosslinguistic study of language acquisition: Vol. 5. Expanding the contexts* (pp. 199–263). Mahwah, NJ: Erlbaum.

Lin, A. (1993). The child as conversational partner. Unpublished doctoral dissertation, Department of Psychology, Clark University, Worcester, MA.

Miller, P. (1986). Teasing as language socialization and verbal play in a white working-class community. In B.B. Schieffelin & E. Ochs (eds), *Language socialization across cultures* (pp. 199–212). Cambridge: Cambridge University Press.

Miller, P. (1996). Instantiating culture through discourse practices: Some personal reflections on socialization and how to study it. In R. Jessor & A. Colby (eds), *Ethnography and human development: Context and meaning in social inquiry* (pp. 183–204). Chicago, IL: University of Chicago Press.

Miller, P.J., & Hoogstra, L. (1992). Language as tool in the socialization and apprehension of cultural meanings. In T. Schwartz, G.M. White, & G.A. White (eds), *New directions in psychological anthropology* (pp. 83–101). New York: Cambridge University Press.

Miller, P.J., Mintz, J., Hoogstra, L., Fung, H., & Potts, R. (1992). The narrated self: Young children's construction of self in relation to others in conversational stories of personal experience. *Merrill-Palmer Quarterly*, 38, 45–68.

Miller, P.J., Potts, R., Fung, H., Hoogstra, L., & Mintz, J. (1990). Narrative practices and the social construction of self in childhood. *American Ethnologist*, 17, 292–311.

Miller, P.J., & Sperry, L.L. (1988). Early talk about the past: The origins of conversational stories of personal experience. *Journal of Child Language*, 15, 293–315.

Miller, P.J., Wiley, A., Fung, H., & Liang, C. (1997). Personal storytelling as a medium of socialization in Chinese and American families. *Child Development*, 68 (3), 557–568.

Moissinac, L., & Budwig, N. (2000). The development of desire terms in early child German. *Psychology of Language and Communication*, 4 (1), 5–25.

Nehrlich, B., & Clarke, D. (1996). *Language, action and context: The early history of pragmatics in Europe and America, 1780–1930*. Amsterdam: Benjamins.

Nelson, K. (1996). *Language in cognitive development: The emergence of the mediated mind*. New York: Cambridge University Press.

Nicolopoulou, A. (1997). World making and identity formation in children's narrative play-acting. In B.D. Cox & C. Lightfoot (eds), *Sociogenetic perspectives on internalization* (pp. 157–187). Mahwah, NJ: Erlbaum.

Nicolopoulou, A., Scales, B., & Weintraub, J. (1994). Gender differences and symbolic imagination in the stories of four-year-olds. In A.H. Dyson & C. Genishi (eds), *The need for story: Cultural diversity in classroom and community* (pp. 102–123). Urbana, IL: National Council of Teachers of English.

Ochs, E. (1986a). Introduction. In B. Schieffelin & E Ochs (eds), *Language socialization across culture* (pp. 1–13). Cambridge: Cambridge University Press.

Ochs, E. (1986b). From feelings to grammar: A Samoan case study. In B. Schieffelin & E. Ochs (eds), *Language socialization across culture* (pp. 251–272). Cambridge: Cambridge University Press.

Ochs, E. (1988). *Culture and language development*. Cambridge: Cambridge University Press.

Ochs, E. (1996). Linguistic resources for socializing humanity. In J. Gumperz & S. Levinson (eds), *Rethinking linguistic relativity* (pp. 407–437). Cambridge: Cambridge University Press.

Ochs, E., & Schieffelin, B. (1984). Language acquisition and socialization: Three developmental stories and their implications. In R. Shweder & R. LeVine (eds), *Culture theory: Essays on mind, self, and emotion* (pp. 276–320). New York: Cambridge University Press.

Palmer, G. (1996). *Toward a theory of cultural linguistics*. Austin, TX: University of Texas Press.

Platt, M. (1986). Social norms and lexical acquisitions: A study of deictic verbs in Samoan child language. In B.B. Schieffelin & E. Ochs (eds), *Language socialization across cultures* (pp. 127–152). Cambridge: Cambridge University Press.

Reddy, M. (1993). The conduit metaphor: A case of frame conflict in our language about language. In A. Ortony (ed.), *Metaphor and thought* (pp. 164–201). New York: Cambridge University Press.

Richner, E.S., & Nicolopoulou, A. (2001). The narrative construction of differing conceptions of the person in the development of young children's social understanding. *Early Education and Development*, 12, 393–432.

Sapir, E. (1970). *Culture, language, and personality: Selected essays edited by D. Mandelbaum*. Berkeley, CA: University of California Press. Original works published 1924, 1929, 1933.

Sapir, E. (1993). *The psychology of culture: A course of lectures* (ed. J.T. Irvine). Berlin: Mouton de Gruyter. Original work published 1934.

Schieffelin, B. (1986). Teasing and shaming in Kaluli children's interactions. In B. Schieffelin & E. Ochs (eds), *Language socialization across cultures* (pp. 165–181). Cambridge: Cambridge University Press.

Schieffelin, B. (1990). *The give and take of everyday life: Language socialization of Kaluli children*. Cambridge: Cambridge University Press.

Schieffelin, B., & Ochs, E. (eds) (1986). *Language socialization across cultures*. Cambridge: Cambridge University Press.

Shweder, R.A., Goodnow, J., Hatano, G., LeVine, R.A., Markus, H., & Miller, P. (1997). The cultural psychology of development: One mind, many mentalities. In W. Damon & R. Lerner (eds), *Handbook of child psychology, 5th edn: Vol. 1. Theoretical models of human development* (pp. 865–937). New York: Wiley.

Silverstein, M. (1976). Shifters, linguistic categories, and cultural descriptions. In K. Basso & H. Selby (eds), *Meaning in anthropology* (pp. 11–56). Albuquerque, NM: University of New Mexico Press.

Sinha, C. (in press). Cognitive linguistics, psychology, and cognitive science. In D. Geeraerts & H. Cuyckens (eds), *Handbook of cognitive linguistics*.

Slobin, D. (1973). Cognitive prerequisites for the development of grammar. In C.A. Ferguson & D. Slobin (eds), *Studies of child language development* (pp. 175–208). New York: Holt, Rinehart, & Winston.

Slobin, D. (1985). Crosslinguistic evidence for the language-making capacity. In D. Slobin (ed.), *The crosslinguistic study of language acquisition* (Vol. 2, pp. 1157–1256). Hillsdale, NJ: Erlbaum.

Slobin, D. (1997). The origins of grammaticizable notions: Beyond the individual mind. In D. Slobin (ed.), *The crosslinguistic study of language acquisition: Vol. 5. Expanding the contexts* (pp. 265–323). Mahwah, NJ: Erlbaum.

Stern, C., & Stern, W. (1928). *Die Kindersprache: Eine psychologische und sprachtheoretische untersuchung (The language of children: A psychological and linguistic-theoretical investigation)*. Darmstadt: Wissenschaftliche Buchgesellschaft. Original work published in 1907.

Stern, C., & Stern, W. (in progress). *The language of children* (ed. and trans. N. Budwig & M. Bamberg). Mahwah, NJ: Erlbaum.

Stern, W. (1906). *Person und Sache: System der philosophischen Weltanschauung*. Leipzig: Barth.

Stern, W. (1911). *Differentielle Psychologie*. Leipzig: Barth.

Stern, W. (1918). *Grundgedanken der personalistischen Philosophie*. Berlin: Reuther & Reichard.

Stern, W. (1938). *General psychology from a personalistic standpoint* (trans. H. Davies Spoerl). New York: Macmillan. Original work published in 1935.

Tardif, T., & Wan, C. (2001). Learning to say 'no' in Chinese. *Early Education and Development*, 12 (3), 303–323.

Taylor, C. (1985). *Human agency and language: Philosophical papers 1*. Cambridge: Cambridge University Press.

Tomasello, M. (ed.) (1998). *The new psychology of language*. Mahwah, NJ: Erlbaum.

Tomasello, M. (1999). *The cultural origins of human cognition*. Cambridge, MA: Harvard University Press.

Valsiner, J. (1989). *Human development and culture: The social nature of personality and its study*. Lexington, MA: Lexington Books.

Valsiner, J. (1998a). The development of the concept of development: Historical and epistemological perspectives. In W. Damon & R. Lerner (eds), *Handbook of child psychology, 5th edn: Vol. 1. Theoretical models of human development* (pp. 189–232). New York: Wiley.

Valsiner, J. (ed.) (1998b). The pleasure of thinking: A glimpse into Karl Bühler's life. *From Past to Future: Clark Papers on the History of Psychology*, 1 (1), 15–35.

Vinden, P. (2001). Who's in control? The language of requests, parenting style, maternal education, and children's understanding of mind. Poster presented at the Society for Research in Child Development, Minneapolis, MN, April.

Wellman, H. (1990). *The child's theory of mind*. Cambridge, MA: MIT Press.

Werner, H. (1957). The concept of development from a comparative and organismic point of view. In D.B. Harris (ed.), *The concept of development: An issue in the study of human behavior* (pp. 125–148). Minneapolis, MN: University of Minnesota Press.

Werner, H., & Kaplan, B. (1984). *Symbol formation*. Hillsdale, NJ: Erlbaum. Original work published 1963.

Wertsch, J.V. (1991). *Voices of the mind*. Cambridge, MA: Harvard University Press.

Wiley, A. (1997). Religious affiliation as a source of variation in childrearing values and parental regulation of young children. *Mind, Culture, and Activity*, 4, 86–107.

Wiley, A., Rose, A., Burger, L., & Miller, P. (1998). Constructing autonomous selves through narrative practices: A comparative study of working-class and middle-class families. *Child Development*, 69, 833–847.

Wootton, A.J. (1997). *Interaction and the development of mind*. Cambridge: Cambridge University Press.

11

Social Development in Cultural Context: Cooperative and Competitive Interaction Patterns in Peer Relations

ANGELA BRANCO

INTRODUCTION

> A socialized individual is one whose concern or responsibility for others commits him or her to something more than self-gratification. (McClintock, 1978, p. 176)

The relevance and role of sociogenetic processes in the co-construction of the multiple and intertwined aspects of human development have progressively attained increasing importance in contemporary psychology. In both the empirical and theoretical domains, researchers are seeking to analyze and better understand the mechanisms involved in the dynamic processes through which the ontogenesis of psychological functioning, at cognitive and socio-emotional levels, takes place within a continuous process of systemic organization. Kurt Kreppner (Chapter 9 in this volume) has analyzed the emergence of social relations and affective development in the first two years of life, while (Nancy Budwig (Chapter 10) has contributed to our understanding of the central significance of language for human development.

In this essay I will emphasize the usefulness of adopting a hermeneutic and systemic paradigm to make sense of the dynamic and multifaceted nature of human social developmental processes. I will also argue for the fundamental role played by culturally situated early peer interactions in the co-construction of differentiated patterns of social interactions and relationships commonly known as cooperation and competition.

I will begin with issues of definition of polysemic terms like cooperation and competition, particularly drawing on well-known traditions from social psychology (e.g. Deutsch, 1949; 1982) and anthropology (e.g. Mead, 1937; Triandis, 1991; 1995). After situating the general topic of social interdependence, I will point out why early peer interactions have progressively deserved special attention by developmental scientists, as and why they play a key part in understanding important dimensions of child development (e.g. Bornstein & Bruner, 1989; Hartup, 1983; 1992; 1993; Hinde, 1976; 1996; Rubin & Ross, 1982; Stambak & Sinclair, 1993).

At both theoretical and empirical levels, various projects have been carried out to examine in detail the role of peer social interactions in the co-constructive processes of different aspects of human development. The definition of human development as a situated and constructive dynamic process of continuous change will be the cornerstone of the analysis, allowing for a theoretical contextualization of the themes under investigation. Numerous aspects of child development such as play (e.g. Bloch & Pellegrini, 1989; Bornstein & Bruner, 1989; Camaioni, 1980; Cohen, 1987; Vygotsky, 1978), imitation (e.g. Eckerman & Peterman, 2001; Eckerman & Stein, 1982; Eckerman, Davis, & Didow, 1989), conflict (e.g. Asher & Coie, 1990; Shantz, 1987; Shantz & Hartup, 1992; Valsiner & Cairns, 1992), collaboration in problem solving situations (e.g. Azmitia, 1988; Doise & Palmonari, 1984; Ellis & Gauvain, 1992; Forman, 1992; Le Mare & Rubin, 1987; Piaget, 1961; Tudge & Rogoff,

1989), communication (e.g. Brockmeier, 1996a; Eckerman, 1992; Eckerman & Peterman, 2001; Erickson, 1987; 1991; Wallat & Green, 1979), and children's cooperation and competition in different contexts (e.g. Branco, 1998; 2001; Hartup, 1996; Johnson & Johnson, 1989, Slavin, 1991; Smith, 1996), will be considered in the assessment of children's social development, which encompasses and integrates socio-affective and cognitive processes along the co-constructive processes of personality formation.

A selection of studies will be examined in order to evaluate their specific contribution to knowledge construction concerning human developmental processes, as I highlight some of the epistemological premises at the foundation of their theoretical and methodological orientations. The present chapter will address the implications of the adoption of traditional paradigms, and the need for the construction of new epistemological bases for developing projects aiming at contributing to the elaboration of relevant knowledge to both theory and practice.

The emergence in peer interactions of patterns of cooperation, competition, and related psychological constructs will be discussed, with an emphasis on issues like individualism and prosocial/antisocial interactions (e.g. Dumont, 1985; Eisenberg & Mussen, 1989; Hoffman, 1989; Shantz, 1987; Staub, 1991). The evolutionary perspective (e.g. Krebs, 1996; LaFrenière & MacDonald, 1996; Wilson, 1975), as well as the emergence, developmental functionality and systemic meaningfulness (e.g. Ford & Lerner, 1992) of cooperative and competitive patterns, will be analyzed from an interpretive and cultural perspective (e.g. Bruner, 1990; Cole, 1992; Gaskins, Miller, & Corsaro, 1992; Parker & Scott, 1992). The notions of individual agency and the concept of 'cultural canalization' processes of convergent and divergent patterns of interactions will be stressed as they assume a central explanatory role in relation to the quality and dynamics of human interdependence patterns (Branco & Valsiner, 1992; 1997; Valsiner, 1989; 1994; 1997; 1998). Last, but not least, I will conclude by reifying the necessity of a paradigm shift for the explanation of the development of complex systems within the framework of a hermeneutic approach.

The interplay between the major impact of cultural social suggestions and the active, constructive participation of each individual child in the co-construction of his/her own development constitutes, therefore, the epistemological grounds on which the critical appraisals of past and recent studies will take place. Suggestions for future research, and some practical consequences of scientific findings, will also deserve special consideration.

Cooperation and Competition: Conceptual and Theoretical Trends

The Analysis of Human Interdependence

One of the most serious problems faced by researchers in the social sciences is the widespread utilization of terms drawn from current or common-sense language. Such terms are selected (or simply used) to represent specific categories relevant to describe and analyze phenomena. However, precisely because they are semiotically open linguistic constructs, they pose enormous difficulty when a specific meaning has to be assigned to them to provide the clarity of definition needed for consistent theoretical elaborations. Cooperation and competition are prime examples of categories charged with such polysemic quality. Hence, the investigation of social interdependence phenomena of cooperation and competition demands a significant appraisal of the conceptualization issues implied by the utilization of the terminology.

Cooperation and competition represent the most basic qualities of human interactive coordinations, expressed and complexly organized at multiple levels. This multiplicity ranges from the structuring of sociocultural contexts and activities, through a broad range of dynamic characteristics of human relationships, to the realms of intra-individual levels, encompassing the continuous constitution of personal motivational systems.

The search for an acceptable definition takes us first to the dictionary. There, under *cooperative* we find: 'to act or work together with another or others for a common purpose' (*Webster New World Dictionary*, third college edition, 1991, p. 306). *Competition* is described as a 'striving for the same object, position, prize etc., usually in accordance with certain fixed rules' (p. 284). These general definitions, nonetheless, are extremely simplistic. On one hand, they cover an immense variety of situations or events, and on the other, they exclude the complexities of multi-dimensional interactions between the above-mentioned pluralities of human interdependence.

Traditionally, cooperation and competition are pictured as antithetical concepts, where cooperation refers to the achievement of a common goal leading to mutual benefits or profits, while competition is viewed as the struggle to achieve a desired goal that, once achieved, necessarily entails the failure of others. Hence, cooperation suggests the existence of shared efforts and mutual supporting, whereas competition implies different sorts of rivalry, where knocking the other down brings a better chance to succeed in accomplishing one's goal.

In most ordinary situations, however, the intertwined character of complex, or even contradictory, motivations at play demands a detailed analysis of the way different goal orientations of the participants interact with the structure or the rules underlying each specific context (Valsiner, Branco, & Dantas, 1997). Deutsch (1949), Harcourt (1992), Triandis (1991) and many others acknowledge the occurrence of such mixed structures, but only a few researchers have seriously considered the complex arrangements involved in most situations (Johnson & Johnson, 1989).

For example, when we watch a soccer match and try to make sense of the dynamics of social interactions and relationships connecting the players in the field, we may find collective (cooperative) efforts by one team to beat the opposite team (competition), but we can also find other sorts of competitiveness among one team's players. Some players may try to outshine their peers (competition) in order to gain a reputation that will enhance their market value. In many cases that may lead to individual initiatives that jeopardize team performance, but some solo efforts are allowed because a lucky strike might win the game. If we take a closer look at the network of affiliative and antagonistic relationships between the players, we realize how subjective experiences during the match might even have a far-reaching impact on each participant's social motivations and personal development.

The ample scope of possible meaning constructions under the labels of cooperation and competition explain why researchers cannot reach a consensus in conceptualizing the phenomena, especially when we know they approach the subject from very different epistemological and theoretical frameworks (Rey, 1997). Feger (1991) stresses his concern with the conceptual divergence among scientists dedicated to investigate cooperation and competition. Definitions of cooperation range from individual self-sacrifice (Boyd & Richerson, 1991) – which is closer to the notion of 'altruism' (Eisenberg & Mussen, 1989) – to the achievement of shared goals within positively structured interdependence contexts (Slavin, 1991). The obvious conclusion is the urgent need to make explicit the theoretical framework within which concepts are being defined and utilized, and consequently, the grounds on which methodological strategies are derived to investigate particular aspects of social interdependence phenomena.

The theoretical tradition in studying cooperation and competition, in the domain of social psychology, can be found in the work of Morton Deutsch. In his 1949 paper, Deutsch refers to cooperation when there are 'promotively interdependent goals' between the individuals, and to competition when 'contriently interdependent goals' are found. Cooperative and competitive social interdependence rules can be objectively structured within the context itself, by implicit or explicit rules establishing the way individuals' behaviors should relate to each other. These rules or 'social participation structures' (Erikson, 1984) define an 'objective' dimension (Deutsch, 1949) that can be revealed by a structural analysis of each activity context. But Deutsch also referred to another dimension that he named 'subjective', which probably refers to intrapersonal experiences and representations. From our perspective, this dimension, together with the dimension of intersubjectivity, that is, the interpersonal interpretive ground that allows for a kind of mutual understanding, plays a very important role in the constitution of individual motivational systems.

Those two levels – 'structural' and 'subjective/intersubjective' – are frequently interrelated, as many studies carried out since the 1970s and 1980s will demonstrate (see Johnson & Johnson, 1989, and Slavin, 1991, for a meta-analysis of relevant research). The structure of the activity usually induces corresponding goals at the psychological level, that is, cooperatively organized contexts tend to promote cooperative goal orientations and so on (Branco & Valsiner, 1993; Johnson & Johnson, 1989). Nonetheless, although the underlying contextual structure tends to 'canalize' the pathways through which personal goal orientations are constructed, individuals may actively introduce particular goal orientations resulting from historical, dynamic processes of co-construction of personal values, as well as from a particular sense of 'self' (or 'selves': Fogel, 1993). The interplay between 'cultural canalization' processes (Valsiner, 1997) and individuals' agency will be further analyzed later in this chapter.

In most of the research and theory, cooperation and competition follow a common-sense understanding, and are seen as opposites. In some circumstances they can even be observed within the same context (see Mead, 1937), but according to many theorists they still maintain an antithetical relationship with one another, despite the warnings by other authors that stress their interrelated quality (e.g. Branco, 1998; Kruger, 1993). From a developmental systemic approach, however, the 'exclusive partitioning' of classical logic in the definition of psychological constructs has been criticized by theorists like Valsiner and Cairns (1992), as they argue for a conceptual redefinition of the term 'conflict'. Given the complexity of psychological phenomena, any simplification of the processes involved (even when those are proposed for well-intended analytical purposes) inevitably reduces the study of the intricacies of human meaningful, and multidetermined, actions into a fruitless and ineffectual investigation built on explanatory models composed of a set of nonsensical dichotomies. From a systemic perspective, the only productive way to analyze multifaceted phenomena is to consider the 'inclusive separation' of the partitioned parts, which enables the researcher to examine the dialectical tensions between the whole and its components. The idea is to preserve the systemic organization of the whole (in our case, the systemic organization of social interdependence) while recognizing the qualities and characteristics of the differentiated, or even apparently contradictory, parts.

Social Interdependence in Different Cultures

Margaret Mead's book *Cooperation and competition among primitive peoples* (1937) is a basic reference concerning the occurrence of distinct social interdependence patterns within the contexts of various cultures. In her book, she brings together ethnographic studies developed in 13 cultures, presenting a notable effort to organize all data along the faces of a triangle representing the general categories of cooperation, competition and individualism. Mead is quite careful in her analysis, and alerts the readers about the dangers of generalizations. She acknowledges the complexities involved in the existence of multiple factors that are active at all levels in each society (political, economic, sociocultural and psychological) but, despite the awareness she herself prescribes, we find in her text a consistent tendency to overgeneralize the information collected in those cultures.

As she locates each culture along the lines of cooperation, competition and individualism, each of which touches the others (the above-mentioned triangle), the Bathonga are considered the most cooperative, the Kwakiutl the most competitive, and the Eskimo, together with the Ojibwa, the most individualistic. The criteria for doing this are manifold, but Mead stresses the centrality of the way goods are distributed (and not produced), and the principal ends (or objectives) found in the directions taken by group activities. An important finding of her analysis is the absence of any significant relationship between social interdependence patterns and relevant factors such as economic characteristics (food gathering, hunting, agricultural or pastoral systems), geographical and cultural areas, technological abilities, or even the presence or absence of scarcity of food or any other valuable goods.

Mead exemplifies this point as follows:

> In other fields of life besides that of obtaining a wife, there is similar lack of correlation between competition for goods and actual supply. The Ifugao base their competition upon an actual scarcity of land, the Kwakiutl in the midst of plenty build their equally fierce competition on an artificially constructed scarcity of titles and prerogatives. Here the artificial limitation of a desired good is just as powerful an element in the competitive emphases of the culture as is the actual limitation of natural resources. (1937, p. 466)

This is an interesting observation, because it strengthens the importance of the historical co-construction of meanings, which represents, from our perspective, the cornerstone of the development of psychological processes and social patterns of interaction within culturally structured contexts. The role of semiotic redefinitions becomes clear when Mead refers to Fortune (1932):

> The Dobuans, not discussed in this study, furnish a useful contrast. They create situations in which the objectively unlimited supply is redefined as being fixed and limited in quantity. No amount of labor can therefore increase the next year's yam crop, and no man can excel another in the number of his yams without being accused of having stolen (magically) his extra yams from someone else's garden. (1937, p. 466)

The diversity of structural organization of the group (almost none in the Eskimo case, for instance) and the multiplicity of motives and values interrelated in a network of meanings in each group seem to serve different purposes that, in the end, make the studied cultures more or less closer to each of the three categories proposed by Mead. Among interesting mechanisms to promote cooperation, for example, Mead alludes to: the Dakota's way of treating pride and self-enhancement as shameful; to Zuni's sanctions against competition, aggression, pride and assertiveness; and, also, to Samoa's sanctions against noncooperativeness among group members. On the other hand, Mead suggests that competitiveness is more likely in cultures that promote, in one way or another, individuals' initiatives and prestige-seeking characteristics (like the Kwakiutl, Manu and Ifugao).

Unfortunately, a substantial part of Mead's interpretive statement about the studies analysed in her book also relies on categories such as 'ego development' and 'sense of security' that ultimately provide the reader with flagrant overgeneralizations based on weakly defined constructs. Her contribution, though, is worthy of consideration, particularly because it brings to light the variety and multiplicity of cultural structures and values, and their complex role in the construction of plural arrangements concerning social interdependence within human societies.

From a holistic and anthropological perspective, Graves and Graves (1985) argue for the significance of cultural-historical changes introduced by modernization in non-Western societies that used to live at the level of subsistence agricultural economies. They carried out a very interesting study in the Cook Islands investigating the impact of technological novelties on the lives of people who traditionally shared their fish surplus with each other. The authors affirm: 'Under the traditional social-economic system it had been adaptive to work together cooperatively to share resources for common survival' (1985, p. 403). People shared the catch among kin and neighbors, and the appearance of gasoline outboard motors made this sharing even more significant, because then it was usual to catch lots of fish. After electricity, though, surplus fish became stored into freezers, and 'Bonds of reciprocity and mutual dependence break down; people can now afford to fight with their extended family and neighbours; social skills diminish through disuse' (1985, p. 404).

Graves and Graves continue:

> Through many seemingly unrelated avenues, the transition from a traditional interdependent community to an

individualistic and highly competitive modern system gradually occurs, just as it has over the past 300 years in Western nations (cf. Merchant, 1980; Stone, 1975). (1985, p. 404)

The authors analyze the school environment, and conclude that both students and teachers tend to favor competitive strategies when asked to play a structured game developed to measure individuals' preferences for cooperative or competitive tactics to win. They compare New Zealand urban children to children living in the traditional villages of Aitutaki, and again find higher scores for urban children. Graves and Graves stress the developmental impact school exerts over the students: sixth and seventh graders, when compared to younger peers, obtained the highest evaluations on rivalry and competitiveness. The powerful effects of formal schooling, and what we now call 'globalization', are emphasized in the production of such transformations:

> Those raised in modern, nuclear households with formally educated, wage-earning parents were more egocentric and individualistic (as we in the West have come to expect to be typical of preschoolers) than those who were raised in traditional families with extended kin and who lived on the side of the island where most people still engage in subsistence agriculture and fishing. (1985, p. 404)

Whiting and Whiting (1975; Whiting & Edwards, 1988) carried out an extensive ethnographic study in six different cultures, where they integrated data from various methodological approaches such as direct observations, interviews, etc. They also deduced from the analysis that rural and traditional sociocultural groups are much more cooperative than urban and modern societies. They emphasized the role played by extended families (as opposed to nuclear families) and the active cooperative participation of children in adult activities. Participation in such contexts is considered to promote the development and maintenance of cooperative patterns of social interactions.

One topic that has recently attracted a lot of attention is the possibility of classifying different cultures into the supposedly opposite categories of collectivism and individualism (e.g. Jurberg, 2000; Triandis, 1991; 1995). Triandis (1995) provides plentiful information concerning the characteristics and correlated attributes of cultures that, according to the author, apply in different degrees (quantitatively expressed in terms of percentage) to one of the two categories (individualism or collectivism). Triandis presents the historical background of the scientific utilization of the constructs to describe the various cultures, and refers to philosophical, anthropological and psychological dimensions of social interdependence patterns characterizing each culture. He shows the intrinsic links existing between aspects of a 'subjective culture' (like beliefs, norms and values) and other dimensions of psychological phenomena such as self-definition, perception, cognition and motivation.

Nevertheless, despite his reference to the existence of a polysemic quality in the terms used, which can even jeopardize the usefulness of the constructs, Triandis does not take this problem into consideration as he proceeds with his analysis (Branco, 1996). He ends up treating culture as a relatively fixed, structural category prone to be described through traditional test assessments of psychological attributes, with the utilization of standardized instruments that definitely cannot account for the complexity of the phenomena. The great heterogeneity and the transformational nature of human social groups, allied with systemic patterns of mutual influences, give rise to original, unique versions of cultural constructions within each social context, rendering Triandis' classification efforts basically impossible. The elaboration of a cultural approach to social development thus requires a lot more epistemological, conceptual and theoretical redefinition and scientific work, as I shall argue.

Evolutionary Approach to the Emergence of Cooperation and Competition

The analysis of the contributions of a phylogenetic perspective to cooperation and competition necessarily starts by mentioning the work of E.O. Wilson. Wilson (1975) presents a powerful case concerning the occurrence of altruistic behavior in numerous species, from termites to birds and to primates. The evidence and arguments analyzed in his book, and further developed by many researchers (e.g. Dawkins, 1976), demonstrate the existence of genetic predispositions that may facilitate either altruism/cooperation or aggression/competition between species members, depending on the particular circumstances. The main point, cleverly defended by many sociobiologists, is that the actual competition always occurs at the gene level, while at the individual level both tendencies can be activated in specific contexts (Smith, 1996).

Based on such ideas and scientific analysis, evolutionary theory has found its way into the literature. A couple of examples of its contribution to the study of cooperation and competition among peers will now be considered. LaFrenière and MacDonald (1996) argue for the heuristic value of evolutionary theory in conceptualizing basic forms of peer interactions. The authors emphasize the existence of evolutionary mechanisms that favor both cooperation and competition. The crucial aspect that determines, from their perspective, which strategies will actually be used by peers is the adaptive value of the social behaviors in the specific context within which their interactions take place.

From an evolutionary perspective, cooperation developed through kin relations, in which context critical affective and cognitive dimensions of reciprocity were particularly selected. In parallel, reciprocity started to spread among group members in those species where individuals could be recognized by each other, and where there was a significant possibility of future encounters between them. The formation of alliances and mutual help expanded altruistic strategies beyond the limits of kin and similarity, even though, according to LaFrenière, 'friendship choice is rooted in behavioral compatibility and perceived psychological and physical similarity' (1996, p. 42). Reciprocity is, therefore, constructed via mutual confidence based on repeated encounters that limit the possibilities of deception between group members.

LaFrenière emphasizes the quality of attachment to later social development:

> Most developmentalists agree that the infant's relationships with the primary attachment figure(s) lay a foundation for subsequent relations because the attitudes, expectations and interpersonal skills that the child acquires are carried forward and reintegrated into emerging developmental contexts . . . [the child may] internalize this basic pattern of relationships and generalize and maintain it outside the circle of kin *on the condition of reciprocity*. (1996, pp. 43, 45, author's emphasis)

Comparing the behavior of pairs of boys (friends versus familiar versus troublesome kids), through teachers' and experts' ratings in a structured competitive situation, the author finds the positive value of affective strategies (particularly observed among friends) in promoting and maintaining cooperation in the dyads.

The crucial adaptive merit of cooperation in the development of human species is also underlined by Krebs, who asserts, 'helping others gain access to the resource is a means to the ultimate end of gaining access to the resource oneself' (1996, p. 76). He also claims that moral beliefs have evolved out of the need to consolidate reciprocity, by the prevention of cheating and as a way to control the greed of others. Edwards, based on the principle of genes' expansion, stresses how cooperation and competition can actually be the two sides of the same coin of 'self-interest' (1991, p. 81)

In the next section, the way young children begin to coordinate their actions with each other within ontogenesis will be examined. One of my points in this chapter is to propose the creative integration of different theories of development – those focusing upon phylogenetic, ontogenetic, and microgenetic (the here-and-now) *dimensions of time* – into a broader systemic theoretical framework.

Peer Interactions, Relationships, and Human Development

Human Development as a Dynamic Process

Conceptualizing human development as a dynamic process has recently become a relatively widespread enterprise (e.g. Baltes, 1987; Bronfenbrenner, 1989; 1993; Cole, 1992; Fisher & Bidell, 1998; Fogel, 1993; Ford & Lerner, 1992; Valsiner, 1997; 1998; 2000). Fortunately, at the end of the twentieth century we witnessed a productive re-examination of the most brilliant ideas of authors like James Baldwin, William James and Lev Vygotsky concerning human development, in an effort to integrate them with new findings and theoretical advances in the field of natural sciences, such as physics and biology. Such an integration leads to the elaboration of sophisticated models for the development of complex living systems (e.g. Ford & Lerner, 1992), inspired by the breakthrough in scientific thinking provided by theorists like Heisenberg, von Bertallanfy, and Prigogine, among others.

Contextualizing the historical trends of psychology over the twentieth century partially explains why we moved away, for such a long time, from a more dynamic conceptualization of human development (as proposed, for example, by Baldwin, 1906). The appeal of the prestigious hard physical sciences, with their rigorous principles of scientific investigation (which almost always included some sort of quantification of 'data'), drove psychological thinking towards the respected norms and principles of 'objective' and analytical investigation based on a positivist epistemological framework (Rey, 1997). This positivist tendency is easily recognized in most of the studies on child development that were carried out through decades of investigation, some of which are mentioned in this present account.

Notwithstanding, the nature of human developmental phenomena is extremely complex, as it is tied to the irreversibility of time (e.g. Prigogine, 1996), to the historically structured sociocultural contexts where it takes place (e.g. Bruner, 1990; Shweder, 1991; Vygotsky, 1978; 1987; Wertsch, 1997), and to the systemic quality of the complex network of interdependences among the multiple factors that contribute to its occurrence (e.g. Bronfenbrenner, 1989; 1993; Fisher & Bidell, 1998; Ford & Lerner, 1992; Morin, 1996).

The definition of human development proposed by Ford and Lerner comprises most of the basic principles necessary to envision development as a dynamic process:

> Individual human development involves incremental and transformational processes that, through a flow of interactions among current characteristics of the person and his or her current contexts, produce a succession of

> relatively enduring changes that elaborate or increase the diversity of the person's structural and functional characteristics and the patterns of their environmental interactions while maintaining coherent organization and structural-functional unity of the person as a whole. (1992, p. 49)

Human development must, therefore, be seen as a complex and dynamic coordination of change processes that occur along the continuous interactions between the individuals and the sociocultural contexts within which they actively experience and co-construct their personal characteristics and identities. This is the standpoint from which I examine some of the traditions in the investigation of peer social interaction development and the emergence of cooperative, competitive and individualistic orientations, and from which I will propose new trends for future research.

The Study of Peer Relations

Developmental psychology had a long historical tradition of studying adult–child (particularly mother–child) relationships, considered by most influential theorists of the time as the cornerstone for all development. For example, Cole (1992) elaborates a critical analysis of the numerous studies on mother–child attachment and its presumed overwhelming impact on human development. More recently, however, research on peer interactions has emerged as an important topic for investigation. Almost forgotten between the 1940s and the 1960s, the observation of child–child interactions seemed to be the ideal approach to understand the emergence of social patterns of behavior such as aggression (see Blurton-Jones, 1972; Patterson, 1990; Shantz, 1987; Shantz & Hartup, 1992) and prosocial modes of interaction (e.g. Eisenberg & Mussen, 1989; Radke-Yarrow & Zahan-Waxler, 1991). The study of peer interactions also proved to be a context for the study of cognitive development, which has encouraged researchers to investigate in experimental situations the relationships between peer collaboration and cognitive development. The renewed interest in studying peer interactions (first expressed during the 1930s; see Hartup, 1983, for a review) was based on the growing concern with socialization and its relevance for the future of our species, as well as on the recognition, plus empirical evidence, that peer interactions exert a powerful effect over different dimensions of cognitive development (e.g. Doise & Palmonari, 1984; Hartup, 1985; Perret-Clairmont, 1981; Piaget, 1961; Rogoff, 1990; Tudge & Rogoff, 1989).

Traditional lines of research on peer interactions can generally be divided into three groups. One group has been oriented towards explaining the contingencies that facilitate the manifestation of diverse social forms of behavior, particularly agonistic and affiliative interaction patterns within nursery and preschool settings (e.g. Montagner, 1978; Rubin, 1991; see Hartup, 1983, for a review). The second group, more developmentally oriented, encompasses two different tendencies. One is devoted to analyze children's interactions from simple social directed behaviors to highly complex and sophisticated interactive patterns (e.g. Brenner & Mueller, 1982; Brownwell & Carriger, 1990; Eckerman & Peterman, 2001; Farver, 1992); the other group consists of experimentally oriented projects searching for statistically significant relations that would indicate the superiority of joint work over individual efforts in problem solving situations (e.g. Kruger, 1993; Tudge & Rogoff, 1989; Verba, 1994). The third group examines, from an interpretive approach, children's growing abilities concerning their active participation in processes of co-construction of meanings (e.g. Brockmeier, 1996b; Corsaro & Schwarz, 1991; Corsaro & Molinari, 1990; Stambak & Sinclair, 1993).

Mostly, the studies have been very effective in illuminating certain aspects of child development. They show how specific antecedents, consequents and characteristics of the context are particularly linked to different behavior patterns, revealing developmental pathways to a growing coordination of social abilities, and demonstrating the value of joint work for improved performance in cognitive tasks (Verba, 1995) and for promoting social development (Johnson & Johnson, 1989). The studies, in general, provided data for a better understanding of the occurrence of patterns of social relationships that certainly have short- and long-term relevance for both parents and teachers. Many projects stemmed from a reconsideration of Piaget's (1965) ideas about the importance of children's cooperation and socio-cognitive conflicts (Doise & Palmonari, 1984) for the achievement of decentration and more advanced reasoning. Moreover, the impact of Vygotsky's (1978, 1987) theory about the axiomatic role played by social interactions in the development of higher mental processes has also proved to be a powerful influence over research on peer interactions.

Most projects carried out in the 1970s and 1980s were definitely more concerned with establishing a taxonomy of social behaviors and patterns of interactions, as well as finding significant relationships between environmental variables and social behavior categories. An excellent example of a systematic investigation of the relationship between contextual characteristics and patterns of peer interaction was the work of Smith and Connolly (1980). Over a 3-year period, they investigated the relations between many variables (such as physical space, number of children in the group, degree of adult intervention and structure of activities – free play versus structured context), and the amount and quality of peer interactions among young boys and girls. Twenty-two children, aged between 32 and 50 months, divided into two groups, participated in the study. The results indicated numerous interesting trends, like how free play, compared to structured activities, favoured various forms of peer interaction, among which were affiliative exchanges. Other illuminating findings refer to how smaller groups, less play equipment and bigger toys tended to facilitate peer contacts, while constraining (reducing) space and structured activities (that also reduced the amount of pretend play) promoted higher levels of aggression among children.

Many other creative studies were designed to examine aggressive (see Shantz, 1987, for a review) and prosocial behaviors (see Eisenberg & Mussen, 1989; Radke-Yarrow & Zahan-Waxler, 1991). Concerning aggression, for example, the distinction between aggressive behaviors and rough and tumble play was made possible by careful observations carried out from an ethological perspective (Blurton-Jones, 1972). As for prosocial behaviors, many studies aimed at finding the main factors related to their acquisition and development (Bar-Tal, 1976; Branco & Mettel 1995; Staub, 1991).

Eisenberg et al. (1981), for instance, examined 33 children aged between 4 and 5 years old in two different classrooms. They videotaped peer interactions during free play for 6 hours and 45 minutes, over a 9 week period, and demonstrated how so-called prosocial behavior can have its roots in completely different motivations. They identified children who exhibited a high level of either spontaneous or compliant prosocial behaviors, showing how heterogeneous were the patterns of antecedents and consequents of such behaviors, and how distinct were the personal characteristics of each group of children. Those exhibiting spontaneous prosocial behaviors were popular, independent kids that responded with positive feedback to peers' prosocial initiatives. Compliant children, however, were usually of low status, did not interact as much with their peers, and appeared to show compliance as a strategy to avoid conflict with others. For all children, most prosocial acts (about 70%) did not receive positive feedback, and those showing higher levels of spontaneous behavior were not privileged regarding such positive feedbacks. Eisenberg et al. (1981) detected the existence of a reciprocity principle guiding peer interactions that perfectly aligns with evolutionary claims about the importance of reciprocal interactions in organizing human relationships within the context of societies.

The search for significant correlations among apparently similar patterns of behavior soon pointed to the complexities of social interdependence among children. Many authors started to acknowledge the immense difficulties in precisely defining each pattern (that is, elaborating a consistent taxonomy of social behavior) and, also, in actually finding substantial consistency in the kind of relations between behavioral patterns (e.g. Eisenberg & Mussen, 1989). Some of the important issues were, for instance, how should 'aggression' be defined? By its consequences, by inferred hostile intentions, by contextual clues? And prosocial behaviors? How can anyone define 'altruism' (as it was usually defined in several studies not too long ago)? Is altruistic conduct a kind of action supposedly 'free' from any self-interested motivation (see Branco, 1998, Edwards, 1991, and Eisenberg & Mussen, 1989, for conceptual discussions)? Should we not first try to define crucial concepts such as 'self', and motivational constructs such as 'intentions', 'interests' and 'goals'?

The diverse and sometimes contradictory results concerning behavior correlations, though surprising to many researchers, did not alert them to the basic problem lying at the level of their assumptions about the very nature of psychological phenomena. What was completely ignored and left aside from the explanatory frameworks utilized by most scientists was the constitutive, fundamental role played by culture in the definition and co-construction of peculiar motivational systems underlying the actual manifestation of behaviors. A significant amount of children's or individuals' actions frequently were considered as similar, or belonging to a same category, exclusively on the basis of topographical criteria. The issue of 'meaning' and 'meaning construction' has not been yet considered to be a relevant or necessary topic, deserving special attention in the attempts carried out to explain empirical evidence. Even worse, the issue of meaning co-construction has rarely been thoroughly discussed in most studies and in their tentative elaborations to provide theoretical accounts for the phenomena.

Reviewing some of the methods often utilized to investigate peer interactions and children's goals and strategies to achieve them, Brown, Odom, and Hollombe (1996) argued for the need to make use of multiple methods to face the complexities involved in social interactions. Brown, Odom, and Hollombe certainly went a step beyond a mere assessment of behavior frequencies when they included the investigation of both goals and action strategies, recognizing the need to integrate the different levels of psychological processes. Nevertheless, they insisted on the adoption of a 'social competence' model, where fixed and well-defined categories of both goals and related actions were expected to be found, and eventually result in the construction of a 'taxonomy' for observing and recording communicative behaviors (1996, p. 35). This insistence well demonstrates how many researchers in the field still rely on epistemological grounds that alienate culture from its central place in the constitution of human development. According to the authors, the information created by the use of such a taxonomy is necessary for the establishment of 'normative standards' and calculations of probabilities of success or failure in achieving social goals. The information would then turn into software to help parents and teachers in their struggle to promote child development, independently of any considerations about *cultural meanings* or relevance. When the concept of 'meaning' is seriously taken into account, though the idea of setting 'normative standards' is evidently useless either to understand or to actually promote human development.

Such obvious neglect of the crucial part played by sociocultural contexts is widespread in the literature concerning the study of peers and child development (e.g. Hartup, 1983; Mize, Ladd, & Price, 1985). Urie Bronfenbrenner (1989; 1993) has always reminded us to avoid the study of human behaviors 'in strange situations, with strange people during the shortest period of time'. His claim for contextualization, criticizing most of the work produced in developmental psychology, resulted in an increased awareness of the cultural significance of human action (sometimes to the cost, as he himself pointed out, of overemphasizing context to the detriment of individual development). Michael Cole and his group at the Laboratory of Comparative Human Cognition (e.g. Cole, 1992; Cole, Engestrom, & Vasquez, 1997) have also provided extensive empirical evidence and developed thoughtful theories to account for the constitutive function of culture. This conceptualization of culture is completely at odds with culture as just another 'variable' to be related to human development, as though it could provide a measurable amount of specific influences over such development (also see Branco & Valsiner, 1997). I will come back to this issue when proposing a constructivist sociocultural approach to the study of social interdependence, later suggesting a paradigm shift towards a systemic perspective on human development.

Developmental Perspectives and Cultural Contextualization

Pathways to Child Development through the Analysis of Peer Interactions

An impressive number of studies have been conducted to systematically trace the developmental pathways of progressive levels of coordination of young children's social actions (e.g. Brenner & Mueller, 1982; Camaioni, 1980; Eckerman & Stein, 1982; Eckerman, Davis, & Didow, 1989; Eckerman & Peterman, 2001; Howes & Stewart, 1987; Musatti & Mueller, 1985; Verba, 1994). Such studies are usually conducted in free play situations, where toddlers or young children interact with each other, showing different degrees of coordinated action at different ages. Some researchers use cross-sectional methodologies, comparing distinct groups of children along a relatively short period of time, but others follow the same group as they grow older, in the context of longitudinal designs. Even though the results do not necessarily coincide, due to researchers' diverse conceptual, theoretical and methodological frameworks, it is clear that there exists a gradual tendency from parallel play in the earlier years, to imitation, to complementary actions, and finally to the emergence of sophisticated reciprocal interactions already detected in pretend play among children around 3 years old (Farver, 1992).

Eckerman and Peterman (2001) present an excellent analysis of this literature, referring to the abundant evidence revealing the progressive organization of young children's play, particularly addressing the functional dimensions of imitation. The emergence of positive social interactions (like smiles, vocalizations, gestures, etc.) occurs as early as 6 months (Hay & Rheingold, 1983), and coordinated actions with objects (like show and give) appear early in the second year of life (e.g. Ross & Goldman, 1977; Eckerman, Whatley, & Kutz 1975). Also peers as young as 30 months old seem to prefer positive peer interactions (24% of the time in daycare observations) to conflict (1%) (Rubenstein & Howes, 1979). Eckerman and Peterman (2001) differentiate between socially directed behaviors, interactions (peers mutually influencing one another) and communication (when they share some understanding of what they are doing together). Presenting a detailed analysis of evidence showing the pathways of early peer behavior coordinations, they argue for the importance of imitation – which tends to emerge around the 24th month – as an outstanding all-purpose strategy used by the child to form a thematically related response to another's actions. According to the authors, the connectedness seems especially perceptually salient, and the clear similarities in the overt actions exert a powerful and effective role in bringing peers to shared attention and coordinated actions.

Eckerman and Peterman (2001) particularly stress the role of preverbal coordinations, as they demonstrate the key contribution of such coordinations to the ontogenesis of language and communication:

> Nonverbal imitative acts form much of the substance of [children's] coordinated action, and their verbalizations are closely related to these nonverbal acts and seem to both highlight the nonverbal actions (e.g. 'I get it' as the child moves to retrieve that ball) and communicate further how these nonverbal acts are to be done (e.g. 'Watch!').

The importance of imitation for the development of language, cognition and socio-affective dimensions is also made evident and underlined by many other researches (e.g. Nadel & Baudonnière, 1981). Cooperation, drawn on the progressive complexities of joint action, also seems to play a central role in child development. Brownwell and Carriger (1990) present a longitudinal study of young peer interactions, from 12 to 30 months, where they show that children at the 24th month are also capable of achieving goal collaboration. According to them, joint coordination of related behaviors is 'at the heart of cooperation whether in play or in joint problem solving' (1990, p. 1165).

Verba (1994), reviewing the literature and analyzing her own data, presents an account of how peer collaboration develops, distinguishing three types of cooperative coordinations as children grow older: 'observation-elaboration', 'co-construction mode' and 'guided activity', each successively involving a more sophisticated pattern of cognitive strategies used to achieve common goals. Farver (1992), studying the sequences observed during children's pretend play, shows how peers as early as 18 months succeed in sharing the meaning of pretend activities with objects, being able to superimpose story lines and scripts upon their activities by the age of 36 months. His investigation is particularly interesting due to the integration of quantitative and interpretive approaches. Farver analyzed the behavior of 40 children, 5 pairs per age group of 2, 3, 4, and 5 years. Same-sex pairs' interactions were audiotaped for 20 minutes. His goal was to identify different linguistic strategies used by children to establish metacommunicative frames to create and maintain pretend play activities. Seven strategies were identified by the method used, namely, paralinguistic cues, descriptions of action, repetitions, semantic tying, calls for attention, directives, and tags. His results showed the prevalence of 'repetition' in 2-year-olds' dyads, 'paralinguistic cues' in 3-year-olds, 'calls for attention' in both ages (2 and 3), and a lot more 'semantic ties', 'descriptions' and the use of 'tags' among 4- and 5-year-old children. The use of a videotape, though, would have been much more effective, had he wanted to expand his objectives to find and integrate with linguistic information the immense variety of nonverbal communication strategies usually observed among young peers.

Sims, Hutchins, and Taylor (1997) draw our attention to the need to scientifically understand the development of peer interactions, and therefore provide productive knowledge for those fostering child development. They argue, based on relevant literature, that peer relationship difficulties can provoke later problems, including deficits in motor development, language and other cognitive skills. Such difficulties can also negatively affect, as well as endanger, abilities to recognize and display the affect, physical health and well-being of the child. Among the issues to be further studied, Sims, Hutchins, and Taylor suggest investigations of the meanings of conflict for child development.

Many definitions of 'conflict' are found in the literature. Malloy and McMurray refer to 'a relationship where two people have incompatible goals and use a variety of prosocial and anti-social strategies to influence each other's behavior' (1996, p. 186). The interesting thing about this definition is that it exposes the tremendous complexity of the interconnections between cooperative and competitive behaviors mentioned earlier in this chapter. The authors were searching for different sorts of goals motivating peer conflicts, and identified seven reasons for conflictual interactions. Unfortunately, they did not seem to be aware of the cultural context dependence of their findings. Moreover, they did not take into account the developmental meanings of the so-called conflicts to human development (Valsiner & Cairns, 1992). Sims, Hutchins, and Taylor only briefly consider that 'conflicts can serve as extremely useful learning opportunities as they provide the impetus for children to question their assumptions and to attempt to see others' perspectives' (1997, p. 249).

In his analysis of conflict, Kruger (1993) emphasizes the danger of classifying social interdependence patterns into exclusively defined categories. The meaning and the particular and integrated functions of social coordination of convergent and divergent kinds are cleverly addressed by the author, despite his controversial suggestion of a clear-cut distinction between 'self' and 'other' orientations. Again, this reveals an unawareness of the fact that the very nature of such concepts (as the 'self') is, indeed, culturally constructed. In the analysis of his data concerning joint problem solving by 48 pairs of 8-year-old girls, Kruger thoughtfully reminds us that:

> It would be misleading to characterize the dyadic discussion presented here as simply conflictual or simply cooperative . . . Collaboration is organized by the consideration of multiple perspectives, and consequently it is conflictual as well as cooperative . . . By being in conflict with each other's ideas, but not necessarily with each other, they discover together a more coordinated view of the dilemma . . . conflict [is] linked with cooperation, and both [are] linked with development. (1993, pp. 177–179)

It is important to incorporate the study of social, emotional and cognitive aspects of child development into investigations of the ways in which preverbal and verbal modes of communication, and cooperative-convergent and competitive-divergent orientations, constitute a broader and dynamic system in active, and permanent, interaction with ever-changing cultural contexts.

Social Construction of Cooperation and Competition within Cultural Contexts

As discussed above, the notion of cooperation and competition encompasses both structural and dynamic dimensions of social interdependence. Depending on the author's theoretical framework, the definition of the constructs may emphasize perceptual, behavioral, relational or context-structural components of social interdependence (e.g. Hinde & Groebel, 1991; Johnson & Johnson, 1982; 1989; Slavin, 1991). The diverse aspects of human social interdependence and the patterns of their interrelationships, therefore, must always be kept in mind. In the present section I will address the issue of cooperation and competition, focusing particularly upon the *intersubjective 'frames' created by the constructive emergence of dynamic coordinations between human goal orientations within specifically structured sociocultural contexts*. The idea is to highlight the intrinsic connections between cultural values and beliefs as they are created by and reflect upon organized activities made available for the child. Here I stress the transformational nature of children's goal orientations as they surface along the flow of peer interactions and continuous negotiations.

The social constructive (or co-constructive) theoretical framework is simultaneously grounded on processes of 'cultural canalization' or cultural suggestions (Valsiner, 1997), and on the active transformation of such messages by the individual. The dialectics between the two poles – the collective culture and the individual – can be found in the operation of internalization/externalization processes (Lawrence & Valsiner, 1993; Valsiner, 1997; 1998) that may also give birth to novel meanings and motives for action. From this standpoint, cooperation and competition are transitory results of a continuous dynamics that reflects specific states of coordination of individuals' goal orientations at a certain time. The term 'goal orientation' is found in recent literature to designate the fluid and ever-changing characteristics of human motivational systems, traditionally defined as 'goals' (e.g. Staub, 1991). Valsiner and Branco (1997) define goal orientation as 'a kind of internal constraining system, semiotically mediated, that, by projecting into the future, constrains actions, feelings, and thoughts in the present time'.

When individuals' goal orientations are compatible, a 'frame' of convergence is usually created as a result of such a pattern of coordination. When individuals' goal orientations are incompatible, a divergent 'frame' is likely to emerge. The concept of 'frame', formerly utilized by Goffman (1974) and Bateson (1972), has also become popular in some areas of contemporary developmental psychology, as well as in sociolinguistic and communication studies, to designate the *relational context co-constructed by individuals in interaction that serves as the basis for the interpretation of meanings* (e.g. Branco, 1998; 2000; Leeds-Hurwizt, 1989; 1995; Fogel & Branco, 1997). In our definition of convergence and divergence, though, it is not sufficient that a certain pattern of goal coordination is detected by external observers. The observed coordination must be evaluated as a modality of convergence or divergence by the participants, allowing for the emergence of intersubjective states that can be characterized as convergent or divergent frames. Quite often, one or more participants do not achieve a clear-cut identification, which makes the task of interpretation extremely complicated or even impossible. The label 'ambivalence' has mostly been used to refer to such cases of frame ambiguity.

Cooperation, according to this conceptual landscape, consists of a special case of goal orientation convergence, where individuals' efforts are directed to accomplish a shared goal. Competition, on the other hand, constitutes a special instance of divergence, precisely because no more than one individual can accomplish the goal; that is, if one person achieves the goal, the other necessarily will not.

Frames of convergence and divergence, as previously defined, include a number of possible coordinations other than cooperation and competition. These range from solidarity, sophisticated joint interactive work, to individualistic goals, and all the way down to mortal rivalries that result in severe losses even for the winner. Nonetheless, difficulties are not limited to the existence of a vast and complex multiplicity of coordinations between individuals' goal orientations. If we add cases where groups also have to be considered as units of analysis, or as sites for intersubjectivity construction, the situation becomes even more puzzling. Another important complication derives from the recognition that there exists an infinite network of conceivable interrelationships between all the different structural levels of human interdependence, as mentioned before. Here I am referring to the fabric resulting from the intertwining of subjective experiencing of a particular interaction, mutual co-constructions of meanings in the here-and-now by individuals in interaction, social participation rules (or expectations) implicit or explicit in the activity context, cultural conventions for action interpretations, and so on and so forth.

Consider, again, what may happen in planned or organized competitions, such as in the soccer game example earlier discussed. Besides the existence of intra-group cooperation *and* competition, and intergroup competition *and* cooperation in following the rules to play a fair game, at every single interactive moment in the field, or in any other context, players will permanently be negotiating their personal relationships. They will be co-creating, along the flow of their interactions and self-dialogues, multiple and sometimes fuzzy relational frames, resulting from such negotiations. The negotiations will derive from a set of intermingled goal orientations that constitute each player's singular, subjective, hierarchically constructed and yet dynamic motivational system. Each player's motivational system brings together all sorts of incitements or purposes created along life experiences, out of personality characteristics, values and beliefs, biological and situational predispositions, and particularly, out of the ongoing emergence of novel states and necessities in the very context of the present interaction.

This being said, the best avenue to approach the issue of cooperation and competition is the analysis of communication processes, particularly the analysis of relational metacommunicative interactions, that involve communication *about* individuals' interactions and relationships, occurring within sociocultural contexts. In the analysis of communication and relational metacommunication, the investigator's aim is to identify the characteristics of the dynamic processes reflecting the expectations and values created by historical traditions and by the here-and-now negotiations of the participants (see the notion of 'frames' presented earlier). On the one hand, this entails the need for a microgenetic view of the processes involved, and on the other, it requires a permanent awareness of the diverse forms in which life contexts, in their multiple levels, are organized and structured, making use of the cultural fabric that is constantly generated within the realms of our cultures.

Branco and Valsiner, in an experimental study carried out in Brasilia (Branco & Valsiner, 1997; Branco, 1998), addressed the issue of cooperation and competition from a social construction perspective, analyzing the flux of interactions among 3-year-olds. Children were organized in two triads composed of two boys and one girl. Each triad was observed within contexts differently structured in terms of the materials available, their spatial arrangement, and the rules orienting the activities (each context was carefully organized to be either cooperative or competitive). One triad was invited to play under cooperative suggestions encoded in the organization of the play material and in the expectations expressed by a young adult female supervisor, during 25 minute sessions. The other triad was also invited to play, except in the context of competitively organized situations. Both triads played in six consecutive sessions during a 3-week period. After that, they were invited to participate in a seventh session, where they were to try to accomplish a cooperative task that included carrying a big doll around to participate in a few suggested pretend activities (like bathing it, taking it to the doctor, etc.). All sessions were videotaped, and then analyzed from a microgenetic viewpoint. Diagrams representing the sequences of goal oriented coordinations among participants (including the adult) through the sessions were constructed, based on detailed transcriptions of verbal and nonverbal behaviors, and representing a starting point for the analysis.

Quantitative analysis of the amount of time spent by children in individual activities, frames of social attention, convergence (particularly cooperation) and divergence revealed a strong and consistent effect of cooperative and competitively structured contexts over children's patterns of goal oriented coordination (Branco, 1998). The efficiency of contextual organization in producing compatible effects over goal oriented coordination was detected throughout the six sessions, but was especially evident during the test session (the seventh session). The interactive episodes that were qualitatively analyzed were those that included transitions between the frames, that is, those that allowed for the identification of the strategies used by children to establish, avoid or change the quality of the frames characterizing their ongoing interactions.

The argument I want to develop here is that the co-creation and negotiation of frames between individuals constitute the essence of relational metacommunication processes. As mentioned before, metacommunication is that important part of communicative processes concerned with relational contents; it is the *communication about the nature or quality of the communication* between the participants, which will serve as the frame for interpretation of actions and creation of meanings within determined contexts. Branco and Valsiner's study revealed the continuous flow of nonverbal metacommunicative strategies, punctuated by the occurrence, here and there, of linguistic forms of relational metacommunication, as when one boy said to the other 'I am not your friend anymore!', or when another used the tag '*amigo*!' – which means 'friend!' in Portuguese – during their conversation.

Branco and Valsiner's (1992; 1997) investigations were designed to go beyond the identification of specific strategies linked to the co-construction of different frames (see Farver, 1992, Le Camus, 1985, Montagner, 1978, for an analysis of such strategies; also see Bateson's observations of play indicators in the context of children's interactions). It also demonstrated the function of conflicts (or divergence) in the co-construction of convergent frames, as conflicts very often led to the negotiation of meanings (here including goal orientations, values and possible constraints). The study provided evidence that allowed for the understanding of how different social strategies combine and are co-created within particular segments of the interactive flow. This was possible by taking into account contextual clues, the history of children's interactions (in the here-and-now) and relationships (the quality of interactions through time), together with investigators' familiarity with the analysis of children's play interactions, as well as their familiarity with the specific group of children being investigated.

Referring to the need for the adoption of an interpretive approach to the investigation of young children's development, Corsaro and Molinari state that:

> Studies of peer relations among toddlers in daycare settings are rare and primarily have been restricted to recent work in Italy and France. Stambak and Verba

> (1986; Stambak, Barrière, Lezine, Rayna & Verba, 1983) have verified the existence of numerous and lengthy episodes of common activities among children from 13 to 26 months in French crèches. (1990, p. 216)

Corsaro and his collaborators (e.g. Corsaro, 1997; Corsaro & Miller, 1992; Corsaro & Molinari, 1990; Corsaro & Schwarz, 1991) have carried out very interesting research on the examination of what they designate as 'peer culture'. The concept of peer culture encompasses the 'routines, artifacts, values and concerns that children produce and share in interaction with peers' (Corsaro & Molinari, 1990, p. 214). Stressing the primary role of language and social routines in child development (Corsaro & Rosier, 1992), they also underline the fact that 'children discover a world that is endowed with meaning and help to shape and share in their own developmental experiences' (Corsaro & Molinari, 1990, p. 214). Corsaro and his collaborators' work offers, therefore, thoughtful insights on the origins, characteristics and development of peer cultures in different contexts.

From a microethnographic perspective, Corsaro and Schwarz (1991) analyzed teachers' participation in the construction of specific contexts for young children's social development in the United States and Italy. After three weeks of non-intrusive observations in class, followed by a period of participant observation, they videotaped group interactions for 25 hours over a period of 5 months. Interviews with teachers, parents and children were also carried out. They found that in the United States most projects were individualistically oriented, whereas in Italy most activities aimed at developing group projects. They described and commented on interactive episodes showing teachers' adequacy to handle situations, and detected interesting cultural differences, like the way adults in Italy were more likely to send children to settle their dispute on their own, in contrast with American teachers who actively used various suggestions and strategies to promote negotiations.

The remarkable complexities of 3-year-olds' negotiations in pretend play contexts were cleverly studied by Bonica (1993). She particularly focused her micro-analysis on the

> transitions between agreement and conflict as well as processes of dissociation between self and others . . . [with the expectation that] their study should clarify the function of pretend play in the regulation of interpersonal relationships. (1993, pp. 55–56)

She highlights the importance of metacommunication processes as she selected and analyzed, from 10 hours of videotaped peer interactions occurring in the playground, one specific episode involving two girls and one boy. The episode is divided into four different phases. The first two phases set the scenario that engenders ambiguities, which cause communication between children to break down. In the third phase, children abandon participating in the play project in order to discuss and reach an agreement concerning their differences and what to do. The last phase reveals the success of the negotiations that had taken place before. By investigating the way children in the pretend play situation work on the reciprocal acceptance of self and other, facing the dilemma 'I desire to do what I want but I also want to stay with you', she identifies numerous sophisticated strategies used by children to metacommunicate their intentions (or goal orientations). In a particular moment, the girl that was resisting the cat role in the story (imposed on her by the other girl) finally accepts being a cat by 'barking like a dog', what was immediately acknowledged by the other as she being a 'cat-dog'!

Parker and Scott (1992) also provide us with an intriguing research adopting a hermeneutic approach to peer relations. Criticizing the 'social competence' approach, particularly to explain why some children are rejected by the group, they argue that what really matters are not the social skills involved but the main 'concerns' or basic motivations with which the child enters and participates in peer social interactions. They studied two cohorts of children during a 2 year stay in a single preschool kindergarten class. As a revealing example, among others, Parker and Scott present in full detail the analysis of Ann, a young girl who was extremely unpopular among her peers. The episodes were all videotaped in the playground. On different and varied occasions, Ann clearly demonstrated that she was extremely sophisticated and skillful in her social abilities. Notwithstanding, she did everything 'wrong', from a social acceptance perspective. Her voice was bossy; she liked to lecture her peers and assign them roles; many times she exhibited ambiguous responses to others' approaches; and, above all, she wanted to be the center of attention, displaying an authoritarian role in relation to peers. Another aspect discussed in the paper was the fact that the more Ann failed using such strategies, the more she insisted on using them. The result was that Ann's peers either ignored or rejected her most of the time. The authors' reasoning concerning the importance of assuming a hermeneutic framework to interpret individuals' conduct on the basis of their main interests and motivations ('concerns') brings to the fore this essential dimension of human phenomena, in order to make sense of the intrinsic and necessary integration between social motivation and social development.

Paradigm Shift: From Behavioral Categories and Competence to Dynamic Co-Constructions of Social Interdependence in the Context of a Hermeneutical Science

'What is the academically legitimate epistemology of psychology?' asks Brockmeier (1996a, p. 289). The answer to this question has caused intense debates over the scientific status of different epistemological approaches. However, for the most part, the main point of the controversy has been ignored by those defending particular conceptualizations of science. The point I initially want to emphasize is the intrinsic relationships found between epistemology, theory, methods, the phenomena under investigation, and the process of knowledge construction (Branco & Valsiner, 1997; Winegar, 1998).

Traditionally founded on an essentialist and non-developmental approach, psychology struggled to keep its roots in the epistemological assumptions that conferred prestige to the natural sciences.

Valsiner stresses the fact that psychology is part of the collective culture, and therefore it creates different kinds of 'socially desirable myths under the halo effect of science' and 'often advances on the basis of social utopias that dominate the given society at the given time' (1997, pp. 65, 15). The strong temptation to provide (as the natural sciences did to a significant extent) useful knowledge to develop advanced technologies lured researchers into the ambitious project of revealing the universal laws governing human behavior. Once unveiled, such laws would allow for full explanations and, consequently, successful prediction, management and control of human conflicts, deficiencies, pathologies, and all sorts of psychological – and, possibly, social – problems.

The myth of finding such universal laws lies at the basis of what Shweder (1991) calls the central project of a 'general psychology'. Such myth, however, cannot hold within the realms of a science that aims at understanding human conduct and activities situated in intentional worlds (Bruner, 1990). If our goal is to identify and understand the existence of possible regularities in developmental processes, we need to abandon an essentialist epistemology (based on Plato and Aristotle), and start building our theories not on the 'hard core' building blocks used to construct old edifices, but instead on the 'softer' but firmer grounds of an epistemology prepared to face the ever-changing nature of our object of study. According to Heraclitus (*c.* 500 BC), *change* is the only permanent characteristic of nature, and the acknowledgment of this fact necessarily requires a developmental approach to reality in order to make sense of it in systematic, knowledgeable and scientific ways. Knowledge construction is a social enterprise that takes place along the continuous interactions between the subjectivity of the culturally situated individual and the aspects of nature (or reality) that resist previous accounts, and invite the individual to new interpretations or re-elaborations of the phenomena under investigation.

Geertz alleges 'there is no such a thing as human nature independent of culture' (1973, p. 49). The constitutive nature of culture in the dynamics of meaning construction, in addition to the crucial role played by time and its irreversibility (e.g. Prigogine, 1996) renders completely ineffectual the search for mutually exclusive categories concerning, among others, the phenomena of human social interdependence. Single aggregations of frequencies presumably referring to events of the same kind (or category) fails to consider their cultural and contextualized meaning. This approach, usually found in cross-cultural psychology literature, does not provide significant information about either the structure or the functionalities that are active in the phenomena under study. As mentioned before, scientific knowledge construction must result from a coherent integration of epistemology, theory and methods. Questions of a non-developmental kind can always be examined by the adoption of causal explanatory models, but issues related to human social co-constructions of interactional patterns, values and related matters inevitably call for a hermeneutic interpretive approach. The adequacy of this approach, demonstrated by important theorists (e.g. Bruner, 1990; Brockmeier, 1996a; Corsaro, 1997; Corsaro & Miller, 1992; Harré, 1983; Rey, 1997; Shweder, 1991; Valsiner, 1997; 1998), thus implies the need to create methodologies that allow for knowledge constructions according to a whole new set of criteria to assess the consistency, coherence and relevance of the quality of the specific interpretations of the phenomena (Chen & Pearce, 1995; Gaskins, Corsaro, & Miller, 1992).

Returning to human interactions and relationships, the metatheoretical and theoretical sociocultural constructivist framework that has been orienting the present analysis points to a redefinition of concepts such as cooperation and competition that reflect the multiplex and dynamic nature of social interdependence patterns. The notion of 'frames', therefore, seems to consist of a productive unit of analysis. It reflects the transitory structures that fluctuate, as meaning co-constructions and negotiations continuously change in human interactions. Analytical inferences of goal orientations, intentions and, to a large extent, values and beliefs orientations may prove useful to account for the dialectical and simultaneous occurrence of specific structures and processes of change, both consisting of key characteristics of the development of living open systems.

Conclusions and Perspectives for Future Research

Throughout this chapter, I have presented arguments to support the view that scientific knowledge construction concerning the emergence and development of the varied patterns of social interdependence among human beings must necessarily be grounded on a systemic, sociocultural and hermeneutic approach that also takes into account the active and constructive participation of individuals in the process of their own development. Given the fact that meaning construction consists of the very foundation of psychological processes, the search for universal categories or social competences to explain human interdependence in its numerous dimensions definitely does not fit the complex nature of the phenomena. Research aimed at unveiling significant correlations among such categories is thus unproductive, and cannot contribute to a better understanding of the issue of social development.

The acknowledgment of such constraints and limitations leads investigators to a paradigm shift that privileges the study of processes instead of outcomes, and the use of qualitative methodological approaches to analyze the phenomena. It is exactly in this direction that researchers should devote their efforts to understand the complex interpersonal negotiations already observed in very young children. This will particularly include the identification and interpretation of the sophisticated strategies utilized by children to co-create meanings out of their joint participation in culturally impregnated activities, as they face the often contradictory goal orientations that coordinate their situated interactions.

Graves and Graves (1985), among many others, alert us to the urgent need to promote cooperative values and activities, simply referring to the inevitable realities of modern societies. Our societies demand an increasing struggle to work and live together, as individuals and nations in a globalized world. We should not underestimate the importance of establishing a reciprocal recognition of each other as persons (Bonica, 1993), and the significance of a deep-rooted acceptance of ethnic and cultural differences which will enhance the possibilities of mutual respect and the co-construction of a plural, richer, more abundant society in terms of creative alternatives to solve the difficult problems to come, and, above all, increase the possibilities of a peaceful world. I will end by quoting Erwin Staub, who wisely recommends:

> We must strive for an ideal of individuals with strong, independent identities who are also supported by their connections to others and rootedness in a community. Connectedness that extends beyond one's group to all human beings is an important building block of a world in which groups turn toward, not against, each other. (1989, p. 270)

References

Asher, S.R., & Coie, J.D. (1990). *Peer rejection in childhood.* New York: Cambridge University Press.

Azmitia, M. (1988). Peer interaction and problem solving: When are two heads better than one? *Child Development*, 59 (1), 87–96.

Baldwin, J.M. (1906). *Thought and things: A study of the development of meaning of thought, or genetic logic. Vol. 1. Functional logic, or genetic theory of knowledge.* London: Swan Sonnenschein.

Baltes, P.B. (1987). Theoretical propositions of life-span developmental psychology: On dynamics between growth and decline. *Developmental Psychology*, 23 (5), 611–626.

Bar-Tal, D. (1976). *Prosocial behavior: Theory and Research.* New York: Wiley.

Bateson, G. (1972). *Steps to an ecology of mind.* New York: Chandler.

Bloch, M.N., & Pellegrini, A.D. (1989). *The ecological context of children's play.* Norwood, NJ: Ablex.

Blurton-Jones, N. (1972). *Ethological studies of child behavior.* New York: Cambridge University Press.

Bonica, L. (1993). Negotiations among children and pretend play. In M. Stambak & H. Sinclair (eds), *Pretend play among 3-year-olds.* Hillsdale, NJ: Erlbaum.

Bornstein, M.H., & Bruner, J.S. (1989). *Interaction in human development.* Hillsdale, NJ: Erlbaum.

Boyd, R., & Richerson, P.J. (1991). Culture and cooperation. In R.A. Hinde & J. Groebel (eds), *Cooperation and prosocial behavior* (pp. 27–48). New York: Cambridge University Press.

Branco, A.U. (1996). Constraints on the universality of psychological constructs: Comments on 'Individualism and collectivism', *Culture & Psychology*, 4 (2), 477–484.

Branco, A.U. (1998). Cooperation, competition, and related issues: A co-constructive approach. In M.C. Lyra & J. Valsiner (eds), *Child development within culturally structured environments: Vol. 4. Construction of psychological processes in interpersonal communication.* Norwood, NJ: Ablex.

Branco, A.U. (2001). Contextual, interactional and subjective dimensions of cooperation and competition: A co-constructivist analysis. In S. Chaiklin (ed.), *The theory and practice of cultural-historical psychology.* Aarhus, Denmark: University of Aarhus.

Branco, A.U., & Mettel, T.P.L. (1995). O processo de canalização cultural das interações criança-criança na pré-escola. *Psicologia: Teoria e Pesquisa*, 11 (1), 13–22.

Branco, A.U., & Valsiner, J. (1992). Development of convergence and divergence in joint actions of preschool children: The emergence of cooperation and competition within structured contexts. Paper presented at the 25th International Congress of Psychology, Brussels, Belgium, 19–25 July.

Branco, A.U., & Valsiner, J. (1997). Changing methodologies: A co-constructivist study of goal orientations in social interactions. *Psychology and Developing Societies*, 9, 1, 35–64.

Brenner, J., & Mueller, E. (1982). Shared meaning in boy toddlers' peer relations. *Child Development*, 53 (2), 380–391.

Brockmeier, J. (1996a). Explaining the interpretive mind. *Human Development*, 39, 287–294.

Brockmeier, J. (1996b). Raccontare 'ciò che è veramente accaduto': Tecniche di persuasione e di giustificazione nel conflitto tra bambini. *Scienze dell'Interazione: Rivista di psicologia, psicosociologia e psicoterapia* (*The Science of Interaction: Journal of Psychology, Psychosociology, and Psychotherapy*), 3, 31–41.

Bronfenbrenner, U. (1989) Ecological systems theory. *Annals of Child Development*, 6, 185–246.

Bronfenbrenner, U. (1993). The ecology of cognitive development: Research models and fugitive findings. In R. Wozniak & K. Fisher (eds), *Development in context: Acting and thinking in specific environments* (pp. 3–44). Hillsdale, NJ: Erlbaum.

Brown, W., Odom, S., & Hollombe, A. (1996). Observational assessment of young children's social behavior with peers. *Early Childhood Research Quarterly*, 11, 19–40.

Brownell, C.A., & Carriger, M.S. (1990). Changes in cooperation and self–other differentiation during the second year. *Child Development*, 61, 1164–1174.

Bruner, J. (1990). *Acts of meaning*. Cambridge, MA: Harvard University Press.

Camaioni, L. (1980). *L'interazione tra bambini*. Roma: Armando.

Chen, V., & Pearce, W.B. (1995). Even if a thing of beauty, can a case study be a joy forever? A social constructionist approach to theory and research. In W. Leeds-Hurwizt (ed.), *Social approaches to communication*. New York: Guilford.

Cohen, D. (1987). *The development of play*. New York: New York University Press.

Cole, M. (1992). Culture in development. In M.H. Bornstein & M.E. Lamb (eds), *Developmental psychology: An advanced textbook* (3rd edn, pp. 731–788). Hillsdale, NJ: Erlbaum.

Cole, M., Engestrom, Y., & Vasquez, O. (1997). *Mind, culture, and activity: Seminal papers from the Laboratory of Comparative Human Cognition*. New York: Cambridge University Press.

Corsaro, W.A. (1997). *The sociology of childhood*. Thousand Oaks, CA: Pine Forge.

Corsaro, W.A., & Miller, P.J. (1992). *Interpretive approaches to children's socialization*. San Francisco: Jossey-Bass.

Corsaro, W.A., & Molinari, L. (1990). From *seggiolini* to *discussione*: The generation and extension of peer culture among Italian preschool children. *Qualitative Studies in Education*, 3 (3), 213–230.

Corsaro, W.A., & Schwarz, K. (1991). Peer play and socialization in two cultures: Implications for research and practice. In B. Scales, M. Almy, A. Nicolopoulou, & S. Ervin-Tipp (eds), *Play and the social context of development in early care and education*. New York: Teachers' College Press.

Dawkins, R. (1976). *The selfish gene*. Oxford: Oxford University Press.

Deutsch, M. (1949). A theory of cooperation and competition. *Human Relations*, 2, 129–152.

Deutsch, M. (1982). Interdependence and psychological orientation. In V.G. Derlega & J. Grzelak (eds), *Cooperation and helping behavior: Theory and research*. New York: Academic.

Doise, W., & Palmonari, A. (1984). *Social interaction in individual development*. Cambridge, MA: Cambridge University Press.

Dumont, L. (1985). *O individualismo: uma perspectiva antropológica da ideologia moderna*. Rio de Janeiro: Rocco.

Eckerman, C.O. (1992). Imitation and toddlers' achievement of co-ordinated action with others. In J. Nadel & L. Camaioni (eds), *New perspectives in early communicative development* (pp. 116–138). New York: Routledge.

Eckerman, C.O., Davis, C.C., & Didow, S.M. (1989). Toddlers' emerging ways of achieving social coordinations with a peer. *Child Development*, 60, 440–453.

Eckerman, C. & Peterman, K. (2001). Peers and infant social/communicative development. In G. Bremner & A. Fogel (eds), *Blackwell handbook of infant development*. Oxford: Blackwell.

Eckerman, C.O., & Stein, M.R. (1982). The toddler's emerging interactive skills. In K.H. Rubin & H.S. Ross (eds), *Peer relationships and social skills in childhood* (pp. 41–71). New York: Springer.

Eckerman, C., Whatley, J.L., & Kutz, S.L. (1975). Growth of social play with peers during the second year of life. *Developmental Psychology*, 11 (1), 42–49.

Edwards, J. (1991). Cooperation and competition: Two sides of the same coin? *The Irish Journal of Psychology*, 12 (1), 76–82.

Eisenberg, N., Cameron, E., Tryon, K., & Dodez, R. (1981). Socialization of prosocial behavior in the preschool classroom. *Developmental Psychology*, 17, 773–782

Eisenberg, N., & Mussen, P.H. (1989). *The roots of prosocial behavior in children*. New York: Cambridge University Press.

Ellis, S., & Gauvain, M. (1992). Social and cultural influences on children's collaborative interactions. In L.T. Winegar & J. Valsiner (eds), *Children's development within social context* (pp. 155–180). Norwood, NJ: Erlbaum.

Erickson, F. (1987). Transformation and school success: The politics and culture of educational achievement. *Anthropology and Education Quarterly*, 18, (4), 335–356.

Erickson, F. (1991). Microethnography in the classroom. Paper presented at the course 'Microethnography', University of Brasília, Brazil.

Farver, J.A. (1992). Communicating shared meanings in social pretend play. *Early Childhood Research Quarterly*, 7, 501–516.

Feger, H. (1991). Cooperation between groups. In R.A. Hinde & J. Groebel (eds), *Cooperation and prosocial behavior*. New York: Cambridge University Press.

Fisher, K., & Bidell, T.R. (1998). Dynamic development of psychological structures in action and thought. In W. Damon & R.M. Lerner (eds), *Handbook of child psychology, 5th edn: Vol. 1. Theoretical models of human development* New York: Wiley.

Fogel, A. (1993). *Developing through relationships: Origins of communication, self and culture*. Chicago: University of Chicago Press.

Fogel, A., & Branco, A.U. (1997). Metacommunication as a source of indeterminism in relationship development. In A. Fogel, M. Lyra, & J. Valsiner (eds), *Dynamics and indeterminism in developmental and social processes*. Hillsdale, NJ: Erlbaum.

Ford, D.H., & Lerner, R.M. (1992). *Developmental systems theory: An integrative approach*. London: Sage.

Forman, E.A. (1992). Discourse, intersubjectivity and the development of peer collaboration: A Vygotskian approach. In L.T. Winegar & J. Valsiner (eds), *Children's development within social context* (pp. 143–160). Hillsdale, NJ: Erlbaum.

Gaskins, S., Miller, P.J., & Corsaro, W.A. (1992). Theoretical and methodological perspectives in the interpretive study of children. In W.A. Corsaro & P.J. Miller (eds), *Interpretive approaches to children's socialization* (pp. 5–24). San Francisco: Jossey-Bass.

Geertz, C. (1973). *The interpretation of cultures*. New York: Basic.

Goffman, E. (1974). *Frame analysis: An essay on the organization of experience*. Cambridge, MA: Harvard University Press.

Graves, N.B. & Graves, T.D. (1985). Creating a cooperative learning environment: An ecological approach. In R. Slavin, S. Sharan, S. Kagan, R. Hert-Lazarowitz, C. Webb & R. Schmuck (eds), *Learning to cooperate, cooperating to learn* (pp. 403–436). New York: Plenum.

Harcourt, A. (1992). Cooperation in conflicts: Commonalties between humans and other animals. *Politics & the Life Sciences*, 11 (2), 251–259.

Harré, R. (1983). *Personal being*. Cambridge, MA: Harvard University Press.

Hartup, W.W. (1983). Peer relations. In P.H. Mussen (ed.), *Handbook of child psychology: Vol. IV. Socialization, personality and social development*. New York: Wiley.

Hartup, W.W. (1985). Relationships and their significance in cognitive development. In R.A. Hinde, A. Perret-Clermont & J. Stevenson-Hinde (eds), *Social relationships and cognitive development* (pp. 66–82). Oxford: Clarendon.

Hartup, W.W. (1992). Conflict and friendship relations. In C.U. Shantz & W.W. Hartup (eds), *Conflict in child and adolescent development* (pp. 186–215). Cambridge, MA: Cambridge University Press.

Hartup, W.W. (1996). Cooperation, close relationships, and cognitive development. In W.M. Bukowski, A.F. Newcomb, & W.W. Hartup (eds), *The company they keep: Friendship in childhood and adolescence* (pp. 213–237). New York: Cambridge University Press.

Hay, D.F., & Rheingold, H.C. (1983). The early appearance of some valued social behaviors. In D.L. Bridgeman (ed.), *The nature of prosocial development: Interdisciplinary theories and strategies*. New York: Academic.

Hinde, R.A. (1976). Interactions, relationships, and social structures. *Man (NS)*, 2, 1–17.

Hinde, R.A. (1996). Describing relationships. In A.E. Auhagen & M. Salisch (eds), *The diversity of human relationships* (pp. 7–35). New York: Cambridge University Press.

Hinde, R.A., & Groebel, J. (1991). *Cooperation and prosocial behavior*. New York: Cambridge University Press.

Hoffman, M.L. (1989). Empathy and prosocial activism. In N. Eisenberg, J. Reykowski, & E. Staub (eds), *Social and moral values: Individual and societal perspectives*. Hillsdale, NJ: Erlbaum.

Howes, C. (1996). The earliest friendships. In W.M. Bukovski, A.F. Newcomb, & W.W. Hartup (eds), *The company they keep: Friendship in childhood and adolescence* (pp. 66–86). Cambridge, MA: Cambridge University Press.

Howes, C., & Stewart, P. (1987). Child's play with adults, toys, and peers: An examination of family and child-care influences. *Developmental Psychology*, 23 (3), 423–430.

Johnson, D.W., & Johnson, R.T. (1982). Effects of cooperative, competitive, and individualistic learning experiences on cross ethnic interaction and friendship. *Journal of Social Psychology*, 118, 47–58.

Johnson, D.W., & Johnson, R.T. (1989). *Cooperation and competition: Theory and research*. Minnesota: Interaction.

Jurberg, M.B. (2000). Individualismo e coletivismo na psicologia social. In *Paradigmas em psicologia social: A perspectiva latino-americana*. Petrópolis, Rio de Janeiro: Vozes.

Kindermann, T., & Valsiner, J. (1989). Research strategies in culture-inclusive developmental psychology. In J. Valsiner (ed.), *Child development in cultural context* (pp. 13–50). Toronto: Hogrefe & Huber.

Krebs, D.L. (1996). The value of evolutionary perspectives on social relations among children: A commentary. *International Journal of Behavioral Development*, 19 (1), 75–80.

Kruger, A.C. (1993). Peer collaboration: Conflict, cooperation or both? *Social Development*, 2 (3), 165–182.

LaFrenière, P.J. (1996). Cooperation as a conditional strategy among peers: Influences of social ecology and kin relations. *International Journal of Behavioral Development*, 19 (1), 1–5.

LaFrenière, P.J., & MacDonald, K.B. (1996). Evolutionary perspectives on children's resource-directed behaviour in peer relationships: An introduction. *International Journal of Behavioral Development*, 19 (1), 1–5.

Lawrence, J., & Valsiner, J. (1993). Conceptual roots of internalization: From transmission to transformation. *Human Development*, 36, 150–167.

Le Camus, J. (1985). *Les relations et les interactions du jeune enfant*. Paris: ESF.

Leeds-Hurwitz, W. (1989). *Communication in everyday life: A social interpretation*. Norwood, NJ: Ablex.

Leeds-Hurwitz, W. (1995). *Social approaches to communication*. New York: Guilford.

Le Mare, L.J., & Rubin, K.H. (1987). Perspective taking and peer interaction: Structural and developmental analysis. *Child Development*, 58 (2), 306–315.

Malloy, H.C., & McMurray, P. (1996). Conflict strategies and resolutions: Peer conflict in an integrated early childhood classroom. *Early Childhood Research Quarterly*, 11, 185–206.

McClintock, C.G. (1978). Social values: Their definition, measurement, and development. *Journal of Research and Development in Education*, 12 (1), 121–137.

Mead, M. (1937). *Cooperation and competition among primitive peoples*. New York: McGraw-Hill.

Mize, J., Ladd, G.W., & Price, J.M. (1985). Promoting positive peer relations with young children: Rationales and strategies. *Child Care Quarterly*, 14 (4), 221–237.

Montagner, H. (1978). *L'enfant et la communication*. Paris: Stock.

Montagner, H. (1990). *A vinculação: a aurora da ternura*. Lisboa: Instituto Piaget.

Morin, E. (1996). Epistemologia da complexidade. In D.F. Schnitman (ed.), *Novos paradigmas, cultura e subjetividade*. Porto Alegre, Brasil: Artes Médicas.

Musatti, T., & Mueller, E. (1985). Expressions of representational growth in toddlers' peer communication. *Social Cognition*, 3 (4), 383–399.

Nadel, J., & Baudonnière, P.M. (1981). Imitação, modo preponderante de intercâmbio entre pares durante o terceiro ano de vida. *Caderno de Pesquisa da Fundação Carlos Chagas (São Paulo)*, 39, 26–31.

Packer, M.J., & Scott, B. (1992). The hermeneutic investigation of peer relations. In L.T. Winegar & J. Valsiner (eds), *Children's development within social context* (pp. 75–111). Hillsdale, NJ: Erlbaum.

Patterson, G.R. (1990). *Depression and aggression in family interaction*. Hillsdale, NJ: Erlbaum.

Perret Clairmont, A. (1979). *La construction de l'intelligence dans l'interaction sociale*. Berne: Peter Lang.

Piaget, J. (1961). *Psicologia da inteligência*. Rio de Janeiro: Fundo de Cultura.

Piaget, J. (1965). *The moral judgement of the child* (1932). New York: Free Press.

Prigogine, I. (1996). O fim da ciência? In D.F. Schnitman (ed.), *Novos paradigmas, cultura e subjetividade*. Porto Alegre, Brasil: Artes Médicas.

Radke-Yarrow, M., & Zahan-Waxler, C. (1991). The role of familial factors in the development of prosocial behavior: Research findings and questions. In D. Olweus, J. Block, & M. Radke-Yarrow (eds), *Development of antisocial and prosocial behavior*. New York: Academic.

Rey, F.G. (1997). *Epistemología cualitativa y subjetividad*. São Paulo: EDUC.

Rogoff, B. (1990). *Apprenticeship in thinking: Cognitive development in social context*. New York: Oxford University Press.

Ross, H.S., & Goldman, B.D. (1977). Establishing new social relations in infancy. In T. Alloway, L. Krames, & P. Pliner (eds), *Advances in communication and affect* (Vol. 4). New York: Plenum.

Rubenstein, J.L., & Howes, C. (1979). Caregiving and infant behavior in day-cares and in homes. *Developmental Psychology*, 15 (11), 1–24.

Rubin, J.Z. (1991). Changing assumptions about conflict and negotiation. In R. Hinde & J. Groebel (eds), *Cooperation and prosocial behavior* (pp. 268–280). New York: Cambridge University Press.

Rubin, K.H., & Ross, H.S. (1982). *Peer relationships and social skills in childhood*. New York: Springer.

Shantz, C.U. (1987). Conflicts between children. *Child Development*, 58 (2), 283–305.

Shantz, C.U., & Hartup, W.W. (1992). *Conflict in child and adolescent development*. New York: Cambridge University Press.

Shweder, R. (1991). *Thinking through cultures: Expeditions in cultural psychology*. Cambridge, MA: Harvard University Press.

Sims, M., Hutchins, T., & Taylor, M. (1997). Conflict as social interaction: Building relationship skills in child care settings. *Child & Youth Care Forum*, 26 (4), 247.

Slavin, R. (1991). Synthesis of research on cooperative learning. *Educational Leadership*, February, 71–82.

Smith, P. (1996). Strategies of co-operation: A commentary. *International Journal of Behavioral Development*, 19 (1), 81–87.

Smith, P., & Connolly, K. J. (1980). *The ecology of preschool behaviour*. Cambridge, MA: Cambridge University Press.

Stambak, M., Barrière, M., Bonica, L., Maisonnet, R., Musatti, T., Rayna, S., & Verba, M. (1982). *Les bébés entre eux*. Paris: PUF.

Stambak, M., & Sinclair, H. (1993). *Pretend play among 3-year-olds*. Hillsdale, NJ: Erlbaum.

Staub, E. (1989). *The roots of evil: The origins of genocide and other group violence*. Cambridge, MA: Cambridge University Press.

Staub, E. (1991). A conception of the determinants and development of altruism and aggression: Motives, the self, and the environment. In C. Zahan-Waxler, E.M. Cummings, & R. Iannotti (eds), *Altruism and aggression: Biological and social origins* (pp. 135–154). Cambridge: Cambridge University Press.

Triandis, H.C. (1991) Cross-cultural differences in assertiveness/competition vs. group loyalty/cooperation. In R.A. Hinde & J. Groebel (eds), *Cooperation and prosocial behavior*. New York: Cambridge University Press.

Triandis, H.C. (1995). *Individualism and collectivism*. San Francisco: Westview.

Tudge, J., & Rogoff, B. (1989). Peer influences on cognitive development: Piagetian and Vygotskian perspectives. In M.H. Bornstein & J.S. Bruner (eds), *Interaction in human development* (pp. 17–40). Hillsdale, NJ: Erlbaum.

Valsiner, J. (1989). *Human development and culture: The social nature of personality and its study*. Lexington, MA: Lexington.

Valsiner, J. (1994). Culture and human development: A co-constructivist perspective. In P. van Geert & L. Mos (eds), *Annals of Theoretical Psychology* (Vol. 10). New York: Plenum.

Valsiner, J. (1997). *Culture and the development of children's actions* (2nd edn). New York: Wiley.

Valsiner, J. (1998). *The guided mind.* Cambridge, MA: Harvard University Press.

Valsiner, J. (2000). *Culture and human development.* London: Sage.

Valsiner, J., Branco, A.U., & Dantas, C. (1997). Socialization as co-construction: Parental belief orientations and heterogeneity of reflection. In J.E. Grusec & L. Kuczynski (eds), *Parenting and children's internalization of values.* New York: Wiley.

Valsiner, J., & Cairns, R. (1992). Theoretical perspectives on conflict and development. In C.V. Shantz & W.W. Hartup (eds), *Conflict in child and adolescent development.* New York: Cambridge University Press.

Verba, M. (1994). The beginnings of collaboration in peer interaction. *Human Development*, 37, 125–139.

Vygotsky, L.S. (1978). *Mind in society.* Cambridge, MA: Harvard University Press.

Vygotsky, L.S. (1987). *Thinking and speech* (ed. and trans. N. Minick). New York: Plenum.

Wallat, C., & Green, J. (1979). Social rules and communicative contexts in kindergarten. *Theory into Practice*, 18 (4), 275–284.

Wertsch, J.W. (1998). *Mind as action.* New York: Oxford University Press.

Whiting, B.B., & Edwards, C.P. (1988). *Children of different worlds: The formation of social behavior.* Cambridge, MA: MIT Press.

Whiting, B., & Whiting, J. (1975). *Children of six cultures.* Cambridge, MA: Harvard University Press.

Wilson, E.O. (1975). *Sociobiology: The new synthesis.* Cambridge, MA: Belknap Press of Harvard University Press.

Winegar, L.T. (1997). Developmental research and comparative perspectives: Applications to developmental science. In J. Tudge, M.J. Shanahan, & J. Valsiner (eds), *Comparisons in human development: Understanding time and context.* New York: Cambridge University Press.

12

Strengths and Weaknesses of Cognition over Preschool Years

EDUARDO MARTÍ

Preschool children are excellent candidates to illustrate the prototypical image of the infantile mind. They are known to be imaginative and playful and also not very rigorous. This picture, however, is only partially true. In contrast with infants, preschool-aged children's cognition is much more comprehensive. New representational capabilities, clearly highlighted by the development of language and symbolic play, enable the child to create a new imaginary world. Although it is a world of fantasy, it also contains a great deal of organized knowledge about reality as well as a mode of reasoning which often surprises adults by being precise in its inventiveness. In contrast with that, when early childhood cognition is compared to school-age children's, the former is fragile as it is undergoing transition. The preschooler's method of reasoning is not always logical, their explanations are often subjective and there is a lack of stability in their knowledge.

The following examples highlight the contrast between the strength and fragility of preschoolers' minds:

- Anna, a 4-year-old girl, prefers that her mother cuts a rectangular piece of cake lengthwise – rather than breadthwise – in order to get bigger pieces.
- Nicholas, a 3-year-old boy, asks his mother why his blood does not come out from his mouth when he opens it.
- Joe, a 3-year-old boy, calls elevators 'flying wardrobes'.
- Isabel, a 4-year-old girl, thinks that the word for car must be longer than the word for banana.
- Carlos, a 3-year-old boy, says that thunders have big mouths because they make a lot of noise
- Nora, a 5-year-old girl, tells her sister that the box of candies is empty because she does not want her to find them.
- Chris, a 3-year-old boy, thinks that guns are alive because they fire.

As a matter of fact, the most productive research on early childhood cognition over recent decades has fluctuated between the Piagetian and the information processing approaches. In the 1960s and the 1970s, the Piagetian view prevailed. Early childhood cognition was defined by a preoperational stage, as a set of incompetences such as precausal reasoning, lack of mobility and egocentrism. Preschoolers' cognition was conceptualized as a transition stage between infants' cognition (of a sensoriomotor and nonsymbolic nature) and the school-age children's cognition, basically understood as the ability to mentally operate in a logical manner (concrete operations).

Piaget's view was very productive, and it revolutionized the field of childhood cognition, although it yielded a negative picture of preschoolers' competencies. Further studies mainly based on the information processing theories showed a more positive picture. Children aged between 2 and 6 years not only learn a great amount of factual knowledge that works as a solid basis for reasoning but also develop a set of complex skills in reasoning and logic. Among these skills, the ability to assign mental states to others and reason about them soon stood out in the research field. The potential to elaborate a theory of mind, understood as the knowledge that enables people to understand some fundamentally human phenomena such as an intention, a lie or a wish, has become a clear characteristic of preschool children.

Although it may apparently seem contradictory, any synthetic view of the main cognitive acquisitions between ages 2 and 6 must include both approaches. Given the complexity and the variety of knowledge available, the goal of this review is not comprehensiveness; instead, we have chosen those aspects that, according to our view, best explain the complexity of the preschooler's mind. Therefore the chapter is organized according to the useful distinction – although too simple for some readers – between structure and content. Since the study of cognition is characterized by many theoretical shades as well as by a broad conceptual diversity, this distinction is very useful for a structured approach to the preschool mind. Contrary to what a naive realistic approach might claim, it is clear to us that all thoughts refer to a content, and therefore content cannot exist unattached to a structure. In spite of that, they may be approached separately. When attention is paid to children's reasoning, to their logic, to the mode of organizing their perception or to their capacity to solve problems, the structural aspect is being prioritized. Most studies within the Piagetian view prioritize this aspect, although they also provide a lot of data about content knowledge. What really matters in these studies is how knowledge is structured rather than the content *per se*. More recent studies on reasoning and problem solving have also contributed to give us a picture of the child as a thinker (DeLoache, Miller, & Pierroutsakos, 1998).

In contrast to that, if the focus is on knowledge acquired by children in different domains, on its organization (categories, scripts) and on how it changes with time, then what is being prioritized is the content of cognition. As a paradigmatic case, and in the section on the content of cognition, we will include the knowledge that preschool children have about people from a theory of mind perspective. The latter view will deal with the conceptualization of the child as a theorist rather than the description of the preschoolers' mode of thinking.

It is only for conceptual and practical reasons that early childhood will be considered a unitary period. It is obvious that there are noticeable differences between a 2- and a 6-year-old child, although these differences become less obvious when both children are compared to a 1-year-old baby or to an 8-year-old boy. Therefore, apart from pointing out the differences between stages, the progress within a stage will also be highlighted when necessary. Also, and as much as possible, we will identify the main change mechanisms that explain the progress of cognition in this period. We will also comment on some of the best known research paradigms used by psychologists to display children's cognition at the preschool stage.

The Child as a Thinker

At the end of infancy, at around 18 months, there is a qualitative change in children's cognition. Although this change is explained differently by different theoretical perspectives, all psychologists agree that such change takes place. It basically consists of a new capacity to represent the real world that enables children to create and manipulate signs and interiorized actions (schemes) which intercede with the relationship between the child and the world. This relationship – direct in the case of infants – becomes mediated through language and symbolic play. Mediation entails representation. Thanks to this new representational capability, children's thinking becomes qualitatively transformed. The child's mind stops being restricted to the here-and-now, and becomes capable of simultaneously representing different situations of the past, future, or other contexts.

Limitations: Preoperational Way of Thinking

In spite of this conclusive progress, preschoolers' thinking presents important limitations when it is compared to older children's. So far, Piaget's work (1973) offers the most comprehensive picture of preschool cognition, although some aspects of his theory are controversial.

Through various dialogues about everyday situations, and especially through simple problem solving events, Piaget demonstrated that preschoolers' thinking is far from showing the logic and accuracy that characterize the thinking of a school-aged child. The explanations – frequently imaginative – offered by preschool children to explain the origin and nature of their dreams, of names, of thoughts, of the wind and the trees are based, according to Piaget (1929), on an illogical and egocentric mode of thinking. For instance, children think that the moon follows them, that there are big mountains for long strolls and small mountains for short strolls, that the shadow of a tree is the same shadow as the shadow of a table, or that we think with our mouth. Along these lines, when children are asked to explain physical phenomena such as forces, weight or movement, they come up with incomplete explanations in which cause and effect are often confounded. Children are closer to magic or finalist explanations than to logical explanations based on clear cause and effect relationships. That's why Piaget (1930) called them 'precausal'.

According to this author, this genuine mode of thinking is explained by the absence of true mental operations. School-aged children are able to think logically and rigorously because their interaction with the real world is mediated by mental operations. Piaget claims that operations are not isolated schemata. They are action schemata organized into a system of relations. The properties of this system, which Piaget called *groupement* (grouping), are the following:

1 Two consecutive actions can be coordinated into one.
2 The action schema becomes reversible.
3 The same point can be reached in different ways.
4 Going back to the starting point enables finding it identical.
5 When the same action is repeated, it can either add nothing or have an accumulative effect (Piaget, 1973).

The power of operational thinking comes from the possibility to relate action schemata among themselves – a relationship that preschoolers are unable to establish.

The main characteristic of operations is their reversible and relational character. A mental action is reversible when it can be related with another operation that compensates or cancels it. For instance, the operation that compares two lengths and establishes the statement that 'the first one is longer' can be related with the reciprocal operation that establishes that 'the second one is shorter'. Likewise, the operation that mentally gathers two sets of objects can be compensated by the operation that separates them. This capability to apply and relate two reversible mental operations – prototypical of older children – facilitates a radically different way of solving problems.

In contrast, preschoolers base their reasoning on intuitions, defined as isolated, nonreversible mental actions that are hardly coordinated. Therefore, preschool thinking presents some peculiarities defined and illustrated as follows.

Centration Focus of attention is only a single, salient aspect of reality. Other features of reality, though important, may be ignored. Thus, when the task requires comparing different features, children's answers are often inaccurate. In contrast, older children tend to make a more complete and a more decentralized perceptual analysis.

For example, when a bunch of flowers with three daisies and two roses is presented to a preschooler in order to compare the class with one of the subclasses, he or she is unable to relate both categories at the same time. When asked, 'Which are there more of, flowers or daisies?', they focus on the subsets only and claim that there are more daisies than flowers. Actually, they compare the two subclasses with each other but not with the class. Preschoolers' thinking does not have enough mobility to take into consideration that daisies and roses are likewise flowers.

Egocentrism The interpretation of the world is done from the point of view of the self. Preschool children tend to think that their point of view is the same as others'. That is to say, they confound their particular and subjective view with a more relativist view because they are not yet aware of their own wishes and ideas. Egocentrism is directly related with the above-mentioned tendency to centration. It consists of a centration subjected (or subdued) to the child's point of view. For Piaget, egocentrism comes from an excessive centration in one's own point of view. It is an unconscious tendency: the child is not aware of his/her own subjectivity. It will be overcome when a higher mobility of the child's thinking relates different ways of looking at the same reality (Piaget, 1973).

For example, in a task that shows a landscape with three cardboard mountains, preschool children have difficulty imagining that another person sitting in front of them can see the mountains differently. Therefore they think that others' points of view agree with theirs.

Importance of Perceptive Appearances Preschool-age children find it difficult to infer relationships that go beyond perceptual appearances. There is a strong tendency to base their thinking on what is apparent rather than just taking it as a starting point to infer new information from there. Preschoolers ensure that things are the way they think they appear to be, and thus their statements are normally based on appearances.

For instance, two sticks of the same length and superposed are presented to the child. As soon as the child says that they are the same length, one of the sticks is moved toward one side and the child is then asked if the sticks are the same length or if one is longer than the other. The prototypical response of a preschool child is to conclude that since one of the sticks gets further to the side and seems longer, it is actually longer.

Importance of States Many of our everyday situations involve static information (about states) only related to processes to explain the change of such states (transformations). Preschool children show a tendency to focus their attention on the states rather than on the transformations that yield these states, and consequently on the present rather than on the past or future states.

For example, in a task to decide what car is faster, preschoolers take their decision based on the final state (i.e. the car that has got further away is the fastest car) and they tend to ignore other conditions of the task (e.g. the car that has driven a further distance or the car that began to move earlier).

According to Piaget, the above-mentioned characteristics of preschool children's thinking are closely related and they provide evidence for an absence of true mental operations.

The Conservation Principle

The best illustration for preoperational thinking is the well known conservation tasks set. With these tasks Piaget showed an essential finding: the conservation principle – very basic in human reasoning – is a very slow construction. Also, with the finding that this construction is achieved at the end of the preschool period, Piaget provided evidence for one of the most important limitations of preschoolers' thinking.

All conservation tasks hold the same logic. A child is presented with two identical magnitudes (matter, liquid, length, number, area or volume). One of the magnitudes is perceptually manipulated and the child is asked whether the magnitude is still the same. In general, preschool children have more difficulty than school children to conclude that the two magnitudes are the same in spite of the manipulation. Figure 12.1 shows some examples of quantity conservation.

Let's take the example of liquid conservation. Although preschool children accept that the two identical beakers contain the same amount of liquid, they tend to focus on the appearances when they have to tell which of the two beakers has more liquid (the thin or the wide). Children at this age normally answer that the thin beaker contains more liquid because it seems to contain more. They centrate in only one dimension (in this example, the height), ignoring the other one (the width). Children do not relate the final state with the initial one. Their thinking does not succeed in compensating the two dimensions (it is higher, but it is narrower, too) or in mentally canceling the transformation (if the liquid is poured back to the first beaker, there will be the same amount of liquid).

One of the unexpected findings in Piaget's theory is that children from the same culture reach the conservation principle at different ages depending on whether it refers to length, weight, volume or surface. For instance, in European societies the conservation of number, length, liquid or mass appears at around age 6, whereas conservation of area and weight

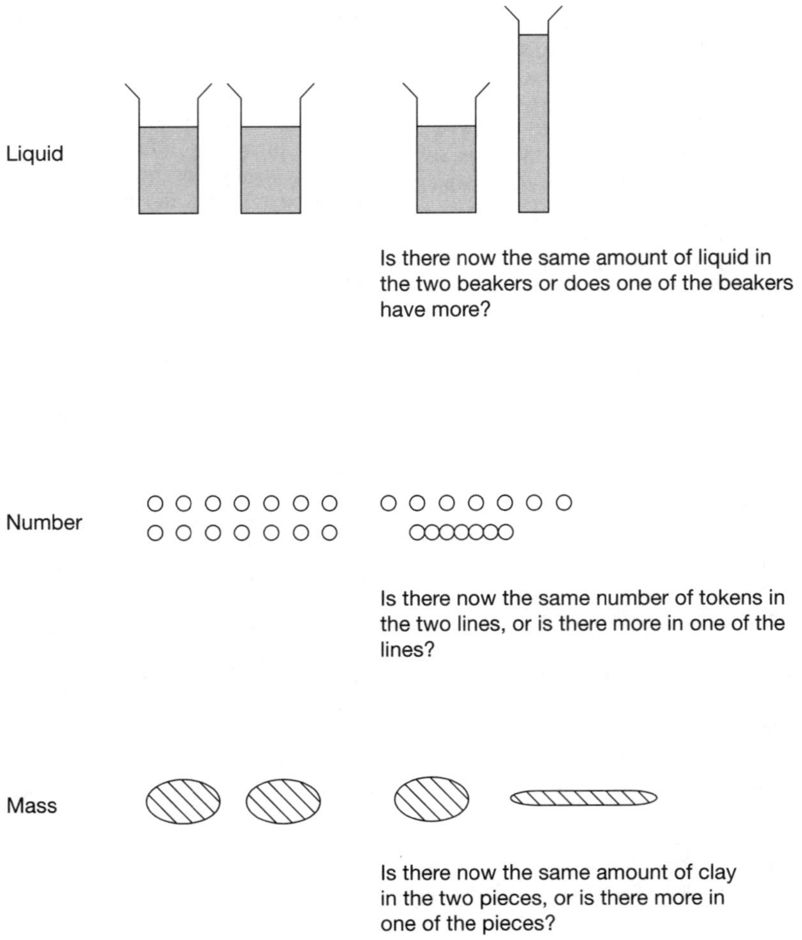

Figure 12.1 *Conservation of quantity*

normally appears at around 8 and finally volume at around 11.

This finding not only points to the general nature of the Piagetian theory, but also reveals that other factors such as children's knowledge about different phenomena can play an important role in development. Later we will analyze the explanation given by other approaches to this finding.

How does Piaget explain the change in the mode of thinking and reasoning between preschool and school children? In contrast with most psychologists, Piaget suggests a general model to explain cognitive changes. According to him, the change mechanisms must be searched for neither in maturational nor in social, cultural or learning factors. Although he does not underestimate these changing factors, Piaget claims the importance of an internal, non-innate factor that would be closely related to the activity involved in the subject's interaction with the world. Piaget (1977) called this factor the equilibration process. The equilibration process must be understood as a set of cognitive regulations activated by subjects to compensate those perturbations that arise in their relation with the world: a new object that cannot be directly assimilated by the action schema, an anticipation disconfirmed by evidence, a new aspect of reality that does not fit with previous theories, etc. In all these cases, new actions are produced in order to eliminate the disequilibrium often taken as a cognitive conflict.

These regulations can be very different depending on the subject's developmental stage. When a baby finds a new object and wants to reach it, s/he will have to regulate his/her action to adapt it to the new object. This new object causes a disequilibrium and the baby's natural tendency to compensate it arises (Piaget, 1952). Older children face another type of disequilibrium. For instance, when a child is presented with a liquid conservation task, s/he thinks there is more in one beaker because it is taller. However, when the child realizes that the beaker is also narrower, a perturbation appears. The cognitive regulation consists in coordinating two relationships: 'taller, then more liquid' and 'narrower, then less liquid'. This possibility to relate two different aspects of reality enables the child to overcome the disequilibrium (Piaget, 1977).

The goal is always the same: to reach a cognitively more stable relationship with the world. The step from an irreversible thinking to a reversible one is a good example of the equilibration process. The capability of the child to understand that any operation can be compensated or canceled by another one is a progress in terms of equilibrium. As soon as children become able to make reversible operations, their understanding of phenomena will become more stable and will not depend so much on perceptual changes.

We hope that this short description may help in an appreciation of the relevance of Piaget's theoretical contribution. The uniqueness of his theory lies in the fact that it breaks the traditional dichotomy between biology and culture. Piaget emphasizes the importance of the activity of the subject, which becomes the leading actor in his/her own development, modeling the biological and sociocultural factors. Contrastingly, the weakness of this argument lies in the fact that the construct is too imprecise and lacks empirical support.

Piaget's approach offers a coherent and theoretically well founded view of the main characteristics of preschool children's thinking and its development. Most of his findings have stood the test of time, although they have been interpreted differently by different perspectives, especially by the information processing approach. Recent studies, improved with more precise and rigorous research designs, offer a more positive picture of preschool children's cognitive competencies. Some empirical studies on the conservation tasks, for instance, show that many preschool children succeed in giving the right answer either when the task is simplified or when it provides some hints (Siegler, 1991). Along this line, a basic comprehension of the causality principle may appear if the experimental situation is presented more concisely (Gelman & Kremer, 1991). Later, we will also discuss how the theory of mind research argues against preschool egocentrism and the difficulties of distinguishing between appearance and reality.

It must be highlighted that, contrary to what many parents, educators and psychologists would like, the main issue is not whether a skill appears at age 4 or at 7 but whether the different variables that contribute to make a skill appear sooner or later. What really matters is to identify the basic cognitive developmental tendencies and to explain them. Piaget himself kept insisting on the negative consequences of treating the cognitive developmental stages too rigidly from a chronological point of view.

Numerous post-Piagetian studies have suggested alternative explanations for Piaget's developmental trends, providing new ways to better understand the preschool mind. Whereas Piaget's view is normative and generalist, recent research indicates a less clear view among researchers. On the one hand, researchers use non-normative explanations which imply less logic in viewing children's competencies. Younger children are not so illogical, and older children's and adults' logic is not so perfect, as previously thought

On the other hand, post-Piagetian studies emphasize the importance of knowledge acquired in specific domains which they claim helps them reach higher success rates when they reason and solve specific domain problems. Contrary to what Piaget pointed out, limitations of the cognition of the preschool child cannot be totally attributed to a weakness in logic due to the absence of mental operations. These limitations can also be attributed to some shortcomings in the amount of knowledge acquired by the child about a given topic. What had been taken as evidence of structural deficits has turned out to stem instead from knowledge deficits.

The information processing approach provides evidence that explains some of the reasoning difficulties displayed in Piaget's research. It offers a different picture – often more precise than the one given by Piaget – of the preschooler's cognitive skills as well as of the change mechanisms.

Achievements in Thinking and Problem Solving: Overcoming the Limitations of Processing

One of the main characteristics of the human mind is its limited capacity to choose and select information. The number of units of information which it can attend to and process simultaneously is limited. Cognitive operations such as coding, comparing and retrieving stored information from memory require time. From this perspective, when a child has to solve a task, the chances to succeed depend not only on structural limitations in his/her mode of thinking, as Piaget suggested, but also on overcoming processing limitations. Differences between the preschool child and the school child might be due to a change in their capacity to overcome these processing limitations. It is possible, for instance, that a 5-year-old child says that the thin beaker has more liquid than the wide one because s/he cannot select and relate the two dimensions (width and height) simultaneously. This interpretation has been made plausible by research that shows that either simplification of those aspects of the task that are not essential, or making the elements of the task more familiar and significant to the child, increases the chances of success (Flavell, 1985). Actually, both actions reduce the task demands and therefore increase the capacity of the child to process information more efficiently.

From the information processing perspective, the preschool- and the school-aged children's cognition entails more continuity than that claimed by Piaget. Also, preschool children's cognitive skills are claimed to depend on many factors and cannot be considered homogeneous, which from Piaget's view would correspond to the preoperational logic. Thus, the cognitive differences between a 4- and an 8-year-old child would not be as clear-cut as Piaget described, since they would depend on how the processing limitations were overcome. This, in its turn, would depend on factors related to the task and previous experience.

Changes in Attention and Perception

It is obvious that attention and perception play a crucial role in solving many cognitive tasks. Selection and control of attention are a prerequisite to succeed in those tasks in which the essential elements must be distinguished from the inessential ones. In addition to that, perception is basic for activities such as categorization, which is essential to introduce a given order in the informational diversity. The important role of attention and perception is easily seen in activities such as reading, language comprehension, spatial orientation, and habit formation.

From a general point of view, both processes – attention and perception – make great progress during the preschool period. In spite of this progress, the preschool child's attention is more whimsical and changeable than the schooler's, which is readily noticeable by parents and educators in their everyday activities with young ones. Preschoolers have difficulty in voluntarily focusing their attention on specific aspects and get easily distracted when other stimuli are present. They are slower and less precise than older children when they have to block their attention to discard non-pertinent stimuli. Also, when they look at a complex stimulus, their exploration process is neither systematic nor complete. In a classic experiment, Vurpillot and Ball (1979) showed these shortcomings when children of different ages had to identify which one of the stimuli representing schematic drawings of houses were identical. They found that it was not until age 9 years that children proceeded with a systematic and exhaustive visual exploration to determine whether the houses were identical or not. The same pattern was found in another study (Enns & Akhtar, 1989) in which children had to identify a series of geometrical symbols that were confounded with other symbols that appeared on a computer screen. A distinguishing aspect of preschool and school-age children's performance is that the former are incapable of anticipating which features of the task are relevant and which are not. This was found in a study in which children of different ages had to fit animal drawings according to different criteria (color, shape, or size) (Pick & Frankel, 1973). In contrast with school-age children, preschool-age children neither improved their performance when they anticipated the criterion, nor showed control in selective attention.

Similarity relationships play an essential role in category formation and inference making. This skill is already present in young babies and it progresses clearly during the preschool period. In this period, children are very imaginative in managing the similarities observed in objects and events seen in their environment to use the same word for different situations or to create new denominations for unknown objects. A 2-year-old boy may call a 'windmill' a 'starfish', and a 3-year-old boy may call a 'hat' a 'lampshade'. This may be taken as evidence for an early skill to build metaphors (Martí, 1986).

Similarity relationships are also basic for making inferences. In some empirical studies (Florian, 1994; López et al., 1992) children of different ages were asked to determine whether different stimuli shared characteristics that were not directly visible. They showed that children from 3 to 6 years of age expect entities that look alike to share other non-obvious characteristics as well. Other studies (Deloache, Miller, & Pierroutsakos, 1998) have shown that the flexibility that preschool children show in selecting which aspect of similarity to attend to depends on the task demands and the contextual variables. The importance of perceptual aspects as a basis to make judgments is consistent with preschool children's cognitive pattern described by Piaget. However, it is not clear that this pattern can be explained by the step from a perceptual to a more conceptual mode of thinking based on more elaborated processes. Some investigations point out that differences in children's reliance on perceptual variables might be attributed to differences in the extent of their knowledge of which attributes are relevant in a domain task (Gelman & Medin, 1993; Jones & Smith, 1993). As knowledge in a given domain increases, children have more resources and criteria to base their judgments on pertinent perceptive relations, and they become more able to discard accidental information. The acquisition of domain specific knowledge plays an important role in children's thinking. As will be discussed in the next section, this knowledge is acquired gradually during early childhood.

Symbolic Relations in Thinking

One of the most important milestones in preschool development is the possibility to understand and use symbols. Symbol systems, whether they are produced by the child or transmitted by culture, constitute powerful means that deeply modify the mode of thinking (Vygotsky, 1978). Symbols expand the realm of thinking by enabling children to represent, draw inferences from, and make predictions about objects and events they have never directly experienced. In this review we will refer to external and nonlinguistic symbols (pictures, small scale models, notations) while other symbolic relations will be considered in other chapters.

During their first year of age, babies do not seem to be interested in images at all. The same applies to other symbols displayed in different formats. They treat them like any other object, more or less interesting depending on their intrinsic properties. It is not until the second half of the second year that symbols are seen differently because they become representative objects. Children's interest increases as they begin to interpret simple graphic images (Perner, 1991). They become aware that symbols have a meaning that goes beyond their physical properties. Symbols represent something that is absent. The comprehension and use of symbols progress spectacularly during the preschool period, setting up an essential basis for most school learning and, from a more general point of view, facilitating children's adaptation to the cultural context.

The understanding of symbols' representational nature is not an easy task. The symbolic relationship is never totally transparent. Its interpretation requires a long elaboration that involves other people capable of making that interpretation. In spite of the fact that the first intuition that something stands for something else may be an early acquisition, younger preschoolers may demonstrate symbol–referent confusion. This confusion is present in both the iconic and the arbitrary symbols (writing or numerical notations). Beilin and Pearlman (1991) reported that preschool children occasionally believe that a picture shares the properties of its referent (a picture of an ice cream cone would be cold, or a photograph of a rose would smell sweet). In another study, Leben and Downs (1991) reported that preschool children rejected many of the experimenter's suggestions about the identity of particular features in a map or in an aerial photograph because they were not sufficiently similar to their referents. Similar symbol–referent confusions occur with respect to writing. For example, preschool children expect the size of an object to be reflected in the size of the word (Bialystok, 1991).

In spite of these difficulties in understanding the representational nature of symbols, preschool children clearly distinguish different symbolic systems and treat them as peculiar objects that present certain formal properties. One of the early distinctions is between iconic and arbitrary symbols. In a recognition and classification task, 3-year-old children clearly set aside drawings from writing and numerals (Martí, 1999). When 4- and 5-year-old children are asked to produce writing, numerals and drawings, although they cannot yet write, they make different marks for drawing and for arbitrary symbols. They are able to capture the regularities that are specific for each system. For instance, the lines in the drawing are continuous whereas the lines in writing and numerals are discontinuous; the marks of the drawing are randomly distributed whereas the writing and numerals are lined up. They become progressively able to differentiate (in classification and production tasks) writing from numerals as they begin to capture the properties that differentiate one system from the other. For instance, (1) repetition of the same element is not allowed in writing whereas the numeral notation system allows it; (2) in the writing notation system there most be a minimal number of elements together for the resulting unit – the word – to have meaning whereas two or three digits together are sufficient to construct a meaningful numeral (Brenneman et al., 1996; Ferreiro, 1988; Sinclair, 1991). This basic knowledge will be essential in the development of literacy, one of the most important acquisitions in the school period.

On the other hand it is worth mentioning that children are able to interpret and use the main symbol systems in their reasoning or for problem solving before they learn them at the school. This is clear in the case of iconic symbols. Some studies have shown that between ages 2 and 3 children begin to use the information in a picture, a drawing or a scale model to infer information about the referent.

In one of these studies, the child watches an experimenter hiding a tiny plastic dog (Little Snoopy) somewhere in a scale model of the room. The child is told that Little Snoopy will be hidden in the same place as in the big room. The child is asked to find Little Snoopy in the room using the information available from the scale model. Three-year-old children were able to solve the task successfully (DeLoache & Burns, 1993). However, the rate of success depends on both the type of symbol used (picture, drawing, scale model) and the perceptual characteristics that relate the symbol with the referent. Around 3, children are able to use iconic symbolic relations to infer new knowledge. The same applies to the arbitrary sign systems, although in this case development is slower because the interpretation of the symbolic relationship is more laborious and needs specific formal learning. Preschool children can use some of the properties of the numerical notation system to infer new information. For example, they know the bus route by its number; they know what direction to go when they see the house number; and they know that a numeral with many digits indicates a bigger amount than a numeral with few digits (Sinclair, 1991). Something similar is claimed to happen with writing (Ferreiro & Teberosky, 1979).

Strategic Thinking: The Case of Number

We have just seen how preschool children use symbols to widen their knowledge about the real world. The use of symbolic means can be seen as a powerful tool to overcome the mind processing shortcomings and preschool children begin to exploit this potentiality. The other way to help overcoming the mind processing limitations is the use of strategies. It is clear that in order to be efficient when we solve a problem, it is necessary to display a sequence of actions – procedures – adapted to the task demands. The use and the variety of strategies depends not only on the task difficulty but also on the knowledge children have about that particular domain. In spite of the fact that this development gets consolidated during the school period and that it is closely related to formal training, children in the preschool period begin to acquire strategies to solve problems in particular domains.

The development of numerical skills in early childhood has always been a central topic for various reasons. On the one hand, it shows the essential nature of human cognition, its great adaptive relevance that leans on different symbolic systems transmitted through culture (the name and the writing of the numerals). It is important to know the development of these skills before the child gets involved in formal school learning which will clearly widen his/her numerical knowledge. On the other hand, previous research along with Piaget's view claims that numerical knowledge acquisition requires the conservation principle. Nevertheless, as we will see further below, there are other specific principles developed during the preschool period that lead to number comprehension and show the great diversity of strategies when children count and solve problems.

At first sight, preschool children seem hardly competent to count and solve numerical problems. They get involved very easily (counting, comparing amounts, showing their age with their fingers, telling what has more objects, etc.), but they tend to make many mistakes. From Piaget's findings, we know now that a simple change in the arrangement of elements is sufficient for a 5-year-old child to deny that there is the same number of elements in both collections. We have all observed how difficult it is for a 3- to 4-year-old child to count a series of elements. They are likely to skip a word in the sequence; they might skip or count twice the same element in the set, and they tend to only count small amounts. However, this is not a real picture. Contrary to the belief that true numerical knowledge does not appear until the school period, different studies have shown an interesting development in early childhood. Around 2 years of age, children begin to use numbers as symbols and they connect words with the elements they count. At the beginning, the relationship between counting actions and words is not guaranteed. Saxe, Guberman, and Gearhart (1987) asked 2½- and 4-year-old children to count two collections of drawn dots (one with five dots and the other with 13). More concretely, they were asked to count the dots and touch them one by one as they counted them. The younger kids could understand the task, but they made many errors. They forgot pointing out many of the dots and they also applied rigid and insufficient sequences of words to both collections. To contrast with that, all 4-year-old children could perfectly count the five-dot set, although they made a few errors in the 13-dot set (a mean of two errors in both pointing out and verbal counting conditions).

What are the principles on which 4-year-old children's numerical skills are based that enable them to count so efficiently? In a classic study, Gelman (1982; Gelman & Gallistel, 1978) claims that the principles that lead preschoolers' numerical competencies are displayed in tasks in which the child is asked to count under given conditions. For instance, in one of the tasks (Gelman, 1980), children between 3 and 6 had to compare collections of mice and decide which had more elements ('the winner set'). In some conditions, same-length files had to be compared, one containing two mice and the other containing three. In other conditions, the distance between mice was identical so the file with three mice was longer than the file with two. The initial task was to decide which file was the winner (always

Table 12.1 *Five basic counting principles*

The one-by-one principle
The child successively assigns the name of a different number, and only one name to each one of the items counted. Although preschool children make some errors that violate this principle due to information processing overload (especially when they count long series), there is evidence that they have some implicit comprehension of the principle.
The stable order principle
Children always recite the names of the numbers in the same order. Although preschool children can recite names that do not correspond to the exact number (they may count, for instance, 'one, two, three, four, eight, ten, eleven'), they normally follow the same order in different counting activities.
The cardinal principle
The name of the uttered number at the end of a sequence corresponds to the cardinal value of the series. As with the first principle, the processing demands when they count can interfere with the correct use of this principle. If these demands are controlled (for instance asking another person to count), 3-year-old children know how many items are in a set by correctly identifying the last word uttered with the amount.
The abstraction principle
All discrete quantities are susceptible of being counted, whether it be events, animate objects, inanimate objects or abstract entities. When preschool children start counting, they do not seem to exclude any object, and they are not concerned with the heterogeneity of the things they count. They are treated as if they were identical.
The order irrelevance principle
When counting, the order in which the objects are numbered does not matter. Three-year-old children already have a certain implicit knowledge of this principle, although it is not until they are 5 that they display their explicit knowledge and can count series of items in any order.

Source: Gelman (1982)

the file with three mice) and which one was the loser (always the one with two mice). After a few tests, the experimenter changed the winner file before showing it to the child (she would either take a mouse off the winner file, making the two files identical, or shorten or enlarge the winner file). Unexpectedly, even 3-year-old kids judged the winner and the loser files in terms of number rather than length or density. According to Gelman, the numerical competency displayed in this task, as well as in other tasks in which children had to count small collections, is based on five principles (see Table 12.1).

Along with these principles, preschool children develop other principles related to numerical reasoning. They know that a simple change in color, identity or position of an item in a collection cannot alter the numerical value of the collection. They also learn that the addition of items increases the numerical value; removing items decreases it; and adding one first and removing it later keeps it identical. Older preschoolers can even use various strategies in problems similar to those encountered at school. Siegler and Jenkins (1989) reported a variety of strategies for solving problems of addition with two addends. Five-year-old children were able to display different strategies according to the type of problem. One of these strategies, the min strategy, involves counting up from the larger of two addends to reach the sum, rather than starting from number one and counting up both addends. After a concentrated experience in solving addition problems, 5-year-old children showed different strategies for adding numbers and were able to generalize their use depending on the type of problem presented. For example, once the min strategy was discovered it was particularly likely to be used on problems (such as 2 + 21) where it saved most of the work.

With development, children become able to elaborate more flexible thinking and successfully solve a greater variety and complexity of problems. Thanks to experimental designs more rigorous than those used by Piaget, we have achieved a more competent picture of preschool children's cognition. In particular, the emphasis on the information processing itself and its limitations has made it possible to determine with greater detail the causes of progress and the reasons for insufficiencies.

The Child as a Theorist

When the emphasis is not on thinking and reasoning but on the content of preschool thoughts, we get a different picture. In this case, the emphasis is on the knowledge and theories about different aspects of reality held by children and on how this knowledge is organized and how it changes. These issues are obviously related to what we have seen so far. As a matter of fact, one of the tendencies displayed by research on preschool cognition shows that changes in the knowledge base affect dramatically preschool children's reasoning and problem solving. Reciprocally, it could be said (although it would be difficult to find empirical evidence) that changes in thinking structure and logic may affect the likelihood of acquiring new knowledge. What we include in the next section is a synthesis of those aspects that, in our view, better define preschool children's cognition when the emphasis is put on the content on which the mind works.

Changes in Knowledge: Cognitive Consequences

Children between 2 and 6 acquire a great amount of knowledge about different aspects of reality. Long before they organize and increase this knowledge through formal learning in school, their interaction with the physical and social environment in everyday life is an endless source of knowledge. At these ages, children are tremendously curious and their willingness to know new things can surprise many parents. Children ask a lot of questions that involve a great variety of subjects. Some children can become true experts in those topics in which they are interested. In a classic work (Chi, 1978), expertise-related differences have been advanced to account for some of the differences in thinking between children and adults. The same applies when children of different ages are compared. Many studies have yielded findings that show that the acquisition of specific domain knowledge in early childhood exerts powerful effects on cognition. This tendency will be illustrated with three research examples on knowledge organization, memory and planning. These examples show that the knowledge held by subjects in their early childhood may increase their success in skills showing a deficit.

First, knowledge organization in preschoolers can be less complex than in schoolers. This difference can be explained in part by the greater amount of knowledge that school children may have about a specific domain topic. From a general point of view, expert knowledge is better organized than that of a novice. Chi and Koeske (1983) described the knowledge structure of one 4½-year-old dinosaur expert. They showed that this knowledge was much more integrated and cohesive for familiar than for unfamiliar dinosaurs.

Second, young children's memory activities tend to be fragile and are restricted to limited domains. Nevertheless, one of the techniques that has been used to demonstrate early competence is situating the experiment in a familiar context. Somerville, Wellman, and Cultice (1983) explored young children's prospective memory for everyday activities (the ability to plan ahead and keep in mind a particular event). Two- to 4-year-old children were instructed to carry out a particular activity at a specified future time. The event to be remembered was either one that was highly appealing to the child (e.g. getting candy) or one that would be of little interest (e.g. getting the wash out of the washer). There was better memory at all ages for the interesting event.

Third, planning how to solve a problem and monitoring and correcting the solution process tend to be difficult for preschool children. The extent to which young children plan is greatly affected by different factors such as the familiarity of the problem-solving task. Hudson, Shapiro, and Sosa (1995) studied children's event representation of familiar activities such as going to the beach or going grocery shopping. They also asked them how one might remedy various mishaps that might occur in these contexts (forgetting the grocery list, not having enough money, forgetting lunch or having your castle knocked down by the waves). Most 3-year-olds were able to generate a plan to remedy the two beach mishaps, but it was not until age 4 that most children could describe a plan to remedy the two grocery shopping mishaps. This difference can be explained in terms of the frequency with which children at these ages participate in activities related with one of the contexts (grocery and beach).

Knowledge Organization

At first, the knowledge of a preschooler may seem confused, fragile and unstructured. Many data originating in the Piagetian tradition described in the first section of this chapter confirm this impression. However, new findings indicate that preschool knowledge is better organized than was initially thought. Neither of the two extreme pictures is probably right: on the one hand a fragile and confused preschooler, on the other a child whose knowledge is as solid as an adult's. As we have claimed in this chapter, preschool children's cognition includes a very particular mixture of competencies and limitations. The conceptual categories of preschool children help them not only to put the world in order in a stable manner but also to establish new relationships and inferences. Their knowledge in 'scene' or 'script' formats facilitates their memory, and helps to plan their actions and anticipate events. Obviously, if we compare the knowledge organization of the preschooler's mind with the mind of a schooler, we find some differences, but the basic form of knowledge does not seem to be modified from one period to the other. What really changes is the articulation and the flexibility between different types of knowledge as well as the higher conscience, which helps the child assess and regulate his/her cognitive activities more precisely.

Numerous studies on categorization in early childhood show some interesting findings that conform to the taxonomic assumption. During the preschool years, the global categories change. Children form many categories at a basic level (e.g. dog, chair). These categories are at an intermediate level between the superordinate (animal, furniture) and the subordinate categories (e.g. collie, recliner). The grouping of elements in superordinate categories is more difficult than it seems to be in basic-level categories except for those cases in which the elements that have to be classified clearly share common elements (i.e. the case of cow, bear and deer but not the case of cat, fish and snake) (Tversky, 1989). Even 3-year-old children understand that the concept of belonging to a basic category goes beyond simple external appearance. Gelman and Markman (1987) found that it is not even necessary to label the categories. Preschoolers who looked at some drawings without naming them could make inferences about some of the characteristics of the categories beyond the perceptual features. They would attribute common features to a green leaf-shaped insect and to a black beetle although they would not attribute common characteristics to the green insect and the leaf of a tree. However, they are more likely to form categories if the categorization task involves a verbal label. Across a number of different procedures when given a label, preschool children extend it to the object of like kind; without a label, they are more likely to choose a thematically related object (Woodward & Markman, 1998). These findings support the idea – much discussed in the pioneer work on categorization – that preschool children always focus on thematic relations between objects (e.g. dogs and bones, people and cars, babies and bottles). In spite of this interest in thematic relations, young children correctly extend object labels to members of a class, rather than to thematically related objects. These researches yield evidence that young children follow the taxonomic assumption.

In the preschool period, children progress in relating basic categories with superordinate and subordinate ones with increasing confidence. Emergence of knowledge plays an important role in explaining this progress. Other factors are those tied to linguistic learning. Callanan (1989) showed that when parents refer to basic categories, they normally point out the object and name it ('This is a dog'). However, when they name a superordinate category they normally give some additional information ('This is a dog. It is an animal'). These differences were not only noticed by 3-year-old children but also used to decide the category that the new terms of the classification belonged to.

Scripts

Categories are not the only tools used by preschool children to organize their knowledge. There are other methods of organization that develop during the preschool years. Among these, scripts are especially worthy of mention. Many complex and culturally meaningful activities are organized into scripts. These formats of mental organization provide children with a more complex understanding of the culture's basic concepts and ways of doing things. Nelson (1986) suggested that as a result of their participation in routine contexts (lunch, birthday party) preschool children construct a kind of schema for events – scripts – that specify the people who participate in an event, the social role they play, the objects that are used, and the sequence of actions that make up the event. Nelson studied the growth of scripted knowledge by interviewing children and by recording conversations while children play together (see Table 12.2).

Table 12.2 *'Going to the restaurant' (girl aged 4 years 10 months)*

'Okay. Now, first we go to restaurants at nighttime and we, um, and we go and wait for a while, and then the waiter comes and gives us the little stuff with the dinners on it, an then we wait for a little bit, a half an hour or a few minutes or something, and, um, then our pizza comes or anything, and um, . . . Then we eat it, and um, then when we're finished eating the salad that we order we get to eat our pizza when it's done, because we get the salad before the pizza's ready. So then when we're finished with all the pizza and all our salad, we just leave'.

Source: Nelson (1981, p. 103).

The example in Table 12.2 illustrates the general knowledge contained in the script as well as its organization into a general structure similar to that of adults' scripts. An adult's or an older child's script would be more precise and would have additional information (i.e. paying the bill), and it would probably make the goal of some of the actions more explicit (i.e. the reasons for going to a restaurant). However, the general structure is very similar at different ages.

There is evidence that scripts fulfill important cognitive and social functions. Their relevance lies in the fact that they seem to work as guides to action. That is, they are mental representations that tell children what is likely to happen next in familiar circumstances. A second function of scripts is to allow people within a given social group to coordinate more effectively. Scripts are an excellent data base of meanings shared by the members of a given culture. In addition, scripts help children to remember the order of an event sequence and enable them to understand basic causal relations. Remember that the distinction between cause and effect is difficult for preschoolers, especially when the context does not facilitate it. The last function of scripts is to provide a framework within which abstract concepts that apply to many kinds of events can be acquired. When, for example, children acquire scripts for playing with blocks, playing in the sandbox, and playing house, they have the opportunity to subsume the specific examples of play into a general category (Luciarello & Rifkin, 1986).

All these data about knowledge organization show that, in early childhood, children produce a great diversity of knowledge structures – such as the above-mentioned categories and scripts – and they use them to understand and predict the world. The development of these structures improves remarkably during the school period. Therefore, these findings show that the mind of preschool children is more coherent, better organized and less confused than it was thought to be. In addition to that, as we will see in the next section, this knowledge is coordinated in active conceptual systems relative to different foundational knowledge.

Theory of Mind: the Child as a Psychologist

The interest in basic knowledge has been one of the most clear-cut trends in the field of cognitive development in recent years. A claim of this interest is that certain systems of knowledge are especially important to human understanding. Knowledge about plants and animals fosters food gathering, avoiding predators, and maintaining health; knowledge about physical objects allows prediction of the effects of one's own and others' physical actions and the creation and use of tools. The same applies to other foundational knowledge such as language, number, space, morality and psychology. Through the regular and active exploration of the world, preschool children develop complex conceptual systems that contain knowledge as well as specialized explicative principles about different aspects of reality. These conceptual systems that will be deeply transformed through formal learning carried on at the school can be considered as precursors of what is known as lay persons' conceptions: that is, common-sense and intuitive conceptions held by adults about physics, biology or psychology. Piaget and his followers largely contributed to better knowledge of preschoolers' ideas about different aspects of reality (physical, mental, biological or moral reality). Nevertheless, as we have seen in the previous section, Piaget's interest was not so much in the content of this knowledge and its organization but in the general limitations of preschool thinking – limitations that were assumed to be common to any domain of knowledge. According to Piaget, these were the limitations that prevented preschool children from clearly distinguishing different domains (physical, biological and psychological) of knowledge. Many of the explanations given by preschool children and reported in Piaget's work (for instance, the animist explanations) were interpreted as a result of young children's difficulty in clearly distinguishing their inner world (of psychological nature) from the outer world (of physical nature). The preschoolers' egocentrism ends, according to Piaget (1929), as soon as the child becomes able to notice this difference and becomes aware of his/her own subjectivity. At present, preschool children are believed to clearly distinguish between different knowledge domains and to have available explicative principles adapted to each of those domains, especially for psychological knowledge (Wellman & Gelman, 1998).

We have chosen only one of these domains of knowledge, the psychological, to show the spectacular progress children make when they try to understand reality. The development of preschoolers' psychological knowledge is especially interesting for various reasons. First, it is of great adaptive value since it helps children make predictions about other people's behavior that affect their social and communicative skills.

Second, it has been one of the most productive research topics in recent years in developmental psychology. Since the early 1980s, there has been a series of studies grouped under 'theory of mind' whose goal is to investigate young children's understanding of people's mental states (intentions, desires, emotions, beliefs, knowledge) and also the relationships they are able to establish between these mental states and their behavior. These studies have provided surprising data about young children's psychological knowledge.

Third, during the preschool stage the child makes spectacular progress with respect to comprehending the mind in relation to human behavior. Although some of the knowledge and the basic principles about people begin to develop during infancy, it is around 3–4 years that the greatest change is observed (Martí, 1997).

The 'theory of mind' term applied to children's cognition is not free from controversy. Up to what level do 5-year-old children's knowledge and explanatory principles constitute a theory? It is obvious that it is not an explicit scientific theory. It would be absurd to think that preschool children are able to build and manipulate a theory such as the psychological theories held by psychologists. It is more likely to be an everyday 'framework' or 'foundational' theory involving a body of knowledge that has three properties. First, it specifies a set of entities or processes that are found in its domain of application and in no other domain. In effect, entities or processes such as beliefs, desires, emotions, and so forth are found only in the psychological domain. Second, it uses causal principles that are likewise unique to the theory's domain. For example, psychological causality–present in explanations like 'she tried to get it because she wanted it and thought she could get it' – is only relevant in the domain of the psychological; physical objects are not caused to move by such mental states. Third, this body of knowledge comprises a system of interrelated concepts and beliefs rather than just a collection of unrelated contents. In fact, our psychological ideas are organized and richly interconnected with different mental states conceptualized as being causally related to one another, to environmental input, and to behavioral output (Flavell & Miller, 1998). Regardless of how suitable the term 'theory of mind' is when it is applied to preschool children's psychological domain knowledge, it seems that this knowledge complies with the basic conditions just mentioned (Wellman, 1990). Much research since the early 1980s shows that preschool children successfully acquire a body of knowledge with well organized basic principles that are specifically applied to the psychological domain (mental states). Let us examine some examples of this body of knowledge and of the creative research designed by psychologists to investigate it.

Mental states characterize the psychological domain in a peculiar way. It would be practically impossible to make sense of human behavior without relating it to constructs attributed to other people (and to ourselves too): desire, intention, emotion, belief, thought, etc. We know that a person searches for an object in a wardrobe because s/he wants to find that object and knows that it is in the wardrobe. We are able to understand why a woman is sad when we see that she is surprised and unhappy when she realizes that her friend is not at the school, because we associate her state of sadness with her desire to meet her friend and with her disappointment contrasted with her belief that her friend would be there. We would be facing a chaotic world if we did not have the capacity to attribute mental states to other people and relate them to their behavior. Something similar seems to happen to autistic children who, according to some authors, are unable to develop a theory of mind (Frith, 1989). Under normal development, preschool children progress spectacularly in terms of this capacity to attribute mental states to other people and to explain their behavior by means of them. There is a great diversity of mental states (e.g. perception, belief, desire, emotion, intention) whose comprehension gets consolidated during this period. In the present review we have chosen to discuss the most relevant finding with respect to two of them – visual perception and belief – that have become fundamental in the investigation of the theory of mind in the preschool period (Flavell & Miller, 1998; Perner, 1991).

The Understanding of Visual Perception

At the beginning of the preschool period, at around 2 years of age, children already present different knowledge about visual experience. They know that people have inner visual experience and also that this experience follows certain properties (they are very sensitive to the direction of a glance, they know that a look can be blocked, they begin to use words such as 'see' correctly, and so forth). But what do preschool children know about the visual experience as a mental state? Are they able to understand that the visual experience can yield different results when the conditions change? Are they aware that different people can hold different points of view? At around 3 years, the first level of comprehension of the visual experience as a mental state is achieved. Children then understand that the other person need not see something just because they do and vice versa. For instance, they realize that whereas they see what is on their side of a vertically held card, another person, seated opposite, does not. A little later – and this would correspond to a second level of elaboration (Flavell, 1992) – children become aware that other people may be looking at the same thing but may see it in a different way due to their different visual experience. For instance, they realize that they see a drawing of a turtle from the right side, but another person seated opposite may see it from the reverse side.

These data are interesting not only because they provide information about preschool children's clear competencies, but also because they argue against Piaget's pessimism about children's egocentrism. It is very likely that children at this age, as Piaget and Inhelder (1956) showed, find it difficult to know exactly what another person seated in front of them is seeing when they are both looking at the three mountains. From the theory of mind perspective it is argued that the reason for that is not the egocentrism. As several studies show (Masangkay et al., 1974), when the task is simple enough, 4-year-old children are aware that another person looking at what they are looking may have a different visual experience depending on their visual accessibility. It is possible that errors made by preschoolers in the three-mountain task are due not so much to their difficulty in differentiating their own point of view from the other's but to their difficulties in reconstructing what the other person really sees. Some authors suggest that the apparently egocentric responses to tasks in which the goal is to differentiate the child's and the other person's point of view seem to be 'realistic' responses. Preschool children might find it difficult to reconstruct what the other person sees, but they show no preference for their own perspective. They seem to choose a 'good picture' regardless of the fact that such a picture corresponds to their own point of view (Light & Nix, 1983).

An interesting finding that also argues against old beliefs about the limitations in preschool children's cognition refers to the distinction between appearance and reality. Actually, responses based more on apparent perceptual features and less on conceptual features have been attributed to preschoolers' mode of thinking. We have already seen in previous sections that conservation tasks are based on the idea that the young child finds it difficult to constitute the conservation principle beyond perceptual appearances (the child says that there is more because it looks like there is more). The same pattern is found when children must determine whether certain incidental modifications change the identity of an object. Is a square that leans on a vertex still a square? Is a cat that covers its face with a dog mask still a cat? Is a raccoon that shaves and dyes its hair to look like a skunk still a raccoon? Preschool children normally judge in terms of apparent changes and deny the permanence of identity (Perner, 1991). Along with Perner's view, and according to the above mentioned findings, in all these cases the child must acquire sufficient knowledge to be able to distinguish if a change in the object or in the situation modifies the identity or only a property of the phenomenon (i.e. the amount). It is not surprising that preschool children do not yet succeed in the task if their knowledge is not sufficient. It might be possible then that, if the task facilitates the choice between appearance and reality, children will be able to clearly distinguish from one another. Flavell, Flavell, and Green (1983) investigated children's comprehension of deceptive appearances. They showed children a piece of sponge that looked like a rock. All the children said that it was a rock. Once children became aware, after touching the object, that it was really a sponge, they were asked:

1 What is this really? It is really a rock or a piece of sponge?
2 When you look at this directly, right now, does it look like a rock or a piece of sponge?

While 3-year-old children had difficulty distinguishing appearance from reality (in response to the first question they said that it was really a sponge and in response to the second question they said also that it looked like a sponge), most 4-year-old children differentiated their answers. This shows that children at an early age (at around 4) are able to distinguish appearance from reality as long as they can both verify that the visual appearance of the object misleads their judgment and also verify the real object identity. This finding also shows that children are progressing in the basic comprehension of the mental states, something that will probably be used in the future when they need to find that appearances are often deceptive.

Beliefs, False Beliefs and Deception

The clearest evidence that children are able to attribute mental states to other people, to differentiate them from their own, and to interpret behavior according to them was originated in false-belief research. We are constantly attributing beliefs to other people and to ourselves with the aim of understanding human actions. These actions make full sense only when we are able to relate them to mental states about knowledge such as the belief. For instance, we go to the bookshelf to get a book because we know (or believe, depending on the degree of uncertainty) that it is there. We understand that our neighbor goes up the steps intend of taking the elevator because we are able to understand that she knows (or believes) that the elevator is out of order. Young children realize that people have epistemic mental states probably from perceptual signs related to their access to information. For instance, they know that people hold representations of reality and that these representations guide their behavior. Nevertheless, it is difficult to know to what degree children have knowledge about epistemic mental states. In order to answer that, we need evidence showing that what children really attribute is not only a real mental state, but most likely a mental state different to their own. With the false belief, the attribution of a belief to another person or to oneself does not correspond to the facts. In general, researchers consider false-belief tasks to be a better test of the concept of belief than true-belief tasks because children could be correct on true-belief tasks by egocentrically assuming that others know what they themselves know. For this reason, and due to the relevance beliefs have for human behavior, false-belief tasks have become the research paradigm in the field of theory of mind.

Although there are many experimental approaches, the two classic paradigms are presented in Table 12.3. These experiments have been replicated by several researchers and carried out with subjects belonging to different cultural contexts, and there is high agreement in the experimental findings. Whereas very few 3-year-olds succeed in the task questions, 4-year-old children respond without making any mistakes. Neither 3- nor 4-year-old children find it difficult to anticipate where the chocolate is now and where it was at the beginning (first paradigm, unexpected transfer). It is also easy for them to anticipate what class of objects are normally in the Smarties box (second paradigm, deceptive box). These answers attest to an unremarkable bit of physical knowledge that all children have acquired when they turn 3. The different responses to the test questions suggest a remarkable developmental difference in their psychological-cognitive knowledge. It is worth mentioning that the same difficulty arises when children have to attribute to themselves a mental state of false belief.

Everything points to the fact that, at around 4, children reach a better comprehension of what belief mental states are. They begin to understand that a belief state can be discordant with reality and they can interpret people's behavior according to their belief mental states. It is not a random coincidence that the false belief coincides with a better comprehension and an effective use of various deceiving behaviors at this age. To deceive a person requires the manipulation of his/her belief state, inducing a false belief state. To understand that someone is deceiving requires a differentiation between the belief state induced by gestures or words (false

Table 12.3 *False-belief paradigms*

The unexpected transfer
Subjects are told a story in which the protagonist (John) placed an object (e.g. chocolate) in a location (e.g. drawer) before going out to play. In his absence the object was relocated (e.g. to a cupboard) in an unexpected transfer of which the protagonist remained unaware. When the story protagonist returned to the scene, subjects were asked where he would look for the object.

Test questions:
(a) Where does John think the chocolate is?
(b) When John comes home, where will he look for his chocolate?

Control questions:
(a) Where is the chocolate now?
(b) Where did John put the chocolate in the beginning?
(c) Did John see how the chocolate changed its location?

The deceptive-box task
Subjects together with a friend are shown to the experimenter's room with the promise that the experimenter will show them what she has in her box. The friend, however, is told to wait his turn outside the room. Inside the room with doors closed, the subject is shown a Smarties box, a container of desirable candy highly familiar to all subjects. Asked what they think is in the box, they all say 'Smarties'. They are then shown that they are wrong and that the box contain a pencil. The pencil is then put back into the box and the box is closed again. Subjects have to indicate what they expect their friend will think there is in the box. They can also be asked what they thought there was in the box the first time they saw it.

Test questions:
(a) What did you think was in here?
(b) What will (name of friend) think is in here?

Control question:
(a) Can you remember what's inside here?

Sources: Wimmer and Perner (1983), Perner, Leekham, and Wimmer (1987).

belief) and the true belief. Several studies test children's potentiality either to deceive another person or to understand that the other person is deceiving them. They show that around 4 this competency gets consolidated. In one of these studies, Peskins (1989) let children choose one out of four stickers (the favorite). They were told that they could keep the sticker but, before that, they had to let the two dolls choose one sticker each. Also the experimenter explained to the children that the dark dressed doll (the good one) would never choose the sticker chosen by the child but that the light dressed doll (the competitive one) always would. Then, the dark dressed doll appeared in the task scene and, in front of it, the child was asked to choose a sticker. All of the children clearly pointed out their favorite sticker. After that, the light dressed doll (the competitive one) would appear and the children were asked again to choose a sticker. All 3-year-old children and some of the 4-year-olds pointed out their favorite, and became very frustrated and disappointed when the doll chose the same sticker. In contrast, most 5-year-olds were able to deceive the competitive doll by pointing at the sticker they did not really want. Although it is likely that children below 4 are able to interpret some deceit situations based on different behavior signs and can also deceive other people using some regularities of behavior, it is clear that any deceiving that involves a modification of the belief mental state seems very unlikely before 4.

The analysis of the reasons for such neat development of the theory of mind during the preschool years is very difficult. There are probably different types of factors that might explain such progress. Some of these factors, according to Flavell and Miller (1998), are: increasingly powerful information processing capabilities; brain development; imitative, unstructured and collaborative learning; bootstrapping from self-understanding to understanding others; social experiences such as parent language focused on emotion and other mental states; and so forth. From a developmental point of view, it is clear that this new comprehension of the psychological phenomena gets established around 4 and it seems to be related to a new cognitive skill that enables children to understand the main characteristics of mental states. A mental state is a peculiar representation because apart from providing information about reality it shows an attitude (of belief, of desire, of intention) about this reality. Thus, its understanding probably requires an important cognitive achievement. For some authors (Perner, 1991), one of the underlying essential mechanisms is meta-representation: that is, the skill to represent the relationship between a mental state and reality to which it is applied. Only with this skill will the child be able to understand that a person holds a wrong belief about something and to understand as well that this belief will affect his/her behavior.

Regardless of the theoretical explanation, these findings show that preschool children achieve a basic understanding of what the main mental states are, and they succeed in relating them with one another to predict people's behavior. This enables children to be more competent from a social point of view, and it is not surprising to observe preschool children apply this knowledge in various situations: for instance, when they have to convince their parents ('if you buy me a TV set for my room I will not fight with my sister for what to watch'); when they want to comfort a friend by reminding him that his birthday party is coming soon; or when they try to convince a player by making him believe that his game rules are wrong. On the other hand, since mental states are signs and information taken from interactive contexts that enable them to build their theory of mind, social and communicative experiences (either related with adults or with other children) foster their comprehension.

CONCLUSIONS

The picture of the preschool mind drawn in this chapter may be too clear-cut for some readers. In fact, although psychological research has contributed a great deal of data and theoretical explanations, there are still many gaps in the understanding of the preschool mind. Throughout the chapter, we have tried to highlight the contrasts between the competent but at the same time fragile nature of preschoolers' cognition. There are, however, many issues yet to elucidate which will be considered in this section. Also, the main tendencies that psychological research has shown so far will be highlighted.

Variability in Cognition

Our description has intended to be both normative (we have offered a general picture of cognitive competencies) and contrasting (we wanted to show the differences between babies and preschool children and especially those between preschool and school-age children). In the last 30 years, psychological research has highlighted the main cognitive tendencies that differentiate preschool children from children in other age groups. However, these great contrasts must be relativized. On the one hand, cognition may be very different from one child to another. Depending on their cognitive skills and styles, and the physical and social conditions of their development, results can come out very differently. Certainly, these differences will depend on the cognitive aspects being studied. It is very likely that a basic cognitive principle such as conservation or a basic skill like the attribution of a mental state may admit few individual differences, whereas if attention is paid to classification strategies or to the ability to use symbols, the individual differences may get much greater. Given the complexity of cognitive development and its multi-causal nature, it is very plausible that different children belonging to the same age period present different performances in response to the same task. Another important aspect that has not received much attention either is the within-child variability. That is, the same child can perform differently not only across tasks but also within the same task. This within-child variability is a crucial aspect to take into consideration, not only because it offers a more realistic image of children's competencies but also because it helps to understand the circumstances under which cognitive change appears as well as the mechanisms of change involved. For instance, contrary to what was expected, microgenetic analysis has provided evidence that shows that conflict is not always a change factor. In many cases, success and knowledge about a given strategy are sufficient conditions for a more explicit comprehension of the task (Karmiloff-Smith, 1992) or for the strategy to be used in new tasks (Siegler & Jenkins, 1989).

Multiplicity of Change Factors

The most wanted explanation (for the sake of simplicity) in preschoolers' cognitive development would be the one that only refers to one mechanism of change. A comfortable and plausible explanation would be that changes in this period are due either to nervous system maturation, or to an interiorization process of social patterns, or to a representational redescription, or even to a growing processing capacity. Nevertheless, any of these would certainly be an incomplete explanation. Experimental data show that there must be different change mechanisms involved in cognitive development and that these mechanisms interact with one another. For example, Piaget's general explanation given in terms of equilibration, or the social learning theories' idea of modeling, should be replaced by theoretical explanations that integrate different change factors. A challenge not yet resolved in the field is to study whether change mechanisms are different in different knowledge domains. At present, psychological research (Gelman & Williams, 1998) points in this direction, partially due to a reaction to Werner's, Piaget's, and Vygotsky's generalist theories of the beginning of the century. Nevertheless, the reasons why some great developmental trends (such as greater conscious access to knowledge, higher flexibility and generality of knowledge, or greater self-control capacity) appear in all domains remain as yet unexplained. Any development explanation must not only consider various change mechanisms but also investigate the relationship between specific and general mechanisms.

The Importance of Learning

Although as a basic postulate it seems clear that 'to develop' is not the same as 'to learn', we have seen the role played by the acquisition of knowledge in cognition and its effect on development during the preschool years. Unfortunately, in present developmental studies in contrast to classical theoretical approaches such as Piaget's and Vygotsky's, the relation between learning and development is hardly explicated at a theoretical level. This gap is paradoxical in light of the quantity of research that insists on the important role of learning in cognitive development. Numerous examples (some of them mentioned in this chapter) show that changes in the knowledge base affect the mode of reasoning and problem solving. In contrast with that, the reciprocal relation is rarely mentioned: that is, how changes in cognition affect the acquisition of knowledge. During the preschool period, there are many converging factors that make the acquisition of knowledge very important. Among these, we find the new symbolization capacity that enables children to follow an exponential path of language development as well as the development of other symbol systems; the consolidation of representative structures (such as scripts and categories) that enable them to assimilate and organize new knowledge; and the acquisition of explicit theories about different knowledge domains which provide interpretive frameworks for new knowledge. It is not surprising that, in general terms, we come across children that display great curiosity and are strongly willing to discover new things. It thus becomes even more necessary than it was when the complex relation between learning and development was claimed to make clear that this relationship is bidirectional and that it keeps changing depending on the stage of development and the content under study.

Cognition in Context

Something surprising among preschool children, and present in most research findings, is the readiness of children to take advantage of other people's help. This may be a general developmental trend as claimed by some authors (Rogoff, 1998). What seems clear is that during the preschool years, the intervention of an adult or a more skilled child can aid progress by either helping structure the task, or focusing the attention on what is relevant, or even partially assuming the cognitive load. This help may be understood as a factor that reduces the task processing demands and thus allows task resolution. Although this may be an explanation, it is not the only plausible one. These findings show that cognitive development can hardly be considered a solitary and an acontextual construction. In everyday life, preschool children learn from others and with others and share with them important elements of the same culture (not only knowledge or symbolic tools but also values and attitudes). It is not surprising then that when a child receives some help or when research is carried on in the everyday child's context, there is evidence of progress. However, we must not forget that the cultural context is not objective, unchangeable and external to the child's reality. Every subject, according to his/her potentialities and attributed meanings, will assimilate and will create a subjective relation with reality. This relation will be naturally built with other people but it will mainly depend on the subjective view created by the child. In this sense, it could be said that preschool children's development takes place by means of their participation in culture, but also that they constantly recreate their culture according to their own peculiar way of understanding things.

Acknowledgements

Preparation of this chapter was supported in part by DGICYT grant PB95-0963 from the Ministerio de Educación y Cultura (Spain). I am very grateful to Mercè Garcia-Milà for her valuable comments and her editing of the English.

References

Beilin, H., & Pearlman, E.G. (1991). Children's iconic realism: Object vs. property realism. In H.W. Reese (ed.), *Advances in child development and behavior* (Vol. 23). New York: Academic.

Bialystok, E. (1991). Letters, sounds, and symbols: Changes in children's understanding of written language. *Applied Psycholinguistics*, 12, 75–89.

Brenneman, K., Massey, C., Machado, S.F., & Gelman R. (1996). Young children's plans differ for writing and drawing. *Cognitive Development*, 11, 397–419.

Callanan, M.A. (1989). Development of object categories and inclusion relations: Preschoolers' hypotheses about word meanings. *Developmental Psychology*, 25, 207–216.

Chi, M.T.H. (1978). Knowledge structures and memory development. In R.S. Siegler (ed.), *Children's thinking: What develops?* Hillsdale, NJ: Erlbaum.

Chi, M.T.H., & Koeske, R. (1983). Network representation of a child's dinosaur knowledge. *Developmental Psychology*, 19, 29–39.

DeLoache, J.S., & Burns, N.M. (1993). Symbolic development in young children: Understanding models and pictures. In C. Pratt & A.F. Garton (eds), *Systems of representation in children: Development and use* (pp. 91–112). New York: Wiley.

DeLoache, J.S., Miller, K.F., & Pierroutsakos, S.L. (1998). Reasoning and problem solving. In D. Kuhn & R.S. Siegler (eds), *Handbook of child psychology: Vol. 2. Cognition, perception and language* (pp. 801–850). New York: Wiley.

Enns, J.T., & Akhtar, N. (1989). A developmental study of filtering in visual attention. *Child Development*, 60, 1188–1199.

Ferreiro, E. (1988). L'écriture avant la lettre. In H. Sinclair (ed.), *La production de notations chez le jeune enfant* (pp. 18–70). Paris: Presses Universitaires de France.

Ferreiro, E., & Teberosky, A. (1979). *Los sistemas de escritura en el desarrollo del niño*. México: Siglo XXI.

Flavell, J.H. (1985). *Cognitive development* (2nd edn). Englewood Cliffs, NJ: Prentice-Hall.

Flavell, J.H. (1992). Pespectives on perspective taking. In H. Beilin & P. Pufall (eds), *Piaget's theory: Prospects and possibilities*. Hillsdale, NJ: Erlbaum.

Flavell, J.H., Flavell, E.R., & Green, F.L. (1983). Development of the appearance–reality distinction. *Cognitive Psychology*, 15, 95–120.

Flavell, J.H., & Miller, P.H. (1998). Social cognition. In D. Kuhn & R.S. Siegler (eds), *Handbook of child psychology: Vol. 2. Cognition, perception and language* (pp. 851–898). New York: Wiley.

Florian, J.E. (1994). Stripes do not a zebra make, or do they? Conceptual and perceptual information in inductive inference. *Developmental Psychology*, 30, 88–101.

Frith, U. (1989). *Autism: Explaining the enigma*. Oxford: Blackwell.

Gelman, R. (1980). What young children know about numbers. *Educational Psychologist*, 15, 54–68.

Gelman, R. (1982). Basic numerical abilities. In R.J. Sternberg (ed.), *Advances in the psychology of intelligence* (pp. 181–205). Hillsdale, NJ: Erlbaum.

Gelman, R., & Gallistel, C.R. (1978). *The child's understanding of number*. Cambridge, MA: Harvard University Press.

Gelman, S.A., & Kremer, K.E. (1991). Understanding natural cause: Children's explanations of how objects and their properties originate. *Child Development*, 62, 396–414.

Gelman, S.A., & Markman, E.M. (1987). Young children's induction from natural kinds: The role of categories and appearances. *Child Development*, 58, 1532–1541.

Gelman, S.A., & Medin, D.L. (1993). What's so essential about essentialism? A different perspective on the interaction of perception, language, and conceptual knowledge. *Cognitive Development*, 8, 157–167.

Gelman, R., & Williams, E.M. (1998). Enabling constraints for cognitive development and learning: Domain specificity and epigenesis. In D. Kuhn & R.S. Siegler (eds), *Handbook of child psychology: Vol. 2. Cognition, perception and language* (pp. 575–630). New York: Wiley.

Hudson, J.A., Shapiro, L.R., & Sosa, B.B. (1995). Planning in the real world: Preschool children's scripts and plans for familiar events. *Child Development*, 66, 984–998.

Jones, S.S., & Smith, L.B. (1993). The place of perception in children's concepts. *Cognitive Development*, 8, 113–139.

Karmiloff-Smith, A. (1992). *Beyond modularity: A developmental perspective on cognitive science*. Cambridge, MA: MIT Press.

Lieben, L.S., & Downs, R.M. (1991). The role of graphic comprehension in understanding the world. In R.M. Downs, L.S. Lieben, & D.S. Palermo (eds), *Visions of aesthetics, the environment, and development: The legacy of Joachim Wohlwill*. Hillsdale, NJ: Erlbaum.

Light, P., & Nix, C. (1983). 'Own view' versus 'good view' in perspective-taking task. *Child Development*, 54, 480–483.

López, A., Gelman, S., Gutheil, G., & Smith, E.E. (1992). The development of category-based induction. *Child Development*, 63, 1070–1090.

Luciarello, J., & Rifkin, A. (1986). Event representations as the basis of categorical knowledge. In K. Nelson (ed.), *Event knowledge: Structure and function in development*. Hillsdale, NJ: Erlbaum.

Martí, E. (1986). First metaphors in children: A new hypothesis. *Communication and Cognition*, 19 (3–4), 337–346.

Martí, E. (ed.) (1997). *Construir una mente*. Barcelona: Paidós.

Martí, E. (1999). 'Esto no es un dibujo': Las primeras distinciones sobre sistemas notacionales. In J.I. Pozo & C. Monereo (eds), *El aprendizaje estratégico* (pp. 239–250). Madrid: Aula XXI/Santillana.

Masangkay, Z.S., McCluskey, K.A., McIntyre, C.W., Sims-Knight, J., Vaughn, B.E., & Flavell, J.H. (1974). The early development of inferences about the visual percepts of others. *Child Development*, 45, 237–246.

Nelson, K. (1981). Social cognition in a script framework. In J.H. Flavell & L. Ross (eds), *Social cognitive development*. Cambridge, MA: Cambridge University Press.

Nelson, K. (1986). *Event knowledge: Structure and function in development*. Hillsdale, NJ: Erlbaum.

Perner, J. (1991). *Understanding the representational mind*. Harvard, MA: MIT Press.

Perner, J., Leekam, S.R., & Wimmer, H. (1987). Three-year olds' difficulty with false belief: The case for a conceptual deficit. *British Journal of Developmental Psychology*, 5, 125–137.

Peskins, J. (1989). Concealing one's intentions: The development of deceit. Unpublished manuscript, *Center for Applied Cognitive Sciences*, Ontario Institute for Studies in Education, Toronto, Ontario.

Piaget, J. (1929). *The child's conception of the world*. New York: Harcourt Brace.

Piaget, J. (1930). *The child's conception of physical causality*. New York: Harcourt Brace.

Piaget, J. (1952). *The origins of intelligence in children.* New York: International University Press.

Piaget, J. (1973). *The psychology of intelligence.* Totowa, NJ: Littlefield & Adams.

Piaget, J. (1977). *The development of thought: Equilibration of cognitive structures.* New York: Viking.

Piaget, J., & Inhelder, B. (1956). *The child's conception of space.* London: Routledge & Kegan Paul.

Pick, A.D., & Frankel, G.W. (1973). A study of strategies of visual attention in children. *Developmental Psychology*, 4, 348–357.

Rogoff, B. (1998). Cognition as a collaborative process. In D. Kuhn & R.S. Siegler (eds), *Handbook of child psychology: Vol. 2. Cognition, perception and language* (pp. 679–744). New York: Wiley.

Saxe, G.B., Guberman, S.R., & Gearhart, M. (1987). *Social processes in early number development. Monographs of the Society for Research in Child Development*, Vol. 52, no. 2, serial 216.

Siegler, R.S. (1991). *Children's thinking* (2nd edn). Englewood Cliffs, NJ: Prentice-Hall.

Siegler, R.S., & Jenkins, E. (1989). *How children discover new strategies.* Hillsdale, NJ: Erlbaum.

Sinclair, A. (1991). Children's production and comprehension of written numerical representations. In K. Durkin & B. Shire (eds), *Language in mathematical education* (pp. 59–68). Buckingham: Open University Press.

Somerville, S.C., Wellman, H.M., & Cultice, J.C. (1983). Young children's deliberate reminding. *The Journal of Genetic Psychology*, 143, 87–96.

Tversky, B. (1989). Parts, partonomies and taxonomies. *Developmental Psychology*, 25, 983–995.

Vurpillot, E., & Ball, W.A. (1979). The concept of identity and children's selective attention. In G.A. Hale & M. Lewis (eds), *Attention and cognitive development.* New York: Plenum.

Vygotsky, L.S. (1978). *Mind in society: The development of higher psychological processes.* Cambridge, MA: Harvard University Press.

Wellman, H.M. (1990). *The child's theory of mind.* Cambridge, MA: MIT Press.

Wellman, H.M., & Gelman, S.A. (1998). Knowledge acquisition in foundational domains. In D. Kuhn & R.S. Siegler (eds), *Handbook of child psychology: Vol. 2. Cognition, perception and language* (pp. 523–573). New York: Wiley.

Wimmer, H., & Perner, J. (1983). Beliefs about beliefs: Representation and constraining functions of wrong beliefs in young children's understanding of deception. *Cognition*, 13, 103–128.

Woodward, A.L., & Markman, E.M. (1998). Early word learning. In D. Kuhn & R.S. Siegler (eds), *Handbook of child psychology: Vol. 2. Cognition, perception and language* (pp. 371–420). New York: Wiley.

13

Development of Play

ANTHONY D. PELLEGRINI AND PETER SMITH

INTRODUCTION

Disciplinary and Historical Overview

Play has been written about from a number of disciplinary perspectives, including ethology, psychology, sociology, anthropology, and education. The work of Groos, in his volumes *The Play of Animals* (1898) and *The Play of Man* (1901), set a broad comparative approach to the topic, in keeping with the early evolutionary views stemming from Darwin, Spencer, and Hall at the turn of the century. However it was not until the 1970s that a more modern synthesis of studies of animal and human play was attempted. From educational and psychological perspectives, observations of children's play were carried out in North America and elsewhere, in the newly established child development or child welfare institutes, during the 1920s and 1930s (see Arrington, 1943, and Smith & Connolly, 1972, for reviews). They described typical patterns of behaviour, and age and sex differences. A more developmental perspective came from the work of Piaget (1951), who provided a classic descriptive account of the development of play in childhood (based on close observations of his own children). It helped shape succeeding research on children's play, especially concerning play with objects and pretend (which he called symbolic) play. His book also drew links between stages of play, and a child's age and level of cognitive development, a continuing theme in later psychological work.

Smilansky (1968) developed Piaget's stages in play further, distinguishing more strongly constructive play and sociodramatic play. She also argued a decisive role for sociodramatic play in children's cognitive and social development, generating a range of play intervention studies with preschool children designed to test this assertion. Her work had considerable influence in early education.

In anthropology, play was a neglected topic in much field work, being mentioned incidentally in descriptions of childhood. Schwartzmann's (1978) book put it back into the mainstream of anthropological discourse. Since then there has been a lively anthropological contribution to this area (e.g. Lancy, 1996).

Bruner (1972) developed further the links between play and the acquisition of skill in childhood. He argued that play was a necessary part of the extended period of immaturity in humans, allowing flexible exploration of the environment and facilitating the putting together of complex motor skills and action plans from simpler components. This argument focuses mainly on play with objects. Bruner also linked the research on human play with parallel research in animal play, and discussed the role of play in an evolutionary perspective, marking a return to the broader questions and wider interdisciplinary perspective started by Groos and others 70 years earlier.

This brief historical review of the play research indicates rather clearly that the mainstream of psychological research on play has concentrated on studies of constructive, pretend and sociodramatic play – the forms of play encouraged in nurseries, preschools and infant schools, and thought to be valuable for children's development. However, some forms of play can be described as physical activity play – motor activity and rough-and-tumble play or play fighting (Pellegrini & Smith, 1998). These kinds of play show the strongest links to forms of animal play. Animal play was reviewed very thoroughly by Fagen (1981), and synthetic reviews of the animal and human literature have been attempted (Pellegrini & Smith, 1998; Power, 2000; Smith, 1982).

The study of play not only sheds light on its nature and function; it is also arguable that societal values concerning play have shaped the thrust of research. Smith (1988) argued that a 'play ethos', a view that play (constructive and sociodramatic play) was essential for normal development, permeated research through the 1950s to 1980s and led to particular interpretations of intervention studies which however were susceptible to charges of experimenter effects, bias, and inadequate design. Similarly, Sutton-Smith (1986; 1997) takes a broad perspective on what he calls the 'idealization of play', and links between play research and broader trends and ideologies in society.

Basic Issues in this Domain

Some basic issues which have emerged in these strands of work on play include: methods of study; definitional issues; and functional issues.

Most psychological studies of pretend and sociodramatic play have followed an experimental or interventionist paradigm. At times, quite unnatural laboratory situations have been used to study that most natural and unconstrained of human phenomena, play. However there has been some redress of this with naturalistic, longitudinal studies in homes (e.g. Haight & Miller, 1993) and school playgrounds (e.g. Pellegrini, 1995a), as well as more ethnographic approaches from anthropologists and sociologists (e.g. Lancy, 1996).

Problems of definition of play have been tackled by ethologists and students of development for a number of years. Starting at least with Groos (1898;1901), play has been considered a hallmark of the juvenile period. One level of response has been to define play as anything a young juvenile does, separate from primary motivations such as feeding, fighting, sleeping, and numerous corresponding functions (see Martin & Caro, 1985, for a discussion). An important step in understanding play should be defining play.

Many scholars suggest that play serves numerous important developmental functions. For example, play during childhood, according to Groos and numerous subsequent play theorists such as Piaget (1951) and Vygotsky (1978), enables children to learn the skills necessary for successful functioning in adulthood. However children's fantasy and sociodramatic play, especially, has been implicated with many developmental functions, including language, creativity, social role taking, emotion regulation, and theory of mind (Leslie, 1987; Smilansky, 1968). Despite much study, all such functions remain essentially unproven at the current time.

In this chapter we define play from perspectives taken in both the ethological and the psychological literature. From this view, we consider play in terms of its ontogeny, phylogenetic comparisons, and proximal factors influencing its occurrence (Tinbergen, 1963). We then discuss possible functions of play using cost–benefit analysis. This method is helpful not only in determining the possible functions of play, but also in locating that period in development when benefits may be accrued.

What is Play? Issues of Definition

Observers can reliably recognize play when they see it, but have difficulty in finding satisfactory operational definitions. Given the complexity of play, it is generally considered that no one definition of play is necessary or sufficient (Martin & Caro, 1985: Pellegrini & Smith, 1998; Rubin, Fein & Vandenberg, 1983); thus definitions are typically multidimensional. For example, in Rubin, Fein, and Vandenberg's (1983) review of the child development literature, children's play is defined according to three dimensions: psychological disposition, behaviour, and contexts supporting (or preceding) play. Ethologists also advocate defining play along a number of dimensions (Martin & Caro, 1985, p. 62; Pellegrini & Smith, 1998), suggesting structural (behavioural), consequential (those behaviours following play), and contextual criteria (where it is observed). In this section we briefly review these two sets of definitions, noting cases where similar labels are used to describe different phenomena.

One of the most widely agreed upon criteria for defining play is that it does not seem to serve any apparent immediate purpose. More specifically, play behaviours resemble 'serious' behaviours but they do not serve their intended purpose. Play behaviours are often typified by exaggerated motions and vocalizations, relative to their nonplayful counterparts. A common example from children's pretend play would involve the exaggerated walk and voice of a child pretending to be a monster. In Rubin, Fein, and Vandenberg's (1983) scheme this immediate 'purposelessness' criterion also relates to the 'means over ends' dispositional criterion. Attending to means over ends assumes that children are less concerned with the outcome of their behaviour than with the behavioural processes *per se*. For example, in playing with blocks, children are less concerned with the outcome of the construction than with the process of putting it together. The importance of means over ends for a definition of animal play has also been noted by ethologists (Martin & Caro, 1985). For example, in the case of two lion cubs playing with captured prey, they do not kill it, but chase and gently pounce on it (Caro, 1995).

Besides defining play along dispositional dimensions, play has also been defined according to contexts which support play. Rubin, Fein, and

Vandenberg (1983) considered contextual factors antecedent to play, including: (1) an atmosphere that is familiar (in terms of props and people), (2) safe and friendly, (3) a minimally intrusive adult, and (4) children who are free from stress, hunger, and fatigue. Martin and Bateson (1993) invoke a similar method in their use of spatial relations to categorize behaviours; that is, behaviours can belong to the same category if they occur in a specific setting or among a certain group. For example, behaviours in the playground could generally be considered play. Ethologists commonly define play as juvenile behaviours.

Play can also be defined in terms of its immediate consequences, or the behaviours that follow play. This strategy is often employed by ethologists (e.g. Hinde, 1980) and has been used in the child development literature to define specific dimensions of play, such as rough-and-tumble (Pellegrini, 1988) and parallel play (Bakeman & Brownlee, 1980). Rough-and-tumble play is defined in terms of structural dimensions, such as quasi-agonistic behaviours (e.g. open hand hit) and positive affect (e.g. a smile or play face), as well as consequence. A behaviour can be categorized as rough-and-tumble play, not aggression, if, along with other criteria, children stay together after the conclusion of the bout; if they separate it can be defined as aggression (though see de Waal, 1989, for an alternative view). Similarly, parallel play, or behaviour which has children interacting next to but not with each other, can be defined as social, rather than solitary, behaviour because the cooperative interaction follows parallel behaviour at a greater than chance rate (Bakeman & Brownlee, 1980). Consequences can be useful complements to structural definitions of play, as illustrated in the case of rough-and-tumble play.

Such a multidimensional approach to defining play is useful given the possibility for ambiguity. Some studies have examined how observers combine information from a number of cues to decide whether an activity is playful or not (Costabile et al., 1991; Smith & Vollstedt, 1985). However, the antecedents and consequences of behaviours should be considered as elicitors and outcomes, respectively, of those behaviours, rather than as components of the behaviour *per se*. Thus, it is important to keep these dimensions conceptually distinct, especially when we consider the role of play as serving a developmental function.

Ontogenetic Development and Proximal Influences

The fact that play is a multidimensional construct becomes more evident when its different forms are examined during childhood. The different forms of play that occur primarily during the juvenile period have been divided differently by ethologists (see below) and psychologists (see later section on developmental sequences in play).

Ethologists generally consider three forms of play, all of which have the common attribute of purposelessness: locomotor play, social play, and object play (Bekoff & Byers, 1981). Locomotor play involves exaggerated and repetitious movements, which often occur in novel sequences. These movements are the sort of behaviour described by Piaget (1951) and Bruner (1972) which very young children engage in as they are beginning to master the functions of their bodies and the objects which furnish their world.

Social play refers to the goalless behaviour which involves a peer or an adult. In the nonhuman literature most social play occurs among juveniles, while in the literature on humans, social play first appears in adult–infant play and later in terms of peer play (Haight & Miller, 1993; see Pellegrini & Smith, 1998, for review). Object play can be solitary or social and involves manipulation of the material environment in ways that are not epistemic.

These types of play are not considered to be hierarchical in the ethological literature, and they often occur together; for example, rough-and-tumble play involving two children is both social and locomotor. Further, most mammalian species exhibit these forms of play (Bekoff & Byers, 1981; Fagen, 1981). Extensive reviews of the literature on animal play suggest that play accounts for about 10% of animals' time and energy (Byers & Walker, 1995; Fagen, 1981; Martin & Caro, 1985). Estimates of children's play, similarly, suggest that play accounts for about 10% of children's energy expenditure (Pellegrini, Horvat, & Huberty, 1998).

Children's play, on the other hand, is more differentiated than that of nonhumans, to the extent that developmental progressions of different forms of play have been documented. One of the earliest differentiations in children's play begins in infancy where play is differentiated from exploration: exploration is epistemic – objects are manipulated or space traversed so as to gain information – and is thus less clearly goal-directed than is play.

Exploration

Children spend much of their time exploring their environment rather than playing with it, particularly in the period of infancy, though the exact amounts of time and energy spent in exploration have not been documented. Exploration is an information gathering activity and is evident, in its earliest forms, by mouthing and simple manipulation of objects (Belsky & Most, 1981; Hutt, 1966). When exploring, infants are thought to be guided dispositionally by the question, 'What can it do?' This object orientation is different from the more person-centred orientation guiding play, 'What can *I* do with it?'

(Hutt, 1966). Through exploration children come to know their environments. It is this knowledge that provides the basis for play. As such, exploration must be considered separate from play.

Exploration precedes play ontogenetically and microgenetically. Ontogenetically, or during the period of human development, observations of infants interacting with their mother in a laboratory suggest that exploration dominates infants' behaviour for the first 9 months of life; by 12 months, play and exploration occur with near equal frequency; and by 18 months play accounts for more of the child's interactions with the environment than does exploration (Belsky & Most, 1981). During late infancy and early childhood, boys, more than girls, engage in exploration (Bornstein et al., 1999). These sex differences were replicated cross-nationally in Argentina and the USA, suggesting that mothers of boys support object manipulation and explorations. These differences in mother–child play, in turn, predict sex differences in object play with peers.

Microgenetically, or through the process by which the activity of play with objects develops, exploration also precedes play to the extent that children explore an object, or know its properties, before they can play with it (Hutt, 1966). This finding has also been proffered as an explanation for observed social class differences in play (McLoyd, 1982; 1983). Specifically, McLoyd suggested that the toys used in experimental studies of social class differences in play are typically found in middle class homes, but not in the homes of poor children. When poor African American preschoolers were presented with these initially unfamiliar toys, they explored them before they played with them.

Developmental Sequences in Play

Piaget (1951) described a developmental sequence of play, starting with practice play or sensorimotor play, including the circular reactions which embrace the transition from exploration to play in infants' interactions with objects in their environment. He documented the origins of symbolic, or pretend, play from 15 months onward, as characterized by nonliteral actions, object use and vocalizations (for example, his daughter Jacqueline putting her head on a cloth, sucking her thumb, blinking her eyes, and laughing – 'as if' going to sleep). Piaget argued that from 6 to 7 years, children left behind the more private worlds of symbolic play and engaged in games with rules – such as hopscotch, football, marbles – in which playful actions were coordinated within a publicly agreed framework of constraints.

Smilansky (1968) extended this developmental progression view of play even more thoroughly, developing a fourfold sequence of functional play, constructive play, dramatic play and games with rules. The distinctive new element here is the postulation that constructive play – making things with objects – is a transitional phase between the functional (sensorimotor) play of infancy, and the dramatic (symbolic role play) of 4- to 6-year-olds, while allowing some overlap between these stages. This was in opposition to Piaget (1951), who had written that 'constructive games are not a definite stage like the others, but occupy a position halfway between play and intelligent work, or between play and imitation'. However, Smilansky's scheme was taken up by a number of North American researchers, who combined it with Parten's (1932) categories of social participation to create a sociocognitive 'nested play hierarchy' (e.g. Rubin, Watson, & Jambor, 1978).

Although such sequences have attractions for applied, descriptive purposes (for example, estimating the maturity of children's play in different nursery environments), there are shortcomings to the approach (Takhvar & Smith, 1990). As defined by Piaget and Smilansky, practice or functional play could occur well beyond infancy, and indeed would seem to include play-fighting or rough-and-tumble play in middle childhood and adolescence. The special role of constructive play in Smilansky's scheme is even more dubious: constructional play and overtly pretend play seem to coexist through the preschool years, and apparently constructive play may have fantasy elements (as becomes obvious when children are asked about their play). Language play, or play with words (Kuczaj II, 1986; Weir, 1962) also do not fit into this scheme.

Fantasy Play

Fantasy, or pretence, is the paradigm case of play during childhood for many psychologists. Fantasy involves an 'as if' orientation to the world and involves actions, the use of objects, and verbalizations and nonliteral meanings; often, it involves playing a distinct pretend role such as mummy, fireman, doctor. Because of its representational nature and its reliance on language, fantasy play is practically unique to humans.

Pretend play is not obviously seen in animal species. A possible candidate for pretence in other species would be play signals such as the play face, or play bow, which signal playful rather than aggressive intent in mammals such as monkeys, canids, felids, ursids (Bekoff & Allen, 1998; Fagen, 1981; Smith, 1982). However, there is no need to take such signals as evidence of pretend; they can simply be preprogrammed signals, seen only in play, which indicate playful intent by the actor.

There are some accounts of what might count as pretend play in the great apes. In chimpanzees, Morris (1962) recounted how, after a visit to a vet for an injection, a chimpanzee gave itself pretend injections; and Hayes and Hayes (1952) gave a classic account of their chimpanzee Viki apparently having an imaginary pull toy. In bonobos, de Waal (1989) has described games of blind man's bluff, and Savage-Rumbaugh (1986) described how Kanzi would hide and eat imaginary food. In gorillas there are possible examples of simple pretend episodes, including making loud sipping noises while 'drinking' from an empty cup (Byrne, 1995). These accounts are of quite simple types of pretend play, which scarcely develop to role playing or any extended narrative sequences. However they may be sufficiently numerous and consistent to suggest some simple abilities for pretence in the great apes. In this sense, they parallel corresponding evidence for simple abilities in theory of mind, language, and self-recognition (Smith, 1996). There are no documented cases of nonhuman primate fantasy in the wild, the cases cited above having been documented with human-reared great apes (Tomasello & Call, 1998).

Fully developed pretend play, including role play and sociodramatic play, seems universal in human societies, from anthropological accounts. It is seen in hunter-gatherer societies (Eibl-Eibesfeldt, 1989; Konner, 1976), where pretend play occurs in mixed-age peer groups; for example, children using sticks and pebbles to represent village huts, herding cows. Reviews of pretend play in non-western societies by Schwartzmann (1978) and Slaughter and Dombrowski (1989) mention over 40 articles describing pretend play. More recent evidence has been presented by Lancy (1996). There are certainly variations in the amount and type of such play, and it can appear 'impoverished' in some societies (Smilansky, 1968), but its presence appears ubiquitous. Slaughter and Dombrowski suggest that in the light of the anthropological evidence, 'children's social and pretend play appear to be biologically based, sustained as an evolutionary contribution to human psychological growth and development. Cultural factors regulate the amount and type of expression of these play forms' (1989, p. 290).

The great majority of the research studies of children's play, including fantasy, have been carried out in preschool classrooms in western societies. Fantasy begins during the second year of life, peaks during the late preschool years, and declines during the primary school years (Fein, 1981). Estimates of time and energy budgets are limited, but it has been found to account for over 15% of the total in-school time budget (Field, 1994), and for 10–17% of preschoolers' and 33% of kindergartners' play behaviours, subsequently declining (Fein, 1981).

Although most studies of fantasy play have been made in peer groups in school, an intensive observational study in homes of young children shows the important supportive role of mothers in early pretend play interactions (Haight & Miller, 1993). Based on these in-home observations, rates of pretend play began at 0.06 minutes/hour for 12 to 14-month-old children, increasing to 3.3 at 24 months and 12.4 at 48 months. Thus, there is convergence between the observational data from the preschool and the home, indicating that pretend play accounts for 12% to 15% of children's available time.

There are sex differences in fantasy play during the preschool period. Girls engage in fantasy play both more frequently and at more sophisticated levels than do boys. Mothers tend to engage in symbolic play with their daughters more frequently than with sons, and these mother–daughter interactions predict peer fantasy play (Bornstein et al., 1999). While the pretence of girls tends to revolve around domestic, dramatic themes, the pretence of boys tends to be more fantastic and physically vigorous, often co-occurring with play fighting and superhero themes (Fein, 1981; Pellegrini & Perlmutter, 1987; Smith, 1974).

Fantasy play is influenced by social variables as well as play materials. Children who are securely, compared to insecurely, attached to their mothers engage in more sophisticated pretend play. For example, securely attached children initiate more play interactions, and the tenor of their interactions with their mother while playing is more positive than that of insecurely attached children (Bretherton, 1989; Roggman & Langlois, 1987). At the level of peer interaction, children's pretence is more sustained and complex when they are playing with friends, compared to acquaintances (Howes, 1994). The mutuality and emotional commitment of friends may motivate children to sustain cooperative interaction (Hartup, 1996).

Play themes generally follow those inherent in the materials available (Pellegrini & Perlmutter, 1989; Smith & Connolly, 1980). Further, the sex role stereotypicality of the materials moderates boys' and girls' play. Boys' play with female-preferred toys, such as dolls, is less sophisticated than it is with male-preferred toys, such as blocks (Pellegrini & Perlmutter, 1989). These findings indicate that at this young age, children's interactions with peers and objects is influenced by social norms governing sex role.

From the age of 3 onwards, pretend play involves quite sophisticated social role-playing skills with peers. Howes (1994) and Howes and Matheson (1992) have described the way in which both adult–child and peer–peer forms of pretend play develop in complexity, reciprocity and shared understanding of pretence and of roles in the play. Extended social role playing was described by Smilansky (1968) as 'sociodramatic play' and involves acting out quite complex narrative sequences.

Besides giving an authoritative description of sociodramatic play, Smilansky (1968) argued that the play of children from 'culturally deprived' backgrounds was impoverished in terms of content, duration and complexity. This led to a body of research suggesting that children from lower socio-economic class backgrounds showed less fantasy play. These studies were criticized by McLoyd (1982) for poor methodology. Some failed to define social class adequately, or confounded it with other variables such as race or school setting. It is likely that global statements about social class effects on play are unwarranted; but there are related proximal influences such as nature of parent facilitation of play, materials available, material familiarity, etc.

In summary, fantasy play accounts for 12% to 15% of preschool children's time at home and at school. Both sex and social partners in play affect these rates. As will be discussed below, sex differences in time spent in different forms of pretend play as well as social partners in play should also have implications for function.

Locomotor Play

Locomotor play is physically vigorous behaviour, e.g. chasing, climbing, and rough-and-tumble play, which does not appear to serve an immediate purpose. Pellegrini and Smith (1998) argued that there are three distinctive forms of locomotor play: rhythmic stereotypies, exercise play, and rough-and-tumble. Each of these forms of play has distinct inverted-U age curves, and it is possible that they serve different developmental functions. Each is discussed in turn.

Rhythmic stereotypies are gross motor movements without any apparent function and occur in the first year of life, e.g. body rocking and foot kicking (Thelen, 1979; 1980). The onset of rhythmic stereotypies is probably controlled by neuromuscular maturation: they are first observed at birth and peak around the midpoint of the first year of life (accounting for about 40% of a 1 hour observational period: Thelen, 1980), averaging about 5.2% of the time during the first year of life. There are no apparent sex differences in rhythmic stereotypies.

Rhythmic stereotypies can also occur in the context of adult–child interaction. For example, Roopnarine and colleagues (1993) describe instances of parents bouncing children on their knees and throwing them in the air. This sort of activity accounted for 13% of all the play activity of 1-year-olds; object play accounts for another 80%. Thelen (1980) reports similar levels of parent–infant physical play in the form of vestibular stimulation.

Exercise play is gross locomotor movement, such as running and climbing, in the context of play. It is physically vigorous and may or may not be social. Exercise play can start at the end of the first year, and initially much of it (like later aspects of rhythmic stereotypies) takes place in the context of adult–child interaction. Though adult–child exercise play peaks at around 4 years of age (MacDonald & Parke, 1986), there are cases where the adult role is to encourage young children to engage in exercise. For example, Konner (1972) observed that adults in a Botswana foraging group encouraged infants to chase after and catch large insects.

Exercise play is common during the preschool period, though many studies do not differentiate exercise play from rough-and-tumble or pretend play, with which it co-occurs (Pellegrini & Perlmutter, 1987; Smith & Connolly, 1980). Thus, it may be under-reported in the literature. Where it is reported, like other forms of play it follows an inverted-U developmental curve, peaking at around 4 to 5 years (Eaton & Yu, 1989; Routh, Schroeder, & O'Tuama, 1974). The statistics presented below illustrate this pattern. At 2 years, exercise play accounted for about 7% of children's observed behaviour in a day care centre (Rosenthal, 1994), and it increased to about 10% for 2- to 4-year-olds in day care (Field, 1994) and at home (Bloch, 1989). At 5 to 6 years, exercise play accounted for about 13% of behaviour in the home (Bloch, 1989). Two ethological studies of children's behaviour in preschools suggest that exercise play (defined as chase, jump, climb, etc.) accounted for about 20% of all observed behaviour in school (McGrew, 1972; Smith & Connolly, 1980).

As children move into primary school the rates of exercise play decline, though there are fewer studies on which to base this judgement. For 6-year-old children, exercise play accounted for only 13% of all outdoor behaviour at recess (Pellegrini, 1995a). This finding suggests a relative decrease from the preschool period. However, this may represent an underestimate, since the school playground supports this sort of play, whereas the preschool studies were in classrooms which, due to spatial and social policy constraints (e.g. school imposed restrictions on children's rough-and-tumble play are common), are less conducive to exercise play (Smith & Connolly, 1980).

There are reliable sex differences in children's exercise play, with boys engaging in it more than girls (Pellegrini & Smith, 1998). This is probably related to the more general sex difference in physical activity, where differences increase from infancy to mid-adolescence (Eaton & Enns, 1986).

A clear limitation of this work is that children's exercise play has been studied for the most part in schools, particularly in preschools. However, in order to better understand the context of play and make accurate estimates of the time and energy expended in play, expanded efforts must be made to study children in their homes and communities (Barker, 1968; Bronfenbrenner, 1979; Pellegrini & Smith, 1998).

One such effort was mounted by Simons-Morton et al. (1990) in a study of children's (aged 9 to 10 years) exercise and physical fitness. Using self-reported frequencies of moderate to vigorous physical activity across a 3 day period, they found, not surprisingly, that children exercise more before and after school than during school. Over the course of each day, they engaged in one or two bouts of moderate to vigorous physical activity (of 10 minutes or longer).

A number of proximal factors affect exercise play. Spatial density is a major determinant, where more exercise play is observed in spatially less dense environments (Smith & Connolly, 1980); it is obviously easier to move around quickly in a place with lots of space than in one that is restricted.

Degree of prior deprivation can be an important factor. When children (Pellegrini, Huberty, & Jones, 1995; Smith & Hagan, 1980), as well as animals such as deer (Mueller-Schwarze, 1984), are deprived of an opportunity to exercise and then given an opportunity, the level and duration of exercise increase. It may be the case that during the period of childhood, when skeletal and muscular systems are maturing quite rapidly, the body over-compensates for lost opportunities to exercise those rapidly developing systems.

Malnourishment, and ambient temperature, are other factors inhibiting exercise play (Pellegrini & Smith, 1998). When short of food, the body probably uses valuable nutrients for physical growth rather than exercise play. Low levels of exercise play are observed in tropical climates (Cullumbine, 1950); and in playgrounds, high levels of exercise play are observed during cool periods compared to warm periods (Pellegrini, Horvat, & Huberty, 1998). These trends may be related to the thermo-regulative role of exercise (Barber, 1991; Burghardt, 1988).

Play Fighting and Rough-and-Tumble Play

Play fighting involves fighting behaviours – such as kicking, wrestling – which are carried out in a playful context. Often chasing behaviour is included as well, and the generic term 'rough-and-tumble play' is widely used. Rough-and-tumble play is probably the most thoroughly studied aspect of play by investigators with an evolutionary focus. It is commonly observed in most mammal species, and accounts for about 10% of their time and energy budgets (Fagen, 1981).

Rough-and-tumble play, like exercise play, is probably underestimated in the child development literature because most investigators do not include it in their coding schemes, and when it is included it is often subordinated to fantasy play, with which it co-occurs (Pellegrini & Perlmutter, 1987; Smith & Connolly, 1980). For example, in Rubin, Fein, and Vandenberg's (1983, p. 723) review of play, an example of a child enacting a *Star Wars* theme is described, and labelled social pretend. Clearly, such enactments could include aspects of play fighting, and might be coded rough-and-tumble/fantasy play. How different play behaviours get coded is obviously important. Differentiated forms of coding are needed for the estimation of time and energy budgets of play. These estimates, in turn, are important for making functional inferences.

Rough-and-tumble play has been described in many human societies (Fry, 1987; Konner, 1972; Smith, 1997). The cues which separate rough-and-tumble play from actual fighting include smiling and laughter, reversal of roles, withholding of full strength in hitting, as well as the precursors and consequences of the episode (such as staying with friends after the episode is finished). Children themselves are aware of these cues, from the later preschool years onwards (Smith, 1997). A study in Italy and England using video film showed that by 8 and 11 years children were quite expert at distinguishing playful and real fighting, and explaining how they did it: 'It was only a play fight because he didn't hit him hard', or 'That was a play fight as the other boys didn't watch them' (Costabile et al., 1991).

Like exercise play and pretend play, early forms of rough-and-tumble for children take place in the context of adult–child play, and account for about 8% of observed parent–child behaviour (Jacklin, DiPietro, & Maccoby, 1984). Rough-and-tumble play typically involves boys and their fathers (Carson, Burks, & Parke, 1993; Roopnarine et al., 1993).

Observations of rough-and-tumble play with peers, like other forms of play, are usually made in school settings. For the preschool period observations occur primarily in classrooms, while primary and middle school observations take place in school playgrounds. As such, these estimates represent a limited portion of a child's day. Rough-and-tumble play with peers during the preschool period accounts for 3% to 5% of observed classroom behaviour (Pellegrini, 1984), increasing to 7% to 8% at 6 to 10 years (Boulton, 1992; Pellegrini, 1988) and 10% at 7 to 10 years (Humphreys & Smith, 1987). It declines to 5% at 11 to 13 years (Boulton, 1992; Pellegrini, 1995b) and to 3% at 14 years (Pellegrini, 1995b).

There are also robust sex differences in rough-and-tumble play. Boys, more than girls, engage in rough-and-tumble play in virtually all human cultures (DiPietro, 1981; Humphreys & Smith, 1984) and in most mammalian species (Meaney, Stewart, & Beatty, 1985; Smith, 1982). These differences hold for parent–child play (Carson, Burks, & Parke, 1993; Roopnarine et al., 1993) as well as peer play (DiPietro, 1981; Humphreys & Smith, 1987; Pellegrini, 1989). The sex differences are more robust for play fighting than for chasing (Smith & Connolly, 1980), perhaps reflecting the degree to which this sort of behaviour is modelled and reinforced for males. For example, fathers spend more time with sons than with daughters (Parke & Suomi, 1981), and fathers more than mothers engage in rough-and-tumble play, and they do so with sons more than daughters (Carson, Burks, & Parke, 1993). Further, in schools, girls' play is supervised more closely than that of boys (Fagot, 1974), and this may inhibit physically vigorous play, which teachers consider inappropriate for girls (Pellegrini, 1988).

The above noted social learning influences on rough-and-tumble play must be considered in conjunction with hormonal events to obtain a full understanding of sex differences in both rough-and-tumble play and exercise play. Hormonal influences on physical activity and play typically centre on the role of androgens on neural organization and behaviour (Meaney, Stewart, & Beatty, 1985). Normal exposure to androgens during foetal development predisposes males, more than females, towards physical activity generally, and exercise play and rough-and-tumble play more specifically. It has been suggested that excessive amounts of these hormones during foetal development lead to masculinized play behaviour in females (Collaer & Hines, 1995; Money & Ehrhardt, 1972). The experimental literature on mice, hamsters, rats, and monkeys lends support to the androgenization hypothesis (Collaer & Hines, 1995; Quadagno, Briscoe, & Quadagno, 1977).

Such experiments are impossible with humans. Yet we do have 'natural experiments' where human foetuses are exposed to abnormally high does of androgens, e.g. congenital adrenal hyperplasia. These studies, too, support the androgenization hypothesis. Utilizing limited behavioural observations and a combination of questionnaires in which both parents and children are asked to report on behaviours, it has been revealed that androgenized girls, relative to controls, preferred male activities and toys (Berenbaum & Snyder, 1995; Hines & Kaufman, 1994; Money & Ehrhardt, 1972).

These robust sex differences in exercise and rough-and-tumble play should be related to functional benefits of these forms of play. The proximal factors affecting rough-and-tumble play are similar to those affecting exercise, as they are both physically vigorous.

War Play

Although children's play tends to be seen positively by adults, play fighting is not always approved of by teachers, and even more controversial is play with war toys. The term 'war play' has been applied to games with toy guns, weapons and combat figures, as well as pretend fighting or warfare. This kind of play has elicited concern from some writers, and is banned in many kindergartens. Carlsson-Paige and Levin (1987) argue that war toys and combat figures encourage stereotyped, good-versus-evil aggressive scripts in play, which impoverish the child's imagination and encourage actual aggression. They recognize the difficulties in banning such play entirely; for example, if replica guns are banned, children may make them from Lego, or just use their fingers! However they do advocate adults intervening to shape such play toward more constructive and less aggressive ends. By contrast, Sutton-Smith (1988) argues that war play is clearly pretend, and just reflects aspects of real life like other pretend play does.

Functions of Play

What is Meant by Function?

Function has at least two meanings in the social and behavioural sciences, following from Tinbergen's (1963) classic 'four whys'. In its ultimate sense, function can be defined in terms of an evolutionary history of biological adaptation for a given species. A behaviour is functional in this 'ultimate' sense (Hinde, 1980, p. 102) if it has typically added to the survival or reproductive success of individuals (genes) over many succeeding generations.

Functions can also be defined in terms of beneficial consequences during the lifespan of any particular individual, irrespective of the evolutionary history of selection. This meaning of function refers to outcomes during the life of the individual player (Hinde, 1980; Symons, 1978). Benefits may be accrued immediately, during childhood, or deferred until adulthood. For example, social physical activity play might have immediate value in terms of affiliation with a peer group, or it may have deferred benefits and relate to later ability to encode and decode social signals (Pellegrini & Smith, 1998).

Play is typically seen by educators as serving an important function in children's development. Indeed, Smith (1988) has described how a 'play ethos' developed from the 1920s through to the 1980s. The 'play ethos' can be described as an uncritical assumption of the long-term benefits of play. For example, Isaacs (1929) stated that 'Play is indeed the child's work, and the means whereby he grows and develops'; and a Department of Environment Report in the UK (1973) stated that 'the realisation that play is essential for normal development has slowly but surely permeated our cultural heritage'. Psychology textbooks of the period often cited many functions of play, quite uncritically. Smith (1988) argued that this play ethos actually distorted the interpretation of many functional studies of object and pretend play during the 1970s and 1980s.

Given the assumptions of the importance of play for development, it can appear paradoxical that behaviours are often classified as play if they appear to have no immediate benefit to the actor. As noted in the section on definitions of play, play behaviours resemble 'more serious' versions of behaviour but are more exaggerated and more concerned with the means of the activity than the end product. The paradox can be reconciled by supposing that the apparent lack of immediate function actually conceals either a function delayed in development, or an immediate function of which the player (and even the observer) may be unaware. It is also possible that the play ethos is fundamentally mistaken and that play has little or no function; though such a view must contend with the evolutionary ubiquity of exercise and rough-and-tumble play, the universally human aspects of fantasy play, and the general finding that these forms of play take up an appreciable time and energy budget for juveniles, as well as incurring some risks of injury.

Researchers into both animal play (Bekoff & Byers, 1981; 1998; Martin & Caro, 1985) and child play (Pellegrini & Smith, 1998; Rubin, Fein, & Vandenberg, 1983) have discussed the numerous developmental functions proposed for play. They are principally delayed functions; the consideration of immediate functions of play has been largely absent from the child development literature.

Immediate or Delayed Functions

Most theories of play (Groos, 1898; 1901; Piaget, 1951) have proposed that the benefits of play are not immediate to the period of childhood but delayed or deferred until later in development. Correspondingly, the purpose of play, a behaviour that is sometimes used as representative of the juvenile period, is understood in terms of what value it has later in development, not during childhood. In Bateson's (1976) terms this view presents play as a 'scaffolding' metaphor: play functions in the assembly of a skill and then is disassembled when the skill is complete (Bruner, 1972). Although this remains an influential view, it has to be recognized that empirical studies of animal and children's play have not provided strong or unequivocal evidence to support this claim (e.g. Bekoff & Byers, 1981; Byers & Walker, 1995; Caro, 1995; Fagen, 1981; Martin & Caro, 1985; Pellegrini & Smith, 1998; Smith, 1982; 1988).

The above scaffolding view of play presents it as being an imperfect version of the mature version of that behaviour. From this view, rough-and-tumble play would be beneficial in terms of the ways in which it can be used to shape mature behaviour related to establishing and maintaining social dominance. An alternative view is that play is not an incomplete or imperfect version of adult behaviour but is beneficial to the specific niche of childhood. Bateson's (1981) metaphor for the immediate functions of play is that of metamorphosis. Specifically, play behaviour and its beneficial consequences are unique to a specific period of development and the advantages of those consequences for later development may not be readily apparent, e.g. through discontinuity in development.

Immediate function may reflect the usefulness of play to a specific period. In this way we consider play as a specific adjustment to childhood (Bateson, 1976; 1981; Bjorklund & Green, 1992; Gomendio, 1988; Pellegrini & Bjorklund, 1997). From this view, 'immature' behaviours, such as play, may serve important purposes during childhood. Those behaviours, in turn, may have been naturally selected for during the period of childhood, as natural selection does exert pressure at different points in development. For example, the sense of mastery and self-efficacy associated with children's play probably relates to children experimenting with new and different activities. Once activities are chosen they should be sustained; this, in turn, affords opportunities for the learning of specific skills (Bjorklund & Green, 1992). This is in contrast to the view that these playful behaviours are useful in the assembly of adult skills.

Making Functional Inferences

Function can be inferred in a number of ways: cost–benefit analysis, considerations of design and contextual features, and experimental enhancement or deprivation of play components.

Cost–Benefit Analyses

Cost–benefit analyses can be used to establish a prima facie case for functional significance and is commonly used in the ethological literature (Caro, 1995; Pellegrini, Horvat, & Huberty, 1998). This method assumes that in order for a construct to be naturally selected for, benefits should outweigh costs. Thus, we assume a correspondence between cost and benefits: high costs should have high benefits; low costs can imply low or high benefits. Importantly, this principle suggests that in order to be favoured by natural selection, the benefits in relation to the cost do not need to be great. The benefits merely should be greater than the cost incurred (Caro, 1989).

This method could be applied to the generation and testing of functional hypotheses. Costs can be defined in terms of caloric expenditure, time, and survivorship. For example, engaging in vigorous play may be costly in terms of the calories that are consumed, calories that might otherwise have been used to grow and support tissue. Regarding time, play may consume a significant portion of the day (estimates at around 10%), time that might be more efficiently used in direct skills tutorials. Lastly and in terms of survivorship, play might be dangerous. During play children could be hurt, most commonly by falling, or in extreme cases killed, by drowning or falling.

Cost–benefit analyses represent a promising method for studying play, primarily because children can be studied in natural ecologies – or those circumstance in which they develop. Although studies of costs are fundamental, there are surprisingly few of them (Pellegrini, Horvat, & Huberty, 1998); consequently we cannot reliably estimate the magnitude of likely benefits of play according to this method. Basic information on amount of time spent in play is scanty. For example, we do not know the amount of time that the average preschool child spends in pretend and exercise play in the course of the day. Information of this kind has implications not only for theoretical issues related to function, but also for child health. Further, we do not know the extent to which childhood accidents are embedded in play or nonplay contexts. For example, what proportion of the total number of drownings (a major cause of accidental deaths among children) occur while playing? These sorts of information are certainly important for providing adequate services for children. For example, if studies show that children spend more time and calories in vigorous play, schools might be encouraged to increase break times where this sort of activity is high.

Some hints about the probable functions of play according to this model can be hypothesized from the animal play research. Play accounts for a limited portion of an animal's time and energy budgets – around 10% (Martin & Caro, 1985; Pellegrini, Horvat, & Huberty, 1998). Based on these rather low levels, as well of lack of evidence for a large and deferred effect for play, cost–benefit analyses suggest that the benefits of play are probably small and immediate. They should be immediate, rather than deferred, because of the increased probability of the risks encountered during the time from childhood to maturation. Risk in this sense refers to the probability of surviving from childhood to adulthood, and ultimately mating and having surviving offspring. More risks are encountered as time increases to maturation. The probability of reaping these small benefits is maximized if they are accrued during childhood rather than waiting until maturation.

Design Features Arguments

A design features argument involves explanation of the similarities between aspects of play behaviour and similar features in functional behaviour. Take one feature of social play, such as reciprocal role taking: role taking in play at 2 years of age could be related (conceptually and empirically) to the ability to take different, more mature roles later, at 6 years of age, such as the ability to take another person's point of view in a debate. Establishing function, then, involves making logical and empirical connections between the features of play at one period and functions later.

However, there are some problems with the design features approach to the study of function. Any one play behaviour may serve more than one function. Similarly, a behaviour in a mature individual may develop from many different antecedents (i.e. 'equifinality': Martin & Caro, 1985). Design features arguments have been made most frequently for rough-and-tumble play and fantasy play.

Regarding *rough-and-tumble play*, social and physically vigorous dimensions of play (such as running/chasing), respectively, have been linked theoretically to later aggressive/fighting capacity and cardiovascular fitness (Humphreys & Smith, 1987; Pellegrini, 1993; 1995b; Smith, 1982). Empirically, rough-and-tumble play relates proximally to children's vigorous games (Pellegrini, 1988). The role alternation and chasing components are similar to the turn taking and running involved in games such as tag. As children approach adolescence, rough-and-tumble play, especially for boys, appears to be increasingly incorporated into assertion or establishing and maintaining social dominance (Pellegrini & Smith, 1998).

These benefits of rough-and-tumble play are consistent with gender differences, where boys engage in rough-and-tumble play more than girls. Specifically, the forms of behaviours that boys use to establish and maintain dominance are similar to those they exhibit in rough-and-tumble. Further, and more distally, any hunting or fighting benefits in adulthood associated with rough-and-tumble play (Smith, 1982) also reflects males' roles in the environment of evolutionary adaptedness (EEA).

Regarding *social fantasy play*, children typically talk about mental and cognitive states in the process of negotiating roles, e.g. 'doctors can't say that' (Pellegrini & Galda, 1993). De Lorimier, Doyle, and Tessier (1995) found children more intensely involved in negotiations in pretence than in non-pretence contexts. Howe, Petrakos, and Rinaldi (1998) examined play in 40 sibling dyads. Target siblings were 5–6 years old. Frequent pretend dyads were more likely to use internal state terms, especially in high-level negotiations about play. Brown, Donelan-McCall, and Dunn (1996) observed interactions between 4-year-olds and their older siblings, a best friend, or their mother. Mental state terms were used a lot with siblings, and best friends. Mental state term use co-occurred with pretend play.

The ability to talk about language is related specifically to children's phonemic awareness, or their awareness of the rules governing the sound system of English, and to subsequent school-based reading. An important component in learning to read involves children learning letter–sound correspondence (Pellegrini et al., 1995). The awareness of these rules probably develops in social pretence.

The studies just cited make a plausible case for some link between pretend play and theory of mind development – the understanding of others' mental states, or a metarepresentational ability. Leslie (1987) has argued that pretend play is an indicator of metarepresentational abilities as early as 18 months, and is important in developing the ability for understanding that someone else may represent things differently (have different knowledge, or beliefs) from yourself. A number of correlational studies have suggested links between pretend play and theory of mind abilities; for example, Taylor and Carlson (1997) studied 3- and 4-year-olds and found a significant correlation between pretend play and theory of mind scores in the 4-year-old children. They concluded: 'our intuition is that extensive fantasy experiences help children develop an understanding of mind' (1997, p. 452).

However, Lillard (1993) and Jarrold et al. (1994) have reviewed the evidence on pretend play skills and theory of mind, and both studies conclude that the evidence is not strong. Much early pretend play (up to 3 years of age) appears to be largely imitative, as is shown by Howes (1994). There is little reason to suppose that social pretence implies metarepresentational abilities on the part of the child until 37–48 months. The period when pretend play does show evidence for metarepresentation is also the period when first-order theory of mind abilities emerge by most criteria; so there is little reason to postulate that pretend play has a leading role in theory of mind development. Correlational evidence can of course be interpreted in various causal directions.

Experimental Deprivation Studies

Deprivation studies are common in the animal play literature (e.g. Mueller-Schwarze, 1984) but relatively uncommon with children. In these studies, children (or young animals) are deprived of an aspect of play, typically social play and physical activity play. The assumption behind these studies is that deprivation of an aspect of play, if it is developmentally important (i.e. it serves a beneficial consequence), should result in a 'rebound effect' (Burghardt, 1984) when children are given the opportunity to play again. Children compensate for the deprivation by engaging in high levels and longer durations of play. Most deprivation studies can be criticized on the grounds that more than one thing is involved when we deprive children of play. So when children are deprived of social play, they are often at the same time deprived of other forms of social interaction.

The effects of depriving children of play opportunities have largely been limited to studies of locomotor play. In three sets of field experiments, Smith and Hagan (1980) and Pellegrini and colleagues (Pellegrini & Davis, 1993; Pellegrini, Huberty, & Jones, 1995) experimentally deprived a sample of British preschoolers and American primary school children of opportunities for locomotor play. The results were consistent across all the experiments in showing that greater deprivation led to increased levels of play when opportunities became available. Further, with the primary school sample, break time increased children's attention to school tasks when they returned to the classroom. Byers and Walker (1995) argued that children engaged in longer and more intense bouts of locomotor play after deprivation so as to overcompensate for lost opportunities for physical exercise, which serves important training functions. Further, the relatively transient effects of physical training suggest that they are immediate and can occur at any point during the life span. Results on the effect of break time on attention to school tasks are consistent with the cognitive immaturity hypothesis (Bjorklund & Green, 1992) that nonfocused play activities, such as those found at break time, provided a release from more focused school work.

Experimental Enrichment Studies

Enrichment procedures provide children with additional opportunities to engage in play that vary according to theoretically relevant dimensions such as reciprocal role taking (Burns & Brainerd, 1979) or conceptual conflict (Pellegrini, 1984). The effect on, say, perspective taking is then examined. Most of the criterion measures in these studies are taken in close temporal proximity to the training, thus assuming that play has immediate rather than deferred benefits.

There have been a host of experimental enrichment studies involving the effects of object play generally and pretend or sociodramatic play specifically on various dimensions of children's social cognitive status, such as role taking (e.g. Burns & Brainerd, 1979), narrative competence (Pellegrini, 1984), creativity (e.g. Dansky & Silverman, 1973), problem solving (Sylva, Bruner, & Genova, 1976), and theory of mind (Dockett, 1998). Most of these studies showed positive benefits of play; but they must be interpreted cautiously, because laboratory-based experimental manipulations of play can only tell us how certain variables *may* affect behaviour in more natural situations (Bronfenbrenner, 1979; McCall, 1977).

Many play enrichment experiments have serious internal validity problems (Smith, 1988). For example, some confound play treatment with adults tutoring children in play (Pellegrini, 1984; Smith & Syddall, 1978). Additionally, lack of control for experimenter bias in much of this work invalidates many possible conclusions regarding function (Simon & Smith, 1985; Smith & Whitney, 1987). Even if internal validity issues have been controlled, the treatments have often been of such short duration (10 minutes in some cases: Dansky & Silverman, 1973) that we must question their efficacy to change otherwise stable behaviour in a child of 3–5 years of age.

Smith (1988) also argued that the play ethos has led researchers to emphasize findings of marginal significance, and ignore nonsignificant findings or explain them away in terms of *ad hoc* methodological shortcomings. As a recent example, consider the report by Taylor and Carlson (1997) linking pretend play to theory of mind, cited earlier. There was no relationship for 3-year-olds, but a significant relationship for 4-year-olds. The correlation for the whole sample was modest: $r = 0.16$ for the correlation of principal fantasy component with theory of mind – significant, but accounting for only 2.6% of the variance. Taylor and Carlson stated, 'we are not certain why this relation between fantasy and theory of mind was not found for the 3-year-olds. Perhaps our methods for assessing individual differences in fantasy were not as appropriate for younger children as for the older ones', thus blaming methodological inadequacy for an unexpected non-significant finding. They nevertheless concluded that 'the results of this study provide strong evidence that there is a relation between theory of mind and pretend play development in 4-year-old children' (1997, p. 451). This seems a very positive gloss on their findings. In taking this otherwise excellent study as an example, we would point out that these kinds of positive gloss on findings still pervade much of the writing on children's play.

ADULT PLAY

Play is typically seen as a juvenile activity, in both animal and human play. Juveniles, relative to adults, spend more time and energy in play. Yet, adults do engage in some forms of play. Theorists have described the shift from play to organized games in adolescence and adulthood. It is not our intention to review the extensive literature on games and sport in adulthood (see Sutton-Smith & Roberts, 1979). So far as play per se is concerned, the most extensive literature is on parent–child play (MacDonald, 1993a). We have seen how early physical play and pretend play are often facilitated or scaffolded by adults, usually parents in western societies.

MacDonald (1993b) argues that such kinds of adult play are a form of parental investment in offspring. Taking as an assumption that play has longer-term benefits, he argues that, especially in societies or social class groups in which value is put on the quality (rather than quantity) of offspring and their development, parent–child play will bring benefits to the children and is a positive aspect, to be encouraged.

There are other views of parent–child or adult–child play, however. Adults might manipulate children to their own advantage, discouraging rough-and-tumble play, for example, because of costs to themselves (noisy, disruptive) and ignoring benefits to the child. Sutton-Smith (1986) argued that the way we define and idealize play may reflect the needs of adults in organizing and controlling children, rather than children's own needs and wishes; he emphasizes that children's play can at times be anarchic, and rebellious of adult expectations. There is also clearly an adult-dominated market of children's toys, heavily advertised and promoted to increase children's consumption – a manipulation of both parents and children by commercial interests. Kline (1995) has described a 'global toy curriculum' in which particular theme toys and play products are marketed on an international scale, with scant consideration of benefits to the children who consume the products.

The issue of reciprocal relationships between play and society has been taken up most thoroughly by Sutton-Smith (1997). His book on the ambiguity of play discusses a series of 'rhetorics' which, he argues, have dictated the research and writing about play across a range of social science disciplines. His work takes further the links between play and related activities such as games, athletics, gambling, and festivals.

CONCLUSION

Play is something juvenile members of many mammal species do; and humans spend more time as juveniles than any other large animal. In fact, if play were to be used as a defining characteristic of the juvenile period, it would extend well into the reproductive years (and perhaps into senescence) in humans. Although play is characterized by its seemingly 'purposelessness', both animal and human theorists of play concur that it does indeed have a function, perhaps numerous ones. Some functions of play appear to be immediate, including thermoregulation, exercise, and the establishment and maintenance of social relations during childhood. Others appear to be deferred, including the practising of adult roles in a nonthreatening context. Play serves as a way for youth to explore both their physical and social worlds and to modify their neural circuitry in the meantime.

We argue, as have others (Bruner, 1972; Fagen, 1981; Martin & Caro, 1985), that play has been subjected to selection pressures over the course of mammalian evolution. Play in humans is extended and so dominates our impression of childhood because human children have so much to learn that they require, not only a long time to learn it, but also safe environments in which to master their eventual adult roles. The interactions and lessons acquired during play among peers, perhaps more than any other single socialization agent, afford children the opportunity and flexibility to learn what it means to be a man or woman in their society.

The pressures of modern society are, in some cases, minimizing the role of play in children's lives. Recently, for example, in both the UK and the USA, children's break times or recesses during school days are being eliminated or curtailed in the interests of increased school achievement (see Pellegrini & Blatchford, 2000). The arguments for elimination of play are that it minimizes valuable instructional time and that it often supports antisocial behaviour. Evidence does not support these claims: for example, children's achievement is enhanced when breaks are distributed across the school day. Further, children learn to cooperate and regulate their emotions by interacting with peers. Play is one of the many ways in which this can be done.

A major challenge in the study of play involves examining play with an objective scrutiny. As play researchers we recognize the possible importance of play, but we must balance this with the possibility that play may not be very important in the way in which some individuals develop. A century after the seminal work of Groos, we have learnt a great deal about play, but still have much to discover.

Acknowledgments

We acknowledge the comments of D. Bjorklund, K. Connolly, and J. Valsiner at various stages in the development of this chapter. Work on this chapter was supported, in part, by grants from the W. T. Grant Foundation and the Spencer Foundation to the first author.

References

Arrington, R. (1943). Time sampling in studies of social behaviour: A critical review of techniques and results with research suggestions. *Psychological Bulletin*, 40, 81–124.

Bakeman, R., & Brownlee, J. (1980). The strategic use of parallel play: A sequential analysis. *Child Development*, 51, 873–875.

Barber, N. (1991). Play and energy regulation in mammals. *Quarterly Review of Biology*, 66, 129–147.

Barker, R.G. (1968). *Ecological psychology: Concepts and methods for studying the environment of human behaviour*. Stanford, CA: Stanford University Press.

Bateson, P.P.G. (1976). Rules and reciprocity in behavioural development. In P.P.G. Bateson & R. Hinde (eds), *Growing points in ethology* (pp. 401–421). Cambridge: Cambridge University Press.

Bateson, P.P.G. (1981). Discontinuities in development and changes in the organization of play in cats. In K. Immelmann, G. Barlow, L. Petrinovich, & M. Main (eds), *Behavioural development* (pp. 281–295). New York: Cambridge University Press.

Bekoff, M., & Allen, C. (1998). Intentional communication in social play: How and why animals negotiate and agree to play. In M. Bekoff and J.A. Byers (eds), *Animal play: Evolutionary, comparative, and ecological perspectives* (pp. 97–114). New York: Cambridge University Press.

Bekoff, M., & Byers, J.A. (1981). A critical re-analysis of the ontogeny and phylogeny of mammalian social and locomotor play. In K. Immelmann, G. Barlow, L. Petronovich, & M. Main (eds), *Behavioural development* (pp. 296–337). Cambridge: Cambridge University Press.

Bekoff, M., & Byers, J.A. (eds) (1998) *Animal play: Evolutionary, comparative, and ecological perspectives*. New York: Cambridge University Press.

Belsky, J., & Most, R. (1981). From exploration to play. *Developmental Psychology*, 17, 630–639.

Berenbaum, S.A., & Snyder, E. (1995). Early hormonal influences on childhood sex-typed activity and playmate preferences: Implications for the development of sexual orientation. *Developmental Psychology*, 31, 31–42.

Bjorklund, D., & Green, B. (1992). The adaptive nature of cognitive immaturity. *American Psychologist*, 47, 46–54.

Bloch, M.N. (1989). Young boys' and girls' play at home and in the community: A cultural ecological framework. In M. Bloch & A. Pellegrini (eds), *The ecological context of children's play* (pp. 120–154). Norwood, NJ: Ablex.

Bornstein, M., Haynes, O.M., Pascual, L., Painter, K.M., & Galperin, C. (1999). Play in two societies. *Child Development*, 70, 317–331.

Boulton, M.J. (1992). Participation in playground activities in middle school. *Educational Research*, 34, 167–182.

Bretherton, I. (1989). Pretense: The form and function of make-believe play. *Developmental Review*, 9, 383–401.

Bronfenbrenner, U. (1979). *The ecology of human development*. Cambridge, MA: Harvard University Press.

Brown, J.R., Donelan-McCall, N., & Dunn, J. (1996). Why talk about mental states? The significance of children's conversation with friends, siblings and mothers. *Child Development*, 67, 836–849.

Bruner, J.S. (1972). The nature and uses of immaturity. *American Psychologist*, 27, 687–708.

Burghardt, G. (1984). On the origins of play. In P.K. Smith (ed.), *Play in animals and humans* (pp. 5–42). Oxford: Blackwell.

Burghardt, G. (1988). Precocity, play, and the ectotherm–endotherm transition. In E. Blass (ed.), *Handbook of behavioural neurobiology* (Vol. 9, pp. 107–148). New York: Plenum.

Burns, S., & Brainerd, C. (1979). Effects of constructive and dramatic play on perspective taking in very young children. *Developmental Psychology*, 15, 512–521.

Byers, J.A., & Walker, C. (1995). Refining the motor training hypothesis for the evolution of play. *American Naturalist*, 146, 25–40.

Byrne, R. (1995). *The thinking ape: Evolutionary origins of intelligence*. Oxford: Oxford University Press.

Carlsson-Paige, N., & Levin, D.E. (1987). *The war play dilemma: Balancing needs and values in the early childhood classroom*. New York: Teachers' College, Columbia University.

Caro, T.M. (1989). Indirect costs of play: Cheetah cubs reduce maternal hunting success. *Animal Behaviour*, 35, 295–297.

Caro, T.M. (1995). Short-term costs and correlates of play in cheetahs. *Animal Behaviour*, 49, 333–345.

Carson, J., Burks, V., & Parke, R.D. (1993). Parent–child physical play: determinants and consequences. In K. MacDonald (ed.), *Parent–child play*. New York: SUNY Press.

Collaer, J.L., & Hines, M. (1995). Human behavioural sex differences: A role for gonadal hormones during early development. *Psychological Bulletin*, 118, 55–107.

Costabile, A., Smith, P.K., Matheson, L., Aston, J., Hunter, T., & Boulton, M. (1991). Cross-national comparison of how children distinguish playful and serious fighting. *Developmental Psychology*, 27, 881–887.

Cullumbine, H. (1950). Heat production and energy requirements of tropical people. *Journal of Applied Physiology*, 2, 201–210.

Dansky, J., & Silverman, I. (1973). Effects of play on associative fluency of preschool-age children. *Developmental Psychology*, 9, 38–43.

de Lorimier, S., Doyle, A.-B., & Tessier, O. (1995). Social coordination during pretend play: Comparisons with nonpretend play and effects on expressive content. *Merrill-Palmer Quarterly*, 41, 497–516.

Department of the Environment (1973). *Children at play*. Design Bulletin 27. London: HMSO.

de Waal, F.B.M. (1989). *Peacemaking among primates*. Cambridge, MA: Harvard University Press.

DiPietro, J.A. (1981). Rough-and-tumble play: A function of gender. *Developmental Psychology*, 17, 50–58.

Dockett, S. (1998). Constructing understandings through play in the early years. *International Journal of Early Years Education*, 6, 105–116.

Eaton, W.C., & Enns, L. (1986). Sex differences in human motor activity level. *Psychological Bulletin*, 100, 19–28.

Eaton, W.C., & Yu, A. (1989). Are sex differences in child motor activity level a function of sex differences in maturational status? *Child Development*, 60, 1005–1011.

Eibl-Eibesfeldt, I. (1989). *Human ethology*. New York: Aldine de Gruyter.

Fagen, R. (1981). *Animal play behavior*. New York: Oxford University Press.

Fagot, B. (1974). Sex differences in toddlers' behaviour and parental reaction. *Developmental Psychology*, 10, 554–558.

Fein, G. (1981). Pretend play: An integrative review. *Child Development*, 52, 1095–1118.

Field, T. (1994). Infant day care facilitates later social behaviour and school performance. In E. Jacobs & H. Goelman (eds), *Children's play in day care settings*. Albany: SUNY Press.

Fry, D.P. (1987). Differences between play fighting and serious fights among Zapotec children. *Ethology and Sociobiology*, 8, 285–306.

Gomendio, M. (1988). The development of different types of play in gazelles: Implications for the nature and functions of play. *Animal Behaviour*, 36, 825–836.

Groos, K. (1898). *The play of animals*. New York: Appleton.

Groos, K. (1901). *The play of man*. New York: Appleton.

Haight, W.L., & Miller, P.J. (1993). *Pretending at home: Early development in a sociocultural context*. Albany: SUNY Press.

Hartup, W.W. (1996). The company they keep: Friendships and their developmental significance. *Child Development*, 67, 1–13.

Hayes, K.J., & Hayes, C. (1952). Imitation in a home-reared chimpanzee. *Journal of Comparative Physiological Psychology*, 45, 450–459.

Hinde, R.A. (1980). *Ethology*. London: Fontana.

Hines, M., & Kaufman, F.R. (1994). Androgen and the development of human sex-typical behaviour: Rough-and-tumble play and sex of preferred playmates in children with congenital adrenal hyperplasia (CAH). *Child Development*, 65, 1042–1053.

Howe, N., Petrakos, H., & Rinaldi, C.M. (1998). 'All the sheeps are dead. He murdered them.': Sibling pretense, negotiation, internal state language, and relationship quality. *Child Development*, 69, 182–191.

Howes, C. (1994). *The collaborative construction of pretend*. Albany, NY: SUNY Press.

Howes, C., & Matheson, C.C. (1992). Sequences in the development of competent play with peers: social and pretend play. *Developmental Psychology*, 28, 961–974.

Humphreys, A.P., & Smith, P.K. (1984). Rough-and-tumble play in preschool and playground. In P.K. Smith (ed.), *Play in animals and humans* (pp. 241–270). Oxford: Blackwell.

Humphreys, A.P., & Smith, P.K. (1987). Rough-and-tumble play, friendship, and dominance in school children: Evidence for continuity and change with age. *Child Development*, 58, 201–212.

Hutt, C. (1966). Exploration and play in children. *Symposia of the Zoological Society of London*, 18, 61–81.

Isaacs, S. (1929). *The nursery years*. London: Routledge & Kegan Paul.

Jacklin, C.N., DiPietro, J.A., & Maccoby, E.E. (1984). Sex-typing behaviour and sex-typing pressure in child/parent interaction. *Archives of Sexual Behaviour*, 13, 413–425.

Jarrold, C., Carruthers, P., Smith, P.K., & Boucher, J. (1994). Pretend play: Is it metarepresentational? *Mind and Language*, 9, 445–468.

Kline, S. (1995). The promotion and marketing of toys: Time to rethink the paradox? In A.D. Pellegrini (ed.), *The future of play theory*. Albany: SUNY Press.

Konner, M. (1972). Aspects of the developmental ethology of a foraging people. In N. Blurton Jones (ed.), *Ethological studies of child behaviour* (pp. 285–304). Cambridge: Cambridge University Press.

Konner, M. (1976). Relationships among infants and juveniles in comparative perspective. *Social Sciences Information*, 13, 371–402.

Kuczaj, S.A. II (1986). Language play. In P.K. Smith (ed.), *Children's play: Research developments and practical applications*. London: Gordon & Breach.

Lancy, D. (1996). *Playing on the mother ground*. New York: Guilford.

Leslie, A.M. (1987). Pretense and representation: The origins of 'theory of mind'. *Psychological Review*, 94, 412–426.

Lillard, A.S. (1993). Pretend play skills and the child's theory of mind. *Child Development*, 64, 348–371.

MacDonald, K. (ed.) (1993a). *Parent–child play*. New York: SUNY Press.

MacDonald, K. (1993b). Parent–child play: An evolutionary perspective. In K. MacDonald (ed.), *Parent–child play*. New York: SUNY Press.

MacDonald, K., and Parke, R. (1986). Parent–child physical play. *Sex Roles*, 15, 367–378.

Martin, P., & Bateson, P.P.G. (1993). *Measuring behaviour*. Cambridge: Cambridge University Press.

Martin, P., & Caro, T. (1985). On the function of play and its role in behavioural development. In J. Rosenblatt, C. Beer, M. Bushnel, & P. Slater (eds), *Advances in the study of behaviour* (Vol. 15, pp. 59–103). Orlando, FL: Academic.

McCall, R. (1977). Challenges to a science of developmental psychology. *Child Development*, 48, 333–394.

McGrew, W.C. (1972). *An ethological study of children's behaviour*. London: Academic.

McLoyd, V.C. (1982). Social class differences in sociodramatic play: A critical review. *Developmental Review*, 2, 1–30.

McLoyd, V. (1983). The effects of the structure of play objects on the pretend play of low-income preschool children. *Child Development*, 54, 626–635

Meaney, M.J., Stewart, J., & Beatty, W.W. (1985). Sex differences in social play. In J. Rosenblatt, C. Beer, M.C. Bushnell, & P. Slater (eds), *Advances in the study of behaviour* (Vol. 15, pp. 2–58). New York: Academic.

Money, J., & Ehrhardt, A.A. (1972). *Man and woman, boy and girl*. Baltimore, MD: Johns Hopkins University Press.

Morris, D. (1962). *The biology of art*. London: Methuen.

Mueller-Schwarze, D. (1984). Analysis of play behaviour. In P.K. Smith (ed.), *Play in animals and humans* (pp. 147–158). Oxford: Blackwell.

Parke, R.D., & Suomi, S.J. (1981). Adult male infant relationships: Human and nonhuman primate evidence. In K. Immelman, G.W. Barlow, L. Petronovitch, & M. Main (eds), *Behavioural development* (pp. 700–725). New York: Cambridge University Press.

Parten, M.B. (1932). Social participation among preschool children. *Journal of Abnormal and Social Psychology*, 27, 243–269.

Pellegrini, A.D. (1984). Identifying causal elements in the thematic fantasy play paradigm. *American Education Research Journal*, 19, 443–452.

Pellegrini, A.D. (1988). Elementary school children's rough-and-tumble play and social competence. *Developmental Psychology*, 24, 802–806.

Pellegrini, A.D. (1989). Elementary school children's rough-and-tumble play. *Early Childhood Research Quarterly*, 4, 245–260.

Pellegrini, A.D. (1993). Boys' rough-and-tumble play, social competence and group composition. *British Journal of Developmental Psychology*, 11, 237–248.

Pellegrini, A.D. (1995a). *School recess and playground behaviour*. Albany: SUNY Press.

Pellegrini, A.D. (1995b). A longitudinal study of boys' rough-and-tumble play and dominance during early adolescence. *Journal of Applied Developmental Psychology*, 16, 77–93.

Pellegrini, A.D., & Bjorklund, D.F. (1997). The role of recess in children's cognitive performance. *Educational Psychologist*, 31, 181–187.

Pellegrini, A.D., & Blatchford, P. (2000). *The child at school: Interactions with peers and teachers*. London: Arnold.

Pellegrini, A.D., & Davis, P. (1993). Relations between children's playground and classroom behaviour. *British Journal of Educational Psychology*, 63, 86–95.

Pellegrini, A.D., & Galda, L. (1993). Ten years after: A re-examination of the relations between symbolic play and literacy. *Reading Research Quarterly*, 28, 162–175.

Pellegrini, A.D., Galda, L., Shockley, B., & Stahl, S. (1995). The nexus of social and literacy events at home and school: Implications for primary school oral language and literacy. *British Journal of Educational Psychology*, 65, 273–285.

Pellegrini, A.D., Horvat, M., & Huberty, P.D. (1998). The relative costs of children's physical activity play. *Animal Behaviour*, 55, 1053–1061.

Pellegrini, A.D., Huberty, P.D., & Jones, I. (1995). The effects of recess timing on children's playground and classroom behaviours. *American Educational Research Journal*, 32, 845–864.

Pellegrini, A.D., & Perlmutter, J.C. (1987). A re-examination of the Smilansky–Parten matrix of play behaviour. *Journal of Research in Childhood Education*, 2, 89–96.

Pellegrini, A.D., & Perlmutter, J.C. (1989). Classroom contextual effects on children's play. *Developmental Psychology*, 25, 289–296.

Pellegrini, A.D., & Smith, P.K. (1998). Physical activity play: The nature and function of a neglected aspect of play. *Child Development*, 69, 577–598.

Piaget, J. (1951). *Play, dreams, and imitation in childhood*. London: Routledge & Kegan Paul.

Power, T. (2000). *Play and exploration in children and animals*. Mahwah, NJ: Erlbaum.

Quadagno, D.M., Briscoe, R., & Quadagno, J.S. (1977). Effects of perinatal gonadal hormones on selected nonsexual behaviour patterns: A critical assessment of the nonhuman and human literature. *Psychological Bulletin*, 84, 62–82.

Roggman, L., & Langlois, J. (1987). Mothers, infants, and toys: Social play correlates of attachment. *Infant Behaviour and Development*, 10, 233–237.

Roopnarine, J.L., Hooper, F.H., Ahmeduzzaman, M., & Pollack, B. (1993). Gentle play partners: Mother–child and father–child play in New Delhi, India. In K. MacDonald (ed.), *Parent–child play*. New York: SUNY Press.

Rosenthal, M.K. (1994). Social and non-social play of infants and toddlers in family day care. In E.V. Jacobs & H. Goelman (eds), *Children's play in child care settings* (pp. 163–192). Albany: SUNY Press.

Routh, D., Schoeder, C., & O'Tuama, L. (1974). Development of activity levels in children. *Developmental Psychology*, 10, 163–168.

Rubin, K.H., Fein, G., & Vandenberg, B. (1983). Play. In E.M. Hetherington (ed.), *Handbook of child psychology: Socialization, personality, and social development* (Vol. IV, pp. 693–774). New York: Wiley.

Rubin, K.H., Watson, K.S., & Jambor, T.W. (1978). Free-play behaviours in preschool and kindergarten children. *Child Development*, 49, 534–536.

Savage-Rumbaugh, E.S. (1986). *Ape language: From conditioned response to symbol*. New York: Columbia University Press.

Schwartzmann, H. (1978). *Transformations: The anthropology of children's play*. New York: Plenum.

Simon, T., & Smith, P.K. (1985). Play and problem solving: A paradigm questioned. *Merrill-Palmer Quarterly*, 31, 73–86.

Simons-Morton, B.G., O'Hara, N.M., Parcel, G.S., Huang, I.W., Baranowski, T., & Wilson, B. (1990). Children's frequency of participation in moderate to vigorous physical activities. *Research Quarterly for Exercise and Sport*, 61, 307–314.

Slaughter, D., & Dombrowski, J. (1989). Cultural continuities and discontinuities: Impact on social and pretend play. In M.N. Block & A.D. Pellegrini (eds), *The ecological content of children's play* (pp. 282–310). Norwood, NJ: Ablex.

Smilansky, S. (1968). The effects of sociodramatic play on disadvantaged preschool children. New York: Wiley.

Smith, P.K. (1974). Social and fantasy play in young children. In B. Tizard & D. Harvey (eds), *Biology of play*. London: SIMP/Heinemann.

Smith, P.K. (1982). Does play matter? Functional and evolutionary aspects of animal and human play. *The Behavioural and Brain Sciences*, 5, 139–184.

Smith, P.K. (1988). Child's play and its role in early development: A re-evaluation of the 'play ethos'. In A. Pellegrini (ed.), *Psychological bases for early education* (pp. 207–226). Chichester:Wiley.

Smith, P.K. (1996). Language and the evolution of mind reading. In P. Carruthers & P.K. Smith (eds), *Theories of theories of mind* (pp. 344–354). Cambridge: Cambridge University Press.

Smith, P.K. (1997). Play fighting and real fighting: Perspectives on their relationship. In A. Schmitt, K. Atswanger, K. Grammar, & K. Schafer (eds), *New aspects of ethology* (pp. 47–64). New York: Plenum.

Smith, P.K., & Connolly, K. (1972). Patterns of play and social interaction in pre-school children. In N. Blurton Jones (ed.), *Ethological studies of child behaviour* (pp. 65–95). Cambridge: Cambridge University Press.

Smith, P.K., & Connolly, K. (1980). *The ecology of preschool behaviour*. Cambridge: Cambridge University Press.

Smith, P.K., & Hagan, T. (1980). Effects of deprivation on exercise play in nursery school children. *Animal Behaviour*, 28, 922–928.

Smith, P.K., & Syddall, S. (1978). Play and group play tutoring in preschool children: Is it play or tutoring that matters? *British Journal of Educational Psychology*, 48, 315–325.

Smith, P.K., & Vollstedt, R. (1985). On defining play. *Child Development*, 56, 1042–1050.

Smith, P.K., & Whitney, S. (1987). Play and associative fluency: Experimenter effects may be responsible for previous findings. *Developmental Psychology*, 23, 49–53.

Sutton-Smith, B. (1986). *Toys as culture*. New York: Gardner.

Sutton-Smith, B. (1988). War toys and childhood aggression. *Play and Culture*, 1, 57–69.

Sutton-Smith, B. (1997). *The ambiguity of play*. Cambridge, MA: Harvard University Press.

Sutton-Smith, B., & Roberts, J.M. (1979). Play, toys, games and sports. In A. Heron & E. Kroeger (eds), *Handbook of cross-cultural psychology: Vol. 4. Developmental psychology*. New York: Allyn & Bacon.

Sylva, K., Bruner, J.S., & Genova, P. (1976). The role of play in the problem-solving behaviour of children 3–5 years old. In J.S. Bruner, A. Jolly, & K. Sylva (eds), *Play: Its role in development and evolution* (pp. 244–261). New York: Basic.

Symons, D. (1978). *Play and aggression: A study of rhesus monkeys*. New York: Columbia University Press.

Takhvar, M., & Smith, P.K. (1990). A review and critique of Smilansky's classification scheme and the 'nested hierarchy' of play categories. *Journal of Research in Childhood Education*, 4, 112–122.

Taylor, M., & Carlson, S.M. (1997). The relation between individual differences in fantasy and theory of mind. *Child Development*, 68, 436–455.

Thelen, E. (1979). Rhythmical stereotypies in normal human infants. *Animal Behaviour*, 27, 699–715.

Thelen, E. (1980). Determinants of amounts of stereotyped behaviour in normal human infants. *Ethology and Sociobiology*, 1, 141–150.

Tinbergen, N. (1963). On the aims and methods of ethology. *Zeitschrift für Tierpsychologie*, 20, 410–433.

Tomasello, M., & Call, J. (1998). *Primate cognition*. New York: Oxford University Press.

Vygotsky, L. (1978). *Mind in society*. Cambridge: Cambridge University Press.

Weir, R. (1962). *Language in the crib*. The Hague: Mouton.

14

Developmental Disorders: An Action-Based Account

BRIAN HOPKINS

INTRODUCTION

A developmental disorder is any process that affects normal development from conception to adulthood. The problem with this loosely formulated definition is twofold. Firstly, what constitutes normal development has varied across historical time and differs between cultures. Secondly, the demarcation between ordered and disordered development is often based on fallible indicators of deviations from some idealized and arbitrary set of norms, which are then categorized into clinical entities. Once categorized and labelled such entities are added to a listing of developmental disorders that increasingly comes to resemble the index of a book undergoing constant revisions.

This opening salvo serves to remind us that a developmental disorder is, at root, a hypothetical construct derived from current and conventional clinical wisdom. Clearly, there are exceptions to this general state of affairs. These are captured by Kolakowski's (1971) notion of 'elementary situations' in which particular circumstances or events are so clearly incapacitating or life-threatening as to require immediate and unquestioning intervention. Such situations, involving severe developmental defects arising from the embryonic period, include the devastating and wholly predictable effects of neural tube malformations (e.g. anencephaly) and chromosomal abnormalities (e.g. trisomies 13–15, 18 and 21).

Most developmental disorders, however, do not stem from these sorts of situations, but rather from a multitude of potential determinants acting at various times during development. These less devastating disorders, ranging from cerebral palsy to behavioural and learning problems, occur in about 10 per 1,000 live births, with some estimates climbing to 11% and 25% (Haskins, 1986). In these instances, diagnosis and thus treatment are often not possible until after the period of infancy and perhaps only when a child is subjected to the demands of formal education. Quite apart from their aetiologies being largely unknown (a feature shared with severe developmental defects), these more common types of developmental disorders have been construed on the basis of theoretical formulations that are weak in description but strong on prescription in terms of the required treatment.

There are two further problems associated with the study of developmental disorders. The first concerns co-morbidity, the fact that children can present, not one, but multiple disorders – an inevitable outcome of adding to the listing of developmental disorders. This is particularly the case for those disorders covered by the *Diagnostic and statistical manual of mental disorders* (DSM-IV: American Psychiatric Association, 1994) such as developmental coordination disorder (DCD) and the so-called pervasive developmental disorders (severe and persistent deficits across a number of areas of development as in the case of autism). It is also evident in children with cerebral palsy as many of them have manifestations of more than one type of disordered movement control. An issue in such cases is to identify the primary disorder. The second problem arises from attempts at describing and codifying developmental disorders as contained in DSM-IV and the *International classification of impairments, disabilities and handicaps* (ICIDH) published by the World Health Organization (WHO) in 1980. In both cases, an attempt is made to capture the common features of a disorder regardless of age, thus making their enterprises essentially non-developmental in nature. The problem then is that a disorder is the same whether a child is 6 or 16 years of age, an outcome that flies in the face of clinical experience.

These are just a sample of some of the problems that assail the study of developmental disorders. They will surface again in subsequent sections along with other problems including the use of the risk concept, the relationship between assessment and intervention, and, most important, the lack of a coherent framework that addresses this relationship. In doing so, an action-based approach to developmental disorders is emphasized. This refers to a focus on spontaneous rather than elicited movements at younger ages and on perceptual-motor functions used in everyday activities (i.e. natural rather than the contrived actions required by experimental tasks) at older ages. While this approach inevitably restricts the coverage of developmental disorders, it has at least one decided advantage. This is that it forces us to go beyond the so far unproductive task of identifying deficiencies in abstract and unchanging control structures to the realities of how healthy and compromised children actually differ developmentally in organizing their behaviour across space and time. Such an approach, it is argued, will not only improve the description of developmental disorders and thereby their diagnoses, but also supply prescriptions for intervention that match the everyday needs of the individual child. In order to illustrate these claims, examples will be given from research on infants born prematurely and children with cerebral palsy.

THE CONSEQUENCES OF DISORDERS: FROM IMPAIRMENTS TO HANDICAPS

One approach to understanding the consequences of a disorder is provided by the 1980 version of the *International classification of impairments, disabilities and handicaps* (ICIDH). As a hierarchically structured system of classification, it contains four levels of description starting with pathology, then going from impairments to disabilities, and culminating in handicaps. Pathology is synonymous with disease and disorder and amounts to damage or an abnormal process occurring within an organ or organ system. It requires invasive procedures (e.g. biopsy, biochemical assay) for its diagnosis, and how the measures derived are incorporated into the diagnosis is not without its problems (see Carroll, 1989). The next three levels are defined and exemplified in Table 14.1.

Impairments are the direct neurophysiological and behavioural consequences of pathology recorded in terms of signs (objective evidence of a disease) and symptoms (impressions of disease as experienced by the patient). While impairments as registered in a standardized neurological examination are used to deduce pathology, not all pathology leads to impairment and not all impairments can be assigned to a specific and detectable pathology. The same applies to disabilities, which can be the functional consequences of pathology or impairments or both. And like impairments, disabilities are difficult to operationalize and measure quantitatively and to relate to qualitative judgements of either. Both require such judgements based on some concept of what constitutes normality, of which there are a number of interpretations: normality as a 'utopian view', as 'average', as 'health' and as 'transaction' (Offer & Sabshin, 1974). These problems are particularly germane to defining and classifying cognitive disabilities, which are not catered for in the ICIDH, as it only recognizes cognitive impairments. Impairments or disabilities in general, but especially those considered to be cognitive in nature, are the products of either the idea of 'normality as average' (i.e. performance relative to normative age standards) or the idea of 'normality as health' (i.e. based on a clinical judgement about the absence of an impairment or a disability).

At the level of handicaps, we are confronted with the social consequences of a disorder. A handicap can arise directly from an impairment or even from a pathological condition without any impairment as well as from a disability. However, such possibilities are largely irrelevant as a handicap refers specifically to a patient's immediate social context and his or her 'quality of life' (a vague concept at the best of times). More than impairment or disability, it relates to the notion of 'normality as transaction' (i.e. how an individual influences and is influenced by interactions with significant others) and ultimately to a utopian view of normality (i.e. what is valued as an ideal in a particular culture or society). Once again, but more so than impairment and disability, it is difficult to operationalize and measure objectively.

All told, the distinctions between impairment, disability and handicap are not clear-cut and are perhaps best treated as forming a continuum with grey areas in between. Epilepsy is a case in point: should it be regarded as an impairment or a disability? For the present purposes, the distinction between impairment and disability will be taken to be that between an external manifestation of a disorder (i.e. a sign) and some adverse alteration in the normal performance of goal-directed behaviour (i.e. an action). As for that between disability and handicap, it resides in whether or not a person experiences a restriction in social roles such as a child being unable to play with other children. The focus here will be on impairments and disabilities

Table 14.1 *World Health Organization (WHO)* International classification of impairments, disabilities and handicaps *(ICIDH) in accordance with Resolution (WHA 29.35) of the World Health Authority and published in 1980. The ICIDH replaced the WHO* International classification of deaths and diseases *(1977) in an attempt to describe disorders in terms of health status rather than by means of medically defined diseases. In turn, the ICIDH has been subjected to revision in ICIDH-2 (1999) due to changes in health care provision and which is currently being field-tested. However, the distinctions between impairments, disabilities and handicaps still retain some heuristic value in understanding the consequences of disorders. Impairments may consist of negative signs (loss of function) or positive signs (release of function). The latter are referred to as release phenomena in that they involve the withdrawal of inhibitory influences on the normal functioning of interneuronal networks*

	Definition	Level	Examples
Impairment	Any loss or abnormality of psychological, physiological, or anatomical structure or function	Organ	Weakness in muscle power (negative sign); involuntary movements (positive sign)
Disability	Any restriction or lack (resulting from an impairment) of ability to perform an activity in the manner or within the range considered normal for a human being	Functional	Inability to grasp objects; shuffling gait
Handicap	Any disadvantages for a given individual (depending on the age, sex, and social cultural factors) resulting from an impairment or a disability that limits or prevents the fulfilment of a role that is normal for that individual	Social/societal	Inability to manoeuvre wheelchair through a narrow aperture; unable to travel by public transport

and how they relate to the more encompassing concept of a developmental disorder – something entirely missing from the ICIDH.

From a developmental perspective, the focus of attention shifts with age from pathology and impairments (e.g. in infants born prematurely) to disabilities and handicaps (e.g. in children with cerebral palsy). As we shall see, judgements as to severity of a pathology or an impairment may have some prognostic value for disabling outcomes such as cerebral palsy when treated as risk factors. The problem, of course, is to detect those infants at most risk for such outcomes and to understand the pathways or risk mechanisms by which they are attained. Interactions between different impairments add to the difficulties of detection, prognosis and uncovering these pathways. For example, motor impairments in preterm infants may make it difficult or even impossible to assess their cognitive abilities by means of standardized developmental tests such as the Gesell and Bayley scales. This has led to the derivation of tests designed to minimize or remove requirements for the control of posture and prehension. These procedures are based on assessments of perceptual discrimination and use, for example, habituation and recognition memory techniques, which have questionable predictive validity for at-risk infants (McCall & Carriger, 1993). What is probably the case, however, is that motor (and perceptual) impairments in infants lead to handicapping conditions by placing restrictions on their social activities. In turn, a caregiver's inability to cope with an infant's impairment may create a source of social risks such that the infant suffers neglect or becomes a target for physical and psychological abuse.

PREMATURITY AND CEREBRAL PALSY

What Is Prematurity and What Are its Consequences?

The definition of prematurity has undergone considerable change in the last 50 years. In the past, it was based on birthweight alone as there were no objective assessments of gestational age in the frequent cases of mothers without a regular menstrual cycle. When such assessments, based on neurological responses and physical characteristics, became available in the early 1970s, both birthweight and gestational age were taken into account in defining prematurity and for distinguishing between various categories of preterm infants.

Prematurity is now defined as infants born before 37 weeks of gestation, regardless of birthweight. Those delivered at less than 32 weeks are classified as very preterm (VPT) infants. However, they typically have a low birthweight (LBW), defined as being less than 2,500 grams. Due to its easy availability, birthweight is also used to classify preterm infants; those weighing less than 1,500 grams are labelled very low birthweight (VLBW), while less than 1,000 grams is regarded as extremely low birthweight (ELBW). Further classification on the basis of the relationship between birthweight and gestational age results in the distinction between small for gestational age (SGA) and adequate for gestational age (AGA) – this being based on whether the birthweight is below (SGA) or above (AGA) the 10th percentile for gestational age. Those with a birthweight below the 2.3 percentile are considered to be very SGA. These various classifications are shown in Figure 14.1.

The incidence of premature birth varies between 4% to 9.5% of all live births in western countries, with that for a VPT birth being around 0.60%. About 7% of live births are LBW, of whom 10% to 15% are VLBW (Wolke, 1991) – giving an incidence ranging from 0.2% to 2.0% for VLBW infants. Among LBW infants, some 18% to 40% are SGA (Chiswick, 1985). The causes of prematurity are not properly understood, but it is known to be associated with foetal and uterus malformations, infections, antepartum haemorrhage, spontaneous premature rupture of the membranes, excessive amount of amniotic fluid and multiple pregnancies. While it has a higher incidence in young mothers who have a low socio-economic status, there is increasing evidence that hereditary factors may play a role (Livishits, 1990). The eradication of premature birth still evades obstetrical practice and the best preventive strategy so far seems to be the identification of women at high risk for premature delivery who are carefully managed and given extensive bed rest (Papiernik, 1993).

There is an enormous number of follow-up studies on the developmental sequelae of prematurity (see Wolke, 1998). They differ in a variety of ways. Firstly, they may involve classifications based on birthweight, gestational age or both. Secondly, they may make the distinction between low-risk and high-risk infants in terms of the absence or presence of one or more medical complications associated with prematurity. Some of the more prominent complications germane to this distinction are listed and defined in Table 14.2. Thirdly, studies with follow-ups beyond term age can differ as to the inclusion of a control (or reference) group of fullterm infants. If they do include such a group, then further differences

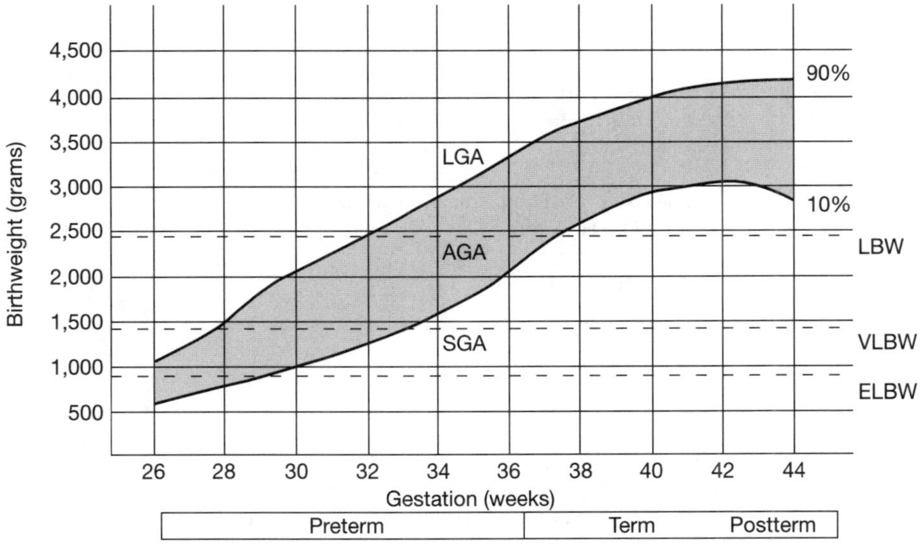

Figure 14.1 *Classification of infants according to birthweight, pregnancy duration or the relationship between the two. Prematurity is birth before 37 weeks gestational age with 23–24 weeks being currently the lower bound for viability. Growth curves with percentiles distinguish between adequate for gestational age (AGA: 10th–90th percentiles), large for gestational age (LGA: above 90th percentile and related to maternal diabetes), and small for gestational age (SGA: below 10th percentile). Most studies on preterm infants are based on birthweight distinctions: low birthweight (LBW), very low birthweight (VLBW) and extremely low birthweight (ELBW). This is because birthweight is more readily available than accurate estimates of gestational age (i.e. ±2 weeks)*

Table 14.2 *Some of the major medical complications associated with prematurity. Their descriptions are necessarily brief and incomplete, but capture their main features. They rarely occur in isolation, but rather in conjunction with other complications (e.g. IUGR and hypoglycaemia). As with prematurity itself, their causes are largely unclear. The risks for abnormal outcomes are generally, but not only, for pervasive neurological disorders, which may be severe (e.g. cerebral palsy) or mild (e.g. DCD). In addition, preterm infants are at risk for persisting health problems such as asthma, upper and lower respiratory infections, and ear infections that sometimes require rehospitalization (a risk factor) and surgical intervention (another risk factor)*

Complication	Description	Developmental risks	References
Intrauterine growth retardation (IUGR)	Two types: type I or proportional (both length and weight affected) and type II or disproportional (only weight affected). Type I is associated with microcephaly and can be due to genetic factors as well as congenital and chromosomal abnormalities. Type II presents with decreased fat and muscle tissue and is thought to be due to placental insufficiency and maternal hypertension. Most studies on preterm SCA infants have concerned type II IUGR	Depend on the severity of GR and degree of prematurity Type I: mental retardation, cerebral palsy[1] Type II: developmental delay,[2] minor neurological problems,[3] and learning difficulties,[4] both at school age	[1] Allen (1984) [2] Vohr & Oh (1983) [3] Hadders-Algra et al. (1988) [4] Low et al. (1982)
Perinatal asphyxia	Any interference with oxygen supply of blood to brain occurring between 7th month of pregnancy and 1 month after birth. Typically results in hypoxic-ischaemic encephalopathy. The most common form is hypoxia, which is 60–70% reduction in oxygen supply. A frequent complication in preterm SGA infants, especially in combination with hypoglycaemia	Abnormal visual evoked responses on first day after asphyxia[1] Major and minor neurological deficits at 1 year[2] Learning and behaviour problems at school age[3]	[1] Pryds et al. (1989) [2] Low et al. (1988) [3] Lindahl et al. (1988)
Hypoglycaemia	A lower than normal level of glucose in the blood. Glucose production for neonatal brain metabolism is mainly a function of the liver, which can be affected in preterm SGA infants. Its supply to the brain via the blood is probably more important than oxygen for brain metabolism as oxygen consumption is relatively low in the neonatal brain and minimal in cerebral	Seizure disorders, below average IQ and cerebral palsy, especially spasticity and ataxia.[1] Even moderate hypoglycaemia present for 3 days or more related to neurodevelopmental sequelae such as developmental delay and cerebral palsy[2]	[1] Fluge (1975) [2] Lucas et al. (1988)

	white matter. In general, it increases vulnerability of brain to ischaemic lesions such as periventricular leukomalacia		
Hyaline membrane disease	Also called idiopathic respiratory distress syndrome (IRDS). Occurs in preterm infants when air spaces of lungs lined with glassy-like membrane. Results in acute breathing difficulty, cyanosis, collapsed alveoli and loss of pulmonary surfactant. Discovered in 1957, its causes are unknown	One of main causes of death in preterm infants during the first 48 hours after birth. Survivors have increased risk of mental retardation and physical disabilities[1]	[1] Hunt (1981)
Bronchial pulmonary dysplasia	One of the most frequent forms of IRDS, it consists of abnormal tissues in bronchi of lungs. Its occurrence related to long-term effects of ventilation and thus is a relatively new complication in preterm infants. Associated with chronic hypoxemia, hypercarbia, bronchospasm and inadequate nutrition in preterm infants	Associated with abnormal movements from about 3rd postnatal month involving limbs, neck, trunk, and oral-buccal-lingual region (and thus related to feeding difficulties).[1] Long-term outcomes: growth and neurodevelopmental problems[2] that appear to be related to length of oxygen supplementation and degree of prematurity[3]	[1] Perlman & Volpe (1989) [2] Bregman & Farell (1992) [3] Robertson et al. (1992)
Hyperbilirubinemia	Bilirubin is a reddish bile pigment thought to be produced by a breakdown in manufacture of haemoglobin. Excessive amount in blood leads to jaundice and crosses blood–brain barrier to damage neurons, rather than glia cells, especially in basal ganglia, brain stem nuclei for oculomotor function and brain stem auditory nuclei	During first year associated with hypotonia, active deep tendon reflexes, persistent tonic neck reflex and delayed motor development.[1] Other motor problems: athetosis in all limbs and difficulties with swallowing, phonation and facial movements.[2] Further problems related to gaze control[3] and hearing loss[4]	[1] Byers et al. (1955) [2] Hayashi et al. (1991) [3] Hoyt et al. (1978) [4] Hyman et al. (1969)
Retinopathy of prematurity (ROP)	Previously termed retrolental fibroplasia. Consists of damage to blood vessels in retina, which may become detached if resulting scar tissue contracts. Linked to hyperpoxia resulting from a too high level of oxygen therapy. Thought to have been eradicated, it has become prevalent again as more VPT infants requiring lung ventilation are kept alive. Severity of ROP graded[1]	Depends on grade. Blindness in VLBW and VPT infants as well as ophthalmic problems such as strabismus, myopia, glaucoma and late-onset retinal detachment in mid-teens or early adulthood[2]	[1] Committee for Classification of Retinopathy of Prematurity (1984) [2] Silverman (1980)

Table 14.2 *(continued)*

Complication	Description	Developmental risks	References
Periventricular leukomalacia (PVL)	First described more than 100 years ago, it is typified by damage to cerebral white matter bordering on lateral ventricles and is usually bilateral. Consists of areas of necrosis that often form cavitating cysts. Resulting lesions can damage corticospinal tracts innervating lower extremities. Causes unknown, but one suggestion is perinatal hypoxic-ischaemic incidents. Occurs more often in VLBW and VPT infants. Extent of PVL graded[1]	Depends on grade. Spastic diplegia most common outcome, but also includes mental retardation, cerebral visual abnormalities and epilepsy[2]	[1] de Vries et al. (1992) [2] Fawer et al. (1987)
Germinal-matrix intraventricular haemorrhage (IVH)	Bleeding in the germinal matrix, a tissue with small, fragile blood vessels situated mainly in periventricular regions of head of caudate nucleus in thalamus. Bleeding can spread into ventricles, which is termed subependymal haemorrhage. A neuropathological consequence is unilateral periventricular haemorrhage (PHI) and frequent accompaniments are hyaline membrane disease and PVL. Causes unclear, but may be due to sudden fluctuations in arterial blood pressure. Frequent in VLBW and VPT infants. Extent of IVH graded[1]	Depends on grade. Range from cerebral palsy, especially spastic diplegia if PHI present,[2] to major and minor cognitive deficits[3]	[1] Papile et al. (1978) [2] McMenamin et al. (1984) [3] Scott et al. (1984)
Necrotizing enterocolitis	Serious gastrointestinal disease, more common in VPT infants, but not confined to them. Results in abdominal distension, vomiting blood and mucus and sometimes bowel perforation. No single cause identified, but associated with hypoxia, bowel infection and blood hyperviscosity. Severity can be reduced by steroids and breast milk feeding	Thought to be involved in cerebral palsy,[1] but little known about its long-term consequences. Some evidence that it is related to persistent health problems (e.g. asthma), strabismus and variety of visual-motor and psycho-social problems[2]	[1] Stanley et al. (2000) [2] Mayr et al. (1994)

CP, cerebral palsy; DCD, developmental coordination disorder; IUGR, intrauterine growth retardation; PT, preterm; SGA, small for gestational age; VLBW, very low birthweight; VPT, very preterm.

can arise with regard to how long age correction needs to be applied in comparing preterm and fullterm infants (see Appendix 1 for an explanation of corrected age and the issues surrounding its use). Finally, studies also differ in the heterogeneity of their samples of preterm infants as well as, for example, in sample size, length of follow-up, selective attrition and outcome measures.

By far the greatest number of studies has involved birthweight distinctions. However, birthweight is related to both gestational age and the rate of intrauterine growth (see Figure 14.1) and therefore such studies inevitably include infants who are VPT or SGA or both. In practice it proves to be difficult to disentangle the respective contributions of these three factors to developmental outcomes in preterm infants such as cerebral palsy.

What Is Cerebral Palsy?

Cerebral palsy (CP) is a general term applied to a group of non-progressive neurological disorders occurring in children and marked by disturbance in the voluntary control of movements (Ingram, 1984). What is 'non-progressive' (i.e. permanent) is the cerebral lesion. However, its functional manifestations change with age as the central nervous system and musculoskeletal system develop, especially during the first five years. The fact that the term covers a group of disorders has given rise to a variety of classifications, most of which stem from that devised by Freud (1897) following Little (1862). The mainstay of current classifications is the distinction between spasticity and the two other principal forms of CP, namely dyskinesia and ataxia. Spasticity, originally defined by Hughlings Jackson (1899) in terms of exaggerated proprioceptive responses, is further classified relative to its distribution or topographical location. Each of these terms is described in Table 14.3, but it should be remembered that the specific details of any one of them varies from one classification system to another.

These descriptions are purely clinical in nature and make no reference to aetiology, pathophysiology and the functional consequences for activities of daily living. Moreover, each type was derived in adult neurology with the consequence that none of them adequately capture the changing manifestations of CP during childhood. This problem is illustrated by the finding that interobserver agreement is only 55%, even with prior training in the use of a six-category classification system (Blair & Stanley, 1985). The picture is further complicated by the fact that children with CP have associated problems: 50–82% have mental retardation and 30–48% epilepsy (Nelson & Ellenberg, 1979), with mental retardation being associated more with spastic quadriplegia than spastic diplegia (Pharoah et al., 1987). In addition, more than 40% have some type of visual impairment (Black, 1980) and about 20% have hearing or language problems. All of this makes the creation of homogeneous groups of CP children well nigh impossible and intervention research fraught with difficulties.

The incidence of CP is about 2 to 2.5 per 100 live births (Gordon, 1976) and, despite fluctuations in the 1970s and 1980s, has remained at the same rate for more than 50 years in developed countries (Hagberg, Hagberg, & von Wendt, 1996). What has changed is an increase in the incidence of spastic diplegia and a decrease in other types such as ataxia and to a lesser extent spastic quadriplegia – changes due to a reduction in the mortality rates of VLBW and VPT infants. The causes (or better the antecedents) of CP are multifactorial for most types. Typically, these are classified as prepregnancy, prenatal, perinatal and postneonatal antecedents or risk factors (Uvebrant, 1988). Examples of each of these sorts of antecedents are given in Table 14.4.

It is not individual antecedents, but rather combinations of them that serve as predictors for CP (e.g. low maternal age and SES together with a VPT infant). However, some evidence suggests that in most fullterm infants CP is related to prenatal antecedents (e.g. severe IUGR) while for preterm infants it is associated with early postnatal events (e.g. hypoxia) or to an interaction between prenatal and perinatal factors (Hagberg & Hagberg, 1984).

Cerebral palsy continues to be portrayed as a disorder consisting of a variety of abnormal motor patterns. The shortcoming of this portrayal is that it overlooks the possibility that problems in the control of movement and posture may engender perceptual impairments, particularly with regard to visual-spatial abilities (Abercrombie, 1964). Recent studies have demonstrated perceptual-motor dysfunctions in CP children for tasks requiring gaze stabilization, the integration of visual and proprioceptive information, and the use of prospective visual information in the control of interceptive actions (reviewed by van der Weel et al., 1996). Others have shown impaired tactile adjustments of fingertip forces when objects with different surfaces have to be lifted using a precision grip (see Eliasson, Gordon, & Forssberg, 1995). These sorts of findings stress that CP is a disorder resulting from impairments in the coupling between perception and action.

Early Detection of Preterm Infants at Risk for Cerebral Palsy

Some 25 years ago, the majority of VLBW and VPT infants died at birth or shortly after. Due to advances in neonatal intensive care, such as surfactant therapy and non-invasive brain imaging techniques, the majority of these infants now survive. These

Table 14.3 *A classification of cerebral palsy (CP). Types are delineated according to motor dysfunctions (spasticity, ataxia, dyskinesia) and with reference to body parts affected (diplegia, hemiplegia, quadriplegia). Other clinical descriptions not included are mixed (e.g. spasticity and dystonia), bilateral hemiplegia (bulbar musculature more severely affected than in right or left hemiplegia) and ataxic diplegia (walking more on toes with a less broad base compared to ataxia). Different types of CP may coexist, but the pattern of coexistence can change over age within any one child*

Type	Description	Comments
Spasticity	Increased resistance to muscle stretch, which is velocity-dependent. Resistance can suddenly diminish (the 'clasp-knife' effect). Tendon reflexes are hyperactive and clonus may be present	Relationship of spasticity to disordered control of voluntary movements unclear. Increased resistance to muscle stretch may in part be due to peripheral changes in muscle stiffness
Spastic diplegia	Increased muscle stiffness mainly affecting the limbs, but more in legs and feet than arms and hands. Minority of patients show involuntary athetoid (writhing) movements of fingers, wrists and forearms and much less frequently occurring choreid (rapid, jerky) movements	Begins with hypotonia, which gives way to rigid/spastic stage. Common type of CP today, accounting for one-third of cases in many large series
Spastic hemiplegia/ hemiparesis	Involvement of one side of body with relative sparing of contralateral limbs. Arms usually more affected than legs. Some patients show athetosis	Right hemiplegia is more common than left hemiplegia. Unlike most other types, it is associated with lower SES. Difficult to diagnose before about 3 years of age. Most common type of CP in children, occurring in upwards of 50% of cases
Spastic quadriplegia/ tetraplegia	Involvement of all four limbs with arms sometimes more affected than legs. Head and trunk also involved	Tends to be diagnosed earlier than other forms of CP
Ataxia	Lack of muscle coordination, particularly in hypotonic trunk and legs, leading to tremulousness, unsteady movements and poor balance	More often recognized than other types of CP. Ataxic CP associated with 'floppy baby' syndrome
Dyskinesia	Consists of two sub-groups: hypertonic (choreathetoid) and dystonic patients. In former, excessive overflow of involuntary movements. In latter, a rigid posture with movement inducing abnormal shifts in muscle power	Both dyskinesias may occur together or independently in same patient and both often associated with spasticity. Thus, dystonia may be confused with spasticity, especially when hypertonia present

survivors, however, have a high risk for acquiring white matter lesions such as intraventricular haemorrhage (IVH) and periventricular leukomalacia (PVL), often associated with hyaline membrane disease or perinatal asphyxia. In turn, these complications, depending on their severity, bear a strong relationship with later major disorders and in particular cerebral palsy, mental retardation, cortical blindness, hearing loss and epilepsy.

One of the consequences of improvements in the paediatric care of preterm infants is that the incidence of CP has changed little in the past 40 years. In a meta-analysis of 85 follow-up studies of VLBW infants, the prevalence of CP during childhood was estimated to be 7.7% with a 95% confidence interval ranging from 5.3% to 9.0% (Escobar, Littenberg, & Pettiti, 1991). Given a population prevalence of about 2 to 3 per 1,000 births, and assuming this estimate to be a reliable one, then the risk of suffering CP is increased by a factor of 25 to 40 in VLBW infants. Developmental risk, however, is a population concept. Thus, it is uninterpretable with regard to the probability of a particular individual in a clinically identifiable group succumbing to some later occurring problem or set of problems. How then can one distinguish the potentially problematic cases from their relatively unproblematic counterparts in such groups? More specifically, how can one identify

Table 14.4 *Prepregnancy, prenatal, perinatal and postneonatal antecedents of cerebral palsy (CP). The first three sets of antecedents are associated with what is referred to as 'congenital CP' while those labelled postneonatal are related to 'acquired CP'. Early prenatal antecedents occur during the first trimester of pregnancy and later ones during the second and third trimesters. Thus, there is considerable overlap in the timing of later prenatal and perinatal antecedents and the boundary between them is an arbitrary one made for pragmatic reasons. Postneonatal antecedents are events that affect a neurologically normal infant after the newborn period, the earlier part of which overlaps with the perinatal period. The age limit for the postneonatal period ranges from 2 to 10 years across relevant studies*

Pregnancy
Chronic maternal illness (e.g. diabetes mellitus)
Long-lasting use of alcohol and/or drugs
Maternal age at delivery (< 20, > 35 years)
Maternal mental retardation
Maternal parity (1st and 4th or more birth)
Maternal SES
Prenatal
Early:
Cell migration and aggregation disorders
TORCH infections[1]
Iodine deficiency
Vitamin deficiencies
Later:
Vascular disorders (e.g. hypoxia)
Pre-eclampsia[2] (and other factors related to IUGR arising from foetoplacental dysfunction)
Perinatal
Placental haemorrhage
Maternal infections (e.g. bacterial vaginosis)
Rupture of membranes > 24hours before delivery
Gestation < 32 weeks
Birthweight < 1800 g
Birth asphyxia[3]
Other medical complications associated with prematurity (see Table 14.2)
Postneonatal
Cerebral infections
Head injury
Cerebrovascular accident
Convulsions
Gastroenteritis
Near-miss SIDS

[1] TORCH infections: *t*oxoplasmosis, *r*ubella, *c*ytomegalovirus and *h*erpes simplex complex.
[2] Pre-eclampsia: pregnancy-induced hypertension, which also includes generalized hypertension and in severe cases proteinuria. Can lead to placental failure and thus to IUGR.
[3] Birth (or perinatal) asphyxia: indicated by signs such as abnormal foetal heart rate (FHR) and lack of FHR.

IUGR, intrauterine growth retardation; SES, socioeconomic status; SIDS, sudden infant death syndrome.

individual differences between preterm infants in terms of their vulnerability for acquiring developmental disorders such as CP?

It is a common clinical experience that two preterm infants with the same history of perinatal complications can have radically different outcomes (Rademaker et al., 1994). Thus, simply knowing the medical status of a preterm infant at birth defined in terms of risk factors provides little certitude about that infant's condition in the long term. With the introduction of routine cranial ultrasonography in the 1980s, prognostic improvements accrued (Hellström-Westas, Rosén, & Svenningen, 1991). However, this innovation has been found to predict only 50% of those preterm infants who become afflicted with CP (Pino-Martin et al., 1995). What this tells us is that the long-term prognosis of preterm infants is complicated by a variety of extracerebral factors such as infections, pulmonary immaturity and chronic forms of bronchial pulmonary dysplasia. The need is for instruments of early detection that in some way assess the functional integrity of the developing nervous system in preterm infants. There are two approaches that fulfil this need: a standardized neurological examination or a specific focus on the evaluation of spontaneous movements.

Neurological examinations appropriate for preterm infants before term such as that devised by Dubowitz and Dubowitz (1981) have undoubted value as tools of early detection. Nevertheless, they have their shortcomings: they are invasive and time consuming and require the existence of stable behavioural states in order to elicit and interpret an array of age-appropriate responses, all of which mitigate against their use with preterm infants who are in poor health. Based on direct observation with the unaided eye, the assessment of spontaneous movements described for the healthy foetus (de Vries, et al. 1982) and the fullterm infant (Hopkins & Prechtl, 1984) offers a means of overcoming these shortcomings. Moreover, assessments made about the quality with which these movements are expressed appear to make a clearer distinction between high- and low-risk preterm infants than simply registering their quantitative output (Prechtl & Nolte, 1984). Such discrimination is particularly evident for the most frequently occurring and complex category of spontaneous movements, namely, general movements.

General Movements

General movements (GMs) consist of gross movements varying in speed and amplitude and involving the whole body, but which lack a particular sequencing of body parts (Hopkins & Prechtl, 1984). Normal GMs also give the impression of waxing and waning in intensity and appear to have gradual onsets and offsets. In healthy foetuses and infants, they are performed in an apparently fluent and elegant manner. Abnormal GMs, in contrast, are strikingly monotonous and cramped with almost no variation

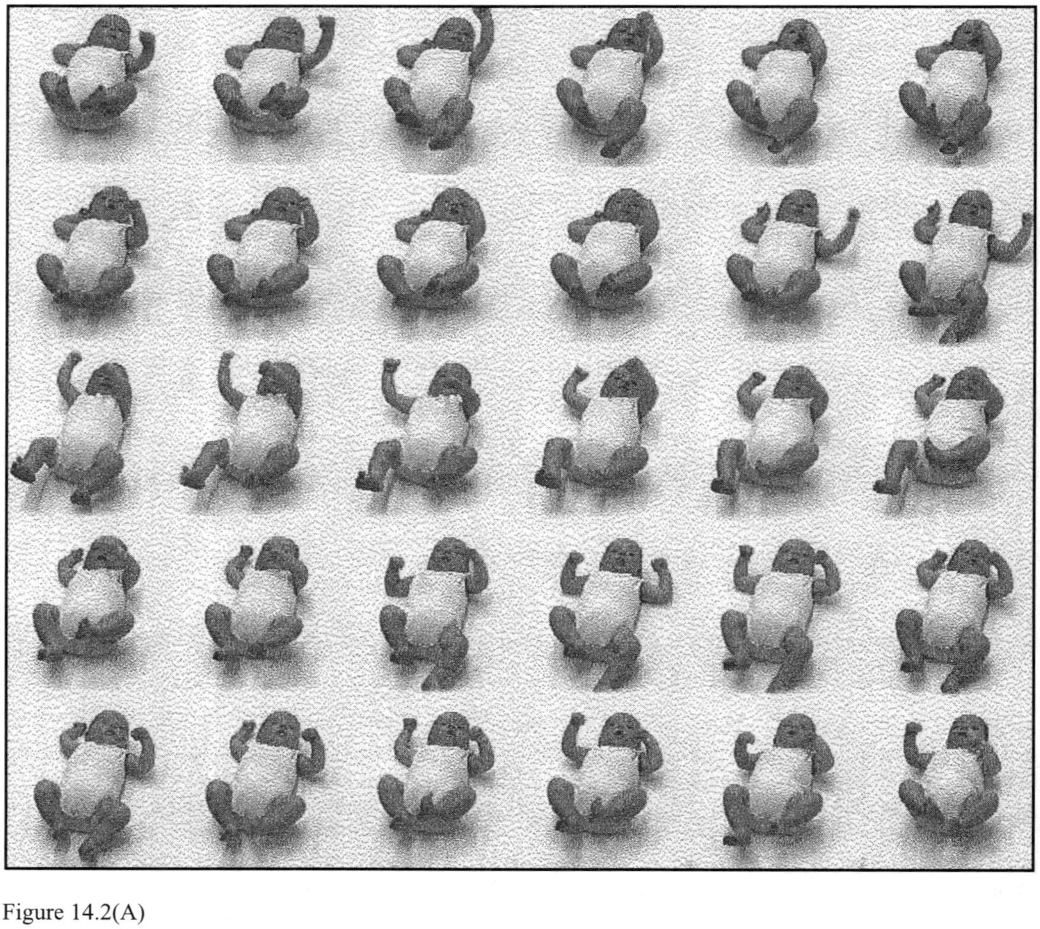

Figure 14.2(A)

in speed and amplitude, and as a consequence they lack the normal fluent and elegant character (Geerdink & Hopkins, 1993a; see Figure 14.2).

The developmental course of normal GMs undergoes two main qualitative changes in the first few months after birth: following on from so-called preterm GMs typified by excessive variation and complexity and many movements of the trunk (Hadders-Algra et al., 1997), they assume first a 'writhing' quality and then one that has a 'fidgety' appearance (Hopkins & Prechtl, 1984). Writhing GMs consist of slower and more forceful movements, but with less involvement of the trunk. Disappearing some 6 to 8 weeks after birth, they are replaced by fidgety GMs that involve a continuous stream of small, rounded movements occurring irregularly over the whole body. Present until about 4 months of age, they in turn give way to goal-directed actions such as reaching and grasping. Surface EMG recordings have shown that the changes from preterm to writhing to fidgety GMs are accompanied by a decrease in tonic background activity together with a reduction in the amplitude and duration of phasic bursts (Hadders-Algra et al., 1992; see Figure 14.3). These findings suggest an increase in Renshaw inhibition, a decrease in motor unit excitability and a regression in the polyneural innervation of muscles – the latter being supported

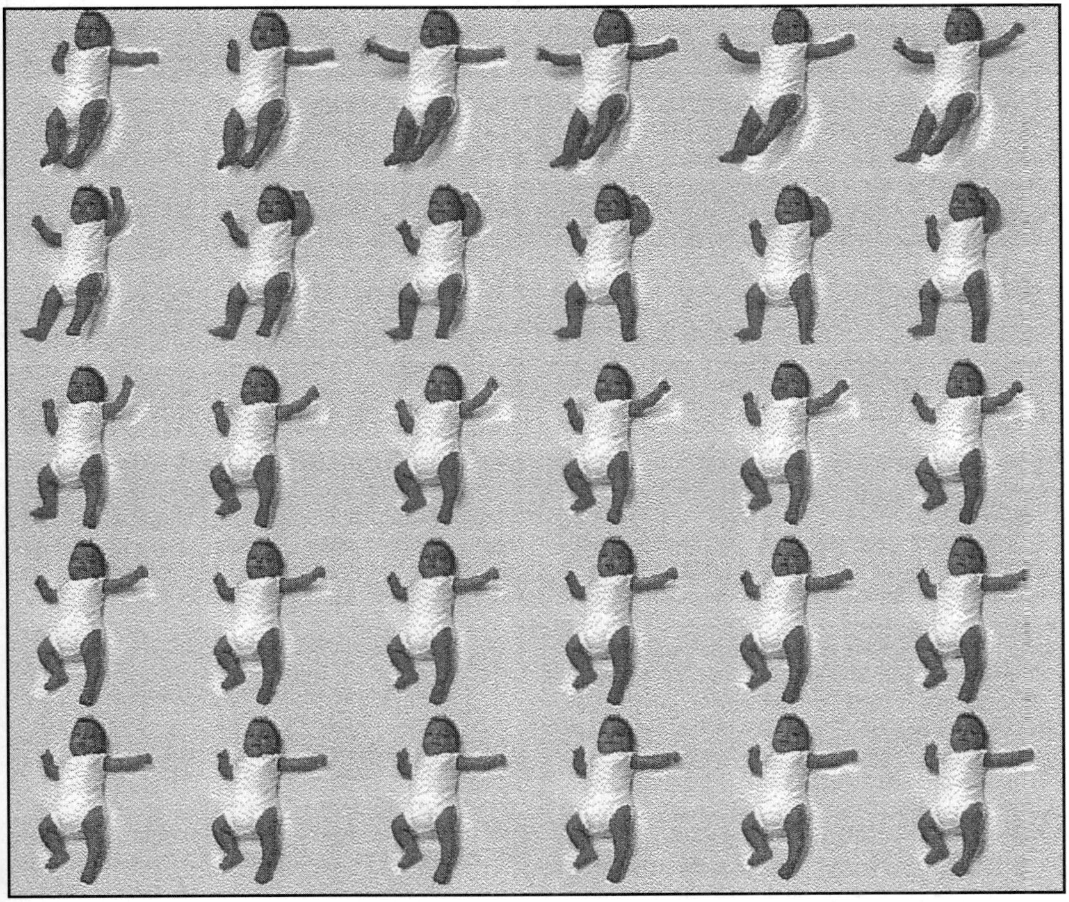

Figure 14.2 (B) *Fragments from video recordings depicting general movements (GMs) in two 3-month-old infants. Both fragments contain 5 rows, each with 6 frames. Each row should be scanned from left to right, starting with the upper left frame and proceeding from top to bottom. The duration of each fragment is 8.16 s with the interval between frames being 0.24 s. Fragment (A) displays normal 'fidgety' GMs performed by a fullterm (FT) infant. Fragment (B) shows abnormal 'fidgety' GMs made by a preterm (PT) infant born after a pregnancy duration of 28 weeks. As can be seen, the movements of the FT infant appear to be more complex and variable. Those for the PT infant have a more stereotyped appearance such that most of the frames are the same with the arms and legs moving in only one plane (reproduced with permission from Hadders-Algra, 1997, Nederlands Tijdschrift voor Geneeskunde)*

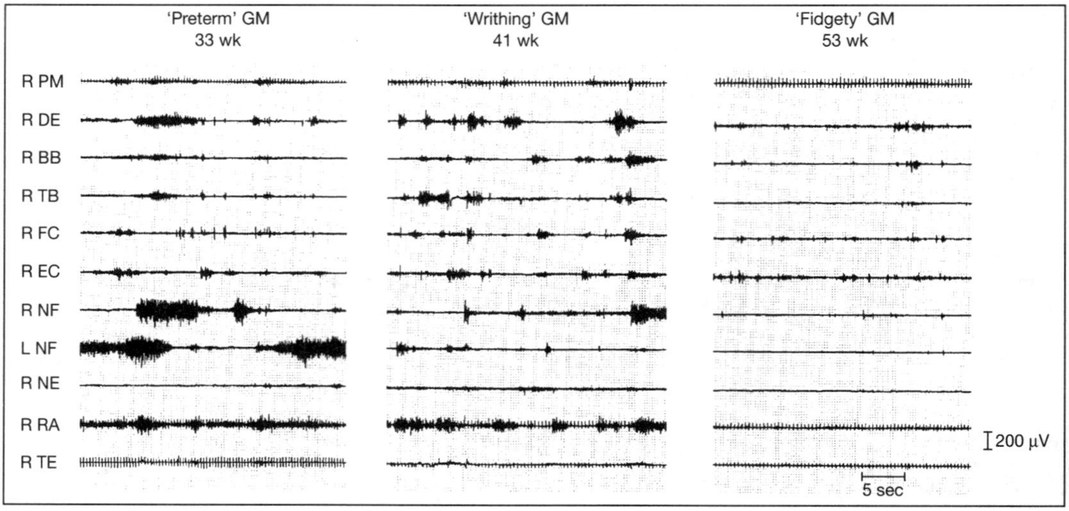

Figure 14.3 *Patterns of EMG activity during normal general movements (GMs) classified as being 'preterm', 'writhing' and 'fidgety' at the postmenstrual ages of 33, 41 and 53 weeks, respectively. Note the changes in EMG patterns from 33 to 53 weeks, which include reductions in phasic bursts and their amplitudes, especially with the changes from writhing to fidgety GMs. While there is evidence of large coactivations of antagonistic muscles for all three types of GMs, there is also a decrease in tonic background activity from writhing to fidgety GMs (reprinted with permission from Hadders-Algra et al., 1997 Developmental Medicine & Child Neurology)*

L, left; R, right; PM, pectoralis major; DE, deltoid; BB, biceps brachii; TB, triceps brachii; FC, flexor carpi; EC, extensor carpi; NF, neck flexor; NE,: neck extensor; RA, rectus abdominis; TE, thoracic extension

by the finding that mononeural innervation in human infants becomes evident at around 3 months of age (Gramsbergen et al., 1997).

There is a growing body of literature demonstrating that assessments of the quality of GMs can provide impressive predictions of developmental outcomes in preterm infants. Table 14.5 presents a sampling of some of the relevant studies, all of which relate GM assessments to outcomes by means of indexes of efficacy (Feinstein, 1977). Explanations of each index are given in Appendix 2 together with the distinctions between true/false positives and negatives.

Three main conclusions can be drawn from the studies reported in Table 14.5. Firstly, abnormal GMs are more evident in high-risk infants compared to their low-risk coevals. Secondly, the assessment of GM quality greatly facilitates the prognosis of later outcomes, especially those classified as abnormal, and seemingly better than brain scans alone. In this respect, it is interesting to note the claim that this form of assessment also provides better predictions of outcome than an infant neurological examination, particularly with regard to CP (Cioni et al., 1997a; 1997b). Thirdly, predictive values improve from about 12 weeks corrected age onwards such that there is an increase and a decrease in true positives and false negatives, respectively – the latter being crucial benchmarks for any instrument of early detection. This improved predictability carries with it both theoretical and practical implications for such instruments, both of which stem from the concept of ontogenetic adaptations.

Ontogenetic Adaptations

Briefly, this concept holds that certain structures and functions are appropriate for survival during one phase of development, but are unnecessary or even incompatible with the adaptations required for later phases (Oppenheim, 1981). As a consequence, they must be eliminated, suppressed or reorganized in the course of normal development. GMs may fit this depiction in that they could be based on transient foetal mechanisms that subserve adaptations to life in the womb, but which continue postnatally to be replaced by functions better adjusted to the extrauterine environment some 2 to 3 months after birth (Prechtl, 1984). This concept offers a theoretical explanation for the recurrent finding that abnormal neurological signs in the newborn have only limited predictive value as they may disappear

Table 14.5 *Examples of follow-up studies involving preterm (PT) infants and the assessment of general movements (GMs) at PT and postterm ages. Outcomes in terms of cerebral palsy (CP), classifications based on neurological evaluations (e.g. normal, abnormal), developmental assessments (e.g. moderate, severe mental retardation), and minor dysfunctions in one study. In all relevant studies (1, 2, 4, 6), infants with an abnormal course of GMs tended to have developmental quotients indicative of moderate to severe mental retardation. Two studies (2, 4) present a range of index values from the youngest to the oldest age at which predictions were calculated. Two other studies (4, 5) compare GM assessment and infant neurological examination in terms of predicting outcomes*

Study	Participants	Outcomes	Main findings	Indexes of efficacy
1 Ferrari et al. (1990)	14 low-risk and 29 high-risk PT infants, latter having brain damage (grade I–IV IVH and/ or PVL) verified by CU	Presence/absence of CP. Neurological assessment up to 2 years CA	28 high-risk infants had abnormal GM quality during PT period versus 1 in the low-risk group. 19/28 developed CP. Developmental course of GMs better predictor of neurological outcome than nature and localization of brain damage	For CP: Sensitivity: 100% Specificity: 59% PPV: 70% NPV : 100% Accuracy: 79%
2 Geerdink & Hopkins (1993b)	18 FT and 35 PT infants, latter consisting of 12 classified as SGA and 23 as AGA. No infant had any major neurological problems during neonatal period	Neurological and developmental assessments at 1 year CA	All FT infants had normal course of GMs and good neurological outcomes. Differences in GM quality between PT SGA and AGA infants became less evident with age. More infants with gestational ages less than 32 weeks maintained abnormal GMs. Prediction of outcomes improved after 12 weeks CA	For neurological outcome in PT infants: Sensitivity: 60–100% Specificity: 58–100% PPV: 75–100% NPV: 47–71% Accuracy: 70–83%
3 Albers & Jorch (1994)	22 PT infants still in acute phase	Neurological assessment at 1 year CA	Infants with abnormal SM persisted with them after acute phase. 4/22 died. Prediction improved after term age	For neurological outcome: Sensitivity: 78% Specificity: 100% PPV: 73% NPV: 100% Accuracy: 91%
4 Cioni et al. (1997a; 1997b)	66 PT infants, 10 normal and 56 with grade I–IV IVH and grade I–IV PVL verified by CU	Neurological and developmental assessments at 2 years CA	Percentage of abnormal GMs decreased with age. 29/56 developed CP. Prediction of outcome improved after term age. Better prediction when developmental trajectories consistently or transiently abnormal. Neurological assessments better predictions after term age, GM quality more consistent predictions across all ages	For neurological outcome (as well as from infant neurological examination): Sensitivity: 91–100% (75–94%) Specificity: 58–91% (49–98%) PPV: 68–97% (59–91%) NPV: 86–100% (67–92%) Accuracy: not available

Table 14.5 *(continued)*

Study	Participants	Outcomes	Main findings	Indexes of efficacy
5 Hadders-Algra et al, (1997)	6 FT and 10 PT, all classified as having abnormal GMs on some of initial assessments. All had some form of brain damage verified by CU with most PT infants having grade I–III IVH or PVL	Presence/absence of CP and MND as well as WHO classification at 18–32 months CA	GM quality before about term age related to ultrasound scans. Improved predictions after about 12 weeks CA, especially when fidgety GMs absent. 7/16 and 6/16 developed CP or MND, respectively. Developmental course of GMs better predictor of outcome than concurrent neurological examination or CU	For CP and MHD (and WHO classification): Sensitivity: 88% (89%) Specificity: 88% (100%) PPV: 88% (100%) NPV: 88% (88%) Accuracy: 88% (94%)
6 Prechtl et al. (1997)	38 FT and 92 PT infants classified as low- or high-risk (grade II–IV IVH and/or PVL) verified by CU	Presence/absence of CP. Neurological and developmental assessments up to 2 years CA	67/70 with normal fidgety GMs had normal neurological outcomes. 57/60 with abnormal or absence of fidgety GMs had abnormal outcomes, 49 with cerebral palsy. Developmental course of GMs better predictor of outcomes than assessments based on CU	For neurological outcome: Sensitivity: 95% Specificity: 96% PPV: 95% NPV: 96% Accuracy: 95%
7 Hadders-Algra & Groothuis (1999)	28 low-risk and 24 high-risk infants, latter consisting of 18 PT infants, 14 with grade I–III PVL	Neurological assessments and parental evaluations of behavioural problems, based in part on DSM-IV, from 4–9 years	GM quality changed frequently. Abnormal GMs related to CP, mildly abnormal ones to MND, ADHD and aggressive behaviour. 8/24 developed CP. Prediction of outcome improved after 12 weeks, especially for CP	For (1) CP, (2) MND and (3) ADHD from fidgety GM quality (as well as from infant neurological examination): Sensitivity: (1) 88% (75%), (2) 85% (38%), (3) 79% (7%) Specificity: (1) 100% (100%), (2) 58% (94%), (3) 57% (80%) PPV: (1) 100% (100%), (2) 46% (71%), (3) 46% (46%) NPV: (1) 98% (96%), (2) 90% (78%), (3) 85% (35%) Accuracy: (1) 98% (96%), (2) 66% (77%), (3) 64% (57%)

ADHD, attentional deficit hyperactivity disorder; AGA, adequate for gestational age; CA, corrected age: CU, cranial ultrasonography; FT, fullterm; IVH, intraventricular haemorrhage; MND, minor neurological dysfunction (in muscle tone regulation, balance, coordination, fine manipulation); NPV, negative predictive value; PPV, positive predictive value; PVL, periventricular leukomalacia; SGA, small for gestational age; SM, spontaneous motility (same as GMs).

together with the transient neural mechanisms. It also emphasizes that abnormalities persisting after 3 months in, for example, the expression of spontaneous movements should be treated as signs indicative of a poor prognosis. A practical implication is that therapeutic intervention before about 3 months of age may incur iatrogenic effects due to it preserving ontogenetic adaptations that would otherwise disappear in the normal course of development. In this way, physical therapy and programmes of sensory stimulation devised for preterm infants could unnecessarily constrain the emergence of alternative developmental pathways if applied before the corrected age of 3 months.

Leg Movements

Another feature of the spontaneous behavioural repertoire of young infants concerns kicking movements in the supine position (Thelen, 1981). Consisting of flexion and extension phases and evident already in the second trimester foetus (Prechtl, 1986), they undergo three distinct changes postnatally: a decline in alternating movements of the legs and an increase in unilateral kicking (1–4 months), a predominance of bilateral kicking (from about 5 months onwards), and subsequently by marked dissociations between movements of the hip, knee and ankle joints (Vaal, van Soest, & Hopkins, 2000a). As revealed by kinematic analyses, these dissociations are preceded by an initial phase of tight interjoint couplings within each leg (Thelen, 1985). Derived from pairwise cross-correlations between movements of the three joints, this measure of intralimb coordination has figured predominantly in studies on spontaneous kicking in preterm infants following the pioneering work of Heriza (1988a). Measures of interlimb coordination have been less prominent in such studies, some of which are reviewed in Table 14.6.

Examination of Table 14.6 reveals a number of clinically relevant findings. To begin with, low-risk preterm infants tend to develop differently up to about 3 months of corrected age, but some then become indistinguishable from their fullterm counterparts. Brain-damaged infants display less variability in the temporal parameters of kicking and persist with more rigid interjoint couplings after 3 months. In contrasting quantitative measures of intra- and interlimb coordination, it appears that the former provides clearer distinctions between healthy and brain-damaged infants, particularly after 3 months of age. This also appears to be the case in comparisons between fullterm and low-risk preterm infants if leg asymmetries in intralimb coordination are taken into account. Thus, interlimb couplings seem to be less affected by additional exposure to the postnatal environment associated with prematurity or by brain damage than do those between joints within a limb. One explanation offered for the greater sensitivity of intralimb coordination to such effects is that dissociations between the movements of joints requires the increasing involvement of the corticospinal tracts (Vaal et al., 2000b). In those infants with white matter lesions such as PVL, these tracts may be damaged, thus giving rise to cerebral palsy and in particular spastic diplegia (Volpe, 1997).

Tables 14.5 and 14.6 also raise another, more general, issue about detection and prognosis in the case of infants at most risk for developmental disorders. Applicable to diagnosis as well, it concerns the respective roles of quantitative (i.e. dimensional) and qualitative (i.e. categorical) methods of assessment (Widiger & Trull, 1991). Qualitative assessments of, for example, GMs and spontaneous kicking are less time consuming, are simpler to use and more readily match clinical practice and its predilection for treating disorders as qualitatively distinct entities. However, for their application, such assessments require extensive clinical experience and clear standards of what constitutes the normal range of behaviour at any one age. Without these requirements, qualitative assessments run the danger of producing arbitrary and artifactual boundaries in separating 'normal' from 'abnormal' and the creation of catch-all categories to cover any uncertainties between these two extreme judgements. Quantitative assessments such as those derived from kinematic analyses can assist in reducing these problems and at the same time enable underlying pathology in control mechanisms to be identified more precisely. A good example of the latter advantage can be seen in the gait analyses of children with cerebral palsy (Gage, 1991). As for prognosis, it is to be expected that qualitative assessments should perform better as by their very nature they reduce a broad spectrum of individual differences to a few prototypical categories for both predictors and outcomes. In general, early detection and prognosis, as well as diagnosis and treatment evaluation, will be improved through combinations of repeated qualitative and quantitative assessments. Together with the serial use of brain imaging techniques, they serve as sources of information, each with their own strengths and weaknesses, from which clinical judgements can be made.

From Prematurity to Cerebral Palsy and Other Outcomes

In general, the lower the birthweight, the shorter the gestation and the greater the severity of medical complications, the more chance there is of an infant developing a disability such as cerebral palsy. What then are the causal pathways that link these biological risk factors to such an outcome? Without doubt, this is one of the most outstanding and largely unanswered questions on the developmental sequelae of prematurity. Some speculative answers are available with regard to VPT birth and PVL. Even more difficult to answer is how biological and social risk factors interrelate in the development of preterm infants.

Very Preterm Birth

Little (1862) and Freud (1897) put forward contrasting explanations of why preterm infants are at risk for cerebral palsy. According to Freud, CP was the consequence of the same events that gave rise to preterm birth. Thus, prematurity was

Table 14.6 *Studies on spontaneous kicking involving preterm infants. Two (1, 2) were carried out before term age, the rest from term age onwards. It is indicated whether a study included measures of intralimb coordination, interlimb coordination or both. Kinematic analyses were used in all except one study (5), sometimes combined with qualitative assessments of kicking (2) or GMs (2, 6, 7) or both (2, 7). Only one study (8) made 3-D kinematic analyses, which allows movements outside the saggital plane to be tracked*

Study and coordination type	Participants	Main findings	Conclusions/comments
1 Heriza (1988a; 1988b) Intralimb	15 FT and 10 low-risk PT infants born at 34–36 weeks GA. Comparisons between 2 groups made at 40 weeks term age	PT infants had increase in kick frequency, movement amplitude and peak velocity during flexion and extension with age. Both groups showed tight interjoint couplings	Coordination of leg movement is not influenced by the additional extrauterine experience of PT infants
2 Droit et al. (1996) Intra- and interlimb	12 low-risk and 12 high-risk PT infants, the latter having brain damage (IVH and/or PVL) verified by cranial ultrasonography. Comparisons made at 31–39 weeks GA	No group differences in temporal parameters except longer intrakick and shorter interkick pauses in brain-damaged infants at 37–39 weeks GA. In terms of interlimb coordination, these infants showed fewer alternating movements and more 'semi-both-leg kicking' (simultaneous flexion and non-simultaneous extension). 11/12 brain-damaged infants developed CP	GM quality assessed in same infants better predictor of neurological outcome than quantitative measures of kicking
3 Heriza (1991) Intralimb	15 FT, 10 low-risk and 24 high-risk PT infants with IVH (grade I, 5; II, 8; III, 5; IV, 6). PT infants born at < 34–36 weeks GA. Comparisons between PT and FT infants made at 40 weeks term age	High-risk PT infants had longer extension and flexion phases and more variability in amplitude and velocity of kicks at 40 weeks. Tight intralimb in all infants	No statistical analyses presented for individual infants or group comparisons
4 Heriza (1991) Intralimb	1 PT infant with grade IV IVH followed from term age to 12 months	Tight interjoint coupling at 40 weeks term age, decrease at 4 months with increases in intralimb coordination at 8 and 12 months	Inability to dissociate intralimb coupling after 4 months indicative of poor motor outcomes. No statistical analyses presented for individual infants or group comparisons
5 Yokochi et al. (1991) Interlimb	3 FT and 46 PT infants selected on the basis of having developed spastic diplegia, and 70 PT infants with normal outcomes at 18 months. Comparisons of qualitative assessments of leg movements made at 3–11 months CA	Simultaneous flexion and extension of hips and knees, with occasional hip movements, only seen in diplegic infants. Leg elevation and isolated knee movements only in PT control infants, both patterns indicating relative loose interjoint couplings	Absence of leg elevation and isolated knee movements after 3 months CA predictive of spastic diplegia. Study was retrospective and thus more likely to find abnormal signs than a prospective study

Table 14.6 *(continued)*

Study and coordination type	Participants	Main findings	Conclusions/comments
6 Geerdink et al (1996) Intralimb	13 FT and 10 low-risk PT infants, the latter consisting of 5 classified as SGA and 5 as AGA. Comparisons made at 6, 12 and 18 weeks CA	Durations of flexion and extension did not differ between FT and PT groups, but PT infants had much higher initial kick rates, especially those classified as SGA. Initially, lower degree of interjoint coupling in PT SGA and those less than 32 weeks GA, but by 18 weeks no differences with FT infants. GM quality related to kick rate and hip–ankle cross-correlation	Different developmental courses for FT and PT infants, but all differences between them resolved after 12 weeks
7 van der Heide et al. (1999) Intra- and interlimb	12 FT, 12 low-risk PT and 11 PT infants with PVL. Comparisons made at 1 and 3 months CA	No persistent group differences for quantitative measures including those for intra-and interlimb coordination. Differences in quality of kicking (fewer segmental foot movements in PVL infants) and GMs (no PVL infant had normal quality). 7/11 PVL infants developed CP	Mechanisms for kicking hardly influenced by extrauterine environment or supraspinal factors, and GM quality gives better prediction of outcome. However, study was cross-sectional and did not go beyond 3 months CA
8 Piek & Gasson (1999) Intra- (both legs) and interlimb	7 FT and 7 low-risk PT infants. Comparisons made at 4–24 weeks CA	No marked differences between groups as a function of age for both intra-and interlimb coordination measures. However, ankle/knee coupling increased for right leg and decreased for left leg in PT infants	Leg asymmetries in PT infants point to need for registering movements of both legs when studying development of intralimb coordination
9 Vaal et al. (2000b) Intra- and interlimb	8 FT and 2 PT healthy infants, 1 FT and 18 PT infants with PVL. Comparisons made at 6, 12, 18, and 26 weeks CA	Less variability in temporal parameters (e.g. peak velocity during flexion) shown by infants with moderate to severe PVL. In severe cases, tight interjoint coupling still present at 18 and 26 weeks, all of whom developed CP. No differences between PVL and healthy infants in developmental course of interlimb coordination	Intra- and interlimb coordination follow different developmental courses, with corticospinal tracts involved in regulation of joint dissociations between 4 and 6 months. Inability to do so in this age range indicative of poor outcomes

GA, gestational age. Other abbreviations as in Table 14.5.

another effect of the same brain-damaging event. For Little, the medical complications associated with preterm birth were the causal agents responsible for CP. Consequently, prematurity resulted in a brain vulnerable to physiological disturbances triggered by medical complications. Both Little and Freud were concerned with preterm infants regardless of gestational age and birthweight. Today, the concern is for outcomes in VPT and VLBW infants, with increasingly more attention being paid to those classified as ELBW (see Hack & Farnoff, 1999, for a recent review). Nevertheless, the explanations proposed by Little and Freud still remain as competitors in attempts to uncover the causal pathways to cerebral palsy (see Figure 14.4).

Pathway A closely resembles Freud's explanation and thus that preterm birth itself is not on the causal route to CP (Stanley, Blair, & Alberman, 2000). Possible complications that cause preterm delivery and CP independently of each other include maternal infections arising from rupture of the membranes and placental haemorrhage (see Table 14.4). Pathway B reflects Little's explanation: preterm birth is caused by an antenatal factor or a combination of factors and the immature brain of the VPT infant is irreversibly damaged by subsequent medical complications (see

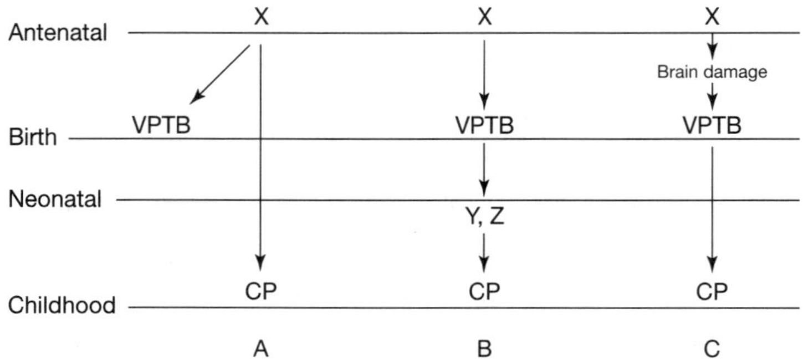

Figure 14.4 *Three possible pathways between very preterm birth (VPTB) and cerebral palsy (CP). Pathway A involves one or more antecedent events that independently cause preterm delivery and CP. It is thus antenatal events X and VPTB that cause CP. Pathway B presents the claim that VPT infants may be more susceptible to neonatal (Y) or perinatal (Z) medical complications than fullterm infants, which in turn give rise to CP. Pathway C holds that antenatal events X cause brain damage associated with CP and that the damage itself is also responsible for VPTB. What is common to all three pathways is that antenatal events X cause VPTB (reproduced with permission from Stanley et al., 2000)*

Table 14.2). Pathway C is potentially possible, but there are no clear-cut examples (Stanley, Blair, & Alberman, 2000). What it suggests is that preterm delivery is caused by antenatal brain damage, which in turn leads to CP. Returning to pathway B, still the most favoured explanation even though it has been questioned (Nelson & Ellenberg, 1985), cerebral white matter damage such as PVL is the most common brain pathology in VPT infants and a potent predictor of CP, especially spastic diplegia.

Periventricular Leukomalacia

PVL is also referred to as parenchymal echodensities, multifocal necrosis of cerebral white matter or cystic changes. It has an overall incidence of 9.2% in VPT infants, but varies according to gestational age (Zupan et al., 1996). There is a peak in incidence at 28 weeks (15.8%) and the lowest at 32 weeks (4.3%). A frequent pathological accompaniment of IVH, it does not appear to be caused by the haemorrhage itself (Rushton, Preston, & Durbin, 1985). Generally consisting of symmetrical damage in the periventricular white matter leading to cystic lesions located at the corners of the lateral ventricles in the frontal, parietal and, less frequently, occipital regions, its causes are unclear (see Table 14.2). Its long-term outcome is spastic diplegia in the majority of VPT infants with cystic PVL and in some with non-cystic PVL (Volpe, 1995).

How does PVL create a pathway leading to spastic diplegia? One hypothesis concerns the site of the lesion produced by PVL relative to the somatotopic organization of the corticospinal tracts (see Figure 14.5). The bilateral lesion is situated in a part of the cerebral white matter through which the tracts descend from the motor cortex. Its locus in the medial part of the corona radiata before the fibres form bundles in the internal capsule means that the legs will be more affected than the upper extremities. Lateral extensions of the lesion into the corona radiata and the centrum semiovale will affect the upper extremities as well and possibly give rise to severe mental retardation (Volpe, 1995).

The cause and effects of PVL are subjects of considerable controversy in the paediatric literature. Thus, the hypothesis that it arises from hypoxic/ischaemic insults has been challenged (Kuban & Gilles, 1985) as has its role in spastic diplegia, which could be due to a 'dying back' neuropathy of distal cortical tracts rather than PVL (Crawford & Hobbs, 1994). All told, however, cerebral white matter damage associated with a very preterm birth for whatever reason clearly constitutes a major biological risk for the development of cerebral palsy. Nevertheless, even preterm infants free of such major medical complications may be at risk and show functional delays relative to fullterm controls or test norms at corrected ages during the period of infancy. This is particularly the case for motor abilities (e.g. Gorga, Stern, & Ross, 1985) and the development of communication (e.g. van Beek, Hopkins, & Hoeksma, 1994), with delays in language functions possibly persisting beyond the second year (e.g. Largo, Molinari, & Cominale Pinto, 1986). Recent evidence, derived from magnetic resonance imaging, suggests that healthy preterm and fullterm infants also differ in structural brain development at term: preterm infants at term age have less grey/white differentiation and myelination (Hüppi et al., 1996) as well as reduced cortical folding (Ajayi-Obe et al., 1999).

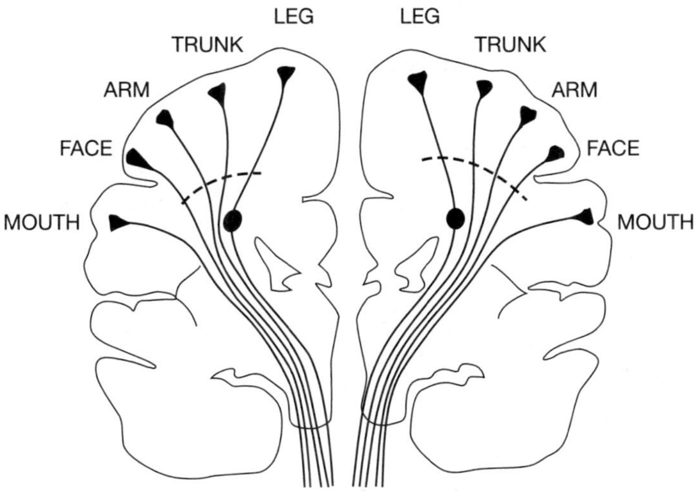

Figure 14.5 *Periventricular leukomalacia (PVL) and spastic diplegia. Shown are the descending corticospinal tracts from the motor cortex that innervate muscles in the lower and upper extremities, the trunk and the facial region. Initially, they are dispersed as corona radiata (fibres between cortex and internal capsule: dashed line), which course through the centrum semiovale (centre of cerebral white matter). Subsequently, they form into bundles when descending through the internal capsule (large white matter tract between thalamus and basal ganglia containing both motor and sensory axons). The site of the PVL lesion in the corona radiata or the centrum semiovale means that it will damage medial fibres more than lateral fibres, and thus affect the lower rather than the upper extremity, thereby leading to spastic diplegia. Note that this is only one hypothesis about the causal pathway between PVL and spastic diplegia (adapted from Volpe, 1995)*

These two sets of evidence could be related, but it may also be the case that the functional delays create additional social risks for the developing preterm infant.

Biological and Social Risks

Preterm infants who are otherwise relatively healthy at birth often display impairments in the control of posture and voluntary movements at later ages (e.g. see van der Fits et al., 1999). Given that modulations in posture and movement are among the earliest means of communication available to the preverbal infants (Hopkins, 1983), impairments in motor control may trigger latent social risks that serve to further exacerbate the potential for deviant developmental outcomes. In addition to such impairments, preterm infants are physically different from their fullterm counterparts, something which can still be evident in late adolescence (Nilsen et al., 1984). Differences in physical appearance, together with motor impairments, may strengthen the prematurity or 'what is premature is bad' stereotype (Stern & Hildebrandt-Karraker, 1990). Being a set of biased beliefs or negative appraisals about infants born prematurely, such a stereotype can represent a potential social risk to the optimal development of preterm infants. On the one hand, it might promote overprotection and the 'vulnerable child syndrome' (Green & Solnit, 1964), and on the other hand, 'interactional failures' (Papousek & Papousek, 1983) that in turn enhance the risk for child neglect and abuse. There is long-standing evidence that this risk is higher for preterm infants in general (Fontana, 1973). A hypothetical developmental pathway incorporating this complex combination of biological and social risk factors is illustrated in Figure 14.6.

The developmental pathway depicted is a gross oversimplification of how biological and social risks may interrelate in determining the fate of a preterm infant. It does not include, for example, the potentially deleterious effects of some neonatal intensive care unit practices (Gottfried & Gaiter, 1984), the aversive crying sounds of preterm infants (Frodi et al., 1978), their poorer state regulation (Watt & Strongman, 1985) and, of course, the mediating influences of SES and associated variables (Censullo, 1994). Nevertheless, it gives a sense of the diversity of factors that have to be accounted for in understanding the pathways to developmental outcomes other than disabilities such as cerebral palsy in preterm infants.

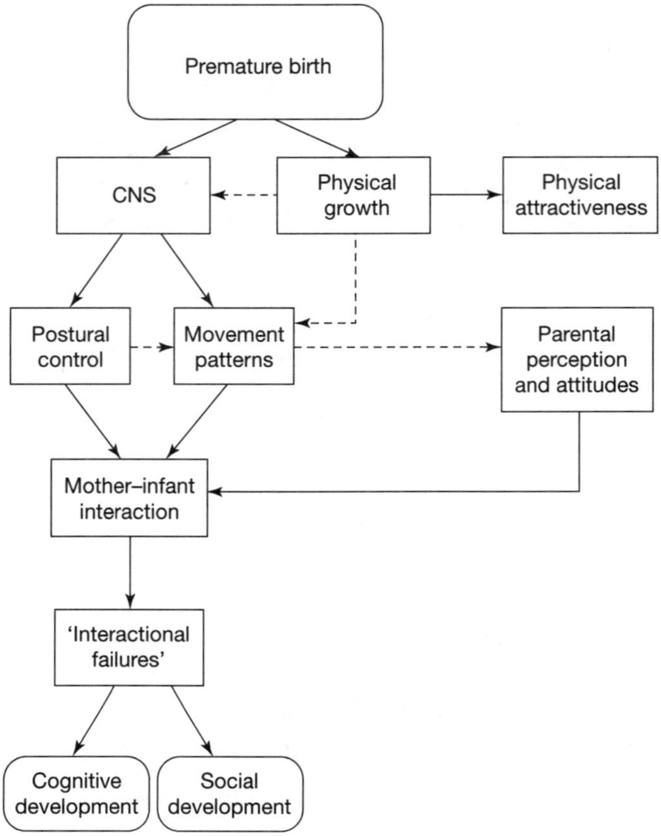

Figure 14.6 *A hypothetical developmental pathway connecting premature birth to later outcomes other than cerebral palsy. Prematurity can have adverse influences on the developing central nervous system (CNS), which can be expressed as delays in the acquisition of posture and movement control. In turn, these delays may create problems in social interaction, which if severe enough may lead to interactional failures. Such failures may not only have negative consequences for social development, but also remove the necessary conditions for the promotion of cognitive development while at the same time increasing the risks for neglect and abuse. Prematurity is also associated with differences in physical growth relative to fullterm infants and which can diminish the perceived attractiveness of preterm infants. This might add to the social risks faced by preterm infants and thus to later occurring problems. Dashed lines indicate other possible connections in the developmental pathway (e.g. effects of intrauterine growth retardation on the developing CNS)*

Developmental Intervention: Is It Efficacious?

Efficacy refers to the desired effect of a treatment relative to an appropriate control. Ideally, assignments to the treatment or control group are made by random allocation. This term is contrasted with efficiency: whether or not a treatment works after it is implemented in clinical practice (see Feinstein, 1977). The two terms are often used interchangeably in intervention research. Here, the concern is with the efficacy of intervention studies involving preterm infants and children with cerebral palsy.

Broadly speaking, there are three types of intervention: primary intervention (to reduce the incidence of a disease *before* it occurs), secondary intervention (to treat a disease *while* it is becoming established) and tertiary intervention (to treat a disease *after* it is established). Intervention research with preterm infants can be of the primary or secondary variety depending on the absence or presence of verifiable brain pathology. Intervention with cerebral palsied children is both secondary and tertiary in nature. Secondary intervention is typically directed towards the treatment of impairments and tertiary intervention towards disabilities or handicaps. A major, but so far unfulfilled role, for primary intervention is to reduce the incidence of premature births and thereby that for cerebral palsy and other disabilities.

An important point to bear in mind is that the medical care of preterm infants has been subject to periodic and rapid change that can consign a study (with or without intervention) to being one with little more than historical interest. Given that such change has been particularly marked in the last 20–30 years, findings published before the middle of the 1970s (and perhaps even since the beginning of the 1990s) should be viewed with caution. The same probably applies to research with CP children, although to a lesser degree as the standard treatment methods have not fundamentally changed in the last two or three decades. The following overview of developmental intervention research with preterm infants and children with cerebral palsy reflects this concern in avoiding studies published before 1980, especially for the former.

Intervention with Preterm Infants

Studies of interest concern what has been termed 'supplemental stimulation' (Field, 1980) with infants before term age and a broad range of intervention strategies typically involving parents in a therapeutic role after term age. Those pursuing the efficacy of supplemental stimulation have mainly employed randomized control trials, and to a lesser extent crossover designs, the latter consisting of within-subject comparisons between two or more treatments (see Feinstein, 1977). In the sorts of studies reviewed by Field (1980), 'stimulation' was either auditory, oral (non-nutritive sucking), tactile or proprioceptive and vestibular in nature or some multimodal combination (with vestibular and proprioceptive stimulation providing inseparable effects as in the case of oscillating or non-oscillating water beds; see Korner & Schneider, 1983). Other studies have examined the effects of maternal education (e.g. Affleck et al., 1989), prone versus supine positioning (e.g. Aebi et al., 1991), individualized developmental care (e.g. Als, 1992), and even reduced (visual) stimulation (e.g. Shirowa, Komiya, & Uchibari, 1986).

A review of studies published in peer-review journals between 1980 and 1990 initially considered 81 (Lacy & Ohlson, 1993). However, only 29 complied with its inclusion criteria devised to exclude poorly designed studies (e.g. those without a control group). All 29 studies were begun before term age and covered the various forms of stimulation and other strategies mentioned previously. Only 9 of them included post-discharge measures varying in time from minimally 6 to maximally 48 months after leaving hospital. The findings make for sober reading, given that only about one-third of the original set of studies was considered suitable for inclusion.

Short-term benefits were claimed by 26 studies, but all contained methodological flaws. In contrast, the three best-designed studies, which also had the largest samples, reported no beneficial effects of intervention on the outcome measures. These seemingly counter-intuitive findings have featured in previous reviews of supplemental stimulation (Ottenbacher et al., 1987) and for medical intervention in general (Williamson, Goldschmidt, & Colton, 1986). But perhaps they are not so counter-intuitive since poorly designed studies will omit the essential controls that inevitably temper what justifiable conclusions can be drawn. If journals are biased towards publishing studies with positive outcomes, then the danger is that research on the effects of early intervention will continue to lack scientific credibility with costs outstripping benefits.

In recent years, there has been a growing tendency for hospital-based intervention programmes involving VPT infants to include what has become known as the Kangaroo Mother Method (Anderson, 1999). Originating in Bogotá, Columbia as an alternative to the prohibitively high costs of neonatal intensive care (Rey & Martinez, 1983), it involves periods of skin-to-skin contact between infant and parent by means of the parent carrying the infant in a sling. The recipient of much optimism regarding its potential benefits, it has been subjected to few controlled trials. A well-designed study carried out in Ecuador found that LBW infants in the treatment group had lower rates of serious illness and fewer readmissions, but did not differ from controls with regard to mortality and growth (Sloan et al., 1994; see also Whitelaw et al., 1988).

Recently, there has also been an increasing trend for hospital-based intervention programmes involving VPT infants to adopt individualized forms of developmental care. One study, which generated a lot of discussion, attempted to evaluate such care using a phase lag design with random assignment to treatment and control groups (Als et al., 1994). In the treatment group, there was, among other things, a reduced incidence of intraventricular haemorrhage and chronic lung disease as well as higher developmental quotients at 9 months corrected age. There are, however, a number of problems with the study (e.g. a lack of adequate matching between the two groups as revealed by the high morbidity rates in the control infants) and so far its effects have not been replicated. Intervention geared to the individual needs of infants has been a common strategy in studies conducted with preterm infants after term age (see Table 14.7 for examples of relevant studies).

As one would expect, parental involvement with some degree of supervised guidance is a feature common to such intervention studies. From the examples listed in Table 14.7, it is clear that gains are

Table 14.7 *Selected examples of intervention studies with preterm (PT) infants after hospital discharge. While all were home-based, some started in the hospital setting (3, 5, 8). Others incorporated a reference group of fullterm infants (2, 5, 6). Only one set of studies consisted of a direct comparison between different methods of intervention (6, 7)*

	Study	Participants	Design	Intervention	Length follow-up	Main findings
1	Bromwich & Parmelee (1979)	63 PT infants varying in SES and ethnic background	QE with expt. ($n = 30$) and control ($n = 33$) groups. Matching on SES, ethnic background and severity of neonatal problems	Health care (both groups) and individualized approach to promote parent–infant interaction (expt. group)	24 months	Expt. group: more positive parental behaviour and infant play. No differences on standardized tests
2	Field et al. (1980)	60 PT infants born to teenage mothers, low SES, black mothers	RA to expt. ($n = 30$) and control ($n = 30$) groups	Sensorimotor exercises and interaction games	8 months	Expt. group: more optimal developmental level and interaction at 4 months. More optimal mental, but not motor, scores at 8 months
3	Minde et al. (1980)	57 PT infants, severe neonatal problems excluded	AA to expt., self-help ($n = 28$) and control, routine care ($n = 29$) groups	Weekly group meetings with experienced mother of PT infant and nurse	3 months	Expt. group: mothers visited, looked at, talked to and touched infants more often
4	Ross (1984)	80 PT infants, all low SES	QE with expt. ($n = 40$) and control ($n = 40$) groups. Matching on SES, ethnic background, birthweight and severity of neonatal problems	Caretaking activities to promote cognitive, motor and social development	12 months	Expt. group: higher mental scores, but not motor, scores. Higher ratings of home environment. No differences on infant temperament and maternal attitudes to child rearing
5	Nurcombe et al. (1984)	78 LBW infants, severe neonatal problems excluded	RA to expt. ($n = 38$) and control ($n = 40$) groups	Mothers taught to focus on infant behaviour and sensitivity/responsivity during interaction	6 months	Expt. group: easier infant temperament and more positive maternal attitude to child rearing. No differences on mental and motor scores. Subsequent follow-ups: at 4 years (Rauh et al., 1988) higher on cognitive score and at 7 years (Achenbach et al., 1990)
6	Barrera et al. (1986a)	59 PT infants, blocked on SES, sex, birthweight and peri/postnatal problems	RA to 2 expt. and 1 control ($n = 12$) group. Expt. groups: infant-focused developmental intervention ($n = 16$) and parent–infant interaction intervention ($n = 22$)	Developmental: parents instructed to promote ability on specific tasks. Parent–infant: enhancing parental sensitivity/responsivity during interaction	16 months	Expt. groups: both higher mental, but not motor, scores. Interaction group: higher ratings on home environment. Subsequent follow-up: at 28 months interaction group higher motor, but not mental, scores as well as better ratings of home environment (Barrera, 1987)

7	Barrera et al. (1986b)	Same as in study 6, but distinctions in terms of VLBW ($n = 20$) and LBW ($n = 39$) infants	RA to same groups as in study 6: developmental ($n = 19$), interaction ($n = 21$) and control ($n = 19$)	As in study 6	16 months	Expt. groups: no differences on any outcome measure, but VLBW (not LBW) in expt. groups had gains on mental (not motor) scores and ratings of home environment. Subsequent follow-up: at 5 years no differences on standardized tests, but better ratings of home environment for expt. groups (Barrera et al., 1990)
8	Resnick et al. (1987)	221 infants less than 1850 g, all low SES	AA to expt. ($n = 17$) and control ($n = 14$) groups	Supplemental multimodal stimulation with subsequent coaching of parent and developmental activities including interaction	24 months	Expt. group: higher mental and motor scores as well as lower incidence of developmental delay
9	Brooks-Gunn et al. (1992) See also Ramey et al. (1992); Bradley et al. (1994)	985 LBW infants varying in SES and ethnic background	RA to expt. ($n = 377$) and control ($n = 608$) groups	Parental group meetings and instruction in age-appropriate games and activities as well as support for management of problems identified by parents	36 months	Expt. group: gains across various cognitive domains, most pronounced for receptive language, visual-motor and spatial abilities. Subsequent follow-up: at 8 years group differences no longer present (McCarton et al., 1997). All studies part of multisite IHDP (1990)

AA, alternate assignment; IHDP, Infant Health and Development Program; QE, quasi-experimental design; RA, random assignment; SES, socioeconomic status.

registered in one or more aspects of parenting, perhaps in part as a consequence of enabling caregivers to overcome self-fulfilling prophecies associated with the prematurity syndrome. In contrast, the gains for infants in terms of a variety of developmental outcomes appear to be less striking although they are more pronounced for mental, rather than motor, abilities. However, at least for the period of infancy, the distinction between mental and motor abilities is dubious at best. This is because the infant tests used in these studies rely heavily on actions performed on objects in judging the level of mental development.

The main problem in evaluating the efficacy of developmental intervention with preterm infants is to know what has produced the effects. Such is particularly the case with studies conducted after hospitalization as they incorporate a plethora of potentially influential factors that are often inadequately defined. Another criticism levelled at early intervention studies with at-risk infants is that they fail to demonstrate long-term benefits. While there are exceptions to this criticism (see Table 14.7), it is questionable whether such benefits should be expected once an intervention has stopped. Any effects it has engendered may be subsequently negated by, for example, changes in family circumstances or by the use of later outcome measures that have little bearing on the original aims of the intervention. As Korner (1987) aptly put it, early intervention is not analogous to immunization. Finally, it should be noted that the non-medical forms of intervention under consideration here have rarely focused on infants at most risk for developing disabilities such as CP. This situation may change, however, given the improvements in brain-imaging and other (non-invasive) methods of early detection discussed previously.

Physical Therapy and Other Forms of Intervention with Cerebral Palsied Children

The two foremost impairments underlying disabilities in children with CP are agonist/antagonist muscle co-contractions and contractures (i.e. alterations in the mechanical properties of muscles and connective tissue resulting in the tightening of tendons, ligaments and skin). Together with disturbances in perceptual abilities, both contribute to a functional decline in children with CP. All physical therapies for such children aim to prevent, or at least ameliorate, this decline in some way through the training of normal movement patterns and the inhibition of abnormal ones, the normalization of muscle power, and the prevention of deformities arising from contractures. Most of them assume that the emerging impairments are due to the failure of the damaged cortex to establish inhibitory influences over the activity of spinal circuits.

The most frequently used method of physical therapy in the treatment of children with cerebral palsy is that devised by the Bobaths (Bobath & Bobath, 1984) and now referred to as Neuro-developmental Therapy (NDT). Also advocated for use with Down's syndrome infants (Harris, 1987) and children with developmental coordination disorder (Schoemaker, Hijkema, & Kalverboer, 1994), it assumes that movement disorders associated with CP arise from impairments in the reflex control of posture. In turn, they lead to the persistence of 'primitive' reflexes and thereby to the absence of, or delay in, the ability to make the postural adjustments required for righting and equilibrium reactions. Therapy is, therefore, directed towards the inhibition of such reflexes, the facilitation of postural reactions and the modification of muscle power, using vestibular-proprioceptive stimuli while guiding the child through various movement sequences.

There is a controversial claim made by NDT and related (eponymous) therapies such as Ayre's Sensory Integration Therapy, the Doman–Delacato Pattern Therapy, the Petö Method of Conductive Education, the Rood Sensorimotor Approach and the Vojta Method (see Scrutton, 1984, for descriptions of these therapies). This is that the therapy enables the non-damaged parts of the brain to assume functions normally performed by the damaged areas (a less controversial claim is that disuse atrophy can be avoided by functional training). The theoretical inspiration for this claim was derived from deprivation, ablation and lesion experiments carried out on a variety of mammalian species within the context of classical neurophysiology (e.g. see Windle, 1956). These experiments revealed that, when damaged, the mammalian central nervous system has considerable restorative powers such as collateral sprouting and the selective re-innervation of nerve fibres, the mechanisms of both being poorly understood (see Lund, 1978). Quite apart from the question of whether such neuroanatomical changes confer any functional benefits, there is simply no scientific evidence that NDT and similar therapies applied to brain-damaged children alter the development of their nervous systems in these ways. Physical therapies of any kind cannot 'undo' brain damage, but may in fact prove to be efficacious in ways that are not predicted by the associated theory, as can be seen from some of the studies reported in Table 14.8.

The studies in Table 14.8, all of which focus on the treatment of impairments rather than disabilities or handicaps, were selected on the basis of the following criteria: a prospective study involving a pretest/posttest design or alternate/random assignment to groups or both. Using these rather basic standards of design, another 10 studies were excluded from consideration. The eight studies surviving the selection process do not add to our confidence about the efficacy of physical therapy for children with CP. Few provide sufficiently detailed descriptions of

Table 14.8 *Selected examples of studies evaluating the effects of physical therapy. Studies 5, 6 and 7 involved infants at risk for cerebral palsy (CP). Four studies (2, 5, 6, 7) incorporated a home-based treatment component with parental involvement. The oldest study (1) is one of the better designed in that it catered for RA, blind assessment and a crossover design for group B. It reported no real benefits from physical therapy except the unpredicted outcome that some children became more sociable and required less help and support than those who did not receive treatment (see also 3)*

	Study and therapy	Participants	Design	Length follow-up	Main findings	Comments
1	Wright & Nicholson (1973) Centre-based NDT	47 CP children, all less than 6 years of age. 19 mentally retarded	RA to 1 of 3 groups: A: NDT for 1 year ($n = 16$) B: no NDT for 6 months, then NDT for 6 months ($n = 16$) C: control group ($n = 15$)	2 years	No differences between groups, but functional improvements in quadraplegic infants between developmental ages of 6–12 months. Some children more sociable and required less help and support as consequence of NDT	No report of length and frequency of treatment sessions. Matching by CA not functional level. Additional treatments (including drugs). No statistical analyses
2	Scherzer et al. (1976) Centre-based/ home-based combination of NDT, PNF and RSA	22 infants initially diagnosed as CP at ages 5–17 months	RA to expt. ($n = 14$) and control ($n = 8$) groups	7–12 months	Expt. group had greater improvements (% change) in outcomes labelled 'motor stature', 'social maturation' and 'home management'	No report of length of each treatment session. No check on parental compliance with home-based programme of therapy. No statistical analyses of group differences
3	Chee et al. (1978) Centre-based focus on main feature of ASIT (vestibular stimulation)	23 preambulatory children at ages 2–6 years	No RA but group matching on basis of pretest scores on motor and reflex tests. 3 groups: T: semicircular canal stimulation (SCS) and handling ($n = 12$) CH: only handling ($n = 6$) CNH: no handling or SCS ($n = 5$)	4 days	Differences in T versus CH and T versus CNH on posttreatment composite scores for motor and reflex tests. Some mothers reported improvements in motor and social-emotional behaviour for children in T group	No report of length of each treatment session. Unclear what is meant by 'handling'. Lack of details on outcome of matching
4	Sellick & Over (1980) Same therapeutic focus as study 3	20 children with CP at ages 8–56 months	RA to expt. group ($n = 10$) and control ($n = 10$) groups with matching on CA, developmental level and CP type	12 weeks	No group differences on any outcome measure	Failure to replicate study 3
5	Piper et al. (1986) Centre-based/ home-based NDT	115 infants at risk for neurological sequelae. Ages at start of therapy unclear	RA after classification according to neurological optimality and birthweight to expt. ($n = 56$) and control ($n = 59$) groups	12 months	No group differences on any outcome measure even when accounting for differences in neurological optimality and birthweight	Question as to whether RA was successful as more infants neurologically abnormal at 12 months in expt. group. Check on parental compliance with home-based programme of therapy described in a booklet

Table 14.8 *(continued)*

	Study and therapy	Participants	Design	Length follow-up	Main findings	Comments
6	Palmer et al. (1988) Centre-based/ home-based NDT	48 infants with CP at ages 12–19 months	RA after classification according to developmental level to 2 groups: A: NDT B: NDT (6 months), then infant stimulation programme (6 months)	12 months	No advantages for group A infants. Higher mental and motor scores for Group B	Tentatively concluded: (a) infant stimulation more beneficial than NDT; (b) NDT may require more frequent contact with therapist for any effects to be realized
7	Mayo (1991) Centre-based/ home-based NDT	29 infants at risk for CP with ages 7–18 months. 20 eventually diagnosed as CP, 6 with non-specific motor delays and 3 as normal	RA to weekly intensive ($n = 17$) and monthly basic ($n = 12$) therapy	6 months	Mean performance of intensive group better on various composite motor scores, but not specific abilities such as walking	Higher levels of education for mothers in intensive group. No check on parental compliance with home-based programme of therapy described in a booklet
8	Bower et al. (1996) Centre-based eclectic form of therapy	44 children with CP at ages 3–11 years	RA after classification on basis of functional severity to different types of therapy defined as conventional ($n = 22$) or intensive ($n = 22$)	2 weeks	Intensive therapy had 'slightly greater effect' on gross motor functioning, especially when specific treatment goals were set	No details on differences between groups in terms of family background or IQ (latter being common shortcoming in post-infancy studies). Informative discussion of logistical problems in carrying out evaluations of therapy for CP children

ASIT, Ayre's Sensory Integration Therapy; CA, chronological age; NDT, Neurodevelopmental Therapy; PNF, Proprioceptive Neuromuscular Treatment (similar to RSA, but involves different planes of movement); RSA,: Rood Sensorimotor Approach.

how the therapy was carried out and few give clear indications that it is beneficial in any meaningful way. The latter problem may have to do with the choice of outcome measures that bear little relationship to the goals of the therapy. Most appear to be directed towards the impractical goal of 'normalizing' development relative to some standardized (or more often unstandardized) test. This brings with it the potential for teaching-to-the-test, a long-standing problem in intervention research known as the Schmidt effect (Kirk, 1948).

Despite the lack of convincing evidence for the efficacy of physical therapy with CP children, therapists and sometimes parents regard it as an effective medium of treatment. The reasons for this state of affairs are unclear, but they may reside in the way therapists and parents approach a child with CP. Rather than holding a deficit model about the child, they may regard what are considered to be impairments as functional adaptations to, for example, the dynamical requirements of locomotion. To pursue this example further, the gait of children with spastic diplegia sometimes appears to be more like running than walking in that they have a higher frequency of strides per minute than do those without CP (Olney, Costigan, & Hedden, 1987). As such, running instead of walking may help the diplegic child to compensate for the lack of propulsive force in the gastrocnemius-soleus muscles by means of recruiting their greater elastic recoil at higher stride frequencies (Holt, Osbuek, & Fonesca, 1996). Thus, given the available dynamical resources, the gait pattern can be viewed as effective and one that enables disabilities associated with locomotion to be overcome. A similar argument can be put forward in the case of co-contractions. Typically regarded as an impairment, they could function to compensate for weak muscles as well as preventing muscle atrophy and circulatory problems in the extremities (Latash, 1993). Such examples of functional adaptations are generally not acknowledged in studies designed to test the efficacy of physical therapy, but they are in its everyday practice.

Space does not permit coverage of evaluations of other, more invasive, forms of therapy for the treatment of CP. These include selective dorsal rhizotomy, the surgical lengthening of muscles or tendons or both, electrical muscle stimulation, the administration of pharmacological agents and the use of orthopaedic appliances such as splints and casts. Often used as an adjunct to physical therapy, especially splinting and casting, their efficacy is a matter of considerable debate. Some of the studies concerned with evaluating these sorts of interventions relative to outcomes in terms of gait in CP patients are reviewed in Gage (1991).

A Common Denominator: Parents and Families

It has now become almost an article of faith that the active participation of parents and other family members is an essential ingredient in achieving the goals of a treatment plan. This conviction applies to both early intervention with preterm infants and physical therapy for children with CP. While adding further layers of complexity to the task of evaluating what actually contributes to the efficacy of a therapeutic intervention, such participation does ensure that the rights and needs of families are being met. In addition to providing parents with concrete instructions about functional training and handling techniques, current interventionist approaches encourage them to become active problem-solvers in caring for their at-risk infants or disabled children (e.g. Barrera, Cunningham, & Rosenblum, 1986; Barrera, Rosenblum, & Cunningham, 1986). Accordingly, parents are taught to identify the problems a child presents and then to devise appropriate problem-solving strategies using the information and techniques they have been supplied with. The short-term goal of this problem-solving model of parental education is to endow parents with some degree of shared control in treating their own child. A longer-term goal is to equip them for dealing with medical and educational specialists so as to get better services for their children. There is little empirical evidence on how parents put such a model into practice, how they experience it and what they perceive its benefits to have been.

The pitfalls associated with indirect forms of intervention in which some degree of therapeutic responsibility is delegated to the parents are considerable. For example, if parents perceive their child not to be improving, this may induce irremediable feelings of guilt, which in turn result in a premature cessation of the teaching programme. Conversely, they may lead to an increase in intensification that is detrimental to the well-being of the child and of the family in general. Prior to initiating the process of delegation, the following questions need to be considered (Ferry, 1988). Would the child be best left alone with caring parents with whom he is allowed to progress at his own rate? Are these parents really the best therapists for their own child or should they just be parents and not therapists? Does time in therapy detract from activities with other members of the family?

While parents have been depicted as 'the keystone of the therapeutic arch' (MacKeith, 1976, p. 285), the role of other family members has been rather neglected. This is particularly the case for the siblings of a child with CP. Given the right guidance, they can provide supportive as well as challenging interactions and even sometimes be more effective than parents in minimizing the CP child's disability.

These claims are supported by at least one study (Craft et al., 1990). The intervention, directed at the brothers and sisters of a child with cerebral palsy, had two aims: to help them understand more fully the effects of CP and to teach them over a four-month period how to use reinforcements in their interactions. Improvements in the CP siblings were found not only at the level of impairments (namely increased range of motion in the joints of the shoulder, elbow and wrist), but also at the disability level (namely in terms of ambulation, personal hygiene, dressing and feeding).

Concluding Comments

This chapter has focused on prematurity and on cerebral palsy as one of its major sequelae in order to illustrate some of the issues and problems associated with the study of developmental disorders. Other conditions known to be the result of dominant or recessive gene defects such as Williams syndrome and phenylketonuria could have been considered. The same applies to autism and chromosomal abnormalities, sex-linked or not, such as fragile X syndrome and Down's syndrome. The reason for their exclusion has to do with their relatively low rates of occurrence set against the details required to describe their aetiologies. Other sequelae associated with prematurity such as attentional deficit hyperactivity disorder and developmental coordination disorder have not been considered because of the continuing difficulties in capturing their essential signs and distinguishing them as clear-cut clinical entities.

An implicit theme running through the essay has been the concept of developmental risk. There has also been a plea for a more action-based approach to the study of developmental disorders. Both raise important theoretical issues concerning research on developmental disorders.

The Concept of Developmental Risk

Broadly speaking, this concept makes a distinction between biological and social (or environmental) risk factors. Biological risk factors include the prepregnancy, prenatal, perinatal and postnatal antecedents of cerebral palsy listed in Table 14.4. The mental states of the parents, the lack of an extended family system and poverty are typical examples of social risk factors. In most cases, both are at best probability judgements that development will be in some way compromised. There are, of course, exceptions such as chromosomal anomalies that have incontrovertible risks (e.g. mental retardation). Such exceptions, together with the probabilistic nature of most developmental risks, have given rise to the distinction between children with established risks (e.g. Down's syndrome) and those 'at risk' (e.g. preterm infants) for a range of possible developmental disorders (Tjossem, 1976).

In practice, such distinctions between classes of risk factors prove to be quite arbitrary. For example, an adverse perinatal event like hypoxia has been traditionally treated as a biological risk in that it affects the foetus through organic mechanisms. It does, however, amount to an environmentally induced risk if it is triggered by the mother smoking during the second half of pregnancy. A further example concerns established risks: they may give rise to fully predictable problems, but also to additional ones that are much more difficult to anticipate (e.g. conduct disorders). And another set of caveats is raised by the fact that what constitute developmental risks will vary across age, cohort and cultures.

There is an interesting twist to the edifice of developmental risk, namely, risk-taking behaviour (Rauh, 1989). In adults, it involves traits such as drug-taking, fast driving and gambling – not ones typically associated with infants. Imported into infant development, it can be conceptualized as a manifestation of heightened levels of curiosity and exploratory behaviour, and as a source of individual differences. It is lack of risk-taking behaviour depicted as such that may differentiate between children at risk and which serves to add to the problems already confronting those with established risks (e.g. making them appear passive in the face of challenging experiences). If present, risk-taking behaviour may be conceived as a protective factor, a concept introduced by Rutter (1979) as a positive countervalence to the effects of risk factors. In the past, protective factors have been portrayed as residing in the child (e.g. in terms of a 'resilient' personality), in the caretaking milieu (e.g. the availability of persons as sources of social support) or in some combination of both (see Werner, 1986).

The distinction between protective and risk factors is also not without problems. For example, illness and hospitalization, relatively common among children born prematurely, can be considered to present developmental risks. However, it has been suggested that such events, under certain circumstances (e.g. if the illness is not life threatening), may promote prosocial behaviour and social competence in general (Parmelee, 1986). For children from dysfunctional families, a period of hospitalization could be a beneficial experience if it involves care and attention that accounts for the individual needs of the patient.

If the concept of risk applied to development is to continue to have any value, then it needs to move beyond problematic distinctions like biological and social risk factors. One step in this direction might be a search for what have been referred to as 'vulnerability markers' (Masten & Garmezy, 1984). In the present context, such markers can be sought initially in various expressions of movement and postural control and their subsequent effects on processes of learning and communication – an approach depicted in Figure 14.6 as an elaboration on the more medically based model portrayed in Figure 14.4. What is required is not more studies searching for multivariate predictors of later outcomes, but rather studies that track the pathways from a well-defined array of initial conditions to some equally well-defined set of outcome measures, with both arising from the same overarching theoretical perspective.

Further Theoretical Considerations

Neural and cognitive approaches to motor control are similar in treating the central nervous system as hierarchically organized. Accordingly, higher levels specify the parameters to be controlled at the lower levels. Applied to the treatment of disorders in motor control, they focus on the inhibition of pathological behaviour and the learning of new movement patterns, which are incorporated into more complex abilities once they have become automatized. Their success in achieving their treatment goals is rather limited as witnessed, for example, by studies evaluating the efficacy of physical therapy. Moreover, they have offered little insight into how disorders in the control of movement or posture actually develop. In an attempt to overcome such shortcomings, dynamical systems approaches to action and perception have been increasingly adopted (see Hopkins & Butterworth, 1997, for an introduction to dynamical systems thinking applied to the development of action). In the study of pathological behaviour, these approaches are reflected in what has been called the dynamical diseases perspective (DDP) by Glass and MacKey (1988).

The term 'dynamical diseases' originally referred to disorders with an abnormal temporal organization. Applied to motor disorders, they are a consequence of abnormal spatio-temporal organization in movement coordination and in the coupling between perception and action. A starting point for the DDP was a ground-breaking study of ambulatory electrocardiograms in patients with severe heart disease (Goldberger, Kobalter, & Bhargava, 1986). Prior to this study, it was believed that normal heart rate was best described as regular sinus rhythm. However, the application of non-linear dynamical models to the time-series of heart beat revealed that such a rhythm was more evident in the presence of cardiopathology. In contrast, the healthy heart rate displayed considerable variability even at rest and fractal structures reminiscent of chaotic dynamics. Extrapolated to movement disorders, the DDP would predict a loss of variability (e.g. a reduction in biomechanical degrees of freedom) and the appearance of pathological periodicities as, for example, revealed in the running-like gait of children with spastic diplegia.

The application of the DDP to movement disorders can be discerned in some of the studies concerned with spontaneous kicking movements (e.g. Vaal et al., 2000b). It has been more fully implemented, however, in research with adult patients. In a comparison of healthy and hemiplegic subjects, speed of walking on a treadmill was increased and decreased in a continuous fashion (Wagenaar & Beek, 1992). In the velocity range of 0.25–0.75 m/s, the healthy participants displayed a much greater between-subject variability in the phase relation between transversal pelvic and thoracic rotations. With increasing walking speed, the rotations became more tightly coordinated in an approximately 120° phase relation between transversal and thoracic rotations for both groups, with the gait of the hemiplegic patients assuming a less asymmetrical pattern. In another study, the provision of external auditory rhythms at walking speeds of 0.36 and 0.75 m/s led to improvements in the coordination of pelvic and thoracic rotations in hemiplegic patients, but only at the latter velocity and when the arms were moved in synchrony with the rhythms (Wagenaar & van Emmerik, 1994). Systematically scaling walking speed has also been shown to reduce some of the pathological features of gait in patients with Parkinson's disease (van Emmerik & Wagenaar, 1996).

The message to be gained from these studies is twofold. Firstly, pathological behaviour represents a state of reduced dimensionality, which constrains the possibilities for reacting to both internal and external perturbations in a flexible and adaptive manner. Secondly, if the aim of therapeutic intervention is to engender such reactions, then the task is to destabilize the old state through systematic manipulations once the pathological patterns of coordination have been identified in terms of low-dimensional descriptors such as relative phase. By 'systematic manipulation' is meant the scaling up and down of a control parameter (e.g. walking speed), which at some critical value induces a change or phase transition in an order parameter (i.e. a low-dimensional descriptor). Whether or not the old state is becoming destabilized can be measured by fluctuations in the order parameter or by local relaxation times. The latter refers to recovery time following an external perturbation: stability is indicated by a long recovery time, while it is much shorter when a system is becoming destabilized and on the verge of making a transition to a new state. Relevant definitions and illustrations of dimensionality in action systems, order and control parameters, relative phase as well as other concepts used in dynamical systems appraoches such as the DDP can be found in Hopkins and Butterworth (1997). Scholz (1990) provides an insightful discussion of how such approaches can be incorporated into physical therapy for children with cerebral palsy.

Given that most therapies focus on the treatment of impairments, a major concern is that any effects will generalize to activities of daily living and to minimizing disabilities and handicaps. There is little evidence to suggest that physical therapies achieve such goals. One approach to assessment and intervention at the level of disabilities has been labelled ecological task analysis (ETA) and derives its theoretical inspiration from a combination of dynamical and allied approaches such as Gibson's (1979) ecological psychology (Burton & Davis, 1996; Davis & Burton, 1991).

Without going into detail, ETA is based on the claim that are many possible solutions to performing activities of daily living and which are determined by relationships between a performer's attributes, environmental conditions and the goal or intent of a particular action. Performance is assessed not by reference to extrinsic or normative measures, but by means of ones that are intrinsic or performer-scaled. In short, a relevant task parameter (e.g. object size) is scaled to a specific performer attribute (e.g. hand size) to give a task/performer ratio or a dimensionless number (see Savelsbergh et al., 1998, for an example of how CP children use such body-scaled information in a locomotion task).

As pointed out by Burton and Davis (1996) and by Wagenaar and Beek (1992), dimensionless numbers provide a means of quantifying the attributes of an individual's action system and thereby an alternative way of classifying patients according to similarities in performance. In this way, intervention can be geared towards the needs of individuals within the same category. Such an analytical approach might be beneficial for research with cerebral palsied children and especially those with developmental coordination disorder as both display considerable heterogeneity in performance with so far limited success in being able to classify them into different functional subtypes.

Ecological task analysis brings with it an important, but neglected, consideration. Unlike many other strategies of assessment and intervention, it is not prescriptive in the sense that it is founded on the view that there are many potential solutions to a particular task. In contrast to more traditional therapies, solution and task are separated such that task performance is no longer compared with some desirable outcome prescribed by modal or normative age-based standards. It offers a set of heuristic guidelines by which developmental disorders can be observed, investigated and treated in ways that take into account each individual's capabilities to discover task-specific solutions that suit them best. In this respect, it promotes a closer match between assessment and intervention, and a more realistic appreciation of what a particular child can be expected to achieve. This sort of appreciation has been noticeably lacking in the more usual forms of assessment and intervention and supplies an ongoing challenge for both the diagnosis and treatment of developmental disorders.

Appendix 1: The Use of Corrected Age

Definition

Calendar (postnatal) age – number of weeks born before a gestational age of 40 weeks.

Example

Infant born at 30 weeks gestation and assessed at 20 weeks after birth has a corrected age of 20–(40–30)= 10 weeks. This preterm infant can then be compared to fullterm infants with a postnatal age of 10 weeks.

Rationale

Development is a function of time since conception, not time from birth. Therefore corrected age matches preterm and fullterm infants in terms of 'level of maturity'.

Issues Involved

(See Lems, Hopkins, & Samson, 1993).

1 How long after birth should corrected age be used?
Answer: in general, up to 18–24 months postnatal age.
2 Should full or partial (e.g. half) corrected age (or some combination of the two) be used?
Answer: no convincing evidence for use of partial correction.
3 Should corrected age be applied to the development of some or all functions?
Answer: some evidence to suggest that correction is more important in the second half of the first year for mental development. For motor development, corrected age is required beyond first year.
4 Should corrected age be used beyond the first year with VLBW and VPT infants?
Answer: little investigated, but findings suggest a prolonged application of corrected age in such infants, dependent on the developmental domain.

Clinical Implications

1 Corrected age may obscure evidence of developmental delay as well as leading to late-occurring diagnosis of neurological sequelae, and thus to referral for therapeutic intervention beyond the time when it is really needed.
2 Uncorrected age can lead to overdiagnosis and unnecessary referral.

Appendix 2: Indexes of Efficacy

Definitions

- Sensitivity: proportion of individuals with an abnormal outcome who were previously classified as abnormal.
- Specificity: proportion of individuals with a normal outcome who were previously classified as normal.
- Positive predictive value: proportion of individuals classified as abnormal who subsequently have an abnormal outcome.
- Negative predictive value: proportion of individuals classified as normal who subsequently have a normal outcome.
- Accuracy: proportion of individuals from whom a correct outcome is predicted.

Derivations

		Neurological outcomes		
		Abnormal	Normal	Total
GM quality	Abnormal	*a* True positives	*b* False positives	m_1
	Normal	*c* False negatives	*d* True negatives	m_2
	Total	n_1	n_2	*N*

- Sensitivity = a/n_1 = true positives/(true positives + false negatives).
- Specificity = d/n_2 = true negatives/(true negatives + false positives).
- Positive predictive value = a/m_1 = true positives/(true positives + false positives).
- Negative predictive value = d/m_2 = true negatives/(true negatives + false negatives).
- Accuracy = $(a+d)/N$= (true positives + true negatives)/all individuals.

Definitions

- True positives: individuals classified initially as abnormal who eventually turn out to be abnormal.
- False positives: individuals classified initially as abnormal who eventually turn out to be normal.
- False negatives: individuals classified initially as normal who eventually turn out to be abnormal.
- True negatives: individuals classified initially as normal who eventually turn out to be normal.

Acknowledgements

Thanks are expressed to Paul Mork and the editors for their comments on a previous draft of the chapter. Mijna Hadders-Algra showed great generosity in supplying copies of Figures 14.2 and 14.3, previously published in two of her papers.

References

Abercrombie, M.L.J. (1964) *Perceptual and visuo-motor disorders in cerebral palsy: A survey of the literature*. London: Heinemann.

Achenbach, T.M., Phares, V., & Powell, C.T. (1990). Seven-year outcome of the Vermont intervention program for low-birthweight infants. *Child Development*, 61, 1672–1681.

Aebi, U., Nielsen, J., Sidiropoulos, D., & Stucki, M. (1991). Outcome of 100 randomly positioned children of very low birthweight at 2 years. *Child, Care, Health and Development*, 17, 1–8.

Affleck, G., Tennen, H., Rowe, J., Roscher, B., & Walker, L. (1989). Effects of formal support on mothers' adaptation to the hospital-to-home transition of high-risk infants: The benefits and costs of helping. *Child Development*, 60, 488–501.

Ajayi-Obe, M., Saeed, N., Rutherford, M., & Edwards, D. (1999). Quantification of cortical folding by magnetic resonance imaging using image segmentation and cortical contour folding. *Early Human Development*, 54, 84.

Albers, S., & Jorch, G. (1994). Prognostic significance of spontaneous motility in very immature preterm infants with brain lesions. *Biology of the Neonate*, 66, 182–187.

Allen, M.C. (1984). Developmental outcome and follow up of the small for gestational age infant. *Seminars in Perinatology*, 8, 125–156.

Als, H. (1992). Individualized, family-focused developmental care for the very low birthweight preterm infant in the NICU. In S.L. Friedman & M.D. Sigman (eds), *Advances in developmental psychology: The psychological development of low birthweight children* (pp. 341–388). Norwood, NJ: Ablex.

Als, H., Lawhon, G., Duffy, F.H., McNulty, G.B., Gibes-Grossman, R., & Blickman, J.G. (1994). Individualized developmental care for the very low birth weight preterm infant: Medical and neurofunctional effects. *Journal of the American Medical Association*, 272, 853–858.

American Psychiatric Association (1994). *Diagnostic and statistical manual of mental disorders* (4th edn). Washington, DC: APA.

Anderson, G.C. (1999). Kangaroo care of the premature infant. In E. Goldson (ed.), *Nurturing the premature infant: Developmental interventions in the neonatal intensive care nursery* (pp. 131–160). New York: Oxford University Press.

Barrera, M.E. (1987). Stability of early home environment effects with preterm infants: One-year follow-up. *Early Child Development and Care*, 27, 635–649.

Barrera, M.E., Cunningham, C.E., & Rosenblum, P.L. (1986a). Low birth weight and home intervention strategies: Preterm infants. *Journal of Developmental and Behavioral Pediatrics*, 7, 361–366.

Barrera, M.E., Kitching, K.J., Cunningham, C.C., Doucet, D.A., & Rosenblum, P.L. (1990). A 3-year early home intervention follow-up study with low birthweight infants and their parents. *Topics in Early Childhood Special Education*, 10, 14–28.

Barrera, M.E., Rosenblum, P.L., & Cunningham, C.E. (1986). Early home intervention with low-birth-weight infants and their parents. *Child Development*, 57, 20–33.

Black, P.D. (1980). Ocular defects in children with cerebral palsy. *British Medical Journal*, 281, 487–488.

Blair, E., & Stanley, F. (1985). Interobserver agreement in the classification of cerebral palsy. *Developmental Medicine and Child Neurology*, 27, 615–622.

Bobath, K., & Bobath, B. (1984). The neurodevelopmental treatment. In D. Scrutton (ed.), *Management of the motor disorders of children with cerebral palsy* (pp. 6–18). London: Heinemann.

Bower, E., McLellan, D.L., Arney, J., & Campbell, M.J. (1996). A randomised controlled trial of different intensities of physiotherapy and different goal-setting procedures in 44 children with cerebral palsy. *Developmental Medicine and Child Neurology*, 38, 226–237.

Bradley, R.H., Whiteside, L., Mundform, D.J., Casey, P.H., Kelleher, K.J., & Pope, S.K. (1994). Contribution of early intervention and early caregiving experiences to resilience in low-birthweight, premature children living in poverty. *Journal of Clinical Child Psychology*, 23, 425–434.

Bregman, J., & Farrell, E.E. (1992). Neurodevelopmental outcome in infants with broncopulmonary dysplasia. *Clinics in Perinatalogy*, 19, 673–694.

Bromwich, R.M., & Parmelee, A.H. (1979). An intervention program for pre-term infants. In T.M. Field, A.M. Sostek, S. Goldberg, & H.H. Shuman (eds), *Infants born at risk: Behavior and development* (pp. 389–411). New York: SP Medical & Scientific Books.

Brooks-Gunn, J., Liaw, F.-G., & Klebanov, P.K. (1992). Effects of early intervention on cognitive function of low birth weight preterm infants. *Journal of Pediatrics*, 120, 350–359.

Burton, A.W., & Davis, W.E. (1996). Ecological task analysis: Utilizing intrinsic measures in research and practice. *Human Movement Science*, 15, 285–314.

Byers, R.K., Paine, R.S., & Crothers, B. (1955). Extrapyramidal cerebral palsy with hearing loss following erythroblastosis. *Pediatrics*, 15, 248.

Carroll, B. (1989). Diagnostic validity and laboratory studies: Rules of the game. In L. Robins & J. Barrett (eds), *The validity of psychiatric diagnosis* (pp. 229–244). New York: Raven.

Censullo, M. (1994). Developmental delay in healthy premature infants at age two years: Implications for early intervention. *Journal of Developmental and Behavioral Pediatrics*, 15, 99–104.

Chee, F.K.W., Kreutzberg, J.R., & Clark, D.L. (1978). Semicircular canal stimulation in cerebral palsied children. *Physical Therapy*, 58, 1071–1075.

Chiswick, M.L. (1985). Intrauterine growth retardation. *British Medical Journal*, 291, 845–848.

Cioni, G., Ferrari, F., Einspieler, C., Paolicelli, P., Barbani, M.T., & Prechtl, H.F.R. (1997a). Comparison between observation of spontaneous movements and neurological examination in preterm infants. *Journal of Pediatrics*, 130, 704–711.

Cioni, G., Prechtl, H.F.R., Ferrari, F., Paolicelli, P.B., Einspieler, C., & Roversi, M.F. (1997b). Which better predicts later outcome in fullterm infants: Quality of general movements or neurological examination? *Early Human Development*, 50, 71–85.

Committee for Classification of Retinopathy of Prematurity (1984). An international classification of retinopathy of prematurity. *Archives of Ophthalmology*, 102, 1130–1134.

Craft, M.J., Lakin, J.A., Oppliger, R.A., Clancy, G.M., & Vanderlinden, D.W. (1990). Siblings as change agents for promoting the functional status of children with cerebral palsy. *Developmental Medicine and Child Neurology*, 32, 1049–1057.

Crawford, C.L., & Hobbs, M.J. (1994). Anatomy of diplegia: An hypothesis. *Developmental Medicine and Child Neurology*, 36, 513–517.

Davis, W.E., & Burton, A.W. (1991). Ecological task analysis: Translating movement behavior theory into practice. *Adapted Physical Quarterly*, 8, 154–177.

de Vries, J.I.P., Visser, G.H.A., & Prechtl, H.F.R. (1982). The emergence of fetal behavior: Qualitative aspects. *Early Human Development*, 7, 301–322.

de Vries, L.S., Eken, P., & Dubowitz, L. (1992). The spectrum of leukomalacia using cranial ultrasound. *Behavioural Brain Research*, 49, 1–6.

Droit, S., Boldrini, A., & Cioni, G. (1996). Rhythmical leg movements in low-risk and brain-damaged preterm infants. *Early Human Development*, 44, 201–213.

Dubowitz, L., & Dubowitz, V. (1981). *The neurological assessment of the preterm and fullterm newborn infant*. London: Heinemann.

Eliasson, A.-C., Gordon, A.M., & Forssberg, H. (1995). Tactile control of isometric fingertip forces during grasping in children with cerebral palsy. *Developmental Medicine and Child Neurology*, 37, 72–84.

Escobar, G.J., Littenberg, B., & Pettiti, D.B. (1991). Outcome among surviving very low birthweight infants: A meta-analysis. *Archives of Disease in Childhood*, 66, 204–211.

Fawer, C.L., Diebold, P., & Calame, A. (1987). Periventricular leucomalacia and neurodevelopmental outcome in preterm infants. *Archives of Disease in Childhood*, 62, 30–36.

Feinstein, A.R. (1977). *Clinical biostatistics*. St Louis: Mosby.

Ferrari, F., Cioni, G., & Prechtl, H.F.R. (1990). Qualitative changes of general movements in preterm infants with brain lesions. *Early Human Development*, 23, 193–231.

Ferry, P.C. (1988). Infant stimulation programs: A neurologic shell game? *Archives of Neurology*, 43, 281–282.

Field, T. (1980). Supplemental stimulation of preterm neonates. *Early Human Development*, 4, 301–314.
Field, T., Widmayer, S., Stringer, S., & Ignatoff, E. (1980). Teenage, lower class mothers and their preterm infants: An intervention and developmental follow-up. *Child Development*, 51, 426–436.
Fluge, G. (1975). Neurological findings at follow-up in neonatal hypoglycaemia. *Acta Paediatrica Scandinavica*, 64, 629.
Fontana, V.J. (1973). The diagnosis of the maltreatment syndrome in children. *Pediatrics*, 51, 780–782.
Freud, S. (1897). *Die infantile cerebralahmung*. Wien: Holder.
Frodi, A.M., Lamb, M.E., Leavitt, L.A., Donovan, W.L., Neff, C., & Sherry, D. (1978). Mothers' and fathers' responses to the faces of and cries of normal and premature infants. *Developmental Psychology*, 14, 490–498.
Gage, J.R. (1991). *Gait analysis in cerebral palsy*. London: MacKeith.
Geerdink, J.J., & Hopkins, B. (1993a). Effects of birthweight status and gestational age on the quality of general movements in preterm newborns. *Biology of the Neonate*, 63, 215–224.
Geerdink, J.J., & Hopkins, B. (1993b). Qualitative changes in general movements and their prognostic value in preterm infants. *European Journal of Pediatrics*, 152, 362–367.
Geerdink, J.J., Hopkins, B., Beek, W.J., & Heriza, C. (1996). The organization of leg movements in preterm and fullterm infants after term age. *Developmental Psychobiology*, 29, 335–351.
Gibson, J. J. (1979). *The ecological approach to visual perception*. Boston: Houghton Mifflin.
Glass, L., & MacKey, M.C. (1988). *From clocks to chaos: The rhythms of life*. Princeton, NJ: Princeton University Press.
Goldberger, A.L., Kobalter, K., & Bhargava, V. (1986). 1/*f* scaling in normal neutrophyl dynamics: Implications for hematologic monitoring. *IEEE Transactions on Biomedical Engineering*, BME-33, 874–876.
Gordon, N. (1976). *Paediatric neurology for the clinician*. London: Heinemann.
Gorga, D., Stern, F.M., & Ross, G. (1985). Trends in neuromotor behavior of preterm and fullterm infants in the first year of life: A preliminary report. *Developmental Medicine and Child Neurology*, 27, 756–766.
Gottfried, A.W., & Gaiter, J.L. (1984). *Infant stress under intensive care: Environmental neonatology*. Baltimore: University Park Press.
Gramsbergen, A., Ijkema-Paasen, J., Nikkels, P.G.J., & Hadders-Algra, M. (1997). Regression of polyneural innervation in the human psoas muscle. *Early Human Development*, 49, 49–61.
Green, M., & Solnit, A.J. (1964). Reactions to the threatened loss of a child: A vulnerable child syndrome. *Pediatrics*, 34, 58–66.
Hack, M., & Farnoff, A.A. (1999). Outcomes of children of extremely low birthweight and gestational age. *Early Human Development*, 53, 193–218.
Hadders-Algra, M. (1997). De beoordeling van spontane motoriek van jonge baby's: Een doeltreffende methode voor de opsporing van hersenfunctiestoornissen. *Nederlands Tijdschrift voor Geneeskunde*, 141, 816–820.
Hadders-Algra, M., & Groothuis, A.M.C. (1999). An abnormal quality of general movements in infancy is related to the development of neurological dysfunction, attention deficit hyperactivity disorder and aggressive behaviour. *Developmental Medicine and Child Neurology*, 41, 381–391.
Hadders-Algra, M., Huisjes, H.J., & Touwen, B.C.L. (1988). Preterm or small-for-gestational-age infants. Neurological and behavioural development at the age of 6 years. *European Journal of Pediatrics*, 147, 273–278.
Hadders-Algra, M., Klip-van den Nieuwendijk, A.W.J., Martijn, A., & van Eykern, L.A. (1997). Assessment of general movements: Towards a better understanding of a sensitive method to evaluate brain in young infants. *Developmental Medicine and Child Neurology*, 39, 88–98.
Hadders-Algra, M., van Eykern, L.A., van den Nieuwedijk, A.W.J., & Prechtl, H.F.R. (1992). Developmental course of general movements in early infancy: II. EMG correlates. *Early Human Development*, 28, 231–251.
Hagberg, B., & Hagberg, G. (1984). Prenatal and perinatal risk factors in a survey of 681 Swedish cases. In F. Stanley & E. Alberman (eds), *The epidemiology of the cerebral palsies* (pp. 116–134). Oxford: Blackwell.
Hagberg, B., Hagberg, G., & von Wendt, L. (1996). The changing panorama of cerebral palsy in Sweden: VII. Prevalence and origin in the birth year period 1987–90. *Acta Paediatrica*, 85, 954–960.
Harris, S.R. (1987). Early intervention for children with motor handicaps. In M.J. Guralnick & F.C. Bennett (eds), *The effectiveness of early intervention for at-risk and handicapped children* (pp. 175–212). Orlando: Academic.
Haskins, R. (1986). Social and cultural factors in risk assessment and mental retardation. In D. Farran & J. McKinney (eds), *Risk in intellectual and psychosocial development* (pp. 29–60). Orlando: Academic.
Hayashi, M., Satoh, J., & Sakamoto, K. (1991). Clinical and neuropathological findings in severe athetoid cerebral palsy: A comparative study of globo-Luysian and thalamo-putaminal groups. *Brain Development*, 13, 47–51.
Hellström-Westas, L., Rosén, I., & Svenningen, N.W. (1991). Cerebral function monitoring during the first week of life in extremely small low birthweight (ESLBW) infants. *Neuropediatrics*, 22, 27–32.
Heriza, C.B. (1988a). Organization of leg movements in preterm infants. *Physical Therapy*, 68, 1340–1346.
Heriza, C.B. (1988b). Comparisons of leg movements in preterm infants at term with healthy full-term infants. *Physical Therapy*, 68, 1687–1693.
Heriza, C.B. (1991). Implications of dynamical systems approach to understanding infant kicking behavior. *Physical Therapy*, 71, 222–235.
Holt, K., Obsuek, J.P., & Fonesca, S.T. (1996). Constraints on disordered locomotion: A dynamical systems perspective. *Human Movement Science*, 15, 177–202.

Hopkins, B. (1983). The development of early communication: An evaluation of its meaning. *Journal of Child Psychology and Psychiatry*, 24, 131–144.

Hopkins, B., & Butterworth, G. (1997). Dynamical systems approaches to the development of action. In G. Bremner, A. Slater, & G. Butterworth (eds), *Infant development: Recent advances* (pp. 75–100). Hove: Psychology Press.

Hopkins, B., & Prechtl, H.F.R. (1984). A qualitative approach to early movement development. In H.F.R. Prechtl (ed.), *Continuity of neural functions from pre- to postnatal life* (pp. 179–197). Oxford: Blackwell.

Hoyt, C.S., Billson, F.A., & Alpins, N. (1978). The supranuclear disturbances of gaze in kernicterus. *Annals of Ophthalmology*, 10, 1487.

Hughlings Jackson, J. (1899). On the comparative study of diseases of the nervous system. *British Medical Journal*, 2, 355–362.

Hunt, J.V. (1981). Predicting intellectual disorders in childhood for preterm infants with birthweights below 1501 gm. In S.L. Friedman & M. Sigman (eds), *Preterm birth and psychological development* (pp. 329–351). New York: Academic.

Hüppi, P.S., Schuknecht, B., Boesch, C., Bossi, E., Felblinger, J., Fusch, C., & Herschkowitz, N. (1996). Structural and neurobehavioral delay in postnatal brain development of preterm infants. *Pediatric Research*, 39, 895–901.

Hyman, C.B., Keaster, J., & Hanson, V. (1969). CNS abnormalities after neonatal hemolytic disease or hyperbilirubinemia. *American Journal of Diseases of Childhood*, 117, 395.

Infant Health and Development Program (1990). Enhancing the outcomes of low birth weight, premature infants: A multisite, randomized trial. *Journal of the American Medical Association*, 263, 3035–3042.

Ingram, T.T.S. (1984). A historical view of the definition and classification of the cerebral palsies. In F. Stanley & E. Alberman (eds), *The epidemiology of the cerebral palsies* (pp. 1–11). Oxford: Blackwell.

Kirk, S. (1948). An evaluation of the study by Bernadine G. Schmidt entitled 'Changes in personal, social, and intellectual behavior of children originally classified as feebleminded'. *Psychological Bulletin*, 45, 321–333.

Kolakowski, L. (1971). *Marxism and beyond: Historical understanding and individual responsibility*. London: Paladin.

Korner, A. (1987). Preventive intervention with high-risk newborns: Theoretical, conceptual, and methodological perspectives. In J.D. Osofsky (ed.), *Handbook of infant development* (2nd edn, pp. 1006–1036). New York: Wiley.

Korner, A.F., & Schneider, P. (1983). Effect of vestibular-proprioceptive stimulation on the neurobehavioral development of preterm infants: A pilot study. *Neuropediatrics*, 14, 170–175.

Kuban, K.C., & Gilles, F.H. (1985). Human telencephalic angiogenesis. *Annals of Neurology*, 17, 539–548.

Lacy, J.B., & Ohlson, A. (1993). Behavioral outcomes of environmental or care-giving hospital-based interventions for preterm infants: A critical overview. *Acta Paediatrica*, 82, 408–415.

Largo, R.H., Molinari, L., & Cominale Pinto, L. (1986). Language development of term and preterm children during the first five years to seven years. *Developmental Medicine and Child Neurology*, 28, 333–350.

Latash, M.L. (1993). *Control of human movement*. Champaign, IL: Human Kinetics.

Lems, W., Hopkins, B., & Samson, J.F. (1993). Mental and motor development in preterm infants: The issue of corrected age. *Early Human Development*, 34,113–123.

Lindahl, E., Michelsson, K., & Donner, M. (1988). Prediction of early school-age problems by a preschool neurodevelopmental examination of children at risk neonatally. *Developmental Medicine and Child Neurology*, 30, 723–734.

Little, W.I. (1862). On the influence of abnormal parturition, difficult labours, premature birth, and asphyxia neonatorium on the mental and physical conditions of the child, especially in relation to deformities. *Transactions of the Obstetrical Society of London*, 3, 293–344. Reprinted in *Cerebral Palsy Bulletin*, 1958, 1, 53–36.

Livishits, G. (1990). Premature baby delivery: Some genetic epidemiological aspects. *American Journal of Human Biology*, 2, 571–585.

Low, J.A., Galbraith, R.S., Muir, D.W., Killen, H.L., Pater, E.A., & Karchmar, E.J. (1982). Intrauterine growth retardation: A study of long-term morbidity. *American Journal of Obstetrics and Gynecology*, 170, 670–677.

Low, J.A., Galbraith, R.S., Muir, D.W., Killen, H.L., Pater, E.A., & Karchmar, E.J. (1988). Motor and cognitive deficits after intrapartum asphyxia in the mature fetus. *American Journal of Obstetrics and Gynecology*, 158, 356–361.

Lucas, A., Morley, R., & Cole, T.J. (1988). Adverse neurodevelopmental outcome of moderate neonatal hypoglycaemia. *British Medical Journal*, 297, 1304–1308.

Lund, R.D. (1978). *Development and plasticity of the brain: An introduction*. New York: Oxford University Press.

MacKeith, R. (1976). The restoration of the parents as the keystone of the therapeutic arch. *Developmental Medicine and Child Neurology*, 18, 285–286.

Masten, A.S., & Garmezy, N. (1984). Risk, vulnerability, and protective factors in developmental psychopathology. In B.B. Lahey & A.E. Kazdin (eds), *Advances in clinical child psychology* (Vol. 8, pp. 1–52). New York: Plenum.

Mayo, N.E. (1991). The effect of physical therapy for children with motor delay and cerebral palsy: A randomized clinical trial. *American Journal of Physical Medicine and Rehabilitation*, 70, 258–267.

Mayr, J., Fasching, G., & Höllwarth, M.E. (1994). Psychosocial and psychometric development of very low birth weight infants with necrotizing enterocolitis. *Acta Paediatrica*, Supplement, 396, 96–100.

McCall, R.B., & Carriger, M.S. (1993). A meta-analysis of infant habituation and recognition memory performance as predictors of later IQ. *Child Development*, 64, 57–79.

McCarton, C.M., Brooks-Gunn, J., Wallace, I.F., Bauer, C.R., Bennett, F.C., Bernbaum, J.C., Broyles, R.S., Casey, P.H., McCormick, M.C., Scott, D.T., Tyson, J., Tonascia, J., & Meinert, C.L. (1997). Results at age

8 years of early intervention for low-birth-weight premature infants: The Infant Health and Development Program.*Journal of the American Medical Association*, 277, 126–132.

McMenamin, J.B., Shackelford, G.D., & Volpe, J.J. (1984). Outcome of neonatal intraventricular hemorrhage with periventricular echodense lesions. *Annals of Neurology*, 15, 285–290.

Minde, K., Shosenberg, N., Marton, P., Thompson, J., Ripley, J., & Burns, S. (1980). Self-help groups in a premature nursery: A controlled evaluation. *Journal of Developmental and Behavioral Pediatrics*, 96, 933–940.

Nelson, K.B., & Ellenberg, J.H. (1979). Neonatal signs as predictors of cerebral palsy. *Pediatrics*, 64, 225–232.

Nelson, K.B., & Ellenberg, J.H. (1985). Antecedents of cerebral palsy: Univariate analysis of risk. *American Journal of Diseases of Children*, 139, 1031–1038.

Nilsen, S.T., Finne, P.H., Bergsjo, P., & Stamnes, O. (1984). Males with low birth weight examined at 18 years of age. *Acta Paediatrica Scandinavica*, 73, 168–175.

Nurcombe, B., Howell, D.C., Rauh, V.A., Teti, D.M., Ruoff, P., & Brennan, J. (1984). An intervention program for mothers of low-birthweight infants: Preliminary results. *Journal of the American Academy for Child Psychiatry*, 23, 319–325.

Offer, D., & Sabshin, M. (1974). *Normality: Theoretical and clinical concepts of mental health*. New York: Basic.

Olney, S.J., Costigan, P.A., & Hedden, D.M. (1987). Mechanical energy patterns in gait of cerebral palsied children with hemiplegia. *Physical Therapy*, 67, 1348–1354.

Oppenheim, R. (1981). Ontogenetic adaptations and retrogressive processes in the development of the nervous system and behaviour: A neuroembryological perspective. In K.J. Connolly & H.F.R. Prechtl (eds), *Maturation and development: Biological and psychological perspectives* (pp. 73–109). London: Heinemann.

Ottenbacher, K.J., Muller, L., Brandt, D., Heintzelman, A., Hojem, P., & Sharpe, P. (1987). The effectiveness of tactile stimulation as a form of early intervention: A quantitative evaluation. *Journal of Developmental and Behavioral Pediatrics*, 8, 68–76.

Palmer, B.P., Shapiro, B.K., Wachtel, R.C., Allen, M.C., Hiller, J.E., Harryman, S.E., Mosher, B.S., Meinert, C.L., & Capute, A.J. (1988). The effects of physical therapy on cerebral palsy: A controlled trial in infants with spastic diplegia. *New England Journal of Medicine*, 318, 803–808.

Papiernik, E. (1993). Prevention of preterm labour and delivery. *Ballière's Clinical Obstetrics and Gynaecology*, 7, 499–521.

Papile, L.A., Burstein, J., Burstein, R., & Koffler, H. (1978). Incidence and evolution of subependymal and intraventricular hemorrhage: A study of infants with birthweights less than 1,500 g. *Journal of Pediatrics*, 92, 529–534.

Papousek, H., & Papousek, M. (1983). Biological basis of social interactions: Implications of research for an understanding of behavioural deviance. *Journal of Child Psychology and Psychiatry*, 24, 117–129.

Parmelee, A.H. (1986). Children's illnesses: Their beneficial effects on behavioral development. *Child Development*, 57, 1–10.

Perlman, J.M., & Volpe, J.J. (1989). Movement disorder of premature infants with severe broncopulmonary dysplasia: A new syndrome. *Pediatrics*, 84, 215–218.

Pharoah, P.O.D., Cooke, T., Rosenblum, L., & Cooke, R.W.I. (1987). Trends in birth prevalence of cerebral palsy. *Archives of Disease in Childhood*, 65, 379–384.

Piek, J.P., & Gasson, N. (1999). Spontaneous kicking in fullterm and preterm infants: Are there leg asymmetries? *Human Movement Science*, 18, 377–395.

Pino-Martin, J.A., Riolo, S., Cnaan, A., Holzman, C., Susser, M.W., & Paneth, N. (1995). Cranial ultrasound prediction of disabling and non-disabling cerebral palsy at age two in a low birth weight population. *Pediatrics*, 95, 249–254.

Piper, M.C., Kunos, V.I., Willis, D.M., Mazer, B.L., Ramsay, M., & Silver, K.M. (1986). Early physical therapy effects on the high-risk infant: A randomized control trial. *Pediatrics*, 78, 216–224.

Prechtl, H.F.R. (ed.) (1984). *Continuity of neural functions from pre- to postnatal life*. Oxford: Blackwell.

Prechtl, H.F.R. (1986). Prenatal motor development. In M.G. Wade & H.T.A. Whiting (eds), *Motor development in children: Aspects of coordination and control* (pp. 53–64). Dordrecht: Martinus Nijhof.

Prechtl, H.F.R., Einspieler, C., Cioni, G., Bos, A.F., Ferrari, F., & Sontheimer, D. (1997). An early marker for neurological deficits after perinatal brain lesions. *Lancet*, 349, 1361–1363.

Prechtl, H.F.R., & Nolte, R. (1984). Motor behaviour in preterm infants. In H.F.R. Prechtl (ed.), *Continuity of neural functions from pre- to postnatal life* (pp. 79–92). Oxford: Blackwell.

Pryds, O., Trojaborg, W., & Carlsen, J. (1989). Determinants of visual evoked potentials in preterm infants. *Early Human Development*, 19, 117–125.

Rademaker, K.J., Groenendaal, F., Jansen, G.H., Eken, P., & de Vries, L. (1994). Unilateral haemorrhagic parenchymal lesions in the preterm infant: Shape, site and prognosis. *Acta Paediatrica*, 83, 602–608.

Ramey, C.T., Bryant, D.M., Wasik, B.H., Sparling, J.J., Fendt, J.J., & LaVange, L.M. (1992). Infant health and developmental program for low birth weight, premature infants: Program elements, family participation, and child intelligence. *Pediatrics*, 3, 454–465.

Rauh, H. (1989). The meaning of risk and protective factors in infancy. *European Journal of Psychology of Education*, 4, 161–173.

Rauh, V.A., Achenbach, T.M., Nurcombe, B., Howell, C.T., & Teti, D.M. (1988). Minimizing adverse effects of low birthweight: Four-year results of an intervention program. *Child Development*, 59, 544–553.

Resnick, M., Eyler, F., & Nelson, R. (1987). Developmental intervention for low-birth-weight infants: Improved early developmental outcome. *Pediatrics*, 80, 68–74.

Rey, E.S., & Martinez, H.G. (1983) Manejo racional del niño prematuro from conferencias. *I curso de Medicina Fetal y Neonatal, Bogotá, Colombia*, 137–151.

Robertson, C.M.T., Etches, P.C., Goldson, E., & Kyle, J.M. (1992). Eight-year school performance, neurodevelopmental and growth outcome of neonates with bronchopulmonary dysplasia: A comparative study. *Pediatrics*, 89, 365–372.

Ross, G. (1984). Home intervention for premature infants of low-income families. *American Journal of Orthopsychiatry*, 54, 263–270.

Rushton, D.J., Preston, P.R., & Durbin, G.M. (1985). Structure and evolution of echodense lesions in the neonatal brain: A combined ultrasound and necropsy study. *Archives of Disease in Childhood*, 60, 708–808.

Rutter, M. (1979). Protective factors in children's responses to stress and disadvantage. In M.W. Kent & J.E. Rolf (eds), *Primary prevention of psychopathology* (Vol. 3, pp. 49–74). Hanover, NH: University Press of New England.

Savelsbergh, G.J.P., Douwes Dekker, L., Vermeer, A., & Hopkins, B. (1998). Locomoting through apertures of different width: A study of children with cerebral palsy. *Pediatric Rehabilitation*, 2, 5–13.

Scherzer, A.L., Mike, V., & Ilson, J. (1976). Physical therapy as a determinant of change in the cerebral palsied infant. *Pediatrics*, 58, 47–52.

Schoemaker, M.M., Hijkema, M.G., & Kalverboer, A.F. (1994). Physiotherapy for clumsy children: An evaluation study. *Developmental Medicine and Child Neurology*, 36, 143–155.

Scholz, J.P. (1990). Dynamic pattern theory: Some implications for therapeutics. *Physical Therapy*, 70, 827–843.

Scott, D.T., Ment, L.R., Ehrenkranz, R.A., & Warshaw, J.B. (1984). Evidence for late developmental deficit in very low birth weight infants surviving intraventricular hemorrhage. *Child's Brain*, 11, 216–269.

Scrutton, D. (ed.) (1984) *Management of the motor disorders of children with cerebral palsy*. London: Heinemann.

Sellick, K.J., & Over, R. (1980). Effects of vestibular stimulation on motor development of cerebral-palsied children. *Developmental Medicine and Child Neurology*, 22, 476–483.

Shirowa, Y., Komiya, Y., & Uchibari, S. (1986). Activity, cardiac and respiratory responses of blindfold preterm infants in a neonatal intensive care unit. *Early Human Development*, 14, 259–265.

Silverman, W. (1980). *Retrolental fibroplasia: A modern parable*. New York: Grune & Stratton.

Sloan, N.L., Camacho, L.W.L., Rojas, E.P., & Stern, C. (1994). Kangaroo method: Randomized controlled trial of an alternative method of care for stabilized low-birthweight infants. *Lancet*, 344, 782–785.

Stanley, F., Blair, E., & Alberman, E. (2000). *Cerebral palsies: Epidemiology and causal pathways*. London: MacKeith.

Stern, M., & Hildebrandt-Karraker, K. (1990). The prematurity stereotype: Empirical evidence and implications for practice. *Infant Mental Health Journal*, 11, 3–11.

Thelen, E. (1981). Kicking, rocking and waving: Contextual analysis of rhythmical stereotypies in normal human infants. *Animal Behaviour*, 29, 3–11.

Thelen, E. (1985). Developmental origins of motor coordination: Leg movements in human infants. *Developmental Psychobiology*, 18, 1–22.

Tjossem, T. (1976). *Intervention strategies for high-risk infants and children*. Baltimore: University Park Press.

Uvebrant, P. (1988). Hemiplegic cerebral palsy: Aetiology and outcome. *Acta Paediatrica Scandinavia*, Supplement, 345, 1–100.

Vaal, J., van Soest, A.J., & Hopkins, B. (2000a). Spontaneous kicking behavior in infants: Age-related effects of unilateral weighting. *Developmental Psychobiology*, 36, 111–122.

Vaal, J., van Soest, A.J., Hopkins, B., Sie, L.T.L., & van der Knaap, M.S. (2000b). Development of spontaneous leg movements in infants with and without periventricular leukomalacia. *Experimental Brain Research*, 135, 94–105.

van Beek, Y., Hopkins, B., & Hoeksma, J.B. (1994). Prematurity, posture and the development of looking behaviour during early communication. *Journal of Child Psychology and Psychiatry*, 35,1093–1107.

van der Fits, I.B.M., Flikweert, E.R., Stremmelaar, E.F., Martijn, A., & Hadders-Algra, M. (1999). Development of postural adjustments during reaching in preterm infants. *Pediatric Research*, 46, 1–7.

van der Heide, J.C., Paolicelli, P.B., Boldrini, A., & Cioni, G. (1999). Kinematic and quantitative analysis of lower-extremity movements in preterm infants with brain lesions. *Physical Therapy*, 79, 546–557.

van der Weel, F.R., van der Meer, A.L.H., & Lee, D.N. (1996). Measuring dysfunction of basic movement control in cerebral palsy. *Human Movement Science*, 15, 253–283.

van Emmerik, R.E.A., & Wagenaar, R.C. (1996). Dynamics of movement coordination and tremor during gait in Parkinson's disease. *Human Movement Science*, 15, 203–235.

Vohr, B.R., & Oh, W. (1983). Growth and development in preterm infants small for gestational age. *Journal of Pediatrics*, 103, 941–945.

Volpe, J.J. (1995). *Neurology of the newborn* (3rd edn). Philadelphia: Saunders.

Volpe, J.J. (1997). Brain injury in the premature infant: Neuropathology, clinical aspects, pathogenesis, and prevention. *Clinics in Perinatalogy*, 24, 567–587.

Wagenaar, R.C., & Beek, W.J. (1992). Hemiplegic gait: A kinematic analysis using walking speed as a basis. *Journal of Biomechanics*, 25, 1007–1015.

Wagenaar, R.C., & van Emmerik, R.E.A. (1994). The dynamics of pathological gait: Stability and adaptability of movement coordination. *Human Movement Science*, 13, 441–471.

Watt, J.E., & Strongman, K.T. (1985). The organization and stability of sleep states in full-term, preterm, and small-for-gestational-age infants. *Developmental Psychobiology*, 18, 151–162.

Werner, E.E. (1986). The concept of risk from a developmental perspective. *Advances in Special Education*, 5, 1–23.

Whitelaw, A., Heisterkamp, G., Sleath, K., Acolet, D., & Richards, M. (1988). Skin-to-skin contact for very low birth weight infants and their mothers. *Archives of Disease in Childhood*, 63, 1377–1381.

Widiger, T., & Trull, T.J. (1991). Diagnosis and clinical assessment. *Annual Review of Psychology*, 42, 109–133.

Williamson, J.W., Goldschmidt, P.G., & Colton, T. (1986). The quality of medical literature: An analysis of validation assessments. In J.C. Bailar & F. Mosteller (eds), *Medical use of statistics* (pp. 370–391). Waltham, MA: NEJM Books.

Windle, W.F. (1956). Regeneration of axons in the vertebrate nervous system. *Physiological Review*, 36, 426–440.

Wolke, D. (1991). Annotation: Supporting the development of low birthweight infants. *Journal of Child Psychology and Psychiatry*, 32, 723–741.

Wolke, D. (1998). Psychological development of prematurely born children. *Archives of Disease in Children*, 78, 567–570.

World Health Organization (1977). *International classification of deaths and diseases*. Geneva: WHO.

World Health Organization (1980). *International classification of impairments, disabilities and handicaps*. Geneva: WHO.

World Health Organization (1999). *ICDH-2: International classification of functioning and disability* (Beta-2 draft). Geneva: WHO.

Wright, T., & Nicholson, J. (1973). Physiotherapy for the spastic child: An evaluation. *Developmental Medicine and Child Neurology*, 15, 146–163.

Yokochi, K., Inukai, K., Hosoe, A., Shimabukuro, S., Kitzazumi, E., & Kodama, K. (1991). Leg movements in the supine position of infants with spastic diplegia. *Developmental Medicine and Child Neurology*, 33, 903–907.

Zupan, V., Gonzalez, P., Tacaze-Masmonteil, T., Boithias, C., d'Allest, A.-M., Dehan, M., & Gabilan, J.-C. (1996). Periventricular leukomalacia: Risk factors revisited. *Developmental Medicine and Child Neurology*, 38, 1061–1067.

PART FOUR: DEVELOPMENT IN MIDDLE CHILDHOOD

15

Contemporary Families as Contexts for Development

PETER STRATTON

In the early 1970s Kevin Connolly invited me to a series of seminars of developmentalists from Sheffield, Oxford and Cambridge. As we were discussing developmental principles arising from a predominantly unintrusive ethological methodology Jerome Bruner said, 'If you think you understand something, try changing it. Then you will find out if your understanding works.' This comment connected powerfully with my belief that we have an ethical responsibility to make our science as useful as possible, but it also connected to my frustration that, although the social constructionist approach to developmental psychology being introduced during the 1970s was theoretically appealing, it was difficult to see how the approach would make a difference in practice. The major practical issues of family dysfunction, neglect and child abuse received very little attention from developmental psychologists. In the textbooks from which I taught at the time, Nash (1970) explained that applied issues were the province of 'child psychology' not of 'developmental psychology', the title of his text. Meanwhile Reese and Lipsitt (1970) explained that 'experimental child psychology' (the title of their text) did not deal with applied issues: that was the job of developmental psychology. During this time an approach to helping disturbed children and adults by treating the whole family as a system was being created. Psychiatrists were the leading profession, in collaboration with anthropologists, social workers, sociologists and social psychologists, but not developmentalists.

Over the last thirty years family therapy and developmental psychology have had remarkably little contact. Although some attempts have been made to bring developmental knowledge into family therapy (Strand, 1997; Stratton, 1988a) and family therapy findings to child psychologists (Stratton, 1992), the two areas have progressed largely without reference to developments in the other (attachment theory is the major exception). As a result, family therapy theory and research are in a position to offer perspectives and knowledge from a different vantage point. This chapter capitalizes on the understanding of family processes that has been created within systemic family therapy and presents some of the main principles as offering the developmentalist insights into the workings of the family – the main context within which child, and to a large degree adult, development in all societies occurs.

Because the work to understand family processes has operated in a clinical rather than a research context, it is strong on the kind of theory that can guide action, but less strong on carefully controlled research. We are now at a stage where the theory is sufficiently developed to provide a platform for productive empirical work. An aspiration for this chapter is to extend the basis for research that will create a developmental psychology of the family, while recognizing the major initiatives already taken by such as Wozniac (1993) and van Geert (Chapter 28 in this volume).

In 1986 Bruner suggested that

> when and if we pass beyond the unspoken despair in which we are now living . . . a new breed of developmental theory is likely to arise. It will be motivated by the question of how to create a new generation that can prevent the world from dissolving into chaos and destroying itself . . . Its central concern will be how to

> create in the young an appreciation of the fact that many worlds are possible, that meaning and reality are created and not discovered, that negotiation is the art of constructing new meanings by which individuals can regulate their relationships with each other. (1986, p. xxx)

In this statement Bruner is taking the constructivist thinking characteristic of family theorists who have been inspired by Maturana's claim that we must work not with a universe but with multiversa (Maturana & Varela, 1980). Bruner then goes beyond the claim (e.g. Wozniac, 1993) that psychologists must adopt this paradigm, to suggest that the people who must understand and thereby bring about change are the family members. In particular a constructionist perception should become a natural part of the ways that children understand their role in their families and in society.

Overview

Developmental psychology has always generated information that is relevant to understanding how families operate. For example, findings from the large-scale child rearing studies of the mid twentieth century are still useful even though they were based on the assumption that parental behaviour is a given, with linear causal consequences for the child. It is also possible to chart a progression in thinking that converges somewhat with family systems thinking. We could start, as many do, with Bell's (1968; 1979) argument for recognizing the independent contribution that the child's characteristics bring to parent–child functioning. This theme was picked up by Lewis and Rosenblum (1974) among others, and is still an issue. For example Neiderhiser et al. (1999) claim to identify the child's genetic contribution as the major factor in the relationship between parental behaviour and adolescent adjustment.

The study of dyadic parent–infant relationships achieved what seems now like a paradigm shift with the change from 'dependency' to 'attachment' (Ainsworth, 1972). The unidirectional and supposedly quantifiable physical and psychological dependence of the child on the caregiver was replaced by an attempt to describe a qualitative relationship. However, Bowlby's (1968) original formulation was primarily concerned with the evolutionary function of attachment. Because of this it did not pay attention to the processes by which attachment occurred and so it was easy to come to describe it as a quality of the child. Then Ainsworth's observations led her to a classification of children in terms of *their* style of attachment and which readily became seen as identifying good and bad attachments. It was only when serious attention was paid to understanding the process (Schaffer, 1971) that the reciprocal nature of attachment formation entered the descriptions. Progressively, attention has spread beyond the mother–infant dyad to take account of siblings, peers, and fathers, and to struggle with triadic relationships. This history is described by Kreppner (Chapter 9) and others in this volume.

The early history of attachment theory followed a familiar route in describing characteristics of the child as deficits (for example, 'the affectionless psychopath': Bowlby, 1951) and then accounting for these in terms of unilateral influences on the child ('maternal deprivation'). Stratton (1977; 1982) proposed that the processes should instead be seen in terms of adaptations which equipped the child for some environments and not others. Thus: 'Confronted with a situation in which the formation of attachments repeatedly leads to the trauma of having the bond abruptly broken, the child makes a highly adaptive adjustment of resisting further deep relationships. The adjustment remains adaptive so long as the individual remains in an environment where the formation of attachments carries a high risk of traumatic disruption' (1982, p. 10). From this perspective the child is not intrinsically damaged by deprivation, but may come to be disadvantaged if the adaptation excludes him or her from forming relationships during adolescence when the context has become more secure. From such considerations a framework for thinking about adaptation was developed.

Some Characteristics of Adaptation

First, adaptations are short-sighted, especially for younger children and for anybody under stress. So when a child is put under pressure within their family, they will adapt in whatever way is within their repertoire to minimize the immediate impact. The adaptation will quite naturally not take account of long-term consequences.

Second, adaptations almost always involve payoffs between different benefits and disadvantages. So adaptations are not usually intrinsically good or bad; their value has to be judged in relation to how they will lead the child to function in whatever environments they are likely to inhabit in the future.

Third, parenting (and therapy and education) can best be evaluated in terms of the adaptations that it provokes. Both positive and negative aspects should be viewed not as parental action having a unidirectional effect on the child, but as parental behaviour setting a context for adaptation. For example, the everyday scene of a young child sitting on a parent's lap to identify words in a picture book is valued differently by the two participants. For the child, the adaptation is to engage in a fairly meaningless task in exchange for positive attention from the parent. From the adult perspective the adaptations that the situation will induce in the child are valued because they work towards the acquisition of reading skills which are judged to be of value in future contexts.

These three aspects of adaptations by individual children have close parallels with species adaptation through natural selection. In that context it is easy to see that a response to a demand is not specified in terms of long-term objectives; that most advantages have some kind of corresponding cost; and above all, that adaptations are not good or bad in themselves, but have to be evaluated in terms of how well equipped they leave the organism for coping with its future environment.

Two further aspects of adaptations become progressively available as the child develops. One is selecting the context in which to function. Here the self-concept comes into play in telling the child which contexts to select and which to avoid – what has been called 'niche-picking'.

The other is knowing that behaviours call forth adaptations from other people. This is what produces the most complex transactions: when each participant is aware of the effects of their responses on the other. As the child begins to be seen as a partner, and not just a recipient of influence, there was a move to conceptualize the processes not simply as interaction but as transactions (Sameroff and Fiese, 1990). The concept of transaction captured not just the reciprocity of interaction, but the continuous unfolding of the process in time. Stratton (1982) extended the notion to one of 'transactional adaptation' so as to go beyond the descriptions provided by 'transactions' to include the processes by which the infant incorporates and acts on the family system, the parents, and the social and physical environments. By the age of 6 children have this ability well developed and use it progressively more consistently in their transactions (Wellman, 1992). It is with this aspect of transactions that we are beginning to get to the core of why families seem to function as entities in their own right, rather than just the sum of their individual members.

Transactional Adaptation

All participants co-create their relationships. Each event provokes an adaptation in participants which reflects their history, their current objectives, and their perception of the event, and this response defines the context in which others are responding, so that no behaviour can usefully be seen in isolation. The conceptualization of such processes as transactions goes beyond interaction in recognizing that each person is, through their effects on the others, creating the environment in which their next adaptations will be made.

The concept also allows for the differences in conceptual breadth and time frame of professional carers, parents, and children of different ages. The concept of transactional adaptation maps readily onto the systemic concepts described below. It also provides a framework for working effectively within constructionist theory.

Constructionism

Developmental psychology has a long history of including constructivist and constructionist thinking (Werner, Vygotsky, Piaget, Shotter). As the interpretivist/relativist position is now also the basis for most branches of family systems theory (McNamee & Gergen, 1992), it constitutes the most likely contact between developmentalists and family systems thinkers. There is no universally accepted distinction between constructionism and constructivism, but Leppington (1991) points to major consequences of adopting one rather than the other. Useful definitions here are:

> *Constructivism*: The position that cognition is about constructing a coherent system of meaning within the person, rather than about understanding reality. Constructivists are likely to regard reality as unknowable and also of less significance for the social sciences than the meaning systems that people create. However they do not claim that reality does not exist, just that it is a more effective strategy to study how we construct our meanings.
>
> *Social constructionism*: The position taken by some social psychologists that social reality is constructed between people, rather than being an objective phenomenon of which there can only be one true description. More broadly it is a position in the social sciences that meaning is socially constructed through interaction, especially through discourse. Therefore it is more useful to study the social construction of meaning than to attempt to study the 'reality' that our meanings are about. (Stratton & Hayes, 1998, p. x)

The constructionist position has led Kogan and Gale (1997) to the following distinctions which indicate something of the difference between an individualist modernist psychology and the current systemic way of thinking:

- Self is not a social product but a social accomplishment.
- Personal identity is an activity, rather than a thing.
- Context is not a bucket, but a performance: we accomplish who we are and what we are on an ongoing basis through interpretive practices.

Another point of convergence between developmental psychology and systemic family therapy is the ecological approach (Bronfenbrenner, 1979; 1993). It incorporates a constructivist concern with conceiving the human organism as a functional whole, while taking on the task of researching its development within its immediate settings (the family) and 'the larger contexts in which the settings are embedded' (1993, p. 7).

In summary, the overall framework offered for understanding the psychological development of children within the family is as follows. First, it is necessary to use both a constructivist conceptualization of the child as a coherent meaning system, and also a constructionist conceptualization of meaning arising as a social product of interaction. For the specific issue of development within the family, the concept of transactional adaptation provides a concrete framework for working out the constructionist and constructivist stances. This position shifts attention away from explanations in terms of normative built-in characteristics of the child, with inevitable interest in the extent to which each is genetically or environmentally determined. Instead it leads to conceptualizing a continual process of mutual influence in which all participants have a degree of awareness of their effects on each other and guide their adaptations partly in relation to these expectations. The position is consistent with the systemic approach that has informed systemic family therapy and so enables the findings from working therapeutically with families to be used to interpret contemporary family functioning.

We can learn much about family forms and processes from the very many viable forms around the world (Valsiner, 2000). However, in this chapter I concentrate on what we have learned through systemic family therapy which has developed primarily within Western culture. The formulation that I have developed has used cultural comparisons to widen the perspective, but our direct experience with cultural variation comes primarily from minority groups living in England. As systemic theory has not been extensively tested on families in other cultures, the claims in this chapter are restricted to European and American contexts. This is not a claim that the principles will not apply more widely, but a recognition of how easy it is to slip into attributing meanings to processes in other cultures that incorporate assumptions from our own (Cecchin, Lane, & Ray, 1994).

FAMILIES PAST, PRESENT AND FUTURE

The monogamous nuclear family has probably always been a dominant form throughout human history, and around the world. However, *polygamy* is also an extremely widespread form especially in hunter-gatherer societies. Whatever form the family takes it is intended to maintain a commitment between members, and mutual social and economic support as a framework for bringing up children. It is the main route by which children learn about their culture and acquire its values. In the process each child develops an identity, a definition of their gender, and a concept of the kind of person they are through feedback from other family members. In fact this process continues throughout life, and most people's identity continues to be influenced by their experiences as they move through the life cycle of partner, parent, grandparent and so on.

In order to give a context for the theoretical ideas in this chapter I will work in terms of a fictitious family called the Smiths. I also invite the reader to relate general concepts introduced in the chapter to the specifics of this family. Every aspect and event described here has been reported by a family in therapy and all data are taken from actual families, but confidentiality is assured by combining aspects of many families, with limited detail from any one of them.

John and Mary Smith live with their four children in the north of England. They came to family therapy because of the fights between their two daughters. Figure 15.1 shows the provisional genogram (family tree) we might have constructed from the referral information. Mary, the mother, was the youngest of five children who was very much cared for during childhood but in adolescence fought with her parents and left home at 17. There is reference to an older cousin who 'led her astray'. John is an only child whose father was authoritative and stern. John believes that children must obey their parents. If any compromise is necessary it is the child who must adapt. He says 'I know how things should be, it is up to the child to fit in.' The first insights into this family may well come from relating Mary's and John's approach to parenting to their experiences and models of their families of origin. Another early task will be to check the assumptions we have made about family structure against the facts.

Our ideas of family have built up over thousands of years as family forms have slowly developed to meet the needs of survival and society (see Burguière et al., 1996 for a detailed history). More immediately, our own images of family are strongly influenced by previous generations, so each family is likely to be repeating patterns from people who were children early in the twentieth century. Western ideas of the family are still shaped by a 'folk image' from the nineteenth century of the family as a stable structure with well defined roles, which related to the role of family members in the outside world. Men worked

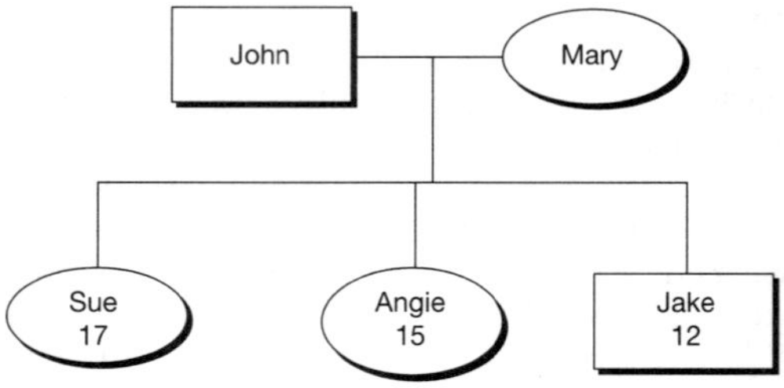

Figure 15.1 *Preliminary genogram of the Smith family*

and women tended the home. McGoldrick points out that 'U.S. society is organized to accommodate [this] type of family structure that represents only 6 per cent of the population' (1998, p. 133). Whether we are aware of it or not, our image of family, and of what it is to be a mother, grandfather, daughter, is strongly influenced by earlier generations of our family. Beliefs from the past become built into the way family members think about themselves. It is useful to think in terms of each family having a set of stories about itself which guide it in knowing what to do. Within family therapy the stories have been discussed in terms of 'stories lived and stories told; of family myths' (Byng-Hall, 1988) and of family narratives (White & Epston, 1990).

During the increasing prosperity of nineteenth century Europe, boys were educated for careers or, in the aristocracy, for cultivated leisure (Burguière & Lebrun, 1996; Harris, 1969). Girls, if they received any education at all, were trained for domestic accomplishments. This produced what is now called the 'conventional nuclear family'. Working class families retained the framework of an 'economic unit' in which all family members contributed, though industrialization brought about changes in the pattern of work for men, women and children. But in keeping with the powerful wish for upward mobility within the nineteenth century middle class, it is their supposed pattern of stability, prosperity and serenity that forms our image of a golden age of the family. The dominance of that image has led many people to assume that the family has been in continual decline ever since and, for some, to regret the passing of a time in which people – men, women, children, the poor – 'knew their place'.

In fact, as we see in this chapter, the family is still an influential and robust institution, but a much more complex and flexible one than images of the past would lead us to expect. It is, however, still operating under legal and other frameworks designed for nuclear families with traditional sex roles. Rules about the inheritance of property, and pens on structures that assume couples stay married for life and the male is the main earner, are just one group of issues that encounter problems with other family structures. But then, as Kessen (1993) points out, our knowledge of developmental psychology has been overwhelmingly constructed through research conducted on white American children, who make up only about 1% of the world's population. In this chapter I argue that developmental psychology has failed to take proper account of the family context of even this 1%. The systemic work drawn on in this chapter has made strenuous attempts to overcome cultural assumptions, especially when working with families from ethnic minorities and with those with less common structures. But such assumptions are difficult to detect (Stratton, 1998) and it remains the case that the work has been primarily located within Europe and America.

Returning to the Smiths, we learn early on that the three children come from Mary's earlier relationships, that Mary and John have a 3-year-old son Mark, and that John has two children from a previous marriage but has no contact with them. The new genogram (Figure 15.2) shows how much more interesting this family is than the family created originally from our cultural assumptions. The structure is far from unusual for our clinic, and is characteristic of reconstituted families.

Deconstituted and Reconstituted Families

It is well known that divorce is becoming progressively more common in most Western countries. The UK, with Europe's highest divorce rate in 1991, has remained stable up to 1996; Spain, with one of the lowest, has seen an increase of almost 30%; and Germany, with a medium level of divorce, has risen

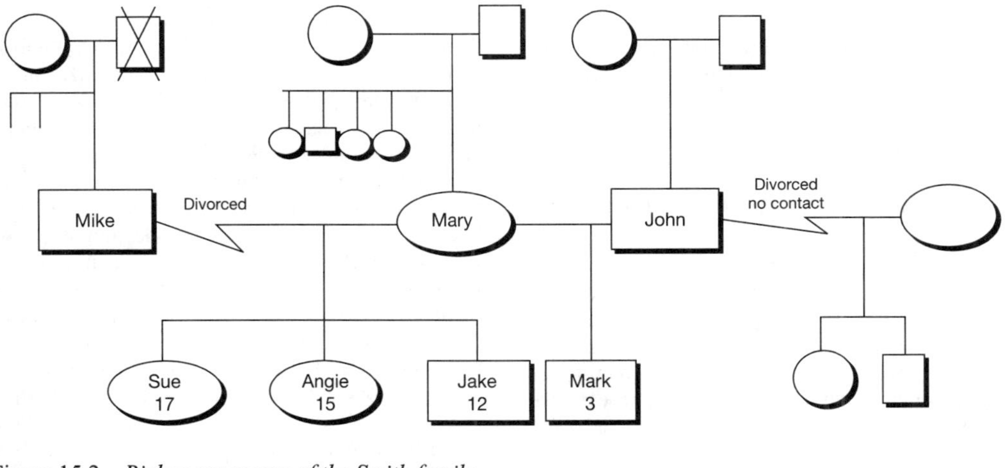

Figure 15.2 *Richer genogram of the Smith family*

by more than 20%. In the United States the rate of divorce peaked in the early 1980s at 5.3 per thousand inhabitants, but dropped to 4.6 per thousand by 1993 (Dreman, 1999). Meanwhile the numbers of people getting married have fallen in nearly all countries (Denmark is one example of an exception). The combined effect is to slightly reduce the number of people living in the average household in most European countries, but the increasing trend to set up families without the formality of a marriage makes it difficult to estimate the full extent of stable family relationships. Although it is difficult to be precise about numbers, other forms of separation are also common: it is estimated that in the USA there are currently 1 million runaway children and a total of 8 million 'runaway' fathers. One consequence of divorce has been an increased likelihood that the children will themselves divorce in due course (Feng et al., 1999). If this pattern continues the recent high frequencies of divorce could become self-fuelling. From the perspective of the (largely mythical) normative intact nuclear family, divorce has to be seen as destructive of 'the family'. From a wider perspective Western society can be seen to be opening up a greater variety of viable family forms and in some respects it is coming to accept aspects of family structure that are common throughout most of the world.

Less widely recognized than family separation is the high frequency with which new families form following break-up. Most single parents will form a new relationship before the children have left home and so create a reconstituted family. It is now quite common to find families in which both parents have children from previous long-lasting relationships. As divorce becomes more common, and sometimes less acrimonious, there is also an increasing likelihood that the adults will be able to keep a reasonable relationship. It is then more likely that parents will have contact with their children and with the parents of their ex-partner. So now we have many children who participate in more than one family, and share the lives of half-sisters and half-brothers, and other children with whom they have no biological relationship at all. Some of these children are no longer sure what these relationships are, and are more concerned with who they spend time with and who they like.

Flexibility in Family Forms

As this century progresses we will see increasing variety in family structures and functions. Solo father and solo mother families may become more common and this may be a voluntary decision in an increasing proportion of cases. The uncoupling of single parenthood from poverty will help researchers to unscramble causal processes but already the evidence seems to indicate that 'neither mothers nor fathers are essential to child development' (Silverstein & Auerbach, 1999). Golombok (1999) reached a similarly positive conclusion in relation to lesbian families. She also reaches a generally positive position from the available evidence on families created through assisted reproduction. However, research has concentrated on measurable group differences in overall developmental outcome. These are a crude indicator of the varieties of adaptation the children in such families are making, and tell us little about the distinctive processes of such families. The versatility of the family in adopting varied forms, and hopefully the flexibility of children in negotiating useful transactions within these family forms, challenges us to develop conceptual models that can encompass such complexity. Edgar calls for 'a more complex set of outcome measures . . . rather than continuing to pursue simplistic models based on biased and culturally myopic assumptions and definitions' (1999, p. 123). This is still a call to prioritize, and wait for, more sensitive measures of outcome that could do justice to the capacity of the family to operate in a rich variety of forms. The Smith family structure indicates how unlikely it is that we will be able to create a simple taxonomy of family structures that could be related to outcome measures. An additional strategy is to use what has been learned from working with families to build a rich concept of how families function. With a sufficiently rich description we should be able to make informed judgements about how novel forms of family will operate; to specify action at various levels to support such families; and formulate research questions that are more productive.

How Families Work

The framework for understanding families that I am proposing is derived from various forms of family therapy. These approaches to treating families have their origin in the application of cybernetics (Weiner, 1948) and general systems theory (von Bertalanffy, 1968) as developed by Bateson (1973) and colleagues, and will be labelled throughout as the systemic approach to understanding families. Although the approaches were developed for the purpose of therapy, the concentration here is on the concepts that have proven most useful in understanding how families function. The account does not follow the history, but is structured to meet the needs of providing a perspective on the development of children within the family. Historical accounts of systemic family therapy are available in sources such as Dallos and Draper (2000) and Carr (2000).

Systemic family therapy has been driven by a belief that problems of individual children are best seen as an outcome of the family system and are most easily resolved by working on the beliefs and relationships by which the family functions. In the process many useful principles of family operation have emerged, and are sketched here as a resource in reviewing research into specific aspects of contemporary families. They are interpreted where appropriate in terms of the concept of transactional adaptation. This formulation was developed within a framework of constructionist thinking specifically to provide a language that could bridge the apparent gap between systemic thinking and the mainstream of work on social development.

The Basic Framework

Systemic family workers find it most helpful to think of the family as a complex system regulated by the stories it creates about itself. In this kind of system, all the parts are closely interconnected so that any movement by one component has an effect on all the others, and causes them to adjust to the new pattern. Symptomatic behaviour by children has been seen as an adaptation to the system. In some cases, consistent behaviour of a child is an adaptation to a previous condition of the system that no longer applies – a 'redundant solution'.

When something goes wrong it is natural to assume that it is caused by someone doing something wrong, or having something go wrong within them. Systemic family therapists have found it more useful to see problems as arising out of the way the whole family works, and to recruit the whole family to help in tackling the problem. Therapy may take account of three levels of system (Figure 15.3):

1. Patterns across generations, how these create myths and how each generation repeats certain of the patterns.
2. The household, with therapy focusing on how relationships are managed.
3. Wider systems within which families have to operate: school, work, health services, financial, etc. When a family encounters problems the connections become even more complex and the family therapy clinic is just one among many systems that the family must interact with. Therapists who work with these 'eco-systems' may spend more time consulting to the professional helping agencies than with the family themselves.

The first, 'intergenerational' focus provides insight into why the family acts as it does; the second, 'here-and-now' approach is likely to find solutions within the family; while the third, with its effort directed to ecosystems, is more likely to achieve practical improvements in the family's circumstances.

Circularity in Family Functioning

The feature of families that brings the above processes together is that influence always works in many directions. Parents bring together stories of family life from their previous experiences, but children have their own characteristics that influence the operation of the stories. Family systems theorists find it most useful to map family beliefs and behaviours in patterns of circular influence. In such continually developing patterns, the way each person gives meaning to what goes on in the family shapes

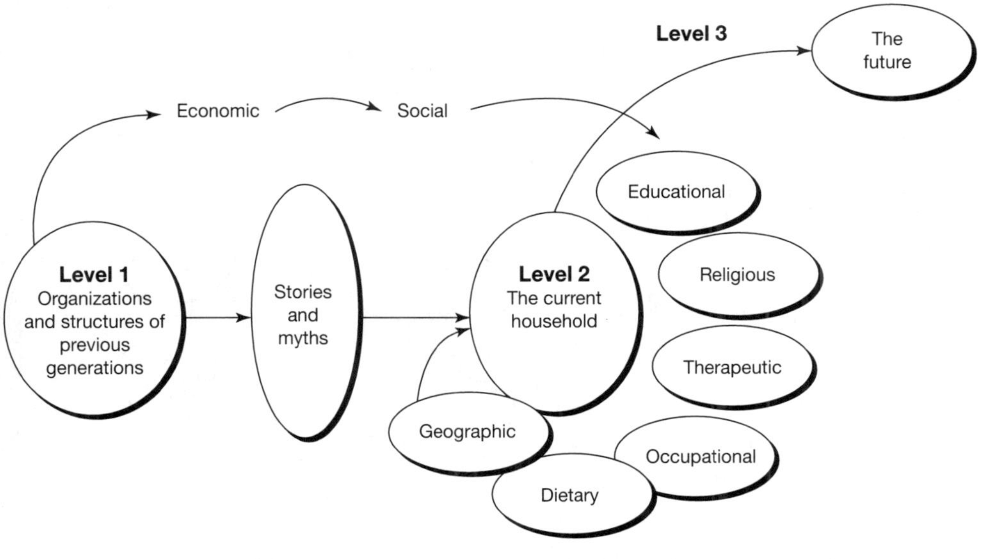

Figure 15.3 *Three levels of family context*

their response, and the others' perceptions and reactions to them (Stratton, 1988b). The notion of circularity within family therapy holds that linear causal sequences cannot be combined to adequately describe complex systems such as families, which are characterized by the mutual influence of their interacting members and the wider systems in which these members participate (Nichols & Schwartz, 1995).

Within systemic family therapy, three circular sequences have been described. The first, labelled *symmetry*, refers to sequences in which a given form of behaviour by one person produces a corresponding form from the other. If John gets cross with Jake, Jake may respond by being aggressive back. John, adopting a linear punctuation, sees aggression as an appropriate response to Jake's behaviour, and so the cycle can continue indefinitely.

Complementary sequences occur when a behaviour elicits its opposite. If Mary responds to Jake's aggression with submissiveness, and Jake regards submissive behaviour as a trigger for aggression, we may again have a continuing cycle of behaviour.

Both symmetrical and complementary cycles have a tendency to continue, but they will only be stable while the responses are roughly at the same level as the one before. If the response is stronger than the preceding behaviour then we have an escalating sequence that will eventually get out of control: a glare produces an insult which is responded to with verbal abuse which provokes a blow which requires a harder blow and so on. Eventually in such sequences a limit is reached: one person is incapacitated; both become exhausted; an outside influence (say a parent) intervenes; or one of the pair switches to the other kind of sequence.

In many relationships, people find it possible to switch between symmetrical and complementary responses in a way that keeps the sequence moving, but within safe limits and without either person losing out. This kind of sequence is called *reciprocal*, and can clearly be expected to be healthier. This concept introduces the dimension of time in family transactions, which has led us to extend systemic family therapy's mapping of circles to descriptions of spirals (Stratton, 1988a). Transactional sequences can be configured as developing spirals, which may be stable or escalating (Figure 15.4). They have the characteristic that a cross-section ('punctuation' in systemic family therapy terms) at any time describes a circular process. It is then apparent that a transactional process that appears to be a fixed circle is actually likely to be a stage in a developmental process.

If we are to conceptualize in terms of 'the family', and not just of the people and interactions within the family, then we need a meaningful basis from which to speak of the family as an autopoietic (self-

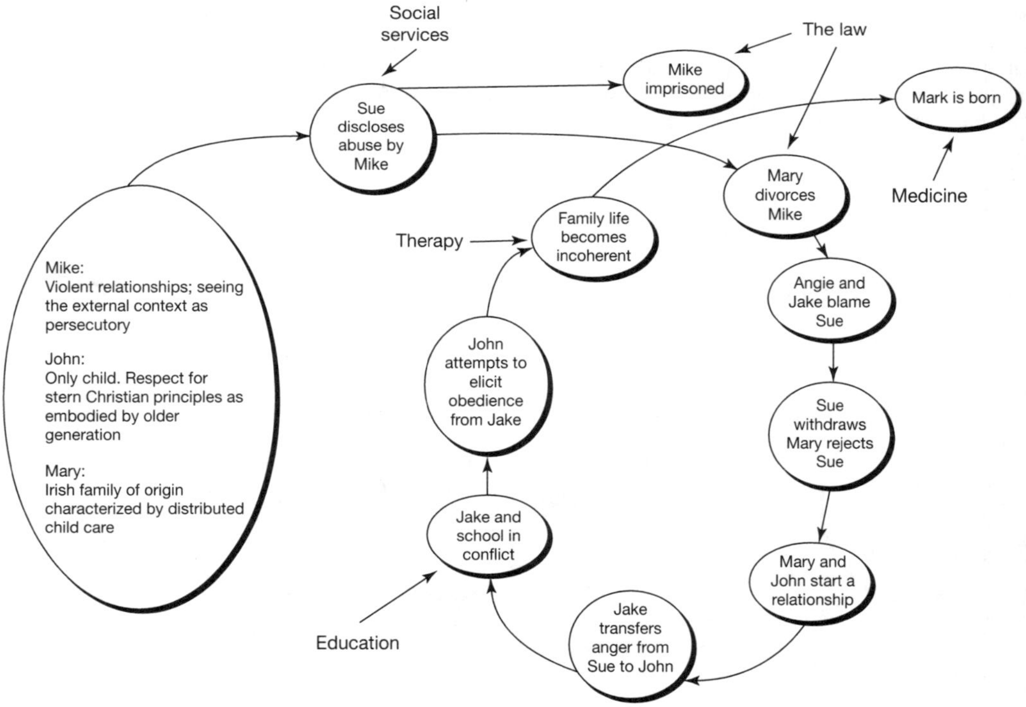

Figure 15.4 *Aspects of the influence of Level 1 (families of origin) on the spiral of events at Level 2 (the household) and the involvement of Level 3 agencies*

building) entity (Maturana & Varela, 1980) rather than a collection of individuals.

The Family as an Entity

A useful starting point is the form of constructivism that draws on the notion of internal representational models as developed in attachment theory (Bowlby, 1968) and in schema theory in general.

People regulate their relationships in terms of models that they develop. These models at their simplest are representations of other significant people. Attachment theorists are more likely to talk in terms of models of relationships, but this may be a distinction without a difference. It is probably the case that these are alternative descriptions that could in principle be translated into each other. However, it seems likely that people have much more elaborate and varied schemata to apply to people than they have for relationships, and so the discussion that follows is in terms of models of people.

One of the sources of complexity of our models of other people is that they incorporate ideas about how those people view others. In other words, we have some ideas about their models of other people. We have called this phenomenon of models within models 'nesting', and have distinguished between horizontal and vertical nesting (Stratton et al., 1993).

Horizontal Nesting of Representational Models

Sue has a model of her sister Angie. Within this model is her understanding of what Angie thinks about their brother Jake. Sue will only be interested in certain aspects of Angie's perception of Jake, so this second level model will be simpler than her own model of Jake.

Horizontal nesting easily reaches through several stages. Consider Sue saying: 'Angie reckons that Mum thinks Jake is too modest.' Being modest is an evaluation of – part of a model of – yourself. So Sue is talking about Jake's model of himself, or rather, Mum's model of Jake. Except that she is reporting Angie's belief – that is, a part of Angie's model of Mum. But we are working from Sue's perceptions. So this innocent little statement is Sue's model of Angie's model of Mum's model of Jake's model of himself. A systemic story should not leave anyone out so perhaps we have to imagine that it was in fact Dad who was telling us that Sue is always saying that Angie reckons . . . and so on.

We propose that the models of other people are a powerful factor in regulating our own feelings and actions. Family living requires a constant process in which the transactions take account of the anticipated reactions of other family members. The anticipations are based in the models each has of the others as well as stories of the form of different family relationships, preferred attribution strategies (Munton et al., 1999) and other knowledge. The parents whose model of their small child is that she is deliberately being naughty to spite them will experience anger, frustration, and inadequacy. The child who feels his parents despise him and want rid of him will function in a constant background of shame and dread. It is possible that a child who feels that his parents have unrealistically high expectations of him, and that their love is dependent on his living up to these standards, could have similar feelings. The child who witnesses a brother or sister being physically abused, or favoured while being sexually abused, will have a model of their parent's model of children which will be very difficult to assimilate, or apply usefully in other relationships.

Therapists, and sometimes researchers, bring to their encounters with clients a set of feelings derived from their past, which are primed to be provoked by anyone who resembles their more powerful models. When a patient taps into an aspect of a model which has strong previous associations, the therapist will experience a counter-transference reaction (Stratton et al., 1993). Only if they are aware of their own models and the associated feelings will they be able to work backwards from their emotional reaction to the patient to gain an understanding of which aspects of people in their past the patient has activated.

But the experience of a counter-transference reaction is more personal, maybe even intrusive, than just a matter of transfer of identification. A fuller picture is obtained from the second form of nesting.

Vertical Nesting of Representational Models

Perhaps the most intriguing aspect of our models of other people is the component which contains our understanding of their model of ourselves. Jake's model of his biological father (Mike) includes a representation of Mike's model of him (Figure 15.5). He may think that his Dad finds him childish, lazy, irresponsible, quite bright, and affectionate. He will use this model to predict how his father will interpret actions like hitting his sister or going into a pub. These models are important in any relationship: for example a social worker will take account of a family's assumptions about them; a researcher, or a therapist, will often work to ensure that the model the other has of them falls within certain boundaries, and is left undefined in certain ways.

Within families, these vertical models have a special status. The final kind of model – the self-concept or identity – is partly derived from the person's understanding of the models that family members have of them. If Jake thinks that his mother, his father, and his sisters all see him as unreliable, this will be a very powerful story about himself that he is likely to come to believe and behave consistently within. Typically, Jake will choose some

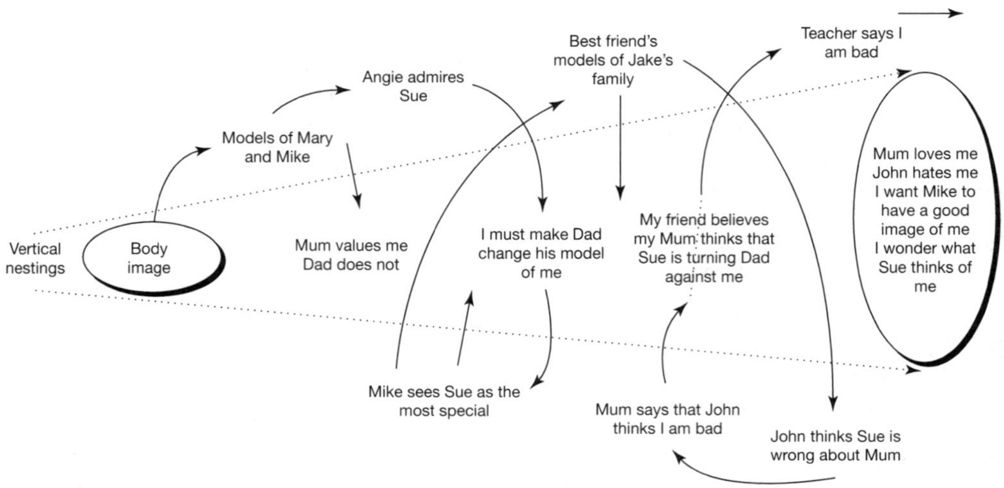

Figure 15.5 *Horizontal and vertical nestings of Jake's internal representational models*

aspects of the story to rebel against, but will overlook many other aspects to which he is conforming. The rich pattern of models that develop within a family means that Jake credits Sue with having a number of different models of him. Think then of Jake having horizontally nested models involving all of his family in different combinations, but at each stage the model incorporates a model of himself. He is provided with a mass of ideas about himself that he has somehow to integrate into his concept of his own identity.

The concept of identity brings us to the final aspect of internal models: that each person carries a model of themselves. This is not just an image of the kind of person they are, but a representation that enables them to interpret their sensations, behaviours, feelings and physiological responses.

Now we need to go back to where Jake's models come from. Over the years he has seen his family responding to him in certain ways, and has developed his ways of construing people's behaviour. It is within this framework that he creates his model of himself. Various aspects of developmental psychology give us clues about how this process operates at various ages. Object relations theory speaks of the earliest stages of integration of internal sensations with perception of the actions of others. Attachment theory now gives us a detailed story about how the interactions required in eliciting and receiving caregiving foster the development of the infant's cognitive system in such a way that this intense reciprocal relationship can develop. Studies of sibling and peer relationships (Dunn, 1993) are coming to show us just how powerfully children influence each other. The recent work on the child's theory of mind (Dunn, 1996; Harris, 1989) has demonstrated that children around 4 to 6 years develop an extensive understanding of other people's emotions and thinking as different from their own.

As each family member achieves adaptation through transactions that take account of their own and the others' representational models, they set up a complex web of mutual influence. It is this that results in the family operating as a system and allows us to conceptualize each family as an entity. The conceptualization of models presented here is a start towards understanding why the mutual influence goes beyond interactions. It is the fact of anticipation of the meaning that an action will take on in another person's thinking, and the change to their models of yourself and of others in the family that may result from these meanings, that makes the process truly transactional.

There are many factors influencing how models affect the transactions. First, the capacities of individuals to follow through nested models will vary (it is said that politicians can operate seven nested levels). Developmental level will clearly be relevant, as well as more transient processes such as the effect of emotional state. In particular, strong negative feelings about someone seem to produce predictable effects.

Causal Attributions as Indicators of Internal Representational Models

We have found that the attribution of responsibility to self and others in the family is a significant indicator of internal models that can be effectively studied through the causal attributions made during therapy and research interviews (Stratton et al., 1986). Consistent patterns of attribution style have been found in relation to the quality of the relationship. For example, Fincham, Beach, & Baucom (1987) reviewed research on attributions in marital relationships and found a consistent pattern that in poor relationships negative events were attributed to significant characteristics of the partner whereas good events were attributed to incidental circumstances. The opposite patterns were found for good relationships. Stratton and Swaffer (1988) and Silvester and Stratton (1991) found a consistent pattern in mothers who physically abused their young children that we called the attributional discrepancy. For bad outcomes, attributions about the child were discrepant from those the mother made about herself and others in the family, for example by describing the child as having much more control over outcomes. Silvester et al. (1995) showed that the degree of attributional discrepancy could be used to predict the response of families to therapy. These findings applied to physical abuse but not consistently to sexual abuse.

The Family Life Cycle

Systemic family therapists have found great value in talking through the family's intergenerational history (Carter and McGoldrick, 1989; Lieberman, 1979). Repeated patterns across generations can often be identified, and genograms can be used to identify relationships that have been left undefined or ambiguous.

Carter and McGoldrick (1989) draw on Beavers (1982) and Beavers and Voeller (1983) who define concepts of centripetal and centrifugal family styles to explain the position of the individual. During a centripetal phase, both the individual members and the structure of the family emphasize a closeness of internal life, and family teamwork is enhanced. During centrifugal periods the opposite will be achieved: individual goals by the family members will be pursued, and there will be increased exchange with the external world. In the Smiths, John and Jake both want a centripetal phase but Jake feels this will be best achieved by John staying out, thus preserving the previous family closeness. John wants a close family that includes himself, and feels it should be achieved through Jake accepting him. Meanwhile, the centrifugal forces are working on Sue because the blame for the loss of Mike is attributed to her. The outcome was that the centrifugal process typical of young adulthood was accelerated for Sue, who thereby repeated her mother's experience of leaving home at 17. John joined the family but Jake continued to regulate closeness in the family by his opposition.

Structures, Boundaries and Regulation of Relationships

A major component of the history of family therapy has been a structural approach (Minuchin, 1974). Out of his work with severely disadvantaged families, Minuchin developed a system of therapy based on defining appropriate communications and boundaries within families. Dysfunctional patterns are seen where, for example, one of the parents is marginalized; a child is operating at a parental level (the 'parentified child'); or conflict between the parents is detoured through a child ('triangulation'), producing symptoms in the child which are then blamed for the family's problems. Elements of this theory have become basic to many forms of systemic family therapy. Perhaps the most important is the recognition that symptomatic behaviour will have an important function in regulating relationships within the family. Typically, childhood disturbance will focus parental attention and effort onto the child, thus enabling them to regulate the emotional distance between them, and avoid too much intimacy or the risk of drifting too far apart. Jake's 'hyperactivity' and criticisms of John were undoubtedly having powerful effects on the relationship between Mary and John, and had in fact delayed John's entry into the household by more than a year.

Constructing the Family through Stories

Myths

Families, over the years, develop strong sets of beliefs which constitute a kind of 'inner image' of family life. Myths may take generations to build up, and they may never be clearly stated, but they tend to have the following characteristics:

1. The whole family participate in them.
2. They exert an influence on all family members and on their relationships.
3. They go unchallenged despite the fact that they do not square with reality.

A simple and very common myth is 'we are a happy family'. Everyone in the family knows that it is essential to maintain this belief, and so indications of unhappiness have to be classified as symptoms of illness. Arguments can be stopped rather than resolved, by recourse to the myth, and in general moves towards growth may be stultified if they contain an implicit message of dissatisfaction.

Scripts

Family life often has the flavour of a drama, and family therapy provides a stage for the re-enactment of familiar scenes. Family members can be thought of as having acquired a script, primarily as it was jointly constructed within their family of origin, which tells them what their role is and how the family play should develop in its various functions. Not only is everyone casting the rest of the family in their personal inner world script, but they are also simultaneously playing roles in everyone else's scripts.

Families enter into transactions with each other, and in relation to wider systems, so that their scripts become compatible, and when a couple come together to set up a family they often adopt one of the two commonest scripts:

- the replicative script, which aims to repeat the past
- the corrective script, which attempts to alter past experience.

If both parents left home at 17, they may build this into their assumptions about how families work and create a family which incorporates this event in everyone's script. An over-protected child may grow up to be an adult who is determined to correct this script in their own parenting. Both kinds of script allow the past to determine the future, and lead to the same patterns being repeated over and over again.

Families that develop a strong belief system that they feel has to be protected from the outside world become closed to information and influence from the wider society. Closed systems tend to become progressively more extreme in their functioning until they break down. Fortunately, most families are keen to, or at least have no choice but to, engage with people and activities outside.

Myths and scripts combine in the stories that families create about themselves and by which they live (Byng-Hall, 1988, 1998). Systemic family therapy has a long-standing interest in family stories, both the stories told and the stories lived. Pearce and Pearce (1998) talk of family therapy as a process of 'joining with clients in the co-construction of new stories' and also claim:

> We believe that stories are the basic technology by which members of the species *Homo sapiens* (as physical entities) become human beings. (1998, p. 172)

The formulation in terms of stories brings together many themes of systemic thinking. Family stories, or narratives, are co-constructed within the family and between family members to make sense of their worlds and to guide their feelings and behaviour:

> stories are not simply mirrored reflections of life that are *post hoc*; they are structures that shape actual lives and prefigure action. (Tomm, 1993, p. 76)

The stories will incorporate the history of previous generations, and therapists have extended the use of factual genograms to the concept of a cultural genogram (Hardy & Laszloffy, 1995). The stories can be seen as the route by which aspects of the wider social systems are brought into the family operation. Systemics then has the rather contradictory notion of 'untold stories' and, more recently, 'subjugated stories' (White & Epston, 1990, drawing on Foucault, 1980), and these concepts allow the practitioner to think, with the family, in terms of there being a coherent underlying account that generates the family rules. The developing capacity of children to regulate and expand their lives through stories (Bruner, 1986; Uccelli et al., 1999) is one area of developmental psychology that could be much more extensively used by family therapists.

Roles and Rules

Families generally benefit from having an agreement about roles. Parents need to be seen to have responsibility and be in control, however much their children and adolescents want to challenge these rules. However, the challenges provided by children as they grow up can be a healthy route to re-examining the rules. Families often find it interesting and useful to sit down together and try to work out what rules and assumptions have developed. Of course, there is always the risk of turning up a previously unstated rule like 'men do not wash up' which might then get questioned. Rules are known to operate at different levels. A family is likely to have rules about when it is good to compete; how someone should show when they are upset; how the family shows love; having different rules for different ages or sexes. Sometimes rules conflict but, because they operate in different aspects of thought (technically, at different logical levels), the contradiction may not be recognized (Bateson, 1973). Within family theory the process is known as a double bind (Sluzki & Ransom, 1976), though it is very similar to a 'catch 22'.

The Double Bind

Family researchers have identified this problematic pattern, which seems to develop very easily within families (Watzlawick, 1963). In a typical double bind a person is apparently offered alternatives but in fact whatever they do will be wrong. For example Mike might forbid Jake to climb a tree because it is dangerous. If the boy climbs the tree he is punished for disobedience, but if he doesn't, his father indicates that he is disappointed in him for being so soft. Whatever Jake does he is going to feel inadequate and guilty: he has done the wrong thing again and disappointed his parents. But the bind leaves him with a belief that if only he had tried harder he would have got it right. Components of the bind may develop in different ways at different times. For example, a man may grow up with an image of masculinity that is highly macho and with a model of a good marital relationship as being sensitive and caring. Within his marriage, any move to satisfy one definition will create problems for the other. He may have to get hurt through provoking fights in bars so he can show his vulnerable side and need to be looked after at home. People do not usually create double binds in a deliberate attempt to harm each other. They arise through having definitions of roles at different logical levels so that the contradictions are difficult to recognize. Often the contradictions arise from discrepancies between family values and those of the outside world.

The Co-ordinated Management of Meaning

A final framework for systemic understanding comes from the co-ordinated management of meaning (CMM: Pearce, 1989). This theory proposes that meaning is structured in a hierarchy of contexts, with higher logical levels defining the meanings given to lower levels (the contextual force), but with events at lower levels affecting the perceptions and beliefs about the higher levels of context (implicative force). A typical hierarchy would be as in Figure 15.6.

While it is easy to see how each higher context frames and provides a causal basis for lower levels, it is also clear in the example that telling Jake off will contribute to Jake's, Angie's, and John's definition of the episode; confirm disobedience as an aspect of the parent–Jake relationship; affect the definition of the parent as effective; and possibly impinge on the cultural belief that fights should be stopped. CMM theory then points out that at different times, the levels may change position. So the relationship may be of such importance that at that time it defines the person's self-concept. A double bind such as that described above will often involve a confusion or reversal of contextual levels, which is why it will be difficult to recognize.

It is important to mention two approaches which are having a major current impact on therapeutic practice but which do not figure explicitly in this attempt to understand how families work. The 'solution focused therapy' of De Shazer (1988; Berg, 1994) is representative of an approach that identifies and cultivates the existing strengths and solutions in the family's repertoire and specifically excludes any attempt to understand how the family or individual achieved their difficulty. It has, however, created an increased alertness to the potential resources and a focus on the positive aspects of even the most troubled families. Another major development has been the narrative approach (White & Epston, 1990). This works on the basis that families that seek help for problems they have failed to resolve are usefully thought of as being constructed by that problem. They have created a narrative of their family which guides and limits their operation, and the task of therapy is to help them create a new account of their lives that opens up new possibilities. The concentration in this approach on the sense in which the problem creates the family system (rather than the system creating the problem) makes it less likely to generate useful descriptions of families that are not structured by their problems. The dominant use of verbal and written narrative limits its usefulness for those whose major interest is in infants and young children, and its attempt to operate with a post-modern basis makes its practitioners reluctant to generalize beyond each specific case. Its contribution has been a strengthening and enriching of concepts around family myths and stories.

With a basic framework for interpreting family functioning in place, we now turn to review some of the major developments in Western families that provide the context for these processes.

FORMS AND VARIETY IN CONTEMPORARY FAMILIES

Family Diversity

Western society is increasingly confronting new family forms. Some are genuinely novel, while others, such as 'single parents', have always existed but have only recently been given a label. Once a label exists it is easier to talk about 'the problem of single parents'. Then researchers can more easily get funding to study this problematic group. In fact, the strength of negative reactions to all of these variations indicates how strongly the old images of family still operate.

One consequence of the operation of evaluative labels in the wider society is that they readily become incorporated into the stories of individual families. It is, for example, quite common for a family member to announce during an assessment session that 'we are a dysfunctional family', following recent media use of the term.

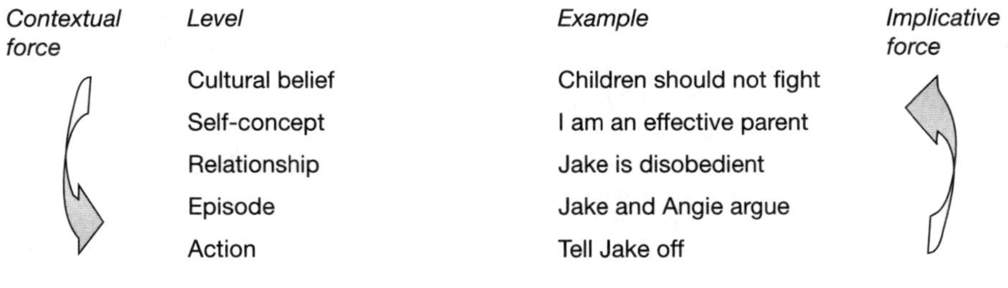

Figure 15.6 *Levels of context and forms of influence*

Single Parents

In the past, single parent families existed primarily because one parent, usually the father, had died. Today they result primarily from divorce. Bradley and Corwyn (1999) estimate that in the US 70% of white children and 96% of black children will live in a single parent family at some time during their childhood. Apart from childless couples, the rate of divorce is highest when couples are in their twenties and have young children. Because Western society has such a strong belief that children must be brought up by mothers, it is still the case that the great majority of single parents are mothers.

There is some evidence that children do less well educationally and in their future careers if they are brought up by a single parent. It is difficult to separate out the relevant factors. Divorce and single parenthood bring with them economic disadvantage, in some cases straightforward poverty. If they are not to do so, then the parent is likely to have to spend most of their time and energy earning, and will have less time for the children. The burden of parenting is not shared, and the benefit for the parent of supportive adult company, which most couples manage to some extent, may be missing. This is perhaps one area in which the search for patterns of linear causality is hopelessly confusing. Starting from the systemic perspectives that value diversity, reject oppositional formulations and above all take total interconnection and reciprocal influence as a fundamental assumption, would generate a different kind of research into issues such as single parenting. It would also directly counter the damaging consequences of a neoconservative perspective that asserts paternal rights by disparaging mothers and any variation from parenting by heterosexual couples (Silverstein & Auerbach, 1999).

Step Families

> Our society offers stepfamilies a choice of two conceptual models, neither of which works: families that act like the intact family next door . . . and the wicked stepparents of the fairy tales. (Carter & McGoldrick, 1989, p. 23)

Reconstituted families require considerable adjustment from all members, and difficulties may continue for many years after a step-parent moves into the family. Inevitably, the choice of new partner is made by the birth parent for their own reasons. While these reasons may well include ensuring a parent of the other sex for the children, the choice of partner is made by the parent, not by the children. As well as having no choice, the children usually have to adjust to the loss of time spent with their parent, and changes in household routine. They may also feel some loyalty to the departed parent which conflicts with forming a close relationship with the step-parent. At the same time the step-parent has to form an appropriate relationship with the children. Becoming a parent may not have been a prime motivation in forming the relationship, and they have not had the benefit of a relationship with the children since birth, which helps, or trains, the biological parents in finding ways to interact with their children. In some cases they will have had no previous experience of parenting. In others they will bring their own children into the household, creating a complex web of new relationships.

In the example of the Smiths, issues of the stepfather are brought into sharp focus because he has brought into the family some very definite views about relationships and discipline. The children had adjusted to having mother as the only parent and were now being required to adapt to a completely different style from their stepfather. But it was a one-way process with all of the adaptation being demanded from the children. Nearly all of the transactions to find a mutual accommodation fell on Mary who had to demonstrate her commitment to the new relationship by agreeing with John but at the same time try to buffer her children from this sudden imposition of new demands.

Families without Children

Another Western hangover from the past is the myth that the natural and desired status for adults is to be married and have children. In the nineteenth century women who did not get married suffered exclusion from all the benefits of society. And if you were married the only reason for not having children was (shameful) infertility. With increasing choice these attitudes are changing, but slowly. More people are deciding to stay single through choice, and couples are now taking an active decision whether to have children or to pursue other forms of satisfaction in their lives. This tendency raises interesting questions about the definition of family. Childless couples may form strong and supportive relationships with families with children, and become regarded as part of the extended family (see below). But they have no formal status, and are unlikely to be granted legal rights of access or to be entitled to absence from work for family commitments. Meanwhile, of course, and usually uncomplainingly, they support families with children through taxation and family oriented working arrangements. Such inequalities can be seen as a further example of the ways that societal definitions of family are based on unrealistic images and lag behind the flexible arrangements that real families are capable of creating. But perhaps our theories of adult development will also need to more flexibly account for lifespan development without the impetus that adults have traditionally had through contact with their children.

Technology of Conception

Novel forms of conception, which have opened up new combinations of genetic relatedness within families, are raising interesting issues about parenthood. Artificial insemination, reimplantation of fertilized eggs, and surrogacy are forcing a re-examination of assumptions about genetic inheritance, and who 'owns' a child. The major studies in this area have found a greater, rather than lesser or more tentative, approach to parenting when children have been conceived through assisted reproduction (Golombok, 1999). It is however notable that none of the parents in these studies had yet told the child about the nature of their conception. It will take time and research to learn about the long-term consequences of these newly available practices. Any speculation at present must take account of the reflexive processes that will occur as assisted reproduction becomes more commonplace so that new generations will not find that it violates their assumptions about family formation.

Homosexual couples generally do not have children, but as discrimination weakens, more lesbian and gay couples are choosing to become parents through adoption or conception. Concerns are expressed about how children will acquire 'appropriate' gender identities in these families, but an early British study found the children of lesbian couples to have better capacities to relate to people of both sexes than children from heterosexual parents (Golombok, Spencer, & Rutter, 1983).

Polygamy

Family structures in which men have more than one wife (polygyny) or women have more than one husband (polyandry) are not unknown in the US and Europe, though usually they are illegal. Some married couples also tolerate a similar arrangement in which one or both have stable long-term relationships outside the marriage. While these arrangements can be made to work, they do not have the same stability as in societies in which polygamy is part of the social structure.

Polygamy serves a useful function in preserving genes in some circumstances. Where one sex is in short supply, for example after a war, it gives all of the majority sex a chance to reproduce. Polygyny usually works by being available to the higher status men. Since status is associated in many societies with aspects of reproductive fitness (health, strength, skill), it will have the effect of increasing the genes for these characteristics.

The Extended Family

Technically, an extended family is one in which kin outside the nuclear family (such as grandparents, uncles or nieces) share in the family tasks. Sharing the same living space is certainly the pattern in many societies around the world and is not uncommon (estimated around 10%) in the West. Many cultures are built around the idea of extended families. In others, including most cultures and subcultures in Europe, it is practical reasons that lead to close contact and interdependence of relatives. Here, extended families are most common in groups with limited income and having low status in the community. These are also the groups with the highest incidence of young single mothers. When the mother is immature and inexperienced, the availability of grandparents to share the burden, so that the mother can continue her education or work, and to provide an additional (often more tolerant) form of childcare, is extremely valuable.

Extending the definition of one's family to include a wider range of relatives and even non-relatives has many advantages. Resources and problems can be shared, childcare is shared and the children benefit from a wider range of contacts and models. Increasing ease of communication and travel have allowed the family to extend to a wider network without living together. At the same time the importance given by society to genetic relationships has diminished so that many people no longer make clear distinctions between blood relatives and other people involved with the family. The involvement of parents in wider networks protects children from the effects of poverty, parental incompetence, and maltreatment. It does not seem to matter whether this wider network is provided by relatives, a religious group, or friends and neighbours.

While the definition of who is family becomes looser, physical changes that are resulting in progressively earlier fecundity are creating families containing an increasing number of generations.

Multigenerational Families

One consequence of the extension of healthy life is that it is now not uncommon for four or even five generations of a family to be actively participating. With improved health and diet there has also been a substantial reduction in the age of onset of puberty over the last century. In families in which teenage pregnancies are common, a grandmother can now be aged under 30 years. Very often in such families the grandmother takes the role of mother. When there are healthy great-grandparents and the grandparents are working it is likely to be the older couple who take the traditional grandparenting role. In one family of six generations it was found that the grandmothers were refusing to care for the new babies, so that this became the job of the great-grandmothers. Meanwhile the oldest, at 91, was living on her own. Even in five-generation families it ceases to be clear who has responsibility for the care of the elders.

Multigenerational families will become more common. They provide opportunities for richer sets of relationships; the different generations can bring experience and wisdom from a wide range of contexts, and the process of making use of this complexity can call forth productive adaptations from all of the generations. However, they also risk such complexity that roles, responsibilities and identities become confused, especially when they are combined with a high frequency of divorce and reconstituting of families.

The trends reviewed in this section indicate some of the changes taking place in Western families. With (hopefully) increasing health and prosperity in many other parts of the world, comparable changes are likely. However, each culture will have a different starting point and the processes can be expected to work out differently. The next section briefly reviews some of the major current influences on Western families.

The Impact of Modern Life on the Family

Working Parents

A number of social changes such as increasing gender equality, rising aspirations and other sources of economic need have resulted in a steep increase in the number of women in work. At the same time, changing work patterns and relaxation of restrictions on, for example, shop opening hours, result in more parental absence from the home. These changes are having substantial effects on the family.

Traditional gender roles are being progressively abandoned, such that the nineteenth century ideal described above feels quite immoral. But while attitudes change, the evidence is that behaviour lags behind. Even in Northern Europe where attitudes have changed most, women still do the great majority of housework and childcare, while men are likely to describe themselves as 'helping'. Children are increasingly likely to come home from school to an empty house, or to be part of a complex set of arrangements for sharing transport and childcare. In turn, children are in some ways becoming self-sufficient for both their physical needs and their entertainment.

As a result of modern lifestyles, e.g. prepared food that can be heated in a microwave and automatic washing machines, children can undertake a lot of their own care. This is beginning to produce a change in children's role in the family. Unlike most other cultures, where children participate in family chores from as young as 4 or 5, Western culture does not require children to work in the home: their work is done within the educational system. But we do try to develop independence and autonomy in our children and this is beginning to have an effect in children using their technical competencies to take charge of more aspects of their lives.

Changes in Family Eating

A major area of contemporary change is in eating habits. The availability of food from all round the world, no longer seasonally limited, potentially offers much greater variety in the available diet. Families no longer need to share the same food at mealtimes, and it is now quite common for each family member, adults and children, to eat according to their individual preferences. The ease of preparing different kinds of food makes this quite workable and it is not usually a source of conflict within the family (Stratton & Bromley, 1999). Our research has found the majority of mothers very pragmatic, and quite willing to provide whatever food their children are most likely to eat. Meanwhile, television within the home and complicated social lives outside are working to encourage people to eat at different times. The traditional family meal is in danger of extinction.

Much may be lost if family meals become uncommon. When things are going well a meal is a pleasurable process which facilitates positive interaction. It is an occasion in which parents are seen to provide, and where children can copy adult activities and so feel that they are participating helpfully. The activities at the table provide a structure for many varied small-scale interactions, and the pleasure of eating can facilitate other forms of positive interaction. Even conversations about school are expected to be more positive during a meal. Each culture has been found to have its own rules about mealtimes which ensure they meet the needs of the culture. For example, Erikson (1963) reports that the Yoruk Indians train their children to never take food without asking, to eat slowly, and to maintain silence so that everyone can think about salmon and becoming rich. Mealtimes can enrich the experience and expand the social repertoire of all the family.

When things are going badly a meal can become a battleground in which each person uses the power of their situation to attempt to win wars over control, independence, recognition and guilt. Refusing to eat is not the only source of power for a child. If sufficiently distressed they can ensure that their distress is shared by everyone else. They will then find it easier to get the family to accept that they should eat separately and thereby change the whole pattern of family eating. Paradoxically, the increased choice can result in some children eating highly restricted diets.

Sibling and Peer Relationships

Siblings learn from each other and also influence the care and quality of interaction that each gets from the parents (Brody, 1996). Many of the characteristics of children that relate to the family structure, and their position in that structure, seem to result from the amount of attention the parents can give them. But a child with siblings has the opportunity for social learning that parents cannot provide. They have opportunities for imitation, caring and fighting within the relative safety of the family.

There is increasing scope for complexity of relationships with two, three, or more children. Apart from the interactions in which they are actively involved, the only interpersonal processes that an only child can observe are between the parents. Two children gives the opportunity to watch a parent interacting with another child, but it is only when there are three children that there is an opportunity to observe two other children interacting within the family. We would expect to see much greater richness in the internal models of relationships as family size increases.

Friendship

By the time they enter their first school, children who have siblings are likely to have spent twice as long in their company as in the company of their parents. Throughout childhood, prosocial and play-oriented interactions are most common. The importance of sibling friendship is shown by the strong connection to popularity and friendships with peers. When an older sibling is playing with a friend, the younger child is much more likely to imitate their sibling than to imitate the friend. Children tend to escalate conflicts with siblings, whereas they try to resolve disputes with friends.

Although sibling relationships are undoubtedly important, there is recent evidence that peers are also extremely important influences on social development (e.g. Parke & Ladd, 1992). While most of the available research follows the traditional developmental interest in the effects of parents on the child's social interactions, Parke and O'Neil (2000) point to an increasing interest in the processes within the child that mediate the parental influence.

Conflict and Aggression

Disputes between siblings are extremely common. They serve a useful function in helping the children learn techniques of reasoned argument, and to work out the rules of the family. Most conflict centres around issues of rights, personal boundaries, and possessions. Resolution of conflict is often achieved by involving the parents. In this sense, sibling arguments are ways of getting interaction with parents, and provide learning opportunities for doing so. But depending on what conclusions parents draw from the fighting, and how they handle it, it can become a well established aspect of the children's models (Patterson, 1986). Conflict is more likely to happen when the home lacks methods of conflict resolution and in which there is parental conflict, or divorce.

The Smith family provide a typical example of these processes. The fights between Sue and Angie were the reason for referral to therapy, but it rapidly became clear that these related to attempts to recruit the parents to their beliefs about the abuse, and that the more serious conflict between Jake and John was primarily about the models that they each wanted Mary to have of themselves and each other.

The Effect of Family Position

Older siblings are more dominant towards their younger brothers and sisters, and usually want to look after them. By the time the younger sibling starts on adolescence the relationship becomes more equal. However, the older sibling will continue to influence by power assertion, while the younger must use low-power strategies. This pattern seems to be related to the fact that children with older siblings tend to be more popular with their peers. An older child who has too much responsibility for younger siblings, called a 'parentified child', will take on adult roles too early; lose their status as a child; and miss out on childhood experiences (Jurkovic, 1997). To adults they will appear mature and responsible and the deficits may not appear until later.

Being born first gives the child a special status. In many countries the firstborn (though in some cases the first male to be born) carries the family lineage, takes over the family business, inherits the main property, and most often is given a family name. Firstborns have been shown to do more household chores in single parent families, and when both parents work, they do more baby sitting. Research in many countries has shown that children who have to care for younger siblings are more helpful in relationships with others outside the home. But helping with chores does not have this effect. The special position of the firstborn gives them a more adult orientation but puts them under greater pressure. They have been shown to be responsible, mature, conforming and self-controlled. Parents demand more, and the child becomes more focused on adult concerns than siblings who have an older child to interact with in the home.

Children with older siblings have been found to experience a wider range of neighbourhoods. This is one aspect of the greater freedom a middle child may have by playing with, and being looked after by, their older sibling. Older siblings are able to engage in sophisticated forms of interaction like teasing, cheating and tricking. Perhaps as a result, younger siblings have been found to have a better understanding of other people, and to be better at understanding how different people may have different beliefs (Ruffman et al., 1998). The child's 'theory of mind' develops most rapidly between 4 and 6 years (Harris, 1989). Middle children are more likely to use this understanding to comfort a younger sibling – or to use it to provoke them in a way that gets them into trouble with the parents.

The last child may encounter an unwillingness of the parents to let them go. Sometimes parents who have focused on bringing up the children worry about how they will get on as a couple on their own.

Sometimes they have concerns about their health. It is easy to slip into strategies that keep the 'baby of the family' at home so that they can care for their parents.

Very Large Families

In many societies, having a large number of children helps to overcome high rates of infant and childhood mortality and provides security for the parents' old age. The industrialised West has only recently moved away from this pattern, and large families during the twentieth century have become associated with aspects of social exclusion such as poverty and unintegrated immigrant families. Earlier research found that children in large, closely spaced families had lower intelligence and poorer health. This effect is no longer found, but the research has been carried out primarily in North America. It is probable that the effects of family size are closely bound up with issues of class, education, and wealth. In a society in which poverty and low social status correlate with large family size, the children in large families will be found to do less well.

Most societies in which women give birth to large numbers of children also have more flexible family boundaries. Children then not only have more siblings, especially as more survive as a result of modern hygiene and medicine, but also more of other kin. Kinship relationships are very important in such societies and children will interact much more closely with cousins, aunts, grandparents and, if the society is polygamous, a range of mothers and fathers. Children in such societies, who also contribute from an early age to the work of the society, have been found to be more socially responsible and caring than children of small nuclear families.

Indicators of Family Problems

It is widely believed that families are under increasing strain and that in the Western world the whole viability of the family is under threat. The evidence does not support these gloomy predictions but the rising figures for divorce and reporting of domestic violence are signs that distress is no longer being contained within the family.

Violence and Abuse

A clear indicator of family distress and failure to cope is the amount of abuse and violence within the home. Murder is more likely to be perpetrated by members of one's own household than by strangers, while we are slowly and reluctantly recognizing the full extent of physical, emotional and sexual abuse of children within their families. Although sexual abuse of children is currently receiving the greatest attention it is not the most common, and may not be the most damaging, form of maltreatment. From a careful review of 16 studies, after adjusting for potential response and definitional biases, Gorey and Leslie (1997) concluded that the best estimate for prevalence of abuse in the US was 14.5% for girls and 7.2% for boys. Wolfner & Gelles (1993) recorded self-reports by parents of minor violence towards children of 62%, with 11% admitting severe violence. A parallel study of Chinese families in Hong Kong found a slightly lower incidence of minor violence, but 46% reporting severe violence, with children aged 3–6 years being especially vulnerable (Tang, 1998). Neglect is the commonest form of reported child maltreatment in the US, accounting for 49% of substantiated cases of abuse. In the UK it is also responsible for 42% of the deaths from abuse (Hobbs, Hanks, & Wynne, 1999, Chapter 6). These facts challenge assumptions about the family being a safe environment within which adults and children thrive. Hobbs, Hanks, and Wynne (1999) report that 68% of sexual abuse perpetrators were a member of the child's family. Proven abuse is likely to represent the extreme of a continuum in which there is an even greater frequency of less serious but still distressing dysfunction within ordinary families. It is also worth noting that, although physical abuse only started being realistically reported from the mid 1960s, and sexual abuse from the early 1980s, there is no reason to suppose that rates of abuse were significantly lower before these times. Current estimates of the overall incidence of child maltreatment range from 10% to 50% depending upon definition. We therefore have to accept that our conclusions from child development research throughout the last century, except where the sampling techniques happened to exclude abused children, are based on groups of children which included many who were experiencing high levels of maltreatment within their families.

Violence is one of the clearest examples of how societies, families and individuals are connected. It has been well understood that parents provide the models for their children, and if violence is part of the family dynamic then children will internalize it and conduct their relationships in the same way. It becomes difficult to break the cycle when the family, neighbourhood and society also practise violence as a means of communication and control and so perpetuate the cycle. Families that readily resort to violence generally have low levels of verbal communication. Providing them with better techniques of conflict resolution is effective in preventing the development of violence but has less effect when patterns of violent interaction are already established.

At present there are many factors which work against being able to make even an approximate evaluation of the effects of abuse. The history of child abuse has been one in which clear medical evidence has been the first, and necessary, indicator before the problem was accepted. But the resistance to recognizing the full range and severity of the effects of abuse goes much deeper. Abuse is a painful reality and everybody, given the chance, would prefer to avoid the pain of recognizing it. We are also likely to take a restricted view of abuse if we continue to regard the child as just being subjected to, and responding to, influence. It is especially difficult in this area to apply the recognition that children are active participants in creating their worlds. Perhaps we are afraid of blaming the victim; perhaps it is just easier to see things from an adult's point of view. But damage is not primarily something that can be put into a child to be carried around, invisible inside them. Damaging environments are places in which children function and grow. The important effects of abuse are at least as likely to be in the kinds of transactional adaptations the child comes to make as in simple direct consequences (Stratton & Hanks, 1991). Within the abuse literature these adaptations are called the 'accommodation syndrome' (Summit, 1983).

From this point of view the behaviour of the child is not a 'symptom' but the best response they could make for their own protection. Think of a child who flinches every time someone moves suddenly anywhere near them. Classifying this as a symptom of twitchiness, or as a neurotic behaviour, is not only unhelpful; it is disparaging the child. Seeing it as an adaptive response to an environment in which you might be suddenly assaulted without warning makes more sense and also opens up ideas of what might be done about it.

The prevalence of child maltreatment throughout the last century, and its relative invisibility in child development research, mean that our images of children may have been distorted and incomplete. Our models of parenting styles have not included any of the common forms of abuse. Developmental theories have underestimated the demands for adaptation imposed on many children. Many of the children who participate in research studies are living in families under considerable stress. Developmental research can either attempt to exclude such children, which will result in a developmental psychology of a small and unrepresentative section of the population, or address the issues directly. A further option, of course, is to avoid awareness of the powerful sources of influence in the family backgrounds of the children being researched. We will briefly review some of the major stressors which can be expected to demand highly focused adaptations from the children within these families. We might best regard the children in such families as having acquired a specialism in coping with the particular demand, but thereby risking limiting other potentials.

Common Family Stressors

Poverty

Poverty and social exclusion affect the development of more children than any other factor. Huston (1999) refers to poverty in the United States as 'a social problem of epidemic proportions'. In the US approximately 20% of children live in poverty and 9% in extreme poverty (family income below 50% of the poverty threshold) (US Bureau of the Census, 1997). As Huston (1999) points out, we have clear correlational data connecting poverty to developmental deficits, and also good evidence that intensive early interventions can be effective (McLoyd, 1997). But poverty correlates with many other aspects of family life, from amount of time watching television, through increased exposure to racism, to father absence (McGoldrick, 1998; Phares, 1996). Rather than seeing these correlates as intervening variables to be controlled for in the research, a systemic view would be to deconstruct the concept of poverty as a rich set of cultural assumptions of Western society, and to attempt the child's perspective on just what exclusion can mean.

Psychological Problems

The family is expected to carry many of the burdens that arise in society. One major source of stress is when a family member suffers from a diagnosable psychiatric condition. Depression is four times as common in women, and most common in adulthood, which means the commonest case is for the mother (or grandmother) to be depressed. Children often adapt initially by taking over the work of the depressed person, and by giving them extra attention. Sometimes this works to increase their feelings of worthlessness, helplessness, and being a burden, and so can make the depression worse.

Siblings of a child suffering serious psychological problems are often not told the nature of the problem and so become confused and resentful. The commonest reaction is an increase in affection and concern, but an increase in hostility is also common. Quite often the sibling, and sometimes a parent, feels both emotions and responds inconsistently as a result. Children who are negotiating their family role in relation to psychological difficulties of others in the family become part of the whole cycle of disturbed process and may come to be seen as the major cause of problems.

Drug Addiction

An increasing problem for families is drug addiction, and the most common form is alcoholism. Apart from the financial damage, alcohol is often a factor in family violence. While it may have arisen in the first place because of unresolved family distress, it also has the consequence that intoxication prevents the person from tackling and resolving difficulties in positive ways. When the addiction is to illegal substances there is the added burden of cost and risk. Addiction readily leads to secretiveness and criminality which have damaging effects on the whole family, and the children as well as the adults may become involved in criminally supporting the habit.

Disability and Chronic Illness

A common source of stress within families is the variety of serious chronic disabling conditions in childhood, whether a physical or a psychological disability. External help may also be needed when a parent has a disability and finds it difficult to look after a child that does not have similar problems. A blind or deaf parent may not readily appreciate the experiences of a sighted and hearing child. One task is alerting the disabled parent to recognize the needs of the children, which may not be apparent to that adult. Also children may sometimes take on greater responsibilities, far beyond those appropriate to their actual age, and so miss out on age-appropriate learning and social skills acquisition.

Like disability, chronic illness in a child or adult puts considerable strain on a family. Parents with chronically ill children often work so hard that their relationship sinks to a low level of contextual importance. Other children in the family may also be called on to make sacrifices and, while this can be a growth experience and increase their capacity for concern, it can also put a strain on all of the relationships involved.

Rolland (1994) and Altschuler (1997) have reviewed the development of the individual and the course of relationships within the family when a child has a chronic illness. They conclude that the consequences for development are dependent on stages of the life cycle and the nature of the illness. In the systemic field there has been a focus on therapy and change rather than the development of self. For example, Altschuler (1997) holds that young people become caught in a double bind, making up for the sick child and providing public accounts of coping which may conflict with the private account of guilt and fear. Rolland (1994), in a review of the literature, concluded that although siblings can easily become forgotten family members when another child is ill or disabled, especially if the illness is a severe or life-threatening condition, direct and clear information and supportive reassurance from parents were often the determining factors in how siblings adjusted to the ill or disabled child.

Bereavement

Every family has to cope with death and dying at some point. Some families work through these events in their lives while others fall apart and do not recover fully. The emotional scars of these events may then be carried by the children into adulthood and influence their parenting patterns. Deaths of children and untimely deaths of other family members, suicides and homicides can have profoundly disturbing effects on a family from which they have difficulty recovering. One form of bereavement that has been found to be especially damaging is when a child is aware of the death of a parent but the death is not openly acknowledged or discussed. The bereaved parent may find it easier to pretend that the other has gone away, and then discourage talk about them.

Aspects of Families That Can Lead to Problems

This chapter started with a review of characteristics of the modern family. All of the features described there can contribute to family problems, but there are other intrinsic aspects that are likely to lead directly to distress.

Problems with Balance

People are usually good at understanding relationships between pairs of people, but have great difficulty when thinking about three or more, as in a family. The rapid increase in the complexity of models of relationships required as more children are added to a family has been discussed above. With this complexity, family members adopt a variety of strategies to control their interactions. One aspect is called 'distance regulation': individuals use the practicalities of family life to maintain a comfortable emotional distance from each other. If an uncomfortable degree of closeness or separateness is threatened, an argument may start up, or a problem with the washing machine or the pocket money may become a priority. Closeness is thereby renegotiated to a more comfortable level. Sometimes a person becomes ill and so gets looked after in a way that everyone finds suitable. Where there are different perceptions of how much closeness is appropriate, as in the Smiths' case, the emotional distance may be achieved through overt conflict.

Another aspect of balance is between cohesion and independence. A family that puts a high value on keeping together may be threatened by an adolescent's moves to independence, and with the first child may have no easy way of letting go of them. Issues of boundaries such as the time the adolescent must come home at night come to symbolize such things as parental caring, the dangers of life outside the home, and the loyalty to peers of the young person.

Secrets

Families have a powerful tendency to define topics as not to be discussed or even mentioned (Imber-

Black, 1993). This tendency enables beliefs that seem quite bizarre when they are finally expressed, to exist without being challenged. Child sexual abuse is almost always accompanied by powerful demands for secrecy, but often the belief itself is perfectly straightforward, and it is just the fact that it is defined as a secret that is damaging. For example, in one family during family therapy the father stated that John was adopted but that he did not know. John, who was 6 years old (and not deaf), listened to this statement without comment. He clearly knew that he was adopted, but he also knew that the important thing about this was that it was not discussed within the family.

Power

Power, and its relationship to race and gender, has become a central issue for societies in Western countries and at a different level for families as well. Families, more than most contexts, incorporate enormous differences in the power that individuals can wield. In most civilizations the children are either the property or the responsibility of the parents. This position makes parents powerful people within families, and when families don't understand how to use this power wisely they may resort to physical and emotional punishment and manipulation of the children within the family.

However, there are many sorts of power and not all can be used. For many people, superior physical strength is not something to be exploited within the family, so it is not a source of power. On the other hand, a greater verbal facility, or ability to manipulate emotions, or stronger religious or political conviction, or the dependency that may come from physical disability, may all be used to control the behaviour of other family members. Sometimes financial power is used; sometimes it is the contact with an outside world that enables one person to be dominant in defining reality.

Scapegoating and Blaming

A very common pattern in distressed families is for one person to be seen as the cause of the problems. Quite often the blamed person accepts this role and comes to believe that all of the family's problems would be solved if only he/she were different. This is an unhelpful belief because there is no way that they can turn into a different person. A child in this position will have low self-esteem and the dysfunctional behaviour this brings will prevent the family from searching for alternative and less damaging solutions. The blaming process often involves a belief by parents that the child has more control over bad events than the parents do, and that there is something about the child's personality that makes them want to cause distress in the family.

Implications for Developmental Psychology of Systemic Family Therapy

We know from developmental research that there are many ways in which the family affects the development of children: marital conflict, sibling relationships, poverty, abuse, eating and TV watching arrangements, and so on. All such findings have a problem in dealing with the direction of effects. The reason for this problem is not some technical difficulty in research design. Each family is a system in the most complete sense. Each component is highly attuned to actions and changes in the others; the physical context of the family means that adaptations are continuous and immediate; and the social context holds the family members together far more resolutely than other human systems such as work teams, so that systemic processes have to be worked through rather than abandoned. And the contextual levels at which the family operates cover an enormous range. We cannot just work with family members as counters manipulated within the system. We must take account of the ways they incorporate their history – of how their thoughts, feelings, digestions and finances transact and adapt within the family. And just as parents are not the given context that works on the child, society is not a given context that works on the family. Historically, it is claimed, it has been the family that creates society in its own image (Stein, 1985). But that image is the one that society has of its families, inaccurate and idealized as it may be: 'Society is the macrocosm of the family (not conversely). This situation in turn stabilizes the family dynamics that constitute its source' (1985, p. 221).

Systemic therapists are learning how to pay appropriate attention to cultural issues of race, gender, religion and other sources of difference. When such differences are ignored, we inevitably attribute meaning to family stories in ways that derive from our own, unconsidered, cultural base (Mock, 1998; Stratton, 1998). Researchers into child development all have in common that they are adults, and will inevitably find it easier to identify with parents so that children become the objects of study. Throughout their history both developmental psychology and systemic family therapy have had to struggle to make the continuing effort to take the child's perspective rather than research the child as an object. There are some recent examples, which, like this chapter, attempt to bridge the gap between the two disciplines. Andreozzi's (1996) formulation of 'Child-centred structural dynamic therapy', which is in turn based on Kantor and Lehr's (1986) conceptualization of family process, specifically deals with the child in family development. The dynamic systems approach (Thelen & Smith, 1994; van Geert, Chapter 28 in this volume) is an ambitious attempt to create non-linear models of development as an emergent product of transactions within the system. Young (1997) gives an intriguing account of acculturation of the individual as a process that builds cultural assumptions into their thinking, by combining neo-Piagetianism and neo-Vygotskyism with a strong basis in Michael White's narrative approach (White & Epston, 1990). Another interesting development has been the formulation of 'multi-systemic therapy', deriving from Bronfenbrenner's theory of social ecology (Randall & Henggeller, 1999). Meanwhile there are techniques in family therapy that could be used by developmentalists to develop their own thinking. An example is Karl Tomm's (1992) technique of the 'internalized other' in which, following a careful induction procedure, the client answers questions from the position of their internalized model of the other person. The technique has been found to be extremely effective and has been used to get parents to adopt the perspective and emotional responses of their child. It would be interesting to have developmentalists undergo this procedure in relation to the children who take part in their research.

CONCLUSIONS

I suggest we consider the proposition that developmental psychology has seen the task of understanding 'the family' as too difficult. Systemic therapy has shown that, as with Maslow's hierarchy of motivation, if some goal is seen as too distant, with no practical way of achieving it, it is not construed as a goal at all. My contention is that the achievements of systemic family therapy can now be used by developmental psychologists both to know how their findings can most usefully be applied for the benefit of children within their families, and to take full account of the family context in designing and interpreting their research.

In a random sample of 1,000 children recruited as a control group for research, there are likely to be between 10% and 50% (depending on definition) who are being or have been abused; around 10% with a chronic illness or disability; 28% living in a single parent household, while a further 16% of those living with a married couple will be stepchildren; and up to 20% whose families are living in poverty. Excluding children who are undergoing treatment will still leave the great majority of these children in the sample. In addition a large proportion of the sample will be experiencing conflict within their families. Although frequencies will vary considerably depending on the society involved and the ages of the children, there are three clear implications:

1 The family, in all its variety, must be studied in its own right if we want to understand the psychological development of the child. Its contribution to development cannot be assessed, let alone eliminated as a covariate, by combining demographic measures with scores on tests of parenting.
2 Ignoring the family context within which 'normal' children are growing up is to ignore a major influence on research assessments of their cognitive, physical, and social functioning. For example, how often do cognitive tests conducted in school take account of whether the last time the child ate was some junk food early the previous evening?
3 The most urgent context for the application of developmental psychology is within the 'normal' family. It is strange to be attempting to have a science of the child that has rarely studied the context that creates children and gives us and them the meanings that they embody. It is even stranger to be training family therapists to work with children but having to admit that the scientific base has largely overlooked the task of constructing a psychology of adequately functioning families.

An old joke has a traveller stopping to ask for directions to their destination and being told, 'If I wanted to get there I wouldn't start from here.' Developmental psychology has the functioning of, and influences on, the individual child as its starting point. I have suggested that different starting points – those of the child in the family system, and of the family system in the child – might lead in other, more fruitful directions. But for a traveller to set off in new directions they need some form of map. I believe that the ways of understanding family functioning that have been created within systemic family therapy, some of which have been described in this chapter, offer usable maps. They are only a start but perhaps they will offer a secure enough base to launch, or at least a transitional object to accompany, research which will contribute to tackling the urgent issues that are calling forth adaptations from today's children.

REFERENCES

Ainsworth, M. (1972). Attachment and dependency: A comparison. In J. Gewirtz (ed.), *Attachment and dependency*. Washington, DC: Winston.

Altschuler, J. (1997). *Working with chronic illness*. London: Macmillan.

Andreozzi, L.L. (1996). *Child centred family therapy*. New York: Wiley.

Bateson, G. (1973). *Steps to an ecology of mind*. London: Paladin.

Beavers, W.R. (1982). Healthy, midrange and severely dysfunctional families. In F. Walsh (ed.), *Normal family processes*. New York: Guilford.

Beavers, W.R., & Voeller, M.M. (1983). Family models: Comparing and contrasting the Olson circumplex model with the Beavers systems model. *Family Process*, 22, 85–98.

Bell, R.Q. (1968). A reinterpretation of the direction of effects in studies of socialisation. *Psychological Bulletin*, 75, 81–95.

Bell, R.Q. (1979). Parent, child and reciprocal influences. *American Psychologist*, 34, 821–826.

Berg, I.K. (1994). *Family-based services: A solution-focused approach*. New York: Norton.

Bowlby, J. (1951). *Maternal care and mental health*. Geneva: WHO.

Bowlby, J. (1968). *Attachment and loss: Vol. 1. Attachment*. London: Hogarth.

Bradley, R.H., & Corwyn, R.F. (1999). Parenting. In L. Balter & C.S. Tamis-LeMonda (eds), *Child psychology: A handbook of contemporary issues*. Philadelphia: Psychology Press.

Bronfenbrenner, U. (1979). *The ecology of human development*. Cambridge, MA: Harvard University Press.

Bronfenbrenner, U. (1993) The ecology of cognitive development: Research models and fugitive findings. In R.H. Wozniak & K. Fischer (eds), *Development in context* (pp. 3–44). Hillsdale, NJ: Erlbaum.

Brody, G.H. (1996). *Sibling relationships: Their causes and consequences*. Norwood, NJ: Ablex.

Bruner, J. (1986). *Actual minds, possible worlds*. Cambridge, MA: Harvard University Press.

Burguière, A., Klapisch-Zuber, C., Segalen, M., & Zonabend, F. (eds) (1996). *A history of the family*. Cambridge: Polity.

Burguière, A., & Lebrun, F. (1996). The one hundred and one families of Europe. In A. Burguière, C. Klapisch-Zuber, M. Segalen, & F. Zonabend (eds), *A history of the family*. Cambridge: Polity.

Byng-Hall, J. (1988). Scripts and legends in families and family therapy. *Family Process*, 27, 167–179.

Byng-Hall, J. (1998). Evolving ideas about narrative: re-editing the re-editing of family mythology. *Journal of Family Therapy*, 20, 133–141.

Carr, A. (2000). *Family therapy: Concepts, process and practice*. Chichester: Wiley.

Carter, B., & McGoldrick, M. (1989). *The changing family life cycle* (2nd edn). Boston: Allyn & Bacon.

Cecchin, G., Lane, G., & Ray, W.L. (1994). *The cybernetics of prejudices in the practice of psychotherapy*. London: Karnac.

Dallos, R., & Draper, R. (2000). *An introduction to family therapy*. Oxford: Oxford University Press.

De Shazer, S., (1988). *Clues: Investigating solutions in brief therapy*. New York: Norton.

Dreman, S. (1999). The experience of divorce and separation in the family: A dynamic systems perspective. In E. Frydenberg (ed.), *Learning to cope: Developing as a person in complex societies*. Oxford: Oxford University Press.

Dunn, J. (1993). *Young children's close relationships*. London: Sage.

Dunn, J. (1996). Studying relationships and social understanding. In P. Barnes (ed.), *Personal, social and emotional development of children*. Oxford: Oxford University Press.

Edgar, D. (1999). Families as the crucible of competence. In E. Frydenberg (ed.), *Learning to cope: Developing as a person in complex societies*. Oxford: Oxford University Press.

Erikson, E.H. (1963). *Childhood and society*. New York: Norton.

Feng, D., Giarrusso, R., Bengtson, V.L., & Frye, N. (1999). Intergenerational transmission of marital quality and marital instability. *Journal of Marriage and the Family*, 61, 451–463.

Fincham, F., Beach, S.R., & Baucom, D.H. (1987). Attribution processes in distressed and nondistressed couples: 4. Self–partner attribution differences. *Journal of Personality and Social Psychology*, 52, 739–748.

Foucault, M. (1980). *Power/knowledge: Selected interviews and other writings, 1972–1977* (ed. and trans. C. Gordon). New York: Pantheon.

Golombok, S. (1999). New family forms. In L. Balter & C.S. Tamis-LeMonda (eds), *Child psychology: A handbook of contemporary issues*. Philadelphia: Psychology Press.

Golombok, S., Spencer, A., & Rutter, M. (1983). Children in lesbian and single-parent households: Psychosexual and psychiatric appraisal. *Journal of Child Psychology and Psychiatry*, 24, 551–572.

Gorey, K.M., & Leslie, D.R. (1997). The prevalence of child sexual abuse: Integrative review adjustment for potential response and measurement biases. *Child Abuse & Neglect*, 21, 391–398.

Hardy, K.V., & Laszloffy, T.A. (1995). The cultural genogram: Key to training culturally competent family therapists. *Journal of Marital and Family Therapy*, 21, 227–237.

Harris, C.C. (1969). *The family*. London: Allen & Unwin.

Harris, P. (1989). *Children and emotion*. Oxford: Blackwell.

Hobbs, C.J., Hanks, H.G.I., & Wynne, J.M. (1999). *Child abuse and neglect: A clinician's handbook*. London: Churchill Livingston.

Huston, A.C. (1999). Effects of poverty on children. In L. Balter & C.S. Tamis-LeMonda (eds), *Child psychology: A handbook of contemporary issues*. Philadelphia: Psychology Press.

Imber-Black, E. (1993). *Secrets in families and family therapy*. New York: Norton.

Jurkovic, G.J. (1997). *Lost childhoods: The plight of the parentified child*. New York: Bruner/Mazel.

Kantor, D., & Lehr, W. (1986). *Inside the family: Toward a theory of family process*. San Francisco: Jossey-Bass.

Kessen, W. (1993). Rumble or revolution: A commentary. In R.H. Wozniak & K. Fischer (eds), *Development in context* (pp. 269–279). Hillsdale, NJ: Erlbaum.

Kogan, M., & Gale, J.E. (1997). Decentering therapy: Textual analysis of a narrative therapy session. *Family Process*, 36, 101–126.

Leppington, R. (1991). From constructivism to social constructionism and doing critical therapy. *Human Systems*, 2, 79–103.

Lewis, M., & Rosenblum, L.A. (1974). *The effect of the infant on its caregiver*. New York: Wiley.

Lieberman, S. (1979). Transgenerational analysis: The geneogram as a technique in family therapy. *Journal of Family Therapy*, 1, 51–64.

Maturana, H.R., & Varela, F.J. (1980). *Autopoeisis and cognition*. Dordrecht: Riedel.

McGoldrick, M. (1998). *Re-visioning family therapy: Race, culture, and gender in clinical practice*. New York: Guilford.

McLoyd, V.C. (1997). Children in poverty: Development, public policy, and practice. In W. Damon (series ed.) & I.E. Sigel & K.A. Renninger (eds), *Handbook of child psychology, 5th edn: Vol. 4. Child Psychology in Practice*. New York: Wiley.

McNamee, A., & Gergen, K. (1992). *Therapy as social construction*. London: Sage.

Minuchin, S. (1974). *Families and family therapy*. London: Tavistock.

Mock, M.R. (1998). The imperatives of cultural competence: Acknowledging culture in psychotherapy. *Human Systems*, 9. 159–165.

Munton, A., Silvester, J., Stratton, P., & Hanks, H. (1999), *Attributions in action*. Chichester: Wiley.

Nash, J. (1970). *Developmental psychology*. Englewood Cliffs, NJ: Prentice-Hall.

Neiderhiser, J.M., Reiss, D., Hetherington, E.M., & Plomin, R. (1999). Relationships between parenting and adolescence over time: Genetic and environmental contributions. *Developmental Psychology*, 35, 680–692.

Nichols, M.P., & Schwartz, R.C. (1995). *Family therapy: Concepts and methods* (3rd edn). Boston: Allyn & Bacon.

Parke, R.D., & Ladd, G.W. (1992). *Family–peer relationships: Models of linkage*. Hillsdale, NJ: Erlbaum.

Parke, R.D., & O'Neil, R.L. (2000). Neighborhoods of southern California children and families. *Future of Children*, 9, 58–63.

Patterson, G.R. (1986). The contribution of siblings to training for fighting. In D. Olweus, J. Block, & M. Radke-Yarrow (eds), *Development of antisocial and prosocial behaviour* (pp. 235–261). New York: Academic.

Pearce, W.B. (1989). *Communication and the human condition*. Carbondale, IL: Southern Illinois University Press.

Pearce, W.B., & Pearce, K.A. (1998). Transcendent story-telling: Abilities for systemic practitioners and their clients. *Human Systems*, 9, 167–184.

Phares, V. (1996). *Fathers and developmental psychopathology*. New York: Wiley.

Randall, J., & Henggeller, S.W. (1999). Multisystemic therapy. In S.W. Russ & T.H. Ollendick (eds), *Handbook of psychotherapies with children and families*. New York: Kluwer/Plenum.

Reese, H.W., & Lipsitt, L.P. (1970). *Experimental child psychology*. New York: Academic.

Rolland, J.S. (1994). *Families, illness, and disability: An integrated treatment model*. New York: Basic.

Rolland, J.S. (1999). Parental illness and disability: a family systems framework. Journal of Family Therapy, 21, 242–266.

Ruffman, T., Perner, J., Naito, M., Parkin, L., & Clements, W.A. (1998). Older (but not younger) siblings facilitate false belief understanding. *Developmental Psychology*, 36, 161–174.

Sameroff, A.J., & Fiese, B.H. (1990). Transactional regulation and early intervention. In S.J. Miesels & J.P. Shonkoff (eds), *Handbook of early childhood intervention*. Cambridge: Cambridge University Press.

Schaffer, H.R. (1971). *The growth of sociability*. Harmondsworth: Penguin.

Silverstein, L.B., & Auerbach, C.F. (1999). Deconstructing the essential father. *American Psychologist*, 54, 397–407.

Silvester, J., Bentovim, A., Stratton, P., & Hanks, H. (1995). Using spoken attributions to classify abusive families. *Child Abuse and Neglect*, 19, 1221–1232.

Silvester, J., & Stratton, P. (1991). Attributional discrepancy in abusive families. *Human Systems*, 2, 279–296.

Sluzki, C.E., & Ransom, D.D. (1976). *Double bind: The foundation of the communicational approach to the family*. New York: Grune & Stratton.

Stein, H.F. (1985). Values and family therapy. In J. Schwartzman (ed.), *Families and other systems: The macrosystemic context of family therapy*. New York: Guilford.

Strand, P.S. (1997). Toward a developmentally informed narrative therapy. *Family Process*, 36, 325–339.

Stratton, P.M. (1977). Criteria for assessing the influence of obstetric circumstances on later development. In T. Chard & M. Richards (eds), *Benefits and hazards of the new obstetrics* (pp. 139–156). London: SIMP.

Stratton, P. (1982). *Psychobiology of the human newborn*. Chichester: Wiley.

Stratton, P. (1988a). Spirals and circles: Potential contributions from developmental psychology to the practice of family therapy. *Journal of Family Therapy*, 10, 207–231.

Stratton, P. (1988b). Parents' conceptualisation of children as the organiser of culturally structured environments. In J. Valsiner (ed.), *Child development within culturally structured environments*. Norwood, NJ: Ablex.

Stratton, P. (1992). Integration of developmental concepts with systemic techniques for intervention with families. *Journal of Educational and Child Psychology*, 8, 28–41.

Stratton, P. (1998). Culture in systemic practice. *Human Systems*, 9, 155–158.

Stratton, P., & Bromley, K. (1999). Families' accounts of the causal processes in food choice. *Appetite*, 33, 89–108.

Stratton, P., & Hanks, H. (1991). Incorporating circularity in defining and classifying child maltreatment. *Human Systems*, 2, 181–200.

Stratton, P., Hanks, H., Campbell, H., & Hatcher, S. (1993). Countertransference in systems thinking and practice. *Journal of Social Work Practice*, 7, 181–194.

Stratton, P., & Hayes, N. (1998). *A student's dictionary of psychology* (3rd edn). London: Arnold.

Stratton, P., Heard, D.H., Hanks, H.G., Munton, A.G., Brewin, C.R., & Davidson, C. (1986). Coding causal beliefs in natural discourse. *British Journal of Social Psychology*, 25, 299–313.

Stratton, P., & Swaffer, R. (1988). Maternal causal beliefs for abused and handicapped children. *Journal of Reproductive and Infant Psychology*, 6, 201–216.

Summit, R. (1983). The child sexual abuse accommodation syndrome. *Child Abuse and Neglect*, 1, 177–193.

Tang, C. So-kun (1998). The rate of physical abuse in Chinese families: A community survey in Hong Kong. *Child Abuse and Neglect*, 22, 381–391.

Thelen, E., & Smith, L.B. (1994). *A dynamic systems approach to the development of cognition and action*. Cambridge, MA: MIT Press.

Tomm, K. (1992). Interviewing the internalized other: Toward a systemic reconstruction of the self and other. Workshop at the California School for Professional Psychology.

Tomm, K. (1993). The courage to protest: A commentary on Michael White's work. In S. Gilligan & R. Price (eds), *Therapeutic conversations* (pp. 62–80). New York: Norton.

Uccelli, P., Hemphill, L., Alexander, B., & Snow, C. (1999). Telling two kinds of stories: Sources of narrative skill. In L. Balter & C.S. Tamis-LeMonda (eds), *Child psychology: A handbook of contemporary issues*. Philadelphia: Psychology Press.

US Bureau of the Census (1997). *Poverty in the United States 1997*. Washington, DC: USBC.

Valsiner, J. (2000). *Culture and human development*. London, Sage.

von Bertalanffy, L. (1968). *General system theory*, New York: Brazillier.

Watzlawick, P. (1963). A review of the double bind theory. *Family Process*, 2, 132–153.

Weiner, N. (1948). *Cybernetics: Or control and communication in the animal and the machine*. Cambridge, MA: MIT Press.

Wellman, H.M. (1992). *The child's theory of mind*. Cambridge, MA: MIT Press.

White, M., & Epston, D. (1990). *Narrative means to therapeutic ends*. New York: Norton.

Wolfner, G.D., & Gelles, R.J. (1993). A profile of violence towards children: A national study. *Child Abuse and Neglect*, 17, 197–212.

Wozniac, R.H. (1993). Co-constructive metatheory for psychology: Implications for an analysis of families as specific social contexts for development. In R.H. Wozniak & K. Fischer (eds), *Development in context*. Hillsdale, NJ: Erlbaum.

Young, G. (1997). *Adult development, therapy and culture: A postmodern synthesis*. London: Plenum.

16

Schooling and the Development of Literacy

DAVID OLSON
and
JANETTE PELLETIER

Arguably no social practice has so pronounced an effect on the intellectual and social development of children as the acquisition of the various forms of literacy that make up schooling. On the personal level, literacy involves not only the acquisition of a basic competence with such notational systems as written language and number, but also the sophisticated uses of such notational systems in the specialized discourses of science and literature. But on the social level, literacy is a defining characteristic of modern bureaucratic societies, that is, those societies in which institutions such as law, government, economics, science and literature are organized around written documents. Personal literacy is that competence required to participate in such institutional practices. In turn, these literate or 'textual' institutions determine to a large extent the specific nature of the intellectual competencies that are to be acquired by individuals. Schools are those institutions designed to play this mediating role.

Literacy is sufficiently high on the political agenda of both developed and developing countries that it, along with defense and health, consumes a major proportion of national budgets. Free public school has been government policy for well over a century in Western democracies and is increasingly so in developing ones. Despite this commitment to literacy via public education, the consequences and implications of literacy remain the object of much research and theory.

Vygotsky (1986, pp. 174ff) set the stage for much of this discussion by raising the argument that many of the properties of mind that we take to be the product of universal developmental processes are, rather, the product of particular enculturation. Vygotsky's view may be described as a metarepresentational view, in that schooling was seen as the instrument of all 'higher functions' which have in common 'awareness, abstraction, and control' (p. 179). In the present vocabulary, this could be expressed as the claim that what schooling in general and literacy in particular bring to cognition is a new kind or level of consciousness. In the case of consciousness of language, what we would now call 'metalinguistic knowledge', he suggested that 'the signs of writing and methods of their use are acquired consciously. Writing in its turn, enhances the intellectuality of the child's actions. *It brings awareness to speech*' (p. 183, italics added). The metarepresentational nature of literacy is central to much of the recent research in the field (Ferreiro & Teberosky, 1979/1996; Karmiloff-Smith, 1992; Olson, 1994). In this chapter we first examine the nature of a literate society and then consider the development of literate competence, primarily the ability to read and write. We conclude with some discussions of the cognitive and social implications of literacy.

Literate Institutions

A modern society may be thought of as a network of institutions which are organized around the production, interpretation and use of written texts or documents. So social theorists (Smith, 1990) refer to such societies as 'textual' or 'document' societies in that social practices are organized around written documents. This handbook is a case in point, as is every contract, receipt, recipe, invoice, and computer program. It is an open question as to why writing and documents have come to have such a 'pride of place' in modern societies. Among the reasons are the fixity and permanence of written artifacts which allow them to be read and reread and to be shared over time and space in ways quite different from speech (Innis, 1950).

The fixity of the written record, itself a historical achievement (Johns, 1998), is a critical factor in understanding writing (Harris, 1986). Every reading and rereading appeals to the same text. Even if unread, written documents are assumed to be fixed.

The fixity of documents, in turn, invites the distinction between the document and its interpretation. While interpretations, which in a reversal of usage have come to be called 'readings', vary greatly, they all appeal to a fixed document. It is the fixity of these documents that has made them such ideal instruments for the accumulation of improvements to the growth of knowledge so heralded in modern societies. Science, as Karl Popper (1972) once noted, is a branch of literature. It is concerned with the growth of a literature, a documented archive, which both preserves the past and makes the recognition of an 'original' possible. On the other hand, this documented archive is enormously conservative as it preserves a limited set of traditions; it controls entry to those traditions, while excluding both the people and the ideas that fall outside those traditions.

It is this document culture that provides an important incentive for learning to read and write. It is the existence of something worth reading, something which gives a learner power or access, that provides both the incentive to the learner and the mandate to the schools to focus on literacy. Further, the fact that knowledge and power in a modern society are organized through literate institutions is the reason that literacy is not just a matter of learning to read and write. It is, rather, a matter of learning how to participate in and contribute to those literate institutions whether in science, law, economics, or literature.

How knowledge is tied up in literate institutions may be illustrated by reflecting briefly on our knowledge of geography or music. In both cases we have some local knowledge of how we get to the corner store or how we recognize a tune. But again in both cases, our knowledge is enhanced and transformed by our knowledge of maps on one hand and musical scores on the other. Maps and musical scores have long histories in Western culture. People's conceptions of space are dramatically reorganized when they begin to locate themselves on a map: 'You are here' (Liben, 1981; Olson, 1994). Similarly, their conceptions of music are transformed when they learn to represent pitch and duration of notes and even more substantially when they begin to represent 'rests' – the silence that makes up an important part of the music (Bamburger, 1991; 1996).

Conceptions of language are similarly affected when children are introduced to a written script, ordinarily in the first years of schooling. Although the world's scripts differ importantly (Sampson, 1985), all of the major writing systems of the world are representations of linguistic form and not of meanings or of things directly. Logographs, syllabaries and alphabets all represent, in their various ways, certain properties of speech. An alphabet, for example, is an evolved notational system, a script, which developed through time, largely through borrowing from earlier writing systems, to represent the lexical and phonological properties of the surface structure of speech. The script represents the form of an utterance and only indirectly the meanings or intentions of the writer. There is nothing in the script to indicate, for example, an ironic tone of voice; special lexical devices have to be invented to make up for what is lost in the act of transcription (Olson & Astington, 1990). Other notational systems such as tallies or numerals represent counting or numbering without representing the linguistic or surface form of the utterance expressing those numbers. For example, the numeral '4' can be read as 'four' or 'quatre'; the circle with an oblique line through it can be read as 'No' in 'No smoking' or as 'Do not enter' if posted on a door. Further, modern alphabetic scripts represent other aspects of the surface form of an utterance in addition to its phonological form (how the word sounds). It represents discrete words by means of spaces, it represents sentences by means of capital letters and periods, it represents mood by question marks and exclamation marks. In consequence, the technology, the script, already has embedded in it graphic signs which children have to learn to interpret as indicating these implicit properties of utterances.

One of the more important advances in our understanding of reading in this century has been the progressive realization that the knowledge represented by these various graphic features does not exist, as such, in children's knowledge prior to their learning to read. That is, although in most cases children are speakers of the language in question, the knowledge organized in the service of speaking is importantly different from that required for reading.

Shankweiler and Liberman were among the first to point out this fact in relation to sound patterns, that is, the phonology of English:

> In reading an alphabetic language like English, the child must be able to segment the words he knows [orally] into the phonemic elements that the alphabetic shapes represent. In order to do this; he needs to be consciously aware of the segmentation of the language into units of phonemic size . . . His competence in speech production and speech perception is of no direct use to him here. (1972, p. 309)

Ferreiro and Teberosky (1979/1996) and Olson (1994) have made a similar argument about words, namely, that competence in speech perception and speech production is of little use in segmenting grammatical strings into an itemizable set of lexical units we literate people think of as words. And yet children are expected to 'recognize' words in learning to read. Again, children's knowledge of language acquired in learning to speak is not organized in such a way as to directly map on to writing. In learning to read and write, children must learn not only to read and write but also to 'hear' and think differently about their own speech in a new way. That is why learning to read is both somewhat difficult and extremely important.

Learning to be Literate

Learning to read and write is essential if children are to come to understand and participate in the literate institutions of our culture. Our conception of schooling is closely tied to a formal writing system, one which is to be mastered not only as proof that one is versed in a discipline, but also as a model of thinking (Gardner, 1999). Literacy is a valued enterprise both as a model of thinking and as evidence of participation in the schooled culture; thus its worth is promoted to our learners. Adults' literacy practices may provide one model of enculturation: that is, by witnessing literate individuals engaged in the enterprises of reading and writing, children 'become aware' of literacy. Through processes of cultural learning (Kruger & Tomasello, 1996; Tomasello, Kruger, & Ratner, 1993), or through folk psychological processes of coming to share beliefs, goals and intentions (Olson & Bruner, 1996), learners acquire the habits of mind (Keating, 1996), understanding of school (Pelletier, 1998) and language of learning (Astington & Pelletier, 1996) determined by their teachers, be they mothers, fathers, siblings or educators in the school.

Another way that literacy is promoted in modern cultures is to legislate that children be schooled in literate activity. In Canada and the United States this means that children will be introduced to the alphabetic script in the first few years of schooling. How this is best done remains a topic of considerable theoretical debate (Adams, 1990; Collins, 1997; Stahl & Miller, 1989).

Despite the arguments about how to teach children to read and write, the important point is that generations of children in literate cultures have continued to be motivated to read and write. That is, the majority of children who have been exposed to books, signs and the like understand that interaction with text is something that they are to do, and furthermore, that this activity is worth doing. Individual differences among children in relation to emergence of motivation as well as capability will influence the degree to which this understanding is demonstrated. In general, we argue it is not a question of whether children come to read and write, but rather, how and to what degree they do so. The question of 'how' cannot be as easily answered as the question of 'why'. We know why children begin to engage with print: it is a valued cultural enterprise. What we are still trying to explicate is how children do so. This latter challenge cannot be answered through simplistic notions that claim children learn to read simply by observing and imitating literate models. Indeed, imitating adults is precisely what children try to do; yet they do not learn to read by doing so. Nor can we say that children learn to read simply by being told or shown. Children must build on prior understandings and address the challenges that come with experience and instruction.

Some milestones in this development are clear. For example, children begin to notice text while looking at storybooks. Adults' literate talk about words, 'What does it say?', shows children that meaning is to be found not only in the pictures but in the print as well. Children soon distinguish print from pictures, and to know what can be read and what cannot (Ferreiro, 1994; Ferreiro & Teberosky, 1979/1996). In their landmark book, Ferreiro and Teberosky (1979/1996) detail discrete steps in children's knowledge building about text. For example, early on children may form theories about formal aspects of the graphic system such as the number of characters in a text that are required to make it readable and such as the distinction between punctuation and letters. Gradually children begin 'reading' with pictures and later understand that one can read without pictures. Writing often begins with learning to write one's own name, learning to draw representational pictures, and making marks on a page that 'stand for' something such as an object. It is often at this developmental point that children begin to enter the school system. In order to understand the transition to literacy, that is, children's growing competence with and use of notational systems such as written text, it is critical to know precisely what children must understand about script in order to read and what they actually do understand as they begin schooling.

The distinction between form and meaning

As children enter school they are generally good users of their oral language. Some children come to produce utterances by learning 'names' for things and words for actions which are pieced together in an agent–action or action–object referential format.

Other children come to speak in what is termed a more 'expressive' style, by producing single strings of sounds that contain more pronouns, with relatively fewer nouns and verbs (Nelson, 1973). Oral language may provide the foundation for reading, that is, seeing the written images helps children to connect what is heard with what is written and that words convey meaning (Eliason & Jenkins, 1999). In this view, children need only learn a system of notation that corresponds with the language they already know (Ziegler, 1986, cited in Adams, 1990). Indeed, the prevailing belief about the early stage of literacy is that children recognize that the purpose of print is communication. While this may be true, the added assumption is that as children are already orally competent, they have only to learn how the written word expresses that meaning. While children do initially grasp the relation between oral language and the written word, at first they look for relations between print and meaning, that is, ideas and referents. Only later, when they understand that sounds and letters are related in text, do they begin to look for patterns of relations between what is said and what is written.

Earlier, the claim was made that children must come to understand that script represents the form of what is communicated, and not only the meaning. But as children are entering school, they are not looking for the property of text; they are looking for meaning. This makes sense given their experiences up to this point. What schooling does is to help children to make the transition from looking for meaning to looking for form. Once this understanding has been made, children will learn that the meaning is derived through the form. In fact, they are able to make very good guesses about meaning, employing, in Kress' (1997) terms, 'whatever they have available'. This may include looking at the size or shape of the script, examining the number of discrete parts (letters) or the spaces between the scripted items. In this way, then, children are looking for meaning, but it is not the meaning that is encoded in the form.

Some examples from Ferreiro and Teberosky (1979/1996) will illustrate this point. Children are shown the sentence 'Dad kicks the ball' and asked about the location of specific words in the text. For example, 'Where does it say "Dad"?' One 5-year-old points to the words 'kicks the' because 'it's longer'. A 4-year-old claims that the entire utterance 'Dad kicks the ball' is located in the written word 'Dad', and that the rest of the written words are labels for compatible nouns, that is, words which might be associated with Dad kicking the ball, for example, 'the field', 'the trees', and 'the dirt ground' (1996, p. 127). In reading the word 'boat' (in Spanish 'barco'), children may ask, 'But which part is the back of the boat?' In becoming attentive to the linguistic form, children learn to analyze the script into components, including sound, word and sentence, that they recognize as constituents of their speech. Learning to read, consequently, is a metalinguistic activity (Olson, 1994).

SCHOOLING: THE EARLY STAGES OF LITERACY

Children need to understand first that print represents the linguistic form including the discrete sounds of what is said, not the more global message of what is meant. To reiterate, children first look to text to find meaning, they do not look to find what is said. They are unable to do this until they grasp the notion that print is a representation of form, not meaning *per se*. This is particularly interesting in light of claims that children must show signs of 'reading readiness' prior to formal reading instruction (Wolfgang & Wolfgang, 1999). Granted, reading readiness consists of signs, determined by an educational system, that children are able to begin to read. These signs include knowing what a letter is, what a word is, the function of the space, use of punctuation (Clay, 1979). Indeed, many educational institutions in Canada, the United States and other countries carry out literacy screening tests to determine children's readiness for reading instruction. Readiness in educational terms may include: (1) the ability to match the spoken word to the printed word using one-to-one correspondence, (2) a graphophonic understanding of words, that is, attending to the initial/final sounds, and (3) the concept of a word. Such readiness indicators are misleading in that rather than readiness, these measures indicate an early familiarity with print; children develop an understanding of these signs through literacy and not prior to literacy. Ferreiro (1994) similarly complains that school asks children to learn codes for sounds and to know the mechanical functions of the alphabet before they have learned 'the intelligent use of it'. It is through exposure to and familiarity with print that children come to understand what a word is or what a sentence is.

What is the basis for this claim? First, there exists a rich literature on young children's early understanding of print prior to becoming literate. For example, Ferreiro and Teberosky (1979/1995) describe their detailed analyses of Spanish preschoolers' interpretations of print. They report that children construct their own formal characteristics or rules about print: to be readable, a notation must have a minimum of three letters and must have a variety of characters. Thus a single letter 'a' cannot be read, nor can 'cccc' because they do not fit these implicit rules. Furthermore, when children encounter text with illustrations, the meaning of the illustration is then attributed to the text. Children expect to find similar meanings attached to both picture and text

(1996, p. 164). Initially children may claim that the picture and the text say exactly the same thing. Thus a child looking at a picture of a bear with accompanying text may claim that the print says, 'This is a bear'. Later the text may be seen as a 'label' for the picture, for example, 'Bear'. Children then begin to examine the size or shape of the text to infer meaning: for example, a child may say that a text written in small font could not say 'Big bear' because the size of words is too small.

Second, our own line of research has examined children's developing conception of print in relation to the understanding of one's own and others' mental states (Pelletier, 2002; Pelletier & Astington, 1998; 1999). That is, we have been particularly interested in how Ferreiro's descriptions of children's entry into literacy might be considered in light of other forms of representational understanding, such as mental state understanding. While this research is ongoing, preliminary results with young English-speaking children show remarkable similarity to those obtained by Ferreiro and Teberosky in terms of literacy development between 3 and 6 years of age. Specifically, 3-year-olds attend to the size and shape of symbols in their attempt to infer meaning, whereas by 5 years, after most children have been in kindergarten, children pay more attention to 'letters' and sounds. Almost all of these children are prepared to claim that a string of same letters, such as 'cccc', cannot be a word. Almost all children believe that a nonsense word that looks like a word ('apud') must be a word. Only the fluent readers are able to say that 'apud' is probably not a word, although even they are not sure, since it might be a word for which they do not know the meaning. In another task we examined children's referential understanding of number and words. Children were presented with the phrase 'Ten little monkeys jumping on the bed' and asked, 'What does it say now?' when the last four words had been covered. Younger children typically say that it now says, 'Three little monkeys jumping on the bed'. Older children typically know that only words, not monkeys, have been removed and these children are more likely to say correctly, 'Ten little monkeys'.

One of our more remarkable findings involves the children's own writing. Among other items, children were asked to write, 'Daddy has three hockey sticks'. Three-year-olds generally scribble, occasionally scribbling three separate notations. Older 5-year-olds and many 6-year-olds attempt to use phonological cues to sound out the sentence, sometimes just writing the first letter of each word, 'D H 3 H S'. Older and more advanced 6-year-olds are better able to write longer phonetic versions of this. The interesting responses come from the 4- and 5-year-olds who seem to be in a transition phase between writing symbols that represent objects and writing symbols that represent linguistic form. So, for example, many of these children write 'D H 3 LLL' (L here stands for a picture of a hockey stick) (see Figure 16.1).

In his discussion of the origins of writing, Harris (1986) claimed that the most important step in the invention of full-scale writing systems was the move from token-iterative to emblem-slotting representations, which Olson (1994) characterized as a shift from emblematic to linguistic representation (Olson, 1997). Children's development appears to replicate this development in that these early signs represent events, and the later ones linguistic form.

Figure 16.1 *'Daddy has three hockey sticks'*

Similar findings have been reported by Levin and Tolchinsky-Landsmann (1989) who, following the Piagetian methodology of Ferreiro and Teberosky (1979/1996), found that young Hebrew-speaking children seek referential links between print and object to infer meaning. Children are likely to attend to the graphic features of the written word, such as number, size of signs or shape, accepting a long curvy line to represent 'snake' and many diverse elements to represent 'butterfly'. Later, especially when they engage in their own writing, children begin to develop an understanding that the number of signs (letters) is related to the length of the utterance. That is, a long utterance will have more signs than a shorter one (Levin, Korat, & Amsterdamer, 1996). Further, Levin and Korat (1993) explore the notion of stage-like literacy development. They conclude that children do not pass through discrete stages, but rather, come to understand that written words are determined both by phonological length and by quantitative differences according to their referents. With time, phonological cues win out over referential cues, so they come to recognize that writing represents not the world, but linguistic representations about the world. We may attribute this change to the effect of schooling.

SCHOOLING: LETTER, WORD AND SENTENCE RECOGNITION

Children in a North American culture are currently exposed to a system of schooling that encourages more attention to phonological cues and less to semantic cues. This move back to systematic phonics instruction follows a decade or more of more holistic or 'whole language' approaches to early literacy education. Advocates of the skills-based approach are pleased that the rest of society has caught up with their thinking which was highly acclaimed 30 years ago (e.g. Chall, 1999). While the benefits of phonological approaches have been widely publicized, particularly in Chall's (1967) early work, we are nevertheless cautioned not to completely dismiss the holistic approaches either (Adams, 1990). Adams highlights the need to help children to develop grapheme–phoneme understanding within a meaningful context: 'graphemes and their phonological correspondences are meaningless, perceptually sparse, and piecewise confusable. Because of this, letter–sound pairings are not very easy to remember, and they are very easy to forget or confuse' (1990, p. 239). Adams' report was based on a meta-analysis of reading practices across the US with English speakers. However, these points can well be made for other alphabetic languages such as French. It appears that the Great Debate continues.

Given that young children in a literate society already know a great deal about print before they begin formal schooling, and given that approaches to literacy instruction are not consistently applied, how exactly does schooling contribute to change in literacy development? One answer to this question is that literacy experiences in school, such as talk about the printed alphabet, help children to pay attention to the letters of the alphabet, to the words that are made up of these letters, and to the sentences that are made up of these words. In the process, children are learning to take these concepts (letters, words, sentences) as objects of reflection (Goodman, 1984; Olson, 1994). This enables children to see print as form rather than just as content. Another perspective is Gombrich's metaphor: knowledge becomes a kind of formulary in terms of which any real event is represented (Gombrich, 1960, cited in Olson, 1994). The representation – in this case the printed word, in Gombrich's example the pictured flower in a school science book – becomes the conceptual entity for perceiving and classifying information. Drawings, maps, words become conceptual models; it is through them that we perceive the world. The flower in the school science book with all its labeled parts looks nothing like the real flower. It is only an artifact or a representation that permits reflection about the real flower. Print similarly is an artifact or a representation, one that permits reflection. Schooling treats language as an artifact (Olson, 1984); it uses written language to teach about oral language, for example, to explain what the word 'word' means.

Additionally, schooling builds on and exploits children's 'explanatory biases' (Keil & Silberstein, 1996) so that children learn to connect their own understandings with what is guided by instructional practice. While Keil promotes the study of natural kinds using this methodology, the same case can be made for the study of literacy. Earlier work has claimed that emergent readers' and writers' knowledge of print conventions enables them to understand the concept of a word, left-to-right progression, spaces between words, that letters and words have uniform sizes and that there are predictable patterns in print (Heller, 1991). This new understanding is that these concepts are entirely dependent upon the ability to analyze and reflect on the properties of speech that these patterns in print represent, such as words and sentences. Smith adds: 'Learning [the] mechanics would be pointless and difficult unless a child had already developed a foundation of insights into the nature and functions of written language' (1984, p. 143).

Involvement with reading is not the only way that children may arrive at these metalinguistic insights. Olson (1994) suggested that through both oral games and literate activities with parents, many young children acquire the metalinguistic concepts necessary for literacy prior to formal schooling. Other children, who do not experience such word games and literacy events at home, must learn this as concepts at school. Children's knowledge of the metalinguistic concepts expressed by the terms 'sentence', 'word', 'letter', 'sound' is related to their progress in learning to read and write. Children who are explicitly taught how to talk learn not only how to talk but also how to talk about talk (Olson, 1984; Yaden, 1986). While some children are first taught by parents, others are first taught in school; children's implicit understanding of language acquired through use becomes explicit when it, the language, becomes the object of discourse (Nelson, 1991). The environment 'scaffolds' the child's implicit understandings, gradually bringing them into explicit awareness. The environment may be an educational system or a parent–child system (Nelson, 1996). Knowledge that exists in the environment is incorporated into the mind of the child. One explanation is that this occurs through 'participatory interactions' (1996, p. 19): children participate in activities without necessarily having explicit understanding of those activities, but through participation, children become aware of the activity as an object of reflection. We suggest that this is the case for language use. Critically, children must come to see how linguistic terms map onto their own experience of spoken language, whether they do so by talking about talk or explicitly through talking about text. As children move through the grades in school, formal spelling and word study provide direct teaching of what to attend to in one's own speech. Reading provides the vocabulary to be studied; writing provides the means to elaborate word knowledge (Henderson, 1992).

Many preschoolers learn to recite the alphabet prior to school entry. Based on previous research that claims knowledge of alphabet letters to be a predictor of future reading performance, Treiman, Tincoff, and Richmond-Welty (1997) examined whether children pick up understanding of the phonological structure of letter names while learning the alphabet. From the results of two experiments, these authors concluded that preschool children have some knowledge of the vowel sounds that occur naturally when saying letter names (for example that 'gi' is a letter but that 'ig' is not). Furthermore, young children have knowledge of the phonological structure of the letter names. The authors claim that alphabet learning sensitizes children to the phonological aspects of letters and to the metalinguistic term 'letters' so that children are able to talk about the relation between sounds and letters.

WHAT IS A WORD?

Studies of young children's understanding of the metalinguistic term 'word' generally show this to be a difficult concept for those who are pre-literate (Ferreiro & Vernon, 1992; Homer & Olson, 1999). In other work we have found that 3-, 4-, 5- and 6-year-olds are able to respond to the question 'Is this a word?' and that they have clear notions about whether or not something is a word. Younger children tend to confound metalinguistic terms such as letters, numbers and words, whereas older children are more able to correctly use these terms. For example, 3- or 4-year-olds may say something is a word 'because it has words in it', whereas 5- and 6-year-olds are more likely to say something is a word 'because it has letters in it' (Pelletier, 2002). Interestingly, children's first concept of a word is as something written, not as something spoken (Francis, 1975).

In order for children to understand the metalinguistic notion of a sentence, they first need to understand how to segment an utterance into word-like units. We know that prior to 5 years of age, even children exposed to alphabetic scripts do not use 'words' to segment their written products. The number and type of marks they use do not reflect the segmental structure of the sentence (Tolchinsky & Teberosky, 1998). Evidence from kindergarten and grade 1 classrooms clearly demonstrates that children do not segment sentences into words in their own writing. Often, children employ the 'scripta continua' formula in their early attempts to produce extended text (see chapters in Pontecorvo, 1997). For example, Claire Blanche-Benveniste (1997) highlights the difference between words in utterances and words in 'the system' organized around print. Words in utterance cannot be separated; however, words in print can be treated in isolation. In the same volume, Hartmut Günther (1997) provides a historical account of the move from writing on papyrus to long scrolls and finally to readable pages. He suggests that children's lack of page sense in their early writing parallels the historical development of writing.

Gradually historically, and in children's writing, written texts become adapted to the needs of the reader. As children gain more experience with the system of reading and writing, they begin to segment into syllables or words, sometimes separating the lexical units by a period or a dash. To summarize this varied body of research, it seems fair to conclude that only through experience with reading and writing within a given culture do children come to understand the concept of letter, word and sentence and how these concepts represent the implicit properties of speech. At every level of analysis, writing serves as a model for thinking about speech (Olson, 1994).

SCHOOLING: THE LATER STAGES OF LITERACY

Jeanne Chall (1983) once divided the child's school years into two literacy-based periods: 'learning to read', the first three years; and 'reading to learn', the remainder. That is, from the period of early kindergarten until about the end of the second grade in school, reading instruction time is devoted to teaching children the discrete skills associated with learning to read. These skills involve the three cueing systems of phonology, semantics and syntax. As children become able to read independently, often by the second grade in school, reading becomes a means to learning. Reading enables one to learn about content such as history or geography, as well as about form, the understanding of writing itself. At this stage, children are no longer learning to read *per se*, but rather are reading to learn. But since literacy is not definable by a single skill that improves with age (Snow et al., 1991), it will be evident in different ways for children of different ages. Nevertheless, there are some generalizations that cut across ages and stages of literacy development; these are discussed in the following sections of this chapter. Specifically, literacy and literacy development play three important roles in children's subsequent intellectual development in addition to providing access to a broad range of information (Anderson et al., 1985). All three are metalinguistic: thinking about words, about sentences and about genre.

Thinking about Words

Vocabulary development is, as is well known, the best correlate of school achievement. Biemiller (1999), for example, provides evidence that reading comprehension in particular is determined by the child's vocabulary development. Vocabulary knowledge is not merely the ability to produce and understand utterances employing a wide diversity of lexical items. Rather, it is knowledge of the relations between words, including synonymy, antonymy, paraphrase and the like – knowledge which is derivative from thinking about words rather than thinking about things, that is, a form of metalinguistic knowledge. For example, children's growing ability to substitute one word for another, such as 'qualm' for 'uneasiness' or 'fluid' for 'liquid', indicates a heightened understanding of words as linguistic properties rather than as properties of objects. Literacy is an essential means for turning language from use into an object of reflection.

Thinking about Sentences

Sentences are linguistic forms used in generating utterances with communicative intention. Sentences, then, are linguistic abstractions. Utterances are what we use in ordinary discourse. Sentences are not only linguistic abstractions, they are abstractions sponsored to a large extent by our experiences with literacy. It is in reading and writing that one learns to divide discourse into complete sentences, to employ punctuation, and even to 'parse' sentences into grammatical categories. Such strategies are important to learning the official standard language of bureaucratic institutions such as law, science and literature, and are therefore of central concern to the school. Although critics are correct in insisting that meaning is often lost in the attempt at analysis, it is nonetheless important that in the later school years students understand the important relations between form and meaning, relations that make both logic and metaphor possible. Children's growing competence in understanding the relations between form and meaning shows up in at least three ways: the recognition of the notion of paraphrase, the recognition of the say–mean distinction, and the recognition of logical necessity.

In an early study, Robinson, Goelman, and Olson (1983) found that, if preschool children knew the thoughts or wants of a speaker who then expressed that desire by means of an ambiguous statement such as 'Give me the blue flower' – when in fact there were two blue flowers and the speaker wanted the larger of the two – they tended to report that the speaker had said 'Give me the large blue flower'. This was taken as evidence that these children conflated what was said with what was meant. Other studies (summarized in Winner, 1988) have shown that, although children recognize falsity and deception from about 4 years of age, they continue to have difficulty with sarcasm and irony. Therefore, although they may recognize an ironic remark – saying 'Beautiful' when someone spills milk – as false, they fail to recognize that the remark is intentionally false and intends the listener to think that the act was far from beautiful. Literacy heightens this distinction.

This system of understanding is greatly elaborated when students acquire the more complex set of speech act and mental state concepts and terms that are so important in talking about text. Verbs such as 'say' and 'think' are part of ordinary language. But in talking about text it becomes important to characterize more explicitly how one is to interpret a statement. Thus, 'to affirm' is quite different from 'to hypothesize' although both are expressions of one's 'attitude' to a statement. These more complex forms of saying and thinking make up what may be called the Literate Standard language, borrowed as they are from scholarly Latin (see Table 16.1). Learning to be literate is, in part, learning to think about complex intentions and interpretations.

Thinking about Genre

A third framework for understanding schooling and the development of literacy is to consider 'genre' as modes of thought. Genres can be thought of as

Table 16.1 *Date of first known use in English of some speech act and mental state verbs.*

Germanic		Latinate	
believe	OE[1]	assert	1604
know	OE	assume	1436
mean	OE	claim	ME
say	OE	concede	1632
tell	OE	conclude	ME
think	OE	confirm	ME
understand	early ME[2]	contradict	1570
		criticize	1649
		declare	ME
		define	ME
		deny	ME
		discover	ME
		doubt	ME
		explain	1513
		hypothesize	1596 (Greek)
		imply	ME
		infer	1526
		interpret	ME
		observe	late ME
		predict	1546
		prove	ME
		remember	ME
		suggest	1526

[1] OE = Old English (before 1150).
[2] ME = Middle English (1150–1350) (late ME 1350–1450).

Source: *The Oxford English Dictionary*; from Olson and Astington (1990).

categories of narrative that help readers to make sense of text (Feldman & Kalmar, 1996); without a framework of genre, narrative events would be open to misinterpretation. Text may even be unintelligible. Consider receiving a joke via e-mail. Without an understanding of the genre, the recipient might react in ways in which the sender had never intended. Apart from the traditional literary genres known to the educated minority, other genres are implicit in the daily lives of children in school. Feldman and Kalmar suggest that teacher–student discourse involves a special classroom genre. Yet teachers may fail to make this genre explicit and recognizable. Consequently, children may not be aware of the genre they are dealing with in school and the particular requirements for dealing with it. Whereas middle-class children are exposed to a greater range of genres at home including this classroom genre, other children may have to learn this special use of language at school if they are to learn it at all. It has been shown, for example, that children from low-income families perform poorly in reading achievement, in contrast to their middle-class peers (Biemiller, 1999; Snow et al., 1991), a difficulty that may be attributed to limited exposure to school and literate genre. Snow et al. (1991) attribute a significant part of this finding to differences in the discourse and literacy environment of the home, mother's educational expectations, income, and parent–school involvement. Furthermore, children from middle-class homes are more likely to come to school with a discourse of mind and mental representations, of thoughts, beliefs and reasons for believing and other theory of mind concepts, than are children from less educated families (e.g. Astington & Jenkins, 1995; Astington & Pelletier, 1996). An important function of schooling is to teach the special genre for thinking and talking about language and mind. Forms of instruction are based on assumptions about the learners' minds (Bruner, 1996a). Similarly learning is affected by the learner's notion of the teacher's mind; by directing children's attention to the processes of thinking, teachers facilitate children's understanding of language itself (Astington & Olson, 1990). In particular, the elaboration of metacognitive and metalinguistic terms raises consciousness of classroom discourse. This in turn contributes to an awareness of discourse genre.

To be able to relate what is being read to knowledge previously acquired requires automaticity in making letter–sound correspondence, recognizing root words as well as the complex rules regarding emphasis in written language. To be able to write competently requires one to consider different audiences and different genres, for example, modifying their language for particular readers (Snow et al., 1991). Thus, an awareness of genre contributes both to understanding of the written word and to informed production of the written word.

Understanding genre is essential to recovering the author's intentions, for example, to know the difference between an autobiographical and a fictional account. When reading, the child comes to understand not only the author's words, but also the author's intentions. When writing, the child must express her own intentions, while simultaneously considering the reader's perspective, whether giving an autobiographical account or writing a fictional narrative. Thus the experience of literacy in school fosters both cognitive and metacognitive understanding (Francis, 1987), that is, understanding of the content and understanding of the authorial intention. Furthermore, explicit talk about genre in the context of classroom activity, including making marked distinctions between, for example, math talk and history talk (Feldman & Kalmar, 1996), gives children clearer notions about 'core facts' as well as opportunities to engage in talk about core facts. In Bruner's terms, genres represent both events and ways of thinking and talking about those events, what they 'stand for' (Bruner, 1996b, p. 98). For Olson, written genres represent both the utterances themselves and the ways in which we 'take' utterances. Consciousness of the 'very words' in relation to intended meaning is 'at the heart of literate thinking' (Olson, 1996, p. 149). Knowing the difference between an utterance and its literal meaning requires an understanding of the 'very words' – the difference between what is meant and what is said, or inference/content. Olson cites Luria's example of the following syllogism: 'In the far North, where there is snow, all bears are white. Novaya Zemlya is in the far North and there is always snow there. What colour are the bears there?' One non-literate subject responded, 'I don't know . . . There are different sorts of bears.' In this case, the subject was not treating the 'very words' of the text as a logical premise, but rather the conversational import of such an utterance. Without an understanding of this literalist genre, the subject is unable to draw inferences from the words alone; instead he falls back on his beliefs about the content. An understanding of text as a fixed entity permits one to treat it according to its linguistic properties, and not only according to its putative reference. It is this aspect of genre that children must come to know in the decontextualized prose of the classroom.

Societal Literacy

As was mentioned at the outset, in acquiring these specialized forms of literate knowledge, students are learning to cope with the demands of modern bureaucratic societies. Elwart (2001) has advanced the concept of 'societal literacy' to describe the kind of literacy that is embedded in large-scale institutions of a modern society. Law, commerce and science are all institutions based on access to and use of written documents and written procedures such as laws, contracts and wills, and the appropriate institutional structures for enforcing them. A 'literate mentality' is the specialized mode of thought required to participate in and to understand a society organized, in part, around these complex institutional forms with their historical, written archival resources. Each institution has its decisive ways in which documents are formed, consulted, interpreted and applied. Each formulates and implements explicit procedures for ordering activities by means of rules, norms, formal procedures or algorithms set out in codes, documents and manuals. Rules are of no importance without institutions for enforcing them. Personal honor will do in small-scale interactions; the full weight of the law is required for others. Literate minds in literate societies involve a new consciousness not only of language but also of forms of argument, understanding evidence, and the appropriateness of genre to economics, law, science and literature. Formal education is the primary means for introducing learners to the specialized competencies required to participate in such documentary, text-based institutions.

References

Adams, M.J. (1990). *Beginning to read: Thinking and learning about print*. Cambridge, MA: MIT Press.

Anderson, R., Hiebert, E., Scott, J., & Wilkinson, I. (1985). *Becoming a nation of readers: The report of the commission on reading*. Champaign, IL: Center for the Study of Reading.

Astington, J., & Jenkins, J. (1995). Theory of mind and social understanding. *Cognition and Emotion*, 9, 151–165.

Astington, J., & Olson, D. (1990). Metacognitive and metalinguistic language: Learning to talk about thought. *Applied Psychology*, 39 (1), 77–87.

Astington, J.W., & Pelletier, J. (1996). The language of mind: Its relation to teaching and learning. In D. Olson & N. Torrance (eds), *Handbook of psychology in education: New models of learning, teaching and schooling* (pp. 593–620). Oxford: Basil Blackwell.

Bamburger, J. (1991). *The mind behind the musical ear: How children develop musical intelligence*. Cambridge, MA: Harvard University Press.

Bamburger, J. (1996). Turning musical theory on its ear. *International Journal of Computers for Mathematical Learning*, 1, 33–55.

Biemiller, A. (1999). *Language and reading success*. Cambridge, MA: Brookline.

Blanche-Benveniste, C. (1997). The unit of written and oral language. In C. Pontecorvo (ed.), *Writing development: An interdisciplinary view* (pp. 21–45). Philadelphia: Benjamin.

Bruner, J. (1996a). Frames for thinking: Ways of making meaning. In D. Olson & N. Torrance (eds), *Modes of thought: Explorations in culture and cognition*. New York: Cambridge University Press.

Bruner, J. (1996b). *The culture of education*. Cambridge, MA: Harvard University Press.

Chall, J. (1967). *Learning to read: The great debate. An inquiry into the science, art, and ideology of old and new methods of teaching children to read*. New York: McGraw-Hill.

Chall, J. (1983). *Stages of reading development*. New York: McGraw-Hill.

Chall, J. (1999). Some thoughts on reading research: Revisiting the first-grade studies. *Reading Research Quarterly*, 34 (1), 8–10.

Clay, M. (1979). *The early detection of reading difficulties: A diagnostic survey with recovery procedures*. Exeter, NH: Heinemann.

Collins, J. (1997). How Johnny should read. *Time Magazine*.

Eliason, C., & Jenkins, L. (1999). *A practical guide to early childhood curriculum* (6th edn). Upper Saddle River, NJ: Prentice-Hall.

Elwart, G. (2001). Societal literacy: Writing culture and development. In D.R. Olson & N. Torrance (eds), *The making of literate societies* (pp. 54–67). Malden, MA: Blackwell.

Feldman, C., & Kalmar, D. (1996). Some educational implications of genre-based mental models: The interpretive cognition of text understanding. In D. Olson & N. Torrance (eds), *Handbook of psychology in education: New models of learning, teaching and schooling* (pp. 434–460). Oxford: Basil Blackwell.

Ferreiro, E. (1994). Literacy development: Construction and reconstruction. In Dina Tirosh (ed.), *Implicit and explicit knowledge: An educational approach* (pp. 169–180). Norwood, NJ: Ablex.

Ferreiro, E., & Teberosky, A. (1979/1996). *Literacy before schooling*. Portsmouth, NH: Heinemann.

Ferreiro, E., & Vernon, S. (1992). La distinction de palabra/nombre en ninos de 4 y 5 anos (The differentiation between word/name in four to five year olds). *Infancia–y–Aprendizaje*, 58, 15–28.

Francis, H. (1975). *Language in childhood: Form and function in language learning*. New York: St Martin's Press.

Francis, H. (1987). Cognitive implications of learning to read. *Interchange*, 19 (1–2), 97–108.

Gardner, H. (1999). *The disciplined mind: What all students should understand*. New York: Simon & Schuster.

Gombrich, E. (1960). *Art and illusion: A study in the psychology of pictorial representation*. New York: Bollingen/Pantheon.

Goodman, Y. (1984). The development of initial literacy. In H. Goelman, A. Oberg, & F. Smith (eds), *Awakening to literacy*. Victoria, BC: Heinemann.

Günther, H. (1997). Aspects of a history of written language. In C. Pontecorvo (ed.), *Writing development: An interdisciplinary view* (pp. 129–147). Philadelphia: Benjamins.

Harris, R. (1986). *Signs of writing*. New York: Routledge.

Heller, M. (1991). *Reading–writing connections: From theory to practice*. New York: Longman.

Henderson, E. (1992). The interface of lexical competence and knowledge of written words. In S. Templeton & D. Bear (eds), *Development of orthographic knowledge and the foundations of literacy: A memorial Festschrift for Edmund H. Henderson* (pp. 1–30). Hillsdale, NJ: Erlbaum.

Homer, B., & Olson, D. (1999). Literacy and children's conception of words. *Written Language and Literacy*, 2, 113–137.

Innis, H. (1950). *Empire and communications*. Oxford: Oxford University Press.

Johns, A. (1998). *The nature of the book: print and knowledge in the making*. Chicago, IL: University of Chicago Press.

Karmiloff–Smith, A. (1992). *Beyond modularity: A developmental perspective on cognitive science*. Cambridge, MA: Bradford Books/MIT Press.

Keating, D. (1996). *Habits of mind for a learning society: Educating for human development*. In D. Olson & N. Torrance (eds), *Handbook of psychology in education: New models of learning, teaching and schooling* (pp. 461–482). Oxford: Basil Blackwell.

Keil, F., & Silberstein, C. (1996). Schooling and the acquisition of theoretical knowledge. In D. Olson & N. Torrance (eds), *Handbook of psychology in education: New models of learning, teaching and schooling* (pp. 621–645). Oxford: Basil Blackwell.

Kress, G. (1997). *Before writing: Rethinking the paths to literacy*. New York: Routledge.

Kruger, A., & Tomasello, M. (1996). Cultural learning and learning culture. In D. Olson & N. Torrance (eds), *Handbook of psychology in education: New models of learning, teaching and schooling* (pp. 369–387). Oxford: Basil Blackwell.

Levin, I., & Korat, O. (1993). Sensitivity to phonological, morphological, and semantic cues in early reading and writing in Hebrew. *Merrill-Palmer Quarterly*, 39 (2), 213–232.

Levin, I., Korat, O., & Amsterdamer, P. (1996). Emergent writing among Israeli kindergartners: Cross-linguistic commonalities and Hebrew-specific issues. In G. Rijlaarsdam, H. van den Bergh, & M. Couzijn (eds), *Theories, models and methodology in writing research*. Amsterdam: Amsterdam University Press.

Levin, I., & Tolchinsky-Landsmann, L. (1989). Becoming literate: Referential and phonetic strategies in early reading and writing. *International Journal of Behavioral Development*, 12 (3), 369–384.

Liben, L. (ed.) (1981). *Spatial representation and behavior across the life span: Theory and application*. New York: Academic.

Nelson, K. (1973). *Structure and strategy in learning to talk. Monographs of the Society for Research in Child Development*, Vol. 38, nos 1–2, serial 149.

Nelson, K. (1991). Remembering and telling: A developmental story. *Journal of Narrative and Life History*, 1 (2–3), 109–127.

Nelson, K. (1996). *Language in cognitive development: The emergence of the mediated mind*. New York: Cambridge University Press.

Olson, D. (1984). See! Jumping! Some oral language antecedents of literacy. In H. Goelman, A. Oberg, & F. Smith (eds), *Awakening to literacy* (pp. 185–192). Victoria, BC: Heinemann.

Olson, D. (1994). *The world on paper*. New York: Cambridge University Press.

Olson, D. (1996). Literate mentalities. In D. Olson & N. Torrance (eds), *Modes of thought: Explorations in culture and cognition*. New York: Cambridge University Press.

Olson, D. (1997). Critical thinking: Learning to talk about text. In G. Phye (ed.), *Handbook of academic learning: Construction of knowledge* (pp. 493–510). San Diego, CA: Academic.

Olson, D., & Astington, J. (1990). Talking about text: How literacy contributes to thought. *Journal of Pragmatics*, 14, 705–721.

Olson, D., & Bruner, J. (1996). Folk psychology and folk pedagogy. In D. Olson & N. Torrance (eds), *Handbook of psychology in education: New models of learning, teaching and schooling* (pp. 9–27). Oxford: Basil Blackwell.

Pelletier, J. (1998). Children's understanding of school in English first language and French immersion kindergartens. *The Canadian Modern Language Review*, 55 (2), 239–259.

Pelletier, J. (2002). Children's 'clever' misunderstandings about print. In J. Brockmeier, M. Wang, & D. Olson (eds), *Literacy, narrative & culture* (pp. 245–265). Surrey: Curzon.

Pelletier, J., & Astington, J. (1998). Representation of mind and print. Poster presented at the annual meetings of the Jean Piaget Society, Chicago, July.

Pelletier, J., & Astington, J. (1999). Theory of mind and representational understanding in early childhood. Paper presented at the annual meetings of the American Educational Research Association, Montreal, Quebec, Canada, April.

Pontecorvo, Clotilde (ed.) (1997). *Writing development: An interdisciplinary view*. Philadelphia: Benjamins.

Popper, K. (1972). *Objective knowledge: An evolutionary approach*. Oxford: Clarendon.

Robinson, E., Goelman, A., & Olson, D. (1983). Children's relationship between expressions (what was said) and intentions (what was meant). *British Journal of Developmental Psychology*, 1, 75–86.

Sampson, G. (1985). *Writing systems*. Stanford, CA: Stanford University Press.

Shankweiler, D., & Liberman, I. (1972). Misreading: A search for causes. In J. Kavanaugh & I. Mattingly (eds), *Language by ear and language by eye: The relationship between speech and reading* (pp. 293–317). Cambridge, MA: MIT Press.

Smith, F. (1984). Literacy and cognition. In H. Goelman, A. Oberg, & F. Smith (eds), *Awakening to literacy* (pp. xiii–xiv). Victoria, BC: Heinemann.

Smith, F. (1990). *To think*. New York: Teachers' College Press, Columbia University.

Snow, C., Barnes, W., Chandler, J., Goodman, I., & Hemphill, L. (1991). *Unfulfilled expectations: Home and school influences on literacy*. Cambridge, MA: Harvard University Press.

Stahl, S., & Miller, P. (1989). Whole language and language experience approaches for beginning reading: A quantitative research synthesis. *Review of Educational Research*, 59 (1), 87–116.

Tolchinsky, L., & Teberosky, A. (1998). The development of word segmentation and writing in two scripts. *Cognitive Development*, 13, 1–24.

Tomasello, M., Kruger, A., & Ratner, H. (1993). Cultural learning. *Behavioral and Brain Sciences*, 16, 495–552.

Treiman, R., Tincoff, R., & Richmond-Welty, D. (1997). Beyond zebra: Preschoolers' knowledge about letters. *Applied Psycholinguistics*, 18, 391–409.

Vygotsky, L. (1986). *Thought and language* (rev. and ed. A. Kizulin). Cambridge, MA: MIT Press.

Winner, E. (1988). *The point of words*. Cambridge, MA: Harvard University Press.

Wolfgang, C., & Wolfgang, M. (1999). *School for young children: Developmentally appropriate practices*. Needham Heights, MA: Allyn & Bacon.

Yaden, D. (1986). Reading research in metalinguistic awareness: A classification of findings according to focus and methodology. In D. Yaden & S. Templeton (eds), *Metalinguistic awareness: Conceptualizing what it means to read and write*. Portsmouth, NH: Heinemann.

Ziegler, E. (1986). Why our children aren't reading. Foreword to R. Flesch, *Why Johnny can't read* (2nd edn, pp. viii–ix). New York: Harper & Row.

17

Memory and Knowledge Development

WOLFGANG SCHNEIDER
and
DAVID BJORKLUND

Although scientific research on memory development has nearly as long a tradition as the scientific study of psychology, the majority of studies have been conducted within the past three decades, stimulated by a shift away from behaviorist theories toward cognitive theories, a shift that has emphasized information-processing considerations (Schneider & Pressley, 1997). Those who are not specialists in memory development can easily be overwhelmed by the extent and diversity of the literature. It is impossible to discuss the great range of relevant topics in this chapter, so we shall restrict our overview of memory development to a discussion of major trends in the field, as we see them, thereby focusing on the age period between childhood and adolescence (i.e. approximately ages 5 to 15). Before getting to the bulk of research carried out with children in this age range, we first briefly explain our conceptualization of 'knowledge' and its relation to memory development, and then shortly summarize the state of the art regarding early signs of (verbal) memory.

'Knowledge': Problems with a Fuzzy Concept

One of the major factors in the development of memory, we believe, is children's acquisition of knowledge. Generally speaking, the term 'knowledge' refers to information about various aspects of the world. Unfortunately, numerous conceptualizations of knowledge can be found in both the developmental and educational literatures (Dochy & Alexander, 1995; Schneider & Weinert, 1990). The long list of knowledge components includes terms such as semantic knowledge, episodic knowledge, conceptual knowledge, prior knowledge, the knowledge base, content knowledge, and domain-specific knowledge. Given this inconsistency in terminology, it is understandable that even experts in the field get confused about possible denotations and connotations of the concept. The definitions found in the literature suggest that world knowledge, semantic knowledge, and conceptual knowledge are perceived as synonymous concepts, and that the same is true for terms such as prior knowledge, content knowledge, domain-specific knowledge, and the knowledge base. However, how do these two classes of terms relate to each other?

The common denominator of all these definitions is, we consider, the belief that knowledge should be conceptualized in terms of information in a modified network model of semantic memory (see Bjorklund, 1987; Bjorklund, Muir-Broaddus, & Schneider, 1990). The term 'semantic memory' refers to a lexicon of words, rules, and concepts that builds up in the brain from early childhood on. Each item in semantic memory is defined by a node that is connected to other nodes. In addition to connections with other items (concepts), each node has features that characterize it. In development, the number of nodes changes, as does the number and strength of connections among items. Also, the number of features associated with an item changes (increases) as a function of everyday experiences. Terms such as 'world knowledge' or 'conceptual knowledge' concern the total amount of information stored in an individual's semantic network. When referring to a 'domain' of knowledge, we refer to semantic knowledge that is highly interrelated, such as knowledge of the game of tennis or knowledge in the fields of physics or medicine. It can be shown that experts in a given domain retrieve information from a semantic network that contains an enormous number of nodes for that domain and also strong and frequent interconnections among these nodes. As shown below, the richness of the knowledge base and the 'density' of the semantic network will significantly influence the speed and accuracy of memory processes related to this domain.

Note that the picture can be totally different when these experts remember information from domains about which they have little knowledge. In such cases, there are fewer nodes and interrelations among nodes, which means that information-processing speed and accuracy of memory performance may be considerably lower. Accordingly, information about the sheer amount of available 'world knowledge' a person possesses may prove less predictive of memory performance than information about the person's specific knowledge about a particular domain. For the purpose of this chapter, it is important to keep in mind that a single set of encoding and storage processes builds up the semantic network, indicating that world knowledge and domain-specific knowledge are based on the same mechanisms.

The Memory System

Explicit versus Implicit Memory

Memory can refer both to the contents of one's mind (one's memories) and to the processes responsible for bringing information to awareness. Two broad distinctions for the contents of memory have been made: *explicit* or *declarative memory*, and *implicit* or *procedural memory* (sometime known as nondeclarative memory). Explicit memory refers to memory with awareness, or the conscious recollection of facts and events, and can be tested directly using free recall, cued recall, and recognition tests. Implicit memory refers to memory without awareness, and is reflected in memory for routinized skills (i.e. procedural memory), priming, and operant as well as classical conditioning. Explicit memory is composed of two different types of interacting systems, *episodic* and *semantic* memory. Episodic memory corresponds to a person's record of past experiences, whereas semantic memory refers to our world knowledge, that is, knowledge of language, rules, and concepts (Tulving, 1985).

The distinction between implicit and explicit memory is more than one of conceptual convenience. There is evidence indicating that these two memory systems are neurologically distinct, as illustrated by the performance of patients with specific types of brain damage (e.g. Schacter, 1992). For example, patients with damage to the hippocampus are unable to transfer new, explicit information to their long-term memories, but can retain implicitly acquired information. In one study, a patient with hippocampal damage was given a mirror-drawing task over several days, in which he had to trace figures while watching his hand in a mirror. Although his performance on this task was quite poor initially, it improved after several days, although he had no recollection of ever performing the task before. The improvement over repeated testings is a reflection of implicit (procedural) memory, whereas his failure to recall previously performing the task is a reflection of a lack of explicit memory (Milner, 1964).

The focus of this chapter will be on children's explicit memory although, as we'll see, the content of children's semantic memories, or their knowledge bases, influences greatly what and how children remember. It is also important to keep in mind that explicit and implicit memory reflect different memory systems, and as such, we should not be surprised if their development follows different paths.

The Short-Term Store and Working Memory

Conventionally, the memory system has been viewed as consisting of two related but distinct components. The *short-term store* (STS) holds small amounts of information (7 ± 2 for adults) for relatively brief periods of time (seconds). The short-term store has been referred to as the contents of consciousness, for information held in the STS can become available to awareness, and we can implement deliberate strategies to help solve problems or to facilitate memory. The *long-term store* (LTS), in contrast, is the permanent repository of information, and is presumed infinite with respect to how much it can hold and for how long. What factors are responsible for getting information into the LTS, and, most important, getting it out when needed? Most of this chapter will involve age differences relating to the long-term store. However, developmental differences in the capacity and processes involved in the STS greatly influence most other aspects of cognitive performance (including retrieval from the LTS) (see Case, 1992; Kee, 1994; Siegel, 1993), and we will discuss some of these issues in this section.

Age differences in the capacity of the short-term store (how much information children can retain in it) has traditionally been assessed by *memory-span tasks*, in which participants must repeat, in exact order, a series of rapidly presented items (usually at a rate of about one per second). Age differences in digit span (memory span using digits as stimuli) are very stable, to the extent that digit-span tasks are used on both the Stanford–Binet and Wechsler intelligence tests. In an extensive review of the literature, Dempster (1981) reported that the memory span of 2-year-olds is about two items; of 5-year-olds about four items; of 7-year-olds about five items; and of 9-year-olds about six items. The average memory span of adults is about seven items. Tests of working memory are similar to memory-span tasks in that participants must remember a series of items in exact order, but they are embedded in an additional task in which participants must transform information held in the STS (e.g. Case, 1985; de Ribaupierre & Bailleux, 1995; Siegel & Ryan, 1989). For instance, children may be given a set of sentences for which they must add the final word (e.g. 'Sometimes we see tigers at the . . .'). After hearing a number of such sentences, they are asked to recall the final word from each sentence in the order they were presented (Siegel & Ryan, 1988). In general, working-memory tasks show the same developmental pattern as memory-span tasks, although the absolute level of performance on the working-memory tasks is usually about two items less than for memory-span tasks (Case, 1985).

Knowledge Base Differences and Age Differences in the STS

Despite the robustness of age differences in memory span, research over the past 25 years has clearly demonstrated that differences in what children know about the task stimuli (i.e. their *knowledge base*) contribute significantly to performance on memory-span tasks (e.g. Chi, 1978; Dempster, 1977; Schneider et al., 1993). As we mentioned previously, knowledge base refers to the long-term representation of world knowledge. Although knowledge base includes aspects of semantic memory (e.g. how language terms are defined and related to other language terms), procedural memory (e.g. rules for playing chess, baseball), and episodic memory (e.g. declarative 'facts' about any topic), it can best be defined in terms of information in a modified semantic memory network (see Bjorklund, 1987 and discussion above). Children use what they know about typical events (e.g. what happens when one goes to a fast-food restaurant) or about things (e.g. what a dog looks like and how it behaves) to make sense of experiences (e.g. a visit to a new restaurant or an encounter with an unfamiliar animal) and later to remember those experiences.

The effects of knowledge base on memory span has been most impressively illustrated by contrasting the performance of chess-expert and chess-novice children and adults for chess positions on a board and for other, nonchess, stimuli (usually digits). In this research, chess-expert children recall well the positions of chess pieces in game-possible positions on a chess board, far in excess of nonexpert adults. Chess-experts' performance on digit-span tasks, however, is much lower, and usually comparable to that of nonexpert agemates (e.g. Chi, 1978; Roth, 1983; Schneider et al., 1993). When generalizing these results to the larger population of children, the robust age differences in memory span can be attributed to the correlated differences in knowledge base. Older children usually know more about the things they are asked to remember (e.g. digits, words) than younger children, and this age difference in knowledge translates to age differences in memory span (see Dempster, 1985 for an extended discussion).

Capacity Differences in the STS

Despite these findings, there is recent evidence of some developmental differences in the absolute capacity of the STS. Cowan et al. (1999) evaluated age differences in the *span of apprehension*, a term coined by Sperling (1960) to refer to the amount of information that people can attend to at a single time or the number of items that people can keep in mind at any one time. Span of apprehension can be assessed only when factors such as focused attention, knowledge for the target items, and encoding strategies can be eliminated, factors that are not eliminated on memory-span or working-memory tasks. Sperling reported that adults had a span of apprehension of about four items. In the study by Cowan et al. (1999), 7- and 10-year-old children and adults played a computer game and heard a series of digits presented through earphones that they were told to ignore. Participants were occasionally and without warning signaled to recall, in exact order, the most recently presented set of digits they had heard. Because participants were not explicitly attending to the digits, it is unlikely that they were using any encoding strategies to remember them, making the task an appropriate one for assessing span of apprehension. Cowan and his colleagues reported that the average span of apprehension increased significantly with age (2.41, 3.13, and 3.56 digits for the 7-year-old, 10-year-old, and adult participants, respectively), and interpreted these differences as reflecting a true developmental difference in the capacity of the short-term store. Although factors such as knowledge base may influence performance on memory-span tasks, age differences in how much children and adults can apprehend during a brief period serve as the foundation for age differences on memory-span tasks.

Speed of Processing and Age Differences in the STS

The effect of knowledge on memory span seems to be exerted via speed of processing. Knowledge that is more elaboratively represented in the long-term store can be activated more quickly. As a result, it requires less time to process, and more information can be retrieved and retained before a child reaches his or her capacity limit (e.g. Bjorklund, Muir-Broaddus, & Schneider, 1990; Case, 1985; Kail, 1991; Kail & Salthouse, 1994). Consistent with this perspective, Dempster (1981), in an extensive review of the extant literature, concluded that ease, or speed, of item identification was the only factor needed to account for developmental differences in memory-span performance.

One model of working memory that places substantial emphasis on speed of processing is that presented by Baddeley, Hitch, and their colleagues (e.g. Baddeley, 1986; Baddeley & Hitch, 1974; Hitch & Towse, 1995; see Gathercole, 1998; see Figure 17.1). In this model, age differences in verbal memory span are primarily the result of age differences in a phonological subsystem called the *phonological loop*. Verbal information is stored in the phonological loop, and these traces decay rapidly if verbal rehearsal is not performed. Although some researchers have reported age differences in the rate at which information decays (e.g. Engle, Fidler, & Reynolds, 1981; see Cowan, 1997), most researchers propose that age differences in rehearsal rate are primarily responsible for developmental differences in memory span. (Baddeley and his colleagues also discuss a visuo-spatial sketch pad, which functions much as the phonological loop does but for visual material. However, there has been less developmental research on the visuo-spatial sketch pad, and for that reason it will not be discussed here.)

One factor that influences rehearsal rate is word length. Baddeley and Hitch assume that the phonological loop involves a literal subvocalization process, with people saying the items to themselves. Longer words require more time to say, thus leaving less time to rehearse other words before they decay and are lost from working memory (see Baddeley, 1986 for an extensive review of evidence in support of this hypothesis for adults). Several child studies have reported age differences in the speed with which words can be articulated and corresponding differences in memory span and working memory span (e.g. Case, Kurland, & Goldberg, 1982; Henry & Millar, 1991; Hitch & Halliday, 1983; Hitch & Towse, 1995; Hulme et al., 1984). Further support for this position comes from experiments that show the articulation rate of adults comparable to that of children. When adults identify the target items at the same rate as younger children (6-year-olds, for example), they display comparable memory spans (e.g. Case, Kurland, & Goldberg, 1982).

Differences in articulation rate may be responsible for differences in digit span that have been reported for children and adults from different cultures and language groups. For instance, Chinese speakers have, on average, significantly longer digit spans than English speakers, and this difference is apparent as early as 4 years of age (e.g. Chen & Stevenson, 1988; Geary et al., 1993). This cultural difference is related to the rate at which number words (e.g. 'one', 'two', 'three', and so on) can be articulated. For example, the terms for the digits 1–9 in Chinese are shorter and can be articulated more rapidly than the corresponding digits in English (Chen & Stevenson, 1988). Although there may be some absolute differences in the capacity of the short-term store, levels of performance for any given child will vary as a function of that child's knowledge of the to-be-remembered information and the speed with which that information can be identified (e.g. Dempster, 1981) or articulated (e.g. Hitch & Towse, 1995). Age differences in speed of processing influence a wide range of tasks and may represent a cognitive primitive (see Kail, 1991; 1993; Kail & Salthouse, 1994). Age differences in speed of processing are influenced by maturational factors (e.g. Lecours, 1975), placing biological limits on how quickly children can process information, and thus on how much information they can retain in their short-term stores. However, speed of processing is also influenced by experiential factors (e.g. knowledge base), making it clear that development of basic

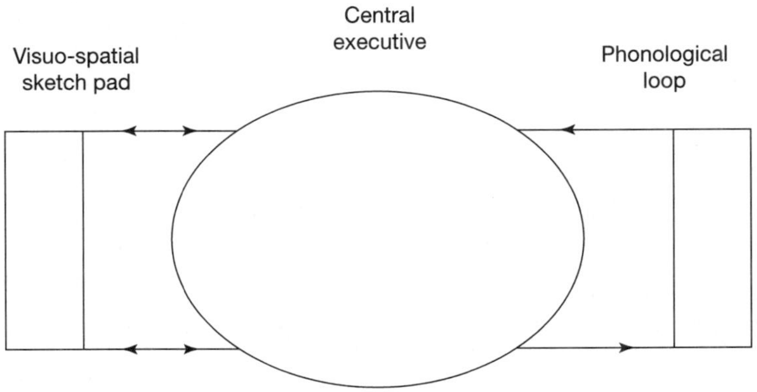

Figure 17.1 *A simplified representation of working memory system as conceptualized by Baddeley (adapted from Baddeley, 1986)*

memory abilities is a result of the dynamic interaction between biological and experiential factors that vary over time. Unfortunately, at this time we are unable to specify how the various endogenous and exogenous factors influence the development of speed of processing and its influence on cognitive task performance.

Memory Development in Very Young Children

Since the early 1970s, numerous studies have shown that infants can remember things (e.g. faces, pictures, objects) for long periods of time (several weeks or months). When only a few days old they demonstrate recognition memory (Slater, 1995). Moreover, they also remember and reinstate memory for activities that they had performed at an earlier point in time (Fagan, 1984; Rovee-Collier & Gerhardstein, 1997). For instance, Rovee-Collier and her colleagues used conditioning techniques to demonstrate that infants as young as 2 months can display memory for actions (kicking their feet in order to control the movement of a mobile) over a period of several weeks. Research focusing on older infants (between 10 and 20 months of age) has used deferred-imitation techniques to measure memory (for reviews, see Bauer, 1997; Meltzoff, 1995). In several of these experiments, infants watched as an experimenter demonstrated some novel, unusual behavior with an unfamiliar toy. The fact that the infants later imitated such behaviors shows that they can form a long-term memory representation of such events, sometimes lasting as long as one year. This finding seems important from a theoretical point of view because it questions a basic assumption made by Piaget (1962), namely that deferred (delayed) imitation requires the retrieval of a mental (symbolic) representation, appearing usually between the ages of 18 and 24 months. However, the work by Meltzoff and colleagues (see Meltzoff, 1995) indicates that even younger children (from about 11 months on) can reproduce behaviors they had earlier observed. Although levels of deferred imitation are typically greater for older than younger infants, the findings indicate that the neurological systems underlying long-term recall are present at the beginning of the second year of life.

As Bauer (1997) emphasized, although maturational processes related to chronological age may place a lower bound on on the capacity for long-term recall of specific events, age does not seem to be the primary determinant of whether or for how long an event will be remembered once the capacity is in place. Rather, the literature indicates that the organization of event representations and the availability of cues or reminders of to-be-remembered events predict young children's long-term retrieval of events. Numerous studies have illustrated the importance of these two aspects and have also explored the mechanisms that regulated the development of event memory.

Regarding the *organization of event memories*, both the nature of temporal relations among the features of an event and the familiarity, that is, repeated experience of the event, influence the organization of an event representation. For instance, Katherine Nelson and her colleagues have demonstrated that young children tend to organize events in terms of *scripts*. These are a form of schematic organization with real-world events organized in terms of their causal and temporal characteristics (Fivush, 1997; Nelson, 1993, 1996). Scripts develop for routine, repeated events. Children learn what usually happens in a situation, such as what happens at a birthday party or at a fast-food restaurant, and remember novel information in the context of these familiar events (Farrar & Goodman, 1992). Substantial research during the past decade has demonstrated that even very young children organize information temporally in a script-like fashion. It has also been shown that even preverbal infants use temporal order to remember events (for reviews see Bauer, 1997; Fivush, 1997).

Importance of repetition and cues

Why should young children's memory be so tied to recurring events? One approach to this question is to ask about the function of memory for young children. Nelson (1996) makes the point that memory for routine events makes it possible for infants and young children to anticipate events and to take part in, and possibly control, these events. Given that there is no such payoff for most novel, single events, it seems to make sense to forget them. It should be noted, however, that the empirical evidence is equivocal. For children in the second year of life, repeated experience is not necessary for the recall of single events over the short term (e.g. one week: Bauer, Hertsgaard, & Wewerka, 1995). Nonetheless, repeated experience clearly facilitates long-term recall in preverbal and early verbal children, and considerably more than for older children and adults.

Additionally cues or reminders also result in an advantage in the recall of very young children. As shown by Fivush, Hudson, and colleagues, the effects of reminding operate both on storage and on retrieval (Fivush, 1997; Hudson & Fivush, 1991; Hudson & Sheffield, 1999; Hamond & Fivush, 1991). For instance, Hudson and Sheffield (1999) demonstrated that exposure to some types of representations of previously experienced events (e.g. exposure to a videotape of another child performing similar activities) was effective for reminding 18-month-olds of the event after short delay intervals (about a day). Furthermore, verbal narration alone was effective in preserving memories in 3-year-old children (Hudson, 1993). Longitudinal research reported by Hamond and Fivush (1991) indicated that reminders also affect information retrieval. These authors interviewed children 6 or 18 months after they had gone to Disney World. Children were either about 3 or about 4 years old when they visited Disney World. Although the older children (i.e. the 4-year-olds) remembered more details, all children recalled a great deal of information about the trip. The main difference between the two age groups was that the younger children (i.e. the 3-year-olds) needed more prompts (retrieval cues) to reconstruct their memories. Thus reminders were particularly helpful for younger children. In fact, young children could remember almost as much information as the older participants but they needed more memory questions in order to do so. Together, these studies demonstrate that young children's recall is facilitated by cues, regardless of whether these are given during a retention interval or at the actual memory test. Young children show low levels of free recall, but can remember much more when specific cues are presented. The research findings reported by Hamond and Fivush (1991) further show that young children's memories for specific events can last for a long time.

Mechanisms of Memory Development in Young Children: The Role of Parents

One interesting finding reported by Hamond and Fivush was that children who talked more about their trip to Disney World with their parents also remembered more. This suggests that parents play an important role in young children's remembering, a point that has been recently emphasized by several researchers (e.g. Fivush, 1997; Nelson, 1996) and is consistent with the theorizing of Vygotsky (1978) and the socio-cultural perspective on cognitive development (Rogoff, 1998). For instance, Hudson (1990) noted that interchanges between parents and their young children predicted children's recall proficiency. Children learn to remember by interacting with their parents, jointly carrying out activities that are later performed by the child alone. Parents begin talking with their young children about things that happened in the past. In particular, parents' repeated questioning helps in understanding how remembering is done. As Hudson (1990) emphasized, parents not only ask the right questions but also give the right answers when the child cannot remember an event. Through these conversations, children learn to notice the important details of their experiences and to store 'to-be-recalled information' in a temporarily organized, script-based way (Ratner, 1984). Together, results of recent research clearly indicate that individual differences in the interactions of parents and young children predict how well children 'learn' how to remember (see also Bjorklund, 2000a).

There is little doubt that young children also discover memory strategies in the context of family interactions, particularly when playing games with their parents. The appearance of strategic memory has been a core issue of memory development research and will be described in more detail below. Before doing so, however, we want to introduce several basic concepts concerning the structure and function of the memory system that have guided developmental research on children's memory.

The Development of Strategic Memory

Strategic memory was at the center of early investigations in memory development (see Harnishfeger & Bjorklund, 1990 for a historical sketch), and continues to be so today, although research on this topic no longer dominates the field as it once did. The reason for the decline in work on strategic memory is because much has been learned about the topic over the preceding decades, and research on the previously neglected topic of autobiographical memory has increased. Despite the decline in research effort, strategic memory development remains an important theoretical topic. On the theoretical side, the development of strategic memory reflects the type of situations in which children gain intentional control over their problem-solving behavior. Much of cognitive developmental research, from Piaget's (1962) description of sensorimotor intelligence to Siegler's (1996) adaptive strategy choice model, has emphasized the importance of understanding the development of goal-directed behavior and the processes underlying such processes (Bjorklund, 2000a).

In most studies examining the development of memory strategies, children are presented with a series of individual items (words, pictures, objects), which they are told to remember for later on. Children are typically given some time in which to study the items (either between the presentation of successive items or after the last item has been presented and before recall is called for), and strategies are identified during these study periods (e.g. rehearsal, sorting into groups) or inferred by the pattern of recall (e.g. by recalling different items from the same conceptual category together). Memory is usually tested via free recall ('Remember as many items as you can in any order you'd like'), although variants of cued recall (e.g. 'Remember all the words that were examples of FRUITS') and recognition are also used. The most frequently examined strategies have been rehearsal (e.g. repeating to-be-remembered items) and organization (grouping similar items together, or 'clustering' related items together in recall).

Production Deficiencies

Perhaps the issue that has generated the most interest in the development of strategies has surrounded the phenomenon labeled *production deficiency* (Flavell, 1970). A production deficiency refers to a person's failure to use (i.e. produce) a strategy when using it would enhance their task performance. In general, young children fail to produce spontaneously a memory strategy, although they can be trained to produce such strategies, usually with corresponding improvements in memory performance (e.g. Kingsley & Hagen, 1969; Ornstein, Naus, & Stone, 1977). However, following successful training, when children are permitted to perform a related memory task 'any way they wish', they typically resort to their earlier, nonstrategic ways (Bjorklund, Ornstein, & Haig, 1977; see Bjorklund & Douglas, 1997). Much research in strategy development has concerned the factors responsible for production deficiencies, the subsequent failure to transfer an acquired strategy to a new situation, and ways in which to improve children's strategy effectiveness (e.g. Pressley & van Meter, 1993; Schneider & Pressley, 1997).

Utilization Deficiencies

More recently, memory researchers have observed that the production-deficiency paradigm has sometimes led to a misreading of some of the data. Specifically, the idea that strategies always benefit children's memory has been questioned, and the concept of *utilization deficiency* was coined by Patricia Miller to capture the fact that children sometimes use a strategy but experience little or no benefit from it (Miller, 1990; 1994; Miller & Seier, 1994). That is, a strategy is implemented but children's level of task performance is not enhanced relative to children who do not use the strategy or to their own performance on a similar task when not using the strategy (e.g. Ackerman, 1996; Bjorklund, Coyle, & Gaultney, 1992; Miller et al., 1986; 1991). Miller and Seier (1994), in a review of 30 years of research, reported strong or partial evidence of utilization deficiencies in more than 90% of all experiments examining children's spontaneous use of memory strategies. Evidence of utilization deficiencies has similarly been found in more than half of memory training studies conducted over a 30-year period (Bjorklund et al., 1997). Earlier researchers rarely discussed their findings of young children using strategies but not benefiting from them, apparently because it represented a deviation from the dominant theoretical perspective. Although there is plenty of evidence supporting the utilization-deficiency paradigm, it is important to note that findings are not always consistent and dependent on task characteristics (cf. Schneider & Sodian, 1997; Waters, 2000; but see Miller, 2000). More longitudinal research, in particular microgenetic studies is needed to explore this phenomenon more carefully.

Developmental Patterns in Strategy Use

Rehearsal

The modern era of research in memory development can be traced to the seminal study by Flavell, Beach, and Chinsky (1966). They developed an innovative technique in which 5-, 7-, and 10-year-old children's spontaneous rehearsal (as reflected by lip movements) for a set of familiar pictures was measured during a study period prior to free recall. They reported that amount of rehearsal increased with age, as did the amount recalled. There were too few 5-year-olds who rehearsed and too few 10-year-olds who did not to evaluate the effects of rehearsal on recall for these children, but about half of 7-year-olds rehearsed during recall and about half did not. Seven-year-old children who rehearsed recalled more than 7-year-old children who did not. Thus was established the canonical result that memory strategy use increases with age and is causally related to levels of recall.

Subsequent research indicated that the relation between frequency of rehearsal and recall was more complex than initially proposed. For example, Ornstein, Naus, and Liberty (1975) required 8-, 11-, and 13-year-old children to rehearse each word on a list at least once in the 5 or 10 second interval between presentation of successive words. Using this technique, Ornstein and his colleagues observed comparable frequency of rehearsal between the youngest and oldest children and greater recall for the older children, counter to the earlier findings of Flavell and his colleagues (1966). However, Ornstein and his colleagues noted developmental differences in the *style* of rehearsal. The youngest children tended to rehearse only one or two unique words during each interval, which Ornstein et al. labeled *passive* or *single-item rehearsal*. In contrast, older children more often rehearsed the target word plus several previously presented words, a style Ornstein et al. labeled as *active* or *cumulative*. Based on these and other data, Ornstein and his colleagues asserted that the important developmental changes are in terms of *style* rather than *frequency* of rehearsal (see also Guttentag, Ornstein, & Siemens, 1987; Kellas, Ashcroft, & Johnson, 1975; Ornstein & Naus, 1985).

Training studies bolstered the causal relation between style of rehearsal and memory performance, with several researchers noting improvements in young children's recall following cumulative-rehearsal training (e.g. Cox et al., 1989; Kingsley & Hagen, 1969; Ornstein, Naus, & Stone, 1977). Yet, rehearsal training for young children rarely eliminated developmental differences, and generalization of the trained strategy was typically weak.

Organization

One possible reason for the beneficial effects of cumulative rehearsal is that it facilitates the recognition of conceptual relations among items, which promotes the contiguous recall of related items (Naus & Ornstein, 1983). Indeed, one of the most frequently studied encoding strategies involves the organization of related items into coherent groups. For example, in sort–recall tasks, children are typically given randomly ordered lists of categorizable pictures or words printed on cards, such as fruit, tools, and the like. Children are told that they are to remember the items for a later test and that they can do anything they'd like with the items during a study period to help them remember. Organization during the study period (sorting) and during recall (clustering) is then assessed.

In general, the developmental pattern observed for rehearsal is also found for organization. Levels of organization, in terms of both sorting and clustering (e.g. Bjorklund, Ornstein, & Haig, 1977; Hasselhorn, 1992; Salatas & Flavell, 1976) increase with age, although young children (e.g. preschool and kindergartners) can be easily trained to use an organizational strategy with corresponding improvements in recall (e.g. Black & Rollins, 1982; Guttentag & Lange, 1994; Lange & Pierce, 1992). Younger children (6 to 7-year-olds) will sometimes use organizational strategies when highly associated items serve as category items (e.g. dog, cat; salt, pepper), but high levels of clustering using less strongly associated categorical items (e.g. goat, deer; shoes, hat) are not typically observed until between 9 and 11 years of age (e.g. Bjorklund & de Marchena, 1984; Schneider, 1986). Again, similar to the findings with rehearsal, such interventions rarely eliminate age differences, and young children will only generalize a trained organizational strategy if training is extensive (e.g. Carr & Schneider, 1991; Cox & Waters, 1986).

Evidence of utilization deficiencies (using a strategy with little or no corresponding benefit to memory) have been found frequently for the strategy of organization, both in preschoolers (e.g. Lange, Guttentag, & Nida, 1990; Lange & Pierce, 1992; Miller et al., 1986) and in school-age children (e.g. Ackerman, 1996; Bjorklund, Coyle, & Gaultney, 1992). Moreover, in some studies, children trained to use an organization strategy generalize it to subsequent transfer trials, but display no corresponding enhancement of recall (e.g. Bjorklund et al., 1994).

Other Strategies

Although rehearsal and organization have been the most frequently studied strategies, other memory strategies have also been investigated, and their age course generally follows those of rehearsal and organization. For example, studies have examined children's *allocation of study time*, evaluating the amount of time children take to prepare for a memory test (e.g. Dufresne & Kobasigawa, 1989; O'Sullivan, 1993). Generally, older children (typically 9 and 10 years old) allocate more time to studying sets of to-be-remembered items and tend to study harder items more than 'easier' items (e.g. Dufresne & Kobasigawa, 1989). Similar age-related patterns are found for *retrieval strategies*. Once children have encoded the target information, they must then focus on getting it out. One robust finding is that young children require a greater number of retrieval cues, or hints, than older children to recall information (e.g. Howe, Brainerd, & Kingma, 1985; Kobasigawa, 1974).

Like rehearsal and organization, allocation of study time and retrieval strategies are both found infrequently in preschool and early school-aged children, but are used in a relatively sophisticated way by children in the 10- or 11-year-old children. Other strategies are more complicated and are typically not used successfully until adolescence. For example, *elaboration* is a form of organization in which a person generates a detailed verbal or visual relation between pairs of items (see Kee, 1994; Schneider & Pressley, 1997, for reviews). For instance, children may be given pairs of items to remember (e.g. milk, car; bananas, coat). At recall, they will be presented with one member of the pair and must recall its mate. A verbal elaboration for the pair 'milk, car' could involve generating a sentence that describes an event involving the two, for example, 'The car ran on milk instead of gas', or thinking of a 'CARton of milk'. A visual elaboration concerning this noun pair could involve creating an image of a cow hooked up on a milking machine that connects directly to the gas tank of a car. Children rarely use elaboration spontaneously, and, although young children can be trained to use elaboration (e.g. Siaw & Kee, 1987), they rarely reach the level of performance of older children (Reese, 1977), reflecting a utilization deficiency.

A similar age-related pattern has been observed in the use of strategies for remembering complex materials, such as text. These strategies involve processes such as identifying, underlining, and summarizing the main ideas of text passages, which develop during the high-school years (see Brown et al., 1983; Pressley et al., 1985) and are usually explicitly taught to children in school. Also, they require prolonged periods of practice before they are used effectively. Like the strategies we described earlier, complicated text-processing strategies can be

Table 17.1 *Approximate ages by which most children display spontaneously various memory strategies effectively for children in schooled cultures*[1]

	6–7 years	8–10 years	11–14 years
Single-item rehearsal	X		
Cumulative rehearsal			X
Organization with highly associated items	X		
Organization with less highly associated items		X	
Effective allocation of study time		X	
Retrieval strategies		X	
Elaboration[2]			X
Strategies for remembering complex text[2]			X

[1] Younger children than listed often display effective strategies when prompted.

[2] These strategies may not be displayed until later and many adults fail to use these strategies effectively.

taught to normal elementary school children (see Gaultney, 1995; Paris & Oka, 1986) and to poor readers (Palincsar & Brown, 1984; Short & Ryan, 1984). However, spontaneous production of strategies for learning and remembering complex text material is the exception rather than the rule, and even adults may fail to use such strategies routinely.

Table 17.1 presents a timetable for the typical age of appearance of various memory strategies for children in schooled cultures.

Factors Affecting Children's Strategy Use and Development

Research in the development of memory strategy presents a relatively clear picture. Young children, although using simple strategies, rarely spontaneously use the more complicated strategies employed by older children. Children can be trained to use such strategies, however (production deficiency), but often fail to demonstrate transfer of training, and sometimes show little gain in memory performance as a result of using the strategies (utilization deficiency). Charting the development of these different strategies and documenting conditions under which strategies can be successfully trained are important, but more critical from a theoretical perspective are the underlying factors responsible for these age-related patterns. In the following sections, we will review research that has sought to discover the factors that influence age differences in children's use of memory strategies and their effectiveness, including efficiency of processing, knowledge base, encoding, and metamemory.

Efficiency of Cognitive Processing

By definition, strategies are effortful cognitive operations. There is a cost to mental resources in using memory strategies. Several theorists have proposed that the principal factor underlying children's strategy use is age differences in *efficiency of processing*. Younger children require more mental effort to execute most cognitive operations relative to older children (e.g. Case, 1985; 1992), and because of this age difference, younger children are less likely to implement a strategy and experience less benefit from its execution than older, more cognitively efficient children (e.g. Bjorklund, 1987; Kee, 1994).

Researchers have used *dual-task procedures* to test this hypothesis, in which children are asked to perform two tasks, both separately and together. The amount of performance reduction on the secondary task (often some simple motor task, such as tapping one's finger as fast as possible) as a result of performing the primary task (usually some measure of strategy performance) is used as an indication of how much mental resources the primary task requires. For example, Bjorklund and Harnishfeger (1987, experiment 2) asked 9- and 13-grade children to tap their index fingers as rapidly as possible on the space bar of a keyboard (secondary task). They were then asked to perform two free-recall memory tasks while tapping their fingers. On the first task, children were asked to recall a set of categorized items in any order they wished (free recall). On the second task, children were instructed in the use of an organizational memory strategy. Children of both ages significantly increased their strategy use on the trained task and displayed a significant reduction in tapping rate on the more effortful trained task relative to the less effortful free-recall task. However, only the older children showed a corresponding increase in recall relative to the free-recall task. This demonstrates that strategy use is effortful, especially for younger children, and, because it consumes a substantial portion of young children's limited mental capacity, strategy use may not always result in enhanced performance (i.e. a utilization deficiency). Similar findings of greater use of mental resources to execute strategies for younger than for older children have been reported for a variety of different strategies (e.g. Guttentag, 1984; Kee & Davies, 1988; Miller et al., 1991).

Knowledge Base

We previously defined knowledge base as children's long-term representations of world knowledge, particularly as it relates to how sets of 'facts' are organized in a modified semantic memory network. Knowledge base refers to what children know about typical (or perhaps atypical) events that occur in their culture (e.g. going to restaurants, going to church, going camping) and about relations among items within a domain (e.g. football, chess, dogs, Pokemon cards). With age, the number of items in a child's knowledge base expands, as do the number and strength of associations and the number and type of features that characterize items (see Bjorklund, 1987). We use the term *elaborated knowledge base* to refer to a domain of knowledge that is highly organized with many strong connections among items within the base (i.e. so that the activation of one item in the domain will make easier the activation of related items).

Age and individual differences in knowledge base have been shown to be important factors in children's memory strategy use and effectiveness (see Alexander & Schwanenflugel, 1994; Bjorklund, Muir-Broaddus, & Schneider, 1990; Hasselhorn, 1995; Kee, 1994; Schneider, 1993). What children know affects how they process information, and older children generally know more about the things they are asked to remember than younger children. The effect of knowledge on memory span was illustrated earlier in this chapter by studies of chess-expert children for positions of chess pieces on a chess board (Chi, 1978; Schneider et al., 1993).

Research using a variety of materials (e.g. categorized words, texts) has consistently demonstrated that children with more detailed knowledge of the to-be-remembered information recall that information better, and typically implement strategies more effectively than children with less detailed knowledge (e.g. Best, 1993; Bjorklund & Zeman, 1982; Schneider, 1986; Schneider, Körkel, & Weinert, 1989). With respect to memory strategies, most researchers propose that knowledge influences the speed with which children can execute a strategy and the subsequent efficiency of that strategy (e.g. Bjorklund, Muir-Broaddus, & Schneider, 1990; Kee, 1994). According to Bjorklund, Muir-Broaddus, and Schneider:

> The primary effect that an elaborated knowledge base has on cognitive processing is to increase speed of processing for domain-specific information. Individual items can be accessed more quickly from the long-term store, as can relations among related items in the knowledge base . . . faster processing is equated with more efficient processing, which results in greater availability of mental resources. These mental resources can then be applied to retrieving specific items (item specific effects . . .), to domain-specific strategies, or to metacognitive processes. (1990, p. 95)

On free-recall tasks on which memory strategies are most useful, children with greater (i.e. more elaboratedly organized) knowledge typically remember more and display greater strategy use that children with less well-developed knowledge for the task material (see Bjorklund & Douglas, 1997). However, in other situations, the greater memory shown by more knowledgeable children is *not* accompanied by increased strategy use in terms of high levels of organization, for example (e.g. Bjorklund & Zeman, 1982; Gaultney, Bjorklund, & Schneider, 1992; Schneider & Bjorklund, 1992; Schneider, Bjorklund, & Maier-Brückner, 1996). For example, in research by Bjorklund & Zeman (1982), children were asked to recall the names of their current school classmates. Recall was high, and most children showed relatively high levels of clustering, based on seating arrangement, reading groups, or sex of child. However, there was little relation between degree of strategy use and recall. And in a subsequent experiment when children were required to recall their classmates by a specified category (seating arrangement or sex of child), children of all ages tested (6, 8, and 10 years) did so almost perfectly, but recalled no more names than children who organized their recall less well (Bjorklund & Bjorklund, 1985). For these children, it seems, most of their elevated levels of recall were attributed to nonstrategic factors associated with an elaborated knowledge base.

In related research, children who were classified as experts in some domain (baseball or soccer) were given sets of domain-related words (e.g. baseball terms) to remember in sort–recall tasks (Gaultney, Bjorklund, & Schneider, 1992; Schneider & Bjorklund, 1992; Schneider, Bjorklund, & Maier-Brückner, 1996). Their performance was contrasted with that of a group of baseball or soccer novices and with their own performance on a set of categorized words (e.g. ANIMALS, FURNITURE, TOOLS). In each of these experiments, the expert children recalled more from the lists that consisted of items from their area of expertise (baseball or soccer terms) than they did from the categorized list of words or than the novices did. However, there were few differences between the novices and experts in terms of organization. The greater recall performance of the expert children was specific to their area of expertise, but was not, apparently, mediated by strategic processes. The effects of knowledge for these experts was rather in terms of item-specific effects. Knowing a lot about the topic enabled them to remember individual terms better (see Bjorklund & Schneider, 1996).

Encoding

Because knowledge base is defined in terms of how information is represented in long-term memory, it is related to the concept of encoding, which refers to the features that children use to represent items for a specific memory task. Younger children use fewer semantic features to encode words on memory tasks than do older children and they require more of the original encoding environment reinstated in order to recall the target information (Ackerman, 1985; 1997). As a result, they remember fewer items, in part because individual items are less elaborately represented and thus more difficult to access than the more elaborately encoded items of older children. Younger children are also less likely to identify common semantic features (such as *dog* and *goat* both being ANIMALS) than are older children (e.g. Bjorklund & Hock, 1982; Howe, Brainerd, & Kingma, 1985), and, as a result, are less likely to use an organizational strategy to remember sets of related items.

Metamemory

Metamemory refers to the knowledge one has of the processes regarding the working and contents of one's memory. There are two general types of metamemory: *declarative* and *procedural*. Declarative metamemory refers to the explicit, conscious, and factual knowledge concerning person and task characteristics and memory strategies (compare with explicit memory). For example, person characteristics would include children's knowledge about their own memory abilities, whereas task characteristics would include information about factors that influence the difficulty of a task (e.g. categorized versus noncategorized list, brief versus longer time for study). Strategy knowledge refers to a child's awareness of what strategies he or she has available and their relative effectiveness. Procedural metamemory refers to the knowledge concerning when strategies are necessary, as well as monitoring how well one is performing on a task (memory monitoring) (see Schneider & Pressley, 1997).

Age Differences in Declarative Metamemory

In general, children's metamemory knowledge, both declarative and procedural, increases with age and is correlated with age-related improvements in memory behavior (see Joyner & Kurtz-Costes, 1997; Schneider, 1999; Schneider & Pressley, 1997 for recent reviews).

Kreutzer, Leonard, and Flavell (1975) queried American children in kindergarten and grades 1, 3, and 5 (approximate ages 6, 7, 9, and 11 years, respectively) about person, task, and strategy variables, and they reported substantial improvements in declarative metamemory knowledge over this age range. For example, 70% of the 6-year-old children did not realize that remembering pairs of opposites (e.g. boy, girl) would be easier than remembering pairs of unrelated words (e.g. Mary, walk). By age 11, 100% of the children said that the opposites would be easier to learn. Only half of the youngest children realized that embedding items in a story would result in better memory than simple list learning, whereas 85% of the oldest children tested believed this. However, young children were not totally out of touch with their memory abilities. For example, a majority of the 6-year-old children knew that using external devices (e.g. writing phone numbers down) helps in remembering information.

Subsequent research confirmed the age-related improvements in declarative metamemory. For instance, young children vastly overestimate their memory abilities (e.g. Schneider, 1998; Yussen & Levy, 1975), allocate their study time poorly (e.g. Dufresne & Kobasigawa, 1989; O'Sullivan, 1993), and fail to realize that recall of gist is easier than verbatim memory (e.g. Rogoff, Newcombe, & Kagan, 1974) and that sets of categorized items are easier to recall than sets of noncategorized items (e.g. O'Sullivan, 1996). In general, it is not until the middle elementary school years that children properly understand the importance of task characteristics to their memory performance (Borkowski et al., 1983; Cavanaugh & Borkowski, 1980; Kurtz & Borkowski, 1984; Schneider et al., 1986; Weinert, 1986). In other studies, kindergarten and young elementary school children are able to judge the greater effectiveness of two strategies only when they produce substantially different levels of performance (e.g. 'just looking' versus grouping by category). Older children, in contrast, are able to make more subtle judgments about the effectiveness of the various strategies (Justice, 1985; Justice et al., 1997).

Age Differences in Procedural Metamemory: Memory Monitoring

The most studied type of procedural metamemory is that of memory (or self-) monitoring, evaluating how well one is progressing. For example, as discussed earlier, young children tend to consistently overestimate their memory abilities and seem only minimally affected by previous experience on such tasks in making their estimates of future tasks (e.g. Schneider, 1998; Yussen & Levy, 1975). However, young children's predictions are more accurate when they are tested using nonverbal as opposed to more traditional verbal measures (e.g. Cunningham & Weaver, 1989), and are greater when tested in a familiar situation rather than in an unfamiliar (i.e. laboratory-type) situation (e.g. Justice & Bray, 1979; Wippich, 1980; see also Ceci & Bronfenbrenner, 1985).

Despite displaying some procedural metamemory competencies in certain contexts, young children are more likely to be out of touch with how they are progressing on a task and the relation between their use of memory strategies and their memory performance than are older children. For example, Ringel and Springer (1980) trained 7-, 9-, and 11-year-old children in the use of an organizational memory strategy. All groups of children learned the strategy and displayed increased levels of recall relative to baseline trials. Following training, children were given transfer trials under one of two instructional conditions. Children in one condition were given explicit feedback concerning their improved performance on the task, whereas children in the other group were not. The 11-year-old children generalized the trained strategy in both transfer conditions, whereas the 7-year-old children failed to transfer the strategy in either condition. Nine-year-old children who did not receive explicit feedback performed like the 7-year-olds, failing to transfer the strategy to the new set of items; in contrast, 9-year-olds receiving explicit feedback behaved more like the older children and transferred the trained strategy to the new context. Apparently, most of these 9-year-old children, despite using and benefiting from an organizational memory strategy, were not aware of the relation between their strategy use and task performance. Making them explicitly aware of this relation resulted in transfer of training. Having procedural knowledge was not enough to permit the 7-year-old children to transfer the strategy. Presumably, these youngest children had additional difficulties (e.g. too little capacity) that limited the likelihood of their transferring the strategy. Other investigators have emphasized the role of metamemory in the effectiveness of strategy use and transfer (e.g. Justice et al., 1997), demonstrating, for example, that training in memory monitoring or other aspects of metamemory is responsible for the effectiveness and maintenance of strategy training (e.g. Leal, Crays, & Moely, 1985; Melot, 1998).

Metamemory–Memory Relations

It has been implicitly assumed that metamemory development was causally related to memory development (e.g. Brown, 1978; Flavell & Wellman, 1977). However, more recent research has demonstrated that the relation between these two factors was not a simple one and varied with the specific behaviors investigated (e.g. Cantor, Andreassen, & Waters, 1985; Cavanaugh & Borkowski, 1980; Schneider, 1985; 1999). For example, in a meta-analysis, Schneider (1985) reported a correlation between metamemory knowledge and memory behavior of 0.41, based on a sample of 27 studies and 2,231 subjects. An updated meta-analysis, increasing the sample size to 60 studies and 7,079 subjects, produced identical results (Schneider & Pressley, 1989). Schneider and Pressley (1989) reported that the strength of relation between the two factors varied with type of task (e.g. organizational strategies or memory monitoring), task difficulty, when metamemory was assessed (before or after the memory task), age, and the interaction of these various factors. For example, studies looking at metamemory/memory relations in organization and elaboration tasks do not yield strong connections between the two factors until the elementary school years (e.g. Lange, Guttentag, & Nida, 1990), and not consistently until about age 10 (e.g. Hasselhorn, 1992). However, when the task is simplified and the metamemory questions are highly related to successful task performance, even preschool children show a significant relationship between metamemory knowledge and memory behavior (e.g. Schneider & Sodian, 1988).

Researchers have understandably believed that good metamemory is the desired state, and that, although good metamemory may not always facilitate task performance, poor metamemory is never an advantage. This perspective has been questioned by a few researchers, who have proposed that, in some situations, children's poor metacognition may be advantageous and lead, eventually, to improved cognitive performance (e.g. Bjorklund, 1997; Bjorklund, Gaultney, & Green, 1993; O'Sullivan & Howe, 1998). For young children, being out of touch with their cognitive abilities (e.g. believing that they are performing better than they actually are) may result in increased task persistence, the avoidance of feelings of failure, and the continued use of currently ineffective strategies (i.e. a utilization deficiency) that will eventually lead to improved performance. Research has shown, for example, that preschool children who overestimate their imitative ability have higher verbal IQ scores than their more accurate peers (Bjorklund, Gaultney, & Green, 1993). Also, one speculation for the phenomenon of utilization deficiencies discussed above is that children are unaware that their use of an effortful strategy is *not* benefiting them; this results in their continued use of the strategy until it becomes effective (Bjorklund & Coyle, 1995; Bjorklund et al., 1997). The timeline for this may be quite brief. For instance, Bjorklund, Coyle, and Gaultney (1992) reported that 44% of the 9-year-old children who were classified as utilizationally deficient in their memory study displayed increases in recall on subsequent trials. From this perspective, the developmental relation between metamemory knowledge and memory behavior is even more complicated than previously believed and may require a reformulation of our ideas about the role of metacognition in cognitive development (see O'Sullivan & Howe, 1998).

Although the relationship between the development of metamemory knowledge and memory behavior is not a simple one, one fact that has become clear is that the relationship between the two factors is bidirectional (e.g. Borkowski,

Milstead, & Hale, 1988; Schneider, 1999; Schneider & Bjorklund, 1998; Schneider & Pressley, 1997). Metamemory competence is as much a cause as a consequence of competent memory behavior, with the relationship varying with age, task variables, and their interaction. For example, as we noted earlier, children who are experts in a domain will remember more in that domain than will less expert children. However, expert children's memory performance will be greatest when they also have substantial metamnemonic knowledge (e.g. Schneider, Körkel, & Weinert, 1990; Schneider, Schlagmüller, & Visé, 1998).

Multiple and Variable Strategy Use

In most studies, researchers have focused on a single type of strategy, noting changes in developmental function or factors that influence the use or effectiveness of that strategy. Although the patterns of development that have been reported in the literature are highly similar for different strategies, research investigating the development of one memory strategy (e.g. rehearsal) rarely also investigates the development of other strategies (e.g. organization), giving the impression that these strategies develop independently, perhaps on different tasks. More contemporary research has seriously questioned this interpretation, however, demonstrating that children of all ages have multiple strategies available to them and use a variety of them on different trials of the same task, and, where appropriate, use several different strategies on a single trial. That is, not only do individual strategies develop, but so too do the combinations and variability of strategies develop (see Bjorklund & Douglas, 1997; Miller & Coyle, 1999; Siegler, 1996).

Research and theory on the development of multiple and variable strategy use have generally followed Siegler's (1996) *adaptive strategy-choice model* of cognitive development. The principal premise behind this model is that of natural selection. As in biological evolution, Siegler assumes that children generate a large number of strategies to solve problems that compete with one another for use. Certain strategies are selected, in that they achieve a desired outcome in a particular problem-solving situation; these strategies increase in frequency. Strategies that produce less desirable outcomes are not selected and thus decrease in frequency, at least in the context in which they are not successful. However, children maintain a variety of strategies, and strategies that are used infrequently do not necessarily die but are occasionally used, particularly in situations where a more dominant strategy is not working.

Recent research that has examined multiple strategy use on memory tasks has consistently reported that children of all ages use a variety of different mnemonic strategies over repeated trials. For example, McGilly and Siegler (1989) assessed strategy use on a serial-recall task for 6-, 7, and 9-year-old children. They reported that the most sophisticated strategy, repeated rehearsal (repeating the entire list continuously during a waiting period) increased in frequency with age (24%, 63%, and 78% for 6-, 7, and 9-year-old children, respectively), but that most children at all ages used at least two different strategies over the course of the experiment (see also McGilly & Siegler, 1990). In other research, Cox et al., (1989) instructed 9-year-old children to sort words into meaningful groups during a study phase of a free-recall experiment. They reported a subsequent improvement in organization and recall as a result of the instruction, and also an increase in the sophistication of rehearsal techniques. That is, improvements in one strategy (organization) led to improvements in another strategy (rehearsal), which in turn led to enhanced levels of memory performance.

In other research, children have been observed to use several different strategies simultaneously (or at least successively) on the same trial (e.g. Coyle & Bjorklund, 1997; Hock, Park, & Bjorklund, 1998; Lange & Pierce, 1992). For example, in a sort–recall study with 8-, 9-, and 10-year-old children, Coyle and Bjorklund reported that children of all ages used multiple strategies (e.g. sorting, category naming, rehearsal, clustering at recall) on most trials, although the use of multiple strategies increased with age. Figure 17.2 presents the mean number of trials (maximum = 5) on which no strategy, one strategy, two strategies, three strategies, or four strategies were used by 8-, 9-, and 10-year-old children. As can be seen, the number of trials on which two or more strategies were used on a trial increased with age, although even the 8-year-old children had more trials on which they used two or more strategies than trials on which they used one or no strategy.

Within an age level, children who used more strategies on a trial generally recalled more words, and children of all ages also showed substantial (and comparable) variability in which strategies they used on the various trials. Strategy variability was measured in three ways. One measure of variability was the number of different combinations of strategies used on a single trial. For instance, a child who used sorting and rehearsal on one trial and rehearsal and category naming on another would be using the same number of strategies on the two trials, but each reflects a unique combination. The average number of different strategy combinations ranged between 2 and 3 for all age groups and did not differ with age. Variability was also measured in terms of (1) the number of adjacent trials on which the combination of strategies changed and (2) the number of strategies that was added or deleted form trial to trial. For example, a child who changed from sorting and rehearsal on one trial to sorting and category

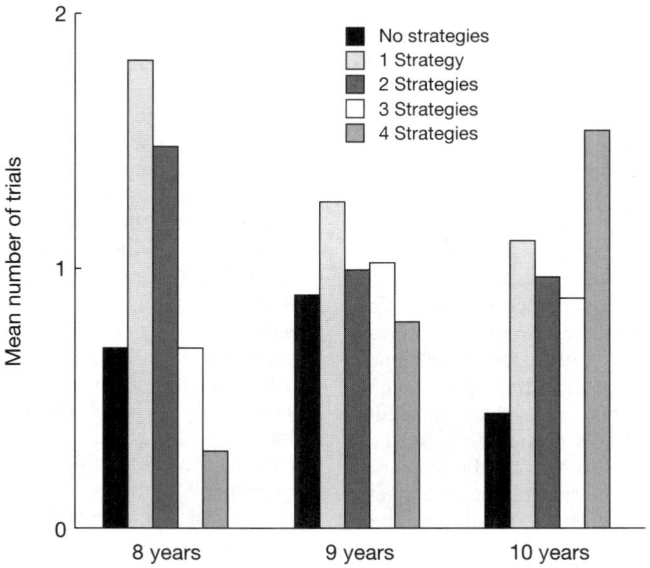

Figure 17.2 *Number of trials on which no strategy, one strategy, two strategies, three strategies, or four strategies were used, by age (adapted from Coyle & Bjorklund, 1997)*

naming on the next trial would be credited with adding one strategy (category naming) and deleting one strategy (rehearsal) for a strategy change score of 2. Again, these measures showed relatively high levels of variability (range from 1.98 to 2.27 for adjacent trials with changes, and 2.81 to 3.37 for number of strategies changed) and did not vary with age. When looking at the relation between variability measures and recall, no consistent pattern was noted for the 8- and 9-year-old children. However, the 10-year-olds showed significant, although moderate, negative correlations between recall and each measures of strategy variability. That is, the more stable the 10-year-old children were in their strategy use, the higher their levels of recall tended to be.

In related research, 8-, 9- and 10-year-old children who had been classified as academically gifted by their schools were found to use multiple strategies as frequently as nongifted children, but recalled more words per trial and displayed lower levels of strategy variability than their nongifted peers (Coyle et al., 1999). Moreover, strategy variability was more consistently (and negatively) related to recall for the gifted than the nongifted children. These patterns of data are consistent with the position that with age, experience, and greater general intelligence, children increasingly use a problem-solving approach that is better fitted to the demands of the task, resulting in higher levels of performance (cf. Siegler, 1996). This research also points to consistent relations between multiple strategy use, strategy variability, and memory performance, making it clear that variability on cognitive tasks is more than just noise.

Memory Development: One Uniform Pattern or Different Developmental Functions?

Developmental studies on verbal memory typically show age-related performance increases across a broad variety of memory measures. Overall, these findings not only suggest that developmental trends can be generalized across different memory functions, but also seem to indicate that there are clear-cut age-related improvements in all of these functions. The goal of this section is to evaluate the generalizability of these basic assumptions. First, evidence of across-task consistency of (verbal) memory performance will be carefully analyzed. Next, more recent research investigating developmental trends in previously neglected areas such as implicit memory and visuo-spatial memory will be presented that gives valuable information on the domain specificity of memory development.

Consistency and Stability of Verbal Memory

A long-standing issue in memory research is whether memory is a single cognitive ability, or whether it represents a variety of abilities. The way to assess this question empirically is to administer different memory tasks and assess the intertask correlations. That is, do those people who do well on one memory task perform well on others, and those who perform poorly on one task also perform poorly on others? Or is there no way to predict performance on one task from performance on another task?

A small number of developmental studies have examined intraindividual variability in children's memory performance. For instance, Cavanaugh and Borkowski (1980) gave 5-, 6-, 8-, and 10-year-old children three laboratory-type memory measures that required memory strategies (e.g. sort–recall). Correlations between recall measures across the three tasks showed a developmental progression. That is, whereas all correlations were nonsignificant for 6-year-olds, intertask correlations were significant and of moderate size for fifth graders, ranging from 0.37 to 0.49. In another study that compared 9- and 12-year-old children's performance on three strategic memory tasks (Kail, 1979), findings were similar in that correlations among tasks were greater for the older than for the younger children. These results based on laboratory tasks seemed to suggest that there is a general verbal memory ability, at least for children 8 years of age and older.

Later research used a wider variety of tasks, including laboratory tasks such as digit span and sort–recall, school-related memory tasks such as story recall, and 'everyday' memory tasks such as memory for a list of shopping items or performance on the game of Concentration (Knopf et al., 1988; Kurtz-Costes, Schneider, & Rupp, 1995; Weinert, Schneider, & Knopf, 1988). For instance, Knopf et al. (1988) assessed the intertask consistency of memory performance in third, fifth, and seventh graders, and in two adult groups ranging in age from 50 to 84 years. When intertask correlations were calculated for children's performance on the four memory measures (sort–recall for both clusterable and nonclusterable items, digit span, and text recall), the coefficients were mostly in the 0.25 to 0.45 range when collapsed across age groups. Correlations decreased markedly when calculated separately for each age group. For adults, about half of the intertask correlations were significant, but only 3 of the 15 correlations exceeded $r = 0.35$. Knopf et al. (1988) concluded that their results provided no strong evidence for the existence of a unitary memory function.

In a subsequent study, Kurtz-Costes, Schneider, and Rupp (1995, study 1) administered a set of 12 memory tasks to 5-, 7-, and 9-year-old children, including laboratory tasks (sort–recall and paired associate), school-related tasks (remembering a geography lesson, recalling a story), and 'everyday' memory tasks (shopping for items at a store). The researchers reported little intertask consistency among the 12 tasks at any age, with only slightly more correlations reaching statistical significance than expected by chance. In a second study with 5- and 8-year-olds, Kurtz-Costes, Schneider, and Rupp (1995) not only replicated these findings but also showed that the low intertask correlations were not due to reliability problems. Both test–retest and parallel-test reliabilities were moderate to good, exceeding 0.70 for most of the tasks.

Confirming evidence for these cross-sectional findings was also provided by recent longitudinal research. Schneider and Weinert (1995) assessed intertask correlations among several memory measures in the same group of children at 4, 6, 8, and 10 years of age. Schneider and Weinert reported few developmental patterns (see Table 17.2). Like Knopf et al. (1988) and Kurtz-Costes, Schneider, and Rupp (1995), these researchers found that intertask consistency was high only for similar memory tasks (i.e. parallel measures of story recall and memory span). Thus the findings of Schneider and Weinert (1995) are consistent with the position that there is no 'unitary' verbal memory construct. Given that intraindividual across-task consistencies were low to moderate for all measurement points, there is reason to assume that the basic pattern does not change as a function of age and experience.

Implicit versus Explicit Memory

Since the late 1980s and early 1990s, researchers interested in adult memory have explored differences between explicit memory, that is, conscious recollections of experiences, and implicit memory, that

Table 17.2 *Synchronous correlations among memory and IQ measures obtained for 10-year-old children (LOGIC sample; N = 202)*

Variables	(2)	(3)	(4)	(5)	(6)	(7)
(1) Word span	0.39	0.46	0.17	0.15	0.35	0.27
(2) Sentence span		0.46	0.32	0.43	0.55	0.40
(3) Digit span			0.23	0.16	0.47	0.31
(4) Recall in sort–recall task				0.26	0.34	0.32
(5) Text recall (fictitious town)					0.44	0.42
(6) Verbal IQ						0.50
(7) Nonverbal IQ						

Note: all correlation coefficients are significant at the 0.05 level.

Source: slightly modified after Schneider and Weinert (1995, p. 270).

is, memory for some information without being consciously aware that one is remembering (e.g. Roediger, 1990; Schacter, 1992). One of the major outcomes of this research is that there are clear dissociations between explicit and implicit memory. For instance, some brain-damaged patients were found to be seriously impaired with explicit memory compared to normals but did not show implicit memory impairment (for a review, see Roediger & McDermott, 1993).

Although there has been relatively little developmental research on implicit memory, some recent studies have addressed this issue. The test commonly used with children involves the use of fragmented pictures, perhaps a dog, that should be identified by the participants. This is very difficult to do initially, but as more of the picture is completed, it becomes increasingly easier to identify the object. After a series of such picture-identification tasks have been given, children are provided with degraded pictures of both previously seen versus unseen objects. The typical finding is that repetition priming is observed. That is, children identify fragmented pictures of previously seen objects significantly faster than fragmented pictures of previously unseen objects (e.g. Ausley & Guttentag, 1993; Drummey & Newcombe, 1995; Hayes & Hennessy, 1996).

Findings from developmental studies further indicate age-related dissociations. That is, age-related differences between younger and older children typically observed on explicit memory tests are greatly reduced with implicit memory testings (Parkin, 1993). More specifically, the priming effects seem comparable for older and younger participants (see Ausley & Guttentag, 1993; Hayes & Hennessy,1996; Naito, 1990). Although older children typically show better explicit memory (i.e. they recognize more pictures than the younger children), no developmental differences in implicit memory are found.

However, one problem with this research is that the majority of studies is based on picture identification tests. For instance, in experiments using the fragmented picture task, children are asked to identify it, which is very difficult to do initially. Children are then shown a series of degraded pictures, and it becomes increasingly easier to identify the object. When a second task involving these and new items is given later, children perform better for those items they had previously seen, regardless of age. In order to draw firm conclusions about the developmental invariance of priming, other types of implicit memory tests are needed. Conceptual priming seems a suitable candidate for an extended validity check. For instance, a conceptual measure of implicit memory provides participants with a list of category names and requires them to produce the first exemplars of the categories that come to mind. The typical finding from studies with adults is that prior presentation of a category exemplar increases the likelihood of that word being named as a category instance (Schumann-Hengsteler, 1995). Given that these tests emphasize the semantic relationships between studied and tested items and thus require conceptually driven processing, one should expect age differences in conceptual priming. Theoretically, older children should show more priming because the semantic categories are more meaningful to them than to younger children.

Contrary to expectation, however, results from the few studies that examined developmental trends in priming based on conceptual measures of implicit memory indicate that priming is age-invariant (see Anooshian, 1997). As noted by Hupbach, Mecklenbräuker, and Wippich (1999), these findings are inconsistent with theoretical accounts of implicit memory and knowledge development. These authors tested the assumption that the unexpected finding of age-invariant conceptual priming demonstrated in previous development studies could be due either to the rather narrow age ranges or to the predominance of familiar semantic categories in those studies. Indeed, Hupbach, Mecklenbräuker, and Wipprich (1999) found reliable age differences in priming effects for atypical but not for typical category exemplars when performances of 4-, 6-, 8-, and 10-year-olds were compared. Accordingly, although there is substantial evidence for the age invariance of priming effects, more studies are needed to explore the generalizability across different task settings.

Overall, the implicit memory results to date point to an independent memory system. It seems that the brain systems mediating perceptual and conceptual priming are fully developed early in life, which clearly contrasts to the continuous development of the explicit memory system (cf. Squire, Knowlton, & Musen, 1993). There is plenty of evidence in cognitive neuroscience of human memory that perceptual and conceptual priming do not depend upon the medial-temporal and diencephalic brain structures that mediate intentional declarative memory (Gabrieli, 1998). Both unintentional and implicit memory fit Geary's (1995) description of biologically primary abilities – ones that have been selected for in evolution and that are found in similar forms across cultures. In contrast, intentional and explicit memory can be classified as biologically secondary abilities, that is, memory skills that are shaped by one's particular culture, especially formal schooling (see Rogoff, 1990).

Developmental Trends in Visuo-Spatial Memory

The vast majority of developmental studies on memory processes and products conducted within the last three decades have focused on issues of verbal memory. Thus, it does not come as a surprise that most sections of this chapter are devoted to problems of verbal memory. Given this, it seems fair to state that the development of visuo-spatial memory represents an interesting but understudied area that deserves more attention in future research.

What do we already know about developmental trends in this field? First of all, it is important to note that there seem to be several visuo-spatial memory systems, and not just one. Although the inclusion of a visual-spatial subsystem ('visuo-spatial sketch pad') in Baddeley and Hitch's (1984) working memory model suggests that the retention of visual and spatial material is organized by the same underlying system, the empirical evidence based on studies with adults does not support this assumption (cf. Logie & Marchetti, 1991). Moreover, the findings indicate that developmental pathways for processing visual and spatial information differ considerably (for a review, see Schumann-Hengsteler, 1995). For instance, Schumann-Hengsteler (1992) used a picture-reconstruction task to disentangle memory for visual and spatial components. Children of different ages (5-, 8-, and 10-year-olds) were first shown large picture frames that contained several small pictures of familiar objects and were then asked to remember the items and their locations. There were clear-cut age effects in the ability to associate a given picture with its location, in that the older children outperformed the younger ones. However, memory for locations (that is, memory for the original positions of the small pictures) was generally well developed and did not vary across age groups. See Ellis, Katz, and Williams (1987) and Mandler and Robinson (1978) for additional evidence supporting the position that there are no major age differences in short-term spatial memory.

The developmental evidence for permanent (long-term) visuo-spatial memory is roughly comparable. We know from many studies that very young children already possess efficient search strategies, as indicated by their performance on hide-and-seek tasks (see DeLoache, 1989; Wellman & Somerville, 1992). Moreover, even preschool children can use maps efficiently and possess relevant route knowledge, that is, represent landmarks and other significant cues in the environment when searching for target locations (Herman, Norton, & Klein, 1986). Although age differences are observed when the task is to estimate the distance between one's own position and the target location, these differences do not seem to affect the outcome of search activities. In fact, knowing whether a place is ahead or behind certain landmarks and its relative distance away is probably sufficient information (Matthews, 1992). All in all, it appears that there is little development in the nature of the spatial knowledge system itself. Developmental changes in permanent visuo-spatial memory mainly reflect an increasing coordination of the knowledge system with action and with spatial markers in the world (Landau & Spelke, 1985).

Although most of the developmental evidence concerns laboratory-type tasks, several studies have focused on the popular game of Concentration, which represents an everyday test of visuo-spatial memory. Most lay people and many developmental psychologists believe that children outperform adults on such a task. In fact, one of the first scientific studies on the topic that compared children with adults (Baker-Ward & Ornstein, 1988) confirmed the impression that children are very good at the game. These authors did not find significant differences between children's and adults' performance. However, Baker-Ward and Ornstein used a reduced number of picture cards (32 instead of 64), and did not include game partners. In a series of well-designed experiments, Schumann-Hengsteler (1995; 1996) assessed developmental differences in three task-relevant skills (i.e. picture identification, relocation of picture cards, and search strategies). In short, her findings, based on comparisons of four age groups (5-, 8-, and 10-year-olds and adults), revealed that adults were actually better players than children, who did not differ from each other. Overall, the older children and adults used more efficient strategies, particularly later during the game. There were no significant age differences in picture recognition. Interestingly, younger children did not make as many location errors (i.e. selecting picture cards adjacent to the target card) as older children and adults.

Although these findings indicate that there are age-related trends in visuo-spatial memory skills, the effect sizes are generally small. Overall, developmental research on visuo-spatial memory has shown that age differences – if noticed at all – are far less pronounced than those observed for verbal memory.

Stability of Memory Abilities over Middle Childhood: Evidence from Longitudinal Studies

More than 99% of the empirical studies on memory development have been cross-sectional in nature. Accordingly, the focus has been on age-correlated *developmental differences* between different age groups. The general result of these studies is that memory performance (e.g. free recall) improves gradually with age and that much of this improvement seems due to increasing efficiency in the use of memory strategies (cf. the section on strategic memory above). The rich data base from cross-sectional investigations on memory development suggests that older children behave more strategically in memory tasks, and that strategy use is more strongly correlated with recall performance in older than in younger children (Bjorklund, 1987; Hasselhorn, 1992; Schneider & Pressley, 1997).

One obvious drawback of the cross-sectional approach to memory development is that nothing is known about intraindividual differences in *developmental changes* over time as well as interindividual differences in intraindividual changes. Because of such limitations, most contemporary models of memory development appear idealistic. For instance, in the field of memory strategy research, the usual research plan that compares aggregated, average strategy scores across age groups supports a tendency to overestimate the universality, intraindividual homogeneity, and interindividual consistency of developmental courses (cf. Schneider & Weinert, 1989, for a more detailed discussion of this problem). Typically, deviations from this ideal sequence have been either ignored or treated as error variance.

One interpretation problem not solvable by cross-sectional research is that, for instance, the age-related increase in memory strategy use typically observed in such studies could be due to the fact either that most children made about the same amount of progress within a given time interval, or that some children made enormous progress whereas other children remained at the same level or even declined. The assessment of *group stability* over time (i.e. test–retest correlations) helps in exploring this issue. For example, overall group stability should be high if – and only if – effects are based on similar strategy and recall improvements in almost all of the children of a given sample. Needless to say, a longitudinal design is needed to evaluate this issue. Such a design also allows for the assessment of *individual stability* or *lability* over time calculated for each individual in a given sample. The variance of individual stabilities in a sample (differential stability) is also informative: for instance, if group stability is low, the analysis of individual and differential stabilities can answer the question of whether such a finding is due to the instability of only some children ('outliers') or is caused by overall low stability in the sample.

To explore the general importance of this basic research problem, findings from longitudinal studies on memory development have to be contrasted with those of cross-sectional research. Unfortunately, the available longitudinal evidence is still very scarce. Below we summarize the findings of the Munich Longitudinal Study on the Genesis of Individual Competencies (LOGIC: see Schneider & Weinert, 1995; Sternberg, 1999; Weinert & Schneider, 1999). Although this study was not restricted to the study of memory development but also included other cognitive domains such as thinking, intelligence, and moral judgments as well as different aspects of personality development and motivation, memory development was particularly thoroughly investigated. The LOGIC study started in 1984 with about 200 children who were about 4 years of age and had just entered German kindergarten. The study is still active. Children were tested annually until 1993 when they were 13 years old. Five years later, they were tested again on a broad variety of cognitive and personality tasks.

The question of whether or not the basic findings of cross-sectional memory studies could be replicated with the LOGIC sample was first addressed by Schneider and Sodian (1990). An attempt was made to validate the findings of an earlier cross-sectional study (Schneider & Sodian, 1988) that dealt with 4- and 6-year-olds' ability to use retrieval cues in a memory-for-location task. One of the most important findings of the cross-sectional study was that substantial interrelationships between children's metamemory (i.e. their knowledge about the utility of retrieval cues), the way they hid the items, the use of retrieval cues, and memory performance were found even for the youngest children in the sample. Schneider and Sodian (1988) concluded that even preschool and kindergarten children can possess task-relevant knowledge and use appropriate strategies when they are familiar with the task.

Schneider and Sodian (1990) compared these findings with those of a longitudinal analysis based on the data of the LOGIC children who were tested on this task at the ages of 4 and 6. Although the intercorrelations obtained from the replication study were somewhat lower than those of the cross-sectional study, the general pattern of the cross-sectional study was basically confirmed. That is, reliable intercorrelations among knowledge, strategies, and memory performance were found at both age levels. However, an unexpected outcome of the replication study concerned group stabilities over the 2-year period. The test–retest correlations varied between 0.01 (metamemory) and 0.24 (recall), indicating almost no stability over time.

One possible reason for this finding is that memory and metamemory data cannot be reliably assessed for children of these young ages. To control for this possibility, Schneider and Sodian (1990) recruited an independent sample of 4-year-olds and presented them with a hide-and-seek task twice within a 2-week interval. As short-term stability was high for all variables, it is unlikely that low long-term stability was due to unreliable measurement. Rather, the instability over time found for this memory task indicates that the young children improved at different rates, thereby considerably changing their relative standing within their reference group between the two measurement points.

Overall, this comparison of cross-sectional and longitudinal evidence makes clear that conclusions about developmental patterns drawn from cross-sectional studies can be inadequate and misleading. Although both the group means and the intercorrelational patterns found for the cross-sectional and longitudinal studies were roughly comparable, the longitudinal findings are not in accord with the assumption that most children progress at about the same pace.

A second major memory paradigm investigated in the LOGIC study concerned the development of organizational strategies and corresponding recal development (Schneider & Sodian, 1991; 1997; Sodian & Schneider, 1999). Children were given a classic sort–recall task at the ages of 4, 6, 8, 10, and 12 years. The task was also used in the 1998 follow-up test when participants were 17 years old. As noted above, many developmental studies have been based on the sort–recall paradigm. Findings from cross-sectional research unanimously suggest that strategy use at encoding (i.e. sorting) and at retrieval (i.e. clustering during recall) increase continuously over the primary and secondary school years, accompanied by increasingly higher levels of recall. Interestingly, the inspection of group means of the longitudinal data for sorting during study, clustering during recall, and recall performance seemed to confirm the cross-sectional findings in that it conveyed the impression of a gradual increase in strategy use and recall performance over the age range under study. However, the generally low long-term stabilities indicated that individual developmental paths did not follow the course suggested by the group data. In fact, individual analyses showed that over 80% of the participants 'jumped' from chance level (i.e. clustering scores < 0.30) to near perfection (i.e. at least 80% of the items sorted conceptually). This indicates that the acquisition of a conceptual clustering strategy is not a process of gradual increase but is an all-or-none, insightful discovery process. Moreover, additional analyses showed that the LOGIC children discovered the strategies at different points in time. Thus, some of the instability in strategic behaviors apparent from the group data analyses can be explained by individual variation in the time of strategy discovery: children go from chance levels of conceptual organization to perfection, but they do so at different ages.

However, a closer look at the longitudinal data suggested that the developmental pattern may be even more complex. That is, children did not always maintain the organizational strategy once they had discovered it. Almost 50% of the total sample showed a U-shaped pattern of strategy acquisition. Two-thirds of these children discovered the strategy at preschool age, lost it subsequently and rediscovered it at the ages of 10 or 12 years. About one-third of the children discovered it at age 8, lost it and rediscovered it at the age of 12. The high incidence of U-shaped developmental curves suggests that early and later organizational 'strategies' may be behaviorally similar, but conceptually unrelated. Two sources of evidence support this assumption. First, there was a (moderate) link between metamemory and the course of strategy acquisition, indicating that children who show U-shaped developmental curves may at first have employed a seemingly strategic behavior without understanding the rationale for its use. Second, performance gains in free recall were not well predicted by strategy gains during the preschool years, but were very well predicted by such gains in elementary school. Overall, then, these data show that generalizations about the developmental course of strategy acquisition that were drawn on the basis of cross-sectional data may obscure individual developmental paths (see Ornstein, 1999, for critical comments on this conclusion).

The performance-gain data also bear on the concept of utilization deficiency discussed above. Clear evidence for a utilization deficiency was demonstrated for the preschool data. Between the ages of 4 and 6 years, 'strategists' (high strategy use at both measurement points), strategy discoverers, and 'nonstrategists' gained about the same amount (about 20%) in recall. This finding indicates that strategy discovery was not functional for recall performance in young strategy users. A completely different pattern emerged for the elementary school period: strategy discoverers clearly had the highest performance gains (between 20% and 30% between two successive measurement points), and strategists' performance gains roughly equaled nonstrategists' (between 5% and 10%) recall performance gains. Thus, children who discovered the organizational strategy between two successive measurement points had performance gains that quadrupled those of both nonstrategists and strategists. These findings suggest that there is less evidence for a utilization deficiency in elementary school children than was previously thought. Of course, given the large time interval (2 years) between successive measurement points, the possibility of shorter periods of utilization deficiency cannot be ruled out based on this longitudinal data set (Ornstein, 1999). However, findings of a recent microgenetic sort–recall study (Schlagmüller & Schneider, 2002) that compared 9- and 10-year-old strategists, nonstrategists, and strategy discoverers repeatedly over a time period of about 9 weeks showed that the transition from nonstrategic to strategic behavior was always accompanied by a significant increase in recall performance.

Can the longitudinal findings obtained for organizational strategies be easily generalized to the acquisition of other memory strategies and developmental changes in various memory skills? The available evidence does not support such a conclusion. For example, Kunzinger (1985) assessed 7-year-old children's strategies in an overt rehearsal task and retested them 2 years later. Group stability for the rehearsal and recall variables was high (r between 0.60 and 0.80). Also, high levels of individual stability were found, indicating that those children who initially rehearsed more maintained their position relative to the group 2 years later. Although these findings should be interpreted cautiously because of the small sample size ($N = 18$), a more recent study (Guttentag, Ornstein, & Siemens, 1987) reported comparable longitudinal stability between 8 and 9 years of age, confirming Kunzinger's results.

Moreover, a more complete analysis of the findings from the LOGIC study indicates that the pattern of individual stabilities is not uniform across memory variables (Weinert, Bullock, & Schneider, 1999). For instance, it was shown that long-term stability of children's autobiographical memory was low to moderate when assessed during the preschool and kindergarten years, and that it increased considerably during the elementary school years (Weber & Strube, 1999). This developmental pattern resembled that found for the verbal and nonverbal intelligence variables, indicating that whereas there was considerable variability in gains during the preschool years, interindividual differences in intraindividual changes were much more stable during the elementary school years. On the other hand, the pattern found for text memory indicated considerable stability of individual differences from the first measurement point on, with 2-year stabilities of about 0.60 (Knopf, 1999). Long-term stability was also rather high, that is, mostly in the 0.40 to 0.70 range, for memory capacity measures such as word-span and sentence-span tasks (Schneider & Weinert, 1995).

Overall, these results from longitudinal analyses support the idea discussed above that memory is not a unitary factor, and that memory functions may differ considerably both between and within individuals. Consequently, these results indicate that individual developmental paths are not only domain-specific but may also vary across different content areas within the same domain. The longitudinal evidence thus suggests that memory is not a single process, but a set of related processes, each having its own developmental function.

The New Interest in Memory Accuracy: The Example of Eyewitness Memory

Research on memory development in the 1970s and 1980s was dominated by basic issues such as the development of strategies or the impact of domain knowledge on memory performance. As noted by Koriat and Goldsmith (1996; Koriat, Goldsmith, & Pansky, 2000), this research paradigm adopted a quantity-oriented conception. In this conception, memory is seen as a storehouse into which items are first deposited and then retrieved. Memory performance is then evaluated in terms of the amount of items correctly recalled. In contrast, the *accuracy-oriented approach* conceives of memory as a representation or reconstruction of past experience. Thus memory is evaluated in terms of *correspondence* or fit with past events, rather than in terms of the mere quantity of information recalled. This correspondence conception is dominant in recent research on autobiographical memory, more specifically, in research on eyewitness memory. During the last decades numerous studies on this feature of event memory have been conducted, stimulated by its relevance for real-life problems. The issue of whether there are age-related differences in the accuracy of eyewitness memory was not only important for theoretical reasons but also the focus of legal scrutiny. The sheer number of developmental studies on eyewitness memory is impressive and difficult to integrate into a coherent organizational scheme. Nonetheless, an attempt will be made to summarize some of the most important findings.

Eyewitness memory represents one specific form of event memory, or autobiographical memory, that emphasizes the accuracy and not so much the amount of information recalled about an experienced event. With children being increasingly called upon to provide testimony in legal cases, issues about how much and how accurately children remember, and the degree to which they are influenced by suggestion and misinformation, has become a high-priority research interest (see Bruck & Ceci, 1999; Ceci & Bruck, 1993; 1998; Doris, 1991; Qin et al., 1997, for reviews). According to Ceci and Bruck's (1998) rough and conservative estimate concerning the situation in the United States, about 100,000 children annually testify in criminal and civil cases. In view of this large number of children giving statements of legal significance, it seems important to know more about the reliability of children's statements. Core issues of interest both to developmental psychologists and to the legal profession include age differences in remembering self-related events, the long-term properties of such memories, and their resistance to misleading post-event information.

Age Differences in Children's Eyewitness Memories

Although there is much variability from study to study, most investigations of children's eyewitness memory begin by showing children a video of some event, having them observe some activity in their school, or involving them personally in some activity. Thus, in many respects, eyewitness memory does not differ from other types of event memory. Children are typically first questioned using general prompts (a request for free recall), usually followed by more specific questions (cued recall).

Consistent with other research on children's event memory, levels of recall to general questions are typically low in preschool and early school-age children and increase with age (e.g. Baker-Ward et al., 1993; Cassel & Bjorklund, 1995; Ornstein, Gordon, & Larus, 1992; Poole & Lindsay, 1995). Despite low levels of recall, what preschoolers recall is usually accurate. When examining the ratio of incorrect to correct information remembered, most studies report no age differences (Howe, Courage,

& Peterson, 1994; Rudy & Goodman, 1991). Also, what young children do recall is highly accurate and central to the witnessed event (Baker-Ward et al., 1993; Goodman, Aman, & Hirshman, 1987; Poole & White, 1995).

As is the case for memory in general, levels of correct recall for an eyewitnessed event increase for people of all ages when more specific cues are provided (Cassel, Roebers, & Bjorklund, 1996; Ornstein, Gordon, & Larus, 1992, Poole & Lindsay, 1995). However, unbiased specific cues can also increase the number of inaccurate answers, although not always (Howe, Courage, & Peterson, 1994; Poole & Lindsay, 1995). Increased error rates to unbiased-cued questions were found in a study by Cassel, Roebers, and Bjorklund (1996) who showed 6-, 8-, and 10-year-old children and adults a video, followed by free recall and then a set of unbiased questions. Cassel and collegues reported that the unbiased cues yielded age-related increases in levels of correct recall for all subjects, but also produced increased levels of inaccurate recall, reducing the overall accuracy of recall particularly for the kindergarten children (see also Bjorklund et al., 1998; Roebers, Rieber, & Schneider, 1995).

Despite age differences, most young children possess the cognitive capacity necessary for accurate testimony. For instance, research assessing children's memory for traumatic and stressful events (e.g. memory for a physical check-up) indicate that even 3-year-olds can provide accurate accounts of personally experienced events (Baker-Ward et al., 1993; Goodman et al., 1991). Age differences may diminish or even disappear under certain conditions. That is, if an event is particularly salient or personally meaningful to young children, this event becomes highly memorable. For instance, Saywitz et al. (1991) examined children's memory for a physical check-up during which half of the 5- and 7-year-old children experienced genital touching. Saywitz and colleagues found age effects in free recall for the children in the nongenital condition but not for the subgroup that had experienced genital touching. Thus, under at least some conditions, even preschoolers can provide relevant and reliable information about their experiences, even though eyewitness memory performance in such situations improves with age. Overall, most studies that included samples of adults illustrate that elementary school children's free recall of witnessed events is comparable to that of adults (Bjorklund et al., 1998; Cassel, Roebers, & Bjorklund, 1996; Roebers & Schneider, 2000).

Developmental Differences in Long-Term Recall and Forgetting Rates

How long do memories of witnessed events last? Certainly not for ever. We know from research on the eyewitness memory of concentration camp survivors (Wagenaar, 1990) that victims can forget about the physical appearance and the names of people who abused them badly and almost caused their death some 40 years earlier. Although most developmental studies on the issue have not assessed the long-term recollections of children, several have investigated children's memories of specific events for periods ranging from several weeks to 2 years (e.g. Flin et al., 1992; Salmon & Pipe, 1997). Although the results of these studies are not totally consistent, they indicate that age differences in the accuracy of recall increase with increasing delays, at least when delays are longer than a month. Most research assessing the effects of delays of 1 month or less reported that the total amount of information recalled and the overall accuracy of recall (that is, the ratio of inaccurate to accurate information) were comparable to what they were when recall was tested immediately after witnessing the event, regardless of age (Baker-Ward et al., 1993; Cassel & Bjorklund, 1995). However, age differences in recall accuracy are found with longer delays. For instance, Poole and White (1993) reported that, although 6-, 8-, and 10-year-olds recalled about as much accurate information as adults following a 2-year delay, they recalled significantly more inaccurate information (about 20%) than the adults (7%), with no differences being observed among the three groups of children (see also Flin et al., 1992). The conclusion from these studies is that age differences in accuracy are found, but only when memory is assessed after extended delays.

How can this pattern of findings be explained? One explanation is offered by fuzzy-trace theory (Brainerd & Reyna, 1998; Reyna & Brainerd, 1995), referring to the greater rate of decay of verbatim (exact) relative to gist traces. Verbatim traces, favored by young children, deteriorate more rapidly than the gist or fuzzy traces preferred by older children, resulting in greater loss of information over delays and corresponding increases in proportions of incorrect recall.

Age Differences in Suggestibility

Perhaps the single most investigated area of eyewitness testimony concerns age differences in suggestibility (see Bruck & Ceci, 1999; Ceci & Bruck, 1993; 1998, for reviews). In most suggestibility paradigms, participants witness an event and are later presented with some post-event information that contradicts events observed earlier (misinformation) or are asked sets of misleading questions, suggesting an inaccurate 'fact'. There is little doubt that people of all ages are susceptible to both misinformation and misleading questions. The primary concern of developmental researchers has been whether or not there are age differences in suggestibility.

Although this has been a controversial area of research, most studies that have looked for age differences in suggestibility have found them, with preschool children being particularly susceptible to suggestion (Ackil & Zaragoza, 1995; Ornstein, Gordon, & Larus, 1992; Poole & White, 1995). Age differences in suggestibility also have been confirmed in studies that used more realistic and externally valid designs by simulating repeated questioning in a legal context. For instance, Bjorklund, Cassel, and their colleagues (Bjorklund, Brown, & Bjorklund, 2002 Bjorklund et al., 1998; Cassel & Bjorklund, 1995; Cassel, Roebers, & Bjorklund, 1996; Roebers & Schneider, in press) simulated a prototypical eyewitness experience over a 1-month period from the time a participant observed a videotaped event through recall of the matter at that trial. Children of different ages and adults went through several questioning sessions, involving free recall and leading questions suggesting either correct or incorrect 'facts', in a way that attorneys might question a witness to a petty theft. Finally, subjects were questioned about 4 weeks after they had observed the event using both correctly leading and misleading questions in the same interview.

As a major result, Bjorklund, Cassel, and their colleagues reported age differences in response to repeated suggestive questioning, with kindergarten children following misleading questions and changing answers more often than older participants. Whereas participants of all ages tended to change their answers when questioned about non-central (peripheral) items, only the kindergarten children showed this pattern for the central items. However, on the final, multiple-choice questions, the kindergarten children were able to provide the correct answer as often as they had to the initial questions, despite intervening errors.

The latter finding indicates that young children's erroneous answers do not necessarily reflect an actual change in memory representation. It is likely that some of the young children's compliance with misleading questions is related to the specific context of the interview, in particular, the social demand characteristics of the situation (Ceci & Bruck, 1998). For example, children may interpret a repeated question as evidence that the (adult) interviewer was not satisfied with their first answer and that another, different answer must be more correct. This is particularly likely in the studies carried out by Bjorklund, Cassel and colleagues discussed earlier with the follow-up question coming immediately after a similarly posed question. In fact, there is evidence that young children are less susceptible to misinformation when given by a child rather than an adult authority figure, and that repeated questioning does not necessarily lead to 'mind changing' and inaccurate recall in young children (Ceci & Bruck, 1993; Poole & White, 1991).

However, as noted by Ceci and Bruck (1993), preschool children are disproportionally more vulnerable to suggestion than either school children or adults. If suggestions are strong and persistent enough, young children may confuse the source of the information, thinking that the misinformation was something they actually experienced and not something they heard someone else say. For instance, Leichtman and Ceci (1995) assessed the effects of negative stereotyping and suggestions on preschool children's recollections of an event that happened at their school. An unfamiliar person, Sam Stone, visited the classroom for a short time, talking to the teacher and listening to a story. Children in the stereotype condition were given misleading background information on Sam Stone before his visit. Children in the suggestion condition were interviewed several times after Sam Stone's visit and given misinformation about the visit. Children in the 'combined' condition received both the negative stereotype and misinformation before the visit and were repeatedly interviewed thereafter. Finally, children in the control condition received neither the stereotyped information nor the misinformation about Sam.

When children were given an open-ended interview 2 weeks after the visit, Leichtman and Ceci found that the highest levels of false reports about Sam's visit came from children who received both the stereotyped information before the visit and the misinformation thereafter. Impressively, the percentage of erroneous answers increased to more than 70% for the younger preschoolers when children were asked specific follow-up questions concerning whether Sam had ripped a book or soiled a teddy bear. Obviously, many children firmly believed that these events actually happened, even after being told that the events were just made up. Thus it seems that false memories of plausible but extraordinary events are relatively easy to put into young children's minds.

Why are younger children so susceptible to the effects of misinformation and suggestion? Again, fuzzy-trace theory (Brainerd & Reyna, 1998; Reyna & Brainerd, 1995) offers an explanation. On the basis of fuzzy-trace theory, young children are more reliant on verbatim (exact) memory traces than older children. Because verbatim traces deteriorate rapidly, they may not be available when post-event information is provided or when suggestive questions are asked. Thus, erroneous information may be incorporated with 'real' memories and become indistinguishable from them. In fact, recent research has shown that false memories can be more resistant to forgetting than real memories (e.g. Brainerd & Mojardin, 1999). It appears, then, that under certain circumstances children can come to believe their implanted memories and treat them as real (e.g. Ceci et al., 1994).

In summary, the available literature indicates that young children's eyewitness memory is typically less accurate than that of older children and adults. However, research findings also show that, in general, young children are capable of providing accurate eyewitness memory about personally significant events in their lives. Although delayed recall has a greater negative impact on preschoolers than on older children (Baker-Ward et al., 1993; Ornstein et al., 1997), the effects of delay are typically not very great. Furthermore, young children are less susceptible to misleading information and better at recalling experienced events when they possess a clearly developed script of the relevant situation. Regardless of age, domain knowledge has a positive impact on eyewitness memory (Ornstein et al., 1997). For instance, Ornstein and colleagues showed that 5-year-old children's knowledge about and understanding of routine pediatric investigations was significantly related to their memory for the visit to the doctor, indicating that domain knowledge influences young children's autobiographical memory.

Facilitating Young Children's Performance

Although this is principally good news, researchers still search to uncover the optimal ways to elicit accurate eyewitness memory from children. For instance, new and promising interview procedures have been developed that enhance accurate memory reports while at the same time decreasing inaccurate reports. Simply asking children to mention everything they have seen and heard seems sufficient to increase levels of accurate recall in young children (Elischberger & Roebers, 2001; Poole & Lindsay, 1995). Also, a warm interpersonal atmosphere in the interview increases children's memory by increasing their accuracy (Goodman et al., 1991). The more open-ended the questions, the less likely that young children report incidents that did not occur. Also, accurate responses are most likely when the interviewer is neutral in tone and does not attempt to mislead the child through suggestive questioning. Taken together, the numerous studies on children's eyewitness memory have not only led to important theoretical advances in our understanding of children's autobiographic memory but also demonstrated their important practical potential for guiding interview procedures in the relevant applied settings.

Future Directions for Memory Development Research

Memory development is a relatively mature field, at least within the realm of psychological development. Researchers over the past 35 years have investigated extensively both strategic and nonstrategic memory and the factors that influence children's encoding, storage, and retrieval of information. However, despite the extent of our knowledge, there is still much to learn, and the centrality of memory to all other aspects of cognition makes it likely that the ontogeny of memory, in one form or another, will continue to be a primary focus of cognitive development.

Some topics deserve more investigation than others, of course, and we would like to suggest several directions that we believe work on memory development should follow over the next decade. The suggested topics include some of those that have received relatively little research attention in the past, along with others that include new approaches to some extensively investigated areas. This list is admittedly a truncated one. Research needs to continue on topics such as infant memory and working memory; and some neglected topics, such as children's nonverbal memory development and the relation between memory development and other higher forms of cognition, such as comprehension (e.g. Kuhn, 2000), also need greater research attention. Our selection of topics reflects only our top five of a list that could have been much longer (see also Hernandez Blasi & Bjorklund, 2001).

Neuropsychology of Memory Development

Cognitive neuroscience has become fashionable in psychology since its emergence in the mid 1980s (see Segalowitz, and Schmidt, Chapter 3 in this volume, for a historical review), and many cognitive developmentalists have recognized that the development of information processing cannot be isolated from development of the brain (e.g. Bjorklund, 2000a; Byrnes & Fox, 1998; Johnson, 1998). In the field of children's memory development, there is an increasing emphasis on the need for greater awareness of and interaction with neuroscience perspectives (e.g. Gathercole, 1998; Nelson, 1997; Schneider & Bjorklund, 1998). However, we still know very little about the neuropsychology of memory development, at the level of both description and explanation (although see summaries of research on the neuropsychology of infant memory, e.g. Nelson, 1995; 1997).

Neuropsychological research can influence memory development research in a number of ways. For example, research contrasting the deferred-imitation abilities of adults with certain types of brain damage has shed light on the nature of infants' and young children's memory (McDonough et al., 1995). Adults with lesions to the hippocampus are unable to acquire new explicit/declarative memories (i.e. memory with awareness), but are able to form new implicit/nondeclarative memories (i.e. memory without awareness). McDonough and her colleagues (1995) administered to a group of amnesics declarative memory tasks (which they failed), and deferred imitation tasks, similar to those passed by 1-year-old toddlers (e.g. Bauer, 1997). The brain-damaged adults also failed these problems, suggesting that the same type of memory system that underlies explicit memory, as reflected by free-recall and recognition memory tasks, also underlies deferred imitation and is functioning, at least in rudimentary form, by the beginning of the second year of life.

Although we believe it is important for memory development researchers to become familiar with neuropsychological techniques and research findings, we also believe that it is important not to lose sight of the cognitive and behavioral levels while examining brain function. Biological levels of explication should not replace psychological-level theories, but should be integrated with them to yield a proper perspective of memory development.

Evolutionary Models of Memory Development

Over the past decade, developmental psychologists have increasingly applied aspects of Darwin's theory of evolution to human development (see Bjorklund, 1997; Bjorklund & Pellegrini, 2000; Geary & Bjorklund, 2000; Surbey, 1998). We will not describe here the assumptions of evolutionary psychology (see e.g. Barkow, Cosmides, & Tooby, 1992; Buss, 1995; 1999), except to point out that evolutionary explanations emphasize adaptive function: that is, what adaptive role some behavior might play today, and also, complementarily, what adaptive role it might have played in our environment of evolutionary adaptedness.

When applying evolutionary thinking to memory development, important questions would be: 'What type of memory functioning might be adaptive for the infant and young child?', or, 'What types of memory ability should develop early in life, and what types might develop later?' From this perspective, it would make sense, for example, for implicit memory to be functioning well early in the life and for explicit memory to develop at a slower pace. Alternatively, one might take models of human cognitive evolution (i.e. cognitive phylogeny) and apply them to cognitive development (i.e. cognitive ontogeny).

Perhaps the best example of this for memory development was proposed by Nelson in her 1996 book *Language in cognitive development.* Nelson's main purpose was to demonstrate that 'language is a catalyst of cognitive change during early and middle childhood', and she explained those changes in terms of memory representations using Donald's (1991) model of cognitive evolution. Basically, Donald (1991) proposed four 'stages' of cognitive evolution (episodic, mimetic, mythic or narrative, and theoretic), expressed in terms of how knowledge could have been represented in memory. Nelson applied these four proposed stages to cognitive development. Table 17.3 presents the four stages from Donald's theory and their corresponding ontogenetic stages from Nelson's theory. It should be noted that Nelson discusses parallels between language and 'cognition' rather than language and 'memory', but given that cognition here is defined in terms of the type of memory representations children can use to 'think', we liberally have considered this a theory of memory.

Implicit Memory Processes in Children

A third challenging area for the future is implicit memory, that is, memory without awareness, which we discussed earlier in this chapter, especially studied simultaneously with implicit learning and the significance of unconscious cognition in general. Implicit learning and memory are relatively new topics to cognitive developmentalists, and, given the

Table 17.3 *Developmental stages mapped onto evolutionary stages*

Stage	Age	Cognition	Language
Infancy: *episodic*	0–1	Event representations (ERs)	Sounds, first 'words'
Early childhood: *mimetic*	1–4	ERs with words	Dialogue
		Games, play, songs, social rituals	Grammar developing, language in mimetic reps
Middle childhood: *narrative*	4–10	Narrative thinking, personal memory, cultural learning	Narrative Beginning reading and writing, math, categorical schemes
Adolescent: *theoretic*	10-adult	Logical abstractions Deductive systems Extensive use of external systems Acquisition of 'scientific' social-conventional knowledge	Logical abstractions, argument and scientific reading and writing, specialization

Source: slightly modified after Nelson (1996, p. 86).

great interest among them, 'it would be surprising if there was not more work on the development of implicit memory in the near future' (Schneider & Pressley, 1997, p. 77). Much research in children's implicit cognition has been led by Karmiloff-Smith's (1992) theory of representational redescription. Basically, she proposes there are several different ways to 'know' something, the most basic being implicit, or knowledge without awareness. This is the level at which most of us know the rules of language, and the way in which a spider knows how to spin a web. Representations become more explicit (conscious and available to awareness) as children rerepresent their knowledge to themselves, something akin to Piaget's (1971) concept of reflective abstraction. In this way, studying implicit processes becomes interesting not only for themselves but also for their potential relations with the development of explicit, conscious processes.

As we noted above, several students of cognitive development have begun systematic programs designed to obtain a better understanding of implicit processes in children (e.g. Drummey & Newcombe, 1995; Vinter & Perruchet, 2000). In general, researchers are reporting smaller and often no developmental differences in implicit, relative to explicit, memory/learning, as well as an independence of the two memory systems (e.g. Hayes & Hennessy, 1996; Russo et al., 1995; Vinter & Perruchet, 2000). It has been proposed also that implicit memory is ontogenetically and phylogenetically an earlier acquisition than explicit memory, based on more basic and primitive brain structures (e.g. Reber, 1992; Ruiz Vargas, 1996).

New Approaches to Strategy Development

We have learned much about strategy development since the pioneering study by Flavell, Beach, and Chinsky in 1966. Despite this success, we believe that there is more to learn, and new models, theories, and perspectives are arising to lead the way. Even in the middle of the rising age of neuroscience and new evolutionary approaches, many things may be better understood at this level of analysis while 'looking at' the brain and other species (Hernandez Blasi, 1999).

Recently, Bjorklund and Douglas (1997, p. 234) suggested four issues for the future of memory strategy research: (1) strategy variability, (2) strategies developed in more naturalistic contexts than school strategies, (3) cross-cultural commonalities and differences in memory strategy development, and (4) teaching of school-type strategies. Each of these is an understudied area, and requires new approaches to some old issues.

Construction and Destruction of Children's Memories

If every single life is itself a personal history, then memory is a personal story, or a narrative. This is an important rule to keep in mind in understanding autobiographical memory because it summarizes two core characteristics of it: autobiographical memory is built within a social context, and it is based on and recalled through a linguistic code. This means that our memories about the past depend on social interaction and language; but it also means that personal memories can be destroyed or modified by language and social influence under certain circumstances (Hernandez Blasi & Bjorklund, 2001). Most research into children's autobiographical memory has, understandably, focused on what and how children remember, with forgetting and intrusions, or false memories, being given less attention (see Bjorklund, 2000b; Ceci & Bruck, 1998; Goodman, Emery, & Haugaard 1998).

From this approach, there are several topics that look especially promising. First, we hope to see more work on the social construction of memory, that is, how parents and other people participate in identifying the critical aspects of an experience and show or help children how to organize them in a temporal and spatial sequence (see e.g. Fivush & Hudson, 1990; Fivush, Haden, & Adam, 1995; Reese & Fivush, 1993). This topic also can be easily linked theoretically to some perspectives not traditionally associated with information-processing approaches, such as the sociocultural perspective, through the idea of shared memories (see e.g. Mistry, 1997; Nelson, 1996; Vygotsky, 1978). A related issue is that of the relationships between children's memory and language, through discourse analysis or narratives (see e.g. Nelson, 1993; 1996). To talk and to remember are likely linked in ways we still do not completely understand. A third topic, discussed in some detail above, concerns children's eyewitness testimony and suggestibility. Although we have certainly learned a lot about this topic over the past decade or so (e.g. Ceci & Bruck, 1998; Goodman, Emery, & Haugaard 1998), there is still much to be learned. We do not know, for example, the duration of true and false memories, the type of false events children and adults are more likely to accept as potentially real, the role of individual differences in suggestibility and false-memory creation, or how to differentiate with reasonable accuracy true from false memories. Moreover, we still do not have a unified and complete theoretical framework for understanding suggestibility in children (Ceci & Bruck, 1998).

CONCLUSION

Research in memory development has played a central role in research and theory in cognitive development since the beginning of the cognitive revolution in academic psychology. We believe that it has been one of the most successful areas in cognitive developmental psychology, with substantial progress being made in fields such as infant memory, working memory, strategic memory, autobiographical memory, and the role that knowledge plays in everyday acts of remembering. Nonetheless, for an faculty that is crucial to every form of higher cognition, children's memory and the factors that contribute to its development continue to justify close attention. We have reviewed some of the research findings in memory development that have consumed developmental psychologists over the past 35 years and have suggested directions for future research. We hope, and expect, that the next 35 years will produce a fuller, clearer picture of memory development and how it affects other aspects of children's developing cognition.

REFERENCES

Ackerman, B.P. (1985). Children's retrieval deficit. In C.J. Brainerd & M. Pressley (eds), *Basic processes in memory development: Progress in cognitive development research* (pp. 1–46). New York: Springer-Verlag.

Ackerman, B.P. (1996). Induction of a memory retrieval strategy by young children. *Journal of Experimental Child Psychology*, 62, 243–271.

Ackerman, B.P. (1997). The role of setting information in children's memory retrieval. *Journal of Experimental Child Psychology*, 65, 238–260.

Ackil, J.K., & Zaragoza, M.S. (1995). Developmental differences in eyewitness suggestibility and memory for source. *Journal of Experimental Child Psychology*, 60, 57–83.

Alexander, J.M., & Schwanenflugel, P.J. (1994). Strategy regulation: The role of intelligence, metacognitive attributes, and knowledge base. *Developmental Psychology*, 30, 709–723.

Anooshian, L.J. (1997). Distinctions between implicit and explicit memory: Significance for understanding cognitive development. *International Journal of Behavioral Development*, 21, 453–478.

Ausley, J.A., & Guttentag, R.E. (1993). Direct and indirect assessments of memory: Implications for the study of memory development. In M.L. Howe & R. Pasnak (eds), *Emerging themes in cognitive development: Vol. 1. Foundations*. New York: Springer.

Baddeley, A.D. (1986). *Working memory*. Oxford: Clarendon.

Baddeley, A.D., & Hitch, G.J. (1984). Working memory. In G. Bower (ed.), *The psychology of learning and motivation: Advances in research and theory* (Vol. 8). New York: Academic.

Baker-Ward, L., Gordon, B.N., Ornstein, P.A., Larus, D.M., & Clubb, P.A. (1993). Young children's long-term retention of a pediatric visit. *Child Development*, 64, 1519–1533.

Baker-Ward, L., & Ornstein, P.A. (1988). Age differences in visual-spatial memory performance: Do children really out-perform adults when playing Concentration? *Bulletin of the Psychonomic Society*, 26, 331–332.

Barkow, J.H., Cosmides, L., & Tooby, J. (eds) (1992). *The adaptive mind: Evolutionary psychology and the generation of culture*. New York: Oxford University Press.

Bauer, P.J. (1997). Development of memory in early childhood. In N. Cowan (ed.), *The development of memory in childhood* (pp. 83–111). Hove: Psychology Press.

Bauer, P.J., Hertsgaard, L.A., & Wewerka, S.S. (1995). Effects of experience and reminding on long-term recall in infancy: Remembering not to forget. *Journal of Experimental Child Psychology*, 59, 260–298.

Best, D.L. (1993). Inducing children to generate mnemonic organizational strategies: An examination of long-term retention and materials. *Developmental Psychology*, 29, 324–336.

Bjorklund, D.F. (1987). How age changes in knowledge base contribute to the development of children's memory: An interpretive review. *Developmental Review*, 7, 93–130.

Bjorklund, D.F. (1997). The role of immaturity in human development. *Psychological Bulletin*, 122, 153–169.

Bjorklund, D.F. (2000a). *Children's thinking: Developmental function and individual differences* (3rd edn). Belmont, CA: Wadsworth.

Bjorklund, D.F. (ed.) (2000b). *False-memory creation in children and adults: Theory, research, and implications*. Mahwah, NJ: Erlbaum.

Bjorklund, D.F., & Bjorklund, B.R. (1985). Organization versus item effects of an elaborated knowledge base on children's memory. *Developmental Psychology*, 21, 1120–1131.

Bjorklund, D.F., Bjorklund, B.R., Douglas, R.B., & Cassel, W.S. (1998). Children's susceptibility to repeated questions: How misinformation changes children's answers and their minds. *Applied Developmental Science*, 2, 101–113.

Bjorklund, D.F., Brown, R.D., & Bjorklund, B.R. (2002). Children's eyewitness memory: Changing reports and changing representations. In P. Graf & N. Ohta (eds), *Lifespan memory development*. Cambridge, MA: MIT Press.

Bjorklund, D.F., & Coyle, T.R. (1995). Utilization deficiencies in the development of memory strategies. In F.E. Weinert & W. Schneider (eds), *Memory performance and competencies: Issues in growth and development* (pp. 161–180). Hillsdale, NJ: Erlbaum.

Bjorklund, D.F., Coyle, T.R., & Gaultney, J.F. (1992). Developmental differences in the acquisition and maintenance of an organizational strategy: Evidence for the utilization deficiency hypothesis. *Journal of Experimental Child Psychology*, 54, 434–448.

Bjorklund, D.F., & de Marchena, M.R. (1984). Developmental shifts in the basis of organization in memory: The role of associative versus categorical relatedness in children's free-recall. *Child Development*, 55, 952–962.

Bjorklund, D.F., & Douglas, R.N. (1997). The development of memory strategies. In N. Cowan (ed.), *The development of memory in childhood* (pp. 201–246). Hove : Psychology Press.

Bjorklund, D.F., Gaultney, J.F., & Green, B.L. (1993). 'I watch, therefore I can do': The development of meta-imitation during the preschool years and the advantage of optimism about one's imitative skills. In M.L. Howe & R. Pasnak (eds), *Emerging themes in cognitive development: Vol. 2. Competencies*. New York: Springer.

Bjorklund, D.F., & Harnishfeger, K.K. (1987). Developmental differences in the mental effort requirements for the use of an organizational strategy in free recall. *Journal of Experimental Child Psychology*, 44, 109–125.

Bjorklund, D.F., & Hock, H.S. (1982). Age differences in the temporal locus of memory organization in children's recall. *Journal of Experimental Child Psychology*, 32, 347–362.

Bjorklund, D.F., Miller, P.H., Coyle, T.R., & Slawinski, J.L. (1997). Instructing children to use memory strategies: Evidence of utilization deficiencies in memory training studies. *Developmental Review*, 17, 411–442.

Bjorklund, D.F., Muir-Broaddus, J.E., & Schneider, W. (1990). The role of knowledge in the development of strategies. In D.F. Bjorklund (ed.), *Children's strategies: Contemporary views of cognitive development* (pp. 93–128). Hillsdale, NJ: Erlbaum.

Bjorklund, D.F., Ornstein, P.A., & Haig, J.R. (1977). Developmental differences in organization and recall: Training in the use of organizational techniques. *Developmental Psychology*, 13, 175–183.

Bjorklund, D.F., & Pellegrini, A.D. (2000). Child development and evolutionary psychology. *Child Development*, 71, 1687–1708.

Bjorklund, D.F., & Schneider, W. (1996). The interaction of knowledge, aptitudes, and strategies in children's memory performance. In H.W. Reese (ed.), *Advances in child development and behavior* (Vol. 26, pp. 59–89). San Diego: Academic.

Bjorklund, D.F., Schneider, W., Cassel, W.S., & Ashley, E. (1994). Training and extension of a memory strategy: Evidence for utilization deficiencies in the acquisition of an organizational strategy in high- and low-IQ children. *Child Development*, 65, 951–965.

Bjorklund, D.F., & Zeman, B.R. (1982). Children's organization and metamemory awareness in the recall of familiar information. *Child Development*, 53, 799–810.

Black, M.M., & Rollins, H.A. (1982). The effects of instructional variables on young children's organization and free recall. *Journal of Experimental Child Psychology*, 33, 1–19.

Borkowski, J.G., Milstead, M., & Hale, C. (1988). Components of children's metamemory: Implications for strategy generalization. In F.E. Weinert & M. Perlmutter (eds), *Memory development: Universal changes and individual differences* (pp. 73–100). Hillsdale, NJ: Erlbaum.

Borkowski, J.G., Peck, V.A., Reid, M.K., & Kurtz, B.E. (1983). Impulsivity and strategy transfer: Metamemory as mediator. *Child Development*, 54, 459–473.

Brainerd, C.J., & Mojardin, A.H. (1999). Children's and adults' spontaneous false memories for sentences: Long-term persistence and mere-testing effects. *Child Development*.

Brainerd, C.J., & Reyna, V.F. (1998). Fuzzy-trace theory and children's false memories. *Journal of Experimental Child Psychology*, 71, 81–129.

Brown, A.L. (1978). Knowing when, where, and how to remember: A problem of metacognition. In R. Glaser (ed.), *Advances in instructional psychology* (pp. 77–165). Hillsdale, NJ: Erlbaum.

Brown, A.L., Bransford, J.D., Ferrara, R.A., & Campione, J.C. (1983). Learning, remembering, and understanding. In J.H. Flavell & E.M. Markman (eds), *Handbook of child psychology* (Vol. 3, pp. 77–166). New York: Wiley.

Bruck, M., & Ceci, S.J. (1999). The suggestibility of children's memory. In J.T. Spence, J.M. Darley, & D.J. Foss (eds), *Annual review of psychology* (Vol. 50, pp. 419–439). Palo Alto: Annual Reviews.

Buss, D.M. (1995). Evolutionary psychology. *Psychological Inquiry*, 6, 1–30.

Buss, D.M. (1999). *Evolutionary psychology: The new science of the mind*. Boston: Allyn and Bacon.

Byrnes, J.P., & Fox, N.A. (1998). The educational relevance of research in cognitive neuroscience. *Educational Psychology Review*, 10, 297–342.

Cantor, D.S., Andreassen, C., & Waters, H.S. (1985). Organization in visual episodic memory: Relationships between verbalized knowledge, strategy use, and performance. *Journal of Experimental Child Psychology*, 40, 218–232.

Carr, M., & Schneider, W. (1991). Long-term maintenance of organizational strategies in kindergarten children. *Contemporary Educational Psychology*, 16, 61–72.

Case, R. (1985). *Intellectual development: Birth to adulthood*. New York: Academic.

Case, R. (1992). *The mind's staircase: Exploring the conceptual underpinnings of children's thought and knowledge*. Hillsdale, NJ: Erlbaum.

Case, R., Kurland, M., & Goldberg, J. (1982). Operational efficiency and the growth of short-term memory span. *Journal of Experimental Child Psychology*, 33, 386–404.

Cassel, W.S., & Bjorklund, D.F. (1995). Developmental patterns of eyewitness memory and suggestibility: An ecologically based short-term longitudinal study. *Law & Human Behavior*, 19, 507–532.

Cassel, W.S., Roebers, C.E.M., & Bjorklund, D.F. (1996). Developmental patterns of eyewitness responses to increasingly suggestive questions. *Journal of Experimental Child Psychology*, 61, 116–133.

Cavanaugh, J.C., & Borkowski, J.G. (1980). Searching for metamemory–memory connections: A developmental study. *Developmental Psychology*, 16, 441–453.

Ceci, S.J., & Bronfenbrenner, U. (1985). 'Don't forget to take the cupcakes out of the oven': Prospective memory, strategic time-monitoring, and context. *Child Development*, 56, 152–164.

Ceci, S.J., & Bruck, M. (1993). Suggestibility of the child witness: A historical review and synthesis. *Psychological Bulletin*, 113, 403–439.

Ceci, S.J., & Bruck, M. (1998). Children's testimony: Applied and basic issues. In W. Damon, (series ed.) & I.E. Sigel & K.A. Renninger (eds), *Handbook of child psychology: Vol. 4. Child psychology in practice* (pp. 713–774). New York: Wiley.

Ceci, S.J., Loftus, E.F., Leichtman, M., & Bruck, M. (1994). The role of source misattributions in the creation of false beliefs among preschoolers. *International Journal of Clinical and Experimental Hypnosis*, 62, 304–320.

Chen, C., & Stevenson, H.W. (1988). Cross-linguistic differences in digit span of preschool children. *Journal of Experimental Child Psychology*, 46, 150–158.

Chi, M.T.H. (1978). Knowledge structure and memory development. In R. Siegler (ed.), *Children's thinking: What develops?* Hillsdale, NJ: Erlbaum.

Cowan, N. (1997). The development of working memory. In N. Cowan (ed.), *The development of memory in childhood*. Hove: Psychology Press.

Cowan, N., Nugent, L.D., Elliott, E.M., Ponomarev, I., & Saults, J.S. (1999). The role of attention in the development of short-term memory: Age differences in the verbal span of apprehension. *Child Development*, 70, 1082–1097.

Cox, B.C., Ornstein, P.A., Naus, M.J., Maxfield, D., & Zimler, J. (1989). Children's concurrent use of rehearsal and organizational strategies. *Developmental Psychology*, 25, 619–627.

Cox, D., & Waters, H.S. (1986). Sex differences in the use of organization strategies: A developmental analysis. *Journal of Experimental Child Psychology*, 41, 18–37.

Coyle, T.R., & Bjorklund, D.F. (1997). Age differences in, and consequences of, multiple- and variable strategy use on a multitrial sort–recall task. *Developmental Psychology*, 33, 372–380.

Coyle, T.R., Read, L.E., Gaultney, J.F., & Bjorklund, D.F. (1999). Giftedness and variability in strategic processing on a multitrial memory task: Evidence for stability in gifted cognition. *Learning and Individual Differences*, 10, 273–290.

Cunningham, J.G., & Weaver, S.L. (1989). Young children's knowledge of their memory span: Effects of task and experience. *Journal of Experimental Child Psychology*, 48, 32–44.

DeLoache, J.S. (1989). Young children's understanding of the correspondence between a scale model and a larger space. *Cognitive Development*, 4, 121–139.

Dempster, F.N. (1977). Memory span and short-term memory capacity: A developmental study. *Journal of Experimental Child Psychology*, 26, 419–431.

Dempster, F.N. (1981). Memory span: Sources of individual and developmental differences. *Psychological Bulletin*, 89, 63–100.

Dempster, F.N. (1985). Short-term memory development in childhood and adolescence. In C.J. Brainerd & M. Pressley (eds), *Basic processes in memory development: Progress in cognitive development research* (pp. 209–248). New York: Springer.

de Ribaupierre, A., & Bailleux, C. (1995). Development of attentional capacity in childhood: A longitudinal study. In F.E. Weinert & W. Schneider (eds), *Research on memory development: State-of-the-art and future directions* (pp. 45–70). Hillsdale, NJ: Erlbaum.

Dochy, F., & Alexander, P.A. (1995). Mapping prior knowledge: A framework for discussion among researchers. *European Journal of Psychology of Education*, 10, 225–242.

Donald, M. (1991). *Origins of the modern mind: Three stages in the evolution of culture and cognition*. Cambridge, MA: Harvard University Press.

Doris, J. (ed.) (1991). *The suggestibility of children's recollections: Implications for eyewitness testimony*. Washington, DC: American Psychological Association.

Drummey, A.B., & Newcombe, N. (1995). Remembering versus knowing the past: Children's explicit and implicit memories for pictures. *Journal of Experimental Child Psychology*, 59, 549–565.

Dufresne, A., & Kobasigawa, A. (1989). Children's spontaneous allocation of study time: Differential and sufficient aspects. *Journal of Experimental Child Psychology*, 47, 274–296.

Elischberger, H.B., & Roebers, C.M. (2001). Improving young children's narratives about an observed event: The effects of nonspecific verbal prompts. *International Journal of Behavioral Development*, 25, 160–166.

Ellis, N.R., Katz, E., & Williams, J.E. (1987). Developmental aspects of memory for spatial location. *Journal of Experimental Child Psychology*, 44, 401–412.

Engle, R.W., Fidler, D.S., & Reynolds, L.M. (1981). Does echoic memory develop? *Journal of Experimental Child Psychology*, 32, 459–473.

Fagan, J.F. III. (1984). The relationship of novelty preferences during infancy to later intelligence and recognition memory. *Intelligence*, 8, 339–346.

Farrar, M.J., & Goodman, G.S. (1992). Developmental changes in event memory. *Child Development*, 63, 173–187.

Fivush, R. (1997). Event memory in early childhood. In N. Cowan (ed.), *The development of memory in childhood* (pp. 139–161). London: London University College Press.

Fivush, R., Haden, C.A., & Adam, S. (1995). Structure and coherence of preschoolers' personal narratives over time: Implications for childhood amnesia. *Journal of Experimental Child Psychology*, 60, 32–50.

Fivush, R., & Hudson, J.A. (eds) (1990). *Knowing and remembering in young children*. Cambridge: Cambridge University Press.

Flavell, J.H. (1970). Developmental studies of mediated memory. In H.W. Reese & L.P. Lipsitt (eds), *Advances in child development and behavior* (pp. 181–211). New York: Academic.

Flavell, J.H., Beach, D.R., & Chinsky, J.H. (1966). Spontaneous verbal rehearsal in a memory task as a function of age. *Child Development*, 37, 283–299.

Flavell, J.H., & Wellman, H.M. (1977). Metamemory. In R.V. Kail & J.W. Hagen (eds), *Perspectives on the development of memory and cognition* (pp. 3–33). Hillsdale, NJ: Erlbaum.

Flin, R., Boon, J., Knox, A., & Bull, R. (1992). The effect of a five-month delay on children's and adult's eye-witness memory. *British Journal of Psychology*, 83, 323–336.

Gabrieli, J.D.E. (1998). Cognitive neuroscience of human memory. *Annual Review of Psychology*, 49, 87–115.

Gathercole, S.E. (1998). The development of memory. *Journal of Child Psychology and Psychiatry*, 39 (1), 3–27.

Gaultney, J.F. (1995). The effect of prior knowledge and metacognition on the acquisition of a reading comprehension strategy. *Journal of Experimental Child Psychology*, 59, 142–163.

Gaultney, J.F., Bjorklund, D.F., & Schneider, W. (1992). The role of children's expertise in a strategic memory task. *Contemporary Educational Psychology*, 17, 244–257.

Geary, D.C. (1995). Reflections of evolution and culture in children's cognition: Implications for mathematical development and instruction. *American Psychologist*, 50, 24–37.

Geary, D.C., & Bjorklund, D.F. (2000). Evolutionary developmental psychology. *Child Development*, 71, 57–65.

Geary, D.C., Bow-Thomas, C.C., Fan, L., & Siegler, R.S. (1993). Even before formal instruction, Chinese children outperform American children in mental arithmetic. *Cognitive Development*, 8, 517–529.

Goodman, G.S., Aman, C.J., & Hirschman, J. (1987). Child sexual and physical abuse: Children's testimony. In C.J. Ceci, M. P. Toglia, & D.F. Ross (eds), *Children's eyewitness memory* (pp. 1–23). New York: Springer.

Goodman, G.S., & Clarke-Stewart, A. (1991). Suggestibility in children's testimony: Implications for sexual abuse investigations. In J. Doris (ed.), *The suggestibility of children's recollections: Implications for eyewitness testimony* (pp. 92–105). Washington, DC: American Psychological Association.

Goodman, G.S., Emery, R.E., & Haugaard, J.J. (1998). Developmental psychology and law: Divorce, child maltreatment, foster care, and adoption. In W. Damon (series ed.) & L.E. Siegel & K.A. Renninger (eds), *Handbook of child psychology: Vol. 4. Child psychology in practice* (pp. 775–874). New York: Wiley.

Goodman, G.S., Hirschman, J.E., Hepps, D., & Rudy, L. (1991). Children's memory for stressful events. *Merrill-Palmer Quarterly*, 37, 109–158.

Guttentag, R.E. (1984). The mental effort requirement of cumulative rehearsal: A developmental study. *Journal of Experimental Child Psychology*, 37, 92–106.

Guttentag, R.E. & Lange, G. (1994). Motivational influences on children's strategic remembering. *Learning and Individual Differences*, 6, 309–330.

Guttentag, R.E., Ornstein, P.A. & Siemens, L. (1987). Children's spontaneous rehearsal: Transitions in strategy acquisition. *Cognitive Development*, 2, 307–326.

Hamond, N.R., & Fivush, R. (1991). Memories of Mickey Mouse: Young children recount their trip to Disneyworld. *Cognitive Development*, 6, 433–448.

Harnishfeger, K.K., & Bjorklund, D.F. (1990). Children's strategies: A brief history. In D.F. Bjorklund (ed.), *Children's strategies: Contemporary views of cognitive development* (pp. 1–22). Hillsdale, NJ: Erlbaum.

Hasselhorn, M. (1992). Task dependency and the role of category typicality and metamemory in the development of an organizational strategy. *Child Development*, 63, 202–214.

Hasselhorn, M. (1995). Beyond production deficiency and utilization inefficiency: Mechanisms of the emergence of strategic categorization in episodic memory tasks. In F.E. Weinert & W. Schneider (eds), *Memory performance and competencies: Issues in growth and development* (pp. 141–159). Hillsdale, NJ: Erlbaum.

Hayes, B.K., & Hennessy, R. (1996). The nature and development of nonverbal implicit memory. *Journal of Experimental Child Psychology*, 63, 22–43.

Henry, L.A., & Millar, S. (1991). Memory span increases with age: A test of two hypotheses. *Journal of Experimental Child Psychology*, 51, 459–484.

Herman, J.F., Norton, L.M., & Klein, C.A. (1986). Children's distance estimates in a large-scale environment. *Environment and Behavior*, 18, 533–558.

Hernandez Blasi, C. (1999). Review of Das, J.P., Kar, B.C., & Parrila, R.K. (1998). *Planificación cognitiva: Bases psicológicas de la conducta inteligente*. Paidós, Barcelona: Infancia y Aprendizaje.

Hernandez Blasi, C., & Bjorklund, D.F. (2001). El desarrollo de la memoria: Avances significativos y nuevos desafíos (Memory devlopment: Accomplishments of the past and directions for the future). *Infancia y Aprendizaje*, 24, 233–254.

Hitch, G.J., & Halliday, M.S. (1983). Working memory in children. *Philosophical Transactions of the Royal Society*, B302, 324–340.

Hitch, G.J., & Towse, J. (1995). Working memory: What develops? In F.E. Weinert & W. Schneider (eds), *Research on memory development: State-of-the-art and future directions* (pp. 3–21). Hillsdale, NJ: Erlbaum.

Hock, H.S., Park, C.L., & Bjorklund, D.F. (1998). Temporal organization in children's strategy formation. *Journal of Experimental Child Psychology*, 70, 187–206.

Howe, M.L., Brainerd, C.J., & Kingma, J. (1985). Development of organization in recall: A stages-of-learning analysis. *Journal of Experimental Child Psychology*, 39, 230–251.

Howe, M.L., Courage, M.L., & Peterson, C. (1994). How can I remember when 'I' wasn't there? Long-term retention of traumatic experiences and emergence of the cognitive self. *Consciousness and Cognition*, 3, 327–355.

Hudson, J.A. (1990). The emergence of autobiographical memory in mother–child conversation. In R. Fivush & J.A. Hudson (eds), *Knowing and remembering in young children*. Cambridge: Cambridge University Press.

Hudson, J.A. (1993). Reminiscing with mothers and others: Autobiographical memory in young two-year-olds. *Journal of Narrative and Life History*, 1, 1–32.

Hudson, J.A., & Fivush, R. (1991). As time goes by: Sixth graders remember a kindergarten experience. *Applied Cognitive Psychology*, 5, 346–360.

Hudson, J.A., & Sheffield, E.G. (1999). The role of reminders in young children's memory development. In L. Balter & C. Tamis-Lemonde (eds), *Child psychology: A handbook of contemporary issues* (pp. 197–214). New York: Garland.

Hulme, C., Thompson, N., Muir, C., & Lawrence, A. (1984). Speech rate and the development of spoken words: The role of rehearsal and item identification processes. *Journal of Experimental Child Psychology*, 38, 241–253.

Hupbach, A., Mecklenbräuker, S., & Wippich, W. (1999). Implicit memory in children: Are there age-related improvements in a conceptual test of implicit memory? In M. Hahn & S.C. Stoness (eds), *Proceedings of the Twenty-First Annual Conference of the Cognitive Science Society*. Mahwah, NJ: Erlbaum.

Johnson, M.H. (1998). The neural basis of cognitive development. In W. Damon (series ed.) & D. Kuhn & R.S. Siegler (eds), *Handbook of child psychology: Vol. 2. Cognition, perception, and language* (5th edn, pp. 1–49). New York: Wiley.

Joyner, M.H., & Kurtz-Costes, B. (1997). Metamemory development. In N. Cowan (ed.), *The development of memory in childhood* (pp. 275–300). London: UCL Press.

Justice, E.M. (1985). Categorization as a preferred memory strategy: Developmental changes during elementary school. *Developmental Psychology*, 21, 1105–1110.

Justice, E.M., Baker-Ward, L., Gupta, S., & Jannings, L.R. (1997). Means to the goal of remembering: Developmental changes in awareness of strategy use–performance relations. *Journal of Experimental Child Psychology*, 65, 293–314.

Justice, E.M., & Bray, N.W. (1979). The effects of context and feedback on metamemory in young children. Paper presented at the biennial meeting of the Society for Research in Child Development, San Francisco.

Kail, R.V. Jr (1979). Use of strategies and individual differences in children's memory. *Developmental Psychology*, 15, 251–255.

Kail, R. (1991). Development of processing speed in childhood and adolescence. In H.W. Reese (ed.), *Advances in child development and behavior* (Vol. 23). San Diego: Academic.

Kail, R. (1993). The role of a global mechanism in developmental change in speed of processing. In M.L. Howe & R. Pasnak (eds), *Emerging themes in cognitive development: Vol. 1. Foundations*. New York: Springer.

Kail, R.V., & Salthouse, T.A. (1994). Processing speed as a mental capacity. *Acta Psychologica*, 86, 199–225.

Karmiloff-Smith, A. (1992). *Beyond modularity: A developmental perspective on cognitive science*. Cambridge, MA: MIT Press.

Kee, D.W. (1994). Developmental differences in associative memory: Strategy use, mental effort, and knowledge–access interaction. In H.W. Reese (ed.), *Advances in child development and behavior* (Vol. 25). New York: Academic.

Kee, D.W., & Davies, L. (1988). Mental effort and elaboration: A developmental analysis. *Contemporary Educational Psychology*, 13, 221–228.

Kellas, G., Ashcraft, M.H., & Johnson, N.S. (1973). Rehearsal processes in the short-term memory performance of mildly retarded adolescents. *American Journal of Mental deficiency*, 77, 670–679.

Kingsley, P.R., & Hagen, J.W. (1969). Induced versus spontaneous rehearsal in short-term memory in nursery school children. *Developmental Psychology*, 1, 40–46.

Knopf, M. (1999). Development of memory for texts. In F.E. Weinert & W. Schneider (eds), *Individual development from 3 to 12: Findings from the Munich Longitudinal Study* (pp. 106–122). Cambridge: Cambridge University Press.

Knopf, M., Körkel, J., Schneider, W., & Weinert, F.E. (1988). Human memory as a faculty versus human memory as a set of specific abilities: Evidence from a life-span approach. In F.E. Weinert & M. Perlmutter (eds), *Memory development: Universal changes and individual differences* (pp. 331–352). Hillsdale, NJ: Erlbaum.

Kobasigawa, A. (1974). Utilization of retrieval cues by children in recall. *Child Development*, 45, 127–134.

Koriat, A., & Goldsmith, M. (1996). Monitoring and control processes in the strategic regulation of memory accuracy. *Psychological Review*, 103, 490–517.

Koriat, A., Goldsmith, M., & Pansky, A. (2000). Toward a psychology of memory accuracy. *Annual Review of Psychology*, 51, 481–537.

Kreutzer, M.A., Leonard, C., & Flavell, J.H. (1975). *An interview study of children's knowledge about memory. Monographs of the Society for Research in Child Development*, Vol. 40, serial 159.

Kuhn, D. (2000). Does memory development belong on an endangered topic list? *Child Development*, 71, 21–25.

Kunzinger, E.L. (1985). A short-term longitudinal study of memorial development during early grade school. *Developmental Psychology*, 21, 642–646.

Kurtz, B.E., & Borkowski, J.G. (1984). Children's metacognition: Exploring relations among knowledge, process, and motivational variables. *Journal of Experimental Child Psychology*, 37, 335–354.

Kurtz-Costes, B., Schneider, W., & Rupp, S. (1995). Is there evidence for intraindividual consistency in performance across memory tasks? New evidence on an old question. In F.E. Weinert & W. Schneider (eds), *Memory performance and competencies: Issues in growth and development*. Hillsdale, NJ: Erlbaum.

Landau, B., & Spelke, E.S. (1985). Spatial knowledge and its manifestations. In H.M. Wellman (ed.), *Children's searching* (pp. 27–52). Cambridge, MA: Harvard University Press.

Lange, G., Guttentag, R.E., & Nida, R.E. (1990). Relationships between study organization, retrieval organization, and general strategy-specific memory knowledge in young children. *Journal of Experimental Child Psychology*, 49, 126–146.

Lange, G., & Pierce, S.H. (1992). Memory-strategy learning and maintenance in preschool children. *Developmental Psychology*, 28, 453–462.

Leal, L., Crays, N., & Moely, B.E. (1985). Training children to use a self-monitoring study strategy in preparation for recall: Maintenance and generalization effects. *Child Development*, 56, 643–653.

Lecours, A.R. (1975). Myelogenetic correlates of the development of speech and language. In e. H. Lenneberg & E. Lenneberg (eds), *Foundations of language development: A multidisciplinary approach* (pp. 75–49) New York: Academic.

Leichtman, M.D., & Ceci, S.J. (1995). The effect of stereotypes and suggestion on preschoolers reports. *Developmental Psychology*, 31, 568–578.

Logie, R.H., & Marchetti, C. (1991). Visuo-spatial working memory: Visual, spatial, or central executive? In R.H. Logie & M. Denis (eds), *Mental images in human cognition* (pp. 105–115). Amsterdam: North Holland.

Mandler, J.M., & Robinson, C.A. (1978). Developmental changes in picture recognition. *Journal of Experimental Child Psychology*, 26, 122–136.

Matthews, M.H. (1992). *Making sense of place*. Hampstead: Barnes & Noble.

McDonough, L., Mandler, J.M., McKee, R.D., & Squire, L.R. (1995). The deferred imitation task as a nonverbal measure of declarative memory. *Proceedings of the National Academy of Sciences*, 92, 7580–7584.

McGilly, K., & Siegler, R.S. (1989). How children choose among serial recall strategies. *Child Development*, 60, 172–182.

McGilly, K., & Siegler, R.S. (1990). The influence of encoding strategic knowledge on children's choices among serial recall strategies. *Developmental Psychology*, 26, 931–941.

Melot, A.-M. (1998). The relationship between metacognitive knowledge and metacognitive experiences: Acquisition and re-elaboration. *European Journal of Psychology of Education*, 13, 75–89.

Meltzoff, A.N. (1995). What infant memory tells us about infantile amnesia: Long-term recall and deferred imitation. *Journal of Experimental Child Psychology*, 59, 497–515.

Miller, P.H. (1990). The development of strategies of selective attention. In D.F. Bjorklund (ed.), *Children's strategies: Contemporary views of cognitive development* (pp. 157–184). Hillsdale, NJ: Erlbaum.

Miller, P.H. (1994). Individual differences in children's strategic behavior: Utilization deficiencies. *Learning and Individual Differences*, 6, 285–307.

Miller, P.H. (2000). How best to utilize a deficiency: A commentary on Waters' 'Memory strategy development'. *Child Development*, 71, 1013–1017.

Miller. P.H., & Coyle, T.R. (1999). Developmental changes: Lessons from microgenesis. In E.K. Scholnick, K. Nelson, S.A. Gelman, & P.H. Miller (eds), *Conceptual development: Piaget's legacy. The Jean Piaget Symposium series* (pp. 209–239). Mahwah, NJ: Erlbaum.

Miller, P.H., Haynes, V.F., DeMarie-Dreblow, D., & Woody-Ramsey, J. (1986). Children's strategies for gathering information in three tasks. *Child Development*, 57, 1429–1439.

Miller, P.H., & Seier, W.L. (1994). Strategy utilization deficiencies in children: When, where, and why. In H.W. Reese (ed.), *Advances in child development and behavior* (Vol. 25). New York: Academic.

Miller, P.H., Seier, W.L., Probert, J.S., & Aloise, P.A. (1991). Age differences in the capacity demands of a strategy among spontaneously strategic children. *Journal of Experimental Child Psychology*, 52, 149–165.

Milner, B. (1964). Some effects of frontal lobectomy in man. In J.M. Warren & K. Akert (eds), *The frontal granular cortex and behavior*. New York: McGraw-Hill.

Mistry, J. (1997). The development of remembering in cultural context. In N. Cowan (ed.), *The development of memory in childhood*. Hove: Psychology Press.

Naito, M. (1990). Repetition priming in children and adults: Age-related dissociation between implicit and explicit memory. *Journal of Experimental Child Psychology*, 50, 462–484.

Naus, M.J., & Ornstein, P.A. (1983). Development of memory strategies: Analyses, questions, and issues. In M.T.H. Chi (ed.), *Trends in memory development research* (Vol. 9, pp. 1–30). Basel: Karger.

Nelson, C. (1995). The ontogeny of human memory: A cognitive neuroscience perspective. *Developmental Psychology*, 31, 723–735.

Nelson, C. (1997). The neurobiological bases of early memory development. In N. Cowan (ed.), *The development of memory in childhood* (pp. 41–82). Hove: Psychology Press.

Nelson, K. (1993). The psychological and social origins of autobiographical memory. *Psychological Science*, 4, 7–14.

Nelson, K. (1996). *Language in cognitive development: The emergence of the mediated mind.* Cambridge: Cambridge University Press.

Ornstein, P.A. (1999). Comments: Toward an understanding of the development of memory. In F.E. Weinert & W. Schneider (eds), *Individual development from 3 to 12: Findings from the Munich Longitudinal Study* (pp. 94–105). Cambridge: Cambridge University Press.

Ornstein, P.A., Gordon, B.N., & Larus, D.M. (1992). Children's memory for a personally experienced event: Implications for testimony. *Applied Developmental Psychology*, 6, 49–60.

Ornstein, P.A., & Naus, M.J. (1985). Effects of the knowledge base on children's memory strategies. In H.W. Reese (ed.), *Advances in child development and behavior* (Vol. 19). New York: Academic.

Ornstein, P.A., Naus, M.J., & Liberty, C. (1975). Rehearsal and organizational processes in children's memory. *Child Development*, 46, 818–830.

Ornstein, P.A., Naus, M.J., & Stone, B.P. (1977). Rehearsal training and developmental differences in memory. *Development Psychology*, 13, 15–24.

Ornstein, P.A., Shapiro, L.R., Clubb, P.A., & Follmer, A. (1996). The influence of prior knowledge on children's memory for salient medical experiences. In N. Stein, P.A. Ornstein, C.J. Brainerd, & B. Tversky (eds), *Memory for everyday and emotional events* (pp. 83–91). Hillsdale, NJ: Erlbaum.

O'Sullivan, J.T. (1993). Preschoolers' beliefs about effort, incentives, and recall. *Journal of Experimental Child Psychology*, 55, 396–414.

O'Sullivan, J.T. (1996). Children's metamemory about the influence of conceptual relations on recall. *Journal of Experimental Child Psychology*, 62, 1–29.

O'Sullivan, J.T., & Howe, M.L. (1998). A different view of metamemory with illustrations from children's beliefs about long-term retention. *European Journal of Psychology of Education*, 13, 9–28.

Palincsar, A.S., & Brown, A.L. (1984). Reciprocal teaching of comprehension-fostering and comprehension-monitoring activities. *Cognition and Instruction*, 1, 117–175.

Paris, S.G. & Oka, E.R. (1986). Children's reading strategies, metacognition, and motivation. *Developmental Review*, 6, 25–56.

Parkin, A.J. (1993). Implicit memory across the lifespan. In P. Graf & M.E.J. Masson (eds), *Implicit memory: New directions in cognition, development, and neuropsychology* (pp. 63–131). Amsterdam: Elsevier.

Piaget, J. (1962). *Play, dreams, and imitation in childhood.* New York: Norton.

Piaget, J. (1971). *Biology and knowledge*. Chicago: University of Chicago Press.

Poole, D.A., & Lindsay, D.S. (1995). Interviewing preschoolers: Effects of nonsuggestive techniques, parental coaching and leading questions on reports of nonexperienced events. *Journal of Experimental Child Psychology*, 60, 129–154.

Poole, D.A., & White, L.T. (1991). Effects of question repetition on the eyewitness testimony of children and adults. *Developmental Psychology*, 27, 975–986.

Poole, D.A., & White, L.T. (1993). Two years later: Effects of question repetition and retention interval on the eyewitness testimony of children and adults. *Developmental Psychology*, 29, 844–853.

Poole, D., & White, L. (1995). Tell me again and again: Stability and change in the repeated testimonies of children and adults. In M.S. Zaragoza, J.R. Graham, C.N. Gordon, R. Hirschman, & Y.S. Ben Porath (eds), *Memory and testimony in the child witness* (pp. 24–43). Newbury Park, CA: Sage.

Pressley, M., & van Meter, P. (1993). Memory strategies: Natural development and use following instruction. In R. Pasnak & M.L. Howe (eds), *Emerging themes in cognitive development: Vol. II. Competencies*. New York: Springer.

Pressley, M., Forrest-Pressley, D.J., Elliott-Faust, D.J., & Miller, G.E. (1985). Children's use of cognitive strategies, how to teach strategies, and what to do if they can't be taught. In M. Pressley & C.J. Brainerd (eds), *Cognitive learning and memory in children*. New York: Springer.

Qin, J.M., Quas, J.A., Redlich, A.D., & Goodman, G.S. (1997). Children's eyewitness testimony: Memory development in the legal context. In N. Cowan (ed.), *The development of memory in childhood* (pp. 301–341). Hove: Psychology Press.

Ratner, H.H. (1984). Memory demands and the development of young children's memory. *Child Development*, 55, 2173–2191.

Reber, A.S. (1992). The cognitive unconscious: An evolutionary perspective. *Consciousness and Cognition*, 2, 93–133.

Reese, H.W. (1977). Imagery and associative memory. In R.V. Kail & J.W. Hagen (eds), *Perspectives on the development of memory and cognition*. Hillsdale, NJ: Erlbaum.

Reese, E., & Fivush, R. (1993). Parental styles for talking about the past. *Developmental Psychology*, 29, 596–606.

Reyna, V.F., & Brainerd, C.J. (1995). Fuzzy-trace theory: An interim analysis. *Learning and Individual Differences*, 7, 1–75.

Ringel, B.A., & Springer, C.J. (1980). On knowing how well one is remembering: The persistence of strategy use during transfer. *Journal of Experimental Child Psychology*, 29, 322–333.

Roebers, C., Rieber, F., & Schneider, W. (1995). Zeugenaussagen und Suggestibilität als Funktion der Erinnerungsgenauigkeit: Eine entwicklungspsychologische Studie (Eyewitness testimony and suggestibility as a function of memory accuracy: A developmental study). *Zeitschrift für Entwicklungspsychologie und Pädagogische Psychologie*, 27, 210–225.

Roebers, C.M., & Schneider, W. (2000). The impact of misleading questions on eyewitness memory in children and adults. *Applied Cognitive Psychology*, 14, 509–526.

Roediger, H.L. (1990). Implicit memory: Retention without remembering. *American Psychologist*, 45, 1043–1056.

Roediger, H.L., & McDermott, K.B. (1993). Implicit memory in normal human subjects. In H. Spinnler & F. Boller (eds), *Handbook of neuropsychology* (Vol. 8, pp. 63–131). Amsterdam: Elsevier.

Rogoff, B. (1990). *Apprenticeship in thinking: Cognitive development in social context*. New York: Oxford University Press.

Rogoff, B. (1998). Cognition as a collaborative process. In W. Damon (series ed.) & D. Kuhn & R.S. Siegler (eds), *Handbook of child psychology: vol. 2. Cognition language, and perceptual development* (pp. 679–744). New York: Wiley.

Rogoff, B., Newcombe, N., & Kagan, J. (1974). Planfulness and recognition memory. *Child Development*, 45, 972–977.

Roth, C. (1983). Factors affecting developmental changes in the speed of processing. *Journal of Experimental Child Psychology*, 35, 509–528.

Rovee-Collier, C., & Gerhardstein, P. (1997). The development of infant memory. In N. Cowan (ed.), *The development of memory in childhood* (pp. 5–39). Hove: Psychology Press.

Rudy, L., & Goodman, G.S. (1991). Effects of participation on children's reports: Implications for children's testimony. *Developmental Psychology*, 27, 527–538.

Ruiz Vargas, J.M. (1996). *La memoria humana: Función y estructura (Human memory: Function and structure)*. Madrid: Alianza.

Russo, R., Nichelli, P., Gibertoni, M., & Cornia, C. (1995). Developmental trends in implicit and explicit memory: A picture completion study. *Journal of Experimental Child Psychology*, 60, 566–578.

Salatas, H., & Flavell, J.H. (1976). Behavioral and metamnemonic indicators of strategic behavior under remember instructions in first grade. *Child Development*, 47, 81–89.

Salmon, K., & Pipe, M.-E. (1997). Props and children's event reports: The impact of a 1-year delay. *Journal of Experimental Child Psychology*, 65, 261–292.

Saywitz, K., Goodman, G., Nicholas, G., & Moan, S. (1991). Children's memory for genital exam: Implications for child sexual abuse. *Journal of Consulting and Clinical Psychology*, 59, 682–691.

Schacter, D.L. (1992). Understanding implicit memory. *American Psychologist*, 47, 559–569.

Schlagmüller, M., & Schneider, W. (2002). The development of organizational strategies in children: Evidence from a microgenetic lomgitudinal study. *Journal of Experimental Child Psychology*, 81, 298–319.

Schneider, W. (1985). Developmental trends in the metamemory–memory behavior relationship: An integrative review. In D.L. Forrest-Pressley, G.E. MacKinnon, & T.G. Waller (eds), *Cognition, metacognition, and human performance* (Vol. 1, pp. 57–109). Orlando, FL: Academic.

Schneider, W. (1986). The role of conceptual knowledge and metamemory in the development of organizational processes in memory. *Journal of Experimental Child Psychology*, 42, 218–236.

Schneider, W. (1993). Domain-specific knowledge and memory performance in children. Educational Psychology Review, 5, 257–273.

Schneider, W. (1998). Performance prediction in young children: Effects of skill, metacognition and wishful thinking. *Developmental Science*, 1, 291–297.

Schneider, W. (1999).The development of metamemory in children. In D. Gopher & A. Koriat (eds), *Attention and performance: XII. Cognitive regulation of performance: Interaction of theory and application*. Cambridge, MA: MIT Press.

Schneider, W., & Bjorklund, D.F. (1992). Expertise, aptitude, and strategic remembering. *Child Development*, 63, 461–473.

Schneider, W., & Bjorklund, D.F. (1998). Memory. In W. Damon (series ed.) & D. Kuhn, & R.S. Siegler (eds), *Handbook of child psychology: Vol. 2. Cognition, language, and perceptual development* (5th edn, pp. 467–521). New York: Wiley.

Schneider, W., Bjorklund, D.F., & Maier-Brückner, W. (1996). The effects of expertise and IQ on children's memory: When knowledge is, and when it is not enough. *International Journal of Behavioral Development*, 19, 773–796.

Schneider, W., Borkowski, J.G., Kurtz, B.E., & Kerwin, K. (1986). Metamemory and motivation: A comparison of strategy use and performance in German and American children. *Journal of Cross-Cultural Psychology*, 17, 315–336.

Schneider, W., Gruber, H., Gold, A., & Opwis, K. (1993). Chess expertise and memory for chess positions in children and adults. *Journal of Experimental Child Psychology*, 56, 328–349.

Schneider, W., Körkel, J., & Weinert, F.E. (1989). Domain-specific knowledge and memory performance: A comparison of high- and low-aptitude children. *Journal of Educational Psychology*, 81, 306–312.

Schneider, W., Körkel, J., & Weinert, F.E. (1990). Expert knowledge, general abilities, and text processing. In W. Schneider & F.E. Weinert (eds), *Interactions among aptitude, strategies, and knowledge in cognitive performance* (pp. 235–251). New York: Springer.

Schneider, W., & Pressley, M. (1989). *Memory development between 2 and 20*. New York: Springer.

Schneider, W., & Pressley, M. (1997). *Memory development between 2 and 20* (2nd edn). Mahwah, NJ: Erlbaum.

Schneider, W., Schlagmüller, M., & Visé, M. (1998). The impact of metamemory and domain-specific knowledge on memory performance. *European Journal of Psychology of Education*, 13, 91–103.

Schneider, W., & Sodian, B. (1988). Metamemory–memory behavior relationships in young children: Evidence from a memory-for-location task. *Journal of Experimental Child Psychology*, 45, 209–233.

Schneider, W., & Sodian, B. (1990). Gedächtnisentwicklung im Vorschulalter: 'Theoriewandel' im kindlichen Verständnis des Lernens und Erinnerns? (Memory development in preschool children: 'Conceptual change' in the understanding of learning and memory?). In M. Knopf & W. Schneider (eds), *Kindheit: Festschrift zum 60. Geburtstag von Franz Emanuel Weinert* (pp. 45–64). Göttingen: Hogrefe.

Schneider, W., & Sodian, B. (1991). A longitudinal study of young children's memory behavior and performance in a sort–recall task. *Journal of Experimental Child Psychology*, 51, 14–29.

Schneider, W., & Sodian, B. (1997). Memory strategy development: Lessons from longitudinal research. *Developmental Review*, 17, 442–461.

Schneider, W., & Weinert, F.E. (1989). Universal trends and individual differences in memory development. In A. de Ribaupierre (ed.), *Transition mechanisms in child development: The longitudinal perspective* (pp. 68–106). Cambridge: Cambridge University Press.

Schneider, W., & Weinert, F.E. (1990). The role of knowledge, strategies, and aptitudes in cognitive performance: Concluding comments. In W. Schneider & F.E. Weinert (eds), *Interactions among aptitudes, strategies, and knowledge in cognitive performance* (pp. 286–302). New York: Springer.

Schneider, W., & Weinert, F.E. (1995). Memory development during early and middle childhood: Findings from the Munich Longitudinal Study (LOGIC). In F.E. Weinert & W. Schneider (eds), *Memory performance and competencies: Issues in growth and development* (pp. 263–279). Hillsdale, NJ: Erlbaum.

Schumann-Hengsteler, R. (1992). The development of visuo-spatial memory: How to remember location. *Inter-*

national Journal of Behavioral Development, 15, 445–471.

Schumann-Hengsteler, R. (1995). *Die Entwicklung des visuo-räumlichen Gedächtnisses* (*Development of visuo-spatial memory*). Göttingen: Hogrefe.

Schumann-Hengsteler, R. (1996). Children's and adults' visuo-spatial memory: The game Concentration. *Journal of Genetic Psychology*, 157, 77–92.

Short, E.J., & Ryan, E.B. (1984). Metacognitive differences between skilled and less skilled readers: Remediating deficits through story grammar and attribution training. *Journal of Educational Psychology*, 76, 225–235.

Siaw, S.N., & Kee, D.W. (1987). Development of elaboration and organization in different socioeconomic-status and ethnic populations. In M.A. McDaniel & M. Pressley (eds), *Imagery and related mnemonic processes: Theories, individual differences, and applications* (pp. 237–273). New York: Springer.

Siegel, L.S. (1993). The cognitive basis of dyslexia. In R. Pasnak & M.L. Howe (eds), *Emerging themes in cognitive development: Vol. 2. Competencies* (pp. 33–52). New York: Springer.

Siegel, L.S., & Ryan, E.B. (1988). Development of grammatical-sensitivity, phonological, and short-term memory skills in normally achieving and learning disabled children. *Developmental Psychology*, 24, 28–37.

Siegel, L.S., & Ryan, E.B. (1989). The development of working memory in normally achieving and subtypes of learning disabled children. *Child Development*, 60, 973–980.

Siegler, R.S. (1996). *Emerging minds: The process of change in children's thinking*. New York: Oxford University Press.

Slater, A. (1995). Visual perception and memory at birth. In C. Rovee-Collier & L.P. Lipsitt (eds), *Advances in infancy research* (Vol. 9, pp. 107–162). Norwood, NJ: Ablex.

Sodian, B., & Schneider, W. (1999). Memory strategy development: Gradual increase, sudden insight, or roller coaster? In F.E. Weinert & W. Schneider (eds), *Individual development from 3 to 12: Findings from the Munich Longitudinal Study* (pp. 61–77). Cambridge: Cambridge University Press.

Sperling, G. (1960). *The information available in brief visual presentations. Psychological Monographs*, Vol. 74, no. 11.

Squire, L.R., Knowlton, B., & Musen, G. (1993). The structure and organization of memory. *Annual Review of Psychology*, 44, 453–495.

Sternberg, R.J. (1999). After Piaget, the Deluge. Essay review of individual development from 3 to 12: Findings from the Munich Longitudinal Study, edited by F.E. Weinert and W. Schneider. *Human Development*, 42, 220–224.

Surbey, M.K. (1998). Developmental psychology and modern Darwinism. In C.B. Crawford & D. Krebs (eds), *Handbook of evolutionary psychology: Ideas, issues, and applications*. Hillsdale, NJ: Erlbaum.

Tulving, E. (1985). Memory and consciousness. *Canadian Psychology*, 26, 1–12.

Vinter, A., & Perruchet, P. (2000). Implicit learning in children is not related to age: Evidence from drawing. *Child Development*, 71, 1223–1240.

Vygotsky, L.S. (1978). *Mind in society: The development of higher psychological processes* (trans. M. Cole, V. John-Steiner, S. Scribner, & E. Souberman). Cambridge, MA: Harvard University Press.

Wagenaar, W.A. (1990). The memory of concentration camp survivors. *Applied Cognitive Psychology*, 4, 77–87.

Waters, H.S. ((2000). Memory strategy development: Do we need another deficiency? *Child Development*, 71, 1001–1012.

Weber, A., & Strube, G. (1999). Memory for events experienced and events observed. In F.E. Weinert & W. Schneider (eds), *Individual development from 3 to 12: Findings from the Munich Longitudinal Study*. Cambridge, UK: Cambridge University Press.

Weinert, F.E. (1986). Developmental variations of memory performance and memory-related knowledge across the life-span. In A. Sörensen, F.E. Weinert, & L.R. Sherrod (eds), *Human development: Multidisciplinary perspectives* (pp. 535–554). Hillsdale, NJ: Erlbaum.

Weinert, F.E., Bullock, M., & Schneider, W. (1999). Universal, differential, and individual aspects of child development from 3 to 12: What can we learn from a comprehensive longitudinal study? In F.E. Weinert & W. Schneider (eds), *Individual development from 3 to 12: Findings from the Munich Longitudinal Study* (pp. 324–350). Cambridge: Cambridge University Press.

Weinert, F.E., & Schneider, W. (eds) (1999). *Individual development from 3 to 12: Findings from the Munich Longitudinal Study*. Cambridge: Cambridge University Press.

Weinert, F.E., Schneider, W., & Knopf, M. (1988). Individual differences in memory development across the life-span. In P.B. Baltes, D.L. Featherman, & R.M. Lerner (eds), *Life-span development and behavior* (Vol. 9, pp. 39–85). Hillsdale, NJ: Erlbaum.

Wellman, H.M., & Somerville, S.C. (1982). The development of human search ability. In M.E. Lamb & A.L. Brown (eds), *Advances in developmental psychology* (pp. 41–84). Hillsdale, NJ: Erlbaum.

Wippich, W. (1980). Meta-Gedächtnis und Gedächtnis-Erfahrung (Metamemory and memory experience). *Zeitschrift für Entwicklungspsychologie und Pädagogische Psychologie*, 12, 40–43.

Yussen, S.R., & Levy, V.M. (1975). Developmental changes in predicting one's own span of short-term memory. *Journal of Experimental Child Psychology*, 19, 502–508.

PART FIVE: DEVELOPMENT IN PRE-ADOLESCENCE AND ADOLESCENCE

18

Children's Relationships and Development of Person–Context Relations

THOMAS KINDERMANN

Developmental psychologists aim to describe and explain the developmental pathways of individuals as they interact with the changing contexts of their world (cf. Baltes, Reese, & Nesselroade, 1988; Cairns, 1979). Although contexts feature as prominently in these goals as individuals, much less attention has been paid to conceptualizing their nature and organization. Theorists advocate conceptions of ecological systems (Bronfenbrenner & Morris, 1998; Ford & Lerner, 1992; Sameroff, 1983), environmental systems (Friedman & Wachs, 1999; Wachs, 1992), cultural systems (Valsiner, 1989), relationships between people and environments (Hinde, 1992; Maccoby, 1992), or co-constructive processes in development (Valsiner, 1994). Common to these approaches are efforts to acknowledge that developmental contexts are highly complex, as well as efforts to specify how they can be conceived as components of a system of multiple influences (Cairns & Cairns, 1994; Wachs, 2000; see Gottlieb, Chapter 1 in this volume).

The current chapter reviews and attempts to build on such efforts, suggesting conceptual elaborations of the defining characteristics of developmental contexts, analyzing their psychologically 'active' processes, and identifying methodological strategies for the study of their influences on development. A basic assumption is that the way in which we describe and explain human development depends on our understanding of what social contexts are, how individuals and contexts become influential for one another, what individuals and their contexts do to and for one another, and how reciprocal influences between people and their contexts change across time. The central argument is that key contexts of development are embedded in the *relationships* that children form with specific partners (Hinde, 1997) and that *interactions* among these partners constitute the 'engines of development' (M. Baltes, 1996; Bronfenbrenner & Morris, 1998).

How Do We Understand Developmental Contexts?

Individuals are well-defined units of psychological study. We know some of their basic characteristics, such as genes, behaviors, emotions, and thoughts, and scientists have experience in mapping the role of these characteristics in organisms' development. However, there is no natural unit of analysis for studying environments (Wachs, 1992). At best, we are able to differentiate multiple levels of complexity in environmental systems (e.g. Ford & Lerner, 1992), to identify specific settings in which we find individuals at specific points in time and to describe their theoretically most important features (e.g. Friedman & Wachs, 1999), or to identify those people who serve as environmental agents for target individuals at specific points in time (e.g. Hinde, 1992). All too often, context accounts are solely based on 'social addresses' (Bronfenbrenner, 1989), simply referencing the presence or absence of specific features, objects, or philosophies, indicating 'stimulus soup' that is 'full of causes of behavior' (Thorngate, 1995, p. 44) and an 'amorphous and haphazard collection of forces' (Dannefer, 1992, p. 90).

In their efforts to conceptualize the 'nature of nurture' (Wachs, 1992), developmentalists have followed two general perspectives. One avenue is characterized by efforts to conceptualize the essential features of *environments* by capturing the key characteristics of the settings in which individuals are found across the life-span. A recent volume edited by Friedman and Wachs (1999) describes such efforts with regard to home environments (Bradley, 1999), child care settings (Friedman & Amadeo, 1999), school and after-school settings (Talbert & McLaughlin, 1999; Vandell & Posner, 1999), work settings (Schooler, 1999), and living arrangements in old age (Lawton, 1999). The second avenue focuses on interpersonal aspects. The *relationships* that people form with social partners are regarded to be key contexts that shape individuals' development (e.g. Hartup & Laursen, 1999; Hinde, 1997; Reis, Collins, & Berscheid, 2000). Relationship contexts consist of people who do specific things to and for one another in social interactions (Cairns & Cairns, 1994), who themselves have personal characteristics (Kindermann & Skinner, 1992), and who often hold 'directive beliefs' for the developing individuals (Bugenthal & Goodnow, 1998). Thus, children's developmental pathways are seen as a function of the complex interconnections and relationships that exist between children and the members of their contexts. Development is understood as the result of reciprocal processes that involve children and social contexts as *co-determinants* of individual change (cf. Collins, 1999; Lerner, 1991).

Both avenues are not mutually exclusive; rather, they complement each other. Both highlight the idea that if environments are to have an impact on individuals, they cannot just coexist, but they must actually do something to, with, or for the individual. Nevertheless, while environmental approaches tend to highlight 'built-in' features, often seen to exist independently of target individuals under study, relationship approaches insist that it is other people who are most influential. While environmental approaches tend to focus on what people do and people's experiences as influential for development, relationship approaches suggest that the quality of interactions also plays a central role. Finally, while environmental approaches aim to construct inventories and taxonomies that allow researchers to compare contexts according to specific features (e.g. whether specific provisions exist that are supportive of development), relationship approaches tend to focus on the personal characteristics of specific partners who are involved.

A perspective of *person–context relations* has promise for integrating the key features of both perspectives. The term denotes an affinity with relationship approaches, but without implications that the most important contexts would be dyadic (e.g. Hinde, 1997) or that quality of these relationships would be the 'engine' of development. The emphasis is on interactions among people. Social interactions are cumulatively seen as 'proximal processes' (Bronfenbrenner & Morris, 1998), and relationship qualities are considered features of the microsystem in which these processes unfold. Thus, person–context relations are aggregates of social partners' interactions across an extended amount of time (Cairns, 1979; Hartup & Laursen, 1999). The emphasis on *development* in these relations highlights that at the time an individual develops, his or her context partners change as well. Although it is a central tenet of most developmental theories, the notion that contexts change is often of little consequence in terms of empirical research (Hetherington & Baltes, 1988; see also Boyce et al., 1998). All too often, contexts are seen as static frames that surround an individual. However, when interactions are seen as the primary contexts of development, social partners need to be assumed to have the same human qualities as the developing individuals themselves.

Three kinds of childhood relationships will be discussed: relationships with *parents*, with *teachers*, and with *peers*. All three exist universally across cultures. Sibling relationships, although likely of similar importance, are not included and neither are imaginary companions, idols, pets, or grandparents. It is not assumed that these are unimportant. However, if the three relationships described in this chapter can be considered in some ways as prototypical examples of relationship contexts, then it is possible that many of the key issues can be exported to the study of other relationships as well.

ARE SOCIAL RELATIONSHIPS ESSENTIAL FOR CHILDREN'S DEVELOPMENT?

Relationships with close partners are central themes of most developmental theories, including those of Baldwin, Erikson, Freud, and Piaget (cf. Cairns, 1998). Developmentalists assume that from the beginning, a child is embedded in a network of relationships. With increasing age, these expand, become more complex, and include new partners. Despite the many differences in the nature and functions of relationships, there are reasons to believe that they are not just common to children's experiences but *essential* for their development.

Strong support for this position is found in research on *parenting*. Harlow's classic studies on the consequences of mother–child separation in Rhesus monkeys (e.g. Cairns, 1972; Harlow & Mears, 1979) indicate that for infants, a relationship with a caretaker is essential, over and above assistance for survival. Similarly, research on institutionalized children after World War II (cf. Bowlby, 1969) showed increased incidence rates of retardation, abnormal behavior, and depression, as well as high death rates. These effects occurred despite the fact that children's basic physiological needs were met by the caretaking environments. Bowlby's (1969) conceptualization of an *attachment* framework concluded that a consistent and secure relationship with one specific caretaker was missing for these children (for review, see Thompson, 1998). This assertion was supported by findings that such severe effects were not found in high quality institutions (e.g. with little caretaker turnover: cf. Rutter, 1979).

Similar support for the assumption that social relationships are essential is found in the literature on *peer relationships* (cf. Harris, 1995). The importance of peers was dramatically shown in Rhesus monkeys by Suomi and colleagues (cf. Suomi & Harlow, 1975). Monkeys who were raised with their mothers but had no contact with peers showed abnormal social behavior when they were subsequently allowed to be with agemates. Peer-deprived monkeys rarely engaged in playful interactions, were highly aggressive, and seemed to lack the social skills necessary for appropriate interactions with agemates. Although one can ask whether the effects would be of similar magnitude with human babies (since human infants may be able to adapt to a wider range of environmental variations), such findings nevertheless suggest that peer relationships are critical for children's development. In addition, they indicate that relationships with peers can serve functions to 'repair' the consequences of early adverse conditions. For example, in an experiment by Novak and Harlow (1975), monkeys who were raised in total isolation were (after 6 months) paired with 'therapist' peers who were several months younger. Over time, such interactions did lead to a reduction in abnormal behavior.

Typically, children's relationships do not just extend to caretakers and other children. Children also have *teachers* with whom they form relationships. Of course, school is not essential for a child's survival or integration into society. However, most cultures have found it useful to provide some kind of formal education in order to foster children's potential, and virtually every culture has established some form of schooling for children and adolescents. This may be in the form of institutionalized schools, as in cultures that follow Western educational philosophies; in the form of religiously based apprenticeship procedures, as in many Eastern and African cultures; or in the form of clan-, caste-, or profession-specific apprenticeship programs. On the surface, the purpose of school is transmission of knowledge to new generations. However, it is also a social institution and a place where children learn to get along with adults who hold a specific developmental agenda, as well as with agemates. Although differences exist in the level of professionalization and formalization of education across the world, it appears to be a ubiquitous phenomenon that teachers emerge as relationship partners for a child.

Common Features of Relationships with Parents, Teachers, and Peers

Relationships with a caregiver, teachers, and peers are typically present for a child, and all three may be necessary for healthy development. Traditionally, however, these relationships have been studied along almost entirely separate lines. When they are mentioned together, it is usually to contrast them to highlight their differences, or to analyze their complementary functions (cf. Hartup & Laursen, 1999; Hinde, 1997; Laursen & Bukowski, 1997). A review of their main characteristics aims to show that their conceptualizations, despite the differences, are based on similar assumptions. An analysis of their commonalities may be useful for building general hypotheses about how relationship contexts influence children's development.

Five main features are common to the three contexts (see Table 18.1). First, all three are characterized by *shared affection* among partners, expressed by warmth and mutual acceptance. Second, they are characterized by high levels of *mutual participation*, shared time, or involvement.

Table 18.1 *Five common features of children's social relationships and of key constructs from empirical investigations*

Common feature	Relationships with parents	Relationships with teachers	Relationships with peers
Shared affection	Warmth, acceptance, harmony	Pedagogical caring, relatedness	Acceptance, mutual liking and regard
Shared time	Time spent, involvement	Involvement, class time	Time spent in interactions
Assortativeness	Genetic similarity	Similarity due to cultural/ institutional assignment	Similarity due to self-selection processes
Developmental adjustment	Directive beliefs, agendas, developmental timetables	Curricula, assignments, autonomy support	Symmetry, homophily
Reciprocity	Evocation, participation, selective help-seeking	Evocation, participation, selective help-seeking	Selective participation, peer context creation

Third, they do not occur at random but are characterized by *assortativeness*: each is created in a way that relationship partners share similarities in certain features. Fourth, they are characterized by *developmental adjustment* among the partners, and fifth, by high levels of *reciprocity*: relationships are contexts in which individuals develop simultaneously with relationship partners. All five features reflect processes of how relationships are formed and maintained as well as facilitative influences among partners. They capture critical features that are needed for describing how relationships can have an impact on individual development. In the following sections, each of the five characteristics is defined and evidence for its centrality to each kind of relationship is briefly reviewed. A final section explores the implications of these common features for our methodological strategies to study how relationships influence development.

Shared Affection: Warmth, Acceptance, and Relationship Quality

Warmth, mutual liking, and acceptance are seen as the 'glue' that holds a person and his or her context together, and as a key factor that allows relationship partners to influence each other (see Table 18.1). Warmth and acceptance in caretakers are key ingredients for the development of secure attachments (Thompson, 1998) as well as key categories of child-rearing styles (Bugenthal & Goodnow, 1998). Both factors have also become variables for conceptualizing relationships between students and teachers in theories on individual differences in student motivation and achievement (e.g. Deci & Ryan, 1991; Ryan & Powelson, 1991). Finally, warmth, acceptance, and mutual liking are also central constructs in many approaches to peer relationships.

Relationships with Parents

Attachment researchers define the quality of children's relationships with caretakers as the extent of security that children feel in the relationship. The first year of life is seen as a sensitive period for the development of attachments (cf. van IJzendoorn, 1995), and interindividual differences in attachment security are assumed to be based on caretakers' sensitivity and responsiveness to the child's needs. Warmth and acceptance are seen as key determinants of caretakers' sensitivity (MacDonald, 1992); sensitivity is regarded to be adults' 'core contribution' to relationship quality (Thompson, 1998, p. 49). During the second and third year of life, attachments stabilize into goal-corrected partnerships, and there are indications that securely attached infants are able to maintain more harmonious relationships with mothers (Matas, Arend, & Sroufe, 1978). Finally, secure attachment appears to be related to a wide variety of positive developmental outcomes, within children themselves as well as in their social relationships (cf. Thompson, 1998), and these effects are stronger when the early caregiving characteristics remain consistent over time (Lamb, 1998).

Socialization research has also highlighted warmth as a key characteristic (in addition to control and involvement: cf. Bugenthal & Goodnow, 1998; Maccoby & Martin, 1983; Parke & Buriel, 1998). Parents who are warm are accepting of their children and able to maintain a nurturing environment characterized by high amounts of responsiveness, praise, and positive affect. Warmth and acceptance are assumed to reduce parents' needs for power assertive discipline and to heighten children's readiness to conform to parents' demands (Kochanska, 1997; Maccoby & Martin, 1983). Warmth is also a key construct in Baumrind's (1967; 1989) conceptualization of parenting styles: across time, parental warmth is related to children's self-reliance and adjustment, as well as to the development of positive relationships with agemates and teachers (e.g. Baumrind, 1967; Steinberg et al., 1992).

Relationships with Teachers

Research on development in educational settings has taken a long time to see interactions between teachers and students as relationship processes. Decades of research have focused on teachers' behavior, expectations, or overall classroom environments without much attention to relationships (Connell & Wellborn, 1991; Deci et al., 1991; Valsiner, 1998; Wentzel, 1999). However, like parents, teachers are partners in social interactions and socialization agents. Conceptualizations of relationships have typically 'borrowed' from the attachment and parental socialization frameworks (e.g. Birch & Ladd, 1998; Skinner & Wellborn, 1994). For example, Silberman (1969) classified teacher–student relationships into categories of attachment, concern, indifference, and rejection; teacher's involvement is assumed to differ for students from different categories. Howes and colleagues (e.g. Howes & Matheson, 1992) classified relationships as secure, avoidant, or resistant-ambivalent, and Lynch and Cicchetti (1992) as optimal, versus deprived, disengaged, confused, or average. Nevertheless, contrary to attachment research, there are no assumptions that a child's relationship with his or her first teacher would be qualitatively different from later relationships.

A key construct is *teacher-relatedness* or 'pedagogical caring' (Wentzel, 1997) which highlights interpersonal closeness and mutual regard in interactions. Teachers' caring is assumed to be a determinant of children's adjustment in school, their school motivation, and academic achievement

(Connell & Wellborn, 1991; Ryan & Powelson, 1991). Teachers are assumed to promote children's feelings of relatedness through warmth and involvement in interactions, while hostility and rejection would undermine relationships. For example, teachers' perceptions of the quality of their relationships with individual students have been found to be predictors of kindergartners' school performance and their liking of school (Birch & Ladd, 1997). At later ages, children's own perceptions of their relationships with teachers are indicative of their autonomy and engagement in the classroom (cf. Ryan, Stiller, & Lynch, 1994; Wentzel, 1997).

Relationships with Peers

Acceptance, liking, and warmth are also key variables in most approaches to children's peer relationships. Three major research strands have traditionally been followed: the study of children's sociometric status, the study of friendship affiliations, and the study of their social networks among each other (for reviews, see Hartup, 1983, Rubin, Bukowski, & Parker, 1998). All three can be traced back to Moreno's (1934) conceptualization of a sociometric framework for the study of interpersonal relationships.

Sociometric methods were originally developed to assess individuals' preferences for social contact. The goals were to identify those partners whom individuals would choose for specific activities, and to use this information as an indicator of individuals' integration into social systems and as a diagnostic tool for the system's own viability (Moreno, 1934). Today, the goals of these approaches have changed considerably; the primary goal of peer relationships research has become to examine children's actual interpersonal relationships.

Current sociometric approaches have changed their emphasis further. In his 1934 book *Who shall survive*? Moreno outlined more than 100 specific hypotheses for a program of sociometric studies. Contemporary sociometry (e.g. Asher & Coie, 1990) follows roughly 20% of these questions. Most importantly, sociometric research has moved away from a focus on individual relationships towards a focus on children's overall social standing in a setting, usually a classroom. The target phenomenon has become the extent to which a child is liked or disliked (or both or neither) across *all* peers in the setting (Coie, Dodge, & Coppotelli, 1982). Based on their overall likeableness, children are grouped into categories of popular, controversial, average, rejected, or neglected students. These categories are still assumed to indicate a child's social success or failure and to be a marker for a set of socializing experiences by which he or she is included and liked or disliked and excluded from participation in the peer context (for reviews, see Asher & Coie, 1990; Newcomb, Bukowski, & Pattee, 1993). However, the quality of specific relationships is seen as less important than the child's overall standing.

In contrast, interpersonal relationships have remained central for research on *friendships*. The defining variable is also liking, but liking that is mutual among (at least) two friends. Studies target durable dyadic peer relations that are characterized by reciprocal affective bonds, and affective quality is assumed to heighten influences that emerge from these relationships; often, mutual influences are expected to be strongest among children who are best friends (cf. Berndt & Keefe, 1996; Hartup & Stevens, 1997). Friendships are considered to be key contexts for social and personality development, as well as for adjustment to school (e.g. Berndt, Laychak, & Park, 1990; Birch & Ladd, 1996; Ladd, 1990).

However, as a unit for a peer context, friendship is quite restrictive. The context is restricted to a child's best friends, often to one single best friend, and across time, just to stable dyads. These may be very special relationships (cf. Kindermann, 1996) because they are most intimate and partners are exposed to one another for a long time. However, they may also be least powerful in generating developmental change (cf. Epstein, 1983) because it is likely that the friends were already most similar to one another when the relationship was formed.

A third research tradition, the study of children's *social networks*, aims to examine peer affiliations beyond the dyadic level. Network approaches have traditionally been used in sociology and anthropology (e.g. Wellman & Berkowitz, 1988), but they are increasingly prominent in psychological research (for reviews, see Cairns & Cairns, 1994; Rubin, Bukowski, & Parker, 1998). The term encompasses approaches to study groups of friends (e.g. Urberg et al., 1995), social support networks (Kahn & Antonucci, 1980), children's identification with cliques or crowds (e.g. Brown, 1999), as well as groups of children who frequently associate with one another (e.g. Cairns, Xie, & Leung, 1998).

In comparison to sociometric or friendship approaches, social network studies place less emphasis on acceptance, warmth, or relationship quality. Partly, this may be due to the fact that dyadic bonds are seen as less important than connections among multiple partners. The main focus is on interactions among members of networks, on the specific kinds of activities that they undertake, and the influences that interactions may have on development (e.g. Cairns & Cairns, 1994). Thus, the relationship 'content' (Hartup & Stevens, 1997) is of more interest than emotional quality. Nevertheless, assumptions are that children who spend much time in shared activities at least tolerate each other, and that some members of some networks share closer relationships than others (Farmer & Rodkin, 1996; Gest, Graham-Berman, & Hartup, 2001).

Shared Time in Relationships

A second feature of conceptualizations of all three relationships is the assumption that those people who spend the most time with a child become most important for his or her development (see Table 18.1). This has also been called the dimension of 'involvement' of relationship partners (Dunn, 1993; Hinde, 1992). (Note that this term has qualitative as well as quantitative meanings; it is used here to denote the amount of time spent in interactions.)

Relationships with Parents

A key assumption of attachment and parental socialization theorists is that the caretaker who spends the most time with a child will become most influential for him or her. Usually, this person is assumed to be a child's mother, but recently, increased attention has been paid to fathers (Lamb, 1997), to groups of caretakers who practice 'conjoint' parenting (Johnson, Shulman, & Collins, 1991; Schneider-Rosen & Burke, 1999), and to professional caretakers (Cassiba, van IJzendoorn, & D'Odorico, 2000; Lamb, 1998).

To pay attention to relationship partners other than mothers accords well with the fact that, although the nuclear family has been the dominant model in the Western world for some time, this predominance seems to be waning. In the US today, almost every third family consists of just one parent. Many mothers continue to work outside the home, and many children spend a considerable amount of time in care provided by non-family members. However, even among single-parent households in the US, about 85% are headed by mothers (Lamb, 1998). Mothers continue to be the most frequent caretakers. In addition, there has been a marked decline in family size during this century, and the historic increase in mothers' work outside the home may have replaced the amount of time that was previously spent on work within the home (which has been taken over by household appliances). Despite the demographic trends, it is not clear whether a mother's rate of interaction with an individual child has historically decreased.

Across cultures, mothers also seem to be universally most important. Children typically grow up within networks of caretaking relationships, usually including their parents, and often the parents share close relationships with other caretakers (e.g. grandparents, friends, servants, siblings: cf. Roopnarine & Carter, 1994). Although not all cultures regard the two-parent family as the ideal constellation, the most frequent alternative provides a child with more than one 'mother'. Polygyny is estimated to be an option in about 80% of the world's cultures and monogamy is only the second most common form (other forms, e.g. polyandry, are rare: cf. Valsiner, 1989, p. 79). Because there is usually some economic burden associated with polygyny, only a minority of the people in cultures that approve of it as a viable family constellation actually practice it; often, the practice is a sign of wealth of a family. Finally, the drastic decrease in maternal death rates during this century has made it overall less likely that a child's mother is not a member of this child's network of caretakers.

Thus, it is a universal feature that mothers are centrally involved in taking care of a child. However, given the considerable diversity of child care arrangements, parenting researchers have become more interested in the extent to which mothers are *actively involved* in child care interactions. Along with warmth in the relationship and control exerted by parents, parent involvement is considered to be one of the key characteristics that determines the strength of socialization influences (Caldwell & Bradley, 1984; Maccoby & Martin, 1983). Parents' involvement in children's activities has been shown to play a role in their social (Patterson & Strouthamer-Loeber, 1984) as well as academic development (e.g. Connors & Epstein, 1995; Grolnick & Slowiaczek, 1994; Steinberg et al., 1992).

Relationships with Teachers

It is unlikely that there is a sensitive period for the establishment of a relationship after infancy (Savin-Williams & Weisfeld, 1989). Rather, relationships will be formed because teachers spend much time with children and because they see it as their role to provide developmental guidance and support (cf. Ryan & Powelson, 1991).

In the US, the majority of children between the ages of 5 and 7, and 99% of the children between the ages of 7 and 13, attend school (Hernandez, 1997). During the elementary years, many children spend almost as much time in school as they do with family members, and often, most time is spent with one single teacher. With increasing age, the child's context broadens to include multiple teachers, and students spend more time with some teachers than with others. Thus, studies (e.g. Skinner & Belmont, 1993) tend to focus on core teachers as students' most frequent interaction partners. Although teachers are assigned to classrooms, and in principle thus spend roughly the same amount of time in the presence of the members of a class, there are nevertheless differences in interaction frequencies with different kinds of students. For example, Dweck and Goetz (1978) reported gender differences in teacher involvement, noting that teachers interact more often with male than female students (although much of the difference is based on discipline issues). The extent to which teachers are involved with particular students is seen as influential for these students' academic development. Students who see their teacher as more involved with them were found to show higher school motivation and academic outcomes (e.g. Skinner & Belmont, 1993; Wentzel, 1997).

Finally, with increasing age, student–teacher relationships become also less confined to the classroom. Mentoring relationships develop between individual students and teachers, based on more casual contacts and students' own efforts to seek support for their specific activities. Thus, students become more able to select 'favorite' teachers among the pool of available candidates with whom they prefer to spend time.

Relationships with Peers

Frequency of contact is one of the most important elements in conceptualizations of peer contexts. Frequent contact defines much of a child's peer context. *Sociometric approaches*, with their focus on a child's overall acceptance, depict popular children as having most access to peer interactions and as being included in a wide variety of peer experiences, while neglected and rejected children would experience restrictions in access and exclusion from many activities (cf. Asher & Coie, 1990). For *friendship* researchers, frequent contact among friends is seen as a defining variable for the relationship (at least during childhood), and interactions among friends are expected to lead to socialization influences that are specific to the particular friendship (e.g. Berndt & Keefe, 1996).

Social network approaches vary in the extent to which they emphasize shared time in interactions. Common to all network approaches is an interest in the structure of social networks, the personal characteristics and interactions of their members, and the developmental consequences of these interactions. Thus, processes of group formation and the criteria that play a role in member selection processes have received much attention (cf. Epstein, 1989).

On the one hand, approaches focusing on friendship groups (e.g. Urberg et al., 1995) or social categories (e.g. Brown, 1999) do not emphasize shared time much. It is considered more important that groups of friends undertake specific activities together or that children identify with prototypical social categories (e.g. 'jocks' or 'nerds'), even if actual interactions among individuals are relatively rare. On the other hand, there is (at least) one approach to peer networks that explicitly uses shared time as the defining criterion of the context. Robert Cairns and colleagues (e.g. Cairns, Perrin, & Cairns, 1985; Cairns et al., 2001; see also Strayer & Santos, 1996) have developed a method of *composite social-cognitive mapping* that explicitly focuses on children who are publicly known in a setting to spend much time together in a variety of activities.

Assortativeness among Relationship Partners

A third common feature of social relationships is that some kind of *similarity* exists among affiliates (see Table 18.1). The feature has also been called 'assortativeness' (Murstein, 1976), 'homophily' (Kandel, 1978), 'synchrony' (Cairns, Neckerman, & Cairns, 1989), or 'mesh' among partners (Hinde, 1992). Relationships do not occur at random, but among people who typically have specific characteristics in common when the relationship is formed. This may be more obvious in peer relationships in which partners tend to self-select one another than in 'obligatory' relationships (Laursen, 1997) with parents or teachers. Nevertheless, attachment and child-rearing researchers also study relationships in which partners are (genetically) assorted to one another; educational researchers study partners who are institutionally assigned to students.

Of course, similarity among partners can be coincidence or transitory in nature. However, when initial similarity exists, even if it is transitory, correlations between partner characteristics and children's developmental outcomes do not necessarily denote that influences have occurred; they also denote outcomes of assortiveness. In nearly all studies in which correlations have been shown between the characteristics of individuals who share a relationship, prior similarity is an alternative explanation that rivals interpretations in terms of mutual influences.

Relationships with Parents

Similarity between parents and their children has not been of much concern for parenting or attachment researchers. It is taken as a given that parents and children are biologically related (even for adopted children, some level of similarity should be assumed because adoption agencies tend to match children to families that fit to the background of the child's biological parents). Behavior genetics researchers, however, have pointed out that much of what can be seen as an outcome of socialization can also be an outcome of pre-existing similarities between parents and children (cf. Harris, 1995). Thus, for parenting researchers, the task is to show that socialization produces changes in children over and above these initial similarities (Collins et al., 2000).

Moreover, genetic similarity may just be a special case of assortativeness in person–context relations. It may be easier for social partners to have mutual regard for one another, to spend much time together, and to form a secure relationship when partners are highly similar. If genetic assortativeness increases the likelihood that close relationships are formed, and if these relationships foster socialization processes, then similarities among siblings (e.g. Hoffman, 1991), intergenerational similarities between parents and children in attachment patterns (e.g. van IJzendoorn, 1992), as well as intergenerational similarities in behavior characteristics (Cairns et al., 1998; Caspi & Elder, 1988) should be higher in families in which relationships are close and enduring. In contrast, the similarities should be relatively small in those (perhaps less frequent) families in which relationships were never close or dissolved across time. In other words, it may be a question whether all implications of assortativeness in parent–child relationships necessarily need to be seen as genetic in nature (see also Gottlieb, Chapter 1 and Wahlsten, Chapter 2 in this volume).

Relationships with Teachers

Similarity between teachers and students has not been much of an issue for studies of educational processes. Teachers are institutionally assigned to students, and one is inclined to think the assignments are more or less random. However, there are reasons to expect that they are not. Because relationships with teachers occur later in life than attachment relationships, and because they are formed in addition to existing relationships (not as replacements), we need to assume that the partners who have established earlier relationships with a child will also be involved in selection of further partners. During the toddler and preschool ages, parents decide whether additional caretakers become involved; from the elementary school years onwards, parents select (to some extent) the institutions of formal schooling which assign children to professional educators. Thus, parents have some influence on the kinds of teachers their children will have, and researchers comparing the effectiveness of different schools (cf. Bryk & Raudenbush, 1992) caution that such differences can be based on effects of assortativeness as well as school factors.

In addition, school practices of 'tracking' students into specific classrooms can produce matches of specific teachers with specific students. If some students are more similar to their teachers than others (e.g. in terms of SES or value of academic achievement), these students may be more likely to form close relationships with them. Thus, findings that close relationships with teachers have positive developmental effects (e.g. Ryan & Powelson, 1991) may also indicate outcomes of assignment to schools, classrooms, or teachers. Finally, from the elementary years onwards, students have access to several teachers with whom they can form differentially close relationships. As with parent–child relationships, it may not just be warmth, mutual regard, or time spent in interactions, but also similarity in specific characteristics, which make it likely that a particular teacher emerges as influential for a child.

Relationships with Peers

Similarity among relationship partners (homophily) has traditionally been most emphasized in peer research. Typically, a child's peer affiliates are self-selected from a pool of (often pre-assigned) candidates. It may be seen as a specific merit of peer research that interpersonal similarity in relationships has received increased attention. Nevertheless, the concept is almost void of accounts for psychological processes. Although researchers have stressed interpersonal similarity, little effort has been made to conceptualize the actual processes of how peer selection proceeds. Often, peer similarity is treated as a nuisance that needs to be controlled in order to study socialization processes.

Because sociometric studies focus on overall acceptance of children in a setting, assortativeness has not received much attention. Classifications of children into rejected, popular, or average students represent social categories, not necessarily affiliative groups. Nevertheless, because selection brings children into specific kinds of schools or classrooms, a child's overall popularity or rejection can denote his or her overall 'fit' in a setting (Boivin, Dodge, & Coie, 1995). In particular, intercultural studies have noted that a child's social standing may greatly depend on the cultural expectations that are held by the majority of children in a classroom (e.g. Chen, Rubin, & Sun, 1992).

In contrast, friendship and peer network researchers have been most attentive to issues of interpersonal similarity (for review, see Epstein, 1989; Hamm, 2000). Kandel (1978) used the term 'selection', and Dishion, Patterson, and Griesler (1994) the terms 'foraging' or 'shopping', to denote children's efforts to seek out similar partners. Similarity in a wide variety of attributes is seen as the single most important criterion for the formation of both kinds of relationships.

Of course, children's selection of affiliates occurs in addition to parents' and teachers' efforts to structure peer relationships. For example, adults decide which agemates are invited to visit their house, to which agemates a child will be brought for a visit, which children will be invited for parties, and (often) which children are assigned to one another for workgroups in school (cf. Parke & Ladd, 1992). Institutions and adults typically provide the pool of agemates from which children select preferred affiliates, and selection criteria appear to be somewhat tied to the specific settings in which affiliations are formed. Thus, academic characteristics appear to play a role in school settings (e.g. Berndt & Keefe, 1996; Kindermann, 1993a; Kindermann, McCollam, & Gibson, 1996). Overall, however, similarities are stronger with regard to SES, ethnicity, gender, and behavior characteristics like smoking, drinking, or tendencies for aggressive behavior (Cairns et al., 1988; Dishion et al., 1996; Urberg, Degirmencioglu, & Tolson, 1998).

Developmental Adjustment: Directive Beliefs, Agendas, and Complementarity

A fourth characteristic common to all three relationships is that the respective partners are typically attuned to a child's developmental level (see Table 18.1). Partners tend to hold expectations, directive beliefs, and specific agendas, and to tailor interactions such that they are in accordance with their goals for the relationship. In order to study partners' developmental influences, it is helpful to know what they expect from children. Developmental agendas can be seen as descriptors of the nature of relationships, as markers of guidance and canalization processes that partners initiate, as well as predictors of the direction of children's developmental processes (see also Valsiner, 1998). For most relationships with adults, these agendas will be complementary in nature; for most peer relationships, developmental adjustment will lead to more symmetrical relationships (e.g. Hartup & Stevens, 1997).

Relationships with Parents

Attachment theorists have not greatly emphasized caretaker agendas or directive beliefs. Developmental adjustment and complementarity are regarded as evolutionary built-in components of interactions. Because attachment is seen as the species-typical outcome of early interactions, mothers are assumed to have natural inclinations to attend to their children in a responsive and sensitive manner (e.g. Papoušek & Papoušek, 1995). By nature, parents' behaviors are attuned to a child's developmental level, and parents themselves adopt the role of making sure that the needs of the dyad are met.

In comparison, socialization researchers have been more explicit about parental agendas. Parents are seen as holding strong expectations for children's development and to assume it as their own role to make it possible that children develop accordingly. Such expectations have been conceived as 'timetables' for when children are expected to show certain accomplishments (Goodnow, 1985), as 'directive beliefs' about their developmental progress (Bronfenbrenner & Morris, 1998), or as developmental 'agendas' (Kindermann & Skinner, 1992) for the relationship. There are differences across cultures, and dramatic changes have occurred across generations (cf. Harkness & Super, 1995). It is assumed that such expectations translate into specific patterns of parent–child interactions. At least at times when developmental tasks emerge for a child, socializing interactions become adjusted to the child's developmental level (e.g. Kindermann, 1993b), resulting in patterns of scaffolding (Heckhausen, 1987), apprenticeship (Rogoff, 1990), or co-constructive interactions in which more experienced partners guide the development of novices (Valsiner, 1998).

Relationships with Teachers

Developmental agendas are most pronounced in children's relationships with teachers. There is not just an implicit timetable, but an explicit *curriculum* for students' development. Teachers are trained to support children's progress according to this plan and their success is evaluated accordingly. Teachers are assigned to classrooms because of their expertise with the respective age range, and classroom size and everyday activities are adjusted to children's developmental level. In the classroom, teachers are 'purposeful' social partners (Valsiner, 1998) whose actions are closely attuned to children's learning processes.

In addition, teachers also tend to hold directive beliefs about individual students. Their expectations of students' abilities and academic potential are predictive of students' success in school (for review, see Brophy, 1985), which has often been taken to indicate 'self-fulfilling prophecies'. By assuming that these effects are analogous to those found in experimental studies, teachers are seen to interact with students according to their expectations and to influence students' classroom behavior in such a way that expectations are met. However, in contrast to the parenting literature, the focus is on underestimations of children's potential and expectations of detrimental effects; with parents, overestimations of competencies are seen as developmentally facilitative (cf. Rogoff, 1990).

This interpretation may reflect the fact that educational processes are usually not seen from a relationship perspective. As Brophy suggested and Jussim and Eccles (1992) have reasserted, instead of holding biases, teachers may often have *accurate* expectations of students' potential, because they spend much time with them and know them well. Thus, teacher perceptions can be outcomes of relationship factors, and experimental simulations that disregard how expectations are formed in relationships may not examine the same phenomenon.

Similarly to attachment and parenting studies, relationships with teachers have also been examined with regard to *how* teachers interact as socialization agents in the classroom. Valsiner (1998) discusses approaches to regard interactions between students and teachers as situated within children's 'zone of proximal development' (Vygotski, 1978). Studies suggest that when teachers' agendas foster children's intrinsic interests, this can lead to positive developmental outcomes (Deci & Ryan, 1985). For example, when teachers adopt a more 'child-centered' (versus didactic) mode of instruction, they foster positive self-perceptions and motivation (Stipek et al., 1995), and when teachers support students' autonomy, they foster self-regulation, interest, and engagement in academic activities (Connell & Wellborn, 1991; Deci et al., 1991; Skinner & Wellborn, 1994).

Relationships with Peers

Peer affiliates are typically not assumed to hold directive beliefs or developmental agendas. Because of self-selection, the relationships tend to be more symmetrical than complementary in nature (Hartup & Stevens, 1997). Group expectations and norms are assumed to be negotiated among partners and to be more concerned with concurrent behavior than with guidance for the future. Of course, peer relationships can also exist among partners who are differentially competent, as, for example, in sibling relationships (e.g. Dunn, 1993) or groups in which partners are assigned to collaboration tasks (e.g. Tudge, 1992). The differences in competencies can have favorable developmental outcomes. However, typically, peer relationships consist of (almost) equally competent partners who share similarities in a variety of characteristics (Kandel, 1978) and have formed the relationship because of their compatibility.

Complementary processes have been of interest to friendship approaches. For example, friendships have been examined with regard to how children's perceptions of themselves are related to their perceptions of their friends (Tesser, Campbell, & Smith, 1984). Children tend to see themselves as more competent in those areas that are central to their identity while they depict their friends as more competent in features that they do not view as central. Epstein (1983) reports that such discrepancies can lead to academic gains in the lower scoring friend. Complementarity (in the form of anticipation) can also play a role when children try to establish affiliations, before an actual relationship is formed (e.g. Corsaro & Rizzo, 1988).

Finally, complementarity has also been examined in social networks. Attention has focused on social hierarchies and dominance (Strayer & Trudel, 1984), as well as on the centrality of specific networks and the centrality of specific members (Gest, Graham-Berman, & Hartup, 2001). For example, central members of groups that hold a central position in a classroom can have exceptional roles (e.g. Farmer, Pearl, & van Acker, 1996; Farmer & Rodkin, 1996), and individual members of a network can adopt specific roles for the functioning of their group (e.g. Cairns & Cairns, 1994). Thus, group socialization processes may be directed towards homogeneity among group members, as well as towards differentiation into complementary roles within a group (see also Harris, 1998; Moreno, 1934).

Reciprocity in Relationships

Since Richard Bell's (1968) assertion that correlations between parents' and children's behavior can be interpreted in terms of children's influences on their parents as much as in terms of classical socialization expectations, developmental psychologists have become much aware of children's contributions to socialization processes. Because socialization agents are other people, reciprocal influences are seen as important as influences from these partners on children.

Reciprocal influences can be studied from several angles (see Table 18.1). One way is to see reciprocal influences as 'evocative' (Cairns, 1972) and to examine children's antecedents (social behavior, temperament, or emotional tone) as contributors to attachment, parental socialization, teacher–student interactions, or peer relationships. Peer relationships, however, suggest also a second route. By selecting specific others as friends or members of their groups, children exert 'choice' (Cairns, 1979; Moreno, 1934) and *create* their own contexts. Selection of socialization agents is an additional process by which children can influence their contexts reciprocally.

Researchers studying the effects of children on parents or teachers typically do not mention selection effects. However, even in these relationships, selection may be expressed in terms of selective initiation of and differential participation in specific activities. Children may choose which parent or teacher to go to for advice, help, or comfort, or may even choose to avoid interactions with a parent (at least in specific situations). The extent to which children actively participate in specific activities with parents or teachers (and avoid others) needs to be regarded as an additional mode of reciprocal influences.

Relationships with Parents

Parenting research has paid much attention to evocative reciprocity. For example, a current debate in attachment research is about the extent to which attachment patterns are determined by children's temperament in addition to mothers' sensitivity and responsiveness (Kochanska, 1997; 1998; Thompson, 1998). A similar debate exists about children's contributions to socialization processes; again, temperament is seen as a key variable (e.g. Scarr, 1992). Overall, children's contributions to interactions have been shown to be as powerful in predictions of socialization outcomes as maternal behaviors (e.g. Grusec & Kuczynski, 1980). For example, children who are more active, less responsive, and less compliant tend to evoke negative parenting behavior as well as negative affect (Bell & Harper, 1977). Patterson and colleagues (e.g. Patterson & Bank, 1988) have elaborated one particular model of how children can shape family interactions. In interactions, children's contingencies for mothers' behavior can operate synergistically with mothers' contingencies for child behavior, and lead to escalating coercive cycles that are fueled by the contributions from both partners.

A focus on relationships and on the extent to which children actively reciprocate in a relationship also raises the question of who, among a child's network of caretakers, would be sought out most by a child, and for which kinds of activities. For example, processes by which children select specific partners, even among their parents, are documented in the literature on gender development (cf. Fagot,

1995). Similarly, interaction behaviors of a child (e.g. low cooperation or responsiveness) with one caretaker may be a marker of stable child characteristics, but they may also indicate that the child selectively participates in one relationship less than in others (cf. Rutter, 2000). Harmony in a relationship and active participation of a child should affect a caretaker's well-being; relationship quality should influence the extent to which caretakers can learn from (as well as adjust to) children. In turn, this should influence socialization outcomes. Overall, to pay attention to reciprocity and selection processes in socialization studies makes it necessary to examine the extent to which patterns of child-rearing styles differ across the caretakers of a child (e.g. Johnson, Shulman, & Collins, 1991) as well as to include children's affiliations with relatives or professional caretakers (e.g. Cassiba, van Ijzendoorn, & d'Odorico, 2000).

Relationships with Teachers

Researchers interested in development in schools have also begun to examine reciprocal processes. For example, kindergartners' behavior at the beginning of a school year was found to be related to the quality of their relationships with teachers (Birch & Ladd, 1998). Similarly, students' behavior and emotional tone in the classroom has been shown to affect teachers' reciprocal behavior (Skinner & Belmont, 1993). Students who are more engaged in classroom activities seem to experience more positive and developmentally facilitative interactions with teachers, whereas passivity in students is often perceived as aversive, often leading teachers to feel incompetent or disliked by students (Deci & Ryan, 1985).

Similar to relationships with parents, children's reciprocal effects on teacher behavior appear to magnify, rather than minimize, earlier interindividual differences (e.g. Skinner & Belmont, 1993). Among students' own characteristics, their selective participation in interactions seems to be influential. Again, one can expect that children will choose to engage more in relationships characterized by high teacher involvement, mutual regard, similarity, and considerable developmental attunement to the developmental level of the child. In turn, quality of the relationship should influence teachers' own satisfaction and motivation in the classroom.

Finally, reciprocal processes are not just confined to children's participation in existing relationships. At the high school level, but probably even earlier, students can find favorite teachers (or mentors) outside their pool of pre-assigned teachers. Thus, based on their own interests and preferences, children can choose whether to ask a specific teacher for help or advice (Nelson-LeGall, 1985; Newman, in press), and longer-lasting relationships can be established based on these (initially) more casual contacts.

Relationships with Peers

Because a child's peers are also children, peer relationship researchers have been most attentive to reciprocal processes. Sociometric researchers have focused much on detailing how children's own behavior contributes to their emerging status in the classroom. Crick and Dodge (1994) have outlined an information processing model suggesting that rejected children process social information differently than other children and, consequently, engage in social behavior that makes social rejection likely. Characteristics are a hostile attribution bias, misinterpretations of social cues, and a high likelihood to respond with inappropriate or aggressive behavior. Overall, aggressive and socially inappropriate behavior tendencies appear to be prominent predictors of peer rejection (e.g. Asher & Coie, 1990).

Friendship and peer network researchers have focused on reciprocal influences when friendships are established, children become new members of a group, or friendship or group affiliations change (e.g. Berndt, 1989; Cairns & Cairns, 1994; Gottman, 1983; Ladd, 1990). A key variable appears to be children's social competence: high competence tends to heighten a child's chances to be accepted and to establish and maintain close relationships. In turn, high relationship quality is also expected to increase the reciprocal influences a child can have on his or her peer partners.

Friendship and network researchers have highlighted selection processes as being guided by frequency of contact, proximity, and similarity among candidates in a variety of characteristics (e.g. Hamm, 2000; Kandel, 1978; Kindermann, 1996). Proximity and similarity make it likely that a child participates actively in peer interactions and thus creates his or her own peer context. Thus, reciprocal processes among peers are seen as the basis for the formation of relationships and, consequently, for all emerging influence processes.

However, beyond findings of assortativeness, not much is known about how peer selection processes proceed and about the individuals' reciprocal contributions (cf. Epstein, 1983). Although peer relationships are highly fluid and friends and members of peer networks are typically exchanged at rapid rates (Cairns et al., 1995; Dishion, Patterson, & Griesler, 1994), there are also indications that the criteria of how children select relationship candidates may not change at the same pace. For example, in a study on peer group influences on children's school motivation in elementary school classrooms, after peer groups had been formed, reselection processes occurred in a way that the groups' motivational composition remained intact (e.g. Kindermann, 1993a). Individuals were exchanged at a rapid pace, but seemingly in a way that did not affect the groups' psychological characteristics.

This suggests that stability of a context, at least in the case of peer relationships, needs to be seen in relative terms. Stability can exist in terms of group members (and can be low), but it also exists in terms of the context's psychological characteristics. Both are affected by reciprocal processes. Because developmentalists have traditionally focused most of their attention on assigned and obligatory contexts, children's own role in creating contexts for themselves has not received much attention. However, the reciprocal influences that are typical for peer relationships suggest that it would be worthwhile to study individual differences and developmental change in how children select (and reselect) friends and peer group members. A particularly promising conceptualization can be borrowed from life-span researchers. Baltes and Baltes (1966) have proposed a model of 'selective optimization' for conceptualizing processes by which individuals arrange their circumstances of living and daily routines in a way that allows them to maximize their efficacy in activities that are central to their own identity. This model may also be useful for describing children's efforts to design their social contexts and thus influence their own development. For example, some children may succeed increasingly well in selecting peer environments that support their own intrinsic interests in academic activities in school. Overall, examinations of children's reciprocal contributions to relationships and their own role in creating these contexts may lead to new insights into the nature of context influences on development.

Key Characteristics of Relationship Contexts Make Them Different from Other Contexts

Five features of children's relationships have been identified in order to advance the idea that relationship contexts have common characteristics that make them different from other developmental contexts – especially from environments that exist independently of the children under study. Parent–child, teacher–student, and peer relationships are characterized by high contact among partners who share mutual regard, are created not at random but through assortative processes, are adjusted according to partners' developmental expectations, and are characterized by reciprocal influences. These features have implications for the designs used to study relationships as well as for the methods used to capture their effects on development.

A first implication is that experimental strategies to study relationship influences need to include attention to these five relationship factors. For example, experiments showing that specific child-rearing techniques, teaching styles, or peer collaboration arrangements, when induced in partners who do not share a pre-established relationship with each other (i.e. using random assignment), produce changes in child behavior, just show that they *can* do so, not that they do so in naturally existing relationships. Influences from social agents who do not share a pre-established relationship with children, have not spent much time with them, are not more similar to them than strangers, and are not developmentally attuned to them much (even if reciprocal processes occur) are very strong, as indicated from studies using experimental social groups (e.g. Asch, 1955). However, for developmentalists, the more interesting questions about relationship influences in childhood do not concern effects from random strangers. Of interest is socialization in natural parent–child dyads, real classrooms, and actual friendships or peer groups; these effects cannot be studied outside the relationships in which they occur (cf. Hinde, 1997).

Experiments in which interaction patterns *within* established relationships are changed do provide evidence of relationship effects. For example, intervention studies indicate that positive changes in caretakers' sensitive and responsive behaviors can influence the development of a secure relationship (van IJzendoorn, Juffer, & Duyvesteyn, 1995). Interventions aimed at a variety of socializing behaviors in mothers or teachers also showed that their behavior change can influence children to change (e.g. Cowan, Powell, & Cowan, 1998; Minuchin & Shapiro, 1983). With regard to peer relationships, the studies by Sherif and colleagues (e.g. Sherif et al., 1961) have shown peer influence effects in children who were initially randomly assigned to groups in a summer camp and *then developed* natural peer relationships.

Such interventions show that natural relationship contexts, if altered, *can* have positive influences on children's behavior and development. However, it is a different question whether the same factors that are active in interventions would also operate naturally and whether their effects persist across time. Such questions can typically only be examined with correlational studies that examine outcomes of natural socialization *across time*. In designing such studies, four questions need to be addressed in order to minimize problems that result from the five characteristics of childhood relationships. Who are the partners who can be assumed to be most influential for a given child at a point in time? What kinds of outcome patterns are expected to indicate socialization processes? How can 'proximal processes' be examined across time? How can reciprocal processes of change be included in analyses of developmental pathways?

Identifying Relationship Partners

Research on parental relationships, on teacher–student relationships in elementary school, and on dyadic friendships has typically focused on just one single context agent who is considered to be most important for a child. Whether this is adequate or whether more context agents need to be identified is a matter of theoretical assumptions about the kinds of relationship that are studied. For example, when children spend much of their time in daycare, when they are often cared for by fathers or relatives, or when child care is shared among parents, attachment theorists point out that the emotional quality of the relationships with the various partners would need to be considered in addition to mere interaction frequency (cf. Lamb, 1998; Thompson, 1998). Similarly, newer conceptions of teacher–student relationships highlight that among several teachers, those would become most influential with whom a child shares a maximum of interpersonal closeness (Ryan & Powelson, 1991). Finally, friendship and sociometric researchers also argue that warmth and mutual regard are the most influential factors (Hartup & Stevens, 1997), while social network researchers tend to focus on time spent and extent of contact in interactions (cf. Cairns & Cairns, 1994; Kindermann, 1996).

To identify a child's most influential social partners is especially difficult when many caretakers, many teachers, or many agemates are involved. Key candidates have (likely) differing amount of contact with a child, share different levels of closeness, are differentially similar to him or her, have different agendas or plans, and show different levels of developmental adjustment and reciprocity. Even in family relationships, it is not always obvious who is the most important partner. For example, the current *Handbook on parenting* (Bornstein, 1995) contains five chapters on the question 'Who is the parent?' Researchers have pointed out that parents' differences in child-rearing styles can be related to differences in children's developmental outcomes (Johnson, Shulman, & Collins, 1991). Larson and Richards refer to 'multiple realities' (1994, p. 189) in children's lives that are shared with different social partners.

However, researchers studying peer relationships are faced with an even more complex task. Most peer contexts are not as well defined as other contexts. Peer contexts tend to be larger than dyads, are typically organized around common activities as well as affective bonds, and can include a child's friends as well as non-friends. Peer contexts can be 'cliques' (Dunphy, 1963), 'crowds' (R. Brown, 1988; B.B. Brown, 1999), friendship groups (Urberg et al., 1995), or social networks (Cairns & Cairns, 1994). In peer contexts, children can divide their time and activities among different combinations of peers, and the partners can differ in terms of social status (Asher & Coie, 1990), position in social hierarchies (Strayer & Trudel, 1984), friendship affiliations (Berndt, 1989), as well as closeness to one another (Farmer & Rodkin, 1996).

Composite Social Maps: Robert Cairns' Approach to Social Networks

Peer relationship researchers often aim to capture complex contexts that consist of many social partners. However, at the same time, they are often skeptical about the extent to which they can rely on children's self-reports about who their most important partners would be (cf. Leung, 1996) and see a need for methods to define such groups objectively. One particular strategy has been developed by Robert Cairns and colleagues (Cairns, Perrin, & Cairns, 1985; Cairns et al., 2001). The focus is on public knowledge about affiliations that is shared among many children who frequently interact in a setting. Multiple children, in a classroom for example, are asked to report about the classmates who are known to frequently 'hang around' with one another. From these reports, maps of social networks of the entire classroom are formed. Similarly to Moreno's sociograms, these maps depict connections among children who are identified as sharing affiliations with one another (see an example in Figure 18.1).

A specific advantage of this method is that not just individuals' own views about their contexts are obtained, but also children's reports about social configurations in the entire classroom. Children participate as expert observers, and because many observers report about the same setting, it is possible to determine their consensus (Kindermann, 1996). A second practical advantage is that, if public consensus exists, not each and every student in a classroom needs to be interviewed. With self-reports, information on the contexts of those children whose respective peer partners did not participate in assessments would be lost; these children can appear to have fewer friends and smaller social groups. A method that targets public knowledge will not miss these contexts. Reports from about 60% of the students in a classroom seem to be sufficient to yield a reliable social map as long as the sample of reporters is fairly representative.

Profiles of Partner Characteristics

When actual relationships (and not just perceptions) are studied, context accounts should also reflect partners' actual characteristics that are measured independently from the scores of target children. When more than one potential socialization partner is involved, these context accounts will need to be based on actual characteristics of all of the partners. Since most peer group researchers expect that influences from the members of a child's social networks would be synergistic, aggregate context profiles (averages across context members) appear to be useful (Kindermann, 1996; alternatives can account for variation across partners or attach weights to specific partners, e.g. according to levels of closeness or stability of the relationship). If it is

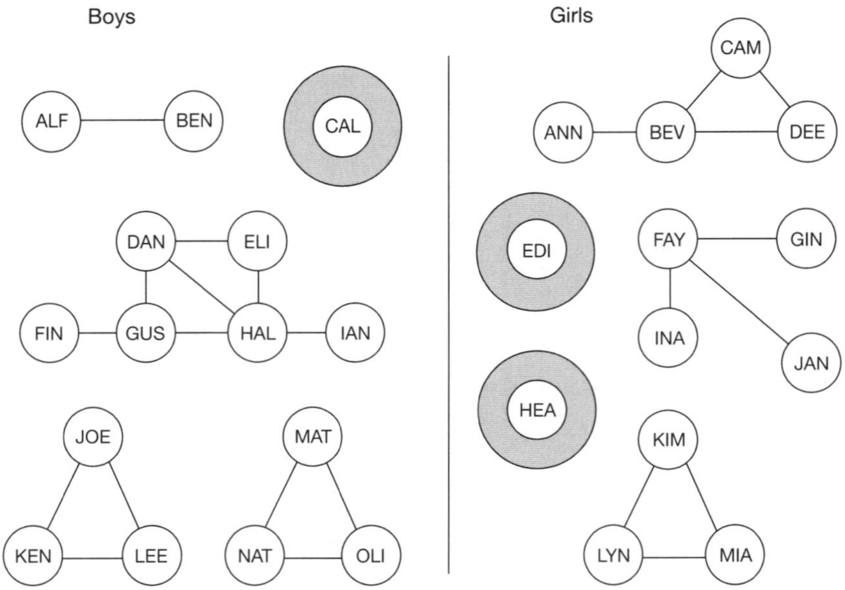

Figure 18.1 *Example of a composite social-cognitive map of peer network affiliations among children in a fourth grade classroom. Individual children's positions are arbitrary and based on drawing convenience*

assumed that partners would differ in their developmental influences, their characteristics can be contrasted. To contrast socialization agents (e.g. mothers and fathers: Johnson, Shulman, & Collins, 1991) appears to be more typical for research on obligatory relationships.

Conceptualizing Socialization Influences

When a child's most important partners and their characteristics are identified, the next task is to model how, analytically, influences from these agents should be shown. Usually, influences that emerge from social interactions are conceived as *socialization processes*. The concept dominated the psychological and sociological literatures between the late 1940s and the early 1970s, but since then has almost 'gone out of fashion' (Bronfenbrenner, 1994, p. xi). Partly, this is due to sobering conclusions about the magnitude of correlations between parental child-rearing characteristics and child outcomes (e.g. Maccoby & Martin, 1983). Partly, this is also due to an increased prominence of organismic perspectives (cf. Sameroff, 1983) which contributed to a shift in focus from contents of interactions towards quality of relationships.

Rather than abandon usage of the concept of socialization, it is possible to argue that the concept would need to be broadened. The traditional understanding of socialization often implied that processes of influence were unidirectional (from a socialization agent to a child) and that the influence would 'make' the child more similar to some socialization ideal. If socialization processes are used more broadly to refer to processes by which social interactions are actively changing something about a person (and in various directions), then issues of strength of effects, assortativeness, and reciprocity in patterns of change can be tackled separately. In particular, socialization can be contrasted to processes whereby individuals influence their own development, such as through selection of developmental partners and selective participation.

Modeling Developmental Outcomes

Contrary to traditional beliefs, one can doubt whether all social influences make people similar. Rather, context influences can occur in at least three different ways. First, children can become *similar* to a cultural norm (and hence to one another as well as to socialization agents) through socialization processes when they share the same contexts. In fact, they can all become so similar so that they appear indistinguishable from one another. Processes by which children, due to socializing influences from families, classrooms, friendships, or peer groups, become so similar to one another that the remaining differences are negligible (compared to children socialized according to different norms) can be seen as processes of *acculturation* or convergence. Such expectations are often held in cross-cultural studies (e.g. LeVine et al., 1994) that focus on the extent to which cultural-specific socialization practices guide children so that they become accepted members of a culture. Similar expectations are found in studies on cultural canalization processes in family interactions (e.g. Kindermann & Skinner, 1988; Valsiner, 1989), on processes of students' learning in school (Valsiner, 1998), or on social convergence in *ad hoc* social groups (Asch, 1955). For example, it can be expected that all children in a specific culture learn to eat with a spoon, that all children learn to multiply efficiently, or that all members of a peer group learn to take turns. Analytically, there is no correlation between antecedent context characteristics and children's later developmental outcomes. However, the absence of a correlation does not imply that there was no influence.

A second developmental outcome is *relative similarity*. Children in a family, classmates who have the same teacher, friends, or members of a peer group can become relatively more similar to one another due to socialization influences. The standard is not absolute, and socialization leads towards relative homogeneity. Variability in socialization outcomes is expected among children who share a context, and it can be examined whether children who grow up in the same contexts become more similar to one another than children who grow up in different contexts. Thus, correlations between context antecedents and individual outcomes become meaningful. Such studies have examined similarities between adopted children and their biological parents (e.g. Scarr & Weinberg, 1983), among siblings in the same family (e.g. Dunn, 1993; Hoffman, 1991), among children who attend the same school environment or have the same teacher (cf. Bryk & Raudenbush, 1992), and among children who share friends or are members of social groups (e.g. Dishion, Andrews, & Crosby, 1995; Ennett & Bauman, 1994).

However, relative similarity is affected by assortativeness. Thus, expectations that relative similarity between parents and children would indicate socialization processes have been criticized by behavior geneticists (cf. Harris, 1995; see Gottlieb, Chapter 1 and Wahlsten, Chapter 2 in this volume). If parental socialization made siblings similar to one another, it should make them more similar than could be expected based on prior similarity. With regard to peer relationships, expectations of relative similarity have received the same criticism (Ennett & Bauman, 1994; Kindermann, 1996), because similarities among friends or members of a peer group can be outcomes of selection processes as much as of socialization. In short, one has to be cautious with taking similarity between relationship partners as indicating socialization processes, because assortativeness provides an alternative interpretation.

Rather than giving up on the notion that relations between environmental characteristics and individual outcomes can be results of socialization processes, researchers have proposed that socialization processes should produce *change* in children (e.g. Kindermann & Valsiner, 1995; Steinberg et al., 1994). Instead of examining similarity (or change thereof) across time, it may be more useful to focus on intra-individual change (see also Nesselroade and Molenaar, Chapter 27 in this volume). Thus, socialization influences from peer affiliates are investigated in such a way that change within friends or individual members of a group is examined as an outcome of earlier peer characteristics, over and above pre-existing similarities that may be due to assortativeness. Similarly, family socialization processes can be investigated so that change in children across time is examined over and above pre-existing (genetic) similarities. Finally, teacher socialization processes can also be examined in terms of within-student change, over and above initial similarities between students that are due to assignment of children to classrooms. Overall, inter-individual differences in how children change may indicate effects of socialization processes most appropriately.

A perspective on socialization processes in terms of change across time can also open up research avenues for examining a third pattern of socialization processes: influences from families, teachers, and peer affiliates, at least under some circumstances, at some points in time, and for some children, may lead children to become increasingly *different* from one another (e.g. Skinner & Belmont, 1993), even if they share the same context. Favorable contexts may not just be advantageous to children's development, they may also encourage increasing differentiation and autonomy (e.g. Deci & Ryan, 1985). At least, it appears hard to reconcile beliefs that relationships are intimate, mutually supportive, and developmentally adjusted contexts with the expectation that they would produce uniform outcomes in the form of a social 'mold'. In relationships, decreases in similarity may (at least sometimes) denote not an absence of socialization, but rather an influence towards increased differentiation.

Identifying Mechanisms of How Socialization Processes Occur

The key question of socialization centers on *how* developmental influences are exerted from one person to another (Lawrence & Valsiner, 1993; Valsiner, 1998). This question will likely go beyond the scope of correlational analyses. Interpretations of correlational analyses will often not be specific enough and will likely not be able rule out alternative interpretations.

One way to strengthen theoretical assumptions is to focus on specific *mechanisms* of social influence that are expected to occur as part of socialization processes. The goal is to show that socialization agents show specific action patterns that are theoretically able to produce the kind of effects that are indicated by correlational studies. A particularly strong case can be made if mechanisms are targeted that are known to have powerful effects in experimentally controlled situations. This strategy follows Donald Baer's (1973; see also Baltes, 1996) proposal for *convergent operations* in the study of socialization processes. That is, if correlation patterns indicate the possibility of socialization influences, and if experimental findings suggest that specific mechanisms can produce similar influence under controlled conditions, naturalistic studies should examine whether the same mechanisms, embedded in natural interactions, can produce the same kind of change. Thus, examining socialization mechanisms can help to narrow the explanatory gap that often remains from correlational analyses.

Theories of socialization processes suggest a variety of candidates for mechanisms that operate as 'proximal processes' (Bronfenbrenner & Morris, 1998). Some of these capture what contexts provide for children, for example, in terms of parental guidance or discipline techniques (cf. Bugenthal & Goodnow, 1998), contingencies in learning processes (e.g. Dishion, Patterson, & Griesler, 1994; Dishion et al., 1991; Sage & Kindermann, 1999), or discussion and persuasion (Berndt & Keefe, 1996; Berndt, Laychak, & Park, 1990; Corsaro & Rizzo, 1988). Others specify children's own efforts to 'extract' specific features from their contexts, as, for example, in processes of imitation (Hall & Cairns, 1984), identification (e.g. Whiting & Whiting, 1975), internalization (e.g. Valsiner, 1989) or social comparison (e.g. Tesser, Campbell, & Smith, 1984). Particularly influential has become the Vygotskian notion of 'participatory appropriation' (Rogoff, 1990; Tudge, 1992; Valsiner, 1998) as a mechanism that enables children to function on developmentally advanced levels when they interact with more competent social partners.

To examine socialization processes directly will likely involve direct observations of interactions among relationship partners. For example, Patterson and colleagues (e.g. Patterson & Bank, 1988) have shown that the same learning theoretical mechanisms that were effective under controlled conditions in altering children's (as well as parents') behavior also coexist in children's natural family relationships. Interventions in natural family relationships targeting these mechanisms were also successful in changing children's developmental outcomes. With regard to teacher relationships, Brophy's (e.g. 1986) 'process–product' research proposal on teacher influences on student motivation followed the same strategy. Specific teacher behaviors that were effective teaching mechanisms under controlled conditions (e.g. specific ways of questioning or classroom management techniques) were also found to be influential for student learning in classrooms. Finally, mechanism studies have also been conducted to study peer relationships. Berndt, Laychak, and Park (1990) examined the role of specific mechanisms by which friends influence each other in processes of decision making about academic matters. The findings corroborated correlational indications that friends would influence students' academic development (e.g. Kandel, 1978). Sage and Kindermann (1999; 2000) presented observational data on everyday classroom interactions between children, members of their peer group(s), and non-affiliated classmates. The results suggest that learning theoretical mechanisms can also provide explanations for correlational findings that have suggested peer group influences on children's engagement in classroom activities (cf. Kindermann, 1993a; Kindermann, McCollam, & Gibson, 1996).

However, studies targeting specific socialization mechanisms appear to be comparatively rare. With the exception of the Vygotskian perspective, assumptions that specific interaction mechanisms influence children's development in socialization processes have lost much of their appeal for developmentalists. One reason is that assumptions about mechanisms seem to compete with an organismic perspective that accords children a more active role in socialization processes. According to the organismic viewpoint, warmth and mutual acceptance are the developmentally facilitative factors in relationships, 'nutriments' that allow a child to do well and to develop his or her intrinsic interests. The focus is typically on aggregates of relationship quality, as for example attachment security, teacher relatedness, or friendship quality. The role of contexts is to provide sensitivity and responsive interactions (Ainsworth et al., 1978), autonomy, support and involvement in the classroom (Deci & Ryan, 1985), or acceptance and peer support (Hartup & Stevens, 1997). From this perspective, socializing interactions are assumed not to directly guide development, but to foster development by providing a supportive environment that facilitates mastery of developmental tasks as well as self-actualization.

However, adopting an organismic perspective does not necessarily preclude attention to specific socialization mechanisms. Rather, an organismic perspective can augment a focus on such mechanisms. Key relationship features, as, for example, time spent, warmth and acceptance, similarity, and developmental adjustment among partners, can be expected to have moderating effects on the strength of direct influences, so that influences from relationship partners would be heightened (cf. Kochanska, 1997). In addition, the specific mechanisms can be seen as contributing to a child's experiences, also depending on the overall relationship characteristics. For example, contingencies in interactions can be perceived as coercive (e.g. Deci & Ryan, 1985), but they can also contribute to children's experiences of responsiveness (e.g. MacDonald, 1992). Thus, time spent among partners, mutual regard, similarity, and developmental attunement may foster experiences of influence mechanisms as benign and helpful, instead of as coercive or as undermining a child's autonomy.

CONCLUSION

The central thesis of this chapter has been that relationship contexts are different from other contexts. Relationships come as a 'package' or set of interrelated features. Some of the features, like warmth, frequency of interaction, or reciprocal influences, can magnify the effects of relationships on children's development. Others, like assortativeness and developmental agendas, can give children's development a direction. Consideration of all of these features has implications for the design of studies intended to capture the effects of relationships on development.

The specific focus of this chapter was on children's relationships with parents, teachers, and peers. It was argued that social interactions with these relationship partners are embedded in ongoing relationships that are characterized by these five features. These features make these three relationships different from more casual social contexts (e.g. acquaintanceship) as well as from contexts that are adverse in nature (e.g. relationships with enemies: cf. Hinde, 1997).

Although these features have been depicted as central aspects of children's relationships, it was argued that they would not necessarily constitute the 'proximal processes' through which relationship partners influence each other. 'Proximal processes' are the mechanisms of influence that relationship partners generate in social interactions, and studies of socialization processes in relationships may want to include attention to such mechanisms of influence. This means that researchers who target the role of specific socialization mechanisms, such as contingencies in interactions or the use of disciplinary techniques like power assertion, may want to examine how these operate in contexts that differ with regard to the features of relationships. For example, specific interactions may have different effects when they occur in relationships that are characterized by warm and frequent interactions, compared to contexts that are cold or distant.

Even for researchers who focus on the features of relationships themselves, for example, on warmth or developmental agendas, the implications are that these are likewise embedded in the other relationship features. The effect of warmth may be mitigated (or magnified) by shared time and assortativeness; the consequences of developmental expectations may be moderated by frequency of contact and mutual acceptance; the consequences of reciprocal influences may depend on developmental agendas and assortativeness.

The five features discussed in this chapter can certainly be refined in both their definitions and their implications. Some may turn out to be less important than they have been portrayed, and additional commonalities may need to be identified. Regardless of the specifics, however, researchers need to be aware that the study of socialization in relationships without attention to these features, or the study of some of these features without attention to the others, may influence their target phenomenon under study.

It was not intended to argue that relationships with parents, teachers, and peers were the same or that they have identical effects on children's development. The goal was to attempt to integrate core features of the three relationships, to borrow lessons learned from the study of each relationship, and to the extent that they are applicable, to use them to enrich the study of the neighboring social partners. For example, warmth has been considered a central feature of parenting for over fifty years; only in the last decade has it been systematically included in empirical work on teaching. Similarly, the identification of a child's peer context(s) has been recognized as a thorny issue for peer researchers, probably since before Moreno's time, but only recently has this issue also been discussed in research on parenting and teaching. Finally, genetic similarity has been identified as a problem for socialization studies by behavior geneticists for some time; it was peer relationship researchers who pointed out that assortativeness is also a problem in relationship contexts that children create themselves.

An important aspect that this chapter could not address is the fact that these relationships do not occur in isolation. Just as social interactions with a given partner are embedded in the features of the relationship with that partner, so too is the relationship with a given partner experienced in combination with those of other relationship partners. Stated simply, the vast majority of children have relationships with caregivers, teachers, *and* peers. In childhood, all relationships coexist. It is likely that the developmental effects of one relationship depend on the nature of the others, that one relationship is affected by changes in others, and that developmental outcomes of one relationship have influences on socialization processes in others (cf. Laursen & Bukowski, 1997). Thus, children's development may be more influenced by the cumulative and synergistic (as well as antagonistic) effects of a variety of relationships than by any particular relationship alone (see also Kurdek & Sinclair, 2000; Mounts & Steinberg, 1995; Wentzel, 1998; 1999). In consequence, the study of the interrelations among the many processes that co-occur in children's developing person–context relations may be the most challenging but also a most fascinating task for developmental researchers.

ACKNOWLEDGMENTS

This chapter is dedicated to the memories of Margret M. Baltes and Robert B. Cairns, who passed away unexpectedly during 1999. The context of their mentorship is sorely missed. I want to thank Ellen A. Skinner from Portland State University for her invaluable support and S. Kristen Hillier for her help with editing of the chapter. The work on this chapter was supported by an AREA grant from NICHD (1-R15 HD37848-01).

REFERENCES

Ainsworth, M.D.S., Blehar, M.C., Waters, E., & Wall, S. (1978). *Patterns of attachment*. Hillsdale, NJ: Erlbaum.

Asch, S.E. (1955). Opinions and social pressure. *Scientific American*, 193, 31–55.

Asher, S.R., & Coie, J.D. (eds) (1990). *Peer rejection in childhood*. New York: Cambridge University Press.

Baer, D.J. (1973). The control of developmental processes: Why wait? In J.R. Nesselroade & H.W. Reese (eds), *Life-span developmental psychology: Methodological issues* (pp. 187–193). New York: Academic.

Baltes, M.M. (1996). *The many faces of dependency*. New York: Cambridge University Press.

Baltes, P.B., & Baltes, M.M. (1996). Selective optimization with compensation: Basic definitions. Unpublished manuscript, Max Planck Institute for Human Development and Education and Free University Berlin, Germany.

Baltes, P.B., Reese, H.W., & Nesselroade, J.R. (1988). *Life-span developmental psychology: Introduction to research methods*. Hillsdale, NJ: Erlbaum.

Baumrind, D. (1967). Child care practices anteceding three patterns of preschool behavior. *Genetic Psychology Monographs*, 75, 43–88.

Baumrind, D. (1989). Rearing competent children. In W. Damon (ed.), *Child development today and tomorrow* (pp. 349–378). San Francisco: Jossey-Bass.

Bell, R.Q. (1968). A reinterpretation of the direction of effects in studies on socialization. *Psychological Review*, 75, 81–95.

Bell, R.Q., & Harper, L.V. (1977). *Child effects on adults*. Hillsdale, NJ: Erlbaum.

Berndt, T.J. (1989). Friendships in childhood and adolescence. In W. Damon (ed.), *Child development today and tomorrow* (pp. 332–348). San Francisco: Jossey-Bass.

Berndt, T.J., & Keefe, K. (1996) Friends' influence on school adjustment: A motivational analysis. In J. Juvonen and K.R. Wentzel (eds), *Social motivation: Understanding children's school adjustment* (pp. 248–278). New York: Cambridge University Press.

Berndt, T.J., Laychak, A.E., & Park, K. (1990). Friends' influence on adolescents' academic achievement motivation: An experimental study. *Journal of Educational Psychology*, 82, 664–670.

Birch, S.H., & Ladd, G.W. (1996). Interpersonal relationships in the school environment and children's early school adjustment: The role of teachers and peers. In J. Juvonen and K.R. Wentzel (eds), *Social motivation: Understanding children's school adjustment* (pp. 199–225).

Birch, S.H., & Ladd, G.W. (1997). The teacher–child relationship and children's school adjustment. *Journal of School Psychology*, 35, 61–79.

Birch, S.H., & Ladd, G.W. (1998). Children's interpersonal behaviors and the teacher-child relationship. *Developmental Psychology*, 35 (5), 934–946.

Boivin, M., Dodge, K.A., & Coie, J.D. (1995). Individual–group behavioral similarity and peer status in experimental play groups of boys: The social misfit revisited. *Journal of Personality and Social Psychology*, 69, 269–279.

Bornstein, M. (ed.) (1995) *Handbook of parenting: Vol. 3. Status and social conditions of parenting*. Mahwah, NJ: Erlbaum.

Boyce, W.T., Frank, E., Jensen, P., Kessler, R.M., Nelson, C.A., Steinberg, L., & The MacArthur Foundation Research Network on Psychopathology and Development (1998). Social context in developmental psychopathology: Recommendations from the MacArthur Network on Psychopathology and Development. *Development and Psychopathology*, 10, 143–164.

Bowlby, J. (1969). *Attachment and loss* (Vol. 1). London: Hogarth.

Bradley, R.H. (1999). The home environment. In S.L. Friedman & T.D. Wachs (eds), *Measuring the environment across the life span: Emerging methods and concepts* (pp. 31–58). Washington, DC: American Psychological Association.

Brophy, J. (1985). Teachers' expectations, motives and goals for working with problem students. In C. Ames & R.E. Ames (eds), *Research on motivation in education: The classroom milieu* (Vol. 2, pp. 175–214). Orlando, FL: Academic.

Brophy, J. (1986). Teacher influences on student motivation. *American Psychologist*, 41, 1069–1077.

Bronfenbrenner, U. (1989). Ecological systems theory. In R. Vasta (ed.), *Annals of child development* (pp. 187–249). Greenwich, CT: JAI Press.

Bronfenbrenner, U. (1994). Foreword. In R.A. LeVine, S. Dixon, S. LeVine, A. Richman, P.H. Leiderman, C. Keefer, & T.B. Brazelton, *Child care and culture: Lessons from Africa*. New York: Cambridge University Press.

Bronfenbrenner, U., & Morris, P.A. (1998). The ecology of developmental processes. In W. Damon (series ed.) & R.M. Lerner (ed.), *Handbook of child psychology: Vol. 1. Theoretical models of human development* (5th edn, pp. 993–1028). New York: Wiley.

Brown, B.B. (1999). Measuring the peer environment of American adolescents. In S.L. Friedman & T.D. Wachs (eds), *Measuring the environment across the life span: Emerging methods and concepts* (pp. 59–90). Washington, DC: American Psychological Association.

Brown, R. (1988). *Group processes: Dynamics within and between groups*. Cambridge, MA: Blackwell.

Bryk, A.S., & Raudenbush, S.W. (1992). *Hierarchical linear models: Applications and data analysis models*. Newbury Park, CA: Sage.

Bugenthal, D.B., & Goodnow, J.J. (1998). Socialization processes. In W. Damon (series ed.) & N. Eisenberg (ed.), *Handbook of child psychology: Vol. 3. Social, emotional, and personality development* (5th edn, pp. 389–462). New York: Wiley.

Cairns, R.B. (1972). Attachment and dependency: A psychobiological and social-learning synthesis. In J.L. Gewirtz (ed.), *Attachment and dependency* (pp. 29–95). New York: Wiley.

Cairns, R.B. (1979). *Social development: The origins and plasticity of interchanges*. San Francisco: Freeman.

Cairns, R. B. (1998). The making of a developmental science. In W. Damon (series ed.) & R.M. Lerner (ed.), *Handbook of child psychology: Vol. 1. Theoretical models of child development* (5th edn, pp. 25–105). New York: Wiley.

Cairns, R.B., & Cairns, B.D. (1994). *Lifelines and risks: Pathways of youth in our time*. New York: Cambridge University Press.

Cairns, R.B., Cairns, B.D., Neckerman, H.J., Gest, S., & Gariépy, J.-L. (1988). Social networks and aggressive behavior: Peer support or peer rejection? *Developmental Psychology*, 24, 815–823.

Cairns, R.B., Cairns, B.D., Xie, H., Leung, M.-C., & Hearne, S. (1998). Paths across generations: Academic competence and aggressive behaviors in young mothers and their children. *Developmental Psychology*, 34, 1162–1174.

Cairns, R.B., Gariépy, J.-L., Kindermann, T.A., & Leung, M.-C. (2001). Social cognitive mapping procedures. In R.B. Cairns, T. Farmer, & T.A. Kindermann (eds), *Handbook of cognitive social mapping strategies and related techniques*. New York: Cambridge University Press.

Cairns, R.B., Leung, M.-C., Buchanan, L., & Cairns, B.D. (1995). Friendships and social networks in childhood and adolescence: Fluidity, reliability, and interrelations. *Child Development*, 66, 1330–1345.

Cairns, R.B., Neckerman, H.J., & Cairns, B.D. (1989). Social networks and the shadows of synchrony. In G.R. Adams, R. Montemayor, & T.P. Gullota (eds), *Biology of adolescent behavior and development* (pp. 275–305). Newbury Park, CA: Sage.

Cairns, R.B., Perrin, J.E., & Cairns, B.D. (1985). Social structure and social cognition in early adolescence: Affiliative patterns. *Journal of Early Adolescence*, 5, 339–355.

Cairns, R.B., Xie, H., & Leung, M.-C. (1998). The popularity of friendship and the neglect of social networks: Toward a new balance. In W. Damon (series ed.) & W.M. Bukowski & A.H.N. Cillessen (eds), *New directions for child development: Vol. 80. Sociometry then and now: Building on six decades of measuring children's experiences with the peer group* (pp. 25–53). San Francisco: Jossey-Bass.

Caldwell, B.M., & Bradley, R.H. (1984). *Home observation for measurement of the environment*. Little Rock, AK: University of Arkansas.

Caspi, A., & Elder, G.H. Jr (1988). Childhood precursors of the life course: Early personality and life disorganization. In E.M. Hetherington, R.M. Lerner, & M. Perlmutter (eds), *Child development in life-span perspective* (pp. 115–142). Hillsdale, NJ: Erlbaum.

Cassiba, R., van IJzendoorn, M.H., & d'Odorico, L. (2000). Attachment and play in child care centres: Reliability and validity of the attachment Q-sort for mothers and professional caregivers in Italy. *International Journal of Behavioral Development*, 24, 241–255.

Chen, X., Rubin, K.H., & Sun, Y. (1992). Social reputation and peer relationships in Chinese and Canadian children. *Child Development*, 63, 1136–1343.

Coie, J.D., Dodge, K.A., & Coppotelli, H. (1982). Dimensions and types of social status. *Child Development*, 59, 815–829.

Collins, W.A. (1999). Willard W. Hartup and the new look in social development. In W.A. Collins & B. Laursen (eds), *The Minnesota Symposia on Child Psychology: Vol. 30. Relationships as developmental contexts* (pp. 3–11). Mahwah, NJ: Erlbaum.

Collins, W.A., Maccoby, E.E., Steinberg, L., Hetherington, E.M., & Bornstein, M.H. (2000). Contemporary research on parenting. *American Psychologist*, 55, 218–232.

Connell, J.P., & Wellborn, J.G. (1991). Competence, autonomy, and relatedness: A motivational analysis of self-system processes. In M.R. Gunnar & L.A. Sroufe (eds), *The Minnesota Symposia on Child Psychology: Vol. 23. Self processes in development*, (pp. 43–77). Hillsdale, NJ: Erlbaum.

Connors, L.J., & Epstein, J.L. (1995). Parent and school partnerships. In M.H. Bornstein (ed.), *Handbook of parenting: Vol. 4. Applied and practical parenting* (pp. 437–458). Mahwah, NJ: Erlbaum.

Corsaro, W., & Rizzo, T. (1988). Discussion and friendship. *American Sociological Review*, 53, 879–894.

Cowan, P.A., Powell, D., & Cowan, C.P. (1998). Parenting interventions: A family systems perspective. In W. Damon (series ed.) & I.E. Siegel & K.A. Renninger (eds), *Handbook of child psychology: Vol. 4. Child psychology in practice* (5th edn, pp. 3–72). New York: Wiley.

Crick, N.R., & Dodge, K.A. (1994). A review and reformulation of social information processing mechanisms in children's social adjustment. *Psychological Bulletin*, 115, 74–101.

Dannefer, D. (1992). On the conceptualization of context in developmental discourse: Four meanings of context and their implications. In D.L. Featherman, R.M. Lerner, & M. Perlmutter (eds), *Life-span development and behavior* (Vol. 10, pp. 83–110). New York: Academic.

Deci, E.L., & Ryan, R.M. (1985). *Intrinsic motivation and self-determination in human behavior*. New York: Plenum.

Deci, E.L., & Ryan, R.M. (1991). A motivational approach to self: Integration in personality. In R. Dienstbier (ed.), *Nebraska Symposium on Motivation: Vol. 38. Perspectives on motivation* (pp. 237–288). Lincoln, NE: University of Nebraska Press.

Deci, E.L., Vallerand, R.J., Pelletier, L.J., & Ryan, R. (1991). Motivation and education: The self-determination perspective. *Educational Psychologist*, 26, 235–346.

Dishion, T.J., Andrews, D.W., & Crosby, L. (1995). Antisocial boys and their friends in early adolescence. *Child Development*, 66, 139–151.

Dishion, T.J., Patterson, G.R., & Griesler, P.C. (1994). Peer adaptations in the development of antisocial behavior: A confluence model. In L.R. Huesman (ed.), *Aggressive behavior: Current perspectives* (pp. 61–95). New York: Plenum.

Dishion, T.J., Patterson, G.R., Stoolmiller, M., & Skinner, M.L. (1991). Family, school, and behavioral antecedents to early adolescent involvement with antisocial peers. *Developmental Psychology*, 27, 172–180.

Dishion, T.J., Spracklen, K.M., Andrews, D.W., & Patterson, G.R. (1996). Deviancy training in male adolescent friendships. *Behavior Therapy*, 27, 373–390.

Dunn, J. (1993). *Young children's close relationships: Beyond attachment*. Newbury Park, CA: Sage.

Dunphy, D.C. (1963). The social structure of urban adolescent peer groups. *Sociometry*, 26, 230–246.

Dweck, C.S., & Goetz, T. (1978). Attributions and learned helplessness. In J. Harvey, W. Ickes, & R. Kidd (eds), *New directions in attribution research* (pp. 157–179). Hillsdale, NJ: Erlbaum.

Ennett, S.T., & Bauman, K.E. (1994). The contribution of influence and selection to adolescent peer group homogeneity: The case of adolescent cigarette smoking. *Journal of Personality and Social Psychology*, 67, 653–663.

Epstein, J.L. (1983). The influence of friends on achievement and affective outcomes. In J.L. Epstein & N. Karweit (eds), *Friends in school: Patterns of selection and influence in secondary schools* (pp. 177–200). New York: Academic.

Epstein, J.L. (1989). The selection of friends: Changes across the grades and in different school environments. In T.J. Berndt & G.W. Ladd (eds), *Peer relationships and child development* (pp. 15–45). New York: Wiley.

Fagot, B.I. (1995). Parenting boys and girls. In M.H. Bornstein, (ed.), *Handbook of parenting: Vol. 1. Children and parenting* (pp. 163–183). Mahwah, NJ: Erlbaum.

Farmer, T.W., Pearl, R., & van Acker, R.M. (1996). Expanding the social skills deficit framework: A developmental synthesis perspective, classroom social networks, and implications for the social growth of students with disabilities. *The Journal of Special Education*, 30, 232–256.

Farmer, T.W., & Rodkin, P.C. (1996). Antisocial and prosocial correlates of classroom social positions: The social network perspective. *Social Development*, 5, 174–188.

Ford, D.H., & Lerner, R.M. (1992). *Developmental systems theory: An integrative approach*. Newbury Park, CA: Sage.

Friedman, S.L., & Amadeo, J.-A. (1999). The child-care environment: Conceptualizations, assessments, and issues. In S.L. Friedman & T.D. Wachs (eds), *Measuring the environment across the life span: Emerging methods and concepts* (pp. 127–166). Washington, DC: American Psychological Association.

Friedman, S.L., & Wachs, T.D. (eds) (1999). *Measuring environment across the life-span: Emerging methods and concepts*. Washington, DC: American Psychological Association.

Gest, S.D., Graham-Berman, S.A., & Hartup, W.W. (2001). Peer experience: Common and unique features of number of friendships, social network centrality, and sociometric status. *Social Development*, 10, 23–40.

Goodnow, J.J. (1985). Change and variation in parents' ideas about childhood and parenting. In I.E. Siegel (ed.), *Parental belief systems* (pp. 235–270). Hillsdale, NJ: Erlbaum.

Gottman, J.M. (1983) *How children become friends. Monographs of the Society for Research in Child Development*, Vol. 48, No. 3, serial 201.

Grolnick, W.S., & Slowiaczek, J.L. (1994). Parental involvement in children's schooling: A multidimensional conceptualization and motivational model. *Child Development*, 65, 237–252.

Grusec, J.E., & Kuczynski, L. (1980). Direction of effect in socialization: A comparison of the parents' versus the child's behavior as determinants of disciplinary tactics. *Developmental Psychology*, 16, 1–9.

Hall, W.M., & Cairns, R.B. (1984). Aggressive behavior in children: An outcome of modeling or social reciprocity? *Developmental Psychology*, 20, 739–745.

Hamm, J.V. (2000). Do birds of a feather flock together? The variable bases for African American, Asian American, and European American adolescents' selection of similar friends. *Developmental Psychology*, 36, 209–219.

Harkness, S., & Super, C. (1995). Culture and parenting. In M.H. Bornstein (ed.), *Handbook of parenting: Vol. 2. Biology and ecology of parenting* (pp. 211–234). Mahwah, NJ: Erlbaum.

Harlow, H.F., & Mears, C. (1979). *The human model: Primate perspectives*. New York: Wiley.

Harris, J.R. (1995). Where is the child's environment? A group socialization theory of development. *Psychological Review*, 102, 458–489.

Harris, J.R. (1998). *The nurture assumption*. New York: Free Press.

Hartup, W.W. (1983). Peer relations. In P.H. Mussen (series ed.) & E.M. Hetherington (ed.), *Handbook of child psychology: Vol. 4. Socialization, personality, and social development* (4th edn, pp. 103–196). New York: Wiley.

Hartup, W.W., & Laursen, B. (1999). Relationships as developmental contexts: Retrospective themes and contemporary issues. In W.A. Collins & B. Laursen (eds), *The Minnesota Symposia on Child Psychology: Vol. 30. Relationships as developmental contexts* (pp. 13–36). Mahwah, NJ: Erlbaum.

Hartup, W.W., & Stevens, N. (1997). Friendship and adaptation in the life course. *Psychological Bulletin*, 121, 355–370.

Heckhausen, J. (1987) Balancing for weaknesses and challenging developmental potential: A longitudinal study of mother–infant dyads in apprenticeship interactions. *Developmental Psychology*, 23, 762–770.

Hernandez, D. (1997). Child development and the social demography of childhood. *Child Development*, 68, 149–168.

Hetherington, E.M., & Baltes, P.B. (1988). Child psychology and life-span development. In E.M. Hetherington, R.M. Lerner, & M. Perlmutter (eds), *Child development in life-span perspective* (pp. 1–19). Hillsdale, NJ: Erlbaum.

Hinde, R.A. (1992). Developmental psychology in the context of other behavioral sciences. *Developmental Psychology*, 28, 1018–1029.

Hinde, R. A. (1997). *Relationships: A dialectical perspective*. Hove: Psychology Press.

Hoffman, L. (1991). The influence of the family environment on personality. *Psychological Bulletin*, 110, 187–203.

Howes, C., & Matheson, C.C. (1992). Contextual constraints on the concordance of mother–child and teacher–child relationships. *New Directions for Child Development*, 57, 25–40.

Johnson, B.M., Shulman, S., & Collins, W.A. (1991). Systemic patterns of parenting as reported by adolescents: Developmental differences and implications for psychosocial outcomes. *Journal of Adolescent Research*, 6 (2), 235–252.

Jussim, L., & Eccles, J.J. (1992). Teacher expectations: II. Construction and reflection of student achievement. *Journal of Personality and Social Psychology*, 63, 947–961.

Kahn, R.L., & Antonucci, T.C. (1980). Convoys over the life course: Attachment, roles, and social support. In P.B. Baltes & O.G. Brim (eds), *Life-span development and behavior* (Vol. 3, pp. 253–286). New York: Academic.

Kandel, D.B. (1978). Homophily, selection, and socialization in adolescent friendships. *American Journal of Sociology*, 84, 427–436.

Kindermann, T.A. (1993a). Natural peer groups as contexts for individual development: The case of children's motivation in school. *Developmental Psychology*, 29, 970–977.

Kindermann, T.A. (1993b). Fostering independence in everyday mother–child interactions: Longitudinal changes in contingency patterns as children grow competent in developmental tasks. *nternational Journal of Behavioral Development*, 16, 513–535.

Kindermann, T.A. (1996). Strategies for the study of individual development within naturally existing peer groups. *Social Development*, 5, 158–173.

Kindermann, T.A., McCollam, T., & Gibson, E. (1996). Peer networks and students' classroom engagement during childhood and adolescence. In K. Wentzel & J. Juvonen (eds), *Social motivation: Understanding children's school adjustment* (pp. 279–312). New York: Cambridge University Press.

Kindermann, T.A., & Skinner, E.A. (1988). Developmental tasks as organizers of children's ecologies: Mother contingencies as children learn to walk, eat, and dress. In J. Valsiner (ed.), *Children's development within socio-culturally structured environments* (pp. 66–105). Norwood, NJ: Ablex.

Kindermann, T.A., & Skinner, E.A. (1992). Modeling environmental development: Individual and contextual trajectories. In J.B. Asendorpf & J. Valsiner (eds), *Stability and change in development: A study of methodological reasoning* (pp. 155–190). Newbury Park, CA: Sage.

Kindermann, T.A., & Valsiner, J. (eds) (1995). *Development of person–context relations*. Hillsdale, NJ: Erlbaum.

Kochanska, G. (1997). Mutually responsive orientation between mothers and their young children: Implication for early socialization. *Child Development*, 68 (1), 94–112.

Kochanska, G. (1998). Mother–child relationship, child fearfulness, and emerging attachment: A short-term longitudinal study. *Developmental Psychology*, 34, 480–490.

Kurdek, L.A., & Sinclair, R.J. (2000). Psychological, family, and peer predictors of academic outcomes in first through fifth grade children. *Journal of Educational Psychology*, 92, 449–457.

Ladd, G.W. (1990). Having friends, keeping friends, making friends, and being liked by peers in the classroom: Predictors of children's early school adjustment? *Child Development*, 61, 1081–1100.

Lamb, M.E. (1997). *The role of the father in child development*. New York: Wiley.

Lamb, M.E. (1998). Non-parental child care: Context, quality, correlates, and consequences. In W. Damon (series ed.) & I.E. Siegel & K.A. Renninger (eds), *Handbook of child psychology: Vol. 4. Child psychology in practice* (5th edn, pp. 73–133). New York: Wiley.

Larson, R., & Richards, M.H. (1994). *Divergent realities: The emotional lives of mothers, fathers, and adolescents*. New York: Basic.

Laursen, B. (1997). Close relationships across the lifespan: A symposium. *International Journal of Behavioral Development*, 21 (4), 641–646.

Laursen, B., & Bukowski, W.M. (1997). A developmental guide to the organisation of close relationships. *International Journal of Behavioral Development*, 21, 747–770.

Lawrence, J., & Valsiner, J. (1993). Conceptual roots of internalization: From transmission to transformation. *Human Development*, 36, 150–167.

Lawton, M.P. (1999). Environmental taxonomy: Generalizations from research with older adults. In S.L. Friedman & T.D. Wachs (eds), *Measuring the environment across the life span: Emerging methods and concepts* (pp. 91–124). Washington, DC: American Psychological Association.

Lerner, R.M. (1991). Changing organism–context relations as the basis process of development. *Developmental Psychology*, 28, 1018–1029.

Leung, M.-C.(1996). Social networks and self enhancement in Chinese children: A comparison of self reports and peer reports of group memberships. *Social Development*, 5, 146–157.

LeVine, R.A., Dixon, S., LeVine, S., Richman, A., Leiderman, P.H., Keefer, C., & Brazelton, T.B. (1994). *Child care and culture: Lessons from Africa*. New York: Cambridge University Press.

Lynch, M., & Cicchetti, D. (1992). Maltreated children's reports of relatedness to their teachers. *New Directions for Child Development*, 57, 81–107.

Maccoby, E.E. (1992). The role of parents in the socialization of children: A historical overview. *Developmental Psychology*, 28, 1006–1017.

Maccoby, E.E., & Martin, J.A. (1983). Socialization in the context of the family: Parent–child interaction. In P.H. Mussen (series ed.) & E.M. Hetherington (ed.), *Handbook of child psychology: Vol. 4. Socialization, personality, and social development* (4th edn, pp. 1–102). New York: Wiley.

MacDonald, K. (1992). Warmth as a developmental construct: An evolutionary analysis. *Child Development*, 63, 753–773.

Matas, L., Arend, R.A., & Sroufe, L.A. (1978). Continuity of adaptation in the second year: The relationship between quality of attachment and later competence. *Child Development*, 49, 547–556.

Minuchin, P.P., & Shapiro, E.K. (1983). The school as a context for social development. In P.H. Mussen (series ed.) & E.M. Hetherington (ed.), *Handbook of child psychology: Vol. 4. Socialization, personality, and social development* (4th edn, pp. 197–274). New York: Wiley.

Moreno, J.L. (1934). *Who shall survive? A new approach to the problem of human interrelations*. Washington, DC: Nervous and Mental Disease Publishing.

Mounts, N.S., & Steinberg, L. (1995). An ecological analysis of peer influence on adolescent grade point average and drug use. *Developmental Psychology*, 31, 915–922.

Murstein, B.I. (1976). *Who will marry whom? Theories and research in marriage choice*. New York: Springer.

Nelson-Le Gall, S. (1985). Help-seeking behavior in learning. In E.W. Gordon (ed.), *Review of Research in Education* (Vol. 12, pp. 55–90). Washington, DC: American Educational Research Association.

Newcomb, A.F., Bukowski, W.M., & Pattee, L. (1993). Children's peer relations: A meta-analytic review of popular, rejected, neglected, controversial, and average sociometric status. *Psychological Bulletin*, 113, 99–128.

Newman, R. (2000). Socialization of children's skills and attitudes pertaining to adaptive help-seeking in the classroom. *Developmental Review*.

Novak, M.A., & Harlow, H.F. (1975). Social recovery of monkeys isolated for the first year of life: I. Rehabilitation and therapy. *Developmental Psychology*, 1, 453–465.

Papoušek, H., & Papoušek, M. (1995). Intuitive parenting. In M.H. Bornstein (ed.), *Handbook of parenting: Vol. 2. Biology and ecology of parenting* (pp. 117–136). Mahwah, NJ: Erlbaum.

Parke, R.D., & Buriel, R. (1998). Socialization in the family: Ethnic and ecological perspectives. In W. Damon (series ed.) & N. Eisenberg (ed.), *Handbook of child psychology: Vol. 3. Social, emotional, and personality development*. New York: Wiley.

Parke, R.D., & Ladd, G.W. (eds) (1992). *Family–peer relationships: Modes of linkage*. Hillsdale, NJ: Erlbaum.

Patterson, G.R., & Bank, C.L. (1988). Some amplifying mechanisms for pathological processes in families. In M. Gunnar & E. Thelen (eds), *The Minnesota Symposia on Child Psychology: Vol. 22. Systems and development* (pp. 167–209). Hillsdale, NJ: Erlbaum.

Patterson, G.R., & Strouthamer-Loeber, M. (1984). The correlation of family management practices and delinquency. *Child Development*, 55, 1299–1307.

Reis, H.T., Collins, W.A., & Berscheid, E. (2000). The relationship context of human behavior and development. *Psychological Bulletin*, 126, 844–872.

Rogoff, B. (1990). *Apprenticeship in thinking: Cognitive development in social context*. New York: Oxford University Press.

Roopnarine, J.L., & Carter, D.B. (1994). *Parent–child socialization in diverse cultures*. Norwood, NJ: Ablex.

Rubin, K.H., Bukowski, W., & Parker, J.G. (1998). Peer interactions, relationships, and groups. In W. Damon (series ed.) & N. Eisenberg (ed.), *Handbook of child psychology: Vol. 3. Social, emotional, and personality development* (5th edn, pp. 619–700). New York: Wiley.

Rutter, M. (1979). Maternal deprivation, 1992–1978: New findings, new concepts, new approaches. *Child Development*, 50, 283–305.

Rutter, M. (2000). Some research considerations on intergenerational continuities and discontinuities: Comment on special section. *Developmental Psychology*, 34, 1269–1273.

Ryan, R.M., & Powelson, C.L. (1991). Autonomy and relatedness as fundamental to motivation and education. *Journal of Experimental Education*, 60 (1), 49–66.

Ryan, R.M., Stiller, J., & Lynch, J.H. (1994). Representations of relationships to teachers, parents, and friends as predictors of academic motivation and self-esteem. *Journal of Early Adolescence*, 14, 226–249.

Sage, N.A., & Kindermann, T.A. (1999). Peer networks, behavior contingencies, and children's engagement in the classroom. *Merrill-Palmer Quarterly*, 45, 143–171.

Sage, N.A., & Kindermann, T.A. (2000). Influences socio-structurelles en groupe de pairs sur la motivation scolaire des jeunes enfants (Peer group influences on children's school motivation: An observational study of social learning mechanisms in the classroom). Invited paper in *Revue Canadienne des Sciences de l'Education*.

Sameroff, A. (1983). Developmental systems: Contexts and evolution. In P.H. Mussen (series ed.) & W. Kessen (ed.), *Handbook of child psychology: Vol. 1. History, theory, and methods* (4th edn, pp. 237–294). New York: Wiley.

Savin-Williams, R.C., & Weisfeld, G.E. (1989). An ethological perspective on adolescence. In G.R. Adams, R. Montemayor, & T.P. Gullota (eds), *Biology of adolescent behavior and development* (pp. 249–274). Newbury Park, CA: Sage.

Scarr, S. (1992). Developmental theories for the 1990s: Development and individual differences. *Child Development*, 63, 1–19.

Scarr, S., & Weinberg, R.A. (1983). The Minnesota Adoption Studies: Genetic differences and malleability. *Child Development*, 54, 260–267.

Schneider-Rosen, K., & Burke, P.B. (1999). Multiple attachment relationships within families: Mothers and fathers with two young children. *Developmental Psychology*, 35, 436–444.

Schooler, C. (1999). The workplace environment: Measurement, psychological effects, and basic issues. In S.L. Friedman & T.D. Wachs (eds), *Measuring the environment across the life span: Emerging methods and concepts* (pp. 229–246). Washington, DC: American Psychological Association.

Sherif, M., Harvey, O.J., White, B.J., Hood, W.E., & Sherif, C.W. (1961). *Intergroup conflict and cooperation: The robber's cave experiment*. Norman, OK: University of Oklahoma Book Exchange.

Silberman, M. (1969). Behavioral expression of teachers' attitudes towards elementary school students. *Journal of Educational Psychology*, 60, 402–407.

Skinner, E.A., & Belmont, M.J. (1993). Motivation in the classroom: Reciprocal effects of teacher behavior and student engagement across the school year. *Journal of Educational Psychology*, 85, 571–581.

Skinner, E.A., & Wellborn, J.G. (1994). Coping during childhood and adolescence: A motivational perspective. In D. Featherman, R.M. Lerner, & M. Perlmutter (eds), *Life-span development and behavior* (Vol. 12, pp. 91–133). Hillsdale, NJ: Erlbaum.

Steinberg, L., Lamborn, S.D., Darling, N., & Dornbusch, S.M. (1994). Over-time changes in adjustment and competence among adolescents from authoritative, authoritarian, indulgent, and neglectful families. *Child Development*, 65, 754–770.

Steinberg, L., Lamborn, S.D., Dornbusch, S.M., & Darling, N. (1992). Impact of parenting practices on adolescent achievement: Authoritative parenting, school involvement, and encouragement to succeed. *Child Development*, 63, 1266–1281.

Stipek, D.J., Feiler, R., Daniels, D., & Milburn, S. (1995). Effects of different instructional approaches on young children's achievement and motivation. *Child Development*, 66, 209–223.

Strayer, F.F., & Santos, A.J. (1996). Affiliative structures in preschool peer groups. *Social Development*, 5, 117–130.

Strayer, F.F., & Trudel, M. (1984). Developmental changes in the nature and functions of social dominance during the preschool years. *Ethology and Sociobiology*, 5, 279–295.

Suomi, S.J., & Harlow, H.F. (1975). The role and reason of peer relationships in rhesus monkeys. In M. Lewis & L.A. Rosenblum (eds), *Friendship and peer relations: The origins of behavior series* (pp. 153–186). New York: Wiley.

Talbert, J.E., & McLaughlin, M.W. (1999). Assessing the school environment: Embedded contexts and bottom-up research strategies. In S. Friedman & T.D. Wachs (eds), *Measuring the environment across the life span: Emerging methods and concepts* (pp. 197–228). Washington, DC: American Psychological Association.

Tesser, A., Campbell, J., & Smith, M. (1984). Friendship choice and performance: Self-esteem maintenance in children. *Journal of Personality and Social Psychology*, 46, 561–574.

Thompson, R.A. (1998). Early sociopersonality development. In W. Damon (Series ed.) & N. Eisenberg (ed.), *Handbook of child psychology: Vol. 3. Social, emotional and personality development* (5th edn, pp. 25–104). New York: Wiley.

Thorngate, W. (1995). Accounting for person–context relations and their development. In T.A. Kindermann & J. Valsiner (eds), *Development of person–context relations* (pp. 39–54). Hillsdale, NJ: Erlbaum.

Tudge, J.R.H. (1992). Processes and consequences of peer collaboration: A Vygotskian analysis. *Child Development*, 63, 1364–1379.

Urberg, K.A., Degirmencioglu, S.M., & Tolson, J.M. (1998). Adolescent friendship selection and termination: The role of similarity. *Journal of Social and Personal Relationships*, 15, 704–710.

Urberg, K.A., Degirmencioglu, S.M., Tolson, J.M., & Halliday-Scher, K. (1995). The structure of adolescent peer networks. *Developmental Psychology*, 31, 540–547.

Valsiner, J. (1989). *Human development and culture: The social nature of personality and its study*. Lexington, MA: Heath.

Valsiner, J. (1994). Culture and human development: A co-constructionist perspective. In P. van Geert, L.P. Mos, & W.J. Baker (eds), *Annals of theoretical psychology* (Vol. 10, pp. 247–298). New York: Plenum.

Valsiner, J. (1998). The development of the concept of development: Historical and epistemological perspectives. In W. Damon (series ed.) & R.M. Lerner (ed.), *Handbook of child psychology: Vol. 1. Theoretical models of human development* (5th edn, pp. 189–232). New York: Wiley.

Vandell, D.L., & Posner, J.K. (1999). Conceptualization and measurement of children's after-school environments. In S.L. Friedman & T.D. Wachs (eds), *Measuring the environment across the life span: Emerging methods and concepts* (pp. 167–196). Washington, DC: American Psychological Association.

van IJzendoorn, M.H. (1992). Intergenerational transmission of parenting: A review of studies in nonclinical populations. *Developmental Review*, 12, 76–99.

van IJzendoorn, M.H. (1995). Of the way we are: On temperament, attachment, and the transmission gap: A rejoinder to Fox (1995). *Psychological Bulletin*, 117 (3), 411–415.

van IJzendoorn, M.H., Juffer, F., & Duyvesteyn, M.G.C. (1995). Breaking the intergenerational cycle of insecure attachment: A review of the effects of attachment-based interventions on maternal sensitivity and infant security. *Journal of Child Psychology and Psychiatry*, 35, 225–248.

Vygotsky, L.S. (1978). *Mind in society*. Cambridge, MA: Harvard University Press.

Wachs, T.D. (1992). *The nature of nurture*. Newbury Park, CA: Sage.

Wachs, T.D. (2000). *Necessary but not sufficient: The respective roles of single and multiple influences on individual development*. Washington, DC: American Psychological Association.

Wellman, B., & Berkowitz, S.D. (eds) (1988). *Social structures: A network approach*. New York: Cambridge University Press.

Wentzel, K.R. (1997). Student motivation in middle school: The role of perceived pedagogical caring. *Journal of Educational Psychology*, 89, 41–419.

Wentzel, K.R. (1998). Social relationships and motivation in middle school: The role of parents, teachers, and peers. *Journal of Educational Psychology*, 2, 202–209.

Wentzel, K.R. (1999). Social-motivational processes and interpersonal relationships: Implications for understanding motivation at school. *Journal of Educational Psychology*, 91, 76–97.

Whiting, B.B., & Whiting, J.W.M. (1975). *Children of six cultures: A psychocultural analysis*. Cambridge, MA: Harvard University Press.

19

Morality and Context: A Study of Hindu Understandings

USHA MENON

Introduction

In this chapter, I examine Hindu moral understandings, and I describe the ways in which such understandings develop amongst Hindus. I attempt to show that Hindus view moral development as a process that continues throughout a person's life. The moral values that one acquires as a child undoubtedly guide one's future moral development but, in Hindu thought, a person grows and evolves as a moral being across the life course partly because the sense of self is thought to be continually changing and partly because context is given primacy in determining whether a particular action is moral or not.

In the last four decades, literature on the origins and development of moral understandings has been dominated by three theories: Kohlberg's 'cognitive developmental' theory (Kohlberg, 1969; 1981), Turiel's 'social interactional' theory (Turiel, 1979; 1983) and Shweder's 'social communication' theory (Shweder, Mahapatra, & Miller, 1987). Building upon Piaget's work, Kohlberg postulates that moral understanding develops in a sequence of stages from the lowest, preconventional level when decisions about the morality of an action are taken from the subjective perspective of the self, through the conventional level when social consensus determines the rightness or wrongness of actions, and finally to the most advanced, postconventional level when the idea of natural law and the abstract principles of harm and justice are invoked in deciding what is or is not moral. Thus, as children become cognitively more sophisticated, moral understandings are thought to develop out of conventional understandings. In contrast, Turiel suggests that even very young children understand the differences between the conventional and the moral. He argues that moral and conventional understandings coexist from early childhood. The former, therefore, cannot be thought of as developing out of the latter. However, both understandings are supposed to become further elaborated when children interact socially with their peers and adults. Turiel claims that the moral and the conventional are distinguished from each other in terms of alterability and relativity. Activities and events that are moral, in contrast to those that are merely conventional, are inherently and intrinsically so; they are universally relevant and they cannot be altered through social consensus.

The most severe criticism that has been leveled against both these theories is that they ignore not just variability in moral and cultural understandings (Edwards, 1980; 1985; Gilligan, 1993; Shweder, Mahapatra, & Miller, 1987) but even the possibility of such variability. For instance, both theories assume ontological individualism – the idea that the individual exists prior to society and enters into a voluntary social contract with others in order to secure his self-interest (see Bellah et al., 1996). More importantly, they universalize this assumption, apparently presuming that it has significance and meaning in other cultures as well. Turiel also assumes that in all cultures conventions would constitute a separate domain of understanding. However, in Hindu India, very little would be classified as merely conventional; I think traffic rules would qualify as something that is designated purely by social consensus and therefore alterable, but I can think of few other examples. In all fairness to Turiel and his colleagues, it also needs to be mentioned that they do admit the possibility of context-dependent moral obligations that would be unalterable but relative.

For my part, Shweder et al.'s 'social communication' theory appears to be the most anthropologically informed. This is perhaps not surprising since they deliberately step outside the Western world to include an ethnographic study of a different worldview and a different morality. I employ, in my analysis, the interpretation, elaborated in this theoretical approach, that everyday cultural practices are performances that dramatize indigenous moral values, and I subscribe to the idea that, beginning with childhood and over the life course, people learn about morality through witnessing and participating in such everyday cultural practices. Furthermore, I agree with Shweder et al.'s insight that Hindus rarely invoke conventions, understood as obligations that are both alterable and relative, when judging what is or is not right conduct. In the Hindu world, domain distinctions between conventions and morality are hardly ever made because Hindus do not distinguish ideologically between the social and the natural moral orders.

There are, however, some rather significant differences between Shweder et al.'s representation of Hindu morality and mine. The most important of these, I think, pertains to the salience and significance of contextuality when Hindus evaluate the rightness and wrongness of their own thoughts, words and actions, and those of others. Morality is *not* universalized, as perhaps Shweder et al. seem to claim, but rather is thought to vary, depending on context. Accordingly, each person is supposed to live by the lights of his or her own particular moral code – a code that is determined by many factors: gender, occupation, family role, caste affiliation, phase of life, to mention only the more important. To use Turiel et al.'s vocabulary, Hindu morality exemplifies

> 'epistemologically significant context-dependent moral thinking' (1987: 217n) because, as the examples in this chapter will demonstrate, it does 'demonstrate contextuality in the *prescriptive* ground of an individual's moral judgments'. (ibid, emphasis in original)

Another important difference, and in a sense a corollary to the one outlined above, has to do with Shweder's classification of the Hindu moral code as a 'duty-based' moral code; I think it is more accurate to classify it as a 'goal-based' moral code, with the qualification that the goal that is taken as fundamental is not a societal goal but a personal one. Thus, the overarching and ultimate moral good that every Hindu is supposed to aspire to and strive toward is not 'respect for authority' or 'creating a utopian society' (Dworkin, 1977, p. 169), but rather *moksha*, liberation from the endless cycle of rebirths to which all humans are condemned – I say 'condemned' because in the Hindu world, by definition, each birth is a passport to more suffering. In the Hindu scheme of things, this goal is universally relevant: all humans should strive towards it. But the paths that different people adopt to achieve this universally relevant goal – the customs and practices they follow – are allowed to be different. The underlying assumption is that what is moral in a particular set of life circumstances is not necessarily so in another. There is no effort to impose a universal morality on everyone. Thus, in sharp contrast to what Shweder et al. have to say about a duty-based moral code, in a goal-based moral code such as the Hindu one it is *not* 'incoherent to proclaim: "Do not impose your private morality on other people"' (1987, p. 21).

And this brings me to the third significant difference between Shweder et al.'s representation of Hindu morality and my own – and again, this is related to the importance of contextuality in Hindu moral thinking. Shweder et al. claim that the Hindu moral code is a proper candidate for an alternative postconventional morality because it includes the 'mandatory' features without which a moral code would lose its 'rational appeal' (1987, p. 18). The three mandatory features they identify as crucial to a rationally defensible moral code are the idea of natural law, and the abstract principles of harm and justice. However, I think that the idea of natural law – the idea that there are discrepancies between what is and what ought to be, the idea that an act may be inherently wrong and therefore should never be done – may not be present in Hindu morality (at least not in the way that Shweder et al. conceive of it) because of the central role played by contextuality in Hindu moral thinking: even the most heinous act could be, given the context, morally justified.

The temple town of Bhubaneswar provides the ethnographic foundations for this study. Both insiders and outsiders are likely to assert that the temple town is a stronghold of Hindu cultural traditions, a place where the winds of modernity blow very lightly. For that very reason, the temple town is an appropriate research site for examining Hindu conceptions of morality: the thoughts and behavior of the people who live here highlight the distinctive features of Hindu morality and the ways in which moral understandings develop amongst Hindus. However, these understandings are not unique to the temple town: as most observers would attest, they can be generalized with respect to Hindu communities elsewhere on the subcontinent (Keyes and Daniel, 1983; Roland, 1988).

Hindu Categories, Hindu Concepts

Hindu Transactional Thinking

In Hindu thought, conditions of flux are said to characterize the manifest world, and this includes both the social and the natural, a distinction that

Hindus rarely make. Within this world, varied entities are constantly engaged in transacting, exchanging and transforming. As Marriott has remarked, there is, in Hindu culture, 'explicit, institutionalized concern for givings and receivings of many kinds in kinship, work and worship' (1976, p. 109). While such concern may not be distinctive, in and of itself, Hindu assumptions about the materiality of all phenomena and Hindu preoccupations with questions of rank certainly are.

Thus, Hindus assume that everything in this universe is material. Even apparently non-material things like thought, and gaze, and caste, and space, and time are material, and have substance, because they have relational properties. Thus, for example, 'space' – houses and workplaces – have characters and moods that can affect the natures and fortunes of those who reside or work in them. 'Time' can be auspicious or inauspicious, in that activities performed at auspicious times are fruitful, and those done at inauspicious times are futile; 'time' can also be good or evil, causing humans to act ethically or unethically. At the same time, matter can be, and is, distinguished in terms of its 'grossness' (*sthulata*) and its 'subtlety' (*sukshmata*): 'gross' includes all that is less refined, less capable of transformation, less generative, and therefore less imbued with power (*sakti*) and value (*mulyam*), while 'subtle' refers to all that is less tangible, more refined, more capable of transformation and generation.[1]

From the Hindu perspective, transactions affect the transactors profoundly, transforming them, because it is thought that 'what goes on *between* actors are the same connected processes of mixing and separation that go on *within* actors' (Marriott, 1976, p. 109, emphasis in original). Therefore, Hindu thought about transactions assumes that it is impossible to separate actors from their actions: actors act as they do because of their particular natures (*svabhava*) and because of the particular codes of conduct (*svadharma*) that are inherent in them, but such action is thought to alter not merely the person at whom it is directed but also the actor who originates the action. Thus, different codes of conduct (*dharmas*) are believed to be immanent in actors and to become 'substantialized in the flow of things between actors' (ibid, p. 110). Such thinking implies that Hindus do not make distinctions between 'substance' (*dhatu*) – in the sense of 'nature' – and 'code of conduct' (*dharma*) – in the sense of 'law' (see Schneider, 1968; and also Marriott & Inden, 1977). As Inden (1976, p. 121) has pointed out, in Sanskrit 'substance' (*dhatu*) and 'code' (*dharma*) share the same etymology – the root *dhr*.

In the same vein, Hindus tend not to distinguish between mind and body, between spirit or consciousness and matter, and between the 'moral' and the 'natural'. Thus, moral code books (*dharmasastras*, *nitisastras*) discuss bodily matters and the ways in which exchange of substances affects a person's moral qualities (*gunas*), while medical treatises (the *Caraka samhita*, 1949, the *Susruta samhita*, 1953, and Ayurvedic texts) develop ideas regarding the constituent elements (*bhutas*) and the moral qualities that are thought to predominate in different life-forms, and that are thought necessary for good health, well-being and longevity.[2] Those who give and receive as well as what and how they give and receive are, indissolubly and simultaneously, both substance and code. This 'nonduality' (Marriott, 1976, p. 110) of substance-and-code has to be well understood because only then is it possible to apprehend the meanings of Hindu social institutions, and Hindu cultural reality. Furthermore, substance-and-code are seen as residing in 'particles' that can be exchanged, ingested, reproduced, exuded, excreted – 'particles' that are in constant circulation.

Hindu Definitions of the Human Body and Personhood

This kind of transactional thinking, together with the belief in the materiality of all phenomena and the constant circulation of substance-and-code, leads to a particular definition of the body and a particular understanding of personhood. Hindus conceive of their bodies as relatively unbounded and porous containers which are partially shared and/or exchanged with others, all through life, forming relationships through events like birth and marriage, and acts like sharing food and living together (Daniel, 1984; Inden and Nicholas, 1977; Lamb, 1993; Trawick, 1990). All human bodies are permeable, but those of women are far more so than those of men because women menstruate and reproduce. This greater permeability requires women to be more circumspect in their behavior but, simultaneously, implies the greater potential for transformation that they possess.

While believing that exchanges between people are inherent and inevitable, Hindus also use this theory of the relative permeability of the human body to deliberately manipulate and transform their physical substances. Throughout the life course, therefore, through daily practices (*nityakarma*) and rituals of refinement (*samskaras*), Hindus regulate, manipulate and transform themselves. Because of the continual exchanging that people are engaged in, the consequence of merely living and being in this world, people are always mixed, and Hindus recognize the sheer impossibility of making radical separations or perfect purifications. Impurities are thought to be part of everyday life and all humans alternate between relative purity (*suddhata*) and relative impurity (*asuddhata*).

Corresponding to this understanding of the human body, the Hindu person is conceived of as open and unbounded, constituted of heterogeneous 'particulate' substances and therefore 'dividual and divisible' in nature (Marriott, 1976, p. 111). This conception of the person is clearly distinct from dominant Western notions that think of the person as a relatively bounded, self-contained individual (see Geertz, 1983). For any particular Hindu, personhood fluctuates during the life course, waxing and waning depending on the degree to which the person concerned initiates, controls, or at least regulates the exchanges in which he or she is participating, and therefore the degree to which he or she controls the process of transformation they experience.

The Hindu View of Society and its System of Ranking

Hindus do not believe that human beings exist prior to, or outside of, society. Neither do they believe that society comes into being because humans enter into a voluntary contract so as to maximize their self-interest. Far from subscribing to any idea of 'ontological individualism' (Bellah et al., 1996, p. 143), social arrangements are seen as part of nature and as more enduring and fundamental than the people who participate in them.

The Hindu view of society is organismic: the metaphor most commonly used is that of the human body. No organ, no part of the body, is similar to or the equal of the other; each is separate and unique but all are required for its proper functioning and flourishing. At the same time, Hindu society is very attentive to questions of rank, such ranking being defined in terms of *guna*s, the three primal qualities or attributes that pervade all matter. There are thought to be three *guna*s: *sattva* or goodness, essentiality, vitality, luminosity; *rajas* or passion, power, activity, dust; and *tamas* or error, ignorance, torpor, darkness. Most Hindus claim that *sattva* predominates in gods and heavenly beings, *rajas* in humans and *tamas* in plants.

The theory about *guna*s is hardly esoteric. Medieval texts like the *Bhagavad gita* (13.19, 21) and the *Visnu purana* (1.2.4) certainly discuss the theory, but so do ordinary villagers in everyday conversations, even today (Daniel, 1984, pp. 4–5; Davis, 1983, p. 64). They speak of *guna*s as having existed in an undifferentiated, quiescent form in primeval nature or in a primordial deity. All agree that once their quiescence was disturbed, *guna*s became separate, and differentiated, which then led to their combining and recombining with each other to produce diverse entities. Living beings are thought to vary from each other and change because their actions exhibit varying proportions of *guna*s. Those who are superior, who take care of others, who regulate the conduct of others, tend to have more *sattva*; those who are active and energetic, those who lead others in politics or into war, those (women, for example) who reproduce, have more of *rajas*; and those who are lethargic, ignorant, dull, fearful, are thought to have a preponderance of *tamas*.

Marriott and Inden correctly observe that caste defined as the 'institution of ranked, hereditary, endogamous occupational groups, is a foreign concept' (1977, p. 230). There is no indigenous term that is a perfect synonym. The word that Hindus use is *jati*, which is the Sanskrit cognate of the Latin 'genus' and in fact, since both words share Indo-European roots, they do connote much the same thing: 'class, kind, group sharing essential characteristics'. However, this equivalence between *jati* and genus is only approximate. Hindu genera do not conform to a Linnaean system of taxonomy that defines exclusive, differentiated taxons; instead, Hindu genera branch out and overlap with each other such that no rigid categoric distinctions can be made (1977, p. 230). In this sense, a single person can be a member of many different genera; he or she can belong to various *jati*s, those of gender, caste, occupation, language, region, patrilineage, religion and so on, each membership being simply another facet of his or her multifaceted identity, an identity that he or she does not share completely with any other living being, an index of his or her uniqueness, his or her individuality.

All *jati*s of humans are thought to have descended from Cosmic Man (*purusa*), who sacrificed himself to create human society, different parts of his body becoming the various Hindu *jatis*. Thus, his head became the priestly class or the *Brahman*s, his arms the warriors or the *Kshatriya*s, his torso the merchants or the *Vaisya*s, and his legs the cultivators or the *Sudra*s. In keeping with the indigenous theory of *guna*s, Brahmans are said to have high rank because they are full of *sattva*; *Kshatriya*s are 'active' but of somewhat lower rank because they have both *sattva* and *rajas*; and *Sudra*s are of the lowest rank because they are fearful and ignorant, being dominated by *tamas* (Davis, 1983). Beyond the pale of this ranked society, because of their mixed or heterogeneous origins and/or because of their defiling occupations, are the previously untouchable groups – numbering about 16% of India's population today. Each of these five divisions consists of numerous ranked subdivisions, and every subdivision is continually contesting and negotiating its rank within the division. Society, from the Hindu perspective, therefore, is a living, organic whole that consists of differentially ranked, heterogeneous yet interdependent components.

Dharma

Every *jati* is thought to have its particular substance-and-code (*dravya*), its defining moral qualities, its capabilities (*sakti*) and its activities (*kriya*, the same root in Sanskrit as the word *karma*), and every member of a *jati* is thought to share in these characteristics. The sum total of these characteristics constitutes a *jati*'s *dharma* or its code of conduct; thus, *dharma* is not regarded as transcendent over bodily substance but rather is thought to be immanent within it. When the members of a *jati* comport themselves according to their *jati dharma*, then they are said to be maintaining and sustaining their *jati*. Such codes of conduct – *dharma* – are presumed to inhere in all generic categories: from country (*rajya dharma* or the moral code of the country) to the genus (*jati dharma*), to the lineage (*kula dharma*), to gender (*stri dharma*, women's *dharma*; and *purusa dharma*, men's *dharma*) and finally to the single person (*svadharma*, the *dharma* right for one's station or one's nature). These codes of conduct – *dharmas* – are, in Marriott and Inden's felicitous phrase, 'internal formulas for uplifting conduct, and not imposed imperatives' (1977, p. 231). As they observe, quite accurately, *dharma* 'appears to be *optative* rather than absolutely limiting or binding'; and, even more interestingly, 'it may be modified by action in time' (1977, p. 231, my emphasis). These varieties of *dharma* are best described as the particular laws or the 'inflections of "the law", which are natural to each special species or modification of existence' (Zimmer, 1946/1967, p. 163).

Apart from such varieties of *dharma*, there are those that are appropriate to particular life stages (*asramas*). Hindus have traditionally distinguished four stages – student (*brahmacharin*), householder (*grhastha*), forest-dweller (*vanaprastha*) and renouncer (*sannyasin*) – and each stage has its distinguishing moral code (*asramadharma*). The moral code of the first of these stages, that of student, requires strict chastity (*brahmacharya*), unwavering concentration (*sraddha*), and the will to hear and learn (*susrusa*). As a householder, a person becomes involved in the affairs of the world, he becomes attached to his wife (*kama*), he begets children, and he accumulates wealth (*artha*). During this phase of life, a person also performs the duties he owes society (*dharma*). During the third stage, as a forest-dweller, a person is expected to break his earlier engagement with the world and retreat to the forest, where he is expected to reflect on the meaning of life and meditate on his *atman*.[3] And the last stage, that of renouncer, is when he separates completely from his previous life, becoming a wanderer, 'taking no thought of the future and looking with indifference upon the present' (*Vivekacudamani*, p. 432).

Finally, I would like to discuss another commonly accepted meaning of the term *dharma*. For Hindus, *dharma* implies 'that which upholds', 'that which sustains', 'the natural order of things': *dharma* is the natural law that upholds and sustains the cosmos. Thus, Oriya Hindus in the temple town, when asked to explicate this meaning of *dharma*, are liable to say: 'It is the *dharma* of the rain to fall from the heavens to the earth; it is the *dharma* of the tree to cast its shadow on the ground on a hot, sunny day.' *Dharma* is thought to be ideal justice made alive. For anything in this world to be without its *dharma* is inconceivable: such a thing would be incoherent, it would be 'inconsistent' (Zimmer, 1946/1967). This understanding of *dharma* frames the Hindu perception that the social and natural world is a living organism that consists of heterogeneous, differentially ranked and interdependent *jatis*. There is a convergence between moral and natural orders; a coincidence between what 'is' and what 'ought to be'. As Zimmer (1946/1967) points out, in Sanskrit the word *sat* means 'good, true, virtuous, chaste, worthy'. But *sat* is also the present participle of the verb *as*, 'to be, to exist, to live'. Therefore, *sat* literally means 'being, existing' as well as 'good, true, virtuous'. Thus, in Hindu ways of thinking, what exists is, by virtue of its existence, also good and true.

Karma

The Sanskrit word *karma* means 'doing', 'causing', 'making'. And keeping to these three primary meanings, Hindus employ the concept of *karma* in at least three discernible senses. In the first sense, *karma* refers to the concrete actions that a person does through being and living in this world, and here the 'doing' aspect of *karma* is being emphasized.

In the second sense, it refers to the accumulated rewards and retributions that one carries with one from past lives; as people commonly say, 'When we are born, we bring with us our *karma* from past lives.' Here, past *karma* causes present situations or life circumstances. It is most often used to explain situations that defy common sense and indigenous logic. Thus, when an old woman who has led an exemplary and virtuous life suffers a painful and undignified death, most Oriya Hindus in the temple town would interpret it as a consequence of some debt (*rno*) she acquired in a past life that had to be burned off in this before she could proceed onto the next.

In the third sense, *karma* is employed in a proactive, future oriented way, such use emphasizing the 'making' aspect of *karma*. The following excerpt from a much longer conversation with a young Oriya Hindu woman clarifies this indigenous understanding of the concept:

> What happens in our lives is in our own hands. How many years we will survive, our lifespan [*ayus*], is written in our forehead [*lalato*], and whether we will be more happy than sad or more sad than happy, that depends on our fate [*bhagya*], but our life of work [*karmamoya jiban*] is in our own hands. If a student should appear for an examination without studying for it, he cannot say, 'Whatever will happen, will happen. If it is my fate [*bhagya*] to fail, I'll fail; if it is my fate to pass, then I'll pass.' He is making a mistake behaving like this; he doesn't understand what *bhagya* is, what *karma* is. He has to study for his examination – that is his *karma* as a student, that he has to do. If after studying, he should fail, then . . . then, that is his *bhagya*. One will only pass if one studies; but in cases of failure, when one

> has done one's *karma*, one can say, 'It isn't in my *bhagya* that I should succeed in this examination.' Always in life we get fruit [*phala*] according to the *karma* we do – our health, our bodies, our eating and drinking, our studies, everything is in our own hands.

This perspective highlights the idea that *karma*, like other substance-and-codes, is 'particulate' and material. It can be manipulated. It can transform people and consequently their future *karma*, and it can be transferred between related people, most particularly from parents to children. *Karma*, defined as accumulated reward or retribution from past lives, as a causative agent, sets the limits, draws the boundaries of situations in this life, but it does little else. Such *karma* does not determine the details of one's present life, it only sketches the broad contours; and after that it is one's *karma*, defined in terms of actual concrete work done in the present – the third meaning of the term – that determines the rewards (fruit, *phala*) one receives in this life, the kind of person one becomes and all that this implies for future lives.

In fact, Oriya Hindus of the temple town believe that even the gods envy human beings their capacity to do *karma* – what they describe as the right (*adhikaro*) to do *karma* that humans alone enjoy. Implicit in this is the Hindu belief that gods and humans and animals and plants are all part of a single continuum of living creatures, gods being higher up on the evolutionary scale but always in danger of falling to lower positions as a consequence of doing something immoral (*adharmik*). Doing *karma* properly is the one path available to sentient beings for self-refinement, in this life and in all the others. Here, Oriya Hindus are distinguishing between *Bhagwan*, the Universal Self or Ultimate Reality, who is 'non-qualified' (Hawley, 1996, p. 6), above fate (*bhagya*) and *karma*, and the hundreds of minor gods who are subject to *bhagya* but are unable to improve their nature and their situations through *karma*. Of course, people are aware that *karma* is a double-edged sword and that bad actions (*kukarma*, also referred to as *dushkarma*, *apakarma*) can jeopardize future lives, perhaps even one's evolutionary status as a human being, and older Oriya Hindus will advise the younger generation, 'Don't live this life as if it were your last. Reflect on the consequences of your actions/bad actions before you do anything.'

The Hindu worldview, therefore, by emphasizing the materiality and fluidity of all phenomena in this 'world of constituted things' (Marriott, 1990, p. 8), and the non-duality of substance and code, explicitly denies 'the peculiar Western philosophic burdens of dualism, universalism and individualism' (Marriott, 1976, p. 109). Given this worldview, what then are the contours of the Hindu moral code?

The Hindu Moral Code

The Ultimate Purpose of Life

The ultimate goal for all Hindus, according to texts on moral codes, should be *moksha* or liberation, release from the never-ending cycle of rebirths and redeaths. *Moksha* implies the final union between the *atman* of particular beings and the Universal *Atman* or *Parmatman*. This final goal is in dramatic counterpoint to the other three goals of life in this world – those of pleasure and the fulfillment of sensual desires (*kama*), profit and material prosperity (*artha*) and the performance of the religious and moral duties and rituals of everyday life (*dharma*). Indeed, *moksha* can never be achieved by simply leading a moral life in this world, performing one's duties sincerely and well. Rather, such liberation is achieved only when one finally transcends all social bonds, including those of morality. It requires a complete separation from this world and its affairs – a radical renunciation. And Brahmans, because they embody the most superior physical substance and because they maintain their high ritual status through strict adherence to Brahmanical customary practice, are regarded as furthest along in the attempt to achieve release from this world and its affairs.

But because such consummations, however devoutly hoped for, are rarely proven as occurring, people speak of their chances of achieving release (*moksha*) very infrequently. There are also those who are sufficiently agile, mentally, to argue that even to want to break out of the cycle of rebirths is itself a desire and one more indication that one is still bound to this world of enchantment, infatuation and illusion (*moha-maya*). Nevertheless, renunciation remains the most enduring ideal that animates the Hindu moral code.

Even today, there are Hindus who renounce the world: through performing 'social' suicide, they cremate the clothes they have worn in the past, and, through ritual, they are born anew with no connection to any other person or group or place in this world – no name, no family, no caste, no occupation. Dumont (1960) singles out the Hindu renouncer as the only true 'individual' to be found in Hindu India. But, it is worth noting that he becomes an individual by leaving the world behind, by living in a state apart from society. The person who lives in the world is, by definition, 'dividual and divisible', a composite of diverse gross and subtle substances that are shared and exchanged with others in the world, but the renouncer by abandoning his part in all the transacting and exchanging that characterizes social interactions becomes an 'individual outside the world'; he neither gives to nor receives from others and so maintains his particular combination of substances, qualities and powers.

However, today, as in the past, any astute observer would also discern a strong contradictory impulse in

Hindu thought and behavior. There are those who do *not* consider renunciation to be a viable or practical option at any stage of one's life. Echoing the very different view preserved in the *Rg veda* (*c.* 1200 BC) and other texts, these Hindus claim that the experiences of this world – to be born, to live, to eat, to love, to procreate – are worthy and valuable goals, worth repeating in future lives. Hindus have tried to resolve the tension between these two very different understandings about the purpose of life by developing the ideal of non-attachment, of not being bound to the fruits of one's labor in this world. As Madan observes, non-attachment is what emerges when renunciation is 'translated into the householder's idiom' (1987, p. 3).

This ideal of non-attachment was given its first and fullest elaboration in the *Bhagavad gita* (*The song of the Blessed Lord*), the most popular, widely memorized of all Hindu texts even today. In this text, consisting of 18 verses and part of the Hindu epic *Mahabharata*, Krishna (an incarnation of the god Visnu) tells his protege, Arjuna, the warrior prince, about the ethical principle that requires a person to carry on with his usual duties and activities of life in this world while cultivating an indifference to the possible gains and losses that these will entail. As Krishna says, 'For it is impossible for any being endowed with a body to give up unremitting activity; but he who relinquishes the fruits of his acts is called a man of true renunciation (*tyaagin*)' (*Bhagavad gita*, 18.11).[4] Therefore, one should not look for any reward in the fulfillment of one's duties as a daughter or a wife or a mother, in the performance of worship, or in any other virtuous conduct; one should strive rather to cultivate perfect non-attachment (*nishkama*).

Scholars who study Hindu India have characterized its moral code as 'duty-based' (Shweder, Mahapatra, & Miller, 1987). This appears perfectly reasonable given the moral significance that Hindus themselves attach to the proper performance of their duties. But, by focusing exclusively on the importance of doing one's duties and by not inquiring into the reason why their proper performance carries moral significance, we run the risk of ignoring a very significant element in this code – the value of non-attachment. And highlighting the value of non-attachment allows us to identify what I consider to be the central virtue of the Hindu moral code – self-refinement (*samskriti*). The moral significance attached to the correct and sincere performance of one's duties, however unpleasant one may find them, emerges from the cultural understanding that doing one's duties uncritically and unquestioningly will, in and of itself, lead to self-refinement. Given the Hindu belief in the non-duality of the mind and body, it is believed that doing one's duties and following customary practices – those involving daily ablutions as well as the more formal rituals of refinement – lead to self-refinement, by encouraging the intellect (*buddhi*) to develop, which leads to the acquisition of knowledge and wisdom (*gyaan*) which, in turn, creates the capacity to discriminate (*vivek*) and so allows one to achieve non-attachment (*nishkama*) most successfully.

It is within this framework of (1) the unstated, perhaps distant, but well-understood life goal of release from the cycle of rebirths, (2) the culturally significant theme of renunciation and its translation into the more achievable, this-worldly goal of self-refinement, (3) the pragmatic involvement with this-worldly activities, and (4) the belief that all humans alternate between conditions of relative purity and impurity, that we need to appreciate the moral significance of customary practices. Customs and practices that appear, at first glance, 'opaque or bizarre' (Shweder, Mahapatra, & Miller, 1987, p. 47) – the meticulous performance of daily ablutions (*nityakarma*), the strict observance of menstrual taboos in Brahman households, the practices and prohibitions that surround death pollution and the restrictions placed on Brahman widows – become less so when interpreted as ways to refine the self. The logic appears to be that one achieves non-attachment only through refining oneself because such self-refinement enables one to develop one's ability to discriminate and so avoid becoming entangled in the positive and/or negative consequences of one's actions in this world.

In critiquing the characterization of these practices as moral, Turiel, Killen, and Helwig argue that there may be 'nonmoral institutional, prudential and sociological functions to such practices' (1987, p. 198). However, from the emic upper caste Hindu perspective, such non-moral functions, even if self-evident from the vantage point of an outsider, are hardly relevant. In the following paragraphs, I attempt to frame these customs and practices within the limited and doable moral goal of self-refinement and intend to demonstrate that these practices carry moral significances for Hindus.

Everyday Practices that Refine

The concern for self-refinement makes upper caste Oriya Hindus of the temple town pay special attention to the correct performance of daily ablutions (*nityakarma*). For these men and women performing daily ablutions properly requires, at the least, the following: defecating twice a day, bathing after each defecation, bathing every time one returns home from any excursion outside, offering prayers to the household deity in the morning and again before the evening meal, bathing before eating a meal, washing the body from the waist up after every meal and for men, reciting specific prayers (*Gayatri mantra, Rg veda*, 3.62.10) in the morning. Often, during the day, men and women will chew a *tulasi* (*Basil indicum*) or *bilva* (*Aegle marmalosum*) leaf to purify themselves.

The body is most vulnerable when one is eating and therefore, in orthodox Brahman households in this neighborhood, residents prefer to eat, often one at a time, with just one of the senior wives of the family serving them. They eat either in the kitchen itself or some other room that is located within the center of the house, so as to reduce the chances that while eating they would hear inauspicious sounds – for instance, the widowed mother in the house next door clearing her throat, or a Bauri (a previously untouchable group that weaves mats and baskets) in the street outside calling out his wares.

Apart from these daily observances, there are available culturally defined means to refine oneself. Most of these revolve around two notions: the surrender of one's sense of self (*atma samarpana*) and giving service to others (*sewa*). Surrendering one's sense of self requires enormous self-control because one learns to discipline the importunate cravings of the self through deferring their gratification; fasting or observing other dietary prohibitions is a culturally approved method for trying to give up one's sense of self. And proper service is no less demanding because it requires satisfying the needs and desires of others to the best of one's abilities, something that, as Vatuk reminds us, has both a physical and a 'mental component' (*manasik*) (1990, p. 72) to it. Merely taking care of the physical needs of others in the family is not enough; their peace of mind has also to be ensured and this requires that sincere and thoughtful service be performed.

No Oriya Hindu would suggest that these are easy things to do but many of the explicitly recognized duties of married women, for instance, are encompassed by these notions of 'surrendering one's sense of self' and service. Thus, cooking, serving food, fasting, eating last, eating leftovers, and taking care of the physical and emotional needs of the members of the extended family with little thought to oneself – all are expected of married women and all are thought to help women to control their urges and desires, and become progressively more refined (see Menon & Shweder, 1998), a concrete example of how a strict performance of one's duties enables self-refinement.

In the temple town, upper caste Oriya Hindus see defiance of cultural norms – whether it be marriage by choice ('love marriages' as they are termed locally) or careless performance of one's duties or neglect of one's daily routines/ablutions – not as a sign of freedom, a mere matter of making a choice, but as a mark of one's subordination to the passions and impulses of the moment. In this again, upper caste temple town residents are espousing a traditional viewpoint which views unrestrained satisfaction of the senses, immediate gratification in matters both small and big, as the surest route to pain and suffering.

Samskaras or Rituals of Refinement

In Sanskrit, the word *samskara* means 'making perfect', 'refining', 'polishing', and it refers, in most Indian languages, to the rituals of refinement that upper caste Hindus undergo during the life course. Doniger and Smith (1991) prefer to use the phrase 'transformative rituals', emphasizing the indigenous understanding that the explicit purpose of these rituals is to transform the existing substances of the human body. *Manu*[5] identifies twelve such *samskaras* for the twice-born castes:[6] three of them are oblations for the embryo, and the rest mark various life transitions. An upper caste boy is reborn through the initiation ritual (*upanayana*) that is performed sometime between the eighth and twelfth years, thus attaining the position of the twice-born (*dvija*). The most important ritual of refinement for an upper caste woman is marriage (*vivaha*): the rituals of marriage begin, quite explicitly, a process of 'reconstruction' (Lamb, 1993) of the woman, and the transformation, amongst Brahmans, is symbolized by the new first name that is given the woman by her husband. And, finally, the last such ritual of refinement that people undergo are funeral rites (*antim samskara*) that are performed for them, the final transformation undergone in hopeful anticipation of a post-mortem rise in the next life.

Moral Emotions: *Lajya* and *Kshama*

A discussion of the way in which the two emotions – *lajya* and *kshama* – are understood and experienced in the temple town of Bhubaneswar is useful in that it deepens our understanding about the cultural concern for self-refinement. The first emotion is culturally salient, the second far less so but I have included it in the present discussion because of its salience in Judeo-Christian ethics.

Lajya

Lajya, an emotion term that is translated, rather loosely, as 'shame', is one of the primary moral emotions that upper caste Oriya Hindus are expected to cultivate. *Lajya*, however, encompasses a much broader lexical domain than that indicated by the English emotion term 'shame', and would be more accurately translated as 'modesty', 'deference', 'circumspection', 'being civilized', 'being refined', 'being respectful to elders and superiors', 'not encroaching on others', 'knowing one's place in society'. These are the positive dimensions of *lajya* – the ones that make persons who experience the emotion feel good about themselves, feel virtuous. It also includes the more painful dimension of a sense of 'acute mortification' or 'unbearable distress' that follow when one acknowledges one's dishonorable behavior, or when one recognizes one has failed to measure up to cultural expectations.

The cultural salience of *lajya* as a moral emotion, not just in Orissa but more broadly in the rest of Hindu India, was explicitly evoked many centuries ago in a hymn that Sankaracarya, the Hindu ascetic and philosopher of the ninth century, dedicated to Devi, the Great Goddess of Hinduism. In that hymn, he celebrates the plenitude, the abundance, of her essence that abides in all perishable beings, and when enumerating the various powers and qualities that characterize her essence, he describes one of them as being *lajya*.[7] Yet, not everyone is capable of experiencing *lajya*. People who have a predominance of the *tamas guna* are thought to be incapable of experiencing *lajya* – and there are many who fall into this category. Such people are castigated as being less than human, little more than animals (see Parish, 1994, pp. 199–215).

In indigenous understandings, *lajya* is considered to be a primary moral emotion because it teaches people how to behave morally, how to show consideration to others, how to regulate their conduct so as to maintain social harmony. While these are the social dimensions of experiencing *lajya*, there are other reasons for considering it a moral emotion. Cultivating *lajya*, developing the ability to experience it, is also thought to refine the person, increasing the amount of the *sattva guna* he or she possesses, making the person morally superior to others.

Interestingly enough, in the temple town of Bhubaneswar, the only time there is a cultural prescription against experiencing *lajya* is during the early days of marriage for a newly married woman. During this phase of her life, a woman occupies a lowly position within the extended family into which she has married; she has yet to assimilate into the family and has still to rise within its ranks. As I have mentioned above, during Hindu marriage rituals, the process of transforming a woman's physical substance into that of the patrilineage she has married into is explicitly begun. And she continues this process of assimilation by *not* cultivating *lajya* during this life phase. This allows her to open more completely to the substances and influences of her conjugal family. It enables the process of assimilation to occur more speedily – her principal goal during this phase of her life.

In the temple town, old widows past menopause are also exempt from cultivating and experiencing *lajya*: they say, do and go pretty much where they please with their heads and breasts uncovered, giving no thought to modesty or deference or for their place in society. However, in their case it is not so much that there is a cultural prescription against experiencing *lajya* but rather a complete indifference on the part of the community as to whether they do or not. As old widows they are so completely marginal to the affairs of the household, their activities are so inconsequential, that it matters little what they experience or do. These women feel this indifference most acutely, and they bemoan their loss of centrality within the family constantly. Old men, too, are marginalized but because, at no phase during their lives, are they central to the spiritual well-being and the material prosperity of their families, they do not feel the marginalization so intensely.

It is important to recognize that *lajya*, the way it is understood and experienced by Oriya Hindus, has, as one of its essential elements, self-evaluation. An Oriya Hindu experiences *lajya* not because the group shuns or ostracizes her; rather, it is because she fails to measure up against her internal standards of appropriate behavior for a refined person. It has little to do with whether another person has witnessed the shameful act or not. Thus, if a young woman sneaked a peek at the photograph of the man with whom her marriage was being arranged, she would experience *lajya* even if no one caught her in the act because she knows that a refined person is supposed to be indifferent to the physical appearance of his or her prospective spouse and to display such curiosity indicates that one has succumbed to one's coarser side. According to indigenous discourse, *lajya* is cultivated through exercising self-control, disciplining impulsive urges and sudden desires. And the more one cultivates *lajya*, the more refined one becomes as a human being.

The story that is told in the temple town of Bhubaneswar about the goddess Kali and her experience of *lajya* is particularly illustrative because of the emphasis it places on the internal sources of *lajya*. In a very popular icon, Kali, the most violent and bloodthirsty manifestation of the Great Goddess of Hinduism, Devi, is shown with her right foot placed squarely on the chest of a supine Siva, her husband, and her tongue hanging out. Such raw exhibition of female power is in dramatic contrast to the manner in which human wives are supposed to comport themselves in the real world. However, for Oriya Hindus, the message is clear: they interpret Kali's protruding tongue to mean that the goddess is experiencing and displaying the most acute *lajya* because she has realized for herself that she has violated all canons of wifely modesty and respect that is due to a husband. Oriya Hindus unanimously emphasize that Kali herself recognized the enormity of the transgression that she has committed by stepping on her husband. As the embodiment of all the energy and power of the universe, there was no force capable of stopping Kali. She could have stepped on her husband and carried on with impunity. If she had, it would have meant the end of all life and all morality in the universe. But, her sensitivity to experiencing *lajya* was the internal monitoring device that enabled her to regain control over herself, and re-establish the moral and social order in the world.

Kshama

I would also like to discuss the salience and meanings attached to another emotion – forgiveness – within the Hindu moral order because I think it underscores rather neatly the differences in moral perspective between Hinduism and the Judeo-Christian tradition. In the latter tradition, forgiveness is often defined as 'a willingness to abandon one's rights to resentment, negative judgment, and indifferent behavior toward one who unjustly injured us, while fostering the undeserved qualities of compassion, generosity and even love toward him or her' (Enright, Freedman, & Rique, 1998). When victims forgive those who have caused them injury, they promote social harmony. By being forgiven, perpetrators are absolved of their sins. This understanding of forgiveness is not found in Hindu India.

The Sanskrit term that is most frequently translated as forgiveness is *kshama*, and its primary meanings are forbearance and patience. Given Hindu ideas about the non-separability of actor from action, Hindus do not adopt the Christian notion of hating the sin while continuing to love the sinner; such distinctions are completely alien to the Hindu moral sense. Sin (*paap*), in the Hindu sense, increases the *tamas guna* in a person, the *guna* that means disorder, incoherence, and darkness. And this decline in the moral quality of the person is also thought to transform his physical substance, darkening and coarsening him. Forgiveness, therefore, becomes untenable because the sin and the sinner cannot be separated.

The idea of absolution is even more alien to Hindu thinking. Not even the gods have the power to absolve a sinner. Only when sinners acknowledge, without reservation, the immorality, the untruthfulness (*asat*) of their conduct, does the act of acknowledgment itself re-establish truth or *sat*. The darkness of untruthfulness is replaced by the lightness of truth. Sinners can also atone for their sins by performing the most austere penances (*tapas*). Such penances purify the body, removing the darkness produced by the sin and replacing it with the luminosity generated by the penances. It is only through such atonement that sinners achieve absolution. The following example from the temple town about a 36-year-old married woman who was rejected by her adulterous husband and who has subsequently returned to her father's household illustrates clearly the connotations of the emotion *kshama* as it is understood and experienced by Hindus. This woman is in an unenviable position because as a married woman who has returned to her father's household she is an anomaly in terms of family roles and positions. In an effort to give some meaning to her life, she has become extremely devout and is on the way to becoming a renouncer, the exact date when she will give up this world depending on when her parents – the only people who really care about her, she says – die. However, despite giving her life to the service of her personal deity, her feelings towards her husband are hardly imbued by any sense of Christian forgiveness. She holds back from wishing him ill – she exercises *kshama* – because, if she did not, that would coarsen her, and impede her progress towards self-refinement. To illustrate this point she told me about an incident that had occurred roughly a year before we met. Apparently one day, overwhelmed by the difficulties of her situation and her sense of loss and injury, she allowed herself to wish that something unfortunate would befall her husband. Almost immediately she took back the wish, but the harm had been done and within an hour she had slipped and fallen while walking across the wet courtyard, breaking her leg. That injury kept her from worshipping her god as she was accustomed to doing for more than three weeks, effectively interfering with attempts to refine herself because worshipping and serving one's god are prototypical ways to self-refinement. She interpreted the injury as her god withdrawing from her, indicating his displeasure with her for allowing the evil thought to darken and coarsen her.

Except for that one stray thought, she is forbearing, but she feels no compassion towards her husband, nor does she feel any generosity; if she controls her sense of resentment, it is because she believes that such resentment would only increase the darkness and disorder within her, making her less refined. She is certain that her husband cannot escape the retribution that he justly deserves, and she takes grim pleasure in telling me about the stroke he has recently suffered at the relatively young age of 50 – to her, convincing proof that one can never avoid the consequences of one's actions, whether good or bad. The question of absolution does not even occur to her: I am sure that if asked, her response would be that he can only atone for what he has done to her by working through his retribution and so achieve absolution. Thus, if she is forbearing or patient, if she holds back from wishing him ill, exercising self-control and therefore *kshama*, it is not because she is willing to overlook the grievous harm he has done her but because she knows that he will suffer the retribution that is his in due course.

The Case for Context-Dependent Moral Thinking amongst Hindus

Contextuality pervades Hindu thinking. One sees this sensitivity to context in Hindu texts that discuss esoteric subjects like *moksha*, *dharma*, and the concept of the self or *atman* as well the way ordinary Hindus talk about everyday events and experiences. Thus, even with respect to experiencing the moral emotion *lajya*, a culturally defined index of refinement, there are times when it is advisable *not* to cultivate it. For instance, in the upper caste households of the temple town, during the first few years of marriage when assimilating quickly with the conjugal family is the primary goal, young married women are advised quite explicitly to be without *lajya*. But again, this is not a blanket injunction: young married women are told to be without *lajya* only with respect to the women of the conjugal family – not with the men. With the older men of the family – the husband's father, his elder brother – they have to be, as always, extremely circumspect and modest. Oriya Hindus of the temple town say,

> If the *nua bou* [the son's new wife] thinks, 'Why should I speak of this? I feel too much *lajya* to tell anyone about this, I will keep it in my own stomach' – then she is only doing herself a disservice . . . if she continues to see herself as separate [*poro*] from the family, then others will also treat her as though she is separate. She must treat her husband's mother as she would her own. She must open her mind and heart completely and tell her everything frankly. If she empties herself of all old feelings and thoughts, then the husband's mother too will look on her as a daughter and not as a son's wife.

Many women admit that to try not to experience *lajya*, even in this context-sensitive way, is extraordinarily difficult, and that some women can never manage it. The older women of the family identify such daughters-in-law as having too much of a sense of self, as less able to 'surrender their sense of self', and therefore, less capable of achieving self-refinement in the long run. The women themselves pay the inevitable price of incomplete and unsatisfactory assimilation with their conjugal families, with all the attendant sorrows and discontentments.

Again, this emphasis on the particular was brought home to me rather sharply some years ago. At that time, I was speaking to women in the temple town about their life experiences, gathering data about how they conceptualize the life course. Many women, when asked to talk about the significant or typical events or experiences in an 'ordinary person's' (*sadharano manisoro*) life, told me bluntly that they could hardly speak about the life of such an 'ordinary person':

> Each person's life has its particularity [*bisheshta*]. I can't say this is how life goes for everyone. It depends on what kind of a family you are born into, what your *jati* is, whether you're a boy or a girl, whether you're the eldest child or the second or whatever, what your capabilities are, what *karma* you have brought with you. Each person's life is different from everyone else's. How can I tell you this and this and this happens in everyone's life? What can I tell you about those kinds of things? You know about them, everyone does. You are born, you grow up, you grow old, you die. Do you want to hear that?

And when conversations that I had with both men and women in the temple town turned to relations between the genders, the same sensitivity to context was apparent. Thus, if I asked about whether men and women could be thought of as being the equal of each other, in any sense of that word, the common response was,

> How can they be equal? Don't they belong to two different *jatis* – the only two *jatis* in the world whose differences can never be transcended?

And if I persisted, insisting that they think of possible situations where men and women could be thought of as equal, they answered, saying,

> How old are these men and women you are speaking about? Is the man older or the woman? How are they related – are they mother and son, or husband and wife or brother and sister? What kind of activities are you thinking about – household affairs, or arranging the marriage of children or managing household finances or ritual matters or outside work like shopping, or going to work?'

This context sensitivity is not confined to the people who live in the temple town of Bhubaneswar. It can be found in Hindu texts, like the Hindu epic *Mahabharata*, or the *Manudharmasastra* (*The Laws of Manu*). A.K. Ramanujan (1990) suggests that these texts exemplify the context-sensitive tendency that characterizes so much of Hindu culture. Thus, speaking of the *Manudharmasastra*, he writes,

> One has only to read Manu after a bit of Kant to be struck by the former's extraordinary lack of universality. He seems to have no clear notion of a universal human nature from which one can deduce ethical decrees like 'Man shall not kill', or 'Man shall not tell an untruth' . . . To be moral, for Manu, is to particularize – to ask who did what, to whom and when. Shaw's comment, 'Do not do unto others as you would have they should do unto you. Their tastes may not be the same' (Mackie, 1977, p. 89) will be closer to Manu's view, except he would substitute 'natures or classes' for 'tastes'. Each class [*jati*] of man has his own laws, his own proper ethic, not to be universalized. (1990, pp.45–46)

And referring to the concept of *dharma*, he observes that when one takes into account all the various kinds of *dharmas* that are immanent in the world – that are appropriate to the various stages of life, to one's *jati* or class, to one's station or particular nature, and finally the *dharma* of extremity (*apad*) – it appears, as Ramanujan says, that

> Each addition is really a subtraction from any universal law. There is not much left of an absolute or common [*sadharana*] *dharma* which the texts speak of, if at all, as a last and not as a first resort. They seem to say, if you fit no contexts or conditions, which is unlikely, fall back on the universal. (1990, p. 48)

The *dharma* of extremity – conduct appropriate for conditions of emergency or distress – is an intriguing concept because it allows for every possible exception. In conditions of extremity, those of famine for instance, it is moral for a father to kill his son (*Manu*, 10.105) and for priests to eat dogs (*Manu*, 10.106–108).

Thus, the most striking feature of the Hindu moral order is its lack of moral absolutes. There are no moral imperatives that apply to all people across the board. Hindus would undoubtedly subscribe to the principle of justice that states that like must be treated alike and different cases differently, except that from the Hindu perspective, there are hardly any cases where likeness prevails.

This is where my understanding of Oriya Hindu morality diverges from that presented by Shweder, Mahapatra, and Miller (1987). In that substantial and significant work, the authors suggest that there is 'clear-cut disagreement between Oriya Brahman and American adults about what is right and what is wrong' (1987, p. 52) with respect to 16 of the 39 practices that they identify as representative of a range of social and domestic practices in the temple town. It appears that both groups of subjects – American and Oriya Brahman – hold that their particular view represents a universal moral obligation. I know little about the American participants of the study and therefore have nothing to say about their responses, but I know enough about the temple town to have some reservations about the degree to which Oriya Brahmans see these practices as 'unalterable and universally binding' (1987, p. 52). Even within the temple town, there is substantial variability of custom and practice. The more rigid and constraining practices are, more often than not, observed and followed by the Brahmans – a reflection of the purity (*sattvikta*) of their physical substances and the need to maintain that purity. Again, one needs to be clear that not all practices are uniformly more restrictive to Brahmans. Thus, death pollution taboos are far *less* onerous to Brahmans – shorter periods of death pollution, for instance – because their bodies, being constituted, as I have just said, of more superior substances (more *sattvik*) than those of lower castes, are able to withstand the rupture that death signifies more robustly (see Mines, 1990). But other Hindus – part of caste Hindu society, locally called 'clean castes' (*panichua*[8]) – do not follow Brahmanical practice: they maintain death pollution taboos more strictly but are more relaxed about most other rituals and practices. And Brahmans are well aware of this difference in custom and practice: in fact their claim to high ritual rank is precisely because their lifestyles are so refined. So it is a little hard to imagine that they would want their practices universalized, especially when their ritual position depends on such practices continuing to be their exclusive preserve. And when lower castes do emulate some of the restrictive practices and customs of Brahmans – for instance, secluding their womenfolk, becoming vegetarian, ceasing to consume alcohol – using this shift in practice as a way of claiming higher ritual status within the caste hierarchy, the Brahmans are the first to resist such attempts at caste mobility.

A Brahman widow in the temple town spends her days reading from the sacred books, refrains from wearing colored clothes and from eating non-vegetarian food because she is atoning for the sin of allowing her husband to die. According to Hindu ways of thinking, a married woman holds her husband's life and his physical well-being within the palms of her hands: her chastity and the degree to which she achieves self-refinement are the source of her power over her husband's life and his health. His death is the measure of her failure to refine herself and achieve the requisite power (*sakti*) needed to protect him. In addition, the marriage rituals and the years of marriage have completed her physical transformation so that finally she and her husband are a single entity. Through surviving him, she is violating natural law, her *dharma*; by rights, she should have died with him; she is *asat*, she should not be, she embodies untruth. Brahman widows feel this moral obligation most strongly because as Brahmans, these women embody a particular level of refinement and truthful conduct and their failure disturbs the natural moral order more than if a Hindu woman of a lower *jati* had failed and her husband had predeceased her. Therefore, a Brahman widow's atonement is more severe and requires more austerities. The failure is even more devastating if the Brahman widow is young, and therefore the penances she has to undergo are proportionately more severe. Clearly, this is an example of reasoning in which a particular moral concern – that of preventing harm from befalling one's husband – is an important consideration when judging the conduct of a Brahman widow but it does not apply when judging the behavior of widows from other castes. And even amongst Brahman widows, age is a factor that would have a critical bearing on judgments about appropriate moral conduct. I think this qualifies as, in Turiel, Killen, and Helwig's terms, 'epistemologically significant context-dependent moral reasoning' (1987, p. 217n), because it demonstrates, quite effectively I think, contextuality in the prescriptive ground of moral reasoning.

My understanding of Hindu morality, and this includes Oriya Hindu morality, is that most social practices related to diet, clothing, etiquette, and terms of address would be, not matters of convention, but examples of context-dependent moral obligations: they are unalterable with respect to particular castes, but relative. Most Hindus, when pressed, may say that most people would benefit from such practices: they would become purer, better and more refined. They may even assert that performing such practices will elevate a person in future lives, perhaps help him or her to rise in the evolutionary scale that stretches from gods to plants. But whether adopting such practices is appropriate depends on the person's *dharma*, which in turn, is determined by factors such as gender, *jati* affiliation, one's station in life, one's particular phase of life, one's occupation, and one's life circumstances (whether distress, hunger, adversity prevail). A person's *dharma* is unique to that person and his or her particular context alone; it cannot possibly be upheld or sustained by anyone else. More importantly, a commonplace in Hindu thought is the understanding that it is better to do your *dharma*, however poorly, than it is to uphold another's, however well; this again is an idea articulated in the *Bhagavad gita* that has seeped into popular consciousness. When each person upholds his or her *dharma*, then together they maintain the natural moral order. Hindus are, therefore, unlikely to say that Americans must follow practices and customs that Hindus observe. They may think that it is advisable that Americans follow such practices. They may say that by not following such practices, Americans are condemning themselves to a decline in evolutionary status in the future – perhaps rebirth as plants and animals – but that would be all.

Hindus view conduct and practices as having enormous transformative potential. Furthermore, Hindus rank practices and customs in terms of their potential for either refining or coarsening the human body: widow remarriage, eating beef, sons not observing death pollution taboos for their fathers, all contaminate the persons involved, impeding their refinement, and hindering whatever progress they are making towards final liberation and release (*moksa*). Brahmans tend to see their own practices as the best if one is at all concerned about the future destination of one's *atman*. They enjoy a special advantage because, as Brahmans, embodying the most superior physical substance, they are, as I have already mentioned, thought to be the furthest along in the effort towards achieving release or moksha. If someone not born a Hindu, a Muslim or a Christian, for instance, was to follow upper caste Hindu custom and practice in his daily life – the *nityakarma* (daily routines) outlined above, and the practices that enable one to surrender one's sense of self including giving service to others – he or she would be venerated by Hindus for exemplifying a way of life that is the Hindu ideal. But in no way would Hindus suggest that their particular beliefs and practices have to be universally observed; there is enough diversity within the Hindu world itself for all Hindus to know that different people, constituted differently, having different *gunas*, would have different emergent *dharmas* that suit their different contexts, even if they were all united by the pursuit of a universal goal, that of release from the cycle of endless births.

A Duty-Based or Goal-Based Moral Code: Complex Realities Reconsidered

I am entirely sympathetic to Shweder, Mahapatra, and Miller's position that 'the orthodox Hindu moral code is an example of an alternative postconventional moral understanding' (1987, p. 76). However, I have some difficulty with the way they represent this alternative conception of morality. In describing the distinctive features of the Hindu moral code, they claim that it assumes that all people are 'naturally vulnerable', that they need to be protected from their vulnerabilities, and that 'paternalism and asymmetrical interdependency' are the most effective ways of achieving such protection. They suggest that the Hindu moral code is 'modeled after the family as a moral institution' and is built upon 'status and role obligations': they claim, in other words, that it is a paternalistic, duty-based moral code. I am not sure that I agree. I think that the Hindu moral code would be more appropriately described as goal-based – a code animated primarily by the ideals of self-refinement and non-attachment. Working towards these goals certainly involves the meticulous performance of one's duties, but such performance is hardly the sum and substance of this moral code: it constitutes but one part of it.

Hindu morality does assume that humans are 'naturally vulnerable' (1987, p. 78) – but not, as Shweder et al. suggest, vulnerable to the exploitation of others or to their own impetuous passions, but rather to contamination and pollution. It assumes that within every human body there resides a transcendental essence, the *atman*, and the goal of every human being is to refine the body so as to make it an appropriate container for this essence. The principle of harm, for instance, has a particular connotation in the Hindu moral code: harm is defined in a particular way and has particular consequences. Doing harm is morally wrong not because of the injury one causes another – although that concern is certainly present – but primarily because the harm one does rebounds onto oneself, coarsening one, increasing pollution to the self. The overwhelming moral concern for Hindus is to maintain the body's purity. Performing one's duties, fulfilling one's 'status obligations', is undoubtedly important but only because it enables one to achieve self-refinement and, thus, non-attachment.

Hindus guard against the natural vulnerability to pollution, that all humans are subject to, by adhering to a battery of explicitly defined customs and practices. Thus, for instance, when people in the temple town speak in favor of the institution of 'arranged' marriages, they may say that it is a way of ensuring that people, swayed by intemperate passions, do not get entangled in unsuitable alliances. But there is more to this statement than just a concern for maintaining harmony within the family or protecting people from their own vulnerability. Marriages are arranged through an elaborate process in which couples are matched in terms of their *jati* affiliation, their social class, their educational levels, their horoscopes, their physical appearances, and so on. And the purpose of such elaborate matching is to ensure compatibility between two people and two families, an auspicious compatibility that will lead to the birth of children and the material prosperity of the husband's family and, most importantly, will enable, rather than impede, the attempts of each partner in the marriage to refine him or herself as they move through the life course.

Clearly, the goals articulated in this moral code are personal, transcendental goals – the more proximate goals of self-refinement and non-attachment and the more distant, rarely acknowledged goal of release from the cycle of rebirths, *moksha*. Unlike Dworkin's (1977) goal-based codes that only articulate societal goals – 'creating a utopian society' or 'respect for authority' – the Hindu moral code defines personal goals, those of self-refinement and non-attachment. And each life is viewed ideally as another opportunity to make progress towards the ultimate goal of *moksha*. While the Hindu moral code defines goals that are seen as universally relevant, it allows for the possibility that there could be a multiplicity of paths taken to achieve these related goals, the underlying assumption being that what is moral in a particular set of life circumstances is rarely so in another. Recognizing the uniqueness of every person and his or her life circumstances, the Hindu moral code consists of context-dependent moral obligations. There is no attempt at imposing any one person's or any one group's morality on another person or group.

And far from the moral code being a paternalistic one in which the weak depend on the care and protection of the powerful, Hindu morality requires that every person be responsible for himself or herself in trying to achieve the goals of self-refinement and non-attachment. The notion of personal responsibility for one's own moral development is very explicitly formulated in Hindu moral understandings. In the discussion on *dharma*, I had pointed to the various kinds of *dharma* that a person had to simultaneously uphold – those of country, *jati*, lineage, and the self. But if there is a conflict between these different *dharma*s, such that in trying to uphold the *dharma* of one level of association, a person would inevitably violate that of another, the culture is quite clear about which *dharma* would take precedence – the more narrowly defined *dharma* always takes precedence. Thus, if there is conflict between the *dharma* of the country and that of the *jati*, a person upholds the latter and ignores the former; if there is conflict between the *dharma*s of *jati* and lineage, one upholds the lineage *dharma* (*kula dharma*); and if there is conflict between the *dharma*s of lineage and the self, the *dharma* of the self – *svadharma* – takes precedence. The Hindu moral code, by emphasizing the overarching importance of upholding one's personal *dharma*, makes clear that one's primary responsibility is to oneself, to ensure that one achieves the necessary moral progress towards release from the cycle of endless rebirths.

Dharma and the Idea of Natural Law

Finally, I would like to draw attention to the possibility that the Hindu moral code may not include the three mandatory features that Shweder, Mahapatra, and Miller insist are necessary for any moral code to be 'rationally defensible'. They identify these features as the abstract idea of natural law and the abstract principles of harm and justice. According to them, the first of these – the idea of natural law – is implicated every time 'a discrepancy between what is and what ought to be' is noted. Natural law implies that certain actions are 'inherently wrong' however pleasurable they may be, and even if there are rules that explicitly permit their occurrence: 'it is the idea of an objective obligation' (1987, p. 19). Now, given the importance of contextuality in Hindu moral thinking, there is hardly any action that is inherently wrong: given the right circumstances, even the most heinous act can be morally justified. As the quotations from *Manu*, cited earlier, make clear, under extreme conditions, there is nothing that can be categorically declared as beyond the limits of morality: fathers can kill their sons, and priests – the embodiments of the most superior physical substance – can eat the most defiling of creatures, dogs.

Dharma, as I have stated earlier, is ideal justice made manifest. Such an understanding of *dharma* makes it inconceivable that there can be a discrepancy between what is and what ought to be. By virtue of its existence, everything that exists is 'true' and as it should be. So injustice and inequity is only *apparent* because, as humans, we only have a limited understanding of Ultimate Reality; in the cosmic order of things, there is no inequity or injustice. And for those who appear to be suffering inequity or injustice, the natural recourse available to them is to live their present lives according to their particular *dharma*s so as to refine themselves and achieve non-attachment, in the hope that such good actions will be rewarded in future lives.

With respect to the two abstract principles of harm and justice, the Hindu moral code includes both but with a twist. The harm that the Hindu moral code primarily concerns itself with is not the harm one may do others but the harm that comes to oneself because of actions that coarsen and contaminate. Such actions tend to hinder self-refinement and non-attachment and jeopardize one's chances of breaking out of the endless cycle of births and deaths – if one was to talk in terms of the ultimate meaning of life. As for the principle of justice, the Hindu moral code has no trouble with the statement that 'like cases must be treated alike and different cases differently' (1987, p. 19). However, given the context-sensitive nature of Hindu thought, almost nothing is exactly like another thing, and therefore, the question of similar treatment is not particularly meaningful.

THE DOMINANCE OF PRACTICE OVER PRECEPT: MORAL REASONING AMONGST ORIYA HINDU CHILDREN

In order to speak sensibly about the ways in which moral reasoning emerges amongst the Oriya Hindu children of the temple town, it is necessary to first describe this neighborhood, the tenor of life here and the kinds of influences that predominate (for more on the temple town, see Mahapatra, 1981; Seymour, 1999; Shweder, 1991). Its central focus is the medieval temple (tenth to eleventh century) dedicated to the Hindu god Siva, represented here as *Lingaraj* (Lord of the Phallus). While this is certainly the largest and most impressive of the temples located here, there are numerous others, each having its own presiding god or goddess. In fact, it would not be an exaggeration to say that practically every lane in the temple town has its own shrine with its own resident deity.

The temple town is a pilgrimage center of some note although it cannot compare with Puri, a town about 40 miles further south-east, that has the distinction of being one of Hinduism's four most sacred centers. The community that lives in this neighborhood consists predominantly of families who have hereditary links with the temple, the menfolk serving the deity in various kinds of ways. *Ashrams* (hermitages) are part of the landscape of the temple town and renouncers in their saffron or white add local color. While it would be a mistake to represent the temple town as an isolated rural backwater, untouched by the events and currents of the world outside, its residents do adhere, rather strictly, to orthodox Hindu practice. More importantly, for the purposes of this essay, conclusions drawn about the ways in which a Hindu moral sense is acquired in this community would apply, with little qualification, to other Hindu communities in other parts of the Indian subcontinent.

Indigenous thinking in the temple town holds that young children acquire their moral understandings experientially, through observing customary practice and participating in them. And how could it be otherwise? Given a contextually derived moral code, the list of dos and don'ts would be so long that it would be impossible to instruct anyone in its intricacies. And not just the magnitude, but the subtleties and fine distinctions that define such a moral code would make it impossible to teach it through precept alone.

Oriya Hindus conceive of childhood (*balya avastha*) as continuing from birth till about seven or eight years of age. They idealize the first five years of this phase of life, describing it as a time of complete irresponsibility (*daitvasunya*) and consequently a period of undiluted happiness. Most Oriya children of the temple town grow up in multi-generational households in which child-care responsibilities are shared between many caretakers – grandmothers, grandfathers, aunts, fathers, uncles, older siblings, and older cousins. Child-rearing practices in Hindu households are very different from those that are customary in the West (Seymour, 1999; Trawick, 1990). Children are never overtly denied anything they request; rather, when they become obstreperous, their caretakers seek to entertain them, striving to restore their good humor through diverting their attention. Small children are always in close physical contact with someone: while awake, they are either carried on someone's hip or held in someone's lap; and at night, they sleep with their mothers.

Oriya Hindus view a young child as extremely malleable, and therefore as very susceptible to influences from the environment in which she is raised as well as from the people with whom she comes into contact. According to Oriya Hindus, till five years of age, a child should be pampered and spoilt, not disciplined at all. They say that a child of this age is unformed, not ready, neither physically nor mentally, for instruction (*updesho*) or education (*sikhya*) or discipline (*anushasano*).

Perhaps because of this cultural prescription, in the temple town, against explicitly teaching the child about indigenous values and virtues, practices like breastfeeding and weaning serve to teach the child its first lessons in cultivating self-control. Oriya Hindu infants are fed on demand, and they are rarely weaned before the age of two or three; sometimes, if there is no sibling born after them, they continue to breastfeed till four or five years of age. Most Western observers of such practices are wont to describe them as dangerously over-indulgent (Carstairs, 1967; Roland, 1988). However, as Seymour (1999) reports, although Oriya Hindu mothers breastfeed their children on demand, they are less and less likely to gratify the child completely the older she gets. After the child is introduced to solid food, mothers begin to adopt a distinctive pattern of incomplete gratification punctuated by intermittent frustrations which seems to be telling the child that while no demand will ever be refused, she should voluntarily give up the infantile pleasure of feeding at her mother's breast for the more mature pleasure of eating solid food with the other children of the family. When asked, Oriya Hindus claim that the child usually weans herself. And this is a fair representation because while both mother and child participate, the child experiences the process as one in which she exercises self-control, voluntarily deciding to give up feeding at her mother's breast.

Between the years of five and seven or eight, a child's intellect (*buddhi*) is thought to develop as well as her ability to discriminate between right and wrong (*bibek*). Mothers say,

> Just as when they were very small we told them, 'Learn to walk, learn to eat, eat with your right hand, don't eat with your left hand, do this good work, don't do that bad

> work' . . . just as we tell them about the difference between good and bad, in the same way, their intellect grows and they slowly learn to distinguish between what is good and bad.

Late childhood, between the years of five and seven or eight, is the time when children begin to pray for themselves. Oriya Hindu women say,

> This god we believe in, we tell the children to pray to him in the morning and the evening. Till the child is about five or six, the mother herself has to do the prayers for the child but after this age, the child gradually becomes able to pray for herself.

Such explicit instruction includes teaching children about the proper way to perform their daily ablutions (*nityakarma*). As I have already explained these customary practices are meticulously followed by adults and, after the age of five or six, a child begins to be told about the need for and importance of maintaining these practices, and she is supervised, either by her mother or by an older sister, to make sure that she does follow them. Apart from such explicit instruction, there are other ways in which 'children discern the moral order as it is dramatized and made salient in everyday practices' (Shweder, Mahapatra, & Miller, 1987, p. 73). For instance, all upper caste households of the temple town observe the auspicious days of the Hindu calendar meticulously: *ekadashi*s (the eleventh day of the lunar fortnight), *amabasya*s (the night of the new moon), *sankranti*s (days that mark the passage of the sun from the house of one planetary body to another's) and *purnima*s (full moon nights) and *chandra grhano*s (lunar eclipses). On these days, adults keep fasts and special prayers and worship are offered to the household gods. All these observances are occasions for telling children richly detailed stories about their particular meanings. For a fortnight during the month of *Asvin* (September–October), *pitru paksh* (the fortnight of the ancestors) is observed, and ancestors are worshipped. During this fortnight, children observe the various rituals and gradually absorb the idea of the continuity of life within the family, the idea that ancestors, and present family members, and those not yet born are all connected by familial essences. They learn that the three debts that all Hindus have to repay during their lifetimes are to their teachers (*gurus*), their ancestors, and their parents. Children also learn about the moral order through participating in the rituals of refinement (*samaskaras*) that I have already discussed earlier in this chapter. These rituals of refinement are embedded in elaborate narratives that teach the child about the moral and cultural meanings of Hinduism: the ultimate meaning of life, the value of renunciation and the significance of self-refinement.

Oriya children in the temple town also learn about the Hindu moral order through listening to stories from the Hindu epics (the *Ramayana* and the *Mahabharata*), the *Purana*s and other folk stories that are particular to the temple town and Orissa.[9] They usually hear these stories from their mothers and grandmothers while being hand-fed, a practice that continues till children are seven or eight years old. As Ramanujan has remarked, children in India don't hear bedtime stories, they hear 'food-time stories' (1986, p. 46). While absorbing nourishment, they are also ingesting the predominant values of the culture. They eat and they simultaneously hear about the ideal son Shravan's selfless acts of filial devotion, or about Krishna's exhortation on the battlefield at Kurukshetra to Arjuna to fulfill his *dharma*, or about Sita, the perfect Hindu wife, whose exemplary chastity (*satitva*) enabled her to withstand the test of fire (*agni pariksha*). These stories are reinforced and made part of their conscious memory because Hindu festivals celebrate them, every year, year after year. Thus, every August, sons emulate Shravan's example and rededicate themselves to the service of their parents; and every November, during the festival of Divali, scenes from the *Ramayana* are re-enacted, including that of Sita's test. And every household in the temple town has its copy of the *Bhagavad gita* that consists of Krishna's exhortation to Arjuna to carry out his *dharma*; and Oriya Hindus quote, often and liberally, from this popular and well-known religious text. In this way, almost unwittingly, Hindu moral understandings and the Hindu worldview seep into the consciousness of a child born and raised in the temple town.

The power of touch to pollute is another lesson that is learned early in the temple town. So for instance, small children see adults recoil when a stray dog brushes past them on the street, and observe them returning home, when this occurs, for a purifying bath and change of clothes before proceeding on their errand. They soon learn that when they display distaste at being touched and fondled by others their behavior receives cultural approbation. Such distaste is thought to indicate the child's innate refinement. Oriya Hindus believe that to shun contact, to maintain exclusivity, confers a mark of distinction on the person who shuns.

Shweder, Mahapatra, and Miller (1987) are quite accurate in the way they describe children being directly forewarned about the polluting power of touch by their menstruating mothers who forbid them from coming close. A mother will warn her four- or five-year-old child not to touch her because she is polluted. She explains her pollution by saying, 'I've just stepped in dog excrement!' While this certainly tells children about the dangers of touching, and the vulnerability of humans to pollution, I think that there is an even more significant lesson being taught: the child is learning about contextuality. In particular situations and at particular times, children learn that a mother's body becomes 'untouchable'. She who is usually indulgent, allowing them to stamp on her, lie upon her, to pollute her with their saliva, their vomit, their excrement, cannot be touched – sometimes. And young children quickly learn that all grown women are 'untouchable', in certain contexts. They recognize the signs of a menstruating woman in the household – the unkempt appearance, the orienting of the body away from people, the tendency to stay at the periphery of a group – and, invariably, teasing them becomes a game. Young boys – five and six years old – will play at trying to touch their unmarried menstruating aunts, to see how far the young women will retreat to avoid contact. Such teasing games usually end in the young women getting irritated and the young children finding the entire situation enormously amusing.

There are other daily occurrences that reinforce the idea of contextuality. When a usually tolerant father, bathed and ready to pray, admonishes a child who comes too close, or an always tolerant grandmother refuses to let the child who has just returned home from school near her unless she removes her clothes and washes herself, the child is absorbing the message that appropriateness and inappropriateness of conduct, of attire, of purity, and of tolerable impurity, vary from context to context.

Children are also quick to pick up on the contrasting cultural perceptions regarding married women and widows, and the ways in which contextuality factors in. Married women are seen as embodying auspiciousness (*sri*) while widows are thought to emanate inauspiciousness. Married women, central to the prosperity of the family, are intimately involved in all activities that have to do with nourishing and sustaining the life of the family. But not widows: children see widows, within their own households, helping in household chores – cutting vegetables, grinding spices – but not allowed to either enter the kitchen or touch the cooking pots in which rice for the household is boiled. During lifecycle rituals – the first feeding of solids to an infant, the sacred thread ceremony of upper caste boys, marriages – in which auspiciousness is sought for the future growth and prosperity of the family, married women play a prominent role, while widows hide in the background even when their own children are involved in the ceremonies. Children realize, sooner rather than later, that the stigmatization of widows varies according to context. Whenever the life and sustenance of the family is at issue, widows are kept at a distance; in other family situations, they do pretty much what another woman of the same age would do.

Not to stretch a point too far, but even particular child-rearing practices serve to accustom children to the importance of context. With respect to toilet training, Oriya Hindu children appear to train themselves: from most accounts (Seymour, 1971), children become toilet trained anywhere between the first and fourth and fifth years. Parents neither praise children for exercising proper anal control nor do they blame them when accidents take place, although group teasing by peers does occur in the latter instance. Even if such an accident were to occur in the family prayer room (*puja gharo*), the child would not be scolded but the uproar that would ensue within the household – the cleaning and the purifying, the loud and explicit blaming of caretakers for not having being sufficiently alert to the child's needs, the dislocation of life in the household for that day – more than suffices to teach the child that there are certain places in the house which are sacred and pure, where accidents are never tolerated. The child learns that whether a behavior is appropriate or not depends entirely on the context.

Thus, the aspects of life in the temple town that encourage Hindu moral understandings to develop are varied and multifarious. As I have described, the role of explicit instruction and precept is limited: the influences that guide a child's moral development are subtle, almost insidious. It appears that Hindu children in the temple town acquire their moral sense through observing and through experiencing life as it gets played out in this neighborhood.

Conclusion

Hindus define moral development as a process that continues throughout a person's life. The moral foundations that one acquires as a child are believed to guide the pattern for future moral development. However, the predisposition to view self-understandings as fluid and changing over the life course, and the tendency to identify context as defining what is moral and what is not, imply that moral development is a project that continues over the life course.

Hindus tend to think of morality or *dharma* as a this-worldly concern. While the importance of upholding one's *dharma* cannot be overstated, and although scrupulous observance of one's *dharma* is thought to improve one's ritual status in future lives, simply doing so only guarantees future rebirths. To finally achieve release from the cycle of rebirths requires transcending all social bonds, even those identified as moral. Through moral action, one refines oneself; one increases one's potential for non-attachment, one separates oneself from all desires, even that for *moksa*.

Therefore, the Hindu moral code defines a universal goal – *moksa* – that has meaning for all humans if they wish to escape the tedium of countless rebirths. It is noteworthy that this goal and the subsidiary ones – those of non-attachment and self-refinement – are not necessarily framed in deistic terms. Given that these are the goals that provide a coherent framework to Hindu moral understandings, I think it makes sense to identify this moral code, not as duty-based, but as goal-based.

While the Hindu moral code does postulate universal moral goals that all humans should aspire to, there are no universal moral obligations. All moral obligations are context-dependent, defined very particularly, in terms of one's *jati*, one's character, one's life phase, one's family role, whether one's life circumstances are extreme or not. There is no conduct that is categorically identified as beyond the pale. Given sufficiently dire situations, any conduct is morally permissible. Perhaps it is this looseness of structure, this lack of emphasis on any particular set of moral obligations, that gives the Hindu moral code its resilience – a resilience that is demonstrated in that it remains a faith to live by for millions, even today.

Notes

1 Therefore, in this system of ranking matter according to its subtlety or grossness, Hindus classify knowledge as more subtle and more powerful than wealth, wealth as more subtle than land, land as more subtle than food, which itself is more subtle than garbage (Marriott, 1976).

2 There are five constituent elements (*bhuta*s): ether (*akasha*), air (*vayu*), fire (*agni*), water (*ap*) and earth (*prithvi*).

3 In all six schools of Hindu philosophy, *atman* is defined as the imperishable entity – the self – that resides in all living creatures. *Moksa* or release is achieved when the *atman* of a single entity unites with the *Paramatman* – the Universal Self.

4 'Unremitting activity' refers to the understanding that we are all constantly engaged in doing (*karma*): as long as we inhabit our bodies, we are constantly doing something, whether it be sitting still, thinking, sleeping, dreaming, digesting.

5 *Manu* refers to *The laws of Manu, Manudharmasastra*, a pivotal Sanskrit text composed around the early centuries of the Common Era, consisting of 2,685 verses that deal with the social, moral and ritual obligations of the different castes and of people at various stages of life.

6 The *Brahman*s, the *Kshatriya*s, and the *Vaisya*s.

7 In the words of the Sanskrit hymn: *ya devi sarvabhutesu lajya rupena samsthita* (Devi who abides in all perishable beings in the form of *lajya*).

8 *Panichua* literally stands for 'water touching': that is, *jati*s that can give water to Brahmans.

9 *Puranas* are 18 anthologies containing cosmogonic myths, ancient legends, theological, astronomical and nature lore. It is generally agreed by textual scholars that the *Puranas* date back to the medieval period.

References

Bellah, R.N., Madsen, R., Sullivan, W.M., Swidler, A., & Tipton, S.M. (1996). *Habits of the heart*. Berkeley, CA: University of California Press.

Bhagavad Gita (1969). *The Bhagavad-gita* (trans. R.C. Zaehner). London: Oxford University Press.

Caraka (1949) *The Caraka samhita* (6 vols). Jamnagar: Shree Gulab Kunverba Ayurvedic Society.

Carstairs, G.M. (1967). *The twice born: A study of a community of high-caste Hindus*. Bloomington, IN: Indiana University Press.

Daniel, E.V. (1984). *Fluid signs: Becoming a person the Tamil way*. Berkeley, CA: University of California Press.

Davis, M.G. (1983). *Rank and rivalry: The politics of inequality in rural West Bengal*. Cambridge: Cambridge University Press.

Doniger, W., & Smith, B.W. (1991). *The laws of Manu*. Harmondsworth: Penguins.

Dumont, L. (1960). World renunciation in Indian religions. *Contributions to Indian Sociology*, 4, 33–62.

Dworkin, R. (1977). *Taking rights seriously*. Cambridge, MA: Harvard University Press.

Edwards, C.P. (1980). The development of moral reasoning in cross-cultural perspective. In R.H. Munroe, R. Munroe, and B.B. Whiting (eds), *Handbook of cross-cultural human development*. New York: Garland.

Edwards, C.P. (1985). Another style of competence: The caregiving child. In A.D. Fogel & G.F. Melson (eds), *Origins of nurturance*. New York: Erlbaum.

Enright, R.D., Freedman, S., & Rique, J. (1998). The psychology of interpersonal forgiveness. In R.D. Enright & J. North (eds), *Exploring forgiveness*. Madison, WI: University of Wisconsin Press.

Geertz, C. (1983). 'From the native's point of view': On the nature of anthropological understanding. In *Local Knowledge*. New York: Basic.

Gilligan, C. (1993). *In a different voice: Psychological theory and women's development*. Cambridge, MA: Harvard University Press.

Hawley, J.S. (1996). The goddess in India. In J.S. Hawley & D.M. Wulff (eds), *Devi*. Berkeley, CA: University of California Press.

Inden, R.B. (1976). *Marriage and rank in Bengali culture*. Berkeley, CA: University of California Press.

Inden, R.B., & Nicholas, R.W. (1977). *Kinship in Bengali culture*. Chicago: University of Chicago Press.

Keyes, C.F., & Daniel, E.V. (1983). *Karma: An anthropological inquiry*. Berkeley, CA: University of California Press.

Kohlberg, L. (1969). Stage and sequence: The cognitive developmental approach to socialization. In D.A. Goslin (ed.), *Handbook of socialization theory and research*. New York: Rand McNally.

Kohlberg, L. (1981). *The philosophy of moral development: Moral stages and the idea of justice*. San Francisco: Harper & Row.

Lamb, S. (1993). Growing in the net of Maya. Unpublished PhD dissertation, University of Chicago.

Mackie, J.L. (1977). *Ethics: Inventing right and wrong*. Harmondsworth: Penguin.

Madan, T.N. (1987). *Non-renunciation*. Delhi: Oxford University Press.

Mahapatra, M. (1981). *Traditional structure and change in an Orissa temple town*. Calcutta: Punthi Pustak.

Marriott, M. (1976). Hindu transactions: Diversity without dualism. In B. Kapferer (ed.), *Transaction and meaning in the anthropology of exchange and symbolic behavior*. Philadelphia: Institute for the Study of Human Issues.

Marriott, M. (1990). Constructing an Indian ethnosociology. In M. Marriott (ed.), *India through Hindu*. New Delhi: Sage.

Marriott, M., & Inden, R.B. (1977). Towards an ethnosociology of South Asian caste systems. In K.A. David (ed.), *The new wind*. The Hague: Mouton.

Menon, U., & Shweder, R.A. (1998). The return of the 'white man's burden': The moral discourse of anthropology and the domestic life of Hindu women. In R.A. Shweder (ed.), *Welcome to middle age!* Chicago: University of Chicago Press.

Mines, D.P. (1990). Hindu periods of death 'impurity'. In M. Marriott (ed.), *India through Hindu categories*. New Delhi: Sage.

Parish, S.M. (1994). *Moral knowing in a Hindu sacred city*. New York: Columbia University Press.

Ramanujan, A.K. (1986). Two realms of Kannada folklore. In S.H. Blackburn & A.K. Ramanujan (eds), *Another harmony*. Berkeley, CA: University of California Press.

Ramanujan, A.K. (1990). Is there an Indian way of thinking? An informal essay. In M. Marriott (ed.), *India through Hindu categories*. New Delhi: Sage.

Roland, A. (1988). *In search of self in India and Japan*. Princeton, NJ: Princeton University Press.

Schneider, D.M. (1968). *American kinship: A cultural account*. Englewood Cliffs, NJ: Prentice-Hall.

Seymour, S.C. (1971). Patterns of child rearing in a changing Indian town: Sources and expressions of dependence and independence. PhD dissertation, Harvard University.

Seymour, S.C. (1999). *Women, family and child care in India*. Cambridge: Cambridge University Press.

Shweder, R.A. (1991). *Thinking through cultures*. Cambridge, MA: Harvard University Press.

Shweder, R.A., Mahapatra, M., & Miller, J. (1987). Culture and moral development. In J. Kagan & S. Lamb (eds), *The emergence of morality in young children*. Chicago: University of Chicago Press.

Susruta (1963). *An English translation of the Susruta samhita* (3 vols, 2nd edn). The Chowkamba Sanskrit Studies 30. Varanasi: The Chowkamba Sanskrit Series Office.

Trawick, M. (1990). *Notes on love in a Tamil family*. Berkeley, CA: University of California Press.

Turiel, E. (1979). Distinct conceptual and developmental domains: Social-convention and morality. In C.B. Keasy (ed.), *Nebraska Symposium on Motivation* (1977, Vol. 25). Lincoln: University of Nebraska Press.

Turiel, E. (1983). *The development of social knowledge: Morality and convention*. New York: Cambridge University Press.

Turiel, E., Killen, M., & Helwig, C.C. (1987). 'Morality: Its structures, functions and vagaries. In J. Kagan & S. Lamb (eds), *The emergence of morality in young children*. Chicago: University of Chicago Press.

Vatuk, S. (1990). 'To be a burden on others': Dependency anxiety among the elderly in India. In O.M. Lynch (ed.), *Divine passions: The social construction of emotion in India*. Berkeley, CA: University of California Press.

Visnu Purana (1972). *The Visnu Purana, a system of Hindu mythology and tradition* (trans. H.H. Wilson). Calcutta: Punthi Pustak.

Vivekacudamani (1932). *Vivekacudamani of Sankaracarya* (3rd edn, trans. Swami Madhavananda). Almora: Mayavati.

Zimmer, H. (1946/1967). *Philosophies of India*. New York: Bollingen.

20

From Early Attachment Relations to the Adolescent and Adult Organization of Self

HARKE BOSMA and COBY GERLSMA

INTRODUCTION

Some of the founding fathers of psychology (e.g. Baldwin, 1895; James, 1890) showed a strong interest in the organization and development of self. This interest was lost while behaviourism dominated psychology. In the second half of the twentieth century a revival of questions concerning self occurred. Next to the traditional drive perspective within psychoanalysis, new perspectives came to the fore: a relational perspective with a focus on the development of self in early attachment relations, and an ego-psychological perspective with an emphasis on social and cultural influences and the development of identity across the lifespan. Moreover, the cognitive revolution opened the way to study self as a set of mental representations. The theoretical and research traditions that have resulted from these developments – attachment, self-representations, and ego-identity research – are central to this chapter.

The traditions differ in various respects: historical origin, conceptualizations and content, methodology, main research findings, focal age range, etc. Each tradition has its limitations, internal debates and subtraditions. Because of these differences, our knowledge of the development of the organization of self is fragmented. Moreover, the domain as a whole is beset with definitional issues and meta-theoretical concerns.

Definitional Issues: Self, Self-Concept and Identity

The noun 'self' is a general and broad construct. In the *Concise Oxford Dictionary* (7th edn, 1982) it is defined as (1) the person's own individuality or essence, and (2) the person as object of introspection or reflective action.

Within psychology similar definitions are used (for overviews see Baumeister, 1995; van der Werff, 1990). In some personality theories self is characterized as the essence or 'inner core' of an individual's personality, but opinions on whether such a core really exists are completely at odds: compare humanistic psychology which posits such a core ('the very me', 'one's true self'), and Sartrean existentialism which assumes a 'nothingness', 'an inner vacuum'. Several authors attribute motivational and integrating functions to the self ('self as agent').

Self can also refer to the individual's experience of him or herself ('the person as object of introspection'), in a general sense ('a sense of self') as well as in a specified sense (e.g. one's perceived self, one's remembered self). In the latter case self is mostly used as prefix, hence 'self-concept,' 'self-image'. These concepts refer to the individual's mental representations of him or herself. An individual can have different self-concepts in different situations/roles, e.g. as a father, as a husband, as an employee at work, etc. The evaluative aspect of one's self-concept(s) is often referred to as 'self-esteem', e.g. how does one value oneself as a sportsman, positive or negative? 'Self' is also used in combination with 'organization', denoting the organization (or structuring) of self.

'Self-organization', however, is also a technical term within dynamic systems theory, referring to the process of the emergence of order in systems. Here we will only use 'self-organization' in the latter sense (compare Lewis & Granic, 1999); in other cases we will use 'organization (or structure) of the self'.

The *Oxford Dictionary* offers two definitions of identity: (1) absolute sameness; individuality, personality; condition of being a specified person; and (2) from mathematics, any transformation that leaves an object unchanged.

In psychology these definitions link to two aspects of a person's identity: (1) characteristic and distinctive features that (2) change, yet remain the same (see for example van der Werff, 1990). Identity in this sense is often described as an issue of 'sameness and continuity'. A person is characterized by and distinguishable from another person by all kinds of features such as physical characteristics, name, date of birth, social security number, biographical descriptions, IQ, attitudes, needs, personality traits, interests, commitments, etc. Individuals can be more or less objectively identified by these characteristics. The compilation of them could be described as a person's 'objective identity', in general, the attributes which are used to identify the holder (compare, 'being a specified and unique person'). 'Subjective identity' is the experiental side of objective identity, i.e. the awareness of oneself with these specific characteristics. Subjective identity ('a sense of identity') is the experience of a sense of being one and the same unique person, a sense of personal coherence and unity. There can be a tension between someone's objective (e.g. how a person is seen by others) and subjective (e.g. how the person sees him or herself) identity. Moreover, across the lifespan, some identifying characteristics will remain the same (e.g. gender) but others can change, in some cases even drastically (e.g. appearance). The concept of identity thus refers to the dynamic relationships between sameness and change and between a subjective and an objective perspective.

Identity is used in different theoretical traditions within psychology. It is a central concept for developmental researchers working in the Erikson tradition (see below), but researchers within personality and social psychology use it as well, even if they focus on what more correctly would be referred to as the self-concept (Bosma, 1995). Especially when 'self' and 'identity' are used in a general sense they are often treated as synonyms (e.g. Ashmore & Jussim, 1997). The theoretical and research traditions in the domains of self and identity development, discussed below, differ with regard to the constructs and the meanings of the constructs they use. We will therefore first let these traditions speak for themselves and work with the constructs as they are used within each tradition. We shall return to questions of complementarity and overlap of the central concepts as we go through the chapter.

Meta-Theoretical Concerns

The theoretical and empirical approaches to self and identity can differ markedly in their focus. In some cases the focus is on the content and structure of a person's self/self-concept/identity (the 'topography of self' as Breakwell, 1986, called it), for example, on the content and organization of one's various self-concepts. A different focus concerns issues of function and process: what is the psychological function of one's self, or more specifically, of a high self-esteem? How is a sense of identity maintained despite changes?

Each focus has its advantages and disadvantages. When self, self-concept, and identity are seen as internal, intrapsychic structures it is difficult to explain how these structures behave and change under the influence of (short-term) changes in the individual's context or long-term changes due to developmental growth. Conceptualizations in terms of change and function present difficulties in understanding stability and continuity. The juxtaposition of these static and dynamic approaches is one of the major themes in this chapter.

Another recurring theme is the issue of the ontological nature of self and identity and the related question of their ontogenetic origins. Folk psychological accounts of self and identity tend to stress individuality and uniqueness. Several authors, however, see these individualistic views as an outcome of historical change that has occurred since the Renaissance in western, industrialized society, and consequently as one-sided and culturally biased. In such views the social nature and social origins of self and identity are ignored. According to Baumeister and Muraven, for example, 'the modern Western individual often perceives a moral imperative in the pursuit of self-interest and self-actualization that is largely unprecedented. According to this new view, one has a moral right, and even a duty, to do what is good for the self, such as learning to understand oneself and cultivating one's talents and abilities' (1996, p. 410). This imperative suggests that one's identity, one's inner self, one's individuality and uniqueness have to be emphasized in order to adapt to the demands of modern life. Authors like Baumeister and Muraven, thus, see self and identity as a form of adaptation between person and context, as the outcome of the interaction between what they call 'the basic nature of selfhood' and the social and cultural context.

A social, interactionist perspective on the origins of self and identity is almost as old as psychology. About a century ago it had already been advocated by Baldwin and Cooley (see Harter, 1999, and Ashmore & Jussim, 1997, for concise historical overviews). Such a perspective suggests that self and identity are social constructions. In these constructions knowledge of oneself and knowledge of the other are intrinsically linked; aspects referring to oneself and aspects referring to (the relationship with) others go hand in hand. Both stem from social interactions. Such a social perspective, however, has not always been acknowledged. It is only recently that authors began to argue that self and identity comprise individuality *as well as* relatedness (e.g. Grotevant & Cooper, 1986; Guisinger & Blatt, 1993; Ryan, 1991). Ryan warned: 'Once acknowledging that the overall direction of life is toward interdependence and synthesis, we can see that conceptions that overly reify the self run the risk of disembedding it from its nature as a set of organizational *processes* within and between persons' (1991, p. 233).

One-sided perspectives have dominated the empirical approaches to self and identity. They were either overly individualistic and decontextualized (see below), or overly social (e.g. social identity theory: see Tajfel, 1982; Turner, 1982). This duality will also become evident from the reviews in the three main sections in this chapter. Self-concept research has traditionally concerned the individual's self-representations, which mostly have been studied in isolation from the context. The study of identity development started from a clearly psychosocial theoretical orientation, but also narrowed to a rather individualistic empirical approach. In attachment research, on the other hand, relationships form the basis of the organization of self, but the self-aspect remained under-exposed in this tradition. In the last two decades, attempts to integrate the individual and social aspects of self and identity in each of these three traditions have become prominent.

The Development of the Organization of Self: Three Main Traditions

Attachment theory (Bowlby, 1969; 1973; 1980) 'arose from the encounter between the new science of ethology and that phase in the history of psychoanalysis in which it was moving from drive towards the relational perspective embodied in the work of Balint, Winnicott, Fairbairn, and Melanie Klein' (Holmes, 1997, p. 232; for a detailed description on the origins of attachment theory, see van Dijken et al., 1998).

In this encounter, Bowlby firmly places the development of the organization of self in relational perspective. Evolution equipped humans with the need to seek proximity to caregivers in the face of threat. Although this need for attachment is innate, individuals' strategies for dealing with their attachment needs are learned through relational experience. Usually when responded to in a sensitive and favourable fashion, the individual will feel 'free' to experience attachment needs and act upon them without qualms, whereas non-responsiveness may leave doubts as to others' availability, or to the avoidance of others altogether. Such attachment experiences not only shape perception and understanding of the social environment but are, to an equal extent, a source of information about self. As Bowlby put it:

> Confidence that an attachment figure is, apart from being accessible, likely to be responsive can be seen to turn on at least two variables: (a) whether or not the attachment figure is judged to be the sort of person who in general responds to calls for support and protection; (b) whether or not the self is judged to be the sort of person toward whom anyone, and the attachment figure in particular, is likely to respond in a helpful way. (1973, p. 238)

The past two decades have seen a steady growth of theoretical and empirical research on attachment, in which several principal streams can be discerned. Pertaining to attachment in infancy and early childhood, there is a flourishing research tradition that followed the ideas developed by Bowlby and his closest colleague, Mary Ainsworth. In their footsteps but with a focus on the nature and role of attachment in adult life a second stream of research developed in the 1980s, which received great impetus from the work of Mary Main and her colleagues. Finally, the discovery of romantic love as an attachment process (Hazan & Shaver, 1987) inspired a good deal of research with a predominantly social psychological approach. In their seminal paper, Hazan and Shaver (1987) not only introduced attachment theory as a suitable and fruitful framework for the study of adult relationship functioning. They also made an important contribution with the introduction of the self-report method for the assessment of adult attachment. Although decidedly more practical and easy to administer, the construct validity of the self-report measures that were subsequently developed is still controversial (see, for instance, Baldwin & Fehr, 1995), whereas their convergence with developmental psychological measures of attachment quality appears to be problematic (e.g. Crowell, Treboux, & Waters, 1999; Stein et al., 1998). This hampers a direct comparison of empirical findings in the different lines of research. Moreover, and in contrast to the mainstream of work in developmental psychology, only scant attention is paid to developmental pathways. We consider a detailed discussion of this line of research beyond the scope of this chapter, and therefore decided to limit our description of the organization of self from an attachment theoretical perspective to a discussion of the two developmental psychological mainstreams.

From the review of the attachment literature it is evident that empirical knowledge of the model of self within this tradition is limited. More on this can be found in the literature on the study of the development of the self-concept (or, more generally, a person's self-representations) and its evaluative part, a person's self-esteem. This research tradition is rooted in the ideas of William James. James (1890) was the first psychologist to systematically study how people perceive and evaluate themselves and he introduced the seminal distinction between 'I' (self as agent, as 'knower') and 'Me' (self as 'known'). Calkins (1900) further elaborated the idea of different selves. The first to study the development of self in the young child was Baldwin (1895). He saw it as a dialectical process between self and other. Cooley (1902) introduced the notion of a 'looking glass self' by which he meant that individuals know themselves by what they learn from significant others. This notion was further elaborated by Mead (1934) in his symbolic interactionism. According to Baldwin, Cooley, and Mead, self is a social construction. This is evident in the recent notion that self is rooted in and regulates relationships.

The study of self lingered on through the decades of radical behaviourism and gained momentum again in the second half of the twentieth century with the growth of cognitivism. What then became the study of the self-*concept* has a strong cognitive orientation with a focus on (static) internal structures and content. Recent self-concept approaches (e.g. Baumeister, 1987; Higgins, 1987; Markus & Wurf, 1987), however, show a shift towards more contextual, dynamic, and motivational conceptualizations. The bulk of self-concept and self-esteem research has been done within personality and social psychology. Within developmental psychology Harter's (1999) work on the development of self is the most notable. Her work covers the development of self-concept and self-esteem from birth through adulthood (see below).

The study of identity development has been strongly inspired by Erikson's (1950; 1968) lifespan developmental theory, which is built on Freud's psychoanalytic theory of personality development in infancy and childhood, while emphasizing person–context interactions. According to Erikson, adolescence is a crucial phase in identity development because adolescents face the task of defining themselves and their position in adult society. Consequently, most identity research concerns adolescents and young adults and has a strong focus on how adolescents commit themselves to adult responsibilities. The most popular empirical approach to identity in adolescence, Marcia's identity status model (Marcia et al., 1993), however, is essentially a typology of individuals, which loses the interactionist quality of Erikson's theory.

The so-called second separation–individuation process is seen as part of the development of identity in adolescence. The small body of research on this aspect of adolescent development is also grounded in Freud's theory (see below).

The Development of Attachment

Theoretical Background

Holmes described attachment theory as 'not so much a single theory as an overall framework for thinking about relationships, or, more accurately, about those aspects of relationships that are shaped by threat and the need for security' (1997, p. 231). In his seminal work on human attachment, Bowlby (1969; 1973; 1980) proposes that threat or distress (felt insecurity) activates an innate attachment system, that is, affect, cognitions, and behaviour. These are aimed at seeking proximity to someone able to provide comfort, protection, and support, with the goal of regaining a sense of security and the ability to meet another, antithetical human urge, i.e. 'the urge to explore the environment, to play, and to take part in varied activities with peers' (Bowlby, 1988, p. 3). The default, innate strategy for dealing with attachment system activation in any human being is to sense a need for closeness to one's selected attachment figure and go for it; this is the primary, secure attachment strategy. Secondary attachment strategies develop when the primary one appears to fail. With the accumulation of adverse experiences in the attachment relationship (e.g. bids for proximity are met with non-responsiveness, rejection, abuse) individuals are likely to lose their confidence in their attachment figure's availability and responsiveness, and take refuge in one of two insecure strategies for dealing with their attachment need. In the hyperactivating strategy the individual becomes preoccupied by the attachment need itself, in an ever increasing effort to restore contact with and regain proximity to the attachment figure; in the deactivating strategy individuals actively deny their need for attachment so as to be able to avoid the attachment figure and the anticipated painful consequences (Bowlby, 1973; Dozier & Kobak, 1992). Bowlby proposed that 'confidence in the availability of attachment figures, or the lack of it, is built up slowly during the years of immaturity – infancy, childhood, and adolescence – and that whatever expectations are developed during those years tend to persist relatively unchanged thoughout the rest of life' (1973, p. 235). Gradually security of attachment becomes a feature of the individual's personality structure, thus contributing to behavioural stability, both in time and across different relationships.

Stability of attachment strategies is carried by the concept of the internal working model of attachment which organizes attachment representations, i.e. memories of past attachment experiences and expectations about future ones. Working models are assumed to consist of two interrelated components, i.e. a model of the attachment figure (with all the relevant information relating to the question 'whether or not the attachment figure is judged to be the sort of person who in general responds to calls for support and protection': 1973, p. 238) and a model of self ('whether or not the self is judged to be the sort of person towards whom anyone, and the attachment figure in particular, is likely to respond in a helpful way': 1973, p. 238). The interrelationship between the model of self and of other is defined as follows:

'Logically these variables are independent. In practice they are apt to be confounded. As a result, the model of the attachment figure and the model of the self are likely to develop so as to be complementary and mutually confirming' (1973, p. 238). Hence, it is not surprising that researchers on attachment have generally interpreted the working model of self as a social product (West, 1997).

Experiences in attachment relationships shape the individual's internal working models; once established, working models tend to persist and affect future relationship functioning as well as psychological and physical health (e.g. Bowlby, 1973), or, as Bowlby put it:

> Evidence shows that during the first 2 or 3 years the pattern of attachment is a property of the relationship . . . As a child grows older, however, clinical evidence shows that both the pattern of attachment and the personality features that go with it become increasingly a property of the child himself or herself and also increasingly resistant to change. This means that the child tends to impose it, or some derivative of it, upon new relationships. (1988, p. 5)

Psychological and physical health is affected as attachment insecurity increases the individual's vulnerability to adverse life events and situations:

> it is necessary to think of each personality as moving through life along some developmental pathway, with the particular pathway followed always being determined by the interaction of the personality as it has so far developed and the environment in which it then finds itself . . . So long as family conditions are favorable, the pathway will start and continue within the bounds of healthy and resilient development, but should conditions become sufficiently unfavorable at any time, it may deviate to a lesser or greater extent toward some form of disturbed and vulnerable development. (1988, p. 6)

Figures 20.1 and 20.2 illustrate developmental pathways as the product of interactions between personality and environment. Note that in these illustrations, Bowlby deliberately set aside innate individual differences:

> True, neonates differ from each other in many ways. Yet the evidence is crystal clear from repeated studies that infants described as difficult during their early days are enabled by sensitive mothering to become happy, easy toddlers. Contrariwise, placid newborns can be turned into anxious, moody, demanding or awkward toddlers by insensitive or rejecting mothering. (1988, p. 5).

There seems to be a paradoxical relationship between, on the one hand, the assumption of stability of working models throughout life and their predictive power with regard to psychosocial development, and, on the other hand, the assumption of working models being the product of relational experiences. This paradoxical, or at the very least strained, relationship between the two assumptions is highlighted by some sharp questions that have been troubling writers on attachment for some time, such as the following.

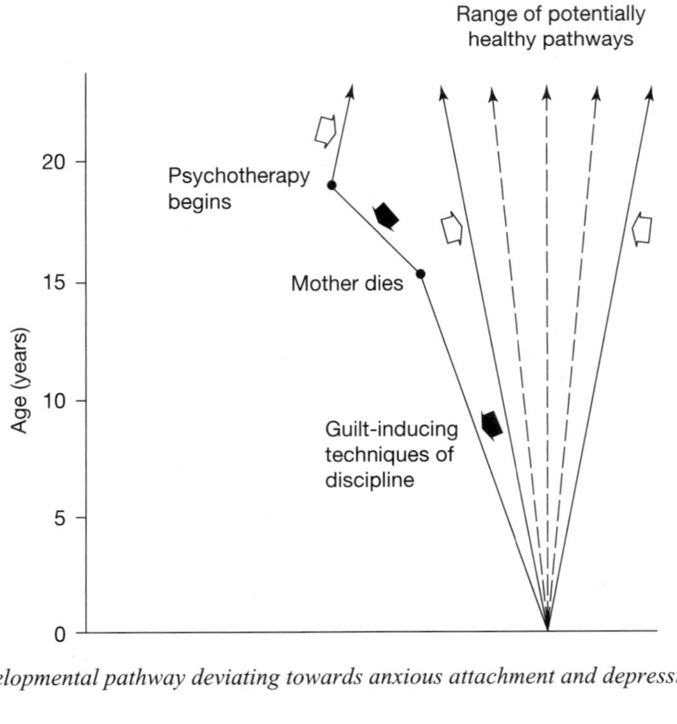

Figure 20.1 *Developmental pathway deviating towards anxious attachment and depression*

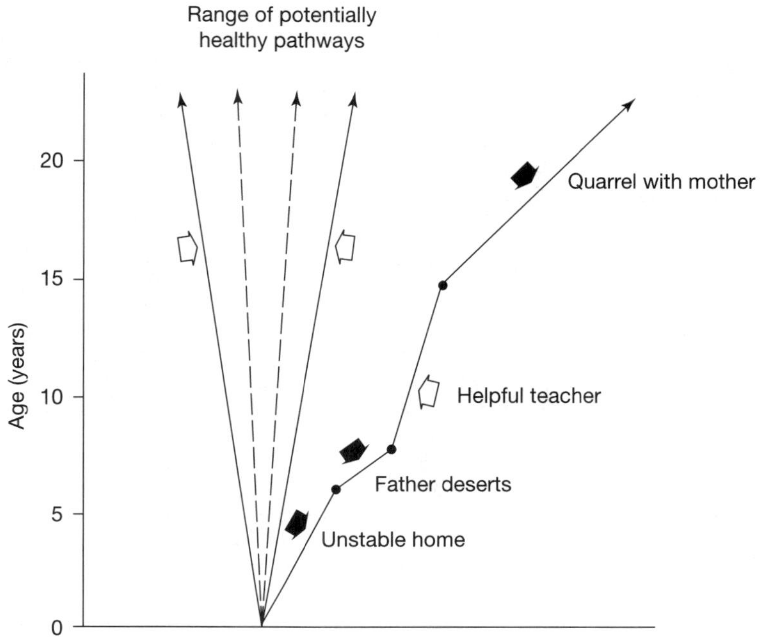

Figure 20.2 *Developmental pathway deviating towards hostility and delinquency*

First of all, it is unclear what exactly happens to the working model (i.e. its self and other components) if the relationship changes. Working models organize memories of past experiences, expectations regarding future encounters, attachment needs and goals, and strategies to meet those (e.g. Collins & Read, 1994) with the primary purpose being to guide the individual's relational functioning. Besides relative stability, attachment theory assumes that working models of attachment are amenable to adaptive change: in order to enhance smooth functioning, new information regarding the relationship must be incorporated (Bowlby, 1988; Main, 1991). How does this change come about; does it affect the self component as much as it does the other component; does the new working model replace the former, or is a new chapter added?

Most individuals are involved in various attachment relationships (e.g. with mother, father, best friend, partner). It is generally assumed that experiences in different relationships are organized in a hierarchical network (e.g. Collins & Read, 1994; Main, 1991) or tangled web (Baldwin et al., 1996) of interrelated general (e.g. self and 'others', self and family) and specific (e.g. self and mother, self and partner) working models. Attachment needs might activate any one of these working models to guide behaviour, dependent on the situation at hand (Collins & Read, 1994). The question then is, how information from various working models becomes integrated into a structure or process that gives the individual's behaviour the stability and predictability proposed by attachment theory: 'does the most important relationship predominate, is there a balance between differing relationships, or does one secure relationship compensate for insecurities in others? No satisfactory explanation has been found and tested' (Rutter, 1995, p. 554).

Furthermore, there is the, fortunately not uncommon, observation that individuals may have secure strategies for dealing with their attachment needs despite decidedly adverse experiences in their attachment relationships (e.g. Fonagy et al., 1994; Main & Goldwyn, 1998; Rutter, 1995; West, 1997). Given his concern for those who have to grow up in unfortunate family environments, it is easy to see why Bowlby (1988) dealt with the phenomenon by considering these resilient individuals as exceptions to the rule (comparing them to heavy smokers who do survive); others (e.g. Main and colleagues, Fonagy and colleagues, West), however, have moved the issue into the spotlight in their efforts to tackle the question as to what, exactly, accounts for this 'security against the odds'.

Finally, empirical studies generally prove attachment security to be an inconsistent, if not poor, predictor of subsequent psychosocial development and psychopathology (e.g. Liable & Thompson, 2000; Oatley & Jenkins, 1996). Yet psychiatric populations show a distinct overrepresentation of individuals classified as insecurely attached (van IJzendoorn & Bakermans-Kranenburg, 1996). Although such findings are in accord with Bowlby's view that 'we need to picture each personality as moving through life along its own unique pathway' (1988, p. 6), there is still much confusion about the factors, conditions, and mechanisms contributing to healthy and deviant pathways. A number of questions arise: what is the role of temperamental differences (Fox, 1995); what promotes 'repair' of initial damage (Collins & Read, 1994; Main & Goldwyn, 1998); does attachment insecurity contribute to the development of psychopathology, or is it an epiphenomenon of the experience of relational disturbances and/or psychiatric conditions (e.g. Gerlsma, 2000; Pielage, Gerlsma, & Schaap, 2000)?

Theoretical dilemmas such as these described above, together with the steady growth of studies on adult attachment as well as the historically older tradition of infant research, moved the nature and role of internal working models to the centre of attention. In recent developments, elaborations of Bowlby's internal working model concept have evolved that generally emphasize the role of the individual's active thought processes (Mace & Margison, 1997; Rutter, 1995), i.e. (re)constructive powers in autobiography, including metacognitive monitoring (Main, 1991), narrative styles (Holmes, 1997; Main & Goldwyn, 1998), and reflective self-capacity (Fonagy et al., 1991; 1993; 1994). Within these elaborations the capacity to (re)construct and manipulate the meanings of experiences and their implications for self depends in large part on the quality of attachment relationships in early childhood (Fonagy et al., 1991; 1993; 1994; Holmes, 1997; Main, 1991).

On the basis of theories and findings with regard to metacognitive processes, Main (1991) elaborated Bowlby's suggestion that 'unfavourable interaction patterns with attachment figures may render the young child vulnerable to the development of multiple models of the attachment figure, and, relatedly, to the development of multiple models of the self' (1973, p.136). The multiple (or incoherent) model notion refers to the existence of multiple and contradictory models of the same object (e.g. self), that is, models that cannot be true at the same time. Multiplicity or incoherence is contrasted with singularity, that is, integration and coherence, of working models. The development of singular, as opposed to multiple, models of others and self largely depends on the metacognitive processing of attachment relevant information: 'where multiple contradictory models of the self or of experience exist, either metacognitive knowledge has yet to develop or there have been failures of corrective metacognitive monitoring' (Main, 1991, p. 134). Metacognitive capacities, i.e. the ability to 'think about thought', to consider one's own feelings and cognitions as the object of thought and reflection, to understand representational diversity and change, only start to develop around the age of 3 years, which makes young children especially vulnerable to the development of multiple models. Once developed, the organization of representations in multiple, implicitly contradictory models hampers metacognitive functioning: 'metacognitive monitoring will almost certainly be more difficult when models are difficult to access, or when information is distorted or disorganized' (1991, p. 146). In short, without the necessary metacognitive capacities, infants and young children cannot but defensively construct multiple models of self in the face of adverse or contradictory attachment experiences; once established, the existence of multiple models hampers the metacognitive processing necessary to reintegrate and reconcile the contradictory selves. The existence of multiple models is enacted in insecure attachment behaviour by infants and young children, and reflected in the incoherent narrative styles of adults in their discussion of attachment themes.

Fonagy et al. (1991; 1993; 1994) delineate a specific metacognitive ability to account for security of attachment, i.e. reflective self-capacity. They also describe reflective self-capacity, among others, as the individual's 'capacity to think of their own and others' actions in terms of mental states, in the specific context of attachment relationships' (1994, p. 241). Holmes called it 'insight in a researchable guise' (1997, p. 237). The level and quality of reflective self-capacity depends primarily on the quality of parent–child interactions in childhood and adolescence, and involves a shift in the level of attachment representations as children develop from a pre-reflective stage to a reflective or psychological stage. In the pre-reflective stage of early childhood, attachment representations will be based on 'physical attributes, superficial categorizations of people over concrete interpretations of their actions', whereas in the reflective stage such representations involve 'mental experiences, feelings, perceptions, beliefs and so on, as well as reflections upon these experiences in mental state terms' (1994, p. 247). Reflective self-capacity develops as children carefully monitor their caregiver's mental states, i.e. the caregiver's perception, interpretation, attribution, and organization, in short understanding, of themselves. Hence, development of reflective self-capacity depends, to a large extent, on the caregiver's ability to provide the child with a 'creative social mirror,' which, in turn, depends on the caregiver's own reflective self-capacity.

Theoretical developments such as described above, together with findings from the empirical studies they generated, have led to yet other formulations that await empirical examination. For instance, Holmes postulates a 'triangle of attachment' built around the concepts of attachment (the product of secure base experiences in childhood and the starting point of intimacy in adulthood), detachment (the capacity to experience and express healthy protest and the basis of autonomy), and non-attachment, with 'the capacity to reflect on oneself, and so to disidentify with painful or traumatic experience' (1997, p. 231). The latter, closely resembling Fonagy's reflective self-capacity, is responsible for the integration of the individual's many (aspects of) different selves. It derives from early experiences becoming internalized as self-narratives (Meares, 1993): sensitivity on the part of the caregiver, i.e. responsiveness without intrusiveness combined with the ability to accept healthy protest, enhances the acquisition of inner speech, as it, 'in a typical Winnicottian paradox, enables the child to forget [the parent], and to concentrate on the self-exploration that is the essence of solitary play. If, on the other hand, the [parent] is unavailable, or inconsistent, or unattuned, the child will be forced to think about her parent, and so be liable to forget herself' (Holmes, 1997, p. 238).

West (1997), on the other hand, points out that in their efforts to work out the Winnicottian paradox (parental presence and attunement as a prerequisite for autonomy and the development of true self), writers on attachment have generally tended to overaccent the relational origins of the organization of self, in line with Bowlby's view of the working model of self as inextricably interwoven with the working model of others and, hence, of self as an essentially social self. Both the 'security against the odds' phenomenon (i.e. individuals who develop coherent working models despite gross negligence or abuse in their attachment relationships) and the emphasis on narrative and autobiographical competence in recent attachment research show that 'the experience of self may be creatively transformed from within'. While writers on attachment (e.g. Bretherton, 1985; Fonagy et al., 1994) do recognize a biologically based, innate need to construct and maintain coherence of self, which underlies the development of capacities such as reflective self-capacity and metacognitive monitoring, they tend to focus on the relational experiences that mediate the development of coherence promoting capacities rather than the need for coherence *per se* and the self-generative nature of self. These considerations have led West (1997) to call attention to the role of the 'private self' in the construction of working models of self.

An entirely different approach has been suggested by Liable and Thompson (2000). Picturing 'each personality as moving through life along its own unique developmental pathway' (Bowlby, 1988, p. 6) calls for a dynamic systems approach that allows attachment patterns to be conceptualized as 'dynamic and thus more flexible, adaptive, and context-specific than traditional attachment theory would suggest' (Liable & Thompson, 2000, p. 318); it also allows relationships among individual, dyadic and contextual influences to be non-linear (see also Granic, 2000). Based on the idea that order emerges through the coupling of basic interdependent elements of, say, parent–child interactions into a higher-level order, a dynamic systems approach can account for stability of attachment behaviour as well as rapid and radical change. Stability in the parent–child system arises on the basis of feedback processes that reinforce the coupling of basic elements into recursive patterns of interaction; however, at particular points (so called bifurcation points) in the parent–child system's development (e.g. maturation, birth of a sibling, starting school, a change in mother's work arrangements) 'small fluctuations have the potential to disproportionally affect the status of other elements, leading to the emergence of new forms' (Granic, 2000, p. 275). In a similar vein, a dynamic systems approach can account for relationship specificity of attachment patterns; the interactional pattern 'entrained' in the parent–child system may never be elicited in other, new relationships due to their unique constellation of basic elements. This view implies that Bowlby's view of the social self that develops on the basis of interactional patterns in attachment relationships may come in different guises and may be subject to radical change.

Attachment Research: Methodology and Measurement

Attachment needs and strategies for dealing with it are with us for life (e.g. Bowlby, 1973; 1988). Empirical research that traces the development of attachment across the lifespan is hampered by the complexities involved in the development of age-appropriate instruments for assessment (Fox, 1995; Owens et al., 1995). Adding to the complexities involved in any endeavour to construct age-appropriate analogues is, in the case of attachment, the crucial role of stress as an elicitor of attachment behaviour, feelings, and cognitions. In order to assess attachment patterns, the attachment system should be activated by 'felt insecurity', i.e. tiredness or distress, threatening features in the environment, or separation from the attachment figure (Rutter, 1995), so as to ascertain the measurement of *relevant* behaviours, feelings, and cognitions (e.g. Simpson & Rholes, 1994). Furthermore, the measurement domain in terms of (the most) relevant attachment relationship should be carefully defined. In adolescence and adulthood, when relationships can be more a matter of choice, care should be taken to make sure that an apparently close relationship actually is an attachment relationship, that is, a selective dyadic relationship with someone deemed a secure base from which to explore and accept challenge, a safe haven to turn to when in distress or a cooperative partner to seek out when involved in conflict (Kobak & Duemmler, 1994). Meeting these criteria requires different methodologies in different age groups.

Infant Attachment

Attachment in the very young – infants ranging in age from approximately 9 to 24 months – is usually assessed by means of a laboratory procedure called the Strange Situation (Ainsworth & Wittig, 1969; Ainsworth et al., 1978) in which the infant's behaviour is observed and videotaped. The session is divided into seven 3 minute sequences, each of which was designed to elicit a particular behaviour, e.g. explorative behaviour in the presence of the parent, reactions to separations from and reunion with the parent, reactions to a stranger with and without the parent present. While each type of these behaviours is essentially guided by the attachment system (activation of which is assured by the novelty and, indeed, strangeness of the situation), attachment classification is derived primarily from the infant's behaviour upon reunion with the parent after a separation (e.g. Belsky et al., 1996). Infants who are classified secure (group B) actively seek contact and proximity to their parent upon reunion, and, when distressed by the separation, are easily comforted. Insecure-avoidant babies (group A) tend to actively avoid or ignore their parent after separations (deactivating strategy), whereas infants classified as insecure-resistant (group C) are angry and demanding towards their parent yet resist being comforted by them (hyperactivating strategy). Finally, disorganized babies (D) lack a coherent strategy to deal with their attachment needs and show a mixture of the patterns described above, often including a display of contradictory and disoriented behaviours (e.g. freezing, odd movements, dropping to the floor); besides the D classification, a secondary, best fitting A, B, or C classification is chosen for these children.

The Strange Situation procedure is intended to assess behavioural patterns that characterize particular dyadic relationships (e.g. infant–mother, infant–father), in line with the attachment theoretical assumption that the attachment concept applies to selective dyadic relationships so that 'security of attachment reflects, in large part, variations in maternal [*sic*] behaviour' (Schneider Rosen & Rothbaum, 1993, p. 358). Secure attachment is taken to reflect consistent responsiveness on the part of the caregiver; insecure-resistant attachment would be related to inconsistent responsiveness; insecure-avoidant attachment relates to consistent non-responsiveness; and disorganized attachment is considered the consequence of extremely negative, i.e. abusive and traumatic or frightening parenting experiences (van IJzendoorn, Schuengel, & Bakermans-Kranenburg, 1999). Because the caregiver's behaviour is not explicitly rated in the Strange Situation's coding system, additional measures are necessary to corroborate this assumption. Initial studies, in which a wide variety of measures on parental responsiveness were used, were puzzling as they generally found inconsistent and small associations with infant attachment status (see reviews in Goldsmith & Alansky, 1987; Schneider Rosen & Rothbaum, 1993). Only extremely negative forms of parenting, including abusive parenting, appeared to be strongly related to insecurity of attachment (Schneider Rosen & Rothbaum, 1993). An explanation for the lack of a firm and consistent association between parental responsiveness and infant attachment status might, according to Fonagy et al., be that the studies have compounded two rather different processes, i.e. on the one hand the parent's attitude and behaviour towards the child (e.g. more or less positive feelings, warmth, affection, accessibility, acceptance) and, on the other hand, his or her ability 'to envisage the infant as a mental entity, a human being with intentions, feelings, and desires' (1993, p. 246). The latter capacity does seem to capture the individual differences in parental responsiveness that affect infant attachment status (Fonagy et al., 1991; 1993; 1994). As these authors put it:

> Defensive behaviours are probably commonly used by all infants in the face of stressful situations. Their use in the laboratory upon reunion with the primary object may indicate frequent recourse to defensive strategies in the face of repeated and painful failures of past attempts at the communication of distress . . . The defensive-insecure pattern of the Strange Situation may mark the caregiver's history of failure to picture the infant's mental state. (1993, p. 978)

This view builds on the theory and research surrounding the assessment of adult attachment status as initiated by Main and her colleagues.

Adult Attachment

The Adult Attachment Interview (AAI: George, Kaplan, & Main, 1985; Main & Goldwyn, 1998) 'was developed with the aim of differentiating mental representations of attachment-related experiences in parents whose infants had been judged to differ in patterns of attachment behaviour as assessed in the Ainsworth Strange Situation' (van IJzendoorn, 1995, p. 389). It is now used to assess security of attachment from late adolescence. The AAI is a semi-structured interview with a focus on past attachment experiences, that is, daily interactions with primary caregivers in childhood as well as explicit attachment behaviour eliciting events (such as separations, death, divorce, abuse and other traumatic experiences); furthermore, the interview pays attention to individuals' views as to how these early experiences have affected their life. Interviews are transcribed verbatim and coded by expert raters. Classification of individuals in secure and insecure attachment categories is based on psycholinguistic analysis of the transcripts. Central to the distinction between secure and insecure categories is adherence to Grice's (1975) maxims of cooperative discourse, such as the criteria of quality ('be truthful and have evidence for what you say') and quantity ('be succinct and yet complete'). Violations of these psycholinguistic rules are inferred from the extent to which the speaker exhibits particular communicative difficulties with regard to attachment themes, in particular as reflected in the incoherence of his or her narrative and the inaccessibility of his or her attachment representations (Main, 1991; Main & Goldwyn, 1998). Individuals in the 'secure' (F) group feel 'free to evaluate attachment information' (Dozier & Kobak, 1992, p. 1474) and value intimate relationships, irrespective of the nature of their experiences. Hence, 'secure' adults may recall sensitive, responsive parenting (as in 'continuous secure' individuals) or have recollections of adversity (as in 'earned secure' individuals); the decisive factors for their classification as 'secure' are the coherence of their narrative and the relative ease with which they recall childhood experiences. Individuals classified as 'dismissing of attachment' (D) tend to idealize their attachment figures, but fail to recall childhood experiences that might evidence these extremely positive descriptions. Their insistence on an inability to recall attachment experiences and a tendency to downplay adversity and minimize the importance of intimate relationships are taken to reflect a deactivating strategy for dealing with attachment themes. Individuals classified as 'preoccupied' or 'enmeshed' (E) show a hyperactive strategy, which is inferred from their expressions of ongoing anger towards attachment figures and from obvious contradictions in their narrative. Like the 'secure' adults, those with a 'preoccupied' attachment orientation generally have easy access to their childhood memories, but unlike the individuals in the secure category, are likely to get entangled in detail without being able to give the impression of an objective and coherent account of their personal history. Finally, some adults' narratives are given an additional classification resembling the Strange Situation's disorganized category: 'unresolved mourning' (U) is inferred from the individual's expression of signs of continuing disorganization due to the loss of an attachment figure.

It is assumed that the topics addressed by the AAI are sufficiently emotionally involving to ensure attachment system activation. As to the domain of attachment relationships addressed, the AAI emphasizes childhood attachment (primarily parent–child) relationships in order to infer from the interviewee's reconstructed autobiography his or her overall state of mind with regard to attachment (Main, 1991); they have established 'a set of rules for the organization of information relevant to attachment and for obtaining or limiting access to that information' (Main, Kaplan, & Cassidy, 1985, p. 67). Hence, contrary to the Strange Situation, the AAI seems to classify individuals rather than dyadic relationships (e.g. Rutter, 1995), reflecting the assumption that by the time one reaches late adolescence the experiences in one's various attachment relationships have been integrated and internalized into an individual characteristic (Bowlby, 1973).

In order to assess reflective self-capacity, Fonagy et al. (1991) constructed an additional scale that is rated on the basis of AAI transcripts. Low scores are assigned to individuals who seem unwilling or unable to reflect on their own or others' intentions; high scores characterize individuals who clearly demonstrate a capacity to reflect on and understand psychological states, including the conscious and unconscious intentions underlying their own and others' behaviour.

Attachment: Questions of Stability and Change

Working models of attachment are assumed to be stable as well as amenable to adaptive change. Although based on actual (infant, childhood, and adolescent) relational experiences in various attachment relationships, they gradually become a feature of the individual's personality structure (Bowlby, 1973). Once established, the stability of internal working models is promoted by their tendency to function as a self-confirming mechanism. Working models guide the individual's choice of attachment figures, and social situations entered during attachment system activation colour their appraisal of their own and others' behaviour in the attachment relationship, and thereby affect attachment behaviour. All of this helps to reconstruct the kind of situation that confirms earlier experiences and existent expectations, as organized in the working model. Most writers on attachment assume that change is only likely to occur in the case of the experience of a life event with a very strong emotional impact or a relational experience of sufficiently long duration and emotional meaning to challenge the existing working model (Bowlby, 1988; Collins & Read, 1994; Crittenden, 1995; Gerlsma & Luteijn, 2000; Main, 1991; see Liable & Thompson, 2000, and Granic, 2000, for alternative views). Just how stressful or ameliorative these experiences need to be in order to affect a change in attachment status remains unclear (Fox, 1995).

Within a developmental framework these considerations lead to different expectations with regard to the continuity versus change issue for infants and young children, adolescents and adults. Infant attachment classifications are assumed to reflect unique characteristics of the dyadic relationship, and not intrinsic child features or contextual factors. Infants do not yet have the cognitive competence required to represent discrepancies between different relationships (e.g. the infant–mother versus the infant–father relationship) or discrepancies within the same relationship (due to a change in the attachment figure's behaviour towards the child: Main, 1991; Rutter, 1995). Hence, in infancy and early childhood attachment status might be expected to be subject to change and be relatively unstable in time as well as across relationships (cf. Bowlby, 1973;

1988). After early childhood, when cognitive competence increases, experiences in different relationships become increasingly integrated, so that security of attachment becomes a characteristic of the individual rather than a feature of a particular dyadic relationship. In late adolescence and adulthood, continuity of attachment status in time as well as across relationships is expected (cf. Bowlby, 1973; 1988).

In discussing research findings with regard to the continuity versus change issue we will distinguish two type of continuity, i.e. continuity in time and continuity across relationships. Both types have been studied in infant as well as adult attachment research but little is yet known about the actual stability from infancy to adulthood (Fox, 1995; Oppenheim & Salatas-Waters, 1995; Owens et al., 1995; van IJzendoorn, 1995).

Attachment: Main Developmental Findings

Stability in Time

Despite the theoretical considerations described above, infant attachment classifications were generally assumed to be stable from the end of the first year to the end of the second year of life. Belsky et al. (1996) trace this belief to the very first study on this issue, which reported a stability rate of 96% (Waters, 1978); as these authors report, subsequent studies fell some 20% short of this rate, with a weighted average between 67% and 75%. In their own large sample study, Belsky et al. (1996) report non-significant stability rates which ranged from 46% to 55%, a finding that could not be attributed to their participants being at risk for biological or contextual reasons.

Several studies have examined the stability of adult attachment classifications in time, foremost with the aim to assess the instrument's test–retest reliability. Time intervals were therefore generally short, e.g. 1 month interval with a stability rate of 77% (Steele & Steele, 1994); 2 month interval with a stability rate of 78% (Bakermans-Kranenburg & van IJzendoorn, 1993); 3 month interval with a stability rate of 90% (Sagi et al., 1994). In studies that assessed continuity across a longer time interval (18 months), stability rates of 90% (Benoit & Parker, 1994) and 88% (Owens et al., 1995) were reported. Hence, compared to infants, adult attachment status seems to be somewhat more stable.

Stability across Relationships

Stability of infant attachment across different relationships is generally inferred from the concordance of infant–mother and infant–father classifications. For the organized attachment classifications (secure, anxious-resistant, and anxious-avoidant), van IJzendoorn and DeWolff (1997) report a significant but small standardized effect size of $r = 0.17$; for the disorganized attachment category the effect size was non-significant at $r = 0.10$ (van IJzendoorn, Schuengle, & Bakermans-Kranenburg, 1999). These averages suggest that infant attachment classification depends to a large extent on unique dyadic characteristics.

Because the AAI's primary intention is to measure individuals' 'overall state of mind with regard to attachment', the question of stability across relationships seems at first glance irrelevant for adult attachment classifications: the terminology suggests that such classifications as derived from the AAI would, by definition, apply to all one's attachment relationships. Studies by Crowell and her colleagues suggest that this is not the case. As an analogue to the AAI, Crowell (see Owens et al., 1995) developed the Current Relationship Interview (CRI) to assess attachment representations that evolve in the context of the current romantic relationship. In a fashion similar to the AAI, security of attachment in the current relationship is inferred from the interviewee's state of mind (coherence and accessibility of representations) regarding this attachment theme. Owens et al. (1995) reported significant but moderate intraindividual concordance rates between CRI and AAI classifications (64% for the secure/insecure split), indicating that one can be secure as a spouse despite insecurity as one's parents' child (and vice versa of course). In a related vein, Waters et al. (1993) showed that narrative style in the AAI was unrelated to narrative style in the discussion of a non-attachment theme (i.e. job experiences).

Stability of adult attachment status in time as well as across relationships is often inferred from the concordance between parents' AAI classification and their offspring's Strange Situation classification. In a meta-analysis on a total of $N = 854$ parent–child dyads by van IJzendoorn (1995) this concordance amounted to 75% for the secure/insecure split; Fonagy et al. (1991; 1994) showed that reflective self-capacity as coded from parents' AAI transcripts proved an even better predictor of the security status of their (at the time of AAI assessment unborn) children. The way parents view the relationships with their own parents seems to affect the relationships with their child who, subsequently, enacts this relationship specific attachment pattern in the Strange Situation procedure. Given the fact that this particular type of concordance involves different methodologies as well as different people (observation units: Campbell & Fiske, 1959), the correspondence is striking indeed, but, as was cogently argued by Fox (1995), without longitudinal data that trace the development of attachment status from infancy to adulthood, not necessarily indicative of stability: coherence and accessibility of parents' attachment representations may have little to do with their actual experiences in early childhood or with their early attachment status.

Conclusions and Discussion

Overall, instability or change of attachment status appears to be less exceptional than has been generally asserted by writers on attachment. The emphasis on stability of attachment across the lifespan was summarized by Fox (1995) in four basic tenets; we will discuss the literature reviewed above within the framework of this summary.

> (1) The primary attachment relationship develops during the 1st year of life and is a function of the quality of maternal caregiving. (1995, p. 405)

It proved difficult to establish those features of mothers' caregiving that determine their children's attachment quality. The rule of thumb has been to consider secure attachment the consequence of consistent sensitive and responsive parenting, anxious-resistant attachment the consequence of inconsistent parental sensitivity and responsivity, avoidant attachment the consequence of consistent insensitivity and non-responsiveness, and disorganized attachment the consequence of extremely negative, abusive and/or frightening parental behaviour. Efforts to operationalize parental sensitivity and responsiveness have, however, generally yielded inconsistent results. Recent studies suggest that parents' own attachment status and reflective self-capacity are decisive factors in the development of their children's attachment orientation. As before, empirical studies are needed to explore the ways in which these parental characteristics are enacted in the infant–parent interaction.

> (2) The relationship that develops during the 1st year of life is critical to the subsequent cognitive and socioemotional development of the child, and this primary relationship represents the essential working model on which all other models are based. (1995, p. 405)

This tenet implies, among others, that all working models will resemble the model of the infant–mother relationship, at least as far as the features that determine attachment status are concerned. In the literature reviewed above it became apparent that infants and adults show different, that is, discordant, attachment status in different relationships. Such discordance is contrary to the interpretation of the infant–mother model as a blueprint, on the basis of which all subsequent models are simply replicated. To put it differently, models of new relationships may be based on the infant–mother model in the sense that the primary model is the frame of reference for subsequent models, but this does not imply that attachment status with mother determines attachment status in other relationships. Assessment and comparison of individuals' working models of various attachment relationships (e.g. with mother, father, current partner, best friend) will be necessary to elucidate the role of the primary working model in the development of later models (Gerlsma & Luteijn, 2000; Owens et al., 1995).

> (3) The working model of attachment developed in the 1st year of life and seen as so primary or essential to subsequent psychological development remains stable over developmental time. (1995, p. 406)

Infant attachment status appeared to be more volatile than was generally assumed. As Belsky et al. put it: 'it now seems inappropriate to assume that stability rather than instability is the norm' (1996, p. 924). The instability of infant attachment status begs the question as to when exactly, after infancy, the working model emerges that will ultimately remain stable over developmental time: 'there would seem to be more need than ever before for renewed efforts to understand whether instability is "lawful", resulting from things going on in children's lives, or instead reflects simple measurement error or even just maturation' (1996, p. 924).

> (4) Behavior in the Strange Situation is relationship specific; that is, the infant's behavior towards the caregiver, and hence the attachment quality that is derived, is unique for the infant and that caregiver. (1995, p. 408)

The literature reviewed above shows discordance of infant–mother and infant–father classifications, and of adult–parents and adult–romantic partner classifications. This discordance might be taken as evidence for the relationship specificity of attachment quality; indeed, the pertinent empirical studies generally welcome discordance as proof that attachment status originates in relational experience, and not in biological or contextual factors. Although perhaps welcome in this respect, the apparent relationship specificity of attachment quality also suggests a need to follow unique attachment patterns over ontogenetic time. As yet, those working on attachment have shown little interest in doing that, perhaps because relationship specificity is slightly at odds with the second tenet, i.e. that the working model of the infant–mother relationship forms the basis for all other working models.

As to the organization of self, the coexistence of working models of various relationships in both infancy and adulthood seems to corroborate Bowlby's notion of self as a social product, albeit with the note that this idea of self may come in different guises as part of different working models: despite being entangled in the relationship with one's mother or, on the contrary, dismissing childhood adversity as of no consequence, secure (autonomous, free) working models of new relationships can be built. Future studies might benefit from an integrated assessment of the individual's various relevant working models in order to examine the possibility that those with discordant working models of different relationships (and, relatedly, of self) actually recognize and to a certain extent accept discrepancies in their social selves, a cognitive process that seems to be implied by Main's metacognitive monitoring and Fonagy's reflective self-capacity, and is explicated in Holmes' non-attachment concept: 'non-attachment underlies narrative or autobiographical competence, the search for meaning, reaching towards a sense of self, and an ability to observe and accept things as they are without being overwhelmed with envy or destructiveness' (1997, p. 245). Non-attachment refers to a 'space into which to "go" in order to get a perspective on oneself and the environment' (1997, p. 245), and reflects trust in one's own feelings and judgements. It is only when non-attachment cannot be achieved that the sense of self in attachment relationships disintegrates and disappears.

The Development of the Self-Concept

Theoretical Background

The working model of an attachment relationship has two main components: a model of the attachment figure, and a model of self. Different relationships can lead to different working models and consequently to different models of self. A pertinent question in attachment research then becomes the organization of these different models within one person's mind.

Self-representations (self-concept) research already has a long tradition of struggling with such questions. In this research the focus is on the knowledge individuals have with regard to themselves, on how they perceive, understand and evaluate themselves. This knowledge is stored in the self-concept (or self-system), a cognitive system, a structure of self-representations. The literature is replete with ideas on the content, the nature, the organization, and the function of this structure.

One generally accepted differentiation in the self-concept is James' (1890) distinction between 'I' and 'me.' The 'I' refers to the subjective experience of the person, the person who knows, the person who manages and constructs self-knowledge (self as 'knower,' self as 'agent'); the 'me' refers to the knowledge the person has of himself or herself (self as 'known'). James thought that the I as the pure subjectivity of experience was inaccessible for scientific study. The me, in contrast, could be studied with standardized and objective methods. In his idea, the I should not be seen as part of the self-concept. More recently researchers have argued that aspects of the I are accessible through the me, for example, by looking at how individuals experience their subjectivity, how they experience themselves as knowers and agents. According to the same line of reasoning, structural aspects of the self-concept can be seen as resulting from the agency of the person: how is the self-concept structured? Is it internally consistent or full of contrasts? Does it comprise global and diffuse or highly specific self-descriptions? When it comes to such questions, the distinction between I and me is no longer of much use in guiding empirical research. James' distinction also has something in common with the differences between self-concept and ego-identity psychology: self-concept psychology at first tended to focus on me-phenomena while ego-identity psychology studies phenomena which many self-concept researchers have associated with the I.

Next to structural issues researchers can also study the content of the self-concept. Which characteristics do individuals use to describe themselves: physical, social, psychological, etc.? And how strongly are these self-descriptions tied to the situation individuals find themselves in? The content of the self-concept can be situation- and role-specific. For this reason researchers often make a differentiation in self-concepts: how I see my self as a teacher, as a partner, as a mother, etc. This brings us back to the question of the structural integration of these different self-concepts. Most authors tend to think in terms of a hierarchy, at the bottom with very specific and at the top with very abstract and general concepts. Another important differentiation has to do with the emotional values of the self-concept; some aspects of the self are valued positively, some neutral and some (very) negatively. How positive or negative is the self-concept in general? This latter evaluative aspect of the self-concept is often referred to in terms of 'self-esteem'.

Self-concept research is done in the various subdisciplines of psychology, most notably in social and personality psychology (e.g. Ashmore & Jussim, 1997; Baumeister, 1999). Self-concepts can also be studied from a developmental perspective. How does the self-concept develop – in content, in organization – from infancy into middle childhood and adolescence and adulthood? How stable is it? How much does it change across the lifespan? What about the variability and stability of one's self-esteem? In this chapter we will focus on such developmental questions. But first let us turn to issues of methodology and measures.

Development of the Self-Concept: Methodology and Measures

Conceptions and the assessment of the self-concept have changed over time (van der Meulen, 2001). In the 1950s through 1970s the self-concept was seen as a relatively stable and general set of descriptive characteristics that could be assessed with self-report methods. Two types of method dominated in this period (overviews are given by Wylie, 1979; 1989). On the one hand, lists of trait names were used (often in the form of adjectives), sometimes in combination with multiple directions, such as 'How do these traits describe you, *as you are*?' and 'How do these traits describe you *as you would like to be*?' On the other hand, free descriptions elicited by questions such as 'Who are you?', 'How would you like to be?' were used. Differences in directions represent different self-perspectives (e.g. 'how I see myself', 'how I hope to be in the future', 'how I think my parents see me'). With regard to the content of the self-concept, the two approaches yield rather different results. Physical characteristics, or characteristics referring to gender or activities, were often found with the 'who are you?' technique (e.g. 'I am a tall man', 'I am a good soccer player') but hardly ever featured in research using trait lists. The traits in trait lists were usually chosen by the researcher and they almost always focus on psychological qualities which form a minor category in the 'who are you?' data. Factor analyses of trait list data have given insight into the dimensionality and structure of the self-concept. One important dimension is the evaluative one: how positively or negatively individuals evaluate themselves. The study of self-esteem has become an important domain in itself. Several Likert-type paper-and-pencil measures have been developed. Harter's (1982) Self-Perception Profiles for Children and for Adolescents (see below) form good examples. A recent review of self-esteem measures is given by Keith and Bracken (1996).

From the 1980s on the insight grew that situational variation in the self-concept could not be ignored (e.g. Markus & Nurius, 1986; Markus & Wurf, 1987). The idea of a stable and generalized set of beliefs individuals hold about themselves gradually became replaced by more dynamic notions (Markus & Wurf, 1987: the 'working self'). A second change concerned the role of emotions. Purely cognitive conceptualizations were complemented by models in which affect also played a role. In her review of these changes van der Meulen concluded that

> The set of beliefs the person has about him- or herself, (a) is not an exclusively cognitive matter, but something that is in several ways closely associated with affect, (b) does not (solely) concern general, decontextualized beliefs, but beliefs that emerge in close interaction with the physical, social and cultural context, and (c) consists of both more or less enduring, stable beliefs as well as more short-term, variable ones. (2001, p. 29)

These changes have profound implications for the measurement of the self-concept and its development. In repeated measurement designs stable aspects should be differentiated from context-bound variation; next to self-report methods, the study of research participants in situations that evoke emotional responses (with the observation of facial expressions and the assessment of physiological indicators) is necessary. Such data on developmental change and stability of the dynamic self, collected in complex designs and with multiple methods, are still scarce. The developmental findings to be presented in the next section are almost exclusively based on self-report paper-and-pencil measures and observations of the pre-literate child collected in cross-sectionally designed studies.

Development of the Self-Concept: Questions of Stability and Change

When the self-concept was seen as a stable cognitive structure, change was not expected to occur. In most studies the measure of this static property was correlated to other aspects of the person. More recent conceptualizations within social psychology acknowledge the context-dependent variation in the self-concept, and see it as a more dynamic structure. How this structure develops from infancy into adulthood is an entirely different issue. When the self-concept is seen as a cognitive construction, the developmental progression in cognitive competence and skills in childhood and adolescence must strongly influence the various aspects of the self-concept. From this perspective, there is every reason to expect that the content and structure of the self-concept will change with age. Which, indeed, is found in empirical research (see below).

An individual's self-esteem is much less clearly linked to cognitive development. Social, affective and motivational factors probably play a more decisive role in a person's self-evaluation. There are no firm reasons to expect strong and general age-related changes in self-esteem. Data generally confirm this expectation. Young children describe themselves very positively. In middle childhood these self-evaluations become more realistic and less positive (see below). In early adolescence another decline in self-esteem occurs. This decline is related to a number of factors: the educational transition to junior high school; the physical, cognitive, social, and emotional changes of puberty, and the timing of puberty. Later in adolescence, self-esteem tends to rise again. Stable interindividual differences in self-esteem are much more important. They strongly outweigh intraindividual change (Harter, 1998).

Development of the Self-Concept: Main Developmental Findings

According to Harter (1998) only very recently has it become possible to give an integrated account of the development of self in infancy. Earlier accounts (Harter, 1983) gave separate discussions of the models that were then available (e.g. Piaget's work on early cognitive development, Ainsworth's and Mahler's work). Newer approaches to infant self-development share some major assumptions that make an integration feasible. Newborns have a biological predisposition to engage in social interaction, and some organization of self exists at the outset and resides in the system of infant and caregiver. The following account of the development of self-representations from infancy through adolescence follows Harter's (1998) review. Other overviews are given by Damon and Hart (1988) and Demo (1992). The empirically well-established normative developmental changes are summarized in Table 20.1.

Infancy

The idea of Mahler and the early Piagetians that the infant of 0 to 4 months is in an undifferentiated, symbiotic state with the mother is refuted by recent research. Already from birth onwards there is some regulation between caregiver and infant in which both play an active role. A supramodal representational system (not linked to one specific input channel such as hearing or taste) enables infants to perceive self-invariance and other-invariance in their stream of experience. Case (in Harter, 1998) speaks of 'small islands of sensory-affective coherence'. Affect plays a crucial role in these processes (Fogel, 1993; Harter, 1998; Stern, 1985).

The period of 4 to 10 months is characterized by many new achievements. The increase in differentiation from the caregiver forms the basis for new levels of relatedness. The child's behaviour shows indications of separation stress and proximity seeking; processes of separation and attachment are in the making. It also shows clear indications of agency and self-efficacy. All these achievements occur in the context of intensive interactions with a 'self-regulating other' (e.g. games like walking fingers and peekaboo). Internal representations of such interactions that have been generalized (Stern, 1985: RIGs) can be seen as the elementary working models of relationships.

In the period of 10–15 months the self–other differentiation increases but attachment and exploration are still strongly linked: separation/exploration is possible, but caregivers must be available to provide a 'secure base'. A rudimentary 'theory of mind' develops; the child begins to learn that he or she and other persons have a mind of their own. Subjective experiences can be shared: the child, for example, becomes able to follow another's line of vision or gesture of pointing. Toddlers of this age also become able to share intentions and affective

Table 20.1 *Harter's overview of the development of self-representations*

Age period	Structure/organization	Salient content	Valence/accuracy
Toddlerhood to early childhood	Isolated representations; lack of coherence, coordination; all-or-none thinking	Concrete, observable characteristics; taxonomic attributes in the form of abilities, activities, possessions	Unrealistically positive; inability to distinguish real from ideal selves
Early to middle childhood	Rudimentary links between representations; links typically opposites; all-or-none thinking	Elaboration of taxonomic temporal comparisons with own past performance	Typically positive; inaccuracies persist
Middle to late childhood	Higher-order generalization that subsumes several behaviours; ability to integrate opposing attributes	Trait labels that focus on abilities and interpersonal characteristics; comparative assessments with peers	Both positive and negative evaluations; greater accuracy
Early adolescence	Intercoordination of trait labels into simple abstractions; abstractions compartmentalized; all-or-none thinking; don't detect, integrate, opposing abstractions	Social skills/attributes that influence interactions with others or one's social appeal	Positive attributes at one point in time; negative attributes at another, leads to inaccurate overgeneralizations
Middle adolescence	Initial links between single abstractions, often opposing attributes; cognitive conflict caused by seemingly contradictory characteristics	Differentiation of attributes associated with different roles and relational contexts	Simultaneous recognition of positive and negative attributes; instability, leading to confusion and inaccuracies
Lade adolescence	Higher-order abstractions that meaningfully integrate single abstractions and resolve inconsistencies, conflict	Normalization of different role-related attributes; attributes reflecting personal beliefs, values, and moral standards	More balanced, stable view of both positive and negative attributes; greater accuracy

states. Out of the working models of the relationships with different caregivers, models of self and other will begin to develop.

The first indications of a cognitive representation of one's own features develop in the period of 15 to 18 months: children begin to recognize themselves in the mirror. Now they also clearly appreciate themselves as independent agents, as well as the separate agency of others. This might explain the observations of an increase in separation distress.

The period of 18 to 30 months is generally seen as a sort of consolidation phase in the development of the (pre-verbal) self: the child develops a stable and comforting internal representation of the mother (Mahler, Pine, & Bergman, 1975: see below), reaches a 'goal-corrected partnership' with the caregiver (Ainsworth & Wittig, 1969; Ainsworth et al., 1978: see earlier) and achieves a level of 'self-constancy' (Sander, in Harter, 1998) that enables the child to take a stance against the parents in the confidence that his or her 'good self' is recognized and that accommodating interactions can be restored. This stage, however, also means an important new step towards the construction of a set of self-representations because of the emergence of linguistic and symbolic representational competencies. Now the foundations are being laid for the construction of a self-concept in the sense of a set of stable self-traits and the construction of a life story as a more enduring self-portrait. This construction process will take several years and a couple of successive stages. Verbal interactions with caregivers provide a most important means in this process. As Harter rightly warns, though, language is a double-edged sword: the self-representations based on verbal interactions can, for diverse reasons, be at odds with other parts of an individual's experiences and, thus, create a gap between what is said and what is felt with regard to one's self. Below we will come back to this risk and its implications.

Childhood and Adolescence

Early studies on the development of self-representations in childhood and adolescence were descriptive and focused on the content of mostly spontaneously generated self-descriptions. The results of these studies suggested qualitative shifts in these descriptions. Young children show a preference for concrete and observable characteristics; in middle and later childhood the self was mostly described in terms of trait-like constructs (e.g. smart, shy); while in adolescence more abstract psychological processes like thoughts, emotions, and attitudes were used. These shifts could easily be related to respectively the preoperational, the concrete operational and the formal operational stages in Piaget's theory. Given all the criticisms of this theory, however, Piaget's work is no longer seen as an adequate framework for understanding the development of the self-concept in childhood and adolescence. Neo-Piagetian frameworks and information-processing models, according to Harter (1998), are better suited.

Young children (3 to 4 years of age) use representations of very concrete and observable characteristics to describe themselves ('I am a boy', 'I live in a farmhouse', etc.). Fischer (cited in Harter, 1998) refers to such representations as 'single representations' because they are highly differentiated and the child is cognitively still unable to relate such representations to each other. For the same reason, children of this age cannot acknowledge that one can have opposing attributes, or experience two emotions at the same time. Self-evaluations tend to be unrealistically positive because of the inability to differentiate between the actual and the desired self.

Children in early to middle childhood show some ability to coordinate single representations into a set of representations. In such a set a number of characteristics is related to each other on the basis of a common dimension (Harter uses the following example: good at running, jumping, climbing). The links between the representations are unidimensional. A most salient dimension for young children in the description of self and others is the evaluative one; attributes are either good or bad. Since they continue describing themselves with positive attributes, they are unable to acknowledge negative aspects of themselves. Others, though, can be totally bad. The kind of unidimensional sets of self-representations typical for this age group do not yet have a hierarchical structure in the sense that a higher-order generalization integrates lower-order behavioural aspects. Children of this age also begin to incorporate their caregiver's expectations. In this way the viewpoints of others begin to function as 'self-guides' which help children to control their own behaviour with evaluative self-reactions such as self-approval and self-sanctions.

In the period from middle to late childhood, children achieve the competence to integrate opposites. This level of cognitive development is labelled as 'bi-dimensional' (Case), the level of 'representational systems' (Fischer), the level of 'higher-order generalizations' (Siegler: all cited in Harter, 1998). In higher-order generalizations (of concrete behaviours) children can integrate opposing characteristics (e.g. good in English and social studies, but poor in maths and sciences). Generalizations like this will function as relatively stable dispositional traits. As a result, the self-concept becomes more integrated, more balanced and less positively biased. The new cognitive skills also enable children of this age to utilize social comparison information in the service of self-evaluation and further self–other differentiation. The children begin to evaluate themselves as persons; they can now focus on the 'type of person' they think others expect them to be. The concept of 'global self-worth' ('how much one likes oneself as a person': Harter, 1990) emerges. Several studies suggest that experience plays an important role in the construction of the higher-order structures of this age period.

Environments that foster positive as well as negative qualities support the integration, while abusing environments – to use the example elaborated by Harter – tend to strongly reinforce negative self-evaluations, even to the point where children begin to experience 'a profound sense of inner badness, as if they were inherently "rotten to the core"' (Harter, 1998, p. 571). Socialization influences at home and at school probably also explain the more negative self-evaluations of girls as compared to boys of this age.

During early adolescence, with the onset of abstract thinking, the trait labels of the earlier age are integrated in abstractions such as 'intelligent' or 'introvert'. According to Damon and Hart (1988) interpersonal attributes and social skills are quite salient at this age. These abstract representations, though, are still quite distinct from each other. Young adolescents lack 'cognitive control' (Fischer, in Harter, 1998) over such abstractions and see these as isolated self-attributes. They do not yet experience conflicts over contrasts in these attributes.

The experience of conflicts occurs in mid adolescence when youngsters begin to relate one abstraction to another. In the beginning this form of relating is still immature: the adolescent can oppose different abstractions, but cannot yet construct higher-order abstractions in which the apparent contradictions are resolved. Introspection and the preoccupation with how they appear in the eyes of others increase dramatically in mid adolescence. All these changes can cause considerable distress and intrapsychic conflict (e.g. Harter & Monsour, 1992). Consequencently, ambivalence and all-or-none thinking are quite common at mid adolescence. Several empirical studies (Harter, 1998) indicate that the socializing pressure to develop 'different selves in different roles or relationships' (e.g. self with parents, classmates, friends, romantic partners) is a major factor in the emergence of the intrapsychic conflict and confusion.

In late adolescence higher-order abstractions can be constructed in which opposing abstractions can be meaningfully integrated. Harter (1998) uses the example of 'flexible across different social situations' in which one's introversion and extroversion are integrated. Now, an integrated theory of self (Epstein, 1973) becomes possible. Because of further internalization adolescents are less tied to social situations and more and more begin to use their own standards. Damon and Hart (1988) found that the late adolescent self is described as an organized set of beliefs and values.

Development of the Self-Concept: Conclusions and Discussion

Of course, this description of the development of the self-concept in infancy, childhood and adolescence does not do justice to the width and depth of the research and theorizing of the second half of the twentieth century. We will conclude this review by briefly discussing a number of issues that are prominent in the recent literature on the development of the self-concept and self-esteem.

The discrepancy between the so-called real and ideal self-concept is an old issue in psychology, dating back to James' distinction between perceptions of one's actual success and one's aspirations. The ideal self-representations develop in middle childhood. The discrepancy between real and ideal increases with age, probably due to the increase in social-cognitive skills which allow for finer and more realistic differentiations between the real (more realistic) and the ideal (higher standards). Research by Higgins (1987) suggests that different types of discrepancies (real versus ideal, real versus ought) produce different forms of distress. A relatively large discrepancy can be seen as an indication of maladjustment. Discrepancies also have the positive function of motivating behaviour. 'Possible selves', such as the hoped-for or the dreaded self (Markus & Wurf, 1987), give direction to how one wants to be in the future. Self-descriptions can differ strongly in individual importance and relevance. Discrepancies in the important domains have more influence on the person's global self-esteem (Harter and colleagues, in Harter, 1998). This also explains why global self-esteem scores of minority youth do not typically differ from self-esteem scores of majority youth: both groups base their self-esteem on different domains.

Self-evaluations, according to extensive recent data, are best described by multidimensional models. Individuals can best be characterized by a profile of self-evaluations across different domains (for example, with the Self-Perception Profiles for Children and for Adolescents: Harter, 1982). Important domains in the profiles for children are scholastic and athletic competence, peer likeability, physical appearance, and behavioural conduct. For adolescents new important domains are job competence, close friendship, and romantic appeal. For the self-perception profiles of college students and adults, yet other domains are important. Across all age groups, including adults, physical appearance is the domain with the highest correlations with global self-esteem (Harter, 1998).

The differentiation between global (general) and domain- (situation-) specific self-representations has led to diverse ideas about the organization of these representations. Hierarchical models with general at the top and domain-specific self-descriptions at the bottom dominate in the literature (Harter, 1998). Questions about the relationships between the levels in such a hierarchy remain to be answered. A more general but crucial question is whether these statistically derived structures tell us anything about how individuals organize their self-constructs. Evidence suggests that valence is an important organizing principle. In contrast to (static) hierarchical models, some researchers have advocated the use of more dynamic models (e.g. Markus & Wurf, 1987).

Related to the issue of structure is the question of whether self basically should be seen as a coherent and unitary structure or as multidimensional and multifaceted. Nowadays, multiplicity views dominate in the self-concept literature (Harter, 1998). Hermans' notion of a 'dialogical self' is a prominent example of such a view (Hermans & Kempen, 1993; Hermans, Kempen, & Van Loon, 1992). The unity view, though, also has good advocates, especially those working from a narrative perspective (e.g. McAdams, 1997). And, in contrast to the self-concept literature, unity and coherence are seen as a core aspect in the identity literature.

From a developmental perspective, the multiplicity of self starts in middle childhood, where children evaluate themselves differently across domains. This multiplicity grows into a proliferation of role- and situation-related self-representations that cause considerable conflict and confusion in mid adolescence. It, therefore, should not be surprising that adolescents are found to be struggling with the question, 'which is the real (authentic) me?' From recent research by Harter and colleagues (Harter, 1998, gives an overview) it has become evident that adolescents have clear ideas about what they see as their true, authentic self and what they see as their so-called 'false self':

> Adolescents' descriptions of their true selves include: 'stating my true opinion', 'expressing my true feelings', 'saying what I really think and feel', and 'acting the way *I* want to behave and not how someone else wants me to be'. False selves are described as the opposite, namely as 'being phony', 'not saying what you think', 'putting on an act', 'expressing things you don't really believe or feel', and 'changing yourself to be something that someone else wants you to be'. (1998, p. 581)

False self behaviour, thus, indicates a suppression of one's thoughts, values and feelings.

More generally, Harter's research suggests that the regulation of behaviour and feelings becomes of prime importance in adolescence. Important factors related to the expression of false self behaviour are approval (from parents, but also from peers) and emotional support. In the concept of emotion regulation and the important role of parents and peers lie clear links to attachment research. Moreover, the data reported by Harter also form a nice bridge to the work of identity theorists and researchers (e.g. Erikson, 1959; Marcia, 1966) who stress the need for coherence and unity and who see adolescence as a major period for the achievement of a sense of identity.

Object Relations and Ego-identity Development

Studies of the development of self, from the perspective of object relations theorists, directly stem from Freud's work. Research on ego-identity development tends to be based on Erikson's lifespan theory of personality development, but this work is also rooted in Freud's psychoanalytic theory of development.

According to Freud, the basic structure of personality is formed in the first seven years of life. This structure comprises three substructures: the 'id', the 'ego', and the 'superego'. The id represents the complex of biological drives, and the superego (including the ego-ideal) the complex of the internalized dos and don'ts and the norms and ideals of the parents. The ego represents the substructure which mediates between id and superego on the one hand and the context on the other. In Freud's view personality development proceeds on the basis of an innate, genetically determined groundplan. Development in infancy and early childhood is driven by the pleasure principle: the striving for pleasure and the avoidance of pain. The strivings are biologically based. According to Freud's observations the pleasure principle works in a rather crude and uncompromising way: drives tend to seek instant and ruthless gratification. The reality principle explains why children in the course of their development begin to behave differently: they gradually learn to postpone direct gratification of their drives and to use socially more accepted ways of finding pleasure and avoiding pain. One important aspect of this developmental process concerns the gradual and age-related shifts in the objects that serve libidinous gratification. For infants the mother is the prime object and the libido manifests itself primarily in an oral way. Via the anal, the oedipal, and the latency stages this developmental process finally, in adolescence, reaches the adult manifestation of genital expression and gratification. (An excellent and detailed description of Freud's work and subsequent psychoanalytic thinking is given by Munroe, 1955; see also Greenberg & Mitchell, 1983.)

The Development of Self in Object Relations: Theoretical Background

According to Freud, the libidinal drive and conflicts between the pleasure and reality principle play a central role in human functioning and development. Other psychoanalytic theorists gave a central role to relationships. Such a relational perspective inspired Bowlby, and it also gave rise to object relations theory within psychoanalysis. Object relations theorists such as Mahler, Pine, and Bergman (1975) and Blos (1967) have elaborated how the child's and adolescent's self develops within the context of the shifts in object relations (objects that serve libidinous gratification). Greenberg and Mitchell have defined object relations as one's 'interactions with external and internal (real and imagined) other people, and the relationship between . . . internal and external object worlds' (1983, pp. 13–14). Object relations theory asserts that internalized representations of other persons mediate interpersonal interactions. These internal representations of others develop in the first three years of life, in what Mahler and colleagues (1975) have called the separation-individuation process. According to these authors, the foundation for the adolescent and adult identity structure is formed in this process.

The gradual construction of internal representations of the mother enables the infant to feel safe and function on its own when mother is out of sight for a while. Note the similarity with the notion of the internal working model of self and other in attachment theory. But in contrast with this theory, object relations theory emphasizes the development of self.

In the separation-individuation process 'separation' refers to the differentiation of the child from the initial symbiotic relationship with the mother, and 'individuation' refers to the child's realization that the mother is a separate person. The idea of an initial symbiotic relationship is highly implausible, however. Other research has demonstrated that within a few weeks of birth infants show good perceptual and cognitive discriminatory skills and play an active role in interactions with the mother (e.g. Fogel, 1993; Rochat, 1995; Stern, 1985). After 5 to 10 months the baby begins to explore its surrounding world more actively. But the mother (primary caretaker) must remain available as a safe haven. The ambivalence between the need for emotional reunion with the mother and separation-individuation, according to Mahler, Pine, and Bergman (1975), is at its height in the so-called *rapprochement* stage in the separation-individuation process. At this stage (at the age of about one and a half to two years) the child begins to fully realize that he or she and the mother are separate persons and that the earlier state of emotional union (symbiosis) is lost forever. The *rapprochement* stage is therefore characterized by feelings of loss, mourning, and regressive behaviour in the form of clinging to the mother. (Note the similarities with findings in the self-concept literature.) In the third year of life this struggle becomes less intense and settles in the achievement of a sense of autonomy and individuality ('individuation'). The child has then reached a certain degree of constancy in object relations. This 'implies that the child can intrapsychically incorporate both the good and the bad parts of maternal as well as self representations, enabling the child to experience both mother and self as separate whole individuals' (Kroger, 1998, p. 175). This intrapsychic structure forms the basis for the child's identity, at least until adolescence when a major intrapsychic restructuring is called for.

Blos (1967) saw clear parallels between the separation-individuation process in early childhood, and a similar intrapsychic restructuring process in adolescence. In this second separation-individuation process the core issue is the emotional disengagement from the internalized parent representations. According to Blos, this restructuring of the internalized ties with parents is essential for further ego maturation and the emergence of a firm sense of self which is no longer tied to the infantile object relations. In the 1970s and 1980s several authors have further elaborated on Blos' ideas, but mostly theoretically. Measures for separation-individuation were developed in the 1980s. For the 1990s Kroger (1998) observed a strong increase in empirical research on aspects of the intrapsychic restructuring process in adolescence.

The Development of Self in Object Relations: Methodology and Main Findings

The empirical study of separation-individuation in early childhood is based on observations of mother–child interactions. Most of the research on the second separation-individuation process is based on self-report measures. A typical instrument is the Separation-Individuation Test of Adolescence (SITA) developed by Levine, Green, and Millon (1986). The SITA consists of nine scales: separation anxiety, engulfment anxiety, practising mirroring, dependency denial, nurturance seeking, peer enmeshment, teacher enmeshment, healthy separation, and rejection expectancy. Other instruments discussed by Kroger (1998) have scales measuring aspects like: attachment need, individuation capacity, painful tension, hostility, and reality avoidance (the Hansburg Adolescent Separation Anxiety Test); functional independence, emotional independence, conflictual independence, and attitudinal independence (Hoffmann's Psychological Separation Inventory); aspects of differentiation, splitting, and various issues associated with separation-individuation disturbances such as tolerance for aloneness (the Separation-Individuation Process Inventory). All these scales are internally consistent (alphas generally above 0.70) and have shown some discriminant, construct and predictive validity. The psychometric qualities of the SITA have been studied most thoroughly (Kroger, 1998).

As this list of scales in the various measures demonstrates, separation-individuation in adolescence refers to a wide range of emotional, motivational, and social behaviours which all have to do with how intrapsychic processes mediate interpersonal interactions, or, in other words, with how the person copes with the balance between self and other. Since empirical research on the changes in object relations in adolescence is only very recent, the available data about these complex processes are scattered and in need of replication. The main results are as follows (Kroger, 1998, gives a review).

Adolescents who are older and more mature in ego-identity development show more differentiation in self–other representations. This differentiation tends to increase with age. There is a decrease with age of the need to struggle with the actual parents and their internalized representations, but this change is coupled with feelings of aloneness and a sense of rejection by important others. With increasing age peers become more important than parents as sources for support, nurturance and self-esteem. Compared to younger age groups there is an increase in anxiety and ambivalence in adolescence. This can be seen as an indication of the intrapsychic restructuring process. Kroger concludes that the available data are in support of adolescent stages of separation-individuation that seem to parallel the stages in the infant process as described by Mahler and colleagues.

Another line of inquiry concerns the relationship with problem behaviours. Correlations have been found between problems and stagnation in the separation-individuation process in adolescence on the one hand, and borderline symptomatology, suicidal behaviour, and eating disorders on the other. Kroger suggests that these problems seem to be rooted in the separation-individuation process in infancy. A third research area concerns the correlations of the intrapsychic changes with interpersonal behaviour such as parenting practices and styles of intimacy. With regard to the relationship with parents, separation-individuation is seen not as a linear process from dependency to independency but as a process of developing new forms of autonomy and connectedness. Parents who acknowledge and support their adolescent's need for individuality as well as connectedness promote their psychological growth and maturity (Grotevant & Cooper, 1985; 1986). An optimal resolution of the second separation-individuation process is also directly linked to more mature forms of intimacy (see Kroger, 1998, and Marcia, 1994, for overviews).

The Development of Self in Object Relations: Some General Conclusions

Object relations and attachment theory both stem from the rise of a relational perspective in psychoanalysis. They both start from the formative role of relationships in the development of self. In both approaches the internalization of representations of self and other plays a central role. Despite these similarities, attachment and object relations theory have developed in quite different empirical traditions. Object relations theory only recently inspired empirical research and, while the first results are promising, they only form a starting point. Theoretical questions remain (e.g. a detailing of stages in the adolescent separation-individuation process) and several assertions still need to be tested in empirical research (Kroger, 1998).

Relationships form a central aspect of object relations theory, but in its further elaboration it shows a strong focus on intrapsychic processes and the internal representations of self and other. This intra-individual focus is similar to self-representations research discussed earlier, but object relations theory does not limit itself to the cognitive core of self-representations. Emotional, motivational and interpersonal aspects also play an important role, theoretically as well as in the assessment of separation-individuation. When compared to the development of identity in a lifespan context, however, object relations theory can best be seen as referring to the intrapsychic part of a more encompassing process: the achievement and subsequent transformation of a sense of identity in adolescence and adulthood.

Identity Development: Theoretical Background

In contrast with the intrapsychic focus of the object relations theorists, Erikson primarily focused on the mediating function of the ego and the role of the context in personality development. In his classic book *Childhood and society* (1950), Erikson described his theory of human development for the first time. As the title of the book indicates, the interaction between biological maturation and the socializing influences of the culture in which an individual grows up forms a central theme in Erikson's developmental theory.

Human (personality) development is governed by the 'epigenetic principle'. This implies that parts of the human personality develop according to a biologically determined groundplan, each part at its proper time, at the proper rate, and in the proper sequence, until all parts form a functioning whole. This process, however, strongly depends on environmental conditions. Like the maturing foetus which needs the proper biochemical environment, the growth of the human personality needs its proper social environment. Personality, thus, develops as a prescribed sequence of locomotor, sensory, and social capacities for interaction with significant others and institutions in a context that becomes wider with every step in the child's development (from parents and the family, via peers, teachers, and the school, to partners and work in adulthood). Next to (a) the biological and mental growth processes, and (b) the environmental (social, cultural, historical, geographical, etc.) conditions, (c) ego processes form the third important part of Erikson's theory of personality development.

The ego plays a mediating role. The ego refers to the mostly unconscious process in which the biological and cognitive changes in the person's life and the demands and possibilities ('developmental tasks') imposed by society are integrated. The results of this integrating function of the ego (Erikson: 'ego synthesis') are manifest in the domain of self and identity. The following quotation illustrates this process:

> Take for example a child who is learning to speak: he is acquiring one of the prime functions supporting a sense of individual autonomy and one of the prime techniques for expanding the radius of give-and-take. The mere indication of an ability to give intentional sound-signs soon obligates the child to 'say what he wants'. It may force him to achieve by proper verbalization the attention which was afforded him previously in response to mere gestures of needfulness. Speech not only increasingly commits him to his own characteristic kind of voice and to the mode of speech he develops, it also defines him as one responded to by those around him with changed diction and attention. They in turn expect henceforth to be understood by him with fewer explanations or gestures. Furthermore, a spoken word is a pact. There is an irrevocably committing aspect to an utterance remembered by others, although the child may have to learn early that certain commitments (adult ones to a child) are subject to change without notice, while others (his to them) are not. This intrinsic relationship of speech not only to the world of communicable facts, but also to the social value of verbal commitment and uttered truth, is strategic among the experiences which mark ego development . . . Thus the child may come to develop, in the use of voice and word, a particular combination of whining or singing, judging or arguing as part of a new element of the future identity, namely, the element 'one who speaks and is spoken to in such-and-such a way'. This element in turn will be related to other elements of the child's developing identity (he is clever and/or good-looking and/or tough) and will be compared with other people, alive or dead, judged as ideal or evil.
>
> It is the ego's function to integrate the psychosexual and psychosocial aspects on a given level of development and at the same time to integrate the relation of newly added identity elements with those already in existence – that is, to bridge the inescapable discontinuities between different levels of personality development. For earlier crystallizations of identity can become subject to renewed conflict when changes in the quality and quantity of drive, expansions in mental equipment, and new and often conflicting social demands all make previous adjustments appear insufficient and, in fact, make previous opportunities and rewards suspect. (Erikson, 1968, pp. 161–162)

Across the human lifespan the major maturational (somatic and cognitive) changes and/or age-related changes in cultural demands can make 'previous adjustments appear insufficient'. Then, the development of a specific aspect of the personality comes to a critical period. On the basis of his clinical and anthropological observations Erikson has posited eight major stages in the human life-cycle (Erikson, 1950; 1959; 1968; 1980). The timing and order of the stages follows the epigenetic principle. This implies that each part of the human personality is related to all other parts and that each part exists in some form before its critical stage in development is reached. Hence, the process of development can be seen as a process of differentiation and integration of various parts. For each individual person these parts form a unique 'Gestalt' from which the individual derives a sense of identity. This Gestalt is 'a configuration which is gradually established by successive ego syntheses and resyntheses throughout childhood. It is a configuration gradually integrating constitutional givens, idiosyncratic libidinal needs, favored capacities, significant identifications, effective defenses, successful sublimations, and consistent roles' (1968, p. 163).

Adolescence is the critical period in the development of a sense of identity. In this stage a full-grown sense of identity must be achieved. As a result of physiological, psychosexual and cognitive changes the adolescent reaches the adult reproductive and cognitive status. These changes interact with the new societal expectations (e.g. the preparation for the labour market, functioning as an independent person) the adolescent is confronted with. Because of all these personal and contextual changes, the identity configuration built up in childhood is too limited to guide the person's functioning as an adult.

Identity development, according to Erikson (1968), begins in childhood with (the rather passive) processes of introjection and identification. 'Introjection' refers to the internalization of the mother's image. The integration of this image depends on the mutuality and trustworthiness of the mother–infant relationship (compare attachment and separation-individuation theory discussed earlier). Identifications are derived from the available role models in childhood (e.g. 'I want to be like my father, teacher, etc.'). This process also depends on successful interactions with others. Identification becomes less useful in adolescence. Then the process of (active) identity formation starts. Enabled by their new cognitive skills and encouraged to become more autonomous and independent, adolescents begin to build their own identity configuration by actively selecting and discarding earlier and new identifications in the light of their own interests, talents and values, and the demands and affordances of the society. The success of this process depends 'on the process by which a society (often through sub-societies) identifies the young individual, recognizing him as somebody who had to become the way he is and who, being the way he is, is taken for granted' (1968, p. 159). Now, the mutuality between the individual and the wider social and cultural context becomes essential.

Erikson has defined 'a sense of identity' as 'a sense of personal sameness and historical continuity' (1968, p. 17) which 'is based on two simultaneous observations: the perception of the selfsameness and continuity of one's existence in time and space and the perception of the fact that others recognize one's sameness and continuity' (1968, p. 50). In his definition Erikson emphasizes two important things. First, he speaks of 'a sense of identity' and, in this way, gives identity a psychological, experiential meaning. Secondly, he links the perception of one's sameness (unity and coherence) and continuity to the recognition of that sameness and continuity by others. In this way he stresses that a sense of identity refers to the subjective experience of a person's core aspects, as well as to the social recognition of these very same core aspects, and thus to the combination of some very personal, and some very social, contextual processes. It is the task of the ego to attune and integrate these processes.

The outcome of the identity formation process can best be seen as a balance between successful and failed integrations. Erikson usually described the outcome as a balance between a sense of identity achievement and a sense of identity confusion. When integration failures predominate, the adolescent can end up in a state of identity confusion: 'A state of identity confusion usually becomes manifest at a time when the young individual finds himself exposed to a combination of experiences which demand his simultaneous commitment to physical intimacy . . . to decisive occupational choice, to energetic competition, and to psychosocial self-definition' (1968, p. 166). The demands imposed on the adolescent then outweigh his integrative capacities.

The identity formation process does not end in young adulthood. Maintaining and changing a sense of identity are an ongoing and lifelong process. In adulthood and old age, every change can threaten the earlier achieved attunement of person and context, and demand identity renegotiations.

Identity Development: Methodology and Measures

Erikson's theory is not based on systematic empirical studies. The identity status model of Marcia (1966; 1967) is inspired by Erikson's theory and is by far the most often used empirical approach to identity in adolescence and adulthood. The element of actively making identity choices is central in this model.

The identity statuses are 'modes of dealing with the identity issue characteristic of late adolescents' (Marcia, 1980, p. 161). By the end of adolescence, individuals either (a) have actively made identity choices and committed themselves to these choices (achievement), or (b) have not and find themselves in a state of identity diffusion (Marcia prefers to speak of 'diffusion' which, he thinks, better describes the state than 'confusion'), or (c) are still actively exploring identity choices (moratorium), or (d) have firm commitments but have never experienced an exploratory period (foreclosure) (see Table 20.2).

The identity statuses form an extension of Erikson's bipolar description of the outcome of the identity crisis in adolescence. Erikson reasoned in terms of achieving a balance between a sense of identity and a sense of identity diffusion. Marcia, however, differentiated the outcome of the Eriksonian identity crisis on empirical grounds into four categories. The achievement and diffusion category can be directly linked to what Erikson postulated. The moratorium category is used for individuals in the process of exploration, on their way to identity achievement. The foreclosure category as an outcome of the adolescent identity crisis has not explicitly been mentioned by Erikson. It was used by Marcia for individuals who were found to have a firm sense of identity but who never experienced any identity exploration period.

For the assessment of a subject's identity status, adolescents and young adults are interviewed about their exploration and commitments in areas such as vocation, relationships, politics, and religion, and categorized by independent raters of the interview in one of the four identity statuses.

Since Marcia developed the interview in the 1960s, it has been used in a large number of studies. The procedure basically remained the same, but it has been extended to other domains and made applicable to other age ranges (young adolescents, adults), and more elaborated scoring manuals were developed (Marcia et al., 1993, gives complete interview and scoring formats). The inter-observer reliability of the status assignment is acceptable. Next to the identity status interview, paper-and-pencil versions have been developed for the measurement of the participants' identity status (Adams, 1999; Adams, Shea, & Fitch, 1979), or for the separate measurement of exploration and commitment (e.g. Balistreri, Busch-Rossnagel, & Geisinger, 1995; Meeus, 1996). For more detailed reviews of identity status and other measures inspired by Erikson, see Bourne (1978) and Marcia (1993a).

Marcia's identity statuses are based on the subject's exploratory and commitment behaviour.

Table 20.2 *Marcia's identity status model*

	Exploration of alternatives	Commitment
Identity achievement	Present	Present
Moratorium	In process	Present but vague
Foreclosure	Absent	Present
Identity diffusion	Present or absent	Absent

Firm commitments ('identity choices') in important domains of life are seen as the behavioural indications of a sense of identity. In the concept of 'commitment' lies another link to Erikson's theory: commitments indicate an integration of person and context. Bourne says:

> Commitments can of course be of many kinds – vocational, avocational, social, marital, ideological, ethical. From an outside observer's point of view, an individual's commitments would include the domains in which he appears most engaged or involved. From the individual's own point of view his commitments are the matters which he characteristically cares about most or values. From either point of view, these commitments have a social significance and at the same time provide the individual with a definition of himself. (1978, p. 227)

Commitments, thus, provide a person with a self-definition and with recognition by others. To quote Bourne again: 'By my commitments I shall know myself and be known to others' (1978, p. 234).

The identity status model has generated a lot of empirical research over the last three decades. Most of the earlier research aimed at individual differences: individuals in the four statuses were compared on various dependent variables (reviews are given by Bourne, 1978; Marcia, 1980; Waterman, 1982). In his 1993b review Marcia discussed personality characteristics such as authoritarianism, anxiety, self-esteem, locus of control, autonomy, conformity, ego development, cognitive performance and cognitive style, formal operational thinking, and interactive styles, which all have been used as dependent variables. In general this research attests the predictive validity of the statuses: adolescents in the different statuses show systematic differences in the dependent variables. The following summary of Marcia's (1994) research-based prototypical and phenomenological descriptions of adolescents in the four statuses can give a good impression of these differences.

Adolescents in the achievement status are thoughtful and introspective. But their introspection does not paralyse them. They function well under stress, have a sense of humour and are well able to establish intimate relations. They are open to new experiences but are able to evaluate these in terms of their own internal standards. In general they are characterized by flexible strength. Adolescents in the moratorium status are active and competitive. They are conflicted and struggling to gain more autonomy in their relationship with their parents. They are anxious. They are characterized by ambivalence and struggle. Adolescents in the foreclosure status are happy and self-confident, but also narrow-minded and self-complacent. They become dogmatic under stress and threat. Family ties are very important to them. They are law-abiding, and suspicious toward other views. Their strength is rigid and brittle. Adolescents in the diffusion status seem unhappy or superficial. Those who seem superficial are like playboys with few ties with others and a happy-go-lucky attitude towards life. They seem reasonably happy. Those who seem unhappy are loners who have few contacts with others. Adolescents with both types of diffusion show a lack of ideas or have a lot of superficial ideas. They have no real intimate relationships but a lot of superficial contacts. They seem to miss a sense of inner coherence and agency.

Marcia (1993b) has used 'internalization' for a general characterization of the empirically found differences between the statuses. He cited Bourne (1978) according to whom internalization involves 'the development of an increasingly stabilized and internalized capacity for . . . control of internal functioning, particularly in the realms of (1) the regulation of self-esteem . . . (2) the exercise of self-calming functions and containment of affective fluctuations in response to stress, and (3) the autonomous organization of motives and resources to anticipate and meet adaptive demands' (1993b, p. 22). In those terms, Marcia considers diffusions (persons in the diffusion status) as least internalized; they have no sense of identity and let circumstances rule their life. The internalization of foreclosures (persons in the foreclosure status, etc.) is based upon the introjection and identification with authority figures (primarily the parents). These identifications are not their own choice. Moratoriums are in the process of releasing earlier identifications and seeking and internalizing their own standards. Identity achievement persons have constructed their own identities and are considered to be most internalized. Achievements have commitments chosen after a period of exploration of alternatives. The commitments of the identity achieved person tend to be more flexible and adaptive than the foreclosed person's commitments which have an assigned character. Self-chosen commitments are indicative of 'the internalization of self-regulatory processes' (1993b, p. 22) and represent a more mature mode of psychosocial functioning. Assigned commitments can also be strong, but they miss the flexibility and adaptiveness of self-chosen commitments and reflect a less mature form of functioning.

The notion of internalization is linked to the idea that the statuses are indicative of underlying structures. Inspired by Piagetian developmental structuralism, Marcia introduced this idea in his 1980 review of identity status research. He then defined identity as an 'internal, self-constructed, dynamic organization of drives, abilities, beliefs and individual history' (1980, p. 159). The process of internalization leads to identity structures, which, in the case of persons in the achieved identity status, are said to be more flexible and adaptive than in the case of foreclosed persons. The moratorium status indicates that the identity structure is growing and changing. Diffusions are probably characterized by the lack of an internal structure.

The idea of a growing structure is reminiscent of Erikson's idea of an evolving configuration (see earlier). Within circles of identity status researchers, structural ideas are not generally accepted. Some authors see it as the core aspect of identity development (e.g. Berzonsky & Adams, 1999; Kroger, 1993; in press; Marcia, 1993b; van Hoof, 1999a), while other researchers talk about identity and identity development without any reference to structural notions (e.g. Waterman, 1999).

Identity Development: Questions of Stability and Change

Erikson's contention that the end of adolescence is marked by the resolution of the identity crisis has been an important starting point for developmental research. Young adults preferably should have achieved some sense of who they are, where they stand in life and what they want with their future; in Marcia's terms, they should have reached the achievement status, or at least be on their way, via the moratorium status, to that position. Because they are not yet facing the societal demands of committing themselves to adult roles and values, young adolescents probably either are not yet actively considering identity choices (identity diffusion) or are functioning on the basis of conferred commitments (foreclosure).

One approach to developmental research is the comparison of frequency distributions of identity statuses in different age groups, for example, a comparison of early, middle and late adolescents. As could be expected, the frequency of achievements and moratoriums among young adults tends to be much higher than among early adolescents. Young adolescents predominantly are in the foreclosure and diffusion status (e.g. Meilman, 1979). Such cross-sectional research, however, has many limitations (e.g. Bosma, 1992). Most of all, it does not inform us about intraindividual change. For the study of individual trajectories in identity development, a longitudinal design is necessary.

Conceptually, the identity statuses can be used to describe such trajectories. An individual can change from one status to another, or can even go through a sequence of more than one status shift (e.g. a trajectory from foreclosed to moratorium to achievement). Other individuals may remain in the same status for a longer time, and thus evidence stability in development. Waterman (1982) was the first to give an overview of conceptually possible status shifts and trajectories, as in Figure 20.3. This figure does not give a model of identity development. It is merely a heuristic scheme depicting possible shifts and trajectories in identity statuses. Persons can stay in the diffusion (D) status for a long time, but also move out of it into the foreclosure (F) or moratorium (M) status. Persons in the foreclosure status can stay in this status or move into the diffusion or moratorium status. A move into the achievement (A) status is only possible for individuals in the moratorium status. The scheme suggests that almost anything is possible. Because of the definition of the foreclosure status the only conceptual restriction is that persons who once went through a moratorium period can never move into this status. (A more recent but in principle not different formulation of identity status development is given in Waterman, 1999.)

Following Waterman (1982) status shifts and trajectories can be described as progressive (upwards on the continuum of diffusion, foreclosure, moratorium, and achievement) or regressive (downwards on this continuum) or stable in the same status. This pattern of developmental trajectories is based on an assumed continuum of statuses in psychological growth and adaptiveness. This continuum comprises various dimensions: for example the degree to which the identity crisis in adolescence has been resolved successfully (with diffusion at the negative and

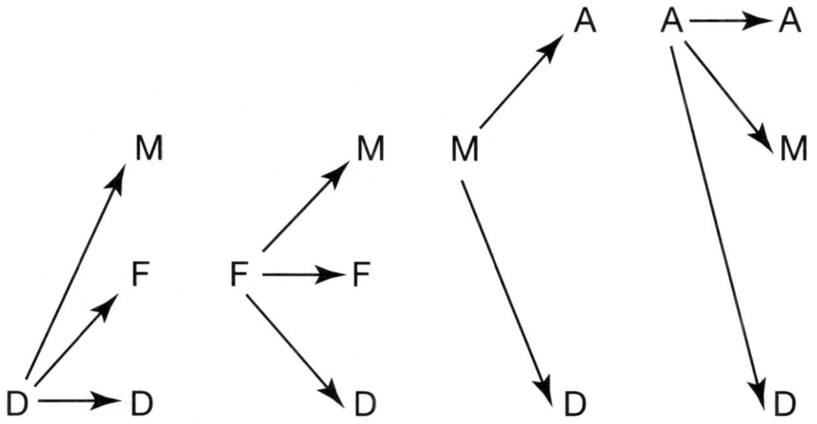

Figure 20.3 *Waterman's model of ego-identity status shifts*

achievement at the positive pole), the degree to which self-chosen values and standards have been internalized (with diffusion and achievement again as the contrasting poles). Comparisons between the statuses on dependent variables have usually led to the same ordering, with the diffusion and foreclosure status as representing less adaptive and the moratorium and achievement status as representing more adaptive behaviour and development (Marcia et al., 1993). The validity of such a continuum for statements about the direction of identity development, however, is nowadays regarded as very limited (e.g. Berzonsky & Adams, 1999; van Hoof, 1999a; 1999b; Waterman, 1999).

Within the framework of Erikson's theory, the status approach has been generalized to other developmental stages as well. The principle is the same: Erikson's bipolar description of each stage is translated into a system of outcome categories. In this way Marcia and coworkers (Marcia, 1998, gives an overview) have successfully operationalized the Eriksonian stages of a sense of industry versus a sense of inferiority (stage IV), a sense of intimacy versus a sense of isolation (VI), a sense of generativity versus a sense of stagnation (VII) and, finally, a sense of integrity versus a sense of despair (VIII). The central hypothesis behind this work is that the resolution of each stage crisis affects the development in each subsequent stage and is affected by the resolution of the crises of each antecedent stage. A positive outcome in one stage increases the chance that the next developmental crisis will also be solved successfully, and vice versa.

Since the operationalizations of the stages later in the life cycle are very recent, only empirical research linking stages V and VI has been done. This research showed indeed that the positive resolution of the identity crisis predicts a positive resolution of the crisis of intimacy versus isolation.

Identity Development: Main Developmental Findings

Status Shifts and Trajectories

The first cross-sectional studies of identity status in adolescence and young adulthood indicated that moratoriums and achievements hardly ever occur before the senior years in the US high school (beyond the age of 16). This was in line with Waterman's (1982; 1993) general hypothesis 'that the transition from adolescence to adulthood involves progressive strengthening in the sense of identity' (1993, p. 42). It received further support from longitudinal research which, in relation to age, showed a predominance of progressive developmental status shifts, i.e. shifts from statuses lower in identity to statuses higher in identity. But there was also evidence for stable (e.g. stable D or F), fluctuating (e.g. DMD; or repeated cycles of moratorium followed by achievement followed by a new moratorium period, and so on, the so-called MAMA cycles) and regressive (from higher to lower statuses) pathways of identity status formation.

A more recent review by Meeus (1996) also gave support to the hypothesis of progressive strengthening of a sense of identity in adolescence. But this evidence appeared to be rather limited: it mostly concerned shifts from one status into another status. Such 'single progressive developmental trends' (out of a lower, into a higher status) occurred often. Progressive shifts involving two upward transitions, as an indication of a more systematic developmental progression, were rare. With regard to the timing of identity change, Meeus and Waterman came to different conclusions. Waterman (1993) found that developmental change mostly takes place during the college years; Meeus concluded that high school samples show more or at least as many progressive developmental shifts.

Other authors (Adams, 1999) have taken the study of identity development a step further with data from longitudinal studies with more than two measurement points. Trajectories involving three consecutive statuses can then be described in terms of two transitions (e.g. progressive–progressive, progressive–regressive, stable, regressive–progressive, regressive–regressive). About half of the trajectories that occurred in this study were progressive, about 15% stable, 10% regressive, 15% progressive–regressive and 10% regressive–progressive. It seems that identity development in terms of status shifts does not proceed in a simple, straightforward, linear way. Cyclical patterns occurred next to progressive, stable and regressive trajectories. Evidence presented by Goossens (1995; Goossens, Marcoen, & Janssen, 1999) led to similar conclusions. Their data came from a longitudinal study of university students with four measurements. They found such a remarkable diversity in identity trajectories that they fundamentally questioned the general developmental continuum of D, F, M and A. In their data continuous progressive development occurred in about one-third of the trajectories; one-third showed stability; and one-third showed patterns of progression and regression. Progressive development is the exception rather than the rule. The developmental process, thus, is far more complex than the developmental continuum and the earlier single developmental progressive trends suggest (see also Meeus et al., 1999).

A most thorough review of the empirical evidence about identity status development has been given by van Hoof (1999a; 1999b). The results of her analysis indicate that stability dominates in identity status shifts (for about 50% of the subjects; van Hoof codes fluctuating patterns as stable too). Moreover, the number of progressive changes is only slightly higher than the number of regressive changes, but lower than could be expected on the basis of chance. While van Hoof interprets this evidence as evidence against the general developmental hypothesis, Kroger (in press) has argued that it supports the general expectation of an increase with age in the frequency of identity achieved individuals (and no decrease), and a general decrease in the frequency of foreclosed and diffuse individuals in late adolescence and young adulthood. It is clear, however, that not everyone has achieved an identity in young adulthood.

There are also other indications that the development of identity proceeds in a much more complex way than was assumed earlier. Kroger (1995) reported longitudinal evidence for two types of foreclosure, namely 'firm' and 'developmental' foreclosure statuses. The firm foreclosures showed a very stable pathway, while the developmental foreclosures progressed towards the higher statuses. A comparable differentiation is reported by Marcia (1989) with regard to the diffusion status: stability versus progressive developmental change (see also Archer & Waterman, 1990). A progressive type of trajectory without status shifts was found by Flum (1994). In a study with high school age adolescents he discovered a distinct group which displayed a so-called 'evolutive style' of identity formation. This group showed a gradual, step-by-step exploration of identity issues. His findings indicate that there might be two different routes toward identity achievement: one is via the moratorium status and involves a more encompassing exploration of identity issues; the other is the pathway characterized by a sequential exploration of 'delimited and circumscribed areas of conflict (as opposed to experiencing a generalized sense of crisis and confusion, like Moratoriums)' (1994, p. 495).

The proliferation of (sub-)statuses and types of developmental trajectories severely undermines the conceptual clarity of the original status model. Future empirical studies of identity trajectories may even show that the identity status model has completely lost its descriptive usefulness and explanatory power for the study of identity development (Goossens, Marcoen, & Janssen, 1999). A cautionary note, however, concerns the validity of paper-and-pencil tests of the identity statuses and of exploration and commitment (e.g. the OM-EIS used by Adams, 1999, and Goossens, Marcoen, & Janssen, 1999, and the U-GIDS used by Meeus, 1996). The question is whether they are able to tap more than the superficial and reasoned aspects of exploratory and commitment behaviour. They have a certain predictive validity but the correspondence of the OM-EIS with the original status interview 'is not as high as one would wish' (Marcia, 1993a, p. 18). It might well be that this behaviour primarily reflects the actual responses of individuals to the options in their situation that are available at the time of measurement, and not the degree of internalization of the self-regulatory processes that are assumed to lie behind the statuses. For this reason, the information gathered with measures aimed at those deeper, intrapsychic structures might give a more valid picture of the development of identity.

Childhood Antecedents and Adult Consequences

Instead of trying to describe and explain identity development in terms of status shifts and trajectories, researchers have also approached the developmental process indirectly by looking at the childhood antecedents and adult consequences of the identity resolution (identity status) in late adolescence. Much stronger than the status shifts literature, this work is framed within the Eriksonian stage model and its psychoanalytic roots: It is assumed that the successful resolution of earlier crises positively influences the successful resolution of the identity crisis. This line of reasoning has indeed found empirical support. In retrospective measures of the earlier stage resolutions, achievements showed most while diffusions showed least positive resolutions (Waterman, 1982). Achievement and moratorium subjects also had better integrated memories of childhood experiences and felt more secure and less anxiously attached than individuals in the other two statuses (Marcia, 1993b).

Another group of antecedent conditions is family characteristics. Although the interpretation of causal effects is problematic in this case, there is a clear relationship with identity status in adolescence. Both connectedness to and separateness from the family are important (Grotevant & Cooper, 1986). The following summary is abstracted from Marcia's (1993b) review. Foreclosures report their families as close, loving and child-centred, with encouragement to conform to the values of the family. Diffusions see their families as distant and rejecting, especially their same-sexed parent. Moratoriums are ambivalent about and struggling with their parents for autonomy. Achievements have families who support their differentiation: the ambivalence of their moratorium period has led to mutuality in the relationship with parents.

Within the Eriksonian framework the outcome of the identity crisis is assumed to influence the outcome of later crises. This idea has found empirical support. After the identity stage comes the intimacy-isolation stage, and several studies have shown that young adults who achieved a sense of their own identity have a higher chance to become engaged in an intimate relationship characterized by mutuality, depth and respect, while foreclosures are most likely to be engaged in more superficial and stereotypic relationships and thus have resolved the intimacy crisis in a less successful way. These studies also suggest that identity seems to precede intimacy in men, but identity and intimacy seem to codevelop in women (Marcia, 1993b; Matteson, 1993).

The process of identity development does not stop when the adolescent has reached adulthood

Nowadays, young adults face a wide range of career and lifestyle options and these can force them to reconsider their earlier, late adolescent identity choices. Kroger (2000) reviewed research which has shown that young adult women in particular have to make 'meta-decisions'. These decisions concern the balances across commitments in the separate identity domains, for example, family and career commitments. Since the research of late adolescence and young adulthood has shown that less than half of the subjects had attained the achievement status when they left college, Kroger suggested that there is 'considerable scope for identity development during young adulthood' (2000, p. 150). Upward identity status shifts, however, are not very common in young adulthood, which according to Kroger could mean that openness to identity exploration is less than in adolescence. This could be due to less social support for identity exploration in young adulthood and/or less willingness of or possibility for the young adult to remain open to new identity alternatives. In the cases where change occurred, the shift from diffusion or foreclosure to moratorium and achievement was most frequent. Another common pattern was the shift from achievement into a new period of exploration (moratorium) and then back to new commitments (the MAMA cycle). Finally, some individuals who were rated as achieved in college appeared to be foreclosed or diffused at a later assessment. Such 'identity closure' (Valde, 1996) is not uncommon in (young) adulthood. Over half of the subjects in Marcia's (1976) follow-up study showed such a change. Theoretically an achievement–foreclosure shift is not possible: individuals in the achievement status have experienced an exploratory period and therefore cannot be categorized as foreclosed. Empirically such changes occur. Although such empirical findings could be due to unreliable categorizations, it is assumed that changes in intrapersonal or contextual conditions for exploration could make such a change plausible as well (Kroger, 1993; Marcia, 1976). The identity statuses must not be seen as strict categories.

Identity Development: Conclusions and Discussion

In his observations and theorizing Erikson has put a sense of identity – a sense of sameness and continuity and the recognition of this sameness and continuity by significant others – at the centre of the ongoing synthesis (by the ego) of person and context-related processes. In adolescence this attunement reaches a critical stage. But, every change in adulthood and old age potentially demands a renegotiation of the sense of identity achieved in adolescence. The identity status model has become the most popular device for the empirical study of identity in adolescence and beyond. The identity statuses are based on an assessment of exploration and commitment and are meant to describe the outcome of the identity crisis in adolescence. Numerous studies have provided evidence for the concurrent and predictive validity of the statuses. However, the model also has its limitations.

While Erikson situated identity at the interface of person and context, identity statuses have primarily been used as individual psychological categories (Côté & Levine, 1988). Recently, identity researchers have therefore argued for more contextualized approaches to identity development (e.g. Adams & Marshall, 1996; Phinney & Goossens, 1996). Studying identity development in context can be done in various ways. Baumeister and Muraven (1996), for example, have shown how historical changes have led to changes in the nature of identity. By rendering more social support for (young) women going through a period of identity exploration, feminism has probably made the moratorium status more adaptive for women (Marcia, 1996). Other evidence (e.g. Adams & Fitch, 1983; Costa & Campos, 1986) suggests that individuals in the different statuses choose the kind of environment that supports and reinforces their way of dealing with identity issues. Moratoriums, for example, often literally move out of a context that does not support their identity exploration (Kroger, 1993).

Another limitation is the rather static connotation of the statuses. The status model is not doing very well in studies of the developmental process. Not only are the findings in terms of status shifts and status trajectories difficult to interpret, but the model also does not inform about the mechanisms and microprocesses involved in the development of identity. For this reason, Grotevant (1987) made detailed suggestions for a more process-oriented approach to identity development. Since then several authors have elaborated process models of identity development (e.g. Berzonsky, 1990; Kerpelman, Pittman, & Lamke, 1997; see Bosma & Kunnen, 2001, for an overview). Kroger (1993; in press; Kroger & Green, 1996) recently started to study identity development in terms of processes of intrapsychic, structural change. Identity transitions (status shifts) in adulthood appeared to be most often associated with internal change processes. While social circumstances set broad limits to probable identity choices, individual personality factors such as openness to experience, ego resilience and cognitive complexity seem to play a key mediating role in one's course of identity development in young and middle adulthood.

A third criticism concerns the fact that the identity statuses are not aimed at the core of identity and only approach a sense of identity indirectly. The status model addresses behavioural indications of identity, i.e. exploration and commitment. According to several authors (Côté & Levine, 1988; van der Werff, 1985; van Hoof, 1999a) it thus misses the core of what Erikson meant, namely, a sense of identity. Blasi and Glodis (1995) have stated this criticism most explicitly and offered an empirical alternative. They have differentiated four aspects of a sense of identity: (a) a sense of agency, (b) a sense of identity with oneself, (c) a sense of unity, and (d) a sense of differentiation from others. On the basis of a questionnaire measure of these aspects they were able to demonstrate an age-related sequence of modes of constructing and experiencing a sense of identity (Blasi & Glodis, 1995, give an overview of this research). Interestingly, this line of work, directly derived from Erikson's theory of identity development, closely parallels recent developments in self-concept research. In later discussion about more integrative research, we will come back to this parallel. Another recent development, starting from the same criticism, is the work of Grotevant (1993; Grotevant & Cooper, 1998). He developed a narrative approach to study a sense of unity, or coherence, as a core aspect of a sense of identity. In his opinion (other authors like Josselson, 1994, and Widdershoven, 1994, think along similar lines) such an approach does more justice to the core aspects and complexities of identity than the identity status approach.

In conclusion, identity researchers are leaving the narrow confines of the once popular identity status approach and are exploring other ways of studying identity development (compare Schwartz, 2001). This brings them into closer contact with methodologies and research questions featuring in the other approaches of the development of the organization of self.

The Adolescent and Adult Organization of Self: Differences and Similarities in the Three Traditions

Conception of Development

In terms of their conceptualization of the developmental process, the four approaches form two groups. Attachment and identity status research yield categorical differences between subjects: the infant, adolescent and adult subjects are categorized into one attachment type or identity status. They have a prime focus on interindividual differences. The main developmental findings with regard to such typologies concern the stability and change across time, and the factors related to this change or stability. Empirical findings mostly support the assumption of interindividual stability in attachment categories: about 70% in infancy and 90% in adulthood. These findings leave room for considerable intraindividual change in infancy and childhood, but how and why this change occurs is not yet clear. Identity status studies report a stability rate of about 50%. More than in attachment research, identity researchers seem to be struggling with the compatibility of a typological approach with the study of intraindividual, developmental change. In a first attempt to use the status typology for a description of intraindividual change, the statuses have been reconceptualized as steps in the developmental process, but this idea is strongly critized on both theoretical and empirical grounds. Other attempts to adapt the status approach to a developmental process model have not met with general agreement amongst researchers either.

In object relations and self-concept research the focus is on intraindividual change – on how individuals change across time. Empirical research from such a perspective tries to document such changes and the factors that determine these age-related changes. The basic assumption is that every individual manifests such age-related changes an assumption amply supported by research. Both object relations and self-concept studies report considerable differences between age groups and change across age. The typological and developmental process approaches thus yield a different kind of information about the construction of self from infancy through adulthood.

These different bodies of knowledge are not incompatible though. It is quite possible that different categories of subjects follow different trajectories of intraindividual change. Person-oriented developmentalists (e.g. Magnusson & Stattin, 1998), for this reason, strongly argue for a differentiation between groups of subjects that may follow different developmental pathways. On the basis of the developmental findings reported in the section on the self-concept, one might for example expect that *all* the children in their development from early childhood into adolescence will manifest changes from more concrete to more abstract in their internal representations of themselves and others. In addition, though, one may expect that there are systematic differences in content, valuation and the kind of organization of the self-concept between children who were securely attached in infancy as compared to, for example, insecure-avoidant children. Moreover, it seems plausible to expect differences between these subgroups in their developmental trajectory from infancy through adolescence.

The point is that up till now self-concept researchers have not studied the development of the self-concept in subgroups differentiated on the basis of their attachment status. Nor have attachment researchers used the self-concept literature to gain insight into changes across age of the working models of self and other in the different attachment groups. Researchers tend to work within one domain; crossing the borders is not popular. Even within domains, though, a person-oriented approach makes much sense. The differentiation by Kroger of foreclosure status adolescents into 'developmental' and 'firm' foreclosures (see earlier) is a good example of a differential developmental study and its potential.

An Internal Structure

There are also other similarities and differences. In each of the four approaches an internal representational structure plays an important explanatory role. In attachment theory this structure explains the stability of attachment strategies. The structure comprises a model of the attachment figure and a model of self. Different relationships yield different models and a pertinent question in attachment research concerns the organization of all these models. Attachment research has provided very limited knowledge about the development of the internal working model of self and other across wider age spans. Within self-concept research the ideas about the structure of self-representations (here a generic term that comprises representations of both self and others) have been elaborated and researched in much greater detail. This research has also generated a fine-grained picture of the age-related changes in self-concept from infancy through adulthood. Object relations theory sees the formation of an internal representation of the caregiver and self in infancy as a necessary step towards individuality and emotional autonomy. The transformation of this structure in adolescence, which comprises cognitive as well as emotional and motivational aspects, is seen a necessary step towards adulthood. In comparison to self-concept research the ideas about the content and organization of this structure on the one hand are less well elaborated and researched in object relations theory, but, on the other hand, more encompassing and less cognitivistic. In Erikson's ego-identity theory and Marcia's identity status research, ideas about the internalization and growth and transformation of an internal structure also play an important role, but within this tradition the elaboration of the organization and age-related changes of this structure is still meagre.

In connection with the views on the organization of the internal structure there is a conspicuous contrast between identity and self-concept research. In terms of James' distinction between I and me, identity research could be seen as referring to I processes (a sense of agency, of continuity and coherence), while self-concept research explores the diversification of a person's me. Both approaches, thus, seem to study contrasting aspects of self. This is not an absolute contrast, though, merely a difference in the aspect of self that a tradition focuses on. And these two aspects probably are inherently related: the stronger are the diversifications and contrasts within the self-concept, the stronger the need could be to maintain a sense of unity. The other two approaches show a similar concern and contrast: attachment research struggles with the multiplicity of self–other models, while object relations theory stresses the need for an increasing self–other differentiation.

Focal Age Ranges

The focal age range is another area of overlap and complementarity. Attachment and object relations are studied in infancy as well as in older age groups: attachment in adolescence and adulthood, and the second separation-individuation process in adolescence. Self-concept research covers the whole age range from infancy into adulthood. Identity research concerns adolescents and adults. In each tradition assumptions are made about the continuities between infant/early childhood development and development in the later stages of childhood, adolescence and adulthood. Longitudinal evidence about the links between the developmental processes in infancy and the later stages in development, however, is lacking. Assumptions and inferences in this regard still need solid empirical support. Of course, there are huge conceptual and methodological obstacles to the study of such comparisons across wide age ranges. The differences in research methods for the study of infant and adult attachment and the question of how findings gathered with such diverse methods can be related across age periods (see earlier) form a nice illustration of such difficulties.

A Relational Perspective

Although there seems to be a growing consensus that self and identity comprise individuality as well as relatedness (e.g. Guisinger & Blatt, 1993), the traditions discussed here are still rather one-sided in this respect.

With their notion that working models of self and other develop in the context of mother–infant interactions, attachment theorists position themselves within the confines of relational perspective. Like Baldwin and Cooley, a century ago, they see self as a social construction. The elaboration of the model of self and others, though, leaves many questions unanswered. It looks as if the development of the individuality part of the model of self and other in particular is hard to understand from an attachment perspective. Attachment researchers have come with rather divergent ideas to tackle this problem. Concepts like 'detachment' and 'non-attachment' (Holmes, 1997; see earlier) give the impression that individuality can only be described negatively, in terms of a *lack* of attachment. At the other extreme one can position the assumption of a 'private self' (West, 1997; also see earlier) in relation to a biologically based, innate need for unity and coherence of self which has no relation whatsoever to the relational base of the model of self and other.

Object relations theory has the same roots (in the relational perspective within psychoanalysis) as attachment theory and a similar focus on the mother–infant/child relationship. Conceptually and empirically, though, it moved in a different direction: it focused on the development of the individuality part of self in the context of the mother–infant relation and tried to describe the young child's steps in the process of achieving a sense of autonomy and individuality. The relatedness aspect of self remains underexposed in this tradition.

Due to its cognitive focus, self-concept research has a strong individualistic orientation. The limitations of cognitivism have been extensively discussed elsewhere; a review of these in the realm of self and identity has recently been given by van der Meulen (2001). Cognitive approaches in general have difficulties accounting for the relationships between the structures of internal representations and contextual influences. How individuals, in their experience of self, feel connected to real persons in the outer world, instead of representations of these other people, is difficult to understand from a cognitive perspective.

In his lifespan developmental theory Erikson advocated a strong interactionist perspective on human development. In this theory the concept of identity refers to a fit between person and context characteristics; a sense of identity concerns the attunement of one's sense of coherence and continuity and the recognition of that sameness and continuity by others. For Erikson individuality and connectedness form the two sides of the same coin. In a sense this relational perspective can be found in the commitment variable in identity status research, but in general the statuses have a strong individualistic ring. The statuses describe categories of individuals who differ in their way of dealing with exploration and commitment. The fact that relationship concerns form part of the domains of exploration and commitment does not change the status approach from an individualistic orientation into a relational one.

Integrative Work, Recent General Trends and New Perspectives

Crossing the Borders

From the overviews in the three main sections of this chapter it must have become evident how separated the four traditions have been over the last decades. There are not many researchers 'crossing the borders'. But times are changing. Despite all the differences, some authors have tried to bridge the gaps between traditions, both theoretically and empirically. They have focused on the similarities in theoretical roots, on the overlapping parts, or on how the traditions complement each other. This work has led to hypotheses and empirical research about the relationships between the central concepts of the different traditions. Moreover, there are some important recent trends in (developmental) psychology that promote similar developments within the traditions. Consequently, the major questions and issues within the traditions become more alike and the areas of overlap larger.

Marcia (1994) has explored the theoretical and empirical links between ego identity (status) and object relations. He uses 'object relations' to refer to attachment theory as well as to object relations theory and suggests the use of 'attachment' as the central concept and fundamental starting point in both approaches. Empirical findings in identity status as well as object relations research support the assumptions about the crucial role of attachment relationships with regard to differences in development and the quality of self–other relationships (see above; Marcia, 1994). Another common ground is the assumption of an internal structure and the social-cognitive processes related to this structure. Here, too, studies indicate that differences in attachment category, separation-individuation, and identity status are related to differences in social-cognitive processes such as information-processing style, the quality of early memories, and the adequacy of thought processes under interfering conditions (Marcia, 1994). Such evidence indicates in an indirect way that the approaches have much in common.

There is also direct evidence of the relationships between separation-individuation, attachment and identity status. Adolescents in the achievement status show much self–other differentiation, while foreclosure adolescents have rather undifferentiated self–other representations. Adolescents in the moratorium status are in the process of transforming their relationships with their parents. Older adolescents and young adults evidence more self–other differentiation and less indications of conflict with their parents and less struggle with their parental introjects than younger adolescents (see Kroger, 1998, for an overview). From his review of research on attachment in adolescence, Rice concluded: 'There appeared to be a consistent positive relationship between attachment and measures of social competence, self-esteem, identity, and emotional adjustment' (1990, p. 534). MacKinnon and Marcia (2002) present further evidence in support of the relationship between identity status and attachment. All this evidence, however, is based on correlations. And it concerns concurrent assessments of attachment and identity.

What about the position of self-concept research with respect to the other three approaches? For decades self-concept research has followed its own cognitivistic course. Despite the incidental use of 'identity', self-concept researchers basically were interested in the person's self-representations, the part that James called 'me'. These self-representations form a structure that motivates and regulates behaviour. As such this idea has much in common with the structural and functional notions within attachment, separation-individuation, and ego-identity theory. However, the approaches differ strongly with regard to the content of this structure. A major difference is whether the content comprises only cognitive material (as in self-concept research) or emotional aspects as well (the other three traditions).

Not every self-concept researcher has followed the exclusive focus on the Jamesian me. Within developmental psychology, Damon and Hart (1988) preferred to use 'self-understanding' because they included in their self-concept research the subject's understanding of himself or herself as a subject; in other words, the I, the part that James deemed inaccessible for empirical research. They distinguished the following aspects of self-as-subject: the sense of agency, the sense of continuity, and the sense of being a unique and distinguishable person. Here lies a bridge: these aspects are also central in the identity literature. Researchers like Blasi and Glodis (1995), Côté and Levine (1988), and van Hoof (1999a) see these aspects as the core of Erikson's definition of identity. A different aspect of Erikson's definition of identity, namely the person's commitments to a society's roles, goals and values, is covered by Marcia's identity status approach. Identity and self-concept research, thus, partly study the same phenomena and partly go different (but sometimes complementary) ways.

A nice example of complementarity lies in the work of van der Werff (1967; 1985; 1990). This work also shows how the gap between self-concept and identity research can be bridged in the notion of 'self-conception problems'.

Self-conception problems are problems people can experience with respect to the multiplicity of their self-representations. Above, examples of such problems were given. People can experience the contrast between how they are and how they would like to be as a painful discrepancy. In a similar way, the discrepancies between how people see themselves and how they think others see them, or between their 'true' and their 'false' selves, can be troublesome and experienced as an obstacle in the achievement of a sense of coherence and unity. Next to suffering from the multiplicity of self-representations, individuals can also experience a lack of reliable and authentic building blocks for their identity. Persons categorized in the status model as identity diffused form an example. In van der Werff's perspective, self-conception problems can be placed in the same category as identity problems. On the basis of the available self-concept and identity literature van Halen (2002) has developed a questionnaire of self-conception problems and studied the nature and occurrence of these problems across four age groups: 17-, 40-, 55-, and 70-year-olds. The results show that all kinds of self-conception problems occur across the lifespan. Problems that have to do with Harter's true–false discrepancies are most prevalent in each age group. Multiplicity problems seem to be typical for adolescents (van Halen, 2002). This research illustrates how self-concept and identity research nicely complement each other under the common denominator of self-conception problems.

Next to the research that crosses borders, there are some general trends in (developmental) psychology that promote further coordination of the traditions reviewed here. A good discussion of these trends as they occur within the domain of self-concept theory and research can be found in van der Meulen (2001). This review focuses on three crucial and general questions with respect to the notion of a relatively stable, generalized system of self-representations: what is the role of emotion? What is the role of the context? How is the situational and temporal variability of the self-concept related to its assumed stability? In one way or another these questions all have to do with the limitations of static, decontextualized, cognitivistic conceptualizations of self and identity and its development. In general, approaches that focus on person–context transactions and that comprise cognitive as well as motivational and social aspects of development are rapidly gaining more influence in developmental psychology (as several chapters in the fifth edition of the *Handbook of child psychology* attest: e.g. Bronfenbrenner & Morris, 1998; Csikszentmihalyi & Rathunde, 1998; Magnusson & Stattin, 1998). Moreover, the study of emotion is a booming business in psychology in general as well as within developmental psychology (e.g. Eisenberg, 1998; Lewis & Haviland-Jones, 2000). As a consequence, theory and research on self and identity begin to show a much stronger concern with motivational and emotional aspects, and with conceptualizations of the developmental process in terms of (chains of) person–context interactions.

Dynamic Approaches

In order to understand and describe the complexities of individual development as a transactional process, several authors have resorted to the use of dynamic systems theory. This has led to a whole new family of approaches, ranging from purely descriptive accounts of developmental processes in terms of dynamic systems theory to simulations of such processes with mathematical models (e.g. Ford & Lerner, 1992; Thelen & Smith, 1994; van Geert, 1991; 1994; 1998). The application of dynamic systems thinking can be found in several developmental domains: motor, cognitive and language development in childhood, emotional and social development, and the development of self and identity. The application of dynamic systems theory has also become popular in social psychology, neuropsychology, and developmental psychopathology (Lewis & Granic, 2000, give examples in the field of emotions research).

A dynamic systems approach is characterized by a number of principles. A phenomenon studied from this perspective has to be defined as an open system of interacting components. The relationships between the components can be linear, but components in living systems often interact in non-linear ways. Dynamic systems show self-organization ('the emergence of order'). This order emerges from the coupling of elementary elements of the system. Positive and negative feedback processes play an important role in self-organization. Development of the system is based on recursive patterns of the moment-to-moment interactions between the components (see Granic, 2000, and Lewis & Granic, 1999, for further elaborations of the principles of self-organization).

Crucial conceptual issues in the application of dynamic systems thinking concern the definition of the system, the definition of the elements and levels of the system ('From which elements at the lower level emerges which organization at the higher level?'), and the reciprocal relationships between the elements (Kunnen et al., 2001). The researcher has to be very explicit about the elements and their interrelationships in the system.

There are many recent examples of the application of the principles of self-organization. Here we will only mention a few, relevant to the topic of this chapter. Granic (2000) has given a heuristic dynamic systems account of the development of parent–child relations. Here the dyadic relationship has been defined as a system. Two different mathematical modelling approaches of parent–child interactions have been explored by Olthof, Kunnen, and Boom (2000). Liable and Thompson (2000) have used dynamic systems thinking to understand and explain the inconsistent findings with regard to the assumed stability of attachment patterns across age and relationships (see earlier). A heuristic dynamic systems account of how communication, self and culture emerge from and through relationships was given by Fogel (1993). Kunnen and Bosma (2000) and Kunnen, Bosma, and van Geert (2001) have applied dynamic systems modelling principles to the study of the development of self and identity. All of these applications of dynamic systems thinking illustrate the growing interest in processes and mechanisms of development. The further empirical elaboration of these promising applications (and the development of appropriate research methods: Kunnen et al., 2001) is one of the greater challenges to future developmental research.

Emotions, Regulation, and Organization

In her introduction to the volume on social, emotional, and personality development of the fifth edition of the *Handbook of child psychology*, Eisenberg (1998) discussed a number of emerging themes in developmental research. Three major themes of her list are very relevant to this chapter: a focus on emotion, a focus on regulation, and a focus on relationships.

Over the last two decades there has been a strong increase in studies of peer–peer relationships alongside parent–child relationships. The findings generally indicate that the quality of peer–peer relationships is determined by the quality of parent–child relationships. Emotions play an important, mediating role in this relationship. An adequate understanding and communication of emotions (i.e. regulation of emotions) is related to positively valued relationships and prosocial behaviour. It is, therefore, plausible to assume that this regulation of emotions is learned in early attachment relationships (Eisenberg, 1998). Securely attached children have learned that it is acceptable to show distress and to look for support and comfort from other people. Insecure-avoidant children have learned to suppress the expression of their emotions and their inclination to seek support and comfort. Parents' responsiveness is related to the ability of children to acknowledge, express, and communicate how they feel, and to how their feelings are incorporated in their self-concept. In trustful relationships, children learn to trust themselves. Intrusive and controlling behaviour of parents will lead to discrepancies between what children feel and what they are supposed to feel; they become detached from their own feelings. In this way, the deep emotional foundations of their internal working model of self and others are laid (Harter: 'lovable or unworthy of love').

The internal working model that is gradually construed out of the repetitive parent–child interactions becomes the main mediating factor in consecutive transactions of the child and others. Eisenberg maintains: 'Obviously, the topic of attachment and early parent–child relationships is a central issue in the study of relationships in developmental psychology. Attachments are hypothesized to affect the development of self, a range of cognitions relevant to quality of relationships, emotion regulation and emotions attached to various relationships, and even personality development' (1998, p. 16). Not only do attachments in their deposit in the form of a working model affect peer relationships, the influence is reciprocal: 'Peer relationships also affect the development of cognitions about the self (including those concerning self-worth and a gender-relevant self-concept) and feelings that are associated with the self and with the social world' (1998, p. 17). While the details of this transactional process are still far from clear, the early (e.g. Bowlby, 1969; 1973) as well as more recent attachment literature (e.g. Cooper, Shaver, & Collins, 1998; Crittenden, 1995; Fonagy et al., 1994; Kobak & Sceery, 1988; Main, 1991; Mikulincer, 1998) assigns a key role to the regulation of emotions.

There is a growing consensus that emotions should be treated as an integral part of the self-concept. But how? There are many ideas but none is generally accepted, yet (see van der Meulen, 2001, for an overview). In the study of ego identity it almost goes without saying that emotional aspects are essential. This insight, however, is not so evident in the empirical research in this tradition. The identity status approach and other popular measures of identity exploration and commitment, for example, primarily tap cognitive and (self-reported) behavioural aspects of identity. Measures of separation-individuation do comprise affective aspects, but authors within this tradition do not refer to the regulation of emotions.

New ways have to be found to include emotions in the study of self and identity. A growing number of authors is trying to do so. Instead of conceptualizing self in terms of self-representations, some of these take recent emotions theory as a point of departure. Emotions researchers (e.g. Lewis & Haviland-Jones, 2000) have argued that emotions indicate that something essential to the individual is at stake. Emotions occur when an individual's concerns (motives, goals, values, ideals, etc.) are threatened. Emotions, when they occur, thus form a royal road to knowledge of the individual; and, when the individual monitors his or her emotions, to self-knowledge. On the basis of recent emotion theory it is argued that the interaction of emotions and cognitive appraisals leads to affective-cognitive structures (Izard, 1984; Lewis, 1995; Magai & McFadden, 1995; Tomkins, 1978), which, in turn, can be seen as the constituting components of a person's identity. Hermans' dialogical self model comprises similar affective-cognitive structures (e.g. Hermans & Hermans-Jansen, 1995).

Recently, these ideas have been developed a step further by combining them with a dynamic systems perspective (Fogel, 2001; Haviland-Jones, Boulifard, & Magai, 2001; Lewis & Ferrari, 2001). This is a combination that offers exciting new prospects.

In Conclusion

Some sort of isolationism characterizes the theoretical and research traditions that have been reviewed here. Each of them has acquired important knowledge about the development of the organization of self, but none offers a complete picture. Even when all the available empirical knowledge is taken together (as far as that is possible in light of all the differences in models of people, world views, theoretical assumptions and methodology) the resulting picture remains fragmented and full of blind spots.

But let us not end overly pessimistic. We see powerful integrative tendencies in the work of authors who focus on processes and mechanisms in the construction of self and other from a dynamical and relational perspective. We see the new prospects of the combination of principles of self-organization and the study of the regulation and organization of affective-cognitive structures. We expect that these ideas will be of great help in further understanding the development of the organization of self, from early attachment relations to the adolescent and adult organization of self. We hope that a growing number of researchers will embrace these ideas.

References

Adams, G.R. (1999). *The objective measure of ego identity status: A manual on theory and test construction*. Department of Family Relations and Applied Nutrition, University of Guelph, Ontario, Canada.

Adams, G.R., & Fitch, S.A. (1983). Psychological environments at university departments: Effects on college students' identity status and ego stage development. *Journal of Personality and Social Psychology*, 44, 1266–1275.

Adams, G.R., & Marshall, S.K. (1996). A developmental social psychology of identity: understanding the person-in-context. *Journal of Adolescence*, 19, 429–442.

Adams, G.R., Shea, J.A., & Fitch, S.A. (1979). Toward the development of an objective assessment of ego identity status. *Journal of Youth and Adolescence*, 8, 223–228.

Ainsworth, M.D.S., Blehar, M.C., Waters, E., & Wall, S. (eds) (1978). *Patterns of attachment: A psychological study of the Strange Situation*. Hillsdale, NJ: Erlbaum.

Ainsworth, M.D.S., & Wittig, B.A. (1969). Attachment and exploratory behavior of one year olds in a strange situation. In B.M. Foss (ed.), *Determinants of infant behavior* (pp. 113–136). London: Methuen.

Archer, S.L., & Waterman, A.S. (1990). Varieties of diffusions and foreclosures: An exploration of subcategories of the identity statuses. *Journal of Adolescent Research*, 5, 96–111.

Ashmore, R.D., & Jussim, L. (1997). Introduction: Toward a second century of the scientific analysis of self and identity. In R.D. Ashmore & L. Jussim (eds), *Self and identity. Fundamental issues* (pp. 3–19). New York: Oxford University Press.

Bakermans-Kranenburg, M.J., & van IJzendoorn, M.H. (1993). A psychometric study of the Adult Attachment Interview: Reliability and discriminant validity. *Developmental Psychology*, 29, 870–879.

Baldwin, J.M. (1895). *Mental development of the child and the race: Methods and processes*. New York: Macmillan.

Baldwin, M.W., & Fehr, B. (1995). On the instability of attachment style ratings. *Personal Relationships*, 2, 247–261.

Baldwin, M.W., Keelan, J.P.R., Fehr, B., Enns,V., & Koh-Rangarajoo, E. (1996). Social-cognitive conceptualization of attachment working models: Availability and accessibility effects. *Journal of Personality and Social Psychology*, 71, 94–109.

Balistreri, E., Busch-Rossnagel, N.A., & Geisinger, K.F. (1995). Development and preliminary validation of the ego identity process questionnaire. *Journal of Adolescence*, 18, 179–190.

Baumeister, R.F. (1987). How the self became a problem: A psychological review of historical research. *Journal of Personality and Social Psychology*, 52, 163–176.

Baumeister, R.F. (1995). Self and identity: An introduction. In A. Tesser (ed.), *Advanced social psychology* (pp. 51–97). New York: McGraw-Hill.

Baumeister, R.F. (ed.) (1999). *The self in social psychology*. Philadelphia: Psychology Press.

Baumeister, R.F., & Muraven, M. (1996). Identity as adaptation to social, cultural, and historical context. *Journal of Adolescence*, 19, 405–416.

Belsky, J., Campbell, S.B., Cohn, J.F., & Moore, G. (1996). Instability of infant–parent attachment security. *Developmental Psychology*, 32, 921–924.

Benoit, D., & Parker, K.C.H. (1994). Stability and transmission of attachment across three generations. *Child Development*, 65, 1444–1457.

Berzonsky, M.D. (1990). Self-construction over the life span: A process perspective on identity formation. In G.J. Neimeyer & R.A. Neimeyer (eds), *Advances in personal construct psychology* (Vol. 1, pp. 155–186). Greenwich, CT: JAI.

Berzonsky, M.D., & Adams, G.R. (1999). Reevaluating the identity status paradigm: Still useful after 35 years. *Developmental Review*, 19, 557–590.

Blasi, A., & Glodis, K. (1995). The development of identity: A critical analysis from the perspective of the self as subject. *Developmental Review*, 15, 404–433.

Blos, P. (1967). The second individuation process of adolescence. *Psychoanalytic Study of the Child*, 22, 162–186.

Bosma, H.A. (1992). Identity in adolescence: Managing commitments. In G.R. Adams, T.P. Gullotta, & R. Montemayor (eds), *Adolescent identity formation* (pp. 91–121). Newbury Park: Sage.

Bosma, H.A. (1995). Identity and identity processes: What are we talking about? In A. Oosterwegel & R.A. Wicklund (eds), *The self in European and North American culture: Development and processes* (pp. 5–17). Dordrecht: Kluwer.

Bosma, H.A., & Kunnen, E.S. (2001). Determinants and mechanisms in ego identity development: A review and synthesis. *Developmental Review*, 21, 39–66.

Bourne, E. (1978). The state of research on ego identity: A review and appraisal. Part I and Part II. *Journal of Youth and Adolescence*, 7, 223–252, 371–392.

Bowlby, J. (1969). *Attachment and loss: Vol. I. Attachment*. London: Hogarth/Institute of Psycho-Analysis.

Bowlby, J. (1973). *Attachment and loss: Vol. II. Separation*. New York: Basic.

Bowlby, J. (1980). *Attachment and loss: Vol. III: Loss, sadness and depression*. New York: Basic.

Bowlby, J. (1988). Developmental psychiatry comes of age. *American Journal of Psychiatry*, 145, 1–10.

Breakwell, G. (1986). *Coping with threatened identities*. London: Methuen .

Bretherton, I. (1985). Attachment theory: Retrospect and prospect. In I. Bretherton & E. Waters (eds), *Growing points of attachment theory and research* (pp. 66–104). *Monographs of the Society for Research in Child Development*, Vol. 50, serial 129.

Bronfenbrenner, U., & Morris, P.A. (1998). The ecology of developmental processes. In W. Damon (series ed.) & R.M. Lerner (ed.), *Handbook of child psychology: Vol. 1* (pp. 993–1028). New York: Wiley.

Calkins, M.W. (1900). Psychology as a science of selves. *Philosophical Review*, 9, 490–501.

Campbell, D.T., & Fiske, D.W. (1959). Convergent and discriminant validation by the multitrait–multimethod matrix. *Psychological Bulletin*, 56, 81–105.

Collins, N.L., & Read, J.R. (1994). Cognitive representations of attachment: Structure and function of working models. *Advances in Personal Relationships*, 5, 53–90.

Cooley, C.H. (1902). *Human nature and the social order*. New York: Scribner.

Cooper, M.L., Shaver, P.R., & Collins, N.L. (1998). Attachment styles, emotion regulation, and adjustment in adolescence. *Journal of Personality and Social Psychology*, 74, 1380–1397.

Costa, M.E., & Campos, B.P. (1986). Identity in university students: Differences in course of study and gender. *Cadernos de Consulta Psicologica*, 2, 5–13.

Côté, J.E., & Levine, C. (1988). A critical examination of the ego identity status paradigm. *Developmental Review*, 8, 147–184.

Crittenden, P. (1995). Attachment and psychopathology. In S. Goldberg, R. Muir, & J. Kerr (eds), *Attachment theory: Social, developmental and clinical perspectives* (pp. 367–406). Hillsdale, NJ: Analytic.

Crowell, J.A., Treboux, D., & Waters, E. (1999). The adult attachment interview and the relationship questionnaire: Relations to reports of mothers and partners. *Personal Relationships*, 6, 1–18.

Csikszentmihalyi, M., & Rathunde, K. (1998). The development of the person: An experimental perspective on the ontogenesis of psychological complexity. In W. Damon (series ed.) & R.M. Lerner (ed.), *Handbook of child psychology: Vol. 1* (pp. 635–684). New York: Wiley.

Damon, W., & Hart, D. (1988). *Self-understanding in childhood and adolescence*. Cambridge: Cambridge University Press.

Demo, D.H. (1992). The self-concept over time: Research issues and directions. *Annual Review of Sociology*, 18, 303–326.

Dozier, M., & Kobak, R.R. (1992). Psychophysiology in attachment interviews: Converging evidence for deactivating strategies. *Child Development*, 63, 1473–1480.

Eisenberg, N. (1998). Introduction. In W. Damon (series ed.) & N. Eisenberg (ed.), *Handbook of child psychology: Vol. 3* (pp. 1–24). New York: Wiley.

Epstein, S. (1973). The self-concept revisited: Or a theory of a theory. *American Psychologist*, 28, 404–416.

Erikson, E.H. (1950). *Childhood and society*. New York: Norton, 1963.

Erikson, E.H. (1959). *Identity and the life cycle*. New York: International University Press.

Erikson, E.H. (1980). *Identity and the life cycle*. New York: Norton.

Erikson, E.H. (1968). *Identity, youth and crisis*. New York: Norton.

Flum, H. (1994). The evolutive style of identity formation. *Journal of Youth and Adolescence*, 23, 489–498.

Fogel, A. (1993). *Developing through relationships: Origins of communication, self, and culture*. New York: Harvester Wheatsheaf.

Fogel, A. (2001). A relational perspective on the development of self and emotion. In H.A. Bosma & E.S. Kunnen (eds), *Identity and emotions: Development through self-organization* (pp. 93–114). Cambridge: Cambridge University Press.

Fonagy, P., Steele, M., Moran, G., & Higgit, A. (1991). The capacity for understanding mental states: The reflective self in parent and child and its significance for security of attachment. *Infant Mental Health Journal*, 12, 201–218.

Fonagy, P., Steele, M., Moran, G., Steele, H., & Higgitt, A. (1993). Measuring the ghost in the nursery: An empirical study of the relation between parents' mental representations of childhood experiences and their infants' security of attachment. *Journal of the American Psychoanalytic Association*, 41, 957–989.

Fonagy, P., Steele, M., Steele, H., Higgitt, A., & Target, M. (1994). The Emanuel Miller Memorial Lecture 1992: The theory and practice of resilience. *Journal of Child Psychology and Psychiatry*, 35, 231–257.

Ford, D.H., & Lerner, R.M. (1992). *Developmental systems theory: An integrative approach*. Newbury Park, CA: Sage.

Fox, N.A. (1995). Of the way we were: Adult memories about attachment experiences and their role in determining infant–parent relationships: A commentary on van IJzendoorn (1995). *Psychological Bulletin*, 117, 404–410.

George, C., Kaplan, N., & Main, M. (1985). Adult attachment interview protocol. Unpublished manuscript, University of California at Berkeley.

Gerlsma, C. (2000). Recollections of parental care and quality of intimate relationships: The role of re-evaluating past attachment experiences. *Clinical Psychology and Psychotherapy*, 7, 289–296.

Gerlsma, C., & Luteijn, F. (2000). Attachment style in the context of clinical and health psychology: A proposal for the assessment of valence, incongruence, and accessibility of attachment representations in various working models. *British Journal of Medical Psychology*, 73, 15–34.

Goldsmith, H.H., & Alansky, J.A. (1987). Maternal and infant temperamental predictors of attachment: A meta-analytic review. *Journal of Consulting and Clinical Psychology*, 55, 805–816.

Goossens, L. (1995). Identity status development and students' perception of the university environment: A cohort-sequential study. In A. Oosterwegel & R.A. Wicklund (eds), *The self in European and North American culture: Development and processes* (pp. 19–32). Dordrecht: Kluwer.

Goossens, L., Marcoen, A., & Janssen, P. (1999) Identity status development and students' perception of the university environment: From identity transitions to identity trajectories. Manuscript under review, University of Louvain.

Granic, I. (2000). The self-organization of parent–child relations: Beyond bidirectional models. In M.D. Lewis & I. Granic (eds), *Emotion, development, and self-organization* (pp. 267–297). Cambridge: Cambridge University Press.

Greenberg, J.R., & Mitchell, S.A. (1983). *Object relations in psychoanalytic theory*. Cambridge, MA: Harvard University Press.

Grice, H.P. (1975). Logic and conversation. In P. Cole & J.L. Moran (eds), *Syntax and semantics: III Speech acts* (pp. 41–58). New York: Academic.

Grotevant, H.D. (1987). Toward a process model of identity formation. *Journal of Adolescent Research*, 2, 203–222.

Grotevant, H.D. (1993). The integrative nature of identity: Bringing the soloists to sing in the choir. In J. Kroger (ed.), *Discussions on ego identity* (pp. 121–146). Hillsdale: Erlbaum.

Grotevant, H.D., & Cooper, C.R. (1985). Patterns of interactions in family relationships and the development of identity exploration. *Child Development*, 56, 415–428.

Grotevant, H.D., & Cooper, C.R. (1986). Individuation in family relationships. *Human Development*, 29, 82–100.

Grotevant, H.D., & Cooper, C.R. (1998). Individuality and connectedness in adolescent development. Review and prospects for research on identity, relationships, and context. In E. Skoe & A. von der Lippe (eds), *Personality development in adolescence: A cross national and life span perspective* (pp. 3–37). London: Routledge.

Guisinger, S., & Blatt, S.J. (1993). Individuality and relatedness: Evolution of a fundamental dialectic. *American Psychologist*, 49, 104–111.

Harter, S. (1982). The perceived competence scale for children. *Child Development*, 53, 87–97.

Harter, S. (1983). Developmental perspectives on the self-system. In P.H. Mussen (ed.), *Handbook of child psychology: Vol. IV* (pp. 275–385). New York: Wiley.

Harter, S. (1990). Causes, correlates and the functional role of global self-worth: A life-span perspective. In J. Kolligian & R. Sternberg (eds), *Perceptions of competence and incompetence across the life-span* (pp. 67–98). New Haven, CT: Yale University Press.

Harter, S. (1998). The development of self-representations. In W. Damon (series ed.) & N. Eisenberg (ed.), *Handbook of child psychology, 5th edn: Vol. 3. Social, emotional, and personality development* (pp. 553–617). New York: Wiley.

Harter, S. (1999). *The construction of the self: A developmental perspective*. New York: Guilford.

Harter, S., & Monsour, A. (1992). Developmental analysis of conflict caused by opposing attributes in the adolescent self-portrait. *Developmental Psychology*, 28, 251–260.

Haviland-Jones, J., Boulifard, D., & Magai, C. (2001). Old-new answers and new-old questions for personality and emotion: A matter of complexity. In H.A. Bosma & E.S. Kunnen (eds), *Identity and emotions: Development through self-organization* (pp. 151–171). Cambridge: Cambridge University Press.

Hazan, C., & Shaver, P. (1987) Romantic love conceptualized as an attachment process. *Journal of Personality and Social Psychology*, 52, 511–524.

Hermans, H.J.M., & Hermans-Jansen, E. (1995). *Self-narratives: The construction of meaning in psychotherapy*. New York: Guilford.

Hermans, H.J.M., & Kempen, H.J.G. (1993). *The dialogical self: Meaning as movement*. San Diego, CA: Academic.

Hermans, H.J.M., Kempen, H.J.G., & van Loon, R.J.P. (1992). The dialogical self: Beyond individualism and rationalism. *American Psychologist*, 47, 23–33.

Higgins, E.T. (1987). Self-discrepancy: A theory relating self and affect. *Psychological Review*, 94, 319–340.

Holmes, J. (1997). Attachment, autonomy, intimacy: Some clinical implications of attachment theory. *British Journal of Medical Psychology*, 70, 231–248.

Izard, C.E. (1984). Emotion–cognition relationships and human development. In C.E. Izard, J. Kagan, & R.B. Zajonc (eds), *Emotions, cognition and behavior* (pp. 17–37). Cambridge: Cambridge University Press.

James, W. (1890). *The principles of psychology*. New York: Dover, 1950.

Josselson, R. (1994). Identity and relatedness in the life cycle. In H.A. Bosma, T.L.G. Graafsma, H.D. Grotevant, & D.J. de Levita (eds), *Identity and development: An interdisciplinary approach* (pp. 81–102). Thousand Oaks, CA: Sage.

Keith, L. K., & Bracken, B.A. (1996). Self-concept instrumentation: A historical and evaluative review. In B.A. Bracken (ed.), *Handbook of self-concept: Developmental, social, and clinical considerations* (pp. 91–170). New York: Wiley.

Kerpelman, J.L., Pittman, J.F., & Lamke, L.K. (1997). Toward a microprocess perspective on adolescent identity development: An identity control theory approach. *Journal of Adolescent Research*, 12, 325–346.

Kobak, R., & Duemmler, S. (1994). Attachment and conversation: Towards a discourse analysis of adolescent and adult attachment. *Personal Relationships*, 5, 121–149.

Kobak, R.R., & Sceery, A. (1988). Attachment in late adolescence: Working models, affect regulation, and representations of self and others. *Child Development*, 59, 135–146.

Kroger, J. (1993). On the nature of structural transition in the identity formation process. In J. Kroger (ed.), *Discussions on ego identity* (pp. 205–234). Hillsdale, NJ: Erlbaum.

Kroger, J. (1995). The differentiation of 'firm' and 'developmental' foreclosure statuses: A longitudinal study. *Journal of Adolescent Research*, 10, 317–337.

Kroger, J. (1998). Adolescence as a second separation–individuation process. Critical review of an object relations approach. In E. Skoe & A. von der Lippe (eds), *Personality development in adolescence: A cross national and life span perspective* (pp. 172–192). London: Routledge.

Kroger, J. (2000). *Identity development: Adolescence through adulthood*. Thousand Oaks, CA: Sage.

Kroger, J. (in press). What transits in an identity status transition? *Identity: An International Journal of Theory and Research*.

Kroger, J., & Green, K.E. (1996). Events associated with identity status change. *Journal of Adolescence*, 19, 477–490.

Kunnen, E.S., & Bosma, H.A. (2000). Development of meaning making: A dynamic systems conceptualization. *New Ideas in Psychology*, 18, 57–82.

Kunnen, E.S., Bosma, H.A., & van Geert, P. (2001). A dynamic systems approach to identity formation: Theoretical background and methodological possibilities. In J.-E. Nurmi (ed.), *Navigating through adolescence: European perspectives*. New York: Garland.

Kunnen, E.S., Bosma, H.A., van Halen, C.P.M., & van der Meulen, M. (2001). A self-organizational approach to identity and emotions: An overview and implications. In H.A. Bosma & E.S. Kunnen (eds), *Identity and emotions: Development through self-organization* (pp. 202–230). Cambridge: Cambridge University Press.

Levine, J.B., Green, C.J., & Millon, T. (1986). The Separation–Individuation Test of Adolescence. *Journal of Personality Assessment*, 50, 123–137.

Lewis, M.D. (1995). Cognition–emotion feedback and the self-organization of developmental paths. *Human Development*, 38, 71–102.

Lewis, M.D., & Ferrari, M. (2001). Cognitive-emotional self-organization in personality development and personal identity. In H.A. Bosma & E.S. Kunnen (eds), *Identity and emotions: Development through self-organization* (pp. 177–198). Cambridge: Cambridge University Press.

Lewis, M.D., & Granic, I. (1999). Who put the self in self-organization? A clarification of terms and concepts for developmental psychopathology. *Development and Psychopathology*, 11, 365–374.

Lewis, M.D., & Granic, I. (eds) (2000). *Emotion, development, and self-organization: Dynamic systems approaches to emotional development*. Cambridge: Cambridge University Press.

Lewis, M., & Haviland-Jones, J.M. (eds) (2000). *Handbook of emotions* (2nd edn). New York: Guilford.

Liable, D.J., & Thompson, R.A. (2000). Attachment and self-organization. In M.D. Lewis & I. Granic (eds), *Emotion, development, and self-organization* (pp. 298–323). Cambridge: Cambridge University Press.

Mace, C., & Margison, F. (1997). Attachment and psychotherapy: An overview. *British Journal of Medical Psychology*, 70, 209–215.

MacKinnon, J.L., & Marcia, J.E. (2002). Concurring patterns of women's identity status, styles and understanding of children's development. *International Journal of Behavioral Development*, 26 (1), 70–80.

Magai, C., & McFadden, S.H. (1995). *The role of emotions in social and personality development: History, theory, and research*. New York: Plenum.

Magnusson, D., & Stattin, H. (1998). Person–context interaction theories. In W. Damon (series ed.) & R.M. Lerner (ed.), *Handbook of child psychology: Vol. 1* (pp. 685–759). New York: Wiley.

Mahler, M.S., Pine, F., & Bergman, A. (1975). *The psychological birth of the human infant*. New York: Basic.

Main, M. (1991). Metacognitive knowledge, metacognitive monitoring, and singular (coherent) vs. multiple (incoherent) models of attachment. In C.M. Parkes, J. Stevenson-Hinde, & P. Marris (eds), *Attachment across the life cycle* (pp. 127–159). London: Routledge.

Main, M., & Goldwyn, R. (1998). Adult attachment scoring and classification system. Unpublished manuscript, University of California at Berkeley.

Main, M., Kaplan, N., & Cassidy, J. (1985). Security in infancy, childhood and adulthood: A move to the level of representation. In I. Bretherton & E. Waters (eds), *Growing points of attachment theory and research* (pp. 66–104). *Monographs of the Society for Research in Child Development*, Vol. 50, serial 129.

Marcia, J.E. (1966). Development and validation of ego-identity status. *Journal of Personality and Social Psychology*, 35, 118–133.

Marcia, J.E. (1967). Ego identity status: Relationship to change in self-esteem, 'general maladjustment', and authoritarianism. *Journal of Personality*, 35, 119–133.

Marcia, J.E. (1976). Identity six years after: A follow-up study. *Journal of Youth and Adolescence*, 5, 145–160.

Marcia, J.E. (1980). Identity in adolescence. In J. Adelson (ed.), *Handbook of adolescent psychology* (pp. 159–187). New York: Wiley.

Marcia, J.E. (1989). Identity diffusion differentiated. In M.A. Luszez & T. Nettelbeck (eds), *Psychological development: Perspectives across the life-span*. Amsterdam: North-Holland Elsevier.

Marcia, J.E. (1993a). The ego identity status approach to ego identity. In J.E. Marcia, A.S. Waterman, D.R. Matteson, S.L. Archer, & J.L. Orlofsky (eds), *Ego identity: A handbook for psychosocial research* (pp. 3–21). New York: Springer.

Marcia, J.E. (1993b). The status of the statuses: Research review. In J.E. Marcia, A.S. Waterman, D.R. Matteson, S.L. Archer, & J.L. Orlofsky (eds), *Ego identity: A handbook for psychosocial research* (pp. 22–41). New York: Springer.

Marcia, J.E. (1994). Ego identity and object relations. In J.M. Masling & R.F. Borstein (eds), *Empirical perspectives on object relations theory* (pp. 59–103). Washington, DC: American Psychological Association.

Marcia, J.E. (1996). The importance of conflict for adolescent and lifespan development. In L. Verhofstadt-Denève, I. Kienhorst, & C. Braet (eds), *Conflict and development in adolescence* (pp. 13–19). Leiden: DSWO.

Marcia, J.E. (1998). Peer Gynt's life cycle. In E. Skoe & A. von der Lippe (eds), *Personality development in adolescence: A cross national and life span perspective* (pp. 193–209). London: Routledge.

Marcia, J.E., Waterman, A.S., Matteson, D.R., Archer, S.L., & Orlofsky, J.L. (eds) (1993). *Ego identity: A handbook for psychosocial research*. New York: Springer.

Markus, H., & Nurius, P. (1986). Possible selves. *American Psychologist*, 41, 954–969.

Markus, H., & Wurf, E. (1987). The dynamic self-concept: A social psychological perspective. *Annual Review of Psychology*, 38, 299–337.

Matteson, D.R. (1993). Differences within and between genders: A challenge to the theory. In J.E. Marcia, A.S. Waterman, D.R. Matteson, S.L. Archer, & J.L. Orlofsky (eds), *Ego identity: A handbook for psychosocial research* (pp. 69–110). New York: Springer.

McAdams, D.P. (1997). The case for unity in the (post)modern self: A modest proposal. In R.D. Ashmore & L. Jussim (eds), *Self and identity: Fundamental issues* (pp. 46–78). New York: Oxford University Press.

Mead, G.H. (1934). *Mind, self, and society*. Chicago: University of Chicago Press.

Meares, R. (1993). *The metaphor of play*. New York: Aronson.

Meeus, W. (1996). Studies on identity development in adolescence: An overview of research and some new data. *Journal of Youth and Adolescence*, 25, 269–598.

Meeus, W., Iedema, J., Helsen, M., & Vollebergh, W. (1999). Patterns of adolescent identity development: Review of literature and longitudinal analysis. *Developmental Review*, 19, 419–461.

Meilman, P.W. (1979). Cross-sectional age changes in ego identity status during adolescence. *Developmental Psychology*, 15, 230–231.

Mikulincer, M. (1998). Adult attachment style and affect regulation: Strategic variations in self-appraisals. *Journal of Personality and Social Psychology*, 75, 420–435.

Munroe, R.L. (1955). *Schools of psychoanalytic thought: An exposition, critique, and attempt at integration*. New York: Holt, Rinehart and Winston.

Oatley, K., & Jenkins, J.M. (1996). *Understanding emotions*. Cambridge, MA: Blackwell.

Olthof, T., Kunnen, E.S., & Boom, J. (2000). Simulating mother–child interaction: Exploring two varieties of non-linear dynamic systems approach. *Infant and Child Development* (previously *Early Development and Parenting*), 9, 33–60.

Oppenheim, D., & Salatas-Waters, H. (1995). Narrative processes and attachment representations: Issues of development and assessment. In E. Waters, B.E. Vaughn, G. Posada, & K. Kondo-Ikemura (eds), *Caregiving, cultural, and cognitive perspectives on secure-base behavior and working models: New growing points of attachment theory and research. Monographs of the Society for Research in Child Development*, Vol. 60, nos 2–3, serial 244.

Owens, G., Crowell, J.A., Pan, H., Treboux, D., O'Connor, E., & Waters, E. (1995). The prototype hypothesis and the origins of attachment working models: Adult relationships with parents and romantic partners. In E. Waters, B.E. Vaughn, G. Posada, & K. Kondo-Ikemura (eds), *Caregiving, cultural, and cognitive perspectives on secure-base behavior and working models: New growing points of attachment theory and research. Monographs of the Society for Research in Child Development*, Vol. 60, nos 2–3, serial 244.

Phinney, J.S., & Goossens, L. (1996). Introduction Identity development in context. *Journal of Adolescence*, 19, 401–403.

Pielage, S., Gerlsma, C., & Schaap, C. (2000). Insecure attachment as a risk factor for psychopathology: The role of stressful events. *Clinical Psychology and Psychotherapy*, 7, 296–302.

Rice, K.G. (1990). Attachment in adolescence: A narrative and meta-analytic review. *Journal of Youth and Adolescence*, 19, 511–538.

Rochat, P. (1995). Early objectification of the self. In P. Rochat (ed.), *The self in early infancy: Theory and research* (pp. 53–72). Amsterdam: Elsevier.

Rutter, M. (1995). Clinical implications of attachment concepts: Retrospect and prospect. *Journal of Child Psychology and Psychiatry*, 36, 549–571.

Ryan, R.M. (1991). The nature of the self in autonomy and relatedness. In J. Strauss & G.R. Goethals (eds), *The self: Interdisciplinary approaches* (pp. 208–238). New York: Springer.

Sagi, A., van IJzendoorn, M.H., Scharf, M., Koren-Karie, N., Joels, T., & Mayseless, O. (1994). Stability and discriminant validity of the Adult Attachment Interview: A psychometric study in young Israeli adults. *Developmental Psychology*, 30, 988–1000.

Schneider Rosen, K., & Rothbaum, F. (1993). Quality of parental caregiving and security of attachment. *Developmental Psychology*, 29, 358–367.

Schwartz, S.J. (2001). The evolution of Eriksonian and neo-Eriksonian identity theory and research: A review and integration. *Identity: An International Journal of Theory and Research*, 1, 7–58.

Simpson, J.A., & Rholes, W.S. (1994). Stress and secure base relationships in adulthood. *Advances in Personal Relationships*, 5, 181–204.

Steele, H., & Steele, M. (1994). Intergenerational patterns of attachment. In K. Bartholomew & D. Perlman (eds), *Attachment processes in adulthood. Advances in Personal Relationships* (Vol. 5, pp. 93–120). London: Kingsley.

Stein, H., Jacobs, N.J., Ferguson, K.S., Allen, J.G., & Fonagy, P. (1998). What do adult attachment scales measure? *Bulletin of the Menninger Clinic*, 62, 33–83.

Stern, D. (1985). *The interpersonal world of the infant*. New York: Basic.

Tajfel, H. (1982). Introduction. In H. Tajfel (ed.), *Social identity and intergroup relations* (pp. 1–11). Cambridge: Cambridge University Press.

Thelen, E., & Smith, L.B. (1994). *A dynamic systems approach to the development of cognition and action*. Cambridge, MA: Bradford/MIT Press.

Tomkins, S.S. (1978). Script theory: Differential magnification of affects. In H.E. Howe Jr & R.A. Dunstbier (eds), *Nebraska Symposium on Motivation* (pp. 201–236). Lincoln: University of Nebraska Press.

Turner, J.C. (1982). Towards a cognitive redefinition of the social group. In H. Tajfel (ed.), *Social identity and intergroup relations* (pp. 15–40). Cambridge: Cambridge University Press.

Valde, G.A. (1996). Identity closure: A fifth identity status. *Journal of Genetic Psychology*, 157 (3), 245–254.

van der Meulen, M. (2001). Developments in self-concept theory and research: Affect, context, and variability. In H.A. Bosma & E.S. Kunnen (eds), *Identity and emotions: Development through self-organization* (pp. 10–32). Cambridge: Cambridge University Press.

van der Werff, J.J. (1967). Contradictions and incompatabilities in the self and the ideal-self concept. *Acta Psychologica*, 26, 249–256.

van der Werff, J.J. (1985). Individual problems of self-definition: An overview, and a view. *International Journal of Behavioral Development*, 8, 445–471.

van der Werff, J.J. (1990). The problem of self-conceiving. In H. Bosma & S. Jackson (eds), *Coping and self-concept in adolescence* (pp. 13–33). Berlin: Springer.

van Dijken, S., van der Veer, R., van IJzendoorn, M., & Kuipers, H.J. (1998). Bowlby before Bowlby: The sources of an intellectual departure in psychoanalysis and psychology. *Journal of the History of the Behavioral Sciences*, 34, 247–269.

van Geert, P.L.C. (1991). A dynamic systems model of cognitive and language growth. *Psychological Review*, 98, 3–53.

van Geert, P.L.C. (1994). *Dynamic systems of development: change between complexity and chaos*. New York: Prentice-Hall/Harvester Wheatsheaf.

van Geert, P.L.C. (1998). A dynamic systems model of basic developmental mechanisms: Piaget, Vygotsky and beyond. *Psychological Review*, 105, 634–677.

van Halen, C.P.M. (2002). Experiencing self-definition problems over the lifespan. Doctoral dissertation, Groningen University.

van Hoof, A. (1999a). The identity status field re-reviewed: An update of unresolved and neglected issues with a view on some alternative approaches. *Developmental Review*, 19, 497–565.

van Hoof, A. (1999b). The identity status approach: In need of fundamental revision and qualitative change. *Developmental Review*, 19, 622–647.

van IJzendoorn, M.H. (1995). Adult attachment representations, parental responsiveness, and infant attachment: A meta-analysis on the predictive validity of the Adult Attachment Interview. *Psychological Bulletin*, 117, 387–403.

van IJzendoorn, M.H., & Bakermans-Kranenburg, M.J. (1996). Attachment representations in mothers, fathers, adolescents, and clinical groups: A meta-analytic research for normative data. *Journal of Consulting and Clinical Psychology*, 64 (1), 8–21.

van IJzendoorn, M.H., & de Wolff, M.S. (1997). In search of the absent father: Meta-analyses on infant–father attachment. A rejoinder to our discussants. *Child Development*, 68, 604–609.

van IJzendoorn, M.H., Schuengel, C., & Bakermans-Kranenburg, M.J. (1999). Disorganized attachment in early childhood: Meta-analysis of precursors, concomitants, and sequelae. *Development and Psychopathology*, 11, 225–249.

Waterman, A.S. (1982). Identity development from adolescence to adulthood: An extension of theory and a review of research. *Developmental Psychology*, 18, 341–358.

Waterman, A.S. (1993). Developmental perspectives on identity formation: From adolescence to adulthood. In J.E. Marcia, A.S. Waterman, D.R. Matteson, S.L. Archer, & J.L. Orlofsky, (eds), *Ego identity: A handbook for psychosocial research* (pp. 42–68). New York: Springer.

Waterman, A.S. (1999). Identity, the identity statuses, and identity status development: A contemporary statement. *Developmental Review*, 19, 591–621.

Waters, E. (1978). The reliability and stability of individual differences in infant–mother attachment. *Child Development*, 49, 483–494.

Waters, E., Posada, G., Crowell, J., & Keng-Ling, L. (1993). Is attachment theory ready to contribute to our understanding of disruptive behavior problems? *Development and Psychopathology* 5 (1–2), 215–224.

West, M. (1997). Reflective capacity and its significance to the attachment concept of the self. *British Journal of Medical Psychology*, **70**, 17–25.

Widdershoven, G.A.M. (1994). Identity and development. A narrative perspective. In H.A. Bosma, T.L.G. Graafsma, H.D. Grotevant, & D.J. de Levita (eds), *Identity and development: An interdisciplinary approach* (pp. 103–117). Thousand Oaks, CA: Sage.

Wylie, R.C. (1979). *The self concept* (Vol. II). Lincoln: University of Nebraska Press.

Wylie, R.C. (1989). *Measures of self-concept*. Lincoln: University of Nebraska Press.

PART SIX:
DEVELOPMENT IN ADULTHOOD

21

Adult Cognitive Development: Dynamics in the Developmental Web

KURT FISCHER, ZHENG YAN and JEFFREY STEWART

Adulthood normally spans more than 60 years, starting from about age 20, and the cognitive changes during those years are vast. Accumulated evidence indicates that cognitive development in adulthood is rich, complex, and dynamic, perhaps even more so than in infancy and childhood, with many factors acting together in various contexts to produce systematic, dynamic variation. For instance, it can be observed that adults frequently show regression performances and move down to lower levels of cognitive skill and then construct higher levels, instead of always following a simple forward progression. This kind of backward transition phenomenon in adult cognitive processes shows an interesting and important cognitive advancement, one that may seem frustrating and counter-intuitive to many intelligent adults.

Backward transition is just the tip of the large iceberg of complex cognitive development in adulthood. In this chapter, we reframe adult cognitive development dynamically, resynthesizing research findings to reveal the complex dynamics behind the variability in adult cognitive development, and reexamine the limitations of traditional cognitive analyses (Fischer, 1980b; Fischer & Bidell, 1998; Valsiner, 1991; van Geert, 1994). A constructed web (like that built in nature by a spider) serves as the meta-metaphor for development, and from the web we elaborate three important types of dynamic patterns in adult cognitive development: dynamic ranges, dynamic strands and networks, and dynamic constructions. With these concepts, we begin to capture the richness and complexity of adult cognitive development and to offer a new story about what, how, and why adult cognitive development takes place over time.

LADDERS AND WEBS: META-METAPHORS OF ADULT COGNITIVE DEVELOPMENT

The history of science shows that different meta-metaphors functioning as central mental models have had tremendous impact on scientific thinking (for example, viewing the earth as the center of the universe, seeing the spiral as the structure of DNA, considering the person as a digital computer). Likewise, different meta-metaphors drive fundamental views of adult cognitive development. We categorize two major types of meta-metaphors for adult development – ladders and webs – which engender different portraits of adult cognitive development.

Developmental ladders characterize development as a simple fixed progression, following monotonic change, with one step following another in a single direction. As shown in Figure 21.1, the developmental ladder-like trajectory has at least three features: (1) development simply follows a single straight line; (2) each step is fixed, following the previous step along the line; and (3) forward progression along the line is the sole form of development.

Piaget's (1983) cognitive developmental model, as it is usually understood, is one of the most common ladder-like models of human cognitive development (although Piaget himself had a more dynamic view, as in Piaget, 1975). According to this model, thinking progresses through a series of stages and then stops at the level of formal operations during adolescence. Many scholars have built upon this Piagetian framework by extending the model vertically or horizontally in adulthood, adding more stages or more unevenness across domains

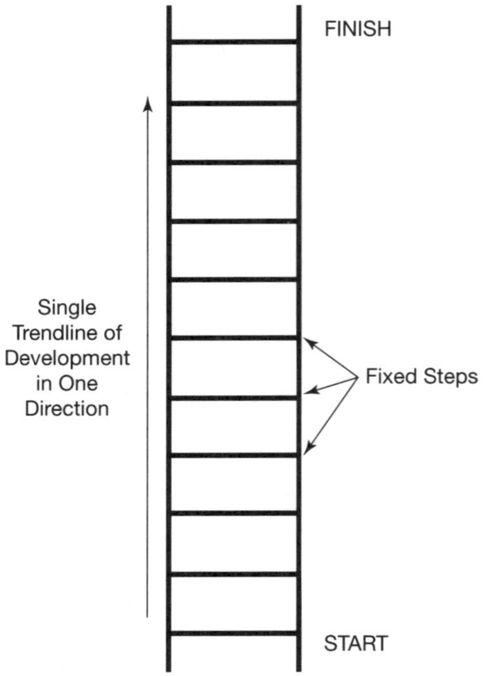

Figure 21.1 *A developmental ladder*

(Alexander et al., 1990; Baltes, 1987; Basseches, 1984; Berg, 2000; Commons et al., 1998; Dawson, 1999; Erikson, 1968; Gardner, 1983; Gruber, 1981; Kegan, 1982; King & Kitchener, 1994; Kohlberg, 1969; 1984; Loevinger, 1976; Sinnott, 1998). These models either have substantially expanded Piaget's model along the vertical dimension by adding higher cognitive stages such as post-formal operations and advanced reflective thinking, or have extended Piagets model along the horizontal dimension by including more cognitive domains such as moral reasoning and self-understanding.

Other models that are grounded primarily in psychometric research, such as standardized ability testing, often have acknowledged phenomena similar to Piagetian stages, but have emphasized certain upward and downward general developmental trends associated with age on standardized tests of abilities (Baltes, 1987; Birren, 1964; 1970; Craik, 1977; Craik & Salthouse, 1991; Horn, 1982; Horn & Cattell, 1967; Salthouse, 1984; 1992; Sternberg, 1985). Some abilities, such as crystallized intelligence, increase well into old age, while others, such as fluid intelligence, begin to decrease by early or middle adulthood.

These various developmental models have substantially added to knowledge of cognitive developmental changes and variations in adults, but all of them, to differing degrees, share an underlying ladder-like meta-metaphor. They treat adult cognitive development, like child cognitive development, as a static progressive process unfolding along a series of fixed ladder steps, either through stages or through linear ability scales. In short, this meta-metaphor does simplify complex developmental phenomena and sketch general developmental trends, but at the expense of neglecting, downplaying, and even misrepresenting the variability and richness of adult cognitive development.

In contrast, *developmental webs* portray adult cognitive development as a complex process of dynamic construction within multiple ranges in multiple directions. As illustrated in Figure 21.2, the developmental web has at least three important features: (1) development occurs in a complex multilevel range; (2) developmental pathways undergo dynamic transformation through multiple strands or network links; and (3) multidirectional construction is the form of development.

Dynamic skill theory (Fischer & Bidell, 1998) analyzes development as involving a constructed web that captures much of the rich variability in human behavior. Central to the variability, it turns out, is the fact that activities take place in specific contexts. People do not act in a void. Growing adaptively in a dynamic world with various social, emotional, technological, and physical challenges means that behavior must fit the immediacy of the situation. For a description of development that aims at both rigor and honesty, these contexts cannot be ignored. A web captures the interconnected complexity of skills in diverse contexts, as shown in Figure 21.2. Each web contains distinct strands for different contexts and activities, sometimes converging through coordination, sometimes diverging through separation or differentiation, always built through specific sensorimotor and mental activities. Emotional states also shape strands, such as the separation of positive and negative activities (good and bad, nice and mean, approach and avoidance). The web metaphor stresses that many components contribute to any activity, producing diverse shapes of development. A person acts interactively, engaged with his or her many environments, and the action process is dynamic and nonlinear because the outcome of an action involves more than adding together the behavior of the individual and the environmental components that contribute to it. Specifically, each person constructs a unique web, while at the same time ordering principles help generalization across individual webs.

The web also incorporates skill variation within each strand. Each strand is structured by a composite of available levels – the developmental range – with reference to the experiences and contextual supports that contribute to its construction. For any single domain of action (single strand), a person's competence is not fixed at a particular point on the strand but can vary along a portion of the strand. Practice and familiarity with a domain, contextual support for

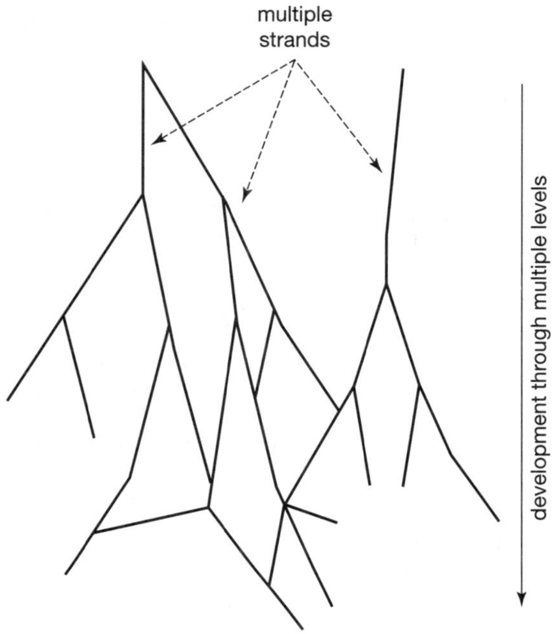

Figure 21.2 *A developmental web*

complex activity, and joint participation with others all affect the level of a person's activities along a strand. Each single strand shows the developmental range in skill and knowledge of the individual for that particular task and domain given varying amounts of experience and contextual support. Later in the chapter we will elaborate how this variability can be integrated into the web metaphor.

Conceptually, the developmental web differs from a developmental ladder in at least six important ways:

1. The web places variation in activity at center stage, whereas the ladder downplays variation, relegating it to marginality as error or individual differences.
2. The web is based on individual cognitive performance, whereas the ladder is primarily based on average group performance.
3. The web includes multiple cognitive levels in each person, whereas the ladder assumes a single level at a time.
4. The web distinguishes multiple tasks and domains, whereas the ladder treats diverse tasks and domains in terms of a single line.
5. The web has inherently complex interconnections within it, whereas the ladder does not include networking among elements.
6. The web shows multiple directions of construction, such as forward consolidation and backward transition, whereas the ladder assumes a single direction of forward progression.

Rethinking adult cognitive development requires establishing new meta-metaphors to replace old meta-metaphors. Developmental webs can capture more of the richness and complexity of adult cognitive development than ladders. As a powerful meta-metaphor, the web can facilitate better understanding of what, how, and why adults' cognition changes in complex situations over the extremely long period of life after childhood.

Dynamic Ranges in the Web

Research shows that the complexity levels of adult cognition continue to change in two important ways. First, for the same cognitive task, an adult often shows multiple levels of cognition under different circumstances. Because of the wide range of levels of which adults are capable, cognitive performance in adults varies much more widely than in children. Adults can think more flexibly, dynamically, and contextually than children, while like children they also continue to make errors, even ridiculous mistakes, and to act in simple, primitive ways. Second, the upper limit of cognitive functioning continues to increase beyond what Piaget called formal operations (Inhelder & Piaget, 1958; Piaget, 1975; 1983). Thus, adults can solve much more abstract and complicated cognitive tasks than children, even while they also can use low-level skills similar to those of children. The lengths of some strands in the web continue to expand into development, representing a continuing increase in adults' optimal cognitive skills and a wide range of variation in the level of skills that adults can use in a domain.

Multiple Levels of Adult Cognitive Development

Along with the increase in overall complexity of adults' cognitive development, both developmental research and everyday observations indicate that adults show multiple levels of cognitive development, not performance at one fixed level. Even very wise adults use simple skills when the situation requires simple action, and from time to time they may make unwise decisions when dealing with complex tasks without sufficient contextual support to them. The dynamics of adults' multilevel performance vary with contextual support, prior experience, and joint action with other people.

Optimal and Functional Levels

A central concept in traditional developmental research is that of 'upper limit': people have an upper limit on a given skill beyond which they cannot go. This concept requires major revision, because even an adult's upper limit varies dynamically with contextual support. Developmental research differentiates two major types of upper limit on skill performance, varying with contextual support: optimal level and functional level. There is no single level of competence in any domain. Instead, in the absence of task intervention or scaffolding by others, individuals show great variation in skill levels in their everyday functioning (Fischer & Bidell, 1998; Fischer, Hand, & Russell, 1984; van Geert, 2002). Optimal levels are attained primarily in those infrequent circumstances when environmental conditions provide strong support for complex performance. Such conditions, including clearly defined tasks, familiar materials, practice, and memory priming of the gist of the activity, are not present in most situations. For this reason, every person shows a persistent gap between the functional level under typical (low-support) conditions and the optimal level afforded by high support.

Functional levels tend to be characterized by slow, gradual, and continuous growth over time, whereas optimal levels exhibit stage-like spurts and plateaus within an upward trend, like those in Figure 21.3. These two trend lines diverge, becoming more disparate with age, because they depend on different sets of growth processes. The functional level results from the steady construction of a skill in a particular domain over time, whereas the optimal level – the upper limit on functioning – is achieved through strong contextual support for a skill combined with organic growth processes that reorganize behavior and brain activity in recurring growth

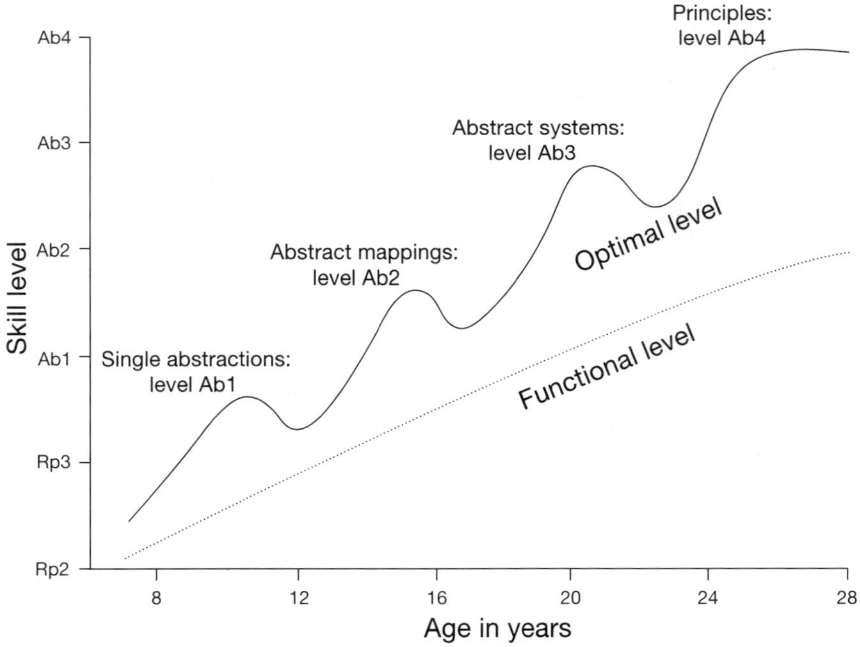

Figure 21.3 *Development of optimal and functional levels in a domain*

cycles. Furthermore, the gap between functional and optimal levels grows with age. Research has found a far larger increase with age in the optimal level for a given skill than in its functional level, and consequently the gap increases from early childhood through adulthood (Bullock & Ziegler, 1994; Fischer, Kenny, & Pipp, 1990; Kitchener et al., 1993; Watson & Fischer, 1980).

An example of optimal and functional levels in abstractions is the development of concepts of self in relationships. In a study of how Korean adolescents (grades 8 through 13, or adolescent through young adult) saw themselves in relationship with others, students participated in the Self-in-Relationships Interview, which included both an open-ended interview about their relationships (low support) and a high-support assessment (Fischer & Kennedy, 1997; Kennedy, 1994). Support was provided through their creation of a detailed diagram of the characteristics of specific relationships. In the high-support assessment, students (a) created descriptions of their characteristics with particular people; (b) placed the descriptions in one of three concentric circles from most to least important; and (c) grouped similar descriptions, drew connecting lines to indicate relations, and added a plus or minus to indicate emotional valence (good, bad, or ambivalent). Then the interviewer asked them a series of questions to elicit explanations of their diagram at different developmental levels. In the low-support assessment students produced only a slight increase over the six years and did not achieve even the level of single abstractions. The same students in the high-support condition started at a higher level, single abstractions, and moved up to the level of abstract systems. In addition, their trajectory showed spurts for the emergence of abstract mappings and abstract systems, similar to those shown in Figure 21.3. Much more sophisticated cognitive skills were called forth with support, while an absence of support led to low-level skills.

Note that optimal level produces a series of spurts in growth followed by plateaus or small drops – a dynamic pattern of change that is common in development (Fischer & Bidell, 1998; Fischer, Kenny, & Pipp, 1990); Thatcher, 1994; van der Maas & Molenaar, 1992). The fact that the functional level shows no such systematic variability underscores the potential for missing the telling dynamics of development by examining performance in only one condition and assuming that it represents the basic nature of cognitive development. Growth patterns differ under different conditions, even for the 'same' skill in the same person, and the dynamics of this variability are fundamental in adult cognitive development.

How do the spurts in optimal level relate to the web of development? Various strands/domains in a web show a cluster of spurts within a concurrent zone, as illustrated in Figure 21.4. Put another way, in the developmental web, the optimal level

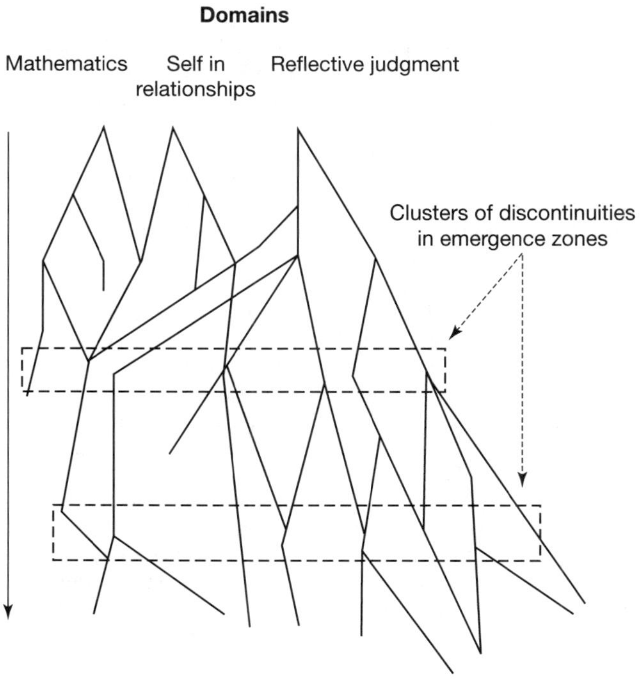

Figure 21.4 *Clusters of discontinuities for two optimal levels across strands and domains*

emerges when clusters of discontinuities appear across many strands in the same time period. This skill phenomenon has a neurophysiological correlate, in that cortical substrates for the increase in ability show developmental changes that mirror the behavioral ones (Fischer & Rose, 1994; Thatcher, 1994). That is, patterns of cortical activity show spurts that are approximately concurrent with the spurts in optimal skill level.

Automatization and Co-Participation

Optimal and functional levels are only two of the many skill levels that adults routinely use. For example, when people act automatically (without thinking or consciously choosing), they typically act at a low level, as when someone steps on the brake automatically when a child runs in front of the car. Researchers have not directly assessed the developmental level of such automatic actions, but they exist in every domain, and usually they are relatively simple and primitive.

On the other hand, people frequently act together with other people, cooperating to accomplish a task together – telling a family story, putting together a jigsaw puzzle, playing poker, or building a house. One person scaffolds the actions of another, sometimes in expert and novice roles as with teacher and student (Wood, Bruner, & Ross, 1976) and sometimes as more equal collaborators (Granott, 1993b; Valsiner, 1996). In actuality, many situations that psychologists often treat as individual are naturally social. Many children prefer to play video games with their friends, either directly sharing them or talking about them on the phone. Many scholars write papers with the help of other people, even when only one author is listed. In co-participation in general, people co-construct complex skills that often go beyond their individual capacity, as Vygotsky (1978) emphasized with his concept of the zone of proximal development, and Wood, Bruner, and Ross (1976) elaborated with the concept of scaffolding. Indeed, the importance of such social construction has been recognized for the entire history of modern psychology and child development, but it continues to be neglected in most research and theory (Valsiner & van der Veer, 1988), which is especially puzzling in elaborations of explicit theories of social construction such as Erikson's (1963). Co-constructive processes are at least as important in adults as they are in children.

In addition, people move up and down in the level of their performance, adapting to the situation, goal, task, emotional state, and their co-participants. Real-time analysis of ongoing activity shows how level varies dynamically with these factors, even more in adults than in children (Bullock & Ziegler, 1994; Fischer & Granott, 1995; Granott, 1993a; 2002; Kuhn et al., 1995; Roberts, 1981; Siegler, 2002; Vaillant, 1977). As a strand in a person's web grows longer, he or she has a wider range of skills to use across portions of the strand. Figure 21.5 shows how the four levels that we have described are evident in the web. Automatized skills, marked by thick solid lines, mostly occur early in each strand. Functional skills, performed thoughtfully but without support, are marked by thin solid lines. Optimal skills, which usually depend on contextual support, occupy later portions of the strand and are marked by dashed lines. Scaffolded skills, in which people jointly perform a complex activity, are most complex and are marked by dotted lines.

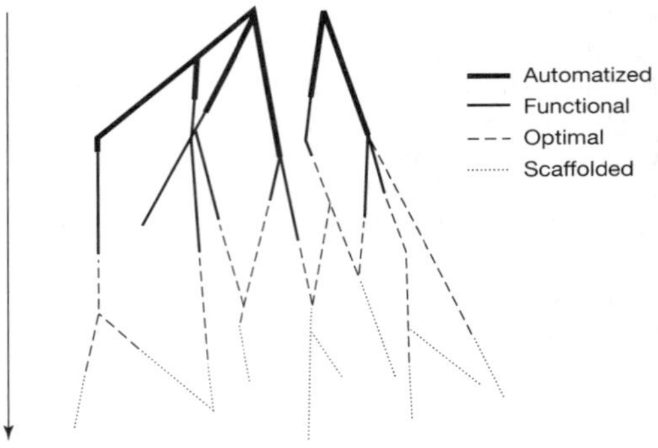

Figure 21.5 *Developmental range in a web*

Levels of Optimal Cognitive Development

Adult development must be understood in terms of the whole scope of development from infancy, both because later skills are built on earlier ones and because adults routinely use skill levels that first emerge in infancy and childhood (especially when they move down in a strand of the web to use automatized skills, or make backward transitions to build new skills). Dynamic skill theory describes the context-based constructive process of building from reflexes to actions, from actions to representations, and from representations to abstractions (Fischer, 1980b; Fischer & Bidell, 1998). Cognitive activity undergoes massive restructuring during the years of infancy and childhood, gradually building toward concrete skills and conceptual categories. In adolescence and early adulthood, people restructure their activities again, moving from representations to abstractions. Much of the rest of adulthood involves consolidation, elaboration, integration, synthesis, and extension of these abstract skills.

The skill hierarchy not only describes cognitive development, but provides a ruler for assessing and studying dynamic variations in adult activities. This ruler allows comparison of levels across conditions and tasks, such as optimal, functional, and scaffolded levels (Figures 21.2 and 21.3), and it makes possible analysis of the dynamics of real-time learning and problem-solving, as in backwards transitions and forward consolidation. Dynamic analysis of skill requires such a scale to assess variability and to model it. Cognitive development research has been hampered by the absence of such scales for coding activity across tasks, domains, and trials, except in the arena of motor activity, where Cartesian coordinates provide ready-made scales for dynamic analysis (Rose & Fischer, 1998; Thelen & Smith, 1994; van Geert, 1994).

Hierarchy of Adult Skill Levels

From birth to 30 years of age, an individual develops skills through four sequential *tiers* in a nested hierarchy. Early *reflexes* become coordinated into *actions*, actions are coordinated into *representations*, and representations into *abstractions*. Each of these qualitatively different behavioral repertoires cycles through a similar pattern of coordinations – the four *levels* of each tier. Movement is from an initial *single* expression of an ability (the first level of a given tier), to a *mapping* of two elements (the second level of a tier), to a *system* that relates multiple elements (the third level), and finally to a *system of systems* (the final level). Each level arises from the gradual combination of two or more skills from the prior level in a process of coordination and differentiation. Taken together, the four tiers produce a scale of 13 levels that increase in complexity and integration – a 13-point interval scale for assessing the dynamics of development and variation. Reorganizations of neural networks seem to help catalyze development of a wide range of skills at each new level (Fischer & Rose, 1994; 1996).

The levels that characterize the final tier move through single abstractions, abstract mappings, abstract systems, and abstract systems of systems, or principles. We will describe this development of increased complexity of abstract thinking from middle childhood through adulthood, as shown in the left-hand part of Table 21.1, and we will explicate the levels through discussions of reflective judgment, moral judgment, identity development, and Darwin's construction of the theory of evolution.

The optimal level of representational systems (Rp3) usually emerges around the age of 6 years in middle-class children with high contextual support, and is elaborated and consolidated over the next 3

Table 21.1 *Levels of development of representational and abstract skills*

	Tier		
Level	Representations	Abstractions	Age[1]
Rp1 single representations	$[Q]$		18 – 24 months
Rp2 representational mappings	$[Q \text{——} R]$		3.5 – 4.5 years
Rp3: representational systems	$[Q^U_V \longleftrightarrow R^U_V]$		6–7 years
Rp4/Ab1: systems of representational systems, which are single abstractions	$\begin{bmatrix} Q^U_V \longleftrightarrow R^U_V \\ \Updownarrow \\ S^W_X \longleftrightarrow T^W_X \end{bmatrix}$	$\equiv [\mathbb{Y}]$	10–12 years
Ab2: abstract mappings		$[\mathbb{Y} \text{——} \mathbb{Z}]$	14–16 years
Ab3: abstract systems		$[\mathbb{Y}^{\mathbb{C}}_{\mathbb{D}} \longleftrightarrow \mathbb{Z}^{\mathbb{C}}_{\mathbb{D}}]$	19–20 years
Ab4: systems of abstract systems, which are principles		$\begin{bmatrix} \mathbb{Y}^{\mathbb{C}}_{\mathbb{D}} \longleftrightarrow \mathbb{Z}^{\mathbb{C}}_{\mathbb{D}} \\ \Updownarrow \\ \mathbb{A}^{\mathbb{E}}_{\mathbb{F}} \longleftrightarrow \mathbb{B}^{\mathbb{E}}_{\mathbb{F}} \end{bmatrix}$	24–25 years

Note: Italic letters designate representational sets, and outline letters abstract sets. Subscripts and superscripts designate differentiated subsets. Long straight lines and arrows designate a relation between sets or systems. Brackets mark a single skill. Note also that structures from lower tiers continue at higher levels (representations in abstract skills, etc.), but the formulas are omitted because they become so complex.

[1] Ages are modal for the emergence of optimal levels based on research with middle-class American and European children. They may differ across cultures or social groups.

or 4 years. (The earlier representational levels are shown for completeness and because they appear in adult problem-solving, discussed below.) This level is the core of much adult functioning, because for many activities people need only concrete actions and representations, not sophisticated abstract thinking. With a skill at this level, a person can coordinate two or three different aspects of several representations. For instance, a child Kara and her mother Jane can play teacher and student, where the child/teacher interacts simultaneously and reciprocally with the mother/student:

$$\overset{\textit{Play}}{\begin{bmatrix} \textit{STUDENT} & \textit{TEACHER} \\ \textit{JANE} \longleftrightarrow & \textit{KARA} \\ \textit{MOTHER} & \textit{CHILD} \end{bmatrix}} \quad (1)$$

Children especially enjoy reversing conventional roles to assume more powerful and independent adult roles in play; and adults frequently cooperate in this pretense. The mother and the child both act with a similar representational system, as shown in formula 1, but the mother's skill may include an additional component for scaffolding her child's skill. The category relations usually remain fully concrete, even when the story becomes complex.

The optimal level of single abstractions (Rp4/Ab1) emerges at about age 10, when youngsters begin to understand abstract concepts commonly used by adults. At this first level of abstract thinking, the ability to relate different explicit instances of representations to an intangible concept becomes commonplace. For a 12-year-old girl, traveling with friends to a parade, buying her own lunch, and choosing her own new clothes can all be related in the concept of independence. The representational systems for the parade, the lunch, and the clothes, which each have a structure similar to that in formula 1, are richly coordinated in a new skill, which is an achievement of representational complexity (Rp4). A diagram for the coordination of two systems to form an abstraction is shown in Table 21.1. The coordination of parade, lunch, and clothes systems gives them the power to broadly unify the three contents into a single abstract concept, independent:

$$\begin{bmatrix} \text{SELF} \\ \text{INDEPENDENT} \end{bmatrix} \quad (2)$$

At this initial level, abstractions are somewhat fuzzy because they are single: without comparison, abstractions cannot be easily differentiated from each other. The 12-year-old may use the same three examples for both independence (formula 2) and individualist:

$$\begin{bmatrix} \text{SELF} \\ \text{INDIVIDUALIST} \end{bmatrix} \quad (3)$$

When asked how the two differ, she muddies them together, not clearly articulating a difference: 'They're the same thing. Both of them involve being free.' Imagine how complex and confusing it is when a third concept such as liberty is added to the pot! The same kinds of confusion create difficulties in coordinating one's own identity with another person's, often leading to a kind of merging or globbing of identities with a close friend or partner (Erikson, 1968). Adults as well as adolescents show this globbing together of distinct abstractions, and it takes many different forms (Fischer, Hand, & Russell, 1984). At least adults are capable of building higher-level skills to compare and differentiate related abstractions.

The optimal level of abstract mappings (Ab2) appears when adolescents are first able to coordinate two or more abstractions, beginning at about age 15. Much sophisticated adult activity involves this level of simple relations of abstractions (Colby et al., 1983; Commons et al., 1998; Cook-Greuter, 1999; Dawson, 1999; King & Kitchener, 1994). Being able to use one abstraction in comparison with another is a great help in making thinking more precise. Independence and individualism are related but distinct, with independence involving the freedom to do things on one's own, and individualism involving a commitment to freely choosing who one wants to be:

$$\begin{bmatrix} \text{SELF} & \text{———} & \text{SELF} \\ \text{INDEPENDENT} & & \text{INDIVIDUALIST} \end{bmatrix} \quad (4)$$

In tandem with the increase in cognitive clarity at this level is a jump in social facility because of the capacity to coordinate and differentiate one's own abstractions with someone else's. In identity, a person can coordinate an abstraction about themselves with one about a close friend or partner, allowing for a new kind of intimate relationship, such as how my independence is similar to and different from my friend's, especially in our close relationship:

$$\begin{bmatrix} \text{SELF} & \text{———} & \text{FRIEND} \\ \text{INDEPENDENT} & & \text{INDEPENDENT} \end{bmatrix} \quad (5)$$

(Erikson, 1968; Fischer & Ayoub, 1996; Kegan, 1982; Loevinger, 1976; Noam et al., 1990).

At around the age of 19 or 20, the optimal level of abstract systems (Ab3) emerges, as individuals coordinate multiple abstractions and begin to understand the subtleties and nuances in abstract relations in many domains, including understanding of self and others. For instance, the young adult can compare and relate the subtleties of abstractions like conformity and independence. At the prior level, relating different forms of conformity and independence in different situations is difficult, but with abstract systems it is easier to see: for example, that both at school and with friends I show mixtures of both conformity and independence. Similarly with identity coordination, a mother and father can understand how their two identities differ with their son and daughter, and a person can more readily coordinate his or her own conformity and independence with a friend's or partner's:

$$\begin{bmatrix} \text{CONFORMING} & & \text{CONFORMING} \\ \text{SELF} & \longleftrightarrow & \text{FRIEND} \\ \text{INDEPENDENT} & & \text{INDEPENDENT} \end{bmatrix} \qquad (6)$$

The optimal level of abstract systems of systems (Ab4), or principles, is the final developmental level predicted by skill theory. Emerging under high-support conditions around the mid-20s, this highest cognitive level allows a person to coordinate several abstract systems together, as diagrammed in Table 21.1. How does my own personal identity relate to moral dilemmas that I have faced, or career choices I have made, or different intimate relationships I have had (Erikson, 1963; 1968)? By coordinating two or more abstract systems, a person can construct and use a general principle that goes across systems, such as the Golden Rule in morality and Reflective Judgment in knowledge dilemmas. We will describe in some detail how Darwin built his level Ab4 principle of evolution by natural selection:

$$\begin{bmatrix} \mathit{EVOLUTION} & \\ & \mathit{SELECTION} \end{bmatrix} \qquad (7)$$

Once constructed, such a principle can be extended to many different abstract systems, as we will illustrate later. People do not remain at this level for long periods, but only use it as needed, with environmental and social supports required to sustain it in the day-to-day activities of living.

These skill levels provide a complexity scale with which to assess the variability in people's activities and to look for patterns of stability and order. People do not act stably at one skill level, as in the ladder metaphor for development. Instead they range widely over many levels, sometimes changing almost instantaneously in adapting to different challenges. The range extends from low levels of action and representation (far below those shown in Table 21.1) to the highest level of abstraction (Brown & Reeve, 1987; Bullock & Ziegler, 1994; Fischer & Bidell, 1998; Fischer & Granott, 1995; Granott, 1993a; 1998; Kuhn et al., 1995; van Geert, 2002). Much of what we describe in this chapter is the rules for order in this pervasive variation in adult cognitive development.

Development beyond Abstractions?

Is there any evidence from these studies that might point to the development of levels and tiers beyond the level of principles (Ab4) – perhaps relating principles to each other or changing skill capacities in some other way? Sound and sufficient empirical evidence is required to answer this question, and we know of little that has been decisive beyond the level of principles for newly emerging optimal levels. Perhaps adults have enough to do simply generalizing and consolidating the abstractions required of them. However, some interesting work by Francine Benes (1984) on myelination of neurons in the brain suggests a possible major reorganization at mid-life. Myelin is the insulation around neural axons that greatly improves the speed and efficiency of neural transmission. After years of only slow change in myelin, adults in their 40s and 50s show myelin growth spurts for neurons connecting the prefrontal cortex to the limbic system. One speculation is that this change creates more refined control of emotional impulses, perhaps in relation with the mastery of the highest levels of abstraction that many adults achieve by these ages. With the capacity to sustain complex abstract and principled thinking without contextual support (at least in areas of expertise) comes a greater opportunity to bring wisdom to bear on emotional equilibrium and self-control. Perhaps this change is relevant to Erikson's (1963) suggestion that wisdom is the central issue in his final stage of identity development.

Development of Reflective Judgment and Moral Judgment

The foundations of knowledge are a fundamental issue in cognitive science and philosophy, and John Dewey (1910) described a model for the development of understanding the bases of knowledge. The goal of education is what he called *reflective judgment*, the 'active, persistent, and careful consideration of any belief or supposed form of knowledge in the light of the grounds that support it, and the further conclusions to which it tends' (1910, p. 6). Key elements include the use of evidence and reasoning, the frameworks for knowledge and belief, and justifications for conclusions. Developing reflective thinking is one of the important tasks and intellectual challenges in adult cognitive growth.

The foundations of moral reasoning are even more important than reflective judgment in human society, especially for socially responsible adults. Moral evaluation and judgment are one of the intellectual challenges that adults face in a world with multiple, often conflicting moral standards and decisions. Good moral reasoning not only requires abstract thinking, but also complex value judgments and emotions. The influential work of Lawrence Kohlberg (1969; 1984) on moral reasoning reveals how people move in their thinking from an authoritarian notion of morality through a gradual relativizing of their judgments, and then to an established value system (a process generally analogous to that for reflective judgment). Indeed, the research on reflective judgment was based directly on the research and methods that Kohlberg devised for moral judgment.

A rich research program led by Kitchener and King has investigated the development of reflective judgment in adults, as well as adolescents, including tests of optimal and functional levels (King & Kitchener, 1994; Kitchener et al., 1993), whereas the research on moral judgment has not assessed these two distinct levels. Kitchener and King start by asking people about difficult dilemmas and how they know something is either true or false for such a dilemma. One of their standard dilemmas concerns chemical additives: are they good things because when added to food, they prevent some illnesses; or are they bad because they may cause cancer? Depending on the response to this dilemma, people can vary over seven stages of understanding, with the optimal stages emerging from, roughly, 2 years of age up to 25 years and beyond (Fischer & Pruyne, 2002). The stages map exactly onto the skill levels outlined in Table 21.1 (Kitchener et al., 1993).

At the first stage, responses reflect only an absolute kind of thinking: a fact or conclusion is either right or wrong. In moral judgment, the first several stages reflect a similar concrete approach to morality: an action is simply good or bad. By stage 4 of reflective judgment (the middle stage) people have moved to a relative type of thinking: the truth of a statement varies with the perspective. Whether something is true 'depends on your bias'. This stage involves the construction of single abstractions (Ab1) for relative knowledge, and, as is typical for this level in general, people have difficulty moving beyond the confusion of single, uncoordinated abstractions. A person knows simply that knowledge is a variable thing, and even though an attempt is made to justify a decision about chemical additives, the justification is neither coordinated conceptually with the decision nor differentiated from it.

The nature of relativism in moral judgment remains a question in the research. It is unclear whether there is a distinct stage of relativism. Two candidates are stage 3, where moral judgment is based on one's social group norms, or an additional stage between 4 and 5, where the relativity of moral judgment to society and culture is recognized (Dawson, 2002; Fischer, Hand, & Russell, 1984).

In stage 5 of reflective judgment (the level of abstract mappings, Ab2) people begin to compare arguments, evidence, and viewpoints, recognizing that some arguments and conclusions are better than others. Arguments and justifications are linked to a certain context or viewpoint, and there is certain logic relating to the conclusions, but still people take a mostly relativistic stance. At stages 6 and 7, Dewey's goal of reflective judgment comes into play: the truth of the proposition depends on the specific arguments made and the supporting evidence for the arguments. With sufficient evidence and argument, a conclusion can be firmly reached that goes beyond a relativistic dependence of viewpoint. Stage 6 arguments (abstract systems, Ab3) recognize that knowledge is not always certain but that strong, justified conclusions can be made with sufficient evidence. Stage 7 arguments (principles, Ab4) move to fully reflective judgment, including formulation of a principle that strong, justified conclusions rest on their evidence, and that different kinds of evidence depend on the situation and viewpoint from which they were collected.

In moral judgment, Kohlberg's stages 5 and 6 constitute what he called *principled moral reasoning*, analogous to the principle of reflective judgment. General principles are held to apply across cultures, along with local variations, and are used to guide judgments of lawful and moral activities. Empirical evidence supports the existence of a social-contract principle, which Kohlberg characterized as stage 5, in which people argue that values established by norms in order to promote social harmony for the good of everyone are subject to modification according to the will of the people. The universal ethical principles that Kohlberg hypothesized for stage 6, such as the Golden Rule (do unto others as you would have them do unto you), remain controversial because research to date has found few people who consistently function with such principles (Colby et al., 1983). We propose that research on dynamic variation in moral judgment, such as optimal and functional levels, will resolve this dispute.

One study of reflective judgment suggests a kind of order in the variation behind the emergence of optimal levels. When a level or stage first emerges, people do not quickly generalize the new skill across all tasks but work slowly and painstakingly to create the general skill. For instance, when the level of abstract systems first emerged in the students in this study at about age 20, they produced only about 50% of their arguments at stage 6 (Figure 21.6). Not until the next level emerged at about age 25 did they produce nearly 100% of their arguments at stage 6. In general, each optimal level produces a spurt in performance, as shown in the line for the general reflective judgment score in Figure 21.6. But that level does not become powerfully generalized until some years later, with the emergence of the next level (or even a further level beyond the next). For the functional level, the process is much longer yet, reaching 50% only in the late 20s. In general, functional consolidation of optimal skills requires many years of adult development.

An important finding about both reflective judgment and moral judgment is that higher education plays a central role in their development and consolidation. All the people in the study in Figure 21.6 were students, either graduate students, college students, or college-bound high school students. Research shows strongly that education plays a more important role than age alone in producing movement to sophisticated judgments about moral issues and the nature of knowledge (Colby et al., 1983; Dawson, 2002; King & Kitchener, 1994; Rest et al., 1999). The emergence of a new optimal level is not enough to produce the stable development of a sophisticated

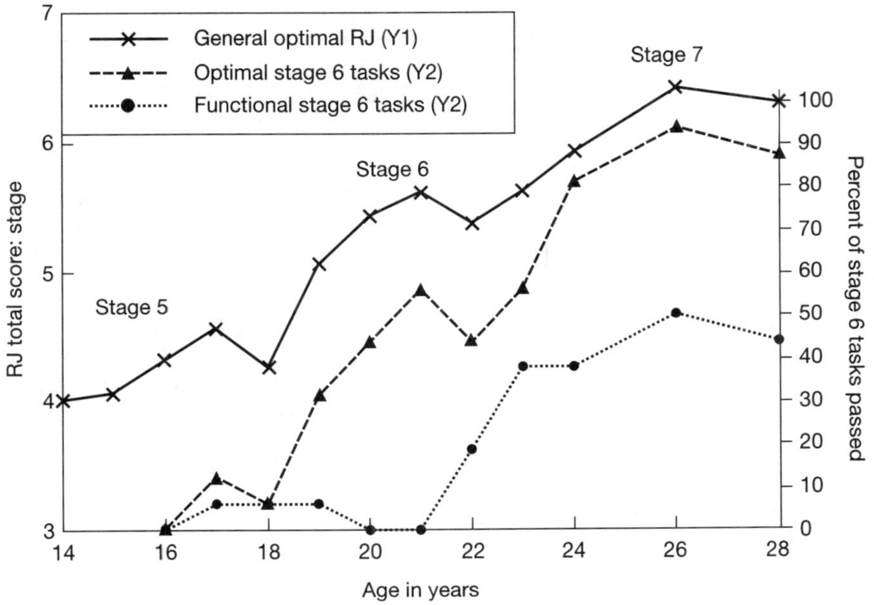

Figure 21.6 *Development of reflective judgment (data from Kitchener et al., 1993)*

skill. A stimulating environment must catalyze the development of the highest stages of moral and reflective judgment, and it may be essential for other domains of adult development as well.

Dynamic Strands and Networks in the Web

Adults develop not only deeply but also broadly. To deal with complex natural, social, and spiritual worlds, adults apply, extend, and expand their sophisticated cognitive skills in a wide variety of distinctive tasks and domains that they encounter in both academic settings and their everyday lives, including job, profession, health, family relationships, child rearing, home purchase and maintenance, self-understanding, emotion regulation, moral reasoning, religion, and politics (Baltes & Staudinger, 1993; Erikson, 1978; Fischer, Hand, & Russell, 1984; Gardner, 1983; Kegan, 1994; Neugarten, 1968; Sternberg, 1990). In all phases of adulthood, people need to update their skill repertoire in multiple domains constantly in order to adapt themselves to change. Adults must develop multiple specialized cognitive skills, such as critical reading, academic writing, moral judgment, household management, business practices, emotional intelligence, and religious practices, to meet challenges they face. The dynamics and complexity of strands in the web provide a model of the richness and complexity of this breadth in adult cognitive development.

The complex interconnections among skill components and domains in a web remind us of a neural network, especially of the many dendrites that can proliferate from a single neuron within a network. With complex networking among multiple skills in multiple domains, adults manifest phenomena that occur not at all or in much reduced form in children, such as complex multiple identities, interdisciplinary expertise, creativity, and wisdom. Moreover, dynamic networks of strands constantly change over time and context, and produce emergent and complicated cognitive processes and products. Examples of how adults develop in multiple domains include strands of identity in adulthood, Darwin's construction of the theory of evolution, and the pluses and minuses of cognitive aging.

Strands of Adult Identity Understanding

Observing, analyzing, and understanding oneself is one of the most difficult lifelong intellectual challenges that each adult has to face. Erik Erikson (1963; 1968), in his classic work on identity development over the life course, had the insight that identity always develops in *relationship* with other people, especially in family, friendship, and work. Erikson described a developmentally ordered sequence of crises that reaches its pivotal point at the end of childhood with the emergence of identity in adolescence. Identity is a person's sense of who she or he is and wants to be, a self-constructed organization of emotions, beliefs, values, goals, and individual history. It is not fully achieved and finished in adolescence or early adulthood but continues to be woven across multiple life strands gradually as we grow older.

From the first formation of identity as the climax of childhood, adults extend and coordinate their own identities with other people's identities across contexts and time periods, progressing through three further stages, according to Erikson. This concept of identity has permeated modern society, so that it is almost a truism today, although everyday use of the concept is often superficial. Most of the empirical work on identity development has unfortunately not focused on the full scope of identity development during adulthood but has instead considered primarily microdevelopment (substages) within the emergence of identity in adolescence and early adulthood (for example, Marcia, 1980; 1994; Matteson, 1977; Phinney, 1989; Turkle, 1995). This research also neglects the importance of social coordination of one's own identity with other people's. As a result, considerable confusion has reigned about the degree to which the crises in fact form stages, although this research has not actually tested the stages themselves. Fortunately a few studies have gone beyond the stage of emergence of identity (versus role diffusion) to examine the full set of stages Erikson described, especially through case analyses and clinical material (Erikson, 1969; 1978; Gilligan, 1982; Loevinger, 1976; Neugarten, 1968; Noam et al., 1990; Vaillant, 1977).

We propose an important differentiation of the identity framework through cognitive analysis of the skills involved in identity formation and coordination with others. Articulating identity development through this skill analysis illuminates the ways that multiple strands of identity develop systematically in a person's web and how people construct identity skills hierarchically in a way that correlates with Erikson's stage crises. The stages are shaped by basic human tasks and issues that people share across cultures, such as learning skills for home and work, choosing a romantic partner, making a living, raising children, and growing old. Individual circumstances differ widely across cultures and families, yet the general pattern of crises (tasks and issues) remains similar. In addition, later crises build up more complex demands in life situations and the need for integration of strands of one's life web – an important cognitive challenge (Kegan, 1994).

Each of the identity stages beyond the first requires co-construction of one's own abstract identity with those of other people, and in each case this challenging task requires a minimum skill level. Table 21.2 lists Erikson's stages, beginning with identity, and shows how each one depends on a skill structure at a particular level to afford the coordination that the stage requires. The earlier levels before the emergence of identity are also shown, because they lay the groundwork for identity through

Table 21.2 *Development of identification and identity: relation to Erikson's stages and generalized skill diagrams*

Erikson's stages of identity: first emergence	Skill level	Representational tier: identification	Abstract tier: identification
↑	Rp1	$[ME_A > YOU_B]$	
Concrete identifications	Rp2	$[ME_A — YOU_B]$	
↓	Rp3	$[ME^C_A \longleftrightarrow YOU^D_B]$	
Stage 5: identity versus role diffusion	Rp4 Ab1	$\begin{bmatrix} ME^C_A \longleftrightarrow YOU\,1^D_B \\ \Updownarrow \\ ME^G_E \longleftrightarrow YOU\,2^H_F \end{bmatrix}$	$\equiv [\mathbb{SELF}_{\mathbb{W}}]$ or $[\mathbb{OTHER}_{\mathbb{V}}]$
Stage 6: intimacy versus isolation	Ab2		$[\mathbb{SELF}_{\mathbb{W}} — \mathbb{OTHER}_{\mathbb{V}}]$
Stage 7: generativity versus stagnation	Ab3		$[\mathbb{SELF}^{\mathbb{Y}}_{\mathbb{W}} \longleftrightarrow \mathbb{OTHER}^{\mathbb{X}}_{\mathbb{V}}]$
Stage 8: ego integrity versus despair	Ab4		$\begin{bmatrix} \mathbb{SELF}^{\mathbb{Y}}_{\mathbb{W}} \longleftrightarrow \mathbb{OTHER}^{\mathbb{X}}_{\mathbb{V}} \\ \Updownarrow \\ \mathbb{SELF}^{\mathbb{T}}_{\mathbb{Z}} \longleftrightarrow \mathbb{OTHER}^{\mathbb{S}}_{\mathbb{U}} \end{bmatrix}$

Note: People develop specific skills, not global ones. These formulas must be filled in with specific content to capture a real skill.

A to *H* are concrete personal characteristics. $\mathbb{S}$ to $\mathbb{Z}$ are abstract identity characteristics.

the formation of concrete identifications that characterize oneself (*ME*) in relation to important others (*YOU*). These identifications are coordinated with a minimum of single abstractions to create the beginnings of identity in early adolescence. The skill formulas in Table 21.2 are listed with general components (letters for variables to be filled in) to make the point that a similar skill structure develops across strands/domains in the web. For application to real people, note that the general variables need to be specified with concrete content. There are no instantly general and generalizable skills.

The creation of multiple concrete identifications during childhood sets the stage for the emergence of identity at the end of childhood and the beginning of adolescence. For example, Kara played a teacher game with her mother Jane, as described in formula 1. With just a minor change in that representational skill (level Rp3), she identifies with Jane as both a teacher and a mother:

$$\left[\begin{array}{ccc} & \textit{Identification} & \\ \textit{TEACHER} & & \textit{TEACHER} \\ \textit{JANE} & \longleftrightarrow & \textit{KARA} \\ \textit{MOTHER} & & \textit{MOTHER} \end{array}\right] \qquad (8)$$

She tries to act like a teacher and mother herself, not only in play but in real-life choices that she makes, such as helping another child with homework similar to the way that she sees Jane teach students and care for a younger sibling and similar to the way Jane takes care of Kara's brother. With many such concrete identifications, a child builds material for the creation of an abstract identity.

The stage of identity versus role diffusion involves abstract answers (not just one) to the question, 'Who am I?' A young person brings together at least two concrete representational systems like formula 8. Coordinating that identification with her identification with her father as physician and parent,

$$\left[\begin{array}{ccc} & \textit{Identification} & \\ \textit{PHYSICIAN} & & \textit{PHYSICIAN} \\ \textit{WALTER} & \longleftrightarrow & \textit{KARA} \\ \textit{FATHER} & & \textit{PARENT} \end{array}\right] \qquad (9)$$

as shown for level Ab1 in Table 21.2, she creates an identity of herself as caregiver:

$$\left[\begin{array}{c} \text{SELF} \\ \text{CAREGIVER} \end{array}\right] \qquad (10)$$

At the same time she builds up many other specific identities, such as self as independent (formula 2), and she constructs her own conceptions of other people's identities in a similar way, such as that her best friend Isabelle is independent:

$$\left[\begin{array}{c} \text{FRIEND} \\ \text{INDEPENDENT} \end{array}\right] \qquad (11)$$

Much of the confusion of early identity formation comes from the multiplicity of strands of identity formation and the difficulty in relating different abstract identity characteristics to each other at this optimal level. To do comparisons of two personal characteristics of her own identity with that of Isabelle, Kara must drop down to concrete characteristics, using a representational system. The coordination of her own abstract identity with that of her friend's thus remains out of reach.

Erikson's next stage of intimacy versus isolation involves the coordination of one's own identity with that of a friend or partner, and the cognitive minimum is abstract mappings, as shown in Table 21.2. When Kara focuses on her own independent tendencies, then she can easily coordinate her own identity with that of Isabelle as she sees it, in a repeat of formula 5:

$$\left[\begin{array}{ccc} \text{SELF} & \text{———} & \text{FRIEND} \\ \text{INDEPENDENT} & & \text{INDEPENDENT} \end{array}\right] \qquad (5)$$

A challenge of intimacy is to have her own abstractions about Isabelle matching well enough with Isabelle's actions and abstractions to sustain a close relationship. Contradictions also come easily at this optimal level, because people have difficulties dealing with multiple abstractions about self and other. When Kara focuses on her own caregiving, for example, there may be a conflict with Isabelle's independence. Within herself too, her own caregiving can seem to contradict her independence – an example of the sense of contradiction and conflict that many adolescents and adults experience (Fischer & Kennedy, 1997; Harter & Monsour, 1992).

Issues of intimacy, like the issues of every one of Erikson's stages, exist throughout life, long before the years of early adulthood and long after them. The reasons that they belong especially to early adulthood are primarily two: (1) people commonly seek intimacy at this age, especially sexual intimacy and long-term partnership; and (2) at this age, cognitive capacities make it possible to truly coordinate abstract identities in intimate relationships. In many cultures and life situations, young adults face the challenge of deepened relationships, involving either sex or work, where the coordination of identities is paramount. Intimate relationships require holding a sense of self, but also an openness toward the uniqueness and depth of another; they require learning the major components of another identity, with the two people becoming a dynamic unit, especially for the ideal intimate partnership that Erikson describes, in which both partners grow together toward fulfillment in a stable relationship.

Intimacy of identities can be much easier with higher levels, because then one skill can readily incorporate more than one or two abstract characteristics of self and other. Marriage partners with children, for example, can share the identities of caregiving and independence, working together to support each other as parents and as independent persons with their own separate needs in an abstract system (Ab3):

$$\begin{bmatrix} \text{CO-PARENT} & & \text{CO-PARENT} \\ \text{SELF} & \longleftrightarrow & \text{SPOUSE} \\ \text{INDEPENDENT} & & \text{INDEPENDENT} \end{bmatrix} \qquad (12)$$

Just as identity only begins to develop with the level of single abstractions (Ab1), intimacy only begins with the level of abstract mappings (Ab2). That is why Table 21.2 refers to the first emergence of Erikson's stages at a specific developmental level.

For the last two stages Erikson depicts even more complex life tasks. The stage of generativity versus stagnation requires meeting the challenges of productivity and creativity, in contrast to feelings of lack of purpose, direction, or self-worth. The most obvious generativity is having children, but generativity involves much more than procreation. This process emerges with abstract systems, because with them one can coordinate multiple abstract identities in self and others, as in the example of parenting and independence. However, the challenges of generativity are enormous: people must coordinate their identities with those of not only their partners, co-workers, or friends, but also children, aging parents, and other people. The abstract thinking at this stage has to accommodate a rich web of interdependence, relating a strong sense of personal identity and its changes over time with the identities of others, both younger and older, whom one seeks to guide in ways commensurate with their own needs for identity and change.

Bernice Neugarten emphasized how cognitive development contributed to the process of generativity in a group of successful middle-aged people: 'We have been impressed with the central importance of what might be called the executive processes of personality in middle age [including] the stock-taking, the heightened introspection, and above all, the structuring and restructuring of experience – that is, the conscious processing of new information in the light of what one has already learned' (1968, p. 98). As one woman from the study stated, 'It is as if there were two mirrors before me, each held at a partial angle. I see part of myself in my mother who is growing older, and part of her in me. In the other mirror, I see part of myself in my daughter.' Kara's mother Jane in such a situation considers her focus on parenting in relationship to her mother and daughter, as well as the independence that she sees in different forms in all three of them. That kind of comparison, going beyond the concrete particulars of one set of actions to general identity analysis, involves a highly complex abstract system:

$$\begin{bmatrix} \text{CAREGIVER} & & \text{PARENT} & & \text{PARENT} \\ \text{DAUGHTER} & \leftrightarrow & \text{SELF} & \longleftrightarrow & \text{MOTHER} \\ \text{INDEPENDENT} & & \text{INDEPENDENT} & & \text{INDEPENDENT} \end{bmatrix} \qquad (13)$$

Erikson's final stage involves ego integrity versus despair, with the challenge of putting the great expanse of one's life into a meaningful synthesis, and with the potential achievement of what may properly be called *wisdom*. Understanding that one is many identities, in interdependence with many other people, as well as with the social and cultural roles required for the meaningful participation in a historical time and place – all these strands coalesce into what Erikson calls *integrity* as one approaches the end of life. Failure to accomplish this synthesis may bring depression and despair at midline or in old age. Achievement of such a grand synthesis requires not only the highest level of abstract thinking, systems of abstract systems (Ab4) and the broad integrative principles about one's life that they can create, but also years of experience relating one's own identity to those of intimate partners, friends, co-workers, children, as well as cultural groups and historical epochs. This is truly a grand cognitive achievement!

Networks in Darwin's Development of the Theory of Evolution

We have described identity development globally, outlining a process that most people develop through, taking many different pathways with common themes (issues, crises). Now we switch to a different perspective: analysis of a case of one person's construction of a multistrand, networked web. The case of Charles Darwin's construction of the theory of evolution portrays the dynamics of strands and networks in the web. Dynamic analysis is at its richest in analyzing individual growth in detail (van Geert, 1994), and Darwin unintentionally provided a great source of data for analyzing how he created the theory of evolution by natural selection. Darwin kept a series of notes between 1832 and 1839 in which he recorded his observations and ideas as they developed into his theory of evolution by natural selection.

The way Darwin constructed his revolutionary understanding is tantamount to a case study of building complex knowledge networks in adult cognitive development. At the age of 22, in December of 1831, Darwin set out on a five-year voyage around the world on the ship *HMS Beagle*, during which he recorded observations and thoughts about the natural phenomena he encountered. Toward the end of this time, between 1837 and 1839, he kept a series of specific notebooks on his thinking about 'the transmutation of species'. In 1839 at the age of 30, he had constructed what became his general theory, although he would not dare release it to the world at large for another 20 years, when he finally published *The origin of species* in 1859. Because of his notes and notebooks we can peer over his shoulder to see the steps he took in building the theory and creating the principle of evolution by natural selection (level Ab4). Table 21.3 outlines some of the major steps in Darwin's web, showing several separate strands (distinct skills for different domains) at each level. Detailed exposition can be found in several other sources, especially Gruber (1973) and Fischer and Yan (2002).

Before his voyage on the *Beagle*, Darwin held a view of the world informed by conventional religious belief, like other scientists at that time. God had created two separate worlds, the Physical World of substances and the Organic World of plants, animals, and people. The fact that these worlds hardly interacted was accepted as God's law. In terms of skill level, the concept for each of these two worlds required only a single abstraction for each world, with little need for a higher level because of the lack of interaction between the two. It was Charles Lyell's *Principles of geology*, which Darwin avidly read on his voyage, that opened up for him the question of interaction. Inspired by Lyell's description of gradual change in the physical world, Darwin was at great pains to record the supporting evidence he found.

Darwin began to realize that the physical changes he saw might relate to the common observation that creatures ill-suited to their environment by some defect tended to die, such as birds with defective wings or fish with defective gills. This phenomenon suggested how the physical world can influence the organic world by getting rid of ill-adapted organisms. Darwin's knowledge of the practices of selective breeding of animals also contributed to the development of his insight about the action of physical forces on the viability and adaptation of organisms. His thinking moved beyond single abstractions to construct abstract mappings – lawful interactions between the worlds of the physical and the organic, as illustrated for level Ab2 in Table 21.3.

Darwin's notes portray his years of following this insight in organizing the countless observations he had gathered on his voyage. One especially important example is his work on the various species of Galapagos finches: he discovered that the different species' feeding habits were closely related to the shapes of their beaks (a level Ab3 system insight). He realized that the form of the beak matched the way the particular finch obtained its most common kind of food. This adaptive match pointed to the finely honed adaptation of the organism to its environment. In another strand/domain, Darwin used his knowledge of fossils to analyze how species had changed (evolved) over long time periods – how characteristics of current species could be related to characteristics of earlier species through concepts of change overtime. In this way, he built systems of abstractions in several independent strands, which he soon wove together to create the theory of evolution by natural selection.

In attempting to build his understanding into a comprehensive explanatory network, Darwin tried out a number of concepts before discarding them as inadequate. Darwin's reading of an essay by Thomas Malthus, concerning how populations can reproduce at much higher rates than their environments can support, played a central role in his formulation of the final theory. Based on his notebooks, it seems that Darwin hit upon his eventual theory several times, but he was not able to generalize it fully until he had reconstructed it repeatedly. This is a common occurrence in the construction of new knowledge, perhaps even more so for complex knowledge networks. Darwin not only had to coordinate a number of complex relationships (coral reefs, finches' beaks, species change over eons), but also had to generalize these coordinations into a principle – evolution by natural selection. Repeated construction is often essential to new understanding: indeed it constitutes generalization, with components being worked into the new fabric of a general skill, such as Darwin's evolutionary principle. In sum, Darwin's construction of the final form of his famous theory illustrates an extremely complex process of organization and reorganization of connections across multiple domains in order to build the coherent, innovative, and powerful knowledge network of evolutionary theory.

Older Adults' Cognitive Ageing

Most adults do not create a new principle that revolutionizes human thinking, but most do deal with the challenges of cognitive and physical ageing, including the growth of wisdom, at least for some domains, and the loss of some speed and facility, especially late in life. When conceptualized in terms of dynamic developmental webs, ageing involves growth combined with decline, wisdom along with slowing down.

The cultural stereotype, at least in many Western countries, is that cognitive ageing means cognitive decline and intellectual deterioration: 'The older, the dumber.' Other common false beliefs are that people become less happy and more lonely with age. Happily, research data paint a more optimistic portrait. Most adults experience more positive emotions and more numerous social connections as they grow older, with early adulthood being one of the loneliest and least happy life periods, on average (Carstensen, 1993; 2000). Likewise for cognition: research does not support the proposition of an overall decline in intelligence during adulthood in concert with the general physical ageing process (Wechsler, 1972). Horn and Cattell's (1967) classic research shows the interweaving of gain and loss with cognitive aging. Many kinds of intellectual skills increase slowly but consistently with age, even in research limited to standardized psychometric tests.

Table 21.3 *Development of Darwin's theory of evolution (1831–1839): a general overview*

Level	Skill	Major events	Dates
Ab1: single abstractions	[WORLD ORGANIC] or [WORLD PHYSICAL]	From adolescence: musings about creation and species; separation of organic and physical worlds	Before 1831
Ab2: abstract mappings	[WORLD —deviant— WORLD PHYSICAL ORGANIC]	Physical world eliminates deviant organisms	
	[WORLD —breed— WORLD HUMAN ORGANIC]	People selectively breed animals and plants for desired characteristics	
		Voyage of *Beagle*: mastering Lyell's *Principles of geology* and collecting observations	1831–1836
	[WORLD —reef— WORLD ORGANIC PHYSICAL]	Beginning of coral reef theory: corals vary with changes in physical world	
Ab3: abstract systems	[ORGANIC X reef PHYSICAL X WORLD ⟷ WORLD ORGANIC Y PHYSICAL Y]	Final coral-reef theory: coral reefs grow as corals adapt to changing ocean depths by growing upward to reach light	1835–1837
	[ORGANIC X match PHYSICAL X WORLD ⟷ WORLD ORGANIC Y PHYSICAL Y]	Variations in Galapagos species match species characteristics with physical niche	
	[ORGANIC R1 time ORGANIC R2 WORLD ⟷ WORLD ORGANIC T1 ORGANIC T2]	Many species show systematic change over long time periods	
		Struggling with idea of multiple creations	
Ab4: systems of abstract systems, which are principles	[monad creation ORGANIC X1 PHYSICAL X1 WORLD ⟷ WORLD ORGANIC Y1 PHYSICAL Y1 tree of ⇕ change ORGANIC X2 PHYSICAL X2 WORLD ⟷ WORLD ORGANIC Y2 PHYSICAL Y2]	Inadequate process of evolution: monad theory, branching tree	1837
		Hybridization (instead of natural selection)	
	[evolution ORGANIC X1 PHYSICAL X1 WORLD ⟷ WORLD ORGANIC Y1 PHYSICAL Y1 natural ⇕ selection ORGANIC X2 PHYSICAL X2 WORLD ⟷ WORLD ORGANIC Y2 PHYSICAL Y2]	Emergence of theory of evolution by natural selection (heredity, variation, natural selection)	1838–1839

Note: Skill structures in this table emphasize relations between physical and organic worlds in the various phases of Darwin's work. Fischer and Yan (2002) describe the actual skills, specifying the components from physical and organic worlds that Darwin actually coordinated.

Sources: Table adapted from Fischer & Yan (2002). Sources for historical information: Barrett (1974), Darwin (1859), Keegan (1989), and especially Gruber (1981).

These reflect what is called *crystallized intelligence*, composed of skills that benefit from accumulated experience, such as vocabulary and general knowledge. On the other hand, many skills also decline with age, especially from middle adulthood, and these reflect what is called *fluid intelligence*, composed of skills that depend on novel activities and information. Most of the activities that adults need to do involve accumulated knowledge and crystallized intelligence, and they get better with age. For example, Schaie's (1996) longitudinal data indicate that inductive reasoning rises slightly through middle adulthood, with a gradual decline beginning only in late adulthood. On the other hand, there are clear, small declines in speed and physical strength beginning in middle age (Horn, 1982; Salthouse, Hambrick, & McGuthry, 1998). Illness is also an important factor, producing powerful declines in skill at any age and becoming more likely in old age.

Cognitive ageing is clearly multidimensional and multidirectional (Baltes, 1987; Baltes & Baltes, 1990; Berg, 2000; Birren, 1970; Craik & Salthouse, 1991; Schaie, 1983; Sternberg, 1985). Research that seems to show one simple factor underlying ageing (or development) is based on assumptions and statistical techniques that force complex webs into single, monolithic dimensions and preclude consideration of the textured richness of developmental webs (e.g. Gottlieb, Wahlsten, & Lickliter, 1998).

The standardized tests used in most ageing research do not assess the complex skills that develop at the highest levels of abstraction, or the integration of emotional and cognitive strands that ground wisdom. Even the reduction in speed with age sometimes comes from the increased sophistication of adult cognitive skills and their thinking processes: more complex webs and networks take longer to process information (Atkinson & Shiffrin, 1968; Fischer & Rose, 1994; Gruber, 1973; Schacter, 1999). What might be called *cognitive pragmatics*, or the culture-based software of mind and body, actually improve with age, as evidenced by numerous studies of adult development (Baltes & Baltes, 1990; Colby et al., 1983; Dawson, 2002; Erikson, 1969; 1978; Levinson, 1978; Loevinger, 1976; Neugarten, 1968; Noam et al., 1990; Vaillant, 1977; 1986). One of the most telling findings is the age at which productivity reaches its maximum in creative people working in highly complex fields, such as historians and novelists (Dennis, 1958; Simonton, 1991; 2000). People in these fields become most productive and creative in their 40s, 50s, and even 60s. In contrast, people in less complexly textured fields, such as mathematicians and poets, often peak in their 20s and 30s.

How can the complex interconnections among these features in cognitive ageing be analyzed and understood? Obviously, they are not totally separate features moving in different directions. With multiple elements interacting with each other over time, a dynamic process of self-organization occurs in which adults actively organize their limited mental resources into dynamic skill networks to adapt to their complex life needs. While some components, such as speed of activity and speed of processing information, reduce the richness of the network past middle age, other components, such as synthetic thinking and interpersonal wisdom, can increase the richness. Through this process, both ageing and aged adults build dynamic cognitive networks to meet various complex life challenges. Two examples from research involve the specific motor skill of typing and the broad cognitive-emotional skill of wisdom.

For the motor skill of typing, older adults organize their skills differently, anticipating a wider span of letters and compensating for lower perceptual-motor speed in simple tasks such as reaction time and tapping (Salthouse, 1984). In a sample of 19- to 72-year-olds, older adults maintained typing speed by more precisely controlling the sequencing of keystrokes across larger spans of characters than did younger typists. For many skills besides typing, dynamic interconnection and compensation play a similar critical role in changes during adulthood. Dynamic compensation and adjustment within complex cognitive networks are widely observed in domains of memory (Barrett & Watkins, 1986, p. 129), chess playing (Charness, 1981), social interaction (Carstensen, 1993), emotional understanding (Labouvie-Vief, De-Voe, & Bulka, 1998), and job change (Sternberg, 1990).

Wisdom is very different from typing, yet it too involves building complex cognitive networks to adapt to needs in life. Wisdom requires integration of multiple types of knowledge and skill about practical and ethical issues in human life (Baltes & Staudinger, 1993; Dawson, 1999; Erikson, 1963; Sternberg, 1990). It requires an implicit, complex, effective knowledge network combining multiple domains over long time periods and extensive experience, and it seems to require special coordination of emotional and cognitive processes. Wisdom seems to compensate for physical slowing in middle and old age, enabling many adults to perform synthetic thinking about self and others in the complex world, often making people especially effective as, for example, political leaders, judges, moral leaders, and scholars.

In summary, adults can develop deeply and broadly in their skills – building complex identities with their family, friends, and colleagues, creating new ideas, practices, or products that shape their society, and building wise ways that go beyond self-interest and immediate response. All these outcomes depend on development of networks connecting multiple strands in the web of skill and emotion.

Dynamic Backward and Forward Constructions in the Web

Besides multiple levels, strands, and connections, development in adults also moves in multiple directions for cognitive construction. The complete picture includes not only complex variations in the strands and networks but also dynamic construction processes within the web. Dynamically, adult cognitive development moves forward, backward, and in various other directions. It forms a dynamic web, and even each separate strand is dynamic (and fractal), not a linear ladder (Fischer & Granott, 1995). Traditionally development is defined as forward progression, but cognitive development moves backward as well as forward. 'Progress' results from a combination of backward and forward movement, with much backward movement preparing the way to move forward through the construction of new adaptive skills. Through thus constructing skills in multiple directions, adults can handle complex tasks effectively and flexibly and advance their competence. Adults' backward directions of cognitive construction are sometimes treated as an indicator of failure and malfunction, especially in old age, but instead, flexible use of simpler and more complex skills reflects maturity and wisdom. Two developmental phenomena show some of the order in the multidirectionality of adult development: backward transition and forward consolidation.

Backward Transition

One important principle of dynamic construction is backward transition, a movement of activity from higher-level skills down to lower-level ones followed by gradual movement in fits and starts back up to higher-level, new skills (Duncker, 1945; Fischer, 1980b; Fischer & Granott, 1995; Granott, 1993a; 1998; 2002). Backward transition or regression seems to be a universal strategy that people use when they are trying to construct new skills, as reflected in explicit problem-solving strategies such as 'breaking a problem down into its simplest units' and 'starting again from the beginning'. When people encounter a task that they do not have the skills to perform, they fall down to low-level activity – even sensorimotor actions similar to those of an infant – so that they can figure out the task and gradually build toward high-level skills. Recent microdevelopmental research indicates that backward transitions are pervasive in adulthood and play such an important role that supposedly inadequate, lower levels of performance need to be reexamined and reevaluated. Backward transition leads adults to perform flexibly and to devise ways of solving complex tasks that are initially beyond them.

Nira Granott (1993a; 2002) devised a methodology that allows a focus on both realtime skill construction and the generalization and consolidation that accompany it. She had teams of adults interact with a small Lego robot called a wuggle. The wuggle, which was about the size of a toy truck, was programmed to respond to changes in light/shadow, sound, and touch by altering its movements. The dyads were given the task of figuring out what the wuggle did, while video cameras recorded interactions and discussions. Granott (1993b) reasoned that because most human cognition takes place in the social arena, observing dyads will provide useful insight into spontaneous learning and problem-solving and the social interaction will make overt many learning processes. Participants began in a small group in a room containing several wuggles that moved or sat among common objects such as tables and boxes, and they formed dyads spontaneously during the observation session.

In analyzing videotapes of this session, Granott and her coders easily reached agreement on what constituted an *interchange*, a single dyadic interaction with the wuggle, and each interchange was scored for complexity using the skill scale. For instance, when a dyad understood that making a loud noise led the wuggle to change direction, the level was coded as an *action mapping* – that is, the second level of the action tier (Sm2), connecting making or hearing a sound with seeing a change in movement.

In a typical initial encounter, the subjects were at first confused, then more engaged as their experimentation brought responses from the wuggle. Granott (1993; 2002) used the dyad of Ann and Donald to illustrate this process. Encountering a wuggle for the first time, they had to learn how it changed its movement in response to a sound. In 148 interchanges over 27 minutes, they started with mere observation of the wuggle's movement (the lowest level of single actions, Sm1) and gradually built up through higher levels as they tried to understand the wuggle. The sequence from action to representation unfolded as follows. Seeing the wuggle move is a single action, and hearing a sound is another single action (level Sm1). A mapping of actions (level Sm2) is noticing that hearing a loud sound goes with seeing the wuggle change movement. A system of actions (level Sm 3) is combining several movements and sound situations. A single representation – the wuggle reacts to sound – emerges from coordinating several action systems (level Sm4/Rp1). And so forth: microdevelopment continues with relating and differentiating representations of the wuggle and sound.

Among the dyads, however, such construction of a representation did not proceed directly through the levels in a ladder-like manner. As shown in Figure 21.7, progress toward a skill for understanding the wuggle went in fits and starts – a series of backwards transitions and reconstructions, not one consistent upward construction. Initially Ann and Donald fell

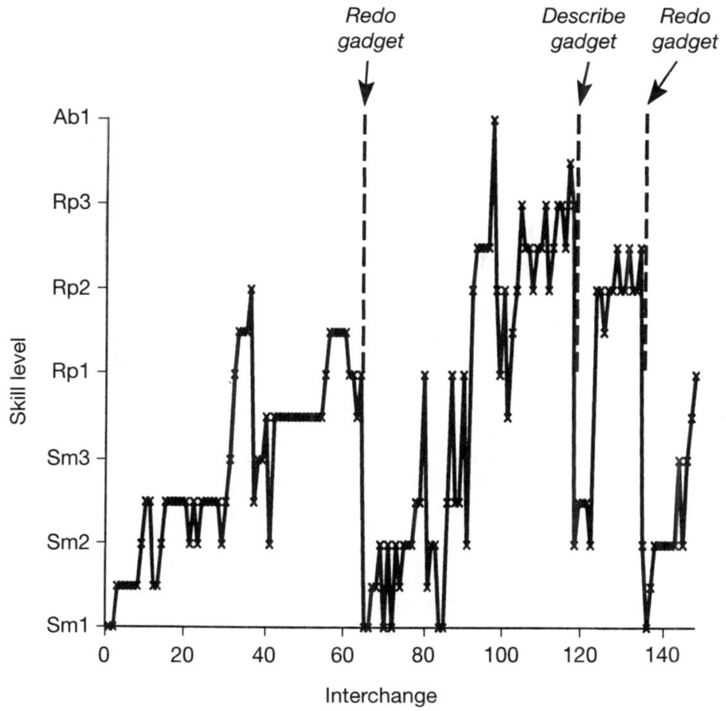

Figure 21.7 *Backward transition and microdevelopment in understanding a wuggle: Ann and Donald (Granott, 1993a; 2002)*

down to a level far below their capacity, producing several level 1 actions and then building up a more complex skill over several minutes. They interacted with the wuggle and made sounds and other actions to explore it, in a faltering way gradually building their first representation that the wuggle reacts to sound (level 4). But then at interchange 65 something interesting happened: a wire had fallen out of the wuggle, and when they placed it back (in a different hole, by mistake), the wuggle acted differently. In the face of this task change their fragile skill collapsed, dropping back immediately to a level 1 action. Over the next several minutes they once more rebuilt more complex skills, gradually returning to a representation that the wuggle reacts to sound (level 4) and then going further to higher levels still, relating several representations to each other.

This process of backward transition and reconstruction happened two more times in the 27 minutes of problem-solving. At interchange 118 Ann and Donald encountered another variation in the task: they set out to summarize what they knew, and again the change in task led to a drop in their skill – this time level 2 mappings of actions followed by again rebuilding skills to reach representations (levels 4 and 5). Then at interchange 134 Ann and Donald changed the wiring of the wuggle again, and they showed backward transition to low-level actions followed by reconstruction of complex actions and representations.

The repeated fall and rise of skill levels in the construction and generalization of new knowledge is a common feature of microdevelopment. Adult learners also showed this scallop-shaped growth in Yan's (1998; 2000) recent study of learning to use a computer program to do simple statistical operations. Participants were graduate students who varied widely in their expertise, both with computers and with statistical operations. Each student worked at a computer, with a teacher at her or his side to answer questions and to intervene when help was needed. Students with intermediate background experience showed clear scalloping in their learning graphs – a low level of skill followed by a gradual increase and then an abrupt drop when a new task element was introduced, as illustrated in Figure 21.8. For students with little background, skill level showed wide fluctuation initially, and scalloping gradually appeared as they became more familiar with the tasks, concepts, and computer operations. Students with a high degree of knowledge (experts), on the other hand, showed little scalloping, staying generally at the upper limit of skill required by the task, with occasional transient drops.

Another important finding of these studies is that adults function at a level appropriate for the task at hand, which may be far below their upper limit (either optimal or functional level). In Figure 21.8, for example, a highly intelligent adult graduate

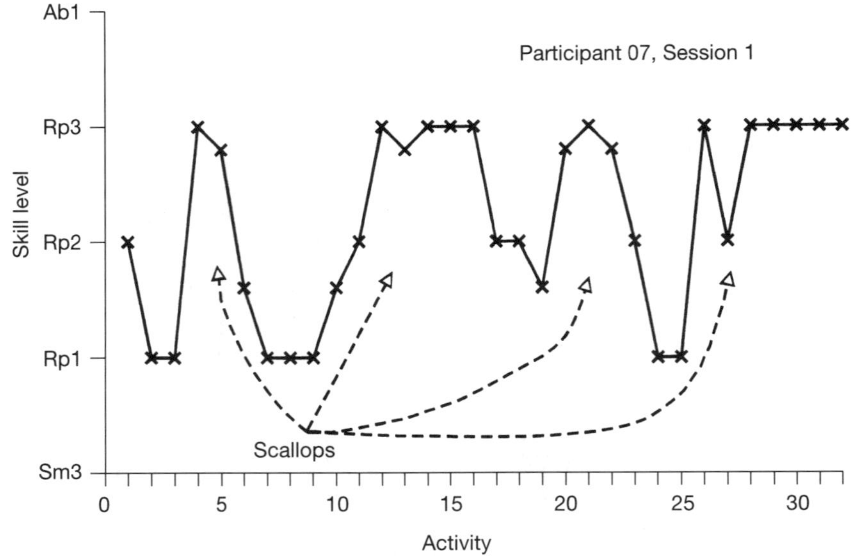

Figure 21.8 *Scalloping in learning a statistics operation (Yan, 1998; 2000)*

student performed with skills that at maximum were only representational systems (Rp3). This optimal level first emerges at 6 or 7 years of age, and the adult student was capable of much more sophisticated activity, including high levels of abstraction, which she regularly demonstrated in other class activities. The reason for the low level that she and all other students demonstrated in this study is that the task required only this level – nothing more!

Yan further asked how interaction with the teacher affected learning. He found that the upward arc of the scallop often followed the teacher's response to a relevant question, especially for the intermediate-level students: the scaffolding provided by the teacher's response allowed the student to build up understanding of the task. The support offered by the instructor through clues and priming facilitated the temporary rises in skill level evident in scalloping.

Just as a teacher can provide a scaffold to support a student's construction of understanding, people can support their own skill construction through a recently discovered mechanism called *bridging* (Fischer & Bidell, 1998; Granott, 1993a; Granott & Parziale, 2002; Parziale, 1997). A bridging shell allows people to bootstrap themselves to new knowledge by creating a temporary target or open-ended shell for what is as yet unconstructed. The shell is a framework (an attractor in dynamic systems terms) for guiding a current level of performance through the search space to the next higher level – like an algebraic skill formula with unknown variables that a person uses to guide discovery during problem-solving. In the wuggle task, dyads continually created shells that helped bridge their exploration of the wuggle to higher levels. For example, the dyad Kevin and Marvin noted that their wuggle showed a 'reaction' to something that they did, but they could not articulate either the cause of the reaction (unknown variable $\mathbf{X}_a$) or the nature of the wuggle's change in activity (unknown variable $\mathbf{Y}_b$) (Granott, Fischer, & Parziale, 2002). They used a sketchy mapping skill as a shell to bridge their construction of an understanding of these two factors:

$$[(\mathbf{X}_a) \xrightarrow{\text{Reaction}} (\mathbf{Y}_b)] \qquad (14)$$

Exploration of the wuggle guided by this shell led them to a series of more explicit skills based on the shell, starting with the realization: 'When it comes over here and as soon as it gets underneath part of the shadow there, it starts changing its behavior.' This statement of a causal relationship began to fill in the shell:

$$\begin{bmatrix} \textbf{SHADOW} & \text{———} & \textbf{IT (WUGGLE)} \\ \textbf{(ON WUGGLE)} & & \textbf{CHANGE(S)} \\ & & \textbf{BEHAVIOR} \end{bmatrix} \qquad (15)$$

As with all new knowledge, the new skill remains a temporary one until it can be reconstructed several times with sufficient variation so that it stabilizes. In a similar manner, adults use bridging frequently to guide their own learning. This process of bridging cries out for research to unpack how adults guide their own learning and development. (Note that bold font indicates sensorimotor skills, which are based in action. The levels prior to representations involve actions, which form the basis for representations.)

The examples with wuggles and computer programs demonstrate that knowledge is not simply a stable accomplishment. In both studies, people moved to high skill levels in a short time, but when they encountered a small change in the task, they instantly fell back to lower levels. General skills must be built through this repetitive process of doing and redoing a task to stabilize and generalize it. Whenever a task is changed, there is backward transition and reworking, gradually leading to a more stable representation (Bever, 1982; Duncker, 1945; Fischer, 1980a; 1980b; Fischer & Bidell, 1998; Granott, 1993a; 1998; Granott, Fischer, & Parziale, 2002; Werner, 1948). The point here is that people do not simply work up to a level of skill and then keep it available for all similar circumstances. For knowledge to become readily accessible across tasks and domains, it has to be reconstructed multiple times, probably with its flexibility determined in large part by the range of variations in the tasks when a person has to reconstruct it.

Knowledge disappears easily and has to be reconstructed. It is unstable. Relatively stable knowledge comes only with extensive generalizing reconstruction for familiar tasks and situations. (Knowledge can be stable in the community without being stable in the individual.) With so little research on the naturally dynamic variation in individual activities and knowledge in the real world, scientists and educators have too easily treated knowledge as stable, even fixed – thus perpetuating a myth of stable individual knowledge that permeates human language and culture (Lakoff & Johnson, 1980).

Forward Consolidation

The phenomenon of forward consolidation involves a different pattern of movement during adult development: The optimal performance that comes with high contextual support is gradually consolidated into functional performance without contextual support. Most cognitive-developmental research examines only conventional forward progression within the same contextual condition: from lower optimal performance to higher, or from lower functional performance to higher, or from lower performance on a standardized test to higher. When young adults face, for example, a difficult dilemma, such as whether chemical additives to food are helpful or harmful, or whether an unwed, poor, young woman who is pregnant should consider giving up the child for adoption, they will show a higher level of reasoning with optimal contextual support than without it. They cannot sustain the optimal level on their own, but they can remember it vaguely and build a bridging shell that eventually leads them to consolidation and mastery of the higher level skill without support. As shown in the developmental web in Figure 21.5, forward consolidation takes place along the strands so that the optimal portion will gradually be turned into the functional portion. This kind of forward consolidation is pervasive in adulthood and plays an important role in adults' cognitive development.

One demonstration of forward consolidation is the pattern of emergence of performance of skills at a given level. The skills that emerge at one optimal level predominate not when they emerge, but years later, often upon emergence of the next optimal level, or even the one after that (Fischer, Kenny, & Pipp, 1990; Kitchener et al., 1993). In other words, the consolidation of skills at a given level takes place with the emergence of the next level. In reflective judgment, skills for stage 6 first spurted at age 20, the usual age when the optimal level of abstract systems (Ab3) emerges. However, students at that age only produced about half of their arguments at stage 6, as shown in Figure 21.6. Not until five years later at age 25 did stage 6 performance jump to nearly 100%. (Age 25 was also when stage 7 performance jumped to 50% as the optimal level of principles, Ab4, emerged.)

The number of years that it takes adults to move from optimal level to consolidation of functional level varies greatly across domains and individuals. For reflective judgment, Table 21.4 describes the age range between emergence of an optimal level for a stage and the consolidation of that skill at functional level. These ages are based mostly on research with American students who have a college education or plan to attend college, and of course they vary for people from other cultural or educational groups. For example, stage 5 reasoning emerges in many students as early as 15 years of age under high support, but in low support (functional) situations, it is not seen until somewhere between 18 and 30 years of age. Similarly, stage 6 may appear at 20 years under optimal support, but it is not consolidated at functional level until 25 to 40 years. Note that the ages for functional level involve only adults who actually showed those stages in research. Many adults never reach the highest stages in any particular domain, as evidenced even in research with college-educated adults.

It takes years for an individual adult to move from emergence of an optimal performance to consolidation of a functional performance. Darwin took several years of intense thinking with high self-scaffolding and long immersion to move from the theory of coral reefs to the principle of evolution by natural selection, even though the coral-reef theory was later seen as an instance of the principle (Fischer & Yan, 2002). The extension of that theory to hundreds of problems in biology went on for the rest of his life. Forward consolidation is both a challenging cognitive journey and a significant intellectual accomplishment, whether for an extraordinary thinker or an ordinary adult.

Why are there such gaps in the timing and performance of reflective judgment and other skills? Catastrophe theory (a kind of dynamics) helps to explain these nonlinear processes. When a number of influences act together, they can produce a

Table 21.4 *Approximate ages for optimal and functional levels of reflective judgment*

Stage of reflective judgment	Emergence of optimal level	Emergence of functional level[1]
Pre-reflective judgment		
Stage 3 (level Rp3)	6 to 7 years	Middle school and high school age 12 to 17 years
Quasi-reflective judgment		
Stage 4 (level Ab1)	10 to 12 years	Late high school, college, and above 16 to 23 years Never for many people and domains
Stage 5 (level Ab2)	14 to 16 years	Early graduate school 19 to 30 years or older Never for many people and domains
Reflective judgment		
Stage 6 (level Ab3)	19 to 21 years	Advanced graduate school 23 to 40 years or older Never for many people and domains
Stage 7 (level Ab4)	24 to 26 years	Advanced graduate school 30 to 45 or older. Never for many people and domains.

Note: this table includes only the last five of the seven stages, which are the ones that adults use most.

1 Ages for emergence of functional level vary widely, and so these estimates are coarse.

Sources: reviews and research by King and Kitchener (1994), Kitchener and Fischer (1990), Kitchener et al. (1993), as well as Basseches (1984), Colby et al. (1983), Cook-Greuter (1999), Dawson (2002), Fischer, Kenny, and Pipp (1990), Perry (1970), Rest et al. (1999), and Vaillant (1977).

nonlinear pattern with a complex shape that includes powerful discontinuities called *catastrophes* (van der Maas & Molenaar, 1992; Zeeman, 1976). Catastrophe theory describes how a developing pathway can bend back on itself over time as it progresses, giving a distinctive scalloped shape to the ascending pathway. This backward bending shows a remarkable parallel to the spikiness and gappiness in the development of optimal level in a given domain or in the confluence of integrating domains, as shown in Figures 21.3 and 21.6 (Fischer & Bidell, 1998; Rose & Fischer, 1998). In a sense, the cognitive capacities pressed into service under high-support conditions are unstable until the person has consolidated them through extensive experience and practice. The instability takes two forms: (1) development of optimal performance shows sudden jumps and drops; and (2) the level appears and disappears with variation in contextual support.

Backward transition and forward consolidation as well as other growth processes form foundations for the dynamic phenomena of adult development. These dynamic processes operate within the strands of the developmental web, and they create the wide range of levels of everyday skill. Skills range from large drops to basic levels in backward transition to high levels of new skill constructed on these basic actions. They range from low levels of automatized actions to functional levels of unaided actions and further up to optimal levels of supported actions. They even extend to the high reaches of collaborative action. The range of variation is especially broad and pervasive in adulthood, even more so than in childhood.

At least three reasons account for this broad variation. First, adults have a wider range of skills available because they are capable of going all the way from elementary sensorimotor actions to complex abstractions. Second, the high-level abstractions of which adults are capable are especially subject to the influences of culture and education, even more than the basic skills of childhood. Third, adults tend to specialize in particular domains, based on their life choices and situations – entering one job and not another, one avocation and not another, one family role and not another.

Conclusion: Richness and Complexity of Adult Development

Accumulated evidence indicates that Piaget's formal operations is not the end of human cognitive development. Instead, development over the 60 years of adulthood is an important part of the whole picture of human cognition. Adult cognitive development is rich and dynamic, like a complex web that is constantly changing with multiple levels, strands, networks, and directions. The wisdom and intelligence of an adult cannot be captured by one developmental level, one domain, one pathway, or one direction. During adulthood, intelligence commonly moves to become more sophisticated, flexible, synthetic, constructive, and socially oriented – more complex and dynamic. Cognitive development in adulthood takes a number of different shapes, and it occurs through a set of fine-grained mechanisms for building and adapting skills. Specific skills emerge at one level but require long periods of consolidation before they predominate in ordinary contexts. They emerge abruptly as new optimal levels for a given domain, but develop more slowly and gradually as functional levels of everyday action. An important mechanism for construction of new knowledge is backward recursion to lower levels of actions and representations followed by repeated rebuilding of a skill until it is consolidated and stabilized as available and generalizable. A major impetus to the work of constructing new approaches to the challenges of a rapidly changing world is through learning with others – colleagues, friends, mentors, parents, relatives, and even their children. Research in the future will need to unpack further the richness, complexity, and dynamics of adult cognitive development, building knowledge of the developmental webs and dynamic processes that we have begun to describe. By opening up the scope of research and theory to analysis of the dynamics of variability and change, we can better understand the true richness and complexity of each adult's adaptive construction of knowledge. This new knowledge of what, how, and why adult cognition changes can eventually help millions of adults to meet new challenges from their complex natural, social, and spiritual worlds more successfully and enjoyably.

REFERENCES

Alexander, C.N., Davies, J.L., Dixon, C.A., Dillbeck, M.C., Druker, S.M., Oetzel, R.M., Muehlman, J.M., & Orme-Johnson, D.W. (1990). Growth of higher stages of consciousness: Maharishi's Vedic psychology of human development. In C.N. Alexander & E.J. Langer (eds), *Higher stages of human development: Perspectives on adult growth* (pp. 286–341). New York: Oxford University Press.

Atkinson, R.C., & Shiffrin, R.M. (1968). Human memory: A proposed system and its control processes. In K.W. Spence & J.T. Spence (eds), *The psychology of learning and motivation: Advances in research and theory* (Vol. 2, pp. 89–195). New York: Academic.

Baltes, P.B. (1987). Theoretical propositions of life-span developmental psychology: On the dynamics between growth and decline. *Developmental Psychology*, 23, 611–626.

Baltes, P.B., & Baltes, M.M. (eds) (1990). *Successful aging: Perspectives from the behavioral sciences*. New York: Cambridge University Press.

Baltes, P.B., & Mayer, K.U. (ed.) (1999). *The Berlin aging study: Aging from 70 to 100*. New York: Cambridge University Press.

Baltes, P.B., & Staudinger, U.M. (1993). The search for a psychology of wisdom. *Current Directions in Psychological Science*, 2, 75–80.

Barrett, G.V., & Watkins, S.K. (1986). Word familiarity and cardiovascular health as determinants of age-related recall differences. *Journal of Gerontology*, 41, 222–224.

Barrett, P.H. (1974). *Darwin's early and unpublished notebooks*. New York: Dutton.

Basseches, M. (1984). *Dialectical thinking and adult development*. Norwood, NJ: Ablex.

Benes, F. (1994). Development of the corticolimbic system. In G. Dawson & K.W. Fischer (eds), *Human behavior and the developing brain* (pp. 176–206). New York: Guilford.

Berg, C.A. (2000). Intellectual development in adulthood. In R.J. Steinberg (ed.), *Handbook of intelligence* (pp. 117–140). New York: Cambridge University Press.

Bever, T.G. (ed.) (1982). *Regressions in mental development: Basic phenomena and theories*. Hillsdale NJ: Erlbaum.

Birren, J.E. (1964). *The psychology of aging*. Englewood, NJ: Prentice-Hall.

Birren, J.E. (1970). Toward an experimental psychology of aging. *American Psychologist*, 25, 124–135.

Brown, A.L., & Reeve, R. (1987). Bandwidths of competence: The role of supportive contexts in learning and development. In L.S. Liben (ed.), *Development and learning: Conflict or congruence?* (pp. 173–223). Hillsdale, NJ: Erlbaum.

Bullock, M., & Ziegler, A. (1994). *Scientific reasoning*. Research report. Munich: Max Planck Institute for Psychological Research.

Carstensen, L.L. (1993). Motivation for social contact across the life span: A theory of socioemotional selectivity. In J.E. Jacobs (ed.), *Nebraska symposium on motivation* (pp. 209–254). Lincoln: University of Nebraska Press.

Carstensen, L.L., Pasupathi, My., Mayr, U., & Nesselroade, J.R. (2000). Emotional experience in everyday life across the adult life span. *Journal of Personality and Social Psychology*, 79, 644–655.

Cattell, R.B. (1963). Theory of fluid and crystallized intelligence: A critical experiment. *Journal of Educational Psychology*, 54, 1–22.

Charness, N. (1981). Aging and skilled problem solving. *Journal of Experimental Psychology: General*, 110, 21–38.

Colby, A., Kohlbeing, L., Gibbs, J., & Lieberman, M. (1983). *A longitudinal study of moral development. Monographs of the Society for Research in Child Development*, Vol. 48, no. 1, serial 200.

Commons, M.L., Trudeau, E.J., Stein, S.A., Richards, F.A., & Krause, S.R. (1998). Hierarchical complexity of tasks shows the existence of developmental stages. *Developmental Review*, 18, 237–278.

Cook-Greuter, S.R. (1999). Postautonomous ego development: A study of its nature and development.

Unpublished doctoral dissertation, Harvard Graduate School of Education, Human Development & Psychology, Cambridge, MA.

Craik, F.I.M. (1977). Age differences in human memory. In J.E. Birren & K.W. Schaie (eds), *Handbook of the psychology of aging* (pp. 384–420). New York: Van Nostrand Reinhold.

Craik, F.I.M., & Salthouse, T.A. (eds) (1991). *The handbook of aging and cognition*. Hillsdale, NJ: Erlbaum.

Darwin, C.R. (1859). *The origin of species*. New York: Penguin.

Dawson, T.L. (1999). 'A good education is . . .': A life-span investigation of developmental and conceptual features of evaluative reasoning about education. *Dissertation Abstracts International: Section B. The Sciences & Engineering*, 60 (3–B), 1329.

Dawson, T.L. (2002). New tools, new insights: Kohlberg's moral reasoning stages revisited. *International Journal of Behavior Development*, 26, 154–166.

Dennis, W. (1958). The age decrement in outstanding scientific contributions: Fact or artifact? *American Psychologist*, 13, 457–460.

Dewey, J. (1910). *How we think*. Amherst, NY: Prometheus Books, 1991.

Duncker, K. (1945). *On problem solving. Psychological Monographs*, Vol. 58, serial 270.

Erikson, E.H. (1963). *Childhood and society* (2nd edn). New York: Norton.

Erikson, E.H. (1968). *Identity: Youth and crisis*. New York: Norton.

Erikson, E. (1969). *Gandhi's truth: On the origins of militant nonviolence*. New York: Norton.

Erikson, E. (ed.) (1978). *Adulthood*. New York: Norton.

Fischer, K.W. (1980a). Learning and problem solving as the development of organized behavior. *Journal of Structural Learning*, 6, 253–267.

Fischer, K.W. (1980b). A theory of cognitive development: The control and construction of hierarchies of skills. *Psychological Review*, 6, 477–531.

Fischer, K.W., & Ayoub, C. (1996). Analyzing development of working models of close relationships: Illustration with a case of vulnerability and violence. In G.G. Noam & K.W. Fischer (eds), *Development and vulnerability in close relationships* (pp. 173–199). Hillsdale, NJ: Erlbaum.

Fischer, K.W., & Bidell, T.R. (1998). Dynamic development of psychological structures in action and thought. In R.M. Lerner (ed.), *Handbook of child psychology: Vol. 1. Theoretical models of human development* (5th edn, pp. 467–561). New York: Wiley.

Fischer, K.W., & Granott, N. (1995). Beyond one-dimensional change: Parallel, concurrent, socially distributed processes in learning and development. *Human Development*, 38, 302–314.

Fischer, K.W., Hand, H.H., & Russell, S.L. (1984). The development of abstractions in adolescence and adulthood. In M. Commons, F.A. Richards, & C. Armon (eds), *Beyond formal operations* (pp. 43–73). New York: Praeger.

Fischer, K.W., & Kennedy, B. (1997). Tools for analyzing the many shapes of development: The case of self-in-relationships in Korea. In K.A. Renninger & E. Amsel (eds), *Processes of development* (pp. 117–152). Mahwah, NJ: Erlbaum.

Fischer, K.W., Kenny, S.L., & Pipp, S.L. (1990). How cognitive processes and environmental conditions organize discontinuities in the development of abstractions. In C.N. Alexander & E.J. Langer (eds), *Higher stages of human development: Perspectives on adult growth*, (pp. 162–187). New York: Oxford University Press.

Fischer, K.W., & Pruyne, E. (2002). Reflective thinking in adulthood: Development, variation, and consolidation. In J. Demick (ed.), *Handbook of adult development*.

Fischer, K.W., & Rose, S.P. (1994). Dynamic development of coordination of components in brain and behavior: A framework for theory and research. In G. Dawson & K.W. Fischer (eds), *Human behavior and the developing brain* (pp. 3–66) New York: Guilford.

Fischer, K.W., & Rose, S.P. (1996). Dynamic growth cycles of brain and cognitive development. In R. Thatcher, G.R. Lyon, J. Rumsey, & N. Kinasnegor (eds), *Developmental neuroimaging: Mapping the development of brain and behavior* (pp. 263–279). New York: Academic.

Fischer, K.W., & Yan, Z. (2002). Darwin's construction of the theory of evolution: Microdevelopment of explanations of species variation and change. In N. Granott & J. Parziale (eds), *Microdevelopment: Transition processes in development and learning* (pp. 294–318). Cambridge: Cambridge University Press.

Gardner, H. (1983). *Frames of mind: The theory of multiple intelligences*. New York: Basic.

Gilligan, C. (1982) *In a different voice: Psychological theory and women's development*. Cambridge, MA: Harvard University Press.

Gottlieb, G., Wahlsten, D., & Lickliter, R. (1998). The significance of biology for human development: A developmental psychobiological systems view. In W. Damon (series ed.) & R.M. Lerner (ed.), *Handbook of child psychology: Vol. 1. Theoretical models of human development* (5th edn, pp. 233–274). New York: Wiley.

Granott, N. (1993a). Microdevelopment of coconstruction of knowledge during problem solving: Puzzled minds, weird creatures and wuggles. Unpublished doctoral dissertation, MIT, Cambridge, MA. *Dissertation Abstracts International*, 54 (10B), 5409.

Granott, N. (1993b). Patterns of interaction in the coconstruction of knowledge: Separate minds, joint effort, and weird creatures. In R.H. Wozniak & K.W. Fischer (eds), *Development in context: Acting and thinking in specific environments* (pp. 183–207). Hillsdale, NJ: Erlbaum.

Granott, N. (1998). We learn, therefore we develop: Learning versus development – or developing learning? In M.C. Smith & T. Pourchot (eds), *Adult learning and development: Perspectives from educational psychology* (pp. 15–34). Mahwah, NJ: Erlbaum.

Granott, N. (2002). How microdevelopment creates macrodevelopment: Reiterated sequences, backward transitions, and the zone of current development. In N. Granott & J. Parziale (eds), *Microdevelopment: Transition processes in development and learning* (Chapter 8). Cambridge: Cambridge University Press.

Granott, N., Fischer, K.W., & Parziale, J. (2002). Bridging to the unknown: A transition mechanism in learning and problem-solving. In N. Granott & J. Parziale (eds), *Microdevelopment: Transition processes in development and learning* (pp. 131–156). Cambridge: Cambridge University Press.

Granott, N., & Parziale, J. (eds) (2002). *Microdevelopment: Transition processes in development and learning.* Cambridge: Cambridge University Press.

Gruber, H.E. (1973). Courage and cognitive growth in children and scientists. In M. Schwebel & J. Raph (eds), *Piaget in the classroom*. New York: Basic.

Gruber, H.E. (1981). *Darwin on man* (2nd edn). Chicago: University of Chicago Press.

Harter, S., & Monsour, A. (1992). Developmental analysis of conflict caused by opposing attributes in the adolescent self-portrait. *Developmental Psychology*, 28, 251–260.

Horn, J.L. (1982). The aging of human abilities. In B.B. Wolman (ed.), *Handbook of developmental psychology*. Englewood Cliffs, NJ: Prentice-Hall.

Horn, J.L., & Cattell, R.B. (1967). Age differences in fluid and crystallized intelligence. *Acta Psychologica*, 26, 107–129.

Inhelder, B., & Piaget, J. (1958). *The growth of logical thinking from childhood to adolescence* (trans. A.P.S. Seagrim) New York: Basic. Originally published 1955).

Keegan, R.T. (1989). How Charles Darwin became a psychologist. In D.B. Wallace & H.E. Gruber (eds), *Creative people at work: Twelve cognitive case studies* (pp. 107–125). New York: Oxford University Press.

Kegan, R. (1982). The evolving self: Problem and process in human development. Cambridge, MA: Harvard University Press.

Kegan, R. (1994). *In over our heads: The mental demands of modern life*. Cambridge, MA: Harvard University Press.

Kennedy, B.P. (1994). The development of self-understanding in adolescents in Korea. Unpublished doctoral dissertation, Harvard University, Cambridge, MA. *Dissertation Abstracts International: Section B. The Sciences & Engineering*, 55 (7–B), 3036.

King, P.M., & Kitchener, K.S. (1994). *Developing reflective judgment: Understanding and promoting intellectual growth and critical thinking in adolescents and adults*. San Francisco: Jossey-Bass.

Kitchener, K.S., & Fischer, K.W. (1990). A skill approach to the development of reflective thinking. In D. Kuhn (ed.), *Developmental perspectives on teaching and learning thinking skills. Contributions to Human Development*, 21 (4), 48–62. Basel, Switzerland: Karger.

Kitchener, K.S., Lynch, C.L., Fischer, K.W., & Wood, P.K. (1993). Developmental range of reflective judgment: The effect of contextual support and practice on developmental stage. *Developmental Psychology*, 29, 893–906.

Kohlberg, L. (1969). Stage and sequence: The cognitive developmental approach to socialization. In D.A. Goslin (ed.), *Handbook of socialization theory and research* (pp. 347–480). Chicago: Rand, McNally.

Kohlberg, L. (1984). Moral stages and moralization: The cognitive-developmental approach. In L. Kohlberg (ed.), *The psychology of moral development: The nature and validity of moral stages* (pp. 170–205). San Francisco: Harper & Row.

Kuhn, D., Garcia-Mila, M., Zohar, A., & Andersen, C. (1995). *Strategies of knowledge acquisition. Monographs of the Society for Research in Child Development*,Vol. 60, no. 4, serial 245).

Lakoff, G., & Johnson, M. (1980). *Metaphors we live by*. Chicago: University of Chicago Press.

Labouvie-Vief, G., De-Voe, M., & Bulka, D. (1998). Speaking about feelings: Conceptions of emotion across the life span. In L.M. Powell & T.A. Salthouse (eds) (1998). *Essential papers on the psychology of aging* (pp. 481–510). New York: New York University Press.

Levinson, D.J. (1978). *The seasons of a man's life*. New York: Knopf.

Loevinger, J. (1976). *Ego development: Concepts and theories*. San Francisco: Jossey-Bass.

Marcia, J.E. (1980). Identity in adolescence. In J. Adelson (ed.), *Handbook of adolescent psychology*. New York: Wiley.

Marcia, J.E. (1994). The empirical study of ego identity. In H.A. Bosma, T.L.G. Graafsma, H.D. Grotevant, & D.J. de Levita (eds), *Identity and development: An interdisciplinary approach* (pp. 67–80). Thousand Oaks, CA: Sage.

Matteson, D.R. (1977). Exploration and commitment: Sex differences and methodological problems in the use of identity status categories. *Journal of Youth and Adolescence*, 6, 353–374.

Neugarten, B.L. (ed.) (1968). *Middle age and aging*. Chicago: University of Chicago Press.

Noam, G.G., Powers, S.J., Kilkenny, R., & Beedy, J. (1990). The interpersonal self in life-span developmental perspective: Theory, measurement, and longitudinal case analyses. In P.B. Baltes, D.L. Featherman, & R.M. Lerner (ed.), *Lifespan development and behavior* (Vol. 10, pp. 59–104). Hillsdale, NJ: Erlbaum.

Parziale, J. (1997). Microdevelopment during an activity based science lesson. *Dissertation Abstracts International: Section B. The Sciences & Engineering*, 58 (5–B), 2723.

Perry, W.G. Jr (1970). *Forms of intellectual and ethical development in the college years*. New York: Holt, Rinehart, & Winston.

Phinney, J.S. (1989). Stages of ethnic identity development in minority group adolescents. *Journal of Early Adolescence*, 9, 34–49.

Piaget, J. (1975). L'équilibration des structures cognitives: Problème central du développement (Equilibration of cognitive structures: Central problem of development). *Études d'Épistémologie Génétique*, 33.

Piaget, J. (1983). Piaget's theory. In P.H. Mussen (series ed.) & W. Kessen (ed.), *Handbook of child pyschology: Vol. 1. History, theory, and methods* (pp. 103–126). New York: Wiley.

Rest, J., Narvaez, D., Bebeau, M.J., & Thoma, S.J. (1999). *Postconventional moral thinking*. Mahwah, NJ: Erlbaum.

Roberts, R.J. Jr (1981). Errors and the assessment of cognitive development. In K.W. Fischer (ed.), *Cognitive development: New directions for child development* (Vol. 12, pp. 69–78). San Francisco: Jossey-Bass.

Rose, S.P., & Fischer, K.W. (1998). Models and rulers in dynamical development. *British Journal of Developmental Psychology*, 16 (Pt 1), 123–131.

Salthouse, T.A. (1984). Effects of age and skill in typing. *Journal of Experimental Psychology: General*, 113, 345–371.

Salthouse, T.A. (1992). *Mechanisms of age–cognition relations in adulthood*. Hillsdale, NJ: Erlbaum.

Salthouse, T.A., Hambrick, D.Z., & McGuthry, K.E. (1998). Shared age-related influences on cognitive and noncognitive variables. *Psychology & Aging*, 13, 486–500.

Schacter, D.L. (1999). The seven sins of memory: Insights from psychology and cognitive neuroscience. *American Psychologist*, 54, 182–203.

Schaie, K.W. (1983). Consistency and changes in cognitive functioning of the young-old and old-old. In M. Schmidt-Scherzer (eds), *Aging in the eighties and beyond*. New York: Springer.

Schaie, K.W. (1996). *Intellectual development in adulthood: The Seattle longitudinal study*. New York: Cambridge University Press.

Siegler, R.S. (2002). Microgenetic studies of self-explanation. In N. Granott & J. Parziale (eds), *Microdevelopment: Transition processes in development and learning* (Chapter 1). Cambridge: Cambridge University Press.

Simonton, D.K. (1991). Creative productivity through the adult years. *Generations*, 15, 13–16.

Simonton, D.K. (2000). Creative development as acquired expertise: Theoretical issues and an empirical test. *Developmental Review*, 20, 283–318.

Sinnott, J.D. (1998). *The development of logic in adulthood: Postformal thought and its applications*. New York: Plenum.

Smith, M.C., & Pourchot, T. (ed.) (1998). *Adult learning and development: Perspectives from educational psychology*. Mahwah, NJ: Erlbaum.

Sternberg, R. (1985). *Beyond IQ: A triarchic theory of intelligence*. New York: Cambridge University Press.

Sternberg, R.J. (ed.) (1990). *Wisdom: Its nature, origins, and development*. New York: Cambridge University Press.

Tennant, M. (1997). *Psychology and adult learning* (2nd edn). New York: Routledge.

Thatcher, R.W. (1994) Cyclic cortical reorganization: Origins of human cognitive development. In G. Dawson & K.W. Fischer (eds), *Human behavior and the developing brain* (pp. 232–266). New York: Guilford.

Thelen, E., & Smith, L.B. (1994). *A dynamic systems approach to the development of cognition and action*. Cambridge, MA: MIT Press.

Turkle, S. (1995). *Life on the screen: Identity in the age of the internet*. New York: Simon & Schuster.

Vaillant, G.E. (1977). *Adaptation to life*. Boston: Little, Brown.

Vaillant, G.E. (ed.) (1986). *Empirical studies of ego mechanisms of defense*. Washington, DC: American Psychiatric Press.

Valsiner, J. (1991). Construction of the mental: From the 'cognitive revolution' to the study of development. *Theory & Psychology*, 1, 477–494.

Valsiner, J. (1996). Co-constructionism and development: A socio-historic tradition. *Anuario de Psicologia*, 69, 63–82.

Valsiner, J., & van der Veer, R. (1988). On the social nature of human cognition: An analysis of the shared intellectual roots of George Herbert Mead and Lev Vygotsky. *Journal for the Theory of Social Behaviour*, 18, 117–136.

van der Maas, H., & Molenaar, P. (1992). A catastrophe-theoretical approach to cognitive development. *Psychological Review*, 99, 395–417.

van Geert, P. (1994). *Dynamic systems of development: Change between complexity and chaos*. London: Harvester Wheatsheaf.

van Geert, P. (2002). Developmental dynamics, intentional action, and fuzzy sets. In N. Granott & J. Parziale (eds), *Microdevelopment: Transition processes in development and learning* (chapter 12). Cambridge: Cambridge University Press.

Vygotsky, L.S. (1978). *Mind in society: The development of higher psychological processes*. Cambridge, MA: Harvard University Press.

Watson, M.W., & Fischer, K.W. (1980). Development of social roles in elicited and spontaneous behavior during the pre-school years. *Developmental Psychology*, 16, 484–494.

Wechsler, D. (1972). 'Hold' and 'don't hold' test. In S.M. Chown (ed.), *Human aging*. New York: Penguin.

Werner, H. (1948). *Comparative psychology of mental development*. New York: Science Editions.

Wood, D., Bruner, J.S., & Ross, G. (1976). The role of tutoring in problem solving. *Child Psychology and Psychiatry*, 17, 89–100.

Yan, Z. (1998). Measuring microdevelopment of understanding the VMS-SAS structure: A developmental scale pilot. Unpublished qualifying paper. Harvard Graduate School of Education, Cambridge, MA.

Yan, Z. (2000). Dynamic analysis of microdevelopment in learning a computer program. Unpublished doctoral dissertation, Harvard Graduate School of Education, Cambridge, MA.

Yan, Z., & Fischer, K.W. (2002). Always under construction: Dynamic variations in adult cognitive development. *Human Development*, 45, 141–160.

Zeeman, E.C. (1976). Catastrophe theory. *Scientific American*, 234 (4), 65–83.

22

Goal-Directed Activities and Life-Span Development

JEANETTE A. LAWRENCE and AGNES E. DODDS

> To desire to strive and to attain our goal is as natural as falling off a log, and with such telelogical causation, we are entirely familiar; we have more intimate understanding of it than of mechanistic causation. (McDougall, 1945, pp. 449–450)

Much personal activity has this teleological, purposive focus, making it natural to assume that people have some definite purposes for their everyday and future lives. With a goal in mind, a person's activities gain direction and meaning in relation to the desired goal. While purposive activity is not the exclusive prerogative of humans, and while not all human activity is purposeful, it makes good intuitive sense to take a teleological perspective on human activity, as McDougall (1945) argued strongly at the beginning of this century.

As the philosopher Bratman (1987) pointed out, a good common-sense psychology admits intentions as functional states of mind which motivate people to act, allowing us to characterize many occasional and everyday human activities as things done under the direction of goals. It is not unreasonable, therefore, to expect psychology also to make good theoretical sense of this commonly understood experience: to seek to explain how purposive activity has a special place in human endeavors.

Since the time of Miller, Galanter, and Pribram's (1960) seminal work on plans and behaviors, the significance of goals has attained respectability in contemporary psychology. Miller et al. observed how in the 1940s 'teleology' and 'unscientific' were synonymous terms in psychology (1960, p. 42). This is no longer the case (see Pervin, 1989, for a perceptive overview of the history of the goal in psychology). Although there are many accounts of how goals relate to different aspects of human experience, there is little in psychology by way of close theoretical analysis of what is meant by the goal-directedness of human activity, and little by way of examining the role of goal-directed activities in personal development. Accordingly, in this chapter we focus on the meaning of goal-directed activities in relation to the course of personal development across the life-span. First, we examine concepts of purposive, goal-directed behavior, analyzing how these teleological concepts have been used to explain human activities. Then we address the place of goal-directed activity within a life-span developmental framework, examining how developmental experience influences goals and their directed activities and vice versa. We argue that personal goals are central to understanding the connections between the past, present and future in a person's life-course, and central to understanding the dynamic interactions between the personal and the social that issue in change. Finally, we suggest that goal-directed activities deserve a special place in discussions of how person–environmental dialogs lead to transformational change in the adult years.

THE GOAL-DIRECTEDNESS OF HUMAN ACTIVITY

Goals have been studied in a wide range of activities (Austin & Vancouver, 1996), across broad cognitive, affective and behavioral domains of functioning (e.g. in: infancy, Gergely & Gergely, 1997; academic learning, Volet & Lawrence, 1990; everyday adaptation, Cantor & Blanton, 1996; life planning, King, 1998; Smith, 1996; 1999; well-being, Emmons & Kaiser, 1996; attention to the self, Deci & Ryan, 1995; achievement, Gollwitzer, 1993; Gollwitzer & Brandstätter, 1997; care for others, Stein et al., 1997; social communication, Berger, 1997). In these and many other studies, the goal of human activity has meant different things – ranging from vague wishes and desires, to central elements of self-definition and to concrete, short-term formulations of intentions to act. Yet, any account of goal-directed behaviors that is likely to add to explanations of developmental change across the life-span will need first to specify what goal-directedness means in people's lives, and then how goal-setting and goal maintenance function in relation to the pathways and turning points that people experience.

In search of the meaning of goal-directedness, we start from Woodfield's (1976) identification of the ambiguity that lies hidden in many descriptions of goal-directed behavior, linking it to Weir's (1984) call for a teleological explanation of goal-directness that covers the several elements of a goal-directed behavioral system. Considerable ground can be made towards clarifying the meaning of goal-directedness by attending to McDougall's elements of purposive psychology. This is especially persuasive, because his theory was linked to Russell's original, biological formulation of the concept of goal-directed behavior. Together, their individual analyses of activities centered on goals provide a foundation for examining how goal-directedness may be related to the developmental experience of transformational change. Activities that are governed by people's purposes for their future are able to speak to how their development has been constructed over time. In turn, goal-governed activities can help us understand how development is likely to proceed to personal futures. In short, goals and the activities serving them have a significant place in the working out of past, present and future in the individual life-course.

Conceptual Ambiguities

Unfortunately, the concept of goal-directed activity carries with it certain ambiguities that can easily lead to confusion in how it is used to explain purposive and changing behavior. While Heckhausen and Kuhl (1985, p. 137), for instance, observed that the goal concept is 'notoriously ill-defined', Woodfield (1976, pp. 42, 43) had already shown a decade earlier how people can be confused in their reference to goals. It is possible, he claimed, to think about the directiveness of a goal in one of two ways:

> It [goal-directed] could mean 'directed to a goal', rather as 'homeward-bound' means 'bound for home'; or it could mean 'directed by a goal' in the way that 'hand-made' means 'made by hand'. On the second interpretation the goal causally influences the direction, whereas the first leaves the causal influence open. (1976, pp. 42–43)

On the basis of this distinction, it can be asked where a theorist locates the generating purpose that sets the processes of change in motion, and how much and what kind of energy the goal supplies in that system. Woodfield distinguished between the varying strengths that can be attributed to a goal in a system of activities. Ambiguities center around the characteristics and functions attributed to the goal. Does an account of goal-directed activity, for instance, mainly focus on an end-state that only vaguely affects the chain of behavior preceding it, so that it simply serves as the end to be achieved? Alternatively, is the focus directed at how the goal actually governs the behavioral system that works towards it as the end-state? For psychology, the distinction involves the difference between saying that a sequence of activity has a discernible end (i.e. is 'homeward bound'), and saying that a directing force comes from its goal, such that, once generated, the goal sets in motion and directs the sequence for its own achievement (i.e. intentionally crafting and maintaining its whole production like a 'hand-made' piece of work). Woodfield, for his part, affirmed the causal significance of the goal, along with its directive force, while attributing the generating creative impetus behind the goal to the desire/belief states of the human mind. Thus, he affirmed the driving force of goals in human activities, and attributed them to internal, purposive states.

The distinction in emphasis is not trivial. Rather, disparate orientations become clearer if we ask about the specific role and energy that is ascribed to a goal in any given paradigm. Social psychologists who ground goal-directedness in theories of the self, for example, seem to be following Woodfield's first, weaker case where the goal is simply a part of a behavioral system. The goal constitutes an end or a valued state towards the achievement of which the person orients attention and effort. The forcefulness and effectiveness of the goal are not as salient as the fact that the goal is conceived and owned by a person with particular characteristics (e.g. with a stronger or weaker sense of self). The focus is on the content of the person's goal rather than on the goal-related processes by which that person acts in the service of the goal (Ford, 1992). What is significant in the case of content is the nature of the goal: what the actual goal expresses, rather than how it works as a directive force in the person's life. Emmons and Kaiser (1996), for instance, categorized sets of goals in terms of approach and avoidant strivings (e.g. 'spend time with others' compared with 'avoid being lonely'). People with predominantly avoidance goals reported less positive mood states and poor life satisfaction, but high levels of anxiety and physical ill-health. This kind of taxonomic approach to understanding the goals people hold has been popular in psychology (see Austin & Vancouver, 1996). It leaves unexplained, however, the dynamic significance for a person's life of having one pattern of goals as opposed to another.

In contrast to a general approach describing the content of people's goals, a problem solving paradigm assigns significant directive power to the goal in specific situations, showing how immediate problem solutions or plans for the future are developed in the service of the goal. Duncker's (1926) account of goal-directed, situated problem solving is a prime example of the situated, specific function of a goal. In this account, the goal is generated within a particular problematic situation and is designed to resolve a problem that arises in the situation (e.g. killing a tumor by X-ray, without destroying surrounding healthy tissue: Duncker, 1926). The problem is resolved only when that particular goal is achieved. Indeed, for Duncker, the problem solution and the realization of a goal were the same thing. Achieving the goal required the person to engage in a series of cognitive activities that concretely linked the problem situation to its goal (see Lawrence & Dodds, 1999). Some goals naturally stimulate more activities than others. Earley and Perry (1987), for example, found that an adolescent was more likely to work on planning how to save money if the goal was to buy a car rather than saving to go to college. In analyzing the prominence of goals, it is important to ask about the specific role that any goal is asked to fulfill in a behavioral system. In Ford's (1992) terms, that requires linking the content of the goal to the processes that work towards its achievement.

Working from a cybernetics orientation and seeking to demonstrate how machines can generate sequences of activity that could rightly be called goal-directed, Weir (1984) threw further light on the ambiguities of goal-and activity connections. He constructed a thorough philosophical and computational analysis of goal-directed behavior, making a careful critique of a series of positions that, he argued, could be found in many philosophical accounts. Most accounts pinned their explanations on only one of three crucial contributors to any goal-directed system (type of behavior, nature of goal, presence of goal director).

> The behaviour itself might be distinctive, the ends might be distinctive (e.g. goals as opposed to *de facto* ends), or there might be a director implied (e.g. a God or agent). (Weir, 1984, p. 68)

Weir's analysis reveals how, by their single-mindedness, different accounts of teleological behavior actually add to the confusion surrounding goal-directedness, by exclusively relying on any one of these three elements. In a real sense, Weir fills out Woodfield's notion of why the concept may be addressed differently. While a theory's general orientation to explaining the strength of the purposive human activity constitutes one aspect of the problem (Woodfield's point), the confusion may also be related to which of Weir's three elements of goal-directedness is asked to carry the burden of the teleological explanation. In such cases, the single emphasis is used as the basis for understanding why and how a goal-directed system is said to function as it does.

Now Weir argued that the distinctiveness of goal-directed behavior does not lie in the types of behaviors that may be used to achieve the teleological end. His point is important if we are to relate the different dimensions of goal-directedness to developmental change. The presence of one form of activity in contrast to another does not mark out a sequence of activities as definitively teleological, or even as part of a causal chain. People use a variety of actions when they are trying to achieve a particular end, or even the same end at different times in their lives. Consequently, an observer is not able to reliably impute goal-directedness to one form of activity over and above another. In a given situation, for instance a catastrophe, neither the effort expended, nor the speed of action, nor the strategy used by different people would allow the observer to infer that one person's activity was goal-governed and another person's was not. Some people, for example, respond to catastrophic events with effective strategies to reduce the danger. Others take panic-filled actions that exacerbate the danger. Yet, it cannot be claimed that one of these responses to catastrophe is more goal-directed than the other. One is simply more effective than the other. People may be following their own goals in idiosyncratic ways without leaving indelible traces of the strength of those goals. The catastrophe example illustrates the diversity of activities that people may use in the service of the same overriding goal of surviving in the same difficult circumstances.

Neither, according to Weir's analysis, does goal-directedness attain distinction from the nature or quality of the goal that is served by particular behaviors. Personal goals, for instance, may not be beneficial or noble, but they can still command diligent pursuit and maintenance. They do not even need to be fulfilled in order to function as powerful motivators of activity. Consequently, the description of a goal-directed sequence of action does not suffer simply because the goal is not reached. In the case of athletic striving, for example, the last runner across the line may be no less purposively motivated than the first. Similarly, in interpersonal communication, one person's goal of influencing the other is not diminished by the fact that that goal cannot be achieved without the consent and cooperation of the other person in the conversation (cf. Berger, 1997).

There is, in fact, as much diversity in the goals that people devise for both their long-term and short-term behaviors as there is diversity in the people who generate the goals and in the situations in which they act teleologically. Goals can be idiosyncratic, so that several people may be seeking to achieve different ends, for example, when students in the same class generate and pursue different goals in relation to the objectives for their assessment published by their instructors (Volet & Lawrence, 1990). Similarly, the same person may have different goals for applying to different situations (e.g. sometimes wishing to be dominant in a conversation, sometimes wishing to be passive). Indeed, if the developmental perspective has any force, a person is likely to rearrange priorities among a set of working goals as s/he moves in and out of different experiences and situations.

If the nature of the goal or the behavior does not definitively identify an activity system as goal-directed, neither does the environmental situation in which the goal is generated. While the power of environmental feedback serves a special function in goal development and revision, especially negative feedback according to Weir, the feedback loop itself does not define goal-directiveness. It has to be used by the recipient as a means of modifying previously held goals. The feedback from the environment must be incorporated into the goal structure if it is to become part of the total goal-oriented activity, and that integration is done by the person who is generating the goal. A vocational goal is likely to be modified in the light of current experience, such as when a young man surrenders his dreams of college and professional life, and drops out of school, because of the possibility of earning money to contribute to pressing family needs (Bühler, 1968). Throughout life, experiences of situation-specific constraints give people the kind of feedback that Weir saw as crucial for goal modification as well as for goal development. Receiving the feedback is only the first step towards altering current activities. Acting on the feedback involves developing an intention to act in a certain way, then following through on the intention.

In relation to that intentional aspect, Weir conceded that a 'special kind of internal state is necessary in accounting for how the distinguishing behavioral characteristics come about' (1984, p. 103). It involves intentional beliefs and motivations that generate goals. Regardless of how they are characterized, mindful, intentional activities are usually understood in terms of purpose, and purpose is usually focused on action situations where goals are likely to make a difference. The purpose, nevertheless, needs to be linked to the action sequence. The desire/belief states that Woodfield saw as purposive must exert some 'control' over the behavior (1984, p. 104) for the behavior to be considered goal-directed in the stronger sense. Thus, the belief states behind the goal and its associated activities are not a sufficient explanation, alone, of the way that goal-directiveness works. Belief states are implemented in situation-specific goals, and as Duncker (1926) showed, by being focused on the peculiar potentials and difficulties of specific situations, goals productively generate certain courses of action (Lawrence & Dodds, 1999). So while internal beliefs are important for the goal-directed system, they also are not, in themselves, sufficient explanation of the system. They need to be expressed in forms that can be translated into action. These forms are the goals that relate intentions to situations and action.

Overall, Weir's emphasis on the total goal-directed system (involving: generating purpose; concrete goal; activities to serve that goal; directing internal states) culminated in the need to construct a teleological explanation that would account for the whole as a connected system:

> As a form of explanation of goal-directed behavior, teleological explanation is distinctive. It necessarily involves explaining the behavior that occurs by reference to some behavior being perceived to bring about the goal. And if the behavior is brought about because of this perception, then the behavior is goal-directed. (1984, p. 121)

Thus, making a statement about goal-directed activity involves proposing that the behavioral system within which that activity is constructed is teleological in its intent and in its execution. There is a goal, and this goal gives the behavioral sequence its meaning, its focus, its driving force and its finality. In addition to the goal and its associated set of behaviors, there is some kind of mindful goal director who forms the underlying intention of specifying and working towards the goal. It would seem that all these elements must work together to designate a behavioral sequence as teleological. Abstract desires and wishes exert little power over a person's activities until they are translated into goals that can be achieved by behaving in particular ways. Gollwitzer and Brandstätter (1997) called the concrete translations of intention 'implementation intentions' that carry with them action plans. The plans they generate also direct attention to situational cues that allow the person to instantiate the goal and the activities that are likely to lead to its achievement. Casting the whole enterprise into a teleologically explanatory statement, however, does not remove the need to deal with the motivating intentions that are part of the system in an account of the developing person. Rather, it puts the person and personal intention within the framework of a total behavioral system.

In the developmentally oriented account that we are proposing, the significance of goal-directed activity can be identified in one of two ways. We can refer to the goal-directiveness of the total behavioral system, in this case the system that is the developing person, as having a goal that is part of its very nature. This is the kind of general position Woodfield identified. Alternatively, we can go further to endow that developing system with purposeful intent, thus giving a special significance to the agentic nature of the person's cognitive and motivational structures. In the second position, a stronger claim is being made about the person's contribution to personal development, where the directiveness bears the sense of intention and purpose, and also the sense of effective action geared towards achieving the specific, intended end. This does not mean, however, that the goals and activities of the person are the sole determinants of his or her development. As we will argue, the life-span approach to understanding development firmly places the goal-generating, goal-directed personal system in an ongoing dialog with other systems operating in the natural world. As in this life-span perspective, the general and the specific senses of the goal-directedness of organic life were not antithetical in the original use of goal-directed activity by the biologist E.S. Russell. Rather, the second, intentional sense serves as a special case of the general position. In the special case, the human mind gives the goal and its associated activities a deliberative quality that is a part of the natural world.

Roots of The Meaning of Goal-Directed Activity

By going back to Russell's original use of the concept of goal-directed activity, it is possible to forge a strong link between the goal as a natural end-state and the striving effort of the activity that is directed towards its achievement. It is significant, also, that Russell, for all his claims of a non-teleological approach, reserved a special place for purposive human thought in his general biological account of goal-directed activity. From Russell's theory of the goal-directiveness of organic life, it is a shorter step than may be imagined to McDougall's thoroughgoing purposive psychology. In fact, Russell constructed that bridging step himself, by acknowledging the higher directive striving that belonged to purposive human thought and behavior.

Russell's Goal-directed Organismic Life

Russell identified directed activity as the irreducible characteristic of organismic life ('we must regard directiveness as an attribute, not of mind but of life': 1945, p. 179). Such an organic, life-expressing directiveness could not be reduced either to physico-chemical mechanisms or to conscious purposiveness. Goal-directed activity involved

> action directed towards end-states or goals which are normally related to the biological ends of self-maintenance, development or reproduction. This we may call directive activity. (1945, p. 3)

Russell emphatically claimed this directed activity of organismic life could not be interpreted as implying consciousness. Instead, he argued, he was using 'directive' as a neutral term with no implications of conation, and he asserted this position throughout his monograph. In its final section, however, Russell admitted how difficult he had found it to describe the kind of goal-directed activity he was ascribing to all living things, without using words heavy with psychological meaning, for example, 'effort', 'perseverance' and 'urge' (1945, p. 191). He needed such words to convey the sense of the striving by which he believed organismic life in any form moved towards its specific endstates. The weaker idea of a naturally occurring sequence of activities was not strong enough to describe his understanding of the movement of living organisms towards their larger biological functions (maintenance, development, reproduction) through intermediate goals.

In Weir's terms, Russell accounted for both the goal and the directed action in his explanation of what we may regard as the life force (that which maintains life as a 'going concern': 1945, p. 187). The goal represented the end or terminus of specified activity, but it also gave a natural focus to the mode of activity striving towards its achievement in spatial-temporal processes. By such focused and energized striving processes, the 'potential' for the organism becomes 'actualized' (1945, p. 190).

Theoretically, these naturally directed activities had for Russell 'the general or normal characteristics of all goal-directed activities' (1945, p. 111). Goal-directed activity: ceases when it is achieved, 'completed' or 'actualized' (e.g. fibre tissue regeneration stops after a severed motor nerve is reconnected); persists until that end is achieved (e.g. when birds continue to lay eggs until a given complement of eggs is produced); can lead to variation of action, including compensatory action (e.g. when cantaloup seedlings react with greater rather than less vigorous growth when the part of the seed containing the food reserves is artificially reduced); is more variable than the goal; and is limited, but not determined, by conditions (e.g. a dissected, starving worm will still reconstitute as two new wholes despite the prevailing poor food supply). In this fashion, although carefully avoiding anthropomorphizing, Russell insisted on the autonomy of organic life and its ability to overcome environmental conditions to maintain life.

Despite this non-purposive theory of biological life, Russell did not only borrow psychological terminology. By describing the purposive, motivating human mind as 'the highest form of the natural striving of all life' (1945, p. 144), he both linked it to other forms of organismic life, and also differentiated its special status. The goals that the person devises for himself, and the consciously planned routes to achieving those goals, are part of the natural world. They simply function at a different (higher) level.

Concerning human activity, Russell made two points that have direct relevance for an exposition of human goals, one to do with constructivism, the other to do with purposive psychology. In his treatment of the constructive nature of organic life, he drew on an analogy of the ability of humans to construct, for example, in building a house. He explicitly added purpose to the explanation of human constructive effort, 'all his constructions are easily explicable in terms of physics and chemistry – and purpose' (1945, p. 169):

> Human purpose must come into the story as an essential element. The building of a house is in fact a typical example of human purposive activity, arising out of a need or desire, guided by forethought and a definite plan, which is adaptable to circumstances. There is persistence of effort until the end is reached, and, if necessary, variation in the method of attaining it. (1945, p. 170)

It was consistent with his position to give purpose its special place in the human scheme of things. In doing so, his theorizing anticipated the concepts and features found in later accounts of human goal-directed activity (e.g. need, desire, plan, variable means to reaching a goal). Thus, the kinds of cognitive and motivational components of goal-directed activity that later attracted the attention of developmental and social psychologists were not only envisaged in the general biological model, but also explicitly seen as a special dimension of the use of the goal-directed concept at its outset. Psychology did not need to invent its own uses of the concept by wresting it from a non-psychological foundation and giving it psychological meaning, but had only to take account of the prior theorizing. That psychological meaning was present at its inception as a working concept.

Further evidence of Russell's inclusion of the psychological aspects of goal-related behaviors can be found in the direct and explicit connections he made between his understanding of goal-directiveness and McDougall's psychology of purposive behavior. Russell deliberately drew links between his characteristics of goal-directed activity and McDougall's:

> It is interesting to note that the characteristics of goal-directed activity which we have distinguished are very similar to those which William McDougall has singled out as characteristics of behavior. (1945, p. 145)

In this comment, Russell was referring to McDougall's 1923 volume *An outline of psychology*. In the 1936, 23rd edition of his *Social psychology*, McDougall identified these characteristics as 'expressive of mind, of hormic, or, in the widest sense, purposive action or striving' (1945, p. 411). This was an explicit dimension of McDougall's theorizing that, actually, had much in common with Russell's.

McDougall, in turn, was aware of Russell's theory, and referred to it as part of a development amongst biologists to move away from exclusively mechanistic explanations of life. He drew attention to Russell's insistence on end-states and striving. In their own disciplines, both these theorists were trying to characterize the kind of activity that is linked to a definable goal and that involves action towards that goal. From a psychological perspective, McDougall's theory focused on the purposive element that Russell had acknowledged and admitted into his scheme, while at the same time covering instinctual behaviors that were more like Russell's general biological directiveness.

McDougall's Psychology of Hormic, Purposive Life

McDougall, as one of the early psychologists to tackle the purposiveness of human activity, derived his concept of 'hormic psychology' from the Greek 'to strive', with due acknowledgments to Nunn and Jung. Most of his contemporaries were wary of anything that smacked of a theological worldview. In coining the concept of 'hormic', he was trying to:

> denote the energy that seems to find expression in purposive striving, in conation of every kind; and the adjective 'hormic' to denote such strivings or activities and also the psychology, which in opposition to the mechanical psychology, regards this conception of the hormic striving as its most fundamental category. (1945, p. 409)

The 1936 account of this form of purposive behavior was partly in response to criticisms of McDougall's earlier work on intention and volition, and partly the expression of the development of his thinking over three decades. In the refined theory, he proposed seven characteristics of purposive action or striving that distinguished it from the activities of the inorganic world, and in the process, identified it as 'expressive of mind, of hormic, or in the widest sense, of purposive action or striving' (1945, p. 411). Thus, while he was referring to something like Russell's biological striving, purposive mental life was at the forefront of McDougall's theorizing.

The seven characteristics of this purposive action involved: (1) the spontaneity and power of the initiative of the person; (2) the tendency of the person to persist in purposive behavior; (3) the variety of persistent movements that people may employ; (4) cessation of activity with the attainment of the goal, that is, 'in effecting a change of situation of a particular kind' (1945, p. 411); (5) anticipation and preparation for the goal; (6) improvement of the process of purposive action with continuing activity; and (7) the involvement of the total organism in the genuinely purposive activity, that is, everything else is subordinated to it. It can be seen how these elements of purposive activity are teleological both in the sense of being forward-looking and in describing the active striving towards achievement of a specific end.

We take these markers as pertinent to the discussion of the person's contribution to personal development, because they draw attention to how the person's goals work within the dialogic encounters with the external world that issue in change. They suggest, for instance, we should expect to find in purposive activities a certain amount of spontaneity, persistence, plasticity, anticipatory awareness and monitoring, and also that we should expect the person's efforts to stop when the particular goal is reached to the person's satisfaction.

While this terminal aspect of goal-directed activity was important for McDougall and Russell, from a contemporary viewpoint it seems mostly significant as an indicator of the meaning and value ascribed to particular goals within the intentions of the goal director, and an indicator of the nature of the activities that are used in the process of striving towards the goal. If we know that a person's persistent striving for a vocational goal ceases, for instance, we know that she has either achieved the goal, modified it or been satisfied with an alternative, or has accepted goal failure (Brunstein & Gollwitzer, 1996). Striving has its impact precisely because it is directed to a certain end. It is neither random nor aimless. When that end is reached, when the goal is achieved or actualized, the reason for the activity no longer exists.

There has been little take-up of this idea in contemporary accounts of personal goals, but in the problem solving paradigms of Duncker (1926) and Newell and Simon (1977) among others (see Lawrence & Dodds, 1999) the achievement of the given goal marks the resolution of a problem and the cognitive satisfaction of the problem solver's intent. For Simon (1957), 'satisficing' is the personally sufficient solution of the original problem that gains its significance in an individualized approximation of the intended end. McDougall had already understood the possibility of this personalized and partial resolution process: 'The anticipation of the end of action is, then, always more or less incomplete; its adequacy is a matter of degree' (1945, pp. 308–309). In effect, the cessation characteristic is a definitive mark of the teleological nature of an action. In short, in relation to the psychology of human activity, McDougall paved the way for considering the purposeful involvement of an agent in teleological activity, because the agent engages in acting on situations and phenomena with the intent of making changes to them to accomplish a goal.

Picking up on his third marker of the variety of activities by which instinctual behavior can be described as purposive and teleological, we note that McDougall eliminated those simple situations in which a person or animal attains a goal easily, by working routinely, directly or repetitively. Purpose is not so significant in such situations, because, in them, responses can be automated. Anderson (1993) provides an elaborated analysis of what McDougall understood as the distinction between automated and deliberate problem solving. Individualized goals are manifested where there is no direct, obvious, automated move to be made. The person has to generate a goal.

This idea of the person's contribution is worked out further in McDougall's explanation of what he meant by the involvement of the whole organism. It was meant to convey the sense of 'a total reaction':

> The energies of the whole organism seem to be bent towards the one end. It may perhaps be questioned whether this last character can properly be asserted of all hormic processes, but it seems to be true of those which are conative in the sense defined by Professor Nunn, or truly purposive in that they involve or imply foresight of the goal to be achieved. (1945, p. 412)

Thus there are conative, intentional activities that bear the sense of not only moving towards the goal, but also being absorbed by it. Some kind of planning ('foresight') demands the attention of that system as part of its conscious moving forward to the accomplishment of the goal. This is a strong statement about the cognitive and motivational aspects of purposive directedness. McDougall, along with Russell, thus reserved a special form of directive striving for that which involved intent. He also agreed with Russell in applying a less conscious form of striving to all organic life systems, and in seeing that striving as environmentally adaptive.

> The adaptability of instinctive action to the circumstances of the moment is its very essence; and this adaptability consists mainly in bringing into action first one, then another, motor mechanism, according as the circumstances of each moment require. (1945, p. 415)

In summary, we may ask what can be gained from the analysis of these two early accounts of goal-directed activities, apart from a general historical and etymological interest. There are at least four implications for an account of the developmental significance of goal-directed activities: (1) the way that the activities associated with goals are said to be directed, with a genuine sense of striving, energy-using movement towards the goals as their ends; (2) the basic biological and instinctual functions that lie behind the organic behavioral system involving goals and goal-directed activities; (3) the adaptability of these goal-related behavioral systems; and (4) the special significance of conscious, purposive goal generation and pursuit, at least for persons.

Undoubtedly, in each account, goals carried more than the vague 'homeward-bound' sense of Woodfield's (1976, pp. 42, 43) weaker form. They were seen as distinctive and definable terminuses of activities. If we are to consider goals as integral parts of people's lives, as Russell and McDougall claimed, we should be looking to the significance of the goals people generate for their lives and looking to the impact of goals on what people think and do. If there is any credence to Russell's invocation of the underlying biological functions that give goal-directed striving its meaning, then it is also possible to see in his theory precursors of the position that goal-directed activities have meaning as they relate to the outworking of the total life-course of the person. Although these early theorists' anti-mechanistic assumptions colored their ways of describing life-force and instinctual behaviors, their perspectives are consistent with developmentally oriented accounts that see the inner life of the person as part of, and linked to, the larger scheme of organic life. They also are consistent with seeing organic life as part of the natural order.

In the work of both Russell and McDougall, there are early indicators of the adaptability principle in which adaptation is worked out in different activities and developmental pathways over the life-course (Baltes & Baltes, 1990; Freund, Li, & Baltes, 1999; Ryan, 1993). Within that adaptability principle, conscious, purposive actions find their strongest expression in persons' agentic capabilities for contributing to their own development. Ryan, for instance, argued that regardless of how development is construed, 'it is still done by some*one* through moment-to-moment intentions, willing and motives' (1993, p. 4, author's emphasis). Across the decades it would seem, Ryan and McDougall were in agreement in assigning effective agency to the developing person, and in attributing to personal agency the intention and purpose that allow some aspects of environmental adaptation to remain under personal control.

Russell and McDougall each had the sense of the person's ability to make some conscious decisions about the future course that personal development might take, and about the activities likely to influence changes and transformations that move the person towards the goal. Of course, not all life movement and change are deliberately and cognitively controlled and monitored. The person acts and develops in a system of mutually constraining internal and external forces (Valsiner & Lawrence, 1997). Nevertheless, the possibility of the agentic consciousness to which Ryan referred was an important part of the early accounts of goal-directed life.

Life-Span Development, Goals and Goal-Directed Activities

The preceding analysis of the meaning of goal-directed activities raises two questions for accounts of the goals that people set for their life directions and accounts of how those goals are worked out over time. One is to do with strength of goal, the other is to do with processes of adaptation.

First, Woodfield's (1976) analysis indicates that we should ask about the directive strength of people's goals in relation to the activities that supposedly serve those goals. Do goals simply function as vague wishes or dreams for the future, or do they actually direct people's choices and actions, and consequently direct the pathways and turning points that their lives take? Drawing on Weir's (1984) insistence that teleological explanations of behavior should relate goals, directed activities and the directing mind, and paying attention to Woodfield's warning about conceptual ambiguities, we need to address how goals are said to function within the total behavioral system. In the present case, that system is the ontogenetically developing person.

The directive strength question, however, seemed to have less relevance to the theories of goal-directed activities developed by Russell and McDougall. For them, the relationship between natural life and goal-directed activities was a given, a feature of organic life. Their question for developmentalists focuses on adaptation: how do goals make a difference to the way people live out their lives, and how do goals facilitate adaptative development? We need to know how goals function as the mediators between agentic consciousness and environmental constraints. By giving direction and focus to the person's activities, goals give impetus to certain actions that take motivating purposes out of the realm of intellectual and emotionally charged intention and into the phenomenal environment.

Lawrence (1991), for instance, presents the example of a young adult student who becomes a paraplegic and needs to address how to incorporate the goal of being independent into a set of normative life goals. Her multiple goals are likely to lead to changes in practical behaviors (e.g. whether to navigate her own way around campus or allow a parent to assist her), with dominant goals setting priorities for her efforts and for her practical expression of the firm intention to remain autonomous. Subsequent to working through the implications of goal-directedness in such a situation, we were able to talk with a student who actually found herself in that position after a car accident. She explained how her aims to achieve independence had led her to move out of home and take a six week overseas holiday on her own in her wheelchair. She was acting in a way that would dramatically help her establish her independence from the family, and assert her personal autonomy. The overseas holiday with its practicalities of finding wheelchair ramps and manipulating doors, for example, constituted goal-directed activities that led her to acquire new skills and greater confidence.

Working on a similar idea of adaptability, Freund, Li, and Baltes (1999) developed an elaborate model of selection, optimization and compensation in old age. Their examples of compensation are similar to the case we have described, analyzing how people can compensate after the loss of the means for accomplishing everyday and longer-term goals. People were able to use different means to achieve their ends, by substitution (e.g. dictating manuscripts when unable to type because of arthritis), or by increasing effort and energy (e.g. trying harder to run as fast as possible in a marathon after losing time because of cramp: 1999, p. 410). Their compensatory activities provide a special window on the control that goals can exert over distinct patterns of behavior. If the goal is strong, in Woodfield's sense, people will search for alternative means for realizing it when existing means fail.

In light of the acknowledged driving power of goals in classical literature and everyday experience, it seems strange that relatively little attention has been paid in investigations of developmental change to the activities carried out under the direction of goals. Most attention seems to be given, instead, to the existence and content of people's goals for their lives, with some inferences about the difference that certain goals may have on people's well-being and life satisfaction (cf. Emmons, 1996; King, 1998). The picture of the relation of goal-directed activities to personal development would be more powerful if there were greater concentration on the actual activities linking goals to significant transformation and change. We need models of change that incorporate the processes by which goals are put into action in such ways that their implementation contributes to new personal directions.

CONNECTIONS BETWEEN GOALS AND DEVELOPMENT

The connection between goal-directed activity and development was powerfully acknowledged by Weir (1984, p. 9). Although not a developmentalist, he specifically argued that organisms not only are the 'natural producers of teleological behavior', but also develop, and their development affects their goals and their purposes. He also emphasized the processes by which feedback from the environment is incorporated into the behavioral system. The direction of influence in the connection between goals and development is important, because it can be thought about as how developmental experience influences goal formation and pursuit, or it can be thought about in terms of how goals influence the course of development.

From a dialogic perspective, these two approaches do not constitute a problem. Influence works in both directions (cf. Lawrence & Valsiner, 1993; Riegel, 1979). Developmental experience affects the goals that people set for themselves, contributing to their type and content and how they are worked out experientially. Goals affect activities by giving them direction and meaning. The activities involved in striving towards goals take people's experiences along particular routes, with consequences for the different dimensions and directions of development. Piaget (1972) argued, for instance, that differential motivation and aptitude led adults to develop some skills to the detriment of others (e.g. concentrating on developing computational skills to the neglect of artistic skills).

The idea of the bidirectionality of the directive forces operating in the developing person resonates with Weir's (1984, p. 76) notion of the working of feedback loops in any internally controlled system that can be called 'selfdirected' (cf. Gollwitzer & Brandstätter, 1997). Self-directed systems are able to take in and use feedback provided by the environment without surrendering the directive power to the environment providing the feedback (cf. Taylor, 1950). The internal system – the personal realm of meaning and purpose – is able to be environmentally sensitive as it regulates its own behaviors. With few analyses deliberately taking a bidirectional perspective, we turn to some illustrative accounts of the relation of goals to development over time, to show how goals link past, present and future, and also to demonstrate the strength of those links.

Developmental Experience and the Pursuit of Life Goals

Accounts of goals as people's teleological ends for their future deal with them variously as life goals (Bühler, 1968), projects for life and life plans (Smith, 1996; 1999), life tasks (Cantor, 1994) and dreams (Levinson, 1996).

Charlotte Bühler's analysis of *life goals* formed an important part of her proposal that self-integration is the achievement of developmental maturity through the life:

> To live a goal-directed life means to have the desire or even the feeling of obligation to see one's life culminating in certain results. Ideally, these results would represent a fulfilment of the aims towards which a person was striving with a determination that governs him throughout his life. (1968, p. 2)

In this definitely teleological statement, as in her overall approach to the development of personal life, Bühler interpreted intentionality as the desire for purpose in a person's life ('something to live for'), giving life meaning and expressing life's 'expansiveness and creativity' (1968, p. 5). Because goals appropriately gave life purpose, they were used by Bühler as a way of interpreting how a person's life worked towards the effective integration of the past, present and future self: a major life task.

This meant, in Bühler's terms, seeing the setting and pursuit of goals both as a normative developmental activity that proceeds through what she called 'normative motivational stages' (1968, p. 333), and as a function of inherently personal development as a response to individualized experiences. Personal goal-setting arose from a complex array of genetic, dynamic, cultural-ideological and structural age and maturation factors (1968, p. 342). This dynamic complexity consequently actually faced Bühler with the challenge of being able to study goals both macroscopically ('looking at the life as a whole') and microscopically ('to examine individual behavior at certain points in time in certain phases of development': 1968, p. 9).

Normatively, adolescence and early adulthood represented the period in which the formation and testing of life goals directly proceeded from the processes of development. During the adolescent years, a person set goals for life, making decisions that issued in living 'constructively' (handling oneself and one's relationships in ways benefiting others and self) rather than 'destructively' (full of hostilities, determined to damage others and self). Between 15 and 25, however, Bühler believed that life goals were only tentatively and experimentally conceived. They could be set in more definite ways between the ages of 25 and 45. Between 45 and 65, people engaged in the assessment of the fulfillment or failure of their lives, again in relation to goals they had, or had not, previously set for themselves, and in how their activities were, or were not, governed by those goals. Progress between the motivational phases was either favored or hindered by personal experience.

In the business of handling experience, a crucial factor related to how goals provided meaning for the future as well as the past and present. Being able to forge a meaningful continuity between past, present and future, moreover, was the kind of activity that belonged to a healthy person, that is, a person engaged in the processes of personal integration. Thus, Bühler proposed a strong dependence of possible life goals on prior developmental experience, with the goals feeding back into the processes of personal integration and well-being.

Viewing expansive goal-setting and pursuit as the characteristics of healthy development, she also looked for any negative effects of experience on goals, and related the present problems of her clinical patients to the difficulties they experienced in trying to achieve their life goals. She reported, for example, the case of one woman who, in her mid thirties, felt unfulfilled because her poverty-stricken childhood had prevented her from developing her musical talent. Under her father's demands, she had had to work for the family's income. Bühler made the observation that, 'Louise did not have the strength to stand up for the goals and values she believed in' (1968, p. 182). This illustrative case is not remarkable for the circumstances it reports, as much as for the weight Bühler placed on the frustration of Louise's goals, and on her inability to engage in goal-directed activity.

Similarly, she interpreted the experience of a refugee woman of 60 years in terms of failure to realize her goals. The woman was unhappy because she felt she had 'wasted her life'. Bühler's therapeutic treatment, together with her interpretation, was along the lines of helping the woman to see her past in relation to her life goals:

> But gradually, she realized that at several turning points, her own decisions had prevented her from striving towards more satisfactory as well as self-realizing goals. (1968, p. 401)

Not only did Bühler interpret the larger, ontogentic (macrocosmic) dimensions of life in terms of activities directed by goals, but also, in analyzing the everyday experiences of people, she saw goals as extremely important for the organization of daily activities. She distinguished between illustrative examples of well-integrated and poorly integrated persons, where integration related to 'the proper pursuit of the coming day's chores and pleasures' (p. 341). Her account, unfortunately, failed to make explicit the connection between these microcosmic activities and any macrocosmic effects they might have on life goals and experience. There were hints of the influence of the microgenetic on the ontogenetic, for example choices at different points, but the connection was not followed through in a systematic fashion.

From a contemporary viewpoint, Smith's (1996; 1999) exposition of *life planning and life projects* is reminiscent of Bühler's developmental differences in goal generation, within a view of life as a planned and a goal-directed activity. Focusing on people's life projects, another way of describing long-term goals, Smith and her colleagues asked young, middle-aged and older adults about the number of projects (goal-oriented activities) they were planning for their lives. Both the quantity and quality of individual life plans changed from early to late adulthood, with young adults generating more plans, but middle-aged adults bringing more of their plans to completion, and older adults forming and completing fewer new goals for their lives.

Levinson's concept of the *dream* for one's future life was defined variously as, 'a vague sense of self in the world', 'an imaginary possibility that generates excitement and vitality', 'a vision' (Levinson et al., 1978, p. 91), and a life goal of an imagined future self. It functioned as the superordinate purpose behind a variety of subsidiary goals, aspirations and values. Levinson and his colleagues (Levinson, 1996; Levinson et al., 1978) investigated 'the dream' in a series of biographical interviews over several months in which research participants described their present and past dreams of their lives in the future, and then told how earlier dreams had been subsequently modified.

The case study of John Barnes illustrates how the life goal and the life-course undergo adjustment over time in relation to each other. The case involved the development of a promising young biology professor and the effect of his developmental experiences and choices on his dream of becoming a first-rank scientist, with a chance at the supreme prize (the Nobel Prize) and 'saving the world'.

Barnes increasingly experienced the influential constraining of his social world as, at 37 years of age, he became more and more successful in academia. As a consequence of the interface between social pressure and his own personal inadequacy, he was deflected from his dream. He commented retrospectively in the biographical interview about the largely unrecognized 'little boy' in him that still needed to be 'number one' and therefore was vulnerable to collegial recognition and preferment. Becoming chairman of his department, he tried to juggle the conflicting goals of scientific discovery and academic leadership until eventually he learned that another research team actually had solved his scientific problem just two weeks before his own team. In terms of the difference between extrinsic goals related to the American dream of fame and success and intrinsic goals related to personal autonomy (cf. Ryan et al., 1996), Barnes' dream had become a nightmare of conflicting goals.

Realizing his position of conflict, Barnes came to a series of different choices in his vocational and personal life, so that over a decade his life dream and goals radically changed in what Levinson et al. described as 'the waning tyranny of the Dream' and a lessened compulsion 'to do the right thing' in favor of greater inner autonomy (1978, p. 276). He became a selfaccepting, successful scientist, happy in his family life, having relinquished his youthful view of himself as hero. Thus the life goal was changed as he himself developed into what could be called, in Bühler's terms, a more integrated and integrating self.

Although the dreams of Barnes and others of Levinson's men were mostly couched in vocational terms, with personal issues acting as side interests or modifiers, for women the distinction was not so clear. Both Levinson (1996) and an earlier paper by Roberts and Newton (1987) reported that women were able to simultaneously hold relational and vocational dreams. Successful career women made no strong claims about ultimate life dreams, except for one woman whose dream was to be an artist. Deflected from choices that would lead to this dream, she became instead a successful business woman. For her, and all the other successful career women in Levinson's study, there was a sanguine realization that a single, distal goal was not a sensible option. As one successful woman of 36, Amy came to realize, 'I don't buy this whole career thing to the exclusion of the rest of my life. Making money is okay, but it's not the meaning of my existence' (Levinson, 1996, p. 332). She had a more immediate goal of having babies before she was 40, and the goals were in conflict. Whether they concentrated on love relationships or children, each of the successful career women moderated their career goals because of other concerns of the type that Amy expressed.

It is possible to infer that career women's goals and dreams are less clear and single-minded than those of career men's, or alternatively, to interpret the multiple, often conflicting goals of women as a reasonable outcome of their experiences of the cultural construction of gender. While the core experiences of men encourage a sense of agency, the core experiences of women encourage them to relinquish a sense of their own agency and desires in favor of relational needs (Labouvie-Vief, 1996). Women's future goals and goals pursuit also have a shorter time-frame and an element of pragmatism that men's goals lack.

The Goal-Directedness of Development

Compared with these accounts of the influence of developmental experience on goals and their related activities, fewer studies have focused on the effect of goals on development, the other face of the goal and development connection. This lack may be partly due to the scope of interpretations of the meaning of 'development'. It is difficult to consistently follow a broad-based view and show effects on the total developing life system. It is likewise difficult to concentrate on a specific domain where the effect is readily observed and, from there, to make large claims about the development of the whole person.

Consciously adopting a dialogic perspective, and seeing the developing cultural environment and the developing person as acting upon each other in a lifelong *pas de deux* allows a range of experiences to be interpreted as developmental. The individual pieces of a life story (Kenyon & Randall, 1997) gain their meaning within a process of dynamic interaction. Neither the personal nor the environmental holds sway over how the life story unfolds. As interacting systems, the personal and the environmental are constantly acting upon each other, constraining and adjusting the other, and in the process constructing developmental change. For instance, people tend to interpret present aspects of their lives negatively once they have formulated definite goals for changing the overall directions of their lives. In the face of negative feedback, such as failing to meet a life goal (to be a doctor), one is likely to increase striving and the chance of success on the next goal-related test (Brunstein & Gollwitzer, 1996). In such cases, not only do the new strategies developed for accomplishing specific goals become part of the person's repertoire for future use, but in addition the experience of pursuing the goal through those activities can open up new possibilities.

There are indications of how goals and their striving feed back into experience in the narratives from Bühler and Levinson's work. Kenyon and

Randall (1997) add narratives about the activity of 'restorying' one's past life, by reviewing and re-editing material in memory in light of present insights and future desires and plans. The restorying process makes a difference to the way that the personal past can be related to the personal present and future.

More formally related to goal structures, Stein and Trabasso and their associates developed a model of how people use information from situations to make appraisals of events, goals and activities, that is, engage in 'goal processes'. Stein et al. (1997) investigated these aspects of the feedback loop between events, goals and development among a sample of gay men who were caring for partners with AIDS. They showed how these goal processes can be adaptive, such as when people revise their goals that are blocked (e.g. the goal of helping an AIDS suffering partner to recovery) or substitute new, more attainable goals for the unattainable (e.g. making the suffering partner more comfortable). Alternatively, the pursuit of certain goals can be maladaptive, such as when people perseverate with impossible goals. In order to maintain psychological well-being, the person must be able to revise false beliefs and change impossible goals. One means of revision involves recognizing the discrepancy between personal goals and the state of the world and acting specifically to alter goals when they are recognized as unrealistic (Folkman & Stein, 1967).

Although Stein et al. did not deliberately follow a dialectical transformational model of change, they did acknowledge that the challenges to existing beliefs coming from external circumstances often push people to form other beliefs. These new beliefs may have either positive or negative valences. For example, goal processes were significant influences on how caregivers coped with the caring role and with the subsequent experience of bereavement. The outcome measures of carers' well-being, coping and adjustment can be taken as indicators of significant change in perspectives and motivations that came out of the uninvited circumstances of their lives. Goals and plans that, at the time of bereavement, were focused on self and on future possibilities were related to later positive appraisals and consequently constructive future orientations. Caregivers who had these longer-term goals during the partner's illness, experienced greater psychological well-being 12 months after the partner's death than caregivers who focused on short-term goals and plans for their partners rather than for themselves while they were caregiving.

Significant features of this work were Stein et al.'s careful differentiation of beliefs, goal outcomes, plans generated to actualize goals, and emotions in caregivers' accounts of their responses to events. In addition, they tracked the carers' accounts over time, parsing narratives for evidence of the caregivers' appraisals and goal-related statements. Consequently, they could make fine-grained distinctions between past and future goals and between short-term and long-term goals in carers' intentions to handle their difficult situations.

These data indicate connections between being able to form realistic goals and plans for the future and being able to get on with life in that future. One episode from a caregiver's transcript, for instance, clearly shows his understanding of what the researchers called 'self growth from past events':

> I've learned so much from this. He left me with so much. He taught me to accept people. To never pass judgment if possible. I still have a life to live and so many things to learn. I have the chance to say yes or no. To decide what's important. And to celebrate life. (Stein et al., 1997, p. 884)

Although changes in this and other carers' goal processes are described in general terms ('I've learnt', 'to celebrate life'), they are definite indications of experiences of personal change.

In a different domain, our studies of adult students' academic work revealed how personal goals impacted on students' understanding and skill development. One woman studying educational psychology in distance education mode was asked about her study goals and working plans in a series of intensive think-aloud interviews (Dodds & Lawrence, 1983). In contrast to the instructor's sequentially integrated goals and activities to help students gain new perspectives on cognitive theory, this student made clear that she intended to select from the array of topics those that would be useful to her in her own current school teaching. If the materials did not satisfy her personal aims, she would not proceed. Later in the semester, she followed through on her early intentions and actually withdrew from the course, with a turning point decision that blocked off any possibilities for developing a new understanding of the course content.

Data from a student in another study (Volet & Lawrence, 1990) showed how her goals changed over the university semester. At week 4, she simply wanted to pass, and emphasized rote learning as the way to do it. By week 11, however, she was looking for greater understanding and integration of the concepts. She had left behind 'the pass only' goal; she now wanted more. By week 15, she could articulate how her aims had changed over time and also what she had done in the service of her transformed aims of integrating the new knowledge. She had radically changed her usual ways of performing academically:

> Normally I pass and I can look back on that course and I can't remember a thing about it . . . Whereas with this course, I know that's something that, it's still there. Whether I pass or not, it's something that's still, that I'll use. (Lawrence & Volet, 1991, p. 152)

In evaluating her performance, the student explained how her work activities had changed from being ineffective: 'It became very effective, because instead of just learning the bare necessities, it became that I was interested in learning lots of outside stuff' (i.e. relating concepts to experiences outside the lecture: 1991, p. 152). Her change in orientation fell out from her change in goal, and as a consequence her usual patterns of behavior were disrupted.

To this point, it is clear that a life-span developmental perspective on goal-directedness is in accord with the meaning of goal-directed activities developed by Russell and McDougall. Goals and personal development are closely connected in the human experience. People pursue goals with persistence and variability of activity. They modify their goals and also their means of attaining those goals. Goal-directed activities play a large part in interactions with environmental factors, and in adaptations to both internal and external forces. They give coherence and meaning to past, present and future.

Indications of personal changes can be seen in these illustrations from different domains. In neither domain, however, are we party to the specific processes by which the goal-driven activities were worked out in the personal system. We see the outcomes of some significant moves to achieve certain goals, but not how they were devised or acted upon. What is needed is a way of relating significant life changes to goals and goals to life changes. That kind of bidirectional analysis entails, however, being able to see how goals affect activities that then have significance for future development. The lack of this kind of analysis means that, as Haith (1997) pointed out about early development, life-span psychologists have not effectively taken up the challenge of finding ways of describing how people think about the future. Yet we should be able to include in analyses of life stories, not only what people wish to achieve, but also the consequences of the ways they think about what they want to achieve, and then how they go about trying to achieve it. That also means suggesting how the goal-directed, human system functions as a changing life in continual dialog with a changing world.

GOAL-DIRECTED ACTIVITIES IN PERSON–ENVIRONMENT DIALOGS

A prior understanding of the dynamics of the continuing interaction of the psychological with the environmental is important for understanding how goal-directed activities influence the course of development. Riegel (1979), in his dialectical theory of developmental change, gave a distinct place to the inner psychological plane of experience. People are capable of being both initiator and reactor in the inner–outer dialog that is precipitated by asynchronous progressions along different planes of existence (the inner biological, individual psychological, cultural-sociological, outer physical). Developmental 'leaps' (1979, p. 13) arise from transforming attempts to coordinate the opposing forces. For individual people, as for social structures, the movement forward is predicated, in part, on how the psychological and the social perform dialectically. The psychological can initiate change, precipitating actions just as it can respond to initiating environmental forces. Personal goals figure largely in both kinds of psychological contribution to the dialog, initiating and responding.

Riegel, however, did not describe how the psychological actually contributes to the interaction. In our present scheme, that means describing how personal goals are implemented in a phenomenal environment that is not passive and may not be benign. The encounter, for Riegel, was polyphonic, making it contrary to his basic position to try to unravel the thread of one voice out of the interacting dialog. He did not hesitate, however, to acknowledge the possibility of the intention and ability to act as part of the psychological domain. In singling out one person's contribution to a dialog, for instance, Riegel argued that the other party's intentions were always a part of the event: 'the psychological experience of the observer creates the effect of contrapuntal interactions, that is, the interactions between what was, what is, what will be' (1979, p. 169). What the person desires for the future becomes the focal point of what s/he does to attempt to coordinate disruptive forces. Any goal-directed activity is open, however, to the activity of the other party, whether that party be another person, a social group or a natural force. But how are anyone's personal goals implemented to the point that they can act upon and be acted upon in the developing world? The goal must be translated into action.

I may desire above all else, as a paraplegic student, my independence, but find that my loving family wishes to protect me from risk and danger. So the family suggest that one of them accompany me on the overseas vacation. In the asynchronous clash of the implementation of my personal goals with family cosseting, I make an even stronger bid for independence, buy a motorized wheelchair and forbid my family to disrupt my intentions. Thus the leap forward into new levels of independence is greater than even I envisaged.

Implementing Goals: The Role of Plans

Two issues must be addressed when we relate goals and goal processes to development: (1) how intentions are moved across what Norman (1988, pp. 50, 51) called the 'gulf of execution' between the person's goals and overt actions; and (2) how goals work as one component of the dialog between developing and mutually constraining personal and environmental worlds that involve those actions.

Plans bring together the two themes of forward-looking, future-oriented thinking and activities carried out under the direction of goals. That conjunction can be made because planning *is* 'goal-directed preparation for the future' (Lachman & Burack, 1993, p. 134). In fact, the explicit function of a mental plan is to work out how goals can be translated into action. Miller, Galanter, & Pribram opened up the discussion of how goals can be turned into action in the world with their analysis of the plans which they identified as the 'rough sketch(es) of some course of action as well as the completely detailed specification of every detailed operation' (1960, p. 17).

As these sketches or mental blueprints, plans to put a goal into action allow the goal director to walk, in imagination, through the different possibilities that may be used to bring the goal to fruition, trying out different strategies, and adjusting to blockages, as Stein et al's (1997) carers had done. By anticipating what may occur, it is possible, for example, to transform other people's expectations and instructions to make them one's own goals and constraints, and to devise situation-specific ways of integrating several smaller activities into one larger set. This integration brings the goal closer (Chalmers & Lawrence, 1993).

Similarly, when planning to achieve one's life goals, as Smith (1999) pointed out, instantiations of such long-term goals require strategies for managing time and resources (e.g. estimating how long or how much effort will be needed to achieve a vocational aspiration), as well as strategies for managing oneself and others (e.g. capitalizing on long-term financial investments, deciding how to find the most appropriate school for a child). Thus, in the example, I imagine what it would be like to have achieved my independence, because I can mentally traverse experiences of living out that independence, by simulated negotiation of airports and foreign places in my motorized wheelchair. Mental plans serve to bring future events closer, make them more familiar and test constraints on goals. Consequently, they also facilitate fulfilling positive goals and avoiding or accommodating environmental constraints. Forward planning, then, is a definite step in the implementation of goals. Plans are mental goal-directed activities.

Of course, plans are not foolproof, nor are they independent, standalone determinants of present action or life-related change. Imagined conversations need to be tested in actual dialog with the other party (Berger, 1997). Life plans may be asynchronous with cultural-sociological trends (e.g. employment opportunities) or environmental events (e.g. famine, war) (Riegel, 1979). Although they are goal-directed, plans remain one step removed from the overt behavioral activities that are actualized in goal achievement, only in so far as they engage in dialog with environmental forces. The best laid plans of mice and men leave some goals unfulfilled.

Gollwitzer (1996) deals with this problem of possible non-completion of a goal, as well as with the processes of implementation, by proposing a four-phase model of the implementation of goals, moving through: (1) a predecisional, motivational phase in which the person sorts through possible desires and sets a goal; (2) a preactional phase in which plans are devised for implementing the goal; (3) an actional phase in which the person engages in determined and persistent pursuit of goal completion; and (4) postactional evaluation of whether or not to continue. However, Gollwitzer's point about planning is that it 'passes on the control of goal-directed behavior to environmental cues' (1996, p. 294), so that goals are implemented quickly under the direction of the cues and without conscious intent. In this scheme, the goal appears to recede from the crucial point of contact, and to move away from the control of the striving. It may, in fact, take the meaning of the goal back into Woodfield's (1976) weaker sense.

We have established that goals are powerful motivators, as Gollwitzer also argues, but in a non-automated action sequence, they need to be implemented in the environmental world, if they are to be more than vague 'homeward-bound' type desires. As external forces are experienced, the person dialogs with the world, engaging in the overt action, but also engaging in internal dialog that foresees, plans and rehearses what may come next in relation to her own teleological ends (Berger, 1997; Honeycutt, 1991). Then s/he is able to regroup intention and energy, proceed as planned or under revision, or abandon plans and/or goals.

The reason why planning is not sufficient explanation of the relationship between goal-directed activity and development comes from the developmental insight that the personal world is constantly evolving in interaction with the developing world. Forward action is not the exclusive property of the purposing mind. Action and movement are constantly being constrained by factors beyond sole personal control. The materials and tools may not fit the task as mentally sketched out. Other parties may not cooperate (e.g. Barnes' colleagues deflect him from his research; the aspiring musician's father requires her to get a job). Natural forces are not amenable to the plan (e.g. the AIDS suffering partner dies, the famine persists). In such cases, either planned activities for achieving a personal goal have to be modified, or the goal itself has to be revised. As Gollwitzer (1993) has shown, some adjustments may be automated or simply not consciously accessible. In many cases, however, the goal director has to engage in conscious, deliberate goal management and revised planning. Such adjusting and revising activity is part of the adaptive process, and can lead to significant transformations in the person and the environment and in their ways of interacting. This interaction is the scene for the developmental leap that proceeds from the dialog. As Valsiner and Lawrence (1997) demonstrated, personal and external worlds are constantly in the process of constraining each other, canalizing teleological intent and striving, and at times breaking the boundaries of that canalization. While developmental change does not belong entirely to either the personal or the natural system, personal goals are not precluded from exerting a powerful influence on what happens. Goal-directed striving may be exerted in the form of the person's externalizing of her intents, taking the dominant role in the constraining dialectic. It also may be exerted in the form of the interpretation the person internalizes, taking it into the personal realm from the dialectical encounter in a form that can be assimilated (see Lawrence & Valsiner, 1993, for an account of internalization and externalization processes). There the message is worked and reworked to form new goals and new plans and planned actions to achieve the new goals in the next round of encounters. Whatever the case, goals at are the action point, with adaptations depending, to some extent, on goal strength and the direction of the goal director's striving.

CONCLUSIONS

In conclusion, we began by examining the meaning of goal-directed activities, following Woodfield's (1976) identification of ambiguous meanings, and looking for teleological explanations that included the significance of the goal, its activities and the mind directing the whole behavioral enterprise. In tracing meanings back to Russell and McDougall we found that goals are significant aspects of an account of human existence that is organic at heart and purposive at the height of its performance. We asked about the strength and energy and striving emanating from a goal, and how the activities striving towards the goal relate to development. Although the person is the goal director who devises the goal and the plans that will serve it, s/he is only one party in a dialog that leads to developmental change.

We proposed that there is an inextricable link between goals and development, and that the link is bi directional, with goals being influenced by developmental experience, and goals and their activities contributing to developmental change. The analysis of how goals are connected to development took us back to Riegel's (1979) often acknowledged but little applied conception of life-span development as a continuing dialog between personal and external worlds.

In order to have some control over what happens in their future lives in relation to their personal present and past, people generate goals, then work from their goals, making plans that allow their purposes to be tested in the external world. We have left to others investigation of the content of goals, and their affective significance. Instead, we have concentrated on the nature of goal-directed activity in a bi directional behavioral system. Teleologically oriented activity is a characteristic of human behavior that is natural and powerful over the course of a person's life. If the analyses of goal-directed activities made by Russell and McDougall are to be useful to life-span developmentalists, then we should be looking for indications of how people form their goals and strive towards them. The tenacity and persistence with which personal goals are pursued and the variety of activities that are used in their service make them significant for the psychology of the person. For lifespan developmentalists who recognize this significance, the challenge of the analysis of goal-directed activities is to develop ways of demonstrating how goals function as part of the developing person in a developing world. They are more than vague wishes for the future. They are effective contributors to the dialog that issues in change as people initiate and respond to activities in other planes of existence. It is difficult, however, to show how goals lead to different forms and modes of activity as the person experiences the effectiveness of personal goals, or roadblocks to the fulfillment of their dreams. More difficult, and to date generally neglected, is the analysis of how goal-directed activities contribute directly to developmental pathways and turning points. To develop approaches for unraveling the voice of personal goals in the continuing constraining of personal and external worlds, involves attending to the processes of change and the specific role of goals and personal teleology in the continuing dialog of development.

REFERENCES

Anderson, J.R. (1993). Problem solving and learning. *American Psychologist*, 48, 35–44.

Austin, J.T., & Vancouver, J.B. (1996). Goal constructs in psychology: Structure, process, and content. *Psychological Bulletin*, 120, 338–375.

Baltes, P.B., & Baltes, M.M. (eds) (1990). *Successful aging: Perspectives from the behavioral sciences*. New York: Cambridge University Press.

Berger, C.R. (1997). *Planning strategic interaction: Attaining goals through communicative action*. Hillsdale, NJ: Erlbaum.

Bratman, M.E. (1987). *Intentions, plans and practical reason*. Cambridge, MA: Harvard University Press.

Brunstein, J.C., & Gollwitzer, P.M. (1996). Effects of failure on subsequent performance: The importance of self-defining goals. *Journal of Personality and Social Psychology*, 70, 395–407.

Bühler, C. (1968). Introduction. In C. Bühler & F. Massarik (eds), *The course of human life* (pp. 1–10). New York: Springer.

Cantor, N. (1994). Life task problem solving: Situational affordances and personal needs. *Personality and Social Psychology Bulletin*, 20 (3), 235–243.

Cantor, N., & Blanton, H. (1996). Effortful pursuit of personal goals in daily life. In P.M. Gollwitzer & J.A. Bargh (eds), *The psychology of action: Linking cognition and motivation to behavior* (pp. 338–359). New York: Guilford.

Chalmers, D., & Lawrence, J.A. (1993). Investigating the effects of planning aids on adults' and adolescents' organisation of a complex task. *International Journal of Behavioral Development*, 16 (2), 191–214.

Deci, E.L., & Ryan, R.M. (1995). Human autonomy: The basis for true self-esteem. In M.H. Kernis (ed.), *Efficacy, agency and self-esteem* (pp. 31–48). New York: Plenum.

Dodds, A.E., & Lawrence, J.A. (1983). Heuristics for planning university study at a distance. *Distance Education*, 4, 40–52.

Duncker, K.A. (1926). A qualitative (experimental and theoretical) study of productive thinking (solving of comprehensible problems). *Pedagogical Seminary*, 33, 642–708.

Earley, P.C., & Perry, B.C. (1987). Work plan availability and performance: An assessment of task strategy priming on subsequent task completion. *Organizational Behavior and Human Decision Processes*, 39, 279–302.

Emmons, R.A. (1996). Striving and feeling: Personal goals and subjective well-being. In P.M. Gollwitzer & J.A. Bargh (eds), *The psychology of action: Linking cognition and motivation to behavior* (pp. 313–337). New York: Guilford.

Emmons, R.A., & Kaiser, H.A. (1996). Goal orientation and emotional wellbeing: Linking goals and affect through the self. In L.I. Martin & A. Tesser (eds), *Striving and feeling: Interactions among goals, affect and self-regulation* (pp. 79–98). Mahwah, NJ: Erlbaum.

Folkman, S., & Stein, N.L. (1997). A goal-process approach to analyzing narrative memories for AIDS related stressful events. In N.L. Stein, P.A. Ornstein, B. Tversky, & C. Brainerd (eds), *Memory for everyday and emotional events* (pp. 113–137). Hillsdale, NJ: Erlbaum.

Ford, M.E. (1992). *Motivating humans: Goals, emotions and personal agency beliefs*. Newbury Park, CA: Sage.

Freund, A.M., Li, K.Z.H., & Baltes, P.B. (1999). In J. Brandtstädter & R.M. Lerner (eds), *Action and self-development: Theory and research throughout the life-span* (pp. 401–434). Thousand Oaks, CA: Sage.

Gergely, G., & Gergely, C. (1997). Teleological reasoning in infancy: The infant's naïve theory of rational action. A reply to Premack and Premack. *Cognition*, 63, 227–233.

Gollwitzer, P.M. (1993). Goal achievement: The role of intentions. *European Review of Social Psychology*, 4, 141–188.

Gollwitzer, P.M. (1996). The volitional benefits of planning. In P.M. Gollwitzer & J.A. Bargh (eds), *The psychology of action: Linking cognition and motivation to behavior* (pp. 287–312). New York: Guilford.

Gollwitzer, P.M., & Brandstätter, V. (1997). Implementation intentions and effective goal pursuit. *Journal of Personality and Social Psychology*, 73 (1), 186–199.

Haith, M.M. (1997). The development of future thinking as essential for the emergence of skill in planning. In S.L. Friedman & E.K. Scholnik (eds), *The developmental psychology of planning: Why, how, and when do we plan?* (pp. 25–42). Mahwah, NJ: Erlbaum.

Heckhausen, H., & Kuhl, J. (1985). From wishes to action: The dead ends and short cuts on the long way to action. In M. Frese & J. Sabini (eds), *Goal directed behavior: The concept of action in psychology* (pp. 134–159). Hillsdale, NJ: Erlbaum.

Honeycutt, J.M. (1991). Imagined interactions, imagery and mindfulness/mindlessness. In R. Kunzendorf (ed.), *Mental imagery* (pp. 121–128). New York: Plenum.

Kenyon, G.M., & Randall, W.L. (1997). *Restorying our lives: Personal growth through autobiographical reflection*. Westport, CT: Praeger.

King, L.A. (1998). Personal goals and personal agency: Linking everyday goals to future images of the self. In M. Kofka, G. Weary, & G. Sedek (eds), *Personal control of action: Cognitive and motivational mechanisms* (pp. 109–128). New York: Plenum.

Labouvie-Vief, G. (1996). Knowledge and the construction of women's development. In P.B. Baltes & U.M. Staudinger (eds), *Interactive minds: Life-span perspectives on the social foundation of cognition* (pp. 109–130). Cambridge: Cambridge University Press.

Lachman, M.E., & Burack, O.R. (1993). Planning and control processes across the life-span: An overview. *International Journal of Behavioral Development* 16 (2), 131–143.

Lawrence, J.A. (1991). What if the how is a why? In J. Asendorf & J. Valsiner (eds), *Framing stability and change* (pp. 240–248). New York: Sage.

Lawrence, J.A., & Dodds, A.E. (1999). Duncker's account of productive thinking: Exegesis and application of a problem solving theory. *From Past to Future: Insights into life, The Drama of Karl Duncker*, 1 (2), 29–44.

Lawrence, J.A., & Valsiner, J. (1993). Conceptual roots of internalization from transmission to transformation. *Human Development*, 36 (3), 150–168.

Lawrence, J.A., & Volet, S.E. (1991). The significance and function of students' goals. In L. Oppenheimer & J. Valsiner (eds), *The origins of action: Inter-disciplinary and international perspectives* (pp. 133–152). New York: Springer.

Levinson, D.J. (1996). *The seasons of a woman's life*. New York: Knopf.

Levinson, D.J., Darrow, C.N., Klein, E.B., Levinson, M.H., & McKee, B. (1978). *The seasons of a man's life*. New York: Knopf.

McDougall, W. (1945). *Social psychology* (23rd edn, 1936). London: Methuen. Originally published 1908.

Miller, G.A., Galanter, E., & Pribram, K.H. (1960). *Plans and the structure of behavior*. New York: Holt, Rinehart & Winston.

Newell, A., & Simon, H.A. (1977). *Human problem solving*. Englewood Cliffs, NJ: Prentice-Hall.

Norman, D.A. (1988). *The psychology of everyday things*. New York: Basic.

Pervin, L.A. (1989). *Goal concepts in personality and social psychology*. Hillsdale, NJ: Erlbaum.

Piaget, J.P. (1972). Intellectual evolution from adolescence from adulthood. *Human Development*, 15, 1–12.

Riegel, K.F. (1979). *Foundations of dialectical psychology*. New York: Academic.

Roberts, P., & Newton, P.M. (1987). Levinsonian studies of women's adult development. *Psychology and Aging*, 2 (2), 154–163.

Russell, E.S. (1945). *The directiveness of organic activities*. Cambridge: Cambridge University Press.

Ryan, R.M. (1993). Agency and organization: Intrinsic motivation, autonomy, and the self in psychological development. In R. Dienstbier & J.E. Jacobs (eds), *Nebraska Symposium on Motivation, 1992: Developmental perspectives on motivation* (pp. 1–56). Lincoln, NB: University of Nebraska Press.

Ryan, R.M., Sheldon, K.M., Kasser, T., & Deci, E.L. (1996). All goals are not created equal: An organismic perspective on the nature of goals and their regulation. In P.M. Gollwitzer & J.A. Bargh (eds), *The psychology of action: Linking cognition and motivation to behavior* (pp. 7–47). New York: Guilford.

Simon, H.A. (1957). *Models of man*. New York: Wiley.

Smith, J. (1996). Planning about life: Towards a social-interactive perspective. In P.B. Baltes & U.M. Staudinger (eds), *Interactive minds: Life-span perspectives on the social foundation of cognition* (pp. 242–275). Cambridge: Cambridge University Press.

Smith, J. (1999). Life planning: Anticipating future life goals and managing personal development. In J. Brandtstädter & R.M. Lerner (eds), *Action and self-development: Theory and research throughout the life span*. Thousand Oaks, CA; Sage.

Stein, N., Folkman, S., Trabasso, T., & Richards, T.A. (1997). Appraisal and goals processes as predictors of psychological well-being in bereaved caregivers. *Journal of Personality and Social Psychology*, 72 (4), 872–884.

Taylor, R. (1950). Purposeful and non-purposive behavior: A rejoinder. *Philosophy of Science*, 17, 327–332.

Valsiner, J., & Lawrence, J.A. (1997). Human development in culture across the lifespan. In J.W. Berry, P.R. Dasen, & T.S. Saraswathi (eds), *Handbook of cross-cultural psychology: Vol. 2. Basic processes and developmental psychology* (2nd edn, pp. 69–106). Boston: Allyn & Bacon.

Volet, S.E., & Lawrence, J.A. (1990). Adaptive learning in university students. In H. Mandl, E. de Corte, N. Bennett, & H.F. Friedrich (eds), *Learning and instruction: European research in an international context* (pp. 497–516). Oxford: Pergamon.

Weir, M. (1984). *Goal-directed behaviour*. New York: Gordon and Breach.

Woodfield, A. (1976). *Teleology*. Cambridge: Cambridge University Press.

23

Dialogical Processes and Development of the Self

HUBERT J. HERMANS and ELS HERMANS-JANSEN

Dialogues between voices are pervasive in the development of the self through the life-course. Young children vocalize and converse not only with their parents and siblings, but also with imagined interlocutors. Garvey (1984), for example, collected a variety of vocalizations that emerged from 28-month-old Sarah's room during one nap period. Sarah's vocalizations ranged from quiet murmurs to grunts, squeals, and intoned babbles, from humming to snatches of songs, rhymes, and counting. It also included talking with a doll, and a bit of a 'telephone conversation'. These observations suggest that young children are involved not only in real conversations, but also in imagined conversations that are partly rehearsals of contacts with significant others. As Winnicot (1971) has demonstrated, children may create imagined figures – at bed time or when playing alone – by transforming inanimate objects into an animate, loved being that can serve as a companion in the transition from one state to another (e.g. from waking to sleeping). Imaginary playmates may provide company in times of isolation or stress, and can also sometimes be used as a handy scapegoat. By playing and conversing with these playmates, children develop an increasing capacity to differentiate between several positions each with their own narratively structured experiences (Manosevitz, Prentice, & Wilson, 1973).

Play, in particular, enables children to take the attitude of particular others towards themselves. As Mead (1934) has emphasized, children, playing the role of the parent, teacher, or policeman, address themselves as a parent or a teacher, and arrest themselves as a policeman. This means that children have a certain set of stimuli available which call out in the children themselves the responses that these stimuli would call out in others. Play, thus, represents a simple form of representing another in the self.

In adult years imagined others continue to play a central role in people's evaluation of themselves. Baldwin and Holmes (1987), for example, found that a sense of self is often experienced in relation to some audience: people who are present or imagined, specific or generalized, actual or fantasized. These authors proposed the term 'private audience': people respond to a range of different significant others, such as spouse, best friend, religious leader, or business colleague, who often represent distinct ways of evaluating the self. Andersen and Cole (1990) even found that significant other representations are richer (trigger more associations), more distinctive (have more unique features), and are more cognitively accessible (time required for retrieval of features) than the other categories (nonsignificant others, stereotypes, and traits). Taken together, studies on private audience suggest that significant others form rich, unique, and accessible images that watch or listen to the person and respond to him or her with affect-laden evaluations. (For the influence of 'imaginary audience' in adolescence see Elkind & Bowen, 1979, and Gray & Hudson, 1984.)

As the above studies suggest, it is a rough simplification to consider the relation between self and other as mutually exclusive, with the self as 'internal' and the other as 'external'. Rather than being a Cartesian outsider, the other, or even better, the others in plural, develop as integrative parts of the self, playing constructive roles in its organization and evaluation. The purpose of the present chapter is to elaborate on this idea, to demonstrate that the self is a multivoiced and dialogical developmental process, implying that the self can be conceived as a narrative construction and reconstruction of the meaning of events. Following a theoretical discussion of these notions, a concrete method is presented which can not only assess the nature of significant voices in the self but also provide an insight into the nature of their dialogical interrelationship. This assessment and process promotion is then illustrated with an actual case study, in which an adult woman expresses three voices representing three different ways of relating to her environment: she tells her story from the perspective of the child, the masculine person, and the feminine person in herself. Together these voices lead to the construction of a complex, organized meaning system in development.

The Self: From Multiplicity to Multivoicedness

Many developments in the psychology of the self are in one way or another rooted in the fertile soil of James' (1890) original thinking on the subject in his *Principles*. The concept of the multivoiced self was anticipated by James when he talked about the 'rivalry and conflict of the different selves' (1890, p. 309). Elaborating on this phrase he describes the tensions inherent in the self in this way:

> I am often confronted by the necessity of standing by one of my empirical selves and relinquishing the rest. Not that I would not, if I could, be both handsome and fat and well dressed, and a great athlete, and make a million a year, be a wit, a *bon-vivant*, and a lady killer, as well as a philosopher; a philanthropist, statesman, warrior, and African explorer, as well as a 'tone-poet' and saint. But the thing is simply impossible. The millionaire's work would run counter to the saint's; the *bon-vivant* and the philanthropist would trip each other up; the philosopher and the lady-killer could not well keep house in the same tenement of clay. Such different characters may conceivably at the outset of life alike be possible to man. But to make any one of them actual, the rest must more or less be suppressed. (1890, pp. 309–310)

Consistent with James' thesis on the possibility of different selves, there has been an upsurge of developments which have emphasized the self as a multiplicity of elements. The self has been described and analyzed as, for example, a complexity of subselves (Martindale, 1980), subpersonalities (Rowan, 1990), potential selves (Schlenker, 1980), possible selves (Markus & Nurius, 1986), private, public, and collective selves (Triandis, 1989), actual, ought, and ideal selves (Higgins, 1987), or imagoes (McAdams, 1993). All these developments share an avoidance of talking about the self *in toto*, as if it is an undifferentiated or entirely unified whole devoid of any conflict or tension. Rather, they are concerned with the diversity of component elements of the self and some of them (e.g. Higgins' 1987 discrepancy theory) explicitly deal with the ways in which these elements are organized and interrelated dynamically.

As the above examples indicate, there is a massive proliferation of terms and concepts representing various views on the self and resulting from different theoretical or research traditions. Despite their divergent origins, the several concepts have in common the idea that the self is not a unified construct but rather a differentiated and organized diversity of elements.

From Cognitive Psychology to a Psychology of Meaning Making and Dialogue

There is another common element in the literature on the multiplicity of the self: the proposed concepts (subselves, possible selves, etc.) do not postulate the existence of a voice which is able to entertain a dialogical relationship with other (internal or external) voices. However, there are recent developments in psychology which increasingly acknowledge the importance of voice and dialogue for the understanding of the human mind.

One of the main advocates of a narrative approach in psychology, Bruner (1990), argued for a theoretical connection between the notion of voice and the construction of meaning. He suggests that the 'cognitive revolution', as it developed in psychology since the late 1950s, with Bruner himself as one of the instigators, had originally proposed a central place for the concept of meaning in psychology. In this project psychologists were intending to cooperate with anthropologists, linguists, and historians. However, as developments in psychology over the past decades have shown, this enterprise shifted from the construction of meaning to the processing of information. Thirty years after the beginning of the cognitive approach in psychology, Bruner argues for a narrative approach, in which meaning and negotiation are cornerstones of our cultural understandings:

> Now let me tell you first what I and my friends thought the revolution was about back there in the late 1950s. It was, we thought, an all-out effort to establish meaning as the central concept of psychology – not stimuli and responses, not overtly observable behavior, not biological drives and their transformation, but meaning . . . Its aim was to discover and to describe formally the meanings that human beings created out of their encounters with the world, and then to propose hypotheses about what meaning-making processes were implicated. It focused upon the symbolic activities that human beings employed in constructing and in making sense not only of the world, but of themselves. (1990, p. 2)

Becoming aware that in the course of time the cognitive revolution did not fulfill its central original purpose, Bruner proposed a return to its original mission:

> there [cannot] be much doubt on reflection that it [cognitive science] has left largely unexplained and even somewhat obscured the very large issues that inspired the cognitive revolution in the first place. So let us return to the question of how to construct a mental science around the concept of meaning and the processes by which meanings are created and negotiated within a community. (1990, pp. 10–11)

By emphasizing the relation between meaning and community, Bruner avoids the trap of a purely individualistic psychology. By virtue of participation in a culture, meaning is always shared in a particular community. This point of view implies that the child enters the life of his or her community not as a 'private or autistic sport of primary processes', but rather as 'a participant in a larger public process in which public meanings are negotiated' (1990, p. 13).

Cognitive Science: Self as a Community of Voices

Although there is no doubt that Bruner's criticism of cognitive psychology has given an important impetus to the reorientation of psychology in the past decade, cognitive science is a more variegated scientific effort than his description suggests. Some computer scientists have presented models which make explicit use of the notions of society and voice as relevant metaphors for understanding the workings of the brain. Therefore, it makes sense to explore the concept of meaning and dialogue at the interface between narrative psychology and cognitive science.

Computer scientist Minsky (1985) developed a model in which the mind is considered a hierarchically organized network of interconnected parts that together function as a 'society'. He conceptualizes the mind as a host of smaller minds, called agents. Many of these agents, although they are parts of a functioning whole, are often not able to comprehend one another because most pairs of agents are not able to communicate at all. As in a human society, these agents have their own action programs and simply do their job without knowing all the other agents that are part of the community. At the higher levels of organization, however, agents may be involved in direct communication. In describing a computer program for block building, Minsky (1985) analyzes a conflict between two agents at the same level of organization: a *Builder* and a *Wrecker*, who is only interested in breaking down what Builder has achieved. Through their communication, agents at this level may agree or disagree:

> Only larger agencies could be resourceful enough to do such things. Inside an actual child, the agencies responsible for *Building* and *Wrecking* might indeed become versatile enough to negotiate by offering support for one another's goals. 'Please, *Wrecker*, wait a moment more till *Builder* adds just one more block: it's worth it for a louder crash!' (1985, p. 33)

In Minsky's view, conflicts between agents tend to migrate upward to higher levels in the society of mind. If the conflicts are not solved, they tend to weaken the higher-level agent under which they are subordinated. If, in the above example, Builder and Wrecker cannot solve their conflict, they will reduce the strength of their mutual superior (e.g. Play). This superior will then be surpassed by competing agencies on the same level (e.g. Sleep or Eat). If Builder and Wrecker are not able to settle their disagreements, the child doesn't continue its play any longer and wants to sleep.

The play example leads Minsky to formulate his 'principle of noncompromise' in more general terms: 'The longer an internal conflict persists among an agent's subordinates, the weaker becomes that agent's status among its own competitors. If such internal problems aren't settled soon, other agents will take control and the agents formerly involved will be "dismissed"' (1985, p. 33). The principle of noncompromise emphasizes the relevance of cooperation between agents or voices at a lower level for their effective competition with voices on a higher level.

The notions of community and voice are also introduced by another computer scientist, Hofstadter (1986), in his attempts to comprehend the workings of the mind. With its billions of neurons, the mind resembles a community made up of smaller communities, each in turn made up of smaller ones. He refers to the highest-level communities as 'subselves' or 'inner voices'. A hypothetical dialogue may take place between those voices – 'a dialogue between two persons both of whom are inside me, both of whom are genuinely myself but who are at odds, in some sense, with each other' (1986, p. 782). Some of these competing voices may be dormant but still present, saying opposite things about a particular self-relevant subject.

In Hofstadter's view, each inner voice is actually composed of millions of smaller parts, each of which is active as part of a community. Under specific circumstances, these smaller parts all 'point in the same direction' and at that moment an inner voice will crystallize and undergo a 'phase transition', that is, the voice proclaims itself an active member of the community of subselves. If it is powerful enough, it exerts pressure in order to be recognized. Once it has this power, it will not want to relinquish it:

> I have a 'piano-playing subself', who, once he is given the floor, refuses to relinquish it for hours on end – until, say, my back – *his* back? – grows achy, or until he gets sleepy. Or until the phone rings or my watch beeps at me,

telling me that some other facet of life must be attended to. (1986, p. 789)

Hofstadter (1986) and Minsky (1985) both conceived the brain as a community of agents or voices which, on its higher levels, may entertain mutual dialogical relationships with one voice as more dominant or active than the other voice. For our purposes it is relevant that recent computer models are well in agreement with the original formulations by James on the 'rivalry and conflict of the different selves' (1890, p. 309).

It should be kept in mind that computer scientists like Minsky and Hofstadter use the notion of society, voice, and dialogue more as metaphors for comprehending the workings of the brain than as means for understanding the social processes in actual communities of people. In order to address dialogicality in terms not only of 'inner voices' within the individual mind but also of 'external voices' which are at the heart of society and culture, we move to the fertile work of Bakhtin which brings the worlds of internal and external dialogue together in a more integrative theoretical framework.

Bakhtin's Polyphonic Novel and the Dialogical Self

From a theoretical point of view, the notion of dialogue is the kernel of Bakhtin's (1929/1973) metaphor of the polyphonic novel, which resulted from his extensive reading of Dostoyevsky's *oeuvre*. The principal feature of the polyphonic novel is that it is composed of a number of independent and mutually opposing viewpoints embodied by characters involved in dialogical relationships. Each character in this novel is considered as 'ideologically authoritative and independent', which means that each character is perceived as the author of his or her own view of the world, not as an object of Dostoyevsky's all-encompassing, artistic vision. The characters are not treated as 'obedient slaves' in the service of Dostoyevsky's artistic intentions but are capable of standing beside their creator, disagreeing with the author, even rebelling against him. It is as if Dostoyevsky enters his novels wearing different masks, giving him the opportunity to present different and even opposing views of self and world, representing a multiplicity of voices of the 'same' Dostoyevsky. The characters representing these voices may, at times, enter into dialogical relations of question and answer, agreement and disagreement, so that new constructions may emerge. As in a polyphonic composition, the several voices or instruments have different spatial positions, and accompany and oppose each other in a dialogical relationship.

Logical versus Dialogical Relationships

Bakhtin's conception of dialogue can only be fully understood if the difference between logical and dialogical relationships is taken into account. Bakhtin gives the example of two sentences which are completely identical (see also Vasil'eva, 1988): 'life is good' and, again, 'life is good'. In terms of Aristotelian logic, these two phrases are related in terms of *identity*: they are one and the same statement. From a dialogical perspective, however, they may be seen as two remarks expressed by the voices of two spatially separated people in communication, who entertain a relationship of *agreement*. The two phrases are identical from a logical point of view, but different as utterances: the first is a statement, the second a confirmation. Similarly, the phrases 'life is good' and 'life is not good' can be compared. From a logical point of view, one is a *negation* of the other. However, as utterances from two different speakers, a dialogical relation of *disagreement* develops. For Bakhtin, the relationships of agreement and disagreement are, like question and answer, basic dialogical forms.

There is a critical difference between logical and dialogical relationships. Logical relationships are 'closed' because they do not permit any conclusion beyond the limits of the rules that govern the relationship. Once the identity or negation thesis has been applied to a set of statements, nothing is left to be said, nor is an opening created to the domain of the unexpected. In contrast, dialogue can only be conceived as an open process: 'Consciousness is never self-sufficient; it always finds itself in an intense relationship with another consciousness. The hero's every experience and his every thought is internally dialogical, polemically colored and filled with opposing forces . . . open to inspiration from outside itself' (Bakhtin, 1929/1973, p. 26). In other words, whereas logical relationships are closed and finalized, dialogical relationships are open and unfinalized. As Valsiner (1997) has argued, dialogical relationships imply an episodic openness to transformation of the self-system to a new state, resulting in developmental processes of emergence.

Dialogical relationships are not only open, but also highly personal. In contrast to logical relationships which are impersonal and lead to a conclusion irrespective of the personal stance of the individual who might be involved in logical reasoning, dialogical relationships always develop between individual people. Dostoyevsky's world is 'profoundly personalized' (Bakhtin, 1929/1973, p. 7) in that an utterance is never isolated from a particular character. Moreover, in Dostoyevsky's novels, characters are always involved in communication with other characters. Because one particular character is always implicitly or explicitly responding to another character, the context of a particular utterance is always highly personalized. Whereas logicality is impersonalized and decontextualized, dialogicality is both personal and contextual (see also Josephs, 1998).

Spatialization of Characters in Dostoyevsky's Novels

Dialogue has the potential to differentiate the inner world of one and the same individual in the form of an interpersonal relationship as well as to allow for the emergence of polyphony. When an 'inner' thought of a particular character is transformed into an utterance, dialogical relations spontaneously occur between this utterance and the utterance of imagined others. Dostoyevsky's novel *The Double* serves as an illustrative example. In this novel the second hero (the double) was introduced as a personification of the interior thought of the first hero (Golyadkin). The externalization of the interior voice of the first hero in a spatially separated opponent results in a fully fledged dialogue between two independent parties. In Bakhtin's view, spatiality is an intrinsic feature of dialogue: 'This persistent urge to see all things as being coexistent and to perceive and depict all things side by side and simultaneously, as if in space rather than time, leads him [Dostoyevsky] to dramatize in space even the inner contradictions and stages of development of a single person' (1929/1973, p. 23). Along these lines, Dostoyevsky constructs a plurality of voices representing a plurality of worlds that are neither identical nor unified, but rather heterogeneous and opposed. As part of this polyphonic construction, Dostoyevsky creates ever-changing perspectives, portraying characters conversing with the Devil (Ivan and the Devil), with their alter egos (Ivan and Smerdyakov), and even with caricatures of themselves (Raskolnikov and Svidrigailov). (For a discussion of dialogue in novelistic literature, art and psychology, see Hermans & Kempen, 1993.)

The Illusion of the Autonomous Subject and the Relativity of the Word 'I'

The idea that dialogue implies a spatial relation between two bodies puts into question the existence of the pronoun 'I' as referring to a separate identity. In many psychological discussions on the nature of the self, a central organizing ego is typically assumed (Sampson, 1985). Such a central organizing agency, however, is not in accordance with the self as a multiplicity of voices. Why is the notion of the centralized, internally unified self so widespread not only in psychological publications but also in everyday life?

Part of the problem is that in everyday life we use the word 'I', or the equivalents in other Indo-European languages, indiscriminately for a wide range of states of mind which, despite their varieties, contrasts, and contradictions, are thought of as being subsumed by a centralized ego. Certainly, cultural factors, closely related to linguistic practices, play an important part in supporting the idea of the centralized ego that is conceived of as having an existence separate from its environment. Wekker (1994), for example, points to the existence of cultural differences in her discussion of the Sranon Tongo, the language of Afro-Surinam people, who adhere to the African-American Winti religion. Adherents of this religion believe in supernatural forces and are involved in contacts with their ancestors who are believed to play an influential role in the daily affairs of their living offspring. The language of this group contains different words expressing different modalities of the word 'I':

Mi	I
Mi kra	My soul, I
A misi (f'mi)	My feminine part
A masra (f'mi)	My masculine part
Mi misi nanga mi masra	My feminine and masculine part
Mi dyodyo	My divine parents
Mi skin	My body, I
Mi geest	My spirit, I

As these examples suggest, a wide variety of voices are directly associated with the word 'I', including not only singular but also plural voices, not only spiritual but also corporeal ones, and not only internal but also external ones. In this language 'I' is not to be understood as an isolated, sovereign subject, essential in itself, and having an existence apart from the flux of person–situation interactions. Rather, 'I' is conceived of as a relationship and as a shifting from one to another relationship, and from one to another situation, which implies a change in the experiencing 'I' itself. In Holquist's (1990) terms, a relation between two bodies occupying simultaneous but different space is assumed. The parents in Winti religion are not simply outside the individual, they are 'here' and 'there' at the same time and experienced as simultaneously inside and outside. It is certainly not so that such experience is foreign to what we are used to in so-called Western culture. There are moments in which I feel that I'm acting like my father, experiencing my father simultaneously outside and inside myself. In a particular situation I just feel like him, as if he is me and I'm him. In other words, what is explicitly present in Sranon Tongo is implicitly working in any other language.

The implicit or explicit presence in the use of the word 'I' suggests that others may be active in the imagination of the speaker. To what extent is imagination acknowledged as a relevant topic in psychology?

Neglecting Imagined Others in Psychology

Caughey, a social anthropologist, criticizes the identification of 'social relationships' with only 'actual social relationships' and considers this conception as actually representing 'an ethnocentric projection of certain narrow assumptions in Western science' (1984, p. 17). He prefers to speak of an (imaginary) 'social world' rather than a purely 'inner world' in order to emphasize the interaction with somebody who is felt to be 'there'. Indeed, the fact that the experiential world of the individual person is populated by a host of imagined others is reason to unmask the idea of a 'private' inner world or, broader, the existence of an 'inner self' where people can be entirely alone with themselves, as an illusion.

Not only dialogues with actual others, but also dialogues with imagined others challenge the idea of a unified, separate, and centralized self. In her book *Invisible guests*, Watkins (1986) describes how dialogues with imagined others play a central role in our daily lives: interwoven with actual interactions, they constitute an essential part of our narrative construction of the world. She argues that we are never really alone. Even when we are outwardly silent, we find ourselves communicating with our critics, with our parents, our consciences, our gods, our reflection in the mirror, with the photograph of someone we miss, with a figure from a movie or a dream, with our babies, or with our pets.

Despite their invisible quality, imagined others are typically perceived as having a spatially different position. This applies not only to our own culture (e.g. imagined contact with an ideal lover, with a deceased parent or friend, or with a wise advisor), but also to non-Western communities. In a thorough anthropological analysis of mythos, Cassirer (1955) describes that people at the lowest level of primitive belief perceive spirits as external alien forces with demonic power. People typically succumb to these forces unless they can ward them off by magical means. In a later stage, however, when a spirit is not taken as a soul of nature but as a tutelary spirit, a new relation develops. The tutelary spirit stands in a closer, more intimate relation to the person with whom it is associated. It not only dominates and threatens the person but also functions as a guide. It is no longer something purely external and alien but something belonging to individual people and familiar and close to them. In mythical consciousness a tutelary spirit is *not* conceived of as the 'subject' of someone's inner life but as something objective, which is spatially connected with individual people and hence can also be spatially separated from them: 'And even where the closest possible relation exists between the tutelary spirit and the man in whom it dwells, even where the tutelary spirit governs his whole being and destiny, it nevertheless appears as something existing for itself, something separate and strange' (1955, p. 168).

On the basis of field work in several non-Western cultures and in North America, Caughey (1984) concluded that imagined interactions are in no way restricted to non-Western cultures. He estimated that the 'real' social world of most North Americans includes between 200 and 300 people (e.g. family, friends, acquaintances, colleagues). Moreover, an equal or larger number of individuals may exist in people's imagined social worlds. He divides imagined figures into three groups: (a) media figures with whom the individual engages in imagined interactions; (b) purely imaginary figures produced in dreams and fantasies; and (c) imagined replicas of parents, friends, or lovers with whom the person communicates as if they were really present. With this classification Caughey demonstrates that imagined dialogues and interactions exist side by side with real interactions and are strongly interwoven with them (e.g. 'If my wife could see me now . . .') and may or may not have a direct link with reality.

In summary, the linguistic practice of indiscriminately using the word 'I' has the detrimental implication that the self is considered as representing a homogeneous, continuous, and separate entity. As a consequence, its diversity and heterogeneity and its apparent fluctuations and discontinuity across time are neglected. In contrast with the supposition of an isolated I in many psychological publications, the linguistic practices in other cultures illustrate the functioning of the self as a dynamic set of relationships.

Two Cartesian Dualisms

The discussion of the centralized, unified, separate self is reflected in Cartesian philosophy which is generally considered as highly influential in Western thought. In an insightful and critical treatment of the subject, Straus (1958) argues that Descartes' *cogito* implies not only a dualism between mind and body but also a dissociation between self and other. When we nowadays speak about an 'outside world', we are in fact using a Cartesian terminology, implying that the world is outside of consciousness, and that, reciprocally, consciousness, including sensory experience, is outside of the world. According to this philosophy we can be aware of ourselves without necessarily being aware of the world. The Cartesian ego is not able to have *direct* communication with any alter ego. In the realm of consciousness, each one is alone with him- or herself. Certainly, Descartes does not deny, or even seriously doubt, the existence of the so-called outside world. However, he insists that it is never *directly* accessible to us. The existence of the other person is not more than probable; it must be proved. The alter ego, and external reality generally, is the product of reasoning and proof, instead of immediate experience and starting point.

In an earlier publication (Hermans & Kempen, 1993), we have discussed the implications of Descartes' philosophy as characterized by two separations, the one between the body and the mind, and the other between self and other. We argued that the Cartesian conception of a rational, individualistic and disembodied mind is in apparent disagreement with everyday experience. In this experience the body is not simply felt as an object in the world, but as 'mine'. Moreover, the other person is not the result of a reasoning process, but of immediate presence 'to me', even before I start to think explicitly. Straus says: 'In sensory experience I always experience myself *and* the world at the same time, not myself directly and the Other by inference, not myself before the Other, not myself without the Other, nor the Other without myself' (1958, p. 148).

From a theoretical point of view, the two Cartesian dualisms correspond to two features of the dialogical processes discussed above: spatiality and multi-voicedness. For Descartes space is part of *res extensa* (extensive matter) and as such outside *res cogitans* (thinking matter). Similarly, the other voice is outside the thinking mind. As we have discussed, the notion of dialogue has the potential of redressing the Cartesian splits. First, it brings space back to the dialogically functioning self: space is not only outside but also inside the self. Second, it brings back the other to the self: the other is not only outside but also inside the self. As we shall see later, this double restoration will contribute to conceiving the self as a flexible movement in a space. This conception can be seen as an attempt to overcome the Cartesian ego which in Johnson's terms is a 'fixed entity, essentially isolated and disembodied, an ego-logical thing, encapsulated in a machine of corruptible matter' (1985, p. 15). In order to overcome the Cartesian ego, it is necessary to interconnect the concepts of self and dialogue.

James' Self as Transcending Descartes' Ego

In James' (1890) view, the two main components of the self were the *I* and the *Me*. The *I* corresponds to the self-as-knower and continuously organizes and interprets experience in a purely subjective manner. Three features characterize the I: continuity, distinctness, and volition (see also Damon & Hart, 1982). The *continuity* of the self-as-knower manifests itself in a 'sense of personal identity' and 'the sense of sameness' through time (1890, p. 332). A feeling of *distinctness* refers to having an own identity, an existence separate from others. A sense of *personal volition* is expressed by the continuous appropriation and rejection of thoughts by which the self-as-knower functions as an active processor of experience. Implicit in the experience of each of these features (continuity, distinction, volition) is the awareness of self-reflectivity that is essential for the self-as-knower.

Whereas James identified the *I* with the 'self-as-knower', he saw the *Me* as identical to the 'self-as-known'. James discerns three categories in the self-as-known: material characteristics (body, clothes, possessions), spiritual characteristics (thoughts, consciousness), and social characteristics (relations, roles, fame). In doing so he was aware that there is a gradual transition between *Me* and *Mine*, and therefore he identified the *Me* as the empirical self that in its broadest sense includes all that the person can call his or her own, 'not only his body and his psychic powers, but his clothes and his house, his wife and children, his ancestors and friends, his reputation and works, his lands and horses, and yacht, and bank-account' (1890, p. 291). These elements, 'constituents' in James' terms, reflect the extension of the self. That is, the self is not closed off from the world, having an existence in itself, but is extended toward specific aspects of the environment (Rosenberg, 1979).

With his conception of the self James made at least two important steps beyond the Cartesian ego. First, he transcended the dualistic separation between mind and body by assuming an extended self that acknowledged the gradual transition between *Me* and *Mine* (my body). Second, James corrected the Cartesian separation between self and other by including social characteristics (e.g. relations and roles) as belonging to the self. Mead (1934) elaborated on these social characteristics by describing the self's capacity of 'taking the role of the other', thus accounting for the fact that the perspective of the other can be incorporated into the self.

Although James made some significant steps in overcoming the solipsistic Cartesian ego, there are some other parts of his conception of the self which suggest that he did not go far enough. Although the body is central to James' conception of the *Me*, the same body was not fully acknowledged as part of the *I*. The central features of the *I* (continuity, distinctness, and volition) were described primarily in mentalistic terms and not covered with flesh and blood. Moreover, in his description of the *I*, James put more emphasis on time than on space. Spatial characteristics were included in the material Me but they played no central role in the formulation of the *I*. Moreover, although the other person was included in the social characteristics of the *Me*, it was not of *a priori* significance for the emergence of the *I*.

The Self from a Narrative Point of View

Mancuso and Sarbin (1983) and Sarbin (1986) took a significant step towards a dialogical view of the self by translating the *I–Me* distinction into a narrative framework. They argued that the uttered pronoun *I* stands for the author, whereas the *Me* represents the actor or narrative figure. The *I* can imaginatively construct a story in which the *Me* is the protagonist. The self as author can imagine the future and reconstruct the past and describe him- or herself as an actor. In Sarbin's (1986) view, such narrative construction is a way of organizing episodes, actions, and the significance of actions. It brings together facts and fantasies in temporal and spatial constructions. For Sarbin time *and* space are fundamental characteristics of narrative construction.

Another theorist, Jaynes (1976), has contributed to the spatialization of the self by describing the self as a 'mind-space'. The *I* constructs an analog space and metaphorically observes the *Me* moving in this space. When we reflect on our lives, we do this in the form of a life narrative in which we see ourselves as the protagonist moving through the stages of life. In these metaphorical constructions, the *I* is always seeing the *Me* as the main figure in the story of one's life. For Jaynes, not only does narratization give structure to our daily activities, but the assigning of causes to our behavior is also part of narratization. Thieves may narrate their act as being caused by poverty, poets theirs as due to beauty, and scientists theirs as due to truth. In Jaynes' view, self and space do not exclude one another in a Cartesian fashion. Rather, the self is a spatial analog of the world and mental acts are analogs of bodily acts. The self functions as a space where the *I* observes the *Me* and relates the movements of the *Me* as parts of a narrative construction.

The Dialogical Self: From One Author to a Multiplicity of Authors

Whereas Sarbin's (1986) version of self-narrative assumes a *single* author who tells a story about him- or herself as an actor, the metaphor of the polyphonic novel goes one step further. It permits one and the same individual to live in a multiplicity of worlds with each world having its own author telling a story relatively independent of the authors of the other worlds. Moreover, the several authors may enter into dialogue with each other. The metaphor of the polyphonic novel has the capacity of integrating the notions of imaginative narrative and dialogue in a multi-authorial world.

In an attempt to bring the notions of dialogue and self together, Hermans, Kempen, and van Loon (1992) proposed the concept of the 'dialogical self' and defined it in terms of a dynamic multiplicity of relatively autonomous *I*-positions in an imagined landscape. More specifically, this conception was formulated as follows:

> The *I* has the possibility to move, as in a space, from one position to the other in accordance with changes in situation and time. The *I* fluctuates among different and even opposed positions. The *I* has the capacity to imaginatively endow each position with a voice so that dialogical relations between positions can be established. The voices function like interacting characters in a story. Once a character is set in motion in a story, the character takes on a life of its own and thus assumes a certain narrative necessity. Each character has a story to tell about experiences from its own stance. As different voices these characters exchange information about their respective *Me*(s) and their worlds, resulting in a complex, narratively structured self. (1992, pp. 28–29)

The dialogical self goes beyond individualism and rationalism and differs in two essential ways from the Cartesian *cogito*. In order to articulate these differences, two features of the Cartesian conception should be mentioned. First, the expression '*I* think' assumes that there is *one I* responsible for the steps in reasoning. Second, the Cartesian 'I *think*' is based on a disembodied mental process assumed to be essentially different from the body and spatial extensions. In contrast to the individualistic self the dialogical self permits one and the same person to occupy many *I*-positions and shift from one position to another. Moreover, the *I* in the one position can agree, disagree, understand, misunderstand, oppose, contradict, question, persuade, and even ridicule the *I* in another position. The dialogical self, in contrast to the rationalistic self, is always tied to a particular position or combination of positions in space and time and the construction of meaning is equally relative to the positions occupied.

The dialogical self is 'social', not in the sense that a self-contained individual enters into social interactions with other outside people, but in the sense that other people occupy positions in the multivoiced self. The spatial and relative nature of the self implies that it is not only 'here' but also 'there' and through the power of imagination the other is constructed as part of the self. This conception is not the same as Mead's (1934) 'taking the role of the other' as this expression implies that the self takes the *actual* perspective of the other. Rather, the dialogical self permits the construal of another person or being as a position which creates an alternative perspective on the world and myself. This perspective may or may not be congruent with the actual perspective of the actual other (which can be checked by entering into conversation with the other).

Prelinguistic Dialogues: The Self as Embodied

The concept of the dialogical self is conceived of as an embodied self. Two arguments are relevant to this idea. First, the dialogical self assumes that space is not simply outside the self but rather in the self. Spatially located interlocutors are assumed when people are involved in question and answer, and in agreement and disagreement. Even in purely imaginary dialogues, the self functions as a self-space with a variety of positions. Second, dialogical relationships are not limited to verbal dialogues but include also preverbal or prelinguistic dialogical forms.

In his study of mother–infant dyads, Fogel (1993) has analyzed interactive sequences between, for example, the crying infant and the consoling vocalizations of the mother. He observed that the vocalizations of mother and infant are clearly co-regulated in both their pitch and intonation. The mother's vocalizations are tuned into the vocalizations of the infant, and vice versa, so that sequential patterns are produced in which the sounds of mother and infant change concomitantly. Similarly, Fogel studied the process of giving and taking between mother and child. When the mother gives a toy to the infant, she brings the object into the visual field of the child and moves the object in such a way that the infant has the opportunity to open its hands before receiving the toy. It is as if the mother says: 'I offer you a toy, do you want it?' The infant, in turn, orients its body to the toy and opens its hands as if to say: 'Yes, I want it.'

Indeed, the infant is not yet able to use language, but the interaction between mother and child is, without doubt, of a dialogical nature. The crucial point is that dialogue should not be restricted to verbal dialogue. It is evident that the infant does not understand the words produced by the parents, but it understands the intonations. Moreover, the intonations which are exchanged between parent and infant can be understood as sequences of question and answer. Similarly, Fogel observed that when the mother reaches out to help the baby into a sitting position, the relative amount of the forces exerted by both persons wax and wane in a co-regulated manner. For example, when the mother pulling the child into a sitting position feels that the infant's forces increase, she responds by decreasing her own force. In turn, the infant increases its force as a response to the decreasing force of the mother. Such a co-regulated movement can be described as a nonverbal invitation by the mother to the child to change its position and as a cooperative response by the child. (For similar phenomena in infancy, such as imitation, co-awareness, mirror behavior, and intentionality, see Rochat, 2000.)

Special cases in point are the so-called 'pseudo-dialogues' in infancy. Using stop-frame and slow-motion microanalysis of films and videotapes, investigators have observed that mothers in their contact with infants begin to take turns from the moment the infant is born. From birth onward babies suck in a regular pattern of bursts. Mothers, sensitive as they are, tend to respond to this pattern. The mother is quiet when the baby sucks and she talks to it and touches it when the baby pauses. Although the baby initially sucks and pauses independent of the responses from the mother, she treats the baby's bursts of sucking as a 'turn', in this way creating a dialogically structured pattern (Kaye, 1977). During this rhythmic process of turn-taking, the mother listens for an *imagined* response from the baby as Newson (1977) and Stern (1977) have described. She acts *as if* the baby is taking turns in an actual 'conversation'. These interactional patterns are precursors of later, more developed dialogical structures, when pauses are actually filled in by the infant's babbling. Later, the incidence of babbling increases contingent on the mother's responses (Bloom, Russell, & Davis, 1986). Clarke-Stewart, Perlmutter, & Friedman (1988) conclude from these observations that mother and child are engaged in a 'pseudodialogue' on the supposition that the child is still too young to engage in a 'real' dialogue.

It should be emphasized that the notion of 'pseudo-dialogue' presupposes that the infant is *not yet* able to engage in real dialogue. In fact, this presupposition reflects the traditional view that equalizes dialogue with verbal conversation. Consequently, there can be no dialogue preceding the maturation of language. However, as Hermans and Kempen (1995) have argued, there is no convincing reason to restrict dialogue to linguistic dialogue. Such a restriction would deny the fact that much communication between people develops through body language, facial expression, smiling, vocalizations, and intonations. Not surprisingly, Mead (1934) explicitly referred to the workings of 'gestures' as central to his theory of symbolic interactionism, and even actions can be symbolically laden. People can become involved in dialogical actions as they, for example, offer and receive presents, exchange greetings, or close a door for an undesirable visitor. Even when somebody is confronted with another person who intentionally and systematically disregards him or her, the disregarded person may perfectly understand the 'message'.

The Significance of Collective Voices

In contrast to the idea of the Cartesian, separated, individualist, and centralized self, the notion of dialogue opens the realm of collective voices. Bakhtin observed that dialogicality includes, but also extends far beyond, face-to-face contact. He was interested in 'social languages' (e.g. languages of particular groups) within a single national language (e.g. Russian, English), and in different national languages within the same culture. Examples of social languages are professional jargons, languages of age groups and generations, languages of passing fashions, and languages that serve the sociopolitical purposes of the day. Speakers always use social languages when producing unique utterances, and thus social languages shape what individual voices can say, although the speaker may not be aware of this. For this simultaneity of individual and collective utterances Bakhtin uses the term *ventriloquation*, which means that one voice speaks through another voice or voice type as found in social language. 'Multivoicedness' refers not only to the simultaneous existence of different individual voices, but also to the simultaneous existence of the voice of an individual and the voice of a group (Wertsch, 1991).

There is growing interest among psychologists in the relationship between self and collectivity. Miller and Prentice (1994), for example, observe that for many decades the group was considered as something external to the individual and centered around the question 'How do individuals behave when in a group?' A different view was taken when researchers, typically those working on self-classification theory, started to ask 'How do groups behave within individuals?' (Turner et al., 1987). These psychologists assumed that social categories with which people identify, have a profound impact on their psychological functioning. Parallel to the relationship between self and group, a similar shift in the relationship between self and culture can be observed (Miller & Prentice, 1994). Traditionally, culture was perceived as *out there*, as something outside the self. More recently, anthropologists and cultural psychologists have been concerned with culture as structures and processes *in* the self (e.g. Shweder & Levine, 1984).

Once we distinguish between individual and collective aspects of the self, we must ask the question concerning how these aspects are related to one another. Empirical evidence suggests that they function as relatively autonomous parts of the self. Prentice, Miller, and Lightdale (1994), for example, showed that one's attachment to the group can be distinguished from one's attachment to the individual group members. Individual people may have a stronger attachment to their group than to its members or, conversely, some individuals like some other individuals more than the group to which they all belong. The relative autonomy between the personal and the collective parts of the self permits the study of dialogical relations between them. From a personal point of view, people may agree or disagree with the collectivities in which they participate (e.g. 'As psychologists *we* are used to saying . . . but *I* think this is nonsensical because . . .') (Hermans, 1996a).

Although individuals may agree or disagree with the groups to which they belong, collectivities and the relation between collectivities seriously influence *and* constrain the meaning systems which emerge from dialogical relationships. As Sampson (1993) has argued, societal relationships are governed by polar opposites leading to 'social dichotomies', such as male versus female, young versus old, or white versus black. Within these dichotomies, the master term (e.g. male) is defined as possessing particular properties whereas the opposite term (e.g. woman) is negatively defined by the fact that it lacks those properties rather than being defined in its own right. Because such opposites are loaded with power differences, the result is that the voices of some groups have more opportunity to be heard than others. As a result of the merging of individual voices and collective voices, the construction of meaning is formed and, at the same time, constrained on the basis of such dichotomies and their corresponding power differences. Persons do not construct meanings in a free space with equal opportunities to express their views. On the contrary, these meanings are organized and colored by the societal positions represented by the collectivities to which they belong.

From a spatial perspective, the distinction between individual and collective voices corresponds with the distinction between two kinds of positions in which individuals are located: social and personal positions (see also Harré & van Langenhove, 1991, for a comparable distinction). Whereas a social position is directly governed by societal definitions, expectations and prescriptions, a personal position receives its form from the particular ways in which a person constructs his or her own life, sometimes in opposition or protest to the expectations implied by societal prescriptions. For example, when a person in a particular society or culture is defined as a woman, this social position carries specific expectations regarding the person's dress, movements, behavior, and emotion regulation. However, from the same woman's personal point of view, she may feel feminine in some situations (e.g. in dress) and masculine in other situations (e.g. in sexual behavior). In this case, there is a certain discrepancy between a person's social position and one or more of her personal positions.

The distinction between personal and social positions can be better understood by observing that many collective voices precede the life of an individual person and as such prestructure the position repertoire of the individual in question. Typically, collective voices enter the self of an individual via the workings of external positions (e.g. family, educators, and mass media), which are then internalized in the form of social positions (e.g. I as a child at home, I as a pupil at school). Personal positions, (e.g. I as ambitious, I as enjoyer of life, I as independent) then, may conform or not conform to the impact of social positions.

The Developmental Relevance of the Process of Positioning

The dialogical self can be seen as a composite concept, in which the term 'self', in the tradition of James (1890), and the term 'dialogue', in the tradition of Bakhtin (1929/1973), are theoretically combined. In this polyphonic translation of the Jamesian self, there is no place for an overarching

I, organizing, as a separate agent, the constituents of the *Me*. Instead, the spatial character of the polyphonic novel leads to the supposition of a decentralized multiplicity of *I*-positions as authors of a variation of stories. The *I* moves in an imagined space (which is intimately intertwined with physical space) from the one to the other position, creating dynamic fields in which self-negotiations, self-contradictions, and self-integrations result in a great variety of meanings.

In Figure 23.1 the self can be represented as a space composed of a multiplicity of positions, represented by dots in two concentric circles. *Internal* positions, depicted by dots within the inner circle, are felt as part of myself (e.g. I as a father, I as an ambitious worker, I as somebody who likes to engage in sports), whereas *external* positions, depicted by dots within the outer circle, are felt as part of the environment (e.g. 'my children', 'my colleagues', 'my friend John'). External positions refer to people and objects in the environment which are, in the eyes of the individual, relevant from the perspective of one or more of the internal positions. And, in reverse, internal positions receive their relevance from their relation with one or more external positions. In other words, internal and external positions receive their significance as emerging from their mutual transactions over time. From a theoretical perspective, all these positions (internal and external) are I-positions because they are part of a self which is intrinsically extended to the environment and responds to self-relevant domains in the environment. The enlarging dots in Figure 23.1 indicate that specific internal and external positions, at some particular point in time, are relevant to one another as part of a dialogical process. In this field of activity, internal and external positions meet one another in processes of negotiation, cooperation, opposition, conflict, agreement, and disagreement.

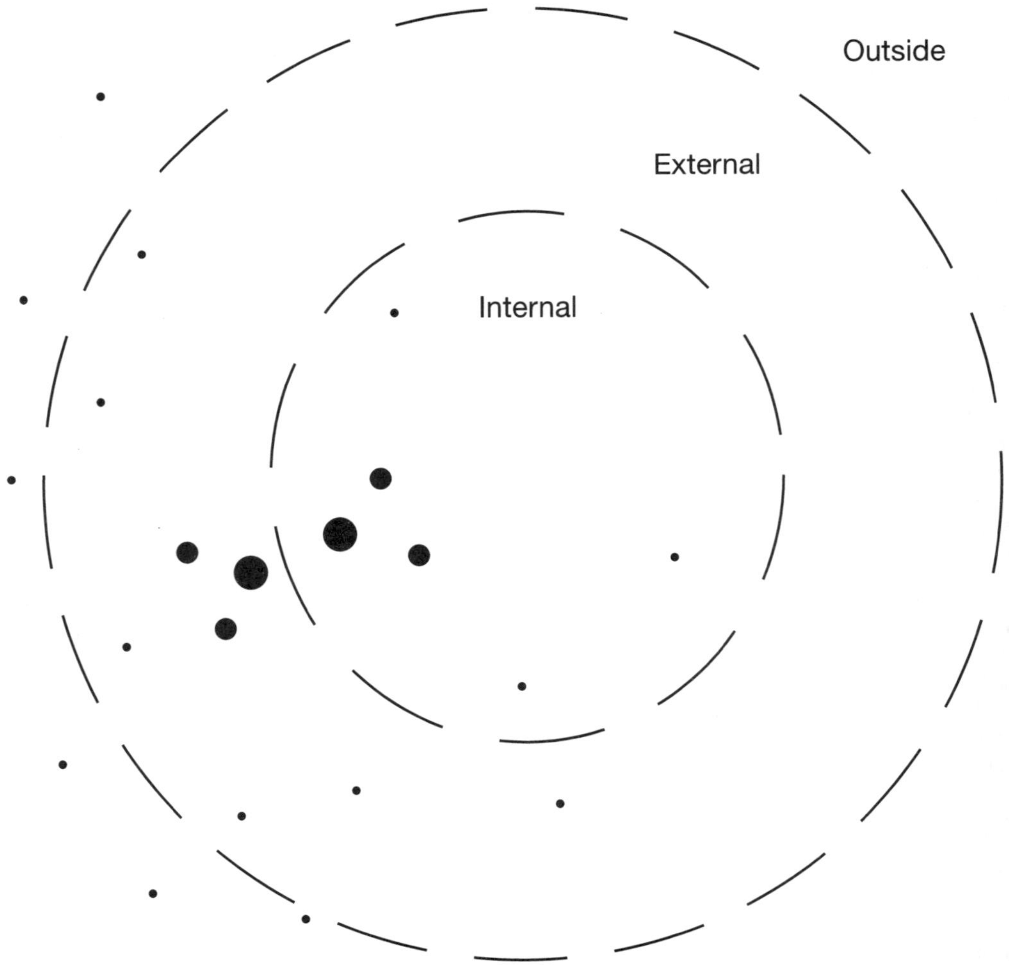

Figure 23.1 *Positions in a multivoiced self*

Dialogical relations typically develop between internal and external positions (e.g. 'As a father I help my children if they need me'). They can, however, also exist between different internal positions ('I disagree with myself because as an ambitious worker I neglect my duties as a father') or between different external positions ('My son and daughter had a terrible argument'). Other positions which show no dialogical relationships in a particular period or at a particular moment are in the background of the system, accessible for dialogical relationships at some other moment in time. The more the positions move to the front of the system, the larger the dots in Figure 23.1.

Some of the positions are represented by small dots in the circles, indicating that these positions are accessible as parts of the self (e.g. 'When my sport mate invites me for a game, the sport fanatic is aroused in myself'). Many positions, however, are simply *outside* the subjective horizon of the self and the person is simply not aware of the existence of these positions. As possible positions, however, they may enter the self-space at some moment in time dependent on changes in the situation. For example, when a child goes for the first time to school, he or she encounters a new teacher (external position) and finds him- or herself in the new position of pupil (internal position). When the person later in life finds a partner and establishes a family, a variety of new external and internal positions will be introduced as part of the self. From a developmental perspective, it is important to note that in some transitional periods in the life-course, the transaction between self and others is more intense than in other periods, which can be seen as relatively stable from a developmental point of view (e.g. Levinson et al., 1974). The presented model also assumes that some positions, that might be relevant in some earlier period of life, disappear from the self in a later period forever or might return later in life (e.g. an older person experiencing a growing affinity with children after an adult life of work and stress).

For a proper understanding of the model presented in Figure 23.1, it should be emphasized that it is based on the idea of moving positions, implying that dots in Figure 23.1 should be seen as moving dots. For example, external positions may move from the external to the internal space: a child may identify with a hero in a story to such a degree that the child *becomes* the hero (internalization). Or, an adolescent may create a new character in a story or a piece of art, in which his or her own self-preoccupations are expressed and materialized (externalization). The interrupted lines of the circles in Figure 23.1 suggest that the internal and external domains of the self are highly permeable and the self is permeable to the outside world.

Moreover, the movement of positions and their mutual relation is dependent on changes in culture. Our present era, often labeled as postmodern, is characterized by an intensified flow and flux of positions moving in and out of the self-space within relatively short time periods. Such a cultural change evokes intriguing questions such as: does this flow lead to an empty self (Cushman, 1990) or a saturated self (Gergen, 1991), or does it lead to a reorganization of the self in such a way that an intensified flow of positions is counteracted by an increasing need for more stable positions which guarantee a basic consistency of the self-system? Although we do not know much about such processes, it seems relevant to devise developmental theories and methods which are sensitive to their exploration.

The Actual Other and the Problem of Dialogical Misunderstanding

For a proper understanding of the presented theory, it should be emphasized that inter-psychological and intra-psychological processes are equally important for dialogicality (Valsiner, 2000). In fact, the two processes are largely intertwined. If I am involved in a conflict with a colleague about a management problem, I rehearse parts of the discussion with him when I'm alone, bringing in new elements and creating more convincing arguments in support of my point of view, thereby anticipating my colleague's response. If I then talk with him about the matter at another time, I'm better prepared to defend my point of view, taking advantage from my preceding imagined dialogues. During the next discussion with my colleague, I have the imaginal discussions with him available so that I can use elements of them if necessary. In other words, internal dialogues with myself or with parts of myself and external dialogues with actual others not only follow each other up, but even go side by side and become intensely interwoven.

Despite the intrinsic relatedness of internal and external dialogicality, it is necessary to make a distinction between the imagined other and the actual other. The actual other, however much a product of my imagination he or she may be, forces me to reconstruct my opinion as the interaction develops. In fact, the actual other questions, challenges and changes existing positions in the self and introduces new ones. The actual dialogue between different selves is represented by the intersecting circles in Figure 23.2, which can be seen as an elaboration of the circles in Figure 23.1. That is, any position as represented by a dot in the external area of Figure 23.1 (e.g. my father, my child, my colleague) is a candidate for an actual dialogue. The idea behind the intersection of the circles in Figure 23.2 is based on the notion of a meaningful dialogue. A meaningful dialogue assumes a certain degree of common understanding of the other and his world with the possibility of misunderstanding and lack of knowledge about the other and his or her view of the world. As a result of the intersection, five areas are to be distinguished:

- Area A represents a *two-way internal sharing* between two people in dialogue. The two people exchange knowledge on the basis of a common understanding of their internal positions. For example, two people recognize in each other a strong need to be honest about their feelings and behavior and want to interact on this basis. 'I as an honest person' is present in both of them and they are aware of the fact that this position is present both in themselves and in the other. This area is not necessarily based on agreement. The two interactional partners may have a common knowledge about their disagreements (e.g. I see life as something to be enjoyed and you see it as an opportunity to achieve something and we both know this).
- Area B refers to a *one-way internal sharing* between two people in interaction. One person positions the other in a particular way and the other is aware of this. For example, a father (represented on the right side in Figure 23.2) may see his son (on the left side in Figure 23.2) as unintelligent and conveys this message to him in verbal and nonverbal ways, so that the son finally believes that he is stupid.
- Area C refers to an *external sharing* of two people in interaction. Two people position somebody or something else in common ways. For example, two people may have a negative attitude towards a minority group and are aware of sharing this attitude.
- Area D represents a *non-sharing internal area* of two people in interaction. One person (on the left in Figure 23.2) positions him- or herself in a particular way but the other person is not aware of this. For example, an adolescent boy (on the left in Figure 23.2) sees himself as quite independent whereas his parents don't know this and continue to see him as dependent.
- Area E refers to a *non-sharing external area* of two people in interaction. One person (on the left in Figure 23.2) positions other people in a particular way but the other person is not aware of this. For example, a married man (on the left in Figure 23.2) has an extramarital relationship but his wife doesn't know about this.

The distinction between overlapping and nonoverlapping areas in the interaction between two people allows for a more articulated comprehension of the problem of dialogical misunderstanding. When people are involved in contact with a particular other, they may act on the basis of common understanding as represented by the areas A, B, and C of Figure 23.2. They are, however, unaware of the positions in the nonsharing areas D and E. Dialogical misunderstanding is caused by faulty assumptions on the nature of the actual dialogical contact. More specifically, misunderstanding exists if there is an actual discrepancy between the dialogical areas in which the partners locate themselves and each other and if they are not aware of this discrepancy. For example,

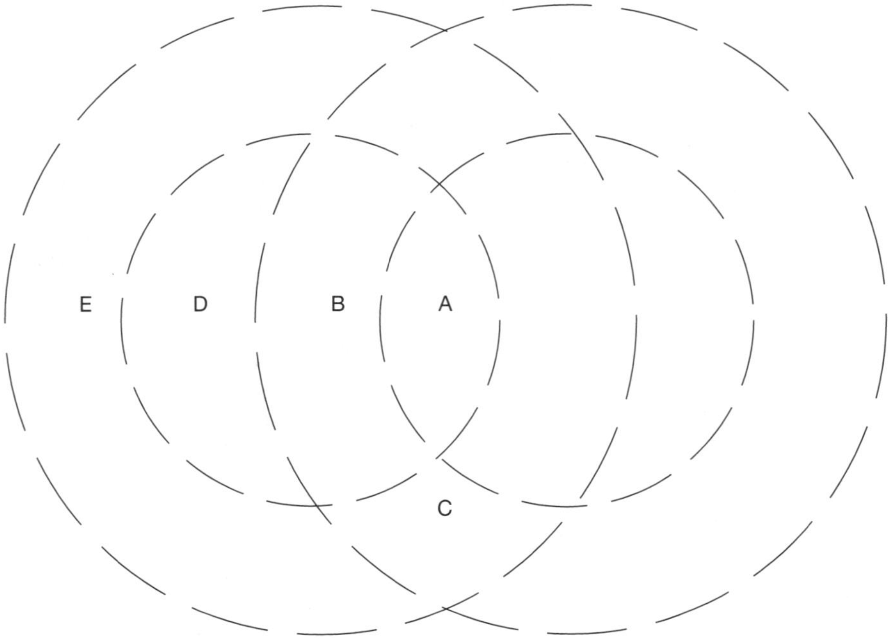

Figure 23.2 *Two actual people in dialogue (see text for explanation of areas A–E)*

a son is a suspect in a criminal case. His mother trusts that he is innocent and that he also sees himself as innocent (she supposes that they are both in area A). In fact, the son is guilty but is afraid to disappoint his mother (he is in area D).

As the interaction between the people continues and they get to know each other increasingly well, the areas which they share will increase in size and the discrepancies will be diminished or removed. It is assumed, however, that there are always areas which the interactional partners do not share because people are involved in interactions with more than one person. The person can be portrayed as being surrounded by other people and his experience in the contact with any of them is not necessarily known to the others. As the result of experiences with different people in different circumstances, our sharing and nonsharing areas with a particular person are very dynamic: they increase and decrease depending on the frequency, depth, and content of dialogical relationships with a variety of other people.

The several interactions, however, are not simply organized as 'dialogical monads'. As explained earlier in this chapter, collective voices are present in the position repertories of interacting people and these voices both organize and constrain the interactions among individuals. The sharing potentials provided by collective voices, however, are limited in a world society with an increasing degree of intercultural communication. Participation in different groups or cultures requires an understanding of the messages originating from different collective voices which may be partly known to the individual. This means that not only on the level of the individual voices, but also on the level of collective voices, the phenomenon of dialogical misunderstanding is inevitable.

As the preceding analysis suggests, dialogical misunderstanding can be considered as an intrinsic feature of dialogue. Cultural factors may even contribute to the importance of dialogical misunderstanding as is suggested by the increasing interest in biculturalism (LaFromboise, Coleman, & Gerton, 1993) and multiculturalism (Fowers & Richardson, 1996). When people are raised in one culture and then migrate to another, this may lead to a self-organization in which two or more heterogeneous internal positions (e.g. I as an Egyptian and I as a Dutch) interact with a heterogeneous multiplicity of external positions (e.g. the family of one's culture of origin and individuals and groups representing the second culture). Such positions (e.g. Egyptian versus Dutch) may be felt as conflicting or they may coexist in relatively independent ways or even fuse so that hybrid combinations in the form of multiple identities (Hermans & Kempen, 1998) emerge. In all these cases, there is a high probability of dialogical misunderstanding because the phenomenon of multiple identities raises the challenging question of how children, adolescents, and adult people, involved in a process of acculturation, are able to organize and reorganize their self-system in such a way that they combine cultural elements which may be highly divergent, partly unknown, and laden with power differences (see also Bhatia & Ram, 2001).

The phenomenon of dialogical misunderstanding and the challenges raised by processes of acculturation and multiple identities require dynamic social-psychological concepts. The spatial terms 'position' and 'positioning' are more dynamic than the traditional term 'role', as Harré and van Langenhove (1991) have argued. Describing and analyzing the self as a process of positioning and repositioning has the advantage of avoiding the reification of the self. As psychologists we are used to talk about 'language', 'speech', 'memory', 'perception', and 'self', as if these phenomena can be understood as 'things' while in their actual workings in everyday life they are processes in time and space. The dynamic nature of positioning is well reflected in Bakhtin's (1929/1973) term 'juxtaposition', which refers to the dynamic relationships among a plurality of voices which are neither identical nor unified, but rather heterogeneous and even opposed. The several positions create a field of tension in which they may cooperate in a process of co-construction of meaning. As involved in this process, the *I* doesn't represent a God's eye view but is intrinsically positioned in time and space. Nevertheless, as part of a process of positioning and repositioning, the I is able to move through a field of internal and external positions leading to the emergence of complex self-structures (Hermans, 1999; see also Kunnen & Bosma, 2000, and Lewis & Ferrari, 2000, who discuss the complexity of the self in terms of self-organizing dynamic systems).

THE CASE OF REBECCA

The preceding theoretical considerations will be illustrated with an actual case study. In describing the case study, attention will be paid to the central notions of the preceding theoretical discussion: the nature of dialogue, the process of positioning and repositioning, the merging of individual and collective voices, and the relation between social and personal positions. The case study concerns a woman, Rebecca, who performed a longitudinal self-investigation during a period in which she had many doubts about herself after a series of broken relationships with different men. The purpose of this case presentation is to show how Rebecca included her doubts, questions, and reflections as part of a organized meaning system and how this meaning system developed over time. A central part of this meaning system is its organization in terms of three *I*-positions: Rebecca as a child, as masculine, and as feminine. Before presenting the case study, the specific theory and method which were used in the study will be described.

Valuation Theory: Multivoiced Meaning Structures

Valuation theory (Hermans, 1987a; 1987b; 1988; 1989; Hermans & Hermans-Jansen, 1995) conceives of the self as an *organized process of valuation*. The 'process' aspect concerns the historical nature of human experience and implies a spatio-temporal orientation. The individual lives in a present situation and is, from this specific position in space and time, oriented to both the past and future and to the surrounding world. This position is voiced, that is, from this particular position (e.g. a significant other, myself as an intellectual, or myself as a dreamer) I can view myself and tell a particular story about the relationship between myself and the world. More significantly, different aspects from the past and different possibilities in the future become salient in different positions. The 'organizational' aspect points to the fact that the individual not only orients to the world from different positions, but also brings the meanings emerging from these positions together in a multivoiced self-narrative. In this narrative the different meanings are placed as parts in a composite whole, in which one meaning or voice is accorded a more influential place than another.

The central concept 'valuation' refers to any unit of meaning which is seen as relevant from a particular position. It has a positive (pleasant), negative (unpleasant), or ambivalent connotation for the individual from the perspective of a particular position. Personal valuations are subjective constructions of personal experiences and refer to a broad range of phenomena such as: a cherished memory, a disappointment in a relationship with somebody else, a good talk with a friend, an exciting project, a physical handicap, an unreachable ideal, etc. Different valuations may emerge in different positions because the individual's reference point changes or alternates from one position to another. As a result of dialogue and self-reflection, the valuations emerging from different positions are organized in a complex, composite self-narrative that develops through time.

A central assumption in valuation theory is that the person is a passionate storyteller; that is, voices do not exchange information in neutral ways but, rather, they express and exchange affect-laden meanings. The implication is that each valuation carries an affective connotation reflected in a particular set of feelings (a particular profile of affect). When we know which types of affect are characteristic of a particular valuation, we know something about the valuation itself. The affective meaning is inherent in a valuation and thus cannot be separated from it.

The voices and their personal valuations, which may vary across time and situations, are on the manifest level of the self. At the latent level, however, there are a limited number of basic motives which are reflected in the affective component of the valuations. An examination of the affective component can therefore reveal the particular motive which is active in a particular valuation. The distinction between valuations and voices on the one hand and basic motives on the other hand permits the reduction of a great variety of surface expressions on the manifest level to a limited set of basic motives on the latent level.

Valuation theory assumes that two basic motives in particular characterize the affective component of the valuations: the striving for self-enhancement or S motive (self-maintenance and self-expansion), and the longing for contact and union with the other or O motive (participation with other people and the surrounding world). This distinction has been proposed by various authors who have dealt with the duality of human experience. Bakan (1966), for example, considered agency and communion as fundamental dynamic principles; Angyal (1965) introduced the concepts of autonomy (or self-determination) and homonomy (or self-surrender); Klages (1948) relied on Bindung (solidification) and Lösung (dissolution) as the two basic human motives; McAdams (1985) has distinguished power and intimacy as fundamental story themes from a narrative perspective.

When a valuation represents a realization of the S motive (e.g. 'When I passed that difficult test, I was more accepted by the group'), the person experiences a feeling of strength and pride in connection with the valuation. Similarly, when a valuation represents a realization of the O motive (e.g. 'I enjoy the moments when I am making music with my friend'), feelings of intimacy and tenderness are associated with the valuation. In other words, the latent motivational base becomes manifest in the affective pattern associated with a particular valuation.

Closely related to S and O feelings, *well-being*, in the form of the relative dominance of positive and negative feelings, plays a central role in valuation theory. The rationale behind these feelings is that people face obstacles on their path towards fulfillment of basic motives. When it is difficult or impossible to overcome obstacles, *negative* feelings emerge. On the other hand, overcoming obstacles and hindrances results in *positive* feelings. Each valuation is associated with a pattern of positive and negative feelings, so that the relative dominance of one of the two types of affect provides information about the extent to which basic motives are fulfilled.

The concept of *generalization* represents the organizational aspect of valuation theory and plays a central role in the methodology presented in the next section. The more a particular valuation generalizes as part of a system, the more it influences the 'general feeling' of a person. When a person tells how he or she feels in general, it is highly probable that certain experiences determine this general feeling more than others. For example, if the person is living in a period of serious conflict with his or her spouse, there is a good chance that the feelings associated with this conflict are more likely to determine the person's general feeling than, for example, the pleasant contact the person may have with his or her colleagues. As this example suggests, not all valuations are equally influential in the system. The more generalizing potential a valuation has, the more influential the affective component of this valuation is in determining the way the person generally feels in a particular period of life. Note that the concept of generalization reflects the organization of the meaning system.

In summary, the multivoicedness of the self is expressed in the supposition that there is a multiplicity of positions or voices, each associated with their particular set of valuations. Each valuation, in turn, is associated with a particular set of feelings, in which basic motives are expressed. It is postulated that a repositioning of the self implies a shift from one voice to another with the possibility of change in the content and organization of valuation and affect.

The Self-Confrontation Method: Exploring a Multiplicity of Meanings

The self-confrontation method is an idiographic procedure based on valuation theory. It is designed to study the relation between valuations and types of affect and the way in which these variables become organized within and between positions (Hermans & Hermans-Jansen, 1995). The procedure involves eliciting a set of valuations for each position and then associating these valuations with a standardized set of affect terms. The result is an individualized matrix in which each cell represents the extent to which a specific affect is characteristic of a specific valuation.

The valuations are elicited through a series of open-ended questions. The main questions, outlined in Table 23.1, are intended to bring out the important units of meaning for the past, the present, and the future. The questions invite individuals to talk about their life situations in such a way that they feel free to mention those concerns that are most relevant from the perspective of a particular position. The subjects are free to interpret the questions in any way they want; they are also encouraged to phrase the valuations in their own terms so that the formulations are as much as possible in agreement with their intended meaning. The typical form of expression is the sentence (i.e. the basic unit of text). In a sentence the subject brings together those events that the person feels belong together as elements of a personal unit of meaning. Typically, each question leads to more than one valuation.

In the second phase of the investigation, a standard list of affect terms is presented to the subject. Concentrating on the first valuation, the subject indicates on a 0–5 scale the extent to which he or she experiences each affect in relation to the valuation (0 = not at all, 1 = a little bit, 2 = to some extent, 3 = rather much, 4 = much, and 5 = very much). The subject, working alone, rates each valuation with the same list of affect terms. The valuations can then be compared on the basis of their affective profiles. Once the affective ratings for the different valuations have been obtained, a number of indices that represent the motivational structure of the valuation system are calculated:

1 Index *S* is the sum of the scores for four affect terms specifically expressing self-enhancement: strength, self-esteem, self-confidence, and pride.
2 Index *O* is the sum of the scores for four affect terms specifically expressing contact and union with the other: love, tenderness, intimacy, and

Table 23.1 *Questions of the self-confrontation method*

Set 1: the past

These questions are intended to guide you in reviewing one or more aspects of your past life that may have been of great importance to you.

- Has there been anything of major significance in your past life that still continues to exert a strong influence on you?
- Was there in the past any person, experience, or circumstance that greatly influenced your life and that appreciably affects your present existence?

Set 2: the present

This set consists of two questions referring to your present life that will lead you, after a certain amount of reflection, to formulate a response.

- Is there anything in your present existence that is of major importance to you or exerts a significant influence on you?
- Is there in your present existence any person or circumstance that exerts a significant influence on you?

Set 3: the future

The following questions referring to your future should again guide you to a response. You are free to look as far ahead as you wish.

- Do you foresee anything that will be of great importance for or exert a major influence on your future life?
- Do you feel that a certain person or circumstance will exert a significant influence on your future life?
- Is there any future goal or object that you expect will play an important role in your life?

caring. Moreover, the *S–O* difference can be calculated for each valuation. When the experience of self-enhancement is stronger than the experience of contact with the other, *S* is greater than *O*. When the feeling of contact with the other prevails, *O* is greater than *S*. When both kinds of experiences coexist, *S* equals *O*.

3 Index *P* is the sum of the scores for 10 general-positive (pleasant) affect terms: joy, happiness, enjoyment, trust, security, energy, inner calm, freedom, inner warmth, and solidarity.
4 Index *N* is the sum of the scores for 10 general-negative (unpleasant) affect terms: powerlessness, anxiety, worry, shame, self-alienation, guilt, loneliness, inferiority, anger, and disappointment. The *P–N* difference can also be examined for each valuation. This indicates the degree of well-being the person experiences in relation to the specific valuation. Well-being is positive when *P* is greater than *N*, negative when *N* is greater than *P*, and ambivalent when *P* equals *N*. (Note that the indices *S* and *O* each range from 0 to 20, and *P* and *N* each range from 0 to 50 for a particular valuation.)
5 The extent of *generalization G* of a valuation within a particular position is assessed by asking the following question at the end of the valuation construction phase: 'How do I generally feel these days?' This question does not ask for a specific valuation but is devised to assess the 'general feeling'. The person answers directly with the list of affect terms that was used for the characterization of the valuations. The product-moment correlation between the pattern of affect that belongs to a specific valuation and the pattern of affect that belongs to the general feeling is a measure of the extent of the generalization of this valuation. The more positive the correlation, the more this valuation is assumed to generalize within a particular position. For example, when a person is, from his or her position as a student, worrying all the time about his or her studies, it is expected that evaluation referring to this problem (e.g. 'Wherever I am, I am always worrying about failing in my studies') has a high degree of generalization within this position. That is, the correlation between the affective profile belonging to this valuation and the affective profile belonging to the general feeling is expected to be high.

Ideally, the self-confrontation method is performed several times across time, typically over a period of several months, so that the developments in the valuation system can be studied. In a second or following investigation the person has the opportunity to modify existing valuations or add new ones depending on the new meanings emerging from the change in person–situation interactions. (For a more detailed description of the self-confrontation method, see Hermans & Hermans-Jansen, 1995.)

Theory and practice of the self-confrontation is based on a collaborative relationship between a subject (or client) and a psychologist (or counselor/psychotherapist). The valuation system and its affective organization are to be seen as a co-construction of two parties involved in a dialogical relationship. In this relationship both parties have their specific expertise. The subjects are knowledgeable in pointing to those meanings which are relevant in their own lives and they are invited to formulate these meanings in their own words. The psychologist is the expert in the theory and the corresponding methodology and has, moreover, experiences with a broad range of subjects which he or she can use in articulating the valuation system of this particular subject. The psychologist co-constructs the subject's valuation system not so much from a content point of view but rather from a methodological point of view. Psychologist and subject work together in the expression and further development of the valuation system.

Rebecca's Situation

Rebecca, a 44-year-old woman, is the mother of two adolescents. At the time of the investigation, she was working in a part-time administrative job. She contacted a counselor (the second author) in a period in which she looked back on several successive relationships with men which lasted typically for some years but were then broken by her or by her partner. She reported that in the beginning of a relationship she liked to give a lot of affection and care for her husband or friend but at the same time felt very dependent on him. She became aware of the fact that by continuously caring for another person, she was distracted from her own needs and wishes. She became gradually aware of a connection between the problems with her husbands and her position in the family in which she was raised. She remembers her father as one who treated her as the 'dumb blonde' and she always felt compared unfavorably with her brothers and sisters. During the course of the investigation she became more and more aware of the similarity between her inferior position in the family and her excessive caring for her husbands and friends. She realized that her caring and giving originated to a great extent from fear of being repulsed or devalued by significant others. When her friend or husband did not give her full attention or did not return the same amount of caring as she gave, she was extremely disappointed. She defended herself by becoming very crude or even breaking off the relationship. The repetitive nature of her disappointments in successive relationships was what brought her to contact a counselor who proposed that she perform a self-investigation with the self-confrontation method.

First Self-Investigation

The self-investigation resulted in a total of 54 valuations. Table 23.2 presents the four valuations with the highest generalizations and the four valuations with the lowest generalizations. The first group is selected because they are most influential in Rebecca's meaning system and the second group because they are least influential in the system. The two groups can be considered in terms of figure and ground, the first group being the (negative) valuations which are most directly influencing Rebecca's well-being, whereas the second group is the (positive) group which is in the background of the system.

As the affective indices in Table 23.2 show, the highest generalizing valuations have low levels of both self-enhancement and contact and union. Moreover, they are associated with higher levels of negative than positive affect. This combination of affective properties indicates the experience of 'powerlessness and isolation' (Hermans & Hermans-Jansen, 1995). Moreover, the content of the formulation explicitly refers to the existence of anxiety (see valuations 2–4). Another feature of the highest generalizing valuations (1 and 2) is that they are inarticulate. Their formulation is quite vague, suggesting that Rebecca doesn't feel able to clearly point to specific events or circumstances which are responsible for her low well-being and for her pervasive anxiety.

In apparent contrast to the highest generalizing valuations, the lowest generalizing valuations are typically associated with high levels of self-enhancement and high levels of contact and union. They express the combination of 'strength and unity' (Hermans & Hermans-Jansen, 1995). Positive feelings are rated higher than negative feelings, indicating that these valuations are associated with high levels of well-being. These valuations indicate that high well-being is related to the experience of self-surrender (valuation 5), genuineness (valuation 6), intimacy (valuation 7), and giving (valuation 8). Apparently, she has organized her valuation system in such a way that her experience of anxiety strongly contrasts with the experience of intimacy and self-surrender, with the former experience being more influential in her valuation system than the latter.

The Period between the First and the Second Self-Investigation

The first self-investigation was an attempt to construct a valuation system with proper attention to its affective organization. As already said, Rebecca was not yet able to clearly articulate the reasons for her anxieties and low well-being. After a series of sessions in which the counselor and Rebecca worked together in exploring her meaning system in close connection with her everyday experiences (for

Table 23.2 *Rebecca's highest and lowest generalizing valuations and their affective indices at investigation 1*

	S	*O*	*P*	*N*	*G*
Highest generalizing valuations					
1 I think a lot about my relationships	4	5	9	16	0.73
2 Where does my anxiety come from?	2	5	1	24	0.72
3 I would like to share my financial concerns with somebody but I'm suspicious of advisors, banks, intermediates and even partners: I'm afraid of being exploited	4	0	4	30	0.72
4 Peter [present friend] is pretending to give me support; yet I'm afraid that he would be better off if he left me; and he always wants to be at the center of attention	2	1	3	28	0.71
Lowest generalizing valuations					
5 I can lose myself in music and dance, I enjoy these activities very much	15	6	33	4	–0.39
6 I feel close to people who are genuine, who don't play tricks or wear masks	13	12	33	3	–0.39
7 I can enjoy physical intimacy, especially giving, if I mean something to somebody	13	13	39	9	–0.37
8 I experience great enjoyment when I succeed in helping someone when I'm asked	16	15	39	4	–0.35
General feeling	5	7	16	23	–

Note: *S* = affect referring to self-enhancement; *O* = affect referring to contact and union; *P* = positive affect; *N* = negative affect; *G* = generalization.

details see Hermans & Hermans-Jansen, 1995), the counselor decided to propose to Rebecca to explore her life more explicitly from the perspective of different positions or voices. In fact, this was a strategic change of the self-investigation. Up till now, Rebecca was asked to construct *one* valuation system from her *one* voice in cooperation with the voice of the counselor. The new strategy was to propose that she consider her life from the perspective of different voices in order to broaden the range of her positions and articulate her valuations. With this purpose in mind, the counselor presented a list of positions to Rebecca and asked her to choose those positions which were of actual relevance to her. The list included a diversity of positions such as: the critic, the optimist, the pessimist, the understanding person, the fighter, the adventurer, the masculine, the feminine, the intellectual, the idealist, the child, etc. Rebecca initially pointed to a rather large number of positions which she considered as relevant to her own life. After a series of sessions in which the chosen positions were discussed in close correspondence with her daily experiences, it became clear that three positions were particularly relevant to her present life: the child, the masculine, and the feminine. (Note that the chosen positions are not simply 'selected'; it is the intention of the procedure that the positions are 'owned' by the client and the discussion with the counselor has the purpose to facilitate this process of owning.)

The position of the child was relevant to Rebecca because she had discovered that her experiences as a child were not simply a memory of past events but were still actual in her present life. As a reaction to the humiliations in her past and the continuous competition with her siblings, she had developed a strong masculine side to compensate for her vulnerability. At times, however, she felt feminine, particularly when she received attention and care from her environment. These positions (child, masculine, and feminine) were central to the second self-investigation.

Second Self-Investigation

The second self-investigation took place 15 months after the first one. This time Rebecca was invited to construct a set of valuations from the perspective of the three positions (child, masculine, and feminine) separately (Table 23.3). In addition, a fourth position was proposed by the counselor, labeled as the 'observing position'. The rationale behind this was the consideration that the links between the three positions could be made explicit by asking Rebecca how she saw the interconnections among the three positions. The observing position required Rebecca to be involved in an intensified process of shifting back and forth between the three positions. In this way the observing position served as a 'meta-position' (Hermans & Kempen, 1993) from which Rebecca had the opportunity to bring to expression her insights into the nature of the interconnections among the several positions.

As the formulations of the valuations from the child suggest, some of Rebecca's experiences were situated in the past (valuations 1–4 in Table 23.3) whereas other experiences were situated in the present (valuations 5–6). The fact that she was able to formulate specific valuations referring to the position of the child in the present corroborates the relevance of this position as more than the mere past. As she formulates in valuation 5: 'I feel treated as a child when somebody does something for me in a gentle way (as if I cannot do it myself).'

As the affective indices in Table 23.3 show, some of the valuations are quite negative (valuations 1–3), others are ambivalent (valuations 4 and 5), and one is positive (valuation 6). Although there are many negative feelings associated with the valuations from the child position, it should be noted that none of the negative valuations have a generalizing influence. The only exception is valuation 6 which has some influence on her general feeling ($G = 0.53$). This means that most of the child valuations have been moved into the background of the self-system.

The most conspicuous feature of the valuations in the masculine position is that they show a relative dominance of self-enhancement affect over contact and union affect. This means that Rebecca's masculine side is systematically associated with self-enhancement, which sometimes is experienced as positive (e.g. valuations 7 and 11) and sometimes as negative (e.g. valuations 9 and 10).

The feminine position comprises the highest generalizing valuations in the system as a whole (valuations 16 and 12). For Rebecca's well-being it is important that these valuations are positive ones and associated with high levels of both self-enhancement and contact and union. Whereas her negative valuations were most generalizing in investigation 1, the positive valuations have the most generalizing power in investigation 2. Another relevant change is that Rebecca, who enjoyed giving care and attention to others in investigation 1 (valuation 8 in Table 23.2), can now permit herself to receive care and attention from others (valuations 13–15 in Table 23.3).

In the observer position Rebecca explains in her own words an insightful connection between the three positions in valuation 17. Here she demonstrates that she is aware of how one position is meaningfully related to another one as part of her personal history. Valuation 18 refers to the importance of another person in relation to her internal positions. She emphasizes that, in order to develop her feminine side, she needs another person who 'takes over' her masculine side. Valuation 19 shows that her anxiety (as associated with her child position) is related to her wish to have intimate

Table 23.3 *Rebecca's valuations for her several positions (child, masculine, feminine, and observer) and their affective indices at investigation 2*

	S	*O*	*P*	*N*	*G*
I as a child					
1 I didn't receive enough love and affection; the only physical contact with my mother was a kiss which she'd withhold as a punishment; I found this very disturbing	4	2	12	24	−0.17
2 The continuous competition among my brothers and sisters made me feel unsafe	5	1	8	30	−0.38
3 When at boarding school I was threatened when I did not do my best	6	3	6	18	−0.18
4 I remember that I often had to find my own way; I could manage by acting tough; I didn't feel safe enough to ask for help	14	4	15	18	0.22
5 I feel treated as a child when somebody does something for me in a gentle way (as if I cannot do it myself)	9	9	19	21	0.07
6 Humor lets me really see and feel the child in myself: the spontaneity without anxieties	19	4	36	2	0.53
I as masculine					
7 I preferred to play with boys and tried to be better than them in wild and risky behavior (e.g. climbing trees)	13	3	27	12	0.40
8 I expressed my leadership by becoming the chairperson of the student council	11	4	18	15	0.22
9 Kevin [present friend] challenges me by transgressing my own boundaries for tolerance, making me express myself in a hard, masculine way	12	2	7	30	−0.26
10 I'm very impatient with weak and indecisive men; I expect more strength from them than I can create in myself	11	2	8	27	−0.23
11 I feel the powerful woman during sex	15	11	22	15	0.53
I as feminine					
12 I felt a complete woman during pregnancy and as a mother	13	13	23	15	0.57
13 I feel like a woman when somebody helps me (e.g. in changing a car tire)	4	7	19	15	−0.02
14 I feel extremely feminine when I'm feeling self-confident and receive a lot of attention (for example, when entering a café)	14	3	25	14	0.38
15 During sex I would like to be the child being protected by an experienced, sweet man	4	17	33	10	0.33
16 I want to be a well-balanced, feminine, self-confident, satisfied woman	12	13	33	12	0.59
I as an observer					
17 Because of a lack of attention, love, and protection, I have developed my masculine side to protect the vulnerable child and the feminine side in myself	10	4	11	18	0.00
18 I want a strong, courageous man around me who gives me the opportunity to develop my feminine side	9	16	37	3	0.50
19 The central question is: do I have the correct intuition and reaction to my friend's selfish behavior (with belly pain as a signal) or is it a deeply rooted anxiety for intimacy and vulnerability?	2	2	4	27	−0.33
General feeling	10	9	22	14	–

Note: S = affect referring to self-enhancement; *O* = affect referring to contact and union; *P* = positive affect; *N* = negative affect; *G* = generalization.

contact (as following from her feminine position). Note that she is much more articulate in the interpretation of her anxiety in the second investigation than she was in the first investigation (see valuation 2 in Table 23.2).

In the preceding analysis, the generalization of the valuations plays a central role. In valuation research this index can be used as one of the indices indicating the movements of the positions and their valuations to the front of the self-system (see Figure 23.1). The assumption is that the more the valuations of a particular position generalize, the more this position moves to the front of the system. During investigation 2 the valuations of Rebecca's feminine position have, relatively speaking, the strongest generalization in the self-system (see Table 23.3). This suggests that this position is close to the front of the system, whereas the other positions, the child position in particular, are somewhat more in the background. If the feminine position is, in the present period, most prominent in the internal domain of the self-system, then this implies that people who appeal to this position are most prominent in the external domain of the system. That is, people who are experienced as contributing to the affirmation of her feminine position are particularly relevant to her self in this particular period.

Innovation of the Self in Human Development

Several theoretical concepts discussed earlier in this chapter play a central role in the case study just described. Foremost, the investigation was based on a dialogical relationship between a psychologist and a client who collaborate in the construction and reconstruction of a meaning system. The psychologist contributes her professional expertise to this construction, the client her personal expertise. Both are considered as knowledgeable in their own field and they combine their expertise with the purpose of developing the client's valuation system and increasing her well-being.

Multivoicedness characterized the collaboration between psychologist and client from the beginning as it developed as an intensive communication between the voices of the client and of the psychologist. Multivoicedness was further elaborated when Rebecca was invited to differentiate her valuation system from the perspective of three positions: child, masculine, and feminine. Whereas the psychologist represented (from the perspective of the client) an external position, her 'subselves' or 'subpersonalities' can be considered as three internal positions which were to some degree interconnected by the client's metaposition (the observer).

The distinction between internal and external positions or voices has two significant theoretical advantages. First, it liberates the literature on subselves and subpersonalities from being closed up in processes which are conceived of as 'inside the self' or 'inside the personality'. When the self is considered as multivoiced and as a dialogical process, then the perspective of the other (including the counselor in Rebecca's case) has much to contribute to the innovation of the self (Hermans, 1999). When psychologist and client cooperate on this basis, their collaboration leads to the elaboration of internal and external positions in their mutual dynamics and innovation. Second, the inclusion of subselves and subpersonalities in the investigation of dialogical processes may enrich the literature on dialogue in the tradition of Bakhtin, which is often of a purely theoretical nature. Just because there is an extensive empirical tradition in the literature of subselves and subpersonalities (see, for example, Rowan & Cooper, 1999) the two traditions (on dialogue and self) may cross-fertilize each other and contribute to each other's theoretical expansion.

The distinction between personal voice and collective voice also plays a central role in our case study. Rebecca was educated as a woman in a traditional milieu implying a set of collective expectations regarding women's behavior and position in society. An unfavorable comparison and the power difference between men and women and between sons and daughters was particularly expressed by her father's humiliating characterization of the 'dumb blonde'. This remark, reflecting a collective voice of this particular social milieu, was, via her father's voice, internalized into Rebecca's self-system (area B in Figure 23.2). This and other devaluing experiences led to Rebecca's particular vulnerability as a child against which she defended herself by developing a masculine side as a protective shield. As a result of this self-protective behavior her feminine side was, according to her own experience, underdeveloped. Her relationship with the counselor can be seen as the introduction of a new voice in the self-system which assisted her to redress an imbalance in her position repertory. The cooperation between Rebecca and her counselor was focused on area B of Figure 23.2: counselor and Rebecca shared some new experiences which led to a correction of the powerful voice of the father in her life. In discussions with her counselor, she gradually gained insight into the nature of the interconnections between her three internal positions. As part of this, she became aware of her need for a particular kind of man (external position) to assist her in the further development of her feminine side (see valuation 18 in Table 23.3). As these aspects of Rebecca's case suggest, there are close interconnections between her (collective) position as a woman, her father as a significant external position, and her internal positions of child, masculine, and feminine. Together these positions are located in the center of her self-space (see Figure 23.1) during the front of her self-investigation. From a theoretical point of view, it should be emphasized that it makes sense to devise theories, methods, and forms of practice which are based on the distinction and interconnection among several kinds of positions (collective versus individual and internal versus external) and which acknowledge the influential role of actual others in the construction and reconstruction of the self.

The innovation of the self is crucial for any developmental process. In the presented theory, innovation results from the introduction of new voices. The voices of parents, caregivers, siblings, peers, teachers, colleagues in the work situation, and many other voices represent new positions in the developing position repertory of the person and all these positions are associated with specific collective voices of the communities in which these persons participate. There are at least two kinds of new voices. First, actual others (parents, peers, etc.) have the potential of introducing new elements in the position repertory of the developing individual. Second, human beings have the unique capacity not only to imaginatively endow a position with a voice, but also to create imaginatively new positions (e.g. writing a novel, creating a story, fantasizing about a new creature) as an internal or external position in the self. Third, the person is able, in close interaction with significant others, to combine existing positions into new combinations or to bring existing positions from the background to the front of the system (e.g. as result of a challenging situation, or therapy, or a discussion with a significant other).

As some of the above examples suggest, the term 'new' should be used with some caution. Often new combinations of positions result from the combination of old ones. The focus in research and practice of the position repertory is more on the organization of positions than on the qualities of separate positions. As dynamic systems theorists (Kunnen & Bosma, 2000; Lewis & Ferrari, 2000) suggest, novel higher-order positions may emerge from recursive interactions among lower-order positions. Particularly, when systems are unstable, these interactions give rise to positive feedback loops that amplify novel coordinations into macroscopic patterns which replace the previous organizational regime. Recurring patterns of coordination change the positions and the connections that give rise to them. These changes facilitate similar coordinations of positions on subsequent occasions, so that active habits grow in strength and replace competing organizations. Finally, during periods of unstable equilibrium, self-organizing systems shift between alternative patterns of coordination which may lead to abrupt changes called phase transitions. These transitions may take the form of 'dominance reversals' (Hermans, 1996b) which refer to dramatic changes in the patterning of positions. Sometimes, small changes caused by a particular event may trigger dramatic changes in the self-system as a whole. This event, however, has not determined the dramatic change because the causation resides within the system itself, that is, in the dialogical relationships within and between internal and external positions.

The developmental implications of the proposed dialogical view can be summarized by referring to some of the fundamental postulates presented by Charlotte Bühler (1968). In her classic work, Bühler proposed that the course of human life can be viewed as a whole composed of a multitude of events experienced by the individual between birth and death. Considering the individual's life as a biography, she says, leads the investigator to collect a large number of events over a longer period of time and to treat them together as parts of an organized whole. In this endeavor it is necessary to know the interrelatedness of events in order to understand them as manifestations of personal history. Moreover, in her biographical approach Bühler gave a central place to the fundamental goal-orientedness of the individual person: 'An effective person has a direction aimed toward certain results, and these results are as eagerly hoped for and expected during the midst of life as they are toward the end' (1968, p. 1).

In line with Bühler's approach, we have proposed to consider the life-span as a multitude of events during the life-course without the necessity of fixed developmental phases or periods. We have elaborated on this basic idea by considering the development of the individual from a dialogical perspective. This assumes not only a person who tells the story of his or her life to a listening audience but also that a story or history is always told from a particular position in time and space. Being multivoiced an individual may even tell different stories from the perspective of different positions. In accordance with Bühler's concern about the fundamental goal-orientedness of the individual, we have included two basic motives which we see as basic orientations which have an organizing influence on the relation between positions and their associated meaning structures. In this chapter we have presented a model which is built on the assumption that the complexity of the process of meaning construction requires a model in which multivoicedness, dialogicality, and goal-orientedness are indispensable theoretical elements.

Toward Three Kinds of History: Individual, Societal, and Evolutionary

As proposed earlier (Hermans & Kempen, 1995) we envision the future of developmental psychology as the study of the individual person from a theoretical framework which incorporates three kinds of history, as originally distinguished by the Russian social scientist Leont'ev (1973): individual, societal, and evolutionary.

Each person goes through an individual history and develops a personal story or self-narrative (Bruner, 1990; Gergen & Gergen, 1988; Hermans & Kempen, 1993; McAdams, 1993; Sarbin, 1986). As we argued earlier in the chapter, the self can be considered as distributed among several positions located in a real or imagined space, with the possibility of moving to and fro among them (Hermans, Kempen, & van Loon, 1992). In this highly dynamic conception of the self, the I has the capacity to move from a particular position to another position *and back* (Marková, 1987). This capacity implies that the same position (e.g. located in another person, real or imagined) can be revisited. This process of positioning and repositioning may result in the clarification and further development of a meaning system.

From a societal point of view, the embodied person is spatially located together with other human beings. This spatio-temporal location implies that the self is prestructured by preceding generations who have produced traditions and institutions that leave their imprint on the individual. This self is speaking not only as an individual voice but also as a collective voice, reflecting the collective values implied in the stories people tell one another as members of the groups and cultures to which they belong. The simultaneity of individual and collective voices contradicts any antinomy of individual and society. Instead, the individual is a micro-society, and society functions as an extended self. As Sampson (1993) has discussed extensively, the differences in societal positions (e.g. men versus women, whites versus blacks, young versus old) are laden with power differences. Given the simultaneity of individual and collective voices, the values implied by the collective voices influence and constrain the personal valuations as expressed by the individual voices.

From an evolutionary perspective, the human body is well equipped to participate in dialogical processes. The hands, in particular, are refined instruments which, in combination with the eyes, provide the biological tools not only for gathering knowledge about the environment, but also for interacting with the world (see, for example, Fogel's 1993 study of giving and taking in mother–infant interactions). The upright position frees the hands to grasp and isolate an object from its context enabling the individual to make new combinations (e.g. combining blocks in building a tower or playhouse). Leont'ev, interested as he was in the division of labor in economic societies, also saw the hand as crucial for higher mental processes: 'The hand, the principal organ for human activity, could only through work reach its perfection' (1973, p. 198). In a similar vein, the Dutch phenomenologist Buytendijk has argued that not only human speech but also the upright position does not develop in an autonomous way but in 'dialogue with the social environment, which calls the child to the venture of standing so that the free use of the hands becomes possible' (1965, p. 42). In other words, in order to understand dialogical processes in a most comprehensive way, the study of the functioning body as emerging from our evolutional history is indispensable.

Another way of incorporating evolutionary processes into future theorizing is to include motivational factors in dialogical models. On the supposition that the person is a passionate storyteller, two basic motives have been discussed in the present chapter, self-enhancement and contact and union, which, as we have seen, have a broad basis in contemporary psychological literature. Other biological and psychological studies imply that similar motives are also found in animals. The self-enhancement motive may find its evolutionary precursor in competitive and aggressive behavior. In a literature review, Walters and Seyfarth (1987) described how male ring-tailed lemurs smear a pheromone on their tails and wave them in the air when competing over access to females; a common squirrel monkey male threatens others by displaying his erect penis; baboons 'flash' their eyelids, revealing a patch of white skin; and gorillas beat their chests. Most primate species accompany such visual threats with vocalizations that can also signal aggression when given alone. The contact and union motive, on the other hand, finds its forerunner in forms of cooperative behavior. The most common form of affinitive behavior in apes is 'grooming', in which one animal, picking through the fur of another animal, removes ectoparasites and cleanses wounds. Other cooperative behaviors include warning calls signaling the presence of predators, mutual tolerance at food sites, and the formation of alliances (Walters & Seyfarth, 1987). The so-called theory of 'reciprocal altruism' (Silk, 1987) also suggests the presence of a contact and union motive in animals. This theory holds that individuals are more likely to receive aid from others if they have previously groomed them. There is sufficient empirical evidence that grooming happens not only between related individuals but also between unrelated individuals. Also in the latter case mutual grooming increases the probability that these animals will subsequently attend to each other's solicitations for aid (Silk, 1987).

The prospect of combining the three kinds of history is that meaning construction and the process of positioning can be studied as being organized along three lines: as emerging from the creative activity of an individual person, as resulting from our collective societal history, and as prestructured by our common evolutionary origin. Dialogue, however cultivated it may be in human societies, is an embodied practice which started long before there was any human development.

Acknowledgments

We thank Ingrid Josephs, Michael Katzko, and Jaan Valsiner for their detailed editorial comments.

References

Andersen, S.M., & Cole, S.W. (1990). 'Do I know you?': The role of significant others in general social perception. *Journal of Personality and Social Psychology*, 59, 384–399.

Angyal, A. (1965). *Neurosis and treatment: A holistic theory*. New York: Wiley.

Bakan, D. (1966). *The duality of human existence*. Chicago: Rand-McNally.

Bakhtin, M. (1929/1973). *Problems of Dostoevsky's poetics* (2nd edn). Trans. R.W. Rotsel. Ann Arbor, MI: Ardis. First edition published in 1929 under the title *Problemy tvorchestva Dostoevskogo (Problems of Dostoevsky's art)*.

Baldwin, M.W., & Holmes, J.G. (1987). Salient private audiences and awareness of the self. *Journal of Personality and Social Psychology*, 53, 1087–1098.

Bhatia, S., & Ram, A. (2001). Rethinking 'acculturation' in relation to diasporic cultures and postcolonial identities. *Human Development*, 44, 1–18.

Bloom, K., Russell, A., & Davis, S. (1986). Conversational turn taking: Verbal quality of adult affects vocal quality of infant. *Infant Behavior and Development*, special issue: abstracts of papers presented at the Fifth International Conference on Infant Studies, 9, 39.

Bruner, J.S. (1990). *Acts of meaning*. Cambridge, MA: Harvard University Press.

Bühler, Ch. (1968). Introduction. In Ch. Bühler & F. Massarik (eds), *The course of human life: A study of goals in the humanistic perspective* (pp. 1–10). New York: Springer.

Buytendijk, F.J.J. (1965). *Prolegomena van een antropologisische fysiologie (Prolegomena of an anthropological physiology)*. Utrecht: Spectrum.

Cassirer, E. (1955). *The philosophy of symbolic forms: Vol. 2. Mythical thought*. New Haven, CT: Yale University Press.

Caughey, J.L. (1984). *Imaginary social worlds: A cultural approach*. Lincoln: University of Nebraka Press.

Clarke-Stewart, A., Perlmutter, M., & Friedman, S. (1988). *Lifelong human development*. New York: Wiley.

Cushman, Ph. (1990). Why the self is empty: Toward a historically situated psychology. *American Psychologist*, 45, 599–611.

Damon, W., & Hart, D. (1982). The development of self-understanding from infancy through adolescence. *Child Development*, 4, 841–864.

Elkind, D., & Bowen, R. (1979). Imaginary audience behavior in children and adolescents. *Developmental Psychology*, 15, 38–44.

Fogel, A. (1993). *Developing through relationships: Origins of communication, self, and culture*. Hertfordshire: Harvester Wheatsheaf.

Fowers, B.J., & Richardson, F.C. (1996). Why is multiculturalism good? *American Psychologist*, 51, 609–621.

Garvey, C. (1984). *Children's talk*. Cambridge, MA: Harvard University Press.

Gergen, K.J. (1991). *The saturated self: Dilemmas of identity in contemporary life*. London: Sage.

Gergen, K.J., & Gergen, M.M. (1988). Narrative and the self as relationship. *Advances in Experimental Social Psychology*, 21, 17–56.

Gray, W.M., & Hudson, L.M. (1984). Formal operations and the imaginary audience. *Developmental Psychology*, 20, 619–627.

Harré, R., & van Langenhove, L. (1991). Varieties of positioning. *Journal for the Theory of Social Behaviour*, 21, 393–407.

Hermans, H.J.M. (1987a). Self as organized system of valuations: Toward a dialogue with the person. *Journal of Counseling Psychology*, 34, 10–19.

Hermans, H.J.M. (1987b). The dream in the process of valuation: A method of interpretation. *Journal of Personality and Social Psychology*, 53, 163–175.

Hermans, H.J.M. (1988). On the integration of idiographic and nomothetic research methods in the study of personal meaning. *Journal of Personality*, 56, 785–812.

Hermans, H.J.M. (1989). The meaning of life as an organized process. *Psychotherapy*, 26, 11–22.

Hermans, H.J.M. (1996a). Voicing the self: From information processing to dialogical interchange. *Psychological Bulletin*, 119, 31–50.

Hermans, H.J.M. (1996b). Opposites in a dialogical self: Constructs as characters. *The Journal of Constructivist Psychology*, 9, 1–26.

Hermans, H.J.M. (1999). Dialogical thinking and self-innovation. *Culture & Psychology*, 5, 67–87.

Hermans, H.J.M., & Hermans-Jansen, E. (1995). *Self-narratives: The construction of meaning in psychotherapy*. New York: Guilford.

Hermans, H.J.M., & Kempen, H.J.G. (1993). *The dialogical self: Meaning as movement*. San Diego: Academic.

Hermans, H.J.M., & Kempen, H.J.G. (1995). Body, mind, and culture: The dialogical nature of mediated action. *Culture & Psychology*, 1, 103–114.

Hermans, H.J.M., & Kempen, H.J.G. (1998). Moving cultures: The perilous problems of cultural dichotomies in a globalizing society. *American Psychologist*, 53, 1111–1120.

Hermans, H.J.M., Kempen, H.J.G., & van Loon, R.J.P. (1992). The dialogical self: Beyond individualism and rationalism. *American Psychologist*, 47, 23–33.

Higgins, E.T. (1987). Self-discrepancy: A theory relating self and affect. *Psychological Review*, 94, 319–340.

Hofstadter, D. (1986). *Metamagical themas*. New York: Bantam.

Holquist, M. (1990). *Dialogism: Bakhtin and his world*. London: Routledge.

James, W. (1890). *The principles of psychology* (Vol. 1). London: Macmillan.

Jaynes, J. (1976). *The origin of consciousness in the breakdown of the bicameral mind*. Boston: Houghton Mifflin.

Johnson, F. (1985). The Western concept of self. In A.J. Marsella, G. de Vos, & F.L.K. Hsu (eds), *Culture and self: Asian and Western perspectives* (pp. 91–138). New York: Tavistock.

Josephs, I.E. (1998). Constructing one's self in the city of the silent: Dialogue, symbols, and the role of 'as if' in self-development. *Human Development*, 41, 180–195.

Kaye, K. (1977). Toward the origin of dialogue. In H.R. Schaffer (ed.), *Studies in mother–infant interaction*. London: Academic.

Klages, L. (1948). *Charakterkunde (Characterology)*. Zürich: Hirzel.

Kunnen, S., & Bosma, H. (2000). A developmental perspective on the dialogical self. Paper presented at the First International Conference on the Dialogical Self, Nijmegen, The Netherlands, 23–26 June.

LaFromboise, T., Coleman, H.L.K., & Gerton, J. (1993). Psychological impact of biculturalism: Evidence and theory. *Psychological Bulletin*, 114, 395–412.

Leont'ev, A.N. (1973). *Probleme der Entwicklung des Psychischen* (*Problems in the development of mind*). Frankfurt: Athenaeum Fischer. Trans. from a text originally published in Russian in 1959.

Levinson, D.J., Darrow, C.M., Klein, E.B., Levinson, M.H., & McKee, B. (1974). The psychosocial development of men in early adulthood and the mid-life transition. In D.F. Ricks, A. Thomas, & M. Roff (eds), *Life history research in psychopathology*. Minneapolis: University of Minnesota Press.

Lewis, M.D., & Ferrari, M. (2000). Cognitive-emotional self-organization in personality development and personal identity. In H.A. Bosma & E.S. Kunnen (eds), *Identity and emotion: A self-organizational perspective*. Cambridge: Cambridge University Press.

Mancuso, J.C., & Sarbin, T.R. (1983). The self-narrative in the enactment of roles. In Th.R. Sarbin & K. Scheibe (eds), *Studies in social identity* (pp. 254–273). New York: Praeger.

Manosevitz, M., Prentice, N.M., & Wilson, F. (1973). Individual and family correlates of imaginary companions in preschool children. *Developmental Psychology*, 8, 72–79.

Marková, I. (1987). On the interaction of opposites in psychological processes. *Journal for the Theory of Social Behavior*, 17, 279–299.

Markus, H.R., & Nurius, P. (1986). Possible selves. *American Psychologist*, 41, 954–969.

Martindale, C. (1980). Subselves: The internal representation of situational and personal dispositions. In L. Wheeler (ed.), *Review of personality and social psychology* (Vol. 1, pp. 193–218). Beverly Hills, CA: Sage.

McAdams, D.P. (1985). *Power, intimacy, and the life story: Personological inquiries into identity*. Chicago: Dorsey. Reprinted by Guilford.

McAdams, D.P. (1993). *The stories we live by: Personal myths and the making of the self*. New York: Morrow.

Mead, G.H. (1934). *Mind, self, and society*. Chicago: University of Chicago Press.

Miller, D.T., & Prentice, D.A. (1994). The self and the collective. *Personality and Social Psychology Bulletin*, 20, 451–453.

Minsky, M. (1985). *The society of mind*. New York: Simon and Schuster.

Newson, J. (1977). An intersubjective approach to the systematic description of mother–infant interaction. In H. R. Schaffer (ed.), *Studies in mother–infant interaction*. London: Academic.

Prentice, D.A., Miller, D.T., & Lightdale, J.R. (1994). Asymmetries in attachments to groups and to their members: Distinguishing between common-identity and common-bond groups. *Personality and Social Psychology Bulletin*, 20, 484–493.

Rochat, P. (2000). Emerging co-awareness. Presentation at the International Conference on Infant Studies, Brighton, July.

Rosenberg, M. (1979). *Conceiving the self*. New York: Basic.

Rowan, J. (1990). *Subpersonalities: The people inside us*. London: Routledge.

Rowan, J., & Cooper, M. (1999). *The plural self: Multiplicity in everyday life*. London: Sage.

Sampson, E.E. (1985). The decentralization of identity: Toward a revised concept of personal and social order. *American Psychologist*, 11, 1203–1211.

Sampson, E.E. (1993). *Celebrating the other: A dialogic account of human nature*. Boulder, CO: Westview.

Sarbin, Th.R. (1986). The narrative as a root metaphor for psychology. In Th.R. Sarbin (ed.), *Narrative psychology: The storied nature of human conduct* (pp. 3–21). New York: Praeger.

Schlenker, B.R. (1980). *Impression management: The self-concept, social identity, and interpersonal relations*. Monterey, CA: Brooks/Cole.

Shweder, R.A., & Levine, R.A. (eds) (1984). *Culture theory: Essays on mind, self, and emotion*. New York: Cambridge University Press.

Silk, J.B. (1987). Social behavior in evolutionary perspective. In B.B. Smuts, D.L. Cheney, R.M. Seyfarth, R.W. Wrangham, & T.T. Struhsaker (eds), *Primate societies* (pp. 318–329). Chicago: University of Chicago Press.

Stern, D.N. (1977). *The first relationship: Infant and mother*. Cambridge, MA: Harvard University Press.

Straus, E.W. (1958). Aesthesiology and hallucinations. In R. May, E. Angel, & H.F. Ellenberger (eds), *Existence: A new dimension in psychiatry and psychology* (pp. 139–169). New York: Basic.

Triandis, H.C. (1989). The self and social behavior in differing cultural contexts. *Psychological Review*, 96, 506–520.

Turner, J.C., Hogg, M., Oakes, P., Reicher, S., & Wetherell, M. (1987). *Rediscovering the social group: A self-categorization theory*. Oxford: Blackwell.

Valsiner, J. (1997). Dialogical models of psychological processes: Capturing dynamics of development. *Polish Quarterly of Developmental Psychology*, 3, 155–160.

Valsiner, J. (2000). Making meaning out of mind: Self-less and self-ful dialogicality. Presentation at the First International Conference on the Dialogical Self, Nijmegen, 23–26 June.

Vasil'eva, I.I. (1988). The importance of M.M. Bakhtin's idea of dialogue and dialogic relations for the psychology of communication. *Soviet Psychology*, 26, 17–31.

Walters, J.R., & Seyfarth, R.M. (1987). Conflict and cooperation. In B.B. Smuts, D.L. Cheney, R.M. Seyfarth, R.W. Wrangham, & T.T. Struhsaker (eds), *Primate societies* (pp. 306–317). Chicago: University of Chicago Press.

Watkins, M. (1986). *Invisible guests: The development of imaginal dialogues*. Hillsdale, NJ: Erlbaum.

Wekker, G. (1994). Eindelijk kom ik tot mezelf: Subjectiviteit in een Westers en een Afro-Surinaams universum

(Finally, I find myself: Subjectivity in a Western and a Afro-Surinam universe). In J. Hoogsteder (ed.), *Etnocentrisme en Communicatie in de Hulpverlening* (Ethnocentrism and communication in the social welfare system) (pp. 45–60). Utrecht: Landelijke Federatie van Welzijnsorganisaties voor Surinamers.

Wertsch, J.V. (1991). *Voices of the mind: A sociocultural approach to mediated action*. London: Harvester Wheatsheaf.

Winnicot, D.W. (1971). *Playing and reality*. London: Tavistock.

24

Cognitive Processes in Ageing

PATRICK RABBITT, MIKE ANDERSON, HELEN DAVIS and VAL SHILLING

Aims

It has sometimes been uncritically assumed that involution mirrors development, so that individuals regress through developmental stages in a sort of inverse 'decalage'. A useful antidote is to remember that the intellectual and methodological problems of describing growing up and ageing are very different. Understanding how children manage to acquire cognitive skills and modes of representation of the world that they could not previously attempt requires a quite different intellectual approach from understanding how older people cease to be capable of skills and modes of representation at which they once were superbly competent. However recent, reductionist general models for cognitive changes throughout the lifespan, while ignoring questions of changes in representational structure and skill acquisition and loss, propose that at any stage in the lifespan attainable levels of competence at all cognitive skills is limited by the current level of a single global factor which increases with developmental age, maintains a long plateau at maturity, and ebbs in senescence. Simplistic versions of this idea have directly equated this resource with a single, measurable performance index: the maximum speed with which individuals can make correct decisions in easy laboratory experiments. An attraction of this approach has been that it seems to provide a way of linking empirically measurable behavioural competence to a potentially measurable functional property of the cognitive system and even to neurophysiological efficiency, providing, as one author has put it, 'a biological basis for intelligence' (Eysenck, 1986). This chapter considers the historical evolution and current plausibility of this general model in three separate fields of research: individual differences in general intelligence, cognitive ageing and developmental psychology.

Introduction

It is curious that most of the models developed by mainstream cognitive psychologists to describe functional processes supporting cognitive skills are descriptions of unrealistic steady state systems that exist nowhere in reality. They do not account for marked individual variations in competence between different individuals for changes in performance that occur as people grow up and grow old, for marked individual differences between people of the same age or for the substantial improvements that occur with practice.

Differential psychologists, developmental psychologists and cognitive gerontologists cannot evade these problems because they are concerned to model individual variability and changes in cognitive performance. They have approached this task in two different ways. Most have tried to account for individual variability and change by adapting and extending models imported from 'mainstream' cognitive psychology. This has been a fruitful approach, resulting in useful models for age-related changes in specific mental abilities such as verbal memory, decision processes or attention. However all such models share a characteristic weakness of mainstream cognitive psychology: they are derived from disparate experimental paradigms, they consequently are based on different kinds of data and on radically different functional assumptions, and they model quite different functional subsystems and so do not cohere to provide general descriptive frameworks for cognitive development, for cognitive ageing or for individual differences. Such models often risk becoming descriptions of the ways in which people cope with particular, very specific experimental paradigms. In the worst case they may even become models of task demands rather than of the functional processes by means of which these demands are met. The idea of a 'general theory' that is, at once, broad enough to encompass the vast range of observable differences between people and changes in their behaviour over time and yet not so vague as to be incapable of empirical falsification seems to have been shelved, if not entirely abandoned.

Nevertheless some ambitious investigators have tried a different approach to the psychological equivalent of the physicists' dream of 'a general theory of everything'. This involves opting for extreme parsimony by proposing that a single, behaviourally measurable task performance index must directly predict the efficiency with which all cognitive skills can be carried on, and so reflect a corresponding, unique, hypothetical performance characteristic of the functional cognitive system and so, also, of the central nervous system. The most popular candidate for such a 'master performance index' has been the maximum speed with which people can process information. Very similar 'global single factor speed' theories (GSFSTs) have been proposed to account for individual differences in general mental ability (Eysenck, 1986; Jensen, 1980; 1982; Vernon, 1985), for cognitive development during childhood (Kail, 1988; 1991a; 1991b) and for changes in cognitive efficiency in old age (Birren, 1959; 1965; Salthouse, 1985; 1991; 1996).

It is helpful to recognize that the successive steps between empirical data and theoretical constructs that investigators take when proposing GSFSTs involve unacknowledged transitions between logically distinct levels of description (see Rabbitt, 1996a; 1996b). In the study of cognitive ageing the initial impetus for a GSFST was the accumulation of theoretically neutral empirical observations that as people grow old they become markedly slower on all tasks involving simple decisions (Birren, 1965). Similarly, in differential psychology the impetus was the observation that groups of people who achieve higher scores on intelligence tests (Brand & Deary, 1982; Eysenck 1986; Jensen, 1980; 1982) are also consistently faster on simple laboratory tests such as choice reaction time (CRT) or tachistoscopic recognition threshold (inspection time, IT) tasks. In both these cases a further, and logically quite unrelated, step has been to speculate that consistent individual differences in decision speed on very simple tasks must necessarily reflect corresponding differences in the functional efficiency of all cognitive skills. It is important to note that, given the evidence then available, this was quite a daring hypothesis. Groups of older and younger or of more and less able individuals had only been compared on particular, easy CRT tasks (Birren, 1965; 1979; Birren, Woods, & Williams, 1980; Jensen, 1980; 1982) or IT tasks (Brand & Deary, 1982; Deary, 1995). A crucial methodological concept in differential psychology is that individual differences in performance on any given task may be due to relative competence at, or familiarity with, the particular demands that it makes. Thus even consistently positive rank-order correlations between individuals' levels of performance on any single task and their ages or intelligence test scores are insufficient basis for a general theory unless they are replicated across a wide variety of other, similar tasks. That is to say we need to check the construct validity of information processing speed as an explanation for individual differences in performance by examining rank-order correlations between many different kinds of CRT and IT tasks. This has not been systematically attempted, possibly because it has been taken for granted that correlations between levels of performance on superficially similar tasks must necessarily be very strong. However Table 24.1 shows correlations between various measures of information processing speed obtained over the last 10 years in the authors'

Table 24.1 *Correlations between Speed Measures in a variety of Laboratory experiments (Ns = 300 to 1746)*

Pair of Tasks Compared	Bivariate Correlation (Pearson's r)
4 choice Rt and speed of movement detection	.27
4 choice Rt and Word Naming	.39
4 Choice Rt and Trails Task Completion	.39
4 Choice Rt and visual search	.42
4 Choice RT and Letter/Letter Coding Speed	.31
Letter/Letter Coding and Visual Search	.59
Word naming and Movement Detection	.18
Letter Categorisation: 2 sets of 2 vs 2 sets of 4	.71
Letter Categorisation 2 sets of 2 vs 2 sets of 6	.69
Letter Categorisation 2 sets of 4 vs 2 sets of 6	.74

laboratories. While correlations between very similar tasks are, indeed, nearly always positive they are not particularly impressive. Even very similar tasks share only between 0.18% and 0.74% of variance.

While individuals who are fast at one task are also reliably fast at others it seems that differences in levels of performance on apparently very similar tasks are often, equally strongly, determined by differences in the ability to cope with the other, disparate and idiosyncratic, demands that they make. Even on apparently very similar measures of decision speed most of the variance between individuals has to be explained in terms of their relative abilities to cope with incidental task demands. Thus direct tests of the construct validity of speed as a unique factor that entirely determines individuals' efficiency across a wide variety of different tasks are not particularly encouraging.

A problem with all attempts to identify measurable task performance indices with hypothetical and unobservable functional system performance characteristics is that we can compare individuals' relative efficiency at different tasks in only two ways. We can measure how long they take to do something or count the number of errors that they make while doing it. CRT and IT tasks allow us to rank order individuals in terms of the times that they take to make simple decisions. The functional processes by means of which these decisions are made, like all others in this universe, unfold in time, and so have measurable durations. Thus to equate the empirically measurable time taken to make any decision with an unmeasurable and hypothetical functional characteristic of the processes by means of which that decision is made is to confuse different levels of description. In particular it may be very tempting to regard the latencies of behavioural decisions as direct reflections of the durations of the functional processes that underlie them. This may indeed provide useful clues, as when Helmholtz subtracted reaction times to touches on the cheek from times to touches on the foot to estimate speed of neural conduction (Riggs, 1972). However note that even in this apparently very simple and direct case, to estimate the speed of a process from a difference between two reaction times does not tell us anything about the *nature* of the processes of neural conduction that take up this time, but tells us only about their summed durations. Of course we may use this information to estimate boundary conditions for the speeds at which humans or other animals can make decisions of any kind. However measurements of the durations, speed or rates of decisions may set limits to, but should not be identified with, the performance characteristics of the functional processes that underlie them.

A convenient analogy to illustrate this point is that any, or all, of a variety of different functional operating characteristics of various components of elementary connectionist networks may determine the speed with which they make decisions. For example decision speed may be affected by the number and degree of connectivity of units in a network, by their operating thresholds and also by higher order properties of the network such as system temperature. Though such functional system performance characteristics may singly and interactively determine the speeds of all of the different kinds of decisions that a network may make, it would not be useful to try to quantify the efficiency of any one of them in units of rate or time. These difficulties equally apply to the robustly common sense view that CRTs and ITs must necessarily reflect basic differences in the neurophysiological properties of the central nervous system, some of which may potentially be checked by other technologies of measurement, such as electrophysiology or functional MRI. Speculative properties that can vary between individuals and change with age have included synaptic efficiency (Eysenck, 1986) or conduction latencies of neural pathways (Reed, 1993; Reed & Jensen, 1992). The point is that while the overall efficiency of neurophysiological systems may indeed be constrained by the operating characteristics of their component units and structures it is unlikely that any single one of these performance characteristics uniquely constrains the efficiency of all kinds of decisions and processes. It is obviously not impossible, but also not particularly fruitful, to index the efficiency of all neurophysiological system performance characteristics in units of duration or speed.

The main questions therefore are whether the evidence cited in support of analogies between epistemologically distinct levels of description has been properly interpreted (Rabbitt, 1996a; 1996b) and whether these analogies actually advance our understanding of individual differences in cognitive function. This chapter discusses the history of GSFSTs in cognitive gerontology and developmental psychology in order to consider whether some of the theoretical and practical issues that they avoid may not be more important than those that they can resolve.

Mental Speed as a Fundamental Explanatory Construct for Cognitive Ageing

The earliest observations that have led to single factor theories based on 'global' or 'general' slowing in cognitive gerontology were made by Jim Birren and his associates from the 1950s to the early 1980s. Many studies had shown that the elderly are invariably slower than young adults in easy choice reaction time tasks in which participants respond on each of a set of different keys to each of a corresponding set of highly compatible signals. Birren

(1979) and Birren, Woods, and Williams (1980) reviewed data from their own and other published studies to make the further point that there is an 'age × complexity interaction' such that this age difference increases with task difficulty: in this particular and restricted case with the numbers of different signals and responses between which participants must discriminate and choose. Birren concluded that this age-related slowing must reflect a fundamental change in the efficiency of the entire cognitive system which becomes more evident as task demands become more severe. He did not further speculate whether there might also be *qualitative* differences in the effects of task demands such that older people are relatively more slowed on some kinds of tasks than others. This issue is, of course, basic to the question whether age affects all cognitive processes to the same degree or affects some kinds of processes earlier and more severely than others.

When older and younger adults are equally accurate only differences in their performance speeds can tell us whether they differ in efficiency. In this sense, when comparisons of the decision speeds of older and younger people are our only evidence that they differ, it is tautological to maintain that 'general slowing' is a fundamental characteristic of age-related changes in cognitive skills, or of the functional processes underlying these skills. We shall argue that the ubiquity of age × task complexity interactions has been an interesting and theoretically provocative empirical discovery but is not evidence that age affects all, qualitatively different, cognitive functions only, or mainly, in terms of their relative speeds.

Cerella (1985) advanced discussion of age × complexity interactions by a brilliant meta-analysis of data from 146 published studies which had compared mean CRTs from groups of older and younger adults. The tasks used in these studies differed quantitatively in terms of the numbers of signal and response alternatives between which participants had to choose, but also qualitatively in terms of the particular nature of the demands that they made. Using an exploratory graphical analysis first suggested by Brinley (1965), Cerella plotted mean CRTs obtained from older against those obtained from younger groups for each condition of each task. Across all conditions of all tasks these 'Brinley plots' were plausibly linear, with average slopes of between 1.2 and 1.4 units. This meant that although these tasks might be supposed to make demands on functionally independent processes there was no evidence that age affected the efficiency of some of these processes more than others.

Cerella's (1985) theoretical interest stemmed from the idea that Sternberg's (1969; 1975) methodology of subtractive decomposition of decision times could be used to test whether cognitive ageing affects some decision processes earlier and more severely than others. Sternberg (1975) reviewed evidence that changes in task parameters, differences between individuals and differences in state within individuals may have different effects on the intercepts and slopes of memory search functions. For example the intercepts of memory search functions are more markedly affected than their slopes by changes in signal discriminability and their slopes are more affected than their intercepts by the onset of schizophrenia and by the ingestion of alcohol (see Sternberg, 1975). Sternberg therefore assumed that any perceptual-motor decision requires successive and serial processes of perceptual discrimination, memory search and response selection. He concluded that because manipulations that increase the duration of one of them do not affect the durations of the others these processes are also functionally independent of each other. Thus this methodology potentially allows us to test whether differences between the average decision times of groups of older and younger adults are greater when tasks impose demands on putatively age fragile than on putatively age robust processing stages. This line of research was enthusiastically taken up, though with inconclusive results, by cognitive gerontologists such as Anders and Fozard (1973) and Anders, Fozard, and Lillyquist (1972) among others and, for some time, remained a hopeful methodological strategy.

Cerella's (1985) finding that age apparently scales up decision times for all tasks by the same constant, whatever the quantitative or qualitative nature of the demands that they make, forced him to conclude that there was no evidence that age affects the efficiency of any one processing stage more than others. If we accept this conclusion we can propose a neat, albeit simplistic, functional model for changes in decision times with age. If, like Sternberg, we suppose that decisions are made by chains of serially entrained subprocesses we may further suppose that the more complex these decisions become the longer will be the sequences of subprocesses necessary to make them. If age lags the durations of all processes by the same multiplicative constant L, then the difference between the mean completion times T for any component process will be TL and the difference between the mean decision times of older and younger people on a task requiring N successive component processes will be $f(NL)$. This would provide a simple and sufficient explanation for the age × complexity interactions which were first observed by Birren (1979) and Birren, Woods, and Williams, (1980) and have been confirmed by all subsequent investigators.

Note that it would be a methodological misfortune if this tidy description were correct because, in that case, we could never hope to use time measurements to tell us whether age affects some functional processes more than others. Since speed and errors are the only task performance indices that we can measure, this would force us to adopt a 'general slowing theory' as an act of desperation rather than of theoretical parsimony. If we lack task performance indices to tell us whether age affects some processes more than others we cannot discount the possibility that it affects all of them equally, and further behavioural research is blocked. This depressing conclusion has made general slowing theories unproductive of new models for individual differences in the ways in which people represent events, objects and the relationships between them that are necessary to cope with their environments.

Fortunately there are objections to this final solution to behavioural research in cognitive gerontology. Cerella's conclusion depends on the assumption that the Brinley functions he fitted are, indeed, truly linear. Simulation studies by Anderson (1995) and Perfect (1994) have shown that apparently excellent least squares fits can disguise gross departures from linearity. To illustrate this consider one of the simulations of Anderson (1995, simulation 1).

Anderson supposed that a cognitive task could evoke processes as diverse as those involved in letter naming, mental rotation and mental calculation. He further supposed that each of these processes underwent quite different changes with age. Age changes in letter naming were described by a very steep exponential function, age changes in mental rotation by a very shallow exponential function and age changes in mental calculation by a (barely plausible) linear function. The central point is that this represents a case where all the processes undergo quite different developmental changes with age. This is a situation where the Brinley functions should depart from linearity if the clearly false hypothesis of a single global age factor is to be rejected. Table 24.2 presents the correlation coefficients of the 8-year-old children compared with all other ages for this simulation.

Table 24.2. *Fit of linear function (Pearson's r) relating simulations of 8 year old children's reaction times to the simulated reaction times of 9–20 year-olds.*

Age	Pearson's r
9	1.0
10	1.0
11	1.0
12	0.9999
13	0.9998
14	0.9997
15	0.9996
16	0.9995
17	0.9994
18	0.9993
19	0.9992
20	0.9992

Note: The simulation generating the reaction times contained three quite different development functions (see text) for the 3 hypothetical processes contributing to reaction time performance.

As can be seen the correlation (and hence the linear fit) is perfect to at least two decimal places. This shows that the interpretation of a linear fit between reaction times between age groups is likely to be heavily biased towards the single global hypothesis. This shows that Cerella's (1985) analyses could fail to detect that the extent of age-related slowing of decision times may indeed vary with the nature of the tasks on which older and younger groups are compared.

The second issue is that the inadequacy of Brinley functions as descriptions of CRT data is confirmed by empirical evidence that the effects of age on mean CRTs actually does differ between different kinds of tasks. One way to realize this is to consider that because least squares fits are approximate indices of central tendencies they tend to cause us to overlook outlying data points. If these outliers merely reflect random variability this does not affect Cerella's conclusions. However if particular tasks consistently produce data points that markedly depart from the age trends that best fit others this is good circumstantial evidence that the functional processes on which they depend are indeed differentially affected by age.

Figure 24.1 plots the mean CRTs obtained from older against those obtained from younger participants on 15 different tasks. These are well fitted by a simple linear function with a slope of 1.33. Each of the individual data points to which this function is fitted may be regarded as the ratio of mean old CRTs to mean young CRTs for that particular task. These 'Brinley ratios' are shown in Table 24.2. They markedly differ between tasks over the wide range of 1.1 to 1.6. The median value is 1.29 which is, of course, close to the mean of the slope of the Brinley function fitted to these data points in Figure 24.1. Ratios for two tasks that have been widely held to reflect the efficiency of the 'central executive' system, the conflict condition of the colour-word 'Stroop test' and a version of the 'Trails test', are much higher than this median. In contrast ratios for other tasks such as an easy CRT task (1.1) and letter/letter coding (1.15) are much lower than the mean. A single observation of these marked differences between Brinley ratios for different tasks does not, of course, challenge the assumption of a general simple linear scaling of decision times because it may simply reflect the marked random variability between measurements which is characteristic of all psychological experiments. However rank-order correlations between these Brinley ratios are robustly significant so we must conclude that they remain consistent across independent pairs of groups of older and younger people. As Anderson (1995) and Perfect (1994) have shown, the slopes of simple linear regressions fitted across mean decision times obtained from different tasks only very coarsely summarize central tendencies. Evidently this has misled us by disguising the fact that, in fact, age slows some decisions markedly more than others.

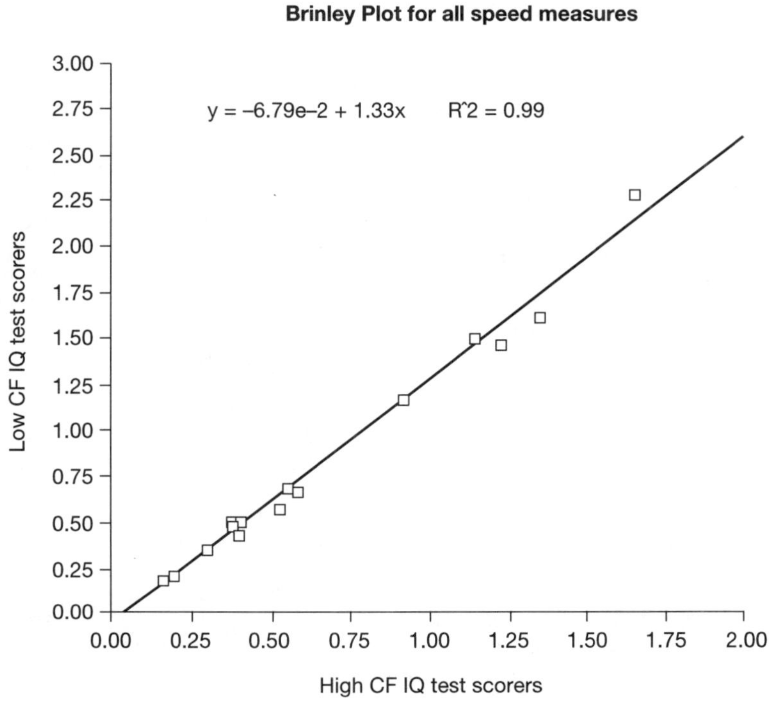

Figure 24.1

Findings that Brinley ratios actually vary widely, and consistently, between tasks would be less interesting if the particular tasks that yield unusually high Brinley ratios (i.e. on which the old are relatively more markedly slowed) were unrelated in their demands and so in their functional bases. However there is growing evidence that tasks that are disproportionately slowed by age tend to be those that involve functions attributed to the 'central executive' system, and supported by the frontal and prefrontal cortex.

This line of research stems from a growing body of opinion that 'normal' or 'usual' ageing produces structural changes earlier and more rapidly in the frontal lobes than in other parts of the cortex even in the absence of pathology (e.g. Haug & Eggers, 1991; Gur et al., 1987; Whelihan & Lesher, 1985). These changes include shrinkage of neurons (Haug & Eggers, 1991), loss of dendritic masses (Scheibel & Scheibel, 1975), reduced cerebral blood flow to the anterior cortex (Gur et al., 1987; Shaw et al., 1984), decline in levels of neurotransmitters such as dopamine (Arnsten et al., 1994), region specific declines in the concentration, synthesis and number of receptor sites for some neurotransmitters (Goldman-Rakic & Brown, 1981) and a loss of myeline (Albert, 1993). A natural speculation then is that cognitive abilities supported by the frontal lobes may be among the first to be affected by increasing age. Tests of the relative efficiency with which younger and older people can inhibit irrelevant stimuli and inappropriate response have been widely used to test this hypothesis (Daigneault, Braun, & Whitaker, 1992; Dempster, 1992). In particular Hasher and Zacks (1988) proposed that much of the decline of cognitive performance in ageing could be explained in terms of inefficient inhibition. Inhibitory mechanisms are thought to be responsible for at least three aspects of attentional control (Hasher, Quig, & May, 1997). One is to determine which of several competing activated perceptual or memorial representations will gain access into working memory so as to ensure that only information which is relevant to the task in hand is further processed. A second is to suppress representations in working memory that have recently been activated but are no longer relevant to current decisions. A third is to prevent salient or recently rejected items from controlling attention before less available alternatives can be considered. If, as Hasher and Zacks (1988) believe, inhibition functions less efficiently in older adults, their selection of information will be incomplete so that irrelevant information will gain access to working memory, information that is no longer relevant will continue to remain active in working memory and attention will frequently be given to inappropriate information.

Hence older people would be expected to be more distractible, to make more inappropriate responses and to take longer to make appropriate responses if inappropriate responses must be suppressed.

Many studies do suggest that older adults show increased distractibility and susceptibility to interference in a broad range of paradigms. An early study by Birren (1959) found that older adults showed the classical pattern of frontal impairment in verbal category generation tasks (verbal fluency tasks). That is, they are more likely to stray from the task of generating words starting with the same letter and less able to inhibit semantic associations that do not fit the experimenter's instructions. Connelly, Hasher, and Zacks (1991) found that older adults are relatively more distracted than younger adults by irrelevant information when reading a text passage. Cohen (1988) found that older adults produce more intrusions from non-presented items in free recall. Shaw (1991) found that old age increases susceptibility to interference in 'flanker' tasks, where relevant and irrelevant information is visually presented in close proximity. Rankin and Kausler (1979) found that in recognition memory tasks older adults are more likely to falsely recognize semantic associates of the words that have actually been presented, and Kausler and Hakami (1982) found that they are less likely to inhibit both well-practised and newly learned response patterns in order to acquire new ones.

In text processing tasks older adults have difficulty suppressing previously generated but no longer relevant inferences (Hamm & Hasher, 1992). They also show heightened memory for irrelevant information under certain circumstances (Hartman & Hasher, 1991). In addition, older adults perform recall tasks poorly compared to young adults; Gerard et al. (1991) suggest that this may be because they suffer from increased competition from irrelevant ideas because they cannot efficiently inhibit them.

Zacks, Radvansky, and Hasher (1996) suggest that further evidence of an inhibition deficit in older adults is their performance in tasks in which items are presented and then cued as 'to-be-remembered' (TBR) or 'to-be-forgotten' (TBF). In such 'directed forgetting' tasks older adults produce more TBF word intrusions on immediate recall, take longer to reject TBF items on a recognition test and recognize more TBF items on a delayed retention test than do younger adults. In all these cases intrusions of TBF items are explained as failures of inhibition. However, as Craik and Jennings (1992) point out, a plausible alternative explanation is that older people may be less able to register or remember the 'remember-or-forget' cues on an item-by-item cueing procedure and so are more likely to forget which items were cued as TBF or TBR.

Perhaps the most intensively studied measure of cognitive inhibition in the elderly has been their performance in the 'negative priming' paradigm. Here, commonly, two items are presented on each of a series of successive displays, one of which is the target to which the participant must respond and the other is an irrelevant distracter. On control trials both the items on the current display (*N*) are different from and unrelated to those on the previous display (*N*–1). On 'negative priming' trials the distracter on trial *N*–1 becomes the target on trial *N*. The general finding with younger adults has been that response latencies are slower on 'negative priming' trials than on control trials. The usual explanation has been that this is because the item presented as a distracter on trial *N*–1 had then to be inhibited and that its involuntary persistence slows a response to it when it immediately recurs as a target on trial *N*. Older adults generally do not show this effect. It has been argued that this is because they cannot fully inhibit the item when it is a distracter so that they do not have to overcome inhibition when it recurs as a target (e.g. Hasher et al., 1991; Kane et al., 1994; McDowd & Oseas-Kreger, 1991).

Finally many experiments have suggested that older are less efficient than younger adults at inhibiting competing channels of information in versions of the Stroop interference paradigm. The original Stroop colour-word task compares time to name aloud the ink colour of 100 coloured squares with time to name aloud the ink colour of 100 words, which were incongruent colour names. (For example, the word 'blue' is printed in red ink; participants are required to name the colour of the ink, i.e. 'red', but are slowed because of interference from the more salient word name, 'blue'.) The inhibition deficit hypothesis (Hasher & Zacks, 1988) would predict that older people should be particularly susceptible to this interference because their inability to efficiently inhibit irrelevant stimuli allows the salient but incorrect colour word access to working memory where it competes for response with the correct colour name.

A number of studies of Stroop interference have found results consistent with this expectation (e.g. Cohn, Dustman, & Bradford, 1984; Comalli, Wapner, & Werner, 1962; Houx, Jolles, & Vreeling, 1993; Panek, Rush, & Slade, 1984). Indeed reviewers have concluded that the Stroop task yields age effects that are 'almost universal' (West, 1996, p. 287) and that the Stroop interference effect is 'highly robust and age-sensitive in that older adults have been found to show more Stroop interference' (Kwong See & Ryan, 1995, p. 459). Nevertheless some well-conducted studies have failed to find significant age differences (e.g. Baumler, 1969; Kieley & Hartley 1997). It does seem that tasks that require people to inhibit attention to or processing of some aspects of stimuli in order to deal with others are, indeed, more difficult for older people and so slow their performance more than others do.

Examining Distributions of Responses Rather than Means and Medians

The problem that summary statistics can disguise informative trends in data is widespread in experimental psychology and particularly evident in comparisons of CRT measurements. A particular issue is that distributions of CRTs are markedly skewed so that their means may only poorly reflect substantial differences between them. Consequently if we compare individuals only in terms of the means and medians of CRTs we discard most of the information available from our data. Current models for the functional processes underlying fast decisions are based on differences between entire distributions of CRTs rather than means or medians alone (Luce, 1986). This makes it pertinent to ask whether differences in the shapes of distributions of CRTs made by young and old people, and perhaps also differences in the ways in which these 'young' and 'old' distributions are altered by task demands, can help us to model how age affects decision processes.

A convenient graphical technique to check whether or not two distributions of CRTs are generated by different transforms is to plot the deciles of one against the deciles of the other as 'Vincent functions'. In Figure 24.2 deciles of CRT distributions from three-choice, four-choice and five-choice CRT tasks obtained from a group of 23 people aged from 50 to 59 years (mean 56, SD 3.5) were plotted against those obtained from a group of 28 people aged from 70 to 79 years (mean 72.8, SD 4.2). All these Vincent plots were well fitted by a common linear function with an intercept of 30.2 and a slope of 1.3 (Stollery, Moore, & Rabbitt, in preparation). This seems *prima facie* evidence that the effects of age are to linearly transform distributions of decision times and that the simple multiplier in this transformation does not alter with the relative levels of difficulty of the tasks on which age groups are compared.

Parenthetically these particular data also illustrate that when we study the effects of age on decision times we do need to consider entire distributions of CRTs rather than simply means or medians. If we consider differences between older and younger groups in terms of each successive decile, in turn from fastest to slowest, there is no age effect for any decile lower then the 5th (median). Another way of putting this is that there is no evidence from this study that age reduces the speed of the fastest responses that people make. Older people's mean and median CRTs are slower not because they cannot make fast correct responses but because they make more slow responses. This sets us the problem of finding a functional model that accounts for the way

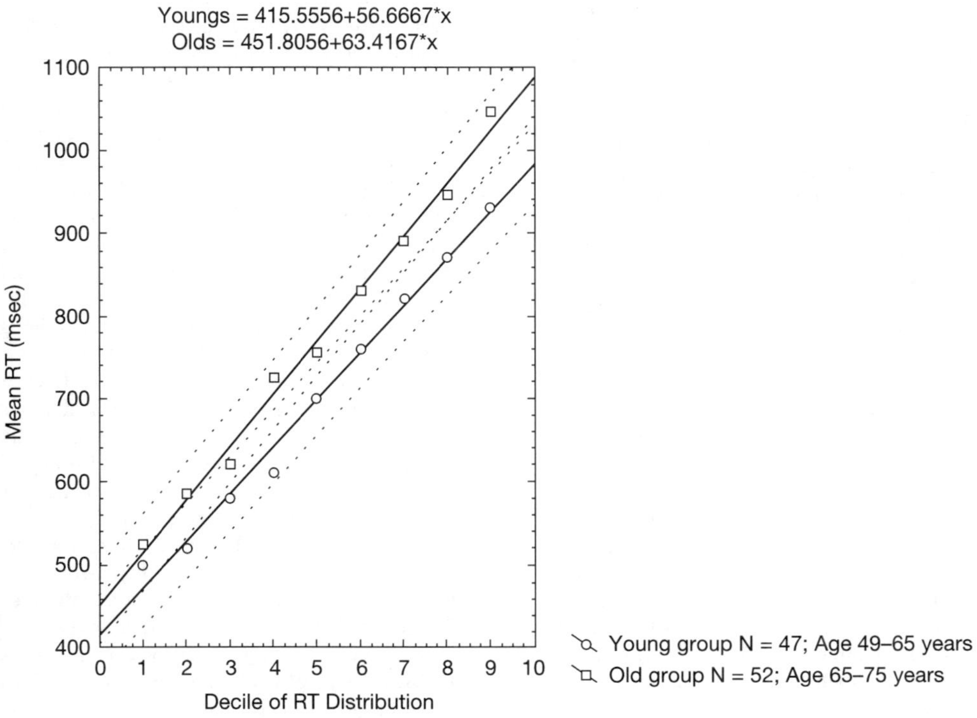

Figure 24.2

in which increasing age transforms CRT distributions to produce this selectively greater effect on slow responses.

An extreme assumption is that fast and slow CRTs may be generated by quite different functional processes and that the processes generating slow responses are more sensitive to the effects of age. This may seem an unlikely hypothesis, but in fact there are precedents in the literature that have provided some employment for cognitive gerontologists.

This pattern of age-related differences in CRT distributions is analogous to findings that fatigue and stress do not increase mean or median CRTs but do markedly increase the numbers of correct responses which are more than 1.5 SD slower than the distribution mean or median. One explanation for these exceptionally slow responses is that they represent lapses of continuous attention which cause 'blocks' or 'gaps' during which information processing is slowed or interrupted (see Broadbent, 1971; Stollery, 1987; 1990; Stollery et al., 1991). In the distributions illustrated in Figure 24.2, if CRTs greater than 1.5 SD are disregarded as being due to interruptions of this kind, the remaining faster deciles do not differ between age groups. In other words, in these very easy CRT tasks the entire effects of age can be explained as an increase in rare, exceptionally slow responses which investigators have considered to reflect brief failures to sustain attention rather than indices of information processing speed. Similar results have been reported by Bunce, Warr, and Cochrane (1993) and others. This possibility raises obvious difficulties for a 'general slowing' model of age-related cognitive change. The main proponent of this theory, Tim Salthouse (1996), was quick to seek a resolution. He replicated the usual finding that the CRT distributions of the elderly were markedly skewed relative to those of the young because they included many more very slow responses. However he analysed his data by running successive hierarchical regression analyses to assess the amount of variance in values of each successive decile which was predicted by individuals' ages after predictions from all faster deciles had been taken into consideration. He iteratively continued entering increasingly slow deciles as predictors and found that as this was done values for slowest deciles were increasingly well predicted. Further, as he included increasing numbers of early deciles the contributions of age to variance in later deciles declined and eventually entirely disappeared. He concluded that the entire effects of age on the slowest deciles of CRT distributions could be accounted for in terms of corresponding differences in the faster deciles of the same distributions.

Because the logical assumptions underlying such comparisons are interesting it is helpful to ignore mathematical anomalies in this particular statistical analysis such as the successive entry as predictors of very highly correlated variables (successive deciles of the same distribution) or the mishandling of multiple regression to partial out age-related variance for which Salthouse has elsewhere received magisterial rebuke (Pedhozur, 1997).

All models for decision processes are based on the assumption that distributions of CRTs are generated by processes whose termination times vary from trial to trial and that it is possible to derive algebraic functions to describe, and so to simulate, this variability. Thus, in this framework of description, all of the CRTs in any empirically observed distributions, even those obtained from populations including both older and younger people, can be well described by at least one function, however complex. The process of making predictions of each successive decile from cumulatively greater numbers of earlier deciles amounts to progressively better extrapolation of the unknown function describing the function, as successive data points are entered. The gradual disappearance of the effect of individual differences associated with age as the extrapolation of the function is improved is as uninformative as it is inevitable. This procedure, at best, confirms that entire distributions of CRTs generated by older and younger people are regular in the sense that there is at least one function that will generate both the faster and the slower CRTs that they contain. The assumption that this analysis can show that the *speed* of faster decisions can completely predict the *speed* of the slower decisions once again illustrates the logical error of confusing the algebraic properties of a particular series of measurements, in this case of speed, with the functional processes that generate particular, complex patterns of that index of measurement that we observe.

This point is well illustrated by a statistically more sophisticated exploration of differences between CRT distributions produced by older and younger adults made by Spieler, Balota, and Faust (1996). These authors compared CRT distributions produced by older, middle aged and younger adults on baseline and interference conditions of a version of the Stroop task. They found that for baseline conditions CRT distributions of older and younger adults could be related by simple transforms but that for the interference condition the best description of the difference between age groups was to assume that distributions were composites of two separate distributions. The difference between the CRT distributions of youngest and the oldest groups tested was best accounted for by a proportionately greater change in the distribution including the slowest responses made. If these results are replicable the mean CRTs of older people are relatively more slowed on the conflict condition of the Stroop test than on other tasks because there are qualititative, rather than merely quantitative, changes in the distributions of CRTs that they produce. This would be further evidence that old age affects some efficient inhibition of intrusive signals and responses more than other functional processes.

Nevertheless the collinearity of Vincent plots illustrated in Figure 24.2 suggests that, at least in some simple tasks, the effects of age are to produce linear rather than complex transformations of CRT distributions. This may be seen as a hopeful outcome since it may help us to identify a particular class of functional models that would produce this particular relationship rather than any other. Let us disregard, for the moment, the difficulties of assuming linearity from least squares fits that we have discussed above in order to consider how some of the many very different functional models for fast decisions might account for simple linear transforms. Note that the models discussed are not chosen because they are the most credible, topical or sophisticated available. They are only selected to show how the same pattern of relationships can be explained by any of a variety of models based on quite different functional assumptions.

Perhaps the simplest possible model for age-related slowing in CRTs derives from Cerella's (1985) landmark paper. This assumes that each signal that occurs during a CRT task activates the same chain of *N* successive information processing units which, acting in series, identify it, and then select and execute an appropriate response to it. If each successive unit has an operating time *t*, observed CRTs will be a function of (*Nt*). That is, CRTs will be slower for difficult decisions that require chains of many units than for easier decisions that require fewer units. These simple assumptions can account for robust findings that, across tasks with very different levels of difficulty and qualitative demands, mean CRTs for groups of older or less able people can be closely estimated by multiplying mean CRTs for groups of younger or more able people by a simple, empirically derived, age or ability constant (Cerella, 1985; Rabbitt & Maylor, 1991; Rabbitt, 1996a; 1996b). If we suppose that greater age or reduced ability lags the operating time for each unit by a constant *L* ms, changes in mean CRT with age and ability will be a simple linear function of *LtN*. In terms of this simplistic description the fact that distributions of CRTs always vary widely about their means can most easily be explained by supposing that the operating time *t* of each unit is not constant, but also varies from trial to trial. In this case observed distributions of CRTs will directly reflect the summed operating times of entrained chains of units and so also the unobservable distributions of the termination times for individual units. On the further assumption that the lag for each unit *L* is constant, additive, and independent of unit operating time *t*, the effect of greater age or lower ability will be to move the entire CRT distribution along the reaction time axis without altering its shape. In this case mean CRTs will increase but with no change in the variance of the CRT distributions from which they are derived. In fact this is not the case and greater age, lower general intellectual ability and the ingestion of alcohol all appear to multiplicatively scale entire CRT distributions with consequently greater effects on slow than on fast CRTs (see Rabbitt & Maylor, 1991). This makes it necessary to assume that the age scaling of distributions of unit operating times *t* is multiplicative rather than additive and so increases slower operating times relatively more than faster operating times. Given these assumptions this simple adaptation of the unit lag model, which is congenial for explanations of individual differences in terms of delayed synaptic transmission or slower neural conduction pathways, can generate the prediction that a change in a single hypothetical neurophysiological system performance parameter, unit lag, will markedly increase the variances, as well as the means, of CRT distributions.

However satisfaction would be premature because the same data can be equally well explained by models derived from many quite different assumptions about the nature of functional processes underlying fast decisions. For example, to account for the logarithmic, or power, functions that characterize improvements with practice in decision speeds on all tasks, Crossman (1958) assumed that, early in practice, decisions may be made by any one of a number of different pathways. Some of these pathways are optimally direct, involve few units and so identify signals and select responses faster than others which entrain more processing units. Early in practice optimal and suboptimal pathways are selected more or less at random with the result that average decision times are slow and trial-to-trial variability is large. As practice continues fast optimal pathways are progressively selected and slow inefficient pathways are progressively discarded with a consequent logarithmic or power function reduction in mean decision times and a directly proportional reduction in trial-to-trial variance.

This model can also account for individual differences in the means and variances of decision times without any assumption of changes in the transmission lags of units. Instead we may suggest that older or less able individuals have impoverished decision networks with a smaller likelihood of maximally efficient pathways, or that they are less able to optimize pathway selection. Note that in this case we appear to lose parsimony because we must invoke not one but several distinct functional system performance characteristics in order to explain individual differences and changes in the forms of CRT distributions. However in return for this we can explain not only individual differences in mean CRTs and CRT variance but also differences in the rates at which people of different ages and levels of ability improve the means and SDs of their CRTs during practice.

Many more recent, elegant and plausible parallel process models are reviewed by Luce (1986). These focus on the fact that CRT distributions can be modelled by Poisson distributions or gamma functions. Such descriptions closely fit the output characteristics predicted for 'distributed parallel self-terminating' systems which assume that to make any decision a number of pathways are simultaneously activated and proceed to termination. A response is chosen by selecting the first pathway to terminate ('first-past-the-post horse-race model') or by averaging of some sample of the outcomes of a subset of these processes. In these cases time-proportionate lagging of all pathways by the same multiplicative constant would predict the same linear scaling of CRT distributions as would the model by Crossman (1958) discussed above. Thus alternative explanations of individual differences to unit lag can be based on the assumptions that decision criteria, or the number of parallel pathways that can be simultaneously activated, vary with age or with general intellectual ability.

Predictions similar to those made by distributed parallel process models can also be derived from quite different functional assumptions than unit lag or pathway selection or alteration of decision criteria. Rabbitt and Vyas (1969) and Smith and Brewer (1995) suggest that people actively control the distributions of their CRTs by varying their response speed from trial to trial so as to locate a region within which both speed and accuracy can be maximized. Individuals are known to make most of their errors because they transgress this optimal trade-off region, but can recognize most of the errors that they make and use this feedback to slow their responses and so improve their accuracy. In contrast people can detect unnecessarily slow responses only by reference to an internal 'clock' or 'timekeeper'. On this model older and younger or more and less able people may differ hardly at all in terms of their speed–error trade-off limits, and so in terms of the fastest correct responses that they can make. They may nevertheless markedly differ in terms of the skews of their CRT distributions and so in their mean CRTs. As we have noted, differences in mean CRTs largely reflect the fact that older people make many more unnecessarily slow responses. Rabbitt and Vyas (1969) suggested that this increased variability may be due to failures of speed monitoring or to imprecision of the internal 'clock' which is used to measure and adjust response speed. Wearden, Wearden, and Rabbitt (1997) found that while older and younger individuals may be equally accurate in the *average* accuracy of time interval duration judgements or of interval generation, older and less able participants show markedly greater variability in these tasks. Thus individual differences in variability of time-estimation and interval production could directly account for the effects of age and ability on CRT variability.

Note that we do not suggest that these models exhaust, or even illustrate, the entire range current in the literature, let alone that they are the best articulated or most plausible available. They are arbitrarily selected only to make the point that models derived from very different functional assumptions can all equally well account for all existing data on consistent individual differences in mean and median decision times and trial-to-trial variance. Unfortunately it cannot be guaranteed that collection of further behavioural data will clarify this issue. Townsend and Ashby (1983) have formally shown that even if such data become available they will be equally well fitted by a variety of very different functional models. We may have to face the predicament that, in principle, data on the means and distributions of CRTs may not uniquely support any single functional model that maps on to a corresponding, uniquely plausible, description of decision-making processes in the human CNS. At present it seems that the best hope is not to search for any single 'master' task performance index or system performance characteristic that can account for individual differences in performance in CRT tasks. It seems more realistic to hope that convergent evidence from advances in techniques such as evoked potential recording, scanning and imaging, or multiple cell recording, make new kinds of data available so that it becomes possible to choose between the many different interpretations that behavioural data leave open.

Conclusions from Consideration of Age Differences in Choice Reaction Times

These discussions of the radically different assumptions that can guide analyses of CRT data are not intended to disparage the clever and sincere attempts of cognitive gerontologists to find the most parsimonious explanations possible. Still less do we intend to suggest that the task must be hopeless. These examples are only offered as an objective illustration of the logical issue raised in the beginning of this chapter: the problems that arise if we mistake entities at one level of description with those at another. In particular, we should not mistake task performance indices such as inspection time or choice reaction time to be the logical equivalents of performance characteristics of hypothetical functional models, let alone of complex neurophysiological systems. We may briefly consider attempts to generalize descriptions in terms of relative processing speed even beyond CRT paradigms, to explain individual differences in memory, in which efficiency is compared in terms of accuracy rather than in speed of processing.

Applications of Global Single Factor Speed Theories to Age Changes in Memory Efficiency

Evidently global single factor speed theories are weak if they can only, tautologously, explain individual differences in tasks in which the only performance index measured is speed, rate or decision time. A suitable test of their generality is their application to memory tasks in which the usual indices of measurement are errors rather than decision times. There are clear findings that age differences in efficiency of list learning are related to the times allowed to enable them to anticipate and study individual items (Arenberg, 1965; Canestrari, 1963; Hulicka, Sterns, & Grossman, 1967; Monge & Hultsch, 1971; Waugh & Barr, 1980; Witte, 1975). This is what we would expect given that the rate at which people can recognize and rehearse material presented to them sharply declines with age. However there has been no suggestion that these relationships are well described by regular scaling related to mean decision times. Nor would models for memory and learning predict this. In contrast to tasks involving decision times it is very clear that the apparently minor differences in the qualitative nature of task demands bring about large differences in the relative efficiency of older and younger people. Current theories of memory are based on differences in task demands which might affect the structure and nature of mental representations of to-be-remembered information rather than speed of information processing. Such task demands have included instructions to recall early or late items in lists, to recall pictures rather than words or vice versa, to recognisze only whether items seem familiar or unfamiliar or to identify them specifically, to deliberately forget some lists while remembering others, to recall the sources as well as the content of information, to overcome interference from earlier to later items in a list or vice versa. As comprehensive reviews show, theories of change in memory efficiency with age are based on changes in sensitivity to these and other task demands, and so are concerned with possible age changes in the ways in which information can be represented in memory (Cohen, 1996; Craik & Jennings, 1992; Kausler, 1982). Changes in information processing speed are not an integral part of these theories and are difficult to incorporate into descriptions of different kinds of representations of events in memory or into the relationships between memorial representations and seem to have nothing useful to add to them.

There is, as yet, no proposal for any single, overarching, general theory of ageing memory, nor has there been any serious suggestion that global changes in memory efficiency must underlie all age-related changes in all mental abilities. On the contrary, there is accumulating evidence that age related changes in memory efficiency may begin earlier than, and proceed separately to, concomitant changes in general mental ability and that these changes are not well predicted by concomitant changes in information processing speed (Rabbitt, 1993). In other words memory seems to depend on a relatively 'modular' system that is more vulnerable to the effects of ageing than other mental abilities.

Attempts to account for age-related changes in memory ability in terms of global single factor speed theories have been based on two kinds of analysis. The first is to make principal components analyses of the scores obtained by older and younger adults on a variety of tasks, including memory tasks and tests of information processing speed. Participant age is also entered as a factor. In analyses of some data sets age has been found to be represented in a first factor together with information processing speed and with memory test scores (Salthouse, 1985; 1991). However in other analyses of data from quite similar tests age is found to load on a second factor, separate from information speed and scores on tests of general mental ability, which load on a first factor (Rabbitt & Yang, 1996). Such failures of replication are unsurprising because the patterns of associations revealed by principal components analyses are notoriously labile to the omission and inclusion of particular task scores. A second technique pioneered by Salthouse (1996) has been to obtain scores on a single memory task and on a number of different tests of information processing speed from the same group of older and younger adults. Participants' ages and scores on tests of decision speed are then entered as predictors of memory test scores in a series of hierarchical regression analyses. A frequent finding is that age ceases to be a significant predictor when scores from a sufficient number of tests of information processing speed have been entered. The argument is that all variance in memory test scores that is associated with age can be accounted for if variance in decision speed is partialled out by this process of cumulative entry.

This procedure is again neither logically nor statistically straightforward (see discussion by Rabbitt & Yang, 1996). It has also been criticized as a misuse of multiple regression (Pedhozur, 1997). However there are also empirical problems because as has often been remarked (e.g. by Burgess, 1998; Weiskrantz, 1992), 'there is no such thing as a pure test'. This is true in two different senses. The first is that our conventional labels for mental abilities are terms such as 'memory', 'attention', 'problem solving' or 'fast decision making' which are borrowed from our common-language descriptions of our interactions with the world. Our understanding of the functional boundaries between the functional processes by means of which we carry out the activities which we differentiate by these labels is imperfect. In this state of ignorance it is reckless to assume that common-language labels for what we perceive as different kinds of task demands also precisely reflect distinctions in the functional processes by means of which these demands are carried out. The second sense in which it is true that no task is pure is the simple empirical problem that it is very difficult to design a task that makes demands on only a single 'mental ability' or 'cognitive skill'. For example even easy, straightforward choice reaction time tasks require participants to remember throughout the task which response key is appropriate to which signals and to continuously sustain attention to a particular display and set of response keys during the testing session. Closer examination of the evidence that age-related variance in memory ability can be entirely accounted for in terms of variance in decision speeds actually provides empirical evidence for the existence of this problem. In all putative demonstrations that age-related variance in memory test scores can be entirely accounted for by progressive partialling out of variance associated with performance on different tests of decision speed, it turns out that this is not achieved unless, and until, speed scores from letter/letter or digit/symbol coding tasks have been entered as predictors. There is now firm evidence that levels of performance on these coding tasks are heavily dependent on memory (Piccinin & Rabbitt, 1999). Thus it is only when scores from a highly memory dependent task are entered that age-related variance in memory test scores is entirely removed.

SINGLE GLOBAL THEORIES AND COGNITIVE DEVELOPMENT

In developmental psychology global speed theories have been much less ambitious, probably because the existence of a much larger, older and richer literature emphasizes issues of mental representations and acquisition of knowledge of the world, language and social responsibilities and interactions to which they obviously cannot make any contribution. However, the last decade has seen a concerted attempt to attribute much of developmental change in cognitive abilities during child development to some sort of single global factor (Hale, 1990; Kail, 1986; 1991a; 1991b; Kail & Park, 1992; Kail & Salthouse, 1994). As in the recent theories of cognitive ageing we have reviewed above, the candidate factor is speed of information processing. While this research ostensibly is restricted to explaining the source of developmental changes in speeded task performance such as reaction time tasks, the implication is that a single fundamental change in information processing can account for the increasing general intellectual competence of the child. Note that a sharp distinction from the global speed theories used in cognitive gerontology has been that no investigators in this research area would claim that changing speed is all that there is to be said about cognitive change in children, or even that changes in information speed underlie developmental changes in all cognitive skills. However many do argue that such a factor can provide the causal basis of change, even though the details might require fleshing out, for example, in one of a variety of working memory models (see for example the cascade model of Fry & Hale, 1996). Before discussing this research in more detail it is worth considering its intellectual predecessors to gain a feel for what kind of explanation of cognitive change it offers.

General theories of cognitive development can still be said to be dominated by the examples set by Piaget in that they hold the twin aims of theory to be the adequate description of the knowledge states of the child and an explanation for developmental change in those knowledge states. To some extent what we see today in the single global research literature is an explicit separation of these two aims, a separation begun by Pascual-Leone 30 years ago.

The Work of Pascual-Leone

Pascual-Leone can be considered the first of those who came to be known as the neo-Piagetians. Pascual-Leone's (1970) structural theory is very Piagetian, positing that the knowledge structure of the child goes through a series of qualitative changes each representing a quite different understanding of central concepts such as space, time and number. The major difference from Piaget is that Pascual-Leone posits that a cognitive 'capacity' called M-space, or central processing space, increases during development. This increasing capacity allows for the increased complexity in representations available to the child. This is both reminiscent of, and interestingly different from, the use of 'information processing speed' as a single, global cognitive resource in the theories of intelligence by Jensen (1980) and Eysenck (1986) or in the theory of cognitive ageing proposed by Salthouse (1985; 1991). In the most general sense, M-space does represent a single common resource whose degree of availability limits both cognitive performance in a range of specific tasks, and the complexity and generality of representations of knowledge and of relationships between aspects of the world. However there is no claim either that this resource can be directly measured by a single class of experimental paradigms, or that it directly reflects any particular functional characteristic of the central nervous system such as 'synaptic conduction rate', 'global neural noise' or number and degree of connectivity of available neural units (see Eysenck, 1986).

The Work of Case

Case (1985) produced perhaps the best-known and most detailed development of the idea that capacity and development are related. Case argued that development could be characterized as the progression through four major qualitatively different developmental stages: sensorimotor, relational, dimensional and vectorial. These stages are in turn characterized as utilizing different kinds of control structures. In turn these control structures utilize a working memory that has associated capacity restrictions, both in a central executive and in a short-term memory store. In order to solve problems the child must perform computations (the nature of which are determined by the control structures). These are implemented in central processing space and use the short-term store to keep track of their intermediate products. The control structures call on different amounts of central executive space and impose different loads on short-term storage space. Thus as central executive space increases with developmental age, older children can implement control structures that are beyond the central processing and memory capacity of younger children. However, the way in which this comes about represents an interesting twist in Case's theory.

Whereas Pascual-Leone argued that capacity increased through development, allowing the increased complexity of control structures to be implemented, Case argues that the total capacity available to the cognitive system is the same throughout development. What changes is not the total capacity available but rather the capacity demands of control structures. Parenthetically we may note that this also is a radical difference from global speed models as used in cognitive gerontology and differential psychology in which the total available resource, defined in terms of information processing speed, declines with age and differs between more and less gifted individuals. The emphasis on 'control structures', and the idea that control structures may be more or less optimal and so solve the same behavioural and representational problems with more or less demand on the available pool of resources, are also sharp insights that have not been developed in cognitive gerontology. The nearest equivalent is, perhaps, the distinction made by Horn (1982) between 'fluid' intelligence, g_f, that declines with age, and 'crystallised' intelligence, g_c, which is age-robust. In this framework g_c is defined as knowledge of the world and of particular problem solving procedures which are acquired over a lifetime and can be maintained by continued practice into old age. It is interesting that, in the Horn model, the learning of the acquired toolkit of crystallized knowledge and procedural skills, and so in some sense its scope, will be determined by the level of g_f available to the person learning them. Case's valuable insight that the more optimal skills and procedures are, the less demanding of central resources they may be, has not been developed in this context. In a sideways step Case links available cognitive capacity to underlying neurophysiology. He argues that the capacity demands of control structures decrease during development because they are processed more efficiently, perhaps because of increased myelinization of the nervous system (to be coherent, increasing myelinization cannot create a concomitant increase in capacity). However, the more general point is that as skills and procedures become better articulated because of practice, so they may reduce the demands that they make on any pool of resources available to support them.

While Case's theory shares much with that of Pascual-Leone, because he denies that cognitive capacity (or central processing space) increases during development, his theory cannot be placed strictly in a single global model camp. However, another theory that takes a fundamentally different structural approach to cognitive development to either Pascual-Leone or Case, shares Pascual-Leone's hypothesis for the mechanism of cognitive change.

The Work of Halford

Halford's theory of the development of thinking (Halford, 1987; 1993) can be considered the most sophisticated development of the idea that change in cognitive structure might be causally related to a change in information processing capacity. Halford's ideas themselves come in two stages. The first stage (Halford, 1987) was based on the match between an information processing analysis of thinking, such as making transitive inferences, and experimental measures of cognitive capacity using dual-task procedures (Halford, Maybery, & Bain, 1986). Halford argues that the problems can be analyzed in terms of their relational structure and that cognitive development involves the ability to process structures of increasing relational complexity. In the initial formulation of the theory there were three levels of relational complexity that required three corresponding levels of what Halford called 'structure mapping'. The following examples should convey the flavour of this approach.

The simplest level of mapping is element mapping. Here a single element of information has to be mapped onto a single element of another representational structure. For example, a name, such as John, has to be mapped onto an element of a structure that represents other features (and relations) of the individual named John. But in element mapping no other relations are affected. So the relation 'X is big' can be modified to 'John is big' when the element information 'John' is mapped to the element 'X' without any constraint of other relations in the representation. So in element mapping a single relation 'X is called John' must be processed. The next level of mapping requires that at least two relational attributes are mapped: 'John is bigger than Mary' requires mapping onto representational structures that contain elements onto which John and Mary are mapped as well as the relation 'bigger than'. The next level of mapping must also preserve not only element and relational mappings but also relations that might be inferred from the system. Solutions to transitive inference problems – 'John is taller than Mary, Mary is taller than Tom, who is taller, John or Tom?' – require system mappings to compute answers. Halford's contention is that each level of mapping imposes a greater load on available cognitive capacity and that cognitive capacity increases through development affording consequently qualitative changes in the reasoning abilities of children. For Halford, capacity (at least in the sense used in his earlier work) can be regarded as a 'resource' and can be measured using, for example, dual-task procedures such as those of Lansman and Hunt (1982). Such procedures can be used to estimate the capacity demands of tasks (by observing the cost on secondary task performance of primary tasks of different mapping complexity) and the resources of individuals (by observing individual differences in 'spare capacity' when processing tasks of the same mapping complexity: see for example Halford, Maybery, & Bain, 1986).

In the second stage of his theory (Halford, 1993; 1999; Halford, Wilson, & Phillips, 1998) this straightforward dichotomy between capacity as a resource and relational mapping as a structural feature of representations has become more blurred. This is probably due to a desire to implement this theory in a connectionist system with a consequent change in the underlying formalism. The three levels of mapping have become three levels of binding between a relation symbol R and its arguments (a, b, c, . . . , n). So the general case for a relation can be written as $R(a, b, c, \ldots, n)$. The complexity of relations is given by the number of arguments which in turn defines the number of problem dimensions (Halford, 1999). In this framework we can view a proposition as a unary relation binding with one argument. For example, the proposition 'John is big' can be expressed BIG(John). A binary relation has two arguments, thus BIGGER-THAN(John, Mary) for John is bigger than Mary; and a tertiary relation such as a love-triangle (Halford, 1999) has three arguments, thus TRIANGLE(John, Mary, Tom). Finally a quartenary relation entails a binding between a relation and four arguments: for example, a proportion such as $a/b = c/d$ can be represented by the relation PROPORTION(a, b, c, d). The new system neatly ties the number of arguments to the number of problem dimensions and to the consequent 'capacity cost'. In this way it provides an interesting theoretical link between the cause of developmental change and the structure of cognition at different ages.

We can see, then, that the capacity theories of developmental change can be regarded as the historical precedent for the single global theories of the late 1980s and 1990s. The point of examining the examples of Case and Halford in detail is to emphasize how much modern research has diverged from these earlier theoretical precedents. In the earlier theories there was an attempt to relate the mechanism of cognitive change to the constructs in the structural theory. Conversely, later research, inspired explicitly by the idea of a single global factor underlying cognitive development, has diverged from this aim by fully divorcing the causal and structural questions. These later theories started from the hypothesis that there was such a causal factor and that this factor might be speed of processing. It was only *after* they had established the plausibility of this hypothesis to their own satisfaction that they sought instantiations of this causal factor within a cognitive structure (e.g. the cascade model of working memory: Fry & Hale, 1996). This strategy has been a mistake for three reasons.

The first mistake is that this shift has constituted, in effect, an unacknowledged change from a cognitive to a pseudo-physiological level of explanation. The cost of this manoeuvre is that it allows no clear way back to theories of cognitive structure. The idea that changes in a single system performance parameter determine the levels of efficiency of all cognitive skills is an unhelpful appeal to a *deus ex machina* unless we also explain precisely how they bring about corresponding changes in higher order representation and computation. As for single factor models in cognitive gerontology, unless these relationships are clearly articulated we are left with the unhelpful tautology 'more' (information processing speed/capacity, etc.) 'is better' (representation/computation of variables and relationships between them).

The second reason why this theoretical manoeuvre has been unsuccessful follows directly from the first. Adoption of single global factor theories may lead to a mind-set in which it may no longer be seen as a requirement of a theory of cognitive development that it can address questions of the structure of cognition at different ages. While in principle this might not be such a bad thing, if the distinction between levels of description of 'single factors' and of their implementation in cognitive structure remains unacknowledged, a global single factor theory may appear to lay claim to be something which it is not – that is, a theory of cognitive development in the spirit of Piaget. Note that this is not to argue that Piaget's specific theory is the correct one, but rather to argue that a single global theory cannot succeed where Piaget failed because it operates at a different level of description. A single global factor theory may be successful only to a limited extent because it has only taken on, at most, half of what is most interesting and has to be explained.

The third reason this strategy might have been a mistake is, as we shall see, that it is by no means clear that it is empirically supported.

The developmental research on the single global factor has used much the same methods and logic that we encountered in the gerontological research described above, particularly in its interpretation of Brinley functions. However, the developmental research has also attempted to answer the specific question of whether speed of processing is the single global factor by measuring speed 'directly'. This has been done, primarily, by measuring inspection times and reaction times in children of different ages. The results leave no doubt that reaction times and inspection times decrease with age and such findings are consistent with the speculation that a global change in information processing speed may underlie developmental changes in cognitive ability. However, as we have seen, measures of the duration, rates or speed of decisions should not be confused with the functional processes that may underlie them. When we look more closely at this literature with this point in mind we can see that a quite different interpretation can be placed on the data.

Changes in Reaction Time and Inspection Time with Age in Children

Reaction time measures of task performance show a regular decrease across a variety of information processing domains, for example letter-name retrieval (Kail, 1986; Keating & Bobbitt, 1978), mental rotation (Kail, 1986; 1988), memory search (Kail, 1986; Keating & Bobbitt, 1978), and numerical calculation (Kail, 1988). Of course, it could be argued that it is children's increasing familiarity with these processing domains that causes faster processing rather than faster processing being a general feature of the older child. However, even simpler, domain-free measures of reaction time have been shown to improve with age. A classical reaction time task is that used to investigate the Hick/Hyman law (Hick, 1952; Hyman, 1953). This law states that reaction time (RT) increases as a logarithmic function (to the base 2) of the number of stimulus–response alternatives. In other words, each doubling of the number of stimulus–response mappings from two-choice to four-choice to eight-choice leads to a constant increase in reaction time. This constant increase in RT has been used by many to indicate rate or speed of processing, indexed by the slope of the linear function of RT on information load (choice), henceforth called the Hick function. Jensen (1982) claims that the slope of the Hick function is related to differences in IQ in adults. Indeed, this is one of the cornerstones of his claim that intelligence is based on individual differences in speed of processing.

The logic of using the slope of these Hick functions as an index of information processing speed can be applied to any individual differences dimension (such as intelligence or age), but has been so only rarely in the case of children (Connolly, 1970). A seminal reaction time study conducted by Fairweather and Hutt (1978) showed that the slopes of Hick functions are steeper for younger than for older children. If we were to take the slope of the Hick function as a measure of the speed of central processing in children, as Jensen does for adults, then we would conclude that the speed of central processing increases regularly with developmental age. Before we examine this claim more closely we should consider how changes in inspection time with age have been interpreted.

Inspection time (the minimum stimulus onset asynchrony, SOA, between a stimulus and a backward mask required by a subject to maintain a certain level of stimulus identification accuracy) correlates about –0.5 with IQ in adult populations (Kranzler & Jensen, 1989; Nettelbeck, 1987) and has been shown to decrease with age during development (Nettelbeck & Wilson, 1985). High IQ subjects have shorter inspection times than lower IQ subjects and older children have shorter inspection times than younger children. But does it follow that what distinguishes children with higher from those with lower IQ, and older children from younger, is the same underlying variable (speed of processing)? It is this question that lies at the heart of much of our criticism of the research on the single global hypothesis: an answer in the affirmative rests on the assumption that inspection time is an acceptable measure of the theoretical construct 'speed of processing' in any sample of children from whom IT data can be obtained. But this in turn necessitates other assumptions, namely (1) that the IT task measures only one process (with the corollary that individual differences in that process bear a one-to-one relationship to individual differences in speed of processing), or (2) that if IT measures more than one process then *all* of these processes are affected by age (or by IQ, or by whatever) to the same degree. Can we claim that this is true for even a relatively simple task like inspection time?

Anderson (1986) argued that younger children may perform more poorly on inspection time tasks for reasons incidental to their speed of processing (defined as the construct related to IQ differences in adults). For example the age difference in IT might occur because younger children are less experienced in doing such tasks (and that, in contrast, individual differences in experience do not contribute to the IT/IQ relationship in adults), or because younger children may have poorer selective attention. Both of these explanations have been refuted (respectively, by Nettelbeck & Vita, 1992, and by Anderson, 1989a). However a third possibility has received some support: Anderson (1989b) found that increasing the perceptual load of an inspection time task increased inspection times equally for older and younger children. This suggests that the speed of stimulus categorization does not change with age. However he also found that increases in the *response selection* demands of the task affected younger more than older children. In other words, even in a relatively simple task like inspection time, we find that two empirically dissociable components of the task are differentially sensitive to ageing. Anderson (1992) subsequently argued that developmental changes in ability to cope with response selection demands might account for developmental differences in speeded task performance and that the functional processes underlying response selection may be unrelated to the speed of processing factor that is correlated with IQ differences in adults. If this is the case, then it is likely that this confound (between IQ-related speed of processing in adults, and age-related response selection in children) would be exacerbated in reaction time tasks. An experiment by Anderson, Nettelbeck, and Barlow (1997) sought to test this hypothesis using two reaction time tasks that differed in their response selection demands.

Jensen's research on the relationship between reaction time and IQ in adults has used a modified version of a Hick procedure and this modification turns out to be important for our investigation of what RT measures in children as opposed to adults. In the Jensen procedure the subject holds down a home button before moving to press a button below one of the stimulus lights. Two components are extracted in Jensen's task: *decision time* to lift the finger off the home button after the appearance of the stimulus, and *movement time* between lifting the finger off the home button and touching the target button. In Jensen's procedure decision time is taken to be equivalent to reaction time in a Hick procedure. Crucially, in the Jensen task the response is made with the same finger, and the lifting of this finger is all that is required to register a reaction time. In other words, the response selection demand of the task (at least in terms of which finger is used to indicate the response choice) is low. If we look again at the classic study of Fairweather and Hutt (1978) described above, we find that this study used a *standard* Hick procedure where each reaction time is registered by a different key press. So as the number of choices increases so does the number of fingers that a child must use to register its response (two choices require two fingers, four choices four fingers, and eight choices eight fingers). This is a much higher response selection demand than the Jensen version of reaction time. Anderson, Nettelbeck, & Barlow (1997) decided to compare performance on high and low response selection tasks to test the hypothesis that speed of processing would decrease with age only in the task with high demand: in other words that Hick functions produced by older children should have shallower slopes than those produced by younger children. The data for 7- and 9-year-old children are shown in Figure 24.3.

The prediction was borne out. The slope of the Hick function only differed between groups when response selection demands were high. Thus whether or not speed of processing can be considered to change with age depends on which task is used to index the Hick function. It seems likely that younger children have more difficulty in selecting and inhibiting responses than older children and that this, rather than changes in overall speed of information

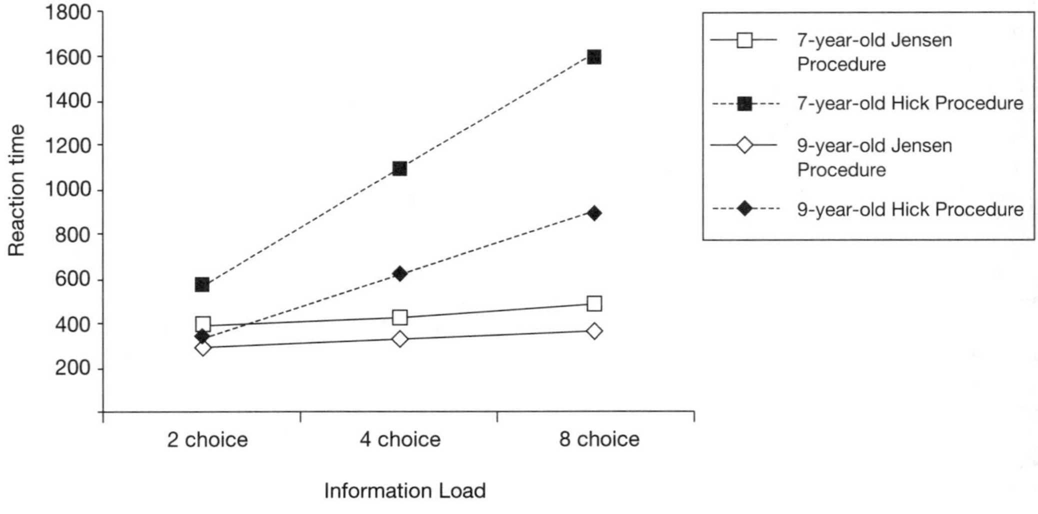

Figure 24.3 *Reaction time as a function of age, information load (choice) and type of task procedure. Adapted from Anderson, Nettelbeck & Barlow (1997), Figure 3.*

processing, may be the source of their longer reaction times. As we shall see this is consistent with conclusions we would draw from the more sophisticated Brinley method of testing the single global hypothesis.

Brinley Plots and the Speed Hypothesis for Developmental Change

As in the gerontological literature Brinley plots or, more accurately, age (1) × age (2) reaction time plots, have emerged as the principal methodology for testing the notion that speed of processing is the single global factor that can account for cognitive change. The typical method is to take adult reaction times on a diverse set of cognitive tasks as a baseline and plot the RTs on the same tasks from children of different ages. The logic of interpreting these functions is the same as in the gerontological literature. If the lines do not significantly differ from linearity then we can conclude that while the tasks may involve many different kinds of cognitive processes a parsimonious explanation is that a single scalar change associated with age can account for age differences in all aspects of task performance. Thus it might be, for example, that the RTs of 8-year-olds can be predicted from the RTs of adults on a wide variety of tasks simply by multiplying the RTs of adults by 1.2 (Hale, 1990). The implication is that developmental changes in reaction time performance can be explained by a simple speeding up of all processes by a factor of 1.2.

There is an additional methodological twist to the developmental studies that does not yet feature in the gerontological literature, but which might very fruitfully be adopted to examine the time-course of involution as a continuous process. Studies that compare more than one successive age group can examine the change in scalar values (the value that is used to multiply the oldest group's RTs to derive the younger group's RT) that is, itself, associated with age. Another way of thinking about this is that the scalar values are equivalent to the slope of the function in the age × age plots. It has been claimed that when this is done the age function in scalar values is fitted best by an exponential rather than a power function (Hale, 1990; Kail, 1988). Since it is also claimed that power functions are better descriptors of performance changes associated with learning and practice and exponential functions are better descriptors of the course of maturational change (Mazur & Hastie, 1978) this can be taken as further evidence that age changes in scalar factors cannot be attributed to age changes in experiential factors. This would further reinforce the hypothesis that, independent of practice and experience, change in speed of processing indexes some fundamental, biological factor that underlies cognitive change

However, in the developmental as in the gerontological literature there are a number of problems with the interpretation of Brinley plots.

The first problem is that it can be shown that many plausible but quite different developmental functions would still generate massively linear functions when the respective RT means of different age groups are plotted against each other (Anderson, 1995; Perfect, 1994). In other words this technique simply is not sensitive enough to detect specificity in developmental functions.

This problem is exacerbated in some of the published studies of Kail (e.g. Kail, 1991a; 1991b; Kail & Park, 1992) who uses the technique of forcing the age × age plots through the origin. Mean RT scores of both age groups can fall in only one possible quadrant (positive x and positive y, as opposed to either, or both, x and y being negative), because any RT mean is necessarily positive. Obviously, then, any straight line of best fit that is forced to pass through the origin will provide a reasonable fit to data that can only appear in the first quadrant (to repeat, the x-axis can only register positive mean reaction times and this is true also for the y-axis). The further from the origin that the set of data points fall the better the fit, regardless of any non-linearity within the data itself. In the case of RTs where means are closer to each other than to the origin (where RT would equal 0), by orders of magnitude this artifact is compounded. Thus, even if you create a set of RT means for an age × age plot that is perfectly negative *within* the first quadrant, the line of best fit through the origin will necessarily have a positive slope and a healthy R^2.

A third problem is that in order to be a fair test of the single global hypothesis each study must include a reasonably diverse set of tasks (allowing, at least in principle, for the possibility that younger children may experience specific difficulty with particular kinds of task demands, such as perhaps those characteristic of prefrontal or 'executive' tasks). Furthermore the age × age comparison must not be confounded by any other relevant group difference. For example, one of Kail's (1986) studies compares young children with young adult subjects who are usually university students. In the latter case age is confounded with differences in IQ test score attainment which would be expected to generate group differences in speed of processing (Anderson, 1992), making any age group difference ambiguous.

We have already discussed the first of these problems (insensitivity) at length in the context of gerontological studies. To illustrate the other two we will look in some detail at a study by Davis and Anderson (2001). They compared the reaction times of 4- to 9-year-old children on tasks measuring processes that from a theoretical perspective were predicted to have different developmental functions (selective attention, verbal and spatial processing). The choice of participants is noteworthy on two counts: first, the age range included children younger (and hence cognitively less mature) than those typically sampled for Brinley plot analysis; and, second, the baseline comparison group consisted of 9-year-olds from the same schools as the younger children, rather than university undergraduates, thus avoiding confounds of age-related and IQ-related differences in performance.

Davis and Anderson compared Brinley plots of the RT data made using Kail's method of allowing slope to vary while fixing the intercept at zero with plots where both slope and intercept were free to vary. These two methods yielded strikingly different lines of best fit and implied correspondingly different interpretations. When Kail's method was employed, his findings were replicated: the single-parameter slopes of the plots for each group produced very high R^2 values and a strong pattern of slope decreasing towards 1.00 as age increased. However, when intercept was allowed to vary slopes showed no change across age groups while intercepts decreased systematically towards zero as group age increased.

Cerella (1990) helps to elucidate the implications of these findings. He argues that the time consumed by RT tasks can be divided into two basic components: central processing time C, which includes the time taken by thoughtful, decision-making processes, and peripheral processing time P, which includes the time taken by perceptual and motor response processes. Davis and Anderson argue that the P component would also include general attentional factors responsible for keeping individuals on task, which would not be expected to vary systematically from task to task or condition to condition. Increasing the information processing load imposed by a task would be expected to increase central processing time while leaving peripheral processing time unchanged. Under global single factor speed models of development it is the C rather than the P component that is supposed to become more efficient with age and to account for cognitive development. If we represent adult RT on a task as $\text{RT(adult)} = P + C$, then we can represent children's RT as $\text{RT(child)} = aP + bC$, where a represents the factor by which children's peripheral processes are slower than adults and b represents the factor by which their central processes are slower than adults. By algebraic manipulation, we can write children's RT as a function of adults' RT: $\text{RT(child)} = b\text{RT(adult)} + P(a - b)$. This function represents the Brinley plot line of best fit. From this, we can see (as argued earlier) that the slope of the Brinley function represents the extent to which children's central processing speed is slower with respect to adults. It can also be seen that the intercept of the Brinley plot indicates the difference in magnitude between the slowing coefficient for peripheral processes and central processes. If $a = b$ then the equation reduces to children's RT being a simple multiplicative function of adults' RT. If central slowing exceeds peripheral slowing then we would expect a negative intercept and, conversely, if peripheral slowing exceeds central slowing then we would expect a positive intercept.

Applying this logic to the findings of Davis and Anderson, the finding that lines of best fit were very different when the intercept was allowed to vary from the origin than when it was fixed at the origin must mean that a and b have different values (central and peripheral slowing coefficients are different). Furthermore, as Davis and Anderson found no evidence of change in Brinley slopes (central processing speed) between 4 and 9 years of age, the systematic age-related decrease in intercept can only be attributed to an increase in peripheral processing speed. Interestingly, the slopes of the Brinley functions in the fixed intercept plot correlate highly and positively with the intercepts of the functions in the free-intercept plots ($r(5) = 0.97, p < 0.01$) while correlating negatively, though not significantly, with the slope of the functions in the free-intercept plots ($r(5) = -0.76$, n.s.). This indicates that the use of one-parameter functions converts large and robust age differences in intercept into apparent age differences in slope. Davis and Anderson conclude that, contrary to the single global hypothesis, attentional and motoric components of reaction time measures are subject to developmental changes but that speed of processing *per se* is not. This was further supported by an examination of task conditions which significantly violated the monotonicity of the Brinley plots, which has been taken as evidence of qualitative differences in performance between age groups (Dunn & Kirsner, 1988). Notably, for 4- and 5-year-olds, the conditions from the selective attention task, in which distracting information was absent or the motor response from the previous trial was to be repeated, stood out as being disproportionately easy for younger as compared to older children. This suggests that selective attention and switching between motor responses make RT tasks particularly difficult for young children. Reminiscent of the gerontological findings presented earlier, these factors appear to demand efficient inhibitory ability as well as, or rather than, faster information processing speed.

In an attempt to obtain a purer measure of central speed by removing peripheral and general attentional factors from the RT measures at an individual level, Davis and Anderson subtracted RTs in the relatively simple from RTs in the more complex conditions. Both Brinley plots and partial correlation analyses showed that despite the fact that IQ groups contained children from the full range of ages, this new difference measure showed no association with age but was systematically related to IQ. Thus it seems that RT tasks measure (at least) two distinct kinds of processing and that the peripheral/attentional component is associated with developmental change while the central speed component is associated with individual differences in intelligence within age groups. This conclusion by Davis and Anderson is consistent with the suggestion by Bjorklund and Harnishfeger (1990) that developmental improvements in decision times may be driven by increasing ability to attend to relevant and to ignore irrelevant stimuli. Equally, the data suggest that if there is a single global factor underlying cognitive development then this is not simple speed of processing. Moreover it is likely that IQ differences have been confounded with developmental age differences in studies in which groups of children with relatively low mean IQs are compared against groups of undergraduates with relatively high IQs.

CONCLUSIONS

The main points from the gerontological research are:

1 'Global' single factor theories of cognitive change with age confuse levels of description. That is, objectively measurable indices of task performance in CRT tasks have been confused with hypothetical constructs in functional models of decision processes, and both indices and constructs have been confused with higher order statistical constructs, akin to g_f in psychometric descriptions of individual differences.
2 These theories rest on the assumption that old age slows performance on all tasks by the same amount. This is not in fact the case. There is accumulating evidence that tasks involving 'central executive' processes, and mediated by frontal or prefrontal cortex, show greater age-related slowing than others and are also earlier and more substantially affected by ageing than others.
3 'Global single factor speed theory' would predict that transforms of CRT and IT distributions are linear rather than non-linear. There is accumulating evidence that transforms of CRT distributions are, in fact, non-linear with differentially greater increases in the numbers of unnecessarily slow responses that individuals make. In any event, it is not clear that behavioural data can distinguish between the range of possible models that can equally well account for the transforms of distributions that are observed in practice.
4 It seems that global single factor speed theories of ageing do not account for age-related changes in memory. This is because evidence that age changes in memory efficiency are entirely predicted by speed changes is methodologically suspect and empirically contradicted. More to the point, age-related changes in memory seem to refer more to qualitative changes in the relative difficulty of forming and retrieving particular kinds of memorial representation than to operations of a single factor relating to all kinds of representations.

The main points from the developmental research are:

1 Originally single global theories were tied to specific theories of cognitive structure. This is no longer so. The central weakness of single factor theories is that they do not discuss cognitive structure.
2 A single global factor signals a shift to a different level of explanation – particularly dangerous given point 1 above. This may make empirical findings uninterpretable.
3 There have been attempts to associate speed with specific tasks (IT/RT) by simply charting their relationship with developmental age. However, as we have made clear these tasks have multiple components and the components may vary in their relationship to individual differences (for example those attributable to developmental age and to age-adjusted IQ).
4 Arguments have been based on age (1) × age (2) Brinley plots. The sensitivity of these plots as analytic tools is now in question. A particular problem in the developmental literature has been the tendency to force the functions through the origin – guaranteeing a linear function. Depending on whether intercepts are fixed or left free we obtain very different results for age and IQ comparisons.
5 When Brinley plots are more carefully examined, and their theoretical rationale is more carefully considered, it appears that decision times can be decomposed into additive components from 'peripheral' and 'central' speed and that development brings about more marked changes in 'peripheral' speed than in 'central' speed. This, of course, contradicts the central tenet of single factor speed theory which is that latencies of all decision processes, whatever their nature, are scaled up by a common constant.
6 Following point 5 and the interpretation of the IT/RT data, this suggests to us that there may be a developmental dimension to cognition related to attentional/inhibitory/executive processes that is related to the growth in cognitive ability and to improved performance on speeded tasks.

REFERENCES

Albert, M. (1993). Neuropsychological and neurophysiological changes in healthy adult humans across the age range. *Neurobiology of Aging*, 14, 623.

Anders, T.R., & Fozard, J.L. (1973). Effects of age upon retrieval from primary and secondary memory. *Developmental Psychology*, 9, 411–415.

Anders, T.R., Fozard, J.L., & Lillyquist, T.D. (1972). Effects of age upon retrieval from short-term memory. *Developmental Psychology*, 6, 214–217.

Anderson, M. (1986). Inspection time and IQ in young children. *Personality and Individual Differences*, 7, 677–686.

Anderson, M. (1988). Inspection time, information processing and the development of intelligence. *British Journal of Developmental Psychology*, 6, 43–57.

Anderson, M. (1989a). The effect of attention on developmental differences in inspection time. *Personality and Individual Differences*, 10, 559–563.

Anderson, M. (1989b). Inspection time and the relationship between stimulus encoding and response selection factors in development. In D. Vickers & P.L. Smith (eds), *Human information processing: Measures, mechanisms and models* (pp. 509–516). Amsterdam: North-Holland Elsevier.

Anderson, M. (1992). *Intelligence and development: A cognitive theory*. Oxford: Blackwell.

Anderson, M. (1995). Evidence for a single global factor of developmental change – Too good to be true? *Australian Journal of Psychology*, 47(1), 18–24.

Anderson, M., Nettelbeck, T., & Barlow, J. (1997). Using reaction time measures of speed of information processing: Speed of response selection increases with age but speed of stimulus categorisation does not. *British Journal of Developmental Psychology*, 15, 145–157.

Arenberg, D. (1965). Anticipation interval and age differences in verbal learning. *Journal of Abnormal Psychology*, 70, 419–425.

Arnsten, A.F.T., Cai, J.X., Murphy, B.L., & Goldman-Rakic, P.S. (1994). Dopamine D1 receptor mechanisms in the cognitive functioning of young adult and aged monkeys. *Psychopharmacology*, 116, 143–151.

Baumler, G. (1969). Decrease in achievement capacity as a result of age with particular reference to the Stroop-interference tendency. *Psychologische Beitrage*, 11, 34–68.

Birren, J.E. (1956). The significance of age-changes in speed of perception and psychomotor skills. In J.E. Anderson (ed.), *Psychological aspects of aging*. (pp. 97–104). Washington, DC: American Psychological Association.

Birren, J.E. (1959). Sensation, perception and the modification of behaviour in relation to aging. In J.E. Birren, H.A. Imus, & W.F. Windle (eds), *The process of aging in the central nervous system* (pp. 143–165). Springfield, IL: Thomas.

Birren, J.E. (1965). Age changes in the speed of behaviour: Its critical nature and physiological correlates. In A.T. Welford & J.E. Birren (eds), *Behaviour, aging and the nervous system*. Springfield, IL: Thomas.

Birren, J.E. (1979). Tutorial review of changes in choice reaction time with advancing age. In H. Baumeister (ed.), *Bayer Symposium no. 6* (pp. 232–247). Bonn: Springer.

Birren, J.E., Woods, A.M., & Williams, M.V. (1980). Behavioural slowing with age. In L.W. Poon (ed.), *Aging in the 1980s: Psychological issues* (pp. 293–308). Washington, DC: American Psychological Association.

Bjorklund, D.F., & Harnishfeger, K.K. (1990). The resources construct in cognitive development: Diverse sources of evidence and a theory of inefficient inhibition. *Developmental Review*, 10, 48–71.

Brand, C.R., & Deary, I.Z. (1982). Intelligence and inspection time. In H.J. Eysenck (ed.), *A model for intelligence*. New York: Springer.

Brinley, J.F. (1965). Cognitive sets, speed and accuracy of performance in the elderly. In A.T. Welford & J.E. Birren (eds), *Behaviour, aging and the nervous system* (pp. 114–149). Springfield, IL: Thomas.

Broadbent, D.E. (1971). *Decision and stress*. New York: Academic.

Bunce, D.J., Warr, P.B., & Cochrane, T. (1993). Blocks in choice responding as a function of age and physical fitness. *Psychology and Aging*, 8, 26–33.

Burgess, P. (1998). Theory and methodology in executive function research. In P.M.A. Rabbitt (ed.), *Methodology of frontal and executive function*. Hove: Psychology Press.

Canestrari, R.E. Jr (1963). Paced and self-paced learning in young and elderly adults. *Journal of Gerontology*, 18, 165–168.

Case, R. (1985). *Intellectual development: Birth to adulthood*. Orlando: Academic.

Cerella, J. (1985). Information processing rates in the elderly. *Psychological Bulletin*, 98, 67–83.

Cerella, J. (1990). Aging and information-processing rate. In J.E. Birren & K.W. Schaie (eds), *Handbook of the psychology of aging* (3rd edn, pp. 201–221). San Diego: Academic.

Cohen, G. (1988). Age differences in memory for text: production deficiency or processing limitations? In L. Light & D. Burke (eds), *Language, memory and aging* (pp. 171–190). Cambridge; Cambridge University Press.

Cohen, G. (1996). Memory and learning in normal aging. In R.T. Woods (ed.) *Handbook of the clinical psychology of ageing* (pp. 43–58). Chichester: Wiley.

Cohn, N.B., Dustman, R.E., & Bradford, D.C. (1984). Age-related decrements in Stroop colour test performance. *Journal of Clinical Psychology*, 40, 1244–1250.

Comalli, P.E., Wapner, S., & Werner, H. (1962). Interference effects of Stroop colour-word test in children, adulthood and aging. *Journal of Genetic Psychology*, 100, 47–53.

Connelly, S.L., Hasher, L., & Zacks, R.T. (1991). Age and reading: The impact of distraction. *Psychology and Aging*, 6, 533–541.

Connolly, K. (1970). Response speed, temporal sequencing and information processing in children. In K.J. Connolly (ed.), *Mechanisms of motor skill development* (pp. 161–192). London: Academic.

Craik, F.I.M., & Jennings, J.M. (1992) Human memory. In F.I.M. Carik & T.A. Salthouse (eds), *The handbook of aging and cognition* (pp. 51–110). Hillsdale, NJ: Erlbaum.

Crossman, E.R.F.W. (1958). A theory of the acquisition of speed skill. *Ergonomics*, 2, 153–166.

Daigneault, S., Braun, C.M.J., & Whitaker, H.A. (1992). Early effects of normal aging in perseverative and non-perseverative prefrontal measures. *Developmental Neuropsychology*, 8, 99–114.

Davis, H., & Anderson, M. (1999). Individual differences in development: One dimension or two? In M. Anderson (ed.), *The development of intelligence*. Hove: Psychology Press.

Davis, H., & Anderson, M. (2001). Developmental and individual differences in fluid intelligence: Evidence against the unidimensional hypothesis. *British Journal of Developmental Psychology*, 19, 181–206.

Deary, I.Z. (1995). Auditory inspection time and intelligence: What is the direction of causation? *Developmental Psychology*, 31, 237–250.

Dempster, F.N. (1992). The rise and fall of the inhibitory mechanism: Towards a unified theory of cognitive development and ageing. *Developmental Review*, 12, 45–75.

Dunn, J.C., & Kirsner, K. (1988). Discovering functionally independent mental processes: The principle of reversed association. *Psychological Review*, 95, 91–101.

Eysenck, H.J. (1986). The theory of intelligence and the psychophysiology of cognition. In R.J. Sternberg (ed.), *Advances in the psychology of human intelligence* (Vol. 3). Hillsdale, NJ: Erlbaum.

Fairweather, H., & Hutt, S.J. (1978). On the rate of gain of information in children. *Journal of Experimental Child Psychology*, 26, 216–229.

Fry, A.F., & Hale, S. (1996). Processing speed, working memory, and fluid intelligence: Evidence for a developmental cascade. *Psychological Science*, 7, 237–241.

Gerard, L., Zacks, R.T., Hasher, L., & Radvansky, G.A. (1991). Age deficits in retrieval: The fan effect. *Journal of Gerontology: Psychological Sciences*, 46, 131–136.

Goldman-Rakic, P.S., & Brown, R.M. (1981). Regional changes of monoamines in cerebral cortex and subcortical structures of aging rhesus monkeys. *Neuroscience*, 6, 177–187.

Gur, R.C., Gur, R.E., Orbist, W.D., Skolnick, B.E., & Reivich, M. (1987). Age and regional cerebral blood flow at rest and during cognitive activity. *Archives of General Psychiatry*, 44, 617–621.

Hale, S. (1990). A global developmental trend in cognitive processing speed. *Child Development*, 61, 653–663.

Halford, G.S. (1987). A structure-mapping approach to cognitive development. *International Journal of Psychology*, 22, 609–642.

Halford, G.S. (1993). *Children's understanding: The development of mental models*. Hillsdale, NJ: Erlbaum.

Halford, G.S. (1999). The development of intelligence includes the capacity to process relations of greater capacity. In M. Anderson (ed.), *The development of intelligence: Studies in developmental psychology* (pp. 193–213). Hove: Psychology Press.

Halford, G.S., Maybery, M.T., & Bain, J.D. (1986). Capacity limitations in children's reasoning: A dual-task approach. *Child Development*, 57, 616–627.

Halford, G.S., Wilson, W.H., & Phillips, S. (1998). Processing capacity defined by relational complexity: Implications for comparative, developmental and cognitive psychology. *Behavioral and Brain Sciences*, 21, 803–864.

Hamm, V.P., & Hasher, L. (1992). Age and the availability of inferences. *Psychology and Aging*, 7, 56–64.

Hartman, M., & Hasher, L. (1991). Aging and suppression: Memory for previously relevant information. *Psychology and Aging*, 6, 587–594.

Hasher, L., Quig, M.B., & May, C.P. (1997). Inhibitory control over no-longer relevant information: Adult age differences. *Memory and Cognition*, 25 (3), 286–295.

Hasher, L., Stoltzfus, E.R., Zacks, R.T., & Rypma, B. (1991). Age and inhibition. *Journal of Experimental Psychology: Learning, Memory and Cognition*, 17, 163–169.

Hasher, L., & Zacks, R.T. (1988). Working memory, comprehension and aging: A review and a new view. In G.K. Bowker (ed.), *The Psychology of Learning and Motivation* (Vol. 22, pp. 193–225). San Diego, CA: Academic.

Haug, H., & Eggers, R. (1991). Morphometry of the human cortex cerebri and cortex striatum during aging. *Neurobiology of Aging*, 12, 336–338.

Hick, W.G. (1952). On the rate of gain of information. *Quarterly Journal of Experimental Psychology*, 4, 11–26.

Houx, P.J., Jolles, J., & Vreeling, F.W. (1993). Stroop interference: aging effects assessed with the Stroop colour-word test. *Experimental Aging Research*, 19, 209–224.

Hulicka, I.M., Sterns, H., & Grossman, J.L. (1967). Age group comparisons of paired associate learning as a function of paced and self-paced association and response times. *Journal of Gerontology*, 22, 274–280.

Hyman, R. (1953). Stimulus information as a determinant of reaction time. *Journal of Experimental Psychology*, 45, 188–196.

Jensen, A.R. (1980). Chronometric analysis of mental ability. *Journal of Social and Biological Structures*, 3, 181–224.

Jensen, A.R. (1982). Reaction time and psychometric g. In H.J. Eysenck (ed.), *A model for intelligence*. Berlin: Springer.

Kail, R. (1986). Sources of age differences in speed of processing. *Child Development*, 57, 969–987.

Kail, R. (1988). Developmental functions for speed of cognitive processes. *Journal of Experimental Child Psychology*, 45, 339–364.

Kail, R. (1991a). Processing time declines exponentially during childhood and adolescence. *Developmental Psychology*, 27, 259–266.

Kail, R. (1991b). Developmental change in speed of processing during childhood and adolescence. *Psychological Bulletin*, 109, 490–501.

Kail, R., & Park, Y.-S. (1992). Global developmental change in processing time. *Merrill-Palmer Quarterly*, 4, 525–541.

Kail, R., & Salthouse, T.A. (1994). Processing speed as a mental capacity. *Acta Psychologica*, 86, 199–225

Kane, M.J., Hasher, L., Stoltzfus, E.R., Zacks, R.T., & Connelly, S.L. (1994). Inhibitory attentional mechanisms and aging. *Psychology and Aging*, 9, 103–112.

Kausler, D. (1982). *Experimental psychology, cognition and human aging*. New York: Springer.

Kausler, D.H., & Hakami, M.K. (1982). Frequency judgements by young and elderly adults for relevant stimuli with simultaneously presented irrelevant stimuli. *Journal of Gerontology*, 37, 438–442.

Keating, D.P., & Bobbitt, B.L. (1978). Individual and developmental differences in cognitive processing components of mental ability. *Child Development*, 49, 155–167.

Kieley, J.M., & Hartley, A.A. (1997). Age-related equivalence of identity suppression in the Stroop colour-word task. *Psychology and Aging*, 12, 22–29.

Kranzler, J.H., & Jensen, A.R. (1989). Inspection time and intelligence: A meta-analysis. *Intelligence*, 13, 329–348.

Kwong See, S.T., & Ryan, E.B. (1995). Cognitive mediation of adult age differences in language performance. *Psychology and Aging*, 10, 458–468.

Lansman, M., & Hunt, E. (1982). Individual differences in secondary task performance. *Memory and Cognition*, 16, 10–24.

Luce, R.D. (1986). Uniqueness and homogeneity of ordered relational structures. *Journal of Mathematical Psychology*, 30 (4), 391–415.

Mazur, J.E., & Hastie, R. (1978). Learning as accumulation: A reexamination of the learning curve. *Psychological Bulletin*, 85, 1256–1274.

McDowd, J.M., & Oseas-Kreger, D.M. (1991). Aging, inhibitory processes and negative priming. *Journal of Gerontology*, 46, 340–345.

Monge, R.H., & Hultsch, D.F. (1971). Paired associate learning as a function of adult age and the length of the anticipation and inspection intervals. *Journal of Gerontology*, 26, 157–162.

Nettelbeck, T. (1987). Inspection time and intelligence. In P.A. Vernon (ed.), Speed of information processing and intelligence. New York: Ablex.

Nettelbeck, T., & Vita, P. (1992). Inspection time in two childhood age cohorts: A constant or a developmental function? *British Journal of Developmental Psychology*, 10, 189–197.

Nettelbeck, T., & Wilson, C. (1985). A cross sequential analysis of developmental differences in speed of visual information processing. *Journal of Experimental Child Psychology*, 40, 1–22.

Panek, P.E., Rush, M.C., & Slade, L.A. (1984). Focus of the age–Stroop interference relationship. *Journal of Genetic Psychology*, 145, 209–216.

Pascual-Leone, J. (1970). A mathematical model for the transition rule in Piaget's developmental stages. *Acta Psychologia*, 32, 301–345.

Pedhozur, E.L. (1997). *Multiple regression in behavioural research: Explanation and prediction* (3rd edn). Fort Worth, TX: Harcourt Brace.

Perfect, T.J. (1994). What can Brinley plots tell us about cognitive ageing? *Journal of Gerontology: Psychological Sciences*, 49 (2), 60–64.

Piccinin, A., & Rabbitt, P.M.A. (1999). Contribution of cognitive abilities to performance and improvement in a substitution task. *Psychology and Aging*, 14, 539–551.

Rabbitt, P.M.A. (1996a). Do individual differences in speed reflect global or local differences in mental ability? *Intelligence*, 22, 69–88.

Rabbitt, P.M.A. (1996b). Intelligence is not just mental speed. *Journal of Biosocial Science*, 28, 425–449.

Rabbitt, P.M.A., & Maylor, E.A. (1991). Investigating models of human performance. *British Journal of Psychology*, 82, 259–290.

Rabbitt, P.M.A., & Vyas, S.M. (1969). An elementary preliminary taxonomy for some errors in laboratory choice RT tasks. *Acta Psychologica*, 33, 56–76.

Rabbitt, P.M.A., & Yang, Q. (1996). What are the functional bases of individual differences in memory ability? In D. Herrman, C. McEvoy, C. Hertzog, P. Hertel, & M.K. Johnson (eds), *Basic and applied memory research: Theory in context* (Vol. 1, pp. 127–159). Mahwah, NJ: Erlbaum.

Rankin, J.L., & Kausler, D.H. (1979). Adult age differences in false recognitions. *Journal of Gerontology*, 34, 58–65.

Reed, T.E. (1993). Effects of enriched (complex) environment on nerve conduction velocity: New data and implications for the speed of information processing. *Intelligence*, 17, 461–474.

Reed, T.E., & Jensen, A.R. (1992). Conduction velocity in a brain-nerve pathway of normal adults correlates with intelligence level. *Intelligence*, 16, 259–272.

Riggs, L.A. (1972). *Woodworth and Schlossberg's experimental psychology*. London: Methuen.

Salthouse, T.A. (1985). *A cognitive theory of aging*. Berlin: Springer.

Salthouse, T.A. (1991). *Theoretical perspectives in cognitive aging*. Hillsdale, NJ: Erlbaum.

Salthouse, T.A. (1996). The processing-speed theory of adult age-differences in cognition. *Psychological Review*, 103, 403–428.

Scheibel, M.E., & Scheibel, A.B. (1975). Structural changes in the aging brain. In H. Brody, D. Harmon, & J.M. Ordy (eds), *Aging* (Vol. 1, pp. 11–37). New York: Raven.

Shaw, R.J. (1991). Age-related increases in the effects of automatic semantic activation. *Psychology and Ageing*, 6, 595–604.

Shaw, T.G., Mortel, K.F., Meyer, J.S., Rogers, R.L., Hardenberg, J., & Cutaia, M.M. (1984). Cerebral blood flow changes in benign aging and cerebrovascular disease. *Neurology*, 34, 855–862.

Smith, G.A., & Brewer, N. (1995). Slowness and age: Speed–accuracy mechanisms. *Psychology and Aging*, 10 (2), 238–247.

Spieler, D.H., Balota, D.A., & Faust, M.E. (1996). Stroop performance in healthy younger and older adults and in individuals with dementia of the Alzheimer's type. *Journal of Experimental Psychology: Human Perception and Performance*, 22, 461–479.

Sternberg, S. (1969). Memory scanning: Mental processes revealed by reaction time experiments. *American Scientist*, 57, 421–457.

Sternberg, S. (1975). Memory scanning: New findings and current controversies. *Quarterly Journal of Experimental Psychology*, 17, 1–27.

Stollery, B.T. (1987). Effects of 50 Hz electric currents on vigilance and concentration. *British Journal of Industrial Medicine*, 44, 111–118.

Stollery, B.T. (1990). Measuring marginal toxicity in industrial environments. In R. West, M. Christie, & J. Weinman (eds), *Microcomputers, psychology and medicine* (pp. 97–120). Chichester: Wiley.

Stollery, B.T., Broadbent, D.E., Banks, H., & Lee, W.R. (1991). Short-term prospective study of cognitive functioning in lead workers. *British Journal of Industrial Medicine*, 48, 739–749.

Townsend, J.T., & Ashby, F.G. (1983). *Stochastic modelling of elementary psychological processes*. Cambridge: Cambridge University Press.

Vernon, P.A. (1985). Individual differences in general cognitive ability. In L.C. Hartledge & C.F. Telzner (eds), *The neuropsychology of individual differences: A developmental perspective*. New York, Plenum.

Waugh, N.C., & Barr, R.A. (1980). Memory and mental tempo. In L.W. Poon, J.L. Fozard, L.S. Cermak, D. Arenberg, & L.W. Thompson (eds), *New directions in memory and aging: Proceedings of the George A. Talland Memorial Conference*, Hillsdale, NJ: Erlbaum.

Wearden, J.H., Wearden, A.J., & Rabbitt, P.M.A. (1997). Age and IQ effects on stimulus and response timing. *Journal of Experimental Psychology: Human Perception and Performance*, 23, 4.

Weiskrantz, L. (1992). Introduction: Dissociated issues. In A.D. Miller & M.D. Rugg (eds), *The neuropsychology of consciousness: Foundations of neuropsychology* (pp. 1–10). London: Academic.

West, R.L. (1996). An application of prefrontal cortex function theory to cognitive aging. *Psychological Bulletin*, 120, 272–292.

Whelihan, W.M., & Lesher, E.L. (1985). Neuropsychological changes in frontal functions with aging. *Developmental Neuropsychology*, 1, 371–380.

Witte, K.L. (1975). Paired associate learning in young and elderly adults as related to presentation rate. *Psychological Bulletin*, 82, 975–985.

Zacks, R.T., Radvansky, G., & Hasher, L. (1996). Studies of directed forgetting in older adults. *Journal of Experimental Psychology: Learning, Memory and Cognition*, 22 (1), 143–156.

25

Wisdom: Its Social Nature and Lifespan Development

URSULA M. STAUDINGER and
INES WERNER

Some Historical Background to the Psychological Study of Wisdom

Since the beginnings of human culture, wisdom has been viewed as the ideal endpoint of human development (Baltes & Staudinger, 2000). Historically, wisdom was conceptualized in terms of a state of idealized being (such as Lady Wisdom), as a process of perfect knowing and judgment as in King Solomon's judgments, or as an oral or written product such as wisdom-related proverbs and the so-called wisdom literature. Important to recognize is that the identification of wisdom with individuals (such as wise persons), the predominant approach in psychology, is but one of the ways by which wisdom is instantiated. In fact, in the general historical literature on wisdom, the identification of wisdom with the mind and character of individuals is not the preferred mode of analysis. Wisdom is considered an ideal that is difficult to fully represent in the isolated individual (Staudinger & Baltes, 1994).

Throughout history, interest in the topic of wisdom has waxed and waned (A. Assmann, 1991; Robinson, 1990). In general, two main lines of argument have been at the center of the historical evolution of the concept of wisdom. The first is the distinction between philosophical and practical wisdom often attributed to Aristotle's differentiation between *theoria* and *phronesis*. The second is the question of whether wisdom is divine or human (Baltes & Staudinger, 2000).

In the Western world, these two issues (philosophical versus practical; divine versus human) were at the center of heated discourse during the Renaissance with many important works written on these wisdom topics during the fifteenth through seventeenth centuries (Rice, 1958). An initial conclusion of this discourse was reached during the later phases of the Enlightenment. Wisdom was still critical, for instance, to the thinking of Kant and Hegel. Both understood wisdom as based on the coordination of the world of science and the practical world of humankind. The eighteenth century French *Encyclopedia* of Diderot and others, however, despite its more than 50 volumes, barely mentioned the topic. During the Enlightenment and the process of secularization, wisdom lost its salience as one of the fundamental categories guiding human thought and conduct.

Nevertheless, from time to time, scholars in such fields as philosophy, political science, theology, and cultural anthropology continue to attend to wisdom, although in our view less in a cumulative sense of theory building than in rejuvenating and revisiting its meaning, historical roots, and implications for raising human awareness about the complexities and uncertainties of life. During the last decade, for example, some philosophers have struggled with the definition of wisdom including the polarization between practical and philosophical wisdom, the integration of different forms of knowledge into one overarching whole, and the search for orientation in life (e.g. Kekes, 1983; 1995; Nozick, 1989; Oelmueller, 1989). In Germany, the latter issue has gained special importance in relation to the advent of postmodernity (e.g. Marquart, 1989).

Finally, there is archeological-cultural work dealing with the origins of religious and secular bodies of wisdom-related texts in China, India,

Egypt, Old Mesopotamia and the like (A. Assmann, 1991; Rudolph, 1987). The cultural-historical scholarship is important as we try to understand the cultural evolution and foundation of wisdom-related thought. Proverbs (Mieder & Dundes, 1981), maxims, and fairy tales (Chinen, 1987) constitute a great part of the materials underlying such efforts. It is impressive to realize how wisdom-related proverbs and tales evince a high degree of cultural and historical invariance. This relative invariance in the meaning and cultural importance of wisdom (Baltes & Staudinger, 2000) gives rise to the assumption that concepts such as wisdom with its related body of knowledge and skills have been culturally selected because of their adaptive value for humankind (see also Csikszentmihalyi & Rathunde, 1990).

Baltes and Staudinger (2000) deduced from the analysis of the cultural-historical wisdom literature the following six characteristics of wisdom common to different cultures and historical times: (1) wisdom deals with important and/or difficult matters of life and the human condition; (2) wisdom is truly superior knowledge, judgment, and advice; (3) wisdom is knowledge with extraordinary scope, depth, and balance applicable to specific situations; (4) wisdom is used for one's own good or the good of others; (5) wisdom combines mind and character; and (6) wisdom is very difficult to achieve but more easily recognized.

When psychologists approach the definition of wisdom (Sternberg, 1990a), they like philosophers are confronted with the need to further specify the content and formal properties of wisdom-related thought, judgment, and advice in terms of psychological categories; and also to describe the characteristics of persons who have approached a state of wisdom and are capable of transmitting wisdom to others. These initial efforts by psychologists for the most part were theoretical and speculative. In his pioneering piece on senescence, G. Stanley Hall (1922), for example, associated wisdom with the emergence of a meditative attitude, philosophic calmness, impartiality, and the desire to draw moral lessons that emerge in later adulthood. Furthermore, writers emphasized that wisdom involves the search for the moderate course between extremes, a dynamic between knowledge and doubt, a sufficient detachment from the problem at hand, and a well-balanced coordination of emotion, motivation, and thought (e.g. Birren & Fischer, 1990; Dittmann-Kohli & Baltes, 1990; Hartshorne, 1987; Labouvie-Vief, 1990; Meacham, 1990). In line with dictionary definitions, such writings typically include varied statements that wisdom is knowledge about the human condition at its frontier, knowledge about the most difficult questions of the meaning and conduct of life, and knowledge about the uncertainties of life, about what cannot be known and how to deal with that limited knowledge.

The Social Nature of Wisdom: Offering a First Definition and Some Illustrations

Before we can start to explore the social nature of wisdom, it is necessary to clarify our understanding of culture as well as social interaction. According to cultural anthropology, culture can be defined as a collection of bodies of knowledge or a body of skills transmitted via social interaction of various forms from one generation to the next (e.g. Boesch, 1991; Cole, 1990; d'Andrade, 1981; Shweder, 1991; Valsiner & Lawrence, 1997). Social interactions can be differentiated according to their degree of proximity. The degree of proximity of social interaction ranges from the immediate face-to-face interaction between two or more individuals on the proximal end to the interaction with cultural artifacts of any kind on the distal end. The social-interactive nature of wisdom in the distal sense refers to social interactions within a given human community or society which have been aggregated over individuals and over time, for instance by taking the form of proverbs. One can also conceive of them as 'depersonalized' social interactions. On the other hand, proximal social interaction is defined as referring to any communicative exchange between two or more individuals which can be either directly or symbolically mediated.

The Three Facets of the Social Nature of Wisdom

Staudinger (1996) proposed that the body of knowledge and judgments associated with wisdom is social-interactive in three ways: wisdom involves social interactions with regard to (i) its cultural evolution and ontogenesis, (ii) the activation and application of wisdom in a given social situation, i.e. how wisdom-related knowledge and judgment unfold in a given situation (microgenesis), and (iii) the identification or recognition of a given product (written, verbal, behavior) as wise. The agent or carrier of wisdom in all three cases can be either a culture or an individual.

Social Interaction and the Cultural Evolution of Wisdom

Social interaction is constitutive for the cultural evolution of wisdom. The body of knowledge and heuristics indexed as wisdom can only develop in a community of people, only if and when people interact. Whenever a number of human beings form a community, a body of knowledge dealing with the conduct, interpretation, and meaning of life is constructed which in its highest elaboration is then called wisdom.

According to cultural-historical analyses, knowledge related to the conduct, interpretation, and meaning of life is one of the first bodies of knowledge to develop in any human community (e.g. J. Assmann, 1992; Baltes & Staudinger, 2000; Rudolph, 1987). Especially in the early phases of cultural evolution, this collective knowledge (i.e. knowledge shared by members of a human community) becomes manifest in sayings, proverbs, and tales. The Egyptian and Mesopotamian cultures, and many current African cultures, are examples of this type of wisdom tradition and wisdom literature. With cultural evolution proceeding, that is, with increasing size and complexity of the human community, the number of proverbs increases, and proverbs subsequently become more and more detached from the concrete situations in which they originally were coined. At this later 'stage' of cultural evolution, the key question then becomes when to apply a particular piece of that body of knowledge (Hahn, 1989). Wisdom then is not yet contained in the sayings and proverbs themselves but rather in their insightful application to a given problem situation.

The study of proverbs further exemplifies the collective nature of the development of wisdom-related knowledge. Proverbs are defined as 'a truth based on common sense or the practical experience of mankind' (*Oxford Dictionary of the English Language*, 1933). In this sense, proverbs seem to be a prototypical example of a product of the collective mind. At the same time, the investigation of proverbs also illustrates the delicate dialectic between the individual and the collective which is one of the underlying themes of the present chapter. Taylor (1962), the doyen of proverb studies, has characterized this dialectic with a saying by Lord John Russell: 'One man's wit and all men's wisdom.' Proverbs only become proverbs by confirmation of recurrent action in a given community, by the experience of a community of people thinking and acting together over time (Goodwin & Wenzel, 1981). An individual's mind is needed, however, to integrate and transform this collective experience into a proper metaphor. The 'socio-logic' (Goodwin & Wenzel, 1981) of certain events and relationships needs to be discovered and pinned down by an individual's mind.

The Cultural Activation and Application of Wisdom

When considering the second facet of the social-interactive nature of cultural wisdom, we find that wisdom has a central cultural function. The body of knowledge associated with wisdom is activated when successful solutions to difficult and uncertain problems of life are needed. Successful solutions to life problems, one can further assume, increase the likelihood of the survival or the prospering of a culture. This cultural function of wisdom as a body of knowledge dealing with life problems is well documented in cultural-historical analyses of the so-called wisdom literature of ancient societies and in psychological investigations on the evolutionary functions of aging (A. Assmann, 1991; J. Assmann, 1992; Baltes & Staudinger, 2000; Brent, 1978; Brent & Watson, 1980; Mergler & Goldstein, 1983).

Taking the view of evolutionary hermeneutics, Csikszentmihalyi and Rathunde (1990) have argued that concepts such as wisdom, which have been used for many centuries under very different social and historical conditions to evaluate human behavior, are most likely to have adaptive value for humankind. Beyond the role of wisdom in cultural evolution, there is also an increasing literature which provides evidence for the effect of social interaction even on the phylogenesis of certain cognitive processes (e.g. Barkow, Cosmides, & Tooby, 1992; Gigerenzer & Hug, 1992; Klix, 1993). Gigerenzer and Hug (1992), for example, showed that correct reasoning is facilitated when the task involves cheating detection (i.e. one type of social interaction).

Wisdom is also activated and asked for when the socialization and education of the youth are concerned. In historical studies, wisdom often is described as crystallized in rules which were collected and put down in writing by certain societal subgroups such as priests. Such collections were then, among other purposes, used for the *education of youth* (J. Assmann, 1992; Rudolph, 1987). Another cultural use of wisdom, that is the *exercise of power*, has been the topic of highly controversial discussions (e.g. Baltes & Staudinger, 2000). It is often argued that full access to this body of knowledge was confined to certain societal elites, enabling them to seize and exercise power (Hahn, 1989; Rudolph, 1987).

The Social Embeddedness of the Ontogenesis and the Microgenesis of Wisdom

Most of the recently fast growing literature on social interaction and cognition (e.g. Bornstein & Bruner, 1989; Resnick, Levine, & Teasley, 1991; von Cranach, Doise, & Mugny, 1992; Wozniak & Fischer, 1993) does not differentiate between the social character of the ontogenesis and the microgenesis of a given body of knowledge. Thus, potential differences in the kind, the amount, and the function of social interaction involved in the ontogenesis as compared to the microgenesis of wisdom cannot be investigated.

The distinction between ontogenesis and microgenesis of wisdom-related knowledge and judgment becomes relevant, for example, when considering the question whether the social-interactive nature of wisdom also implies that wisdom or something close to it cannot be observed within an isolated individual. With regard to the ontogenesis of wisdom this is highly likely. The lifespan development of wisdom-related knowledge and judgment is dependent on proximal and distal social influences. In other words, a wise Kaspar Hauser is difficult to imagine. However, it is still an open issue whether a certain amount and a certain kind of proximal social interaction are indispensable in order for wisdom to emerge. On the other hand, when considering the microgenesis of wisdom, i.e. the unfolding of wisdom-related knowledge and judgment in a given situation, proximal social interaction may not be absolutely necessary. Due to processes of socialization and internalization, individuals in the course of their lives accumulate and develop some wisdom-related knowledge and judgment which they can then use in a given situation independently of proximal social interaction.

Like any knowledge acquisition, the *ontogenesis* of wisdom-related performance is highly dependent on social interaction and social-cultural context. Cultural anthropologists and the sociologists of knowledge have argued that a good part (if not most) of what a person knows is learned from other people. A person's knowledge is very much influenced by her interactional history and her social 'fate' (e.g. Berger & Luckmann, 1967; Schütz & Luckmann, 1979; Shweder, 1991). Along this line, wisdom researchers have argued that supportive interpersonal relationships are crucial for the development and maintenance of wisdom. Close relationships and friendships may provide for (1) wisdom-conducive experiences, and (2) a conversational context which allows one to explore the limits and doubts involved in knowing (Kramer, 1990; Meacham, 1990).

Within lifespan developmental theory, several levels or territories of social influences are distinguished. Some of these developmental influences are socially interactive in the proximal sense defined above and others are more distal and mediated through selective exposure to certain experiential settings (Lerner & von Eye, 1992). Underlying any development and 'omnipresent' is the macrostructure of culture which has mediating and regulating power in shaping content, level, and direction of development (Cole, 1990; Schütz & Luckmann, 1979; Shweder, 1991; Valsiner & Lawrence, 1997). Being a member of a human community includes, for example, learning its language and learning about the collectively defined rules of life. On a second level there is the society-driven production of individual differences by age, gender, educational level, professional status, to name just a few (Dannefer, 1984; Featherman & Lerner, 1985). Finally, there is the microenvironment in terms of the family in which we grow up, and our educational or peer group settings (Bronfenbrenner, 1999). These settings often, by means of social interaction in the proximal sense, refine and specify the social influences exerted by the other two levels.

What Is Social about the Identification of Wisdom in an Individual?

Wisdom is usually attributed to others or by others and identified in social context (see also Sternberg, 1990c). In an empirical study of the characteristics of wise nominees and their nominators, Orwoll and Perlmutter (1990) found, for example, that people hold a general belief that wisdom increases with age, and that older people are more likely to be nominated as wise than young people. Subjects, however, did not rate their own wisdom in a manner that was consistent with this general belief of an age-related increase of wisdom. In fact, it is a well-established part of the wisdom literature that it is a characteristic of so-called wise persons to not attribute wisdom to themselves (e.g. Baltes & Staudinger, 2000; Meacham, 1983). The classic Socrates citation, 'I know that I don't know', speaks to this point. With regard to the orientation of wisdom, the analysis of cultural-historical wisdom literature shows that wisdom is oriented towards the interests of others (Baltes, & Staudinger, 2000; Sternberg, 1998). In other words, the intention of wisdom is social-interactive in nature as well.

The social nature of wisdom can be traced in (i) dictionary definitions, (ii) implicit or lay theories of wisdom, and finally (iii) explicit theories of wisdom. These are presented in turn.

The Social Nature of Wisdom in Dictionary Definitions

The social nature of wisdom is reflected, for instance, in its treatment in encyclopedias and dictionaries. The major German historical dictionary (Grimm & Grimm, 1854/1984) defined wisdom as 'insight and knowledge about oneself and the world . . . and sound judgment in the case of difficult life problems'. Similarly, the *Oxford Dictionary* (Fowler & Fowler, 1964) includes in its definition of wisdom: 'Good judgment and advice in difficult and uncertain matters of life.' Both dictionary definitions offer support for the notion of wisdom as an abstract entity which can find different carriers. The *Oxford Dictionary* definition, for example, says: 'the quality or character of being wise *or* something in which this is exhibited' (1933, p. 191, emphasis added). In other words, wisdom may be exhibited in individuals but this is not the only means of expression. Other possibilities are cultural products like law compendiums or constitutions. Second, the definition of wisdom as capacity to judge reflects the communicative, social-interactive aspect of wisdom. And finally, support for the social-interactive nature of wisdom is obtained in such dictionary definitions with regard to its educational function in society that is wisdom is described as being used for 'teaching the young' (1933, p. 191).

THE SOCIAL NATURE OF WISDOM IN IMPLICIT THEORIES

The social nature of wisdom is emphasized even more clearly when we consider results from research on people's subjective beliefs or implicit theories of wisdom (e.g. Clayton, 1976; Clayton & Birren, 1980; Holliday & Chandler, 1986; Orwoll & Perlmutter, 1990; Sowarka, 1989; Sternberg, 1986). The pursuit of answers to questions such as 'What is wisdom?', 'How is wisdom different from other forms of intelligence?', 'Which situations require wisdom?', 'What are the characteristics of wise people?' are prototypical for that kind of research.

These studies in principle build on research initiated by Clayton (1976). In her work three dimensions were typical of wise people: (1) affective characteristics such as empathy and compassion, (2) reflective processes such as intuition and introspection, and (3) cognitive capacities such as experience and intelligence. It seems that one of the three dimensions which she identified in a multidimensional scaling study of people's definitions of a wise person is directly related to the social-interactive nature of wisdom. She referred to this dimension as the affective component of wisdom, which captures adjectives such as empathic or compassionate (Clayton, 1976; Clayton & Birren, 1980). The other two dimensions, reflective and cognitive, are more but not exclusively person-centered. For example, what she labelled the cognitive dimension includes characteristics such as exposure to experiential contexts which usually comprise the interaction with other people.

The focus of a study by Sternberg (1986) investigating implicit theories was the location of wisdom in the semantic space marked by other constructs such as creativity and intelligence. Within that frame of reference, Sternberg found wisdom described by six dimensions: reasoning ability, sagacity, learning from ideas and environment, judgment, expeditious use of information, and perspicacity. The components explicitly related to the social-interactive nature of wisdom are sagacity, perspicacity, and learning from ideas and environment. They are defined by features such as the wise person showing concern for others or considering advice (sagacity), offering right and true solutions (perspicacity), and perceptive learning from mistakes (learning from ideas and environment). The value of prior experience was also reflected in a component called expeditious use of information. Only two of the six components have an emphasis on the individual (reasoning ability, judgment). Sternberg (1990b) used these results and others to specify six characteristics relating to six domains which lead people to label a person as wise: (1) understanding of presuppositions, meaning, and limits (knowledge); (2) resisting automization of own thought but seeking to understand it in others (process), (3) judicial (primary intellectual style), (4) understanding of ambiguity and obstacles (personality), (5) interest to understand what is known and what it means (motivation), and (6) depth of understanding needs to find appreciation in context (environmental context). In later theoretical work, Sternberg defined wisdom as balancing intrapersonal, interpersonal, and extrapersonal interests to achieve a common good through a balance among, adaptation to, shaping of, and selection of environments (Sternberg, 1998). This later theory actually makes the social aspect a constituent part of wisdom.

Another major study on subjective theories of wisdom was conducted by Holliday and Chandler (1986). Their work included an analysis of the words people use to describe wisdom and wise persons and the attributes judged to be most typical indicators of these concepts. Holliday and Chandler (1986) identified five factors: interpersonal skills, judgment and communicative skills, social unobtrusiveness, exceptional understanding, and general competence. Of these five only the last one, 'general competence', has an emphasis on the 'isolated' individual. The other four are all related to the social-interactive nature of wisdom. The factor called interpersonal skill, for example, is described by items like 'sensitive' and 'sociable' and the factor named judgment and communicative skill is characterized by items such as 'is a good source of advice'.

Two studies in the tradition of implicit-theory research involved asking subjects to nominate wise people and subsequently characterize nominees (Orwoll & Perlmutter, 1990; Sowarka, 1989). Sowarka (1989) reported two findings of special importance. First, it seemed that the characterization of wisdom and wise persons was a task readily performed by elderly research participants. Second, subjects emphasized the notion that the persons they had nominated as wise displayed 'excellent character'. Using a similar procedure, Orwoll and Perlmutter (1990) found with respect to their demographic characteristics that wisdom nominees tended to be middle-aged to old, male rather than female, and more highly educated. However, none of these studies, conducted in Germany and the US, respectively, employed heterogeneous, representative samples. Therefore, it may very well be that as such research is systematically applied to nominators from various cultural subgroups, new constellations of person characteristics including different gender and age distributions would emerge.

There is also initial evidence on the implicit theories about wise acts (Oser, Schenker, & Spychiger 1999). Wise acts seem to be characterized by the following seven features: (i) paradoxical, unexpected, (ii) moral integrity, (iii) selfless, (iv) overcoming internal and external dictates, (v) striving towards equilibrium, (vi) implying a risk, (vii) striving towards improving the human condition. A number of these features are social in nature: for instance, the selflessness, the moral aspect and the striving towards improving the human condition clearly transcend the individual.

From this research on implicit theories of wisdom and wise persons, it is evident that people in Western samples hold fairly clear-cut images of the nature of wisdom and its social nature. Four findings are especially noteworthy. First, in the minds of people, wisdom seems to be closely related to wise persons and their acts as 'carriers' of wisdom. Second, wise people are expected to combine features of mind and character and balance multiple interests and choices. Third, wisdom carries a very strong interpersonal and social aspect with regard to both its application (advice) and the consensual recognition of its occurrence. Fourth, wisdom exhibits overlap with other related concepts such as intelligence, but in aspects like sagacity, prudence, and the integration of cognition, emotion, and motivation, it also carries unique variance.

The Social Nature of Wisdom in Explicit Theories

A more recent line of empirical psychological inquiry on wisdom addresses the question of how to measure behavioral expressions of wisdom. Whereas implicit theories are constructions in the minds of people, explicit theories are constructions of scientists that are based or tested with data from people performing tasks presumed to measure wisdom-related functioning (Sternberg, 1990b). Within this tradition, three lines of work can be distinguished: (1) assessment of wisdom as a personality characteristic (e.g. Erikson, Erikson, & Kivnick, 1986; Loevinger, 1976; Orwoll, 1988; Ryff, 1982; Walaskay, Whitbourne, & Nehrke, 1983–84), (2) assessment of wisdom in the Piagetian tradition of postformal thought (e.g. Arlin, 1990; Kitchener & Brenner, 1990; Kramer, 2000; Labouvie-Vief, 1995, Pascual-Leone, 1990), and (3) assessment of wisdom as an individual's problem-solving performance with regard to difficult problems involving the interpretation, conduct, and management of life (e.g. Baltes, Smith, & Staudinger, 1992). We will focus on the explication of the social nature of wisdom with regard to the third explicit theory approach.

Assessment of Wisdom as a Personality Characteristic

Within personality theories, wisdom is usually conceptualized as an advanced if not the final stage of personality development. Wisdom, in this context, is comparable to 'optimal maturity'. A wise person is characterized, for instance, as integrating rather than ignoring or repressing self-related information, as having coordinated opposites, and as having transcended personal agendas and turned to collective or universal issues. Ryff (Ryff & Heincke, 1983) and Whitbourne (e.g. Walaskay, Whitbourne & Nehrke, 1983–84), for example, have undertaken the effort to develop self-report questionnaires based on the Eriksonian notions of personality development, especially integrity or wisdom. In a similar vein, Orwoll (1988) investigated people who had been nominated as wise according to subjective beliefs about wisdom. She found that wise nominees were indeed characterized by high scores on Eriksonian measures of ego integrity and showed a greater concern for the world state or humanity as a whole than the comparison group. Utilizing her widely used sentence completion technique, Loevinger developed a measure of her theoretically postulated stages of ego development (e.g. Loevinger & Wessler, 1978). Loevinger's last stage, labeled 'ego integrity', has been found to be related to other personality dimensions, such as 'competence' from the CPI Inventory (Helson & Wink, 1987) or 'openness to experience' from the NEO-PI (McCrae & Costa, 1980). Recently, wisdom, in the sense of self-development and maturity, was operationalized using various scales of the California Q-sort and was found to predict life satisfaction in old age (Ardelt, 1997).

Assessment of Wisdom in the Neo-Piagetian Tradition of Postformal Thought

Central to neo-Piagetian theories of adult thought is the transcendence of the universal truth criterion that characterizes formal logic. A postformal thinker is able to construct truth criteria against the background of pluralism. According to these models autonomy emerges through recognition of the genuine complexity and relativity of social systems. The transcendence of the universal truth criterion is common to conceptions such as dialectical (Basseches, 1984; Riegel, 1973), complementary (Oser & Reich, 1987), and relativistic thinking (Kuhn, Pennington, & Leadbeater, 1983). Such tolerance of multiple truths, that is of ambiguity, has also been mentioned as a crucial feature of wisdom. Given this definition it is not surprising that studying postformal thought also entails study of the integration of cognition and emotion as it is highlighted in Gisela Labouvie-Vief's work (e.g.. Labouvie-Vief, 1995).

Research in the neo-Piagetian tradition focuses on changes in cognitive structure, particularly in the level of complexity, abstraction, and differentiation people can employ when reasoning about fundamental life problems. Here, researchers nearly always ask for free responses to problems, elicited in interview settings. The resulting responses are then coded, using various schemes, for qualities like the representation and integration of multiple viewpoints. From this perspective, the sophistication of scientific and moral reasoning increases from childhood and adolescence through early adulthood (see Kitchener & King, 1990; Kramer, Kahlbaugh, & Goldston, 1992; Kuhn, 1989; Pratt et al., 1990). After early adulthood, there may be more stability in complex reasoning than change according to cross-sectional studies (age range 35–85 years; e.g. Kuhn, 1989; Pratt et al., 1990). One longitudinal study (covering 4 years) shows declines in complexity or reasoning structure in the oldest group (63–80 years; Pratt et al., 1996). Unfortunately, these cross-sectional and longitudinal results are difficult to compare because of differences in variability and other methodological differences. Labouvie-Vief (1995) and her colleagues have shown that adults' thinking about themselves moves from hardly differentiating between self and other, and heavy influence from social conventions, towards self-defining thoughts that emphasize contextual, process-related, and idiosyncratic features of selfhood.

Assessment of Wisdom as an Individual's Problem-Solving Performance

Besides these measures of wisdom as a personality characteristic and as postformal operation, there is also work that attempts to assess wisdom-related performance in tasks dealing with the interpretation, conduct, and management of life. The Berlin wisdom paradigm is presented next (e.g. Baltes & Smith, 1990; Baltes, Smith, & Staudinger, 1992; Baltes & Staudinger, 1993; Dittmann-Kohli & Baltes, 1990).

The Berlin Wisdom Paradigm

Conceptualization of Wisdom The Berlin wisdom paradigm is based on lifespan theory, the developmental study of the aging mind and aging personality, research on expert systems, and cultural-historical definitions of wisdom. By integrating these perspectives, wisdom is defined as an expert knowledge system in the fundamental pragmatics of life permitting exceptional insight, judgment, and advice involving complex and uncertain matters of the human condition (Baltes, Smith, & Staudinger, 1992).

This is a body of knowledge and judgment which concerns the mastery of difficult and uncertain problems related to life conduct and the meaning of life. Wisdom is defined as *superior knowledge* of how to act for our own good, for the good of others, and the good of the society we live in. Wisdom and wisdom-related knowledge become visible in *sound judgment* and *exceptional insight* into difficult life problems. Note that the concept of wisdom is restricted to expert-level products or performances in the domain of fundamental pragmatics of life. Any lower levels are denoted by the term 'wisdom-related'.

It is further argued that the body of knowledge and judgment called wisdom is a *theoretical* rather than an empirical object. This means that wisdom is conceived of as an 'idea' in the sense that Plato developed in his early writings on geometry, aesthetics, and ethics (Mittelstraß, 1981). Reality by definition falls short of the ideal. In the very early wisdom literature, wisdom is already described as an ideal which the individual or society can only strive for rather than attain (Adler, 1992).

The idea of wisdom, in this sense, can become manifest in an individual's judgment, behavior, and character but it can also be displayed on a societal level in proverbs, tales, religious writings, constitutional texts, and law compendiums (see also Baltes & Smith, 1990). Given this conceptualization of wisdom as a *theoretical object*, as just introduced, it is *not* the specific carrier of wisdom (e.g. person or written product), but rather the structure and function of this body of knowledge associated with the fundamental matters of life and the human condition, which determines the essence of wisdom.

The core features of wisdom-related knowledge and judgment, irrespective of whether it is instantiated in a written text or in the verbal or actual behavior of an individual, have been defined by a family of five criteria: rich factual and rich procedural knowledge about life, lifespan contextualism, value relativism, awareness and management of uncertainty. Table 25.1 describes these five criteria in more detail and provides illustrations of how they can be instantiated in verbal discourse.

The Assessment of Wisdom-Related Performance To elicit and measure wisdom-related knowledge and skills, in the Berlin wisdom paradigm subjects are presented with difficult life dilemmas such as the following: 'Imagine a good friend of yours calls you up and tells you that she can't go on anymore and has decided to commit suicide. What would you be thinking about, how would you deal with this situation?' Participants are then asked to 'think aloud' about such dilemmas. The five wisdom-related criteria introduced above (see Table 25.1) are used to evaluate these protocols. The obtained scores are reliable and provide an approximation of the quantity and quality of wisdom-related knowledge

Table 25.1 *Criteria for features of wisdom-related knowledge and judgment*

	High performances are exemplified by	Instantiation in verbal discourse (Example: a 14-year-old is pregnant; what should she do and consider?)
Basic criteria		
Rich factual knowledge about life	Consideration of general (human condition) and specific (e.g. life events, institutions) features of life matters as well as scope and depth in coverage of issues	Who, when, where? Specific knowledge, examples, variations General knowledge of emotions, vulnerability, and multiple options (parenting, adoption, abortion)
Rich procedural knowledge about life	Consideration of decision strategies, goal selection, choosing means to achieve goals, people to consult with, as well as strategies of advice giving	Strategies of information search, decision making, and advice giving Timing of advice Monitoring of emotional reactions Heuristics of cost-benefit analysis
Meta-level criteria		
Lifespan contextualism	Consideration of past, current, and possible future life contexts and the circumstances in which a life is embedded	Likely age sequence Sociohistorical and idiosyncratic context Coordination of life themes (family, education, work) and temporal changes Contextual conflicts and tensions
Value relativism	Consideration of variations in values and life priorities and the importance of viewing each person within an individual framework, but also the importance of a small set of universal values oriented towards the good of others and oneself	Religious and personal preferences Current/future values, goals, motives Cultural relativism
Awareness and management of uncertainly	Consideration of the inherent uncertainty of life (in terms of interpreting the past and predicting the future) and effective strategies for dealing with uncertainty	No perfect solution Optimization of gain/loss ratio Future not fully predictable Back-up solutions

Source: adapted from Baltes and Smith (1990), Baltes, Smith, & Staudinger (1992).

and skills of a given person (for more information about rating see the manual: Staudinger, Smith, & Baltes, 1994). When using this wisdom paradigm to study people who were nominated as wise according to nominators' subjective beliefs about wisdom, it turned out that wisdom nominees also received higher wisdom scores than comparable control samples of various ages and professional backgrounds (Baltes et al., 1995).

Indicators of Reliability and Validity In multiple studies interrater consistency ranged from very good to moderately high for the five wisdom-related criteria scales (Baltes et al., 1995; Smith & Baltes, 1990; Smith, Staudinger, & Baltes, 1994; Staudinger, 1989; Staudinger, Smith, & Baltes, 1992). No systematic differences in interrater consistency between different tasks were found. The five criteria consistently demonstrated moderate to high intercorrelations. Thus, they form a positive manifold. Patterns of convergent and discriminant validity followed the theoretical expectations. That is, in the adult age range, our measure of wisdom was found to correlate most highly with measures representing joint personality and cognitive functioning, such as creativity or cognitive style. Only low correlations were identified with indicators of fluid and crystallized intelligence and the big five personality characteristics (see Staudinger, Lopez, & Baltes, 1997, for detail). In adolescence the complementary pattern was found (Staudinger & Pasupathi, 2002). In the following, it will be explored to which degree the social nature of wisdom is represented in the Berlin wisdom paradigm.

The Social Nature of Wisdom as Illustrated in the Berlin Wisdom Paradigm

Social Interaction and the Ontogenesis of Wisdom

We have developed a general framework outlining the conditions for the development of wisdom as it is instantiated in persons (Baltes & Smith, 1990; Baltes & Staudinger, 1993). The model (see Figure 25.1) presents a set of factors and processes which need to 'co-operate' for wisdom to develop. We postulate cognitive and emotional-motivational processes as well as certain experiential factors associated with the interpretation, conduct, and management of life to be important antecedents of wisdom.

First, as shown on the left-hand side of Figure 25.1, there are general individual characteristics related to adaptive human functioning such as intelligence and personality. Second, the model presumes that the development of wisdom is advanced by certain expertise-specific factors, such as practice and being guided by a mentor. Third, the model implies the operation of macro-level facilitative experiential contexts. For instance, certain professions and historical periods are more facilitative than others. In the center of Figure 25.1, some of the organizing processes (life planning, life management, and life review) which may be critical for the development of wisdom-related performance are identified. And finally, on the right-hand side certain theoretical assumptions about where the five criteria fall in the course of the development of wisdom are depicted. Applying general models of expertise development (e.g. Anderson, 1987), individuals first may reach good performance levels on the two basic criteria, factual and subsequently procedural knowledge about life. Good performance on the three meta-criteria of lifespan contextualism, value relativism, and awareness and management of uncertainty is expected to emerge in later phases of the acquisition process.

The social nature of wisdom is represented in this model, for instance, by the experiential settings related to socialization, such as family background, schooling, peer groups, or later professional training. Society-driven interindividual differences like age and social class can be interpreted as allocating distinct bodies of wisdom-related experience by means of age-specific roles, expectations, and access to spheres of life (e.g. Riley, 1985). Finally, historical periods can be considered as one concrete example of the cultural macrostructure. In addition, culture certainly provides the general framework (e.g. language, knowledge) within which wisdom-related development takes place.

Age by Experience Paradigms

The empirical work based on the Berlin measurement paradigm and the ontogenetic model demonstrated that advanced chronological age is not a risk factor for wisdom-related performance. In contrast to cognitive performances that draw primarily on the fluid mechanics of the mind, for which aging-related losses are the hallmark (for a review, see Lindenberger & Baltes, 1994; Salthouse, 1991), older adults (up to 75–80 years of age) were among the top scorers in wisdom-related performance (for review see Staudinger, 1999a). It seems that

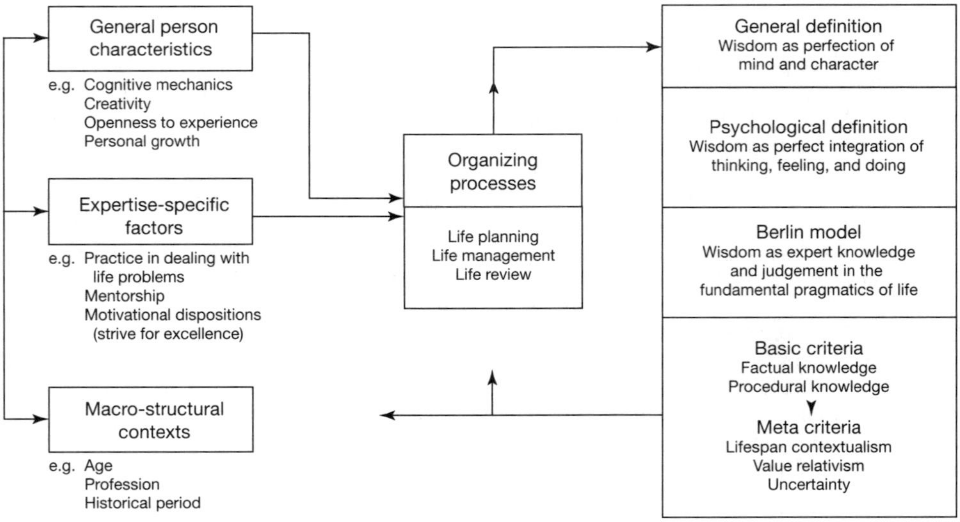

Figure 25.1 *A working model of the antecedents and correlates of the development of wisdom-related knowledge and judgment (after Baltes, Smith, & Staudinger, 1992)*

wisdom-related knowledge and judgment emerges between the age of 14 and 23 years (Pasupathi, Staudinger, & Baltes, 2001). During that time, normative age-related increase of wisdom-related performance is found. After age 20–25, increase in wisdom-related performance is no longer normatively related to age. Rather, a complex pattern of person characteristics as well as experiences and their 'digestion' determines further increases in wisdom-related knowledge and judgment.

Living longer (i.e. age) only increases the *probability of encountering* potentially wisdom-conducive experiences. In adulthood, age is no guarantee for an actual increase of wisdom-related knowledge and skill. Instead, the accumulation of wisdom-related knowledge may depend on more than chance encounters with wisdom-facilitative life experiences. It may depend on a great number of experiences, on guidance (having a mentor, i.e. social interaction) in dealing with those experiences, and on a certain personality make-up such as an interest in gaining insights into life. Furthermore, later in the development of wisdom-related knowledge, experiences with being a mentor become relevant.

Thus, it was argued that the development of wisdom-related performance is best investigated within a design which examines age as well as exposure to wisdom-facilitative experiential settings. Within such a so-called age by experience paradigm (e.g. Charness, 1989; Salthouse, 1991) three developmental conditions have been specified as especially relevant: (i) extensive experience with a wide range of human conditions; (ii) mentor-guided practice in dealing with difficult issues of life conduct and life interpretation, that is, social interaction with a more experienced person; and (iii) a motivational disposition which would support the endurance of extended periods of 'practice' in fundamental matters of life (see also Ericsson, Krampe, & Tesch-Römer, 1993).

An empirical example of the investigation of the potential facilitative effect of certain experiential and social-interactive contexts is provided by the study of groups with specific professional training and practice. In one study, clinical psychology was selected as a profession which in training and practice is putatively characterized by an above average amount of exposure to fundamental matters of life and to ways of dealing with them, as well as the experience of mentorship in how to interpret and deal with such life issues. It was demonstrated that the experiential context of training and practice in clinical psychology indeed seems to be conducive to higher levels of wisdom-related performance. Clinical psychologists displayed higher levels of wisdom-related performance than comparison groups from other academic professions (Smith, Staudinger, & Baltes, 1994; Staudinger, Smith, & Baltes, 1992). At the same time, however, selection into the profession of clinical psychology because of a certain personality profile may account for some of the clinical psychologists' superiority.

Experiential Settings and Historical Time

This finding of the wisdom-conducive effect of exposure to certain professional contexts was replicated and extended in a study which compared people nominated as wise with old clinical psychologists and control groups. People nominated as wise, among other things, were characterized by an average age of 64 years and by seemingly extraordinary biographies with regard to experiential settings and to interpersonal relationships: 44% had published their autobiographies, 31% had been members of the resistance movement against the Nazi regime or had emigrated during the Third Reich, and 56% had been in leading positions in public administration, the church, the arts, and the sciences. The wisdom nominees, who had been nominated independent of our definition of wisdom, outperformed both the clinical psychologists and the control groups on our measure of wisdom-related performance (Baltes et al., 1995). This finding seems to suggest that besides professional contexts, historical times can also provide for experiential contexts which are – given a certain personality profile – conducive to the development of wisdom-related knowledge and judgment.

Interacting with a Mentor as Part of the Development of Expertise

There is a large body of literature in educational and child psychology about the effect of social interaction on cognitive development (for review see e.g. Azmitia, 1996; Azmitia & Perlmutter, 1989; Slavin, 1980). It is not the intention of this chapter to provide an extensive review of this literature. Rather, more evidence will be provided concerning a small portion of this literature which concerns the role of mentorship in cognitive development. In conjunction with the conceptualization of wisdom as expertise, receiving as well as providing mentorship seems to play a crucial role in the accumulation of wisdom-related knowledge and judgment.

Within the expertise literature, Bloom (1985; see also Ericsson, Krampe, & Tesch-Römer, 1993) has so far provided perhaps the most comprehensive overview of the attainment of exceptional performance in everyday domains of functioning. However, we are only beginning to gain insight into the external and internal support conditions that contribute to the development of expertise. Inspecting evidence across a variety of domains, Bloom distinguished three phases of expertise development. In all three phases, mentorship and social interaction play a crucial role. In the first phase, during the early years of childhood, it is the parents who provide encouragement and support. In the second and third phase, that is, in the middle and later years of training, it seems to be essential that the individual works with a teacher or coach who has also performed at an exceptional level or at least coached other exceptional performers.

Research on mentorship or apprenticeship in adult–child relationships has demonstrated that the *type* of guidance provided plays a critical role in the facilitation of development (e.g. Rogoff, 1993). There must be not just any kind of social interaction with an adult or an individual with higher levels of knowledge; the interactional style has to fit the type of task and the performance capacity of the individual in order to be profitable (see also Tudge, 1992). These findings emphasize how important it is to tailor social interaction to the individual and the task at hand if it is to be supportive.

The Effect of Social Interaction on the Social-Cognitive Processes Involved in the Ontogenesis of Wisdom: The Sample Case of Life Review

The ontogenetic model of wisdom presented in Figure 25.1 makes certain rudimentary assumptions about organizing processes involved in the development of wisdom. Three such processes have been specified: life planning, life management, and life review. They may support the acquisition and refinement of personal as well as indirect life experiences (such as mediated through conversations, observations, or media). These life processes have also been employed to access and measure wisdom-related knowledge and judgment.

Life review – a more adequate term might be life (re)construction – will serve as a sample case to further illustrate the social-interactive nature of the ontogenesis of wisdom-related knowledge (Staudinger, 2001; Staudinger & Dittmann-Kohli, 1994). Most of the life experiences which we collect are dependent on direct or indirect interaction with other people. Beyond this quite obvious fact, however, the process of life (re)construction itself, which organizes such experiences by means of selection, categorization, abstraction, and interpretation, is social-interactive in nature. With regard to knowledge about one's own life, we know at least since James (1890) and later Mead (1934) that identity formation is mediated through feedback by others. In a similar vein, memory research has shown, for example, that the development of autobiographical memory is highly dependent on the development of the ability to communicate with others about what is happening or has happened (Nelson, 1992).

Let's consider some of the possible effects of social interaction on the process and product of life (re)construction (encompassing one's own life and life in general). Social interaction can facilitate as well as hamper this process. On the asset side, insights about life at which we have arrived individually may be tested by talking to other people about them. Or such insights may only be gained through communicative interaction with others. It may be the other who confronts us with undesirable observations about our own behavior, who points to contradictions in our construction of the world and who prevents us from glossing over things. These examples illustrate how certain kinds of communicative interaction may help us to become more self-critical and gain distance from our own behavior. A look at the debit side of social interaction, however, reveals that social transactions may also be dysfunctional and may interfere with the individual's life (re)construction. An example is if a partner, by misusing his or her influence, 'forces' interpretations on the person, or exclusively focuses on the strengths or the weaknesses of the person. The selection of the most suitable partner and the most suitable situation for a given piece of life (re)construction seems to be a crucial determinant of the utility of a given social interaction.

Social Interaction and the Activation of Wisdom

After the role of social interaction in the development of wisdom has been discussed, the social-interactive nature of the activation of individual wisdom-related performance will be considered. Whenever a situation calls for wisdom, most often more than one person is involved. Thus, wisdom very often is activated in situations of advice seeking or giving in view of difficult life problems. For example, when we consider how people deal with life problems, we find that very often they do consult with others, or perhaps with books, before making a decision or coming up with a proper interpretation of events.

Consulting with Others as the Most Important Informational Source

Such anecdotal evidence is supported by the findings from a pilot study in which people were asked how they usually, that is, in everyday life, go about solving fundamental life problems. Specifically, a heterogeneous sample, ranging in age from 19 to 80 years, was asked to what degree they dealt with life problems by (i) thinking about them by themselves, (ii) 'consulting' books or other media, (iii) thinking what other people might say about the problem at hand, and finally (iv) actually consulting with other people (Staudinger & Baltes, 1996). Overall, subjects reported the highest degree of endorsement for the option of consulting with others. Significantly lower in rank were both the option of thinking about the problem by oneself and the option of taking into account what other people might say to this problem.

Again, significantly lower and last in the ranking was the endorsement of 'consulting with' books and other media.

Original empirical efforts within the Berlin wisdom paradigm, however, generally neglected social interaction as part of the activation (microgenesis) of wisdom-related knowledge and judgment. The Berlin wisdom paradigm, like most other research efforts in this area, has been built around a person-centered experimental paradigm. That is, an individual subject has to respond to a given life dilemma. The social-interactive nature of wisdom, of course, was represented in the nature of the wisdom tasks but not in the actual experimental performance setting. Therefore, later empirical efforts concentrated on developing a social-interactive paradigm for the activation of wisdom-related performance.

A Study Implementing a Social-Interactive Paradigm for the Activation of Wisdom

To remedy this shortcoming an empirical study was conducted that aimed at doing more justice to the social-interactive nature of wisdom. Derived from our contention of the social-interactive nature of wisdom and evidence reported above, it was assumed that in most cases people have three ways of dealing with life problems: (1) consulting with other people whom they consider potentially helpful, *or* (2) taking into consideration what other people whose advice is usually sought might say to this problem, *or* (3) 'consulting' with informational sources potentially helpful for the problem at hand, be it books or their long-term memory. These three conditions vary among other things along a dimension which may be labelled 'directness of social interaction'. The dimension 'directness of social interaction' ranged from actual interactions between two people, through symbolic interaction with mental representations of other people's ideas, to interacting with written products of other people. The products of this 'consultation phase' or this interactive cognitive activity may then enter into individual cognition which finally results in a solution to the problem.

Based on such considerations, five experimental conditions were designed which were meant to gain first insights into the effect of social interaction on wisdom-related performance. Findings from research on group problem solving have demonstrated that the gains and losses involved in any social interaction have to form a positive balance in order to support the production of higher levels of performance. Therefore the experimental conditions in this study were constructed such that they allowed us to start teasing apart the facilitative and inhibitory effects of interactive and individual cognition on wisdom-related performance (Staudinger & Baltes, 1996).

In the following, the five performance settings will be described in the order of predicted increase of wisdom-related performance. The highest amount of performance increase was expected for the experimental condition called 'dialogue plus individual appraisal'. This experimental condition first provides for the opportunity of a natural dyad to discuss a wisdom task in any way they wish for 10 minutes. Afterwards each member of the dyad has 5 minutes to think about the task and the discussion by him- or herself before each is asked to respond individually. This condition was expected to result in the highest performance increase because it is characterized by a combination of individual and interactive cognition. Considerable performance increase was also expected for the second condition, called 'inner dialogue'. This condition provided for 10 minutes in which each subject should think about the wisdom task by taking into consideration what other people whose advice they value might have to say about this. Again, one can argue that this condition is characterized by a combination of interactive and individual cognition. Less performance increase was expected for both the conditions 'dialogue' and 'inner monologue'. In the dialogue condition, a natural dyad had 10 minutes to discuss a wisdom task in any way they wished. Immediately afterwards each of the members had to respond individually. The inner monologue condition provided for 10 minutes individual thinking after the subject had been presented with the wisdom task and before he or she had to respond. Finally, lowest wisdom-related performance levels were expected of the traditional standard wisdom procedure which asked the subject to immediately think aloud after being presented with the wisdom task.

These five experimental conditions were applied to a sample of 140 men and women from all walks of life covering an age range from 19 to 80 years. Two wisdom tasks were employed to access wisdom-related knowledge. One was a life-review task which confronted a fictitious person with the meaning of life question, and the other was a non-normative life-management problem which dealt with a young girl that wanted to move out of her parents' home.

Averaged across two wisdom-related tasks, the five performance conditions formed a linear trend with 'dialogue and individual appraisal' being first, 'inner dialogue' second, 'inner monologue' third, 'dialogue' fourth and 'standard' fifth in rank. No interaction with gender was obtained (Staudinger & Baltes, 1996).

This first study using an interactive minds paradigm seems to offer some support for the usefulness of social-interactive paradigms in teasing apart the contribution of individual and interactive cognition to wisdom-related performance. The condition combining individual and actually interactive cognition, that is, the 'dialogue and individual appraisal' condition, increased performance levels as compared to the standard condition by *one standard deviation*. However, the condition 'dialogue', which gives primacy to actual interactive cognition, did not result in a significant increase in performance as compared to traditional person-centered paradigms.

It seems that performance settings, optimally facilitative of wisdom-related knowledge, may be characterized by a balance between interactive and individual cognition. According to the findings of this first study, it does not seem to make a difference whether two people actually interact with each other or whether this interaction is mediated through mental representations of other people's wisdom-related knowledge. Even stronger, one can hypothesize that symbolically mediated interaction provides for more individual freedom in terms of when to 'access' another person's knowledge system.

Social Interaction and the Identification of Wisdom

In the Berlin work on wisdom, the social-interactive nature of the identification and attribution of wisdom and its collective representation has been acknowledged by using a social consensus criterion of wisdom. This has been implemented in two ways. First, people are nominated as wise by a group of nominators who had to reach consensus concerning the nomination in order for the nominee to be included in the final sample (Baltes et al., 1995). Second, the usual procedure of measuring wisdom-related performance involves a panel of raters who are trained to assess the level of wisdom-related knowledge present in a subject's response to our life dilemmas (e.g. Baltes & Smith, 1990; Baltes & Staudinger, 1993). A rating of responses done according to the raters' own conceptions of wisdom, without the provision of a definition, resulted in interrater consistencies of about 0.7 and a correlation of 0.7 with a wisdom rating obtained through the application of the five wisdom-related criteria (Staudinger, Smith, & Baltes, 1992). Additional evidence to support the high social consensus with regard to the identification of wisdom was gained in a study of implicit theories of wisdom (Staudinger et al., 2000). In this study a very high intersubject consistency on how they described a wise person was found.

Another result from this study of implicit theories of wisdom is relevant with regard to the social aspect in identifying wisdom. Although none of the subjects completing the questionnaire was found to be 'wise' when considering their own wisdom-related performance, all were very well able to describe and recognize a wise person. People seem to have representations of the meaning and characteristics of wisdom and wise persons. They themselves are not able, however, to apply those characteristics (which they can recognize in others) to a given life dilemma and thereby generate a high-level wisdom-related performance.

Conclusions

The concept of wisdom represents a fruitful topic for psychological research: (1) the study of wisdom emphasizes the search for continued optimization and the further evolution of the human condition, and (2) in a prototypical fashion, it allows for the study of collaboration among cognitive, emotional, and motivational processes.

From an inspection of dictionary definitions and implicit and explicit theories, wisdom was suggested to be a collective and social-interactive concept. The social-interactive nature of wisdom has been conceptualized as being threefold. The three facets refer to the development (ontogenesis, evolution), the activation in a given situation (microgenesis), and the identification (recognition) of wisdom-related knowledge. As wisdom can become manifest on an individual and a cultural level, all three facets can be identified on both levels as well. Proximal (face-to-face interaction) and distal (interaction with cultural artifacts) forms of social interaction were distinguished. Wisdom cannot develop without distal and proximal social interaction. But when it comes to the activation of wisdom in a given situation, proximal interaction does not constitute but rather facilitates wisdom-related performance.

An empirical study employing for the first time a social-interactive wisdom paradigm provided initial evidence to support the contention that optimal performance conditions for the activation of wisdom-related knowledge may involve a delicate balance between interactive and individual cognition rather than one or the other alone. Furthermore, the increase in performance by one standard deviation demonstrated that wisdom-related performance capacity seems to be quite rich given the right instructional settings.

We expect that future research on wisdom will be expanded in at least three ways: (1) the further identification of social and personality factors and life processes relevant for the ontogeny of wisdom, (2) the exploration of wisdom as a meta-heuristic (Baltes, in preparation; Baltes & Staudinger, 2000), and (3) the contribution of wisdom research to building a psychological art of life (Staudinger, 1999b).

Acknowledgements

Some of the data reported in this chapter were collected as part of the project 'Wisdom and Lifespan Development' conducted at the Max Planck Institute for Human Development and Education, co-directed by Paul B. Baltes and Ursula M. Staudinger (1992–9). The first author also gratefully acknowledges the multiple discussions about wisdom with colleagues at the Max Planck Institute for Human Development, especially Paul Baltes, Jacqui Smith, and Monisha Pasupathi.

REFERENCES

Adler, M.J. (1992). *The great ideas: One hundred two essays*. New York: Macmillan.

Anderson, J.R. (1987). Skill acquisition: Compilation of weak-method problem solutions. *Psychological Review*, 94, 192–210.

Ardelt, M. (1997). Wisdom and life satisfaction in old age. *Journal of Gerontology*, 52B, 15–27.

Arlin, P.K. (1990). Wisdom: The art of problem finding. In R.J. Sternberg (ed.), *Wisdom: Its nature, origins, and development* (pp. 230–243). New York: Cambridge University Press.

Assmann, A. (ed.) (1991). *Weisheit*. München: Fink.

Assmann, J. (1992). *Das kulturelle Gedächtnis: Schrift, Erinnerung und politische Identität in frühen Hochkulturen*. München: Beck.

Azmitia, M. (1996). Peer interactive minds: Developmental, theoretical, and methodological issues. In P.B. Baltes & U.M. Staudinger (eds), *Interactive minds* (pp. 133–162). New York: Cambridge University Press.

Azmitia, M., & Perlmutter, M. (1989). Social influences on children's cognition: State of the art and future directions. *Advances in Child Development and Behavior*, 22, 89–144.

Baltes, P.B. (in preparation). *Wisdom: The orchestration of mind and character*. Boston: Blackwell.

Baltes, P.B., & Smith, J. (1990). Toward a psychology of wisdom and its ontogenesis. In R.J. Sternberg (ed.), *Wisdom: Its nature, origins, and development* (pp. 87–120). New York: Cambridge University Press.

Baltes, P.B., Smith, J., & Staudinger, U.M. (1992). Wisdom and successful aging. *Nebraska Symposium on Motivation*, 39, (pp. 123–167).

Baltes, P.B., & Staudinger, U.M. (1993). The search for a psychology of wisdom. *Current Directions In Psychological Science*, 2, 1–6.

Baltes, P.B., & Staudinger, U.M. (2000). Wisdom: A metaheuristic to orchestrate mind and virtue towards excellence. *American Psychologist*, 55, 122–136.

Baltes, P.B., Staudinger, U.M., Maercker, A., & Smith J. (1995). People nominated as wise: A comparative study of wisdom-related knowledge. *Psychology and Aging*, 10, 155–166.

Barkow, J.H., Cosmides, L., & Tooby, J. (eds) (1992). *The adapted mind: Evolutionary psychology and the generation of culture*. New York: Oxford University Press.

Basseches, M. (1984). *Dialectical thinking and adult development*. Norwood, NJ: Ablex.

Berger, P.L., & Luckmann, T. (1967). *The social construction of reality*. Garden City, NY: Doubleday.

Birren, J.E., & Fischer, L.M. (1990). The elements of wisdom: Overview and integration. In R.J. Sternberg (ed.), *Wisdom: Its nature, origins, and development* (pp. 317–332). New York: Cambridge University Press.

Bloom, B.S. (1985). Generalizations about talent development. In B.S. Bloom (ed.), *Developing talent in young people* (pp. 507–549). New York: Ballantine.

Boesch, E.E. (1991). *Symbolic action theory and cultural psychology*. Heidelberg: Springer.

Bornstein, M.H., & Bruner, J.S. (1989). On interaction. In M.H. Bornstein & J.S. Bruner (eds), *Interaction in human development* (pp. 1–14). Hillsdale, NJ: Erlbaum.

Brent, S.B. (1978). Individual specialization, collective adaptation and rate of environmental change. *Human Development*, 21, 21–33.

Brent, S. B., & Watson, D. (1980). Aging and wisdom: Individual and collective aspects. Paper presented at the annual meeting of the Gerontological Society of America, San Francisco.

Bronfenbrenner, U. (1999). Environments in developmental perspective: Theoretical and operational models. In S.L. Friedman, T.D. Wachs et al. (eds), *Measuring environment across the life span: Emerging methods and concepts* (pp. 3–28). Washington, DC: APA.

Charness, N. (1989). Expertise in chess and bridge. In D. Klahr & K. Kotovsky (eds), *Complex information processing: The impact of Herbert A. Simon* (pp. 183–289). Hillsdale, NJ: Erlbaum.

Chinen, A.B. (1987). Fairy tales and psychological development in late life: A cross-cultural hermeneutic study. *The Gerontologist*, 27, 340–346.

Clayton, V.P. (1976). A multidimensional scaling analysis of the concept of wisdom. Unpublished doctoral dissertation, University of Southern California.

Clayton, V.P., & Birren, J.E. (1980). The development of wisdom across the life-span: A reexamination of an ancient topic. In P.B. Baltes & O.G. Brim (eds), *Life-span development and behavior* (Vol. 3, pp. 103–135). New York: Academic.

Cole, M. (1990). Cultural psychology: A once and future discipline? *Nebraska Symposium on Motivation*, 37, 279–335.

Csikszentmihalyi, M., & Rathunde, K. (1990). The psychology of wisdom: An evolutionary interpretation. In R.J. Sternberg (ed.), *Wisdom: Its nature, origins, and development* (pp. 25–51). New York. Cambridge University Press.

d'Andrade, R.G. (1981). The cultural part of cognition. *Cognitive Science*, 5, 179–195.

Dannefer, D. (1984). Adult development and social theory: A paradigmatic reappraisal. *American Sociological Review*, 49, 100–116.

Dittmann-Kohli, F., & Baltes, P.B. (1990). Toward a neofunctionalist conception of adult intellectual development: Wisdom as a prototypical case of intellectual growth. In C. Alexander & E. Langer (eds), *Higher stages of human development* (pp. 54–78). New York: Oxford University Press.

Ericsson, K.A., Krampe, R.Th., & Tesch-Römer, C. (1993). The role of deliberate practice in the acquisition of expert performance. *Psychological Review*, 100, 363–406.

Erikson, E.H., Erikson, J.M., & Kivnick, H. (1986). *Vital involvement in old age: The experience of old age in our time*. London: Norton.

Featherman, D.L., & Lerner, R.M. (1985). Ontogenesis and sociogenesis: Problematics for theory and research about development and socialization across the lifespan. *American Sociological Review*, 50, 659–676.

Fowler, H.W., & Fowler, F.G. (1964). *The concise Oxford dictionary of current English*. Oxford: Clarendon.

Gigerenzer, G., & Hug, K. (1992). Domain-specific reasoning: Social contracts, cheating, and perspective change. *Cognition*, 43, 127–171.

Goodwin, P.D., & Wenzel, J.W. (1981). Proverbs and practical reasoning: A study in socio-logic. In W. Mieder & A. Dundes (eds), *The wisdom of many: Essays on the proverb* (pp. 140–159). New York: Garland.

Grimm, J., & Grimm, W. (1854). *Deutsches Wörterbuch*. München: Deutches Taschenbuch, 1984.

Hahn, A. (1989). Zur Soziologie der Weisheit. In A. Assmann (ed.), *Weisheit: Archäologie der literarischen Kommunikation III* (pp. 47–58). München: Fink.

Hall, G.S. (1922). *Senescence: The last half of life*. New York: Appleton.

Hartshorne, C. (1987). *Wisdom as moderation: A philosophy of the middle way*. Albany: SUNY.

Helson, R., & Wink, P. (1987). Two conceptions of maturity examined in the findings of a longitudinal study. *Journal of Personality and Social Psychology*, 53, 531–541.

Holliday, S.G., & Chandler, M.J. (1986). *Wisdom: Explorations in adult competence*. Basel: Karger.

James, W. (1890). *The principles of psychology*. New York: Holt.

Kekes, J. (1983). Wisdom. *American Philosophical Quarterly*, 20, 277–286.

Kekes, J. (1995). *Moral wisdom and good lives*. Ithaca, NY: Cornell University Press.

Kitchener, K.S., & Brenner, H.G. (1990). Wisdom and reflective judgment: knowing in the face of uncertainty. In R.J. Sternberg (ed.), *Wisdom: Its nature, origins, and development* (pp. 212–229). New York: Cambridge University Press.

Kitchener, K.S., & King, P.M. (1990). The reflective judgment model: Ten years of research. In M.L. Commons, C. Armon, L. Kohlberg, F.A. Richards, T.A. Grotzer, & J.D. Sinnott (eds), *Adult development: Vol. 2. Models and methods in the study of adolescent and adult thought* (pp. 63–78). New York: Praeger.

Klix, F. (1993). *Erwachendes Denken: Geistige Leistungen aus evolutions-psychologischer Sicht*. Heidelberg: Spektrum Akademischer.

Kramer, D.A. (1990). Conceptualizing wisdom: The primacy of affect–cognition relations. In R.J. Sternberg (ed.), *Wisdom: Its nature, origins, and development* (pp. 279–313). New York: Cambridge University Press.

Kramer, D.A. (2000). Wisdom as a classical source of human strength: Conceptualization and empirical scrutiny. *Journal of Social and Clinical Psychology*, 19 (1), 83–101.

Kramer, D.A., Kahlbaugh, P.E., & Goldston, R.B. (1992). A measure of paradigm beliefs about the social world. *Journal of Gerontology: Psychological Sciences*, 47, 180–189.

Kuhn, D. (1989). Children and adults as intuitive scientists. *Psychological Review*, 96, 674–689.

Kuhn, D., Pennington, N., & Leadbeater, B. (1983). Adult thinking in developmental perspective. In P.B. Baltes & O.G. Brim (eds), *Life-span development and behavior* (Vol. 5, pp. 157–195). New York: Academic.

Labouvie-Vief, G. (1990). Wisdom as integrated thought: Historical and developmental perspectives. In R.J. Sternberg (ed.), *Wisdom: Its nature, origins, and development* (pp. 52–83). New York: Cambridge University Press.

Labouvie-Vief, G. (1995). *Psyche and Eros: Mind and gender in the life course*. New York: Cambridge University Press.

Lerner, R.M., & von Eye, A. (1992). Sociobiology and human development: Arguments and evidence. *Human Development*, 35, 12–33.

Lindenberger, U., & Baltes, P.B. (1994). Aging and intelligence. In R.J. Sternberg (ed.), *Encyclopedia of intelligence* (pp. 52–66). NewYork: Macmillan.

Loevinger, J. (1976). *Ego development: Conceptions and theories*. San Francisco: Jossey-Bass.

Loevinger, J., & Wessler, R. (1978). *Measuring ego development: I. Construction and use of a sentence completion test*. San Francisco: Jossey-Bass.

Marquart, O. (1989). Drei Betrachtungen zum Thema 'Philosophie und Weisheit' (Three observations concerning 'philosophy and wisdom'). In W. Oelmueller (ed.), *Philosophie und Weisheit (Philosophy and wisdom)* (pp. 275–308). Paderborn: Schöningh.

McCrae, R.R., & Costa, P.T. (1980). Openness to experience and ego level in Loevinger's sentence completion test: Dispositional contributions to developmental models of personality. *Journal of Personality and Social Psychology*, 39, 1179–1190.

Meacham, J.A. (1983). Wisdom and the context of knowledge: Knowing that one doesn't know. In D. Kuhn & A. Meacham (eds),*On the development of developmental psychology* (pp. 111–134). Basel: Karger.

Meacham, J.A. (1990). The loss of wisdom. In R.J. Sternberg (ed.), *Wisdom: Its nature, origins, and development* (pp. 181–211). New York: Cambridge University Press.

Mead, G.H. (1934). *Mind, self, and society*. Chicago: Chicago University Press.

Mergler, N.L., & Goldstein, M.D. (1983). Why are there old people? *Human Development*, 26, 72–90.

Mieder, W., & Dundes, A. (eds) (1981). *The wisdom of many: Essays on the proverb*. New York: Garland.

Mittelstraß, J. (1981). Platon. In O. Höffe (ed.), *Klassiker der Philosophie* (pp. 38–62). München: Beck.

Nelson, K. (1992). Emergence of autobiographical memory at age 4. *Human Development*, 35, 172–177.

Nozick, R. (1989). *The examined life: Philosophical meditations*. New York: Simon & Schuster.

Oelmueller, W. (ed.) (1989). *Philosophie und Weisheit (Philosophy and wisdom)*. Paderborn: Schöningh.

Orwoll, L. (1988). Wisdom in late adulthood: Personality and life history correlates. Unpublished doctoral dissertation, Boston University.

Orwoll, L., & Perlmutter, M. (1990). The study of wise persons: Integrating a personality perspective. In R.J. Sternberg (ed.), *Wisdom: Its nature, origins, and development* (pp. 160–177). New York: Cambridge University Press.

Oser, F.K., & Reich, K.H. (1987). The challenge of competing explanations: The development of thinking in terms of complementarity. *Human Development*, 30, 178–186.

Oser, F.K., Schenker, C., & Spychiger, M. (1999). Wisdom: An action-oriented approach. In K.H. Reich, F.K. Oser & W.G. Scarlett (eds), *Psychological studies on spiritual and religious development*. Pabst: Leugerich.

Oxford Dictionary of the English Language (1933). Vol. XII. Oxford: Clarendon Press.

Pascual-Leone, J. (1990). An essay on wisdom: Toward organismic processes that make it possible. In R.J. Sternberg (ed.), *Wisdom: Its nature, origins, and development* (pp. 244–278). New York: Cambridge University Press.

Pasupathi, M., Staudinger, U.M., & Baltes, P.B. (2001). Seeds of wisdom: Adolescents' knowledge and judgement about difficult matters of life. *Developmental Psychology*, 37, 351–361.

Pratt, M.W., Diessner, R., Pratt, A., Hunsberger, B., & Pancer, S.M. (1996). Moral and social reasoning and perspective taking in later life: A longitudinal study. *Psychology and Aging*, 11, 66–73.

Pratt, M.W., Pancer, M., Hunsberger, B., & Manchester, J. (1990). Reasoning about the self and relationships in maturity: An integrative complexity analysis of individual differences. *Journal of Personality and Social Psychology*, 59, 575–581.

Resnick, L.B., Levine, J.M., & Teasley, S.D. (1991). *Perspectives on socially shared cognition*. Washington, DC: American Psychological Association.

Rice, E.F. (1958). *The renaissance idea of wisdom*. Cambridge, MA: Harvard University Press.

Riegel, K.F. (1973). Dialectical operations: The final period of cognitive development. *Human Development*, 16, 346–370.

Riley, M.W. (1985). Age strata in social systems. In R.H. Binstock & E. Shanas (eds), *Handbook of aging and the social sciences* (pp. 369–411). New York: Van Nostrand Reinhold.

Robinson, D.N. (1990). Wisdom through the ages. In R.J. Sternberg (ed.), *Wisdom: Its nature, origins, and development* (pp. 13–24). New York: Cambridge University Press.

Rogoff, B. (1993). Children's guided participation and participatory appropriation in sociocultural activity. In R.H. Wozniak & K.W. Fischer (eds), *Development in context: Acting and thinking in specific environments* (pp.121–153). Hillsdale, NJ: Erlbaum.

Rudolph, K. (1987). Wisdom. In M. Eliade (ed.), *Encyclopedia of religion: Wisdom* (Vol. 15, pp. 393–401). New York: Macmillan.

Ryff, C. (1982). Self-perceived personality change in adulthood and aging. *Journal of Personality and Social Psychology*, 42, 108–115.

Ryff, C.D., & Heincke, S.G. (1983). The subjective organization of personality in adulthood and aging. *Journal of Personality and Social Psychology*, 44, 807–816.

Salthouse, T.A. (1991). *Theoretical perspectives on cognitive aging*. Hillsdale, NJ: Erlbaum.

Schütz, A., & Luckmann, T. (1979). *Strukturen der Lebenswelt* (Vol. 1). Frankfurt am Main: Suhrkamp.

Shweder, R.A. (1991). *Thinking through cultures*. Cambridge, MA: Harvard University Press.

Slavin, R. (1980). Cooperative learning. *Review of Educational Research*, 50, 315–342.

Smith, J. & Baltes, P.B. (1990). A study of wisdom-related knowledge: Age/cohort differences in responses to life-planning problems. *Developmental Psychology*, 26, 494–505.

Smith, J., Staudinger, U.M., & Baltes, P.B. (1994). Occupational settings facilitating wisdom-related knowledge: The sample case of clinical psychologists. *Journal of Consulting and Clinical Psychology*, 62, 989–999.

Sowarka, D. (1989). Weisheit und weise Personen: Common-Sense-Konzepte älterer Menschen (Wisdom and wise persons: Common-sense views from elderly people). *Zeitschrift für Entwicklungspsychologie und Pädagogische Psychologie*, 21, 87–109.

Staudinger, U.M. (1989). *The study of life review: An approach to the investigation of intellectual development across the life-span*. Berlin: Sigma.

Staudinger, U.M. (1996). Wisdom and the social-interactive foundation of the mind. In P.B. Baltes & U.M. Staudinger (eds), *Interactive minds* (pp. 276–315). New York: Cambridge University Press.

Staudinger, U.M. (1999a). Older and wiser? Integrating results on the relationship between age and wisdom-related performance. *International Journal of Behavioral Development*, 23, 641–664.

Staudinger, U.M. (1999b). Social cognition and a psychological approach to an art of life. In F. Blanchard-Fields & B.T. Hess (eds), *Social cognition, adult development, and aging* (pp. 343–375). New York: Academic Press.

Staudinger, U.M. (2001). Life review: A social-cognitive analysis of life review. *Review of General Psychology*, 5, 148–160.

Staudinger, U.M., & Baltes, P.B. (1994). Psychology of wisdom. In R.J. Sternberg (ed.), *Encyclopedia of human intelligence* (pp. 1143–1152). New York: Macmillan.

Staudinger, U.M., & Baltes, P.B. (1996). Interactive minds: A facilitative setting for wisdom-related performance? *Journal of Personality and Social Psychology*, 71, 746–762.

Staudinger, U.M., & Dittmann-Kohli, F. (1994). Lebenserfahrung und Lebenssinn. In P.B. Baltes, J. Mittelstraß, & U.M. Staudinger (eds), *Alter und Altern: Ein interdisziplinärer Studientext zur Gerontologie* (*Old age and aging: An interdisciplinary reader in gerontology*) (pp. 408–436). Berlin: de Gruyter.

Staudinger, U.M., Lopez, D.F., & Baltes, P.B. (1997). The psychometric location of wisdom-related performance. *Personality and Social Psychology Bulletin*, 23, 1200–1214.

Staudinger, U.M., Maciel, A., Sowarka, D., Smith, J., & Baltes, P.B. (2000). *Characteristics of a wise person: Interrelating implicit and explicit theories of wisdom.* Unpublished manuscript, available from first author.

Staudinger, U.M., & Pasupathi, M. (2002). Age-graded paths towards desirable development: Correlates of wisdom-related performance in adolescence and adulthood. Submitted manuscript, available from first author.

Staudinger, U.M., Smith, J., & Baltes, P.B. (1992). Wisdom-related knowledge in a life review task: Age differences and the role of professional specialization. *Psychology and Aging*, 7, 271–281.

Staudinger, U.M., Smith, J., & Baltes, P.B. (1994). *Manual for the assessment of wisdom-related knowledge and judgment.* Technical Report no. 46, Max Planck Institute for Human Development, Berlin.

Sternberg, R.J. (1986). Implicit theories of intelligence, creativity, and wisdom. *Journal of Personality and Social Psychology*, 49, 607–627.

Sternberg, R.J. (ed.) (1990a). *Wisdom: Its origins, and development.* New York: Cambridge University Press.

Sternberg, R.J. (1990b). Wisdom and its relations to intelligence and creativity. In R.J. Sternberg (ed.), *Wisdom: Its origins, and development* (pp. 142–159). New York: Cambridge University Press.

Sternberg, R.J. (1990c). Understanding wisdom. In R.J. Sternberg (ed.), *Wisdom: Its origins, and development* (pp. 3–9). New York: Cambridge University Press.

Sternberg, R.J. (1998). A balance theory of wisdom. *Review of General Psychology*, 2, 347–365.

Taylor, A. (1962). The wisdom of many and the wit of one. *Swarthmore College Bulletin*, 54, 4–7.

Tudge, J.R. (1992). Processes and consequences of peer collaboration: A Vygotskian analysis. *Child Development*, 63, 1364–1379.

Valsiner, J., & Lawrence, J.A. (1997). Human development in culture across the life-span. In J.W. Berry, P.R. Dasen et al. (eds), *Handbook of cross-cultural psychology: Vol. 2. Basic processes and human development* (2nd edn), pp. 69–106. Boston: Allyn & Bacon.

von Cranach, M., Doise, W., & Mugny, G. (eds) (1992). *Social representations and the social bases of knowledge.* Lewiston, NY: Hogrefe & Huber.

Walaskay, M., Whitbourne, S.K., & Nehrke, M.F. (1983–84). Construction and validation of an ego-integrity status interview. *International Journal of Aging and Human Development*, 18, 61–72.

Wozniak, R.H., & Fischer, K.W. (eds) (1993). *Development in context: Acting and thinking in specific environments.* Hillsdale, NJ: Erlbaum.

PART SEVEN: METHODOLOGY IN THE STUDY OF DEVELOPMENT

26

Qualitative Methodology

JONATHAN SMITH AND FRASER DUNWORTH

Over the past decade or so there has been an explosion of interest in qualitative approaches in psychology. This is reflected in the emergence of a number of texts specifically for psychologists (Hayes, 1997a; Murray & Chamberlain, 1999; Richardson, 1996; Smith, in press; Smith, Harré, & van Langenhove, 1995c; Willig, 2001; Yardley, 1997) and a number of special issues/sections of psychology journals (Henwood & Nicolson, 1995; *Journal of Counselling Psychology*, 1994). This is a significant shift in a discipline which has hitherto primarily employed quantitative methodology. This chapter will sketch briefly an introduction to qualitative methods in psychology, describe the different types of qualitative methodology which are available and give a more detailed account of one method, interpretative phenomenological analysis, and its use in development studies.

The Qualitative–Quantitative Distinction

What is qualitative psychology? In terms of dictionary definitions the difference between qualitative and quantitative analysis is that the former is concerned with describing the constituent properties of an entity, the latter with determining how much of the entity there is. And it is the case that much qualitative research aims to provide rich or 'thick' (Geertz, 1973) descriptive accounts of the phenomenon under investigation, while quantitative research is more concerned with counting occurrences, volumes, or the size of associations between entities.

Qualitative and quantitative approaches are clearly different in the principal forms of data employed in analysis. Quantitative research depends on the ability to reduce phenomena to numerical values in order to carry out statistical analyses. Thus while much quantitative research begins with verbal data (e.g. in the form of questionnaire responses), this verbal material must be transformed into numbers for a quantitative analysis to be performed. By contrast qualitative research involves collecting data in the form of verbal reports – e.g. written accounts, interview transcripts – and the analysis then conducted on these is linguistic and textual. Thus the concern is with interpreting what a piece of text means rather than finding a way of capturing it numerically. The interpretation is then conveyed through detailed narrative reports of participants' perceptions, understandings or accounts of a phenomenon. For most qualitative researchers, this approach is consonant with a theoretical commitment to the importance of language as a fundamental property of human communication, interpretation and understanding. Given that we tend to make sense of our social world and express that sense-making to ourselves and others linguistically, qualitative researchers emphasize the value of analytic strategies which remain as close as possible to the symbolic system in which that sense-making occurs.

Qualitative approaches in psychology are generally engaged with exploring, describing and understanding the personal and social experiences of participants and trying to capture the meanings that particular phenomena hold for them. In that sense the quintessential entity for the qualitative researcher is meaning. An attempt is usually made to understand a small number of participants' lived experience or views of the world rather than trying to test a preconceived hypothesis on a large sample. For some qualitative researchers, e.g. discourse analysts, the primary emphasis lies in how meanings are constructed and shaped discursively. Qualitative approaches are particularly useful when the topic under investigation is complex, dilemmatic, novel or under-researched and where there is a concern with understanding process rather than measuring outcomes.

While the above introduction attempts to portray the distinct flavour of qualitative research – and in practice qualitative and quantitative research projects usually differ considerably in terms of research question, orientation and execution – making categorical distinctions between qualitative and quantitative methods proves difficult. The differences are often better expressed as tendencies and one can see degrees of overlap in various ways.

Take the importance of meaning, for example. It is the case that for many qualitative researchers the primary concern is with exploring the meanings of phenomena to participants. However, many quantitative researchers would take issue with the claim that they are not concerned with meaning and argue they too are interested in how participants interpret and construct their social world, i.e. the process of making meaning. The difference is often more a matter of the degree of emphasis on meaning as the central concern, the definition of the level of analysis of meaning and the best way to capture it methodologically. Then take the possible contrast between a qualitative concern with description and a quantitative concern with prediction and explanation. While this holds as a distinction between many qualitative and quantitative research projects, it is by no means an absolute differentiation. Quantitative research can produce descriptive statistical analyses and some qualitative researchers, e.g. grounded theorists, may wish to propose causal accounts to explain the phenomena under question.

At a technical level too, a categorical separation of qualitative and quantitative methods proves difficult to sustain. While it is the case that many qualitative projects eschew counting altogether, others incorporate a degree of quantification at various stages. Thus some research is based on the collection of relatively open-ended verbal, and therefore qualitative, material, but this material is then subjected to systematic quantitative techniques such as content analysis (Krippendorf, 1980) and protocol analysis (Green & Gilhooly, 1996). Other research studies engage in a process of qualitative analysis of the data collected but the resulting themes or categories are then presented in the form of descriptive statistics, indicating the degree of frequency of their occurrence in the corpus of verbal material. Finally Hayes (1997b) makes the interesting point that the process of analysis and presentation in qualitative research often invokes quantitative properties as judgements are made, implicitly or explicitly, of the strength or otherwise of a category or property being reported and individuals are compared with each other on various dimensions. Similarly, of course, one can argue that quantitative research always involves interpretation on the part of the researcher and that this process is essentially a qualitative one. For further discussion of the relation between qualitative and quantitative research methods and the difficulty in making definitive distinctions, see Hayes (1997b), Bryman (1988) and Smith, Harré, and van Langenhove (1995b).

In this section we have attempted to illustrate some of the particular features of qualitative research which set it apart from quantitative work, but also indicate that the boundary between the two may not be as clear cut or absolute as is sometimes presented. A case can be made that all psychological inquiry involves both qualitative and quantitative properties but different approaches and projects prioritize these properties very differently. We are now putting those issues to do with categorical definition to one side and moving to examine the approaches which are generally considered to be qualitative in nature and which have been taken up by psychologists. While we are not concerned here with a strict definition of what is qualitative as opposed to quantitative, we are concerned with pointing to the differences which exist even between researchers who describe themselves as qualitative and yet point to strong differences between themselves and other qualitative psychologists.

Thus it is important to realize that qualitative psychology is not homogenous. There are a number of different approaches, each with overlapping but different theoretical and/ or methodological emphases. The following section gives a brief outline of some of the main qualitative approaches currently in use by psychologists. We shall devote the remainder of the chapter to discussing one particular qualitative approach, interpretative phenomenological analysis, which has been used in a range of different psychological research projects.

QUALITATIVE APPROACHES IN PSYCHOLOGY

Phenomenology

Husserl is usually credited as the key figure in establishing the phenomenological approach to inquiry. Husserl developed a theory of consciousness and subjective experience and described a method for studying it. A number of social scientists (e.g. Blumer, 1969; Glaser & Strauss, 1967) acknowledge a debt to Husserl's phenomenology in their development of qualitative approaches. Phenomenological psychology recognizes that a whole set of factors lead to differences in people's perception of reality and is committed to the exploration of individual lived experience. One of the key writers on phenomenological psychology is Giorgi (1985; 1995) who has articulated an approach to inquiry, developed an accompanying methodology and applied it to a range of research issues. Giorgi's method involves a sequence of steps in analysing the personal accounts provided by participants of their experience of a particular phenomenon. The researcher's views are bracketed during this process as the emphasis is on revealing the implicit structure in the participant's verbal report. The account is read a number of times in order to elicit meaning units. An examination of the meaning units uncovers the central features of the experience. A descriptive account is produced of the person's experience, paying due regard to the particular context in which this phenomenon was experienced. Subsequently by comparing the individual accounts of a number of participants a more generalized account of the experience can be produced. For further reading on phenomenology, see Spinelli (1989), Giorgi (1995) or Giorgi and Giorgi (in press). A useful collection providing guidance on method and examples of phenomenological research studies on learning, thinking and self-deception can be found in Giorgi (1985).

Grounded Theory

Grounded theory is an approach to inquiry first proposed by two sociologists Glaser and Strauss (1967). Their aim was to develop a systematic and rigorous set of procedures for the qualitative analysis of verbal material, which enabled the development of middle level theoretical accounts of particular phenomena. Data collection could take a number of forms, e.g. a researcher's field notes from participant observation or ethnography, interviews with participants or participants' own autobiographical accounts. The analytic sequence begins with line by line coding of transcript material in a primarily inductive fashion. Subsequently the account moves bottom up to a higher level of analysis as the researcher develops a more focused account of the material. Through constant comparison between different sources of data, the account is refined, and new data sources are identified to test the boundaries of the emerging account. Glaser and Strauss describe this process as allowing the discovery of theory which is therefore grounded in the data which have been collected rather than the testing of preconceived hypotheses on new data sources.

Grounded theory, though originating in sociology, is now beginning to interest psychologists. Several versions of grounded theory have been described, and modifications made, in the light of social constructionist concerns with the importance of language and the role of the investigator in the discovery of theory. See Charmaz (1995; in press), Pidgeon and Henwood (1996), and Strauss and Corbin (1990) for discussion of grounded theory and its methodology. See Feldman (1996) for a grounded theory study of enhancing teachers' practice through collaborative action research.

Discourse Analysis

Discourse analysis as developed in contemporary social psychology is a qualitative approach which is concerned with examining how verbal accounts are constructed, the linguistic resources drawn on in their construction, and the social ends served by them. This form of discourse analysis is strongly influenced by social constructionism and sceptical of the ability to examine or uncover conventional psychological constructs – cognitive and affective – from participants' verbal reports. Potter and Wetherell (1987; 1995) place particular emphasis on the variability of participants' reports, arguing that, rather than reflecting underlying stable cognitive entities such as beliefs and attitudes, these reports in fact illustrate contextual and contingent factors influencing their accounts. They also document the interpretative repertoires through which participants construct reality. Parker (1992), influenced by Foucault, is more interested in the pre-existing social discourses which shape participants' construction of the social world. For an example of an empirical project employing discourse analysis, see Wetherell and Potter (1992). See Burman (1996) for a discussion of developmental psychology and discourse analysis.

Co-operative Inquiry

Co-operative inquiry is an approach to research strongly influenced by humanistic psychology and action research. In co-operative inquiry the researcher acts as a facilitator for the research project, inviting a group of individuals to develop a research study in which they all act as co-researchers throughout the project. Thus the co-researchers decide: the topic of the inquiry, what will count as data and who it will be collected from, how the data will be analysed, and how the results will be disseminated. For more on co-operative inquiry, see Reason and Heron (1995) and Reason (in press).

Narrative Analysis

Narrative psychology focuses on the way in which participants' understanding and ordering of experience can be considered as a form of story telling. This can include a concern with the pre-existing cultural patterns available and how individuals use those narrative structures in their own particular accounts. For example Gergen and Gergen (1988) describe narratives of independence and connection which underlie and inform participants' accounts of their personal relationships. For more on narrative psychology, see Crossley (2000) and Murray (1999; in press).

Interpretative Phenomenological Analysis (IPA)

Interpretative phenomenological analysis is a relative newcomer to the qualitative field. It has been specifically developed in psychology and entails a set of procedures for analysing verbal material from a particular theoretical perspective. The aim of interpretative phenomenological analysis is to explore in detail the participant's view of the topic under investigation. Thus the approach is phenomenological in that it is concerned with an individual's personal perception or account of an object or event as opposed to an attempt to produce either an actuarial account of a response category or an objective statement about the object or event itself. At the same time, interpretative phenomenological analysis also makes provision for the fact that the research exercise is a dynamic process. The investigator is trying to get close to the participant's personal world, to take, in Conrad's (1987) words, an 'insider's perspective', but one cannot do this directly or completely. Access depends on, and is complicated by, the researcher's own conceptions; indeed these are required in order to make sense of that other personal world through a process of interpretative activity. Hence the term 'interpretative phenomenological analysis' is used to signal these two facets of the approach.

There is considerable overlap between interpretative phenomenological analysis (IPA) and grounded theory. However, grounded theory, having been in existence for thirty years, has developed in a range of diverse ways. Therefore while some studies using grounded theory may look very similar to IPA, others will differ considerably. In this context, interpretative phenomenological analysis is distinguished by its psychological orientation and origins, and by the crucial place individual accounts have in the analysis and write-up. IPA is idiographic (Smith, Harré, & van Langenhove, 1995a), beginning with particular cases and only slowly working up to more general categorization or statements. However, even when an IPA paper is couched in more general terms, the individual voices of participants are always present. For IPA, the development of theory is not necessary. A rich or 'thick description' (Geertz, 1973) of the phenomenon under investigation can be a satisfactory outcome for an IPA study. However analysis can move to a more explanatory or theoretical level if the data warrant it.

IPA has a very different epistemological position from discourse analysis. While the latter, as exemplified by Potter and Wetherell and by Parker, is sceptical of or antagonistic towards the possibility of a chain of connection between verbal response and underlying cognition, IPA believes in the existence of this chain and is committed to cognitive entities such as beliefs and attitudes. This means that IPA also has common ground with the social cognitive paradigm in psychology, though IPA tends to picture the cognitive entities under investigation, the links between them, and the best way to explore them in rather different ways from conventional social cognitive research. For more on the theoretical underpinning of IPA see Smith (1996a).

Interpretative Phenomenological Analysis in Practice: Exploring the Experience of Mothers of Children with Attention Deficit Hyperactivity Disorder

The aim of this section is to illustrate the stages involved in a project using interpretative phenomenological analysis. Each phase of the research process will be described: constructing an interview schedule; conducting, recording and transcribing the interviews; analysing the transcripts; and writing up the results. The general account will be illustrated with examples taken from a project which employed interpretative phenomenological analysis to discover more about the experience of mothers and their children who were being treated for attention deficit hyperactivity disorder (ADHD) Dunworth, F. (1999). Interpretative phenomenological analysis is not a methodological straitjacket. It is a tool which will be adapted and developed to meet the needs of particular projects with particular aims, carried out by researchers with their unique interpretative styles. Qualitative analysis is inevitably a personal process and the analysis itself is the interpretative work which the investigator does at each stage.

ADHD and this Study

ADHD is a psychiatric diagnosis applied to children who present with significant difficulties in important areas of their lives when these difficulties can be understood as the result of behaviour which is impulsive, overactive and/or inattentive to a degree excessive for the individual's developmental age. Treatment regimes which include the prescription of medication, usually a stimulant such as methylphenidate (Ritalin), are increasingly common. There is evidence that the short-term benefits of such medication can include increased self-control, concentration, co-operation and academic productivity (more work completed), along with a decrease in hostility and behaviour problems. Depression, antisocial behaviour and academic achievement (qualifications and level of education) may be unaffected. Positive effects may not persist when medication is discontinued (see Barkley, 1998, for more on ADHD).

There has been little research into the impact of the diagnosis of ADHD and its treatment on children's understanding of themselves and their behaviour. There has also been little investigation of the experience of the parents of such children. The present study is therefore essentially exploratory. Qualitative approaches have been described as especially suitable for projects of this kind where little is known about the phenomenon under investigation.

For this study, six boys aged 9 to 12 years and their mothers were interviewed. The boys had been receiving Ritalin for ADHD for at least three months. The interviews were recorded and transcribed. The transcripts were then analysed and the analysis written up.

The Interview

The type of interview discussed here, and used in the ADHD study, follows a semi-structured format. With semi-structured interviews the researcher constructs an interview schedule. This schedule may then act as a guide and a reminder during the interview. It does not have to be followed rigidly. The researcher thus remains free to enquire more deeply into particular areas and to follow the priorities and concerns of the interviewee, who can introduce topics the researcher had not thought of. During the interview, time should be devoted to building rapport with the interviewee and the order and form of any questions can be tailored accordingly. In one sense, the participant can be seen as the 'expert' on the subject in question and the idea is to give her/him the best possible opportunity to tell their story.

The interview schedule used with both the boys and their mothers covered three broad areas: the experience of diagnosis and treatment, the experience of self and others, and the experience of attempting to understand and deal with ADHD. The interview schedule constructed for use with the mothers in the study is given in Box 26.1.

Specific questions to address relevant facets of each area should be devised, taking care to use clear everyday language and avoid specialized jargon. The interviewer should be aware of the language used by the respondent and try to communicate in ways that they will be comfortable with. Some consideration should also be given to prompts which could usefully follow on from the answers that might be given. A prompt is a more explicitly focused question which may be helpful when exploring a complex issue or when the original question proves too general for the particular participant (e.g. B1 in Box 26.1). They can also act as reminders for the interviewer to make sure relevant aspects of a topic are covered, for example, after questions A6 and A7 (Box 26.1).

The aim is to construct questions which are specific enough to encourage the respondent to talk about the topic and general enough to encourage them to do it in their own way, from their own perspective and with their own emphasis. Usually the more general and open the questions and the fewer the specific prompts required during any particular interview the better. The order in which topics and questions are raised in the schedule may be decided by what seems logical and by consideration of the potential sensitivity of the various issues, more sensitive matters being left until later in the interview when the respondent has had a chance to relax and become used to speaking to the interviewer.

Before the first interview it is good practice for the interviewer to memorize the schedule. This facilitates its use as a framework and a mental checklist and avoids the interviewer having to refer to it constantly during the interview. It is not necessary to follow a schedule slavishly. A good interview might involve the participant freely discussing their thoughts and experiences regarding all the areas on the schedule, and more besides, without the interviewer asking a single question as it actually appears on the schedule.

There is no fixed procedure for conducting semi-structured interviews. The interviews in the ADHD study lasted for up to an hour and a half and took place in the participants' own homes. The interviewer should take enough time at the outset to establish a relaxed atmosphere and a comfortable relationship with the respondent. Then, during the interview, it is useful to try and set a slow enough pace to enable the respondent to have time to give full and complete answers to questions (for more on qualitative interviewing see Smith, 1995b, and Kvale, 1996).

The transcription of interviews which requires great care and attention is a time-consuming activity. Different qualitative approaches employ different levels of transcription. Thus, for example, conversation analysis (Drew, 1995) is concerned with the micro-analysis of small segments of talk and therefore includes detailed transcription of linguistic and paralinguistic features such as intonation, exact

Box 26.1 Interview schedule: mother's experience of ADHD

A *Diagnosis and treatment*

1. Can you describe your son's problem, as you see it, from its beginnings to diagnosis and treatment commencing?
2. What were your thoughts when the diagnosis was made?
3. What did you feel?
4. What do you think about your son taking Ritalin?
5. What are your feelings about your son's treatment?
6. In what ways does taking Ritalin affect your son's life?
   Prompt: school, friendships, family, activities.
7. How does your son's treatment affect your life?
   Prompt: work, family, relationships, interests.

B *Self and others*

1. How do you see your son?
   Prompt: what sort of person is he? What are his most important characteristics?
2. How has this changed, if at all, since taking Ritalin?
3. How do others see and behave towards your son?
   Prompt: other children, family, teachers, other adults.
4. How has this changed, if at all, since he began treatment?
5. How does your son see and behave towards others?
6. How has this changed, if at all, since he started taking Ritalin?
7. How do you see yourself?
8. How has this changed, if at all, since diagnosis and treatment of your son?
9. How do others see and behave towards you?
10. How has this changed, if at all, since your son began treatment?
11. How does you see and behave towards others?
12. How has this changed, if at all, since your son started taking Ritalin?

C *Understanding and dealing with ADHD*

1. What does ADHD mean to you personally?
2. How do you deal with ADHD?
   Prompt: do you have particular ways of coping? Practical methods? Emotional?
3. How do you see the future for your son?
4. How do you imagine your own future?

pause length and intake of breath. Interpretative phenomenological analysis is more oriented to the meanings in the text. In the investigation of ADHD children, the aim was to reproduce verbatim all that the participant and the interviewer said during the interview, noting, in addition, significant non-verbal events such as laughter and noticeably long pauses in a way which was easy to read.

Analysis

A project may focus on one transcript from a single respondent or it may involve interviews with a number of participants. Even in the latter case, it is advisable to start by examining the transcript of one interview in detail before moving on to others. This follows an idiographic approach to analysis.

In the ADHD study the transcripts were analysed one at a time. The mothers' transcripts were analysed first, then their children's. The process is one of moving from the particular to the general, starting with specific examples of themes in a participant's transcript, gradually developing more generally applicable categories for the themes in that transcript, doing the same with the other participants' transcripts and then deriving overarching themes applicable to the participants as a group. In this study, the mothers and the children were treated as separate groups. The process of analysis from the initial reading of one transcript to the account of the group themes is illustrated with examples from the mothers' transcripts.

If the researcher has not transcribed the tape-recordings, it is helpful for her/him to listen to the tape-recording at least once while first reading the transcript. Mentally hearing the voice of the participant during subsequent readings of the transcript assists with a more complete analysis.

The first stage of analysis involves reading the transcript a number of times and at each reading noting things of importance in what the participant is saying. These initial notes include preliminary summaries and interpretations of the material, attempts to make links with other aspects of the participant's account, or simply represent associations and speculations which occur to the researcher. See Box 26.2, which illustrates the initial analysis of one participant, Pat, who is describing her experience of an initial interview with a Child and Family Mental Health Team.

The researcher then goes through the transcript again and translates the initial notes into emerging themes, that is, words or phrases which seem to capture the gist or essence of what is being said by the participant. These theme labels do not need to be conclusive or very general at this stage and should remain close to the text. One way this can be done is by using the words of the participant, where appropriate. At the same time, inevitably, the process is selective and interpretative as the researcher tries to make sense of what the participant is saying and the process also moves to a slightly higher level of abstraction. Box 26.3 presents the themes which were identified in the extract from Pat's account.

To illustrate this process further, Box 26.4 presents another section of the transcript showing the initial notes, and the themes identified in this passage are shown in Box 26.5.

When the transcript has been worked through in this way, a complete listing of the emergent themes at this 'first level' is compiled. Some themes may appear a number of times throughout the transcript. To help illustrate the sequence of analysis, a list of themes is presented in Box 26.6; however it only

Box 26.2 Making initial notes on the transcript

Initial notes	**Transcript**
Previous experience of not being heard	Well the thing is I'd had this from the doctor anyway, and I thought I'm coming here now and I'm going to
Hope that will be listened to, unburdened	be able to get it all off me chest and somebody's going to listen to me, but I took an instant dislike to her
Defensiveness?	anyway because of her attitude, she, I don't . . . We had conversations about was the marriage stable, um,
Questions seen as hostile, irrelevant?	did you ever hit him, um, well the things she was asking me to do and the things she was telling me what
Advice seen as controlling, unwanted, unsympathetic, unrealistic	I should be doing well I didn't agree with. I got the impression from her that yes I could do that if he was
Child as the problem	an ideal child. It was as though I was getting the blame
Feeling blamed	That was the feeling I got from her.

Box 26.3 Translating initial notes into themes (level 1)

Transcript	**Themes**
Well the thing is I'd had this from the doctor anyway, and I thought I'm coming here now and I'm going to be able to get it all off me chest and somebody's going to listen to me, but I took an instant dislike to her anyway because of her	Desire to be understood
attitude, she, I don't . . . We had conversations about was the marriage stable, um, did you ever hit him, um, well the things she was asking me to do and the things she was telling me what I should be doing well I didn't agree with. I got the impression from her that yes I could do that if he	Getting advice
was an ideal child. It was as though I was getting the blame. That was the feeling I got from her.	Feeling blamed

Box 26.4 Making initial notes on the transcript (another example)

Initial notes	**Transcript**
Pat unsure how teachers view her son Seeing son as naughty obscures nature of his difficulties? Pat's struggle with school Pat does get response from teachers Overwhelmed by advice? Did she try all these things? Was she expected to do it all? Time and effort These 'things' not working	*Pat*: I don't know if the teachers just looked upon him as a naughty child. So I pushed and pushed and pushed at school. Well it was just a case of, er, try this and try that, try a rewarding system. Over the years you get to the point where you think, well this is just not working. All these things they were asking me to do were just not working. *Interviewer*: They were asking you to try different things and you didn't have any success? *Pat*: No I didn't. No. *Interviewer*: How did that make you feel? At the time?
Helplessness Need to feel able to control son Uselessness Feeling a failure as a parent Self-doubt and self-blame	*Pat*: At the time [sighs]. Well basically I just felt like, what can I do? I can't control him. Yeah I felt like a, sort of a useless parent. You get to the point where you think, 'Is it me? Is it the way I brought him up? Have I done something wrong?'

Box 26.5 Translating initial notes into themes (second example)

Transcript	**Themes**
Pat: I don't know if the teachers just looked upon him as a naughty child. So I pushed and pushed and pushed at school. Well it was just a case of, er, try this and try that, try a rewarding system. Over the years you get to the point where you think, well this is just not working. All these things they were asking me to do were just not working.	Different views of son Pat's struggle Advice Failure
Interviewer: They were asking you to try different things and you didn't have any success? *Pat*: No I didn't. No. *Interviewer*: How did that make you feel? At the time?	
Pat: At the time [sighs]. Well basically I just felt like, what can I do? I can't control him. Yeah I felt like a, sort of a useless parent. You get to the point where you think, 'Is it me? Is it the way I brought him up? Have I done something wrong?'	Helplessness Control of son Failure as parent Blaming self

shows a small number of the total themes elicited for this transcript.

The next stage of the analysis involves looking for connections and similarities among the first level themes. Some themes may be near repetitions of the same content; others will be linked by more general, overarching themes. The process is one of gathering themes which seem to belong together into groups, thinking about what links them and what broader categories they might be aspects of. This process can be performed 'manually' by listing themes on paper or cards, or it can be done on a computer where standard 'cut and paste' facilities can be used to cluster the themes. Each cluster is given a label which captures the thematic essence of the group. An example from the analysis of Pat's transcript is given in Box 26.7. Page numbers refer to the original transcript and are used to locate instances of themes.

Box 26.6 Listing of themes (level 1)

Relationship with husband
Isolation
Demands of children
Neglect of daughter
Son not interested
Son seen as selfish
Struggle to meet different demands
Comparison: son and daughter
Son's inertia
Desire to be understood
Getting advice
Feeling blamed
Different views of son
Pat's struggle
Advice
Failure
Helplessness
Control of son
Failure as parent
Blaming self
Pat's struggle to do the right thing
Pat's guilt
Others criticizing
Different views of child-rearing
Son unstimulated
Reference to norms
Pat's sacrifice
Son unenthusiastic
Son not communicating with Pat

The aim of this process is to organize the thematic material into a manageable number of superordinate themes (level 2) which can be said to capture the essence of one's reading of the transcript. This process for this interview still produced a large number of these superordinate themes (approximately 70). Therefore the process of looking for connections and groupings among this list was repeated. In this way, a final list of master themes (level 3) for the interview should emerge, the constituent themes and examples of which can be readily traced back through the analytic process to their occurrence in the text. The table of master themes derived from the transcript of Pat's interview is reproduced in Box 26.8. For brevity's sake the relevant second level themes are given for only two of the master themes. The level 2 themes from Box 26.7 can be seen as items 26, 27, and 28 in this master themes list.

The analysis of a single participant's transcript may form the basis of a case study or the researcher may move on to analyse interviews with a number of different individuals. One possibility is to use the master theme list from interview 1 to begin the analysis of the second interview, looking for more instances of the themes identified from the first interview while being ready to identify new ones that may arise.

Box 26.7 Producing superordinate themes (level 2)

Pat criticized, put down
Husband criticizes Pat p. 5, p. 13
Others criticizing Pat p. 4
Getting advice p. 3, p. 9
Negative experience with psychologist p. 9
Feeling blamed p. 9, p. 11
Pat 'put down' p. 8
Desire to be understood p. 9

Pat rejected by GP
Rejected by GP p. 8
GP dismissive p. 5, p. 8

Pat isolated, unsupported
Pat avoids others due to son p. 6
Isolation p. 3
Absent husband p. 13
Lack of support p. 3
Support not given p. 2
No support for Pat p. 5
No response from professionals p. 6
GP unhelpful p. 8
Lack of progress p. 2

In the ADHD study a different approach was adopted. Here the process of analysis described above for the first interview was repeated for each of the participants' transcripts in turn, i.e. the researcher started from scratch with the second transcript looking for whatever themes were present in that interview. A list of all the master themes from each of the transcripts was then compiled. Thus each transcript generates a table of master themes. The next stage in the analysis involves an examination of connections between each of the individual's theme tables so that they in turn can be clustered together and, from these groupings, master themes emerge which capture the important shared aspects of experience described across the individual transcripts. This system works well with studies within an idiographic paradigm and which employ small samples such as the one presented. With such studies it is possible to retain an overall picture of each of the individual cases and the occurrence of themes within them while, at the same time, searching for connections across cases.

The end product of this systematic iterative process will be a table of master themes for the group of participants (level 4). The exact format of this table will depend on the project, material and researcher. For example, it may be a complete

Box 26.8 Master themes from first transcript (level 3)

1 Sense of responsibility
- 22 Different views of son (from Pat's)
- 26 Pat criticized/put down
- 27 Pat rejected by GP
- 33 Pat helpless/a failure
- 34 Pat depressed
- 36 Pat's guilt/responsibility
- 37 Differences *re* parenting
- 32 Battle to control son
- 18 Son blamed for lack of bond with Pat
- 17 Early separation of Pat and son
- 23 Pat's contradictory views of grand-parents' relationship with son
- 19 Son OK when little
- 20 Pat senses problem early on
- 21 Developmental changes

2 Mother's burden
- 25 Conflict in marriage due to son
- 28 Pat isolated, unsupported
- 29 Burden on Pat
- 30 Pat's needs
- 31 Difficulty balancing needs of children
- 32 Battle to control Pat
- 35 Pat's struggle to get help

3 Negative and contradictory views of son

4 Explaining her son

5 Support

6 Significance of diagnosis

7 Significance of Ritalin treatment (more complex)

8 Uncertain future

mapping of all themes and superordinate themes with identifiers of specific instances. Alternatively, it may be an abbreviated skeletal map showing merely the master entries for each participant, allowing the individual theme tables to be referred to for further detail. In this project, because of the large number of first level themes, the abbreviated mapping approach was employed. A partial version of this is shown in Box 26.9 with the constituent individual master themes for group master themes 1 and 2.

Six group master themes were derived which seemed to capture and organize a great deal of the material present in the interviews with the mothers and therefore represent a mapping of the analysis of

Box 26.9 Master themes for the group (level 4)

1 Mother's sense of responsibility
- Mother takes it personally (Ann)
- Mother's sense of responsibility (Liz)
- Mother's sense of responsibility (Pat)
- Mother's sense of responsibility (Sharon)
- Taking it personally (Jane)
- Mother's sense of responsibility (Val)

2 Mother's burden
- Burden on Liz (Liz)
- Burden (Pat)
- Ann's burden and struggle (Ann)
- Sharon's burden (Sharon)
- Burden on Val (Val)
- Support (Pat)

3 Contradictions in the view/account of the child

4 The struggle to understand and explain the child

5 Uncertainty regarding the future

6 The significance of diagnosis and treatment

the mothers' experience of living with ADHD. These master themes acted as umbrella descriptions under which those aspects of experience which were most important to the participants as a group could be gathered. Once derived, they were used as a 'lens' for a review of each transcript to check that the master themes were significantly present in each account. For example, from the list of group themes, it appeared that *mother's burden* was not an important theme in the account of Jane. However, returning to the transcript revealed that this theme was present in her account and that examples had been clustered under somewhat different headings. At this stage, and throughout the process of writing up, there may be further revision and elaboration of interpretations. As the themes were being written up in the ADHD study, for example, it became clear that the six group master themes could be further integrated and combined into three more unified and inclusive master categories (level 5) (see Box 26.10).

This illustrates the systematic and iterative nature of this type of analysis. The investigator is gradually moving from an initial close reading of each individual transcript to a more abstracted synthesized account of the group of participants as a whole. The link between each level as one moves up should be

> **Box 26.10 Final table of master themes for the group (level 5)**
>
> 1 **Shouldering the burden and responsibility**
> Mother's sense of responsibility
> Mother's burden
>
> 2 **The struggle to understand and explain the child**
> Contradictions in the view/account of the child
> The struggle to understand and explain the child
>
> 3 **The significance of diagnosis and treatment**
> Uncertainty regarding the future
> The significance of diagnosis and treatment

clear and, at each stage, the analysis can be modified by reference back to material from a previous stage.

Writing Up

The aim of writing a narrative account of the group themes is to give the reader a coherent sense of the importance of the themes, to illustrate how they work for individual participants and to suggest how this might relate to existing work in the area. This may be achieved in a variety of ways and there is more flexibility in the format of a qualitative study than in quantitative and experimental work. Sometimes individual themes are introduced, illustrated and related to existing literature in turn in a single analysis and discussion section. In other cases an analysis section presents the thematic material which is then related to the extant literature in the discussion. Whichever organizing structure is chosen, a feature of interpretative phenomenological analysis is that the themes presented in the analysis are always supported by verbatim extracts taken from the transcripts themselves. This serves a number of purposes. It is a good discipline for the researcher who must check the emerging analysis against the raw material which stimulated it. It is also consonant with the rationale of the approach, as the narrative account can be seen to be illustrating different facets of the phenomenological and interpretative endeavour, the different voices of participant and researcher and the dialogical nature of qualitative analysis. This practice also allows the reader to examine the claims being made by the researcher by checking the evidence which has been marshalled to support the case.

In the write-up of the mother's accounts, each master theme was considered in turn. An attempt was made to articulate what was similar in the experiences of the respondents regarding each theme and to do justice to what was different, by noting the range of experiences described and any contrasting perceptions or practices, for example.

A short extract from the analysis section of the ADHD study is shown in Box 26.11. This short extract shows how the interpretative phenomenological analytic account is constructed – introducing, describing and illustrating each theme with instances from the different participants. Within the complete report the analysis would be framed by other sections. The introduction outlines the question which is being explored, provides a brief overview of work on ADHD, and explains why a qualitative methodology was chosen and why interpretative phenomenological analysis in particular. The method section describes the procedures followed, and the discussion, which follows the analysis section, links the themes to the existing literature.

A Further Example of the Application of Interpretative Phenomenological Analysis: Identity Change During the Transition to Motherhood

This section provides an extended example of interpretative phenomenological analysis by describing and illustrating a research project on identity change during the transition to motherhood. The central concern of the work is with women's accounts of how their sense of self or identity changes during their first pregnancy and the transition to motherhood. The study was longitudinal: data were collected at specified intervals and how each woman's account changed over time was examined. To provide the necessary detail the study was multi-method: different kinds of information were collected to help build a richer picture of the woman's experience. Given the purpose of the project a qualitative methodology was judged most appropriate. The project was concerned with how individual women were thinking and feeling over the course of their pregnancy. The aim of the work was to capture this experience from the individual woman's own viewpoint, not to measure the frequency of a particular event or response. At the same time, the study employed an idiographic quantitative instrument – the repertory grid – but those data are not discussed here (see Smith, 1995a, for further details).

Conducting the Study

The women were contacted through a number of sources, for example from general practitioner

Box 26.11 Extract from write-up of analysis

Shouldering the burden and responsibility

For all these mothers, having a son with ADHD was seen as a significant source of additional demands upon their resources as a parent, at least before a diagnosis was made and treatment begun. An important part of this sense of an extra burden was the stress and strain of dealing with the child's challenging behaviour, for example the exhausting level of vigilance and involvement required to keep their sons safe and out of trouble:

> He was hard work, very hard work. Not sleeping at all, which means I can't sleep. He was in hospital cos he jumped off the shed. Split his head, there was blood everywhere. I caught him hanging out of his bedroom window. He'd tried to jump out of the window and got stuck on the window fastenings. It's very tiring. I've got to constantly keep my eye on him, cos he gets himself into dangerous situations he's just not aware of. (Liz)

> To be honest he'd wear me out. He was always up to something. Like one time I caught him pushing straws into the gas fire. Playing with electric appliances, smashing his toys and his sister's toys, you name it. He was always up to some mischief, it never let up. So you had to watch him constantly, you know, watch him like a hawk. (Val)

For Jane the demands on her attention began from the first few months of her son's life:

> Right from the day he was born, he was always a whingey [whining, complaining] baby. He was constantly needing the attention, if you like, you had to be picking him up or cuddling him or carrying him or doing something, occupying him, or again there'd be this constant whining. (Jane)

Jane, Val and Pat each described the effort to deal with their child's behaviour as a battle with few if any peaceful interludes:

> Taking him on holiday and things like that weren't right nice. We'd be sat at the airport and he'd be running around, tearing round like and then you'd be worn out because you'd be so on edge all the time. What's he going to do? Where's he going to go? For all them years it seemed such a battle. (Pat)

This battle could be made all the more debilitating by having to balance the needs of other children:

> I was also having to please another child at the same time. Because with him being like that she got left out quite a lot because I was trying to please him and that made it harder. I was torn between them. (Pat)

> You'd be trying, you know, trying to deal with him, anything that might help, and that meant the others got like left out. Or you'd spend time with them and he'd be all over the place. It was a right juggling act, a nightmare. (Val)

referrals and antenatal clinics. At the first meeting the women were told that this was a study about the relationship between pregnancy and identity and informed of what would be required, before they agreed to take part. Each woman was visited four times, at three, six and nine months into the pregnancy and five months after the birth. Certain minimal criteria for inclusion were chosen to allow some comparability across cases. These were: it should be the woman's first pregnancy, the pregnancy should be planned, and the woman should be in a stable relationship.

Each woman was interviewed at every visit and was asked to keep a diary between visits. The interviews explored how the transition was affecting the woman's sense of personal and social identity. Although a schedule was used, the questions were deliberately open, intended mainly as cues for the women to talk, and the interview proceeded with minimum constraint or comment by the investigator. This followed the procedure outlined above. Each interview lasted between 60 and 90 minutes. The interviews were taped with the woman's permission, and the tapes were transcribed verbatim.

Instructions for keeping the diary were left open. Each woman was asked to record things she thought and felt during the pregnancy which were related to the topics discussed in the first interview. At each subsequent visit the current notebook diary was collected and a new blank one issued.

After the investigator had familiarized himself with the transcripts and texts, they were subjected to interpretative phenomenological analysis, along the lines illustrated earlier in the chapter. Once a preliminary analysis had been conducted, a draft case study was constructed for each woman, drawing on all the differing data sources. Thus this first stage of the project entails drawing on a great deal of material to prepare a detailed case study of each woman's changing sense of identity during the transition to motherhood. The woman's case studies were then examined for shared themes. This analysis has been published in a number of papers, each of which focuses on a different aspect of the analysis (Smith, 1994; 1999a; 1999b).

To illustrate how interpretative phenomenological analysis can be used in a longitudinal developmental project, material collected from one of the women is presented. At the beginning of her pregnancy, Clare is 29 and in full-time employment. She is married to Paul who is considerably older than she is and who is the father of a child from a previous relationship. The names of the woman and members of her family have been changed to protect confidentiality.

Pregnancy as Psychological Preparation for Mothering

Clare seems to use her pregnancy as a time for psychological preparation for childbirth and becoming a mother. We can see this process occurring as we follow her through the pregnancy. Consider the following extract from interview 1, when Clare was three months pregnant (ellipsis indicates editorial elision):

Interviewer: Do you think that being pregnant has made any difference to you as a person?

Clare: I'm seeing things slightly differently in that internal politics of work seem a bit trivial and I can't be doing with them [laughs] and it's reduced if you like and I've had – I have to contain, I'm feeling I'm having to contain myself for what lies ahead . . . I seem to have developed a capacity for sort of sitting and thinking . . . I've always liked time on my own and liked going out walking and just sitting, preferably on a hill, thinking . . . There is a need to, not withdraw within yourself, but just to prepare, and to make ready and to make sure that you are whole.

Here at three months pregnant, Clare is preparing herself for what lies ahead – the birth of the child – so there seems to be a shift in attention inwards rather than outwards. In the above passage Clare is using the words 'contain' and 'capacity' psychologically, but interview 2 at six months pregnant reveals an interesting development:

Claire: I'm beginning to feel my bulk though [laughs] and slowing down and generally very level. I mean whether it's something to do with your sort of physical shape changing and becoming more solid and you begin to feel a bit like a ship in full sail or you know stately as a galleon, you know. So that psychologically it seems to me at the moment that I'm not particularly easily disrupted or swayed. Things aren't, you know, not getting flapped about things or whatever, you just sort of sail on . . . It's not a question of not feeling deeply or as intensely about things, no intensely's the wrong thing, because there's not the same sort of – urgency doesn't come into it but depth is still there, if not more so . . . I've developed more confidence, not in an overt self-confident way. I'm just . . . more self-contained.

These psychological terms seem to have taken on more of their literal, material quality. Perhaps confidence gained from a period of self-containment has helped Clare in her preparation for becoming a 'container'. However this physicality is itself transformed into the metaphor of the sea vessel. Further, notice how Clare's choice of vessel changes from sailing ship to a stately galleon – the weight of which can emphasize its unflappability and seems more appropriate to the state of pregnancy. This sequence shows the development of the theme in action. Thus the galleon metaphor links to the containing theme, acts as a vehicle for Clare's levelness – contradicting the stereotype of emotional volatility in pregnancy – and allows talk of emotional depth. Perhaps physical weight helps prepare for psychological weight and depth.

At nine months pregnant Clare presents herself as more questioning, uncertain and impatient:

Clare: I think impending labour exercises my mind somewhat, fairly cataclysmic . . . This emergence of a new life is very near and impending now, whereas whenever it was back in June, was a sort of floating . . . Having to come out of that, I suppose it's a sort of protection which I'm having to break free of now in order to move on to the next stage . . . You wonder what the contractions are going to be like . . . Will you know what to do? . . . and I suppose a little bit of fear about whether you will come through intact . . . The ground is much more uncertain than it was three months ago. You reach out for it but you wonder and you can't wait for it.

Generally then Clare's focus is shifting outwards again. In terms of the metaphor, she is emerging from containment, and the coming birth seems to be the main catalyst to this change. It would appear that the self-containment acted as a protection which will help strengthen Clare for the next stage but which now needs to be shirked off as Clare is looking uncertainly, and with some trepidation, to the immediate future.

Engagement with Significant Others during Pregnancy and the Development of the Relational Self

There is a growing sense of psychological relationship with significant others during the pregnancy. During the interviews and diaries we see Clare talking more, explicitly or implicitly, about involvement with key others: partner, mother, and sister. Thus for example at three months Clare speaks of how the pregnancy is likely to draw her mother and herself closer:

Clare: I will have entered the elite – no, not the elite, er – the band of women, if you see what I mean. Motherhood is very important to her and I think the fact that I will be sharing that experience will make a difference to her . . . It's almost as if actually having a child makes the relationship much more equal . . . I think there'll be more a feeling of assuredness . . . in my relationship, as an adult, with my Mother.

A key relationship is with her husband and this seems increasingly important through the pregnancy. In her diary when about five months pregnant, Clare writes:

> About five years ago, I remember being quite obsessed with the idea of pregnancy. Looking back it was a very detached sensation, very intense but somehow divorced from the rest of my life. I never told anyone about it, least of all Paul. It bore no resemblance to any of my feelings surrounding this actual pregnancy.

There is a sense in which this previous wish was not quite right – partly because it was not shared. Contrast this with an extract in interview 2 at six months pregnant:

Interviewer: How much difference did feeling the movement make?

Clare: Well the original sensation was a sort of confirmation, if you like, for me. But the real thing to do with establishing this person's identity and individuality came when Paul was able to see the movement.

Interviewer: Why's that?

Clare: 'Cos it was such a secret before [laughs] or it had the feelings of just me and the child . . . Sometimes I think I felt that Paul was left out, was sort of excluded from all that was going on, that he was actually able to witness that and establish for himself that this wasn't just me imagining things.

This seems to indicate the need for confirmation by an important other; the child's identity is only properly established when physically witnessed by Paul. Up till that point the pregnancy may have been like the previous one – a fantasy or secret wish. Paul's witness to the movement is both manifestation and legitimization of the child's identity.

Then at seven months we see Clare describing, in her diary, how she is catching up with her husband:

> I managed to get Paul to go to one of the parentcraft sessions run at the health centre . . . Somehow I wanted the reassurance of public acknowledgement that we're going through this together, it's as if sometimes I feel like I'm running to catch up with him on the experience stakes – pretty inevitable really when you consider the circumstances!

So again we see the importance of external confirmation, which also relates to legitimacy. Now the child has been recognized and accepted by Paul, Clare requires a further level of recognition, the reassurance of public acknowledgement of commitment to the relationship and the mutual production of the child, partly necessary because Paul, unlike Clare, has been through this process before.

What emerges from the interview and diary data is a sense of increasing psychological connections with these significant others and a story of her catching up with them, as she moves to the parent status they have already achieved. Interestingly this experiential sharing is also translated into psychological similarity. The repertory grid data which is not shown here clearly illustrate a convergence between elements representing self and those for significant others (mother and partner) during the pregnancy. This means that for Clare, during pregnancy, she and these significant others come to share more personal constructs, that is Clare sees herself as becoming more like her mother and partner. Thus Clare would seem to have 'caught up' relationally, experientially and psychologically: the relationships are closer, she shares more with Paul and her mother, and she is now more like them psychologically.

The Process of Pregnancy and Changing Identities

These two themes hint at the complex process of pregnancy. On the one hand we see a need to look inwards away from the public world, as preparation for mothering. On the other hand we see increased engagement with family members. Thus it may be for Clare that she needed to turn away from the public world of work, to have a period of self-containment, but that that period of containment also required, or led to, closer contact with those most important to her. The net effect of these processes is, at nine months, some recognition of changing identity, the greater importance to her sense of self of the relationships she is engaged in:

Clare: I'm me but I'm one of two and I'm also one of three . . . and the emphasis is always changing . . . Sometimes you feel as though me is being lost

> or submerged . . . On the whole me is intact but I don't think I want to be me on my own entirely for ever more anyway, I mean, how do you explain it? An irrevocable decision, the steps have been made that mean that my other identities, if you like, as a mother and as a partner make up that essential me now.

The passage makes a strong statement about a shift in Clare's perception of her identity, her roles as mother and partner becoming more central to her sense of self. Perhaps part of moving on and away from self-containment is the growing recognition of the importance of one's role in relation to others. That this is not an easy process is suggested by the ambivalence in Clare's reaction.

The aim in this section of the chapter has been to illustrate how interpretative phenomenological analysis can be used to examine developmental processes in detail. In fuller papers from the transition to motherhood project (Smith, 1994; 1999a; 1999b) other cases are subjected to the same detailed qualitative analysis and then group themes are presented and discussed in relation to concepts in the literature, e.g. developmental processes during pregnancy (Gloger-Tippelt, 1983; Shereshefsky & Yarrow, 1973); the public and private worlds (Antonucci & Mikus, 1988; Rich, 1977); and the relational self (Gilligan, 1982; Mead, 1934).

Interviewing Children

The two studies used to illustrate qualitative psychological methods have presented different developmental topics from the perspective of adults. Of course many developmental studies require the collection of data from children. In this section some issues arising when conducting qualitative research interviews with children will be considered. Various authors have emphasized the importance of focusing on children's own unique perceptions when the aim of research is to develop an understanding of children's experiences (Amato and Ochiltree, 1987; Bernheimer, 1986; Ireland and Holloway, 1996; Yoos, 1991).

The basic principles underlying the use of qualitative research interviews with children are the same as with adults. The aim is to enable the participants to give as rich and detailed an account of their unique perceptions and experience as possible. However, there are two general guidelines which it may be especially useful to bear in mind when carrying out qualitative research with children. First, be flexible in order to meet the needs and respect the capabilities of each individual child. Second, take care when interviewing and when analysing the resulting data to check the accuracy and reliability of your understanding of the child's account.

Although using this approach with children may not differ radically from using it with adults there are a number of particular issues which it is helpful to be aware of. These will be discussed in more detail below and include establishing the relationship and encouraging the child to talk, the length and number of interviews, use of language, and children's cognitive, emotional and social development.

Establishing the Relationship

Children must feel safe and comfortable in their relationship with the researcher. The researcher carrying out the ADHD study tried to facilitate this by arranging an initial informal meeting with the children in their own homes, after interviewing their mothers. Children may feel more secure and relaxed being interviewed in their own homes. In the ADHD study the interviews took place on health service premises. This made it possible for the privacy and confidentiality of the interviews to be emphasized and for parental influence to be kept to a minimum. Care was taken to make the interview room as comfortable and welcoming as possible, with toys and art materials available for the children to use if they wished.

When conducting interviews with children it may be necessary to allow or even encourage them to talk about areas of their lives, such as hobbies or interests, which do not appear to have much direct relevance to the focus of the research. In this way the child's confidence, enthusiasm and commitment to the interview process can be nurtured and they may then be willing to respond more freely and fully to questioning later in the interview. Children's accounts of their experience may be facilitated through the use of painting, drawing or model making or by the provision of puppets or other toys. For example, some of the children in the ADHD study were invited to draw or paint pictures of their ADHD or themselves, before and after taking Ritalin. This seemed to make it easier for some of them to then reflect on and discuss their perceptions and experience of these phenomena.

Length and Number of Interviews

It may be useful to vary the number and duration of interview sessions to match each participant's motivation and capacity to engage in discussion with the researcher. In principle any number of interview sessions of varying duration could be appropriate depending on the needs of the participants and the researcher. The interviews with the children in the ADHD study lasted from 25 minutes to one hour and each child was interviewed twice. The length of each interview was determined by the interviewer's judgment of the child's level of interest and concentration, the aim being to maintain the participant's enthusiasm and commitment. Having more than one opportunity to interview the children allows for greater flexibility; particular topics can be followed up in more depth during the next session and vague or uncertain aspects of the child's account may be checked and clarified.

Use of Language

Care should be taken to ensure that the language used by the interviewer is as simple and concrete as possible. Technical language and professional jargon should be avoided. Using the participant's own words where appropriate may aid the development of trust and understanding between child and researcher. It is useful to take time to become familiar with the child's vocabulary and level of comprehension, for example, through informal conversation before addressing the main topics of the research interview. In the ADHD study this was done during the first, informal, meeting with the child in their own home, which also afforded the opportunity to observe them talking to their mother. At this first meeting the researcher established with the child and mother what terms they would normally use to refer to things such as ADHD and Ritalin.

Cognitive, Emotional and Social Development

There has been relatively little research into the relationship between children's development and the nature and quality of the data which may be obtained through interviewing them (Deatrick & Faux, 1991). Researchers should consider what is known about children's cognitive, emotional and social development at different ages and how this might affect the accounts they give of different phenomena. For example, the age range of the children participating in the ADHD study (9–12 years) was chosen partly because previous work suggests that by that age children have developed the ability to integrate information concerning various domains of their life into a global concept of self (Marsh, Craven, & Debus, 1991) and to reflect upon their self-identity and the subjectivity of others (Damon & Hart, 1988; Selman, 1980). It should be emphasized that there may be considerable variation in the developmental maturity of children within the same age group and the researcher must be alert and sensitive to the individual participant's level of maturity as it is expressed throughout the interview.

Although children's accounts of their experiences and the meaning they make of them may not be as expansive, detailed or complex as those produced by adults, they may nonetheless help the researcher to get closer to an 'insider's perspective' and provide a vivid glimpse into their personal worlds (Gorman, 1980). In the ADHD study, for instance, the thematic concerns and preoccupations which emerged through the analysis of the interviews with the children were often very different from those of their mothers. To take just one example, the children's experience of the changes in their behaviour and relationships following their treatment with Ritalin included a sense that some defining aspects of their self-identity had been lost. As one boy put it: 'I was naughty sometimes, but I was a laugh. My mates thought I was a laugh, really funny, I'd do anything. Now they say I'm no fun, I'm boring [pause] I am.' This contrasted with the views of the mothers who celebrated the changes in terms of what had been gained: 'It's wonderful. He's like a different boy, normal, I've got a normal little boy.'

VALIDITY

There has been considerable debate about the issue of validity in qualitative research over the last decade. This discussion has come about partly from the dissatisfaction felt by qualitative researchers when their work is evaluated according to the criteria used for quantitative research. As a result various suggestions for alternative criteria for assessing the validity of qualitative research have been proposed (e.g. Elliott, Fischer, & Rennie, 1999; Madill, Jordan, & Shirley, 2000; Smith, 1996b; Stiles, 1993; Yardley, 2000).

Part of the discussion concerns whether a single set of criteria can be applied to different types of qualitative research (Elliott, Fischer, & Rennie, 2000; Reicher, 2000). Madill, Jordan, and Shirley's (2000) response is to suggest different indicators of validity for alternative qualitative approaches. However, we suggest that the criteria proposed by Yardley and Elliott are for the most part framed in such a way that they can usefully be considered for qualitative projects arising from very different epistemological approaches. Indeed while no single set of factors has so far been established for evaluating qualitative research, a high degree of overlap exists between the criteria proposed by various authors. At the same time, most authors in this area take pains to present the proposed criteria as a set of guidelines to help researchers and readers review qualitative studies, but are opposed to these suggestions being turned into simplistic and rigid checklists where all items must be satisfied before a report or paper can be considered acceptable for publication.

Yardley (2000) presents her suggested criteria in the form of three broad categories and points out that qualitative studies can satisfy the criteria in a number of different ways. Her first category is sensitivity to context, whereby it is argued that the research should show an awareness of some of the contextual factors which inform it. Possible contexts can include the relevant literature, the data collected, the socio-cultural setting of the study, the relationship between researcher and participant. So for example, one way a study could show sensitivity to context would be by providing a detailed description of the participants and the locale in which the study took place.

Yardley's second category is commitment, rigour, transparency and coherence. Commitment can be measured by prolonged engagement with the topic and immersion in the data, and rigour by the completeness of the data collection, analysis and interpretation. Transparency can be achieved by describing each of those stages for the reader and by presenting verbatim extracts from the corpus of data to help the reader judge the strength of the claims being made. The coherence of a study might include the degree to which the argument is convincing and the fit between data and claims. The premise here is that the more systematic, engaged and transparent the research process, the more likely is the resultant analysis to be valid, in the sense of being meaningful and trustworthy. Yardley's final category is impact and importance. Amongst ways in which studies can meet this criterion are by the extent to which they open up new means of understanding a topic or, if the research has an explicitly social purpose, by the extent to which change has been facilitated by the research.

What should be clear from this brief summary is the degree of flexibility which is possible when considering possible criteria for evaluating qualitative research, and Yardley presents her suggestions in this spirit. A further way of considering quality and validity in respect of qualitative research which we find useful is the independent audit. Yin (1989) suggested that a good discipline for qualitative researchers was to file all the material collected and produced during the research project in such a way that someone else, who had played no part in the research itself, could follow the chain of evidence that led to the final report. Thus if the project is based on semi-structured interviews, the file might contain initial notes on research questions, draft interview schedules, the final schedule, audiotapes, annotated transcripts, lists of themes, codings or categorizations, the draft report and the final report. Filing the material in this way, as if to allow someone else to check the chain of evidence, can, in itself, be useful in demanding that the researcher be systematic and rigorous in the analysis.

It is also possible for someone else to conduct a real independent audit and this was suggested as good practice by Lincoln and Guba (1985). In this case the file of material is given to a researcher, not directly involved in the study, whose task is to check that the final report is credible in terms of the data collected and that a logical progression runs through the chain of evidence. It is important to realize that the independent auditor is assessing whether the claims made in the qualitative study are justified or warranted on the basis of the material collected and filed. The task is not to decide whether the account is the definitive one, and indeed the auditor may have alternative interpretations of some of the material collected. The independent audit is not attempting to suppress alternative readings or force a consensus; its purpose is to validate one particular reading.

CONCLUSION

This chapter has introduced qualitative psychology in relation to quantitative psychology and outlined the different approaches which have been adopted by qualitative psychologists. A fuller description of one particular qualitative methodology, interpretative phenomenological analysis, has been provided along with illustrations of its application to developmental psychology. It is probably true to say that qualitative approaches have excited more interest among social and health psychologists than developmental psychologists, though there are exceptions to this (e.g. Gilligan, 1982). Investigators in life-span psychology and the cognate areas of personology and life history have shown considerable enthusiasm for qualitative approaches (see e.g. Handel, 1987; Josselson & Lieblich, 1995; Levinson, 1978).

Qualitative methods have a particularly valuable role to play in developmental psychology as it has been argued they are especially useful when one is concerned with examining process and change. Thus while a quantitative instrument can give one a snapshot recording at time 1 and time 2, a qualitative study can include a description of what is occurring between the two time points. This can be in the form of (a) the participant's account of the process (b) an observational record of the process, and (c) an interpretation of the process inferred from qualitative reports received at the beginning and end points. This is illustrated in the case study of the transition to motherhood outlined above.

ACKNOWLEDGEMENTS

We would like to thank the editors of this volume for helpful comments on an earlier version of this chapter.

References

Amato, P.R., & Ochiltree, G. (1987) Interviewing children and their families. *Journal of Marriage and the Family*, 49, 669–675.

Antonucci, T.C., & Mikus, K. (1988). The power of parenthood: Personality and attitudinal change during the transition to parenthood. In G. Michaels & W. Goldberg (eds), *The transition to parenthood: Current theory and research*. Cambridge: Cambridge University Press.

Barkley, R.A. (1998). *Attention-deficit hyperactivity disorder: A handbook for diagnosis and treatment*. New York: Guilford.

Berheimer, L.P. (1986). The use of qualitative methodology in child health research. *Child Health Care*, 14, 224–232.

Blumer, H. (1969). *Symbolic interactionism*. Englewood Cliffs, NJ: Prentice-Hall.

Bryman, A. (1988). *Quantity and quality in social research*. London: Unwin Hyman.

Burman, E. (1996). Continuities and discontinuities in interpretive and textual approaches in developmental psychology. *Human Development*, 39, 330–345.

Charmaz, K. (1995). Grounded theory. In J.A. Smith, R. Harré, & L. van Langenhove (eds), *Rethinking methods in psychology*. London: Sage.

Charmaz, K. (in press). Grounded theory. In J.A. Smith (ed.), *Qualitative psychology: A practical guide to research methods*. London: Sage.

Conrad, P. (1987). The experience of illness: Recent and new directions. *Research in the Sociology of Health Care*, 6, 1–31.

Crossley, M. (2000). *Introducing narrative psychology*. Buckingham: Open University Press.

Damon, W., & Hart, D. (1988). *Self-understanding in childhood and adolescence*. Cambridge: Cambridge University Press.

Deatrick, J.A., & Faux, S.A. (1991). Conducting qualitative studies with children and adolescents. In J.M. Morse (ed.), *Qualitative nursing research* (2nd edn). Newbury Park, CA: Sage.

Drew, P. (1995) Conversation analysis. In J.A. Smith, R. Harré, & L. van Langenhove (eds), *Rethinking methods in psychology*. London: Sage.

Dunworth, F. (1999). Mothers' experiences of their son's diagnosis and treatment for ADHD. Doctorate in Clinical Psychology, University of Sheffield.

Elliott, R., Fischer, C., & Rennie, D. (1999). Evolving guidelines for publication of qualitative research studies in psychology and related fields. *British Journal of Clinical Psychology*, 38, 215–229.

Elliott, R., Fischer, C., & Rennie, D. (2000). Also against methodolatory: A reply to Reicher. *British Journal of Clinical Psychology*, 39, 7–10.

Feldman, A. (1996). Enhancing the practice of physics teachers: Mechanisms for the generation and sharing of knowledge and understanding in collaborative action research. *Journal of Research in Science Teaching*, 33, 513–540.

Geertz, C. (1973). Thick description: Toward an interpretive theory of culture. In C. Geertz (ed.), *The interpretation of culture*. New York: Basic.

Gergen, K., & Gergen, M. (1988). Narrative and the self as relationship. *Advances in Experimental Psychology*, 21, 17–56.

Gilligan, C. (1982). *In a different voice: Psychological theory and women's development*. Cambridge, MA: Harvard University Press.

Giorgi, A. (1985). Sketch of a psychological phenomenological method. In A. Giorgi (ed.), *Phenomenology and psychological research*. Pittsburg: Duquesne University Press.

Giorgi, A. (1995). Phenomenology. In J.A. Smith, R. Harré, & L. van Langenhove (eds), *Rethinking psychology*. London: Sage.

Giorgi, A., & Giorgi, B. (in press). Phenomenology. In J.A. Smith (ed.), *Qualitative psychology: A practical guide to research methods*. London: Sage.

Glaser, B., & Strauss, A. (1967). *Discovery of grounded theory*. Chicago: Aldine.

Gloger-Tippelt, G. (1983). A process model of the pregnancy course. *Human Development*, 26, 134–148.

Gorman, G. (1980). The school-age child as historian. *Paediatric Nursing*, Jan./Feb., 39–40.

Green, C., & Gilhooly, K. (1996). Protocol analysis: Practical implementation. In J. Richardson (ed.). *Handbook of qualitative research methods for psychology and the social sciences*. Leicester: British Psychological Society.

Handel, A. (1987). Personal theories about the life span development of oneself in autobiographical self presentation of adults. *Human Development*, 30, 83–98.

Hayes, N. (ed.) (1997a). *Doing qualitative analysis in psychology*. Hove: Erlbaum.

Hayes, N. (1997b). Introduction: Qualitative research and research in psychology. In N. Hayes (ed.), *Doing qualitative analysis in psychology*. Hove: Erlbaum.

Henwood, K., Nicolson, P. (eds) (1995). Qualitative research. *The Psychologist*, special issue, 8, 109–129.

Ireland, L., & Holloway, I. (1996). Qualitative health research with children. *Children and Society*, 10, 155–164.

Josselson, R., & Lieblich, A. (eds) (1995). *Interpreting experience*. Thousand Oaks, CA: Sage.

Journal of Counselling Psychology (1994). Qualitative research in counselling process and outcome. Special section, 41, 427–512.

Krippendorf, K. (1980). *Content analysis*. Beverly Hills, CA: Sage.

Kvale, S. (1996). *Interviews*. Thousand Oaks, CA: Sage.

Levinson, D. (1978). *The seasons of a man's life*. New York: Ballantine.

Lincoln, Y., & Guba, E. (1985). *Naturalistic inquiry*. Beverly Hills, CA: Sage.

Madill, A., Jordan, A., & Shirley, C. (2000). Objectivity and reliability in qualitative analysis: Realist, contextualist and radical constructionist epistemologies. *British Journal of Psychology*, 91, 1–20.

Marsh, H.W., Craven, R.G., & Debus, R. (1991). Self-concepts of young children 5 to 8 years of age:

Measurement and multidimensional structure. *Journal of Educational Psychology*, 83, 377–392.

Mead, G.H. (1934). *Mind, self and society*. Chicago: University of Chicago.

Murray, M. (1999). The storied nature of health and illness. In M. Murray & K. Chamberlain (eds), *Qualitative health psychology: Theories and methods*. London: Sage.

Murray, M. (in press). Narrative psychology. In J.A. Smith (ed.), *Qualitative psychology: A practical guide to research methods*. London: Sage.

Murray, M., & Chamberlain, K. (eds) (1999). *Qualitative health psychology: Theories and methods*. London: Sage.

Parker, I. (1992). *Discourse dynamics*. London: Routledge.

Pidgeon, N., & Henwood, K. (1996). Grounded theory: Practical implementation. In J. Richardson (ed.), *Handbook of qualitative research methods for psychology and the social sciences*. Leicester: British Psychological Society.

Potter, J., & Wetherell, M. (1987). *Discourse and social psychology: Beyond attitudes and behaviour*. London: Sage.

Potter, J., & Wetherell, M. (1995). Discourse analysis. In J.A. Smith, R. Harré, & L. van Langenhove (eds), *Rethinking methods in psychology*. London: Sage.

Reason, P. (in press). Co-operative inquiry. In J.A. Smith (ed.), *Qualitative psychology: A practical guide to research methods*. London: Sage.

Reason, P, & Heron, J. (1995). Cooperative inquiry. In J.A. Smith, R. Harré, & L. van Langenhove (eds), *Rethinking methods in psychology*. London: Sage.

Reicher, S. (2000). Against methodolatory: Some comments on Elliott, Fischer and Rennie. *British Journal of Clinical Psychology*, 39, 1–6.

Rich, A. (1977). *Of woman born*. London: Virago.

Richardson, J. (ed.) (1996). *Handbook of qualitative research methods for psychology and the social sciences*. Leicester: British Psychological Society.

Selman, R.L. (1980). *The growth of interpersonal understanding*. New York: Academic.

Shereshefsky, P.M., & Yarrow, L.J. (eds) (1973). *Psychological aspects of a first pregnancy and early postnatal adaptation*. New York: Raven.

Smith, J.A. (1994). Reconstructing selves: An analysis of discrepancies between women's contemporaneous and retrospective accounts of the transition to motherhood. *British Journal of Psychology*, 85, 371–392.

Smith, J.A. (1995a). Repertory grids: An interactive case study perspective. In J.A. Smith, R. Harré, & L. van Langenhove (eds), *Rethinking methods in psychology*. London: Sage.

Smith, J.A. (1995b). Semi-structured interviewing and qualitative analysis. In J.A. Smith, R. Harré, & L. van Langenhove (eds), *Rethinking methods in psychology*. London: Sage.

Smith, J.A. (1996a). Beyond the divide between cognition and discourse: Using interpretative phenomenological analysis in health psychology. *Psychology & Health*, 11, 261–271.

Smith, J.A. (1996b). Evolving issues for qualitative psychology. In J. Richardson (ed.), *Handbook of qualitative research methods*. Leicester: British Psychological Society.

Smith, J.A. (1999a). Towards a relational self: Social engagement during pregnancy and psychological preparation for motherhood. *British Journal of Social Psychology*, 38, 409–426.

Smith, J.A. (1999b). Identity development during the transition to motherhood: an interpretative phenomenological analysis. *Journal of Reproductive and Infant Psychology*, 17, 281–300.

Smith, J.A. (ed.) (in press). *Qualitative psychology: A practical guide to research methods*. London: Sage.

Smith, J.A., Harré, R., & van Langenhove, L. (1995a). Idiography and the case study. In J.A. Smith, R. Harré, & L. van Langenhove (eds), *Rethinking Methods in psychology*. London: Sage.

Smith, J.A., Harré, R. & van Langenhove, L. (1995b). Introduction. In J.A. Smith, R. Harré, & L. van Langenhove (eds), *Rethinking methods in psychology*. London: Sage.

Smith, J.A., Harré, R., & van Langenhove, L. (eds) (1995c). *Rethinking methods in psychology*. London: Sage.

Spinelli, E. (1989). *The interpreted world*. London: Sage.

Stiles, W. (1993). Quality control in qualitative research. *Clinical Psychology Review*, 13, 593–618.

Strauss, A., & Corbin, J. (1990). *Basics of qualitative research*. Newbury Park, CA: Sage.

Wetherell, M., & Potter, J. (1992). *Mapping the language of racism*. Hemel Hempstead: Harvester.

Willig, C. (2001). *Introducing qualitative research in psychology*. Buckingham: Open University Press.

Yardley, L. (ed.) (1997). *Material discourses and health*. London: Routledge.

Yardley, L. (2000). Dilemmas in qualitative health research. *Psychology & Health*, 15, 215–28.

Yin, R. (1989). *Case study research*. Newbury Park, CA: Sage.

Yoos, H. (1991). Children's illness concepts: Old and new paradigms. *Pediatric Nursing*, 20, 134–145.

27

Quantitative Models for Developmental Processes

JOHN R. NESSELROADE AND
PETER C.M. MOLENAAR

Developmentalists can scarcely be satisfied with the ways their arguably most central concept – 'process' – is represented in the current scientific literature. To a developmentalist, the word 'process' sounds appropriate, natural, and straightforward when it is written or spoken in nontechnical discourse, but as one tries to pin down just what a *developmental process* is, how it is to be recognized, how its progress is to be measured, and what are its concomitants, one quickly realizes just how elusive the concept can be (see e.g. van Geert, 1991). Consider a verbal definition of the concept of process, taken from the *Oxford English Dictionary*: 'A continuous and regular action or succession of actions, taking place or carried on in a definite manner, and leading to the accomplishment of some result.' On the surface, it is easy to agree and say, 'Oh yes, that is what we want to study in developmental research.' If sound and scientifically productive developmental psychology theory and research are to be fostered, however, the working and operational definitions of *process* cannot be purely verbal. In order for developmental science reasonably to aspire to dealing in abstract generalizations, rigorous mathematical definitions of fundamentally important concepts such as process that then, in turn, lead to clear, testable specifications must be developed and used to guide research efforts. In general, such precision has rarely been the case in the study of development.

Objective

The objective of this chapter is to present and discuss a set of rigorously defined quantitative models of process that we believe can be valuably applied to the concerns of developmental psychologists. The chapter is very much a 'work in progress', however, because the examples we will give are by no means exhaustive or complete. Rather, our focus is on presenting and discussing a selected set of mathematical-statistical latent variable models that permit one to describe temporally organized changes and specify and test hypotheses concerning the nature of those changes. Moreover, the models we will present carry the potential for rapid strengthening and improvement over the short run. Thus, in some ways this chapter is written more in the spirit of a progress report than as a 'how to' chapter on modeling developmental processes.

The first step in accomplishing our objective will be to identify a working definition of process, more or less as it is found in the literature. This definition will then be rendered operational in mathematical-statistical modeling terms with concern for building as much developmental veridicality as possible into the models. The models will be specified in terms that make their parameters estimable via currently available computer software such as AMOS, EQS, LISREL, Mx, and a number of others.

To broaden our perspective at the outset, it is useful to point out that one of the more methodologically sophisticated developmentalists (Wohlwill, 1973) fairly well avoided the concept *process* in his classic book on studying behavioral development.

Instead, he emphasized the *developmental function*, which he defined as 'the form or mode of the relationship between the chronological age of the individual and the changes observed to occur in his responses on some specified dimension of behavior over the course of his development to maturity' (1973, p. 32). Identifying the determinants of these developmental functious is a task of the developmental researcher who may use both experimental and nonexperimental methods as appropriate to the nature of the variables. This working definition seems to fit well with the modeling approach discussed subsequently as 'growth curve analysis' (McArdle, 1988; McArdle & Nesselroade, 2002). The Preface by Valsiner and Connolly in this volume deals explicitly with the related process–outcome distinction and its implications.

QUANTITATIVE MODELING OF PROCESSES

The purpose of the present section is to lay groundwork for a subsequent examination of some mathematico-statistical models that we believe can be used to represent process in the way that developmentalists intend to use the term. We focus on some general modeling issues, introduce what is meant by a *multivariate* representation, and provide a more precise definition of process that can be used to structure further discussion of the process concept.

Modeling Occasions versus Lags

Pertinent in the discussion will be an explicit consideration of various foci of modeling efforts, e.g. *occasions* versus *lags*. One important distinction among models is illustrated by contrasting certain time-series representations with growth curve modeling. In the former, one can speak of relationships defined across t_0, t_1, t_2, etc. which allow different strengths of relationship among variables depending on the length of the time interval under consideration. This seems an essential part of any viable notion of 'process'. Growth curve modeling, by contrast, describes one or more idealized trajectories realized across particular, explicit times, e.g. age 2, age 3, age 4, or 1970, 1971, 1972 or trial 1, trial 2, trial 3, etc. Moreover, in some applications, growth curve modeling assigns individuals scores that remain fixed with respect to time (individual differences information) and that describe the similarities of their particular trajectories to the idealized trajectories. An alternative way to conceptualize the distinction is in terms of differential (and difference) equations on the one hand versus their integrated forms on the other. The former gives a much more general picture of the notion of process and it is on such features that the chapter will be focused. Indeed, we believe that the distinction represents an important point of bifurcation in the evolution of model applications in behavioral science (see West, 1985) and that even though the field may not fully be ready to make the transition to more dynamic models, they represent an important advance over the more static models that have tended to be used for representing developmental change. It is crucial that developmentalists understand these general model differences and work toward conducting their theorizing and research to capitalize on the more powerful dynamic modeling possibilities.

Multivariate Representations of Process

Cattell (1963; 1966b; 1979; 1980), probably more than any other behavioral science researcher of the past several decades, argued strongly for a multivariate orientation for the purpose of structuring and measuring changes, including those changes captured by the term 'process'. Baltes and Nesselroade (1973), Baltes, Reese, and Nesselroade (1977), and Nesselroade and Ford (1987) further examined the structuring and analysis of developmental change via multivariate models. Bentler (1973) summarized many of the multivariate approaches to representing developmental change that were available at the time of his review. Since then, the developmental literature has witnessed a proliferation of studies that have involved applying various structural equation modeling (SEM) techniques to multivariate data. For example, in 1987 a special issue of *Child Development* was devoted to SEM applications for studying developmental phenomena.

Among the earliest and perhaps the clearest examples of attempts to follow a rigorous, quantitative schedule in developmental process definition via a multivariate orientation are the efforts to render operational concepts of *integration*, *differentiation*, and *reintegration* in the case of human abilities by means of the factor analytic model (e.g. Burt, 1954; Garrett, 1946). These early attempts to specify processes of differentiation via the factor analysis model, however, were fraught with the ambiguities and uncertainties of the essentially exploratory common factor model available at that time. More recent work involving confirmatory factor modeling approaches has helped greatly to clarify the issues and strengthen the procedures (see e.g. Olsson & Bergman, 1977) in relation to the concept of *differentiation*.

Salient Characteristics of a Process

In his classic chapter on representing change and process, Cattell (1966b) argued that it is naive to think that one can *arbitrarily* and *subjectively* recognize individual processes to be studied. He argued that one might contrive a process by experimental means such as teaching a rat to make a sequence of responses, but even that learning process, controlled by the experimenter, is likely to have parts that are unsuspected by the experimenter such as when rats learning to run a maze also 'learn' to react less shyly to the experimenter. Cattell (1966b) defined the 'natural, recurrent process' as a 'pattern over occasions'. We will take that notion as a starting point but, in line with the effort to move in the direction of dynamic models, we believe a significant advantage will be gained by extending Cattell's definition to include a 'pattern over lags'. This distinction will be made clear below.

Cattell's general notion of the nature of a process is a useful one for further consideration. He identified several characteristics that need to be taken into account in defining the concept more rigorously. These include: (1) the pattern over occasions constituting a process is a configuration rather than a mere profile because sequential ordering of events is important; (2) the variables on which the process is defined can be all-or-nothing or continuous and parametric; and (3) the variables on which the process is defined can have their later values predicted by their earlier ones. This latter idea is a crucial one, because it is related to the key distinction between 'closed' processes that unfold irrespective of the context and 'open' processes in which the sequence of the organism's behavior is, at least in part, dependent on the environment's behavior (Valsiner, 1984).

When one goes a step further and specifies that the later values of the variables on which the process is defined are dependent on the earlier values, the set of variables can be said to exhibit *intrinsic dynamics* which can be argued to represent a *strong* version of the third of Cattell's points above (dependent on, not just predicted by) and thus further exemplifies the process concept.

In very clear ways, the features identified by Cattell dovetail with the verbal definition of process with which we began this section. Our task, then, is to translate these quite consistent verbal definitions into more mathematical-statistical terms. Before doing that, however, we will examine some other aspects that will bear directly on how we render the process concept operational.

Salient Historical Lines of Thought

Multivariate Orientation

In the inaugural editorial of the journal *Multivariate Behavioral Research*, launched in 1966, Raymond B. Cattell argued that significant developments in understanding and modeling behavior would only come from adopting a general approach to studying behavioral phenomena that substantially augmented (if not replaced) manipulative experiment with more naturalistic observation of the behaving organism in context, focusing on measuring many rather than a few variables. Cattell's stance was another example of highlighting the tradeoffs between internal and external research design validity (Campbell & Stanley, 1963). The 'cleaner' results, those that could be obtained by careful manipulation of a few variables and recording of a few others, were less interesting from the standpoint of building an explanatory system than were the 'messy' results obtained from recording both multiple outcomes and multiple putative causes in their more-or-less natural contextual variation and applying the powerful methods of multivariate analyses to structure this information. From this perspective, developmental processes cannot be understood by attending to manipulating a few variables and examining the effects on a few others. Rather, the 'messy' results involving the typically many variables involved are more representative of the systemic organization of processes.

In pursuing the 'multivariate' orientation mentioned earlier, Cattell promoted a variety of 'covariation' designs or data definitions based on such research design modes as persons, variables, and occasions of measurement with the articulation of the general heuristic known as 'the data box' (Cattell, 1952). His aim was to systematize the various possible multivariate covariation designs and their characteristics and interrelationships, thus making them more widely known and accessible to substantively oriented researchers. A representation of the heuristical 'data box' is given in Figure 27.1.

Starting at a very broad conceptual level, highly pertinent to developmentalists was the distinction between intraindividual change and variability (change within an individual over time) and interindividual variability (usually referred to as 'individual differences') (see e.g. Buss, 1979). The relative emphasis placed on these two kinds of variability is closely linked to fundamentally different orientations to the study of behavior (see e.g. Nesselroade & Featherman, 1997; Valsiner, 1984). These distinctions can be extended an important step further with terminology such as inter-intraindividual variability which captures the notion of interindividual differences and similarities in intraindividual change patterns (Baltes, Reese, & Nesselroade, 1977).

This distinction is directly embodied in the two covariation techniques defined by Cattell (1952) in the context of the 'data box' as R-technique and P-technique factor analysis. These centrally important covariation designs are represented explicitly in Figure 27.1. R-technique involves an analysis of the relationships among variables as they are defined

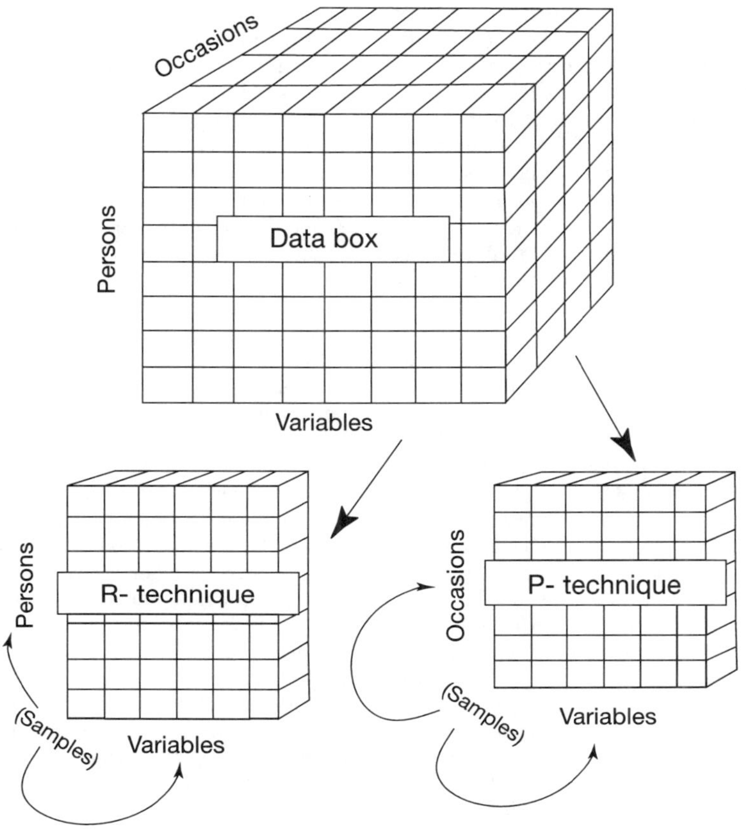

Figure 27.1 *R-technique and P-technique data in the data box context*

across a sample of persons who have been measured on each variable only one time. By contrast, P-technique involves an analysis of the relationships among variables as they are measured on only one individual across a sample of occasions.

At the time of presenting the 'data box', R-technique analysis was by far the most popular kind of factor analysis, largely because many of the questions being asked were simply not developmental in nature. Rather, they tended to reflect a strong belief in highly stable differences among the various 'endowments' of individuals. In marked contrast, P-technique was promoted by Cattell (e.g. Cattell, Cattell, & Rhymer, 1947) for studying 'individual traits', as a promising tool by which process could studied. Bereiter (1963) recognized P-technique as 'the logical way to study the interdependencies of measures' and explicitly pointed out that the more common cross-sectional covariation designs were approximations, for better or worse, to the information obtainable from P-technique studies. Indeed, Bereiter went on to say:

> it will generally follow that at any given time relevant antecedent conditions will vary for different individuals who may be tested at that time. Thus correlations between measures over individuals should bear some correspondence to correlations between measures for the same or randomly equivalent individuals over varying occasions, and the study of individual differences may be justified as an expedient substitute for the more difficult P-technique. Viewed in this way, however, the fact that measures on the same individuals may not correlate the same way on different occasions must be taken as evidence for the inadequacy of individual differences analysis as a substitute for P-technique analysis. (1963, p. 15)

Although they fly in the face of common practice, Bereiter's observations illustrate why some researchers are not satisfied with the way group designs and analyses are usually implemented and their findings interpreted (see e.g. Lamiell, 1981; Molenaar, Huizinga, & Nesselroade, in press)

Elsewhere, Nesselroade and Molenaar (1999) discussed the general matter of uncritically interchanging the information obtained from interindividual variability at one time with that obtained from intraindividual variability across time and raised some cautions regarding its appropriateness. We used a concept from statistical mechanics – ergodicity (see also Jones, 1991) – to identify conditions under which such substitution was not misleading and further explored the matter within the context of identifying subsets of individuals on whom relevant process information appears to be consistent and separating them from others before conducting more refined analysis on the process aspects of their data. More recently, Molenaar, Huizinga, & Nesselroade (in press) examined this matter in the context of evaluating selected aspects of developmental systems theory. Their results raised grave concerns regarding the use of among-persons differences to draw inferences about the course of within-person developmental changes. More will be said about this subsequently.

In the view of the writers, the strong case made for P-technique analysis by Bereiter, Cattell, and others (e.g. Zevon & Tellegen, 1982) signals an important turning point in the rigorous representation of behavioral process as well as other changes, in part because of the explicit distinction between manifest and latent variables. Fitting the factor analytic model to P-technique data, despite acknowledged weaknesses of such application, was a promising way to try to examine and represent psychological processes. The procedure relied on multiple measures: indeed, the factor analyses could include both stimulus and response information (see e.g. Cattell & Scheier, 1961). In the case of response variables, the covariances reflected variation within the individual over time. For stimulus variables, the variance underlying covariances represented changing stimulus values across time.

The straightforward application of the traditional factor analysis model to P-technique data was soon called into question,[1] (e.g. Anderson, 1963; Holtzman, 1963) and for those who wanted to model latent variables in terms of changes over time in the single case, important modifications to the traditional P-technique factor analysis model did not appear until the 1980s (e.g. Engle & Watson, 1981; Geweke & Singleton, 1981; McArdle, 1982; Molenaar, 1985). In various ways, these newer models took into account explicitly the sequential information in the repeated measurements, thereby offering not only more rigor but also some variety in the modeling of process and change.

Temporal Organization and Sequencing

Cattell (1966b) said: 'By a process we mean that kind of pattern which is a configuration rather than a mere profile. That is to say, a sequential order is an essential part of the signatures of the numbers in the profile.' In our view, and in line with Bereiter's valuation of P-technique, the concept of process is one of the most critical examples of interdependencies among measures. The pattern of interdependency involves both (a) covariation over time and (b) sequential organization. Within the context of the P-technique model, the former is illustrated by the covariation over time of measured variables and the resulting patterns of factor loadings while the latter is illustrated by the nature of the changes in factor scores across time, one example of which would be auto- and cross-correlations of the factors. It is these two features which lie at the heart of the modeling efforts that we discuss in the next sections.

With regard to multiple variables, covariation over time and sequential organization in a set of observed variables are each necessary but not sufficient evidence of an underlying process. To illustrate this point, consider the following example. For many of us, as our automobile is driven more and more it gets noisier and noisier while the amount we owe the bank on it becomes less and less. Thus, there is a temporal organization to both noise (increasing) and principal remaining to be paid (decreasing) just as there is a covariation between them over time. When one is high, the other is low and vice versa. But one is scarcely tempted to invoke the notion of a single process to account for this covariation. Both variables may be involved in processes (e.g. deterioration of the car and repayment of the loan) which are occurring at the same time but are not integrally connected. Thus, to paraphrase an old cliché, 'coincidence does not mean causation'.

Idiographic/Nomothetic Relations

Another pertinent line of development that can be traced, in large part, to the operational nature of P-technique factor analysis, is the melding of individual- and group-oriented approaches that were not really feasible earlier. Various researchers (Lebo & Nesselroade, 1978; Roberts & Nesselroade, 1986; Shifrin et al., 1997; Wessman & Ricks, 1966) who used the general P-technique methodology recognized the importance of forestalling the strong criticisms regarding the lack of generalizability in studies of the individual, and applied the logic and power of the intensively measured individual to groups of individuals more or less simultaneously. Zevon and Tellegen (1982; see also Nesselroade & Ford, 1985) formalized the general ideas under the topic of putting an idiographic approach to the service of establishing nomothetic laws. Other authors (e.g. Lamiell, 1981; 1988; Valsiner, 1984) have argued compellingly for the more systematic exploration of individual-level information prior to naively aggregating across individuals in the service of group-based analyses. Nesselroade and Molenaar (1999) used such arguments to develop the rationale for an evaluation of homogeneity of individuals' lagged covariance matrices that fosters selective and informed aggregation of individuals' data for group analysis.

Valsiner and Connolly (Preface in this volume) emphasize that what they call *intrasystemic analysis*, which is cognate with analyzing individual cases over time, is the core of developmental science. They point out that the study of the single case can be done nomothetically when it leads to a generalized formal model that is then tested against other single case data and the model parameters adjusted to reflect mismatches. For Valsiner and Connolly, aggregation of cases into samples becomes useful (and adequate) if and only if the aggregate is the system one wants to study. An alternative proposal aimed at reaching the same conclusion – general lawfulness – was expressed by Meredith (2001) as: 'Growth and development are lawful. All individuals obey the same laws of development. Every individual develops differently from every other. So we need mathematical laws whose parameters can account for individual differences.'

Some Current Models for Process and Change

Out of the milieu described above, although admittedly only a few aspects can be recounted here, which include the seminal contributions by earlier P-technique factor analytic studies initiated by Cattell and his colleagues (e.g. Cattell, Cattell, & Rhymer, 1947), emerged some promising and substantial improvements in the way researchers began to conceptualize and model change, including developmental change (e.g. Baltes, 1973; Cattell, 1966a; Collins & Horn, 1991; Collins & Sayer, 2000; Harris, 1963; Wohlwill, 1973). Before describing some of these models more specifically, however, we will examine a distinction that bears integrally on the matter of 'choosing' among alternative models for representing processes.

Contrast of 'Open' and 'Closed' Models

Earlier, we briefly considered the distinction between 'open' and 'closed' models (see also Valsiner, 1984). This distinction is critical to developmental science because it denotes a central question of developmental theory: what are the nature and relative roles of 'internal' versus 'external' influences on the developing individual? Models that allow for differential openness of the developing system across time sharply contrast with those that don't, and the differences between the two orientations clearly stand with one leg in the methodological realm. In an important sense, 'closed' models lead to the elimination of developmental processes with their unfolding, partially indeterministic nature, in favor of a new classification system of development outcomes – exemplified, for example, by growth curves. 'Open' models allow for developmental outcomes that are well represented not by trajectories or pathways but rather by dynamical formulations in which the outcomes are somewhat constrained, but are not precisely determined. The often used example of not being able to predict where on the ground a particular leaf will land, but being able to predict the probable distribution of fallen leaves around the tree, exemplifies the 'open' model notion. In the 'humans as self-constructing, living systems' theoretical framework, Ford (1987) and Ford and Lerner (1992) discussed developmental processes that integrate both deterministic and probabilistic influences on the developing organism.

Static to Dynamic Models

Natural scientists distinguish among (1) static, (2) kinematic, and (3) dynamic representions. Static models have to do with relations that reside in equilibrium, kinematic models with aspects of change (motion) apart from mass and force, and dynamic models with forces and their relationship primarily to change (motion) and sometimes equilibrium. These distinctions have considerable import for differences among mathematical and statistical models that are invoked to represent process. It may seem contradictory to say that static models are used to represent process but this is very much the case in psychology, including developmental psychology. Unquestioned acceptance of static models is, at least in part, why the measurement of change has been such a problem for behavioral and social sciences (see e.g. Nesselroade & Ghisletta, 2002). West (1985) discussed how the natural progression in evolving scientific disciplines is from static to dynamic representations of their phenomena of interest. Let us illustrate these different levels of models with some examples taken from the lifespan developmental psychology literature.

Static Models

The integration–differentiation–reintegration description of the nature of human ability development illustrates well the use of a static modeling approach to representing developmental change. These analyses can (and generally were) conducted on data representing one-time measurements of individuals. Yet, the implication drawn from these data had to do with describing the course of developmental progression from a less to a more differentiated set of abilities that, in later life, tended again to be less differentiated.

Kinematic Models

Some of the cross-sequential analyses reported in the 1960s and 1970s (e.g. Nesselroade & Baltes, 1974; Nesselroade, Schaie, & Baltes, 1972) illustrate kinematic modeling applications. The descriptive statements that arise (e.g. ability and personality change from 1970 to 1971 to 1972 in the case of the study by Nesselroade & Baltes, 1974) reflect changes across a particular set of time intervals. Extrapolation beyond those intervals is just that – extrapolation. In open systems, especially, predictability much beyond the range of actual observation becomes very tenuous.

Dynamic Models

Time-series and differential equation models with parameters explicating the actions (forces) of previous events on subsequent events illustrate the dynamic models that are receiving more and more attention in the behavioral and social sciences. Notably, interest in dynamical representations has ebbed and flowed for the past several decades. Primarily in the sociological literature, earlier dynamical representations by, for example, Arminger (1993), Coleman (1968), and Tuma and Hannan (1984) looked very promising but seemed to take a back seat to the surge of interest in linear SEM analyses in the 1970s, 1980s, and 1990s. In psychology, more recent examples by, for example, Boker and Graham (1998), Browne (2001), McArdle and Hamagami (2001), and Molenaar (1985) illustrate the power and range of these kinds of process models currently. Technical development in estimation procedures continues also with the stochastic differential equations representations (e.g. Singer, 1993).

Example: Growth

Let us examine how one or the other modeling decision either opens a view on development or closes it. Consider growth, for example. One can fit precisely specified mathematical forms or the more 'free-formed' descriptions generated by variations on principal components or hierarchical linear modeling procedures to describe the data (e.g. Rao, 1958; Tucker, 1958; 1966). In either case, fixed representations of the variable with respect to some index of time are generated, much as in Figure 27.2. Alternatively, a dynamical representation in the form of a differential equation can be used to model various kinds of growth data. One familiar kind of 'growth' is epitomized by the compound interest problem which applies to a variety of change phenomena: principal and interest, radioactive decay, cooling of physical bodies, electrical current reduction, etc. The representation can be expressed as:

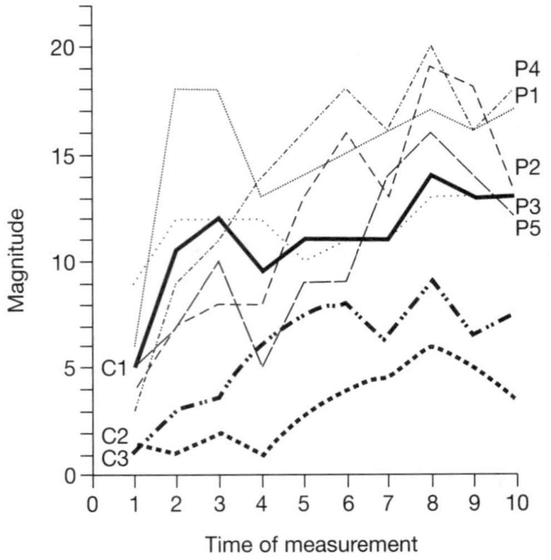

Figure 27.2 *Individual person curves over time (P1, P2, etc.) and component curves (C1, C2, etc.) derived from them* (see Nesselroade & Ghisletta, 2002).

$$\frac{dq}{dt} = kq$$

where q is the amount (principal, mass, difference between the temperature of a body and the surrounding air, amount of electrical current), k is a constant of proportionality, and t is time. The differential equation relates the rate of change to amount, that is, the greater the principal the faster it grows for a given rate of interest, the greater the radioactive mass the longer it takes for it to decay, etc. One can integrate the function and generate a specific curve representing particular values of the variables. As models of developmental processes, the implications of these quantitative representations are remarkably different.

Despite the lead–lag alterations of theory and method over time described by Wohlwill (1973) it is the case at this moment in the history of developmental science that technology is not lagging behind theoretical concerns. A number of computer software packages are available that make the kinds of analyses described here quite feasible for most investigators.[2]

Growth Curve Models

Lest the point be missed, we believe that growth curve modeling (McArdle, 1988; McArdle & Nesselroade, 2002; Meredith & Tisak, 1984; 1990; Rogosa, Brandt, & Zimowski, 1982; Tucker, 1966) has been highly instrumental in reinforcing for developmentalists and other students of process the great strengths of longitudinal data. Cronbach (1957), for example, offered the work of Tucker (1966) on modeling growth and process via his 'generalized learning curves' approach as a possible *rapprochement* between 'the two disciplines of scientific psychology' because it explicitly represented both general and individual differences information within one formulation. McArdle (1988), Meredith and Tisak (1984; 1990) and others advanced the methodology considerably by casting it firmly within a latent variable framework, the parameters of which models could be estimated using readily available software.

McArdle (1988) systematized two general ways of approaching the structuring of multivariate change in distinguishing between *factors of curves* and *curves of factors*. The essence of the distinction had to do with decomposing a sample of manifest variable curves plotted over time (occasions of measurement) versus decomposing the data at each occasion of measurement by the factor analytic model, identifying invariant factors over occasions of measurement and then examining the curves of factor scores plotted across those occasions. On the one hand, the curves of factors approach lends highest integrity to the factors as they are defined to be invariant at each occasion. The focus of a study of change is shifted thereby from the manifest variables to the latent factors, but the issues and problems of measuring change remain to be dealt with. The factors of curves approach, on the other hand, lends highest integrity to the manifest trajectories of variables across time and seeks to identify a parsimonious set of basic components of these manifest trajectories that in some sense are 'idealized' represention of the course of change.

Time-Series Models

For our purposes, we restrict our concerns here to a certain kind of time-series model, namely that tied to the parametric modeling of latent variables. Certainly, the reader is well advised to consider other kinds of modeling of process variables, including multivariate time-series models and sequential analysis of social interaction variables as have been discussed by various writers (see e.g. Bakeman & Gottman, 1997), but these are not the concern of this chapter.

The key idea here is that processes are sequential organizations of events that are related in some larger scheme. As noted earlier, however, sequential events need not necessarily be part of the same process. Moreover, many different levels of process can occur simultaneously and exert their effects on the same variables. School children, for example, are growing physically concurrently with learning to read, write, and calculate as they are undergoing 'socialization' at home, school, etc. A child's *sense of self*, for instance, can be simultaneously influenced by all these processes, some of which are individual, some institutional.

To be able to move beyond static description of what is going on (e.g. what the trajectory of the child's sense of self looks like plotted over age), one needs to develop formulations that incorporate dynamics into the representations. This is simply illustrated. Suppose that at any time t, the rate of change (velocity) in the developing child's sense of self is inversely proportional to the child's current sense of self. This would be a dynamic representation of sense of self and it says that the child with a strong sense of self is changing less rapidly (approaching equilibrium?) than a child with a weak sense of self. Thus, the same general rule fits both the child with a strong sense of self and the child with a weak sense of self but the rate of change differs markedly between the two of them. How to model this kind of system?

As we have discussed elsewhere (Nesselroade & Molenaar, 1999), a focus on modeling process at this stage of evolution of developmental psychology needs to rest on both (1) a multivariate orientation to measurement and analysis (Baltes & Nesselroade, 1973; Cattell, 1966a), and (2) an idiographic emphasis in pursuing nomothetic relationships (Lamiell, 1981; Nesselroade & Ford, 1985; Zevon & Tellegen, 1982). The models that we wish to present are significant elaborations of the basic P-technique approach (Browne, 2001; McArdle, 1982; Molenaar, 1985; Nesselroade & Molenaar, 1999; Nesselroade et al., 2002; Wood & Brown, 1994). These newer models were designed to take into account the lag structure residing in the repeated measurements. For example, suppose a string of measurements obtained daily for 30 days contains the information that on days following a high score the score tends to be low, whereas on days following a low score the score tends to be high. This information was not reflected in regular P-technique factors. However, the newer models directly represent this kind of information in the factor outcomes. Elsewhere, the two general approaches have been referred to as the white noise factor score (WNFS)[3] and the direct autoregressive factor score (DAFS) models (Nesselroade et al., 2002). Browne (2001) has referred to the more generic, parent model as the 'shock' model and to what we are calling the DAFS model as the 'process' model. To tie these two models more directly to the concept of process discussed earlier, consider the following line of argument.

White Noise Factor Score (WNFS) Model

This model, which was presented by Molenaar (1985; 1994; see also Hershberger, Molenaar, & Corneal, 1996; Wood & Brown, 1994) is shown graphically in Figure 27.3. Elsewhere, the details of the WNFS model are presented in the traditional framework of

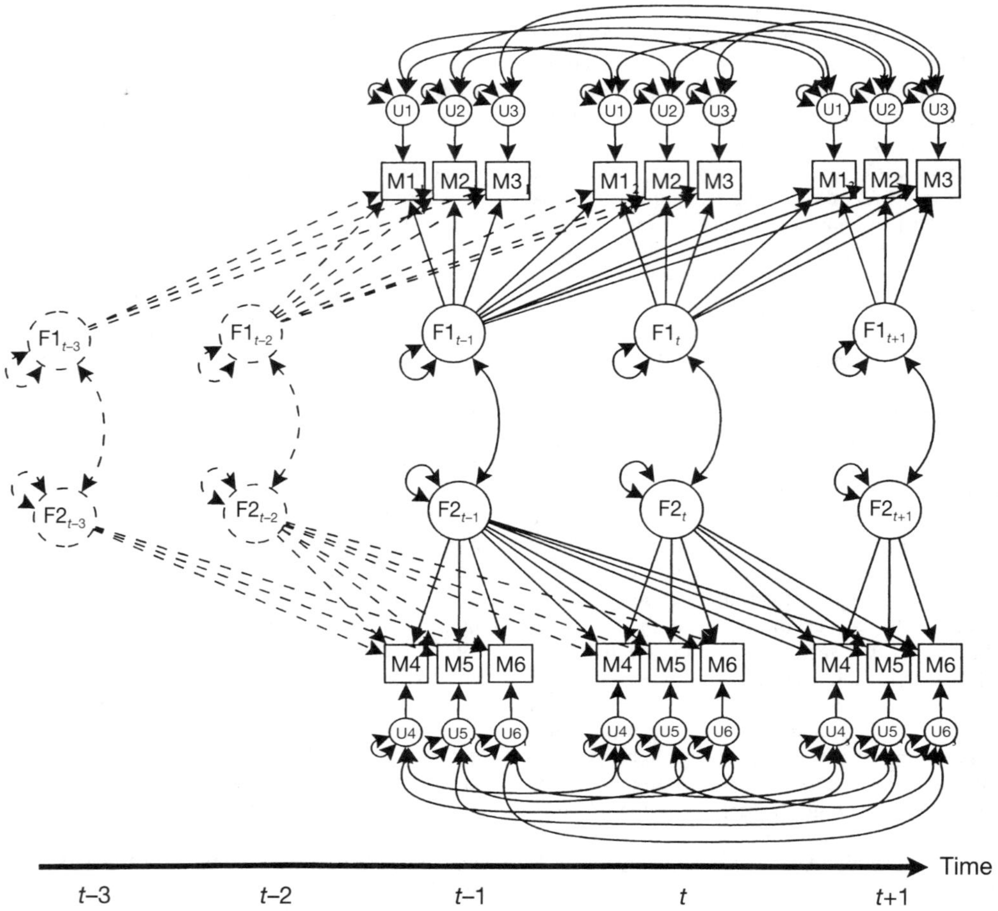

Figure 27.3 *White noise factor score (WNFS) model (see Nesselroade et al., 2002)*

common factor analysis (Nesselroade & Molenaar, in press). The model allows the earlier factor scores to influence directly the later values of the observed, or manifest variables. Thus, the model fits very well with a notion of process in which process is a latent variable that *drives* the manifest variables but the pattern of influence might be different for different variables at different lags. Suppose, for example, that the manifest variables are driven to extreme values at a given time and then they tend to return toward some homeostatic equilibrium point but they return at different rates. Moreover, suppose the return is impeded by different external influences for different manifest variables. The WNFS model allows for such contingencies because *today's* observed scores are influenced by *today's* factor scores, by *yesterday's* factor scores, and by specific factors acting on the variables at particular times.

The WNFS model specification is as follows:

$$\mathbf{y}(t) = \Lambda(0)\eta(t) + \Lambda(1)\eta(t-1) + \ldots + \Lambda(s)\eta(t-s) + \varepsilon(t)$$

where $\mathbf{y}(t)$ is a p-variate observed time-series measured at time $t(t = 1, 2, \ldots, T)$, $\eta(t)$ is a k-variate time-series of (unobserved) factor scores at time t, $\varepsilon(t)$ is a vector of uniquenesses (specificity plus errors of measurement) at time t, and $\Lambda(s)$ is a $p \times k$ matrix of factor loadings at lag s.

Note that Λ carries a lag identifier, e.g. $\Lambda(1)$. Thus, a central identifying characteristic of the WNFS model is that the factor loadings differ according to the lag. Other key features include allowing an autocorrelational structure in the uniquenesses of the variables and, as was noted above, the 'white noise' specification of the factor scores. To reiterate the implications of the model specification: today's value of a manifest variable is jointly determined by *today's* factor scores, *yesterday's* factor scores, etc., *today's* uniquenesses, and, possibly, *yesterday's* specific factor score value for that variable. Thus, the WNFS model is able to represent such temporally defined influences as decay, latency, etc., in the lag-defined patterns of factor loadings and these can be different for different manifest variables. The DAFS model (see below), by contrast, cannot handle differential *return rates* for different manifest variables. Its strict metric invariance for all lags does not permit such flexibility in the relationships between latent and manifest variables.

Direct Autoregressive Factor Score (DAFS) Model

The DAFS model specification proposed by McArdle (1982) explicitly incorporates lagged effects of factors on variables by allowing the factor scores to manifest time-related dependencies in the form of auto- and cross-correlations. *Yesterday's* factor scores, for instance, can directly influence *today's* factor scores by which they have an impact on *today's* observed variable scores. Said another way, earlier factor scores exert only indirect influence on later variable scores through their effect on later factor scores. This is a key point of difference between the DAFS model and Molenaar's (1985) WNFS model presented earlier. The DAFS model is depicted graphically in Figure 27.4. The reader is referred to Nesselroade et al. (2002) for more detail.

The DAFS model specification can be written as the pair of equations:

$$\mathbf{y}(t) = \Lambda f(t) + e(t)$$

$$f(t) = \mathbf{B}_1 f(t-1) + \mathbf{B}_2 f(t-2) + \ldots + \mathbf{B}_s f(t-s) + u(t)$$

Combining these,

$$\mathbf{y}(t) = \Lambda[\mathbf{B}_1 f(t-1) + \ldots + \mathbf{B}_s f(t-s)] + \Lambda u(t) + e(t)$$

where $\mathbf{y}(t)$ is a p-variate observed time-series measured at time t ($t = 1, 2, \ldots, T$), Λ is a $p \times k$ matrix of factor loadings, $f(t\text{-}w)$ ($t = 1, 2, \ldots, T$; $w = 0, 1, 2, \ldots, s$) is a k-variate time-series of (unobserved) factor scores w occasions prior to occasion t, and $e(t)$ is a p-variate time-series of errors or unique parts of

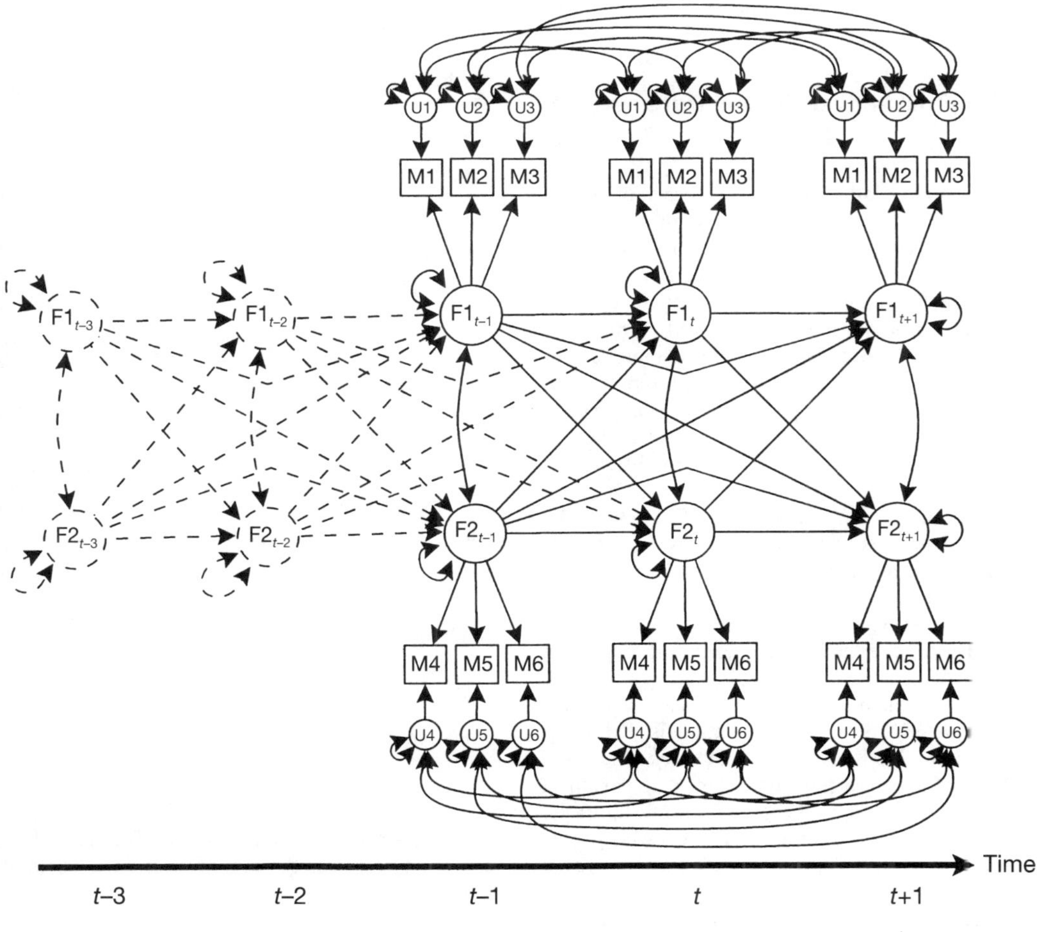

Figure 27.4 *Direct autoregressive factor score (DAFS) model (see Nesselroade et al., 2002)*

the observed scores that may have an autocorrelational structure but have no cross-correlational structure. The matrix $\mathbf{B}k$ is a weight matrix in which element βk_{ij} represents the magnitude of influence of the ith factor from k occasions earlier on the current value of the jth factor, $u(t)$ is a disturbance term signifying concurrent contributions to the factor scores that are not part of the direct autoregressive structure.

Key distinguishing features of the DAFS model are that the factor loadings are invariant with respect to lag and allowances are made for auto-and cross-correlational structure in the common factor scores and for possible autocorrelational structure in the uniquenesses of the variables. Thus, in the case of the DAFS model the *pattern* of influence of the factor on the observed variables does not depend on the lag, but the *magnitude* of the influence does depend on the lag. Although a simple autoregressive model will probably fit many kinds of data if there are strong delayed effects, a large scaling value on the factor scores at some relatively distant lag may be appropriate. Assuming sufficient degrees of freedom, this does not necessarily pose a problem for the estimation of the model parameters.

Conceptual Similarities and Differences of the Two Models

The two models differ from each other in important conceptual and technical ways. From a conceptual viewpoint, they differ fundamentally in the presumed nature of the common factors – especially the nature of the loading patterns at different lags – and thus represent process in distinctly different ways within the constraints dictated by the common factor model. Both models allow for a representation of 'continuity' despite changes over time – a key feature of process – but the mechanisms by which factors 'drive' variables, however, are notably different in the two model specifications.

For both the WNFS and DAFS models, the estimated models apply to the entire time-series. A lag of 5 applies equally to occasions 1 versus 6 and occasions 101 versus 106. Therefore, unique events are 'errors' in regard to both the WNFS and DAFS models but, nevertheless, they exert and impact on the system.

Highly pertinent to our developmental concerns, both the WNFS and DAFS models explicitly represent two kinds of external influences. One is any influence that consistently affects one of the manifest variables but not the others. This shows up in the magnitude of the autoregressive coefficient for the corresponding specific factor. The second are the 'shocks' to the system that occur randomly across the period of repeated measurements but do not occur consistently enough to determine a lag-defined effect. These 'random shock' effects influence the magnitude of the unique variances of the variables and thus reduce the apparent level of lag-defined coherence of the observed variable system. This explicit 'openness' of the system of observed variables to external influence is a desirable feature of the model and a timely reminder that processes do not occur in a vacuum as the contextualists are wont to remind us. Some other, more regular environmental 'shocks' can impact the system but their effects can decay over time without leaving a permanent impact. This illustrates an aspect of the 'stationarity' property of this model – an issue to which we return subsequently.

Technical Similarities and Differences of the Two Models

We will make a brief, more technical comparison of these two models to clarify further their implications for modeling process. We use simplified (first-order lags only) equations for the models, namely:

$$\mathbf{y}(t) = \Lambda(0)\ \eta(t) + \Lambda(1)\ \eta(t-1) + \varepsilon(t)$$

for the WNFS model and

$$\mathbf{y}(t) = \Lambda f(t) + e(t)$$

$$f(t) = \mathbf{B} f(t-1) + u(t)$$

for the DAFS model. We next rewrite

$$f(t) = \mathbf{B} f(t-1) + u(t)$$

as

$$f(t) - \mathbf{BL}f(t) = u(t)$$

where $\mathbf{L}$ is the lag operator defined as:

$$\mathbf{L}f(t) = f(t-1)$$

Now,

$$f(t) - \mathbf{BL}f(t) = u(t)$$

can be written as:

$$(\mathbf{I} - \mathbf{BL})\, f(t) = u(t)$$

which, in turn, can be rewritten as:

$$f(t) = (\mathbf{I} - \mathbf{BL})^{-1}\ u(t)$$

where $(\mathbf{I} - \mathbf{BL})^{-1}$ is the inverse of $(\mathbf{I} - \mathbf{BL})$. $(\mathbf{I} - \mathbf{BL})^{-1}$ can be expressed as the sum of the infinite series of terms

$$\mathbf{I} + \mathbf{BL} + \mathbf{BBLL} + \mathbf{BBBLLL} \ldots$$

so

$$f(t) = (\mathbf{I} - \mathbf{BL})^{-1}u(t)$$

can be expressed as

$$f(t) = u(t) + \mathbf{B}\,u(t-1) + \mathbf{B}^2\,u(t-2) + \mathbf{B}^3\,u(t-3) + \ldots$$

where $\mathbf{B}^2$ denotes the square of $\mathbf{B}$, etc. Substituting this representation of the factor scores into the DAFS equation yields the model:

$$\mathbf{y}(t) = \Lambda\,u(t) + \Lambda\mathbf{B}\,u(t-1) + \Lambda\mathbf{B}^2\,u(t-2) + \ldots + e(t)$$

which is also seen to be a WNFS model in which there are infinitely many lagged loadings:

$$\Lambda, \Lambda\mathbf{B}, \Lambda\mathbf{B}^2, \ldots$$

Now the unique identification can be made:

$$\eta(t) = u(t)$$
$$\eta(t-1) = u(t-1)$$

etc., and $\varepsilon(t) = \varepsilon(t)$. Of course the infinite series of lagged loadings can be truncated at some convenient lag, as is typically done in practice, because the sequence

$$\Lambda, \Lambda\mathbf{B}, \Lambda\mathbf{B}^2, \ldots$$

is strictly decreasing to zero.

A more thorough examination of these relationships between the two models has been presented by Nesselroade et al. (2002). The conclusion reached there was that the WNFS model can be thought of as a general model for any time-series data with a factor analytic structure. The DAFS model is a restrictive version of the WNFS model which, due to additional constraints on the factor structure, may or may not fit a given time-series as well as the latter.

As was pointed out elsewhere (Nesselroade et al., 2002) for a given problem size (number of variables, number of factors, and number of lags) and three or more indicators per factor, the DAFS model generally has fewer parameters than the WNFS model. (One can also count the paths in Figures 27.3 and 27.4). Because the DAFS model has more degrees of freedom in cases where the data meet the proportionality constraints, it will provide a better fit. For example, in cases where the manifest variables change at different rates in response to changes in the factor scores, the WNFS model can accommodate these differences but it costs degrees of freedom to do so in comparison to the DAFS model. However, the loss of degrees of freedom may be worthwhile if the indicators show quite differential lag patterns.

Obviously, many variations on the WNFS and DAFS models described above are possible. To make empirical comparisons between them as informative as possible, we have specified the two models in a way that highlights their similarities. For example, we specified the same uniqueness structure for both models. If the two models account in a similar way for the same data, then the argument of parsimony would favor the model with the fewest parameters. If the two differ in the way they account for the same data then the evaluation has to take into account the parsimony of the model as well as other features. Ultimately, it will be necessary to compare the alternative specifications using many different kinds of data representing different kinds of processes if the further development and use of these models is to be maximally effective.

STATIONARITY AND DEVELOPMENTAL PROCESSES

There remains a major issue with which to deal in making the transition from time-series models with latent variables to the modeling of developmental processes. This is the matter of *stationarity* – a condition regarding the nature of the time-series that is assumed to obtain when fitting models such as the WNFS and DAFS. We have avoided this matter in order to emphasize the time-organized nature of these quantitative models in the most simple and straightforward way. However, by and large, developmental processes are not stationary phenomena. Organisms grow, develop, gain, lose, etc., all of which signify a shift in the level or amount of the attribute being observed over time. To accommodate this notion, extensions of the time-series models must be utilized.

Developmental processes are nonstationary in some essential ways. Not every type of nonstationarity will be considered characteristic of development. For instance, in the econometric sciences, nonstationarity often is understood to refer to processes having a wandering mean, while the structural models that describe such nonstationary econometric processes are themselves invariant in time (the process models concerned are called (co-)integrative models; cf. Maddala & Kim, 1998 for a recent overview). Although the latter models might capture some aspects of developmental processes, they are not considered to be the prime examples of the type of nonstationarity characterizing genuine development. In contrast, the waxing and waning of factors in structural models of multivariate time-series can be considered to be a prime example of nonstationarity that is characteristic of development (e.g. Nesselroade & Ford, 1987).

To specify these general remarks somewhat further, we will use an illustration based on the

DAFS model. Let $\mathbf{y}(t)$ be a p-variate manifest time series obeying the DAFS model in which, for ease of presentation, $f(t)$ is considered to be a univariate latent factor series that has a simple first-order autoregressive structure:

$$\mathbf{y}(t) = \Lambda f(t) + \mathbf{e}(t)$$

with

$$f(t) = bf(t - l) + u(t)$$

This illustrative stationary DAFS model can be generalized to nonstationary instances of several distinct types. First, suppose that the autoregressive coefficient $b = 1$. Then the first-order autoregressive model for the latent factor series $f(t)$ becomes:

$$f(t) = f(t - l) + u(t)$$

and this is an integrated first-order autoregression. The DAFS model then becomes an instance of the nonstationary integrated process models used in econometrics. Because the structural model itself does not change in time, this might not be considered genuine development.

Second, suppose that only the variance of $\mathbf{e}(t)$ is time-varying. This implies that the communal part of the DAFS model also is time-varying or, stated otherwise, that the reliabilities of the measurements $\mathbf{y}(t)$ are time-varying. This may occur in repeated measurements which start shortly after birth (where reliability usually is low) and proceed until a more mature age (where reliability tends to be higher). Such a finding usually would not be considered to be a genuine developmental process, because the systematic communal part of the DAFS, $\Lambda f(t)$, itself stays stationary.

Third, consider the case where the factor loadings in the DAFS are themselves time varying:

$$\mathbf{y}(t) = \Lambda_t f(t) + \mathbf{e}(t)$$

with

$$f(t) = bf(t - 1) + u(t)$$

We now have a type of nonstationarity where a subset of the basic parameters of the DAFS, the factor loadings Λ_t, are time-varying. Consequently, in this type of nonstationarity it is the structure of the DAFS itself that is subject to change (giving rise to lack of measurement equivalence across time points) and therefore we consider this an instance of genuine development.

Fourth, and finally, it also may be the case that the autoregressive parameter b in the first-order autoregression for the latent factor series $f(t)$ is time-varying:

$$\mathbf{y}(t) = \Lambda_t f(t) + \mathbf{e}(t)$$

with

$$f(t) = b_t f(t - 1) + u(t)$$

Again, this can be considered an instance of a genuine developmental process because the structure of the DAFS model itself is subject to change (although of a different kind than in the previous case where the factor loadings are changing in time). An example of such a developmental process is illustrated by McCall's discussion of second-order transitions in intellectual development (McCall, 1983; McCall, Eichorn, & Hogarty, 1977).

In conclusion it should be remarked that to the best of our knowledge there do not yet exist statistical methods to fit cases three and four (involving genuine development) to empirical multivariate time-series. In contrast, there does exists a plethora of statistical methods, especially in the econometrics literature, to fit cases one and two involving nonstationarity not directly characteristic of genuine development. However, Molenaar (1994) has introduced an EM algorithm to fit genuinely developmental nonstationary DAFS of the types three and four mentioned above to empirical multivariate time-series.

Some Further Promising Models for Development and Change

In closing this chapter, we want to present some brief commentary on selected aspects of systems modeling that we believe is pertinent to the aims of representing developmental processes.

Linear and NonLinear Systems Models

In addition to the latent variable time-series models discussed above, there are some other promising approaches to capturing the concept of process in rigorous, quantitative terms that involve the application of difference and differential equations to repeated measurements. The explicit use of time in defining these models (e.g. first and second derivatives taken with respect to time) renders them close to process ideas directly. Such modeling efforts have had a limited but nevertheless important role in the social and behavioral sciences (Arminger, 1986; Boker & Graham, 1998; Boker et al., 1998; Coleman, 1968; McArdle & Hamagami, 2001; Tuma & Hannan, 1984).

The use of explicit mathematical formulations involving derivatives, for example, further expands possibilities for the rigorous testing of hypotheses about the nature of processes against empirical data. One useful, relatively simple dynamical model with which intraindividual variability can be represented is the damped linear oscillator (Beltrami, 1987). The pendulum with friction is an example of a system that can be modeled as a damped linear oscillator. Boker and Graham (1998) and Boker et al. (1998), for example, fit a linear damped oscillator model (which involves both first and second derivatives of system variables) to empirical, adolescent drug use data and to mood data of a sample of rapid cycling bipolar disorder patients. Illustrating the capacity for including external influences in the modeling, in the latter case, weather patterns also were modeled and the mood variations were determined to be coupled to the weather changes to a significant extent.

The damped linear oscillator equation is a differential equation. However, it can be thought of as a case of the familiar multiple regression equation in which the variables are the values of the displacement from equilibrium and the values of the first and second derivatives of the displacement. The equation is a linear differential equation because the relationships between variables are represented as linear combinations. A nonlinear system is one for which the equations cannot be reduced to a linear combination, for instance where products of variables are involved.

The differential equation for a damped linear oscillator similar to a pendulum with friction can be expressed as:

$$\frac{\mathrm{d}^2 x(t)}{\mathrm{d}t^2} + \zeta \frac{\mathrm{d}x(t)}{\mathrm{d}t} + \eta x(t) = 0$$

where $x(t)$ represents the value of a variable x at time t, η represents the frequency of oscillation and ζ represents the damping. To illustrate, let x be the displacement of a pendulum from equilibrium. Then the first derivative of x is velocity and the second derivative of x is acceleration. A variable that is functionally related to its derivatives is said to exhibit *intrinsic dynamics*.

This second-order differential equation can be expressed as a system of two first-order equations (Boker & Nesselroade, 2001) by defining

$$x^*(t) = \frac{\mathrm{d}x(t)}{\mathrm{d}t}$$

$$\frac{\mathrm{d}x^*(t)}{\mathrm{d}t} = -\left(\zeta x^*(t) - \eta x(t)\right)$$

Thus the analogy with multiple regression is manifest in the second equation where $\mathrm{d}x^*(t)/\mathrm{d}t$ (the rate of change in the rate of change in x) is the criterion variable and x^* (the rate of change in x) and x are the predictor variables.

From a more psychological point of view, moods and states are often conceptualized in ways that are compatible with this kind of model as is implied, for example, by the term 'mood swings'. By and large, the organism is quite involved in the regulation of its moods and states – an activity nicely represented by the magnitude and direction of the damping parameter. For instance, Carstensen (1993) has articulated a theory of socio-emotional selectivity that characterizes how individuals selectively use their social contexts and other resources to regulate their emotions across the life-span. This implies that the linkages between contextual variables and damping parameters can be empirically investigated. Somewhat more complex models that represent major shocks as well as 'tickles' can be used to represent mood and state as well.

In a more general vein, the linear damped oscillator bears a considerable amount of 'face validity' in relation to the 'open processes' conception of development in the sense that the continual 'shocks' the system receives from its environment do tend to 'damp out' as the organism seeks to maintain some level of equilibrium. The model also allows for individual differences in the damping parameter which squares with differences in how well different individuals manage to regulate their behavior.

One of the major difficulties in applying such modeling approaches to behavioral development research is obtaining large enough numbers of observations for building differential equation models and then estimating their parameters. Methods to generate local estimates of such parameters (e.g. Boker & Nesselroade, 2001) look promising but remain to be more fully developed and tested. When such methods are available, they will bring to the behavioral science workbench one of the most desirable tools used by the physical sciences to represent processes of change.

CONCLUSION

No goal is more critical to the further evolution and growth of behavioral developmental science at this time in its history than strengthening the ability to explicate concepts of process with rigorous, empirically testable representations. As matters stand currently, there is too huge a gap between the usual practices of substantive developmental theorists and researchers and the availability of advanced tools and methods for rendering their most cherished concepts operational. It is encouraging to note that efforts are being made to bring forward newer methods that seem powerful enough to serve the aim of representing process with rigor and testability. It is also comforting that these tools are gradually being tried out in various developmental research contexts. Obviously more needs to be done to foster these hopeful signs.

From our perspective, an encouraging omen is an increased awareness of and interest in intraindividual variability and change aspects of behavioral phenomena studied by developmentalists. Even more encouraging is that this seems to be the case at both ends of the lifespan (see e.g. Hultsch et al., 1998; Siegler, 1994). We believe that a coalescing of the interests of developmentalists with those of researchers, both substantively and methodologically oriented, who are studying intraindividual variability phenomena will have mutually facilitating effects. Developmentalists can provide those who study 'process' in the abstract with important content-oriented examples crying out for more rigorous expression, and modelers and their kin can have more direct access to substantive areas and examples that 'really matter'.

The modeling tools that we have presented here are meant to offer some encouragement regarding the feasibility of applying the tools of intraindividual variability and change to the explication and testing of ideas regarding developmental process in rigorous ways. Rather than simply describing the course of change either verbally or with simple compilations of average levels across some fixed number of occasions of measurement, mathematical and statistical expressions can be formulated that imply intrinsic mechanisms and dynamics of changes and the fit of such models to empirical data can be evaluated.

In the end, the onus remains on developmentalists; it is their field that is, by definition and by proclamation, focused on process. It is they who are obligated to render the concepts of process as rigorous and empirically testable as possible. However, those who build models for studying intraindividual processes can support the efforts of developmentalists directly and creatively – to the benefit of all.

ACKNOWLEDGMENTS

This work was supported by The Institute for Developmental and Health Research Methodology at the University of Virginia.

NOTES

1 It is somewhat ironic that in defending the then current use of P-technique in 1963 Cattell did not strongly argue for the sanctity of temporal sequence in defining the factor loadings and, just three years later, temporal sequence became a key aspect of his definition of process (e.g. Cattell, 1966b).

2 A far bigger issue, and one of international concern, is how better to train young behavioral scientists in the use of these methods. Graduate training is much better than it used to be concerning teaching graduate students methods that are not dominated by the analysis of variance model, but much remains to be done until the recently trained cohort of PhDs thinks in multivariate/correlational terms as easily as previous cohorts thought in analysis of variance terms in regard to research design and data analysis.

3 Elsewhere, Nesselroade et al. (2002) introduced this term to recognize that Molenaar specified the common factor scores as a 'white noise' time-series. He did this for technical reasons: model identification and other specifications could be used to this end as appropriate.

REFERENCES

Anderson, T.W. (1963). The use of factor analysis in the statistical analysis of multiple time series. *Psychometrika* 28, 1–24.

Arminger, G. (1986). Linear stochastic differential equation models for panel data with unobserved variables. In N. Tuma (ed.), *Sociological methodology 1986* (pp. 187–212). San Francisco: Jossey-Bass.

Arminger, G. (1993). The analysis of panel data with mean and covariance structure models for non-metric dependent variables. In C.M. Cuadras & C.R. Rao (eds), *Multivariate analysis: Future directions 2* (pp. 131–151). Amsterdam: Elsevier.

Bakeman, R., & Gottman, J.M. (1997). *Observing interaction: An introduction to sequential analysis* (2nd edn). Cambridge: Cambridge University Press.

Baltes, P.B. (1973). Prototypical paradigms and questions in life-span research on development and aging. *The Gerontologist*, 485–467.

Baltes, P.B., & Nesselroade, J.R. (1973). The developmental analysis of individual differences on multiple measures. In J.R. Nesselroade & H.W. Reese (eds), *Life-span developmental psychology: Methodological issues* (pp. 219–249). New York: Academic.

Baltes, P.B., Reese, H.W., & Nesselroade, J.R. (1977). *Life-span developmental psychology: Introduction to research methods*. Monterrey, CA: Brooks/Cole.

Bentler, P. (1973). Assessment of developmental factor change at the individual and group level. In J.R. Nesselroade & H.W. Reese (eds), *Life-span developmental psychology: Methodological issues* (pp. 145–174). New York: Academic.

Bereiter, C. (1963). Some persisting dilemmas in the measurement of change. In C.W. Harris (ed.), *Problems in measuring change*. Madison, WI: University of Wisconsin Press.

Boker, S.M., & Graham, J. (1998). A dynamical systems analysis of adolescence substance abuse. *Multivariate Behavioral Research*, 33, 479–507.

Boker, S.M., & Nesselroade, J.R. (2002). A method for modeling the intrinsic dynamics of intraindividual variability: Recovering the parameters of simulated oscillators in multi-wave data. *Multivariate Behavioral Research*, 37, 127–160.

Boker, S.M., Postolache, T., Naim, S., & Lebenluft, E. (1998). Mood oscillations and coupling between mood and weather in patients with rapid cycling bipolar disorder. Unpublished manuscript, Department of Psychology, University of Notre Dame.

Browne, M.W. (2001). Dynamic factor models: Some promising uses and extensions of ARMA time series models. Workshop presentation, Charlottesville, Virginia.

Burt, C. (1954). The differentiation of intellectual abilities. *British Journal of Educational Psychology*, 24, 76–90.

Buss, A.R. (1979). Toward a unified framework for psychometric concepts in the multivariate developmental situation: Intraindividual change and inter- and intra-individual differences. In J.R. Nesselroade & P.B. Baltes (eds), *Longitudinal research in the study of behavior and development* (pp. 41–59). New York: Academic.

Campbell, D.T., & Stanley, J.C. (1963). Experimental and quasi-experimental designs for research on teaching. In N.L. Gage (ed.), *Handbook of research on teaching*. Chicago: Rand McNally.

Carstensen, L. (1993). Motivation for social contact across the life span: A theory of socioemotional selectivity. In J.E. Jacobs (ed.), *Nebraska Symposium on Motivation 40* (pp. 209–254). Lincoln, NB: University of Nebraska Press.

Cattell, R.B. (1952). The three basic factor-analytic research designs: Their interrelations and derivatives. *Psychological Bulletin*, 49, 499–520.

Cattell, R.B. (1963). The interaction of hereditary and environmental influences. *The British Journal of Statistical Psychology*, 16, 191–210.

Cattell, R.B. (1966a). Guest editorial: Multivariate behavioral research and the integrative challenge. *Multivariate Behavioral Research*, 1, 4–23.

Cattell, R.B. (1966b). Patterns of change: Measurement in relation to state dimension, trait change, liability, and process concepts. In R.B. Cattell (ed.), *Handbook of multivariate experimental psychology* (1st edn, pp. 355–402). Chicago: Rand McNally.

Cattell, R.B. (1979). *Personality and learning theory: The structure of personality in its environment* (Vol. 1). New York: Springer.

Cattell, R.B. (1980). *Personality and learning theory: A systems theory of maturation and structured learning* (Vol. 2). New York: Springer.

Cattell, R.B., Cattell, A.K.S., & Rhymer, R.M. (1947). P-technique demonstrated in determining psychophysical source traits in a normal individual. *Psychometrika*, 12, 267–288.

Cattell, R.B., & Scheier, I.H. (1961). *The meaning and measurement of neuroticism and anxiety*. New York: Ronald.

Coleman, J.S. (1968). The mathematical study of change. In J.H.M. Blaylock & A. Blaylock (eds), *Methodology in social research* (pp. 428–478). New York: McGraw-Hill.

Collins, L.M., & Horn, J.L. (eds) (1991). *Best methods for the analysis of change*. Washington, DC: American Psychological Association.

Collins, L., & Sayer, A. (eds) (2000). *Methods for the analysis of change*. Washington, DC: American Psychological Association.

Cronbach, L.J. (1957). The two disciplines of scientific psychology. *American Psychologist*, 12, 71–84.

Engle, R., & Watson, M. (1981). A one-factor multivariate time series model of metropolitan wage rates. *Journal of the American Statistical Association*, 76, 774–781.

Ford, D.H. (1987). *Humans as self-constructing living systems*. Hillsdale, NJ: Erlbaum.

Ford, D.H., & Lerner, R.M. (1992). *Developmental systems theory: An integrative approach*. Newbury Park, CA: Sage.

Garrett, H.E. (1946). A developmental theory of intelligence. *The American Psychologist*, 1, 372–378.

Geweke, J.F., & Singleton, K.J. (1981). Maximum likelihood 'confirmatory' factor analysis of economic time series. *International Economic Review*, 22, 37–54.

Harris, C.W. (ed.) (1963). *Problems in measuring change*. Madison, WI: University of Wisconsin Press.

Hershberger, S.L., Molenaar, P.C.M., & Corneal, S.E. (1996). A hierarchy of univariate and multivariate time series models. In G.A. Marcoulides & R.E. Schumacker (eds), *Advanced structural equation modeling: Issues and techniques* (pp. 159–194). Mahwah, NJ: Erlbaum.

Holtzman, W.H. (1963). Statistical models for the study of change in the single case. In C.W. Harris (ed.), *Problems in measuring change* (pp. 199–211). Madison, WI: University of Wisconsin Press.

Hultsch, D.F., Hertzog, C., Dixon, R.A., & Small, B.J. (1998). *Memory change in the aged*. Cambridge: Cambridge University Press.

Jones, K. (1991). The application of time series methods to moderate span longitudinal data. In L.M. Collins & J.L. Horn (eds), *Best methods for the analysis of change: Recent advances, unanswered questions, future directions* (pp. 75–87). Washington, DC: American Psychological Association.

Lamiell, J.T. (1981). Toward an idiothetic psychology of personality. *American Psychologist*, 36, 276–289.

Lamiell, J.T. (1988). Once more into the breach: Why individual differences research cannot advance personality theory. Paper presented at the annual meeting of the American Psychological Association, Atlanta, GA.

Lebo, M.A., & Nesselroade, J.R. (1978). Intraindividual differences dimensions of mood change during pregnancy identified in five P-technique factor analyses. *Journal of Research in Personality*, 12, 205–224.

Maddala, G.S., & Kim, I. (1998). *Unit roots, cointegration, and structural change*. Cambridge: Cambridge University Press.

McArdle, J.J. (1982). Structural equation modeling of an individual system: Preliminary results from 'A case study in episodic alcoholism'. Unpublished manuscript, Department of Psychology, University of Denver.

McArdle, J.J. (1988). Dynamic but structural equation modeling of repeated measures data. In J.R. Nesselroade & R.B. Cattell (eds), *Handbook of multivariate experimental psychology* (2nd edn, pp. 561–614). New York: Plenum.

McArdle, J.J., & Hamagami, F. (2001). Latent difference score structural models for linear dynamic analysis with incomplete longitudinal data. In L. Collins & A. Sayer (eds), *New methods for the analysis of change* (pp. 139–175). Washington, DC: American Psychological Association.

McArdle, J.J., & Nesselroade, J.R. (2002). Growth curve analysis in developmental research. In J. Schinka & W. Velicer (eds), *Comprehensive handbook of psychology: Vol. II. Research methods in psychology*. New York: Pergamon.

McCall, R.B. (1983). Exploring developmental transitions in mental performance. In K.W. Fischer (ed.), *Levels and transitions in children's development: New directions for child development* (Vol. 21, pp. 65–80). San Francisco: Jossey-Bass.

McCall, R.B., Eichorn, D.H., & Hogarty, P.S. (1977). *Transitions in early mental development. Monographs of the Society for Research in Child Development*, Vol. 42, no. 3, serial 171.

Meredith, W. (2001). Personal communication, October.

Meredith, W., & Tisak, J. (1984). 'Tuckerizing' curves. Paper presented at the annual meeting of the Psychometric Society, Santa Barbara, CA.

Meredith, W., & Tisak, J. (1990). Latent curve analysis. *Psychometrika*, 55, 107–122.

Molenaar, P.C.M. (1985). A dynamic factor model for the analysis of multivariate time series. *Psychometrika*, 50 (2), 181–202.

Molenaar, P.C.M. (1994). Dynamic latent variable models in developmental psychology. In A. von Eye & C.C. Clogg (eds), *Latent variables analysis: Applications for developmental research* (pp. 155–180). Thousand Oaks, CA: Sage.

Molenaar, P.C.M., Huizinga, H.M., & Nesselroade, J.R. (in press). The relationship between the structure of inter-individual and intra-individual variability: A theoretical and empirical vindication of developmental systems theory. In U.M. Staudinger & U. Lindenberger (eds), *Understanding human development*. Dordrecht: Kluwer.

Nesselroade, J.R., & Baltes, P.B. (1974). *Adolescent personality development and historical change: 1970–72* (Vol. 39) (Whole No. 154).

Nesselroade, J.R., & Featherman, D.L. (1997). Establishing a reference frame against which to chart age-related change. In M.A. Hardy (ed.), *Studying aging and social change: Conceptual and methodological issues* (pp. 191–205). Thousand Oaks, CA: Sage.

Nesselroade, J.R., & Ford, D.H. (1985). P-technique comes of age: Multivariate, replicated, single-subject designs for research on older adults. *Research on Aging*, 7, 46–80.

Nesselroade, J.R., & Ford, D.H. (1987). Methodological considerations in modeling living systems. In M.E. Ford & D.H. Ford (eds), *Humans as self-constructing living systems: Putting the framework to work* (pp. 47–79). Hillsdale, NJ: Erlbaum.

Nesselroade, J.R., & Ghisletta, P. (2002). Structuring and measuring change over the lifespan. In U.M. Staudinger & U. Lindenberger (eds), *Understanding human development: Lifespan psychology in exchange with other disciplines*. Dordrecht: Kluwer.

Nesselroade, J.R., McArdle, J.J., Aggen, S.H., & Meyers, J.M. (2002). Alternative dynamic factor models for multivariate time-series analyses. In D.M. Moskowitz & S.L. Hershberger (eds), *Modeling intraindividual variability with repeated measures data: Advances and techniques* (pp. 235–265). Mahwah, NJ: Erlbaum.

Nesselroade, J.R., & Molenaar, P.C.M. (1999). Pooling lagged covariance structures based on short, multivariate time-series for dynamic factor analysis. In R.H. Hoyle (ed.), *Statistical strategies for small sample research*. Newbury Park, CA: Sage.

Nesselroade, J.R., & Molenaar, P.C.M. (in press). Applying dynamic factor analysis in aging research. *Psychology and Aging*.

Nesselroade, J.R., Schaie, K.W., & Baltes, P.B. (1972). Ontogenetic and generational components of structural and quantitative change in adult behavior. *Journal of Gerontology*, 27, 222–228.

Olsson, U., & Bergman, L.R. (1977). A longitudinal factor model for studying change in ability structure. *Multivariate Behavioral Research*, 12, 221–242.

Rao, C.R. (1958). Some statistical methods for the comparison of growth curves. *Biometrics*, 14, 1–17.

Roberts, M.L., & Nesselroade, J.R. (1986). Intraindividual variability in perceived locus of control in adults: P-technique factor analyses of short-term change. *Journal of Research in Personality*, 20, 529–545.

Rogosa, D.R., Brandt, D., & Zimowski, M. (1982). A growth curve approach to the measurement of change. *Psychological Bulletin*, 92, 726–748.

Shifrin, K., Hooker, K.A., Wood, P.K., & Nesselroade, J.R. (1997). The structure and variation in mood in individuals with Parkinson's disease: A dynamic factor analysis. *Psychology and Aging*, 12, 328–229.

Siegler, R.S. (1994). Cognitive variability: A key to understanding cognitive development. *Current Directions in Psychological Science*, 3 (1), 1–5.

Singer, H. (1993). Continuous-time dynamical systems with sampled data, errors of measurement, and unobserved components. *Journal of Time Series Analysis*, 14, 527–545.

Tucker, L.R. (1958). Determination of parameters of a functional relation by factor analysis. *Psychometrika*, 23 (1), 19–23.

Tucker, L.R. (1966). Learning theory and multivariate experiment: Illustration by determination of generalized learning curves. In R.B. Cattell (ed.), *Handbook of multivariate experimental psychology* (pp. 476–501). Chicago: Rand McNally.

Tuma, N.B., & Hannan, M.T. (1984). *Social dynamics: Models and methods*. New York: Academic Press.

Valsiner, J. (1984). Two alternative epistemological frameworks in psychology: The typological and variational modes of thinking. *The Journal of Mind and Behavior*, 5, 449–470.

van Geert, P. (1991). A dynamic systems model of cognitive and language growth. *Psychological Review*, 98, 3–53.

Wessman, A.E., & Ricks, D.F. (1966). *Mood and personality*. New York: Holt, Rinehart, and Winston.

West, B. (1985). *An essay on the importance of being nonlinear*. Berlin: Springer.

Wohlwill, J.F. (1973). *The study of behavioral development*. New York: Academic.

Wood, P., & Brown, D. (1994). The study of intraindividual differences by means of dynamic factor models: Rationale, implementation, and interpretation. *Psychological Bulletin*, 116, 166–186.

Zevon, M., & Tellegen, A. (1982). The structure of mood change: Idiographic/nomothetic analysis. *Journal of Personality and Social Pyschology*, 43, 111–122.

28

Dynamic Systems Approaches and Modeling of Developmental Processes

PAUL VAN GEERT

The notion of development plays an important role in cultural, political and personal discourse. For instance, in the newspaper, we read about the problems of developing countries. At another level, personal development is considered an important issue and people spend considerable effort in promoting their development and that of others for whom they have responsibility.

The notion of development has subtle and diverse meanings, which are reasonably adequately covered by everyday language. Scientific discourse about development as such, apart from the technical aspects of applying it to one or other specific domain of inquiry, is not much better developed, if at all, than its everyday counterpart. It might be interesting, therefore, to look at the intuitive meaning of the notion of development, in an attempt to uncover aspects that might be worth considering in more formal, scientific approaches. One way to do so is to look at the original meaning of the word 'development', its etymology.

THE NOTION OF DEVELOPMENT: AN APPROACH THROUGH ITS ETYMOLOGY

The English word 'development' stems from the Old French *desvoloper*, which means 'to unwrap'. The German and Dutch words *Entwicklung* and *ontwikkeling* are literal translations of that term. In its historical roots, the word 'development' is related to the Latin *evolutio* (to unroll) and the semantically related word *explicatio* (to unfold). The Latin words referred among others to the unfolding or unrolling of book rolls. The latter meaning is still preserved in the word 'explain', which therefore bears an unexpected relationship to the word 'development' (Thomae, 1959; Trautner, 1978).

There is a lot of metaphorical connotation in these semantic forebears of the notion of development that is still preserved in its current use (for a more extensive treatment of this issue, see van Geert 1986a; 1986b; 1988; 1990). The notions of unwrapping and unfolding carry a meaning of something that is inside the wrapping and that is taken out. Another metaphoric meaning contained in those terms is that of a folded structure that is folded out, similar to rosebuds whose petals grow and meanwhile fold out to bring forth the rose's mature shape. The unfolding is a particularly nice metaphor, since it suggests that the form is already there at the beginning in some germinal state and that it is reached in a series of qualitatively different intermediate forms that correspond with each step of the unfolding. Many years ago, Nagel (1957, p. 17) probably hinted at this metaphor when he described development as what happens to a system with a specific structure and initial capacities, characterized by a series of successive changes leading to relatively permanent, new structural properties.

The notion of development as used in colloquial discourse – and scientific discourse too, for that matter – carries the meaning of an internally driven force acting in a specific context. For instance, we speak about developing a photograph or developing a piece of land. The body develops because the person consumes food and exercises its growing capacities; people develop their skills by learning from others and using the skills where appropriate. We speak about the development of logical thinking, of language and so forth. Although we are well aware of the fact that such things will hardly ever develop out of their proper contexts, we also assume that they change because of some internal drive or process. All this is reminiscent of Bergson's notion of the *élan vital*, the vital drive, that governed the processes of life and evolution, at least as was thought around the turn of the nineteenth into the twentieth century. As far as development is concerned, there exists a non-specific relationship between the context and the process of development that takes place in this context (the context is needed, but it does not prescribe or prefigure the development). This is very different from what is supposed to happen in a process of learning, or of cultural transmission, where the environment directly governs – or at least attempts to do so – the internal changes in the learning person (what is learned is what is given or transmitted: van Geert, 1986a).

In addition to this aspect of an internal drive, development has a connotation of progress, of increasing complexity, structure and order. One does not develop to become less or worse. This idea of intrinsic progression is also entailed in theories of development, or more particularly, theoretical models that described the course of the developmental process. Based on the structure of those models, we can make a distinction between retrospective theories and prospective theories. Retrospective theories are those that look at the developmental process from the perspective of an end state and view all preceding states in light of this end state. Under this perspective, the developmental process is like a logically necessary move towards the preset end state. Prospective theories are those that look at development from the perspective of its initial state and the mechanisms that operate on that initial state. They see development as a fundamentally open process (for a more detailed analysis, see van Geert 1987a; 1987b; 1987c; 1987d; 1988). It is interesting to note, however, that the concept of development sometimes entails a notion or progress that creates its own progress criteria. For instance, when we speak about the development of a new artistic style or a new form of philosophical thought, that new form or style sets at least part of the criteria by which it has to be judged. In fact, one can almost distinguish two kinds of approaches to the issue of progress as it relates to development. One is, so to say, more conservative, in that it sees progress as the reaching of some preset standard or criterion (like a person with a well-developed taste, implying that his taste meets some accepted, culturally valued criterion). The other is a more progressive approach, which focuses on the fact that new criteria for judging that progress emerge simultaneously with the progress itself. This latter approach to development emphasizes the aspect of novelty, of development as the creator of something new. Note that, since development is assumed to be internally driven, novelty does not necessarily imply uniqueness. It is conceivable that each and every newborn child develops through a series of structural possibilities – such as the Piagetian stages, for instance – which are entirely new from the child's standpoint, which have neither been transmitted nor been genetically coded, but are nevertheless (almost) similar for all children.

In summary, the notion of development as it features in colloquial speech and general models alike entails a certain tension between opposing traits. Development entails an aspect of predestination – something unfolds that is already there – but also an aspect of coming-into-being that is more than the simple uncovering of what is there already at the beginning. Second, development involves an aspect of self-governed, internally driven change, but also an aspect of context dependency, of the necessity of an external support. It also involves the idea of increasing order and structure, a progress towards higher quality and even the creation of new forms and structures. In summary, development is a highly particular process that cannot and should not be reduced to a simple causal process driven by either internal or external conditions. Its particular nature finds its expression in the rather ambiguous, somewhat unclear nature of the concept as it is used in different forms of discourse.

Scientific Attacks on the Notion of Development

One of the main problems with the notion of development as described in the preceding section is that there exists a lot of common sense evidence for it, but very little real theory to back it up. For instance, parents with some experience of raising children find that educating children requires a lot of effort, while on the other hand, the child's growing up has a logic of its own and is all but directly governed by the parents' goals and actions. Every new organism comes into existence through a somatic developmental process that transforms more or less non-specific energy supplied from outside, in the form of food, for instance, into a highly specific body form. Historically, cultures have changed and developed without a mastermind that governed their paths (wherever such a mastermind took the lead, things went – often dramatically – wrong).

The explanation of development has long since been the endeavor of philosophers more than of natural scientists. Kant (1724-1804), for instance, viewed the organism as a whole of interdependent components and aspects, sustained by its inherent logic. In the late nineteenth and early twentieth centuries, philosophers and historians tried to explain cultures as developing wholes, with their own internal drives and their own life span and developmental stages (see for instance the work of Spengler, 1880-1936, on the decline of western civilization). We have already encountered the French philosopher Bergson (1859-1941), for instance, who conceived of an *élan vital*, which is a vital impulse that governed the unfolding of life's inherent tendencies.

In stark contrast to these mostly philosophical attempts at explaining and describing the process and notion of development, the natural sciences – at least since Newton – have gradually shifted away from the core meanings of development and have become increasingly critical about it.

The second law of thermodynamics, which is a fundamental law of nature, deals with the fate of order and structure in the universe. It says that order can never spontaneously increase. It must decay unless it is driven by some external source, which must have a higher level of order than the order it is able to create. The history of the discovery of the second law of thermodynamics is intimately related to the emergence of industrial society and the massive use of machines (Atkins, 1984). Machines need energy to accomplish something and what they accomplish is always less than the net energy that has been put into them. There exists an analogy to this process of heat transmission in the transmission of information through a channel: there is always more information in the sender than in the receiver, since the transmission through the channel leads to an irreversible and inevitable loss of information. Since the laws of thermodynamics also govern animate nature, development – if viewed as a spontaneous increase of order – must be an illusion.

Not only in physics, but also in biology, the idea of development as an inherent trend towards improvement came under severe attack. Historically, the idea of gradual improvement of successive life forms became known as the *Scalae Naturae*, the ladder of nature or the Great Chain of Being. The idea was that life begins (in a non-historical sense of that word, however) with the most primitive organisms and advances through stages of increasing complexity up to the most complex of them all, man. Although this notion did not entail a concept of time – and thus of evolution or development as we see it today – it did entail a progression towards increasing complexity. The idea was vindicated by the so-called Rational Morphologists, who saw the form of the organisms' bodies as coherent wholes and the relation between the body forms of species as one of an underlying structural logic across the species' boundaries. These concepts were wiped out completely with the advent of Darwinian evolutionary theory. Darwin made an important contribution in that he introduced the notion of time as an inherent factor in the explanation of the forms and properties of biological species and in doing so he introduced the notion of phylogenetic change in addition to the already familiar notion of ontogenetic change (the growth of a single organism). Meanwhile, Darwin's theory of evolution discarded all reference to a notion of development, of progress-directed deployment of inherent structure. The major mechanism is that of selection of accidental variations by an environment that selectively favors some variations over others. Selection leads to increasingly better adaptations of the species to its environment, but this result is not due to the working of some inherent tendency towards betterment. Evolution does not necessarily lead to increase of structure and complexity. If survival is better warranted by loss of complexity and structure than by gain, then loss of complexity is what occurs. Thus, whatever survives is better adapted than anything that does not survive and in that sense the predicate 'fittest' can only be given after the facts (after the selection has taken place). However, if evolution is looked at from a retrospective point of view – that is, given the present state of affairs at the stage of biological species – it seems as if evolution was indeed driven to some highly complex end state, the complex tree of life that we witness today. But this retrospective look is highly deceptive. We should realize that the state of species evolution as we know it today is a highly coincidental matter. The stage could just as well have been populated in a dramatically different way and what we call increasing complexity is nothing but the result of the fact that the only direction evolution could go was to increase complexity in some species, whereas the most successful species are still very close to the 'simplicity' of early life forms (both arguments are strongly defended in Gould, 1989; 1996). The principle of selection is entirely dependent on the mechanism of variation, because if there is no variation there are no differences and if there are no differences it doesn't matter what is selected, because the result will remain the same. Thus, understanding the source and mechanisms of variation is of crucial importance to understanding the course of evolution. Variation is something that applies to the form and properties of the organism, i.e. their morphology, and this morphology is the product of the mechanisms of morphogenesis.

The process of morphogenesis – the growth of a single organism – remained largely a mystery until the discovery of genetics, especially the atomistic approach originally developed by Mendel. It explained the growth of the organism as the result of building instructions contained in the genes. This approach to genetics basically pays tribute to the second law of thermodynamics: the complexity of the developing body is entirely entailed in its genetic starting point. Form and order do not emerge spontaneously but are inscribed in the genetic instruction book. Note that this approach to genetics agrees very well with the notion of development as the unfolding of what is already there, though concealed in the organism's deepest, genetic kernel. However, it differs from the more naive developmental view in that it acknowledges that the end result of morphogenesis is, structurally speaking, nothing more than what was already contained in the genetic instruction. The mechanisms of morphological variation are thus reducible to those of genetic variation, i.e. mutations. In summary, the biological view on the evolution of species – their phylogenetic development, so to speak – seems to be reducible to the principle of instruction sets (the genome), random variation of this genome and selection of the most favorable expressions of the potential genomes. (I say 'seems to be reducible', since I shall argue that modern views on morphogenesis take a somewhat different approach; by and large, however, even today the widespread view on the evolution of species is still very similar to the one just sketched.)

As to developmental psychology, the notion of development has had its strong defenders in scholars that did their main work in the first half of the twentieth century (Piaget, Werner, Vygotsky and others). Later scientific developments, however, gradually moved the field away from its concern with development proper (van Geert, 1998c). One is the adoption of linear statistical modeling, which no doubt increased the methodological rigor of research, but also replaced the notions of wholeness and mutuality characteristic of the older conceptualizations of development with one of asymmetric relationships between variables. As a result, developmental psychology gradually turned into a study of group differences, the groups defined by their ages. A second change in the field had to do with the emergence of a new approach to the study of language, namely Chomskyan linguistics, which was strongly inspired by a centuries-old rationalism. With regard to language development, Chomsky showed that language – *qua* human knowledge – is underdetermined by the input, that is, the language addressed to a language-learning child. That is to say, it is logically impossible to extract the grammar of a language on the basis of the linguistic environmental input alone. Nevertheless, children do acquire the grammar of their language and they do so easily and rapidly. Since the grammar is not transmitted by giving linguistic input, it follows that knowledge of the grammar must be present in the language learner in advance. Language development is therefore basically the unfolding of innately present knowledge, with the innate knowledge actualized in the form of some specific language. This view of language acquisition is highly reminiscent of genetic information transmission as conceived of in the atomistic, Mendelean view. In the 1970s, this view of language acquisition was highly applauded by a group of biologists and geneticists who gathered at the Abbaye de Royaumont to witness a discussion between Piaget and Chomsky. The discussion, which was laid down in a widely cited book (Piattelli-Palmarini, 1980), led to a victory, if one may use that word, of the Chomskyan view and to the defeat of Piaget's developmentalism. Piaget's view was identified with an obsolete vision of change and evolution (de Graaf, 1999).

In summary, the position of development as described in the first section of this chapter, namely as a self-governed process of spontaneous increase in complexity and structure, seems fatally weak. There seems to be no reasonable scientific foundation for such a notion. To the contrary, well-established scientific findings lend support to the conclusion that development should be banned to the realm of romantic philosophical illusions. In the next section, however, we shall see that this conclusion is premature and that the scientific basis of development is stronger than thus far suggested.

In Support of Development: The Dynamic Systems Approach

The Early Years: The Study of Changes Brought About by Interacting Forces

Newton and Leibniz are the fathers of differential calculus, and differential calculus is the mathematical method that allows one to study and formalize continuous change. The fact that motion patterns could be formalized into equations was a major discovery of the seventeenth century. It led to a formalization of the motion of celestial bodies, of pendulums in clocks, of heat transmission in a steam engine. Virtually no domain in which change occurred in some continuous and more or less regular way escaped from study. The common theme was dynamics. *Dynamic* refers to the Greek *dynamikos*, which means 'powerful'. The study of dynamics concerns the way forces apply and how they change and exert an influence on the world. Since Newton, one of the main areas of study was the dynamics of celestial bodies, such as planets or the sun. Planets exert a gravitational influence upon one another – they exchange gravitational force – and by doing so they keep each other in regular orbits, the forms of which were already described by Kepler. Although the dynamics of two interacting bodies, planets for instance, could be formalized and solved without too much effort (speaking in hindsight, that is), the problem of describing the dynamics of three interacting bodies proved notoriously difficult to solve. Two interacting planets form a simple *system* (a word that stems from a Greek verb that means 'to combine') and three planets form a system that is apparently just a little more complicated. However, the truth is that from an explanatory point of view, three planets form a system that is incomparably more complex than two. The so-called three-body problem marked the start of the development of non-linear dynamics as a mathematical discipline. Around the turn of the century, the French mathematician Henri Poincaré developed a set of methods for studying possible solutions of the three-body problem and by doing so laid the foundations of the current science of non-linear dynamics and dynamic systems. Before we proceed, let me point out the possible relations between such vastly differing problems as three planets revolving around each other and the psychological development of human beings. First, both problems concern the mutual relationship between various components that affect one another. Second, both problems concern the evolution of patterns in time – be it spatial patterns or patterns of developing personal properties – that result as a consequence of the interacting forces. The important discovery that Poincaré made was that there exist general methods for approaching those problems, irrespective of their actual content matter. Thanks to these general methods and related insights, dynamic systems theory grew into a general formal approach to the problems of change.

The Study of Stable and Dynamic Equilibria

Further studies in the field of dynamics, both mathematical and physical, demonstrated the existence of spontaneously emerging equilibria. Some systems of interacting forces tend to drive each other to an equilibrium state, that is, a state where the forces involved keep each other at a fixed level or value. This stability is a form of dynamic stability: it is because the forces interact that they keep each other in a locked position. Some forms of stability turned out to be dynamic themselves. For instance, some systems spontaneously evolve towards a cyclical pattern. That is, the pattern of the forces involved keeps changing, but it does so in a cyclical fashion (for instance the so-called van der Pol oscillations that occur in electric and magnetic media). It is even possible for some systems to run into patterns that never repeat but that nevertheless show a high level of regularity. This phenomenon was discovered in the 1960s by a meteorologist by the name of Lorenz who simulated weather phenomena on a computer (although the first experimental evidence for this phenomenon came from the Dutch engineers van der Pol and van der Mark in 1927).

Since the Lorenz model features so prominently in many introductions to chaos and dynamic systems, it is worthwhile to give a little more background information that will also be illustrative of how dynamic systems models operate (see Jackson, 1991b; de Swart, 1990). The weather can be seen as a process of atmospheric circulations (of air with a certain temperature and moisture, for instance) and these circulations can be mathematically represented as the sum of waves with a particular wavelength and amplitude (the fact that a complex wave can be represented as a sum of harmonic waves was discovered by the French mathematician Fourier, 1768-1830, and is used in spectral analysis, which is the basis of the Lorenz and comparable models). In order to provide a reasonably realistic description of the real atmospheric circulation, one needs a model with many such waves. Lorenz wanted to understand the essentials of the interaction between the functions that govern the evolution of such waves and managed to come up with a set of three connected functions. The first describes the magnitude of an atmospheric flow and the second and third describe the magnitude of two temperature waves. It is important to note that this is no longer a model of a real weather system but a model that reduces a weather system (and many comparable systems of flow, such as magnetic flows) to its bare essentials and by doing so tries to understand the fundamental properties of the dynamics. This kind of reduction to the essentials is typical of dynamic systems models, as we will see with the predator-prey model of Lotka and Volterra. The system of equations that Lorenz studied is as follows:

$$\Delta x/\Delta t = \sigma(y - x)$$
$$\Delta y/\Delta t = -xz + rx - y$$
$$\Delta z/\Delta t = xy - bz$$

The parameters σ, r and b are typical of models for dynamic flows; r, for instance, is the so-called Rayleigh number, which is a measure for a temperature difference, for instance the difference between the ground temperature and the temperature at a high altitude.

What is the essential fact or facts about the weather that Lorenz wanted to study with the aid of his three simple equations (and they are indeed very simple, since understanding them requires no more than elementary school mathematics)? A short overview of Lorenz' findings with his three simple equations will show what those essential facts are. First, Lorenz discovered that even simple systems (no more complicated than three mutually interacting variables) could spontaneously settle into regular but never identical patterns, so-called strange attractors (Figure 28.1). Second, he found that such patterns display sudden switches for no apparent reason other than their internal dynamic drive. Third, he found that some interaction patterns – depending on the value of the parameters – are highly sensitive to initial conditions. These are processes we now call by the name 'chaos', although the word chaos itself is quite misleading, since most of what we refer to as 'chaos' are in fact deterministic processes with high apparent irregularity but nevertheless high internal order). If

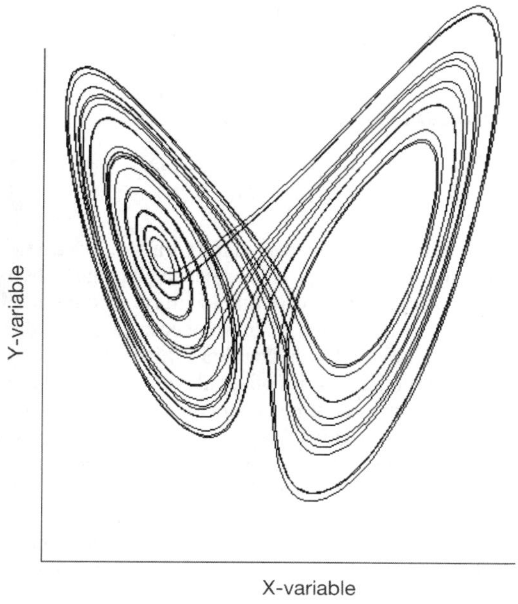

Figure 28.1 *Plotting the position of the* x-*variable against the* y-*variable (or any other combination of the three variables* x, y, *and* z, *for that matter) yields a complicated spatial pattern. The pattern represents the change of the* x- *and* y-*values over time and is known as a 'strange attractor'*

we repeat such a process with only an extremely small difference in its starting conditions, the process trajectory will at first be indistinguishable from that of the first time. But after some time the effect of the minor difference – however minor it may be – will show up in the form of a sudden major divergence between the two dynamic patterns. This is the so-called butterfly effect, which has become almost proverbial: it can be mathematically proven that a butterfly flapping its wings in Singapore, to name just one place, could cause a hurricane in Texas (a finding that puts a heavy burden on the fragile shoulders of innocent butterflies). To put it differently, there exist – simple – systems of interacting forces whose stability is only temporal. After a while they will suddenly diverge and the magnitude of their divergence is in no way proportional to the cause of the divergence. Note that this finding does not imply that all systems of interacting forces are unstable in this particular sense. The point is that some systems tend to stability and will return to that stable point (or pattern) even if they are disturbed – perturbed is the common term – by influences from outside, whereas other systems will vastly diverge if any disturbance occurs, however tiny it may be.

The general lesson that can be learned from these early developments in dynamic systems theory is that systems of interacting forces (can) have a natural tendency to evolve towards some equilibrium state, which is dynamically maintained as soon as it is reached. Some equilibria consist of dynamic patterns, for instance cycles. There exist stable equilibria that are relatively insensitive to perturbations, and unstable equilibria, whose outcomes depend on minute differences in starting conditions or perturbations along the way.

Mathematical Models of Quantitative Biological Processes

Meanwhile, in the 1920s and 1930s, non-linear dynamic modeling was applied to the life sciences, more particularly to biology. The first domains to which dynamic systems ideas were applied were epidemiology – the discipline that deals with the spreading, waxing and waning of diseases – and population biology. Both fields deal with ecological problems, that is, problems relating to the interaction of many different biological species that share an environment. The word 'ecology' is based on the Greek word *oikos*, which means household. An ecological system is characterized by a specific energy flow, by temporal static or dynamic *stabilities* and by long-term change (evolution). Probably the best known example of early dynamic systems modeling is the work of the American ecologist Lotka and the Italian mathematician Volterra. Independently of one another, both scholars discovered the principle of dynamic predator-prey interaction. Volterra's work was based on observations by his future son-in-law, who was a marine biologist. The latter sought an explanation for the finding that during the First World War, when fishing had almost ceased, there was an increase in certain predaceous fish, namely those that lived off prey fish that used to be fished before the war had started. This was an unexpected fact, since one would expect a rise in the population of those prey fish, simply because they were no longer caught in great numbers by fishermen (one could say that the predator fish had taken over the role of the human predators). This question resulted in a simple mathematical model that described the interaction between a predator population and a prey population. Since it is such a nice example of fundamental dynamical thinking, it is worthwhile to go into it a little deeper. Let P be the symbol for the population size of the predator fish (mackerel, for instance) and F the population size of the prey fish (sardines, for instance). If the predators are left without prey, their population will decrease proportionally to a certain death rate, i.e.

$$\Delta P/\Delta t = -aP$$

which one should read as follows: the change in population ΔP over some time interval Δt is equal to the size of the population P multiplied by a rate of dying $-a$ (we could also have set a to a negative number, but this notation is a little more insightful). However, if there is prey to feed on, the predator fish will be able to increase their numbers: the living fish will live longer and newborn predator fish will have a better chance to survive. It is obvious that the increase in the predator population depends on the available prey. If there are a lot of prey fish, considerably more predator fish will survive. Thus, we know that the predator population P increases proportionally to the amount of available prey F and a certain growth rate b, which depends on the predators' natural longevity, their reproductive rate and potentially many other factors that need not be of concern in detail:

$$\Delta P/\Delta t = +bFP$$

In summary, we know that the predators' population is based on two mechanisms, death and survival (including births) and thus we should combine the two equations into one:

$$\Delta P/\Delta t = -aP + bFP = P(-a + bF)$$

However, the predators are not alone in this world: every prey fish they eat affects the food resource on which they thrive. Therefore we must also specify a model of the prey fish population F. We begin with the assumption that the prey fish live off some food source that is independent of the predators and that, thanks to this food source, the prey fish population F increases by a certain survival (maintenance and birth) factor c:

$$\Delta F/\Delta t = +cF$$

Unfortunately, the prey fish are hunted by the predators. The more predators there are around, the more prey fish are caught. Given there are so many predator fish, we can describe the rate of prey catching by a constant d which depends on the predators' hunting skills. It is clear that the more prey fish are around, the more prey fish will be caught, and thus the prey fish population decreases proportionally to the catch rate and the number of predator fish that hunt them:

$$\Delta F/\Delta t = -dPF$$

Similar to the predator fish population, the prey fish population is based on the combination of death and survival, that is, the combination of the decrease and increase factor:

$$\Delta F/\Delta t = +cF - dPF = F(c - dP)$$

We know that the two populations are coupled. Each time a prey fish is caught, the prey fish population changes but so does the predator population, since the eating of the prey fish will increase the chances of the predator to survive. Thus, we have to combine the two equations in a system of equations, where one equation refers to the other and vice versa:

$$\Delta P/\Delta t = -aP + bFP = P(-a + bF)$$
$$\Delta F/\Delta t = +cF - dPF = F(c - dP)$$

This system of coupled equations is a prime example of a dynamic system. It specifies the change in two variables as a function of time, of the preceding state of each variable and of the preceding state of the variable to which it is coupled. This mathematical model results in a series of population sizes over time that show an interesting pattern, which confirmed the Italian observations, namely a series of lagged cyclical changes in the population sizes of both prey and predators (Figure 28.2). The cycles are not caused by some external factor but are entirely based on the dynamic interaction (Hofbauer & Sigmund, 1988; Murray, 1989). This simple model captures an essential element of predator-prey dynamics, namely the cyclical oscillation of populations. It should be noted that it is not meant as an empirical model of actual predator-prey interactions. Rather, it tries to capture the essence of those dynamics by using the smallest and most elementary set of assumptions. A more realistic model can use the Lotka-Volterra model as its starting point and add all necessary assumptions about the populations studied in order to arrive at a model that better fits a chosen part of reality. However, the model illustrates a fundamental feature of dynamic modeling, namely the search for the simplest possible model that is as close as possible to the essence of some dynamic phenomenon.

Another interesting approach concerned the study of the diffusion of certain genes through a population and the potential evolutionary effects of that spreading. An ecological system is a prime example of a self-sustaining, stable and yet developing or changing structure. In spite of its complexity, it is governed by a small number of basic dynamic principles that explain its order and evolution. The dynamic approach to ecological systems may form a source of inspiration for a comparable approach to behavioral and psychological development, as we shall see later.

Computational Approaches to Dynamics and the Emergence of Systems Thinking

During and after the Second World War, an important technological and theoretical breakthrough took place with the development of the digital computer. The study of dynamic systems would be virtually impossible without computers. Many dynamic systems

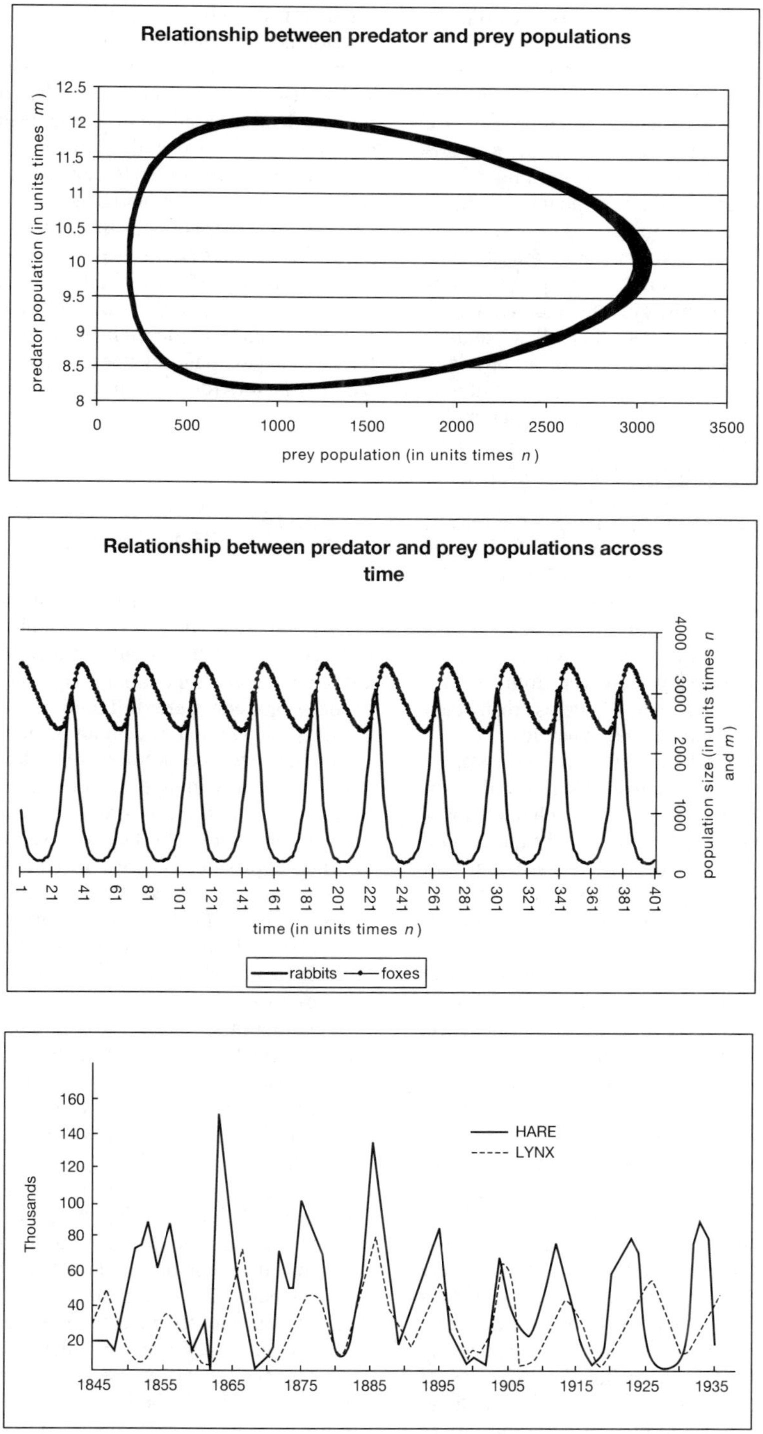

Figure 28.2 *The population dynamics of predator–prey interactions. Relationship (top) between the size of the predator population and the size of the prey population. The egg shape represents the lagged occurrence of (middle) two oscillating patterns. Data (bottom) based on furs of snowshoe hare and lynx (a typical prey–predator species couple) sold to the Canadian Hudson Bay Company in the nineteenth century (Lotka, 1925; Volterra, 1926)*

models cannot be solved analytically. In order to study them, their behavior must be numerically simulated and in order to do so, a computer is an indispensable instrument. Oddly enough, computers are strictly linear and sequential machines and are therefore very different from the dynamic systems that are modeled with them. The coming of the computer also boosted a lot of fundamental ideas about systems in general. In the 1940s and 1950s, researchers like Wiener, von Neuman, Ashby and von Foerster explored topics such as complexity, self-organization, connectionist systems and adaptation. One of their main ideas was that all systems – irrespective of whether they are of a physical, a biological, a social or a psychological nature – display certain general characteristics that capture the fundamental quality of such systems. This idea gave rise to new systems approaches, like cybernetics (Wiener) and general systems theory (von Bertalanffy, Boulding). In psychology, the idea of systems was most notably explored by Herbert Simon (1969), whose work concentrated on hierarchically organized systems that are capable of adaptive information processing. In these earlier systems approaches, the predicate 'dynamic' did not feature as explicitly as it does today. However, from the start, it was clearly acknowledged that systems are, by their very nature, time-dependent and dynamic.

The early and fundamental work on complex dynamic systems diverged into a wide range of topics and approaches. In the 1960s, the French mathematician René Thom (1972) began to study the general properties of sudden changes, more particularly of discontinuities. A good example of a discontinuity from developmental psychology is Piaget's notion of transitions from one stage to another. Thom described a small set of general, elementary discontinuities that he called 'catastrophes' (hence 'catastrophe theory'). The Piagetian-type stage transition, for instance, amounts to a so-called cusp catastrophe, that is, a discontinuous change based on gradual changes in only two control dimensions (van der Maas & Molenaar, 1992) (Figure 28.3).

Another major interest of dynamic systems students is chaos, a theme that became popular with James Gleick's best-selling book (Gleick, 1987). Chaos is a somewhat misleading term, since it refers to patterns that are, on the surface, extremely disorderly and random, but that in reality show a deep underlying order. The most important feature of chaos is probably that it can emerge spontaneously as certain variables that control the behavior of simple, orderly systems cross a specific threshold value. For instance, when the reproduction rate of biological populations that have discrete breeding seasons, insects for instance, exceeds a certain value, the population sizes start to oscillate in a seemingly random, chaotic way (May, 1976). Typically, chaotic systems are highly sensitive to initial state conditions and exhibit the butterfly effect discussed earlier. The discussion about the eventual importance of chaos to developmental psychology has not been settled yet. In order to empirically demonstrate that a process is really chaotic and not just driven by a multitude of independent external factors, one needs quantities of data that are usually beyond the reach of developmental research. However, chaos theory has shown that randomness and chaotic variation do not need to come from outside the system. They can be produced by the system itself if the conditions are right. In development, variability can be an important functional aspect and it is important that such variability can be produced by the developing system itself, i.e. that it is not necessarily dependent on external factors (de Weerth, van Geert, & Hoijtink, 1999).

Epigenesis and the Emergence of Biological Form

In biology, the 1920s and 1930s witnessed the birth of mathematical biophysics, which unraveled a number of interesting dynamic principles. During the 1950s and 1960s, important ideas about the dynamics of development were initiated by a number of biologists interested in developmental biology and embryogenesis (see Gottlieb, 1992, for an overview and discussion with applications to developmental psychology; and see Gottlieb, Chapter 1 in this volume). Probably the best-known representative of this approach is the British biologist and embryologist Conrad Hal Waddington (1905-1975), whose picture of the epigenetic landscape – showing a ball rolling down a landscape of hills and valleys – features in almost every textbook on developmental psychology (Figure 28.4).

Waddington's basic contribution to the dynamic thinking about development can be contrasted to the widespread but simplistic view that genes carry the full description of the organism's form, or more precisely that the genes contain a full set of instructions for how to build a body up to its finest details (for instance, the Habsburg kings all had the same remarkable, somewhat protruded chin; it can be assumed therefore that the building instructions for that chin must be contained in the Habsburg genes: where else could that chin come from?). Waddington showed that genes form the starting point of embryogenesis and that the process of embryogenesis itself creates the conditions under which the organism's body plan comes about. Simply said, genes may code for the production of certain tissue, but once that tissue is formed, it may cause other tissues to develop, or it may cause certain genes to turn on or off. This basic idea, that the form of the body is literally constructed by the construction process itself – and is not specified in some pre-existing full instruction set, design or

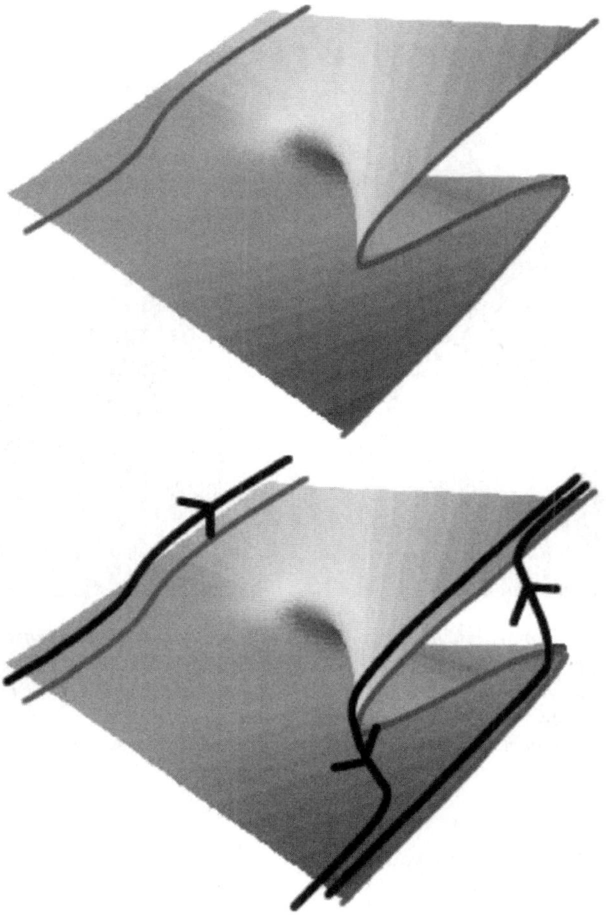

Figure 28.3 *The cusp catastrophe refers to a particular kind of discontinuous change. The folded surface represents different transition possibilities (grey lines). The transition is either continuous (top) or discontinuous (bottom). Which type of transition will occur depends on the values of the control parameters that govern the process at issue. The cusp catastrophe is a general model of processes based on two control parameters*

building plan – is known under the term *epigenesis*. The epigenetic concept from embryology currently features as an important dynamic metaphor for students in the field of developmental psychology (de Graaff, 1999; Gottlieb, Chapter 1 in this volume). A simple example may help to clarify the gist of this approach. Suppose you arrive at the station of some big, unknown city and you have to go to a particular place. You can use a city map to get there. The city map gives a complete description of all the streets you have to go along and so functions as an explicit, predefined instruction set. Suppose you didn't have a street map and you had to ask a passer-by. He or she could sum up all the turns you had to take and all the street names you had to remember in order to get to your destination. Again, the description is a full instruction set but it has one major disadvantage: it is difficult to remember. You'll probably forget the order of the lefts and the rights and you'll get lost. One thing you could do is remember the first half of the instructions, act upon them and when you've reached the last instruction ask another passer-by for the additional instructions. This situation is comparable to dividing the developmental instructions between a set of genetic and a set of environmental instructions. Together they fully define the developmental path. But suppose the city has a number of big squares connected by major streets or avenues. In that case, your informant might say, 'Go straight ahead to Square X, and there take the major avenue to your right and follow that to the next square, and there you do the same thing and you'll automatically get at your destination.' In this particular case, the meaning of the information given

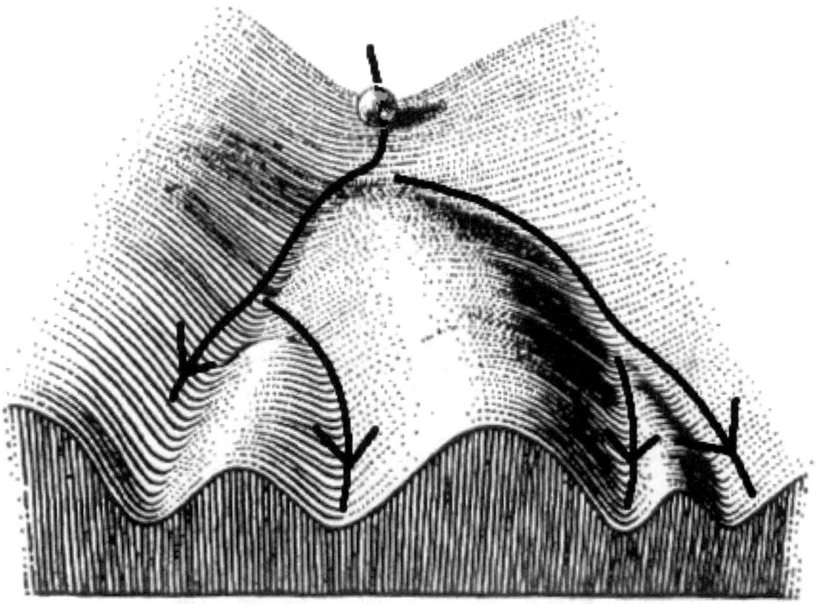

Figure 28.4 *Waddington's epigenetic landscape. The position of the ball represents an organism in a space of developmental (e.g. morphogenetical) dimensions or possibilities. The hills and valleys represent different developmental pathways. Downhill pathways require less energy and will be more common than (slightly) uphill pathways. Steep uphill pathways are in principle non-existent (their probability is too small) (after Waddington, 1956, p. 412)*

depends entirely on what you'll find once you arrive at each of the major squares. You'll have to get there first in order to know what choice of road you'll have to make. The information becomes available as you carry out the simple instruction given at the beginning. This latter situation is somewhat comparable to the epigenetic explanation of development. Each step in the process creates the conditions for the next step. In fact, there exists a kind of *bidirectionality* between the traveler and the city. The traveler follows an instruction, which brings him to some particular place, and once arrived at this place it becomes clear what the next instruction should be.

Note that the traveler can make mistakes, for instance when two avenues he'll have to choose from are about as broad and both to the right. But since he knows the general principle, he can always retrace his steps or make a detour if need be. In other words, the itinerary is defined in a *probabilistic* way. At every point, the traveler has to decide which step is the most probable, given the local circumstances. It is highly likely that another traveler, following the same general instruction, will also reach the same destination but through a somewhat different itinerary. Biologists working in the epigenetic tradition call this *equifinality* – reaching a similar goal through different means or paths.

Note also that the success of the epigenetic solution to finding your way in the city depends very much on the structure of that city, and some cities may be easier to walk through than others. Thus, if someone tries to understand my itinerary, he or she has to take account not only of the instructions given to me but also of the city plan and how it looks to the pedestrian. That is to say, one has to take a holistic view of the problem. This position was defended by the theoretical biologist von Bertalanffy, who coined the term general systems theory, as a general account of problems of complex order. The holistic view is consistent with the bidirectionality mentioned earlier, which implies that traveler and city in fact interact and by doing so produce a successful route to the final destination.

Spontaneous Increase of Order and Structure

One of the recurrent themes in the dynamic biological systems view is that development is characterized by an increase of complexity and by the creation of novel forms, that is, forms (properties) that were not explicitly specified or coded for in the initial state (Gottlieb, Wahlsten, & Lickliter,

1998). The idea of increasing complexity has been pioneered in non-linear thermodynamics, especially in the field of chemistry. In the 1960s and 1970s the Belgian chemist (of Russian descent) Ilya Prigogine studied chemical reactions that self-organized into complex patterns that maintained themselves as long as a sufficient energy supply was administered. We have already met the second law of thermodynamics, which – highly simplified – says that energy spontaneously streams from hotter to colder objects and never the other way around. The second law implies that if one starts with a world with concentrated spots of heat (hot objects, like a cup of fresh coffee on my desk), the result will inevitably be a world with a diminished concentration of heat (with the coffee having the same temperature as the air in my office), or, in the end, a world with a completely uniform distribution of temperature. If one identifies the specific concentration of heat with a high amount of structure (or specificity), it follows that structure must decline spontaneously (the distribution becomes more even). In a technical sense, we can say that the world is characterized by a spontaneous increase of entropy, which, for our purposes, can be simplified as a spontaneous loss of order or structure (note that entropy has a specific physical definition, but explaining this is beyond the scope of the present chapter: see Atkins, 1984). What holds for temperature also holds for information (in the formal, mathematical sense, both notions are highly similar). A practical application of the second law to the field of information is that if one sends a message to someone else – over a phone line, for instance – there is always a spontaneous loss of information. The line is noisy and some words are difficult to understand. The opposite never occurs spontaneously: there is no telephone line that spontaneously transforms a noisy message into crisp, clearly understandable words. One of the major findings of non-linear thermodynamics, as studied by Prigogine and many others, is that there exist processes that appear to contradict the second law: they do result in an increase of order, structure or information. There exist chemical reactions, such as the Belousov-Zhabotinsky reaction, that spontaneously produce complex spatial and temporal patterns. They are the result of an *autocatalytic* process. In such a process, the reactants produce a chemical compound that facilitates the formation of another compound, that eventually either counteracts or facilitates the first, or affects still another one, and so on. As a result, the process oscillates between complex, spontaneously produced states. The only thing we have to do to keep the process going is to give it a constant supply of some basic reactant or temperature.

The output of the process – the spatial or temporal patterns formed by the chemical reactants – is considerably more complex than the input (Figure 28.5). This is a result of *self-organization*: the process organizes itself into complex patterns. There is nothing that instructs the process to do so: it spontaneously creates itself. Self-organization occurs in processes or systems that already have a high amount of structure by themselves. That is, it occurs in complex systems. But don't these systems violate the second law of thermodynamics? In the end, they do not: the spontaneous creation of structure in such systems actually increases the flow of energy through such systems. They exist by virtue of an increasing loss of structure elsewhere in their environment (they dissipate energy, which is also why they are called dissipative systems).

The existence of spontaneous self-organization and the general conditions under which it exists is an important discovery, demonstrating that increase of order is a natural and basic phenomenon of nature. This fact as such does not prove that psychological and behavioral development is also such a process, i.e. one where order and structure are created, but given the generality of such processes, it would be remarkable if development were not self-organizational. It should also be noted that self-organization and an increase of order and structure occur at the cost of increased energy consumption. Development, if it is indeed a self-organizational system, consumes energy (or information, which is basically the same) and is therefore confined by the available energy (or information) in the environment.

The Dynamics of Complexity

Developments in the 1980s and 1990s shifted the interest from the issue of increasing order and structure *per se* to the question of how and why order and novelty emerge. Complexity became the major theme. A complex system consists of a large amount of elements or components that interact with one another. A physical example of a complex system – although it doesn't sound like one – is a heap of sand to which new sand is added (like the heap of sand made by a child who digs a pit on the beach). The grains of sand exert a certain amount of force on one another because they are all subject to the forces of gravity and friction. As a result, the sand in the heap slips down in the form of avalanches of different sizes. It is interesting to note that the study of heaps of sand brought one investigator – Per Bak – to the discovery of an interesting dynamic phenomenon, namely *subcriticality* (Bak & Chen, 1991). Subcriticality is the state that keeps dynamic systems on the verge of changing and that causes sudden changes or discontinuities at different levels of magnitude (Adami, 1995). We have already encountered the issue of sudden changes in our short discussion of catastrophe theory and how it eventually related to stagewise developmental change.

Complex systems are widely studied in the field of biology. An example of a complex system is an

Figure 28.5 *The Belousov–Zhabotinsky reaction, discovered by Belousov in 1958 and described by Zhabotinsky in 1964. The reaction is based on the interaction of four chemicals (sulfuric acid, sodium bromate, malonic acid and ferroin). The chemicals produce a reaction pattern of spatially distributed waves in the form of a chaotic pattern or strange attractor. The reaction is one of the standard examples of self-organization in chemical reactions*

ecosystem: the arrangement of animal and plant species that interact with one another in a particular time and place. Another example is the web of interactions between different biological species. Complexity theory has been used to explain the processes of biological evolution and extinction, particularly by Stuart Kauffman. Kauffman (1993) studied general aspects of evolution in networks of biological species by reducing species to single on–off nodes in a so-called Boolean network. Although this approach amounts to an incredible reduction of the essence of a biological species, it nevertheless captures essential aspects of the evolutionary process. We have already encountered this important aspect of the dynamic systems approach, where a seemingly unacceptable amount of simplification is often the key to understanding the deepest aspects of the processes under scrutiny. An interesting finding in complex systems studies, such as Kauffman's networks of species, is that one gets order and structure for free – that is as a result of spontaneous self-organization – only in complex systems within a certain range of interconnectedness. To see what connectedness means, imagine a social group con-sisting of many people. If all people are in some way interacting with each other, the degree of interconnection is complete. If no person interacts with someone else, connectedness is minimal (zero in fact). If every person interacts with just a few others, connectedness is low, but often sufficient to get interesting self-organizational processes off the ground (more interesting than those occurring with complete interconnectedness, for instance). Although the degree of connectedness seems at first like a rather trivial property of a system, it is nevertheless critical to the emergence of self-organization. This point illustrates another aspect that is often found in dynamic systems, namely that properties that at first seem trivial and irrelevant to the process at issue can nevertheless play an essential role (which is not to say that all trivial properties are essential, of course, or that essential roles are always played by trivial properties).

From Complexity to Connections

Another widely studied biological example of a complex self-organizing system – that is also closely related to the field of psychology – is the brain. The brain consists of a very large network of interacting neurons, each neuron directly connected with only a limited number of other neurons. The study of such networks has led to the development of an exciting new field, namely that of connectionist networks – also called artificial neural networks – that are used to explain and simulate processes of learning and pattern formation (Bechtel & Abrahamsen, 1991). A connectionist network basically consists of a large number of simple components. The role of each component is to receive input from other components and send some output back (or send it to the outside world). The inputs and outputs are simple: they usually consist of an activation level, which can be represented by a number (e.g. an output or input of magnitude 5 represents a higher activation level than an input or output of 2). The output of a component (the activation it sends to other components or to the outside world) is a function of the input it receives (the activation it receives from other components). The total input a component receives is, in principle, a simple sum of the inputs it receives from all the components to which it is connected by an input channel. Thus, a component that receives a total input of, say, 10, will send out a higher activation level than a component that receives a total input of 3, for instance. A central feature of a connectionist network is that every connection between two components carries a specific weight (think of that connection as a channel that links one component to another and through which the activation flows). The function of the weights is to alter the magnitude of the activation levels sent out by the connected component. For instance, if a component A sends out an activation level of 5 to a component B and the A–B connection channel carries a weight of 2, B receives an input of 10; if the weight is –1, B receives an input of –5 (and this input will be subtracted from the inputs coming from other components). The importance of connectionist networks lies in the fact that they are adaptive, that they can learn. A network may receive inputs from the outside world, for instance visual information about forms of objects. In its turn, it may send an output to that outside world, for instance a name of the object it 'sees'. Before it can do so, however, it has to learn which words should be associated with which visual inputs. If the system improves in making the correct association, it shows learning or adaptation. This is exactly what connectionist networks are made for, namely to adapt to the requirements of some environment, i.e. to learn. They do so by altering the weights between the components. The idea is that if an output is consistent with some criterion (e.g. the name of the object chosen by the network, given a specific visual input, is also the name approved by the environment) the weights between the components that have led to this correct output are amplified (if the output is wrong or inconsistent, the weights are diminished). In general, the weights are altered by a function that is proportional to the distance between the given output and the desired output (the bigger that distance, the bigger the error). The most important feature of connectionist networks – or artificial neural nets – is that the learning or adaptation occurs automatically, that is, as a result of self-organization. We don't have to penetrate the system and change the weights and output functions by hand, so to speak, in order to get the system into the right direction. Connectionist systems will find the rules or the patterns by themselves. Furthermore, the input does not need to be entirely consistent. Even if the environment makes mistakes or if it is to a certain extent inconsistent in its corrections or in its inputs, the connectionist network will nevertheless pick up the required rules, associations or adaptations.

Why are connectionist network models important to the study of development? The answer is that these models actually provide a proof of the claim that learning can occur in networks of simple interacting components that have some sort of connection with a structured, outside world (Elman et al., 1996). Superficially, this may seem a trivial accomplishment, were it not that before connectionist modeling became available, we had no proof for the contention that – among others biological – systems could spontaneously construct order and regularity, given an input that exemplified the structure or order in some way or another. That is, knowledge – of whatever sort – does not have to be present or programmed in advance; it can emerge spontaneously, given the right sort of input. Although learning and adaptation seem almost trivial (why would anyone doubt their possibility), connectionist models provide the first real demonstration of the basic 'mechanical' conditions under which those seemingly trivial accomplishments occur. It needs to be said, however, that the fact that connectionist networks represent a form of learning and adaptation does not logically imply that all forms of learning and adaptation must occur by connectionist network principles. An important feature of these models is that they are 'brain-like' in an abstract sense. Both the brain and connectionist networks consist of interconnected units that receive and produce levels of activation and by doing so can accomplish extremely complex processes of pattern recognition, classification, association, and so forth. They operate under conditions that require a high amount of error tolerance, incompleteness, inconsistency and fuzziness, which is characteristic of systems that need to operate under natural, biologically valid circumstances. At present, connectionist networks are among the most studied examples of complex systems, that is, systems consisting of interconnected simple units that self-organize and by doing so perform complex symbolic tasks.

In Support of Development

In the first section we explored the colloquial meaning of the concept of *development*. We found that it entailed aspects of unwrapping inherent potentialities, guidance by an intrinsic tendency towards higher complexity and the construction or production of novelty. In the second section we discussed scientific approaches according to which this image of development is only an illusion. We saw that increase of complexity is impossible and that the emergence of structure must be based on pre-programmed, full instruction sets, such as genes or transmittable contents. In the third section we turned to developments in the field of dynamic systems theory and found that the conclusions of the second section were, at best, preliminary. In complex systems, increase of structure and complexity seems the rule rather than the exception. Self-organization, a process of creating structure and order without explicit instructions or guidance from outside, is a general mechanism and we have now come to understand some of its basic properties and possibilities. The romantic image sketched in the first section did not seem too far off the truth after all; or, to put it differently, there exist no logical or empirical impediments for it. More importantly, dynamic systems theory has provided a number of conceptual, mathematical and methodological tools by which complex, self-organizing processes can be described, explored and studied. The systems approach emphasizes the fact that important properties of systems can be studied irrespective of the actual, physical or other properties of the systems at issue. Principles that govern physical or biological processes can also be applied to social and psychological processes, provided that similar general properties hold. These properties are usually related to the way the components in the system interact and how they change, that is, to the dynamic aspects of those components. In the next section I shall explain how dynamic systems thinking can be applied to the problems of psychological and behavioral development and how dynamic systems models of such developmental processes may be designed.

A Dynamic Systems Approach to Development

Dynamic systems theory is an approach to perceiving, conceptualizing and studying phenomena and events we find of interest. It consists of a collection of general concepts, methods and techniques and of an ever-increasing series of worked-out examples in a variety of fields. In the preceding section, I have introduced a number of those general aspects and examples in an attempt to provide a first, intuitive grasp of what dynamic systems theory is about. As a collection of generally and widely applicable tools, dynamic systems theory can also be fruitfully applied to developmental psychology. This assertion does not imply that its application will lead to results that are comparable to those from fields such as physics, chemistry or biology. The latter are sometimes light years ahead of developmental psychology in terms of data collection and mathematical rigor, but that does not prevent us from making dynamic systems approaches work for developmental psychology too.

What Is a Dynamic System of Development?

The Universe of Discourse

In accordance with the basic principles of dynamic systems theory itself, the best way of explaining the nature of a dynamic system is to show how to get at one. In order to construct a dynamic systems model of development, one starts with selecting a universe of discourse. This universe of discourse is a vaguely confined, highly implicit collection of phenomena, concepts, approaches and so forth that relate to the content matter of developmental psychology. It is basically what the community of developmental psychologists as a whole understands by 'development'. No single person has a copy of this universe of discourse in his or her head, but as a community we understand each other more or less and know more or less what we are talking about. Note that this universe of discourse is considerably vaster than the topics and concepts that developmental psychologists address at this very moment. Some regions, so to speak, are more frequently visited than others (there's more interest in the development of the object concept, for instance, than in the development of dreaming: Breeuwsma, 1993). Some people prefer to stay in one region of the universe of discourse, others prefer entirely different spaces (cognitivists, for instance, consider concepts and representations real entities of development, whereas ecological psychologists and dynamic systems theorists inspired by ecological psychology stick to action and perception in real time and consider concepts and representations a myth). The universe of discourse changes as new insights and viewpoints wax and wane over the years. Currently, for instance, developmental discourse relies heavily on biological, genetic and neurological concepts and phenomena; in the early 1970s it was strongly influenced by the narrative of cultural and social influences. A deliberate choice for a specific universe of discourse is hardly ever made. It is implicit in our research, discussions and theorizing. Nevertheless, it forms a crucial backdrop against which all our efforts at understanding development make sense.

The Dynamic System

A system is basically any collection of phenomena, components, variables or whatever that we take from our universe of discourse that we are interested in. This collection is a system in as much as its components relate to one another. It is a dynamic system if its components affect and change one another in the course of time. In order to make clear what this means I shall start with an example that is not a dynamic system but that is nevertheless recognizable as an example of common theory formation in psychology. Let us assume we are interested in the relationship between social economic level (SES) of families and the intelligence (IQ) of their children. The SES-IQ collection is a system because it consists of components that relate to one another. For instance, it is claimed that higher SES corresponds with higher IQ, on average. Is the SES-IQ system a dynamic system? It is not, in spite of the fact that we can say that, somewhat loosely stated, SES affects IQ. What we mean by that claim, under the standard interpretation, however, is that in a particular population SES relates to IQ in such a way that IQ can be statistically predicted, given SES. It is a static system in that it specifies that for any SES level there exists a certain, loosely confined cloud of IQ levels (and it is this cloudy character that will be expressed in the mathematical format of a correlation, which we are all used to).

How would a dynamic systems theorist look at the SES-IQ model? In order for a system to be dynamic – that is a system where the components affect one another over time – we have to specify a format of actual dynamic influence. SES is a bookkeeping term, basically. It is not something that actually features in real interactions between people. However, we know that SES corresponds with things like schooling, knowledge, interaction style and so forth and that these things correspond with the language used, the quality of intellectual help given to children and so forth. IQ too is basically a bookkeeping term. Yet we know that it relates to actual things such as problem solving, knowing and understanding a wide variety of words and so forth. Let us take a factor that is related – maybe somewhat loosely – to the sociological concept of SES, namely the verbal interaction patterns between parents in children. We now take another factor that is also related to what we usually call IQ, namely language understanding and the ability to reason with verbally presented concepts. It is reasonable to assume that, all other factors being equal, elaborate verbal interactions between parents and children will enhance the child's verbal understanding and verbal skills. Thus, for some arbitrary moment in time we claim that

$$\Delta V_c/\Delta t = aV_cP_p$$

by which we mean that the increase in the verbal skill of a child V_c is a function of the verbal skill the child has already acquired, the verbal performance P_p of the child's parents and some parameter a that regulates the effect of parental verbal performance on the child's verbal skill. If we assume that the parent's verbal performance is a direct product of the parent's verbal skill, we may simplify the equation as follows:

$$\Delta V_c/\Delta t = aV_cV_p$$

It is also reasonable to assume that, all other things being equal, the child's verbal skill will have some effect on the parent's verbal performance, and thus on the parent's verbal skill in the broad sense of the word. Thus, if the child easily understands what the parent says and asks for more justifications of the parent's disciplinary measures, the parent will in many cases, be obliged to adopt a more elaborate style of verbal justification. We can specify this relationship in the following equation:

$$\Delta V_p/\Delta t = bV_cV_p$$

Substituting x for V_c and y for V_p we can write our model as a set of connected equations:

$$\Delta x/\Delta t = axy$$

$$\Delta y/\Delta t = bxy$$

which is a dynamic model that is comparable to those we found in biology (the predator-prey equations) or physics (the Lorenz equation for flows in atmospheric systems). Of course we do not know whether our toy model of mutual interaction between parents and children has anything to do with reality, but that is a different matter. The point is that we have constructed a dynamic systems model consisting of two components, namely the verbal skill or habit of a parent and that of a child. The model says that, first, for every temporary level of verbal skill or habit in a parent and a child, there is some effect on a succeeding state of verbal skill or habit in that parent and child; and, second, that this effect is moderated by two parameters, a and b.

More often than not, this collection of components we are interested in is relatively vaguely specified. For instance, people interested in the development of the early object concept call upon a somewhat loosely specified set of concepts and phenomena, such as object concept, object permanence, hiding and finding objects, reaching and grasping, that are all supposed to relate to the notion 'early object concept'. New research in the field usually results in extending or confining the collection. For instance, when it is found that hiding time and number of objects play a role in the infant's successful retrieval of a hidden object (Wellman, Cross, & Bartsch, 1987), memory and perception become aspects that relate to the object concept in a relevant way.

Once the results of empirical research have to be communicated, however, the loose collection of components is reduced to a strictly confined set of variables that relate to one another in some statistically specified way (for instance, the length of the delay between hiding the object and letting the infant search is correlated to the infants' retrieval success, as specified across a sample of actually studied infants). A similar reduction and specification of the components also results from an attempt to turn the original conceptual model (of the object concept, for instance) into a dynamic systems model that is used for simulation or numerical experimentation.

The Environment

Once we have specified a dynamic system within our universe of discourse we have also implicitly specified another component, namely the system's environment. The system's environment is everything in the universe of discourse that does not belong to the system but nevertheless interacts with it. In our historical overview we have discussed thermodynamic systems that spontaneously increased their internal structure by consuming energy from their ambient environment. By doing so they reduced the amount of order in the wider, ambient environment and so complied with the general entropic principle that governs the whole of nature. It is important to note that both environment and system result from the choices made by the researcher: they are not implicit categories of nature. Take for instance the following specification of a dynamic system. One component of the system is a caretaking adult who is also a mature and competent speaker of a language. The other component is an infant who is not yet in command of that language and will learn it from the caretaker. This two-component system defines an environment, which is basically everything else that affects both the infant and the adult. Note that we shall confine ourselves to only those environmental influences that are related to the dynamic process at hand, which in this case is one of language transmission and appropriation. It goes without saying that the real interactions between the wider environment and the adult–infant system are of incredible complexity. However, we do not need to accommodate all this complexity in order to understand how the system and the environment operate. Systems thinking is basically about finding the right simplifications, that is, those simplifications of reality that are necessary to capture the basic aspects of the dynamics at issue. We have given a biological example – that of a predator–prey relationship – in which the relationship with the broader environment could be reduced to a constant inflow of energy. This energy is whatever the prey population needs to sustain itself. This simplification suffices to specify the most basic and important properties of a predator–prey system.

The same principle holds for the adult–infant system and the environment as defined by that. It suffices that we treat the environment as a source of otherwise unspecified energy needed to let the adult–infant system 'run'. A more appropriate term than energy is the term *resources*. Thus we see the environment as the origin of all the resources required to let the dynamics of the adult–infant system unfold itself. The only thing that we should really reckon with is that the resources are limited or constrained (van Geert, 1991). For instance, in order to transmit and learn language, the adult–infant system requires time, working memory, a language to transmit or learn, attention and effort and so forth. These resource components may be big, but they are also limited. The participants' working memories, for instance, are extremely limited in comparison to the complexity of the content – the language – that is produced in the adult–infant dynamics. The role of limited general resources is not always (in fact, mostly not) accounted for in psychological theorizing and research. It is, however, crucial from a dynamic point of view (Elman, 1994; van Geert, 1991). Since a further discussion of this issue far exceeds the scope of the present chapter, suffice it to say that the intrinsic resource limitation is an important driving force of any dynamics, explaining, among other things, the emergence of equilibria (I shall come back to this later when I present an example of dynamic model building based on principles of resource-dependent growth).

Note that this technical, systems notion of environment differs from what (developmental) psychologists usually call 'environment'. By 'environment' is usually meant the person's objective surroundings: the physical space in which the person lives. In addition, the environment is also often seen as an independent source of influences on the subject, that is, as a collection of forces that can, in principle at least, be freely manipulated. In dynamic systems models, however, the notion of environment is a technical concept, defined, as I explained earlier, by how the system at issue is defined. For instance, if we specify a system consisting of an interaction between two components, namely an immature grammar (for instance that of a 2-year-old language learner) and a mature grammar (for instance the grammar of the language spoken in the community of competent language users), we define the environment as everything that interacts with this two-component system. For instance, the working memory of the language-learning child, which interacts with the language-learning process, is therefore part of the system's environment (in spite of the fact that it is 'inside' the language-learning child). If we split the formerly defined system up in its constituent parts and focus on the former subsystem consisting of the immature grammar, the other former subsystem (the mature grammar) automatically becomes part of the first system's environment. However, since we expect that both former subsystems (the immature and the mature grammar) will actively interact (for instance, the mature grammar will produce a language type called 'Motherese' that is adapted to the learning needs of the immature grammar) it is probably wise to make a distinction between those parts of the environment with which the system actually interacts and those that are basically passive (or that can at least be treated as such for the sake of model building, like working memory, for instance). That is, there is a distinction, in terms of the models employed, between the active environment and the background environment. By making this distinction, we refer to the fact that systems are hierarchically organized (Bronfenbrenner, 1979). The fact that considerable parts of the environment are in close interaction with the developing system implies that the effective environment co-depends, so to speak, on the developmental process. That is, it is not the independent, freely manipulable source of possibilities that it is often seen to be in the standard view. The tendency to view the environment as an objective, independent entity has led to the misrepresentation of family environments, among others. In behavior genetics, for instance, a distinction is made between siblings' shared and non-shared environments, which are nevertheless both part of the same family environment (Pike & Plomin, 1996).

Development in a Dynamic Systems Frame

How Does a Dynamic System Work

A dynamic system – however it is defined – changes because it is affected by other systems (in short, the system's environment) and by itself. The latter aspect is of crucial importance. Let us take as an example of a system a language-learning child. In order to conceive of the child as a dynamic system, we have to follow its changes on a moment-by-moment basis (which is a conceptual choice; it goes without saying that we cannot do so empirically, for instance in the form of a continuous observation of the language acquisition process, which would be just too demanding on the child and the researcher.) At any particular moment, the system is affected by whatever environmental inflow occurs at this particular time, and, equally importantly, by the system's preceding state. This property turns the changes that the system undergoes into what is called an *iterative process*. An iterative process takes the output of its preceding state (that is, the change it underwent in the immediately preceding moment) as the input of its next state. Although it is hard to conceive of a system that is not affected by its preceding state, this iterative property is hardly ever taken seriously in, let us say, standard approaches to development. It is likely that it is considered so trivial that almost no one ever expected anything interesting from it. However, dynamic systems modeling and research has shown that it is exactly this iterative property that explains a lot of the interesting features of changing and developing systems.

For one thing, dynamic systems are (often) non-linear. Mathematically, a linear operator L is defined by the property of linear superposition. This basically means that L is a linear operator if

$$L(ax + by) = aL(x) + bL(y)$$

for a and b constants and x and y functions. A function is a way of associating 'objects' in a set to other 'objects'. For instance, multiplication by 2 is a function that associates a number (an object in the set of numbers) to another object in that set (another number, which is twice the first number). An operator is a symbol that instructs you to do something with what follows the operator. Thus, if 'times 2' is an operator and 'raise to the second power' is an operator, the first is a linear operator and the second is not, since

'times 2'(2 + 3) = 'times 2'(2) + 'times 2'(3)

whereas

'second power'(2 + 3) <> 'second power'(2) + 'second power' (3)

(see Jackson, 1991a, for formal definitions). In short, (non-)linearity is an abstract mathematical property and it should not be identified with the contrast between relationships that can be represented by a straight line and those that can be represented by a curved line, for instance. Nevertheless, it is possible to obtain an intuitive understanding of the non-linearity of dynamic processes. Non-linearity means, among other things, that the effect of a dynamic process differs from the sum of its parts (it can be more but it can also be less, dependent on where in the process the effect is occurring). An alternative and somewhat more intuitive way of defining the property of non-linearity is to say that the effect of a factor that influences the system is not (necessarily) proportional to the magnitude of that factor. For instance, research on the effect of birth weight on later intellectual development has shown that birth weight (e.g. as a consequence of prematurity) has hardly any effect on later development if the infant's weight is above some threshold weight (Wolke & Meyer, 1999). Once it is lower than the threshold, a strong negative effect occurs. This threshold effect is related to the fact that dynamic systems evolve towards some form of (dynamic and often temporal) equilibrium. This means that such systems are 'attracted' towards some end state. The state to which they are attracted, that is, towards which they spontaneously evolve as a consequence of the underlying dynamic principles that govern their behavior, is called the system's *attractor*. Research on dynamic systems in general has demonstrated that attractors can take various forms. The simplest attractor is the point attractor, which implies that the system evolves towards a stable state (like a thermostat that keeps the room's temperature constant). An example of such an attractor is the adult speaker's stable level of linguistic skill. Still another example is the overall developmental state of a person (for instance the concrete operational state that 6- to 12-year-old children are supposed to occupy according to the Piagetian model). Another type of attractor is the cyclical attractor, which implies that the states of the system are running through a cycle. An example of such an attractor can be found in the neo-Piagetian stage theories, which assume that every stage is characterized by a repetitive cycle of substages (Case, 1990). We should realize, however, that the attractors of complex, natural systems are far less regular than those found in mathematically pure systems and that the latter are, at best maybe, only metaphors of the complex equilibria of natural systems.

Dynamic systems are affected by control variables. An example of a control variable in a population of animals is the animals' average reproduction rate or their average longevity. An example of a control variable in a cognitive system is the size of the system's working memory. Limits on working memory size may affect the final stage of cognitive development that the system may reach. Scaling up a control variable – a gradual increase in working memory due to neurological maturation, for instance – may result in the system making an abrupt choice between either of two mutually exclusive states. For instance, children confronted with a Piagetian conservation experiment either understand the conservation principle (state B) or not (state A). It has been hypothesized that a gradual increase in working memory, for instance, will result in a relatively abrupt appearance of conservation understanding. More precisely, a system that had only one possible state (non-conservation A) has now two (non-conservation A, and conservation B). The state the system will actually occupy (A or B) will depend on, for instance, the nature of the conservation problem they are presented with (van der Maas, 1993). Points – or better, conditions – under which such discontinuous switches from one to two possible states may take place, are called *bifurcation points* (and the emergence of the discrete alternatives is called a *bifurcation*). Bifurcations occur wherever the system can be in qualitatively different states or stages. They are characteristic of qualitative change in development.

A final property of dynamic systems that is worth mentioning here is that they are often interlinked on all possible levels. For instance, the system's output may itself affect a control variable that in its turn governs the output. As a rule, the system and its environment stand in a relationship of mutuality: one affects the other and vice versa. This mutuality is often responsible for much of the non-linearity that is so characteristic of developing systems in general.

Systems, Environments and Self-Organization

We have seen that dynamic systems are (often, not always) characterized by an interesting property, self-organization. Lewis (1994; 1996), for instance, has presented self-organization as the hallmark of the dynamic systems approach to developmental processes. Cognitive structures come about as a result of self-organization; basic emotions are not innate but emerge as a result of early and rapid self-organizational processes (Camras, 2000). Although such processes involve extremely complicated self-organizational processes, which we still do not understand, the principle of self-organization itself is relatively simple to explain.

Let us take the case of language acquisition as a process that occurs between an infant and a competent speaker (note that the 'competent speaker' could also be the collection of all competent users of the language that effectively relate to the infant at issue). Define the infant as the system and, hence, the competent speaker as the system's active environment. There exists a constant flow from the environment to the system and vice versa. Since we are dealing with language acquisition, the flow consists, on the one hand, of the language by the mature speaker that is picked up by the child and, on the other hand, of the language by the child that is picked up by the mature speaker (or anyone else; note that what the child itself tells to others is also part of the linguistic input it gets; see Elbers' 1997 input-as-output thesis). These flows have a specific *structure* or *order* (in a system consisting of a steam engine and a heat source, the flow is one of thermal energy from heat source to engine, and the 'order' is the temperature). In the case of language, the structure or order of the environment-system flow (the language addressed to the child) is characterized by a grammar. A grammar is a set of specific, coherent rules necessary to explain the language as spoken to the mature speaker (a grammar is a formal description of the basic properties of a language; it is not a description of the internal mechanism that lets a speaker speak his mother tongue). The old – let us call it the pre-Chomskyan – view on language acquisition was that the environment-system language flow *overdetermines* the structure required to produce it (which is the grammar). By this we mean that the language contains more than sufficient information to reconstruct the grammar. Put differently, according to this view, the system – the language-learning child – receives the language flow (usually called the input) and this flow or input contains more than enough information for the child to reconstruct the grammar of the language. This situation basically complies with the second law of thermodynamics, also known as the entropic principle, which we discussed earlier. The law said that natural processes always show a decline in order or effectiveness. The thermal energy put in a steam engine is always more than the effective labor the engine produces. Similarly, when a message is transmitted, there is always a loss of information. Therefore, the message must be redundant, that is, contain more information than will effectively be retrieved by the receiver. That is, in order for the child to be able to construct the grammar from the input, that input must specify the grammar in a redundant (that is, overcomplete) way.

We have already seen however that Chomsky showed that language, as presented in the flow from adult to infant, *underdetermines* the structure required to produce it (the grammar). That is, the language contains *not enough* (instead of too much) of the information required to reconstruct the grammar. Because the child has not enough information to reconstruct the original grammar, the grammar that is actually constructed will be considerably poorer than the grammar of the adult. If we follow this line of reasoning and imagine the infant growing up to become an adult who addresses language to his or her offspring, the offspring will construct even poorer grammars (it goes without saying that children cannot look into the adults' brains and see the adults' grammars; they can only listen to what the adults are saying). In a few generations, language will be wiped off the surface of the earth. This is of course not what happens. In spite of the linguistic inflow underdetermining the grammar, the child nevertheless reconstructs the grammar required to produce the language. Put differently, the child produces a structure (grammar) that is richer or more complex than the inflow upon which that grammar was based. Thus, contrary to the entropic principle, an *increase in structure* has occurred. We can also say that the organization of the result (the reconstructed grammar) is of higher complexity than the organization of the inflow (the language addressed to the child).

An even more compelling example of spontaneous increase in structure is the emergence of an entirely new language, based on the rudiments of several different languages. For instance, on the basis of highly impoverished Pidgin languages spoken in communities of slaves or laborers speaking different languages, children have built complete and complex new languages – so-called Creoles – in just a few generations (Bickerton, 1991).

It is this increase in order (complexity or structure) that we call self-organization. Self-organization can vary from only a very little increment in the structure provided, to the building of very complex structures, such as bodies of organisms that are massively underdetermined by the information contained in the genetic code alone.

It is worthwhile pursuing the issue of language acquisition because it is related to a major theoretical discussion in developmental psychology. We have seen that, according to Chomsky's analysis, the language input was of lower complexity (showed less specificity) than the grammar produced or learned by the child. Chomsky and many others concluded that there is no known learning mechanism that can explain this miraculous increase in structure (which is right, there is no *learning* mechanism that can do the job). The conclusion must be, therefore, that what the language input lacks in structure must be supplied by some other source of information. The only known source of information, other than the environmental input, is the genome, the collection of human genes. The reasoning was that, since the observed spontaneous increase in structure is logically impossible, the fundamental properties of grammar (that are not contained in the input) must be innate, i.e. genetically determined. Fodor (1975) used a similar reasoning to prove the impossibility of development *à la* Piaget: it is logically impossible for a representation to produce a representation of higher order. Hence, it is impossible for a cognitive system in stage A to produce the more complex properties of the higher stage B.

The problem with this line of reasoning lies with the relationship between the premise and the conclusion. It is correct that there is no known learning mechanism that produces an increase of order relative to the input or inflow. But it does not follow that development or acquisition of structures like language must be based on a *learning* mechanism. We know that there exist many processes that spontaneously increase the order given. We call them self-organizational processes. It is highly likely that language acquisition, similar to many other processes that involve growth and development, is such a self-organizational process. It is true that we do not have even the faintest clue of how this process actually works (but we don't have the faintest clue of how grammar could ever become represented into the genome either). But this lack of understanding does not imply that such a process must therefore be logically impossible.

Dynamics and Self-Organization in Classic Theories

The issue discussed in the preceding section is of central importance to developmental theory building and far exceeds the limits of the example given, namely language development. The discussion focuses on the question of whether development is a process that occurs by design or by a different kind of mechanism that lies in the process of development itself. The view that development occurs by design could mean either of two things.

First, development could be the long-term effect of a process of instruction guided by the environment. What we call development, under this view, is the accumulation of learning processes that come in many different forms: reinforcement and operant learning, respondent learning, imitation, modeling, rehearsal, verbal instruction and so forth. The order and structure inside the developing organism are entirely defined by the order and structure as provided by the environment. In cultural environments, this is the structure of historically evolved skills, knowledge systems, science and so forth. In this view, development is the direct consequence of instruction and education and amounts to a process of acculturation. The internal mechanism needed for such a process of transmission to be successful is relatively simple. It is just a general association-storage-retrieval mechanism characteristic of information processing systems in the most general sense of that term.

The second view that favors the development-by-design explanation puts the prespecified order and structure not in the environment but in the organism itself, namely in the organism's biological make-up as specified by the genes. According to this view, the genes specify the consecutive steps taken by the developing organism. It goes without saying that the genetic design depends entirely on some specific environment to get its work done. However, the environment as such is vastly insufficient to specify the path of development. Such specification lies entirely in the genes.

The developmental issue that is at stake here is usually seen as a fight between two opposites, namely genes (or body) versus environment. The standard solution to the controversy is to admit that both aspects play a role. However, from a dynamic systems point of view, the controversy in fact does not lie between the genes approach and the environment approach, and the solution to whatever the controversy is, is not one of combining the two approaches. The real issue is between both the genes approach and the environment approach, as instances of the development-by-design position, versus a position that sees development as a self-organizing process. Self-organizing processes use whatever possibilities are offered by both genes (and body) and environment, but those possibilities come about as a result of the ongoing dynamic process.

One of the classic theories of development, that of Piaget, has taken a definite stance in this debate. Although Piaget's theory is often and superficially seen as taking an interactionist 'both-genes-and-environment' position, it really focuses on the design-versus-self-organization question. In Piaget's model, the inflow from the environment is entirely defined by the organism's internal structure, that is by its means and tools for taking this input. A similar physical event, like a yellow plastic block entering the visual field of a person, leads to entirely different experiences, depending on whether that person is an adult or a baby. For the baby, the experience is entirely sensorimotor: reaching towards, grasping and holding the object in a firm grip. For the adult, the experience is one of a geometric object that eventually fits in with a broader geometric structure (a wall of plastic bricks for instance). This act of assimilation, as it is called, brings about a complementary act, that of accommodation, which implies that the internal tools that tailor the experience are altered by the experience itself. The magnitude of this alteration, however, depends on the broader structure into which the assimilation is embedded. For instance, with babies that are on the verge of establishing differential grip patterns, the experience of grasping a plastic block may help the infant differentiate between grips suited for angular objects and those for rounded objects. With babies that already possess such grip patterns, the experience does nothing else than consolidate the already established pattern. This differential effect is not trivial, since it hints at another important aspect of Piaget's developmental theory, that of internal organization. Grip patterns, geometric forms or whatever the person is able to grasp literally or figuratively do not come as isolated properties, isolated tools in the cognitive toolbox. The tools are internally organized into higher-order structures. These structures are the result of internal, auto-regulative processes that operate on the properties of the existing cognitive tools and on how they relate to the environment, in terms of assimilation and accommodation. This internal structuring is governed by a tendency towards internal stability, or, in Piaget's terms, equilibrium. This automatic striving towards equilibrium is an intrinsic property of complex organic structures. An unfortunate dog that has lost a paw in a car accident will, after recovery, spontaneously adapt its gait pattern to the number and position of the remaining paws in order to compensate for the loss. Along the same lines, an experience that does not fit in with the existing cognitive structure will either be transformed into one that does not contradict that structure or lead to a change in the structure itself, such that the experience is no longer contradictory (for instance, an experience of the result of action that contradicts the person's expectation of what that action should have brought about). It is important to note that the properties of the internal organization are defined by the organizational process itself and by the contents on which it operates. This will lead to a succession of basic structural organizations, which are better known in the form of Piaget's major stages (sensorimotor, pre-operational, concrete operational and formal operational). The order of those major structures also results from self-organization. For instance, as the sensorimotor organization collapses under the pressure of experiences that no longer fit in with that structure's limitations, a new structural organization emerges. By logical necessity, it must be the pre-operational organization. By 'logical necessity' is meant that, given the properties of the preceding structure (sensorimotor), the nature of the experiences that it brings about and the nature of the organizational processes that operate on cognitive contents, no other form of organization can emerge than the pre-operational organization.

Piaget's view of development as self-organizational rather than occurring by design is highly radical. It focuses primarily on the developing organism itself and sketches a form of self-organization that pervades all aspects of development and leads to global, overarching structures that characterize the child as being in a particular developmental stage (the stage characterized by a single, overarching cognitive structure). Having said this, I do not intend to claim that Piaget's is a dynamic systems theory of development *avant la lettre*. However, in its emphasis on development as a self-organizational process rather than a process-by-design, it does contain a core that is entirely consistent with current dynamic systems theorizing.

Some authors, also working in the dynamic systems approach, have pitted their dynamic theories against the theory of Piaget, thus implying that Piaget's opposes the major dynamic principles of development (Thelen & Smith, 1994; 1998). What these authors are attacking, however, is Piaget's (alleged) representationalism, that is, his idea that actions are based on internal representations and schemes. Those schemes act as if they were internal instructions, ready to be retrieved and used to guide actions. According to Thelen and Smith, action – motor, cognitive or whatever – is not based on prespecified instruction sets in the form of internal representations and schemes. Actions 'self-assemble' on-line as they call it, that is, the structure of an action results from the acting itself and from how the acting brings about changes in the environment. Development alters the conditions of such self-assembly in ways that are not currently understood (connectionist network models may provide reasonable explanations of what happens here). It should be noted, however, that a rich, incomplete and by itself also evolving theory such as Piaget's is not necessarily explicit about all its potential claims. A scheme such as Piaget's does not necessarily imply a form of representationalism that we have been accustomed to since the heyday of information processing theory and cognitive science. By its very nature, a sensorimotor scheme, like the grasping scheme, must be something that is entirely specified in sensorimotor terms and comes into existence only in a sensorimotor act. Identifying such schemes with the internal conditions – whatever they are – that make the self-assembly of grasping acts possible is not necessarily at odds with Piaget's notion of scheme.

Examples of Dynamic Systems Models of Development

Knowledge and Knowledge Development as Dynamic Processes in Real Time

Thelen and Smith (1994, 1998) have presented dynamic systems theory as a theory of development. A good example of their approach is their work on a phenomenon called the A-not-B error (Smith et al., 1999). When infants between 6 and 12 months of age watch an object being hidden under some cover and, after a short delay, are given the opportunity to recover it, they will reach to the place where they saw it hidden. After a few trials in which the object is hidden in one place (called A) the object is then hidden – while the infant watches – in some other place, for instance to the left of the first place (place B). Although the infant has seen the object hidden in place B, he or she will nevertheless reach for it in the original hiding place A. The A-not-B error is a step in the process of the development of the object concept. It has been introduced by Piaget and has been extensively studied ever since (Wellman, Cross, & Bartsch, 1987). Basically, what Thelen, Smith, and co-authors react to is that the A-not-B error shows the manifestation of a – still immature – internal representation of the notion of object. They criticize the widespread standard conviction that this representation is an internal symbolic structure that features in set of internal beliefs and instructions that is supposed to guide the infant's actions. The standard conviction is supposed to be like this. The infant has an immature object concept, which is an internal symbolic structure specifying the properties of objects in general. In infants between 6 and 12 months, the object representation is still tied to the infant's representation of the action it has performed with the object. Hence the infant believes that in order to retrieve the object, he or she must repeat the action that was successful in the first place. This internally represented belief is thought to be the causal impetus behind the action 'reach-towards-A'. In Thelen and Smith's dynamic systems view, however, knowledge – of the object concept for instance – is not some internal symbolic structure that causally guides actions. Knowledge is a process. It is the result of the dynamic process of interaction between a specific context and a specific body (a body with a specific past and history). The process unfolds by the continuous transaction between the context and the body, and both body and context change during that interaction and by so doing provide new conditions for further steps in the process. Consolidated knowledge (as when we say that a 15-month-old child *has* an object concept) means that the contextual and individual conditions are such that the process has zoomed in on some stable, repetitive pattern (e.g. the infant reliably retrieves the object from place B).

According to the analysis of the A-not-B error provided by Thelen, Smith, and co-authors, the phenomenon is not about objects and object concept development, but about 'the dynamics of goal-directed reaching in unskilled reachers when placed in a task that requires them to repeatedly reach to one location and then reach to another' (Thelen & Smith, 1998, 613). In order to explain the error, one should realize that 'activity at any moment will be shaped by the just previous activity at any level' (1998, p. 613). I introduced the general idea that underlies this principle, that of iteration, in the description of the general properties of dynamic systems. In a task like this one, the internal neural coding of the preceding act of reaching still persists after the reach. In skilled reachers, this coding is sufficiently counteracted by a neural coding based on an act of visual attention to the new target (place B). Unskilled reachers need a strong visual attractor and also one that immediately precedes the reaching in order to be able to decouple the looking from the reaching. In the standard A-not-B task, however, the hiding places are not strongly visually distinct from one another, and nor is visual attention to the B-position drawn immediately before the reaching is made possible. The net result of all these conditions is this: with repeated reaching the infant builds up a strong temporary reaching attractor to place A, which implies that the attractor persists after the reaching is finished and thus influences any consequent reaching act; the visual saliency of the B-place is not enough to overcome the reach-to-A pattern and also not enough to decouple the looking (to B) from the reaching (to A). Consequently, the infant looks and reaches to A. If the infant's attention is drawn to B just before reaching is allowed, the infant can decouple the reaching and the looking and then the looking provides a strong enough attractor to guide the reaching to the place he or she is looking at. That is of course also the place where the object was hidden, which means that the infant no longer makes the A-not-B error. However, if we were to conclude that the reaching is now governed by a new internal representation, that of an object whose existence is independent of its movements, we would have made a serious mistake. In other words, what we see is a temporal pattern that entirely depends on the way the components of that pattern interact in time, on how and when they occur in the first place. But the meaning of the components of the pattern entirely depends on the just preceding events and on the internal condition of the reacher. The latter is the long-term product of the reacher's history, his or her preceding experiences with reaching, looking and acting. According to Thelen and Smith, the disappearance of the A-not-B error is primarily based on the emergence of self-locomotion (walking, crawling). Self-locomotion stimulates the decoupling of reaching and looking because it requires that goals (where one is going to) are specified more or less independently of what one is momentarily looking at or what one is momentarily doing.

An important point of Thelen and Smith's dynamic systems theory of development is that they do not make a distinction between short-term and long-term effects of actions. Actions affect the actor during the action by changing the actor's expectations, skills and so forth (or more precisely, whatever internal mechanism corresponds with what we are used to call expectations or skills, for that matter). The short-term effects accumulate, in some way or another, and so correspond with long-term changes we call 'development'.

In summary, the appearance and disappearance of the A-not-B error has nothing to do with the emergence of an internal, symbolic representation of the object that guides the child's activity. It is the result of the dynamic coupling of actions and perceptions in an ongoing stream of context- and self-dependent activity.

Concepts and Representations in a Dynamic Systems Framework

The cognitive revolution in psychology has brought the notions of concepts and representations as explanation of human symbolic action to the fore. Thelen and Smith's dynamic systems approach to knowledge, however, lies in the tradition of non-symbolist approaches to the nature of cognition. They defend the position that concepts and representations do not function as mechanisms of human action and, hence, that they do not exist. However, concepts and representations and similar notions are indispensable in the description of complex dynamic processes such as human action and they are perfectly compatible with a dynamic systems view if correctly interpreted. In my view, the controversy deals with a distinction between the question 'What is it *that* you know?' and the question 'What is it *how* we know?', which are related to the distinction between order parameters and control parameters that will be explained later. The question 'What is it *that* you know?' can be answered by specifying the content or nature of a person's knowledge in some symbolic form. For instance, if asked what an 18-month-old child knows when she solves a Piagetian object retrieval problem, we may answer that she has knowledge about the fundamental nature of objects, that she has an object concept. By so doing, we give a symbolic description of what it is that the infant knows. More precisely, we give a description of what it is that the infant *relates to* whenever he or she is reacting adequately to the object problems with which the infant is presented: we say that in his or her reaching actions the infant relates to *an object*. (This is not a trivial remark. For instance, when I mistakenly hold Mr X for Mr Y and address Mr X as if he were Mr Y, *I* am in fact relating to Mr Y, though for someone else, who knows Mr Y and Mr X, I am relating to Mr X. This kind of relationship is usually explained by referring to beliefs – I believe that Mr X is Mr Y – but it is not implied that a belief must be something separate from the action, something 'in my head' that is independent of my actually relating to the alleged Mr Y.)

However, the – somewhat oddly formulated – question 'What is it *how* we know?' is all too often answered by invoking the answer to the first question (what we know) as a causal mechanism. For instance, when we say that an infant has an object concept, we explain the infant's behavior with objects by assuming that the concept is some kind of behavior-producing engine inside the child. However, this solution amounts to a category mistake, but it is a mistake that seems difficult to avoid, given our tendency to view concepts, representations and so forth as causal, internal entities. The answer to how you know the object concept lies in a description of the actual mechanisms of your behavior. These mechanisms can take the form of connectionist-network-like brain structures, specific problem contexts, dynamic interactions between such contexts and acting persons and so forth. An important merit of Thelen and Smith's approach is that they have tried to show how knowledge is brought about in the actual, dynamic process of action, which is a process that changes the conditions under which such actions are possible (or impossible) and by so doing covers both developmental and action time.

The distinction between 'what is it that I know' and 'how is it that I know' has a counterpart in a distinction made in dynamic systems theory (usually in the approach known as synergetics) between so-called order parameters and control parameters. The order parameters describe the 'order' of the behavior of the process, that is, its structure. The control parameters describe those aspects that cause the process to behave as it does, that is, as described by the order parameters. In complex, meaning-laden behavior such as human action, the order parameters, specifying the structure or nature of the behavior, are described by referring to the nature of what it is that the acting person relates to. Thus, the complex action of an 18-month-old child correctly retrieving a hidden object from a hiding place and who is no longer fooled by the A-not-B phenomenon, is described by saying that the infant 'retrieves an object', hence, that the infant 'has an object concept'. Note that the notions of concept and conceive stem from the Latin *concipio*, which means to take hold of, take up, take in, take or receive. Thus, if we say that an infant has an object concept, we express the fact that the infant takes this-or-that particular entity as an object (and not as something else). The notions of object or object concept are in fact the order parameters of the infant's behavior: the myriad of components that make up the infant's actual, conscious perceptual-motor activity are 'summarized', so to speak, by referring to the fact that the infant relates to an object. This order parameter, however, is different from the control parameter (more exactly, the many control parameters) that causes the behavior to self-organize in a form that we characterize by the order parameter 'object (concept)'. Those control parameters unfold in the form of a complex time-dependent dynamics, as Smith et al. (1999) have shown in their analysis of the infant's A-not-B error. That is, the notion of object concept does not refer to some internal set of representations that cause the infant to correctly retrieve hidden objects or to avoid the A-not-B error. It is in this sense of the word that concepts do not exist, as Thelen and Smith would contend. A similar reasoning applies to the notion of representation, but it would lead too far to pursue this issue here. Finally, it is worth mentioning that the problems with regard to concepts and representations that dynamic systems theory runs into, and cognitive science too, for that matter, were already being extensively discussed by the phenomenological psychologists who were active around the middle of the twentieth century and whose basic inspiration goes back to the philosopher Franz Brentano (1838-1917).

The Dynamics of Mental and Behavioral Ecologies

The present author's work on dynamic systems models of development has been strongly influenced by models from ecological biology. Ecologists study and model the dynamics of ecosystems (Kingsland, 1995). An ecosystem is a distinguishable structure of components – animal and plant species embedded in an environment of physical living conditions – that interact with one another and by doing so alter their presence in the ecosystem. The basic alteration applies to the species' population sizes. Stable ecosystems entertain some kind of dynamic stability that conserves the global structure of the system (the species involved). Ecosystems are explicitly resource dependent. To a particular species, the sum of all the species to which it is functionally connected and the physical living conditions form that species' resources for maintained existence. The study of ecosystems is primarily concerned with the study of how the available resources contribute to the structure of the ecosystem in space and time.

I have argued that psychological systems, in the broadest sense of the word, comply with the general, abstract principles of ecosystems (van Geert, 1991; 1993; 1994). Let us take a child's cognition and language as our universe of discourse and consider the child's linguistic knowledge as the system we are interested in. This system can be divided into various subsystems, for instance, the child's phonological knowledge, knowledge of the lexicon, of syntax, of semantics and so on. Note that this subdivision is just a functional simplification, defining the levels at which we want to study the system at issue (see the section on defining a system). Note also that by defining the subsystems as separable components (lexicon, syntax, semantics) I make no claim whatsoever about those subsystems' underlying forms. The point is that, whatever such components really are in terms of the underlying mechanisms, they can be fruitfully and meaningfully treated as separable but interacting components.

Each component in such a system is further defined as something that is subject to growth (such a component is, somewhat trivially, called a *grower*). For instance, the lexicon (knowledge of words) begins somewhere and sometime with a minimal starting level (metaphorically speaking its germinal state) and grows towards some form of dynamic stability in adulthood (which lies probably around 200,000 lexical entries, i.e. basic words). Its growth is mathematically modeled by a simple equation, the logistic growth equation. This equation specifies growth as the joint product of the component's current growth level (thus obeying the iterative principle that a dynamic system is always governed by its just preceding state) and the available but limited external resources (the component's environment). Any additional component in the system (for instance syntax) to which the current component (the lexicon) is functionally connected forms part of that component's resource structure. The functional relationships are often symmetrical (syntax is a resource component of the lexicon, the lexicon is a resource component of syntax) and sometimes antagonistic (the lexicon positively affects the growth of early syntactic knowledge whereas early syntactic knowledge has a – temporary – negative effect on the growth of syntax).

A dynamic model – in this particular case a model of language growth – consists, first, of a specification of how the components involved in the system affect one another in terms of resource functions (e.g. L has a positive effect of magnitude *m* on S, S has an initial negative effect on L, and so on). Second, it specifies the initial conditions of each component, and third, the eventual conditional dependencies among the components (e.g. a specified minimal level of lexical knowledge is a precondition for the emergence of syntactic structures such as two-word sentences). Even a relatively small number of components easily results in a rather complicated web of relationships and mutual effects. The dynamics of such a web can only be understood by simulating its evolution under various conditions (e.g. stronger or weaker influences among the components involved, different timing of the emergence of components and so on). Simulation studies with those web structures demonstrate that they can spontaneously show qualitative and quantitative properties that are characteristic of development (van Geert, 1991; 1994). For instance, they settle into equilibria, show stepwise change, show stage-like coherence, run into temporary disorder, and so forth. The fact that such models show the required properties does not, of course, provide a proof that real development occurs along the models' principles. Part of the supporting evidence must come from studies that concentrate on specific aspects of the models and actively manipulate the model's control variables. Such manipulation is considerably more easily done in studies of motor development than in studies of language or cognition, for instance.

These models can also be fruitfully applied to specifying relationships between components at a much finer scale of detail. For instance, instead of specifying relations between lexicon, syntax, semantics and so forth, one may focus on specific syntactic rules or structures as components of a web of interactions. For instance, in a study on the emergence of verbs and prepositions, we studied various early preposition structures used by infants (e.g. N-Prep structures, as in 'doll in'). From the patterns of increase and decrease in the frequency with which these patterns occurred, we inferred a sequence of asymmetric relationships among those rules: preceding rules have a positive effect on the emergence of later rules, whereas later rules have a negative, i.e. competitive, effect on earlier ones and lead to the disappearance of the latter (see Figure 28.6).

Note that this pattern of relationships – a positive relationship from a developmentally earlier to a later component, and a negative relationship from a later to an earlier one – is probably quite universal in development. For instance, if applied to various stages of moral reasoning as described in the Kohlberg tradition, these relationships lead to the pattern of appearance and disappearance of moral reasoning styles found in a cross-sectional study by Colby et al. (1983; see van Geert, 1998b).

A disadvantage of these ecological models is that they provide no explanation for the actual emergence of new forms in development (new forms can easily be incorporated, but they are not explained). In an alternative to this ecological model, I introduced notions directly inspired by Piaget's assimilation–accommodation principles (van Geert, 1998a). In this model, environmental inflow is defined by the child's current state of development. The eventual progress the child makes, given this inflow, is based on that inflow and on the child's current developmental state. Stated in this general form, these principles are also present in Vygotsky's notion of the *zone of proximal development*, which implies, among other things, that children acquire new skills and knowledge when given help – by a more competent person – that fits in with their current developmental level. It turns out that a dynamic model based on these general and traditional developmental principles explains not only gradual change, but also discontinuous and stagewise change and changes in the variability of performance. In empirical studies, for instance, we found that day-to-day or week-to-

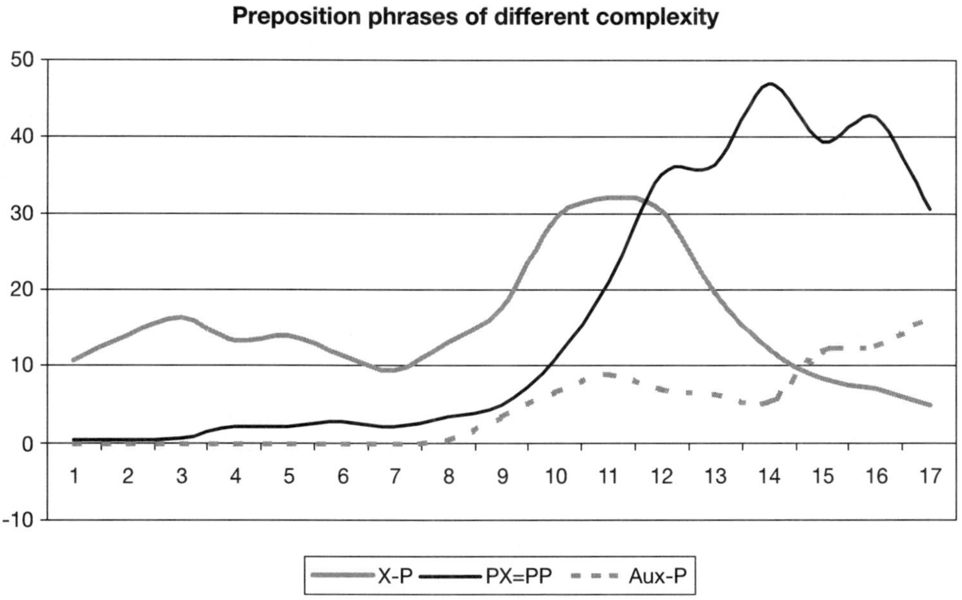

Figure 28.6 *Changes in the frequencies of utterances with prepositions. The utterances are ordered in terms of increasing syntactic complexity (X-P, PX=PP, Aux-P). The least complex form (XP) increases, then decreases as more complex forms emerge*

week variability in performance levels is quite considerable at the beginning of some developmental process and that the range of variation decreases as the process settles into some equilibrium level (de Weerth, van Geert, & Hoijtink, 1999). Note that the pattern of change in variation depends on the nature of the developmental process at issue: in some processes it must, by necessity, be small at the beginning and increase towards the end or increase just before the process jumps to a new equilibrium level (van der Maas & Molenaar, 1992).

Building Your Own Models: A Short Tutorial

Building dynamic models of developmental processes requires some special skills and practice, but those skills are not beyond the reach of anyone who has some experience with computers. There are several software packages on the market that are especially designed for systems modeling. A quick search across the Internet shows how many of such specialized packages have already been developed.[1] Several of those programs (such as Ithink and Modelmaker) provide relatively user-friendly interfaces, free demo-programs and worked examples. For the occasional model builder, they have the disadvantage that they are not always cheap and that they require considerable practice before they can be actually used. A good alternative – if one is aware of the unavoidable disadvantages – is the use of spreadsheet programs such as Excel. Such programs are widely distributed and considerably more versatile than many users think. With some extension of the skills that spreadsheet users mostly already have acquired, interesting demonstrations and explorations of dynamic interactions between variables are possible. Basically, the cells of a spreadsheet are predefined variables. We can specify an equation in each cell (variable) that refers to other variables. If we view every time step as a separate variable, we can use the spreadsheet program to build a (somewhat crude but essentially effective) model of dynamic systems processes. The idea of a time step needs a little more explanation – and caution. If we specify a simple conceptual model – for instance, that social experiences affect social knowledge in children – we are usually not explicit about whether the effect is continuous or discrete. In this particular example, it is likely to be discrete. Each time the child has a particular social experience, some of its social knowledge (whatever that is, in reality) is changed. In our model, each time step corresponds with a discrete event, namely the experience and its effect on knowledge. However, if we zoom in onto the event itself and imagine how a child perceives and evaluates the stream of actions in the social situation and acts him- or herself, the relationship between the variables at interest (the experiences and their effects) is more likely to take the form of a continuous stream of mutual effects. In a computer simulation, such continuous streams are always broken up into discrete steps, but in order to approach the continuous character of the events, the steps are made very small and specific mathematical algorithms are used to correct for the discretization. If one uses a spreadsheet program, continuous processes are best (but still somewhat crudely) approached by cutting the whole process into a (very) large number of steps. Discrete processes should be modeled by taking a number of steps that correspond with the number of discrete events one wishes to model. This, by the way, is just one example of the effect of modeling on theory building: when trying to construct the model, a whole series of decisions need to be made that require further theoretical and empirical analysis of the processes we model and, thus, potentially lead to a better understanding of such processes, even if the modeling itself proves in the end not very successful.

In line with the ecological approach I take with respect to developmental processes, I have often used an ecologically inspired model of increase or decrease in a variable, namely the logistic model (see the section on the dynamics of mental and behavioral ecologies). The logistic model, which describes the growth of populations, but which can also be applied to economic processes or to the growth of scientific publications, to name just two examples, views the increase in a variable as the effect of two sources of influence. The first is the variable itself, the second is the variable's environment, that is, the collection of influences outside the modeled variable (other variables 'inside' the subject and variables 'outside' the subject, i.e. his or her external environment). Take for instance a child's understanding of a simple arithmetic operation such as addition. The effect of information – feedback on an addition error made by the child, for instance – depends on the level of understanding already acquired by the child. The growth of the child's understanding of addition is based on – and therefore also limited by – the total set of resources that operate on that particular understanding. Those resources are internal (the child's knowledge and understanding of numbers, for instance) and external (the kind of help given by the environment, the opportunities given to the child for practicing addition, and so forth). According to the logistic model, any next level of some variable – for instance the child's understanding of addition – can be expressed in the form of the following mathematical equation:

$$L_{t+\Delta t} = L_t + L_t \times \text{rate}_{\Delta t} \times (1 - L_t/K_t)$$

where $L_{t+\Delta t}$ the next state of the variable and L_t is the preceding state; $\text{rate}_{\Delta t}$ is the growth rate that applies to the time interval Δt between the next and the preceding state; and K_t is the carrying capacity, which is the set of resources that apply to the variable at issue. This set of resources is expressed in the form of the equilibrium level K_t that the variable will eventually attain. This equation forms the expression of a simple but powerful dynamic process model. It is iterative in that every next step is the product of the preceding step (and something else). It is dynamic in that it models the change of the variable as a process that takes place over time. In the next section I shall give an example of how this model may be transformed into a spreadsheet model with which we can experiment.

Using Chopsticks To Eat Your Meals

Let us assume we are interested in the growth of a particular skill, namely the ability to eat with chopsticks. I shall assume that we have some kind of ruler against which we can measure an individual's chopsticks manipulation skill (note that we don't need to have such a measure or test in reality, it suffices that it makes sense to assume that such a ruler is available in principle).

First, we have to decide on some initial level, a 'seed' that must be bigger than 0. The 'seed' can be any arbitrarily small number (or a number that is based on empirical observations of initial state conditions). Let us assume that we arbitrarily set the initial level of chopstick manipulation to 1/100th of the average skilled chopstick user (we can try different initial states once we've set up the model). Let us also assume that the effect on the chopstick manipulation skill is based on discrete experiences, namely one meal a day (one meal a day eaten with chopsticks, that is). Assume further that we have observed that most children who begin with chopsticks at an early age take about three months to become really proficient with this equipment. Three months is rounded off to 100 days, which, given there is one practice event a day, gives a total of 100 practice events. Our model should therefore count about one hundred steps. We open a spreadsheet file and dedicate the first one hundred cells in the first column to our chopsticks model. Assuming that we set the level of skilled chopstick manipulation to 1, the initial level must, as agreed, be 0.01. We dedicate the first cell in the column to the initial state and write 0.01 in the first cell, A1 (this should sound quite familiar to spreadsheet users). A2 is the second practice event, A3 the third and so forth, up to A100. If the effect of practice is specified in the form of the logistic growth equation explained above, we can fill in the chopsticks manipulation skill level during the second event (A2, the second meal) by introducing the equation in cell A2, which, in spreadsheet format should look like this:[2]

= A1 + A1 * rate * (1 – A1/carrying capacity)

Recall that we decided that the level of a skilled chopsticks manipulator should be set to 1. That is, 1 is the level that will be achieved, given all the resources present in the environment (by resources I mean the subject's general motor level, muscle strength, eye–hand coordination, etc. in addition to teaching, examples and guidance with regard to chopsticks manipulation by the more experienced users in the environment). Thus, the A1 variable at the end of the equation is divided by the carrying capacity, which is 1, and this division can, of course, be omitted from the equation. Each of the remaining 98 steps in our model must refer to its predecessor (the preceding step) and calculate the level achieved in that step on the basis of the level achieved in the preceding step. In order to accomplish this, we simply copy the content of cell A2 to all the remaining cells in the column (a spreadsheet copy command will automatically make the correct reference of every next cell to its preceding cell). We have now completed our first dynamic model in spreadsheet format. If we graph the data in the column comprising the 100 steps (which is very easily accomplished in a spreadsheet program), we will see that chopsticks manipulation increases in the form of an S-shaped curve, provided the growth rate is not too small – and not too big either. If we set the growth rate to 2.85 for instance (which means that the change per event equals an almost threefold increase of the level, damping factors not taken into account, which is indeed very much), we see that the process turns into a chaotic oscillation. Although it is interesting to see that a change in one parameter can cause a qualitative change in the growth pattern (from a smooth to a chaotic process), there is no reasonable conceptual interpretation for such a high growth rate – and its effect – in the case of a motor skill such as chopsticks use. Thus, the mathematical possibility of a chaotic oscillation does not fit in with the nature of the process we are currently modeling (it may fit in with other processes, though).

Let us now extend the model by assuming that a person can lose his or her skill if the manipulation of the chopsticks is not sufficiently practiced. This is basically what occurs with an occasional visitor of oriental restaurants, who uses chopsticks only once in a while. We use the column right of the skill level column for specifying randomized intervals between events, i.e. between meals in which chopsticks are used. The equation for a randomized interval is as follows:[3]

1 + Int(Rand()* length)

If length is the maximal number of days between meals in which chopsticks are used, the equation produces a random number of days between 1 and the value of 'length'. This random period differs for each step in the process.

We assume that the skill level decays if it is not practiced. The decay is proportional to the level already attained, the length of the period without practice and the decay parameter. Our dynamic model is now expressed in the form of a more extensive equation, namely:

A1 + A1 * rate * (1 – A1/carrying capacity)
– decay * B1 * A1

Assuming that we have defined the parameter name 'decay', the additional part of the equation refers to the level already attained (which, for the second step, is the level attained in the first step, which is in cell A1) and to the number of days between the first and second meal with chopsticks, a value that can be found in the cell right of cell A1, namely cell B1. We copy the new formula and the random period formula to the 98 remaining cells in columns A and B. Each time we let the program recalculate the process, we will calculate new randomized periods and thus find different curves for our chopsticks skill level. With a little experimenting, we will discover an interesting property of our model, namely that the average period between chopsticks meals determines the (approximate) equilibrium level of the chopsticks manipulation skill. That is, the average period between meals turns out to be part of the set of resources and thus determines the equilibrium level of the skill. This is an interesting discovery (although it is a fact that can be mathematically inferred from our equations). Before trying the model out we would probably have thought that the practice intervals would result in a decrease of the learning speed, i.e. that it would take longer before the maximal level is attained. This little example shows that building dynamic models – however simple – and studying their properties based on varying the values of the parameters, may indeed lead to a better understanding of the properties of our models (Figure 28.7).

The preceding example had no other function than to show how a simple model could be built and implemented in the form of a spreadsheet program. Simple though it is, its basic principles can be applied to a host of more realistic examples, such as the growth of the lexicon, the growth of the use of syntactic structures and categories in language, the growth of cognitive skills and so forth.

A Model of Hierarchically Connected Growers

Some time ago, Fischer (see Chapter 21 in this volume) and myself cooperated on an attempt to build a dynamic model of Fischer's skill theory (Fischer, 1980). Skill theory describes domain-specific development in the form of a series of major stages or 'tiers', subdivided into substages or levels. The series forms a hierarchical structure. Each lower level is a precursor to its higher-level successor and

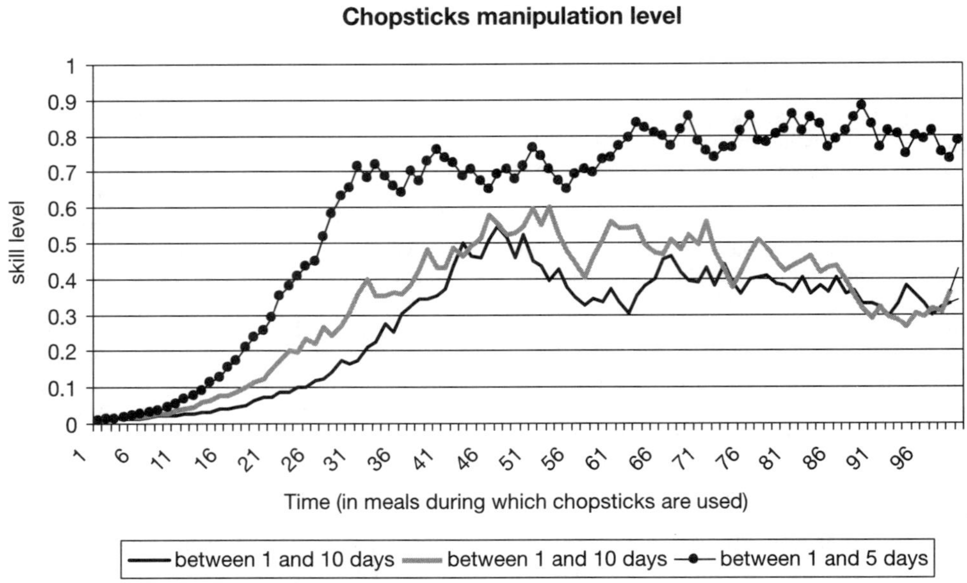

Figure 28.7 *The growth of chopsticks manipulation skill. The model is based on a random factor-driven logistic model. The increase or decrease of the skill level is based on discrete learning events, namely meals eaten with chopsticks. The intervals between the meals are also randomized, with a maximum interval of ten and five days respectively. The five day maximum results in a higher and more constant level of skill than the ten day maximum, all other factors being equal (except for the random variations in the parameters). Random variations in the parameters may cause differences in the rate of growth (see the graphs based on the ten day maximum)*

is integrated into the higher level as soon as the latter has emerged. A simple example of three such levels concerns the understanding of an arithmetic operation such as addition. Level *A* consists of the ability to solve simple addition problems. Level *B* involves an abstract understanding of the addition operation as a combination of smaller units into a larger one. Level *C* involves the abstract under standing of a relationship between arithmetic operations, for instance addition and abstraction. Each level can be conceived of as a 'grower'. A grower is a variable that starts at an initial level and that increases by way of a process described earlier in the form of the logistic growth equation. A model of the three levels described above would consist of three logistic growth equations, one for each level of addition understanding. According to Fischer's theory, the three growers are hierarchically connected. What does that mean in terms of a mathematical relationship between the three equations? First, the connection applies from the lower to the higher level and concerns a conditional relationship. The higher level cannot get off the ground as long as the lower level – the condition or precursor – has not yet reached some minimal, conditional level (i.e. abstract understanding of the addition operation is not possible without a reasonably developed skill in solving simple addition problems). Recall that the logistic growth equation has the following form (it has been written in the form of an equation for level *B*):

$$B_{t+\Delta t} = B_t + B_t \times \text{rate}_{\Delta t} \times (1 - B_t / K_t)$$

We know that *B* cannot get off the ground as long as the level of its predecessor, grower *A*, stays beneath a conditional level, which we will set to A_c (determining this level would normally be a matter of empirical research). We now introduce a parameter C_B and alter the above equation as follows

$$B_{t+\Delta t} = B_t + [B_t \times \text{rate}_{\Delta t} \times (1 - B_t/K_t)] \times C_B$$

C_B is a parameter with only two possible values, 0 and 1. The equation for C_B is as follows:

$$C_B = 1 \quad \text{if} \quad A_t \geq A_c$$
$$C_B = 0 \quad \text{if} \quad A_t < A_c$$

for A_c, the conditional value of the variable *A*. Note that equations like these can be very easily written down in the form of a spreadsheet model. Assuming that the values of variable *A* are in the A-column and those of variable B in the B-column, we use the C-column to calculate the C_B value. We select the second cell of the column, i.e. the first row after the row that contains the initial values of A and B. Assuming this is cell C2, we write down the following equation:

= If (A1 = >0.8,1,0)

This equation should be read as follows: if the value in cell A1 is equal to or bigger than 0.8 (the value that we have taken as the conditional level necessary for variable B to start growing), the value in cell C2 is 1; if the condition is not fulfilled, the value in cell C2 is 0. A different, more abstract way of reading this equation is IF condition A1=>0.8 is true, THEN 1, ELSE 0. In cell B2 (which I assume to be the second step in the calculation of the variable B), we write down the following equation:

$$B2 = B1 + [B1 \times \text{rate}_B \times (1 - B1/K_B)]C2$$

(recall that B2, B1 and C2 refer to the values in the cells B2, B1 and C2 respectively). It is easy to see that as long as the values in the A-column (the A variable) remain below 0.8, the corresponding value in the C-column remains 0. Since $[B1 \times \text{rate}_B \times (1 - B1/K_B)]$ 0 is of course 0, the growth equation amounts to $B_{n+1} = B_n + 0$, which means that every next cell is equal to its predecessor, which simply means that the value of B does not change. As soon as the A value is equal to 0.8 (or any other value we find appropriate), the value in the C-column turns into 1, and the growth equation starts to take effect. Since the conditional relation holds between any level and its successor, it also holds between growers B and C. A similar set of equations can be set up, applying to columns B and C respectively.

We have now modeled the first part of our theory, namely the notion of a conditional or precursor relationship. The second part seems a little bit more complicated. What could we possibly mean by saying that the less complex level is incorporated in the more complex one, or that the less complex level is integrated or incorporated in the more complex one? Since we are dealing with the quantitative aspect of the variables only (we are modeling their level) we must translate this idea of integration into a quantitative relationship. When we say that A, the simple addition skills, have been integrated into B, the more complex level of understanding of what addition actually means, we intend to say that A has changed, that it has become an expression of B rather than the old, limited understanding as expressed in the original skill of solving addition problems. We may argue that this change in the nature of A should lead to an improvement in the expression of A, or, stated more simply, that an understanding of what addition really means should allow a child to solve addition problems (the A skill) more adequately, with fewer errors, or that more complicated addition problems can be solved. Note that this is the theory, not necessarily the empirical reality. But what we are trying to model here is the mechanism or the relationships as postulated by the theory. Whether or not these relationships also cover reality remains to be seen, but that problem is not at stake here. If it is indeed so that an integration of A into B should lead to an improvement in A (this is what the theory says), we could increase the level of A as a function of the level of B. Thus, the higher the level of B, the higher the level of A, or A grows as a function of the growth of B. This relationship can be expressed in the following form:

$$\Delta A = A_t \times B_t \times \text{support}_{BtoA}$$

which should be read as follows: part of the increase of A depends on the level of A at time t, the level of B at time t and a factor that expresses the degree of support from B to A.

Now the full equation for the variable A is as follows:

$$A_{t+1} = A_t + A_t \times \text{rate} \times (1 - A_t/\text{carrying capacity}_A) + A_t \times B_t \times \text{support}_{BtoA}$$

By now, it shouldn't be too difficult to transform this equation into a spreadsheet model. Note that with the equations for the variables B and C the increase component (the part of the equation after the first A_t at the right-hand side of the formula) is multiplied by the conditional factor C_B (or C_c). The resulting graphs show a series of three 'stages'. The first consists of level A only, the second witnesses the emergence of B and an increase in A, and the third involves the emergence of C and an increase in the levels of B and C (Figure 28.8).

Our model has, of course, severe limitations. It confines itself to the quantitative aspects of growth and it does not explain why B emerges, given A (we only show that B will not get off the ground as long as A stays beneath some preset value, but we haven't explained why it is B that grows, and not C or D or E . . .). However, in all its simplicity, it nevertheless demonstrates some interesting properties of the developmental dynamics. For instance, it shows how patterns such as stepwise growth emerge from the nature and the interaction. The timing of growth spurts (and related phenomena such as dips) is not preprogrammed by some internal alarm clock but depends entirely on interactions between variables that are there all the time. Models such as these also allow the researcher to experiment with many different parameter settings in order to investigate the range of possible outcomes that the model allows for. It is usually hardly possible to infer this range of possible patterns on the basis of the conceptual model alone. One needs to turn one's conceptual models of processes into calculation procedures –

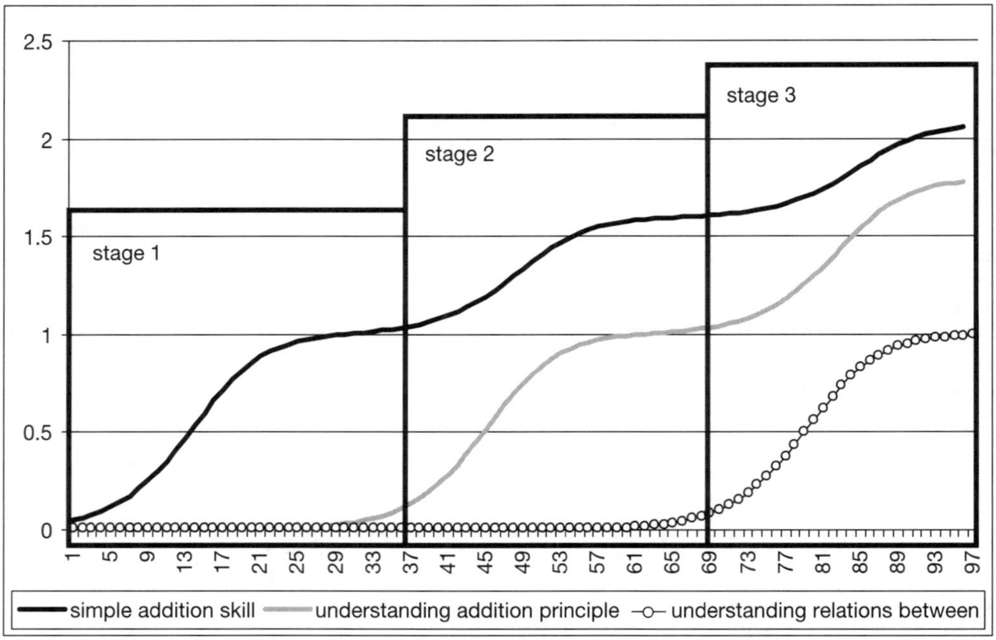

Figure 28.8 *A simulation of three hierarchically coupled growers based on Fischer's (1980) skill model. The first grower is a precursor to the second, and the second to the third. The first grower profits from the growth of the second, and the second profits from the third. The 'profit' is the effect of hierarchical integration of the earlier grower into the more advanced grower (its successor). The result is a series of stepwise increases that resemble a three-stage growth model*

i.e. into dynamic models – in order to obtain an idea about the model's inherent possibilities. If researchers want to use the models to predict or explain empirical phenomena, it is of utmost importance that they know what their models are capable of. In this way, the building of dynamic models is an important, if not essential, step between conceptual theory formation and the empirical testing of the theory. In this regard, I have compared the building of dynamic models with doing experimental theoretical psychology (van Geert, 1994). It is theoretical psychology in that it concerns the researcher's conceptual models, but it is experimental in the sense that it consists of experimenting with possible parameter settings in order to find out what the model will do.

Summary and Conclusion

The notion of development, as an unfolding of inherent properties and a tendency towards increasing order and structure, plays an important role in everyday discourse. As a scientific concept, it was largely discarded by developments in physics and biology, which emphasized that order does not spontaneously increase but only decreases and that evolution does not involve an intrinsic tendency towards more complexity and 'higher' forms. Although these conclusions still hold, they have been explicitly modified and amended by developments in dynamic systems theory, which studied the properties of processes where order and structure are spontaneously increased and gave a new and considerably more exact meaning to the notion of inherent property. With its emphasis on the central importance of interaction in real time, dynamic systems theory forms a natural framework for the study of development. However, dynamic systems theory is not a single theory but a general approach, with many different possibilities. After an overview of the many faces of dynamic systems theory, we proceeded with a discussion of some of its applications in the field of developmental psychology. These applications are still haunted by a host of problems of a methodological, conceptual, modeling and empirical nature. Development itself, however, is a difficult notion and in general a very tough nut to crack. In fact, it is considerably easier to altogether abandon the notion of development and explain developmental phenomena by reference to internal programs or instruction sets, such as the genetic code. If we take development seriously, however, an approach like dynamic systems or something along similar lines will probably be the only way out, however premature and incomplete such an approach at present may be.

NOTES

1 Try for instance http://www.acs.ilstu.edu/faculty/wjyurci/nsfteachsim/simsoftware.html; http://www.idsia.ch/~andrea/simtools.html.
2 I assume that the spreadsheet user has already defined the parameter 'rate' as a name in the spreadsheet; Excel users do this by clicking Insert/Name from the menu.
3 This is how Excel would specify that equation; in another spreadsheet, the equation will probably be a little different from this one.

REFERENCES

Adami, C. (1995). Self-organized criticality in living systems. *Physics Letters A*, 203, 29–32.

Atkins, P.W. (1984). *The second law*. New York: Scientific American Books.

Bak, P., & Chen, K. (1991). Self-organizing criticality. *Scientific American*, 265 (1), 46–53.

Bechtel, W., & Abrahamsen, A. (1991). *Connectionism and the mind*. Oxford: Blackwell.

Bickerton, D. (1991). *Language and species*. Chicago: University of Chicago Press.

Breeuwsma, G. (1993). *Alles over ontwikkeling: Over de grondslagen van de ontwikkelingspsychologie*. Amsterdam: Boom.

Bronfenbrenner, U. (1979). *The ecology of human development*. Cambridge, MA: Harvard University Press.

Camras, L.A. (2000). Surprise! Facial expressions can be coordinative motor structures. In M.D. Lewis & I. Granic (eds), *Emotion, development and self-organization: Dynamic systems approaches to emotional development*. Cambridge: Cambridge University Press.

Case, R. (1990). Neo-Piagetian theories of child development. In R. Sternberg & C. Berg (eds), *Intellectual development* (pp. 161–196). New York: Cambridge University Press.

Colby, A., Kohlberg, L., Gibbs, J., & Lieberman, M. (1983). *A longitudinal study of moral development. Monographs of the Society for Research in Child Development*, Vol. 48, no. 124.

de Graaf, J.W. (1999). Relating new to old: A classical controversy in developmental psychology. Doctoral dissertation, University of Groningen.

de Swart, H.E. (1990). Wordt het weer beschreven door een vreemde aantrekker? Chaos en voorspelbaarheid in atmosferische modellen (Does a strange attractor describe the weather? Chaos and predictability in atmospheric models). In H.W. Broer & F. Verhulst (eds), *Dynamische systemen en chaos: Een revolutie vanuit de wiskunde (Dynamic systems and chaos: A revolution from mathematics)* (pp. 256–285). Utrecht: Epsilon.

de Weerth, C., van Geert, P., & Hoijtink, H. (1999). Intraindividual variability in infant behavior. *Developmental Psychology*, 35, 1102–1112.

Elbers, L. (1997). Output as input: A constructivist hypothesis in language acquisition. *Archives de Psychologie*, 65, 131–140.

Elman, J.L. (1994). Implicit learning in neural networks: The importance of starting small. In C.Umilta & M. Moscovitch (eds), *Attention and performance 15: Conscious and nonconscious information processing* (pp. 861–888). Cambridge, MA: MIT Press.

Elman, J.L., Bates, E.A., Johnson, M.H., & Karmiloff-Smith, A. (1996). *Rethinking innateness: A connectionist perspective on development*. Cambridge, MA: MIT Press.

Fischer, K.W. (1980). A theory of cognitive development: The control and construction of hierarchies of skills. *Psychological Review*, 87, 477–531.

Fodor, J.A. (1975). *Language of thought*. New York: Crowell.

Gleick, J. (1987). *Chaos: Making a new science*. New York: Penguin.

Gottlieb, G. (1992). *Individual development and evolution: The genesis of novel behavior*. New York: Oxford.

Gottlieb, G., Wahlsten, D., & Lickliter, R. (1998). The significance of biology for human development: A developmental psychobiological systems view. In W. Damon & R. Lerner (eds), *Handbook of child psychology* (Vol. 1, pp. 233–273). New York: Wiley.

Gould, S.J. (1989). *Wonderful life: The Burgess Shale and the nature of history*. New York: Norton.

Gould, S.J. (1996). *Full house: The spread of excellence from Plato to Darwin*. New York: Three Rivers.

Hofbauer, J., & Sigmund, K. (1988). *The theory of evolution and dynamical systems*. Cambridge: Cambridge University Press.

Jackson, E.A. (1991a). *Perspectives of nonlinear dynamics* (Vol. 1). Cambridge: Cambridge University Press.

Jackson, E.A. (1991b). *Perspectives of nonlinear dynamics* (Vol. 2). Cambridge: Cambridge University Press.

Kauffman, S.A. (1993). *The origins of order: Self-organization and selection in evolution*. New York: Oxford University Press.

Kingsland, S.E. (1995). *Modeling nature: Episodes in the history of population ecology*. Chicago: University of Chicago Press.

Lewis, M.D. (1994). Cognition-emotion feedback and the self-organization of developmental paths. *Human Development*, 38, 71–102.

Lewis, M.D. (1996) Self-organising cognitive appraisals. *Cognition and Emotion*, 10, 1–25.

Lotka, A.J. (1925). *Elements of physical biology*. Baltimore: Williams & Wilkins.

May, R.M. (1976). Simple mathematical models with very complicated dynamics. *Nature*, 261, 459–467.

Murray, J.D. (1989). *Mathematical biology*. Berlin: Springer.

Nagel, E. (1957). Determinism and development. In D.B. Harris (ed.), *The concept of development*. Minneapolis: University of Minnesota Press.

Piatelli-Palmarini, M. (ed.) (1980). *Language and learning: The debate between Jean Piaget and Noam Chomsky*. Cambridge, MA: Harvard University Press.

Pike, A., & Plomin, R. (1996). Importance of nonshared environmental factors for childhood and adolescent psychopathology. *Journal of the American Academy of Child and Adolescent Psychiatry*, 35, 560–570.

Simon, H. (1969). *The sciences of the artificial*. Cambridge, MA: MIT Press.

Smith, L.B., Thelen, E., Titzer, R., & McLin, D. (1999). Knowing in the context of acting: The task dynamics of the A-not-B error. *Psychological Review*, 106, 235–260.

Thelen, E., & Smith, L.B. (1994). *A dynamic systems approach to the development of cognition and action*. Cambridge, MA: Bradford Books/MIT Press.

Thelen, E., & Smith, L.B. (1998). Dynamic systems theories. In W. Damon & R. Lerner (eds), *Handbook of child psychology* (Vol. 1, pp. 563–634). New York: Wiley.

Thom, R. (1972). *Stabilité structurelle et morphogénèse: Essai d'une théorie générale des modèles*. Paris: InterEditions.

Thomae, H. (1959). Entwicklungsbegriff und entwicklungstheorie. In R. Bergius & H.Thomae (eds), *Handbuch der Psychologie, Band 3: Entwicklungspsychologie*. Göttingen: Verlag für Psychologie.

Trautner, H.M. (1978). *Lehrbuch der Entwicklungspsychologie*. Gottingen: Hogrefe.

van der Maas, H. (1993). *Catastrophe analysis of stage-wise cognitive development: Model, method and applications*. Doctoral dissertation, University of Amsterdam.

van der Maas, H.L., & Molenaar, P.C. (1992). Stagewise cognitive development: An application of catastrophe theory. *Psychological Review*, 99, 395–417.

van Geert, P. (1986a). The concept of development. In P. van Geert (ed.), *Theory building in developmental psychology* (pp. 3–50). Amsterdam: North-Holland.

van Geert, P. (1986b). The structure of developmental theories. In P. van Geert (ed.), *Theory building in developmental psychology* (pp. 51–102). Amsterdam: North-Holland.

van Geert, P. (1987a). The structure of developmental theories: A generative approach. *Human Development*, 30, 160–177.

van Geert, P. (1987b). The structure of Erikson's model of the Eight Ages of Man: A generative approach. *Human Development*, 30, 236–254.

van Geert, P. (1987c). The structure of Galperin's theory of the formation of mental acts: A generative approach. *Human Development*, 30, 355–381.

van Geert, P. (1987d). The concept of development and the structure of developmental theories. In W.J. Baker, M.E. Hyland, H. van Rappard, & A.W. Staats (eds), *Current issues in theoretical psychology* (pp. 379–392). Amsterdam: North-Holland.

van Geert, P. (1988a). A graph theoretical approach to the structure of developmental models. *Human Development*, 31, 107–135.

van Geert, P. (1988b). The concept of transition in developmental models. In W. Baker, H. Stam, & H. van Rappard (eds), *Recent trends in theoretical psychology*. New York: Springer.

van Geert, P. (1990). Theoretical problems in developmental psychology. In P. van Geert and L. Mos (eds), Annals of theoretical psychology: Developmental psychology. New York: Plenum, pp. 1–54.

van Geert, P. (1991). A dynamic systems model of cognitive and language growth. *Psychological Review*, 98, 3–53.

van Geert, P. (1993). A dynamic systems model of cognitive growth: Competition and support under limited resource conditions. In L.B. Smith & E. Thelen (eds), *A dynamic systems approach to development: Applications* (pp. 265–331). Cambridge, MA: MIT Press.

van Geert, P. (1994). *Dynamic systems of development: Change between complexity and chaos*. London: Harvester Wheatsheaf.

van Geert, P. (1998a). A dynamic systems model of basic developmental mechanisms: Piaget, Vygotsky, and beyond. *Psychological Review*, 105, 634–677.

van Geert, P. (1998b). A dynamic systems model of adolescent development. Paper presented at the EARA conference, Budapest, 1998.

van Geert, P. (1998c). We almost had a great future behind us: The contribution of non-linear dynamics to developmental-science-in-the-making. *Developmental Science*, 1, 143–159.

Volterra, V. (1926). Variazioni e fluttuazioni del numero d'individui in specie animali conviventi. *Mem. R. Accad. Naz. dei Lincei. Ser. VI*. 2.

Waddington, C.H. (1956). *Principles of embryology*. New York: MacMillan.

Wellman, H.M., Cross, D., & Bartsch, K. (1987). Infant search and object permanence: A meta-analysis of the A-not-B error. *Monographs of the Society for Research in Child Development*, Vol. 51, pp. 1–51.

Wolke, D., & Meyer, R. (1999). Cognitive status, language attainment, and prereading skills of 6-year-old very preterm children and their peers: The Bavarian Longitudinal Study. *Developmental Medicine and Child Neurology*, 41, 94–109.

Index